Florida

level RED

HOLT SCIENCE & TECHNOLOGY

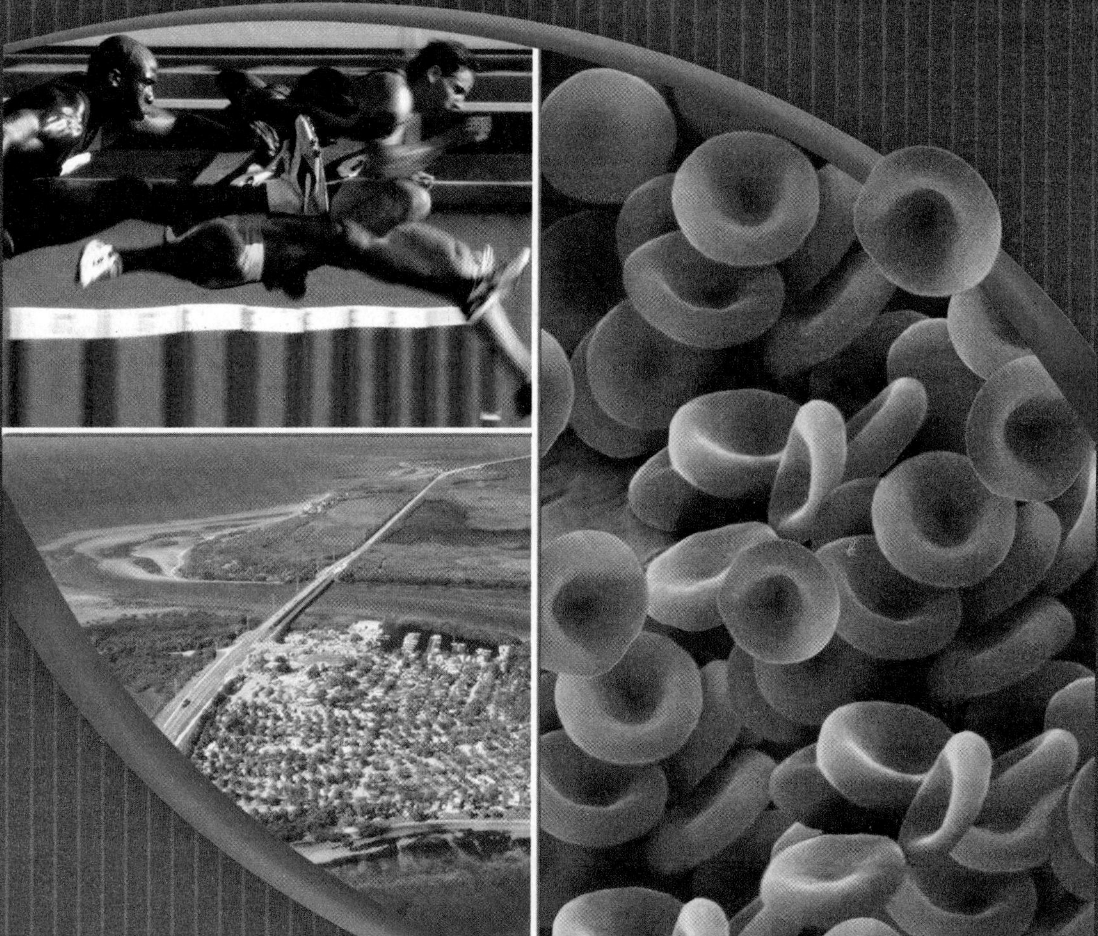

HOLT, RINEHART AND WINSTON

A Harcourt Education Company

Orlando • **Austin** • New York • San Diego • Toronto • London

Acknowledgments

Contributing Authors

Mario Affatigato, Ph.D.
Professor of Physics
Coe College
Cedar Rapids, Iowa

Katy Z. Allen
Science Writer
Wayland, Massachusetts

Linda Ruth Berg, Ph.D.
Adjunct Professor of Natural Sciences
St. Petersburg College
St. Petersburg, Florida

Leila Dumas, MA
Former Physics Teacher
Lago Vista, Texas

Jennie Dusheck, MA
Science Writer
Santa Cruz, California

Steve Feller, Ph.D.
B.D. Sillman Professor of Physics
Coe College
Cedar Rapids, Iowa

Carol A. Fortino, Ph.D.
Instructor in Elementary Education
Department of Elementary Education
University of Northern Colorado
Greeley, Colorado

Teresa Greely
Biological Oceanographer
Director of Education and Outreach Programs
College of Marine Science
University of South Florida
St. Petersburg, Florida

Mary Kay Hemenway, Ph.D.
Research Associate and Senior Lecturer
Department of Astronomy
University of Texas
Austin, Texas

Kathleen Kaska
Life and Earth Science Teacher
Oak Harbor Middle School
Oak Harbor, Washington

John Krupczak, Jr., Ph.D.
Associate Professor & Engineering Program Director
Department of Physics and Engineering
Hope College
Holland, Michigan

William G. Lamb, Ph.D.
Winningstad Chair in the Physical Sciences
Oregon Episcopal School
Portland, Oregon

Karen J. Meech, Ph.D.
Associate Astronomer
Institute for Astronomy
University of Hawaii
Honolulu, Hawaii

Robert J. Sager
Chair and Professor of Earth Sciences
Pierce College
Lakewood, Washington

Lee Summerlin, Ph.D.
Professor of Chemistry
University of Alabama
Birmingham, Alabama

Mark F. Taylor, Ph.D.
Associate Professor of Biology
Biology Department
Baylor University
Waco, Texas

Florida Teacher Consultants

Susan Biehler
Science Teacher
Kernan Middle School
Jacksonville, Florida

Joe Dexter
2004 District Teacher of the Year
Science Teacher
Florida State University School
Tallahassee, Florida

Trisha Elliot
Science Teacher
Chain of Lakes Middle School
Orlando, Florida

Russ Harris
Science Teacher
Addie R. Lewis Middle School
Valparaiso, Florida

Victor Hatfield
Science Department Chair
Union Park Middle School
Orlando, Florida

Denise Hulette
Science Teacher
Conway Middle School
Orlando, Florida

Janet Keskinen
Science Teacher
Green Cove Springs Middle School
Green Cove Springs, Florida

M. R. Penny Kisiah
Science Teacher and Department Chair
Fairview Middle School
Tallahassee, Florida

Rebecca Larsen
Science Teacher
Fernandina Beach Middle School
Fernandina Beach, Florida

Anne Malloch
Science Teacher
Morgan Fitzgerald Middle School
Largo, Florida

Lynne McDaniel
Science Teacher
Stewart Middle Magnet School
Tampa, Florida

Magdalena F. Molledo
Science Department Chair
DeLaura Middle School
Satellite Beach, Florida

Barbara Rapoza
President, Florida Association of Science Teachers
New River Middle School
Fort Lauderdale, Florida

Cary B. Rosillo
Science Teacher
Independence Middle School
Jupiter, Florida

Acknowledgments
continued on page 813

ISBN 0-03-036377-2

2 3 4 5 6 7 048 09 08 07 06

Contents in Brief

Contents

Contents **v**

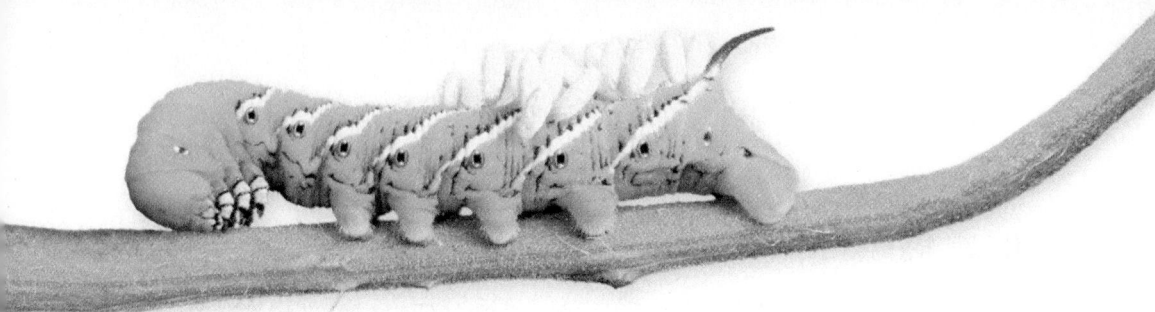

Florida Benchmarks

D.1.3.4 AA, D.2.3.2, G.1.3.4 AA,
G.1.3.5, G.2.3.4 AA

D.1.3.4 AA, G.1.3.4 AA

G.1.3.3 CS, G.2.3.2 CS

D.1.3.3 CS, G.2.3.2 CS

D.1.3.3 CS, D.1.3.4 AA, G.2.3.2 CS

xiii

Chapter Labs

The more labs, the better!

Take a minute to browse the variety of exciting **labs** in this textbook. Labs appear within the chapters and in a special LabBook in the back of the textbook. All labs are designed to help you experience science firsthand. But please don't forget to be safe. Read the Safety First! section before starting any of the labs.

Labs

LabBook Labs

Not all laboratory investigations have to be long and involved. The **Quick Labs** found throughout the chapters of this textbook require only a small amount of time and limited equipment. But just because they are quick, don't skimp on safety.

Quick Labs

Pre-Reading Activities

Start your engines with an activity!

Get motivated to learn by doing the two activities at the beginning of each chapter. The **Pre-Reading Activity** helps you organize information as you read the chapter. The **Start-Up Activity** helps you gain scientific understanding of the topic

Start-Up Activities

Activities

Benchmark Activities

Activities

> ## Make sure you really get it!
> Mastering the benchmarks of the Florida Sunshine State Standards takes practice! The **Benchmark Activity** found in each chapter will help you understand the content of a particular benchmark through hands-on experience.

Internet Activities

Get caught in the Web!

Go to **go.hrw.com** for **Internet Activities** related to each chapter. To find the Internet Activity for a particular chapter, just type in the keyword listed above.

School to Home

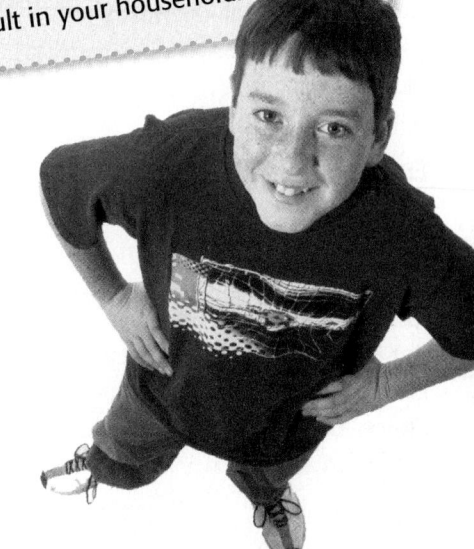

Science brings you closer together!

Bring science into your home by doing **School-to-Home Activities** with a family member or another adult in your household.

Math Practice

Science and math go hand in hand.

The **Math Focus** and **Math Practice** items show you many ways that math applies directly to science and vice versa.

Math Focus

Connection to...

One subject leads to another.

You may not realize it at first, but different subjects are related to each other in many ways. Each **Connection** explores a topic from the viewpoint of another discipline. In this way, all of the subjects you learn about in school merge to improve your understanding of the world around you.

Science In Action

How to Use Your Textbook

Your Roadmap for Success with Holt Science and Technology

Get Organized

Do the **Pre-Reading Activity** at the beginning of each chapter to create a **FoldNote** or a **Graphic Organizer,** which are helpful note-taking and study aids.

Read for Meaning

Start your reading with a warm-up. The **Reading Warm-Up** at the beginning of every section provides you with the section's **Objectives.** The Objectives tell you what you'll need to learn. The red benchmark codes indicate which Objectives meet the Florida Sunshine State Standards for science.

The Reading Warm-Up also lists **Terms to Learn** for each section. The blue icons indicate which terms will appear on the FCAT. Each term is highlighted in the text and is defined at point of use and in the margin.

A **Reading Strategy** provides tips to help you organize and remember the information covered in the section.

STUDY TIP Each **Section Review** includes a **Summary.** You can use this summary to preview or review a section.

SECTION 2

Ecological Succession

Imagine that you have a time machine that can take you back to the summer of 1988 in Yellowstone National Park. There, you would likely see fire all around you, because during that summer, fires raged throughout the park area.

By the end of that summer, large areas of the park were burned to the ground. When the fires were put out, a layer of gray ash blanketed the forest floor. Most of the trees were dead, although many of them were still standing.

READING WARM-UP

Objectives
- Explain how the process of succession results in the cycling of matter. G.1.3.4 AA
- Describe ways in which plants and animals reshape the landscape during succession. D.1.3.4 AA
- Contrast primary and secondary succession.
- Explain how mature communities develop.

Terms to Learn
succession
biodiversity *FCAT VOCAB*

READING STRATEGY

Reading Organizer As you read this section, make a table comparing primary succession and secondary succession.

Regrowth of a Forest

The following spring, the appearance of the "dead" forest began to change. **Figure 1** shows the changes after just one year. Some of the dead trees fell over, and small, green plants grew in large numbers. Within 10 years, scientists reported that many trees were growing and the forest community was coming back. A gradual development of a community over time, such as the regrowth of the burned areas of Yellowstone National Park, is called **succession.** Succession takes place in all communities, not just those affected by disturbances such as fire. Succession is important because it allows matter and nutrients to be recycled within a community.

Benchmark Check How is succession beneficial to a community? G.1.3.4 AA

succession the replacement of one type of community by another at a single location over a period of time

G.1.3.4 AA (partial) knows that the interactions of organisms with each other and with the nonliving parts of their environments result in the flow of energy and the cycling of matter throughout the system.

D.1.3.4 AA knows the ways in which plants and animals reshape the landscape (e.g., bacteria, fungi, worms, rodents, and other organisms add organic matter to the soil, increasing soil fertility, encouraging plant growth, and strengthening resistance to erosion).

Figure 1 *Huge areas of Yellowstone National Park were burned in 1988 (left). By the spring of 1989, regrowth was evident in the burned parts of the park (right).*

342 Chapter 13 Cycles in Nature

↗ Be Resourceful—Use the Web

SciLinks boxes in your textbook take you to resources that you can use for science projects, reports, and research papers. Go to **scilinks.org** and type in the **SciLinks code** to find information on a topic.

Visit go.hrw.com
Check out the **Current Science®** magazine articles and other materials that go with your textbook at **go.hrw.com.** Click on the textbook icon and the table of contents to see all of the resources for each chapter.

Primary Succession

Sometimes, a small community starts to grow in an area where organisms had not previously lived. There is no soil in such an area. And usually, there is nothing but bare rock. Over a very long time, a series of organisms live and die on the rock. As the organisms live and die, the rock is slowly transformed into soil. This process is called *primary succession*, as shown in **Figure 2.** The first organisms to live in an area are called *pioneer species.*

Land Recovery Investigate the process of succession around Mount St. Helens. Go to **go.hrw.com,** and type in the keyword **HL5CYCW.**

Figure 2 An Example of Primary Succession

❶ A slowly retreating glacier exposes bare rock on which there are no living organisms, and primary succession begins.

❷ Most primary succession begins with lichens. Acids from the lichens begin breaking the rocks into small particles. These particles mix with the remains of dead lichens to start forming soil. Lichens are an example of a pioneer species.

❸ Years la... soil for... time, m... Next, o... insects,... die, the... and ad...

Mature Communities and Biodiversity

In the early stages of succession, only a few species grow in an area. These species grow quickly and make many seeds that scatter easily. But all species are vulnerable to disease, disturbances, and competition. As a community matures, it may be dominated by well-adapted, slow-growing *climax species.*

As succession proceeds, more species may become established. The variety of species that are present in an area is referred to as **biodiversity.** A forest that has a high degree of biodiversity is less likely to be destroyed by an invasion of insects. Most plant-damaging insects prefer to attack only one species of plants. The presence of a variety of plants will lessen the impact and spread of invading insects. Not all mature communities are forests. A mature community is simply a community in which organisms are well adapted to living together in the community over time. For example, the plants of the Sonoran Desert, shown in **Figure 4,** are well adapted to the desert's conditions.

Benchmark Check How can an invasion of insects change the landscape of a community? D.1.3.4 AA

Figure 4 *This area of the Sonoran Desert in Arizona is a mature community.*

biodiversity the number and variety of organisms in a given area during a specific period of time
FCAT VOCAB

SECTION Review

Summary

- Succession results in the cycling of matter and nutrients. G.1.3.4 AA
- Organisms can reshape the landscape during succession. D.1.3.4 AA
- Primary succession occurs in an area where no soil is present. Secondary succession occurs in an area where soil is present.
- Mature communities develop slowly as organisms that are well adapted survive.

Using Key Terms
1. Write an original definition for *succession.*

Understanding Key Ideas
2. Describe how lichens can change the landscape of a community. D.1.3.4 AA
3. What is a mature community?
4. Contrast primary and secondary succession.

Critical Thinking
5. **Analyzing Ideas** Explain why soil formation is always the first stage of primary succession. Does soil formation ever stop? Explain your answer.
6. **Making Inferences** How are matter and nutrients cycled during succession? How can succession make a community's soil more fertile? G.1.3.4 AA

FCAT Preparation
7. Wind blew horseweed seeds into an abandoned cropland. How will the seeds change the cropland? D.1.3.4 AA
   A. No change will occur.
   B. Horseweeds will grow and will replace other weeds.
   C. Insects will destroy the cropland.
   D. Conifers will begin to grow.

SciLINKS.
Developed and maintained by the National Science Teachers Association
For a variety of links related to this chapter, go to www.scilinks.org
Topic: Succession
SciLinks code: HSM1475

345

Get Involved

The best way to learn science is to do science. Each chapter has a wide variety of hands-on activities and labs that will help you experience science up close and personal. Activities include **Start-up Activities, School-to-Home Activities,** and **Benchmark Activities.** Labs include **Quick Labs, Chapter Labs,** and additional labs located in the **LabBook** at the back of the book.

Prepare for Exams

It is never too early to start preparing for success. **Reading Checks, Benchmark Checks, Section Reviews,** and **Chapter Reviews** will help you prepare for exams. The **Standardized Test Preparation** located after each Chapter Review will help you practice for the FCAT.

STUDY TIP To make sure you know the material before an exam, take the time to review the Objectives, Terms to Learn, and Summary in each section.

Use the FCAT Study Guide

Your **FCAT Study Guide** contains a variety of resources designed to help you be successful when you take the FCAT. These resources include the **FCAT Glossary, FCAT Science Reference Sheet, Periodic Table,** and **Annually Assessed Benchmark Focus.**

Visit Holt Online Learning

If your teacher gives you a special password to log onto the **Holt Online Learning** site, you'll find your complete textbook on the Web. In addition, you'll find some great learning tools and practice quizzes. You'll be able to see how well you know the material from your textbook.

SAFETY FIRST!

Exploring, inventing, and investigating are essential to the study of science. However, these activities can also be dangerous. To make sure that your experiments and explorations are safe, you must be aware of a variety of safety guidelines. You have probably heard of the saying, "It is better to be safe than sorry." This is particularly true in a science classroom where experiments and explorations are being performed. Being uninformed and careless can result in serious injuries. Don't take chances with your own safety or with anyone else's.

The following pages describe important guidelines for staying safe in the science classroom. Your teacher may also have safety guidelines and tips that are specific to your classroom and laboratory. Take the time to be safe.

Safety Rules!

Start Out Right

Always get your teacher's permission before attempting any laboratory exploration. Read the procedures carefully, and pay particular attention to safety information and caution statements. If you are unsure about what a safety symbol means, look it up or ask your teacher. You cannot be too careful when it comes to safety. If an accident does occur, inform your teacher immediately regardless of how minor you think the accident is.

Safety Symbols

All of the experiments and investigations in this book and their related worksheets include important safety symbols to alert you to particular safety concerns. Become familiar with these symbols so that when you see them, you will know what they mean and what to do. It is important that you read this entire safety section to learn about specific dangers in the laboratory.

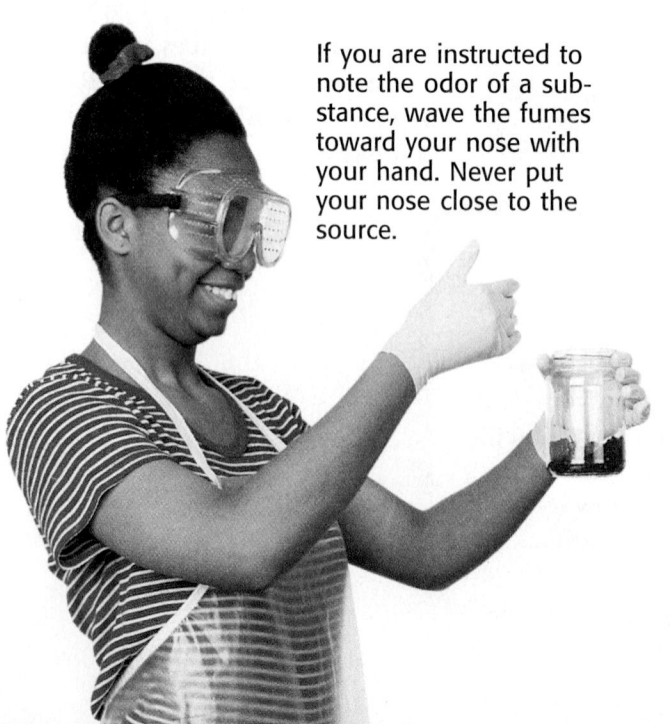

If you are instructed to note the odor of a substance, wave the fumes toward your nose with your hand. Never put your nose close to the source.

Eye protection

Clothing protection

Hand safety

Heating safety

Electric safety

Chemical safety

Animal safety

Sharp object

Plant safety

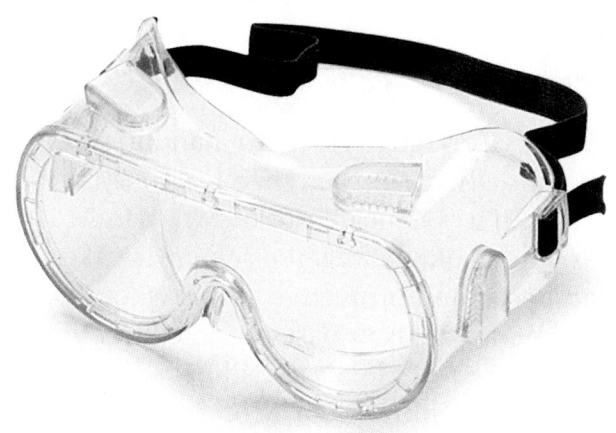

Eye Safety

Wear safety goggles when working around chemicals, acids, bases, or any type of flame or heating device. Wear safety goggles any time there is even the slightest chance that harm could come to your eyes. If any substance gets into your eyes, notify your teacher immediately and flush your eyes with running water for at least 15 minutes. Treat any unknown chemical as if it were a dangerous chemical. Never look directly into the sun. Doing so could cause permanent blindness.

Avoid wearing contact lenses in a laboratory situation. Even if you are wearing safety goggles, chemicals can get between the contact lenses and your eyes. If your doctor requires that you wear contact lenses instead of glasses, wear eye-cup safety goggles in the lab.

Safety Equipment

Know the locations of the nearest fire alarms and any other safety equipment, such as fire blankets and eyewash fountains, as identified by your teacher, and know the procedures for using the equipment.

Neatness

Keep your work area free of all unnecessary books and papers. Tie back long hair, and secure loose sleeves or other loose articles of clothing, such as ties and bows. Remove dangling jewelry. Don't wear open-toed shoes or sandals in the laboratory. Never eat, drink, or apply cosmetics in a laboratory setting. Food, drink, and cosmetics can easily become contaminated with dangerous materials.

Certain hair products (such as aerosol hair spray) are flammable and should not be worn while working near an open flame. Avoid wearing hair spray or hair gel on lab days.

Sharp/Pointed Objects

Use knives and other sharp instruments with extreme care. Never cut objects while holding them in your hands. Place objects on a suitable work surface for cutting.

Be extra careful when using any glassware. When adding a heavy object to a graduated cylinder, tilt the cylinder so that the object slides slowly to the bottom.

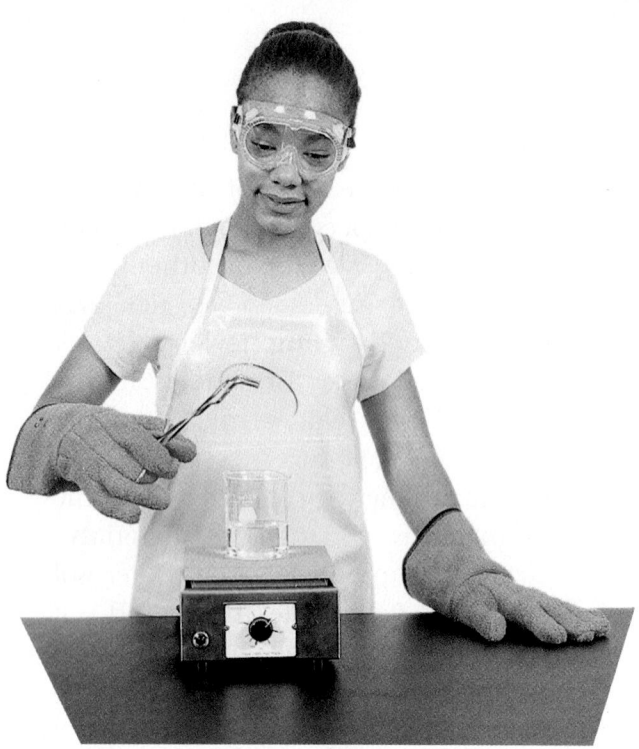

Heat

Wear safety goggles when using a heating device or a flame. Whenever possible, use an electric hot plate as a heat source instead of using an open flame. When heating materials in a test tube, always angle the test tube away from yourself and others. To avoid burns, wear heat-resistant gloves whenever instructed to do so.

Electricity

Be careful with electrical cords. When using a microscope with a lamp, do not place the cord where it could trip someone. Do not let cords hang over a table edge in a way that could cause equipment to fall if the cord is accidentally pulled. Do not use equipment with damaged cords. Be sure that your hands are dry and that the electrical equipment is in the "off" position before plugging it in. Turn off and unplug electrical equipment when you are finished.

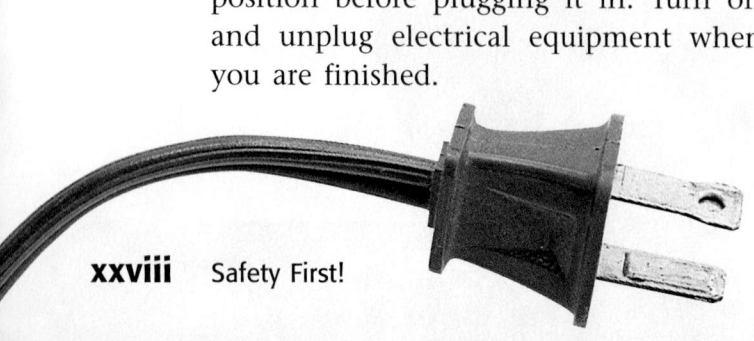

Chemicals

Wear safety goggles when handling any potentially dangerous chemicals, acids, or bases. If a chemical is unknown, handle it as you would a dangerous chemical. Wear an apron and protective gloves when you work with acids or bases or whenever you are told to do so. If a spill gets on your skin or clothing, rinse it off immediately with water for at least 5 minutes while calling to your teacher.

Never mix chemicals unless your teacher tells you to do so. Never taste, touch, or smell chemicals unless you are specifically directed to do so. Before working with a flammable liquid or gas, check for the presence of any source of flame, spark, or heat.

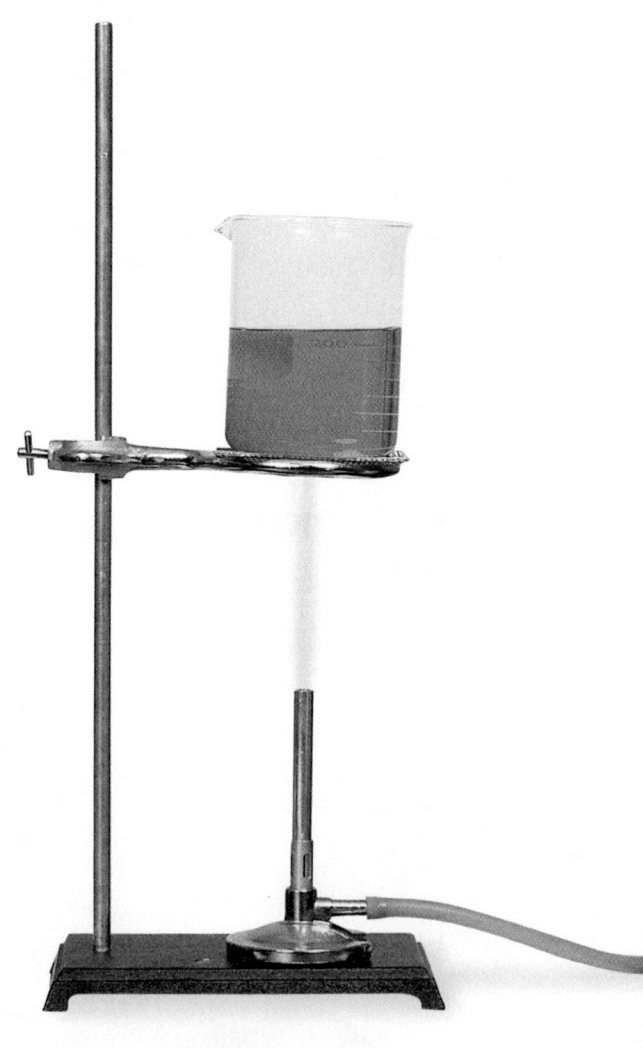

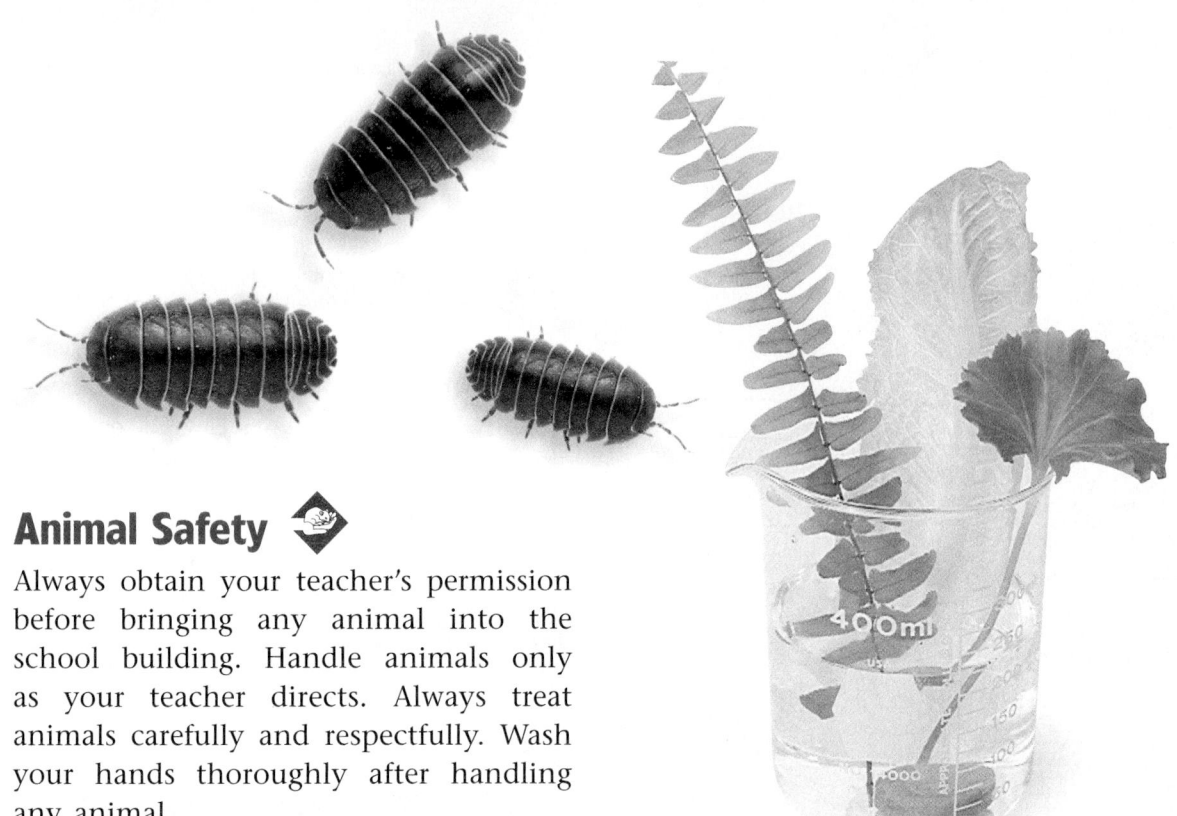

Animal Safety

Always obtain your teacher's permission before bringing any animal into the school building. Handle animals only as your teacher directs. Always treat animals carefully and respectfully. Wash your hands thoroughly after handling any animal.

Plant Safety

Do not eat any part of a plant or plant seed used in the laboratory. Wash your hands thoroughly after handling any part of a plant. When in nature, do not pick any wild plants unless your teacher instructs you to do so.

Glassware

Examine all glassware before use. Be sure that glassware is clean and free of chips and cracks. Report damaged glassware to your teacher. Glass containers used for heating should be made of heat-resistant glass.

UNIT 1

TIMELINE

Science in Our World

People have always searched for answers about the world around them. Science is one way that people learn about the world. Through careful study, scientists have been able to find answers to many of their questions. In this unit, you will learn about the tools that scientists use and will learn to ask your own questions about the world around you.

Many people and events have helped us better understand the world around us. This timeline identifies a few of the people and events that have helped shape science.

Around 2700 BCE

Si Ling-Chi, empress of China, observes silkworms in her garden and develops a process to cultivate them and make silk fabric.

1931

The first electron microscope is developed.

1934

Dorothy Crowfoot Hodgkin uses X-ray techniques to determine the protein structure of insulin.

1970

Floppy disks for computer data storage are introduced.

1983

Dian Fossey writes *Gorillas in the Mist*, a book about her research on mountain gorillas in Africa and her efforts to save them from poachers.

Around 1000

Ibn al Haytham, an Arab mathematician and physicist, discovers that vision is caused by the reflection of light from objects into the eye.

1684

Improvements to microscopes allow the first observation of red blood cells.

1914

His studies on agriculture and soil conservation lead George Washington Carver to perform research on peanuts.

1944

Oswald T. Avery demonstrates that DNA is the material that carries genetic properties in living organisms.

1946

ENIAC, the first entirely electronic computer, is built. It weighs 30 tons.

1967

Dr. Christiaan Barnard performs the first successful human heart transplant.

1984

A process known as *DNA fingerprinting* is developed by Alec Jeffreys.

1998

In China, scientists discover a fossil of a dinosaur that had feathers.

2001

A team of scientists led by Philippa Uwins announces that tiny nanobes that are 20 to 150 nanometers wide have been found in Australia. Scientists debate whether these particles are living things.

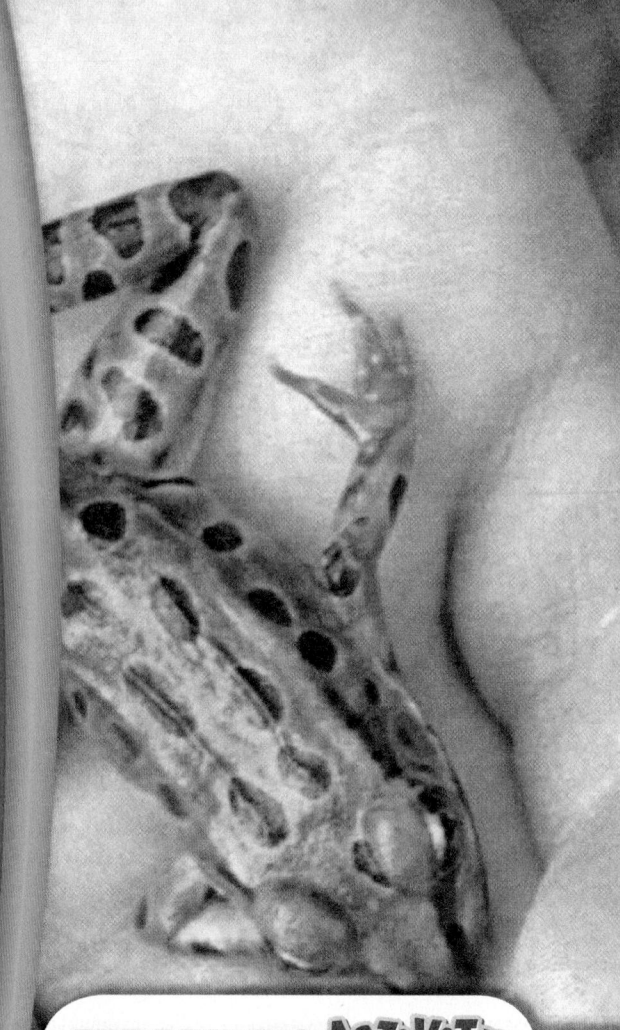

1

The Nature of Science

The Big Idea Scientists use scientific processes to study the patterns of natural events and to solve problems.

About the PHOTO

What happened to the legs of these frogs? Science can help answer this question. Deformed frogs, such as the ones in this photo, have been found in the northern United States and southern Canada. Scientists and students like you have been using science to find out how frogs may develop deformities.

PRE-READING ACTIVITY

FOLDNOTES **Layered Book** Before you read the chapter, create the FoldNote entitled "Layered Book" described in the **Study Skills** section of the Appendix. Label the tabs of the layered book with "Science and scientists," "Scientific methods and inquiry," "Tools and measurement," and "Safety in science." As you read the chapter, write information you learn about each category under the appropriate tab.

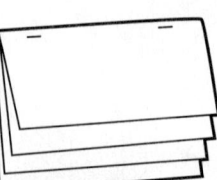

START-UP ACTIVITY

A Little Bit of Science

In this activity, you'll find out that you can learn about the unknown without having to see it.

Procedure

1. Your teacher will give you a **coffee can** to which a **sock** has been attached. Do not look into the can.

2. Reach through the opening in the sock. You will feel **several objects** inside the can.

3. Record observations you make about the objects by feeling them, shaking the can, and so on.

4. What do you think is in the can? List your guesses, and state some reasons for your guesses.

5. Pour the contents of the can onto your desk. Compare your list with what was in the can.

Analysis

1. Did you guess the contents of the can correctly? What might have caused you to guess incorrectly?

2. What observations did you make about each of the objects while they were in the can? Which of your senses did you use?

Science and Scientists

You are enjoying a picnic on a summer day. Crumbs from your sandwich fall to the ground, and ants carry the crumbs away. You wonder, Why do ants show up at picnics?

Congratulations! You just took one of the first steps that a scientist takes. How did you do it? You observed the world around you. Then, you asked a question about your observations. And asking a question is part of what science is all about.

READING WARM-UP

Objectives

● Describe similarities and differences between science disciplines. **H.1.3.3 CS**

● Describe three methods of investigation.

● Identify some benefits of science.

● Describe how scientific knowledge may be modified. **H.1.3.1 AA**

● Describe five jobs that use or contribute to science. **H.1.3.6**

Terms to Learn

science

READING STRATEGY

Prediction Guide Before reading this section, write the title of each heading in this section. Next, under each heading, write what you think you will learn.

Asking a Question

The world around you is full of amazing things. Single-celled algae float unseen in ponds. The newspaper reports that Mars may have had water in the past. And 40-ton whales glide through the oceans. Things such as these may lead you to ask a question. And that is the beginning of science. **Science** is the knowledge gained by observing the natural world.

Science disciplines differ in topic, techniques, and outcomes, but they share a common purpose, philosophy, and enterprise. For example, some biologists use microscopes to study microorganisms, and some astronomers use telescopes to study distant galaxies. But all scientists carefully gather information to answer questions about the natural world.

Benchmark Check How do science disciplines differ from each other, and how are they similar? **H.1.3.3 CS**

In Your Neighborhood and the World Beyond

Look around your home, school, and neighborhood. Often, you take things that you use or see every day for granted. But one day you might look at something in a new way. That's when a question hits you! The student in **Figure 1** didn't have to look very far to realize that he had some questions to ask.

You don't have to stop at questions about things in your neighborhood. Ask questions about atoms and galaxies, pandas and bamboo, or earthquakes. You can even ask questions about places other than those on Earth. Look outward to the moon, the sun, the planets in our solar system, and the universe! There are enough questions to keep scientists busy for a long time.

Figure 1 *Part of science is asking questions about the world around you.*

Why do leaves change color in the fall?

Why did the dinosaurs die out?

How do birds know where to go when they migrate?

Investigation: The Search for Answers

After you ask a question, it's time to look for an answer. How do you start your investigation? Several methods may be used.

Research

You can find answers to some of your questions by doing research, as **Figure 2** shows. You can ask someone who knows a lot about the subject of your question. You can find information in textbooks, encyclopedias, and magazines. You can search on the Internet. You might read a report of an experiment that someone did. But be sure to think about the sources of your information. Use information only from reliable sources.

Observation

You can also find answers to questions by making observations. Be careful in making observations. Sometimes, what people expect to observe affects what they do observe. For example, most plants need light to grow. Does that mean that all plants need bright light? Do some plants prefer shade? Some people might "observe" that bright light is the only answer. To test an observation, you may have to do an experiment.

Experimentation

You might answer the question about light and shade by doing a simple experiment, such as the one shown in **Figure 3.** Your research and your observations can help you plan your experiment. What should you do if your experiment needs something that is hard to get? For example, what do you do if you want to know whether a certain plant grows in space? Don't give up! Try to find results from someone else's experiment.

science the knowledge obtained by observing natural events and conditions in order to discover facts and formulate laws or principles that can be verified or tested

Figure 2 *A library is a good place to begin your search for answers.*

H.I.3.3 CS knows that science disciplines differ from one another in topic, techniques, and outcomes, but that they share a common purpose, philosophy, and enterprise.

Figure 3 *This student is doing an experiment to find out whether this type of plant grows better in shade or in direct sunlight.*

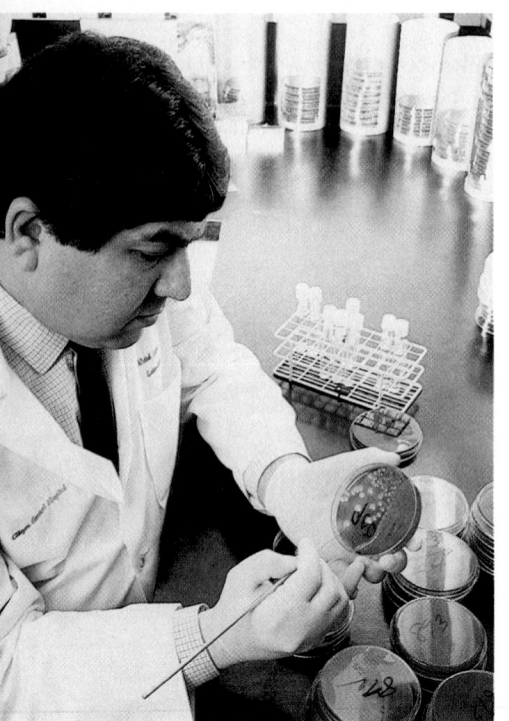

Figure 4 *Abdul Lakhani studies AIDS to find a cure for the disease.*

Why Ask Questions?

Although scientists cannot answer every question immediately, they do find some interesting answers. Do any of the answers really matter? Absolutely! As you study science, you will see how science affects you and society around you.

Fighting Diseases

Polio is a disease that can cause paralysis by affecting the brain and nerves. Do you know anyone who has had polio? You probably don't. But in 1952, polio infected 58,000 Americans. Fortunately, vaccines developed in 1955 and 1956 have eliminated polio in the United States. In fact, the virus that causes polio has been wiped out in most of the world.

Today, scientists are searching for cures for diseases such as mad cow disease, tuberculosis, and acquired immune deficiency syndrome (AIDS). The scientist in **Figure 4** is learning more about AIDS, which kills millions of people every year.

Saving Resources

Science also helps answer the question, How can we make resources last longer? Recycling is one answer. Think about the last time that you recycled an aluminum can. By recycling that can, you saved more than just the aluminum, as **Figure 5** shows. Using science, people have developed more-efficient methods and better equipment for recycling aluminum, paper, steel, glass, and even some plastics. In this way, science helps make resources last longer.

Figure 5 **Resources Saved Through Recycling**

 Compared with producing aluminum from its ore, recycling 1 metric ton (1.1 tons) of aluminum does the following things.

 produces 95% less air pollution

 saves 4 metric tons (4.4 tons) of ore

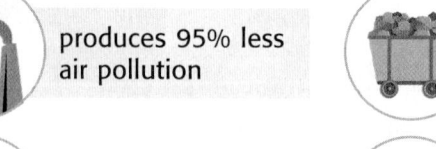 produces 4 metric tons (4.4 tons) fewer chemical products

 uses 14,000 kWh less energy

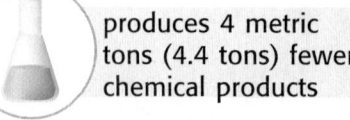 produces 97% less water pollution

Answering Society's Questions

Sometimes, society faces questions that do not seem to have immediate answers. One example is the question of how to reduce air pollution. Car exhaust is one cause of air pollution, but the millions of people who depend on their cars cannot just stop driving. As air pollution has become more important to people, different technologies have been developed to reduce it. Scientists have developed cleaner-burning gasoline and ways to clean up exhaust before it leaves the car. Engineers and scientists have also developed hybrid cars that run on electrical energy as well as gasoline. Others are working on hydrogen-fueled cars that may be available in the future.

Advancing Scientific Knowledge

Asking questions also leads to changes or modifications in scientific knowledge. As scientists do research to answer questions, they may find new information that challenges prevailing scientific theories. New information and new questions may lead to the development of new theories. These new theories cause scientists to look at old observations in a new way. In this way, scientific knowledge is continuously modified.

Benchmark Check How does asking questions lead to modifications in scientific knowledge? **H.1.3.1 AA**

H.1.3.1 AA knows that scientific knowledge is subject to modification as new information challenges prevailing theories and as a new theory leads to looking at old observations in a new way.

H.1.3.3 CS knows that science disciplines differ from one another in topic, techniques, and outcomes, but that they share a common purpose, philosophy, and enterprise.

H.1.3.6 recognizes the scientific contributions that are made by individuals of diverse backgrounds, interests, talents, and motivations.

Scientists All Around You

Scientists work in many different places. Any person who asks questions and looks for answers could be called a scientist! Scientific contributions are made by people of diverse backgrounds, interests, talents, and motivations. Keep reading to learn about a few people who use science in their jobs.

Zoologists

A *zoologist* (zoh AHL uh jist) is a person who studies the lives of animals. Dale Miquelle, shown in **Figure 6,** is part of a team of Russian and American zoologists studying the Siberian tiger. The tigers have almost become extinct after being hunted and losing their homes. By learning about the tigers' living space and food needs, zoologists hope to make a plan that will help the tigers survive better in the wild.

Figure 6 *To learn how much land a Siberian tiger covers, Dale Miquelle tracks a tiger that is wearing a radio-transmitting collar.*

Figure 7 *This geochemist may work outdoors when collecting rock samples from the field. Then, he may work indoors as he analyzes the samples in his laboratory.*

Figure 8 *A mechanic can help keep a car's engine running smoothly.*

H.1.3.3 CS knows that science disciplines differ from one another in topic, techniques, and outcomes, but that they share a common purpose, philosophy, and enterprise.

H.1.3.6 recognizes the scientific contributions that are made by individuals of diverse backgrounds, interests, talents, and motivations.

Geochemists

Some scientists work outdoors most of the time. Other scientists spend much of their time in the laboratory. A geochemist (JEE oh KEM ist), such as the one shown in **Figure 7,** may work in both places. A *geochemist* is a person who specializes in the chemistry of rocks, minerals, and soil.

Geochemists determine the economic value of these materials. They also try to find out what the environment was like when these materials formed and what has happened to the materials since they first formed.

Mechanics

Do you have a machine that needs repairs? Call a mechanic, such as Gene Webb, shown in **Figure 8.** Mechanics work on everything from cars to the space shuttle. Mechanics use science to solve problems. Mechanics must find answers to questions about why a machine is not working. Then, they must find a way to make it work. Mechanics also think of ways to improve the machine by making it work faster or more efficiently.

Oceanographers

An *oceanographer* studies the ocean. Some oceanographers study waves and ocean currents. Others study plants and animals that live in the ocean. Still others study the ocean floor, including how it forms.

While studying the ocean floor, oceanographers discovered black smokers. *Black smokers* are cracks where hot water (around 300°C) from beneath Earth's surface comes up. These vents in the ocean floor are home to some strange animals, including red-tipped tube worms and blind white crabs.

Volcanologists

If black smokers are not hot enough for you, perhaps you would like to become a volcanologist (VAHL kuh NAHL uh jist). A *volcanologist* studies one of Earth's most interesting features—volcanoes. The volcanologist shown in **Figure 9** is photographing lava flowing from Mount Etna, a volcano in Italy. Mount Etna's lava may reach temperatures of 1,050°C. By learning more about volcanoes, volcanologists hope to get better at predicting when a volcano will erupt. Being able to predict eruptions would help save lives.

Benchmark Check What do oceanographers and volcanologists do? **H.1.3.6**

Figure 9 *Volcanologists gain a better understanding of the inside of Earth by studying the makeup of lava.*

SECTION Review

Summary

- Science is a process of gathering knowledge about the natural world.

- Science disciplines differ in several ways but share a common purpose, philosophy, and enterprise. **H.1.3.3 CS**

- A scientific investigation may include research, observations, and experimentation.

- Science can help save lives, save resources, and protect the environment.

- Asking questions leads to modifications in scientific knowledge as new information is gathered and as new theories are developed. **H.1.3.1 AA**

- Scientific contributions are made by individuals of diverse backgrounds, interests, and talents. **H.1.3.6**

Understanding Key Ideas

1. Describe five careers that use or contribute to science. **H.1.3.6**

2. List and describe three methods of investigation.

3. What are three benefits of science?

4. Describe two reasons why scientific knowledge may be modified. **H.1.3.1 AA**

Math Skills

5. Students in a science class collected 50 frogs from a pond. They found that 15 of the frogs had deformities. What percentage of the frogs had deformities?

Critical Thinking

6. **Making Comparisons** Compare two science disciplines, such as zoology and volcanology. List three ways that the disciplines differ and three ways that they are similar. **H.1.3.3 CS**

7. **Identifying Relationships** Make a list of three things that you consider to be problems in society. Give an example of how new technology might solve these problems.

FCAT Preparation

8. According to current atomic theory, an atom is made of a dense, positively charged nucleus that is surrounded by a cloud of negatively charged electrons. Predict what would happen if a scientist found evidence that challenged current atomic theory. **H.1.3.1 AA**

   A. The evidence would be considered to be wrong.

   B. Atomic theory may be modified.

   C. Atomic theory would be considered to be wrong.

   D. The evidence would be ignored.

Scientific Methods and Inquiry

Imagine that your class is on a field trip to a wildlife refuge. You discover several deformed frogs. You wonder what could be causing the frogs' deformities.

A group of students from Le Sueur, Minnesota, actually made this discovery! By making observations and asking questions about the observations, the students used scientific methods.

What Are Scientific Methods?

When scientists observe the natural world, they use the inquiry process. The *inquiry process* is the process of asking questions and using experiments and observations to find the answers. **Scientific methods** are the ways in which scientists follow steps in the inquiry process. The steps used for all investigations are the same. But the order in which the steps are followed may vary, as shown in **Figure 1.** Scientists may use all of the steps or just some of the steps during an investigation. They may even repeat some of the steps. The order depends on what works best to answer the question. By studying the ways that scientists have used scientific methods to make discoveries, you can learn about the inquiry process and its effects.

Benchmark Check What can you learn if you study scientific methods? **H.1.3.2 CS**

READING WARM-UP

Objectives

● Describe scientific methods and what can be learned by studying scientific methods. **H.1.3.2 CS**

◑ Describe why accurate record keeping, openness, and replication of results are important. **H.1.3.4 AA**

● Explain why changing variables affects controlled experiments. **H.1.3.5 AA**

● Explain what happens when similar investigations give different results. **H.1.3.7**

Terms to Learn

scientific methods
hypothesis
controlled experiment
variable **FCAT VOCAB**

READING STRATEGY

Reading Organizer As you read this section, make a flowchart of the possible steps in scientific methods.

scientific methods a series of steps followed to solve problems

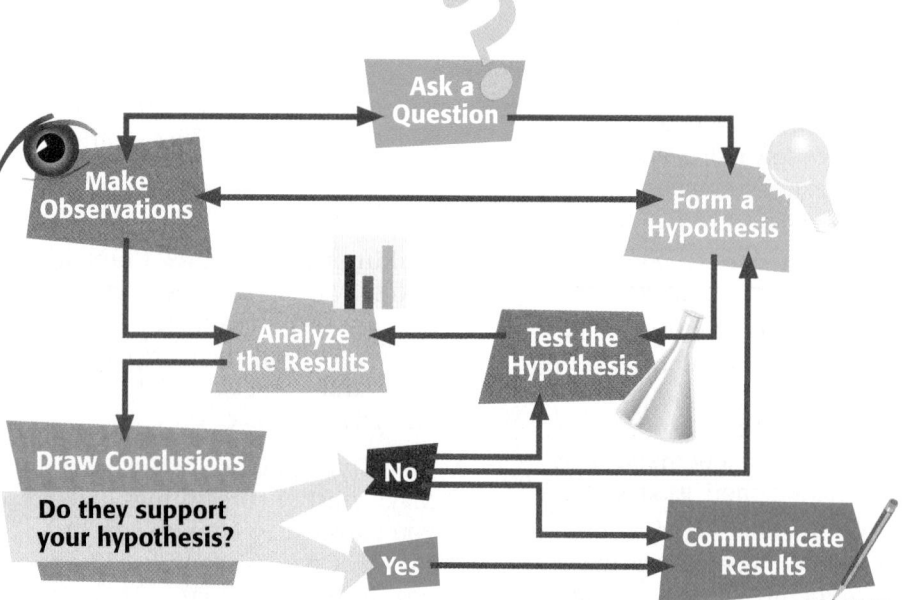

Figure 1 *Scientific methods often include the same steps, but the steps may not be used in the same order every time.*

Ask a Question

Have you ever observed something out of the ordinary or difficult to explain? Such an observation usually raises questions. For example, about the deformed frogs you might ask, "Could something in the water be causing the frog deformities?" Looking for answers may include making more observations.

Make Observations

After the students in Minnesota realized that something was wrong with the frogs, they decided to make additional, careful observations, as shown in **Figure 2.** They counted the number of deformed frogs and the number of normal frogs they caught. They photographed the frogs, took measurements, and wrote a thorough description of each frog. They also conducted many tests on the pond water. The students carefully recorded their data and observations.

Figure 2 *Making careful observations is often the first step in an investigation.*

Accurate Observations

Any information gathered through your senses is an observation. Observations can take many forms. They may be measurements of length, time, or loudness. They may describe the shape or behavior of an organism. The range of observations that can be made is endless. Despite what observations reveal, they are useful only if they are accurately made and recorded. Accurate record keeping is essential to maintaining an investigator's credibility with other scientists and society. Scientists use many tools and methods to make and record observations. Examples of these tools are shown in **Figure 3.**

H.1.3.2 CS knows that the study of the events that led scientists to discoveries can provide information about the inquiry process and its effects.

H.1.3.4 AA knows that accurate record keeping, openness, and replication are essential to maintaining an investigator's credibility with other scientists and society.

Benchmark Check Why is accurate record keeping important?
H.1.3.4 AA

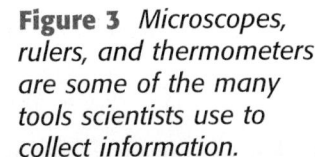

Figure 3 *Microscopes, rulers, and thermometers are some of the many tools scientists use to collect information.*

Careers in Life Science

Investigate an interesting career! Go to **go.hrw.com**, and type in the keyword **HL5LIVW.**

hypothesis an idea or explanation that is based on prior scientific research or observations and that can be tested

Form a Hypothesis

After asking questions and making observations, scientists may form a hypothesis. A **hypothesis** (hie PAHTH uh sis) is a possible explanation or answer to a question. A good hypothesis is based on observation and can be tested. When scientists form hypotheses, they think logically and creatively and consider what they already know.

To be useful, a hypothesis must be testable. A hypothesis is testable if an experiment can be designed to test it. But if a hypothesis is not testable, it is not always wrong. An untestable hypothesis is simply one that cannot be supported or disproved. Sometimes, it may be impossible to gather enough observations to test a hypothesis.

Scientists may form different hypotheses for the same problem. In the case of the Minnesota frogs, scientists formed the hypotheses shown in **Figure 4.** Were any of these explanations correct? To find out, scientists had to test each hypothesis.

Reading Check What makes a hypothesis testable?

Figure 4
More than one hypothesis can be made for a single question.

Hypothesis 1:
The deformities were caused by one or more chemical pollutants in the water.

Hypothesis 2:
The deformities were caused by attacks from parasites or other frogs.

Hypothesis 3:
The deformities were caused by an increase in exposure to ultraviolet light from the sun.

Predictions

Before scientists can test a hypothesis, they must first make predictions. A *prediction* is a statement of cause and effect that can be used to set up a test for a hypothesis. Predictions are usually stated in an if-then format, as shown in **Figure 5.**

Figure 5 lists the predictions made for the hypotheses shown in **Figure 4.** More than one prediction may be made for each hypothesis. After predictions are made, scientists can conduct experiments to see which predictions, if any, prove to be true and support the hypotheses.

Figure 5 *More than one prediction may be made for a single hypothesis.*

Hypothesis 1:
Prediction: If a substance in the pond water is causing the deformities, then the water from ponds that have deformed frogs will be different from the water from ponds in which no abnormal frogs have been found.
Prediction: If a substance in the pond water is causing the deformities, then some tadpoles will develop deformities when they are raised in pond water collected from ponds that have deformed frogs.

Hypothesis 2:
Prediction: If a parasite is causing the deformities, then this parasite will be found more often in frogs that have deformities.

Hypothesis 3:
Prediction: If an increase in exposure to ultraviolet light is causing the deformities, then some frog eggs exposed to ultraviolet light in a laboratory will develop into deformed frogs.

CONNECTION TO Language Arts

WRITING SKILL **"Leading doctors say . . ."** Suppose that you and a friend see an ad for a cold remedy on TV. According to the ad, "Leading doctors recommend this product for their patients." Then, a famous actor comes on and says that he or she uses the product, too. Write a dialogue of the debate you might have with your friend about whether these claims are believable.

Test the Hypothesis

After scientists make a prediction, they test the hypothesis. Scientists try to design experiments that will clearly show whether a particular factor caused an observed outcome. In an experiment, a *factor* is anything that can influence the experiment's outcome.

Under Control

Scientists studying the frogs in Minnesota found many factors that affect the development of frogs, as shown in **Figure 6.** But it was hard to tell which factor could be causing the deformities. To sort factors out, scientists perform controlled experiments. A **controlled experiment** tests only one factor at a time and consists of a control group and one or more experimental groups. All but one of the factors for the control group and the experimental groups are the same. The one factor that differs is called the **variable.** Because only the variable differs between the control group and the experimental groups, any differences observed in the outcome of the experiment are probably caused by the variable. Changing one or more variables usually alters the outcome of an investigation.

Benchmark Check What may happen if you change one or more variables in an investigation? **H.1.3.5 AA**

Designing an Experiment

Every factor should be considered when designing an experiment. Look at the prediction for Hypothesis 3: *If an increase in exposure to ultraviolet light is causing the deformities, then some frog eggs exposed to ultraviolet light in a laboratory will develop into deformed frogs.* An experiment to test this hypothesis is summarized in **Table 1.** In this case, the variable is the length of time the eggs are exposed to ultraviolet (UV) light. All other factors are the same in the control and experimental groups.

Figure 6 *Many factors affect this tadpole in the wild. These factors include chemicals, light, temperature, and parasites.*

controlled experiment an experiment that tests only one factor at a time by using a comparison of a control group with an experimental group

variable a factor that changes in an experiment in order to test a hypothesis *FCAT VOCAB*

Table 1 Experiment to Test Effect of UV Light on Frogs				
	Control factors			**Variable**
Group	**Kind of frog**	**Number of eggs**	**Temperature of water**	**UV light exposure**
#1 (control)	leopard frog	100	25°C	0 days
#2 (experimental)	leopard frog	100	25°C	15 days
#3 (experimental)	leopard frog	100	25°C	24 days

H.1.3.5 AA knows that a change in one or more variables may alter the outcome of an investigation.

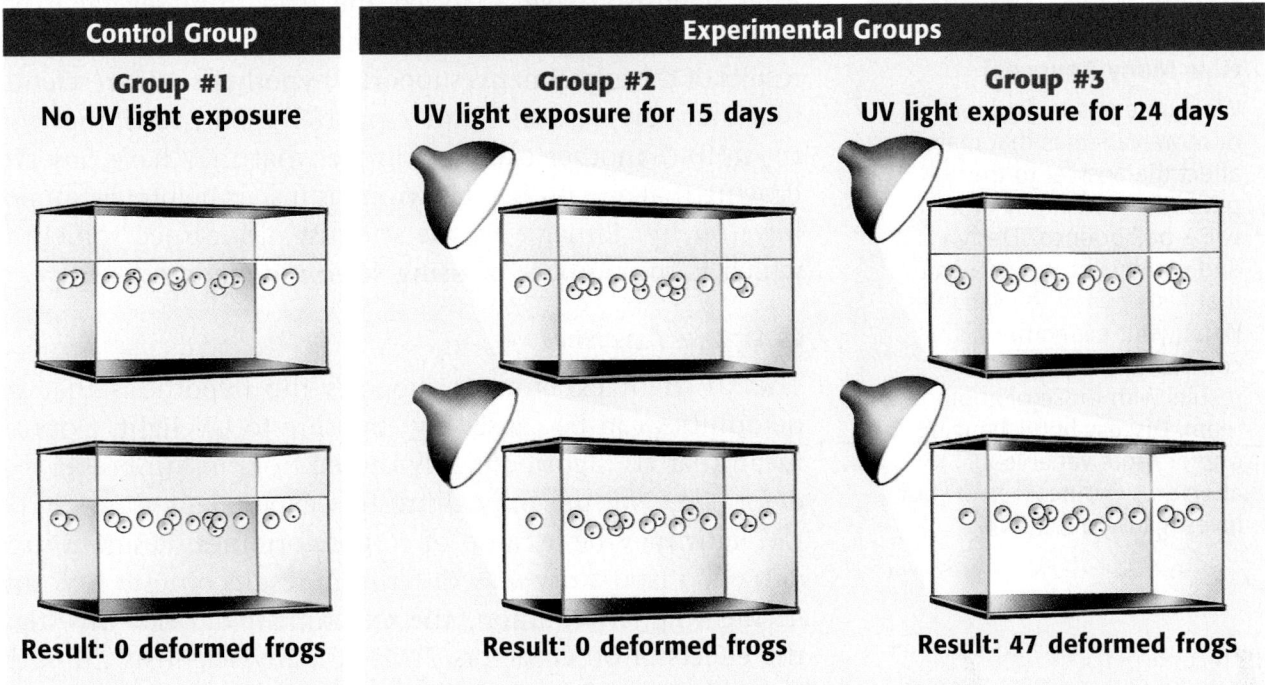

Figure 7 UV Light Experiment

Control Group	Experimental Groups	
Group #1 **No UV light exposure**	**Group #2** **UV light exposure for 15 days**	**Group #3** **UV light exposure for 24 days**
Result: 0 deformed frogs	Result: 0 deformed frogs	Result: 47 deformed frogs

Collecting Data

Figure 7 shows the experimental setup to test Hypothesis 3. As **Table 1** shows, there are 100 eggs in each group. Scientists always try to test many individuals. They want to be sure that differences between control and experimental groups are caused by the variable and not by differences between individuals. The larger the groups are, the more likely it is that the variable is responsible for any changes.

Scientists often replicate experiments. *Replicate* means to repeat. If an experiment gives the same results each time, scientists are more certain about the variable's effect. Scientists keep accurate records and share their data so that other scientists can repeat the experiment and verify the results.

Benchmark Check Why are openness and replication of experiments important? **H.1.3.4 AA**

Analyze the Results

After scientists finish their tests, they must organize their data and analyze the results. Scientists may organize data in a table or a graph. The data collected from the UV light experiment are shown in the bar graph in **Figure 8.** Analyzing the results helps scientists explain and focus on the effect of the variable. For example, the graph shows that the length of UV exposure has an effect on the development of frog deformities.

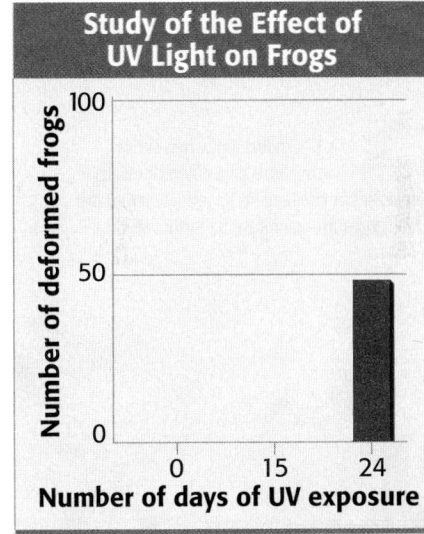

Study of the Effect of UV Light on Frogs

Figure 8 This graph shows that 24 days of UV exposure had an effect on frog deformities, whereas less exposure had no effect.

H.1.3.4 AA knows that accurate record keeping, openness, and replication are essential to maintaining an investigator's credibility with other scientists and society.

40064000656114

Draw Conclusions

After scientists have analyzed the data from several experiments, they can draw conclusions. They decide whether the results of the experiments support a hypothesis. When scientists find that a hypothesis is not supported by the tests, they must try to find another explanation for what they have observed. Proving that a hypothesis is wrong is just as helpful as supporting it. Why? Either way, the scientist has learned something, which is the purpose of using scientific methods.

Is It the Answer?

The UV light experiment supports the hypothesis that frog deformities can be caused by exposure to UV light. Does this mean that UV light definitely caused frogs in Minnesota to be deformed? No, the only thing this experiment shows is that UV light may be a cause of frog deformities. Results of tests done in a laboratory may differ from results of tests performed in the wild. In addition, the experiment did not investigate the effects of other factors. In fact, many scientists think that more than one factor could be causing the deformities.

Sometimes, similar investigations or experiments give different results. For example, another research team may have had results that did not support the UV light hypothesis. In such a case, the scientific challenge is to find out by further study if the differences are important. Often, making that decision requires more experiments, more evidence, and sharing data.

Benchmark Check What happens when similar investigations give different results? **H.1.3.7**

Communicate Results

Scientists form a global community. After scientists complete their investigations, they communicate their results to other scientists. The student in **Figure 9** is explaining the results of a science project.

Scientists regularly share their results for several reasons. First, other scientists may then repeat the experiments to see if they get the same results. Second, the information can be considered by other scientists with similar interests. The scientists can then compare hypotheses and form consistent explanations. New data may strengthen existing hypotheses or show that the hypotheses need to be altered. There are many paths from observations and questions to communicating results.

Benchmark Activity

How Many Bounces?

Work in teams to list four or more variables that may affect the answer to the question, How many times will a ball bounce? Design and conduct an experiment that tests two of the variables. When your experiment is complete, compare your results with those of another team. Discuss how changing one or more variables affected the outcomes of your investigations. H.1.3.5 AA

H.1.3.7 knows that when similar investigations give different results, the scientific challenge is to verify whether the differences are significant by further study.

Figure 9 *This student scientist is communicating the results of his investigation at a science fair.*

SECTION Review

Summary

- Scientific methods are the ways in which scientists follow steps to solve problems.
- Studying scientific methods can provide information about the inquiry process and its effects. **H.1.3.2 CS**
- A controlled experiment tests only one variable at a time and consists of control and experimental groups. Changing variables affect the outcome of the experiment. **H.1.3.5 AA**
- After testing a hypothesis, scientists analyze the results and draw conclusions about whether the hypothesis is supported.
- Accurate record keeping, openness, and replication of results are essential to maintaining an investigator's credibility. **H.1.3.4 AA**
- When similar investigations give different results, the scientific challenge is to verify by further study whether the differences are significant. **H.1.3.7**

Using Key Terms

1. Use *hypothesis, controlled experiment,* and *variable* in the same sentence. **FCAT**

Understanding Key Ideas

2. The steps of scientific methods
   a. are exactly the same in every investigation.
   b. must be used in the same order every time.
   c. are not used in the same order every time.
   d. always end with a conclusion.

3. What is the relationship between variables and the outcome of an investigation? **H.1.3.5 AA**

4. What is the reason for studying scientific methods? **H.1.3.2 CS**

5. Under what conditions might a scientist decide to study a problem further? **H.1.3.7**

Critical Thinking

6. **Analyzing Methods** When scientists report their results, they often publish scientific papers that describe their experiment, list their data, and analyze their results. Why do you think that scientists publish such detailed reports? **H.1.3.4 AA**

7. **Analyzing Processes** Why are there many ways to follow the steps of scientific methods?

8. **Making Inferences** Why might two scientists working on the same problem draw different conclusions?

FCAT Preparation

9. After students in Minnesota found deformed frogs, scientists did experiments to determine what could be causing the deformities. What can you learn by reading about a scientific experiment that tested the link between UV light and frog deformities? **H.1.3.2 CS**
   A. how scientists set up controlled experiments
   B. how scientists catch deformed frogs
   C. whether UV light affects humans
   D. how deformed frogs survive in the wild

10. Two scientists claim to have bred an animal that is half dog and half cat. Predict what would happen if the scientists refuse to explain how the animal was produced or allow others to examine it. **H.1.3.4 AA**

SC LINKS®

NSTA
Developed and maintained by the
National Science Teachers Association

For a variety of links related to this chapter, go to www.scilinks.org

Topic: Scientific Methods; Deformed Frogs
SciLinks code: HSM1359; HSM0383

Tools and Measurement

Would you use a hammer to tighten a bolt on a bicycle? No, you wouldn't. You need the right tools to fix a bike.

Scientists use a variety of tools in their experiments. A *tool* is anything that helps you do a task.

Tools for Measuring

You might remember that one way to collect data is to take measurements. To get the best measurements, you need the proper tools. Stopwatches, metersticks, and balances are tools that you can use to make measurements. Thermometers, spring scales, and graduated cylinders are also helpful tools. Some of the uses of these tools are shown in **Figure 1.**

✓ **Reading Check** Name six tools used for taking measurements.

Tools for Analyzing

After you collect data, you need to analyze them. Perhaps you need to find the average of your data. Calculators are handy tools to help you do calculations quickly. Or you might show your data in a graph or a figure. A computer that has the correct software can help you make neat, colorful figures. Of course, even a pencil and graph paper are tools that you can use to graph your data.

Figure 1 **Measurement Tools**

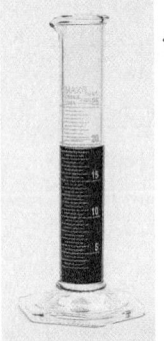

You can use a **graduated cylinder** to measure volume.

You can use a **thermometer** to measure temperature.

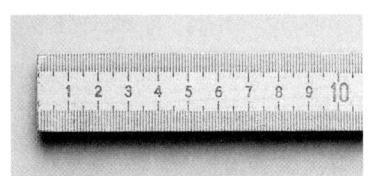

▲ You can use a **meterstick** to measure length.

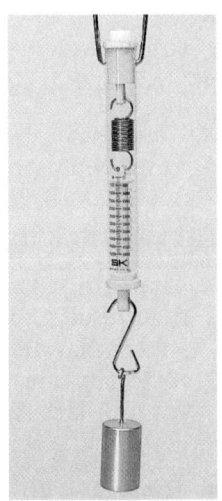

▲ You can use a **spring scale** to measure force.

You can use a **stopwatch** to measure time.

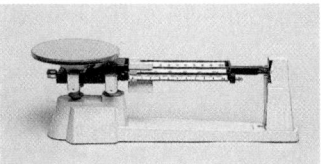

▲ You can use a **balance** to measure mass.

Units of Measurement

The ability to make accurate and reliable measurements is an important skill in science. Many systems of measurement are used throughout the world. At one time in England, the standard for an inch was three grains of barley placed end to end. Other modern standardized units were originally based on parts of the body, such as the foot. Such systems were not very reliable. Their units were based on objects that had different sizes.

The International System of Units

In the late 1700s, the French Academy of Sciences began to form a global measurement system now known as the *International System of Units*, or SI. Today, most scientists and almost all countries use this system. One advantage of using SI measurements is that doing so helps scientists share and compare their observations and results.

Another advantage of SI units is that all units are based on the number 10, which makes conversions from one unit to another easy. **Table 1** contains commonly used SI units for length, volume, mass, and temperature.

No Rulers Allowed

1. Measure the width of your desk, but don't use a ruler.
2. Select another object to use as your unit of measurement.
3. Compare your measurement with those of your classmates.
4. Explain why it is important to use standard units of measurement.

Table 1 Common SI Units and Conversions

Length		meter (m)	
		kilometer (km)	1 km = 1,000 m
		decimeter (dm)	1 dm = 0.1 m
		centimeter (cm)	1 cm = 0.01 m
		millimeter (mm)	1 mm = 0.001 m
		micrometer (μm)	1 μm = 0.000001 m
		nanometer (nm)	1 nm = 0.000000001 m
Volume		cubic meter (m^3)	
		cubic centimeter (cm^3)	1 cm^3 = 0.000001 m^3
		liter (L)	1 L = 1 dm^3 = 0.001 m^3
		milliliter (mL)	1 mL = 0.001 L = 1 cm^3
Mass		kilogram (kg)	
		gram (g)	1 g = 0.001 kg
		milligram (mg)	1 mg = 0.000001 kg
Temperature		kelvin (K)	0°C = 273 K
		Celsius (°C)	100°C = 373 K

Measurement

Scientists report measured quantities in a way that shows the precision of the measurement. To do so, they use significant figures. *Significant figures* are the digits in a measurement that are known with certainty. The Math Focus below will help you understand significant figures and will teach you how to use the correct number of digits. Now that you have a standardized system of units for measuring things, you can use the system to measure length, area, mass, volume, and temperature.

Length

How long is a lizard? Well, a **meter** (m) is the basic SI unit of length. However, a scientist, such as the one in **Figure 2,** would use centimeters (cm) to describe a small lizard's length. If you divide 1 m into 100 parts, each part equals 1 cm. So, 1 cm is one-hundredth of a meter. Even though 1 cm seems small, some things are even smaller. Scientists describe the length of very small objects in micrometers (μm) or nanometers (nm). To see these small objects, scientists use powerful microscopes.

Area

How much paper would you need to cover the top of your desk? To answer this question, you must find the area of the desk. **Area** is a measure of the size of the surface of an object. To calculate the area of a square or a rectangle, measure the length and width. Then, use the following equation:

$$area = length \times width$$

Units for area are square units, such as square meters (m^2), square centimeters (cm^2), and square kilometers (km^2).

Figure 2 *This scientist is using a metric ruler to measure a lizard's length. The unit chosen to describe an object, such as this lizard, depends on the size of the object being measured.*

meter the basic unit of length in the SI (symbol, m)

area a measure of the size of a surface or a region

Significant Figures Calculate the area of a carpet that is 3.145 m long (four significant figures) and 5.75 m (three significant figures) wide. (Hint: In multiplication and division problems, the answer cannot have more significant figures than the measurement that has the smallest number of significant figures does.)

Step 1: Write the equation for area.

$$area = length \times width$$

Step 2: Replace *length* and *width* with the measurements given, and solve.

$$area = 3.125 \text{ m} \times 5.75 \text{ m} = 18.08375 \text{ m}^2$$

Step 3: Round the answer to get the correct number of significant figures. Here, the correct number of significant figures is three, because the value with the smallest number of significant figures has three significant figures.

$$area = 18.1 \text{ m}^2$$

Now It's Your Turn

1. Use a calculator to perform the following calculation: 125.5 km × 8.225 km. Write the answer with the correct number of significant figures.

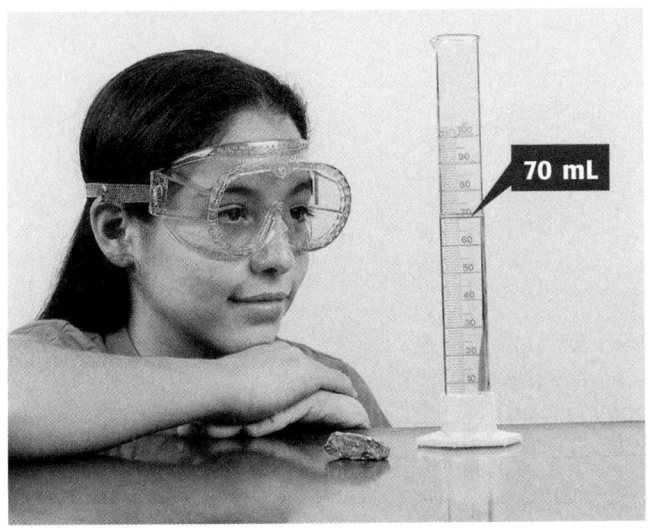 

Figure 3 *Adding the rock changes the water level from 70 mL to 80 mL. So, the rock displaces 10 mL of water. Because 1 mL = 1 cm³, the volume of the rock is 10 cm³.*

Mass

How large a rock can a rushing stream move? The answer depends on the energy of the stream and the mass of the rock. **Mass** is a measure of the amount of matter in an object. The kilogram (kg) is the basic unit for mass in the SI. Kilograms are used to describe the mass of a large rock. Grams are used to measure the mass of smaller objects. One thousand grams equals 1 kg. For example, a small apple has a mass of about 100 g. Masses of very large objects are given in metric tons. A metric ton equals 1,000 kg.

✓ **Reading Check** What is the basic SI unit for mass?

Volume

Think about moving some magnets to a laboratory. How many magnets will fit into a box? The answer depends on the volume of the box and the volume of each magnet. **Volume** is a measure of the size of a body in three-dimensional space. In this case, you need the volumes of the box and of the magnets.

The volume of a large, solid object is given in cubic meters (m³). The volumes of smaller objects can be given in cubic centimeters (cm³) or cubic millimeters (mm³). The volume of a box can be calculated by multiplying the object's length, width, and height. The volume of an irregularly shaped object can be found by measuring the volume of liquid that the object displaces. **Figure 3** shows an example of this measurement.

The volume of a liquid is often given in liters (L). Liters are based on the meter. A cubic meter (1 m³) is equal to 1,000 L. So, 1,000 L will fit into a box measuring 1 m on each side. A milliliter (mL) will fit into a box measuring 1 cm on each side. So, 1 mL = 1 cm³. Graduated cylinders are used to measure the volume of liquids.

mass a measure of the amount of matter in an object
FCAT VOCAB

volume a measure of the size of a body or region in three-dimensional space

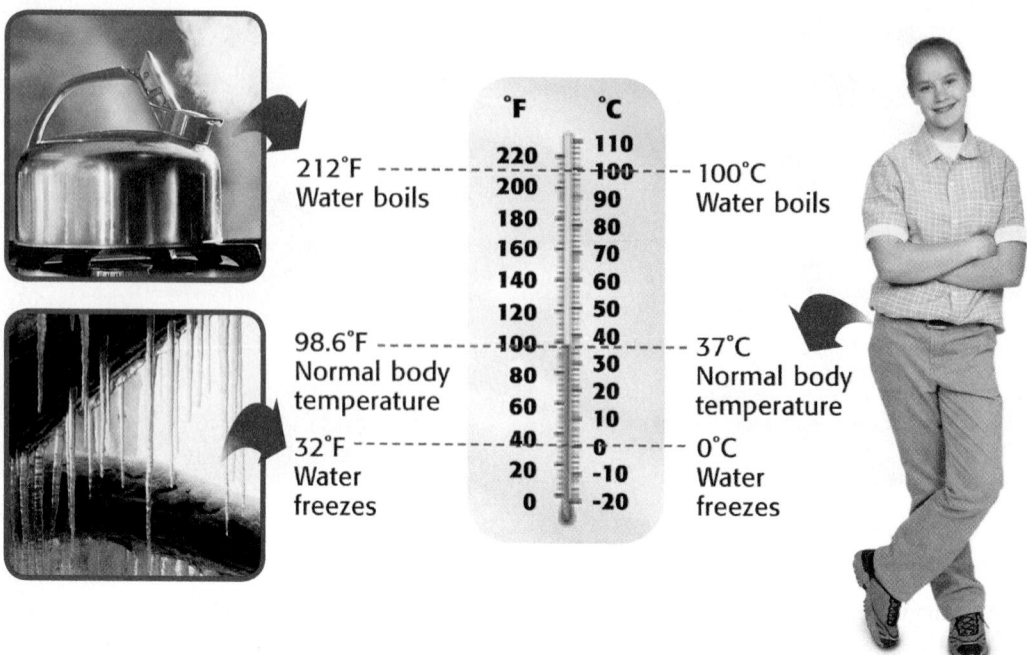

Figure 4 *This thermometer shows the relationship between degrees Fahrenheit and degrees Celsius.*

212°F
Water boils

98.6°F
Normal body
temperature

32°F
Water
freezes

°F
220
200
180
160
140
120
100
80
60
40
20
0

°C
110
100
90
80
70
60
50
40
30
20
10
0
-10
-20

100°C
Water boils

37°C
Normal body
temperature

0°C
Water
freezes

Temperature

temperature the measure of how hot (or cold) something is

density the ratio of the mass of a substance to the volume of the substance

How hot is melted iron? To answer this question, a scientist would measure the temperature of the liquid metal. **Temperature** is a measure of how hot or cold something is. You probably use degrees Fahrenheit (°F) to describe temperature. Scientists commonly use degrees Celsius (°C), although the kelvin (K) is the official SI base unit for temperature. You will use degrees Celsius in this book. The thermometer in **Figure 4** compares the Fahrenheit and Celsius scales.

Density

If you measure the mass and volume of an object, you have the measurements that you need to find the density of the object. **Density** is the amount of matter in a given volume. You cannot measure density directly. But after you have measured the mass and the volume, you can use the following equation to calculate density:

$$density = \frac{mass}{volume}$$

Density is the ratio of mass to volume, so units often used for density are grams per milliliter (g/mL) and grams per cubic centimeter (g/cm^3). Density may be difficult to understand. Think of a table-tennis ball and a golf ball. They have similar volumes. But a golf ball has more mass than a table-tennis ball does. So the golf ball has a greater density.

CONNECTION TO Social Studies

Archimedes Archimedes (287 BCE–212 BCE) was a Greek mathematician. He was probably the greatest mathematician and scientist that classical Greek civilization produced and is considered to be one of the greatest mathematicians of all time. Archimedes was very interested in putting his theoretical discoveries to practical use. Use the library or Internet to research Archimedes. Make a poster that illustrates one of his scientific or mathematical discoveries. **ACTIVITY**

Measurements and Living Things

When making measurements of living things, scientists must take special precautions. If research involves animals, the animals must be treated humanely. When research involves humans, science ethics require that potential subjects be fully informed about the risks and benefits of the research. People must know what they can gain by participating in the study and what problems might occur. The potential subjects should also have the right to refuse to participate. Science ethics also demand that scientists must not knowingly subject coworkers, students, or the community to health risks or property risks.

H.3.3.1 CS knows that science ethics demand that scientists must not knowingly subject coworkers, students, the neighborhood, or the community to health or property risks.

H.3.3.3 knows that in research involving human subjects, the ethics of science require that potential subjects be fully informed about the risks and benefits associated with the research and of their right to refuse to participate.

Benchmark Check What does science ethics require when dealing with human subjects? **H.3.3.1 CS, H.3.3.3**

SECTION Review

Summary

- Scientists use a variety of tools to measure and analyze the world around them.

- The International System of Units (SI) is a reliable and uniform system of measurement that is used by most scientists.

- The basic units of measurement in the SI are the meter (for length), the kilogram (for mass), and the Kelvin (for temperature).

- Science ethics demand that scientists must not knowingly subject others to risk. **H.3.3.1 CS**

- Potential human subjects must be informed of the risks and benefits of the research and have the right to refuse to participate. **H.3.3.3**

Understanding Key Ideas

1. SI units are
   a. based on standardized measurements of body parts.
   b. almost always based on the number 10.
   c. used to measure only length.
   d. used only in France.

2. List three tools that you can use to collect or analyze data.

3. Which SI unit would you use to measure the mass of a fly?

Math Skills

4. What is the area of a field that is 110 m long and 85 m wide?

5. What is the density of silver if a 6 cm³ piece has a mass of 63 g?

Critical Thinking

6. **Applying Concepts** Some people are thinking about sending humans to the planet Mars. Why is it important for scientists around the world to use SI units as they make these plans?

7. **Analyzing Ideas** Why do you think potential human subjects need to be fully informed of a research project? **H.3.3.3**

FCAT Preparation

8. A scientist accidentally spills a poisonous chemical in a lab in which many people are working. What should the scientist do first? **H.3.3.1 CS**
   A. alert other people in the lab
   B. leave the lab
   C. put on safety equipment
   D. call for an ambulance

9. What must researchers tell people who may participate in a drug study? **H.3.3.1 CS**
   F. the name of the drug
   G. possible side effects of the drug
   H. the number of people who will take the drug
   I. who makes the drug

SCILINKS®

NSTA
Developed and maintained by the
National Science Teachers Association

For a variety of links related to this chapter, go to www.scilinks.org

Topic: Tools of Life Science; SI Units
SciLinks code: HSM1535; HSM1390

Safety in Science

While walking by a construction site, you notice a sign on the fence: "Hard Hat Area." When you look through the fence, you can see that all of the construction workers are wearing heavy plastic helmets.

Construction workers wear hard hats to prevent injury if an accident happens. Similar to construction workers, you take precautions to be safe at home and in school. You also take special care when you learn science, as shown in **Figure 1.**

The Importance of Safety Rules

Safety is the state of being free of danger or injury. To be safe while doing science, you must learn some safety rules. Perhaps the most important safety rule is to follow the directions given by your teacher. Following directions will make your work easier, and you will get better results. And, you will be safer!

✓ *Reading Check* **What is safety?**

Preventing Accidents

Following rules may not seem like fun. But following rules is better than getting hurt! The most important reason for obeying safety rules is to prevent accidents. Your teacher will remind you of safety rules, but it's your job to follow them. Accidents are less likely to happen when safety rules are followed.

Preventing Injury

Unfortunately, accidents can happen even when all safety rules are obeyed. When an accident does happen, you or someone nearby could get hurt. Following safety rules can help you avoid or reduce injury. For example, wearing gloves will help protect your skin if you accidentally spill a chemical on your hands.

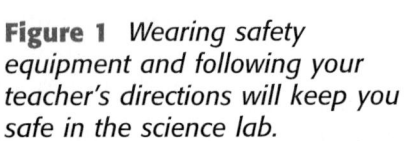

Figure 1 *Wearing safety equipment and following your teacher's directions will keep you safe in the science lab.*

Figure 2   Safety Symbols

◇ Eye protection

◇ Clothing protection

◇ Hand safety

◇ Heating safety

◇ Electrical safety

◇ Chemical safety

◇ Animal safety

◇ Sharp object

◇ Plant safety

Elements of Safety

There are many parts to safety. Recognizing safety symbols can alert you to potential dangers. Reading directions and being neat can prevent accidents. Safety equipment keeps you safe during experiments, and proper clean-up procedures keep your classroom safe after an experiment is over.

Safety Symbols

Most road signs have specific meanings. For example, a stop sign means that cars must stop moving. A one way sign means that cars must travel only in a certain direction. Signs and symbols that have specific meanings are also used in science. **Figure 2** shows the safety symbols that are used in this book. Learning the meaning of and obeying these symbols can help prevent injury or an accident.

In some experiments, such as the one shown in **Figure 3,** you must work with live animals. When you do an experiment with animals or insects, you will see the symbol for animal safety. This symbol tells you to be careful when handling animals. For example, never squeeze or frighten animals. Follow your teacher's directions on how to pick animals up and how to dispose of animal waste. You should handle only those animals provided by your teacher and should never bring wild animals into the classroom. And after working with animals, you should thoroughly wash your hands with soap and water.

Benchmark Check What does the symbol for animal safety tell you? **H.3.3.2**

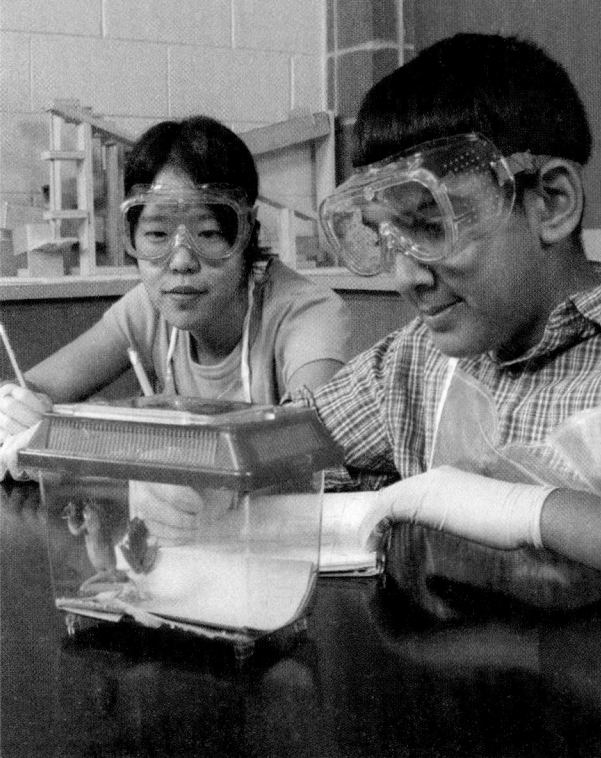

Figure 3 *Always wear protective gloves when handling animals during an experiment.*

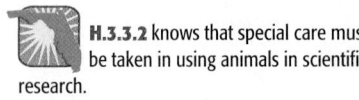
H.3.3.2 knows that special care must be taken in using animals in scientific research.

Reading and Following Directions

If you want to successfully bake a cake, you will probably use a recipe. The recipe tells you what ingredients to use and the proper procedure to follow. When scientists work in the laboratory, they also follow directions. Likewise, you must follow directions given by your teacher and the lab procedure when you work in the laboratory.

Read all of the instructions of every science experiment very carefully before starting it. Reading the directions before starting will help you get better results and will reduce the chance of having an accident. If you don't understand the instructions in a lab procedure, ask your teacher to explain the directions to you in a different way.

While doing an experiment, leave your book open to the page with the instructions. You will then be able to find the instructions quickly if you need to reread them.

Neatness Counts!

Before starting any science activity, clear your work area of books, backpacks, and any other unneeded objects. These objects can get in the way and may cause you to trip or spill your materials. Also, prepare data tables and gather necessary safety equipment, as shown in **Figure 4.**

Neatness also counts when you are doing your experiment. Arrange the lab materials on the desk or table so that you can find them easily. Clearly label all chemicals so that they won't be mixed up. And record your findings carefully in a notebook or data table so you and others can read them.

✓ **Reading Check** Why should you label chemicals in a lab?

Figure 4 *Proper preparation before an experiment will help keep you safe in the laboratory.*

28

Figure 5 *These students are wearing protective gloves when they work with chemicals. But they put on heat-resistant gloves before lifting the beakers off the hot plates.*

Using Proper Safety Equipment

Safety equipment can protect you from injury. Safety goggles, gloves, and aprons are some examples of lab safety equipment. The safety symbols shown next to laboratory instructions indicate what kind of safety equipment to use. For example, when you see the eye protection symbol, you must put on your safety goggles. Goggles should fit comfortably but snugly.

If you see the symbol for hand protection, you need to wear gloves. The kind of gloves that you need depends on the experiment that you are doing. If you are using chemicals or animals, wear protective gloves. But if you are handling warm objects, using a hot plate, or using an open flame, you must wear heat-resistant gloves. Both kinds of gloves can be seen in **Figure 5.**

Proper Clean-Up Procedures

After you finish a science experiment, clean up your work area. Place caps back on bottles, and return everything to its proper place. If you have used burners, be sure that the gas is turned off. Wash all of your glassware, and check for chips and cracks. If you find any damaged glassware, give the glassware to your teacher. If you have any extra or waste chemicals, follow your teacher's directions for disposal. Once your desk or table is clear, wipe it with a wet paper towel. Finally, wash your hands thoroughly with soap and water.

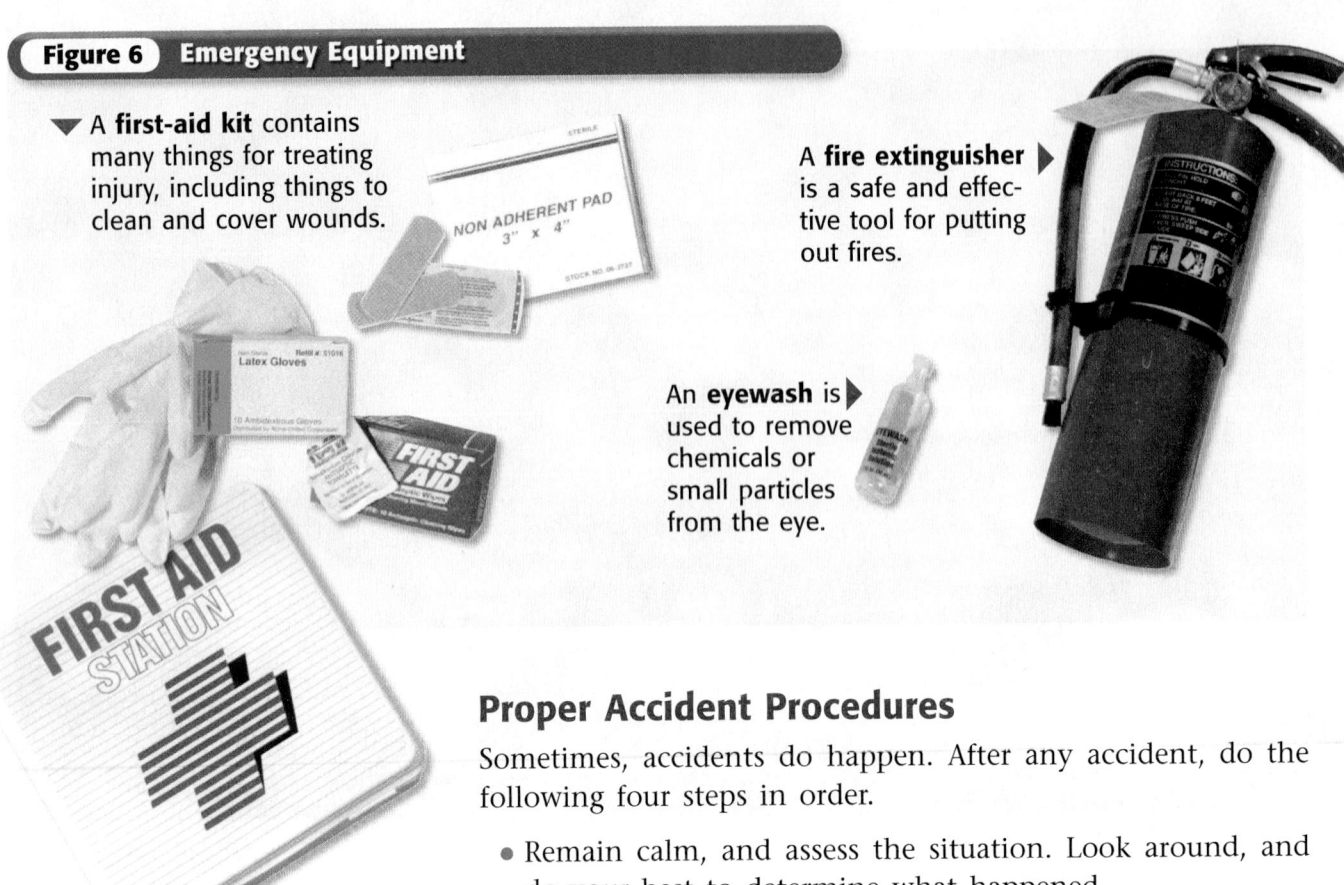

Figure 6 Emergency Equipment

▼ A **first-aid kit** contains many things for treating injury, including things to clean and cover wounds.

STERILE

NON ADHERENT PAD
3" x 4"

STOCK NO. 09-3737

Latex Gloves

FIRST AID

FIRST AID STATION

A **fire extinguisher** ▶ is a safe and effective tool for putting out fires.

An **eyewash** is ▶ used to remove chemicals or small particles from the eye.

first aid emergency medical care for someone who has been hurt or who is sick

Proper Accident Procedures

Sometimes, accidents do happen. After any accident, do the following four steps in order.

- Remain calm, and assess the situation. Look around, and do your best to determine what happened.
- Secure the area around the accident. Make sure that you are safe and that no one else is in danger.
- Tell your teacher, or call for help. Always tell your teacher if an accident happens, even if the accident is very minor.
- Assist your teacher with cleanup or giving aid. Do exactly what your teacher tells you to do.

After an accident, your teacher may need you to get emergency equipment. The emergency equipment shown in **Figure 6** is often found in labs. Study the emergency equipment in your classroom, and learn where it is kept. You may not have time to search for the equipment when an accident happens.

Table 1 Simple First-Aid Procedures

Injury	First-aid procedure
Minor heat-related burn	Hold affected area under cold, running water for at least 15 min.
Small cuts	Clean area, cover with a clean cloth or gauze pad, and apply pressure.
Chemicals on skin	Rinse area with running water for 15 min.
Chemical in eye	Rinse eye with running water or in an eyewash for 15 min, and then see a doctor.

Proper First-Aid Procedures

If an accident results in an injury, it is important that you know what to do. Fortunately, almost all laboratory injuries are minor and are easily treated. When treating an injury in the lab, your teacher will use first aid. **First aid** is temporary emergency medical care for someone who has been hurt.

You should not perform first aid unless you are properly trained. If first aid is not done properly, a victim can be more seriously injured. However, there are a few simple first-aid procedures that you can do without training. These procedures are listed in **Table 1.** Remember that first aid is only temporary care. An injured person should see a doctor for more treatment.

✓ Reading Check What is first aid?

SECTION Review

Summary

- Following safety rules helps prevent accidents and helps reduce injury when accidents happen.

- Five elements of safety are recognizing safety symbols, following directions, being neat, using proper safety equipment, and using proper clean-up procedures.

- Animals used in scientific research require special care. H.3.3.2

- When an accident happens, assess the situation, secure the area, tell your teacher, and help your teacher with cleanup or first aid.

- First aid is emergency medical care. Some first-aid procedures can be done without training.

Using Key Terms

1. Use *first aid* in a sentence.

Understanding Key Ideas

2. Why are safety rules important?
   a. Following safety rules can prevent accidents.
   b. Following safety rules can reduce injuries.
   c. Following safety rules can prevent injuries.
   d. All of the above

3. Describe five elements of safety.

4. What should you do if you spill a chemical on your skin?

5. List the four steps that you should take after an accident.

Critical Thinking

6. **Making Inferences** Suppose that you are doing research to determine how quickly a mouse can learn to run a maze. Explain how you would care for and handle the mouse. H.3.3.2

7. **Applying Concepts** Imagine that your lab partner dropped a glass beaker and cut his finger on the broken glass. Describe what you should do next.

FCAT Preparation

8. Rabies is a viral disease that is often transmitted through the bite of an animal that is infected by the rabies virus. People who get the rabies virus suffer from a variety of symptoms and will die if not treated in time. What precaution should scientists who are studying rabid bats take? **H.3.3.1 CS**
   A. The bats should not be allowed to fly.
   B. The bats should not be in contact with people.
   C. The bats should not be fed.
   D. The bats should be kept under bright lights.

For a variety of links related to this chapter, go to www.scilinks.org

Topic: Safety
SciLinks code: HSM1339

Skills Practice Lab

OBJECTIVES

Apply scientific methods to predict, measure, and observe the mixing of two unknown liquids.

MATERIALS

- beakers, 100 mL (2)
- cylinders, graduated, 50 mL (3)
- gloves, protective
- liquid A, 75 mL
- liquid B, 75 mL
- marker, glass-labeling
- thermometer, Celsius

SAFETY

H.1.3.1 AA knows that scientific knowledge is subject to modification as new information challenges prevailing theories and as a new theory leads to looking at old observations in a new way.

Does It All Add Up?

Your math teacher won't tell you this, but did you know that sometimes 2 + 2 does not appear to equal 4? In this experiment, you will use scientific methods to predict, measure, and observe the mixing of two unknown liquids. You will learn that a scientist does not set out to prove a hypothesis but to test it and that sometimes the results just don't seem to add up!

Make Observations

1. Put on your safety goggles, gloves, and lab apron. Examine the beakers of liquids A and B provided by your teacher. Write down as many observations as you can about each liquid. **Caution:** Do not taste, touch, or smell the liquids.

2. Pour exactly 25 mL of liquid A from the beaker into each of two 50 mL graduated cylinders. Combine these samples in the third graduated cylinder. Record the final volume. Pour the liquid back into the beaker of liquid A. Rinse the graduated cylinders. Repeat this step for liquid B.

Form a Hypothesis

3. Based on your observations and on prior experience, formulate a testable hypothesis that states what you expect the volume to be when you combine 25 mL of liquid A with 25 mL of liquid B.

4. Make a prediction based on your hypothesis. Use an if-then format. Explain the basis for your prediction.

Data Table				
	Contents of cylinder A	Contents of cylinder B	Mixing results: predictions	Mixing results: observations
Volume				
Appearance		DO NOT WRITE IN BOOK		
Temperature				

Test the Hypothesis

5 Make a data table like the one above.

6 Mark one graduated cylinder "A." Carefully pour exactly 25 mL of liquid A into this cylinder. In your data table, record the liquid's volume, appearance, and temperature.

7 Mark another graduated cylinder "B." Carefully pour exactly 25 mL of liquid B into this cylinder. Record the liquid's volume, appearance, and temperature in your data table.

8 Mark the empty third cylinder "A + B."

9 In the "Mixing results: predictions" column in your table, record the prediction you made earlier. Each classmate may have made a different prediction.

10 Carefully pour the contents of both cylinders into the third graduated cylinder.

11 Observe and record the total volume, appearance, and temperature in the "Mixing results: observations" column of your table.

Analyze the Results

1 **Analyzing Data** Discuss your predictions as a class. How many different predictions were there? Which predictions were supported by testing? Did any measurements surprise you?

Draw Conclusions

2 **Drawing Conclusions** Was your hypothesis supported or disproved? Either way, explain your thinking. Describe everything that you think you learned from this experiment.

3 **Evaluating Methods** Explain the value of incorrect predictions.

Chapter Review

USING KEY TERMS

1 Use *science* and *scientific methods* in the same sentence.

2 Write an original definition for *hypothesis*.

For each pair of terms, explain how the meanings of the terms differ.

3 *controlled experiment* and *variable* **FCAT** *VOCAB*

4 *area* and *volume*

UNDERSTANDING KEY IDEAS

Multiple Choice

5 Which of the following is NOT an SI unit?

  a. meter   **c.** liter

  b. foot   **d.** kilogram

6 The steps of scientific methods

  a. must all be used in every scientific investigation.

  b. are always used in the same order.

  c. often start with a question.

  d. always result in the development of a theory.

7 In a controlled experiment,

  a. a control group is compared with one or more experimental groups.

  b. there are at least two variables.

  c. all factors should be different.

  d. a variable is not needed.

8 A scientist repeated an experiment. The results from the second experiment were different from the results of the first experiment. What should the scientist do next? **H.1.3.4 AA** **FCAT**

  a. throw out the results of the first experiment

  b. throw out the results of the second experiment

  c. keep only the results that support the scientist's hypothesis

  d. check for differences between the two experiments

9 Which of the following tools is best for measuring 100 mL of water?

  a. 10 mL graduated cylinder

  b. 150 mL graduated cylinder

  c. 250 mL beaker

  d. 500 mL beaker

10 The directions for a lab include the safety icons shown below. These icons mean that

  a. you should be careful.

  b. you are going into the laboratory.

  c. you should wash your hands first.

  d. you should wear safety goggles, a lab apron, and gloves during the lab.

11 A pencil is 14 cm long. How many millimeters long is it?

  a. 1.4 mm

  b. 140 mm

  c. 1,400 mm

  d. 1,400,000 mm

Short Answer

12 Give an example of how a scientist might use computers and technology. **H.3.3.7**

13 Describe how you would clean up after doing an experiment in class.

14 List three kinds of safety equipment, and describe when they should be used.

CRITICAL THINKING

Extended Response

15 **Making Inferences** Investigations often begin with observation. What limits the observations that scientists can make? **H.1.3.2 CS**

16 **Predicting Consequences** Light is made of particles called *photons*. Physicists generally agree that photons do not have mass. Suppose that a group of scientists found a new particle in light that has mass. How do you think that the other scientists would react to this news? **H.1.3.1 AA** *FCAT*

17 **Expressing Opinions** Your friend says that all scientists are geeks who are good at math. Do you agree with your friend? Explain your opinion. **H.1.3.6**

18 **Analyzing Processes** A student is doing a class project to determine the effect of sunlight, water, and fertilizer on plant growth. Describe a possible controlled experiment that the student could do. What is the reason for changing only one variable at a time during this experiment? **H.1.3.5 AA** *FCAT*

Concept Mapping

19 Use the following terms to create a concept map: *observations, predictions, questions, controlled experiments, variable,* and *hypothesis.*

INTERPRETING GRAPHICS

The pictures below show how an egg can be measured by using a beaker and water. Use the pictures below to answer the questions that follow.

Before: 125 mL   After: 200 mL

20 What kind of measurement is being taken?

a. area

b. length

c. mass

d. volume

21 Which of the following is an accurate measurement of the egg in the picture?

a. 75 cm^3

b. 125 cm^3

c. 125 mL

d. 200 mL

For the following questions, write your answers on a separate sheet of paper.

1 Jana knows that there are many jobs that require the use of scientific knowledge and inquiry. She wants to work in the hotel and restaurant business in a position where she can use science research and the processes of inquiry. Which one of the following careers would be a good choice for Jana?

A. waitress
B. desk clerk
C. bookkeeper
D. bakery chef

2 Dr. Yan wants to test the effectiveness of a new drug he has developed for the treatment of multiple sclerosis. After identifying some people he would like to try his new drug on, he told the subjects what the drug is supposed to do to help their condition. He also told them that some of them would be in the control group and would not receive the drug. Finally, Dr. Yan told them about any risks or dangerous side effects they may experience from the drug. What else should Dr. Yan have told the subjects?

F. the names of the other subjects in the study
G. what year Dr. Yan received his medical degree
H. the detailed chemical composition of the drug
I. that they have the right to refuse to participate

3 If a drug company found from experimental research that cancer cells form and develop in a different way than described in current theories, how should the scientific community react? What should the scientific community do to evaluate the claims made by the drug company?

4   Susan is testing how seaweed fertilizer and fish emulsion fertilizer affect the growth of bean plants. She put three bean plants in a sunny window and waters one with plain water, one with water containing seaweed fertilizer, and one with water containing fish emulsion fertilizer. Every three days she checks the growth of the bean plants. She measures plant growth by comparing the plants to the length of her thumb. In her journal, Susan records the height of each plant in thumb lengths. What change could Susan have made to improve her experiment? Why would this change make the experiment easier for others to verify?

5 Kena concluded her experiment on the cause of deformities in frogs. She tested the hypothesis that deformities are caused by the length of time that frog eggs are exposed to UV light. Her experimental conditions are shown in the table below. The last column in the table shows the number of deformed frogs she found in each sample.

EXPERIMENT TO TEST EFFECT OF UV LIGHT ON FROGS

Group	Control Factors			Variable	Results
	Kind of Frog	Number of Eggs	Temperature of Water (°C)	UV Light Exposure (in Days)	Number of deformed frogs
1 (Control)	Leopard frog	100	25	0	0 frogs
2 (Experimental)	Leopard frog	100	25	15	12 frogs
3 (Experimental)	Leopard frog	100	25	24	47 frogs
4 (Experimental)	Leopard frog	100	25	36	?

Which of the following is the **most** likely number of deformed frogs Kena would find in Group #4?

A. 15 frogs
B. 30 frogs
C. 47 frogs
D. 60 frogs

6 The diagram below shows the steps of scientific methods.

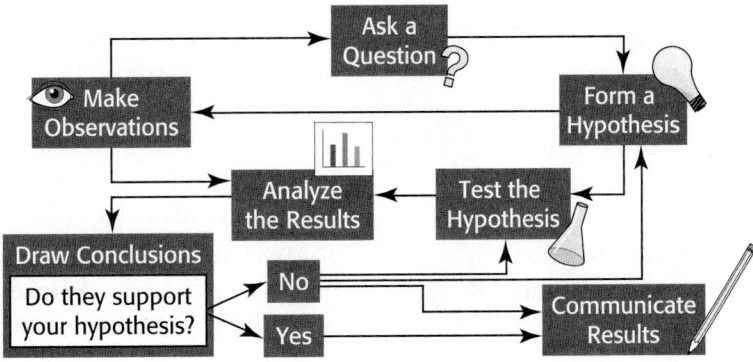

Which step relates to the inquiry process where scientists propose possible answers to questions?

F. Analyze the Results
G. Form a Hypothesis
H. Make Observations
I. Test the Hypothesis

STOP

Science in Action

Scientific Debate

Should We Stop All Forest Fires?

Since 1972, the policy of the National Park Service has been to manage the national parks as naturally as possible. Because fire is a natural event in forests, this policy includes allowing most fires caused by lightning to burn. The only lightning-caused fires that are put out are those that threaten lives, property, uniquely scenic areas, or endangered species. All human-caused fires are put out. However, this policy has caused some controversy. Some people want this policy followed in all public forests and even grasslands. Others think that all fires should be put out.

Science, Technology, and Society

Fighting Coral Bleaching

The coral reefs off the Florida coast are unique and important to the state. But the corals in the Florida reefs, like all corals in the world, are in danger of dying off because of a process called *coral bleaching*. Coral bleaching happens because of changes in the marine environment.

A technological system called the *Coral Reef Early Warning System* (CREWS) is being used to predict and better understand coral bleaching events. CREWS collects data, such as temperature, wind speed, and salinity, from monitoring stations in coral reef areas. The monitoring stations send data via satellite to a central location, where computers analyze the data. Scientists hope that the information learned from CREWS will help fight the problem of coral bleaching.

Social Studies ACTIVITY

WRITING SKILL Research a location where there is a debate about controlling forest fires. You might look into areas with national forests or parks. Write a newspaper article about the issue. Be sure to present all sides of the debate.

Language Arts ACTIVITY

WRITING SKILL Write a short story about a teen who sees evidence of coral bleaching while snorkeling. You may have to research coral reefs before writing your story.

Yvonne Cagle

Flight Surgeon and Astronaut Most doctors practice medicine with both feet on the ground. But Dr. Yvonne Cagle found a way to fly with her medical career. Cagle became a flight surgeon for the United States Air Force and an astronaut for the National Aeronautics and Space Administration (NASA).

Cagle's interest in both medicine and space flight began early. As a little girl, Cagle spent hours staring at X rays in her father's medical library. Those images sparked an early interest in science. Cagle also remembers watching Neil Armstrong walk on the moon when she was five years old. As she tried to imagine the view of Earth from space, Cagle decided she wanted to see it for herself.

Becoming an Air Force flight surgeon was a good first step toward becoming an astronaut. As a flight surgeon, Cagle learned about the special medical challenges humans face when they are launched high above the Earth. Being a flight surgeon had the extra benefits of working with some of the best pilots and getting to fly in the latest jets.

It wasn't long before Cagle worked as an occupational physician for NASA at the Johnson Space Center. Two years later, she was chosen to begin astronaut training. Cagle is looking forward to her first flight into space. Her first mission will likely take her to the *International Space Station,* where she can monitor astronaut health and perform scientific experiments.

Math ACTIVITY

In space flight, astronauts experience changes that affect their bodies in several ways. Because of gravity, a person who has a mass of 50 kg weighs 110 pounds on Earth. But on the moon, the same person weighs about 17% of his or her weight on Earth. How much does the same person weigh on the moon?

To learn more about these Science in Action topics, visit go.hrw.com and type in the keyword **HT6FSF7F.**

Current Science

Check out Current Science® articles related to this chapter by visiting go.hrw.com. Just type in the keyword HL5CS01.

2

Science and Technology

 **The Big Idea** Science, technology, and society are interwoven and interdependent.

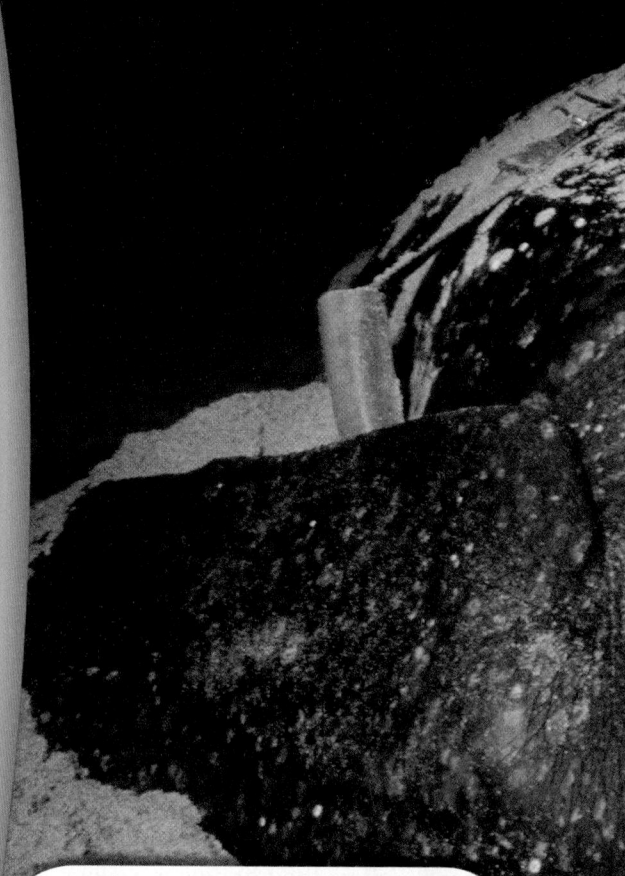

About the PHOTO

Gathering information is important to scientists. In this picture, a marine biologist is using technology to gather information about the behavior of sea turtles. The strange, blue harness attached to the turtle transmits radio signals. Scientists use these signals to track the movement of turtles through the ocean.

PRE-READING ACTIVITY

 **Tri-Fold** Before you read the chapter, create the FoldNote entitled "Tri-Fold" described in the **Study Skills** section of the Appendix. Write what you know about technology and the nature of science in the column labeled "Know." Then, write what you want to know in the column labeled "Want." As you read the chapter, write what you learn about technology and the nature of science in the column labeled "Learn."

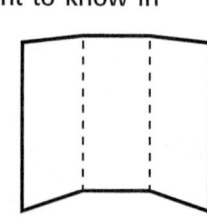

START-UP ACTIVITY

What Does It All Mean?

In this activity, you will use observations to form a question and develop a plan for answering your question.

Procedure

1. Get a **picture or drawing** from your teacher.

2. Make a list of observations about the picture or drawing.

3. From your list of observations, develop a question.

4. Create a plan to answer the question. Your plan should include a list of specific observations needed to answer your question, a description of the kinds of tools needed, and a plan for collecting and making sense of your observations.

Analysis

1. How did your initial observations influence the question that you developed?

2. How important is it for scientists to have a plan for answering a scientific question before they begin their work? Explain your answer.

Gathering Scientific Data

You're waiting for the bus. With your back to the road, you notice the smell of the exhaust and the sound of the engine and brakes. Turning around, you see a big, yellow vehicle waiting to take you to school.

Without any effort, you constantly gather information about the world around you. Just as you do, scientists gather information all of the time. Yet in science, information is gathered for specific reasons and in a particular way.

The Importance of Observations

Why do scientists gather information? Scientists gather information, or make observations, to answer questions about the world. An **observation** is any use of the senses, such as seeing or hearing, to gather information. Scientists ask questions about the world based on observations that interest them. The scientist in **Figure 1** is measuring the beak length of a duckling. What question do you think he is trying to answer with this observation?

Deciding What Information to Collect

How do scientists decide what information to collect? It depends on the question being asked. Some questions can be answered by making observations of nature. Others require information obtained from controlled experiments. Still others can be answered only by building and observing models.

No matter what kind of information is needed, a scientist must gather all of the information related to the question being asked. In addition, a scientist must remain unbiased and must gather observations even if the observations suggest that the hypothesis is incorrect.

Benchmark Check Why are observations important? H.1.3.4 AA

Figure 1 *This scientist is making observations. Gathering information about the size of ducklings can help scientists learn about the growth and development of ducks.*

Figure 2 Qualitative and Quantitative Observations

Observing a Pineapple	
Qualitative observations	**Quantitative observations**
yellow and orange body	body length of 15.2 cm
green leaves	leaf length of 20.3 cm
rigid, sharp leaves	leaf thickness of 0.25 cm
heavy, dense body	total mass of 1.7 kg

Qualitative Observations

Observations can be divided into two categories. The first category is made up of qualitative observations. A **qualitative observation** is descriptive information that is not expressed as a number. Qualitative observations include descriptions of how an event occurs, what an object looks like, or how an organism acts.

Qualitative observations are important to scientists. Often, qualitative observations point scientists toward interesting questions about the world. These questions lead scientists to form new hypotheses and to perform experiments. Even though qualitative observations are open to interpretation, they are important for explaining characteristics of objects or events that cannot be expressed in numbers.

Quantitative Observations

Quantitative observations make up the second category of observations. **Quantitative observations** are expressed in terms of quantity or numbers. **Figure 2** shows how quantitative observations differ from qualitative observations. Quantitative observations are less open to interpretation than qualitative observations are. Three people may describe the color of a pineapple in three different ways. But by using a scale, each person would find that the pineapple has a mass of 1.7 kg.

Quantitative observations have many advantages. Scientists can easily compare and discuss quantitative observations. Also, one scientist can check the quantitative observations made by another scientist. When an observation is expressed as a quantity or number, there are fewer opportunities to misunderstand what the observation means.

observation the process of obtaining information by using the senses

qualitative observation descriptive information that is not expressed as a number

quantitative observation information that is expressed in terms of quantity or numbers

H.1.3.4 AA knows that accurate record keeping, openness, and replication are essential to maintaining an investigator's credibility with other scientists and society.

Figure 3   Making an Estimate

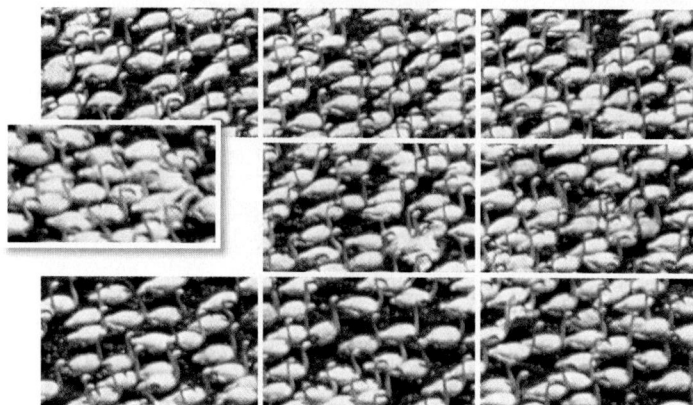

Because an estimate is based on a known quantity, it is not a guess.

❶ Divide the picture into areas that are the same size.

❷ Count the number of flamingos in one area.

❸ Multiply the number of flamingos in one area by the total number of areas.

Estimating

Imagine that you have noticed that flamingo populations have been dwindling in Florida. You need to track how many flamingos are in a large flock. Counting all of the flamingos would be very difficult. How are you going to make this important observation? In situations such as this one, scientists often make an estimate. An **estimate** is an approximate calculation. Scientists estimate by dividing a large sample into smaller areas that are the same size. The image in **Figure 3** has been broken into nine equal boxes. A scientist would count the objects in one of the boxes and would multiply this exact observation by the total number of boxes in the entire sample. Estimating is not the same as guessing. Because the scientist counts the exact number of flamingos in one area of the picture, the estimate is based on a known fact. However, an estimate is not an exact measurement. There will always be a margin of error.

estimate a rough or approximate calculation

H.3.3.7 knows that computers speed up and extend people's ability to collect, sort, and analyze data; prepare research reports; and share data and ideas with others.

Figure 4   A History of Clocks

1500 BCE
Sundial

1656
Pendulum clock

The Tools That Scientists Use

What are the most important tools that a scientist uses? The most important tools for gathering information are the brain and the senses. The brain is perfect for deciding what information to gather and how to gather it. All of the information you gather is filtered through your senses. Technological tools enhance and extend the abilities of your brain and senses.

Extending Abilities

Technological tools act as extensions of a scientist's senses. A scientist can use an electron microscope to see very small things that cannot be seen with the unaided eye, such as viruses. Likewise, the *Hubble Space Telescope* gathers the faint light from objects in space and helps astronomers see the distant stars. Using computers, scientists can process and share large amounts of data in complex ways that would not be possible by hand. Computers are also used to operate equipment and to model experimental conditions.

Benchmark Check How do computers extend a scientist's ability to make and record observations? **H.3.3.7**

Advances in Technology

As technological tools have developed, tools have become more accurate. Accurate tools allow scientists to study events and objects more closely. **Figure 4** shows the development of tools that measure time. People use time in a variety of ways. For example, accurate clocks make it possible for people to arrange meetings with one another or to coordinate travel and delivery schedules. Advanced tools also allow scientists to work with larger groups of data. Scientists can also gather information in places and in ways that they could not before.

INTERNET ACTIVITY

Electrifying Science and Technology Write a biography about a scientist or inventor who worked with electrical energy. Go to **go.hrw.com** and type in the keyword **HP5ELTW**.

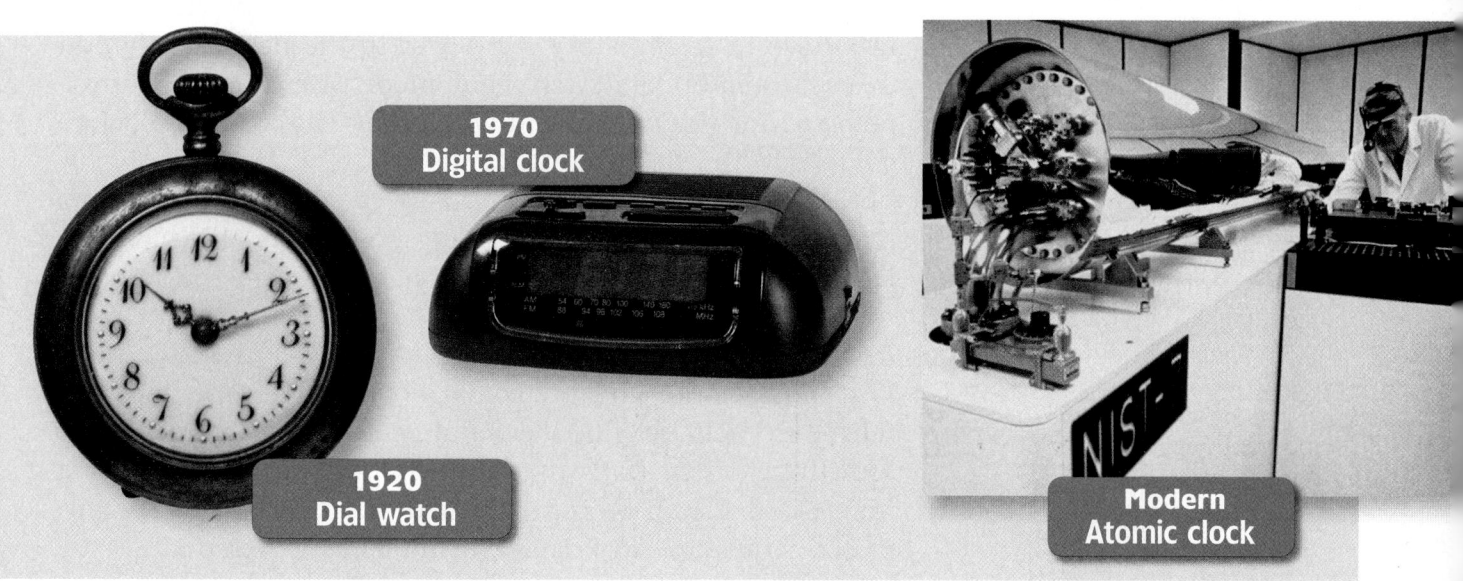

1970 Digital clock

1920 Dial watch

Modern Atomic clock

Figure 5 *This forensic detective is carefully collecting fingerprints from a crime scene.*

Gathering Information in the Field

Not all information is gathered in a laboratory. For many experiments, gathering information will take a scientist outside. Any location outside a laboratory where experiments occur is called the *field.* Often, data or samples are collected in the field and are taken back to a laboratory to be studied in greater detail. Fieldwork is an essential part of the scientific process. Scientists must know how to collect meaningful data from the natural world despite its distractions.

Skills for Fieldwork

The forensic detective in **Figure 5,** like all scientists, received special training for fieldwork. The safety concerns that scientists have in a laboratory carry over to the field. In addition to using appropriate safety equipment, scientists have to be prepared for the unexpected when they work outside. Before going into the field, scientists should know as much as possible about the area. An attitude of care will help scientists remain aware of their surroundings. Scientists also have the responsibility to treat all living things with care and respect.

Scientists must be careful to avoid contamination of data. It is difficult to control experimental conditions in the field. If scientists notice unexpected data, observing the setting carefully may help scientists determine if they were measuring something other than what they intended to measure. Data from the field can be contaminated by many things, such as passing animals, bad weather, or human interference.

Does It Check Out?

How carefully do you observe your surroundings? Test your observation skills by asking a family member to complete this activity with you. Set a timer for 1 min. On a blank piece of paper, write down as many things as you can about the room in which you are sitting. When the time is up, compare your list with your family member's list. Were your lists similar? What kinds of things did each of you observe?

ACTIVITY

Gathering Information Responsibly

All aspects of science are guided by **scientific ethics,** principles of proper scientific conduct. For example, one principle requires scientists to keep accurate, open records of their experiments. When records are open, other scientists have an opportunity to repeat experiments and verify results. Open records reduce the risk that scientists will make false or harmful claims about their discoveries. Having access to accurate, open records makes it possible for the public to make informed decisions. When information is available to the public, people can make decisions considering the benefits along with the risks.

scientific ethics the principles and values of proper scientific conduct

H.1.3.4 AA knows that accurate record keeping, openness, and replication are essential to maintaining an investigator's credibility with other scientists and society.

Benchmark Check Why is accurate record keeping important?
H.1.3.4 AA

SECTION Review

Summary

- Observations form the basis of science.
- Quantitative observations describe information expressed in numbers. Qualitative observations describe information that is not expressed in numbers.
- Tools, such as computers, extend the abilities of scientists to make observations. **H.3.3.7**
- Gathering information in a nonlaboratory setting requires scientists to have special skills.
- Accurate, open records are important to a scientist's credibility. **H.1.3.4 AA**

Understanding Key Ideas

1. What is the difference between a quantitative observation and a qualitative observation?

2. Explain why making observations is an important part of the scientific process.

Math Skills

3. Joaquín needs to estimate the number of ant mounds in a field. He counts three ant mounds in a 100 m^2 area. If the field covers 2,000 m^2, what is the estimated number of ant mounds for the entire field?

Critical Thinking

4. **Applying Concepts** Propose a list of information that would be important to gather if you were testing the ability of Mars to support life.

5. **Applying Concepts** A scientist thinks that the warming of the oceans might be hurting plankton, small organisms that live in the ocean. What information could the scientist gather to test this hypothesis?

FCAT Preparation

6. Lucinda is conducting an experiment to test a new herbal cleaner. The manufacturer claims that the cleaner eliminates bacteria from any surface. Explain what Lucinda must do to make her results scientifically valid. **H.1.3.4 AA**

7. How have computers extended the ability of scientists to collect information? **H.3.3.4 CS**
   A. Access to data has decreased.
   B. Scientists are unable to process data.
   C. Scientists are able to study hard-to-reach places.
   D. Communications between scientists have slow

SCI LINKS
Maintained by the Teachers Association
ated to this
scilinks.org
For

Organizing Your Data

It's Tuesday night, and you have a test tomorrow morning. You have a notebook, the textbook, and flashcards. You have so much information that you feel overwhelmed!

In the same way, you—like the student in **Figure 1**—could be easily overwhelmed with all of the data gathered from scientific experiments. To be useful, scientific data must be organized. But how? In this section, you will see how a group of students organized data. The methods that the students used are the same methods that scientists use to make information easier to interpret and understand.

Creating a Data Table

For five years, a teacher has been taking his class to a grassy prairie at the edge of Big Cypress National Preserve in southern Florida. Each year, the students gather information about the number of plant species that grow so they can monitor the health of the prairie. The first step that the teacher and students take in organizing the data is to fill in a data table.

Organizing: The First Step

It's important to determine what information you are going to gather and to create a data table before the experiment starts. Then, you can be as organized as possible and can be sure not to miss any information that might be important.

READING WARM-UP

Objectives

● Identify key elements of a data table.

● Explain the steps to create a graph by using a set of data.

● Describe how graphs show patterns.
  H.2.3.1 CS

● Explain how technology extends the ability of scientists to organize data.
  H.3.3.7

Terms to Learn

independent variable *FCAT* VOCAB
dependent variable *FCAT* VOCAB
axis

READING STRATEGY

Discussion Read this section silently. Write down questions that you have about this section. Discuss your questions in a small group.

F... at When performing co...nt, you can tha...ch information ove... to become stud... this

and Technology

Figure 2 Creating a Data Table

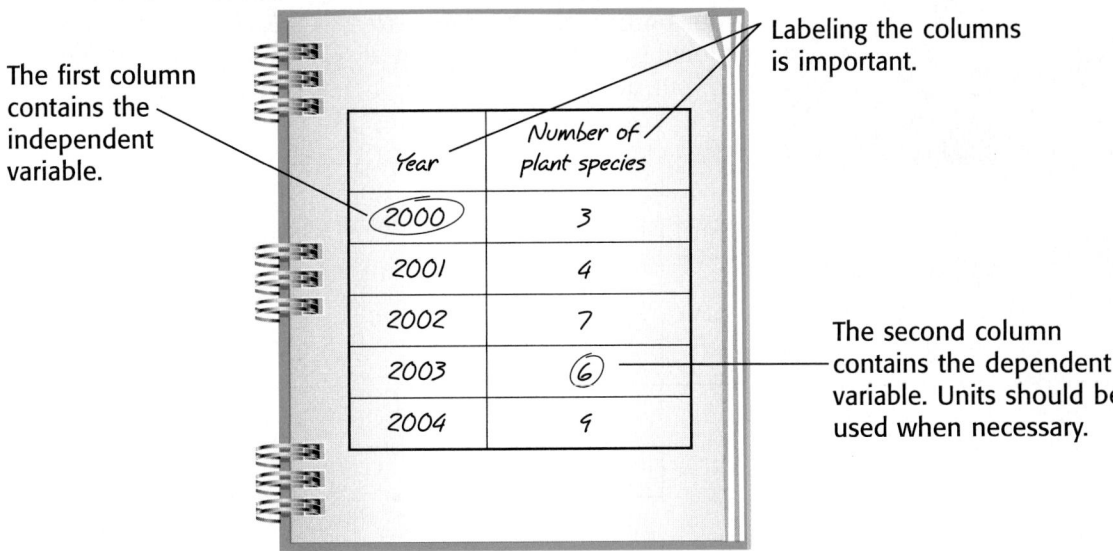

The first column contains the independent variable.

Labeling the columns is important.

Year	Number of plant species
2000	3
2001	4
2002	7
2003	6
2004	9

The second column contains the dependent variable. Units should be used when necessary.

The Independent Variable

A data table has two columns, as **Figure 2** shows. The first column lists the **independent variable,** the factor that the experimenter changes. The word *variable* is used because the numbers in the column are not the same. They vary from row to row. In this case, the class chose to count plant species once per year. So, the independent variable is the year.

The Dependent Variable

The second column in the data table lists the dependent variable. The **dependent variable** is the factor that changes in response to the independent variable. It is the variable that the scientist measures. In **Figure 2,** the dependent variable is the number of plant species. It changes with the independent variable, or changes every year.

Labels and Units

If someone asks you to identify yourself, you might answer by giving your name. Likewise, each part of the data table needs information to help identify what the data represent. Labels and units identify the contents of the data table.

The label at the top of each column tells us what the data in the column represent. The column labels for the data table in **Figure 2** are "Year" and "Number of plant species." If the data in a table represent some type of measurement (such as the mass of a turtle), then the unit of the measurement (such as the kilogram) should be included.

✓ **Reading Check** Why is it important to label your data table?

independent variable in an experiment, the factor that is deliberately manipulated *FCAT VOCAB*

dependent variable in an experiment, the factor that changes as a result of manipulation of one or more other factors (the independent variables) *FCAT VOCAB*

Figure 3 Creating a Graph

Drawing the Axes
Your horizontal and vertical axes should be long enough to fit all of your data.

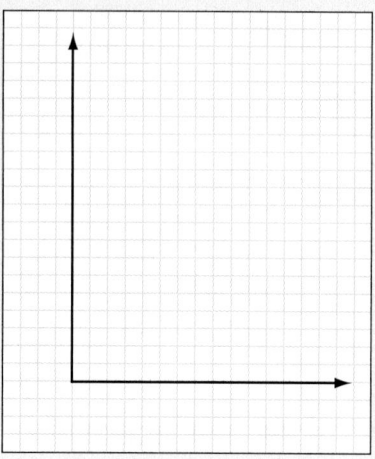

Labeling Your Axes
Each axis should have a label and, when needed, the correct unit.

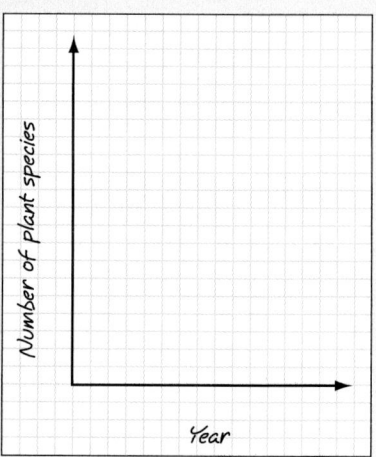

Graphing It!

Data tables help you organize data. Graphs help you understand and use that data. Graphs make it easy to identify trends and make predictions. Students studying plants at Big Cypress National Preserve used their data table to graph the number of plant species observed per year.

axis one of two or more reference lines that mark the borders of a graph

Axes

Figure 3 shows how to make a graph. First, use a data table to determine the graph's axes (singular, *axis*). An **axis** is a reference line that forms one side of a graph. A graph has a horizontal *x*-axis and a vertical *y*-axis. The *x*-axis usually represents the independent variable in the data table. The *y*-axis usually represents the dependent variable. In a graph of the number of plant species observed per year, the *x*-axis represents the year, and the *y*-axis represents the number of plant species. Each axis is labeled with the name of the variable that is represented.

Range

Each axis has its own range. To find the range, subtract the smallest value of a single variable from the largest value of the same variable. For the plant-species data, the range of the independent variable, the year, is 5 years. Therefore, the *x*-axis must cover at least 5 years. The range of the dependent variable, the number of species, is $9 - 3 = 6$. Thus, the *y*-axis must have room for at least 6 plant species.

Height Vs. Arm Span

1. Create a data table with height as the independent variable and arm span as the dependent variable.

2. Use a **meterstick** to measure the height and arm span of five classmates.

3. Graph your data, and describe the relationship you find between the two measurements.

Determining Range and Scale

Each axis on a graph can have its own scale so that the data can be seen easily.

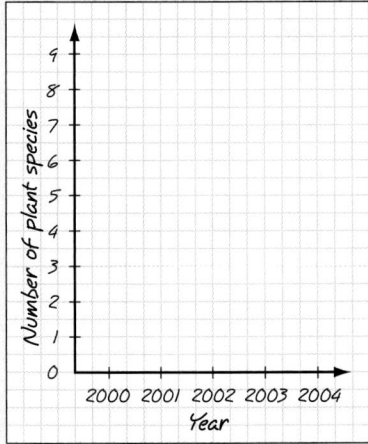

Plotting the Data Points

The easiest part of creating a graph is taking pairs of data and putting them where they belong.

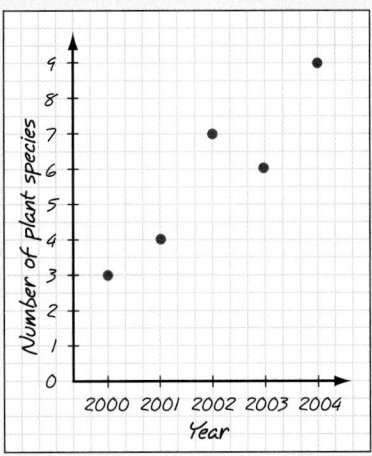

Labeling the Graph

Every graph needs an appropriate title. A good title tells a reader what the graph is all about.

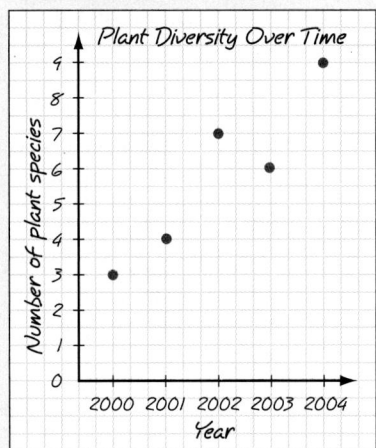

Scale

The next step is to decide the scale of the graph. Each axis has its own scale. The scale is the size that is used for each box or grid mark on the graph. For the plant species data, we can choose a scale of 1 year for each grid mark on the x-axis. For the y-axis, the grid marks can be placed at intervals of 1. The scale should be chosen such that the graph spreads out to fill most of the available space.

Data Points

Now, the data points need to be plotted. You plot the data points by putting a dot on the graph for each pair of data in the data table. Sometimes, a "line of best fit" is needed. Most graphs of data or observations are not drawn dot to dot through the data points. A line of best fit, such as the one in **Figure 4,** is a smooth line that is drawn to "fit," or to include some but not all of the data points. The smooth line without sharp turns or sudden bends shows the pattern described by the data. The line of best fit also shows how the data deviate from the pattern.

Labels

The last step is to give the graph a title. The title helps people recognize what the graph describes. Scientists often include the independent and dependent variables in the title.

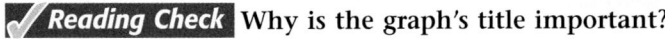 **Reading Check** Why is the graph's title important?

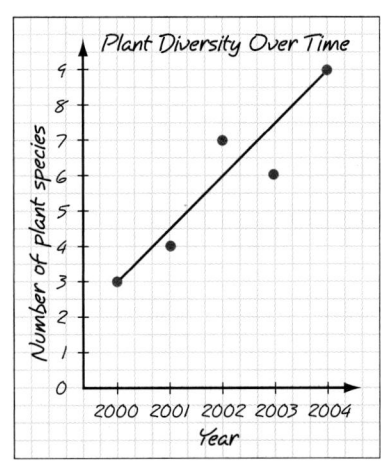

Figure 4 *The "line of best fit" shows the general relationship between the two variables in the graph. It also shows how data vary from the overall relationship.*

Figure 5 Trends in Nonlinear Graphs

Direct Nonlinear Relationship
The dependent variable increases as the independent variable increases.

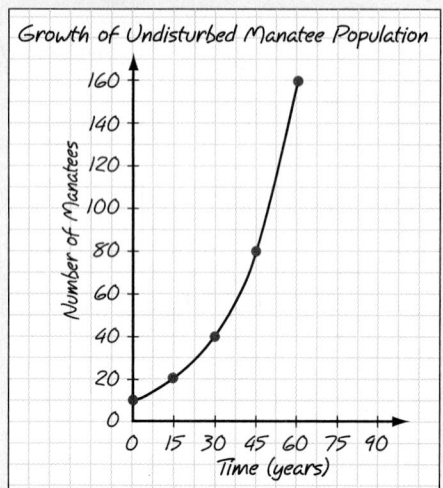

Growth of Undisturbed Manatee Population

Inverse Nonlinear Relationship
The dependent variable decreases as the independent variable increases.

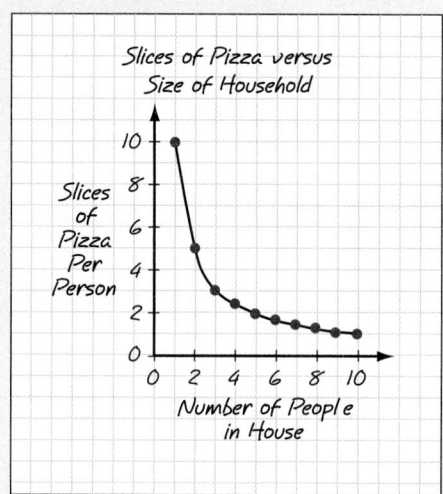

Slices of Pizza versus Size of Household

Patterns Shown by Graphs

When you graph data, you can identify what the pattern, or *trend,* of the data is. A trend shows the relationship between the two variables studied in the experiment. Graphs make it easy to tell if something is increasing, decreasing, or staying the same.

A graph in which the relationship between the independent variable and dependent variable can be shown with a straight line is called a *linear graph.* In a linear graph, a straight line can be used to show the data's trend. Sometimes, the relationship between the independent variable and dependent variable is not a straight line but a smooth curve. Any graph that is not a straight line is called a *nonlinear graph.*

Graphs allow scientists to determine if the relationship between the variables is direct or inverse. If a graph shows that the dependent variable increases as the independent variable increases, the relationship between the variables is direct. If one variable increases while the other variable decreases, the relationship between the variables is inverse. **Figure 5** shows two nonlinear graphs, one of which has a direct relationship and one of which has an inverse relationship. Scientists use graphs to describe their findings to other scientists or to people who are interested in the question under investigation.

H.2.3.1 CS recognizes that patterns exist within and across systems.

H.3.3.7 knows that computers speed up and extend people's ability to collect, sort, and analyze data; prepare research reports; and share data and ideas with others.

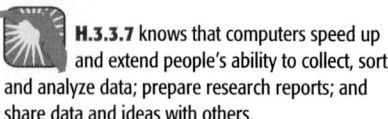 **Benchmark Check** How do graphs show patterns? **H.2.3.1 CS**

52   Chapter 2   Science and Technology

Tools for Organization

Computer technology can be used to make organizing data easier. Computers help scientists collect, organize, process, and display large amounts of data. In **Figure 6,** a doctor is recording data on her hand-held computer. With this tool, she is able to gather and communicate data rapidly and as needed. Computer technology extends our ability to quickly examine observations for patterns. Specially designed software creates visually appealing graphs from lists of data. The instant feedback provided by computer technology allows scientists to use data as they are collected.

Benchmark Check How can technology help scientists organize data efficiently and easily? **H.3.3.7**

Figure 6 *This doctor uses a hand-held computer to help her keep track of patient information and her demanding schedule.*

SECTION Review

Summary

- Scientists use data tables to organize information.
- Labels and units are important parts of data tables and graphs.
- The independent variable is the factor that the experimenter changes.
- The dependent variable is the factor that the experimenter measures.
- The line of best fit shows the trend of a linear graph.
- Graphs help show patterns in data. **H.2.3.1 CS**
- Technology helps scientists organize information and create graphs. **H.3.3.7**

Understanding Key Ideas

1. Why is it important to organize a data table before doing an experiment?

2. Alfonso is conducting an experiment to determine whether temperature affects how fast earthworms move. What is the dependent variable? What is the independent variable?

3. While studying how long it takes milk to warm, Marissa makes the observations below. Use her data to create a graph.

Time (min)	Temperature (°C)
0	25
3	28
5	30

Critical Thinking

4. **Making Inferences** List three reasons that labels and units are important parts of data tables and graphs.

5. **Identifying Relationships** As computer technology becomes faster, how does the ability of scientists to collect and organize data change? Explain. **H.3.3.7**

FCAT Preparation

6. After an experiment, Monica creates a graph that shows a direct linear relationship between the size of a fish and the fish's oxygen use. Which statement is true? **H.2.3.1 CS**

   A. The larger a fish is, the smaller the amount of oxygen that the fish uses.

   B. The smaller the fish is, the smaller the amount of oxygen that the fish uses.

   C. The smaller the fish is, the larger the amount of oxygen that the fish uses.

   D. It is impossible to determine a relationship between the size of a fish and oxygen use.

SCLINKS®

NSTA
Developed and maintained by the
National Science Teachers Association

For a variety of links related to this chapter, go to www.scilinks.org

Topic: Computer Technology
SciLinks code: HSM0334

Mathematics in Science

You're in a race to design the first privately funded, crewed spacecraft. You've spent months perfecting your spacecraft, but when you fly it for the first time, you'll have passengers! How can you be sure that your rocket will fly?

One way is to use mathematics. Mathematical models in the form of computer simulations can answer questions about how rockets, such as the one in **Figure 1,** will fly and react to different conditions before the rockets even leave the ground.

Why Mathematics?

Just like making observations, conducting experiments, and organizing data, mathematics is used to answer questions. Mathematics helps determine important properties of substances, such as area, volume, and density. Mathematics also allows scientists to understand and summarize large quantities of information. As a result, scientists can make predictions. For example, a meteorologist who has gathered data about hurricanes may use mathematics to understand patterns in the data. Then, he or she could use these patterns to predict where future hurricanes will hit land.

There are scientists in every country around the world. They speak every language imaginable. Mathematics is often called the *language of science* because mathematics allows scientists to easily communicate their findings to each other in a language that everyone understands: numbers!

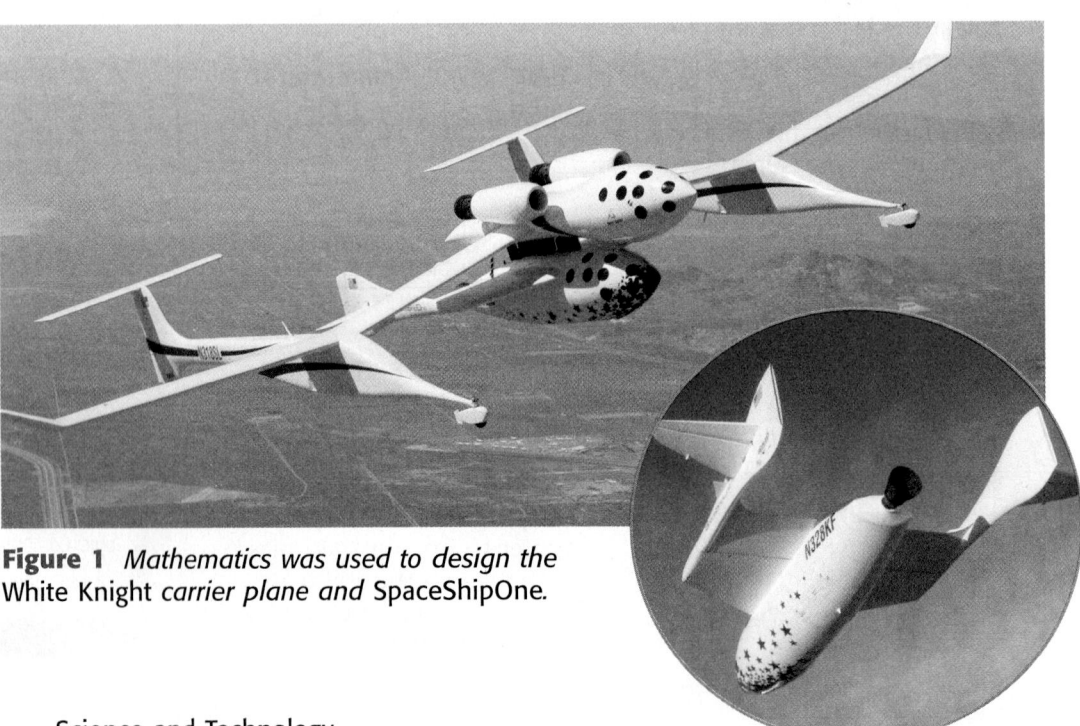

Figure 1 *Mathematics was used to design the* White Knight *carrier plane and* SpaceShipOne.

Figure 2 How Tools Make a Difference

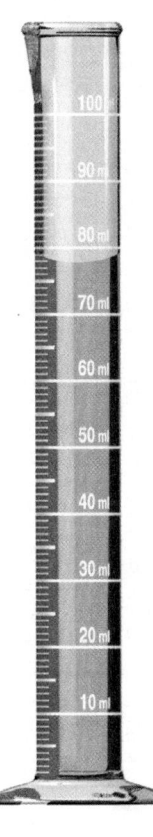

How Certain Are You?

Every measurement has some degree of uncertainty based on what tool was used to make the observation. For example, you know that the beetle in **Figure 2** is longer than 6.8 cm and shorter than 6.9 cm, because the ruler is accurate to a tenth of a centimeter. Although you might be tempted to record your measurement as 6.8 cm, scientists would estimate how far in between 6.8 and 6.9 cm the end of the beetle's body falls and might record 6.85 cm. Because the final number is an estimate, scientists might also interpret the length of the beetle to be 6.83 or 6.88 cm. Regardless of which measurement is recorded, the certain numbers (6.8 in the example) stay the same.

Significant Figures

Scientists assume that when documenting observations, other scientists record all certain numbers as well as one estimated number. A measurement written in this way uses *significant figures*. Using significant figures maintains the validity of a scientist's results. Significant figures also indicate the precision of the tool used by demonstrating the certainty of measurements made with the tool.

The Difference That Tools Make

You may have already used a graduated cylinder like the one shown in **Figure 2.** A graduated cylinder is a measuring device and is more precise than a common measuring cup found in a kitchen. You can be imprecise when you are cooking, but you must be very precise in a lab, especially a medical lab.

Reading Check How are significant figures useful to scientists?

CONNECTION TO Chemistry

The Foundation of Chemistry Chemical measurement is important in many areas of our lives, such as medicine, industry, and manufacturing. Chemists work to find the most accurate measurements of values. As new tools allow chemists to make more-precise measurements, the true value changes, too.

Figure 3 Data Table of Plant Diversity

Plot	Number of plant species
A	8
B	12
C	9
D	12
E	8
F	12
G	9

Seven groups of students counted the number of plant species living in seven different plots.

mean the number obtained by adding up the data for a given characteristic and dividing this sum by the number of individuals

median the value of the middle item when data are arranged in order by size

mode the most frequently occurring value in a data set

Finding the mean.
Add your data together.
Divide the sum by the number of observations in your data set.

A	8
B	12
C	9
D	12
E	8
F	12
G	+ 9
Sum	70

Mean = 70/7 = 10 plant species

Figure 4 *The mean is calculated by adding all of the data points together and dividing the sum by the total number of data points.*

Analyzing Your Data

Graphs are only one tool that scientists use to analyze data. Scientists also use mathematics to understand the information gathered during an experiment. *Averaging,* which is finding the most common measurement within a large set of measurements, is a particularly powerful mathematical tool. It allows scientists to summarize large pools of data into a single point. There are three kinds of averages: mean, median, and mode. We'll use the plant-species data shown in **Figure 3** to learn about the difference between the three kinds of averages.

Mean: Not as Bad as It Sounds!

One way to average data is to find the mathematical mean. The **mean** is found by calculating the sum of the data and then dividing the sum by the number of data points. **Figure 4** shows that the mean of the plant-species data is 10. The mathematical mean is useful when you want an average that represents all of the data points.

However, there are limits to how useful the mean can be. In some cases, just a few data points within a much larger group cause the mean to be either much higher or much lower than the majority of the data. If the students working in plot G had counted 30 plant species instead of 9, the mean of the data—13—would be larger than the majority of the data gathered. Scientists cannot discard data just because some observations were unexpected or difficult to explain. Scientists may decide that the best option is to average this data set by finding the median or mode.

Median: Smack Dab in the Middle

A median is another kind of average. **Figure 5** shows how to find the median. The **median** is the value of the middle item when data are arranged in order by size. If a data set has an odd number of data points, the median is the number in the middle of the data set. If a data set has an even number of data points, you add the two middle numbers and divide the sum by 2. Notice that the median of the plant species data—9—differs from the mean. The median is useful when a few data points are much smaller or much larger than the majority of the data.

Mode

Like the median and mean, the mode is used to help summarize or describe a group of data. Of the three kinds of averages, the mode is the easiest to find. The **mode** is the number that appears most often in a data set. First, you list the numbers in order from smallest to largest. Then, you determine which number appears most often. **Figure 6** shows that the mode of the plant-species data is 12. The mode is quite different from the mean and median. It tells scientists that they are most likely to find 12 species on a single plot.

The mode is useful when you would like to know what is most common. For example, imagine that you are doing an experiment to find the most common number of pairs of shoes that your classmates own. You survey 10 of your classmates and gather the following data: 2, 3, 3, 3, 3, 5, 5, 6, 7, and 10. The most common number of pairs of shoes owned by your classmates is 3. Because the mode is the most commonly occurring number, it is the best measure of the average because it answers the question that you are asking. In contrast, the mean and the median are not the most common datum.

 **Reading Check** Explain the difference between a mean, a median, and a mode.

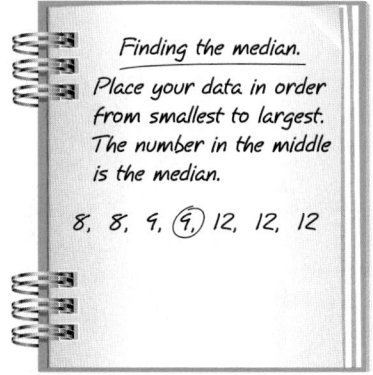

Figure 5 *The median is calculated by arranging the data in order from smallest to largest. The middle entry is the median.*

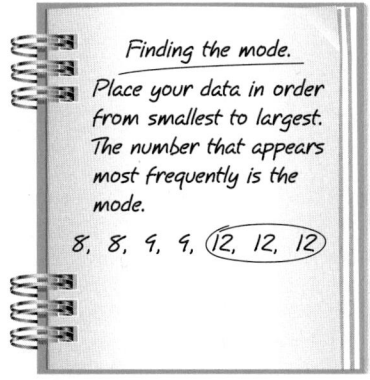

Figure 6 *The mode is calculated by arranging the data in order from smallest to largest. The data point that appears most frequently is the mode.*

MATH FOCUS

Calculating the Mean Find the mean batting average for five baseball players whose individual batting averages are 0.372, 0.366, 0.362, 0.333, and 0.327.

Step 1: Find the sum of the batting averages.

0.372 + 0.366 + 0.362 + 0.333 + 0.327 = 1.760

Step 2: Divide the sum by the total number of items.

1.760/5 = 0.352

Now It's Your Turn

1. David has test scores of 85, 76, 82, and 90. What is his mean test score?
2. The basketball coach has made a list of the number of points scored by each member of the girl's basketball team. What is the mean number of points scored if the coach collected these data: 26, 18, 4, 18, 18, 5, 6, 11, 4, 9, and 8?

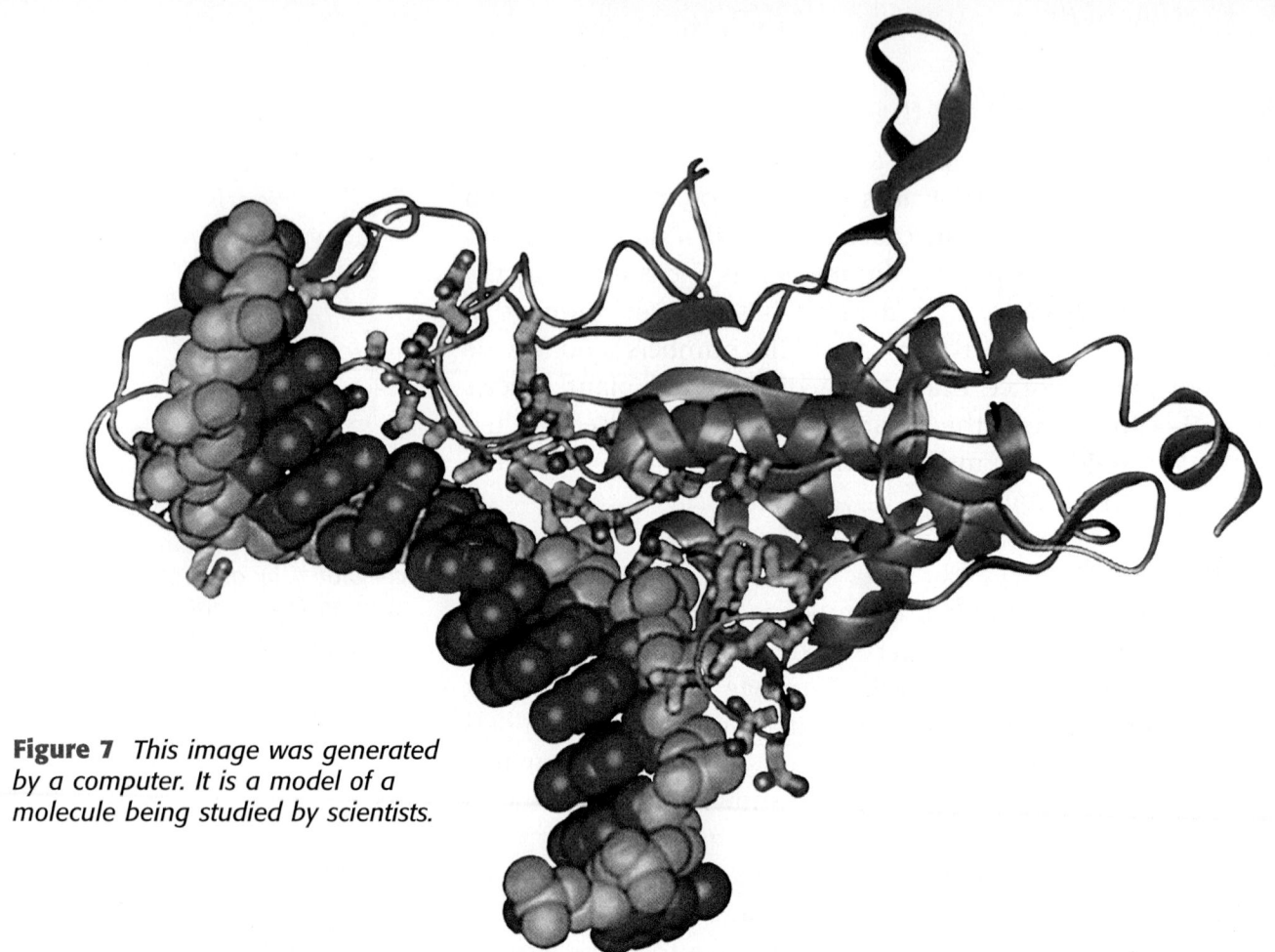

Figure 7 *This image was generated by a computer. It is a model of a molecule being studied by scientists.*

Creating Scientific Models

Although averaging is a powerful mathematical tool, it is not always the best way to analyze information. When scientists need to communicate information that would be difficult to explain, they often create a model, such as the one in **Figure 7.** A **model** is a representation of an object or system. Models are used in the design of many complex objects, such as cars and airplanes. Models are also used to help predict the weather and to study very small objects, such as cells. Mathematics plays an important role in scientific models.

model a pattern, plan, representation, or description designed to show the structure or workings of an object, system, or concept

Mathematical Models

A mathematical model may be made up of numbers, equations, or other forms of data. Some mathematical models are simple and can be used easily. Others are very complex. Scientists often work with computers to develop and use mathematical models. Computers can add, subtract, multiply, and divide more quickly and more accurately than humans can. Computers can also display the results of a model in ways that allow scientists to easily interpret and share the results.

H.3.3.7 knows that computers speed up and extend people's ability to collect, sort, and analyze data; prepare research reports; and share data and ideas with others.

Benchmark Check How does computer technology help scientists create and use models? **H.3.3.7**

The Limits of Models

Models are an important tool for scientists. Mathematical models allow scientists to perform multiple trials of complex experiments rapidly and efficiently. For example, scientists can use models to study how certain drugs might fight diseases without testing the drugs on animals or people.

But it is important for a scientist to remember the limitations of the models that he or she uses. A model is not exactly the same as the real object or system. To make sense of the information gathered, a scientist must know the ways in which a model does not act exactly as the real thing does.

Benchmark Check What is one limitation of a model? H.3.3.7

SECTION Review

Summary

- Mathematics is an important tool for scientists.
- Significant figures communicate the precision of measurements.
- Means, medians, and modes are used to summarize data.
- Models are used to predict and understand natural phenomena.
- Computers enhance the complexity and kinds of models that scientists create. H.3.3.7

Understanding Key Ideas

1. A scientist is measuring the height of water hyacinths on 30 ponds. Why would he use significant figures when recording his observations?

2. Why is mathematics an important tool for scientists?

Math Skills

3. Rachel has gathered information about the guppy population in her fish tank. She has counted the number of living guppies once per month for four months. Her data are as follows: 5, 15, 20, 35, and 55. Calculate the mean, median, and mode for these data.

Critical Thinking

4. **Applying Concepts** Describe a situation in which the median of a data set would be more useful than the mean.

5. **Analyzing Ideas** Give an example that illustrates how models are used in science.

FCAT Preparation

6. Computers perform many important tasks in science. How has the use of computers to create mathematical models most influenced science? H.3.3.4 CS

   A. Computer-generated mathematical models are always three dimensional.
   B. Mathematical models are harder to handle than the real objects or systems.
   C. Computers extend the ability of scientists to create accurate models.
   D. Computers help reduce the amount of paperwork that a scientist must complete.

SCILINKS.

NSTA
Developed and maintained by the National Science Teachers Association

For a variety of links related to this chapter, go to www.scilinks.org

Topic: Using Models
SciLinks code: HSM1588

Technology and Scientists

How long have people been farming? You may be surprised to learn that people have been farming and raising animals for more than 9,000 years!

Agriculture is one of the oldest forms of technology. Since its development, agriculture has changed a great deal. To suit human needs, farmers use many technological processes and tools, including irrigation. These technologies are used in the farm in **Figure 1.**

What Is Technology?

Technology is the use of tools, materials, and processes to meet human needs. Even the clothes that you wear are a result of many technologies working together. Processes such as weaving and tools such as mechanized looms work together to turn raw fibers into cloth quickly and inexpensively. People in all cultures develop technology to meet their needs. As time passes, these processes and tools become available to everyone. As technology spreads, it is adapted to meet the needs of the people who are using it. For example, Teflon was first used to make machine parts for the military. Then, people adapted it for use as a nonstick coating for cookware.

Benchmark Check Who can use technology? **H.3.3.6**

technology the application of science for practical purposes; the use of tools, machines, materials, and processes to meet human needs

Figure 1 *Agriculture is a set of practices that rely on many highly specialized technological processes and tools.*

H.3.3.6 knows that no matter who does science and mathematics or invents things, or when or where they do it, the knowledge and technology that result can eventually become available to everyone.

Figure 2　Computers over the Years

UNIVAC-1 was completed in 1951. It was so large it required an entire room of its own!

This computer was one of the first personal computers and was much faster than UNIVAC-1.

Modern computers can process more than 300 million operations per second.

Technology as a Tool

People have used tools to make their lives easier for thousands of years. You may think that technology is limited to tools such as MP3 players, microscopes, or cars. But pencils, silverware, and bicycles are examples of technological tools, too. Tools that were created to address human needs often influence future human needs and capabilities. For example, the printing press allowed knowledge to be spread quickly. As people had better access to information, building on the knowledge of others became easier. Scientists in particular were able to explore the world in greater depth by building on the discoveries of other scientists. As a result, scientists needed more-accurate tools for making and recording observations.

Computers

One technological tool that has revolutionized science and the world is the computer. Computers are tools that perform complex mathematical operations and can direct the actions of other technological tools. Computers have increased the ability of people to share knowledge and the speed at which they share knowledge. Since the first computers were invented in the 1940s, their ability to process information has grown very quickly, as described in **Figure 2.** Using computers, scientists can collect, sort, and analyze large amounts of data. Some experiments in which thousands of measurements and calculations are performed would be impossible without computers.

Benchmark Check Why is the computer an important technological tool? **H.3.3.7**

H.3.3.7 knows that computers speed up and extend people's ability to collect, sort, and analyze data; prepare research reports; and share data and ideas with others.

Technological Design

How is technology designed? Technology is designed to address human needs. But there are constraints, or limitations, on what can be invented or developed. Scientists and inventors, such as the scientists who designed the surgical process and tools shown in **Figure 3,** are limited by natural laws and the kinds of materials that are available. Scientists and inventors are also limited by the values of the society in which they live. Designs for new technology must consider the cost of the technology as well as the potential political and social impact.

For example, when NASA is designing a new space shuttle, these factors must be considered. The engineers and scientists working on this project should ask several questions about their design. Will the shuttle be able to fly? Do the available materials have the right properties? How much will building and flying this space shuttle cost? Could the money be used in other ways that would benefit society more? Will a new shuttle strain the relationship between NASA and space agencies in other countries? Finally, will this shuttle be aesthetically appealing enough to interest the public? The answer to each question has an effect on the design process.

Benchmark Check What considerations must technological design take into account? **H.3.3.4 CS**

Figure 3 *This doctor is practicing a heart surgery with the assistance of technology.*

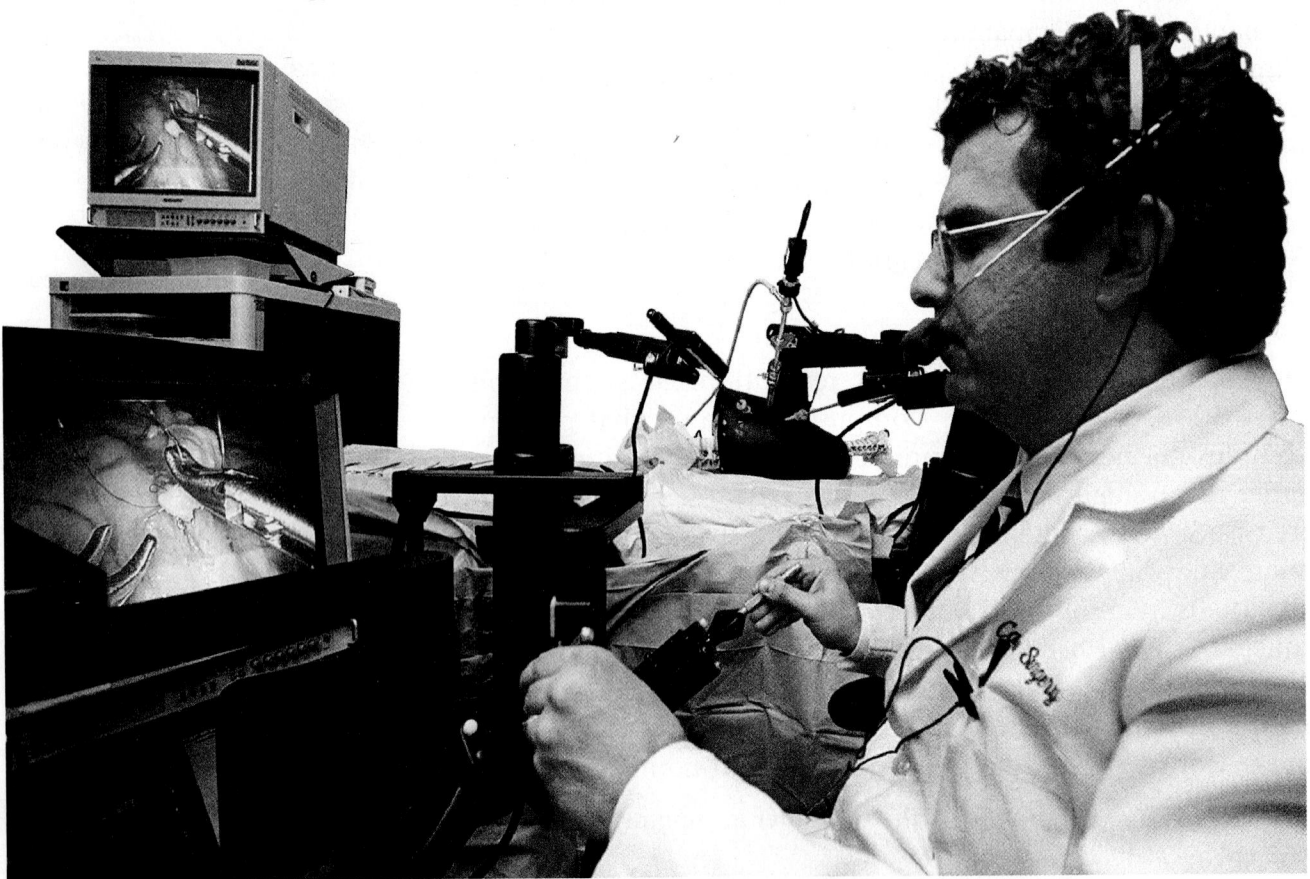

Technology and Ethics

Technology can cause harm if misused. Sometimes, the development of technology occurs faster than people can decide the best use for it. That is why scientific ethics are important. Scientific ethics guide scientists when they design and perform experiments. Scientific ethics also help scientists decide the proper use of technology.

Technology can be used ethically to communicate the risks and benefits of scientific endeavors. The scientists in **Figure 4** are communicating their findings to the public by using video and models. Another ethical use of technology is the use of computer-generated models to replace living subjects in some experiments. But when an experiment must be performed on living subjects, scientists can use technology to determine the risks posed to living subjects before the experiment even begins. Technology can often be used to reduce the amount of dangerous chemicals used in experiments involving animals.

Figure 4 *Scientific ethics demand that scientists communicate their findings to other scientists and to the public.*

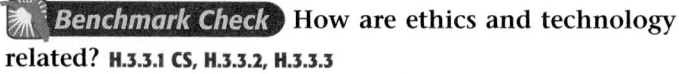 **Benchmark Check** How are ethics and technology related? H.3.3.1 CS, H.3.3.2, H.3.3.3

SECTION Review

Summary

● Technology is developed by people in many cultures and eventually is available to everyone. **H.3.3.6**

● Computers speed up and extend scientists' capabilities. **H.3.3.7**

● Technological design must take the values of society into account. **H.3.3.4 CS**

● Technology can help a scientist be ethical. **H.3.3.1 CS, H.3.3.2, H.3.3.3**

Understanding Key Ideas

1. Which statement about technology is true? **H.3.3.6**
   a. Technology can be used only by the people who develop it.
   b. Technology is developed to address human needs.
   c. Rain is one example of technology.
   d. Technology has been developed only since 1805.

2. List two ways that scientists benefit from computers. **H.3.3.7**

Critical Thinking

3. **Expressing Opinions** How has technology changed the way that experiments involving living subjects are conducted? **H.3.3.1 CS**

4. **Applying Concepts** What questions must a scientist ask while designing a new technology for treating acne? **H.3.3.4 CS**

FCAT Preparation

5. A local college is designing a new inhaler for asthma patients. Which of the following should be considered in the design? **H.3.3.4 CS**
   A. the name of the journal that will publish the research
   B. names of similar diseases
   C. cost of making the inhaler
   D. the number of asthma patients in 1950

SC¡LINKS®   NSTA
Developed and maintained by the National Science Teachers Association

For a variety of links related to this chapter, go to www.scilinks.org

Topic: Science and Technology of Florida
SciLinks code: HSMF14

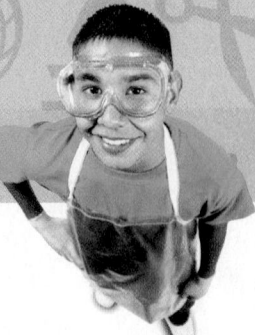

Skills Practice Lab

OBJECTIVES

Analyze a crime scene.

Reconstruct events based on observations.

MATERIALS

- Crime-Scene Processing Kit

Crime-Scene Processing

Someone has been in the classroom. Papers are all over the floor. The room is a mess! But who did it, and why? According to Locard's exchange principle, anyone who enters a room both takes something from the scene and leaves something behind. Using this principle, can you get to the bottom of this mystery?

In this lab, you will be investigating the scene of a crime that occurred in your classroom. Follow the steps below to explore who was in the classroom and why the room was left so messy!

Ask a Question

1 What took place in the room? Why is it such a mess, and why hasn't it been cleaned up yet?

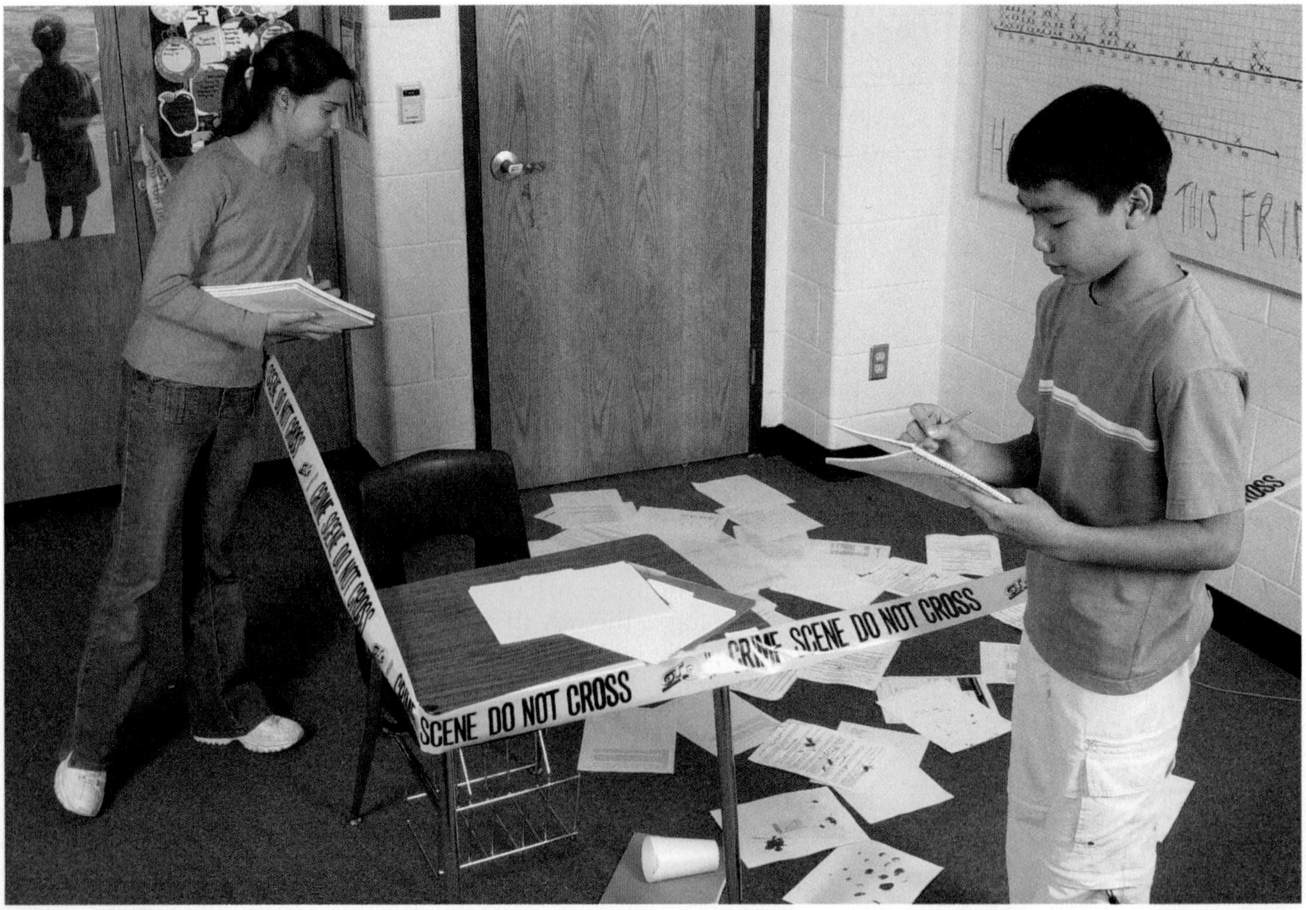

Form a Hypothesis

2 In a small group and from a distance, see if you can guess what has taken place. Write a hypothesis that answers the questions in step 1. Explain your reasoning.

Test the Hypothesis

3 Carefully read the following statement from the custodian:

Yes, I saw the room like this when I came in to clean yesterday at 6:30 P.M. I knew something wasn't right, so I left. This room is never as messy as it was last night. As you can see, there are papers and trash thrown all over. The school was pretty busy yesterday. It's homecoming week. Cheerleaders were painting banners, and people were rehearsing for the talent show. During the day, the school was a very active place.

4 Obtain a crime-scene processing kit from your teacher. Distribute the materials to each person in your group.

5 Determine a use for each object in the kit. Make a data table that lists each object and a description of how each object will be used.

6 When your teacher instructs you to do so, go to the crime-scene area and begin making careful observations. Do not touch anything.

7 Record all of the observations that your group makes.

8 Using your group's observations, determine how closely the data that you collected support your hypothesis.

9 Compare your hypothesis and observations with those of at least two other groups.

Analyze the Results

1 **Examining Data** How do your hypothesis and observations agree or disagree with the hypotheses and observations of the other groups in your class? Explain in as much detail as possible.

2 **Examining Data** Label each observation that you collected as either quantitative or qualitative.

Draw Conclusions

3 **Drawing Conclusions** Write a paragraph explaining what you think happened in the room yesterday. Be as specific as possible. Support your description with the observations and data that you collected. Underline statements included in your description that are not supported by direct observations or evidence.

4 **Applying Conclusions** Using your answer to item 3, create a plan for collecting the information needed to solve this case. Include names of people or groups of people that you would like to interview as well as a list of questions for each interview.

Applying Your Data

How does Locard's exchange principle hold up in your life? For an entire school day, collect observations about each classroom that you enter. What kinds of clues do other students leave in your classrooms? What evidence do you leave behind when you move from one place to another? Write a short paragraph that explains your observations.

Chapter Review

USING KEY TERMS

Use a term from the chapter to complete each sentence below.

1 The ___ is the factor that the experimenter changes.

2 A reference line that forms one side of a graph is called a(n) ___.

3 A(n) ___ is a rough or approximate calculation.

4 The ___ changes in response to the independent variable.

5 ___ is the use of tools, materials, or processes to meet human needs.

6 Scientists often create a(n) ___ when they cannot easily study the real thing.

UNDERSTANDING KEY IDEAS

Multiple Choice

7 Which of the following observations about frog eggs found in a pond is a quantitative observation?

　a. Each egg measures 0.5 cm across.

　b. The center of each egg is black.

　c. The eggs are found near the shore.

　d. Many eggs were stuck together in a group.

8 Why are computers important to scientists? **H.3.3.7**

　a. Computers extend human abilities.

　b. Computers do things faster.

　c. Computers sort information easily.

　d. All of the above

9 In an experiment, the mass of each of five apples is measured. The results are 95 g, 85 g, 90 g, 85 g, and 100 g. What is the median mass?

　a. 85 g

　b. 90 g

　c. 92 g

　d. 95 g

10 Which of the following is the **least** important thing for a scientist to do when she conducts research in which animals are used?

　a. to consider if there are risks or dangers to herself or other living things

　b. to explain her results to other scientists

　c. to treat the animals with care and respect

　d. to use a computer

Short Answer

11 Make three qualitative and three quantitative observations about yourself.

12 A data table shows the age and height of a person on his birthday each year. What is the independent variable?

13 Several scientists are working together to study coral reefs and coastal ecosystems. Describe two ways that they might use computers in their work.

Math Skills

14 Find the mean, median, and mode of the following data set: 8.9 cm, 7.2 cm, 15.7 cm, 5.2 cm, and 15.7 cm.

CRITICAL THINKING

Extended Response

15 **Identifying Relationships** Science has been used to develop technology to meet the needs of human beings. Identify how scientific ethics have determined the use of technology as it is developed. **H.3.3.1 CS**

16 **Predicting Consequences** Scientists are constrained in many ways when designing new technology. Predict how an aluminum shortage might impact the design of new soft-drink containers. **H.3.3.4 CS**

17 **Applying Concepts** A baby's mass is measured when the baby is born and then every month for 6 months. At 3 months of age, the baby was sick, so the baby's mass was not measured. Create a graph by using the data table below. Use the graph to find the likely mass of the baby at 3 months. **H.2.3.1 CS**

Age (months)	Mass (kg)
0	3.2
1	4.2
2	5.1
4	6.7
5	7.3
6	7.8

Concept Mapping

18 Use the following terms to create a concept map: *observation, quantitative observation, qualitative observation, estimate, model,* and *technology.*

INTERPRETING GRAPHICS

The graph below shows average monthly temperatures in Tampa, Florida. Use the graph below to answer the questions that follow.

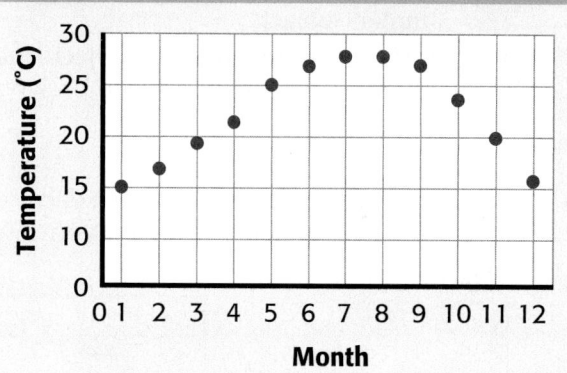

Average Monthly Temperature in Tampa, FL

19 What are the warmest months?

20 Which month has an average temperature of 20°C?

For the following questions, write your answers on a separate sheet of paper.

1  Because scientists are at work all over the world, it is important for them to communicate their observations and results with the rest of the scientific community. One way that scientists can communicate with each other is through mathematics, which is often called the language of science. How is mathematics essential to scientific communication? Give two examples.

2 A medical research scientist is designing an experiment to determine the effectiveness of a newly developed chemical substance that will be used to treat a human disease. The new substance might cause harmful side effects in people. What is the **best** way to address some of the ethical issues that must be considered in the design of the experiment?

    A.   Use animals in the experiment so that no humans are exposed to potential harm.

    B.   Design the experiment to be as cost-effective as possible because funding is hard to find.

    C.   Explore the possibility of a computer-generated model before testing the substance on human subjects.

    D.   Inform potential human subjects that there are risks, but be careful not to reveal too much or they might want to back out as subjects.

3 Because using graphs is such an excellent way to visually communicate data trends, scientists often use them to help them communicate scientific information.

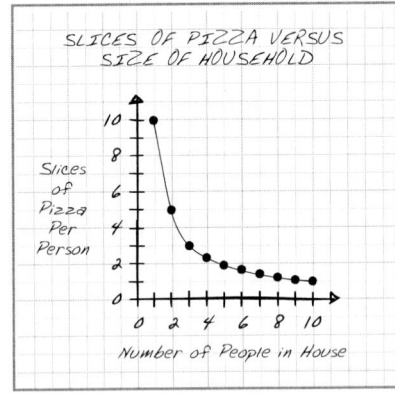

What trend is depicted in the graph?

    F.   There is no relationship between the variables in this graph.

    G.   There is not enough information in the graph to determine the trend.

    H.   The dependent variable decreases as the independent variable increases.

    I.   The dependent variable decreases as the independent variable decreases.

4 Analyzing data is important in scientific investigations because it helps scientists to understand and communicate their results. One way that a data sample can be described is by finding the average of a data set. There are three different ways of calculating the average: median, mean, and mode. The table below records length in meters (m).

Length (m)
115
125
115
150
135
160
120
145
130
155

What is the mode of the data in the table?

A. 115 m
B. 135 m
C. 140 m
D. 160 m

5 Technology is defined as the use of tools, materials, and processes to meet human needs. Throughout history and across the world, people have pursued the development of technology. Which of the following statements describes technology throughout history and across cultures?

F. As technology spreads, it never changes.
G. The technology of the past is of very little use today.
H. As time passes, technology and knowledge become available to everyone.
I. When designing technology, scientists and inventors can use whatever they want.

6 Which of the following lists **best** describes some primary considerations that a scientist should take into account when designing new technology?

A. benefits to corporations or institutions providing funding and costs of materials used
B. costs, benefits to society, properties of materials used, and safety to humans and animals
C. how it will affect the scientist's career and if there is a way to use other scientific research to save time
D. how much time is involved, how much money can be made, and how the technology can be kept secret

Science in Action

Science, Technology, and Society

Kanzi

Did you know that some chimpanzees raised in captivity can learn to understand some parts of human language? These animals cannot speak any human words. But researchers working with Kanzi, a bonobo chimp who has grown up in Georgia, have used technology to help him communicate. Kanzi uses a board that has more than 400 buttons. On the buttons are symbols that represent different words. Kanzi presses a button to communicate the word represented by that button. This board of buttons allows Kanzi to communicate with people.

Weird Science

Dolphins in the Navy

Did you know that some dolphins work for the U.S. Navy? One way that dolphins help the U.S. Navy's Marine Mammal Program is by detecting underwater mines. Underwater mines are bombs that drift underwater. Most mines explode when a large object bumps into them. Dolphins can find mines safely by using *echolocation*, a natural sonar system that allows dolphins to sense their surroundings, even in murky waters. When a dolphin finds a mine and alerts a person, experts can deactivate the mine.

Math ACTiViTY

Suppose that each dolphin in the navy's program is trained for 5 years and each trained dolphin works for 25 years. If 10 dolphins began training each year for 10 years, how many would be working at the end of those 10 years? How many would still be in training?

Language Arts ACTiViTY

WRITING SKILL What would you ask Kanzi if you could speak to him? Think of a question that you would like to ask an animal. Imagine how the animal might respond. In the first person, write this response in a creative essay.

Evan Forde

Oceanographer   You're 2 mi below the water's surface, trapped in a tiny submarine. A small, underwater landslide has partially buried your sub. Ten minutes crawl by. The submarine finally breaks free, and you notice that your heartbeat and breathing begin to slow. You are just 28 years old, but you're already an expert on undersea canyons. When you were a high school student in Miami–Dade County, you never thought that your work would include such exciting experiences!

Evan Forde survived his submarine scare and continues to enjoy being an oceanographer, a scientist who studies oceans. Forde and other oceanographers use a variety of tools to help them explore and understand the oceans. Forde works for the National Oceanic and Atmospheric Association (NOAA), a scientific branch of the U.S. government. His current specialty is using satellites and computers to improve early-warning systems for detecting hurricanes. Forde is part of NOAA's Atlantic Oceanographic and Meteorological Laboratory, which is located in Miami, Florida.

Social Studies ACTIVITY

Research an oceanographer of your choice, and prepare a class presentation on your findings. Focus on the accomplishments of the scientist and the ways that the scientist used technology to study the oceans.

To learn more about these Science in Action topics, visit **go.hrw.com** and type in the keyword **HT6FTF7F.**

Current Science

Check out Current Science® articles related to this chapter by visiting **go.hrw.com.** Just type in the keyword **HP6CS19.**

Cells

Cells are everywhere. Even though most cells can't be seen with the naked eye, they make up every living thing. Living things may be made up of one cell or many cells. Your body alone contains trillions of cells!

In this unit, you will learn about different kinds of cells. You will also learn about what happens in a cell. This timeline shows some of the discoveries that scientists have made about cells. Each discovery has helped people understand more about these tiny, mysterious structures.

1492
Christopher Columbus reaches North America after sailing from Europe.

Around 1595
Zacharias and Hans Janssen build the first compound microscope.

1838
Johannes Muller proves that cancerous tumors are made up of cells.

1869
Friedrich Miescher discovers a special material in the nucleus of a white blood cell. Later research on this material leads to the discovery of DNA.

White blood cell

1999
Elizabeth Gould and Charles Gross discover that cells in the brain can be repaired and regrown. This discovery contradicts previous scientific understanding.

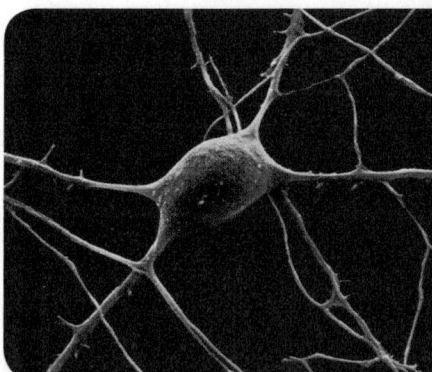

A neuron

1665

Robert Hooke looks at cork under a microscope and uses the name *cells* to describe the small structures that he sees.

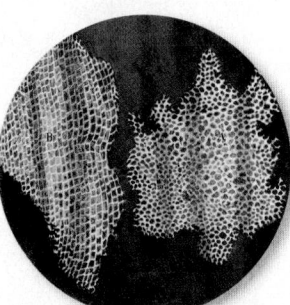

1683

Anton van Leeuwenhoek uses a microscope to observe bacteria living on his teeth. He calls these bacteria *animalcules*.

Streptococcus sanguis found on teeth

1809

Abraham Lincoln, the 16th president of the United States, is born.

1873

Camillo Golgi develops a stain that allows scientists to view the structure of entire nerve cells.

1937

Sir Hans Adolf Krebs discovers how cells produce energy from nutrients through the citric acid cycle.

1967

Ragnar Granit, Haldan Hartline, and George Wald are awarded a Nobel Prize for describing how cells in the eye are sensitive to light.

Rods and cones in the eye

1999

The largest known bacterial species, *Thiomargarita namibiensis,* is discovered near Namibia. The cell of one bacterium is 0.3 mm long!

2001

Two separate groups publish the decoded human genome.

2003

Peter Agre receives a Nobel Prize for discovering water channels in human cells.

Cells: The Basic Units of Life

The Big Idea All living things are made of one or more cells.

About the PHOTO

Harmful bacteria may invade your body and make you sick. But wait—your white blood cells come to the rescue! In this image, a white blood cell (the large, yellowish cell) reaches out its pseudopod to destroy bacteria (the purple cells). The red discs are red blood cells.

 **Key-Term Fold** Before you read the chapter, create the FoldNote entitled "Key-Term Fold" described in the **Study Skills** section of the Appendix. Write a key term from the chapter on each tab of the key-term fold. Under each tab, write the definition of the key term.

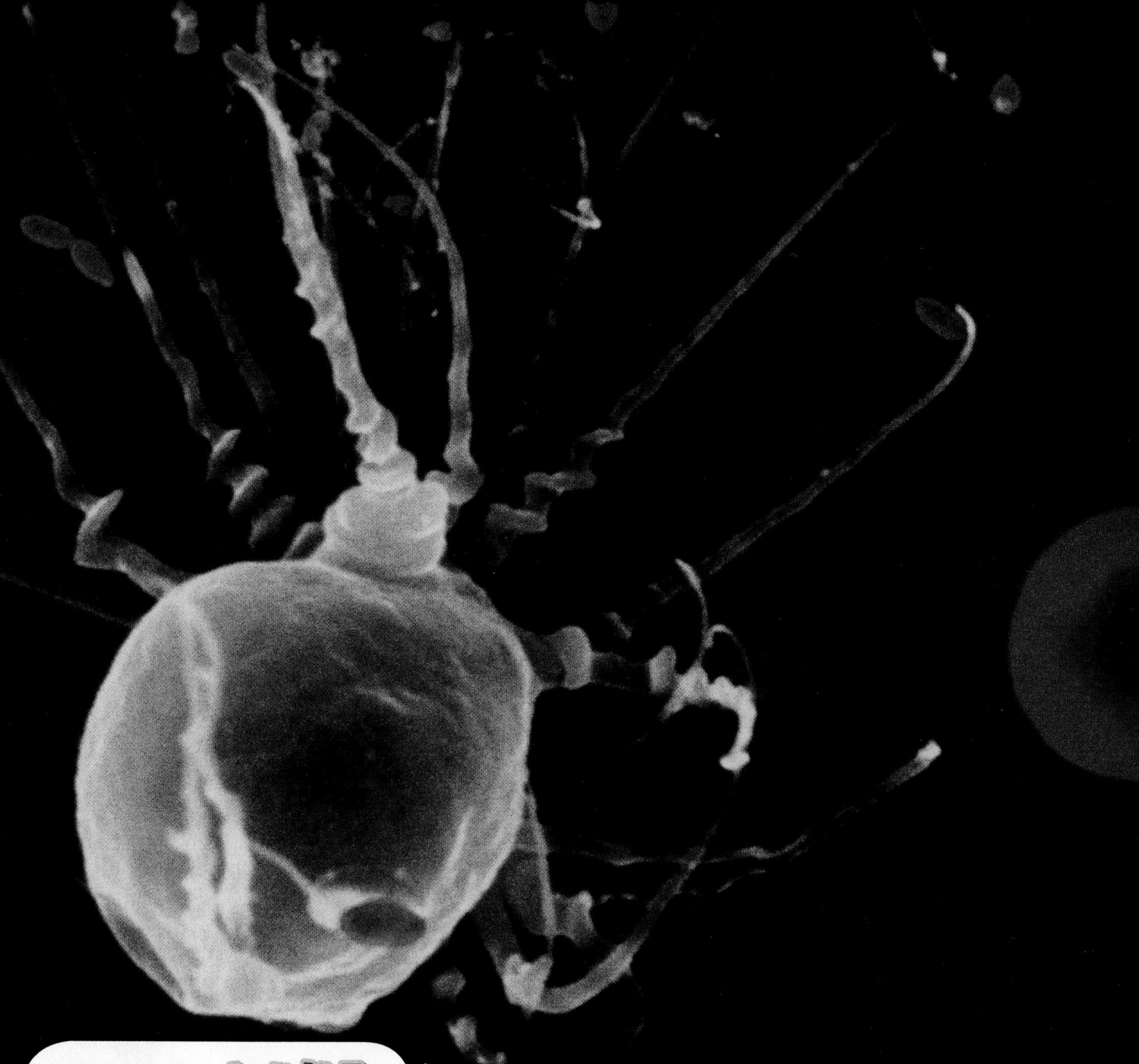

START-UP ACTIVITY

What Are Plants Made Of? F.1.3.2 CS

All living things, including plants, are made of cells. What do plant cells look like? Do this activity to find out.

Procedure

1. Tear off a **small leaf** from near the tip of an **Elodea sprig.**

2. Using **forceps,** place the whole leaf in a **drop of water** on a **microscope slide.**

3. Place a **coverslip** on top of the water drop by putting one edge of the coverslip on the slide near the water drop. Next, lower the coverslip slowly so that the coverslip does not trap air bubbles.

4. Place the slide on your **microscope.**

5. Using the lowest-powered lens first, find the plant cells. When you can see the cells under the lower-powered lens, switch to a higher-powered lens.

6. Draw a picture of what you see.

Analysis

1. Describe the shape of the Elodea cells. Are all of the cells in the Elodea the same?

2. Do you think human cells look like Elodea cells? How do you think they are different? How might they be similar?

SECTION 1

The Diversity of Cells

Most cells are so small they can't be seen by the naked eye. So, how did scientists find cells? By accident, that's how! The first person to see cells wasn't even looking for them.

The structural basis of all living things is the cell. A **cell** is the smallest unit that can perform all of the processes necessary for life. Because of their size, cells weren't discovered until microscopes were invented in the mid-1600s.

Cells and the Cell Theory

Robert Hooke was the first person to describe cells. In 1665, he built a microscope to look at tiny objects. One day, he looked at a thin slice of cork. Cork is found in the bark of cork trees. The cork looked as if it was made of little boxes. Hooke named these boxes *cells,* which means "little rooms" in Latin. Hooke's cells were really the outer layers of dead cork cells. Hooke's microscope and his drawing of the cork cells are shown in **Figure 1.**

Hooke also looked at thin slices of living plants. He saw that the slices too were made of cells. Some cells were even filled with "juice." The "juicy" cells were living cells.

Hooke also looked at feathers, fish scales, and the eyes of houseflies. But he spent most of his time looking at plants and fungi. The cells of plants and fungi have cell walls and thus are easy to see. Animal cells do not have cell walls. The absence of cell walls makes it harder to see the outline of animal cells. Because Hooke couldn't see their cells, he thought that animals weren't made of cells.

READING WARM-UP

Objectives

● State the parts of the cell theory. **F.1.3.2 CS**

● Explain why cells are so small.

● Describe the parts of a cell.

● Explain the difference between prokaryotic cells and eukaryotic cells.

● Identify how scientists classify organisms. **G.1.3.3 CS**

Terms to Learn

cell
cell membrane
organelle
nucleus **FCAT** *VOCAB*
prokaryote
eukaryote

READING STRATEGY

Reading Organizer As you read this section, create an outline of the section. Use the headings from the section in your outline.

cell in biology, the smallest unit that can perform all life processes and cells are covered by a membrane and have DNA and cytoplasm

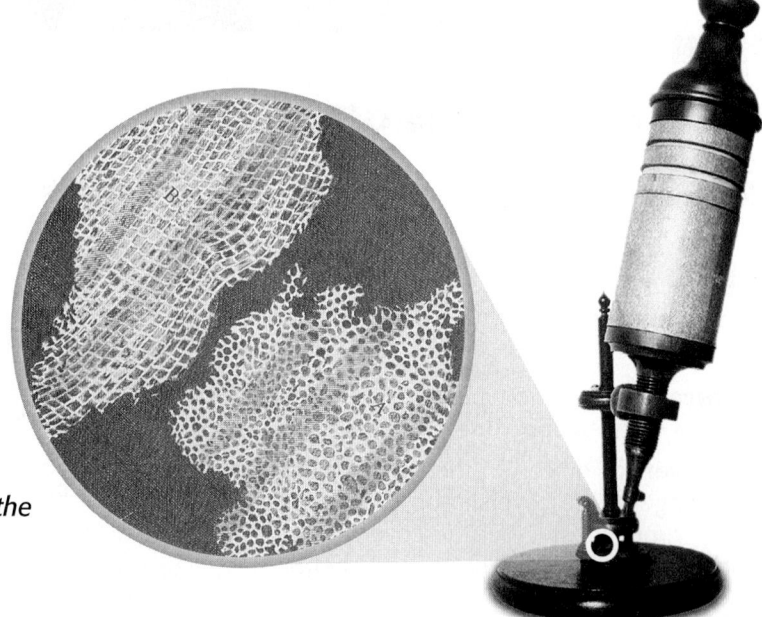

Figure 1 *Hooke discovered cells by using this microscope. Hooke's drawing of cork cells is shown to the left of his microscope.*

Ceratium

Campylodiscus

Symbiodinium

Figure 2 *Protists that are members of the genera* Ceratium *and* Campylodiscus, *live in the water. Protists that are members of the genus* Symbiodinium, *live within organisms such as this kind of brain coral found on the reefs in Florida.*

Finding Cells in Other Organisms

In 1673, Anton van Leeuwenhoek (LAY vuhn HOOK), a Dutch merchant, made his own microscopes. Leeuwenhoek used one of his microscopes to look at pond scum. Leeuwenhoek saw small organisms in the water. He named these organisms *animalcules,* which means "little animals." Today, we call these single-celled organisms *protists* (PROH tists). Protists are found in the water and in other organisms, as shown in **Figure 2**.

Leeuwenhoek also looked at animal blood. He saw differences in blood cells from different kinds of animals. For example, blood cells in fish, birds, and frogs are oval. Blood cells in humans and dogs are round and flat. Leeuwenhoek was also the first person to see bacteria. And he discovered that yeasts that make bread dough rise are single-celled organisms.

The Cell Theory

Almost 200 years passed before scientists concluded that cells are present in all living things. Scientist Matthias Schleiden (mah THEE uhs SHLIE duhn) studied plants. In 1838, he concluded that all plant parts were made of cells. Theodor Schwann (TAY oh dohr SHVAHN) studied animals. In 1839, Schwann concluded that all animal tissues were made of cells. Soon after that, Schwann wrote the first two parts of what is now known as the *cell theory:*

- All organisms are made of one or more cells.
- The cell is the basic unit of all living things.

Later, in 1858, Rudolf Virchow (ROO dawlf FIR koh), a doctor, stated that all cells could form only from other cells. Virchow then added the third part of the cell theory:

- All cells come from existing cells.

Benchmark Check What is the basic structural unit of all living things? F.1.3.2 CS

CONNECTION TO Physics

Microscopes The microscope that Hooke used to study cells was much different from microscopes today. Research different kinds of microscopes, such as light microscopes, scanning electron microscopes (SEMs), and transmission electron microscopes (TEMs). Select one type of microscope. Make a poster or other presentation to show to the class. Describe how the microscope works and how it is used. Be sure to include images.

ACTIVITY

F.1.3.2 CS knows that the structural basis of most organisms is the cell and most organisms are single cells, while some, including humans, are multicellular.

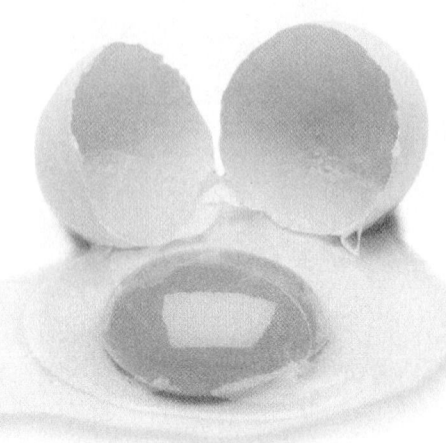

Figure 3 *The white and yolk of this chicken egg provide nutrients for the development of a chick.*

Cell Size

Most cells are too small to be seen without a microscope. It would take 50 human cells to cover the dot on this letter i.

A Few Large Cells

Most cells are small. A few, however, are big. The yolk of a chicken egg, shown in **Figure 3,** is one big cell. The egg can be this large because it does not have to take in extra nutrients.

Many Small Cells

There is a physical reason why most cells are so small. Cells take in food and get rid of wastes through their outer surface. As a cell gets larger, it needs more food and produces more waste. Therefore, more materials pass through its outer surface.

As the cell's volume increases, its surface area grows, too. But the cell's volume grows faster than its surface area. If a cell gets too large, the cell's surface area will not be large enough to take in enough nutrients or pump out enough wastes. So, the area of a cell's surface compared with the cell's volume limits the cell's size. The ratio of the cell's outer surface area to the cell's volume is called the *surface area–to-volume ratio,* which can be calculated by using the following equation:

$$surface\ area\text{–}to\text{-}volume\ ratio = \frac{surface\ area}{volume}$$

F.1.3.2 CS knows that the structural basis of most organisms is the cell and most organisms are single cells, while some, including humans, are multicellular.

✓ **Reading Check** Why are most cells small?

Surface Area-to-Volume Ratio Calculate the surface area–to-volume ratio of a cube whose sides measure 2 cm.

Step 1: Calculate the surface area.

surface area of cube = number of sides × area of side

surface area of cube = 6 × (2 cm × 2 cm)

surface area of cube = 24 cm²

Step 2: Calculate the volume.

volume of cube = side × side × side

volume of cube = 2 cm × 2 cm × 2 cm

volume of cube = 8 cm³

Step 3: Calculate the surface area–to-volume ratio.

$$surface\ area\text{–}to\text{-}volume\ ratio = \frac{surface\ area}{volume} = \frac{24}{8} = \frac{3}{1}$$

Now It's Your Turn

1. Calculate the surface area–to-volume ratio of a cube whose sides are 3 cm long.

2. Calculate the surface area–to-volume ratio of a cube whose sides are 4 cm long.

3. Of the cubes from questions 1 and 2, which has the greater surface area–to-volume ratio?

4. What is the relationship between the length of a side and the surface area–to-volume ratio of a cell?

Parts of a Cell

Cells come in many shapes and sizes. Cells have many different functions. But all cells, including those in multicellular organisms, have the parts discussed below in common.

The Cell Membrane and Cytoplasm

All cells are surrounded by a cell membrane. The **cell membrane** is a protective layer that covers the cell's surface and acts as a barrier. It separates the cell's contents from its environment. The cell membrane also controls materials going into and out of the cell. Inside the cell is a fluid. This fluid and almost all of its contents are called the *cytoplasm* (SIET oh PLAZ uhm).

Organelles

Cells have organelles that carry out various life processes. **Organelles** are structures that perform specific functions within the cell. Different types of cells have different organelles. Most organelles are surrounded by membranes. For example, the algal cell in **Figure 4** has membrane-bound organelles. Some organelles float in the cytoplasm, and some organelles are attached to membranes or to other organelles.

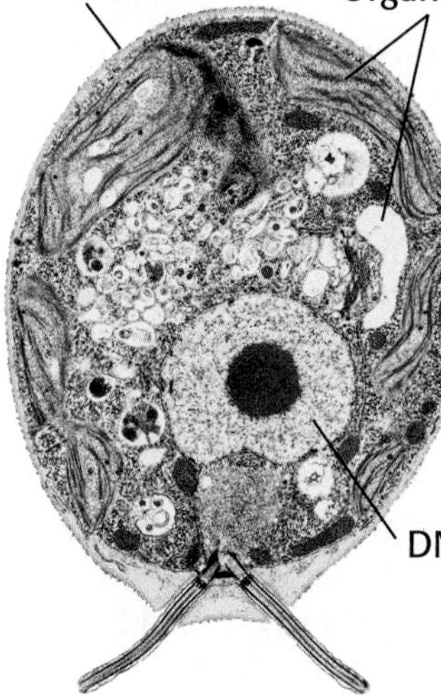

Genetic Material

All cells contain DNA (**d**eoxyribo**n**ucleic **a**cid) at some point in their life. *DNA* is the genetic material that carries information needed to make new cells and new organisms. DNA is passed on from parent cells to new cells and controls the activities of a cell. **Figure 5** shows the DNA of a bacterium.

In some cells, the DNA is enclosed inside an organelle called the **nucleus.** For example, your cells have a nucleus. In contrast, bacterial cells do not have a nucleus.

In humans, mature red blood cells lose their DNA. Red blood cells are made inside bones. When red blood cells are first made, they have a nucleus with DNA. But before they enter the bloodstream, red blood cells lose their nucleus and DNA. They survive with no new instructions from their DNA.

Cell membrane — Organelles

DNA

Figure 4 *This green alga has organelles. The organelles and the fluid surrounding them make up the cytoplasm.*

cell membrane a phospholipid layer that covers a cell's surface and acts as a barrier between the inside of a cell and the cell's environment

organelle one of the small bodies in a cell's cytoplasm that are specialized to perform a specific function

nucleus in a eukaryotic cell, a membrane-bound organelle that contains the cell's DNA and that has a role in processes such as growth, metabolism, and reproduction
FCATVOCAB

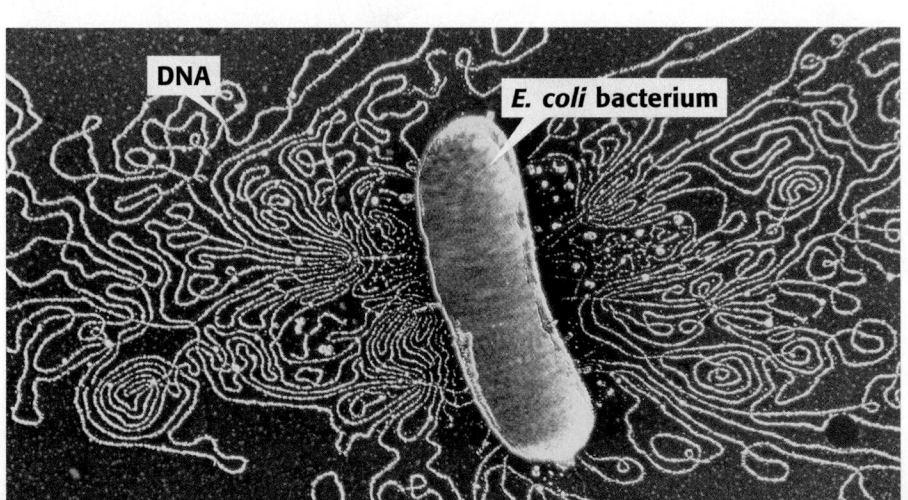

DNA

E. coli bacterium

Figure 5 *This photo shows an* Escherichia coli *bacterium. The bacterium's cell membrane has been treated so that the cell's DNA is released.*

prokaryote an organism that consists of a single cell that does not have a nucleus and has no membrane-bound organelles

Two Kinds of Cells

All organisms are made of one or more cells. All cells have the following structures: a cell membrane, organelles, cytoplasm, and DNA. There are two basic types of cells: prokaryotic (PROH kar ee AHT ik) cells and eukaryotic (YOO kar ee AHT ik) cells. *Prokaryotic cells* are cells that do not have a nucleus. *Eukaryotic cells* are cells that have a nucleus. Organisms that are made up of prokaryotic cells are called prokaryotes (pro KAR ee OHTS). **Prokaryotes** are single-celled organisms that do not have a nucleus or membrane-bound organelles.

Prokaryotes: Bacteria and Archaea

Grouping organisms into different levels of classification, such as domains and kingdoms, is useful in studying organisms. Scientists use many characteristics to classify prokaryotes into two domains: Bacteria (bak TIR ee uh) and Archaea (ahr KEE uh).

Benchmark Check What do scientists use to classify organisms, such as prokaryotes? G.1.3.3 CS

Bacteria

Domain Bacteria is made up of bacteria (singular bacterium). A bacterium's DNA is a long, circular molecule that is shaped like a twisted rubber band. The DNA molecule floats in the cytoplasm of the cell. Bacteria have ribosomes, which are tiny, round organelles that are not membranebound. Bacteria also have a strong, weblike cell wall. This wall helps the cell retain its shape. A bacterium's cell wall lies on the outside of the cell membrane. The cell wall and cell membrane allow materials into and out of the cell. Some bacteria live in soil and in water. Bacteria also live in or on other organisms. For example, bacteria live on your skin and in your digestive system. **Figure 6** shows a typical bacterial cell.

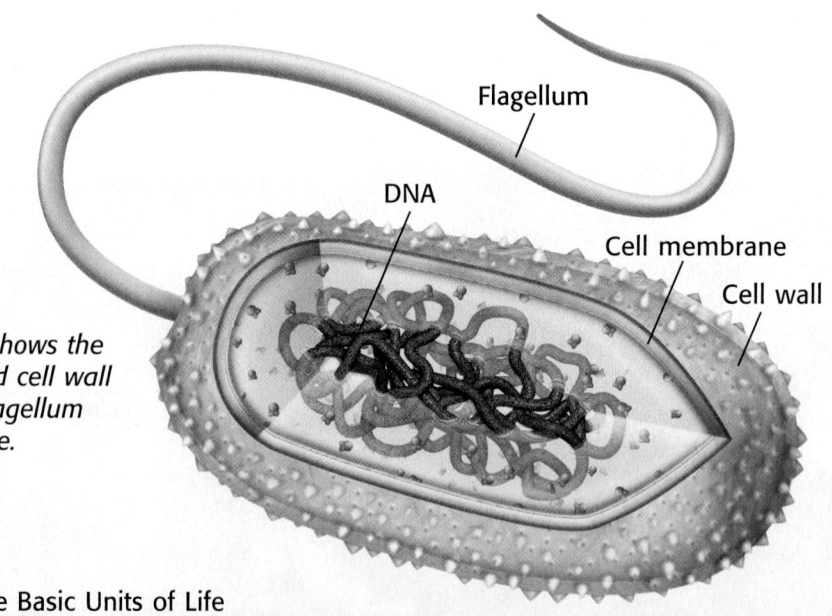

Figure 6 *This diagram shows the DNA, cell membrane, and cell wall of a bacterial cell. The flagellum helps the bacterium move.*

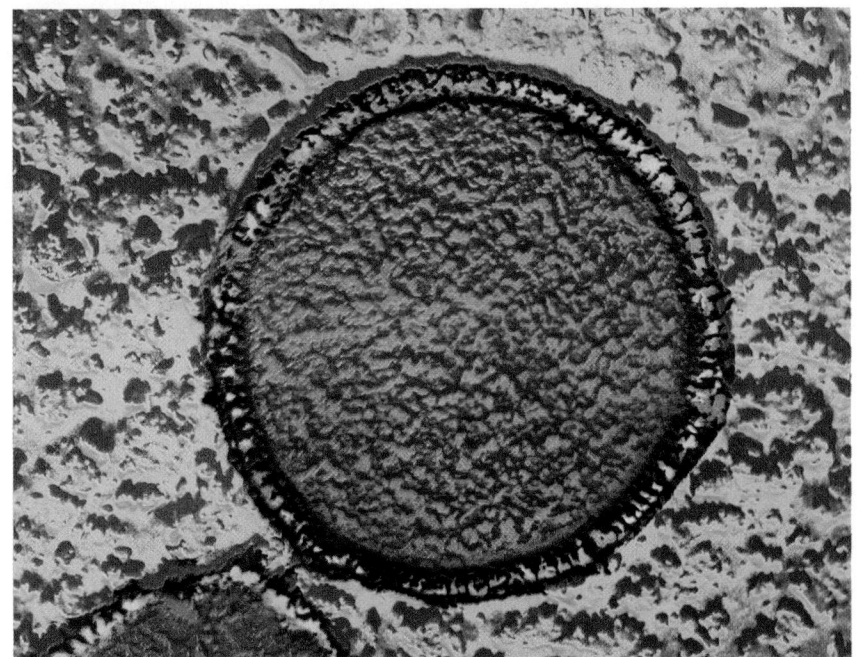

Figure 7 *This photograph, taken with an electron microscope, is of an archaeon that lives in the very high temperatures of deep-sea volcanic vents. The photograph has been colored so that the cell wall is green and the cell contents are pink.*

Archaea

Domain Archaea is made up of archaea (singular archeon). Archaea are similar to bacteria in some ways. For example, both are single-celled organisms. Both have ribosomes, a cell membrane, and circular DNA. And both lack a nucleus and membrane-bound organelles. But archaea differ from bacteria in some ways, too. For example, archaeal ribosomes differ from bacterial ribosomes.

Archaea are similar to eukaryotic cells in some ways, too. For example, archaeal ribosomes are more like the ribosomes of eukaryotic cells than like bacterial ribosomes. But archaea also have some features that no other organisms have. For example, the cell wall and cell membrane of archaea have some unique features. And some archaea live in places where no other organisms are able to live.

Three types of archaea are *heat-loving,* *salt-loving,* and *methane-making* archaea. Methane is a gas that is frequently found in swamps. Heat-loving and salt-loving archaea are sometimes called *extremophiles.* Extremophiles live where conditions are extreme. Some live in very hot water, such as in hot springs, and some live in extremely salty water. **Figure 7** shows a kind of methane-making archaeon that lives deep in the ocean near volcanic vents. The temperature of the water from those vents is above the boiling point of water at sea level. However, scientists believe that archaea live not only in extreme environments but also in plankton of the open sea.

✓ Reading Check **What is one difference between bacteria and archaea?**

CONNECTION TO Social Studies

Where Do They Live? While most archaea live in extreme environments, scientists have found that archaea live almost everywhere. Do research about archaea. Select one kind of archaeon. Create a poster showing the organism's geographical location, describing its physical environment, and explaining how the organism survives in its environment.

ACTIVITY

F.1.3.2 CS knows that the structural basis of most organisms is the cell and most organisms are single cells, while some, including humans, are multicellular.

G.1.3.3 CS understands that the classification of living things is based on a given set of critera and is a tool for understanding biodiversity and interrelationships.

Cell World Invite tourists to visit different parts of the cell. Go to **go.hrw.com** and type in the keyword **HL5CELW**.

eukaryote an organism made up of cells that have a nucleus enclosed by a membrane; eukaryotes include animals, plants, and fungi but not archaea or bacteria

F.1.3.2 CS knows that the structural basis of most organisms is the cell and most organisms are single cells, while some, including humans, are multicellular.

G.1.3.3 CS understands that the classification of living things is based on a given set of critera and is a tool for understanding biodiversity and interrelationships.

Eukaryotic Cells and Eukaryotes

Eukaryotic cells are the largest cells. Most eukaryotic cells are still microscopic, but they are about 10 times larger than most bacterial cells. A typical eukaryotic cell is shown in **Figure 8.**

Unlike bacteria and archaea, eukaryotic cells have a nucleus. The nucleus is one kind of membrane-bound organelle. A cell's nucleus holds the cell's DNA. Eukaryotic cells have other membrane-bound organelles, too. Organelles are like the different organs in your body. Each kind of organelle has a specific job in the cell. Together, organelles, such as the ones shown in **Figure 8,** perform all of the processes necessary for life.

Organisms made of eukaryotic cells are called **eukaryotes.** All eukaryotes are classified into the domain Eukarya. Many eukaryotes are multicellular, which means having "many cells." Multicellular organisms are usually larger than single-celled organisms. So, most organisms that you see with your naked eye are eukaryotes. The domain Eukarya is further divided into four kingdoms. Kingdom Animalia is made up of animals (including humans), which are multicellular. Kingdom Plantae is made up of plants. Kingdom Protista includes amoebas, which are singlecelled and green algae, some of which are multicellular. Kingdom Fungi includes yeasts, which are singlecelled and mushrooms, which are multicellular.

Reading Check How do eukaryotes and prokaryotes differ?

Figure 8   Organelles in a Typical Eukaryotic Cell

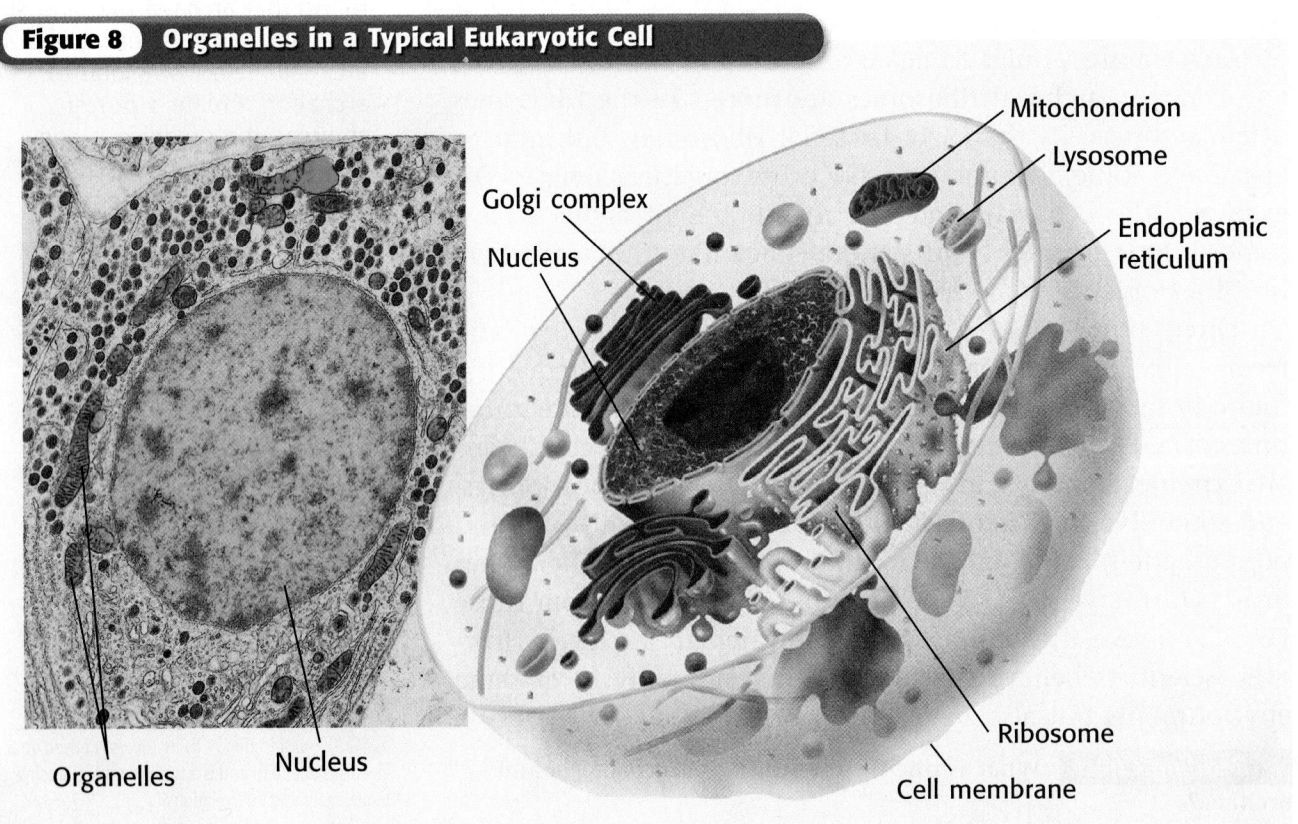

Organelles

Nucleus

Golgi complex

Nucleus

Mitochondrion

Lysosome

Endoplasmic reticulum

Ribosome

Cell membrane

Summary

- Cells were not discovered until microscopes were invented in the 1600s.

- The cell theory states that all organisms are made of cells, the cell is the basic structural unit of all living things, and all cells come from other cells. **F.1.3.2 CS**

- All cells have a cell membrane, cytoplasm, and DNA.

- Most cells are too small to be seen with the naked eye. A cell's surface area–to-volume ratio limits the size of a cell.

- The two basic kinds of cells are prokaryotic cells and eukaryotic cells. Eukaryotic cells have a nucleus and membrane-bound organelles. Prokaryotic cells lack these features.

- Scientists use characteristics to classify prokaryotes into the domains Bacteria and Archaea. **G.1.3.3 CS**

- All prokaryotes are single-celled organisms. Eukaryotes can be singlecelled or multicellular. **F.1.3.2 CS**

- Eukaryotes are classified into the domain Eukarya. **G.1.3.3 CS**

Using Key Terms

1. In your own words, write a definition for the term *organelle*.

2. Use the following terms in the same sentence: *prokaryotic, nucleus,* and *eukaryotic*.

Understanding Key Ideas

3. Cell size is limited by the
   a. thickness of the cell wall.
   b. size of the cell's nucleus.
   c. cell's surface area–to-volume ratio.
   d. amount of cytoplasm in the cell.

4. Name two structures that every cell has.

5. List two ways in which archaea differ from bacteria.

Critical Thinking

6. **Applying Concepts** You have discovered a new single-celled organism. It has a cell wall, ribosomes, and a long, circular DNA. Is it a prokaryote or a eukaryote? In to which domain is the organism classified? Explain. **G.1.3.3 CS**

7. **Identifying Relationships** A classmate brings you a cell that is about the size of the period at the end of this sentence. It is a single cell, but it can form chains. What characteristics will this cell have if it is a eukaryotic cell? if it is a prokaryotic cell? What characteristic will you look for first to determine the cell's type?

FCAT Preparation

8. When scientists were first able to see cells, they looked at all kinds of organisms. Their studies led them to make three main statements about the cell and the relationship between organisms and cells. They called this group of statements the *cell theory*. Which of the following statements is one of the statements that make up the cell theory? **F.1.3.2 CS**

   A. All organisms are made up of many cells.

   B. The cell is the basic unit of all living things.

   C. Archaea and bacteria are single-celled organisms that are prokaryotes.

   D. All cells are prokaryotic cells.

For a variety of links related to this chapter, go to www.scilinks.org

Topic: Prokaryotic Cells
SciLinks code: HSM1225

Eukaryotic Cells

Most eukaryotic cells are small. For a long time after cells were discovered, scientists could not see what was going on inside cells. They did not know how complex cells are.

Now, scientists know a lot about eukaryotic cells. These cells have many parts that work together and keep the cell alive.

Cell Wall

Some eukaryotic cells have cell walls. A **cell wall** is a rigid structure that gives support to a cell. The cell wall is the outermost structure of a cell. Plants and algae have cell walls made of cellulose (SEL yoo LOHS) and other materials. *Cellulose* is a complex sugar that most animals can't digest.

The cell walls of plant cells allow plants to stand upright. In some plants, the cells must take in water for the cell walls to keep their shape. When such plants lack water, the cell walls collapse and the plant droops. **Figure 1** shows a cross section of a plant cell and a close-up of the cell wall.

Fungi, including yeasts and mushrooms, also have cell walls. Some fungi have cell walls made of *chitin* (KIE tin). Other fungi have cell walls made from a chemical similar to chitin. Bacteria and archaea also have cell walls, but those walls are different from plant or fungal cell walls.

✔ **Reading Check** What types of cells have cell walls?

cell wall a rigid structure that surrounds the cell membrane and provides support to the cell

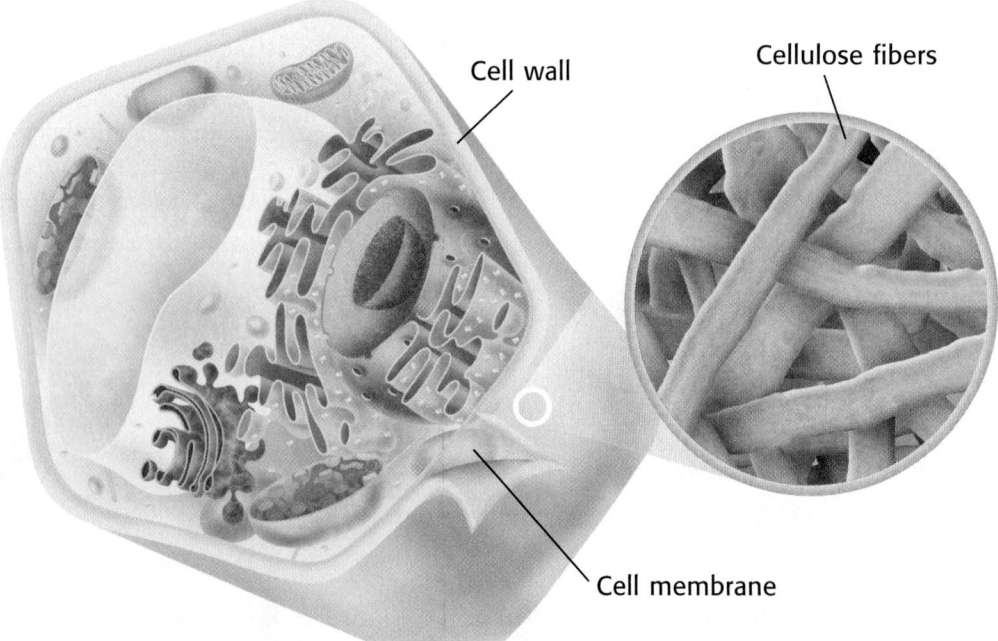

Figure 1 *The cell walls of plant cells help plants retain their shape. Plant cell walls are made of cellulose.*

Cell wall

Cellulose fibers

Cell membrane

Cell Membrane

All cells have a cell membrane. The *cell membrane* is a protective barrier that encloses a cell. It separates the cell's contents from the cell's environment. The cell membrane is the outermost structure in cells that lack a cell wall. In cells that have a cell wall, the cell membrane lies just inside the cell wall.

The cell membrane contains proteins, lipids, and phospholipids. *Lipids,* which include fats and cholesterol, are a group of compounds that do not dissolve in water. The cell membrane has two layers of phospholipids (FAHS foh LIP idz), shown in **Figure 2.** A *phospholipid* is a lipid that contains phosphorus. Lipids are "water fearing," or *hydrophobic.* Lipid ends of phospholipids form the inner part of the membrane. Phosphorus-containing ends of the phospholipids are "water loving," or *hydrophilic.* These ends form the outer part of the membrane.

Some of the proteins and lipids can actively attach to materials to move them into and out of the cell. Other proteins form passageways in the cell membrane. Many materials move into and out of the cell through these protein passageways. For example, nutrients move into the cell and wastes move out of the cell through these protein passageways.

Benchmark Check Why is it important to an organism that its cell membranes allow nutrients into its cells? **F.1.3.5 CS**

CONNECTION TO Language Arts

WRITING SKILL **The Great Barrier** In your **science journal,** write a science fiction story about tiny travelers inside a person's body. These little explorers want to visit the nucleus in a cell, but first they must cross the cell membrane. Research how the cell membrane works. Illustrate your story.

Hydrophilic heads

Phospholipids

Hydrophobic tails

Figure 2 *The cell membrane is made of two layers of phospholipids. It allows nutrients to enter the cell and allows wastes to exit the cell.*

Cell membrane

F.1.3.5 CS explains how the life functions of organisms are related to what occurs within the cell.

Cytoskeleton

The *cytoskeleton* (SIET oh SKEL uh tuhn) is a web of proteins in the cytoplasm. The cytoskeleton, shown in **Figure 3,** acts as both a muscle and a skeleton. It keeps the cell membrane from collapsing. The cytoskeleton also helps some cells move.

The cytoskeleton is made of three types of protein. One protein is a hollow tube. The other two are long, stringy fibers. One of the stringy proteins is also found in muscle cells.

Reading Check What is the cytoskeleton?

Nucleus

All eukaryotic cells have the same basic membrane-bound organelles. The *nucleus* is a large organelle in a eukaryotic cell. It contains the cell's DNA, or genetic material. DNA contains the information on how to make a cell's proteins. Proteins control the chemical reactions in a cell. They also provide structural support for cells and tissues. But proteins are not made in the nucleus. Messages for how to make proteins are copied from the DNA. These messages are then sent out of the nucleus through the membranes.

The nucleus is covered by two membranes. Materials cross this double membrane by passing through pores. **Figure 4** shows a nucleus and nuclear pores. The nucleus of many cells has a dark area called the *nucleolus* (noo KLEE uh luhs). The nucleolus is the place where a cell begins to make its ribosomes.

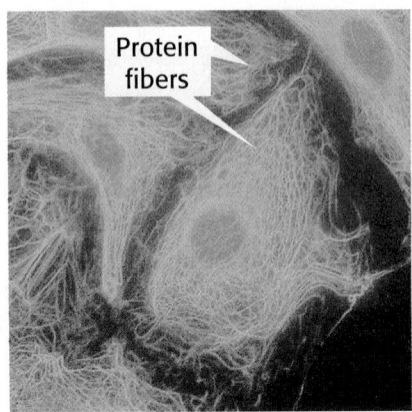

Figure 3 *The cytoskeleton, made of protein fibers, helps a cell retain its shape, move in its environment, and move its organelles.*

F.1.3.5 CS explains how the life functions of organisms are related to what occurs within the cell.

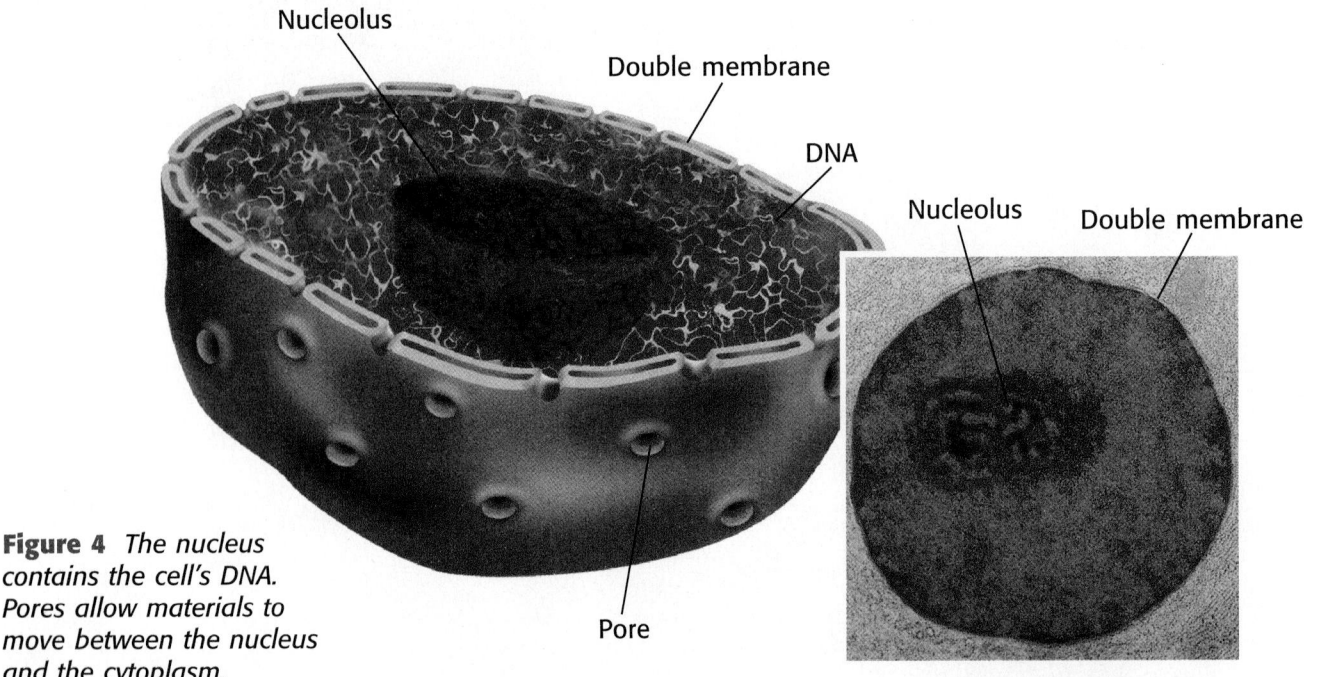

Nucleolus

Double membrane

DNA

Nucleolus

Double membrane

Pore

Figure 4 *The nucleus contains the cell's DNA. Pores allow materials to move between the nucleus and the cytoplasm.*

Ribosomes

Organelles that make proteins are called **ribosomes.** Ribosomes are the smallest of all organelles. And there are more ribosomes in a cell than there are any other organelles. Some ribosomes float freely in the cytoplasm. Others are attached to membranes or the cytoskeleton. Unlike most organelles, ribosomes are not covered by a membrane.

Proteins are made within the ribosomes. Proteins are made of amino acids. An *amino acid* is any 1 of about 20 different organic molecules that are used to make proteins. All cells need proteins to live. All cells have ribosomes.

Endoplasmic Reticulum

Many chemical reactions take place in a cell. Many of these reactions happen on or in the endoplasmic reticulum (EN doh PLAZ mik ri TIK yuh luhm). The **endoplasmic reticulum,** or ER, is a system of folded membranes in which proteins, lipids, and other materials are made. The ER is shown in **Figure 5.**

The ER is part of the internal delivery system of the cell. Its folded membrane contains many tubes and passageways. Substances move through the ER to different places in the cell.

Endoplasmic reticulum is either rough ER or smooth ER. The part of the ER covered in ribosomes is rough ER. Rough ER is usually found near the nucleus. Ribosomes on rough ER make many of the cell's proteins. The ER delivers these proteins throughout the cell. ER that lacks ribosomes is smooth ER. The functions of smooth ER include making lipids and breaking down toxic materials that could damage the cell.

ribosome a cell organelle composed of RNA and protein; the site of protein synthesis

endoplasmic reticulum a system of membranes that is found in a cell's cytoplasm and that assists in the production, processing, and transport of proteins and in the production of lipids

Figure 5 *The endoplasmic reticulum (ER) is a system of membranes. Rough ER is covered with ribosomes. Smooth ER does not have ribosomes.*

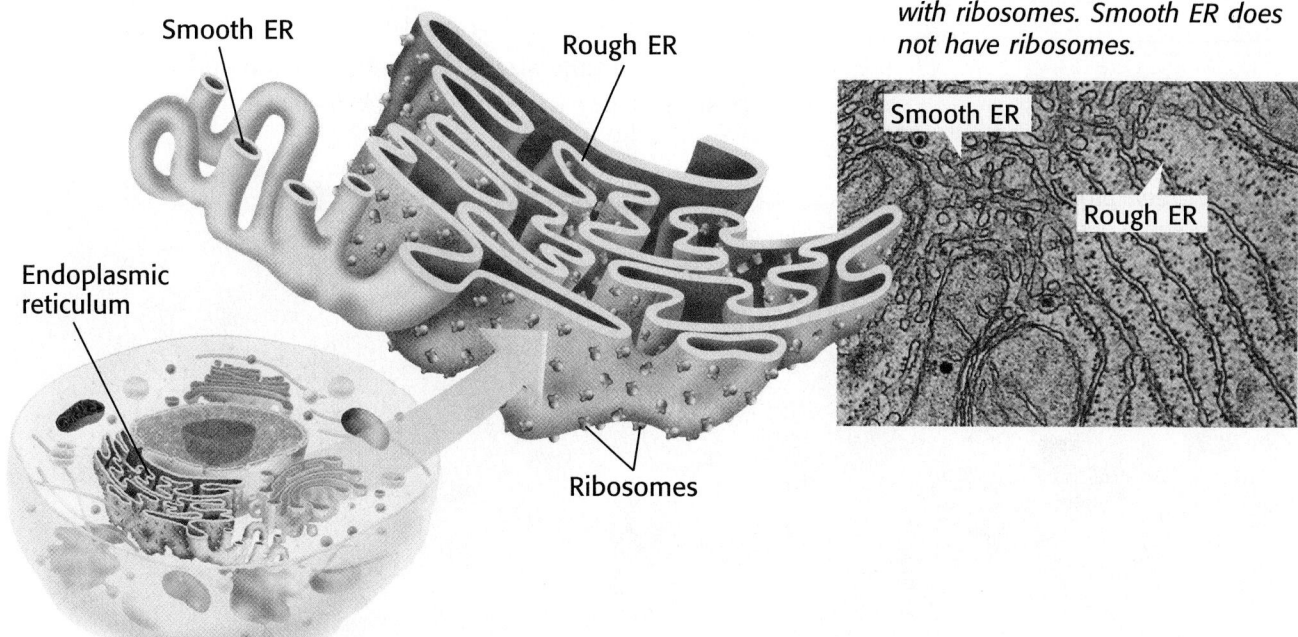

Smooth ER

Rough ER

Endoplasmic reticulum

Ribosomes

Smooth ER

Rough ER

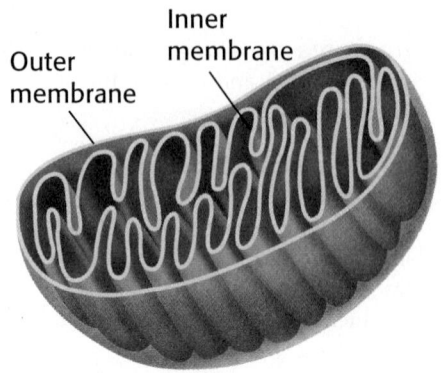

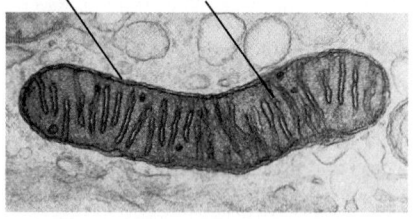

Figure 6 *Mitochondria break down sugar and make ATP. ATP is produced on the organelles' inner membrane.*

mitochondrion in eukaryotic cells, the cell organelle that is surrounded by two membranes and that is the site of cellular respiration

Mitochondria

A **mitochondrion** (MIET oh KAHN dree uhn), the main powerhouse of a cell, is the organelle in which sugar is broken down to produce adenosine **tri**phosphate (ATP). Mitochondria are covered by two membranes, as shown in **Figure 6.** The energy released by mitochondria is stored in ATP molecules. An organism then uses the stored energy to power all of its life functions. ATP can be made at several places in a cell. But most of a cell's ATP is made in the inner membrane of the cell's mitochondria.

Most eukaryotic cells have mitochondria. Mitochondria are the size of some bacteria. Like bacteria, mitochondria have their own DNA, and mitochondria can divide within a cell.

Benchmark Check Why are mitochondria important to the cell and to the organism? **F.I.3.5 CS**

Chloroplasts

Animal cells cannot make their own food. Plants and algae are different. Some of their cells have chloroplasts (KLAWR uh PLASTS). *Chloroplasts* are organelles in plant and algae cells in which photosynthesis takes place. Like mitochondria, chloroplasts have two membranes and their own DNA. A chloroplast is shown in **Figure 7.** *Photosynthesis* is the process by which plants and algae use sunlight, carbon dioxide, and water to make sugar and oxygen.

Chloroplasts are green because they contain *chlorophyll*, a green pigment found inside their inner membrane. Chlorophyll traps the energy of sunlight, which is used to make sugar. The sugar produced by photosynthesis is then used by mitochondria to make ATP.

Figure 7 *Chloroplasts harness and use the energy of the sun to make sugar. A green pigment—chlorophyll— traps the sun's energy.*

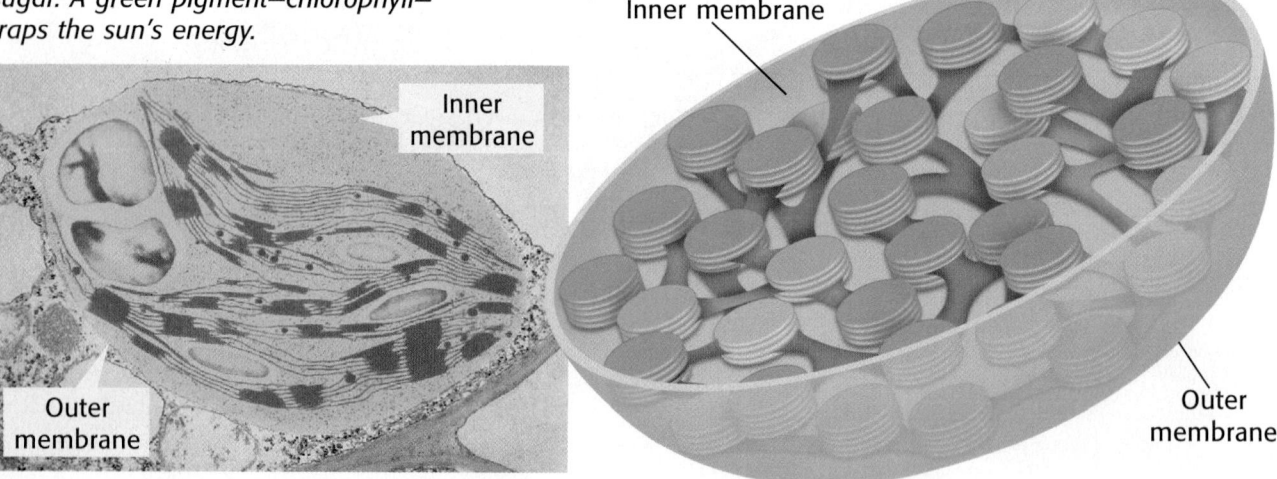

Golgi Complex

The organelle that packages and distributes proteins is called the **Golgi complex** (GOHL jee KAHM PLEKS). It is named after Camillo Golgi, the Italian scientist who first identified the organelle.

The Golgi complex looks like smooth ER, as shown in **Figure 8.** Lipids and proteins from the ER are delivered to the Golgi complex. There, the lipids and proteins may be modified to do different jobs. The final products are enclosed in a piece of the Golgi complex's membrane. This membrane pinches off to form a small bubble. The bubble transports its contents to other parts of the cell or out of the cell.

Cell Compartments

The bubble that forms from the Golgi complex's membrane is a vesicle. A **vesicle** (VES i kuhl) is a small sac that surrounds material to be moved into or out of a cell. All eukaryotic cells have vesicles. Vesicles also move material within a cell. For example, vesicles carry new protein from the ER to the Golgi complex. Other vesicles distribute material from the Golgi complex to other parts of the cell. Some vesicles form when part of the cell membrane surrounds an object outside the cell.

Golgi complex a cell organelle that helps make and package materials to be transported out of the cell

vesicle a small cavity or sac that contains materials in a eukaryotic cell; forms when part of the cell membrane surrounds the materials to be taken into the cell or transported within the cell

F.1.3.5 CS explains how the life functions of organisms are related to what occurs within the cell.

H.1.3.6 recognizes the scientific contributions that are made by individuals of diverse backgrounds, interests, talents, and motivations.

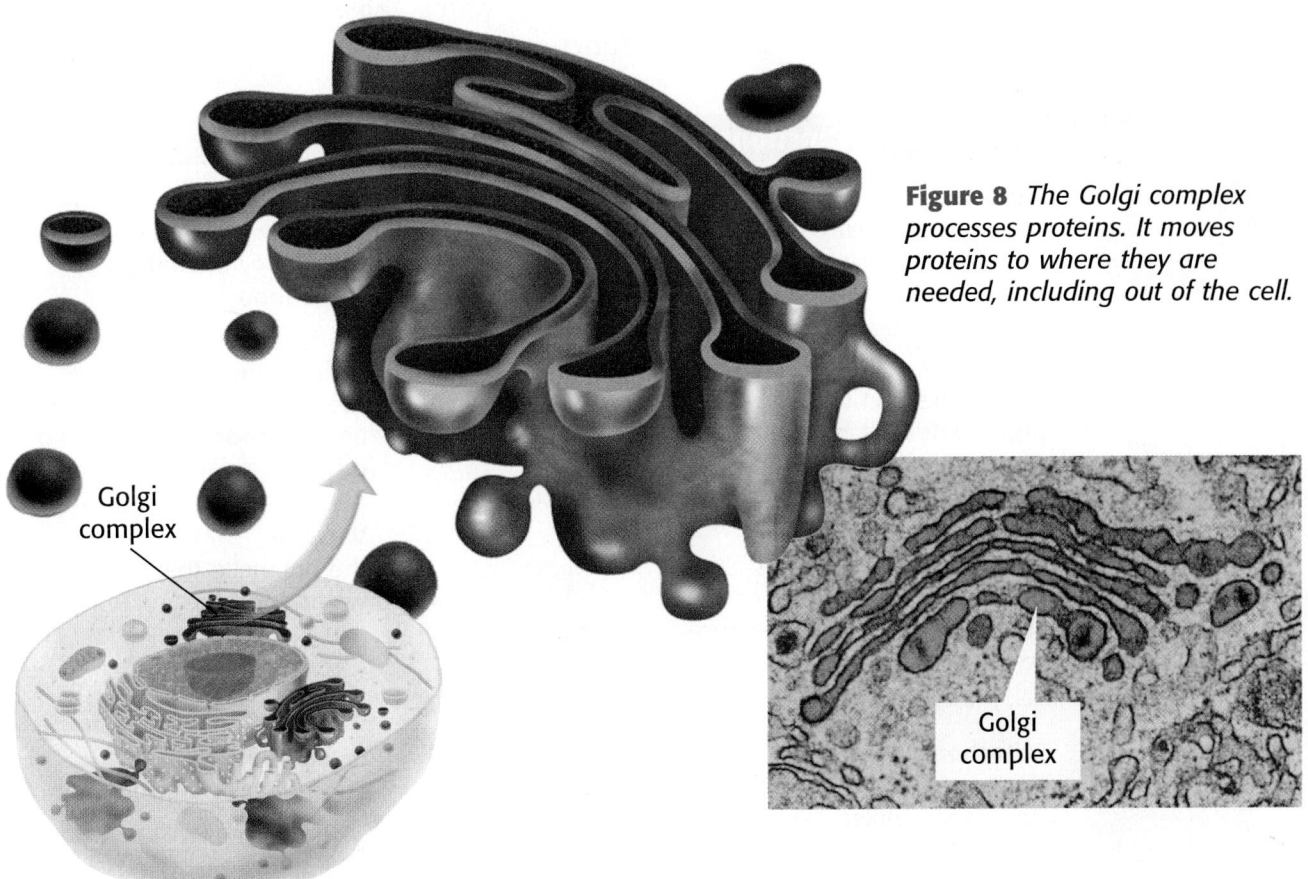

Figure 8 *The Golgi complex processes proteins. It moves proteins to where they are needed, including out of the cell.*

Golgi complex

Golgi complex

lysosome a cell organelle that contains digestive enzymes

Cellular Digestion

Lysosomes (LIE suh SOHMZ) are vesicles that contain digestive enzymes and are responsible for digestion inside a cell. They destroy worn-out or damaged organelles and get rid of waste materials. In addition, they protect the cell from foreign invaders. Lysosomes, which come in a wide variety of sizes and shapes, are shown in **Figure 9.**

Lysosomes are found mainly in animal cells. When eukaryotic cells engulf particles, they enclose the particles in vesicles. Lysosomes bump into these vesicles and pour enzymes into them. These enzymes digest the particles in the vesicles.

Benchmark Check Why are lysosomes important to your body? **F.1.3.5 CS**

Vacuoles

A *vacuole* (VAK yoo OHL) is a large vesicle. In plant and fungal cells, some vacuoles act like large lysosomes. They store digestive enzymes and aid in digestion within the cell. Vacuoles in plant cells also store water and other liquids. Vacuoles that are full of water, such as the one in **Figure 9,** help support the cell. Some plants wilt when their vacuoles lose water. **Table 1** lists some organelles and their functions.

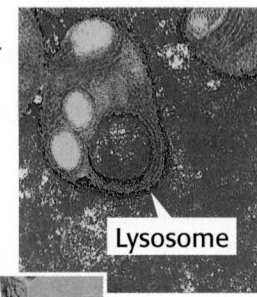
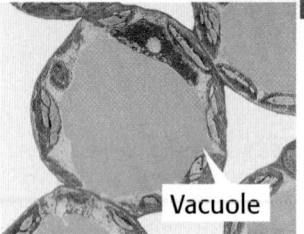

Figure 9
Lysosomes digest materials inside a cell. In plant and fungal cells, vacuoles often perform this function.

Lysosome

Vacuole

F.1.3.5 CS explains how the life functions of organisms are related to what occurs within the cell.

Table 1 **Organelles and Their Functions**	
Nucleus the organelle that contains the cell's DNA and is the control center of the cell	**Chloroplast** the organelle that uses the energy of sunlight to make food
Ribosome the organelle in which amino acids are hooked together to make proteins	**Golgi complex** the organelle that processes and transports proteins and other materials out of cell
Endoplasmic reticulum the organelle that makes lipids, breaks down drugs and other substances, and packages proteins for the Golgi complex	**Vacuole** the organelle that stores water and other materials
Mitochondria the organelle that breaks down food molecules to make ATP	**Lysosome** the organelle that digests food particles, wastes, cell parts, and foreign invaders

SECTION
Review

Summary

- Organelles in eukaryotic cells perform functions that help the cells live. **F.1.3.5 CS**
- All cells have a cell membrane. Some cells have a cell wall. Some cells have a cytoskeleton.
- The nucleus of a eukaryotic cell contains the cell's genetic material, DNA.
- Ribosomes are the organelles that make proteins. Ribosomes are not covered by a membrane.

- The endoplasmic reticulum (ER) and the Golgi complex make and process proteins before the proteins are transported to other parts of the cell or out of the cell.
- Mitochondria and chloroplasts are organelles that provide chemical energy for the cell. **F.1.3.5 CS**
- Lysosomes are organelles responsible for digestion within a cell. In plant cells, organelles called *vacuoles* store cell materials and sometimes act like large lysosomes.

Using Key Terms

1. Write an original definition for *endoplasmic reticulum* and *lysosome*.

Understanding Key Ideas

2. What is the function of a Golgi complex?

Critical Thinking

3. **Making Comparisons** How does a cell wall differ from a cell membrane?

4. **Expressing Opinions** Do you think that chloroplasts give plant cells an advantage over animal cells? Support your opinion. **F.1.3.5 CS**

Interpreting Graphics

Use the diagram below to answer the questions that follow:

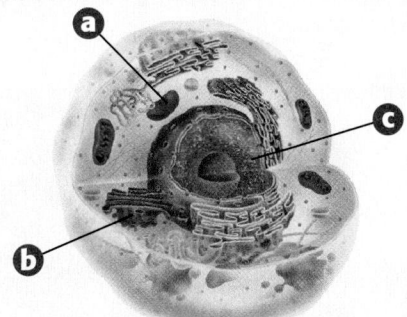

5. What does the organelle labelled *c* store?

6. What organelle does the label *b* refer to?

FCAT Preparation

7. Mitochondria are very important to the cell and are sometimes called the *powerhouses of the cell*. Imagine that a certain virus penetrates a cell and reaches the cell's mitochondria. Predict what would happen to the cell if the virus were able to destroy all of the cell's mitochondria. **F.1.3.5 CS**

   A. The cell would multiply uncontrollably because there is nothing to stop it anymore.

   B. The cell would eventually die without the ATP that it needs for its activities.

   C. The cell would rapidly produce more proteins.

   D. The cell would be unaffected by the loss of mitochondria and would continue to function normally.

For a variety of links related to this chapter, go to www.scilinks.org

Topic: Eukaryotic Cells
SciLinks code: HSM0541

The Organization of Living Things

In some ways, organisms are like machines. Some machines have just one part. But other machines have many parts. Some organisms exist as a single cell. Other organisms have many—even trillions—of cells.

Most cells are smaller than the period that ends this sentence. Yet every cell in every organism performs the processes of life. So, are there any advantages to having many cells?

The Benefits of Being Multicellular

You are a *multicellular organism*. This means that you are made of many cells. Multicellular organisms grow by making more small cells, not by making their cells larger. For example, an elephant is bigger than you are, but its cells are about the same size as yours. An elephant just has more cells than you do. Some benefits of being multicellular are the following:

- **Larger Size** Many multicellular organisms are small. But they are usually larger than single-celled organisms. Larger organisms are prey for fewer predators. Larger predators can eat a wider variety of prey.

- **Longer Life** The life span of a multicellular organism is not limited to the life span of any single cell.

- **Specialization** Multicellular organisms are made of organ systems. Each system has a specialized job, such as reproduction or growth. Specialization makes the organism more efficient. For example, the cardiac muscle cell in **Figure 1** is a specialized muscle cell. Heart muscle cells contract and make the heart pump blood.

Benchmark Check What is one life function performed by an organ system of an organism? F.1.3.1 AA

READING WARM-UP

Objectives

- List three advantages of being multicellular.
- Explain that living things are composed of organ systems that perform their life functions. F.1.3.1 AA
- Describe the specialized cell structures that help cells perform their function. F.1.3.6 CS
- Describe the levels of organization in living things. F.1.3.4 CS
- Explain the relationship between the structure and function of a part of an organism.

Terms to Learn

tissue	organism
organ	structure
organ system	function

READING STRATEGY

Paired Summarizing Read this section silently. In pairs, take turns summarizing the material. Stop to discuss ideas that seem confusing.

F.1.3.1 AA understands that living things are composed of major systems that function in reproduction, growth, maintenance, and regulation.

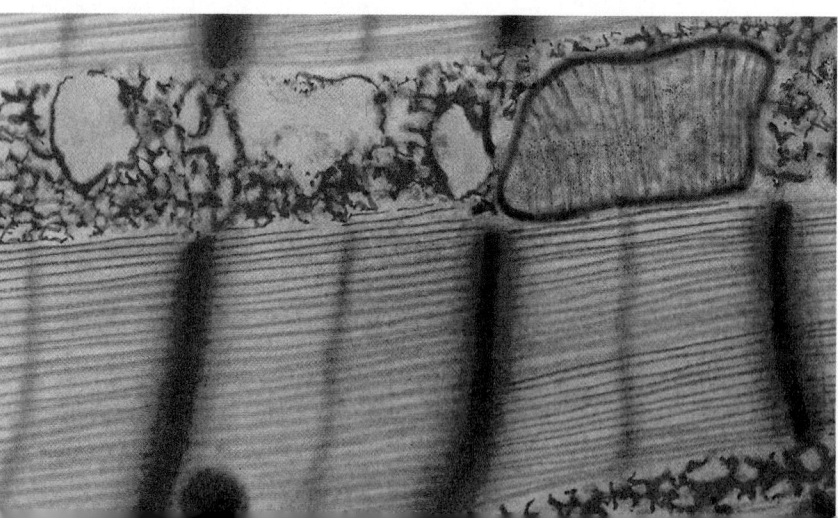

Figure 1 *This photomicrograph shows a small part of one heart muscle cell. The green line surrounds one of many mitochondria, the powerhouses of the cell. The pink areas are muscle filaments.*

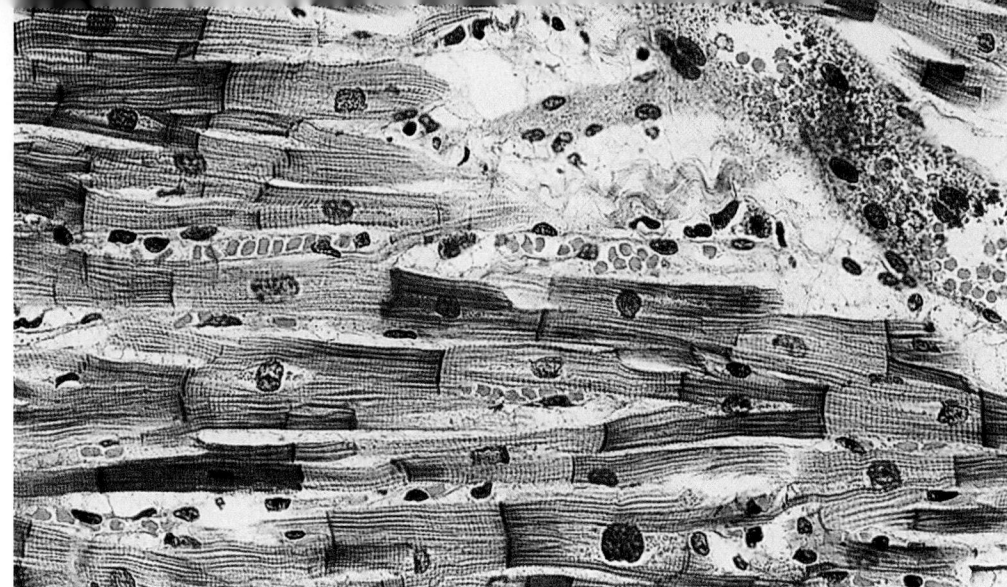

Figure 2 *This photomicrograph shows cardiac muscle tissue. Cardiac muscle tissue is made up of many cardiac cells.*

Cells Working Together

A **tissue** is a group of cells that work together to perform a specific function. Cells that have similar structures perform similar functions. For example, the cardiac muscle tissue, shown in **Figure 2,** is made of many cardiac muscle cells. All of these cells have the same structure. Cardiac muscle tissue is one type of tissue in a heart. Cells of different tissues have different structures that help them perform their particular function.

Animals have four basic types of tissues: nerve tissue, muscle tissue, connective tissue, and protective tissue. In contrast, plants have three types of tissues: transport tissue, protective tissue, and ground tissue. Transport tissue moves water and nutrients through a plant. Protective tissue covers the plant. It helps the plant retain water and protects the plant against damage. Photosynthesis takes place in ground tissue.

Benchmark Check What can you infer about cells that have different structures? **F.I.3.6 CS**

Tissues Working Together

An **organ** is a structure that is made up of two or more tissues that work together to perform a specific function. Your heart is an organ that is mostly made of cardiac muscle tissue. But your heart also has nerve tissue and blood vessel tissues that work together to make your heart a powerful pump.

Your stomach is another organ that is made of several kinds of tissues. It has muscle tissues to move the food through the stomach. Special tissues make chemicals that help digest your food. Connective tissues hold the stomach together. Nervous tissues carry messages between the stomach and the brain.

Plants also have different kinds of tissues that work together as organs. A leaf is a plant organ that contains tissues that trap light energy to make food. Other examples of plant organs are stems and roots.

tissue a group of similar cells that perform a common function

organ a collection of tissues that carry out a specialized function of the body

Benchmark Activity

Hypothermia and Frostbite
How do the tissues and organs in your body respond to exposure to very low temperatures? Research hypothermia and homeostasis. Write a safety pamphlet for hikers and skiers that explains how the body protects itself when exposed to extreme cold. Explain how frostbite occurs and how to prevent it. **F.I.3.1 AA**

F.I.3.6 CS knows that the cells with similar functions have similar structures, whereas those with different structures have different functions.

Organs Working Together

A group of organs working together to perform a particular function is called an **organ system.** Each organ system has a specific job to do in the body. To perform different functions, cells must have structures that are specialized for that function.

For example, the digestive system is made up of several organs, such as the stomach and intestines. Each organ in this system is made of a variety of cell types. Each cell type helps the digestive system do its job of breaking down food into small particles. Other parts of the body use these small particles as fuel. In turn, the digestive system depends on the respiratory and cardiovascular systems for oxygen. The cardiovascular system, shown in **Figure 3,** includes organs and tissues such as the heart and blood vessels. Plants also have organ systems, such as leaf systems, root systems, and stem systems.

Organisms

Anything that can perform life processes by itself is an **organism.** An organism made of a single cell is called a *unicellular organism.* Bacteria, most protists, and some kinds of fungi are unicellular. Although some of these organisms live in colonies, they are still unicellular. Each cell in the colony must carry out all life processes in order for that cell to survive. In contrast, even the simplest multicellular organism has specialized cells that depend on each other for the organism to survive.

Benchmark Check What are organ systems, such as the cardiovascular system composed of? F.1.3.4 CS

F.1.3.4 CS knows that the levels of structural organization for function in living things include cells, tissues, organs, systems, and organisms.

Figure 3 **Levels of Organization in the Cardiovascular System**

Cell
Cells form tissues.

Tissue
Tissues form organs.

Organ
Organs form organ systems.

Organ system
And organ systems form organisms such as you!

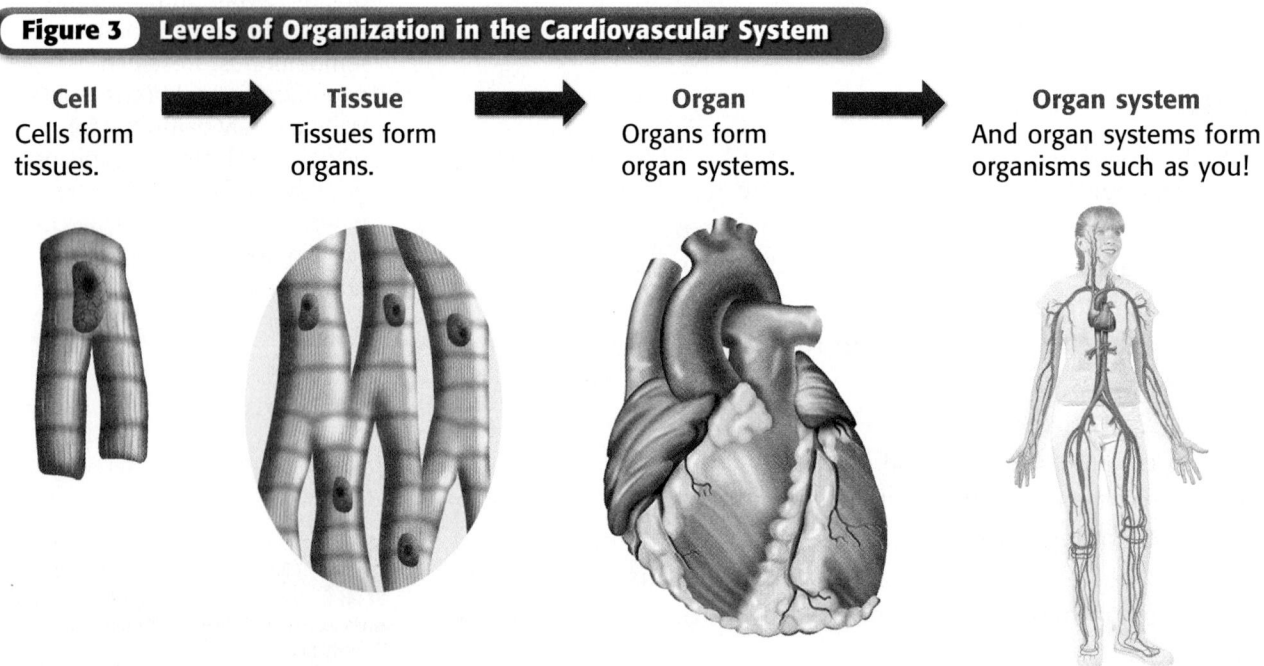

Structure and Function

In organisms, structure and function are related. **Structure** is the arrangement of parts in an organism. It refers to the shape of a part and the material that makes up the part. **Function** is the job that the part does. For example, the structure of a lung is that of a large, spongy organ made up of millions of tiny air sacs called *alveoli*. Blood vessels wrap around the alveoli, as shown in **Figure 4.** Such a structure enables the lungs to perform their function of delivering oxygen to the body and removing carbon dioxide from the body. Oxygen from air in the alveoli enters the blood. Blood carries the oxygen to body tissues. Blood then picks up carbon dioxide, that it carries back to the alveoli, where it is exhaled.

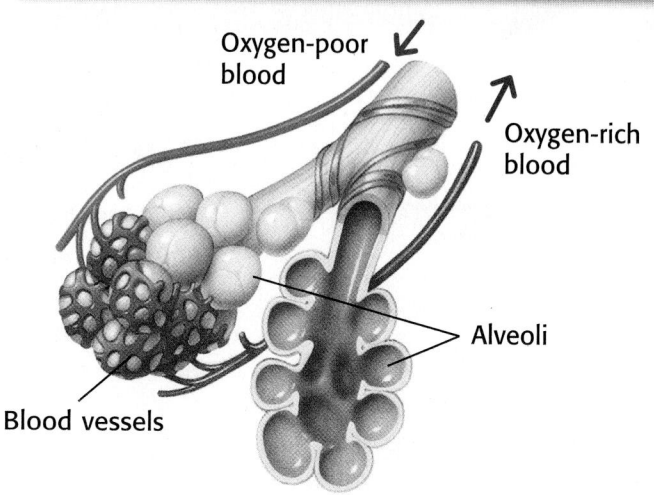

Figure 4 The Structure and Function of Alveoli

Oxygen-poor blood

Oxygen-rich blood

Alveoli

Blood vessels

SECTION Review

Summary

- Advantages of being multicellular are larger size, longer life, and cell specialization.

- Organ systems perform the life functions of living things. F.I.3.1 AA

- Cells have specialized structures to perform specific functions. F.I.3.6 CS

- The levels of organization are the cell, tissue, organ, organ system, and organism. F.I.3.4 CS

- In organisms, a part's structure and function are related.

Using Key Terms

1. Use each of the following terms in a separate sentence: *tissue, organ,* and *function.*

Understanding Key Ideas

2. What are the levels of organization in living things? F.I.3.4 CS
   a. cell, multicellular, organ, and organ system
   b. cell, organism, tissue, and organ
   c. larger size, longer life, specialized cells, and organs
   d. cell, tissue, organ, and organ system

Critical Thinking

3. **Making Inferences** What would you infer about the functions of two similarly shaped cells in a tissue? What would you infer about the functions of two cells whose shapes differed? F.I.3.6 CS

FCAT Preparation

4. Organ systems perform life functions, such as maintenance and growth, for living things. Organ systems are made of many parts. Which answer choice describes an organ system? F.I.3.1 AA
   A. a group of cells
   B. a group of tissues
   C. a group of organs
   D. a group of organelles

SCiLINKS.

NSTA

Developed and maintained by the National Science Teachers Association

For a variety of links related to this chapter, go to www.scilinks.org

Topic: Organization of Life
SciLinks code: HSM1080

Model-Making Lab

OBJECTIVES

Explore why a single-celled organism cannot grow to the size of an elephant.

Create a model of a cell to illustrate the concept of surface area–to–volume ratio.

MATERIALS

- calculator (optional)
- cubic cell patterns
- heavy paper or poster board
- sand, fine
- scale or balance
- scissors
- tape, transparent

SAFETY

Elephant-Sized Amoebas?

An amoeba is a single-celled organism. Like most cells, amoebas are microscopic. Why can't amoebas grow as large as elephants? If an amoeba grew to the size of a quarter, the amoeba would starve to death. To understand how this can be true, build a model of a cell and see for yourself.

Procedure

1 Use heavy paper or poster board to make four cube-shaped cell models from the patterns supplied by your teacher. Cut out each cell model, fold the sides to make a cube, and tape the tabs on the sides. The smallest cell model has sides that are each one unit long. The next larger cell has sides of two units. The next cell has sides of three units, and the largest cell has sides of four units. These paper models represent the cell membrane, the part of a cell's exterior through which food and wastes pass.

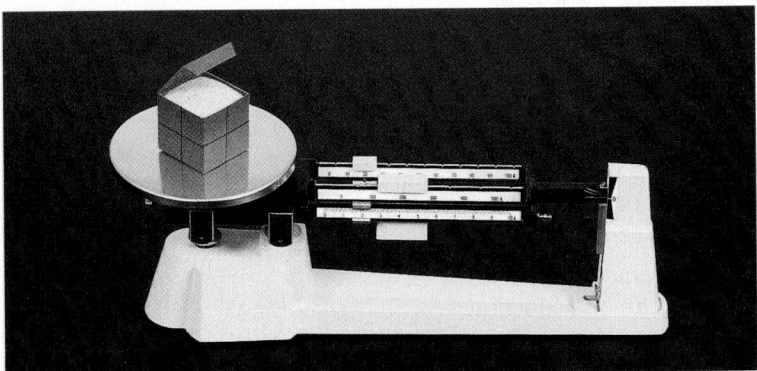

Data Table for Measurements						Key to Formula Symbols
Length of side	Area of one side $(A = S \times S)$	Total surface area of cube cell $(TA = S \times S \times 6)$	Volume of cube cell $(V = S \times S \times S)$	Mass of filled cube cell		S = the length of one side
1 unit	1 unit^2	6 unit^2	1 unit^3			A = area
2 unit						6 = number of sides
3 unit		*DO NOT WRITE IN BOOK*				V = volume
4 unit						TA = total area

2 Copy the data table shown above. Use each formula to calculate the data about your cell models. Record your calculations in the table. Calculations for the smallest cell have been done for you.

3 Carefully fill each model with fine sand until the sand is level with the top edge of the model. Find the mass of the filled models by using a scale or a balance. What does the sand in your model represent?

4 Record the mass of each filled cell model in your Data Table for Measurements. (Always remember to use the appropriate mass unit.)

Analyze the Results

1 **Constructing Tables** Make a data table like the one shown at right.

2 **Organizing Data** Use the data from your Data Table for Measurements to find the ratios for each of your cell models. For each of the cell models, fill in the Data Table for Ratios.

Draw Conclusions

3 **Interpreting Information** As a cell grows larger, does the ratio of total surface area to volume increase, decrease, or stay the same?

4 **Interpreting Information** As a cell grows larger, does the total surface area–to-mass ratio increase, decrease, or stay the same?

5 **Drawing Conclusions** Which is better able to supply food to all of the cytoplasm of the cell: the cell membrane of a small cell or the cell membrane of a large cell? Explain your answer.

6 **Evaluating Data** In the experiment, which is better able to feed all of the cytoplasm of the cell: the cell membrane of a cell that has high mass or the cell membrane of a cell that has low mass? Explain your answer in a verbal presentation to the class, or write a report illustrated with drawings of your models.

Data Table for Ratios		
Length of side	Ratio of total surface area to volume	Ratio of total surface area to mass
1 unit		
2 unit		
3 unit		*DO NOT WRITE IN BOOK*
4 unit		

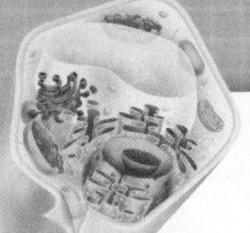

Chapter Review

USING KEY TERMS

Use a term from the chapter to complete each sentence below.

1 A(n) ___ is the basic unit of structure and function in all living things. **F.1.3.2 CS**

2 The job that an organ does is the ___ of that organ.

3 Ribosomes and mitochondria are types of ___.

4 A group of similar cells working together to perform a specific function is a(n) ___. **F.1.3.4 CS**

UNDERSTANDING KEY IDEAS

Multiple Choice

5 Your body has many levels of structural organization. For example, your brain cells work together and form brain tissue. Various types of brain tissues work together and form the brain. The brain is a part of your nervous system. Which of the following best describes your brain? **F.1.3.4 CS** *FCAT*

 a. a group of cells that work together to perform a specific job

 b. a group of tissues that belong to different systems

 c. a group of tissues that work together to perform a specific job

 d. a group of organ systems working separately

6 In eukaryotic cells, which of the following organelles contains the DNA?

 a. nucleus   **c.** smooth ER

 b. Golgi complex   **d.** vacuole

7 What are some of the benefits to being multicellular?

 a. small size, long life, and cell specialization

 b. generalized cells, longer life, and ability to prey on small animals

 c. larger size, more enemies, and specialized cells

 d. longer life, larger size, and specialized cells

8 Just like you, sparrows are multicellular organisms that arise from a single cell. Observations like this one, lead scientists to develop the cell theory. Which of the following statements is part of the cell theory? **F.1.3.2 CS** *FCAT*

 a. All cells suddenly appear by themselves.

 b. All cells come from other cells.

 c. All organisms are multicellular.

 d. All cells have identical parts.

9 Which of the following is limited by the surface area–to-volume ratio of a cell?

 a. the activities that the cell does

 b. the size of the cell

 c. the place where the cell lives

 d. the nutrients that a cell needs

10 Eukaryotes are classified into the domain Eukarya. Which of the following cell parts do eukaryotes have? **G.1.3.3 CS** *FCAT*

 a. a nucleus

 b. ribosomes

 c. cytoplasm

 d. a cell wall

Short Answer

11 When you sleep, your body requires less oxygen to function properly than when you are excersizing. How does your respiratory system help you maintain the levels of oxygen you need? **F.1.3.1 AA** *FCAT*

12 Describe the levels of organization in living things. **F.1.3.4 CS**

13 How does the structure of an organ differ from the function of the organ?

14 Why is cell maintenance important to a multicellular organism? **F.1.3.5 CS**

15 What can you infer about cells whose structures are similar? about cells whose structures differ? **F.1.3.6 CS**

CRITICAL THINKING

Extended Response

16 **Identifying Relationships** Explain how the structure and function of an organism's parts are related. Give an example.

17 **Expressing Opinions** Scientists think that millions of years ago the surface of Earth was very hot and that the atmosphere contained a large amount of methane. In your opinion, which type of organism is the older form of life: a bacterium or an archaeon? Explain your reasoning.

18 **Evaluating Hypotheses** One of your classmates states a hypothesis that all organisms must have organ systems. Is your classmate's hypothesis valid? Explain your answer. **F.1.3.1 AA** *FCAT*

19 **Predicting Consequences** What would happen if your ribosomes disappeared?

Concept Mapping

20 Use the following terms to create a concept map: *cells, organisms, Golgi complex, organ systems, organs, nucleus, organelle,* and *tissues.*

INTERPRETING GRAPHICS

Use the diagram below to answer the questions that follow.

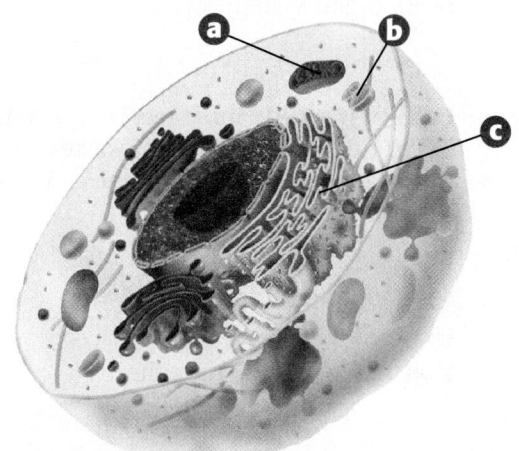

21 What is the name of the structure identified by the letter *a*?

22 What does the structure shown by letter *a* produce, and why is it important to the organism? **F.1.3.5 CS**

23 Which letter identifies the structure that digests food particles and protects the cell from foreign invaders?

24 Which letter identifies the structure that makes proteins, lipids, and other materials and that contains tubes and passageways that enable substances to move to various places in the cell?

For the following questions, write your answers on a separate sheet of paper.

1 Cardiac muscle tissue is found only in the heart. Cardiac muscle tissue contracts to help the heart pump blood throughout the body. The heart is an organ in the cardiovascular system. Describe how this system helps perform maintenance for organisms, such as humans.

2 Organelles are vital parts of cells that carry out specialized functions. Additionally, the body's cells combine to form structures that perform specialized functions. Which of the following body structures is made up of similar cells that work together to perform a specific function?

    A.   organ

    B.   tissue

    C.   organism

    D.   organ system

3 Cells in the body must receive nutrients to perform life processes. Cells must also be able to get rid of their wastes. If wastes could not be removed, they would build up in cells and cause the organism to become sick and die. Which of the following structures helps the cell remove wastes?

    F.   vesicles

    G.   mitochondria

    H.   Golgi complex

    I.   endoplasmic reticulum

4 Diya left her plant near an open window during the day. After a few days, she noticed that her plant was bending towards the window. Why did the plant bend towards the open window?

    A.   The plant was getting sick.

    B.   The plant was responding to the sunlight.

    C.   The plant was not getting watered evenly.

    D.   The plant's stem was weaker on one side than the other.

5 Ahmad has to make a model of a body tissue. He knows that a body tissue is made up of many cells that have specific characteristics. Which of the following statements describes the characteristics of the cells that make up a tissue?

    F.   The cells have similar structures and similar functions.

    G.   The cells have different structures and similar functions.

    H.   The cells have similar structures and different functions.

    I.   The cells have different structures and different functions.

6 Jennifer is learning about cells in her biology class. She knows that organisms can be classified into domains based on the characteristics of their cells. Some cells have a nucleus, such as the one shown below, and some cells do not have a nucleus.

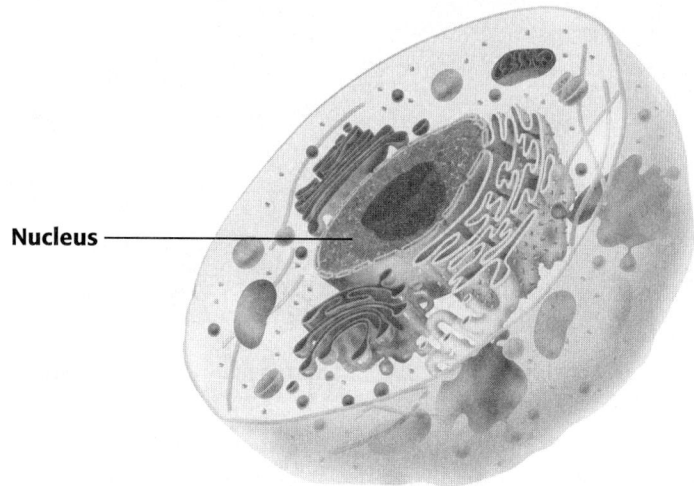

Nucleus

Into which domain would you classify an organism that had a cell similar to the one in the diagram?

A. domain Eukarya
B. domain Archaea
C. domain Bacteria
D. domain Prokarya

7 Antwone examined a single-celled organism in his biology class. He saw an organism similar to the one pictured below.

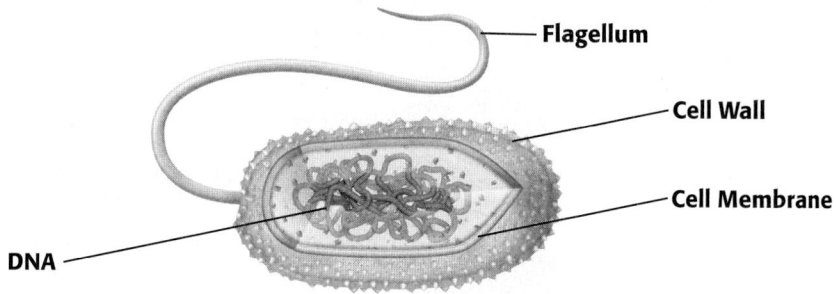

Flagellum

Cell Wall

Cell Membrane

DNA

Which of these conclusions could Antwone make about this organism?

F. This organism is eukaryotic.
G. This organism has many structural levels of organization.
H. This organism undergoes cell division to repair damaged tissues.
I. This organism has special structures to help it perform all its life functions.

Science in Action

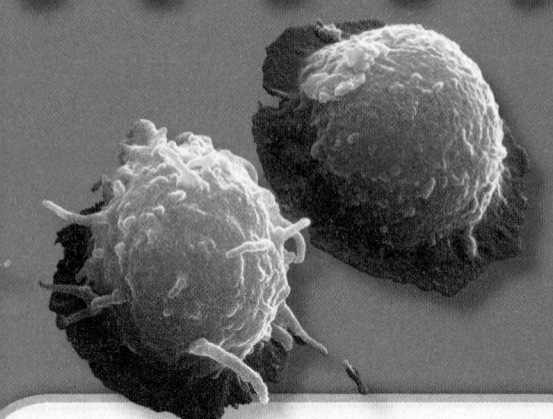

FOCUS ON
FLORIDA

Scientific Discoveries

Discovery of the Stem Cell

What do Parkinson's disease, diabetes, aplastic anemia, and Alzheimer's disease have in common? All of these diseases are diseases for which stem cells may provide treatment or a cure. Stem cells are unspecialized cells from which all other kinds of cells can grow. And research on stem cells has been going on almost since microscopes were invented. But scientists have been able to culture, or grow, stem cells in laboratories for only about the last 20 years. Research during these 20 years has shown scientists that stem cells can be useful in treating—and possibly curing—a variety of diseases.

Weird Science

The Mystery of the Blob on the Beach

What would you do if you saw a huge blob—measuring 21 ft long and 7 ft wide and weighing 7 tons—washed up on a beach? Two boys found a blob near St. Augustine, Florida, in late 1896. In the picture, you can see Dr. DeWitt Webb beside a portion of that blob. Many people thought that the blob was all that was left of a giant sea monster. Others thought that the blob was the remains of an alien. Last summer, another blob—one as big as a school bus—was found in Chile. Sydney Pierce, chair of the Biology Department at the University of South Florida, and his team used DNA testing to solve the mystery of the blob. The blob on the beach is whale blubber!

Language Arts ACTIVITY

Imagine that you are a doctor who treats diseases such as Parkinson's disease. Design and create a pamphlet or brochure that you could use to explain what stem cells are. Include in your pamphlet a description of how stem cells might be used to treat one of your patients who has Parkinson's disease. Be sure to include information about Parkinson's disease.

Social Studies ACTIVITY

Research various types of migratory whales. Choose one species, and make a poster showing what you learned about the migratory path of the species. Include information about where the species can be found at different times of the year and which parts of its life are spent in those areas.

Caroline Schooley

Microscopist Imagine that your assignment is the following: Go outside. Look at 1 ft^2 of the ground for 30 min. Make notes about what you observe. Be prepared to describe what you see. If you look at the ground with just your naked eyes, you may quickly run out of things to see. But what would happen if you used a microscope to look? How much more would you be able to see? And how much more would you have to talk about? Caroline Schooley could tell you.

Caroline Schooley joined a science club in middle school. That's when her interest in looking at things through a microscope began. Since then, Schooley has spent many years studying life through a microscope. She is a microscopist. A *microscopist* is someone who uses a microscope to look at small things. Microscopists use their tools to explore the world of small things that cannot be seen by the naked eye. And using today's powerful electron microscopes, microscopists can study things we could never see before—things as small as atoms.

Math

An average bacterium is about 0.000002 m long. A pencil point is about 0.001 m wide. Approximately how many bacteria would fit on a pencil point?

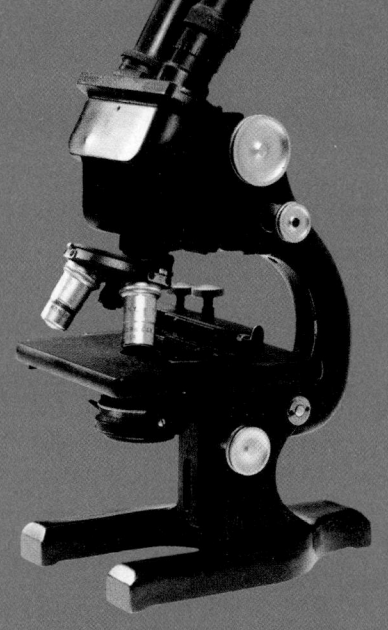

To learn more about these Science in Action topics, visit **go.hrw.com** and type in the keyword **HT6FCF7F.**

Current Science

Check out Current Science® articles related to this chapter by visiting go.hrw.com. Just type in the keyword HL5CS03.

The Cell in Action

The Big Idea The structure of cells allows cells to reproduce, grow, and function in their environment.

About the PHOTO

Katydids are common to Florida. This adult katydid is emerging from its last immature, or nymph, stage. As the katydid changed from a nymph to an adult, every structure of its body changed. To grow and change, an organism must produce new cells. When a cell divides, it makes a copy of its genetic material.

PRE-READING ACTIVITY

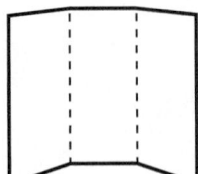

FOLDNOTES **Tri-Fold** Before you read the chapter, create the FoldNote entitled "Tri-Fold" described in the **Study Skills** section of the Appendix. Write what you know about the actions of cells in the column labeled "Know." Then, write what you want to know in the column labeled "Want." As you read the chapter, write what you learn about the actions of cells in the column labeled "Learn."

START-UP ActiViTy

Cells in Action

Yeast are single-celled fungi that are an important ingredient in bread. Yeast break down sugar to release the energy needed for their life functions. This reaction produces carbon dioxide gas. Bakers use this reaction to make bread dough rise.

Procedure

1. Add **4 mL of a sugar solution** to **10 mL of a yeast-and-water mixture**. Use a **stirring rod** to thoroughly mix the two liquids.

2. Pour the stirred mixture into a **small test tube.**

3. Place a slightly **larger test tube** over the small test tube. The top of the small test tube should touch the bottom of the larger test tube.

4. Hold the test tubes together, and quickly turn both test tubes over. Place the test tubes in a test-tube rack.

5. Use a **ruler** to measure the height of the fluid in the larger test tube. Wait 20 min, and then measure the height of the liquid again.

Analysis

1. What is the difference between the first height measurement and the second height measurement?

2. What do you think caused the change in the height of the fluid?

Exchange with the Environment

What would happen to a factory if its power were shut off or its supply of raw materials never arrived? What would happen if the factory couldn't get rid of its garbage?

Like a factory, an organism must be able to obtain energy and raw materials and get rid of wastes. An organism's cells perform all of these functions. These functions keep cells healthy so that they can divide. Cell division allows organisms to grow and repair injuries.

The exchange of materials between a cell and its environment takes place at the cell's membrane. To understand how materials move into and out of the cell, you need to know about diffusion.

Benchmark Check Why do cells exchange materials with their environment? **F.1.3.5 CS**

What Is Diffusion?

What happens if you pour dye on top of a layer of gelatin? At first, where the dye ends and the gelatin begins is clear. But over time, the line between the two layers will blur, as **Figure 1** shows. Why? Everything, including the gelatin and the dye, is made up of tiny moving particles. Particles travel from where they are crowded to where they are less crowded. This movement from areas of high concentration (crowded) to areas of low concentration (less crowded) is called **diffusion** (di FYOO zhuhn). Dye particles diffuse from where they are crowded (near the top of the glass) to where they are less crowded (in the gelatin). Diffusion also happens within and between living cells. Cells do not need energy for diffusion.

READING WARM-UP

Objectives

- Explain how the movement of materials across the cell membrane is related to the survival of an organism. **F.1.3.5 CS**
- Explain the process of diffusion.
- Describe osmosis and its importance to the cell. **F.1.3.5 CS**
- Compare passive transport with active transport.
- Explain how large particles get into and out of cells.

Terms to Learn

diffusion
osmosis
passive transport
active transport
endocytosis
exocytosis

READING STRATEGY

Reading Organizer As you read this section, make a table comparing active transport and passive transport.

diffusion the movement of particles from regions of higher density to regions of lower density

Figure 1 *The particles of the dye and the gelatin slowly mix by diffusion.*

F.1.3.3 CS knows that in multicellular organisms cells grow and divide to make more cells in order to form and repair various organs and tissues.

Figure 2 Osmosis

❶ The side that holds only pure water has the higher concentration of water particles.

❷ During osmosis, water particles move to where they are less concentrated.

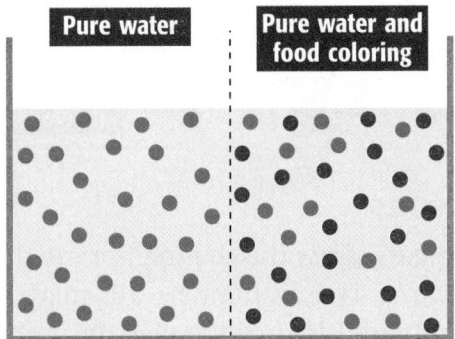

Pure water | Pure water and food coloring

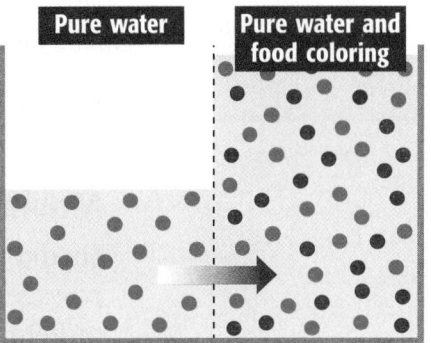

Pure water | Pure water and food coloring

Diffusion of Water

The cells of organisms are surrounded by and filled with fluids that are made mostly of water. The diffusion of water through cell membranes is so important to life processes that it has been given a special name: **osmosis** (ahs MOH sis).

Water is made up of particles, called *molecules*. Pure water has the highest concentration of water molecules. When you mix something, such as food coloring, sugar, or salt, with water, you lower the concentration of water molecules. **Figure 2** shows how water molecules move through a membrane that is semipermeable (SEM i PUHR mee uh buhl). *Semipermeable* means that only certain substances can pass through. The picture on the left in **Figure 2** shows liquids that have different concentrations of water. Over time, the water molecules move from the liquid that has the high concentration of water molecules to the liquid that has the lower concentration of water molecules.

The Cell and Osmosis

Osmosis is important to cell functions. For example, red blood cells are surrounded by plasma. Plasma is made up of water, salts, sugars, and other particles. The concentration of these particles is kept in balance by osmosis. If red blood cells were in pure water, water molecules would flood into the cells and would cause the cells to burst. In a salty solution, the concentration of water molecules inside red blood cells is higher than the concentration of water molecules outside. This difference makes water move out of the cells, and the cells shrivel up. Red blood cells cannot work if they burst or shrivel up, and the organism may die. Osmosis also occurs in plant cells. Osmosis makes a wilted plant firm again.

osmosis the diffusion of water through a semipermeable membrane

Bead Diffusion

1. Put three groups of **colored beads** on the bottom of a **plastic bowl.** Each group should be made up of five beads of the same color.

2. Stretch some **clear plastic wrap** tightly over the top of the bowl. Gently shake the bowl for 10 seconds while watching the beads.

3. How is the scattering of the beads like the diffusion of particles? How is it different from the diffusion of particles?

Benchmark Check Explain why osmosis is important. **F.I.3.5 CS**

F.I.3.5 CS explains how the life functions of organisms are related to what occurs within the cell.

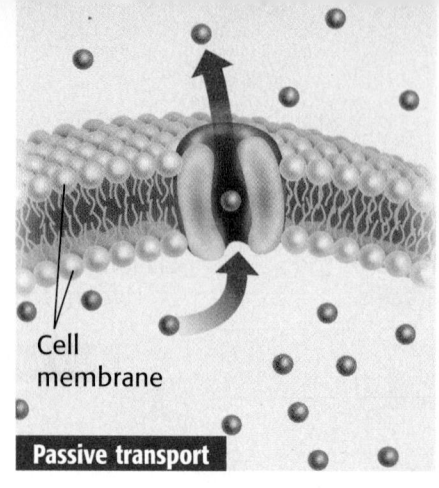
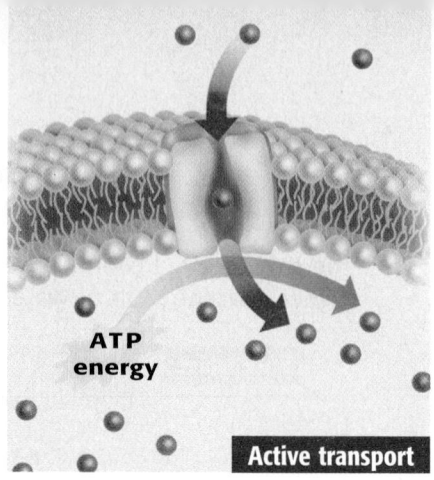

Cell membrane

ATP energy

Passive transport

Active transport

Figure 3 *In passive transport, particles travel through proteins to areas of lower concentration. In active transport, cells use energy to move particles, usually to areas of higher concentration.*

passive transport the movement of substances across a cell membrane without the use of energy by the cell

active transport the movement of substances across the cell membrane that requires the cell to use energy

endocytosis the process by which a cell membrane surrounds a particle and encloses the particle in a vesicle to bring the particle into the cell

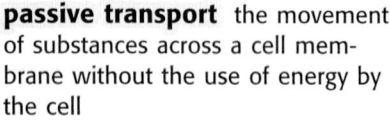

F.1.3.5 CS explains how the life functions of organisms are related to what occurs within the cell.

Moving Small Particles

Small particles, such as sugars, cross the cell membrane through passageways called *channels*. These channels are made up of proteins in the cell membrane. Particles travel through these channels by either passive or active transport. The movement of particles across a cell membrane without the use of energy by the cell is called **passive transport**, shown in **Figure 3.** During passive transport, particles move from an area of high concentration to an area of low concentration. Diffusion and osmosis are examples of passive transport.

A process of transporting particles that requires the cell to use energy is called **active transport.** Active transport usually involves the movement of particles from an area of low concentration to an area of high concentration.

Moving Large Particles

Small particles cross the cell membrane by diffusion, passive transport, and active transport. Large particles move into and out of the cell by processes called *endocytosis* and *exocytosis*.

Endocytosis

The active-transport process by which a cell surrounds a large particle, such as a large protein, and encloses the particle in a vesicle to bring the particle into the cell is called **endocytosis** (EN doh sie TOH sis). *Vesicles* are sacs that are formed from pieces of the cell membrane. **Figure 4** shows endocytosis.

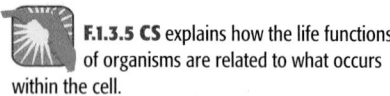 **Endocytosis**

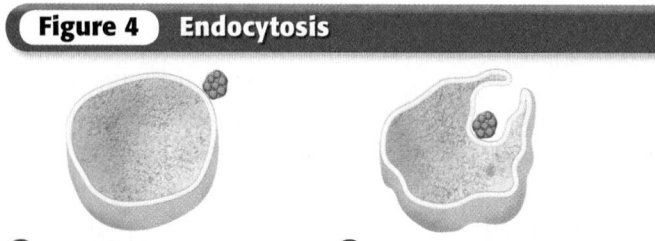
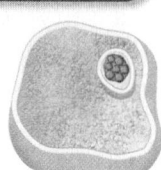
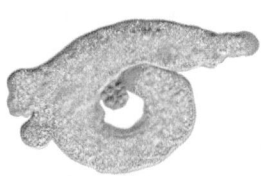

❶ The cell comes into contact with a particle.

❷ The cell membrane begins to wrap around the particle.

❸ Once the particle is completely surrounded, a vesicle pinches off.

This photo shows the end of *endocytosis*, which means "within the cell."

Figure 5 **Exocytosis**

1 Large particles that must leave the cell are packaged in vesicles.

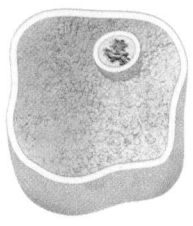

2 The vesicle travels to the cell membrane and fuses with it.

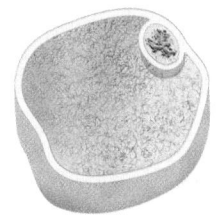

3 The cell releases the particle to the outside of the cell.

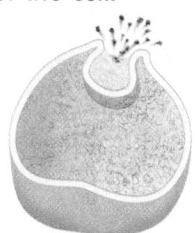

Exocytosis means "outside the cell."

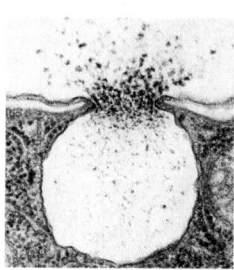

Exocytosis

A cell uses **exocytosis** (EK soh sie TOH sis), another active-transport process, to remove large particles, such as waste. During exocytosis, shown in **Figure 5,** a vesicle forms around a large particle within the cell and carries the particle to the cell membrane. The vesicle then fuses with the cell membrane and releases the particle outside the cell. This process keeps the organism healthy.

exocytosis the process in which a cell releases a particle by enclosing the particle in a vesicle that then moves to the cell surface and fuses with the cell membrane

✓ **Reading Check** How is waste removed from the cell?

SECTION
Review

Summary

- Cells exchange materials with their environment through diffusion, osmosis, passive transport, and active transport to support the organism's life functions. F.I.3.5 CS

- Small particles move across the cell membrane by passive transport and by active transport.

- Large particles enter cells by endocytosis and exit cells by exocytosis.

Using Key Terms

For each pair of terms, explain how the meanings of the terms differ.

1. *active transport* and *passive transport*

2. *endocytosis* and *exocytosis*

Understanding Key Ideas

3. The movement of particles from a crowded area to a less crowded area is called
   a. exocytosis.   c. endocytosis.
   b. diffusion.   d. channeling.

4. Describe a cellular process that allows a plant that has wilted to restore itself. F.I.3.5 CS

Critical Thinking

5. **Predicting Consequences** Explain what would happen to an organism and its cells if its channel proteins stopped transporting particles. F.I.3.5 CS

FCAT Preparation

6. For organisms to remain healthy, cells have many methods to take in nutrients and get rid of waste. Moving these particles can require energy. Which of the following methods uses energy? F.I.3.5 CS
   A. osmosis
   B. active transport
   C. passive transport
   D. diffusion

SCI LINKS.

NSTA
Developed and maintained by the
National Science Teachers Association

For a variety of links related to this chapter, go to www.scilinks.org

Topics: Diffusion; Osmosis
SciLinks code: HSM0406; HSM1090

Cell Energy

Why do you get hungry? Feeling hungry is your body's way of telling you that your cells need energy.

All organisms and their cells need energy to live, grow, and reproduce. Plant cells get their energy from the sun. Many animal cells get the energy they need from food.

From Sun to Cell

Nearly all of the energy that fuels life comes from the sun. Plants capture energy from the sun and change it into food through a process called **photosynthesis.** The food that plants make supplies them with energy. This food also becomes a source of energy for the organisms that eat the plants.

Photosynthesis

Plant cells have molecules that absorb light energy. These molecules are called *pigments*. Chlorophyll (KLAWR uh FIL), the main pigment used in photosynthesis, gives plants their green color. Chlorophyll is found in chloroplasts.

Plants use the energy captured by chlorophyll to change carbon dioxide and water into food. The food is in the form of the simple sugar glucose. Glucose is a carbohydrate. When plants make glucose, they convert the sun's energy into a form of energy that can be stored. The energy in glucose is used by the plant's cells for the plant's life functions. Photosynthesis also produces oxygen. Photosynthesis is summarized in **Figure 1.**

photosynthesis the process by which plants, algae, and some bacteria use sunlight, carbon dioxide, and water to make food

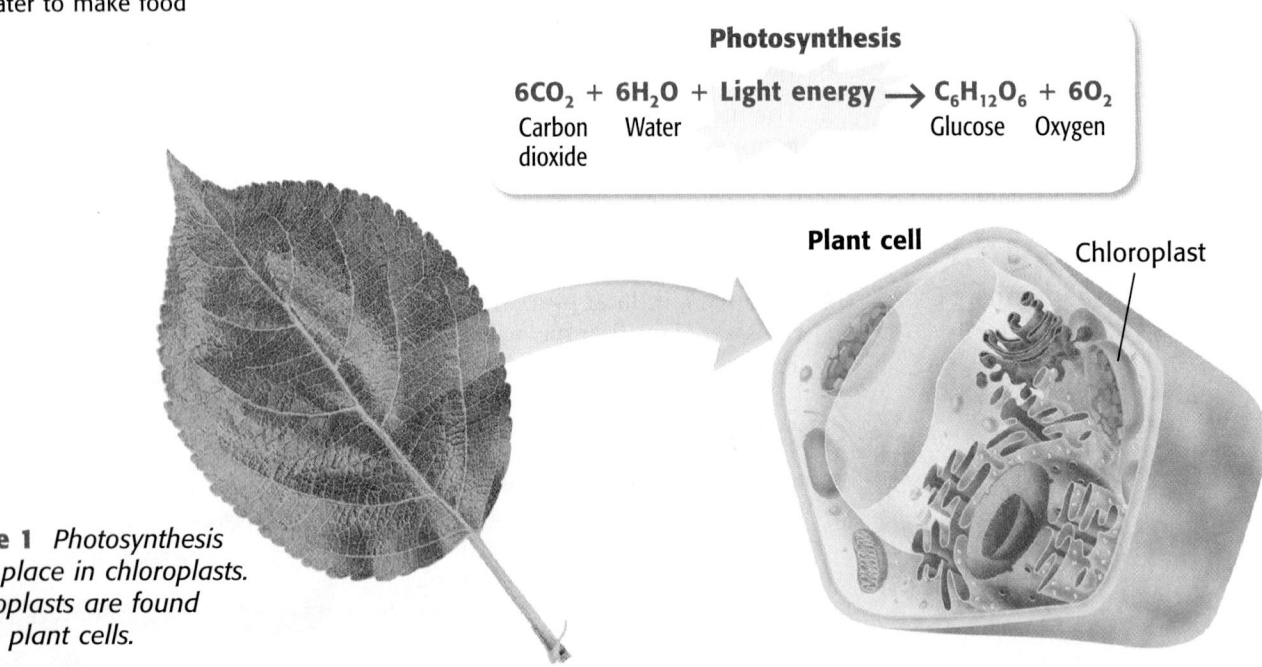

Photosynthesis

$$6CO_2 + 6H_2O + \text{Light energy} \longrightarrow C_6H_{12}O_6 + 6O_2$$

Carbon dioxide   Water   Glucose   Oxygen

Plant cell

Chloroplast

Figure 1 *Photosynthesis takes place in chloroplasts. Chloroplasts are found inside plant cells.*

Getting Energy from Food

Animal cells have different ways of getting energy from food. One way, called **cellular respiration,** uses oxygen to break down food. Many cells can get energy without using oxygen through a process called **fermentation.** Cellular respiration will release more energy from a given food than fermentation will.

Cellular Respiration

The word *respiration* means "breathing," but cellular respiration is different from breathing. Breathing supplies the oxygen needed for cellular respiration. Breathing also removes carbon dioxide, which is a waste product of cellular respiration. But cellular respiration is a chemical process that occurs in cells.

Most complex organisms, such as the cow in **Figure 2,** obtain energy through cellular respiration. During cellular respiration, food (such as glucose) is broken down into CO_2 and H_2O, and energy is released. Most of the energy released maintains body temperature. Some of the energy is used to form adenosine triphosphate (ATP). ATP supplies energy that fuels cell activities.

Most of the process of cellular respiration takes place in the cell membrane of prokaryotic cells. But in the cells of eukaryotes, cellular respiration takes place mostly in the mitochondria. The process of cellular respiration is summarized in **Figure 2.** Does the equation in the figure remind you of the equation for photosynthesis? **Figure 3** on the next page shows how photosynthesis and respiration are related.

Benchmark Check Where does cellular respiration occur in eukaryotes, and why is this process important to them? **F.I.3.5 CS**

cellular respiration the process by which cells use oxygen to produce energy from food

fermentation the breakdown of food without the use of oxygen

Benchmark Activity

Surviving in the Dark

Many organisms live in complete darkness at the bottom of the ocean, near hydrothermal vents. Some of these organisms do not have mouths. How do their cells get the food they need? These organisms rely on bacteria that perform chemosynthesis for food. In chemosynthesis, only chemicals are used to make food. Research the organisms that live near hydrothermal vents. Make a poster that has pictures of these organisms. Label the organisms that rely on chemosynthesis and the organisms that do not. **F.I.3.5 CS**

F.I.3.5 CS explains how the life functions of organisms are related to what occurs within the cell.

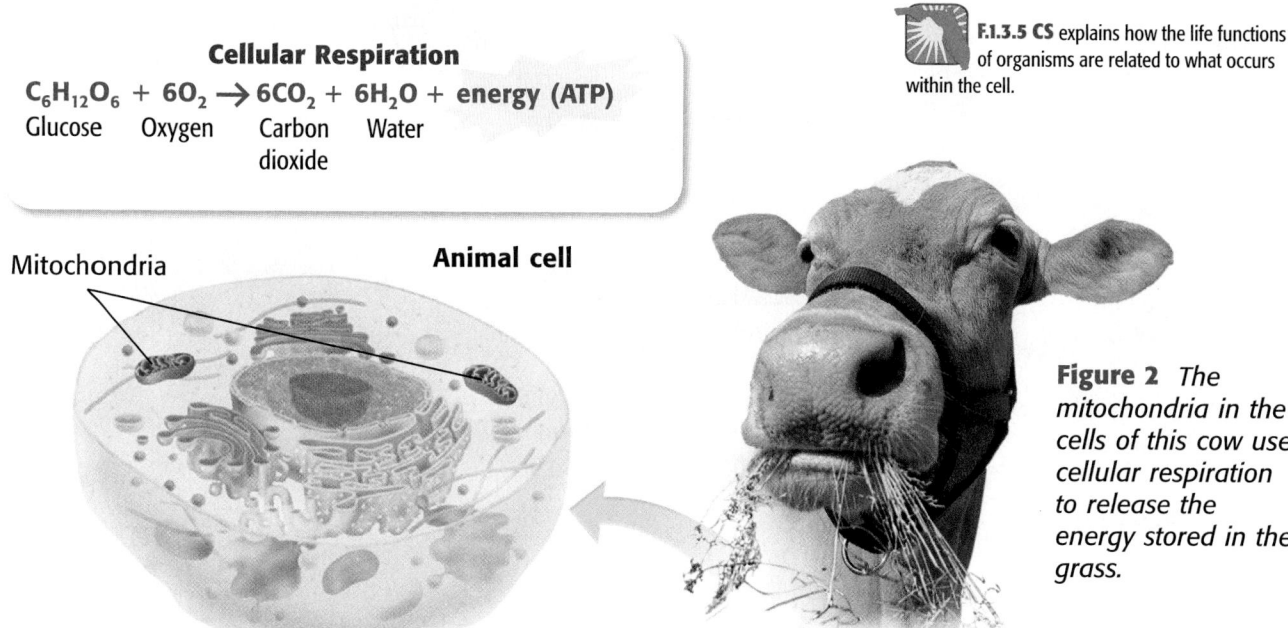

Cellular Respiration

$$C_6H_{12}O_6 + 6O_2 \rightarrow 6CO_2 + 6H_2O + \text{energy (ATP)}$$

Glucose   Oxygen   Carbon dioxide   Water

Mitochondria

Animal cell

Figure 2 *The mitochondria in the cells of this cow use cellular respiration to release the energy stored in the grass.*

Figure 3 The Connection Between Photosynthesis and Respiration

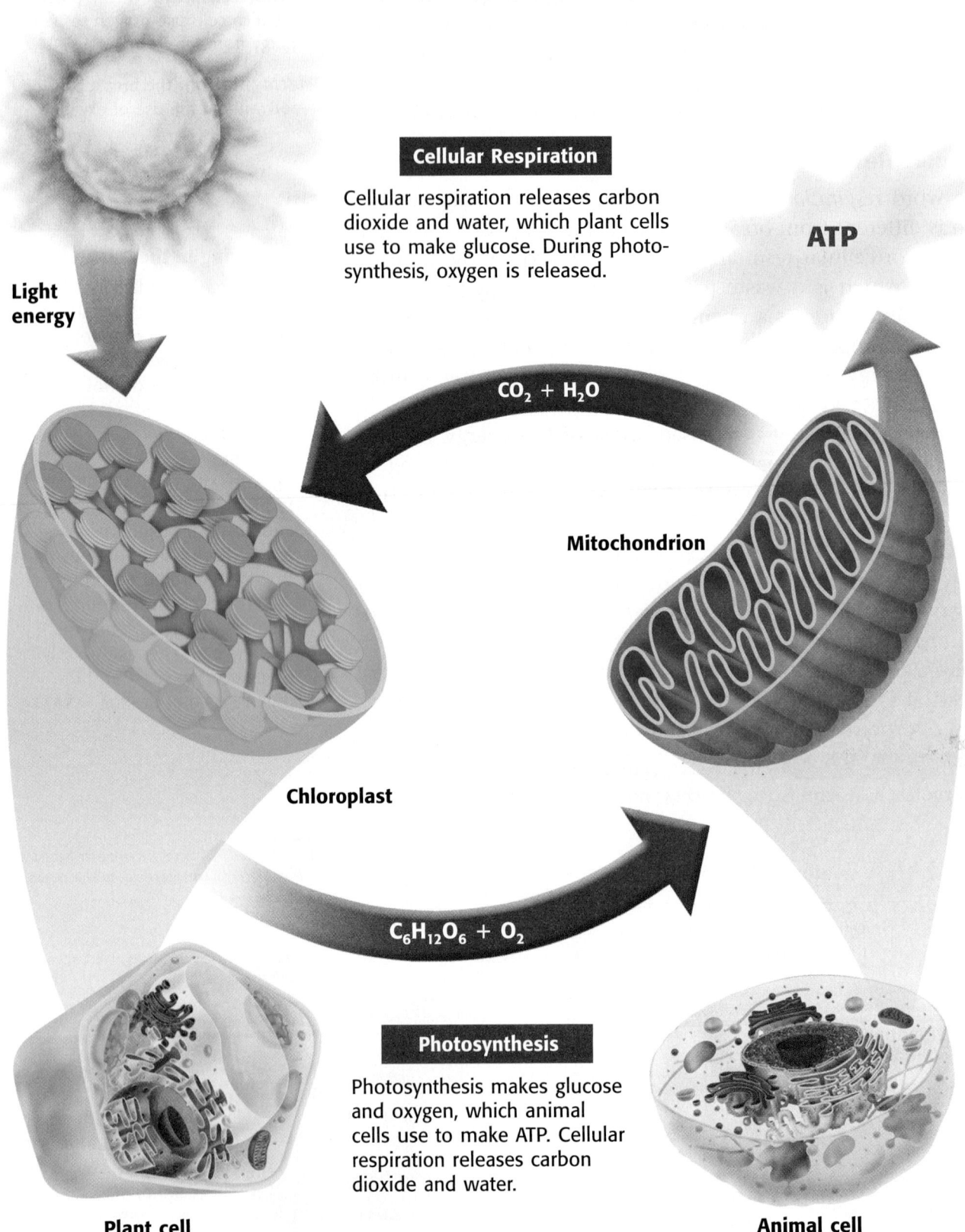

Light energy

Cellular Respiration

Cellular respiration releases carbon dioxide and water, which plant cells use to make glucose. During photosynthesis, oxygen is released.

ATP

$CO_2 + H_2O$

Mitochondrion

Chloroplast

$C_6H_{12}O_6 + O_2$

Photosynthesis

Photosynthesis makes glucose and oxygen, which animal cells use to make ATP. Cellular respiration releases carbon dioxide and water.

Plant cell

Animal cell

Connection Between Photosynthesis and Respiration

As shown in **Figure 3,** photosynthesis transforms energy from the sun into glucose. During photosynthesis, cells use CO_2 and H_2O to make glucose and release O_2. During cellular respiration, cells use O_2 to break down glucose, to release energy, H_2O and CO_2. Each process makes the materials that are needed for the other process to occur elsewhere.

Fermentation

Have you ever felt a burning sensation in your leg muscles while you were running? When muscle cells can't get the oxygen needed for cellular respiration, they use the process of fermentation to get energy. One kind of fermentation happens in your muscles and produces lactic acid. The buildup of lactic acid contributes to muscle fatigue and causes a burning sensation. This kind of fermentation also happens in the muscle cells of other animals and in some fungi and bacteria. Another type of fermentation occurs in some types of bacteria and in yeast, as described in **Figure 4.**

✓ Reading Check What are two kinds of fermentation?

Figure 4 *Yeast forms carbon dioxide during fermentation. The bubbles of CO_2 gas cause the dough to rise and leave small holes in bread after it is baked.*

F.1.3.5 CS explains how the life functions of organisms are related to what occurs within the cell.

SECTION Review

Summary

- Most of the energy that fuels life functions comes from the sun.
- The sun's energy is converted into food through the process of photosynthesis. **F.1.3.5 CS**
- Cellular respiration breaks down glucose into water, carbon dioxide, and energy.
- Fermentation is a way that cells get energy from their food without using oxygen.

Using Key Terms

1. Write an original definition for *fermentation.*

Understanding Key Ideas

2. Explain why photosynthesis and cellular respiration are important to organisms. **F.1.3.5 CS**

3. How are respiration and fermentation similar? How are they different?

Math Skills

4. Cells of plant A make 120 molecules of glucose per hour. Cells of plant B make half as much glucose per hour as plant A does. How much glucose does plant B make every minute?

Critical Thinking

5. **Analyzing Relationships** Why are plants important to the survival of all other organisms?

FCAT Preparation

6. Cells use cellular respiration to release energy when oxygen levels are high and use fermentation when oxygen levels are low. When would your muscle cells use fermentation? **F.1.3.5 CS**

   A. when you are exercising heavily

   B. when you are sleeping

   C. when you are drawing

   D. when you are reading a book

SCILINKS. **NSTA**
Developed and maintained by the National Science Teachers Association

For a variety of links related to this chapter, go to www.scilinks.org

Topic: Cell Energy; Photosynthesis
SciLinks code: HSM0237; HSM1140

READING WARM-UP

Objectives

- Explain why cells produce more cells. **F.I.3.3 CS**
- Compare cell division in prokaryotes and eukaryotes.
- Describe the process of mitosis.
- Explain how cell division differs in animals and plants.

Terms to Learn

cell cycle
chromosome
homologous chromosomes
mitosis **FCAT** *VOCAB*
cytokinesis

READING STRATEGY

Paired Summarizing Read this section silently. In pairs, take turns summarizing the material. Stop to discuss ideas that seem confusing.

cell cycle the life cycle of a cell

chromosome in a eukaryotic cell, one of the structures in the nucleus that are made up of DNA and protein; in a prokaryotic cell, the main ring of DNA

Figure 1 *Bacteria reproduce by binary fission.*

F.I.3.3 CS knows that in multicellular organisms cells grow and divide to make more cells in order to form and repair various organs and tissues.

The Cell Cycle

In the time that it takes you to read this sentence, your body will have made millions of new cells! Making new cells allows you to grow and replace cells that have died.

The environment in your stomach is so acidic that the cells lining your stomach must be replaced every few days. Other cells are replaced less often, but your body constantly makes new cells.

The Life of a Cell

Cells divide to make more cells. In multicellular organisms, cells also divide so that the organism can grow and repair damaged tissues. As you grow, you pass through different stages. Your cells also pass through different stages in their life cycle. The life cycle of a cell is called the **cell cycle.** The cell cycle begins when the cell forms and ends when the cell divides to form new cells. Before a cell divides, it must make a copy of its deoxyribonucleic acid (DNA). DNA is the hereditary material that controls all cell activities, including the making of new cells. The DNA of a cell is organized into structures called **chromosomes.** Copying chromosomes ensures that each new cell will be an exact copy of its parent cell. How a cell makes more cells depends on whether the cell is prokaryotic (without a nucleus) or eukaryotic (with a nucleus).

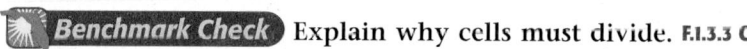

Benchmark Check Explain why cells must divide. **F.I.3.3 CS**

Making More Prokaryotic Cells

Prokaryotes, like bacteria, have one circular DNA molecule. Bacteria divide by *binary fission,* as **Figure 1** shows. Binary fission results in two cells, each of which has one copy of DNA.

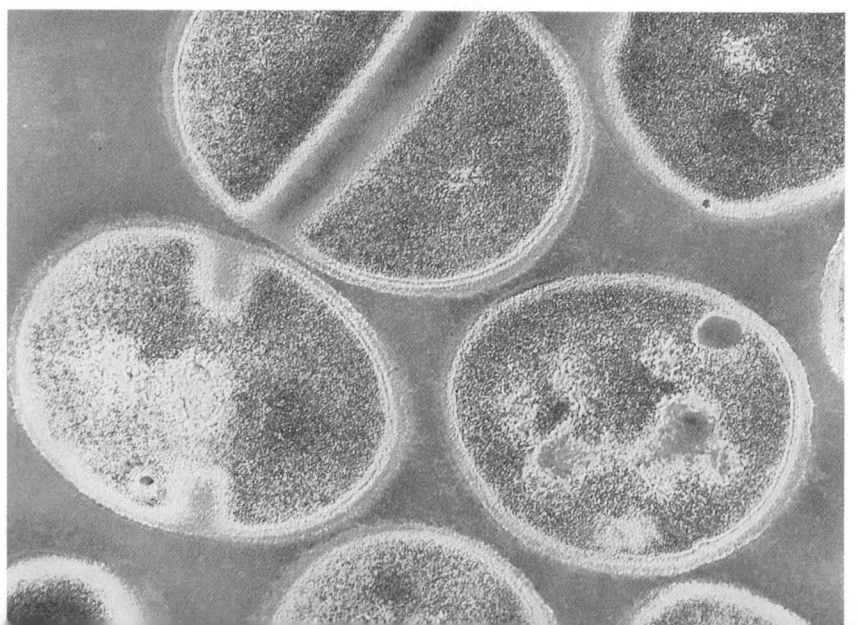

Eukaryotic Cells and Their DNA

Eukaryotic cells are more complex than prokaryotic cells are. The chromosomes of eukaryotic cells contain more DNA than those of prokaryotic cells do. Different kinds of eukaryotes have different numbers of chromosomes. Complex eukaryotes do not necessarily have more chromosomes than simpler eukaryotes do. For example, fruit flies have 8 chromosomes, potatoes have 48, and humans have 46. **Figure 2** shows the 46 chromosomes of a human body cell lined up in pairs. These pairs are made up of similar chromosomes known as **homologous chromosomes** (hoh MAHL uh guhs KROH muh SOHMZ).

✔ **Reading Check** Do complex organisms always have more chromosomes than simpler organisms do?

Figure 2 *Human body cells have 46 chromosomes, or 23 pairs of chromosomes.*

Making More Eukaryotic Cells

The eukaryotic cell cycle includes three stages. In the first stage, called *interphase,* the cell grows and copies its organelles and chromosomes. After each chromosome is duplicated, the two copies are called *chromatids*. Chromatids are held together at a region called the *centromere*. The joined chromatids twist and coil and condense into an X shape, as shown in **Figure 3.** After this step, the cell enters the second stage of the cell cycle.

In the second stage, the chromatids separate. The complicated process of chromosome separation is called **mitosis.** Mitosis ensures that each new cell receives a copy of each chromosome. Mitosis is divided into four phases, as shown on the following pages.

In the third stage, the cell splits into two cells. These cells are identical to each other and to the original cell.

homologous chromosomes chromosomes that have the same sequence of genes and the same structure

mitosis in eukaryotic cells, a process of cell division that forms two new nuclei, each of which has the same number of chromosomes
FCATVOCAB

Figure 3 *This duplicated chromosome consists of two chromatids. The chromatids are joined at the centromere.*

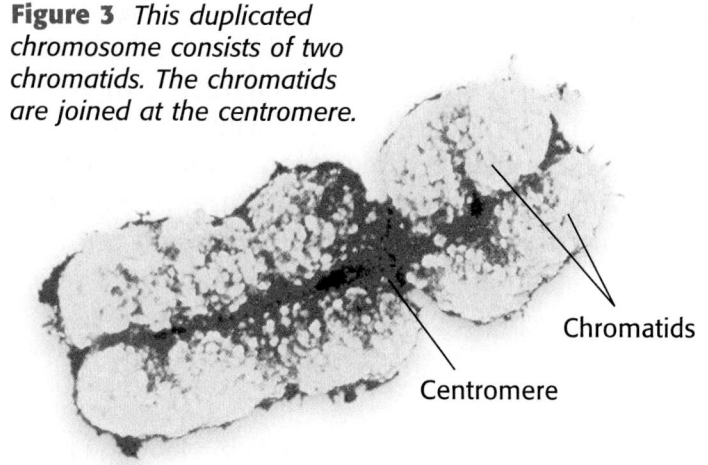

Chromatids

Centromere

Mitosis Adventure Describe cell division from the inside! Go to **go.hrw.com** and type in the keyword **HL5ACTW**.

Figure 4 **The Cell Cycle**

Copying DNA (Interphase)

Before mitosis begins, chromosomes are copied. Each chromosome is then two chromatids.

Mitosis Phase 1 (Prophase)

Mitosis begins. Chromosomes condense into rod like structures.

Mitosis Phase 2 (Metaphase)

The nuclear membrane is dissolved. Paired chromosomes align at the cell's equator.

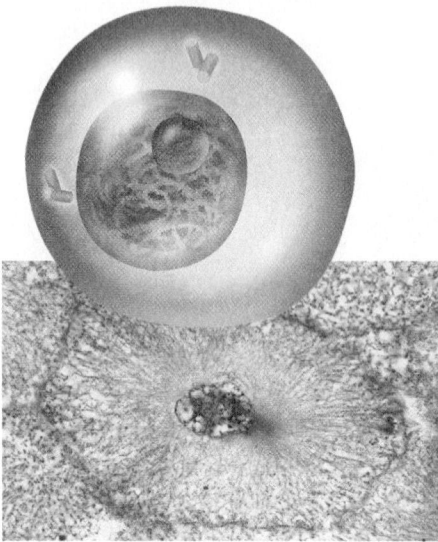
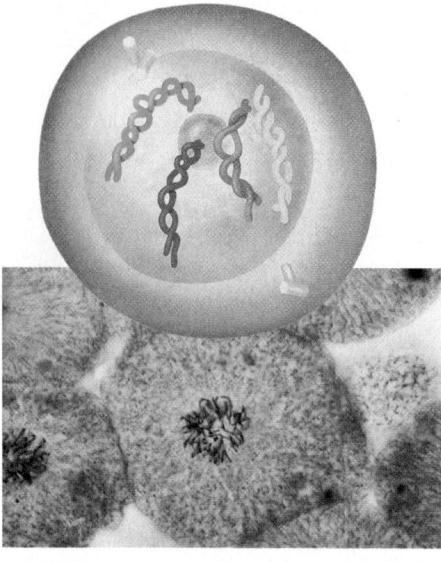
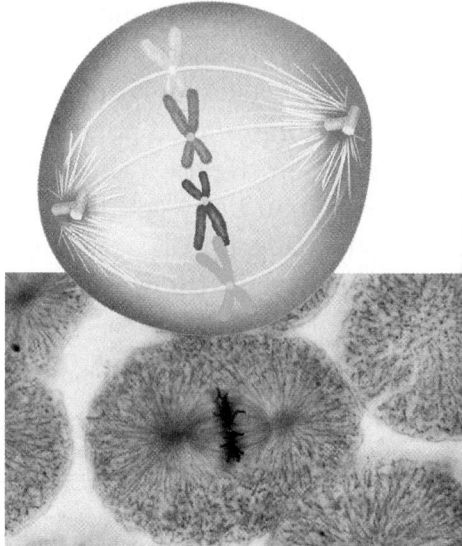

cytokinesis the division of the cytoplasm of a cell

Mitosis and the Cell Cycle

Figure 4 shows the cell cycle and the phases of mitosis in an animal cell. Mitosis has four phases that are shown and described above. This diagram shows only four chromosomes to make it easy to see what's happening inside the cell.

Cytokinesis

In animal cells and other eukaryotes that do not have cell walls, division of the cytoplasm begins at the cell membrane. The cell membrane begins to pinch inward to form a groove, which eventually pinches all the way through the cell, and two daughter cells form. The division of cytoplasm is called **cytokinesis** and is shown at the last step of **Figure 4.**

Eukaryotic cells that have a cell wall, such as the cells of plants, algae, and fungi, divide differently. In these cells, a *cell plate* forms in the middle of the cell. The cell plate contains the materials for the new cell membranes and the new cell walls that will separate the new cells. After the cell splits into two, the cell plate develops into the cell walls and cell membranes of the two daughter cells. The cell plate and a late stage of cytokinesis in a plant cell are shown in **Figure 5.**

Despite these differences, most cells share the need and the ability to divide.

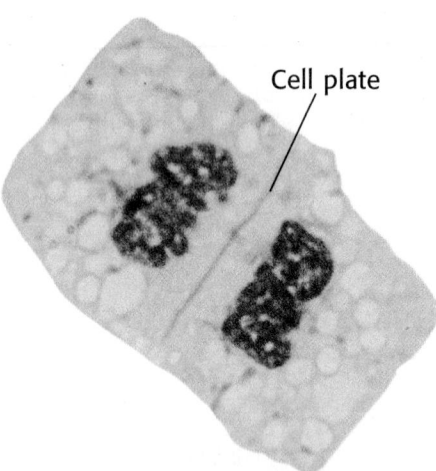

Cell plate

Figure 5 *When a plant cell divides, a cell plate forms in the middle of the cell and the cell splits into two cells.*

F.I.3.3 CS knows that in multicellular organisms cells grow and divide to make more cells in order to form and repair various organs and tissues.

✓ **Reading Check** Compare cytokinesis in plant and animal cells.

Mitosis Phase 3 (Anaphase)

The chromatids separate and move to opposite sides of the cell.

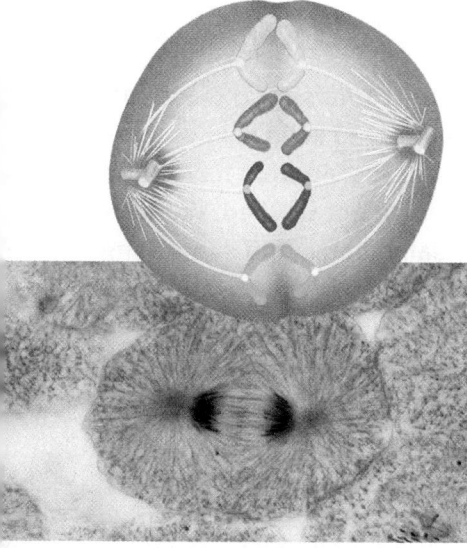

Mitosis Phase 4 (Telophase)

A nuclear membrane forms around each set of chromosomes, and the chromosomes unwind. Mitosis is complete.

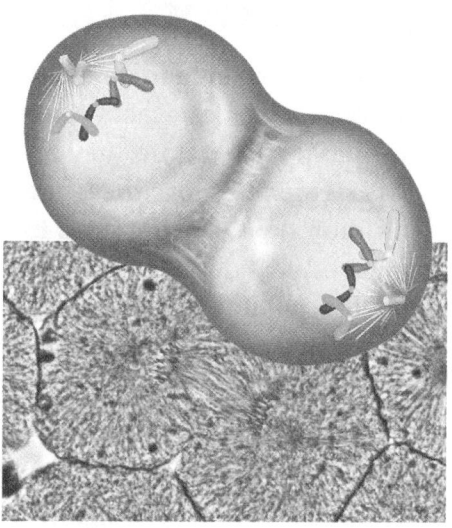

Cytokinesis

In cells that lack a cell wall, the cell pinches in two. In cells that have a cell wall, a cell plate forms and separates the two new cells.

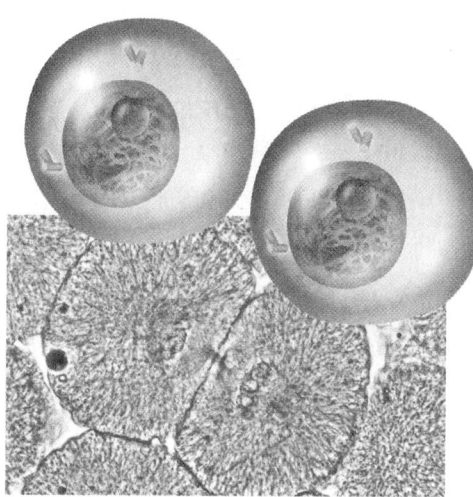

SECTION Review

Summary

- Cells divide to make more cells. Cells also divide to form and repair tissues. **F.1.3.3 CS**
- Prokaryotes divide by binary fission. Eukaryotic cells divide by mitosis.
- Mitosis produces two cells that have an equal number of chromosomes.
- New cells separate by cytokinesis. In animals, a cell pinches in two. In plants, a cell plate separates the two new cells.

Using Key Terms

1. Write an original definition for *cell cycle* and *cytokinesis*.

Understanding Key Ideas

2. Why do cells divide? **F.1.3.3 CS**

3. Describe mitosis. Compare mitosis and binary fission.

Critical Thinking

4. **Predicting Consequences** What would happen if cytokinesis occurred without mitosis?

5. **Applying Concepts** How does mitosis ensure that both new cells have an equal number of chromosomes?

6. **Making Comparisons** Compare the processes that animal cells and plant cells use to make new cells.

FCAT Preparation

7. Cells in multicellular organisms divide to make more new cells. The organism can use the new cells for many different things. Which of the following is a reason for cell division? **F.1.3.3 CS**

    A. to obtain more energy

    B. to enable you to grow

    C. to enable you to play

    D. to obtain more proteins

SCiLINKS®

NSTA
Developed and maintained by the
National Science Teachers Association

For a variety of links related to this chapter, go to www.scilinks.org

Topic: Cell Cycle; Cell Structures
SciLinks code: HSM0235; HSM0240

Inquiry Lab

The Perfect Taters Mystery

You are the chief food detective at Perfect Taters Food Company. The boss, Mr. Fries, wants you to find a way to keep his potatoes fresh and crisp before they are cooked. His workers have tried several methods, but these methods have not worked. Workers in Group A put the potatoes in very salty water, and something unexpected happened to the potatoes. Workers in Group B put the potatoes in water that did not contain any salt, and something else happened! Workers in Group C didn't put the potatoes in any water, and that method didn't work either. Now, you must design an experiment to find out what can be done to make the potatoes stay crisp and fresh.

OBJECTIVES

Examine osmosis in potato cells. F.1.3.2 CS, F.1.3.5 CS

Design a procedure that will give the best results.

MATERIALS

- cups, clear plastic, small
- potato pieces, freshly cut
- potato samples (A, B, and C)
- salt
- water, distilled

SAFETY

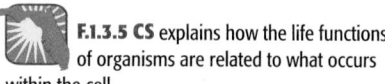 **F.1.3.2 CS** knows that the structural basis of most organisms is the cell and most organisms are single cells, while some, including humans, are multicellular.

F.1.3.5 CS explains how the life functions of organisms are related to what occurs within the cell.

1. Before you plan your experiment, review what you know. You know that potatoes are made of cells. Plant cells contain a large amount of water. Cells have membranes that hold water and other materials inside and keep some things out. Water and other materials must travel across cell membranes to get into and out of cells.

2. Mr. Fries has told you that you can obtain as many samples as you need from the workers in Groups A, B, and C. Your teacher will have these samples ready for you to observe.

3. Make a data table like the one below. List your observations in the data table. Make as many observations as you can about the potatoes tested by workers in Groups A, B, and C.

Observations	
Group A	
Group B	DO NOT WRITE IN BOOK
Group C	

Ask a Question

1. Now that you have made your observations, state Mr. Fries's problem in the form of a question that can be answered by your experiment.

Form a Hypothesis

2 Form a hypothesis based on your observations and your questions. The hypothesis should be a statement about what causes the potatoes not to be crisp and fresh. Based on your hypothesis, make a prediction about the outcome of your experiment. State your prediction in an if-then format.

Test the Hypothesis

3 Once you have made a prediction, design your investigation. Check your experimental design with your teacher before you begin. Mr. Fries will give you potato pieces, water, salt, and no more than six containers.

4 Keep very accurate records. Write your plan and procedure. Make data tables. To ensure that your data are accurate, measure all materials carefully and make drawings of the potato pieces before and after the experiment.

Analyze the Results

1 **Explaining Events** Explain what happened to the potato cells in Groups A, B, and C in your experiment. Include a discussion of the cell membrane and the process of osmosis. Why is osmosis important to potatoes?

Draw Conclusions

2 **Analyzing Results** Explain your experimental method, results, and conclusion to Mr. Fries in a written report. Include a recommendation for how to keep the potatoes fresh and crisp.

Chapter Review

USING KEY TERMS

1 Use *diffusion* and *osmosis* in the same sentence.

Use a term from the chapter to complete each sentence below.

2 Plants use __ to make glucose.

3 During __, oxygen is used to break down food molecules, which releases large amounts of energy.

For each pair of terms, explain how the meanings of the terms differ.

4 *cytokinesis* and *mitosis*

5 *active transport* and *passive transport*

6 *cellular respiration* and *fermentation*

UNDERSTANDING KEY IDEAS

Multiple Choice

7 The cells of all organisms go through cell division. Cell division results in an increased number of cells. What does cell division allow you to do? **F.I.3.3 CS** *FCAT*

  a. to grow

  b. to eat

  c. to sleep

  d. to play

8 Which of the following cells would form a cell plate during the cell cycle?

  a. a human cell

  b. a prokaryotic cell

  c. a plant cell

  d. All of the above

9 Particle movement through a membrane from a region of low concentration to a region of high concentration is called

  a. diffusion.

  b. passive transport.

  c. active transport.

  d. fermentation.

10 Mitosis and cytokinesis results in

  a. two identical cells.

  b. two nuclei.

  c. chloroplasts.

  d. two different cells.

11 Without enough water a person becomes dehydrated. In extreme cases, a person may go to a hospital, where they might be given a saline drip. A saline drip is a solution of chemicals made to match the solution in healthy cells. What may happen if there is not enough water in the drip? **F.I.3.5 CS** *FCAT*

  a. The person will still be dehydrated.

  b. The person will get full.

  c. The person will get stronger.

  d. The person will throw up.

Short Answer

12 Explain why you think cells divide. **F.I.3.3 CS**

13 Why do organisms need to move sugars into their cells? **F.I.3.5 CS**

14 Explain how photosynthesis and cellular respiration are related.

15 Are exocytosis and endocytosis examples of active or passive transport? Explain your answer.

Extended Response

16 **Identifying Relationships** Why do your muscle cells need more food when there is a lack of oxygen than when there is plenty of oxygen? **F.1.3.5 CS**

17 **Making Inferences** Which one of the plants pictured below was given salty water, and which one was given pure water? Explain how you know, and use the word *osmosis* in your answer. **F.1.3.5 CS**

18 **Applying Concepts** A friend told you that cells were dividing to repair your broken leg. State a case that would support or reject your friend's statement. **F.1.3.3 CS**

19 **Making Inferences** You know that cells exchange materials with their environment through the cell membrane. What process does an amoeba use to engulf its food particles? **F.1.3.3 CS**

Concept Mapping

20 Use the following terms to create a concept map: *chromosome duplication, cytokinesis, prokaryote, mitosis, cell cycle, binary fission,* and *eukaryote.*

The picture below shows a cell. Use the picture below to answer the questions that follow.

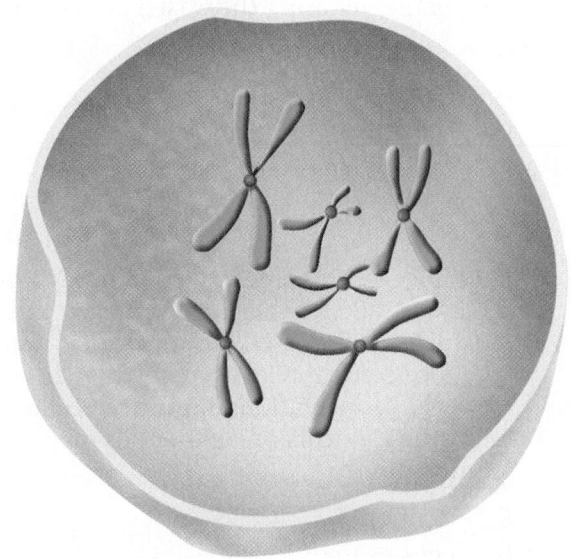

21 Is the cell prokaryotic or eukaryotic?

22 Which stage of the cell cycle is shown?

23 How many chromatids are present? How many pairs of homologous chromosomes are present?

24 How many chromosomes will be present in each of the new cells after the cell divides?

For the following questions, write your answers on a separate sheet of paper.

1 Tiffany watched a video about how wastes are moved out of a cell. First, vesicles form around waste particles. Then, these vesicles move to the cell membrane and fuse with the membrane, releasing the wastes outside the cell. What is this process called?

A. diffusion

B. exocytosis

C. endocytosis

D. passive transport

2 Fruit juice can become wine or vinegar when yeast digests the sugars in the juice. This process is called fermentation. During this process, carbon dioxide is released. Carbon dioxide is also released during cellular respiration. Both fermentation and cellular respiration are processes that release energy that an organism can use to perform its life functions. However, fermentation differs from cellular respiration in one main way. Which of the following elements or compounds plays a role in cellular respiration but is not involved in fermentation?

F. carbon

G. glucose

H. hydrogen

I. oxygen gas

3 All organisms are made of one of two kinds of cells, prokaryotic cells or eukaryotic cells. Both prokaryotic and eukaryotic cells undergo cell division. The two types of cells have very different processes for division, but they both begin the process in the same way. What do both types of cells need to do before they begin cell division?

A. copy their DNA

B. develop a cell plate

C. complete binary fission

D. dissolve the nuclear membrane

4 Anita knows that all cells reproduce. She also knows that each type of cell reproduces for different reasons. What is the main reason that prokaryotic cells reproduce?

F. to repair damaged cells

G. to create new organisms

H. to increase specialization

I. to grow into a larger organism

5 Cells obtain the raw materials they need to keep the organism healthy through many different processes. Many of these processes do not require the cell to use any energy. One process that does require the use of energy is called active transport. Which of the following is an example of active transport?

A. osmosis of water across the cell membrane
B. diffusion of small particles across the cell membrane
C. movement of large particles from an area of low concentration to an area of high concentration
D. movement of small particles from an area of high concentration to an area of low concentration

6 Shawn's biology teacher talked to the class about the cycles of photosynthesis and cellular respiration. Single-celled organisms, such as diatoms and multicellular organisms, such as plants can perform photosynthesis. Celluar respiration releases the energy stored in the sugars that may have been made through photosynthesis. The teacher drew a diagram on the board similar to the one shown below.

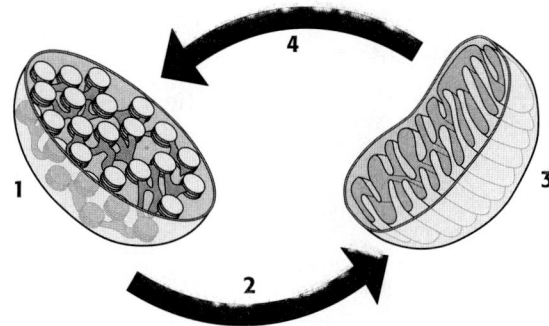

What number in the diagram shows where the process of cellular respiration occurs?

F. 1
G. 2
H. 3
I. 4

FCAT Preparation

Science in Action

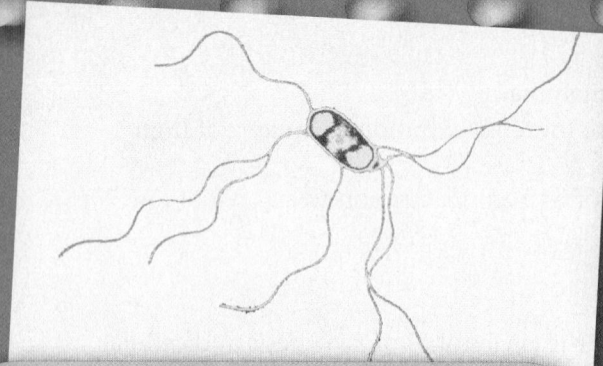

Scientific Discoveries

Electrifying News About Microbes

Your car is out of fuel, and there isn't a service station in sight. This is not a problem! Your car's motor runs on electricity supplied by trillions of microorganisms. Some chemists think that "living" batteries will someday operate everything from watches to entire cities. A group of scientists at King's College in London has demonstrated that microorganisms can convert food into usable electrical energy. The microorganisms convert foods such as table sugar and molasses most efficiently. An efficient microorganism can convert more than 90% of its food into compounds that will fuel an electric reaction. A less efficient microbe will convert only 50% of its food into these types of compounds.

Science Fiction

"Contagion" by Katherine MacLean

A quarter mile from their spaceship, the *Explorer,* a team of doctors walk carefully along a narrow forest trail. Around them, the forest looks like a forest on Earth in the fall—the leaves are green, copper, purple, and fiery red. But it isn't fall. And the team is not on Earth.

Minos is enough like Earth to be the home of another colony of humans. But Minos might also be home to unknown organisms that could cause severe illness or death among the crew of *Explorer*. These diseases might be enough like diseases on Earth to be contagious, but they might be different enough to be very difficult to treat.

Something large moves among the shadows—it looks like a man. What happens next? Read Katherine's MacLean's "Contagion" in the *Holt Anthology of Science Fiction* to find out.

Math ACTIVITY

An efficient microorganism converts 90% of its food into fuel compounds, and an inefficient microorganism converts only 50%. If the inefficient microorganism makes 60 g of fuel out of a possible 120 g of food, how much fuel would an efficient microorganism make out of the same amount of food?

Language Arts ACTIVITY

WRITING SKILL Write two to three paragraphs that describe what you think might happen next in the story.

Felicia Snead

Radiation Oncologist Felicia Snead is a radiation oncologist. Dr. Snead uses X-ray energy to treat cancer patients. She is also a professor at the University of Florida. Dr. Snead always had a strong interest in science and enjoyed helping others. Before going to medical school, she worked as a radiation oncology technologist. Dr. Snead "loved being part of a process that helps people feel better." She also liked the excitement of a field in which technology changes quickly. Radiation oncologists go to medical school before they specialize in radiation oncology. Then, they learn how to use the equipment that makes high-energy radiation waves and how to use this equipment to treat cancer patients. With this knowledge, radiation oncologists can also make scientific advances by developing new ways to help patients. For students interested in radiation oncology, Dr. Snead says to "work hard in math and science and always keep an open mind. This field lives and thrives on innovations and compassion."

Social Studies ACTIVITY

WRITING SKILL Research a famous or historical figure in science. Write a short report that outlines how he or she became interested in science.

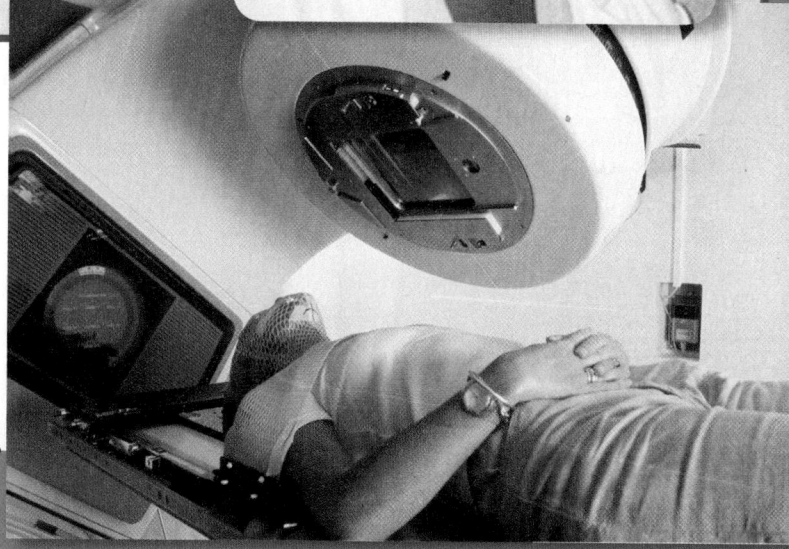

The patient in this photo is receiving radiation treatment. The mesh over her face helps keep her head absolutely still so that the radiation waves hit only diseased areas.

To learn more about these Science in Action topics, visit go.hrw.com and type in the keyword **HT6FACFF.**

Current Science

Check out Current Science® articles related to this chapter by visiting go.hrw.com. Just type in the keyword **HL5CS04.**

Human Body Systems

Like a finely tuned machine, your body is made up of many systems that work together. Your lungs take in oxygen. Your brain reacts to things that you see, hear, and smell and sends signals that cause you to react to those things. Your digestive system converts the food that you eat into energy that the cells of your body can use. And those are just a few things that your body can do!

In this unit, you will study the organ systems of your body. This timeline shows some of the events that have helped us understand the human body.

Around 3000 BCE
Ancient Egyptian doctors are the first to study the human body scientifically.

1824
Jean Louis Prevost and Jean Batiste Dumas prove that sperm is essential for fertilization.

1766
Albrecht von Haller determines that nerves control muscle movement and that all nerves are connected to the spinal cord or to the brain.

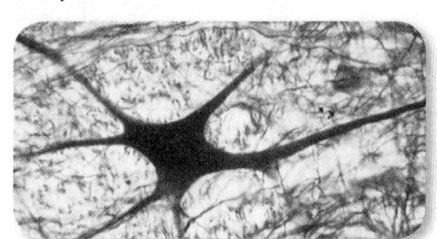

1940
During World War II in Italy, Rita Levi-Montalcini is forced to leave her work at a medical school laboratory because she is Jewish. She sets up a laboratory in her bedroom and studies the development of the nervous system.

Around 500 BCE

Susrata, an Indian surgeon, performs operations to remove cataracts.

1492

Christopher Columbus lands in the West Indies.

1543

Andreas Vesalius publishes the first complete description of the structure of the human body.

1616

William Harvey discovers that blood circulates and that the heart acts as a pump.

1893

Daniel Hale Williams, an African American surgeon, becomes the first person to repair a tear in the pericardium, the sac around the heart.

1922

Frederick Banting, Charles Best, and John McLeod discover insulin.

1930

Karl Landsteiner receives a Nobel Prize for his discovery of the four human blood types.

1982

Dr. William DeVries implants an artificial heart into Barney Clark.

1998

The first successful hand transplant is performed in France.

2001

Drs. Laman A. Gray, Jr., and Robert D. Dowling at Jewish Hospital in Louisville, Kentucky, implant the first self-contained mechanical human heart.

Body Organization and Structure

 **The Big Idea** The human body is composed of major systems that function in reproduction, growth, maintenance, and regulation.

About the PHOTO

Lance Armstrong has won the Tour de France several times. These victories are especially remarkable because he was diagnosed with cancer in 1996. But with medicine and hard work, he grew strong enough to win one of the toughest events in all of sports.

PRE-READING ACTIVITY

FOLDNOTES **Four-Corner Fold**
Before you read the chapter, create the FoldNote entitled "Four-Corner Fold" described in the **Study Skills** section of the Appendix. Label the flaps of the four-corner fold with "The skeletal system," "The muscular system," and "The integumentary system." Write what you know about each topic under the appropriate flap. As you read the chapter, add other information that you learn.

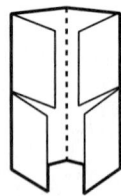

START-UP ACTIVITY

Too Cold for Comfort

Your nervous system sends you messages about your body. For example, if someone steps on your toe, your nervous system sends you a message. The pain you feel is a message that tells you to move your toe to safety. Try this exercise to watch your nervous system in action.

Procedure

1. Hold **a few pieces of ice** in one hand. Allow the melting water to drip into a **dish.** Hold the ice until the cold is uncomfortable. Then, release the ice into the dish.

2. Compare the hand that held the ice with your other hand. Describe the changes you see.

Analysis

1. What message did you receive from your nervous system while you held the ice?

2. How quickly did the cold hand return to normal?

3. What organ systems do you think helped restore your hand to normal?

4. Think of a time when your nervous system sent you a message, such as an uncomfortable feeling of heat, cold, or pain. How did your body react?

Body Organization

Imagine jumping into a lake. At first, your body feels very cold. But eventually, you get used to the cold water. How?

Your body gets used to cold water because your body returns to *homeostasis* (HOH mee OH STAY sis). **Homeostasis** is the maintenance of a stable internal environment in the body. When you jump into a lake, homeostasis helps your body adapt to the cold water.

Cells, Tissues, Organs, and Organ Systems

Maintaining homeostasis is not easy. Your internal environment is always changing. Your cells need nutrients and oxygen to survive. Your cells need wastes removed. If homeostasis is disrupted, cells may not get the materials they need. So, cells may be damaged or they may die.

Cells Form Tissues

Your cells must do many jobs to maintain homeostasis. But each of your cells does not have to do all of those jobs. Just as each person on a soccer team has a role during a game, each cell in your body has a job in maintaining homeostasis. Your cells are organized into groups. A group of similar cells that work together forms a **tissue.** Your body has four main kinds of tissue. The four kinds of tissue are shown in **Figure 1.**

Figure 1 **Four Kinds of Tissue**

Epithelial tissue covers and protects underlying tissue. When you look at the surface of your skin, you see epithelial tissue. The cells form a continuous sheet.

Nervous tissue sends electrical signals through the body. It is found in the brain, nerves, and sense organs.

Figure 2 **Organization of the Stomach**

The stomach is an organ. The four kinds of tissue work together so that the stomach can carry out digestion.

Nervous tissue in the stomach partly controls the production of acids that aid in the digestion of food. Nervous tissue signals when the stomach is full.

Epithelial tissue lines and protects the stomach wall.

Blood and another **connective tissue** called *collagen* are found in the wall of the stomach.

Layers of **muscle tissue** break up stomach contents.

Tissues Form Organs

One kind of tissue alone cannot do all of the things that several kinds of tissue working together can do. Two or more tissues that work together form an **organ.** The stomach, shown in **Figure 2,** uses all four kinds of tissue to carry out digestion.

Organs Form Organ Systems

Your stomach does a lot to help you digest your food. But the stomach doesn't do it all. Your stomach works with other organs, such as the small and large intestines, to digest your food. Organs that work together make up an *organ system*.

Benchmark Check How is the stomach part of an organ system? F.1.3.4 CS

organ a collection of tissues that carry out a specialized function of the body

F.1.3.4 CS knows that the levels of structural organization for function in living things include cells, tissues, organs, systems, and organisms.

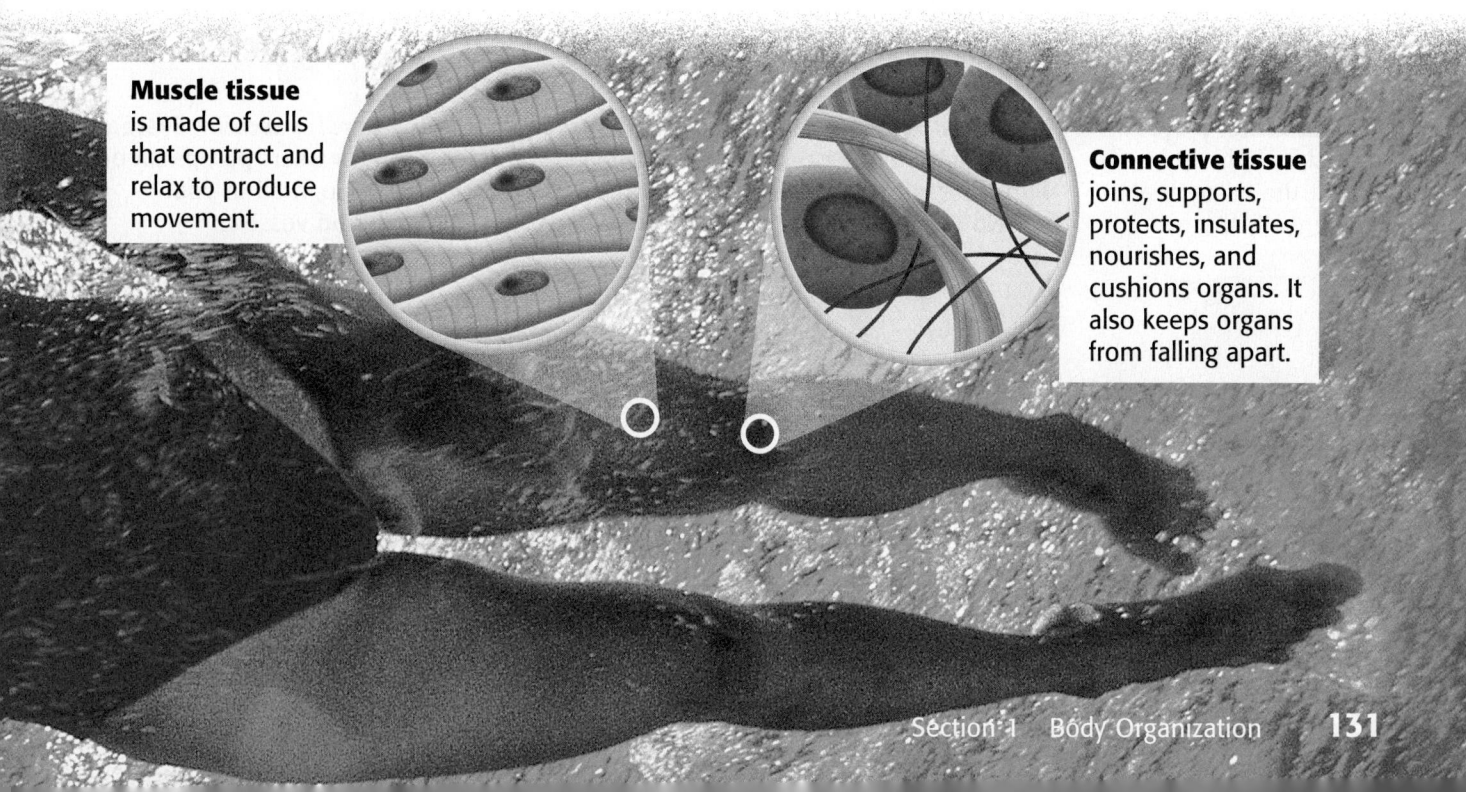

Muscle tissue is made of cells that contract and relax to produce movement.

Connective tissue joins, supports, protects, insulates, nourishes, and cushions organs. It also keeps organs from falling apart.

How Organ Systems Work Together

Your body's 11 major organ systems, as shown in **Figure 3,** work together to maintain homeostasis in an organism. For example, the cardiovascular system, which includes your heart, blood, and blood vessels, works with the respiratory system. Your cardiovascular system picks up oxygen from tiny sacs, called *alveoli,* in the lungs. The lungs are part of the respiratory system. The cardiovascular system delivers materials, such as oxygen, that your cells need to survive.

Benchmark Check What two organ systems in the human body work to deliver oxygen to the cells? What would happen to the body's cells if these two systems stopped working? **F.1.3.1 AA, F.1.3.5 CS**

F.1.3.1 AA understands that living things are composed of major systems that function in reproduction, growth, maintenance, and regulation.

F.1.3.5 CS explains how the life functions of organisms are related to what occurs within the cell.

Figure 3 Organ Systems

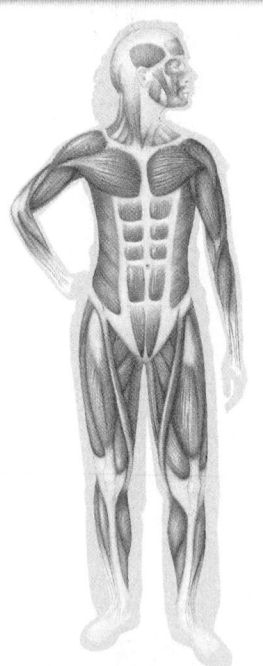

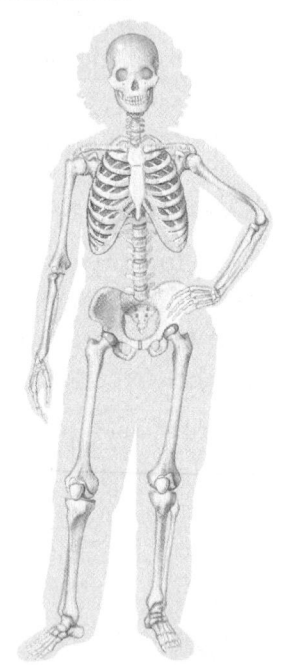

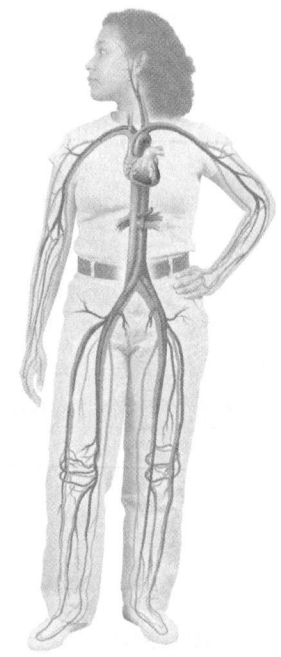

Integumentary System Your skin, hair, and nails protect the tissue that lies beneath them.

Muscular System Your muscular system works with the skeletal system to help you move.

Skeletal System Your bones provide a frame to support and protect your body parts.

Cardiovascular System Your heart pumps blood through all of your blood vessels.

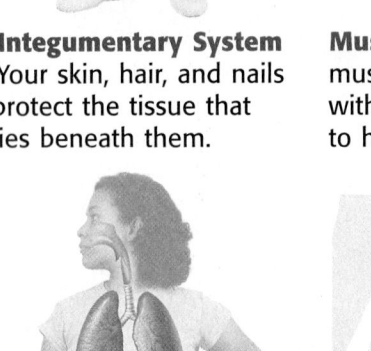

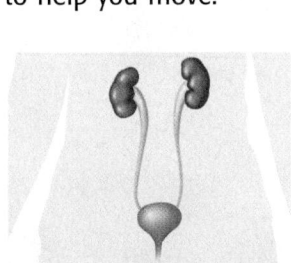

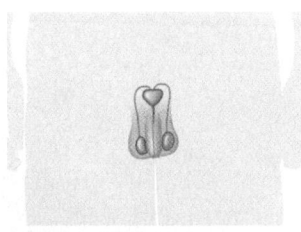

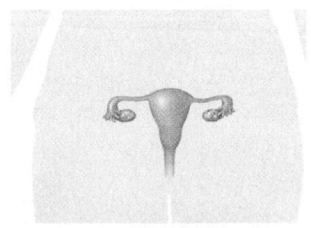

Respiratory System Your lungs absorb oxygen and release carbon dioxide.

Urinary System Your urinary system removes wastes from the blood and regulates your body's fluids.

Male Reproductive System The male reproductive system produces and delivers sperm.

Female Reproductive System The female reproductive system produces eggs and nourishes and protects the fetus.

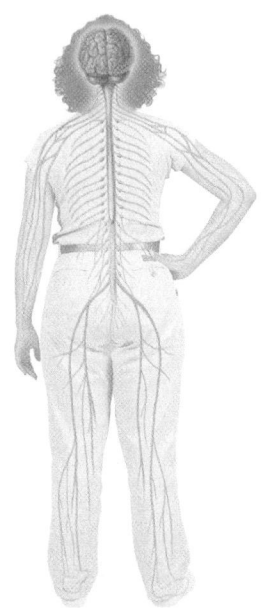

Nervous System Your nervous system receives and sends electrical messages throughout your body.

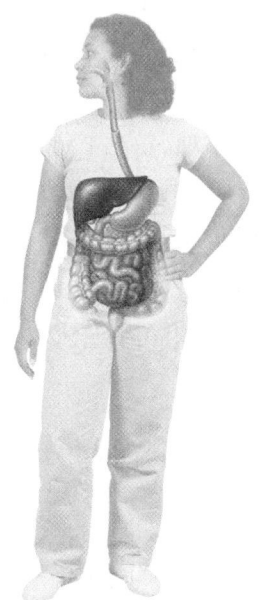

Digestive System Your digestive system breaks down the food you eat into nutrients that your body can absorb.

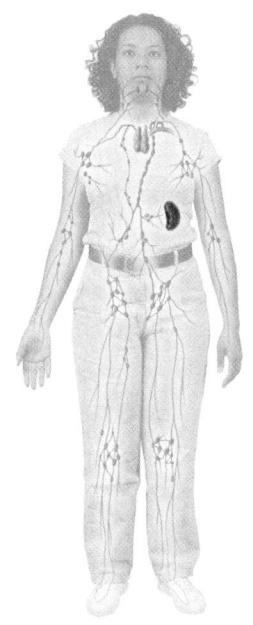

Lymphatic System The lymphatic system returns leaked fluids to blood vessels and helps get rid of bacteria and viruses.

Endocrine System Your glands send out chemical messages. Ovaries and testes are part of this system.

SECTION Review

Summary

- A group of cells that work together is a tissue. Tissues form organs. Organs that work together form organ systems. **F.1.3.4 CS**
- There are four kinds of tissue in the human body.
- There are 11 major organ systems in the human body. **F.1.3.1 AA**
- Organ systems work together to help the body maintain homeostasis.

Using Key Terms

1. Use the following terms in the same sentence: *homeostasis, tissue,* and *organ*.

Understanding Key Ideas

2. List the 11 organ systems. **F.1.3.1 AA**

3. Which organ system works with your muscular system to help you move?

Critical Thinking

4. **Applying Concepts** Tanya went to a restaurant and ate a hamburger. Describe how Tanya used five organ systems to eat and digest her hamburger.

5. **Predicting Consequences** Predict what might happen if the human body did not have specialized cells, tissues, organs, and organ systems to maintain homeostasis. **F.1.3.5 CS**

FCAT Preparation

6. Which of the following statements describes how tissues, organs, and organ systems are related? **F.1.3.4 CS**

   A. Organs form tissues, which form organ systems.

   B. Organ systems form organs, which form tissues.

   C. Tissues form organs, which form organ systems.

   D. Organ systems form tissues, which form organs.

SCiLINKS

NSTA
Developed and maintained by the National Science Teachers Association

For a variety of links related to this chapter, go to www.scilinks.org

Topic: Tissues and Organs; Body Systems
SciLinks code: HSM1530; HSM0184

The Skeletal System

When you hear the word skeleton, *you may think of the remains of something that has died. But your skeleton is not dead. It is very much alive.*

Your bones are alive and active. Bones, cartilage, and the tissues that hold bones together make up your **skeletal system.**

Bones

The average adult human skeleton has 206 bones. Bones help support and protect parts of your body. They work with your muscles so that you can move. Bones also help your body maintain homeostasis by storing minerals and making blood cells. **Figure 1** shows the functions of your skeleton.

Benchmark Check **What are four functions of the skeletal system?** F.1.3.1 AA

skeletal system the organ system whose primary function is to support and protect the body and to allow the body to move

Figure 1 **The Skeleton**

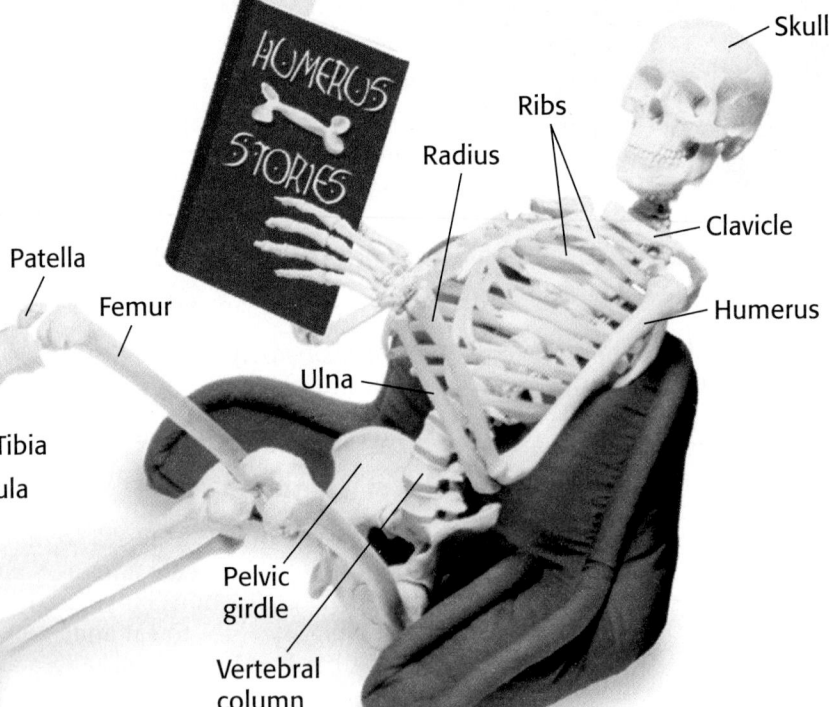

Skull

Ribs

Radius

Clavicle

Humerus

Patella

Femur

Ulna

Tibia

Fibula

Pelvic girdle

Vertebral column

Protection Your heart and lungs are protected by ribs, your spinal cord is protected by vertebrae, and your brain is protected by the skull.

Storage Bones store minerals that help your nerves and muscles function properly. Long bones store fat that can be used for energy.

Movement Skeletal muscles pull on bones to produce movement. Without bones, you would not be able to sit, stand, walk, or run.

Blood Cell Formation Some of your bones are filled with a special material that makes blood cells. This material is called *marrow.*

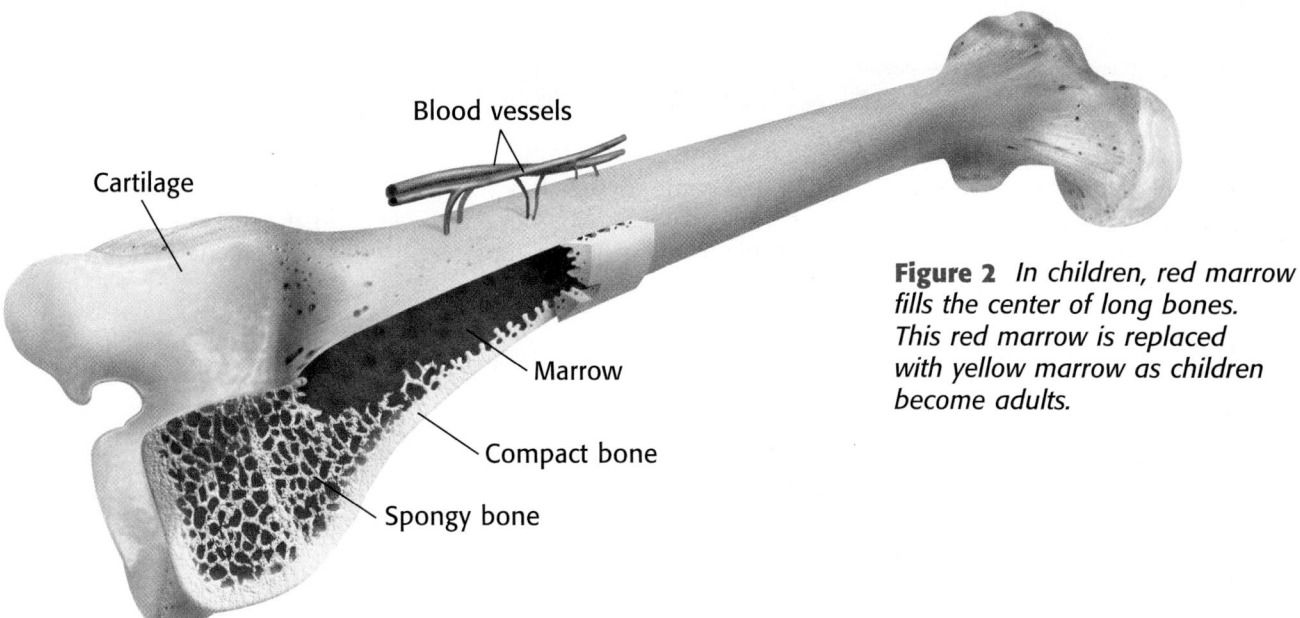

Blood vessels

Cartilage

Marrow

Compact bone

Spongy bone

Figure 2 *In children, red marrow fills the center of long bones. This red marrow is replaced with yellow marrow as children become adults.*

Bone Structure

A bone may seem lifeless. But a bone is a living organ made of several different tissues. Bone is made of connective tissue and minerals. These minerals are deposited by living cells called *osteoblasts* (AHS tee oh BLASTS).

If you look inside a bone, you will notice two kinds of bone tissue. If the bone tissue does not have any visible open spaces, it is called *compact bone*. Compact bone is rigid and dense. Tiny canals within compact bone contain small blood vessels. Bone tissue that has many open spaces is called *spongy bone*. Spongy bone provides most of the strength and support for a bone.

Bones contain a soft tissue called *marrow*. There are two types of marrow. Red marrow produces both red and white blood cells. Yellow marrow, found in the central cavity of long bones, stores fat. **Figure 2** shows a cross section of a long bone, the femur.

Bone Growth

Did you know that most of your skeleton used to be soft and rubbery? Most bones start out as a flexible tissue called *cartilage*. When you were born, you didn't have much true bone. But as you grew, most of the cartilage was replaced by bone as the osteoblasts grew and divided to make more bone cells. During childhood, most bones still have growth plates of cartilage. These growth plates provide a place for bones to continue to grow.

Feel the end of your nose. Or bend the top of your ear. These areas are two places where cartilage is never replaced by bone. These areas stay flexible.

 **Benchmark Check** How do bones grow? **F.1.3.3 CS**

Pickled Bones

1. Place a **clean chicken bone** in a **jar of vinegar.**

2. After 1 week, remove the bone and rinse it with **water.**

3. Describe the changes that you can see or feel.

4. How has the bone's strength changed?

5. What did the vinegar remove?

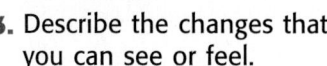 **F.1.3.1 AA** understands that living things are composed of major systems that function in reproduction, growth, maintenance, and regulation.

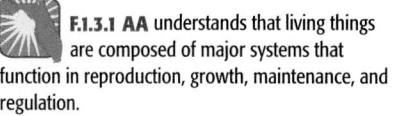 **F.1.3.3 CS** knows that in multicellular organisms cells grow and divide to make more cells in order to form and repair various organs and tissues.

Figure 3 **Three Joints**

Gliding Joint
Gliding joints allow bones in the hand and wrist to glide over one another and give some flexibility to the area.

Ball-and-Socket Joint
As a video-game joystick lets you move your character all around, the shoulder lets your arm move freely in all directions.

Hinge Joint
As a hinge allows a door to open and close, the knee enables you to flex and extend your lower leg.

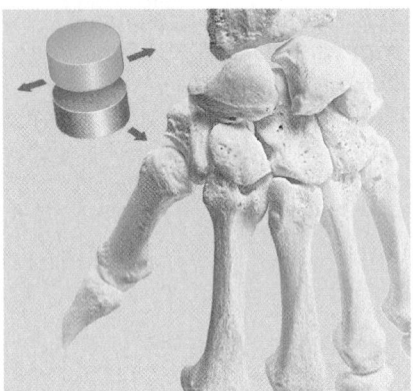

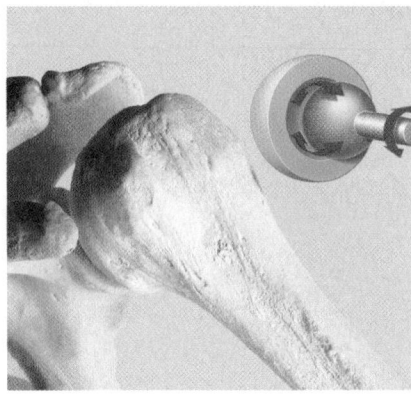

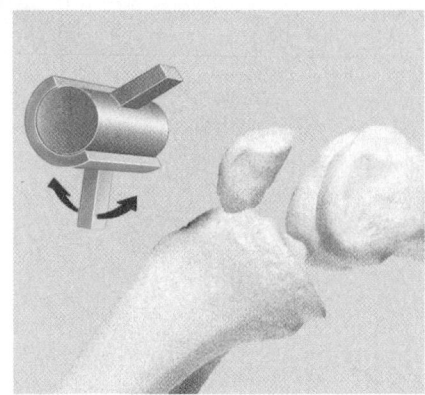

joint a place where two or more bones meet

Joints

A place where two or more bones meet is called a **joint.** Your joints allow your body to move when your muscles contract. Some joints, such as fixed joints, allow little or no movement. Many of the joints in the skull are fixed joints. Other joints, such as your shoulder, allow a lot of movement. Joints can be classified based on how the bones in a joint move. For example, your shoulder is a ball-and-socket joint. Three joints are shown in **Figure 3.**

Joints are held together by *ligaments* (LIG uh muhnts). Ligaments are strong elastic bands of connective tissue. They connect the bones in a joint. Also, cartilage covers the ends of many bones. Cartilage helps cushion the area in a joint where bones meet.

✓ **Reading Check** Describe the basic structure of joints.

INTERNET ACTIVITY

Humans in Space What is the effect of zero gravity and space travel on the human body systems? Go to **go.hrw.com,** and type in the keyword **HL5BD1W** to find out!

CONNECTION TO Physics

WRITING SKILL **Bones in Space** On Earth, your bones are constantly renewing themselves in response to the effects of gravity and other stressors, such as weight bearing exercise. However, in space, your bones would experience microgravity or zero gravity and would not experience the stressors that occur on Earth. The absence of these stressors cause the calcium in bones to be brokendown and released into the bloodstream. Research how the loss of calcium affects bones and bone function. Also research how this information might help cure bone diseases. Write a report discussing your findings.

Skeletal System Injuries and Diseases

Sometimes, parts of the skeletal system are injured. As shown in **Figure 4,** bones may be fractured, or broken. Joints can also be injured. A dislocated joint is a joint in which one or more bones have been moved out of place. Another joint injury, called a *sprain*, happens if a ligament is stretched too far or torn.

There are also diseases of the skeletal system. *Osteoporosis* (AHS tee OH puh ROH sis) is a disease that causes bones to become less dense. Bones become weak and break more easily. Age and poor eating habits can make it more likely for people to develop osteoporosis. Other bone diseases affect the marrow or make bones soft. A disease that affects the joints is called *arthritis* (ahr THRIET is). Arthritis is painful. Joints may swell or stiffen. As they get older, some people are more likely to have some types of arthritis.

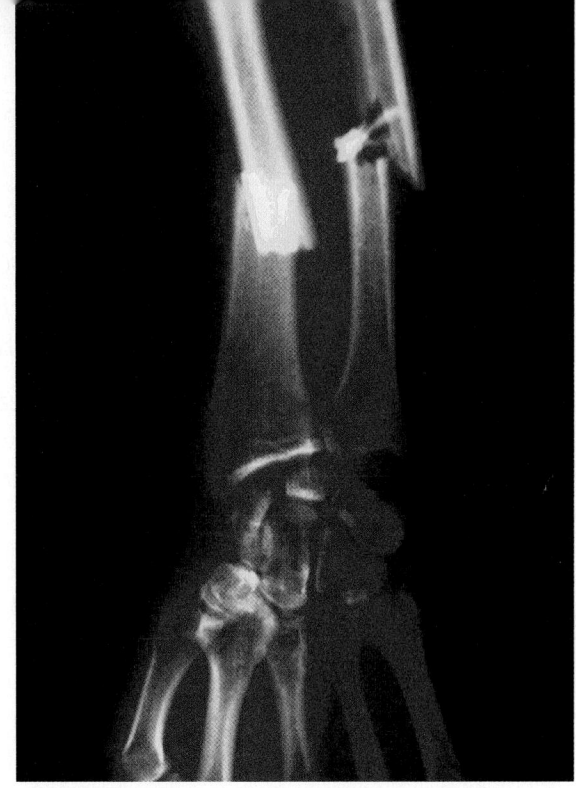

Figure 4 *This X ray shows that the two bones of the forearm have been fractured, or broken.*

SECTION Review

Summary

- The skeletal system includes bones, cartilage, and connective tissues.
- The skeletal system protects the body, stores minerals, allows movement, and makes blood cells. F.I.3.1 AA
- Joints are places where two or more bones meet.
- Bones are repaired and grow because of cell division. F.I.3.3 CS
- Fractures, dislocations, and sprains are skeletal system injuries. Arthritis and osteoporosis are skeletal system diseases.

Using Key Terms

1. In your own words, write a definition for the term *skeletal system.*

Understanding Key Ideas

2. Describe four functions of the skeletal system. F.I.3.1 AA

3. Name three types of joints?

4. Describe two diseases that affect the skeletal system.

Critical Thinking

5. **Identifying Relationships** Red bone marrow produces blood cells. Children have red bone marrow in their long bones, while adults have yellow bone marrow, which stores fat. Why might adults and children have different kinds of marrow? F.I.3.3 CS

FCAT Preparation

6. A broken bone usually heals in about six weeks. Which of the following cells work to repair broken and damaged bone tissue? F.I.3.3 CS

A. neurons

B. osteoblasts

C. lymphocytes

D. muscle cells

SCILINKS.

Developed and maintained by the National Science Teachers Association

For a variety of links related to this chapter, go to www.scilinks.org

Topic: Skeletal System; Medicine in Florida
SciLinks code: HSM1399; HSMF10

The Muscular System

Have you ever tried to sit still, without moving any muscles at all, for one minute? It's impossible! Somewhere in your body, muscles are always working.

Your heart is a muscle. Muscles make you breathe. And muscles hold you upright. The **muscular system** is made up of the muscles that let you move.

Kinds of Muscle

Figure 1 shows the three kinds of muscle in your body. *Smooth muscle* is found in the digestive tract and in the walls of blood vessels. *Cardiac muscle* is found only in your heart. *Skeletal muscle* is attached to your bones for movement. Skeletal muscle also helps protect your inner organs.

Muscle action can be voluntary or involuntary. Muscle action that is under your control is *voluntary*. Muscle action that is not under your control is *involuntary*. Smooth muscle and cardiac muscle are involuntary muscles. Skeletal muscles can be both voluntary and involuntary muscles. For example, you can blink your eyes anytime you want. But your eyes will also blink automatically.

Benchmark Check What are the functions of the muscular system? **F.1.3.1 AA**

Figure 1 Three Kinds of Muscle

Skeletal muscle enables bones to move.

Smooth muscle moves food through the digestive system.

Cardiac muscle pumps blood around the body.

Figure 2 **A Pair of Muscles in the Arm**

muscular system the organ system whose primary function is movement and flexibility

Skeletal muscles, such as the biceps and triceps muscles, work in pairs. When the biceps muscle contracts, the arm bends. When the triceps muscle contracts, the arm straightens.

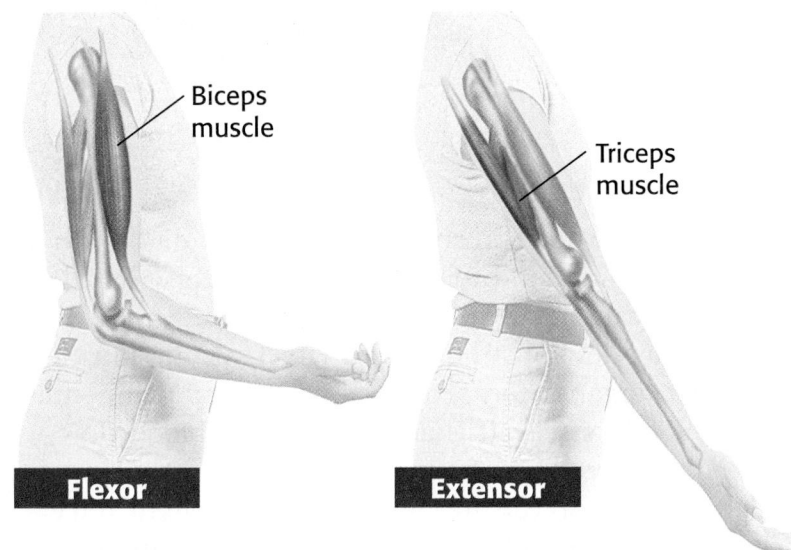

Biceps muscle

Triceps muscle

Flexor

Extensor

Movement

Skeletal muscles can make hundreds of movements. You can see many of these movements by watching a dancer, a swimmer, or even someone smiling or frowning. When you want to move, signals travel from your brain to your skeletal muscle cells. The muscle cells then contract, or get shorter.

F.1.3.1 AA understands that living things are composed of major systems that function in reproduction, growth, maintenance, and regulation.

Muscles Attached to Bones

Strands of tough connective tissue connect your skeletal muscles to your bones. These strands are called *tendons*. When a muscle that connects two bones gets shorter, the bones are pulled closer to each other. For example, tendons attach the biceps muscle to a bone in your shoulder and to a bone in your forearm. When the biceps muscle contracts, your forearm bends toward your shoulder.

Muscles Working in Pairs

Your skeletal muscles often work in pairs. Usually, one muscle in the pair bends part of the body. The other muscle straightens part of the body. A muscle that bends part of your body is called a *flexor* (FLEKS uhr). A muscle that straightens part of your body is an *extensor* (ek STEN suhr). As shown in **Figure 2,** the biceps muscle of the arm is a flexor. The triceps muscle of the arm is an extensor.

Reading Check **Describe how muscles work in pairs.**

SCHOOL to HOME

Power in Pairs

Ask a parent or guardian to sit in a chair and place a hand palm up under the edge of a table. Tell your parent or guardian to apply gentle upward pressure. Feel the front and back of his or her upper arm. Next, ask him or her to push down on top of the table. Feel your parent or guardian's arm again. What did you notice about the muscles when your parent or guardian was pressing up? pushing down?

ACTIVITY

Figure 3 *This girl is strengthening her heart and improving her endurance by doing aerobic exercise. This boy is doing resistance exercise to build strong muscles.*

Use It or Lose It

What happens when someone wears a cast for a broken arm? Skeletal muscles around the broken bone become smaller and weaker. The muscles weaken because they are not exercised. Exercised muscles are stronger and larger. Strong muscles can help other organs, too. For example, contracting muscles squeeze blood vessels. This action increases blood flow without needing more work from the heart.

Certain exercises can give muscles more strength and endurance. More endurance lets muscles work longer without getting tired. Two kinds of exercise can increase muscle strength and endurance. They are resistance exercise and aerobic exercise. You can see an example of each kind in **Figure 3.**

Resistance Exercise

Resistance exercise is a great way to strengthen skeletal muscles. During resistance exercise, people work against the resistance, or weight, of an object. Some resistance exercises, such as curl-ups, use your own weight for resistance.

Aerobic Exercise

Steady, moderately intense activity is called *aerobic exercise*. Jogging, cycling, skating, swimming, and walking are aerobic exercises. This kind of exercise can increase muscle strength. However, aerobic exercise mostly strengthens the heart and increases endurance.

CONNECTION TO Chemistry

Muscle Function Body chemistry is very important for healthy muscle function. Spasms or cramps happen if too much sweating, poor diet, or illness causes a chemical imbalance in muscles. Identify three chemicals that the body needs for muscles to work properly. Make a poster explaining how people can make sure that they have enough of each chemical.

ACTIVITY

Muscle Injury

Any exercise program should be started slowly. Starting slowly means you are less likely to get hurt. You should also warm up for exercise. A *strain* is an injury in which a muscle or tendon is overstretched or torn. Strains often happen because a muscle has not been warmed up. Strains also happen when muscles are worked too hard.

People who exercise too much can hurt their tendons. The body can't repair an injured tendon before the next exercise session. So, the tendon becomes inflamed. This condition is called *tendinitis*. Often, a long rest is needed for the injured tendon to heal.

Some people try to make their muscles stronger by taking drugs. These drugs are called *anabolic steroids* (A nuh BAH lik STER oidz). They can cause long-term health problems. Anabolic steroids can damage the heart, liver, and kidneys. They can also cause high blood pressure. If taken before the skeleton is mature, anabolic steroids can cause bones to stop growing.

✓ Reading Check What are the risks of using anabolic steroids?

MATH PRACTICE

Runner's Time

Jan has decided to enter a 5 km road race. She now runs 5 km in 30 min. She would like to decrease her time by 15% before the race. What will her time be when she reaches her goal?

SECTION Review

Summary

● The muscular system is responsible for movement and is made up of smooth muscle, cardiac muscle, and skeletal muscle. **F.1.3.1 AA**

● Skeletal muscles often work in pairs. They contract to allow movement.

● Resistance exercise improves muscle strength. Aerobic exercise improves heart strength and muscle endurance.

● Strains are injuries to muscles and tendons. Tendinitis affects tendons.

Using Key Terms

1. Write an original definition for *muscular system*.

Understanding Key Ideas

2. Describe three kinds of muscle.

3. List two kinds of exercise. Give an example of each.

4. Describe two muscular system injuries.

Critical Thinking

5. **Applying Concepts** Describe some of the muscle action needed to pick up a book. Include flexors and extensors in your description.

6. **Predicting Consequences** If aerobic exercise improves heart strength, what likely happens to heart rate as the heart gets stronger? Explain your answer.

FCAT Preparation

7. The muscular system is one of the human body's major organ systems. Which of the following tasks is the primary function of the muscular system? **F.1.3.1 AA**

   A. excretion

   B. movement

   C. reproduction

   D. energy storage

SCILINKS **NSTA**
Developed and maintained by the National Science Teachers Association

For a variety of links related to this chapter, go to www.scilinks.org

Topic: Muscular System; Medicine in Florida
SciLinks code: HSM1008; HSMF10

The Integumentary System

What part of your body has to be partly dead to keep you alive? Here are some clues: It comes in many colors, it is the largest organ in the body, and it is showing right now!

Did you guess your skin? If you did, you guessed correctly. Your skin, hair, and nails make up your **integumentary system** (in TEG yoo MEN tuhr ee SIS tuhm). The integumentary system covers your body and helps you maintain homeostasis.

Functions of Skin

Why do you need skin? Here are four good reasons:

- Skin protects you by keeping water in your body and foreign particles out of your body.
- Skin keeps you in touch with the outside world. Nerve endings in your skin let you feel things around you.
- Skin helps regulate your body temperature. Small organs in the skin called *sweat glands* make sweat. Sweat is a salty liquid that flows to the surface of the skin. As sweat evaporates, the skin cools.
- Skin helps get rid of wastes. Several kinds of waste chemicals can be removed in sweat.

As shown in **Figure 1,** skin comes in many colors. Skin color is determined by a chemical called *melanin.* If a lot of melanin is present, skin is very dark. If little melanin is present, skin is very light. Melanin absorbs ultraviolet light from the sun. So, melanin reduces damage that can lead to skin cancer. However, all skin, even dark skin, is vulnerable to cancer. Skin should be protected from sunlight whenever possible.

integumentary system the organ system that forms a protective covering on the outside of the body

F.1.3.1 AA understands that living things are composed of major systems that function in reproduction, growth, maintenance, and regulation.

F.1.3.3 CS knows that in multicellular organisms cells grow and divide to make more cells in order to form and repair various organs and tissues.

Benchmark Check What are the functions of the integumentary system? **F.1.3.1 AA**

Figure 1 *Variety in skin color is caused by the pigment melanin. The amount of melanin varies from person to person.*

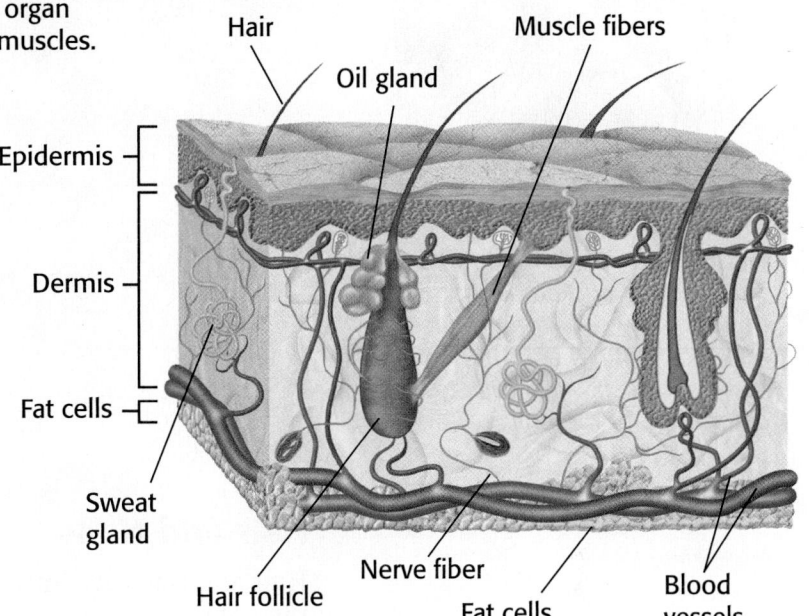

Figure 2   Structures of the Skin

Beneath the surface, your skin is a complex organ made of blood vessels, nerves, glands, and muscles.

Blood vessels transport substances and help regulate body temperature.

Nerve fibers carry messages to and from the brain.

Hair follicles in the dermis make hair.

Muscle fibers attached to a hair follicle can contract and cause the hair to stand up.

Oil glands release oil that keeps hair flexible and waterproofs the epidermis.

Sweat glands release sweat to cool the body. Sweating is also a way to remove waste materials from the body.

Hair · Oil gland · Muscle fibers · Epidermis · Dermis · Fat cells · Sweat gland · Hair follicle · Nerve fiber · Fat cells · Blood vessels

Layers of Skin

Your skin grows with you as cells divide and make more cells. Skin is the largest organ of your body. In fact, the skin of an adult covers an area of about 2 m²! Skin has two main layers: the epidermis (EP uh DUHR mis) and the dermis. The **epidermis** is the outermost layer of skin. You see the epidermis when you look at your skin. The thicker layer of skin that lies beneath the epidermis is the **dermis.**

epidermis the surface layer of cells on a plant or animal

dermis the layer of skin below the epidermis

Epidermis

The epidermis is made of epithelial tissue. Even though the epidermis has many layers of cells, it is as thick as only two sheets of paper over most of the body. It is thicker on the palms of your hands and on the soles of your feet. Most cells in the epidermis are dead. These cells are filled with a protein called *keratin*. Keratin helps make the skin tough.

Dermis

The dermis lies beneath the epidermis. The dermis has many fibers made of a protein called *collagen*. These fibers provide strength. They also let skin bend without tearing. The dermis contains many small structures, as shown in **Figure 2.**

Reading Check Describe the dermis. How does it differ from the epidermis?

Your epidermis is showing!

Hair

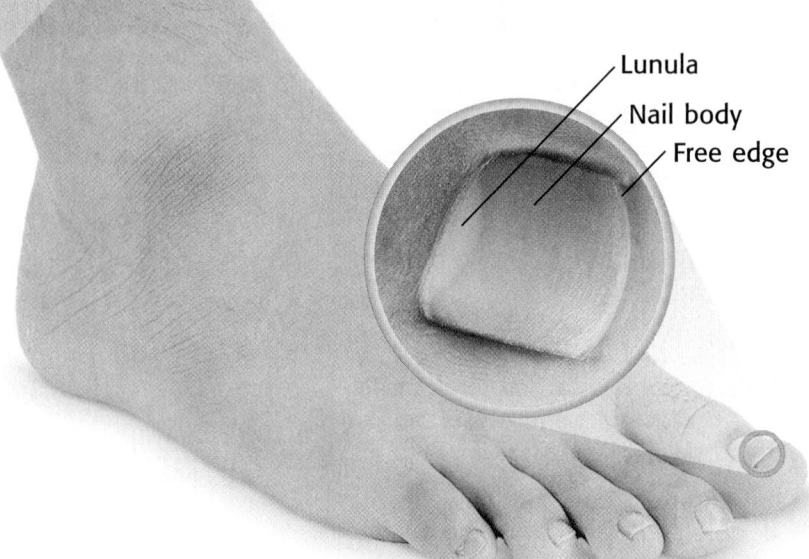

Lunula
Nail body
Free edge

Figure 3 *A hair is made up of layers of dead, tightly packed, keratin-filled cells. In nails, new cells are produced in the nail root, just beneath the lunula. The new cells push older cells toward the outer edge of the nail.*

F.1.3.3 CS knows that in multicellular organisms cells grow and divide to make more cells in order to form and repair various organs and tissues.

Hair and Nails

Hair and nails are important parts of the integumentary system. Like skin, hair and nails are made of living and dead cells. **Figure 3** shows hair and nails.

A hair forms at the bottom of a tiny sac called a *hair follicle.* The hair grows as new cells are added at the hair follicle. Older cells get pushed upward. The only living cells in a hair are in the hair follicle. Like skin, hair gets its color from melanin.

Hair helps protect skin from ultraviolet light. Hair also keeps particles, such as dust and insects, out of your eyes and nose. In most mammals, hair helps regulate body temperature. A tiny muscle attached to the hair follicle contracts. If the follicle contains a hair, the hair stands up. The lifted hairs work like a sweater. They trap warm air around the body.

A nail grows from living cells in the *nail root* at the base of the nail. As new cells form, the nail grows longer. Nails protect the tips of your fingers and toes. So, your fingers and toes can be soft and sensitive for a keen sense of touch.

Skin Injuries

Skin is often damaged. Fortunately, your skin can repair itself, as shown in **Figure 4.** Some damage to skin is very serious. Damage to the genetic material in skin cells can cause skin cancer. Skin may also be affected by hormones that cause oil glands in skin to make too much oil. This oil combines with dead skin cells and bacteria to clog hair follicles. The result is acne. Proper cleansing can help but often cannot prevent this problem.

![Benchmark Check] How do cells help in repairing skin? **F.1.3.3 CS**

Figure 4 How Skin Heals

1 A blood clot forms over a cut to stop bleeding and to keep bacteria from entering the wound. Bacteria-fighting cells then come to the area to kill bacteria.

2 Damaged cells are replaced through cell division. Eventually, all that is left on the surface is a scar.

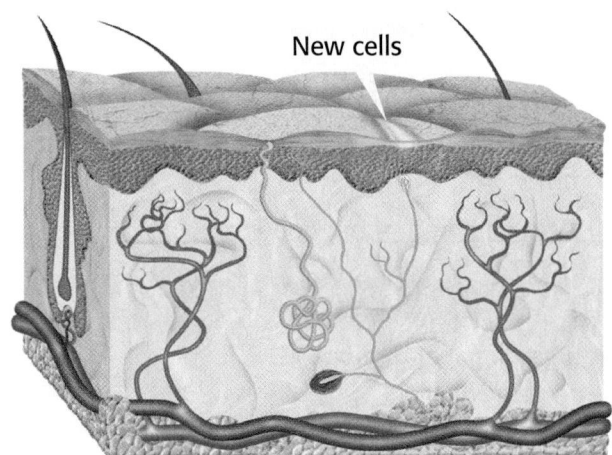

Scab

Blood clot

Bacteria-fighting cells

New cells

SECTION Review

Summary

- The integumentary system keeps water in the body, keeps foreign particles out of the body, lets people feel things around them, regulates temperature, and removes wastes. **F.I.3.1 AA**

- The epidermis contains keratin. The dermis lies beneath the epidermis and contains collagen.

- Hair grows from cell division in hair follicles. Nails grow from cell division in nail roots. **F.I.3.3 CS**

- Cell division allows skin growth and repair. **F.I.3.3 CS**

Using Key Terms

1. In your own words, write a definition for each of the following terms: *integumentary system*, *epidermis*, and *dermis*.

Understanding Key Ideas

2. Which of the following is NOT a function of the integumentary system? **F.I.3.1 AA**

   a. to regulate body temperature

   b. to keep water in the body

   c. to move your body

   d. to get rid of wastes

3. Describe the two layers of skin.

4. Describe how a cut heals. **F.I.3.3 CS**

Critical Thinking

5. **Making Inferences** Why do you feel pain when you pull on your hair or nails, but not when you cut them?

FCAT Preparation

6. As you grow into an adult, your organ systems, such as your integumentary system, are also growing. How are cells involved in repairing damage to your skin and helping it grow with you? **F.I.3.3 CS**

   A. skin cells expand

   B. skin cells divide

   C. skin cells shrink

   D. skin cells die

SCiLINKS.

NSTA

Developed and maintained by the National Science Teachers Association

For a variety of links related to this chapter, go to www.scilinks.org

Topic: Integumentary System; Medicine in Florida

SciLinks code: HSM0803; HSMF10

Skills Practice Lab

Seeing Is Believing

OBJECTIVES

Measure nail growth over time.

Draw a graph of nail growth.

MATERIALS

- graph paper (optional)
- metric ruler
- permanent marker

SAFETY

Like your hair and skin, fingernails are part of your body's integumentary system. Nails, shown in the figure below, are a modification of the outer layer of the skin. Nails grow from the nail bed and will grow continuously throughout your life. In this activity, you will measure the rate at which fingernails grow.

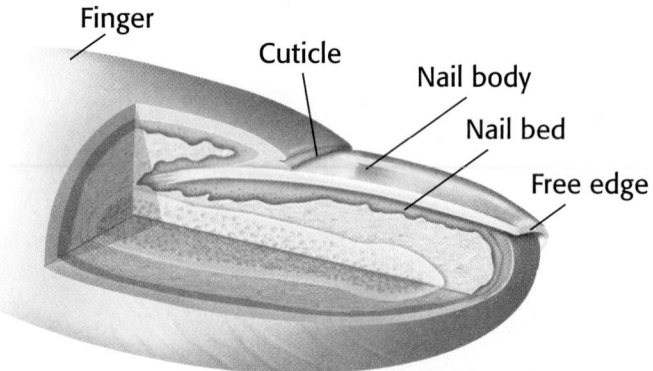

Finger   Cuticle   Nail body   Nail bed   Free edge

Procedure

1 Use a permanent marker to mark the center of the nail bed on your right index finger, as shown in the figure below. **Caution:** Do not get ink on your clothing.

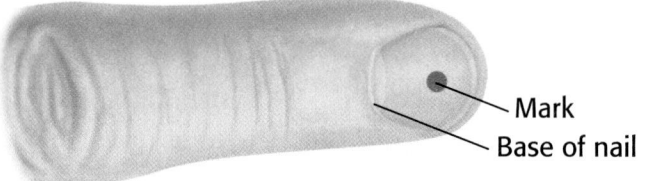

Mark
Base of nail

2 Measure from the mark to the base of your nail. Record the measurement, and label the measurement "Day 1."

3 Repeat steps 1 and 2 for your left index finger.

4 Let your fingernails grow for 2 days. Normal daily activity will not wash away the mark completely, but you may need to freshen the mark.

5 Measure the distance from the mark on your nail to the base of your nail. Record this distance, and label the measurement "Day 3."

6 Continue measuring and recording the growth of your nails every other day for 2 weeks. Refresh the mark as necessary. You may continue to file or trim your nails as usual throughout the course of the lab.

7 After you have completed your measurements, use them to create a graph similar to the graph below.

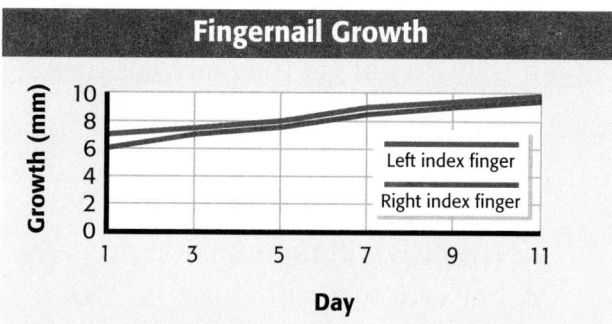

Fingernail Growth

Growth (mm) vs. Day
- Left index finger
- Right index finger

Analyze the Results

1 **Describing Events** Did the nail on one hand grow faster than the nail on the other hand?

2 **Examining Data** Did your nails grow at a constant rate, or did your nails grow more quickly at certain times?

Draw Conclusions

3 **Making Predictions** If one nail grew more quickly than the other nail, what might explain the difference in growth?

4 **Analyzing Graphs** Compare your graph with the graphs of your classmates. Do you notice any differences in the graphs based on gender or physical characteristics, such as height? If so, describe the difference.

Applying Your Data

Do additional research to find out how nails are important to you. Also, identify how nails can be used to indicate a person's health or nutrition. Based on what you learn, describe how your nail growth indicates your health or nutrition.

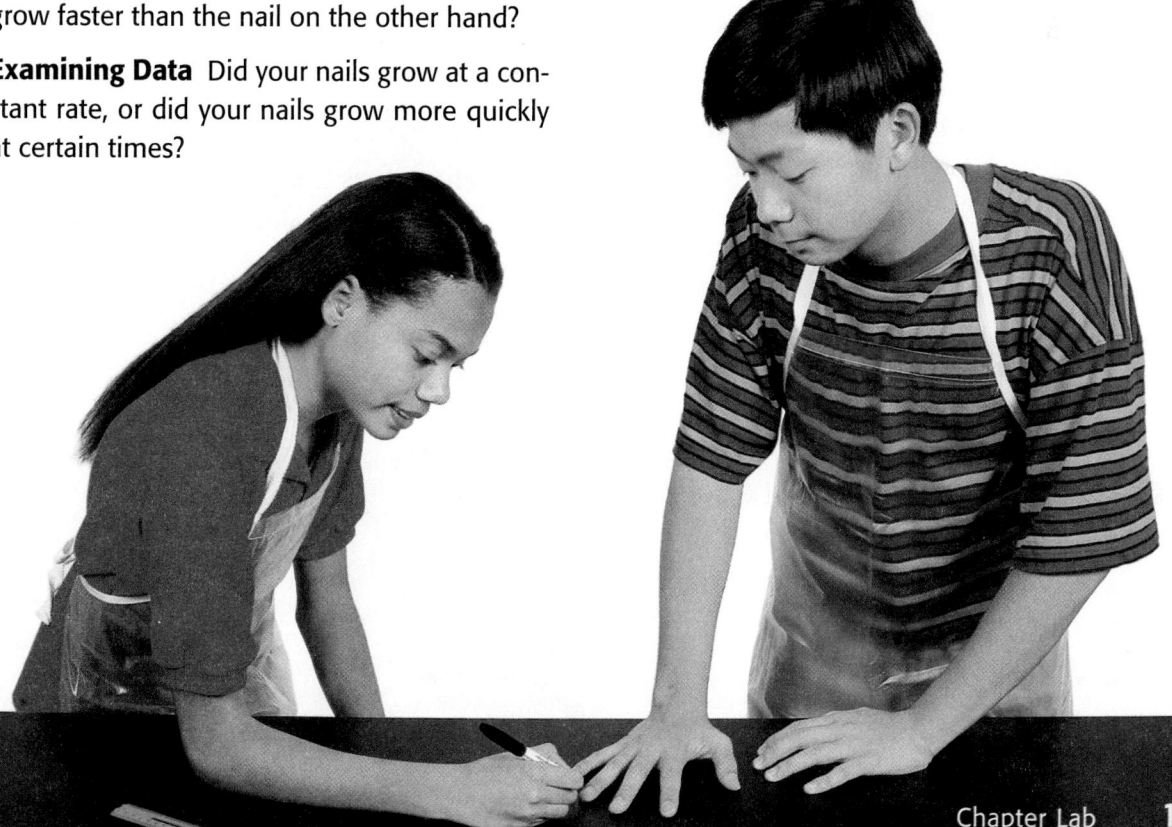

Chapter Review

USING KEY TERMS

Use a term from the chapter to complete each sentence below.

1 A(n) ___ is a place where two or more bones meet.

2 ___ is the maintenance of a stable internal environment.

3 The outermost layer of skin is the ___.

4 The organ system that includes skin, hair, and nails is the ___.

5 A(n) ___ is made up of two or more tissues that work together. **F.I.3.4 CS**

6 The ___ supports and protects the body, stores minerals, and allows movement. **F.I.3.1 AA**

UNDERSTANDING KEY IDEAS

Multiple Choice

7 Muscles receive signals from the brain to move. The muscles need energy to contract. At what level of structural organization do muscles get energy from food? **F.I.3.4 CS** FCAT

  a. cell

  b. tissue

  c. organ

  d. organ system

8 Which muscle tissue can be both voluntary and involuntary?

  a. smooth muscle

  b. cardiac muscle

  c. skeletal muscle

  d. All of the above

9 What is one function of the integumentary system? **F.I.3.1 AA**

  a. It helps regulate body temperature.

  b. It helps the body move.

  c. It stores minerals.

  d. It makes red blood cells.

10 Homeostasis is the maintenance of a stable internal environment in an organism. If homeostasis is disrupted, cells may not get the materials they need. What is likely to happen to cells if they do not get the materials they need? **F.I.3.5 CS** FCAT

  a. The cells will make more ATP.

  b. The cells will not be affected.

  c. The cells will not function properly.

  d. The cells will reproduce.

Short Answer

11 Explain how skeletal muscles move bones.

12 Describe the skeletal system, and list four functions of bones. **F.I.3.1 AA**

13 How does the production of melanin help protect skin cells from sun damage?

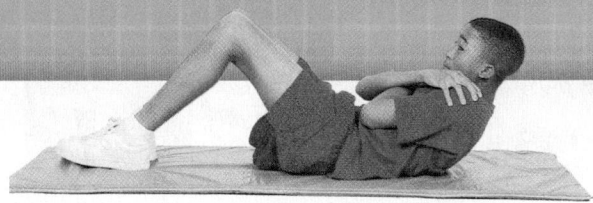

14 Describe the muscular system and its function. F.1.3.1 AA

15 Give an example of how organ systems work together.

16 List three injuries and two diseases that affect the skeletal system.

17 Compare aerobic exercise and resistance exercise.

18 What are two kinds of damage that may affect skin?

19 Describe how damaged skin is repaired. F.1.3.3 CS

CRITICAL THINKING

Extended Response

20 **Predicting Consequences** Cardiac muscle is made of many layers of specialized cells. If a blood vessel that supplies oxygen and nutrients to the cardiac muscle's cells becomes blocked with cholesterol, the cells will die. What will most likely happen once many cardiac muscle cells die? F.1.3.5 CS

21 **Making Inferences** Imagine that you are building a robot. Your robot will have a skeleton similar to a human skeleton. If the robot needs to be able to move a limb in all directions, what kind of joint would be needed? Explain your answer.

22 **Identifying Relationships** Why might some muscles fail to work properly if a bone is broken?

Concept Mapping

23 Use the following terms to create a concept map: *tissues, muscle tissue, connective tissue, cells, organ systems, organs, epithelial tissue,* and *nervous tissue.*

INTERPRETING GRAPHICS

Use the cross section of skin below to answer the questions that follow.

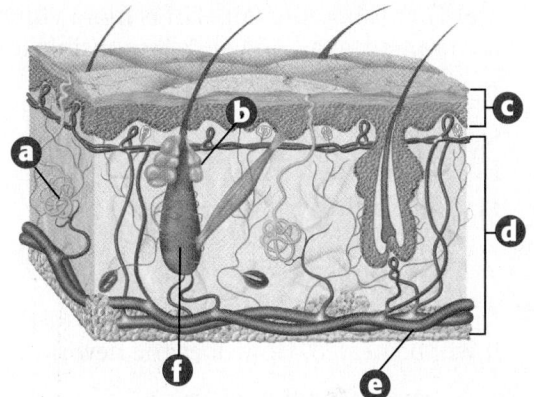

24 What layer does **d** represent? What substance is most abundant in this layer?

25 What is the name and function of **a**?

26 What is the name and function of **b**?

27 Which letter corresponds to the part of the skin that is made up of epithelial tissue that contains dead cells?

28 Which letter corresponds to the part of the skin from which hair grows? What is this part called?

For the following questions, write your answers on a separate sheet of paper.

1 Cells with the same function form tissues in the body. Tissues work together to form the body's organs. There are four kinds of tissues in the body. What kind of tissue forms most of the brain?

   A. muscle tissue
   B. nervous tissue
   C. epithelial tissue
   D. connective tissue

2 Fair-skinned people are more likely to develop skin cancer than dark-skinned people are. That is because fair skin is more vulnerable to the ultraviolet rays of the sun. What component of a skin cell is responsible for blocking ultraviolet rays?

   F. collagen
   G. dermis
   H. epidermis
   I. melanin

3 Donna cut her finger. A scab has formed over the cut. When her scab falls off, the skin below it will be healed. How does the new skin form?

   A. through cell division
   B. from collagen proteins
   C. from bacteria-fighting cells
   D. through keratin production

4 **READ INQUIRE EXPLAIN** Tyrone was running down the hallway and did not see the open door in front of him. He stubbed his toes badly enough to bleed. He also bruised his knee. Many of his 11 major organ systems were directly involved in responding to his injury. Briefly explain what happened to his integumentary system and cardiovascular system.

5 Jaya was playing basketball with her little brother Arun. Arun tried to score, but the basketball bounced off the rim, straight towards Jaya. She immediately moved out of the way. Why is it important that Jaya had the ability to respond to what was happening?

   F. so that she could catch the ball
   G. so that she could test her reflexes
   H. so that she could avoid getting hurt
   I. so that she could chase Arun more quickly

6 The body has many ways of maintaining a stable body temperature. For example, when it is cold, Jamal begins to shiver and the hair on his arms and legs stands up straight to help him keep warm.

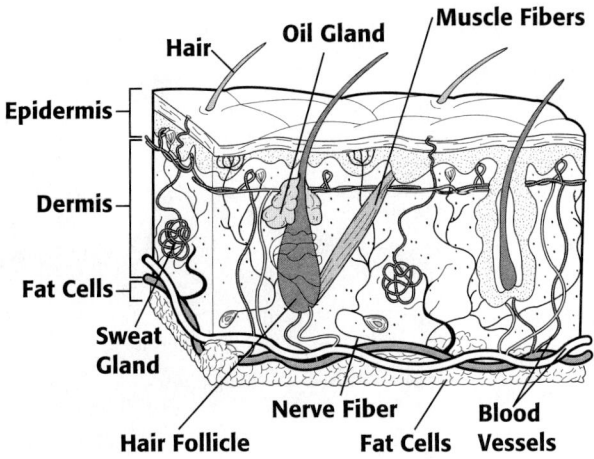

What happens within the skin to make the hair stand up?

A. The oil glands release oil.
B. The muscle fibers contract.
C. The blood vessels constrict.
D. The nerve fibers fire very quickly.

7 This picture shows where the bones of a child's cranium have grown together. This area is called a growth plate. Earlier, this area was made up of tissues that are more flexible than bone. These tissues hold a place for bones to grow as the child matures.

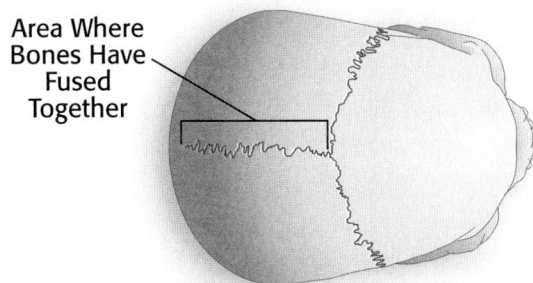

Overhead View of Human Skull

What changes occured as these bones joined together?

F. Bone cells replaced cartilage.
G. Bone cells grew in the marrow.
H. Bone cells formed a gliding joint.
I. Bone cells developed into muscle tissue.

Science in Action

Weird Science

Using Coral for Bone Transplants

What do you think of using coral skeleton to replace a bone? When bones are lost or badly damaged, patients may need a bone transplant. Scientists at Mote's Pigeon Key Marine Research Center in the Florida Keys hope to increase the use of artificially grown coral skeletons as an alternative to human bone transplants. A coral skeleton can be shaped more easily than human bone, is free of disease, is less likely to be rejected by the patient's body than a human bone transplant, and is quickly replaced by new bone. Researchers at the Mote Center also hope to not only produce a better material for bone transplants but to also prevent the harvest of wild coral.

Math ACTiViTY

The staghorn coral shown below can grow at depths of up to 160 ft in the wild. In Florida, its optimal depth range is 3 m to 20 m. What is the difference between this species' maximum depth and the maximum depth of its optimal depth range in meters?

Science, Technology, and Society

Beating the Odds

Sometimes, people are born without limbs or lose limbs in accidents. Many of these people have prostheses (prahs THEE SEEZ), or human-made replacements for the body parts. Until recently, many of these prostheses made it more difficult for many people to participate in physical activities, such as sports. But new designs have led to lighter, more comfortable prostheses that move the way that a human limb does. These new designs have allowed athletes with physical disabilities to compete at higher levels.

Social Studies ACTiViTY

Research the use of prostheses throughout history. Create a timeline showing major advances in prosthesis use and design.

Zahra Beheshti

Physical Therapist A physical therapist is a licensed professional who helps people recover from injuries by using hands-on treatment instead of medicines. Dr. Zahra Beheshti is a physical therapist at the Princeton Physical Therapy Center in New Jersey. She often helps athletes who suffer from sports injuries.

After an injury, a person may go through a process called *rehabilitation* to regain the use of the injured body part. The most common mistake made by athletes is that they play sports before completely recovering from injuries. Dr. Beheshti explains, "Going back to their usual pre-injury routine could result in another injury."

Dr. Beheshti also teaches patients about preventing future sports injuries. "Most injuries happen when an individual engages in strenuous activities without a proper warm-up or cool-down period." Being a physical therapist is rewarding work. Dr. Beheshti says, "I get a lot of satisfaction when treating patients and see them regain their function and independence and return to their normal life."

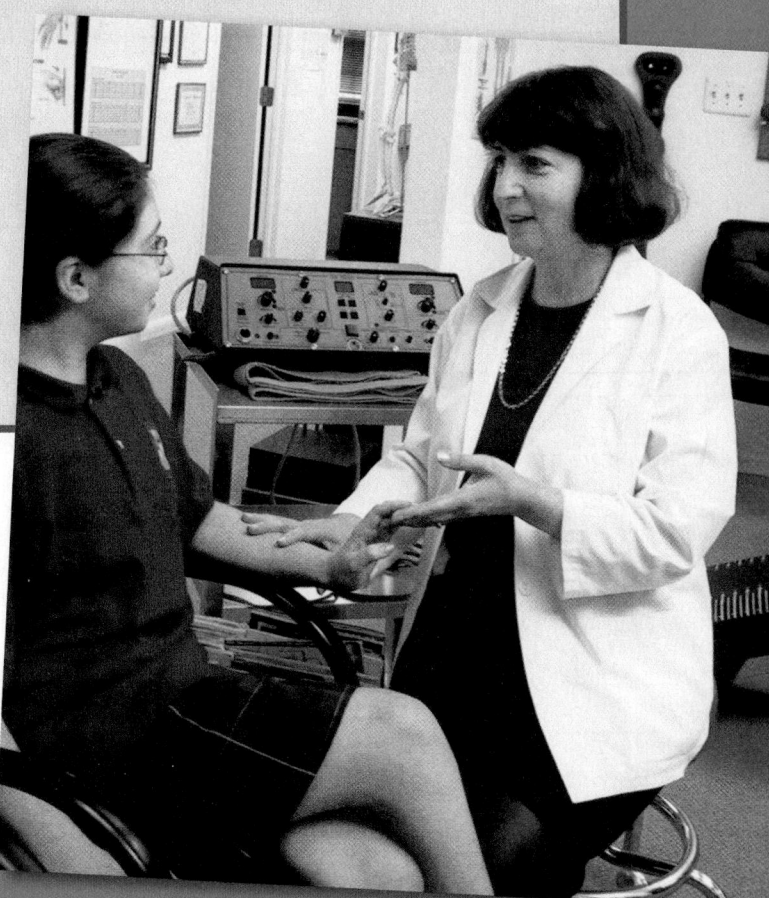

Language Arts
ACTiViTY

WRITING SKILL Interview a physical therapist who works in or near your community. Write a newspaper article about your interview.

To learn more about these Science in Action topics, visit **go.hrw.com** and type in the keyword **HT6FBOFF**.

Current Science

Check out Current Science® articles related to this chapter by visiting go.hrw.com. Just type in the keyword HL5CS22.

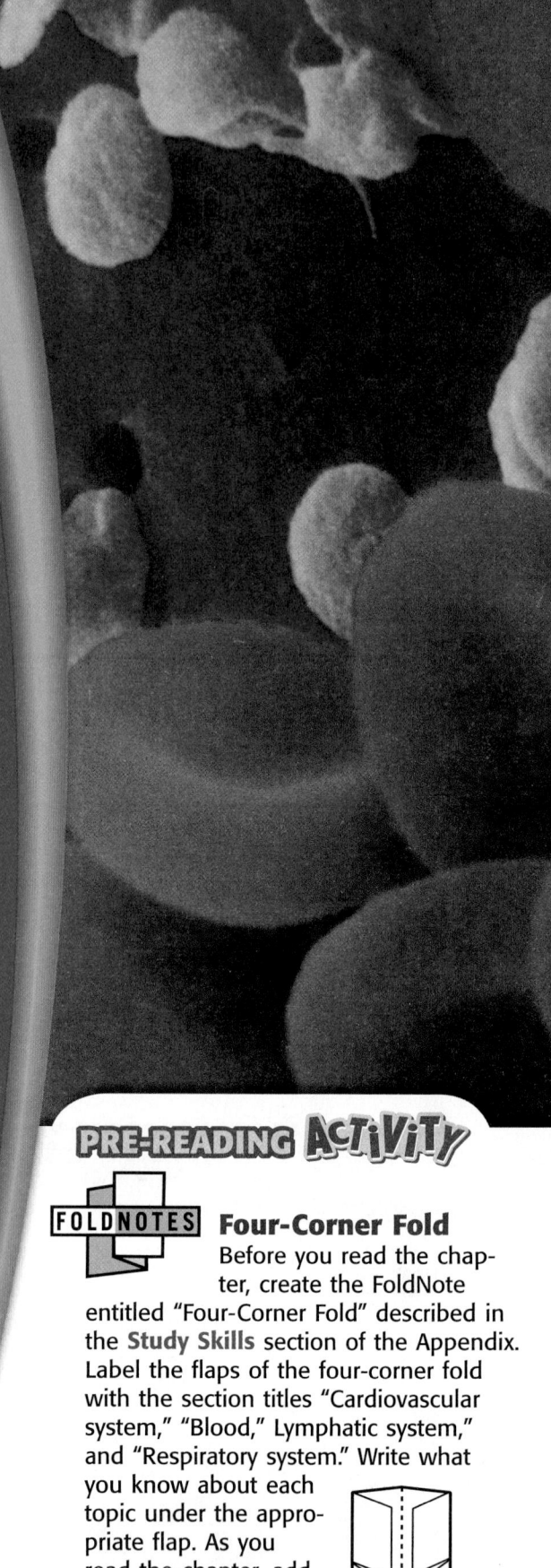

Circulation and Respiration

 **The Big Idea** The human body has systems that transport oxygen, nutrients, and waste.

About the PHOTO

Your cardiovascular system is made up of the heart, blood vessels, and blood. This picture is a colored scanning electron micrograph of red and white blood cells and cell fragments called *platelets*. Red blood cells are disk shaped, white blood cells are rounded, and platelets are the small green fragments. There are millions of blood cells in a drop of blood. Blood cells are so important that your body makes about 200 billion red blood cells every day.

PRE-READING ACTIVITY

FOLDNOTES **Four-Corner Fold**
Before you read the chapter, create the FoldNote entitled "Four-Corner Fold" described in the **Study Skills** section of the Appendix. Label the flaps of the four-corner fold with the section titles "Cardiovascular system," "Blood," Lymphatic system," and "Respiratory system." Write what you know about each topic under the appropriate flap. As you read the chapter, add other information that you learn.

START-UP ACTIVITY

Exercise Your Heart F.1.3.1 AA

How does your heart respond to exercise? You can see this reaction by measuring your pulse.

Procedure

1. Take your pulse while remaining still. (Take your pulse by placing your fingers on the inside of your wrist just below your thumb.)

2. Using a **watch with a second hand,** count the number of heart beats in 15 s. Then, multiply this number by 4 to calculate the number of beats in 1 minute.

3. Do some moderate physical activity, such as jumping jacks or jogging in place, for 30 s.

4. Stop moving, and calculate your heart rate again.
   Caution: Do not perform this exercise if you have difficulty breathing, if you have high blood pressure or asthma, or if you get dizzy easily.

5. Rest for 5 min.

6. Take your pulse again.

Analysis

1. How did exercise affect your heart rate? Why do you think this happened?

2. How does your heart rate affect the rate at which red blood cells travel throughout your body?

3. Did your heart rate return to normal (or almost normal) after you rested? Why or why not?

Circulation and Respiration   **155**

The Cardiovascular System

When you hear the word heart, *what do you think of first? Many people think of romance. Some people think of courage. But the heart is much more than a symbol of love or bravery. Your heart is an amazing pump.*

The heart is an organ that is part of your cardiovascular system. The word *cardio* means "heart," and the word *vascular* means "blood vessel." The blood vessels—arteries, capillaries, and veins—carry blood pumped by the heart.

Your Cardiovascular System

Your heart, blood, and blood vessels make up your **cardiovascular system** (KAR dee OH VAS kyoo luhr SIS tuhm). Your heart creates pressure when it beats. This pressure moves blood throughout the body. **Figure 1** shows your heart, major arteries, and veins.

The cardiovascular system helps perform many life functions. For example, this system helps maintain your body by carrying nutrients to your cells and removing wastes from your cells. This system also helps in regulation by carrying chemical signals called *hormones* throughout the body.

Benchmark Check Describe the cardiovascular system and its role in maintaining the body. **F.1.3.1 AA**

cardiovascular system a collection of organs that transport blood throughout the body

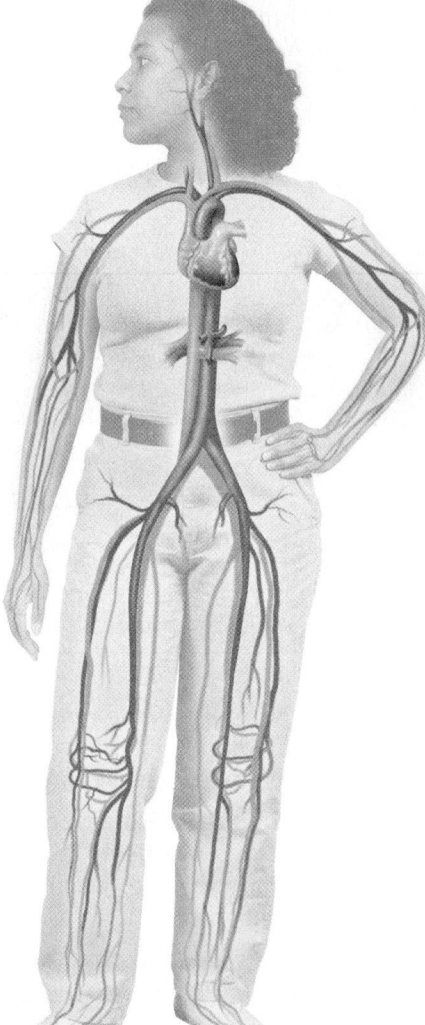

Figure 1 *The cardiovascular system carries blood to every cell in your body.*

F.1.3.1 AA understands that living things are composed of major systems that sfunction in reproduction, growth, maintenance, and regulation.

The Heart

Your *heart* is an organ made mostly of cardiac muscle tissue. It is about the size of your fist and is almost in the center of your chest cavity. Like hearts of all mammals, your heart has a left side and a right side that are separated by a thick wall. The right side of the heart pumps oxygen-poor blood to the lungs. The left side pumps oxygen-rich blood to the body. As you can see in **Figure 2,** each side has an upper chamber and a lower chamber. Each upper chamber is called an *atrium* (plural, *atria*). Each lower chamber is called a *ventricle.*

Flaplike structures called *valves* are located between the atria and ventricles and in places where large arteries are attached to the heart. As blood moves through the heart, these valves close to prevent blood from going backward. The "lub-dub, lub-dub" sound of a beating heart is caused by the valves closing. **Figure 3** shows the flow of blood through the heart.

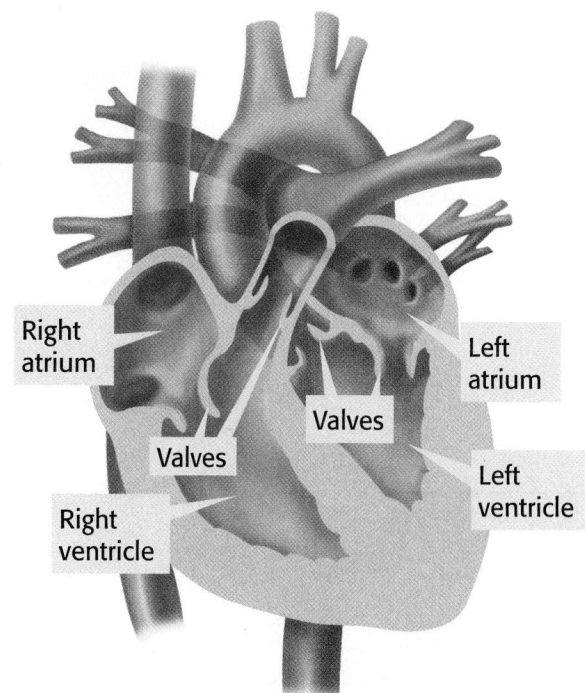

Figure 2 *The heart pumps blood through blood vessels. The vessels carrying oxygen-rich blood are shown in red. The vessels carrying oxygen-poor blood are shown in blue.*

Figure 3   The Flow of Blood Through the Heart

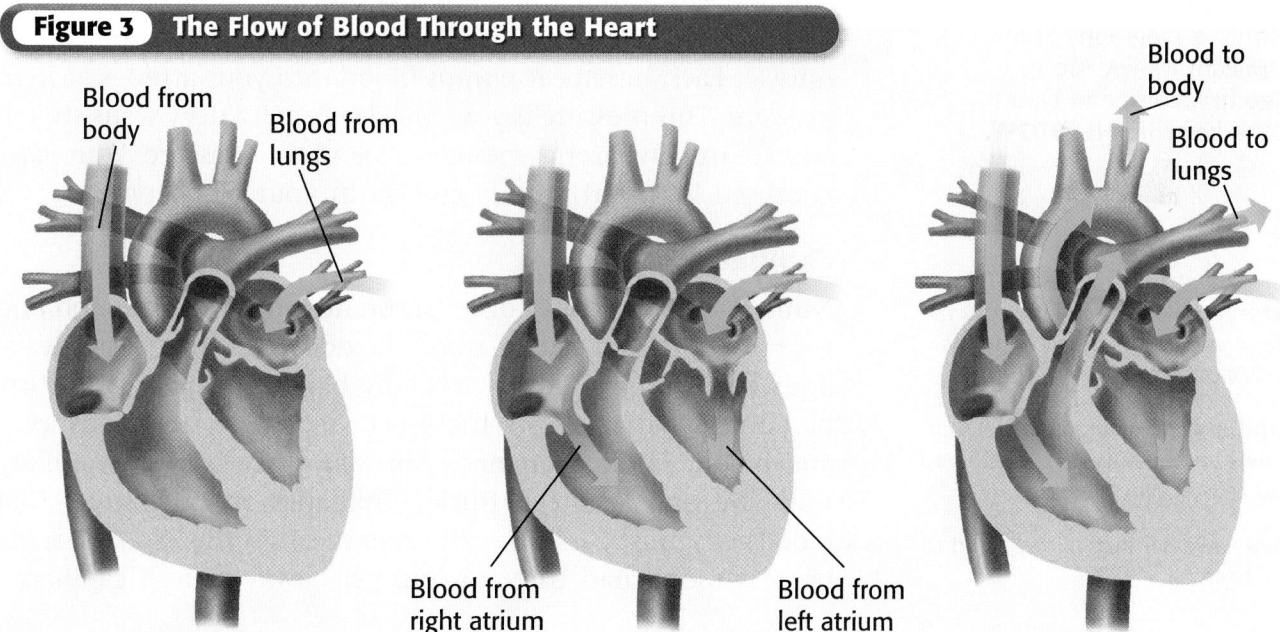

❶ Blood enters the atria first. The left atrium receives oxygen-rich blood from the lungs. The right atrium receives oxygen-poor blood from the body.

❷ When the atria contract, blood is squeezed into the ventricles.

❸ While the atria relax, the ventricles contract and push blood out of the heart. Blood from the right ventricle goes to the lungs. Blood from the left ventricle goes to the rest of the body.

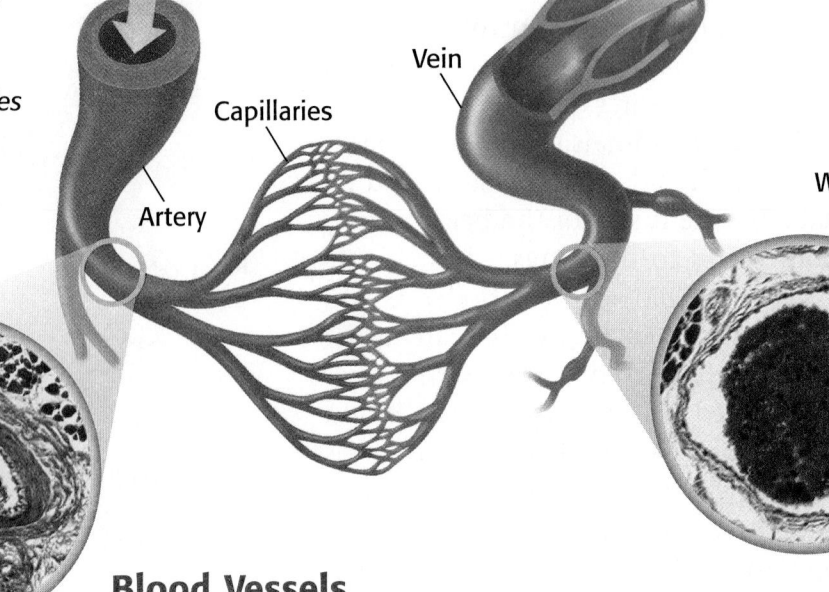

Figure 4 *Large arteries branch into smaller arteries, which branch into capillaries. Capillaries join small veins, which join to form large veins.*

From heart

To heart

Vein

Capillaries

Artery

Wall of vein

Wall of artery

William Harvey Biography
Write a biography about William Harvey. Go to **go.hrw.com,** and type in the keyword **HL5BD2W.**

artery a blood vessel that carries blood away from the heart to the body's organs

capillary a tiny blood vessel that allows an exchange between blood and cells in other tissue

vein a vessel that carries blood to the heart

Blood Vessels

Blood travels throughout your body in hollow tubes called *blood vessels.* The three types of blood vessels—arteries, capillaries, and veins—are shown in **Figure 4.**

Arteries

A blood vessel that carries blood away from the heart is an **artery.** Arteries have thick walls, which contain a layer of smooth muscle. Each heartbeat pumps blood into your arteries at high pressure. This pressure is your *blood pressure.* Artery walls stretch and are usually strong enough to stand the pressure. Your *pulse* is caused by the rhythmic change in your blood pressure.

Capillaries

Nutrients, oxygen, and other substances must leave blood and get to your body's cells. Carbon dioxide and other wastes leave body cells and are carried away by blood. A **capillary** is a tiny blood vessel that allows these exchanges between body cells and blood. These exchanges can take place because capillary walls are only one cell thick. Capillaries are so narrow that blood cells must pass through them in single file. No cell in the body is more than three or four cells away from a capillary.

Veins

After leaving capillaries, blood enters veins. A **vein** is a blood vessel that carries blood back to the heart. As blood travels through veins, valves in the veins keep the blood from flowing backward. When skeletal muscles contract, they squeeze nearby veins and help push blood toward the heart.

Reading Check Describe the three types of blood vessels.

F.1.3.1 AA understands that living things are composed of major systems that function in reproduction, growth, maintenance, and regulation.

Two Types of Circulation

Where does blood get the oxygen to deliver to your body? From your lungs! Your heart pumps blood to the lungs. In the lungs, carbon dioxide leaves the blood and oxygen enters the blood. The oxygen-rich blood then flows back to the heart. This circulation of blood between your heart and lungs is called **pulmonary circulation** (PUL muh NER ee SUHR kyoo LAY shuhn).

The oxygen-rich blood returning to the heart from the lungs is then pumped to the rest of the body. The circulation of blood between the heart and the rest of the body is called **systemic circulation** (sis TEM ik SUHR kyoo LAY shuhn). Both types of circulation are shown in **Figure 5**.

pulmonary circulation the flow of blood from the heart to the lungs and back to the heart through the pulmonary arteries, capillaries, and veins

systemic circulation the flow of blood from the heart to all parts of the body and back to the heart

Figure 5   The Flow of Blood Through the Body

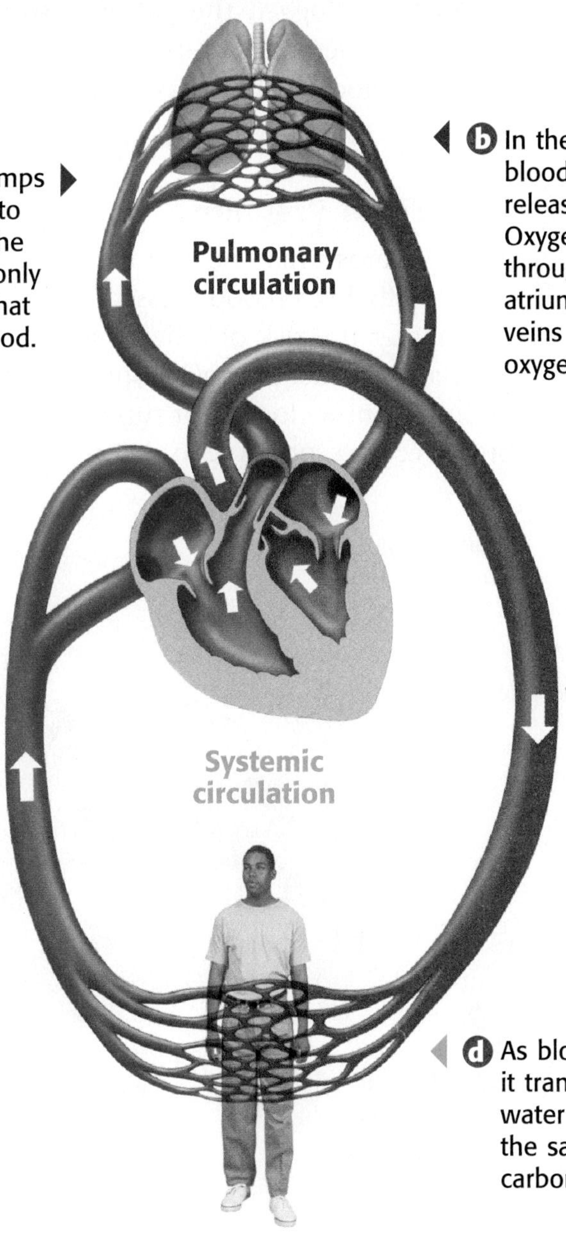

ⓐ The right ventricle pumps oxygen-poor blood into arteries that lead to the lungs. These are the only arteries in the body that carry oxygen-poor blood.

ⓑ In the capillaries of the lungs, blood takes up oxygen and releases carbon dioxide. Oxygen-rich blood travels through veins to the left atrium. These are the only veins in the body that carry oxygen-rich blood.

Pulmonary circulation

ⓔ Oxygen-poor blood travels back to the heart and is delivered into the right atrium by two large veins.

Systemic circulation

ⓒ The heart pumps oxygen-rich blood from the left ventricle into arteries and then into capillaries.

ⓓ As blood travels through capillaries, it transports oxygen, nutrients, and water to the cells of the body. At the same time, waste materials and carbon dioxide are carried away.

Cardiovascular Problems

More than just your heart and blood vessels are at risk if you have cardiovascular problems. Your whole body may be harmed. Cardiovascular problems can be caused by smoking, high levels of cholesterol in the blood, stress, physical inactivity, or heredity. Eating a healthy diet and getting plenty of exercise can reduce the risk of having cardiovascular problems.

Atherosclerosis

Heart diseases are the leading cause of death in the United States. A major cause of heart diseases is a cardiovascular disease called *atherosclerosis* (ATH uhr OH skluh ROH sis). Atherosclerosis happens when cholesterol (kuh LES tuhr AWL) builds up inside of blood vessels. This cholesterol buildup causes the blood vessels to become narrower and less elastic. **Figure 6** shows how clogged the pathway through a blood vessel can become. When an artery that supplies blood to the heart becomes blocked, the person may have a heart attack.

✓ **Reading Check** Why is atherosclerosis dangerous?

High Blood Pressure

Atherosclerosis may be caused by hypertension. *Hypertension* is abnormally high blood pressure. The higher the blood pressure, the greater the risk of a heart attack, heart failure, kidney disease, and stroke. A *stroke* happens when a blood vessel in the brain becomes clogged or ruptures. As a result, that part of the brain receives no oxygen. Without oxygen, brain cells die.

Figure 6 *This illustration shows the narrowing of an artery as the result of high levels of cholesterol in the blood. Lipid deposits (yellow) build up inside the blood vessel walls and block the flow of blood. Lipid particles (yellow balls) are shown escaping.*

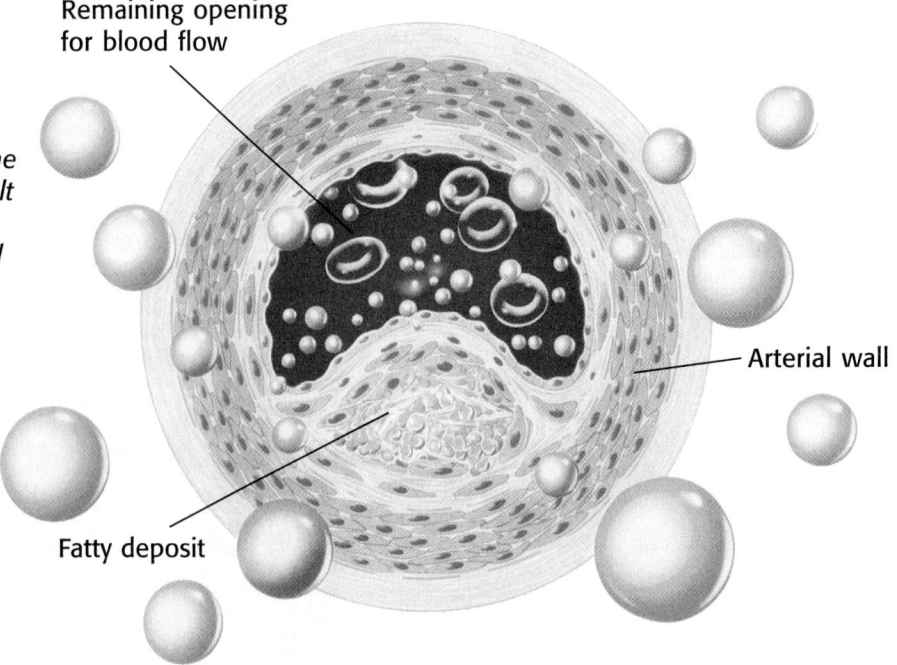

Remaining opening for blood flow

Arterial wall

Fatty deposit

Heart Attacks and Heart Failure

Two other cardiovascular problems are heart attacks and heart failure. A *heart attack* happens when heart muscle cells die and part of the heart muscle is damaged. As shown in **Figure 7,** arteries that deliver oxygen to the heart may be blocked. Without oxygen, heart muscle cells die quickly. When enough heart muscle cells die, the heart may stop.

Heart failure is different. *Heart failure* happens when the heart cannot pump enough blood to meet the body's needs. Organs, such as the brain, lungs, and kidneys, may be damaged by lack of oxygen or nutrients, or by the buildup of fluids or wastes.

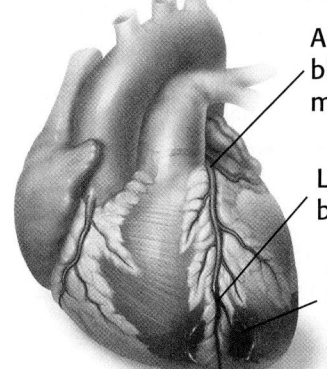

Figure 7 Heart Attack

Artery delivering blood to heart muscle

Location of blocked artery

Area of heart damaged by lack of oxygen to heart muscle

SECTION Review

Summary

- The cardiovascular system is made up of the heart, blood, and three types of blood vessels.

- The cardiovascular system helps perform life functions such as maintenance by distributing oxygen, nutrients, and other needed materials throughout the body and by removing wastes. **F.I.3.1 AA**

- Oxygen-poor blood flows from the heart and through the lungs, where it picks up oxygen.

- Oxygen-rich blood flows from the heart to the rest of the body.

- Cardiovascular problems include atherosclerosis, hypertension, heart attacks, and strokes.

Using Key Terms

1. Use *systemic circulation* and *pulmonary circulation* in separate sentences.

Understanding Key Ideas

2. Which of the following statements about blood in the pulmonary veins is true?
   a. The blood is going to the body.
   b. The blood is oxygen poor.
   c. The blood is going to the lungs.
   d. The blood is oxygen rich.

3. Identify the three parts of the cardiovascular system. Describe the functions of each part.

4. What is the difference between a heart attack and heart failure?

Critical Thinking

5. **Analyzing Ideas** Your body has many veins and arteries, but a pulse is often taken at an artery in the neck or wrist. Explain.

6. **Making Inferences** Andy's cholesterol levels are too high. What cardiovascular problem might Andy develop if he does not lower his cholesterol levels?

FCAT Preparation

7. The cardiovascular system helps maintain the body by carrying oxygen to cells and by removing wastes from cells. Doctors may prescribe aspirin for patients who have had a heart attack. One of aspirin's effects is that it prevents pieces of cells in blood called *platelets* from clotting or sticking to each other, so that the blood flows more easily. Platelets help wounds heal by clotting. **F.I.3.1 AA**

   PART A How might aspirin affect the function of the cardiovascular system?

   PART B Why is aspirin harmful to patients who are healing after surgery?

SCiLINKS

NSTA
Developed and maintained by the
National Science Teachers Association

For a variety of links related to this chapter, go to www.scilinks.org
Topic: The Cardiovascular System; Cardiovascular Problems
SciLinks code: HSM0221; HSM0220

Blood

Blood is part of the cardiovascular system. It travels through miles and miles of blood vessels to reach every cell in your body. So, you must have a lot of blood, right?

Well, actually, an adult human body has about 5 L of blood. Your body probably has a little less than that. All the blood in your body would not fill two 3 L soda bottles.

What Is Blood?

Your *cardiovascular system* is made up of your heart, your blood vessels, and blood. **Blood** is a connective tissue made up of plasma, red blood cells, platelets, and white blood cells. Blood carries oxygen and nutrients to all parts of your body.

✓ **Reading Check** What are the four main components of blood?

Plasma

The fluid part of the blood is called plasma (PLAZ muh). *Plasma is a mixture of water, minerals, nutrients, sugars, proteins, and other substances. Red blood cells, white blood cells, and platelets are found in plasma.

Red Blood Cells

Most blood cells are *red blood cells,* or RBCs. RBCs, such as the ones shown in **Figure 1,** take oxygen to every cell in your body. Cells need oxygen to carry out their functions. Each RBC has hemoglobin (HEE moh GLOH bin). *Hemoglobin* is an oxygen-carrying protein. Hemoglobin clings to the oxygen you inhale. RBCs can then transport oxygen throughout the body. Hemoglobin also gives RBCs their red color.

blood the fluid that carries gases, nutrients, and wastes through the body and that is made up of platelets, white blood cells, red blood cells, and plasma

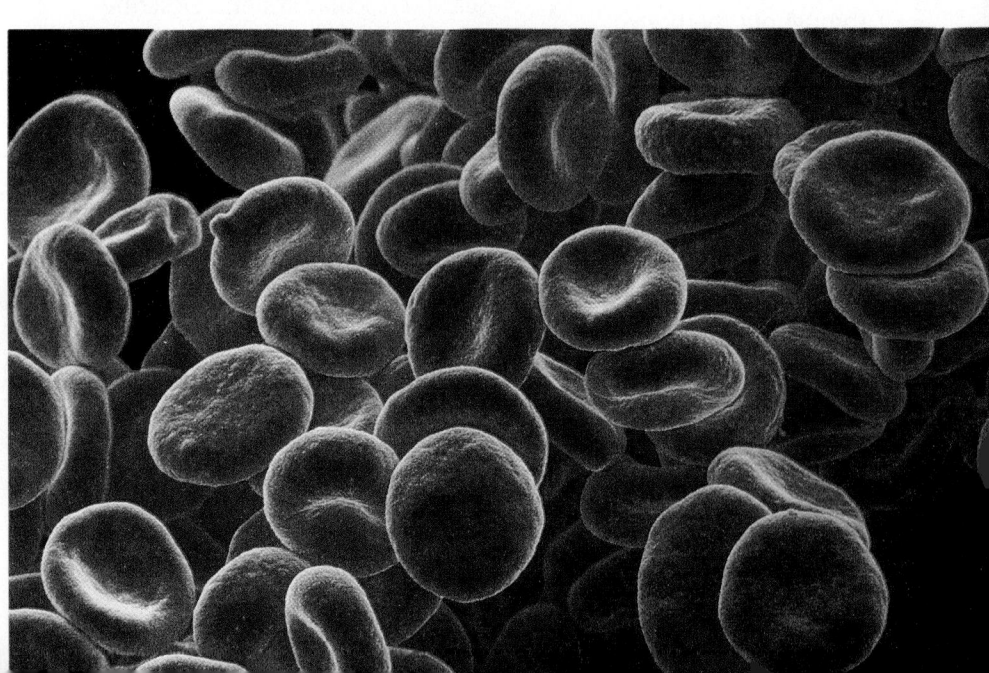

Figure 1 *Red blood cells are made in the bone marrow of certain bones. As red blood cells mature, they lose their nucleus and their DNA.*

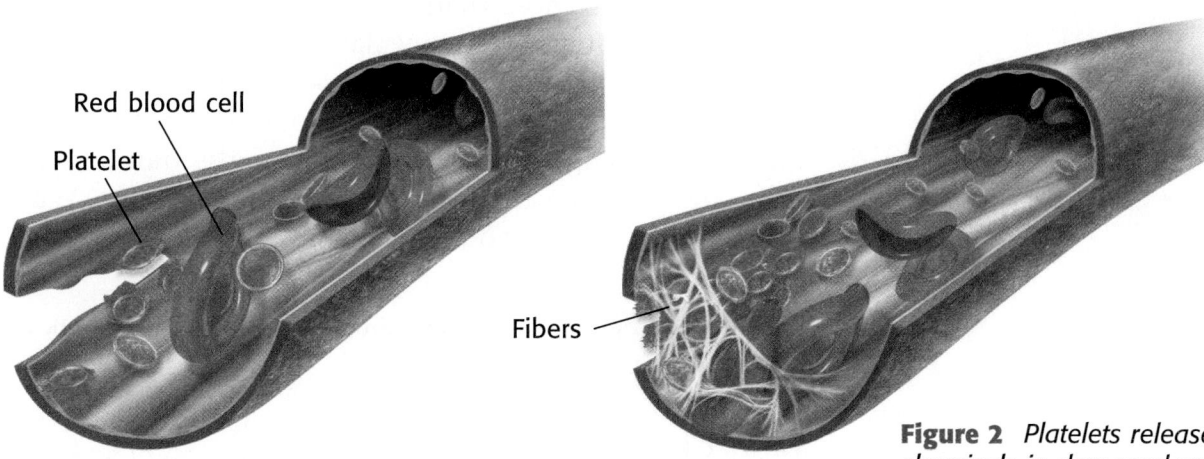

Red blood cell

Platelet

Fibers

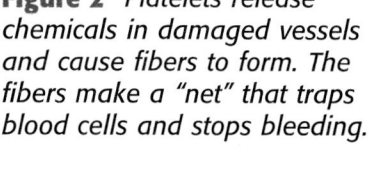

Figure 2 *Platelets release chemicals in damaged vessels and cause fibers to form. The fibers make a "net" that traps blood cells and stops bleeding.*

Platelets

Drifting among the blood cells are tiny particles called platelets. *Platelets* are pieces of larger cells found in bone marrow. These larger cells remain in the bone marrow, but fragments are pinched off and enter the bloodstream as platelets. Platelets last for only 5 to 10 days, but they are an important part of blood. When you cut or scrape your skin, you bleed because blood vessels have been opened. As soon as bleeding starts, platelets begin to clump together in the damaged area. They form a plug that helps reduce blood loss, as shown in **Figure 2.** Platelets also release chemicals that react with proteins in plasma. The reaction causes tiny fibers to form. The fibers help create a blood clot.

White Blood Cells

Sometimes, *pathogens* (PATH uh juhnz)—bacteria, viruses, and other microscopic particles that can make you sick—enter your body. When they do, they often meet *white blood cells,* or WBCs. WBCs, shown in **Figure 3,** help keep you healthy by destroying pathogens. WBCs also help clean wounds.

WBCs fight pathogens in several ways. Some WBCs squeeze out of blood vessels and move around in tissues, searching for pathogens. When they find a pathogen, they destroy it. Other WBCs release antibodies. *Antibodies* are chemicals that identify or destroy pathogens. WBCs also keep you healthy by destroying body cells that have died or been damaged. Most WBCs are made in bone marrow. Some WBCs mature in the lymphatic system.

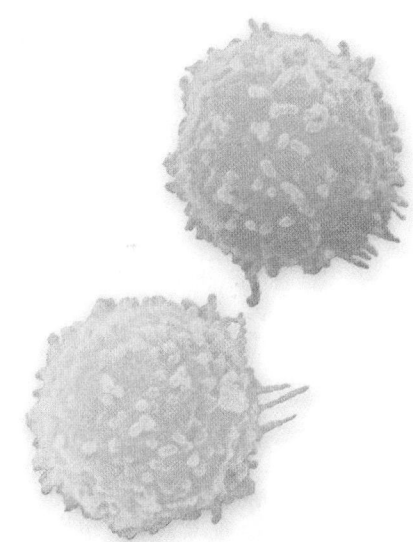

Figure 3 *White blood cells defend the body against pathogens. These white blood cells have been colored yellow to make their shape easier to see.*

F.1.3.1 AA understands that living things are composed of major systems that function in reproduction, growth, maintenance, and regulation.

F.1.3.6 CS knows that cells with similar functions have similar structures, whereas those with different structures have different functions.

Benchmark Check Compare the structures and functions of red blood cells and white blood cells. **F.1.3.6 CS**

Body Temperature Regulation

Your blood does more than supply your cells with oxygen and nutrients. It also helps regulate your body temperature. When your brain senses that your body temperature is rising, your brain signals blood vessels in your skin to enlarge. As the vessels enlarge, heat from your blood is transferred to your skin. This transfer helps lower your temperature. When your brain senses that your temperature is normal, it instructs your blood vessels to return to their normal size.

Benchmark Check Describe how blood helps regulate body temperature. **F.I.3.1 AA**

Blood Pressure

Every time your heart beats, it pushes blood out of the heart and into your arteries. The force exerted by blood on the inside walls of arteries is called **blood pressure.** Blood pressure is expressed in millimeters of mercury (mm Hg). For example, a blood pressure of 110 mm Hg means the pressure on the artery walls can push a narrow column of mercury to a height of 110 mm.

Blood pressure is usually given as two numbers, such as 110/70 mm Hg. Systolic (sis TAHL ik) pressure is the first number. *Systolic pressure* is the pressure inside large arteries when the ventricles contract. The surge of blood causes the arteries to bulge and produce a pulse. The second number, *diastolic* (DIE uh STAHL ik) *pressure,* is the pressure inside arteries when the ventricles relax. For adults, a blood pressure of 120/80 mm Hg or below is considered healthy. High blood pressure can cause heart or kidney damage.

Blood Types

Everyone has one of four blood types: A, B, AB, or O. Your blood type refers to the type of chemicals you have on the surface of your RBCs. These surface chemicals are called *antigens* (AN tuh juhnz). Type A blood has A antigens; type B has B antigens; and type AB has both A and B antigens. Type O blood has neither the A nor the B antigen.

The different blood types have different antigens on their RBCs. They may also have different antibodies in the plasma. These antibodies react to antigens of other blood types as if the antigens were pathogens. As shown in **Figure 4,** type A blood has antibodies that react to type B blood. If a person with type A blood receives type B blood, the type B antibodies attach themselves to the type B RBCs. These RBCs begin to clump together, and the clumps may block blood vessels. A reaction to the wrong type of blood may be fatal.

blood pressure the force that blood exerts on the walls of the arteries

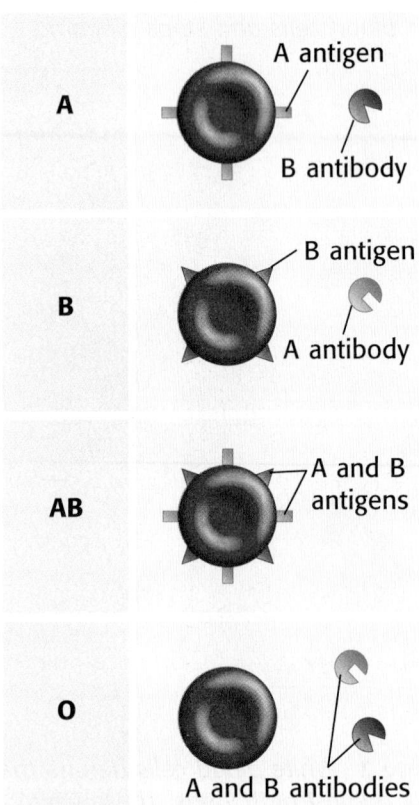

A — A antigen, B antibody

B — B antigen, A antibody

AB — A and B antigens

O — A and B antibodies

Figure 4 *This figure shows which antigens and antibodies may be present in each blood type.*

F.I.3.1 AA understands that living things are composed of major systems that function in reproduction, growth, maintenance, and regulation.

Blood Types and Transfusions

Sometimes, a person must be given a blood transfusion. A *transfusion* is the injection of blood or blood components into a person to replace blood that has been lost because of surgery or an injury. **Figure 5** shows bags of blood that may be given in a transfusion. The blood type is clearly marked. Because the ABO blood types have different antigen-antibody reactions, a person who needs blood must only accept certain blood types. **Table 1** shows blood transfusion possibilities.

✓ **Reading Check** People with type O blood are sometimes called *universal donors*. Why might this be true?

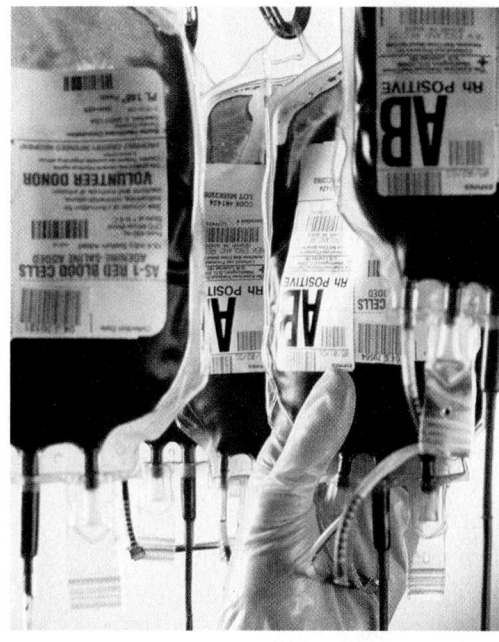

Figure 5 *The blood type must be clearly labeled on blood stored for transfusions.*

Table 1 Blood Transfusion Possibilities

Type	Can receive	Can donate to
A	A, O	A, AB
B	B, O	B, AB
AB	all	AB only
O	O	all

SECTION Review

Summary

- Blood is made up of plasma, red blood cells, platelets, and white blood cells. **F.I.3.6 CS**
- Blood carries oxygen and nutrients to cells, helps protect against disease, and helps regulate body temperature. **F.I.3.1 AA**
- Blood pressure is the force blood exerts on the inside walls of arteries.
- Every person has one of four ABO blood types. Mixing blood types may be fatal.

Using Key Terms

1. Use *blood* and *blood pressure* in separate sentences.

Understanding Key Ideas

2. A person who has type B blood can donate blood to people who have which of the following?
   a. type B or type AB
   b. type A or type AB
   c. type B
   d. all blood types

3. List the four main components of blood, and describe the function of each component. **F.I.3.6 CS**

4. Why is it important for a doctor to know a patient's blood type?

Critical Thinking

5. **Identifying Relationships** How does the cardiovascular system help regulate body temperature? **F.I.3.1 AA**

FCAT Preparation

6. Abnormally shaped RBCs can block capillaries and the flow of oxygen. Which of the following about abnormal and normal RBCs is true? **F.I.3.6 CS**
   A. The abnormal shape affects the cell's function.
   B. Abnormal RBCs function better than normal RBCs.
   C. They both function well.
   D. A cell's shape is unrelated to its function.

SCiLINKS® NSTA
Developed and maintained by the
National Science Teachers Association

For a variety of links related to this chapter, go to www.scilinks.org

Topic: Blood; Blood Donations
SciLinks code: HSM0175; HSM0178

The Lymphatic System

Every time your heart pumps, a little fluid is forced out of the thin walls of the capillaries. Some of this fluid collects in the spaces around your cells. What happens to this fluid?

Most of the fluid is reabsorbed through the capillaries into your blood. But some is not. This fluid moves into your lymphatic (lim FAT ik) system.

The **lymphatic system** is the group of organs and tissues that collects the excess fluid and returns it to your blood. The lymphatic system also helps your body fight pathogens.

Vessels of the Lymphatic System

The fluid collected by the lymphatic system is carried through vessels. The smallest vessels of the lymphatic system are *lymph capillaries*. Lymph capillaries absorb some of the fluid and particles from between the cells. Some of these particles are dead cells or pathogens. These particles are too large to enter blood capillaries. The fluid and particles absorbed into lymph capillaries are called **lymph.**

As shown in **Figure 1,** lymph capillaries carry lymph into larger vessels called *lymphatic vessels.* Skeletal muscles squeeze these vessels to force lymph through the lymphatic system. Valves inside lymphatic vessels stop backflow. Lymph drains into the cardiovascular system at the large veins in the neck.

Benchmark Check How does the lymphatic system function in body maintenance? F.1.3.1 AA

lymphatic system a collection of organs whose primary function is to collect extracellular fluid and return it to the blood

lymph the fluid that is collected by the lymphatic vessels and nodes

Figure 1 *The white arrows show the movement of lymph into lymph capillaries and through lymphatic vessels.*

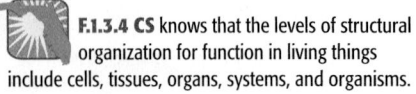
F.1.3.1 AA understands that living things are composed of major systems that function in reproduction, growth, maintenance, and regulation.

F.1.3.4 CS knows that the levels of structural organization for function in living things include cells, tissues, organs, systems, and organisms.

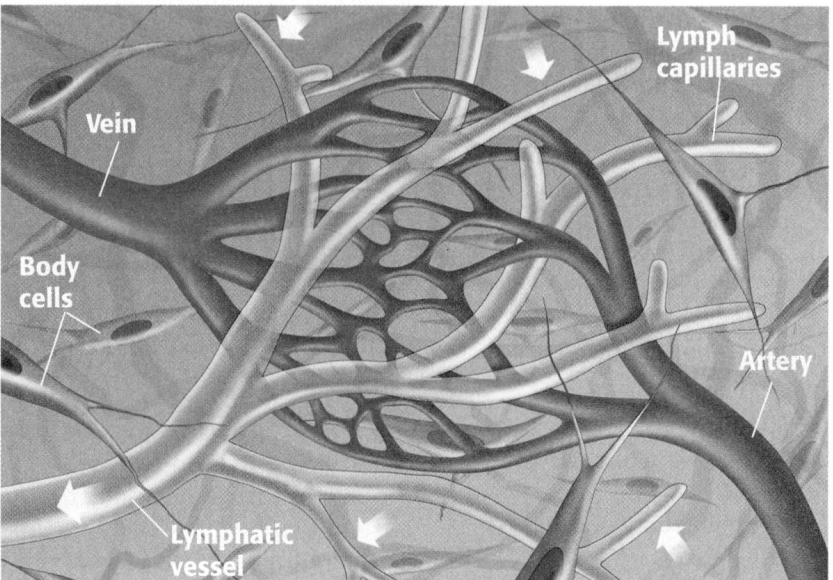

Lymph capillaries

Vein

Body cells

Artery

Lymphatic vessel

Other Parts of the Lymphatic System

In addition to vessels and capillaries, several organs and tissues are part of the lymphatic system. These organs and tissues are shown in **Figure 2.** Bone marrow plays an important role in your lymphatic system. The other parts of the lymphatic system are the lymph nodes, the thymus gland, the spleen, and the tonsils.

Bone Marrow

Bones—part of your skeletal system—are very important to your lymphatic system. *Bone marrow* is the soft tissue inside of bones. Bone marrow is where most red and white blood cells, including lymphocytes (LIM foh SIETS), are produced. *Lymphocytes* are a type of white blood cell that helps your body fight pathogens.

Lymph Nodes

As lymph travels through lymphatic vessels, it passes through organs called *lymph nodes*. **Lymph nodes** are small, bean-shaped masses of tissue that remove pathogens and dead cells from the lymph. Lymph nodes are concentrated in the armpits, neck, and groin.

Lymph nodes contain lymphocytes. Some lymphocytes—called *killer T cells*—surround and destroy pathogens. Other lymphocytes—called *B cells*—produce antibodies that attach to pathogens. These marked pathogens clump together and are then destroyed by other cells.

When bacteria or other pathogens cause an infection, WBCs may multiply greatly. The lymph nodes fill with WBCs that are fighting the infection. As a result, some lymph nodes may become swollen and painful. Your doctor may feel these swollen lymph nodes to see if you have an infection. In fact, if your lymph nodes are swollen and sore, you or your parent can feel them, too. Swollen lymph nodes are sometimes an early clue that you have an infection.

Thymus

T cells develop from immature lymphocytes produced in the bone marrow. Before these cells are ready to fight infections, they develop further in an organ called, the *thymus*. The **thymus** produces T cells that are ready to fight infection. The thymus is also called the *thymus gland*. It is located behind the breastbone, just above the heart. Mature lymphocytes from the thymus travel through the lymphatic system to other areas of your body.

lymph node an organ that filters lymph and that is found along the lymphatic vessels

thymus the main gland of the lymphatic system; it produces mature T lymphocytes

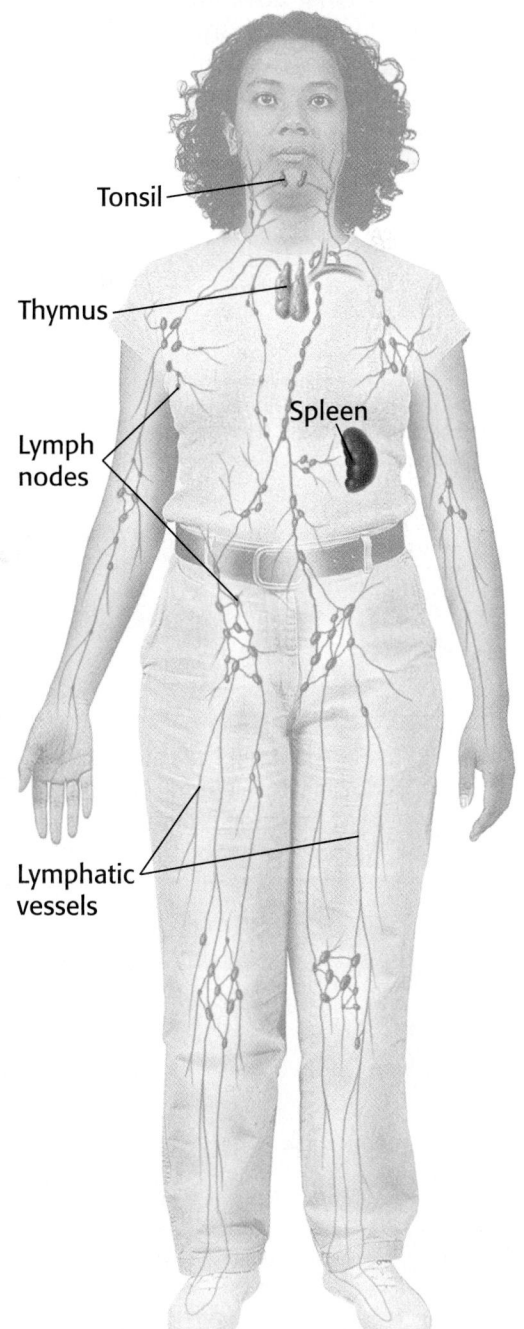

Figure 2 The Lymphatic System

Tonsil

Thymus

Spleen

Lymph nodes

Lymphatic vessels

Spleen

Your spleen is the largest lymphatic organ. The **spleen** stores and produces lymphocytes. It is a purplish organ about the size of your fist. Your spleen is soft and spongy. It is located in the upper left side of your abdomen. As blood flows through the spleen, lymphocytes attack or mark pathogens in the blood. If pathogens cause an infection, the spleen may also release lymphocytes into the bloodstream.

In addition to being part of the lymphatic system, the spleen monitors, stores, and destroys blood cells. When red blood cells (RBCs) are squeezed through the spleen's capillaries, the older and more fragile cells burst. These damaged RBCs are then taken apart by some of the cells in the spleen. Some parts of these RBCs may be reused. For this reason, you can think of the spleen as the red-blood-cell recycling center.

The spleen has two important functions. The *white pulp*, shown in **Figure 3,** is part of the lymphatic system. It helps to fight infections. The *red pulp*, also shown in **Figure 3,** removes unwanted material, such as defective red blood cells, from the blood. However, it is possible to lead a healthy life without your spleen. If the spleen is damaged or removed, other organs in the body take over many of its functions.

Benchmark Check To which of level of structural organization does the spleen belong: cells, tissues, or organs? F.1.3.4 CS

Figure 3 White and Red Pulp in the Spleen

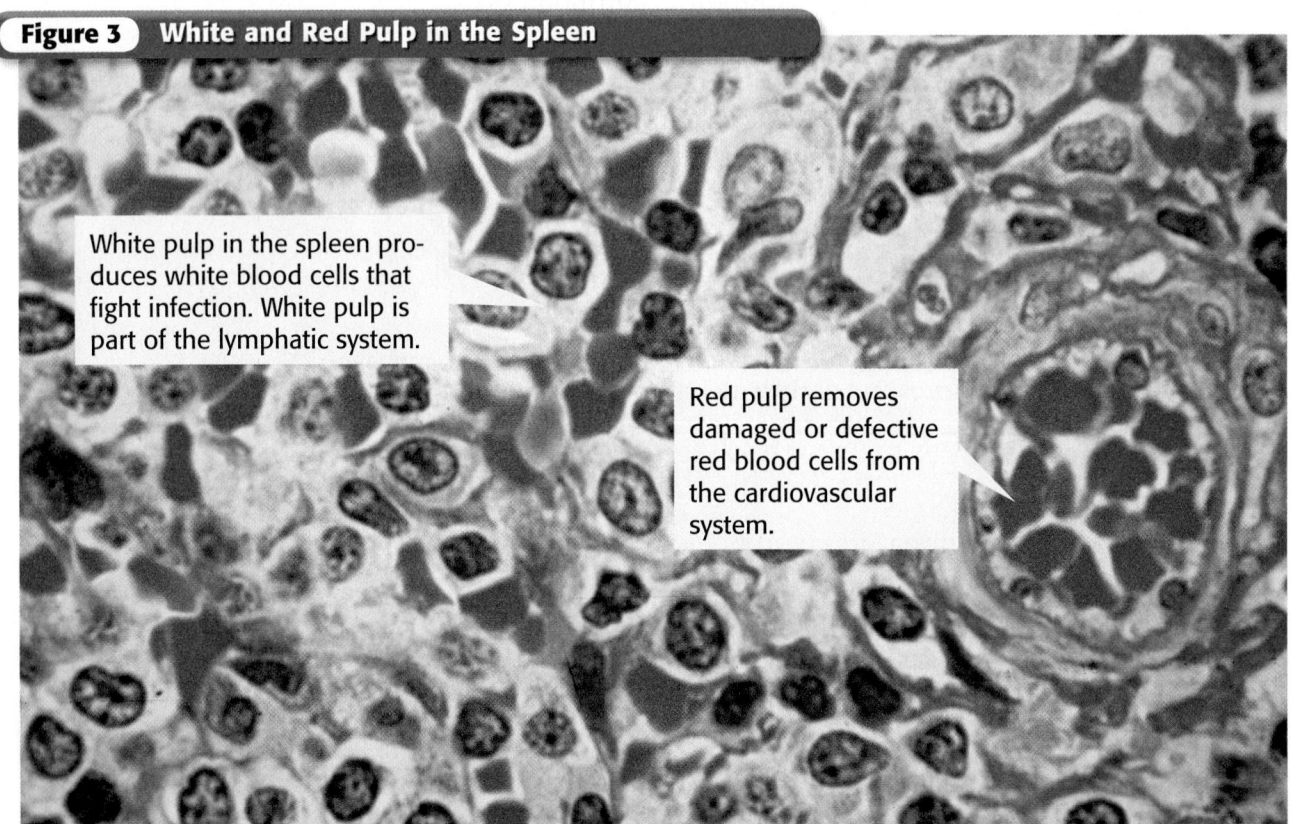

White pulp in the spleen produces white blood cells that fight infection. White pulp is part of the lymphatic system.

Red pulp removes damaged or defective red blood cells from the cardiovascular system.

Tonsils

The lymphatic system includes your tonsils. **Tonsils** are organs that are made up of lymphatic tissue. Tonsils are located in the nasal cavity and at the back of the mouth on either side of the tongue. Each tonsil is about the size of a large olive.

Tonsils help defend the body against infection. Lymphocytes in the tonsils trap pathogens that enter the throat. Sometimes, tonsils become infected and are red, swollen, and very sore. Severely infected tonsils may be covered with patches of white, infected tissue. Sore, swollen tonsils, such as those in **Figure 4,** make swallowing difficult.

Sometimes, a doctor will suggest surgery to remove the tonsils. In the past, this surgery was frequently done in childhood. It is less common today. Surgery is now done only if a child has frequent, severe tonsil infections or if a child's tonsils are so enlarged that breathing is difficult.

tonsils organs that are small, rounded masses of lymphatic tissue located in the pharynx and in the passage from the mouth to the pharynx

Figure 4 *Tonsils help protect your throat and lungs from infection by trapping pathogens.*

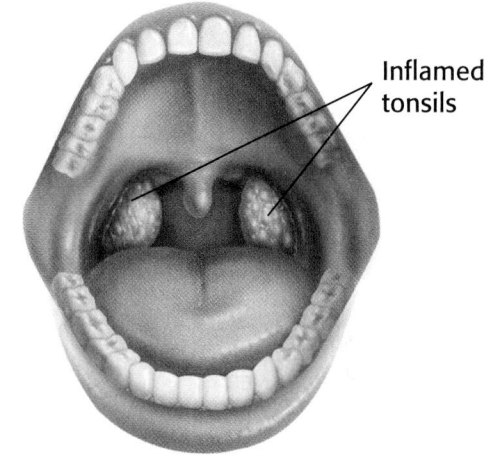

Inflamed tonsils

SECTION Review

Summary

- The lymphatic vessels collect fluid from between cells and return it to the cardiovascular system.
- The thymus, spleen, and tonsils contain lymphocytes that help the body fight disease. **F.1.3.1 AA**
- Lymphocytes are cells of the lymphatic system. Bone marrow are tissues in this organ system. The lymph nodes, thymus gland, spleen and tonsils are organs of the lymphatic system. **F.1.3.4 CS**

Using Key Terms

1. Use *lymph nodes, spleen,* and *tonsils* in separate sentences.

Understanding Key Ideas

2. To which level of structural organization does each component of the lymphatic system belong? **F.1.3.4 CS**

3. How are your cardiovascular and lymphatic systems related?

Math Skills

4. One cubic millimeter of blood contains 5 million RBCs and 10,000 WBCs. How many times more RBCs are there than WBCs?

Critical Thinking

5. **Analyzing Ideas** Why is it important that the lymphatic system is spread throughout the body? **F.1.3.1 AA**

FCAT Preparation

6. Your tonsils are at the back of your mouth. A tonsil is made up of different cells and tissues that help fight diseases that enter your body through your mouth. To which level of structural organization do tonsils belong? **F.1.3.4 CS**

A. Tonsils are organs.

B. Tonsils are cells.

C. Tonsils are organ systems.

D. Tonsils are tissues.

The Respiratory System

Breathing—you do it all the time. You're doing it right now. You hardly ever think about it, though, unless you suddenly can't breathe.

SECTION 4

Then, it becomes very clear that you have to breathe in order to live. But why is breathing important? Your body needs oxygen in order to get energy from the foods you eat. Breathing makes this process possible.

Respiration and the Respiratory System

The words *breathing* and *respiration* are often used to mean the same thing. However, breathing is only one part of respiration. **Respiration** is the process by which a body gets and uses oxygen and releases carbon dioxide and water. Respiration is divided into two parts. The first part is breathing, which involves inhaling and exhaling. The second part is cellular respiration, which involves chemical reactions that release energy from food.

Breathing is made possible by your respiratory system. The **respiratory system** is the group of organs that take in oxygen and get rid of carbon dioxide. The nose, throat, lungs, and passageways that lead to the lungs make up the respiratory system. **Figure 1** shows the parts of the respiratory system.

Benchmark Check Describe the function of the respiratory system. F.1.3.1 AA

READING WARM-UP

Objectives

- Describe the structure and function of the respiratory system. F.1.3.1 AA
- Explain how breathing happens.
- Discuss the relationship between the respiratory system and the cardiovascular system. F.1.3.5 CS
- Identify two respiratory disorders.

Terms to Learn

respiration	trachea
respiratory system	bronchus
pharynx	alveoli
larynx	

READING STRATEGY

Reading Organizer As you read this section, make a flowchart of the steps of the process of respiration.

respiration the exchange of oxygen and carbon dioxide between living cells and their environment; includes breathing and cellular respiration

respiratory system a collection of organs whose primary function is to take in oxygen and expel carbon dioxide

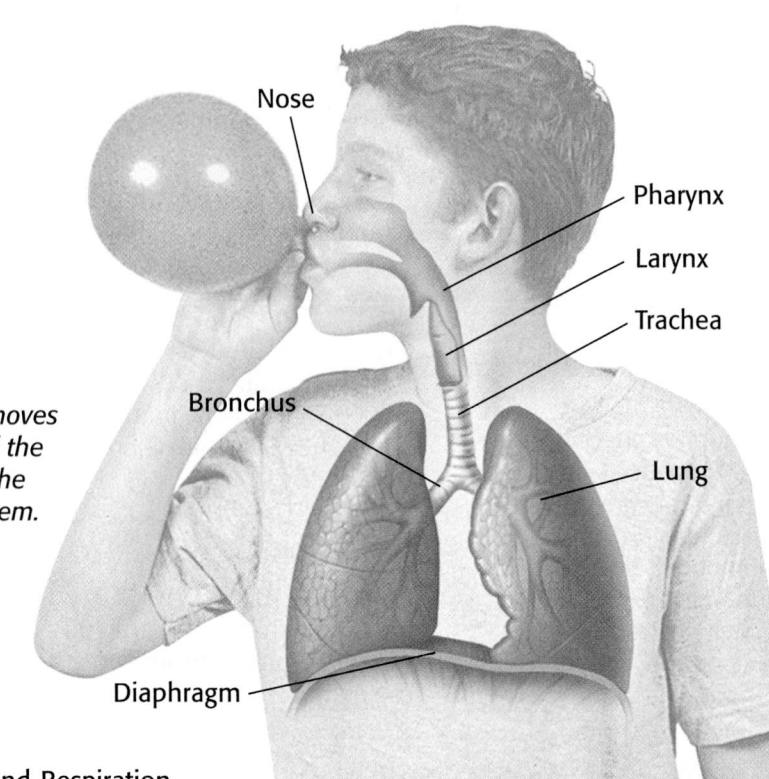

Figure 1 *Air moves into and out of the body through the respiratory system.*

Nose

Pharynx

Larynx

Trachea

Bronchus

Lung

Diaphragm

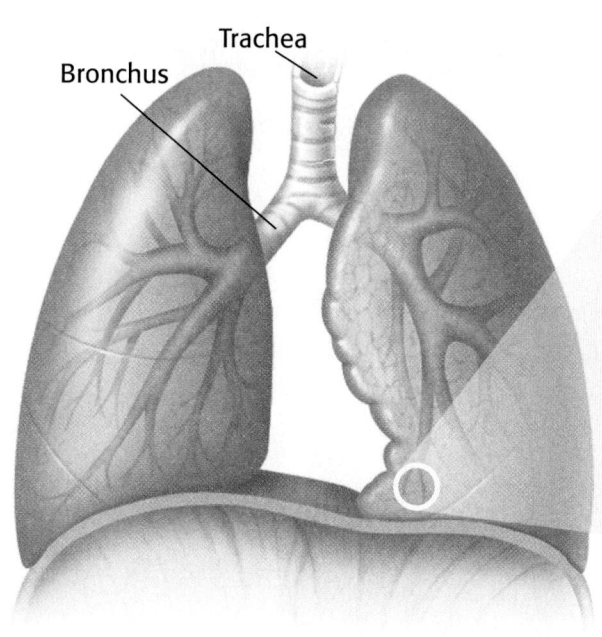

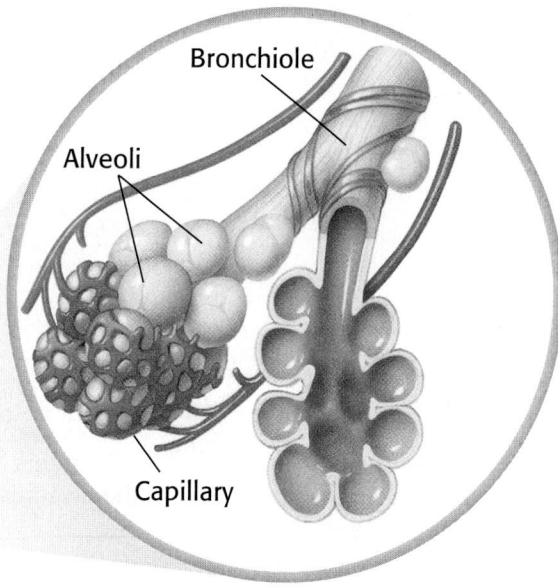

Figure 2 *Inside your lungs, the bronchi branch into bronchioles. The bronchioles lead to tiny sacs called alveoli.*

Nose, Pharynx, and Larynx

Your *nose* is the main passageway into and out of the respiratory system. Air can be breathed in through and out of the nose. Air can also enter and leave through the mouth.

From the nose, air flows into the **pharynx** (FAR ingks), or throat. Food and drink also travel through the pharynx on the way to the stomach. The pharynx branches into two tubes. One tube, the *esophagus,* leads to the stomach. The other tube is the larynx (LAR ingks). The larynx leads to the lungs.

The **larynx** is the part of the throat that contains the vocal cords. The *vocal cords* are a pair of elastic bands that stretch across the larynx. Muscles connected to the larynx control how much the vocal cords are stretched. When air flows between the vocal cords, the cords vibrate. These vibrations make sound.

Trachea

The larynx guards the entrance to a large tube called the **trachea** (TRAY kee uh), or windpipe. Your body has two large, spongelike lungs. The trachea, shown in **Figure 2,** is the passageway for air traveling from the larynx to the lungs.

Bronchi and Alveoli

The trachea splits into two branches called **bronchi** (BRAHNG KIE) (singular, *bronchus*). One bronchus connects to each lung. Each bronchus branches into smaller tubes that are called *bronchioles* (BRAHNG kee OHLZ). In the lungs, each bronchiole branches to form tiny sacs that are called **alveoli** (al VEE uh LIE) (singular, *alveolus*).

✓ Reading Check Describe the flow of air from your nose to your alveoli.

pharynx the passage from the mouth to the larynx and esophagus

larynx the area of the throat that contains the vocal cords and produces vocal sounds

trachea the tube that connects the larynx to the lungs

bronchus one of the two tubes that connect the lungs with the trachea

alveoli any of the tiny air sacs of the lungs where oxygen and carbon dioxide are exchanged

F.I.3.I AA understands that living things are composed of major systems that function in reproduction, growth, maintenance, and regulation.

F.I.3.4 CS knows that the levels of structural organization for function in living things include cells, tissues, organs, systems, and organisms.

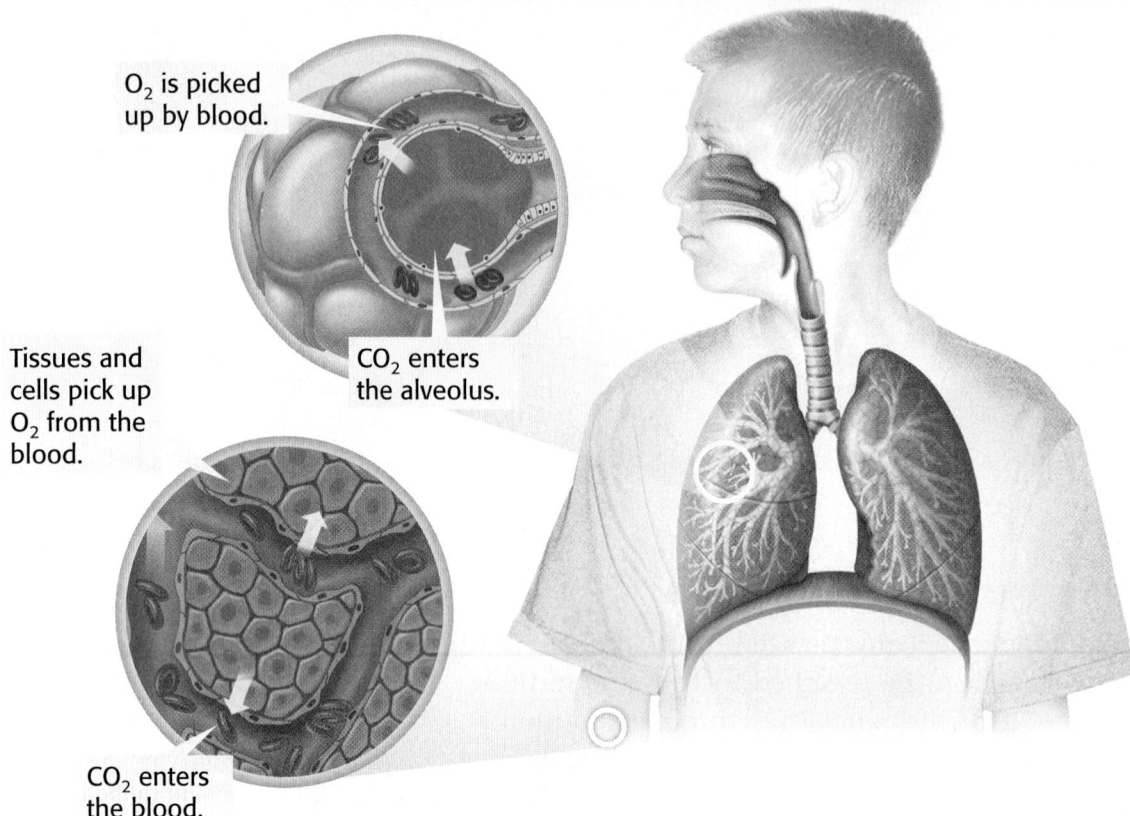

Figure 3 The Role of Blood in Respiration

O₂ is picked up by blood.

CO₂ enters the alveolus.

Tissues and cells pick up O₂ from the blood.

CO₂ enters the blood.

Breathing

When you breathe, air is sucked into or forced out of your lungs. However, your lungs have no muscles of their own. Instead, breathing is done by the diaphragm (DIE uh FRAM) and rib muscles. The *diaphragm* is a dome-shaped muscle beneath the lungs. When you inhale, the diaphragm contracts and moves down. The chest cavity's volume increases. At the same time, some of your rib muscles contract and lift your rib cage. As a result, your chest cavity gets bigger and a vacuum is created. Air is sucked in. Exhaling is this process in reverse.

Breathing and Cellular Respiration

In *cellular respiration,* oxygen is used by cells to release energy stored in molecules of glucose. Where does the oxygen come from? When you inhale, you take in oxygen. This oxygen diffuses into red blood cells and is carried to tissue cells. The oxygen then diffuses out of the red blood cells and into each cell. Cells use the oxygen to release chemical energy. During the process, carbon dioxide, CO_2, and water are produced. Carbon dioxide is exhaled from the lungs. **Figure 3** shows how breathing and blood circulation are related.

Benchmark Check How does breathing affect the function of red blood cells? F.1.3.5 CS

F.1.3.5 CS explains how the life functions are related to what occurs within the cell.

Benchmark Activity

Living with Anemia

Anemia is a condition in which blood cannot carry enough oxygen. Research anemia, and write a paragraph about it. Find out the common causes and symptoms of this condition. Discuss how the life functions of a person who has anemia are affected. F.1.3.5 CS

Respiratory Disorders

Millions of people suffer from respiratory disorders. Respiratory disorders include asthma, emphysema, and severe acute respiratory syndrome (SARS). Asthma causes the bronchioles to narrow. A person who has asthma has difficulty breathing. An asthma attack may be triggered by irritants such as dust or pollen. SARS is caused by a virus. A person who has SARS may have a fever and difficulty breathing. Emphysema happens when the alveoli have been damaged. People who have emphysema have trouble getting the oxygen they need. **Figure 4** shows a lung damaged by emphysema.

Figure 4 *The photo on the left shows a healthy lung. The photo on the right shows the lung of a person who had emphysema.*

 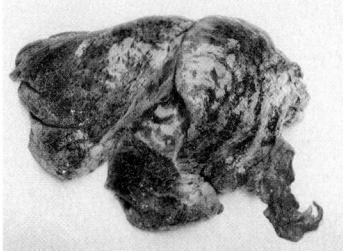

Why Do People Snore?

1. Get a **15 cm² sheet of wax paper.**
2. Hum your favorite song.
3. Then, take the wax paper and press it against your lips. Hum the song again.
4. How was your humming different when wax paper was pressed to your mouth?
5. Use your observations to guess what might cause snoring.

SECTION Review

Summary

- The respiratory system maintains oxygen and carbon dioxide levels in the body. F.1.3.1 AA
- Breathing involves lungs, muscles in the rib cage, and the diaphragm.
- Oxygen enters blood and carbon dioxide leaves blood through alveoli in the lungs. F.1.3.5 CS
- Respiratory disorders include asthma, SARS, and emphysema.

Using Key Terms

1. Write an original definition for *pharynx* and *larynx*.

Understanding Key Ideas

2. Which of the following are respiratory disorders?
    a. SARS, alveoli, and asthma
    b. alveoli, emphysema, and SARS
    c. larynx, asthma, and SARS
    d. SARS, emphysema, and asthma

3. Explain how breathing happens.

4. Describe the structure and function of the respiratory system. F.1.3.1 AA

Critical Thinking

5. **Identifying Relationships** A respiratory disorder causes the lungs to fill with fluid. How does this affect the cardiovascular system and the person? F.1.3.1 AA

FCAT Preparation

6. Carbon dioxide levels are well regulated in the body. How do red blood cells (RBCs) help control these levels? F.1.3.5 CS
    A. RBCs carry carbon dioxide to the lungs to be exhaled.
    B. RBCs break down carbon dioxide.
    C. RBCs carry carbon dioxide to cells.
    D. RBCs use carbon dioxide to release energy.

Developed and maintained by the National Science Teachers Association

For a variety of links related to this chapter, go to www.scilinks.org

Topic: The Respiratory System; Respiratory Disorders

SciLinks code: HSM1307; HSM1306

Skills Practice Lab

OBJECTIVES

Detect the presence of carbon dioxide in your breath.

Compare the data for carbon dioxide in your breath with the data from your classmates.

MATERIALS

- calculator (optional)
- clock with a second hand, or a stopwatch
- Erlenmeyer flask, 150 mL
- eyedropper
- gloves, protective
- graduated cylinder, 150 mL
- paper towels
- phenol red indicator solution
- plastic drinking straw
- water, 100 mL

SAFETY

Carbon Dioxide Breath

Carbon dioxide is important to both plants and animals. Plants take in carbon dioxide during photosynthesis and give off oxygen as a byproduct of the process. Animals—including you—take in oxygen during respiration and give off carbon dioxide as a byproduct of the process.

Procedure

1. Put on your gloves, safety goggles, and apron.

2. Use the graduated cylinder to pour 100 mL of water into a 150 mL flask.

3. Using an eyedropper, carefully place four drops of phenol red indicator solution into the water. The water should turn orange.

4. Place a plastic drinking straw into the solution of phenol red and water. Drape a paper towel over the flask to prevent splashing.

5. Carefully blow through the straw into the solution. **Caution:** Do not inhale through the straw. Do not drink the solution, and do not share a straw with anyone.

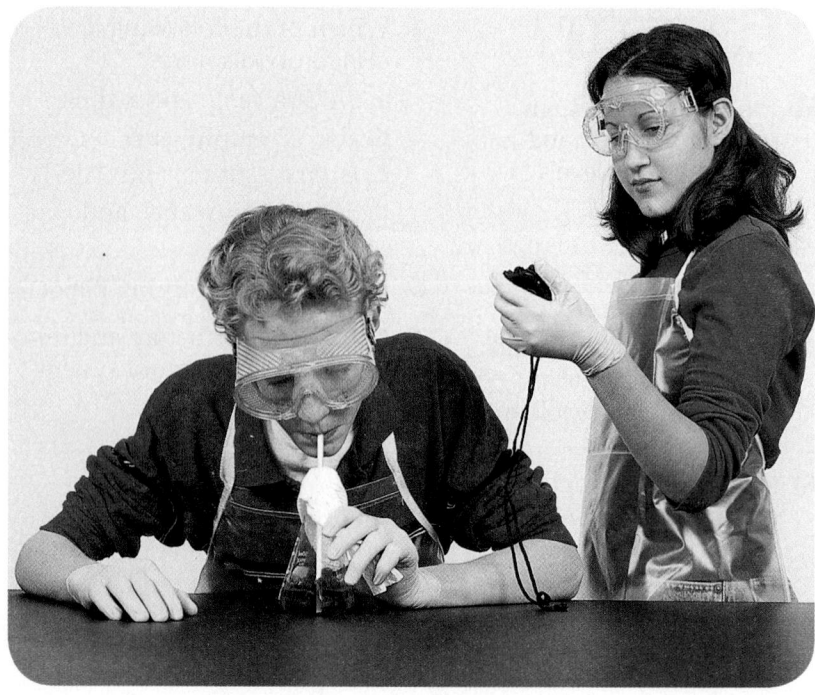

F.1.3.1 AA understands that living things are composed of major systems that function in reproduction, growth, maintenance, and regulation.

6 Your lab partner should begin keeping time as soon as you start to blow through the straw. Have your lab partner time how long the solution takes to change color. Record the time.

Analyze the Results

1 **Describing Events** Describe what happens to the indicator solution.

2 **Examining Data** Compare your data with those of your classmates. What was the longest length of time it took to see a color change? What was the shortest? How do you account for the difference?

3 **Constructing Graphs** Make a bar graph that compares your data with the data of your classmates.

Draw Conclusions

4 **Interpreting Information** Do you think that there is a relationship between the length of time the solution takes to change color and the person's physical characteristics, such as which gender the tester is or whether the tester has an athletic build? Explain your answer.

5 **Making Predictions** Predict how exercise might affect the results of your experiment. For example, would you predict that the level of carbon dioxide in the breath of someone who was exercising would be higher or lower than the carbon dioxide level in the breath of someone who was sitting quietly? Would you predict that the level of carbon dioxide in the breath would affect the timing of any color change in the phenol solution?

6 **Applying Conclusions** Name a body system that expels carbon dioxide from your body. Why is it important that this body system can deal with varying levels of carbon dioxide?

Applying Your Data

Do jumping jacks or sit-ups for 3 minutes, and then repeat the experiment. Did the phenol solution still change color? Did your exercising change the timing? Describe and explain any change.

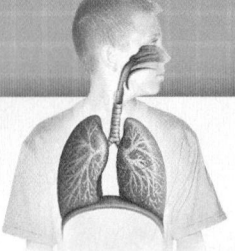

Chapter Review

USING KEY TERMS

Use a term from the chapter to complete each sentence below.

1 ___ deliver oxygen to the cells of the body.

2 ___ carry blood away from the heart.

3 The ___ helps the body fight diseases. **F1.3.5 CS**

4 Air travels through the respiratory system to tiny sacs called ___.

UNDERSTANDING KEY IDEAS

Multiple Choice

5 You are watching a video about blood and its components. Knowing that red blood cells or RBCs have a different function than white blood cells or WBCs, which of the following predictions can you make? **F.1.3.6 CS** *FCAT*

a. RBCs and WBCs have different structures.

b. RBCs and WBCs use carbon dioxide to release energy.

c. RBCs and WBCs carry oxygen.

d. RBCs and WBCs fight diseases.

6 Ajay will need a blood transfusion during his knee surgery. Ajay's blood type is B. People who have type B blood produce antibody A. What blood types can Ajay safely receive? **F1.3.5 CS** *FCAT*

a. type A only

b. types A and B

c. type AB only

d. types B and O

7 A shortage of red blood cells may cause a condition known as anemia. Which of the following could occur as a result of anemia? **F1.3.5 CS** *FCAT*

a. shortness of breath

b. inability to form blood clots

c. loss of antibodies

d. swollen lymph nodes

8 Which of the following activities is a function of the lymphatic system?

a. pumping blood to all parts of the body

b. delivering nutrients to the cells

c. bringing oxygen to the blood

d. returning excess fluid to the cardiovascular system

9 What prevents blood from flowing backward in veins?

a. platelets

b. valves

c. muscles

d. cartilage

10 Air moves into the lungs when the diaphragm muscle

a. contracts and moves down.

b. contracts and moves up.

c. relaxes and moves down.

d. relaxes and moves up.

Short Answer

11 Compare and contrast pulmonary circulation and systemic circulation in the cardiovascular system.

12 Walton's blood pressure is 110/65. What do the two numbers mean?

13 Describe how the cardiovascular system and the lymphatic system work together to keep your body healthy. F1.3.1 AA

14 How is the spleen important to both the lymphatic system and the cardiovascular system? F1.3.4 CS

15 Briefly describe the path that oxygen follows in your respiratory system and your cardiovascular system.

16 Describe four cardiovascular problems.

CRITICAL THINKING

Extended Response

17 **Identifying Relationships** Hypertension and artherosclerosis are very different conditions, but they can both lead to heart attacks. Explain.

18 **Applying Concepts** A healthy person has about 5 million RBCs in each cubic millimeter (1 mm^3) of blood. How many RBCs are in 1 mL of blood? (Hint: One milliliter is equal to 1 cm^3 and to 1,000 mm^3.)

19 **Evaluating Conclusions** Amy is having difficulty breathing because her bronchioles have narrowed. Jane says Amy's condition is caused by emphysema. In your opinion, is Jane correct? Support your answer.

20 **Identifying Relationships** When a person is not feeling well, a doctor may examine samples of the person's blood to see how many white blood cells are present. Why would this information be useful? F1.3.5 CS

Concept Mapping

21 Use the following terms to create a concept map: *blood, oxygen, alveoli, capillaries,* and *carbon dioxide.*

INTERPRETING GRAPHICS

The diagram below shows how the human heart would look in cross section. Use the diagram to answer the questions that follow.

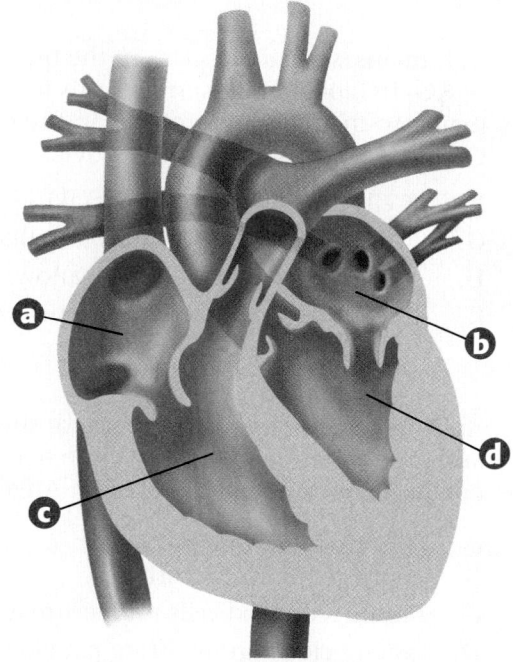

22 Which letter identifies the chamber that receives blood from systemic circulation? What is this chamber's name?

23 Which letter identifies the chamber that receives blood from the lungs? What is this chamber's name?

24 Which letter identifies the chamber that pumps blood to the lungs? What is this chamber's name?

Standardized Test Preparation

For the following questions, write your answers on a separate sheet of paper.

1 The basic level of structural organization in living things is the cell. Cells with similar function and structure work together to form tissues. Tissues that work together form organs, and groups of organs form organ systems. These different levels of structural organization help support the organism. Which of the following parts of the human lymphatic system belongs to the **highest** level of structural organization?

A.   lymph, which is made up of fluid and particles

B.   spleen, which is made up of different kinds of tissues

C.   lymphocytes, which are cells that help fight infections

D.   tonsil cells, which help fight pathogens entering the body through the mouth

2 In humans, special receptors in the brain and in the arteries in the neck monitor the levels of CO_2 in blood. The brain uses this information to adjust the breating rate and depth to maintain the right levels of CO_2 in the body. Which of the following would happen if the CO_2 in blood was not being removed from the body quickly enough?

F.   Cells in the body will start taking up CO_2.

G.   Cells in the body will start to reduce the amount of CO_2 they make.

H.   Breathing would become shallower and slower to breakdown the CO_2.

I.   Breathing would become deeper and faster to get rid off CO_2 from the body.

3 Angelina went to the doctor because she felt very sick. The doctor took a sample of her blood and found that she has many more white blood cells than normal. What other symptoms could the doctor check for to see if Angelina has an infection?

A.   swollen lymph nodes

B.   enlarged veins and arteries

C.   more red blood cells than normal

D.   blood clots forming from platelets

4 White blood cells (WBCs) are cells that are specialized to fight disease-causing agents, or pathogens, that get into the body. Different kinds of WBCs destroy pathogens in different ways. Some WBCs engulf the pathogen and then break it down. Other WBCs make antibodies. Antibodies are special chemicals that will attach themselves to the pathogen. Antibodies help identify the pathogen for destruction. What can you infer about WBCs based on this information?

F.   that different kinds of WBCs have similar structures

G.   that different kinds of WBCs can become pathogens

H.   that different kinds of WBCs have different structures

I.   that some kinds of WBCs are not as effective as others

5   Anthony is studying how breathing helps provide the body with oxygen. He has decided to make a flow chart that shows how oxygen is taken into the body and used by cells to release energy from food. A picture of his flow chart is shown below.

Movement of Oxygen from the Atmosphere to Cells

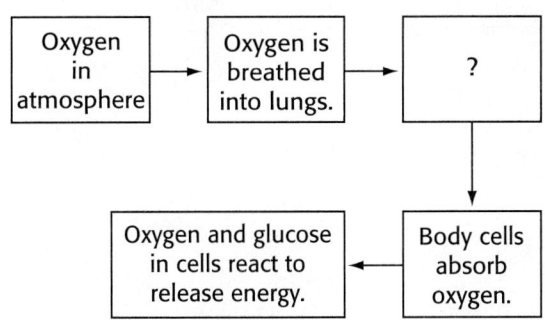

Identify and describe the process that occurs at the missing step in Anthony's flow chart.

6   The cardiovascular system is divided into two kinds of circulation as shown in the diagram below.

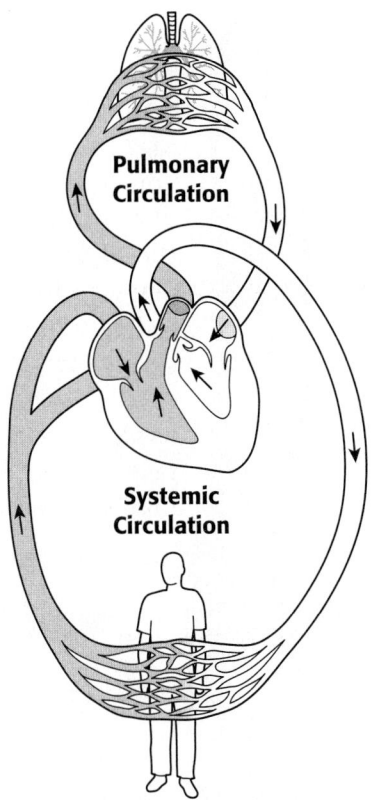

Which kind of circulation provides the cells of the body with oxygen, and through which vessels does the blood travel in this circulation?

Science in Action

Science, Technology, and Society

Artificial Blood

What happens when someone loses blood rapidly? Loss of blood can be fatal in a very short time, so lost blood must be replaced as quickly as possible. But what if enough blood, or blood of the right type, is not immediately available? Scientists are developing different types of artificial blood—including one based on cow hemoglobin—that may soon be used to save lives that would otherwise be lost.

Weird Science

Circular Breathing and the Didgeridoo

Do you play a musical instrument such as a clarinet, flute, or tuba? How long can you blow into it before you have to take a breath? Can you blow into it for one minute? two minutes? And what happens when you stop to breathe? The Aboriginal people of Australia have a musical instrument called the *didgeridoo* (DIJ uh ree DOO). Didgeridoo players can play for hours without stopping to take a breath. They use a technique called *circular breathing* that lets them inhale and exhale at the same time. Circular breathing lets a musician play music without having to take breaths as often. With a little practice, maybe you can do it, too.

Language Arts ACTiViTY

WRITING SKILL Imagine that you are a doctor and one of your patients needs surgery. Create a pamphlet or brochure that explains what artificial blood is and how it may be used in surgical procedures.

Social Studies ACTiViTY

WRITING SKILL Select a country from Africa or Asia. Research that country's traditional musical instruments or singing style. Write a description of how the instruments or singing style of that country differs from those of the United States. Illustrate your report.

Sylvia Earle

Queen of the Deep Sylvia Earle's family moved to Clearwater, Florida, when she was 13. There they encouraged her love of the oceans. At school, a teacher gave her some good advice: the best way to learn about the ocean is to jump in! So she took the plunge, to become a world-famous oceanographer, conservationist, and deep-sea diver. Known as the "Queen of the Deep," Earle has led more than 50 underwater expeditions, spent more than 6,000 hours below the sea's surface, and set a number of diving records. Her passion for the sea has also inspired her to create and test many unique diving technologies. Earle hopes that ever-improving submersible technology will allow deeper exploration of the oceans. Only about 5% of the oceans have been explored, and most of that research has taken place in the top 30 m. Making smaller, personal submersibles could allow more scientists, and even everyday people, to "jump in" and experience the wonder of the sea and all of its creatures. Earle believes that more deep-sea study and exploration can only lead to a greater understanding and appreciation of the oceans—and stronger support for their protection.

Math ACTIVITY

At the surface of the sea, you experience 1 atmosphere of pressure. For every 10 m below the sea surface, you experience on more atmosphere of pressure. How many atmospheres of pressure would you experience at the deepest known point in the ocean, which is at least 11,000 m below the surface?

go.hrw.com

To learn more about these Science in Action topics, visit **go.hrw.com** and type in the keyword **HT6FFCRF**.

Current Science

Check out Current Science® articles related to this chapter by visiting go.hrw.com. Just type in the keyword HL5CS23.

7

The Digestive and Urinary Systems

The Big Idea The human body has systems that break down nutrients and remove wastes.

About the PHOTO

Is this a giant worm? No, it's an X ray of a healthy large intestine! Your large intestine helps your body preserve water. As mostly digested food passes through your large intestine, water is drawn out of the food. This water is returned to the bloodstream. The gray shadow behind the intestine is the spinal column. The areas that look empty are actually filled with organs. A special liquid helps this large intestine show up on the X ray.

PRE-READING ACTIVITY

Graphic Organizer

Chain-of-Events Chart Before you read the chapter, create the graphic organizer entitled "Chain-of-Events Chart" described in the **Study Skills** section of the Appendix. As you read the chapter, fill in the chart with details about each step of the processes that your body uses to digest food.

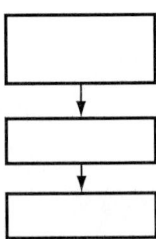

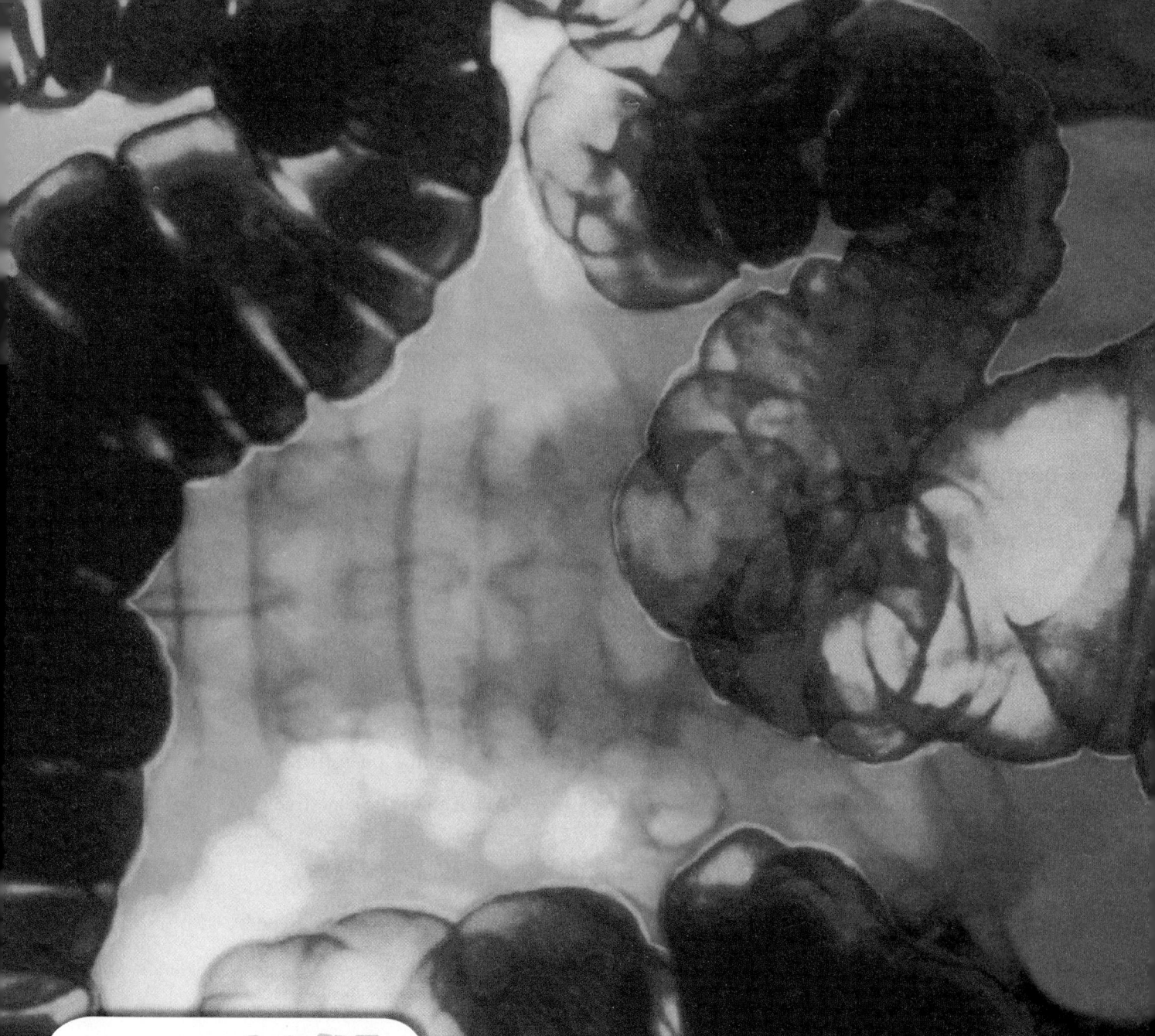

START-UP ACTIVITY

Changing Foods

One of the ways the stomach breaks down food is by squeezing the food. You can model this action of the stomach in the following activity.

Procedure

1. Add **200 mL of flour** and **100 mL of water** to a **resealable plastic bag.**

2. Mix **100 mL of vegetable oil** with the flour and water.

3. Seal the plastic bag.

4. Shake the bag until the flour, water, and oil are well mixed.

5. Remove as much air from the bag as you can, and reseal the bag carefully.

6. Knead the bag carefully with your hands for 5 min. Be careful to keep the bag sealed.

Analysis

1. Describe the mixture before and after you kneaded the bag.

2. How might the changes that you saw in the mixture relate to how your stomach digests food?

3. Do you think that this activity is a good model of how your stomach works? Explain your answer.

The Digestive System

It's your last class before lunch, and you're starving! Finally, the bell rings, and you get to eat!

You feel hungry because your brain receives signals that your cells need energy. Body systems help the body meet its needs. The digestive system helps the body use food to meet its energy needs. Energy from food fuels body functions, such as reproduction, growth, maintenance, and regulation.

Digestive System at a Glance

The **digestive system,** shown in **Figure 1,** is an organ system. This organ system is made up of a group of organs that work together to digest food so that it can be used by the body. A major part of the digestive system is the series of tubelike organs called the *digestive tract.* Food passes through these organs. This path includes the mouth, pharynx, esophagus, stomach, small intestine, large intestine, rectum, and anus. The human digestive tract can be more than 9 m long! The liver, gallbladder, pancreas, and salivary glands are also used in digestion. But food does not pass through these organs.

Benchmark Check What does the digestive system do? **F.1.3.1 AA**

digestive system the organs that break down food so that it can be used by the body

Figure 1 The Digestive System

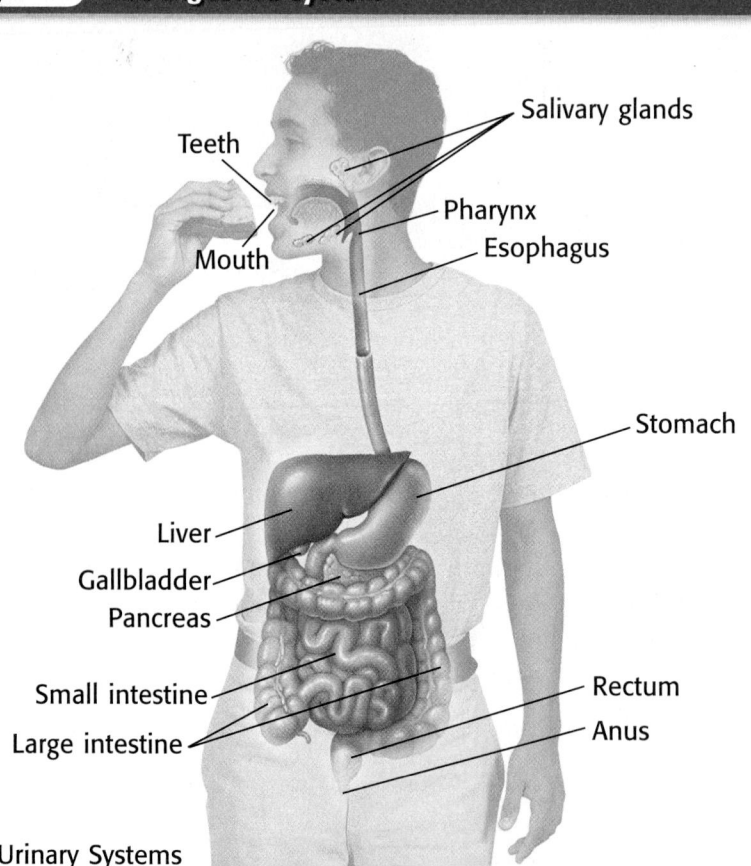

- Teeth
- Mouth
- Salivary glands
- Pharynx
- Esophagus
- Stomach
- Liver
- Gallbladder
- Pancreas
- Small intestine
- Large intestine
- Rectum
- Anus

Breaking Down Food

Digestion is the process of breaking down food, such as a peanut butter and jelly sandwich, into a form that can pass from the digestive tract into the bloodstream. There are two types of digestion: mechanical and chemical. The breaking, crushing, and mashing of food is called *mechanical digestion.* In *chemical digestion,* large molecules are broken down into nutrients. Nutrients are substances in food that the body needs for normal growth, maintenance, and repair.

Three major types of nutrients—carbohydrates, proteins, and fats—make up most of the food that you eat. In fact, a peanut butter and jelly sandwich contains all three of these nutrients. Substances called *enzymes* break some nutrients into smaller particles that the body can use. For example, proteins are chains of smaller molecules called *amino acids.* Proteins are too large to be absorbed into the bloodstream. So, enzymes cut up the chains of amino acids. Amino acids are small enough to pass into the bloodstream. This process is shown in **Figure 2.**

Reading Check How do enzymes help digestion?

Break It Up!

1. Drop **one piece of hard candy** into a **clear plastic cup of water.**

2. Wrap an **identical candy** in a **towel,** and crush the candy with a **hammer.** Drop the candy into a **second clear cup of water.**

3. The next day, examine both cups. What is different about the two candies?

4. What type of digestion is represented by breaking the hard candy?

5. How does chewing your food help the process of digestion?

Figure 2 **The Role of Enzymes in Protein Digestion**

1 Enzymes act as chemical scissors to cut the long chains of amino acids into small chains.

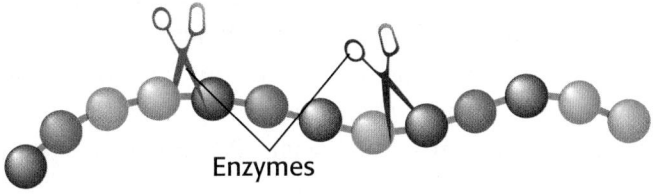

Enzymes

2 The small chains are split by other enzymes.

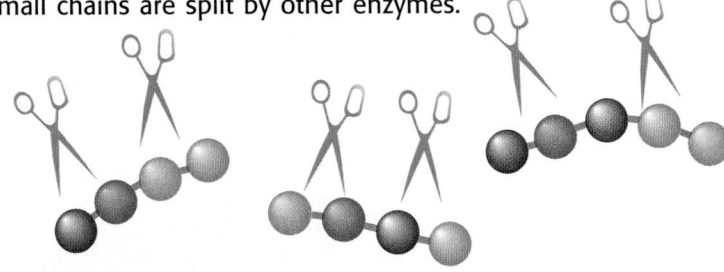

3 Individual amino acids are small enough to enter the bloodstream, where they can be used to make new proteins.

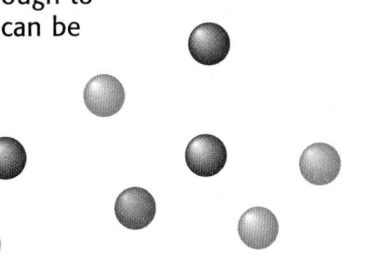

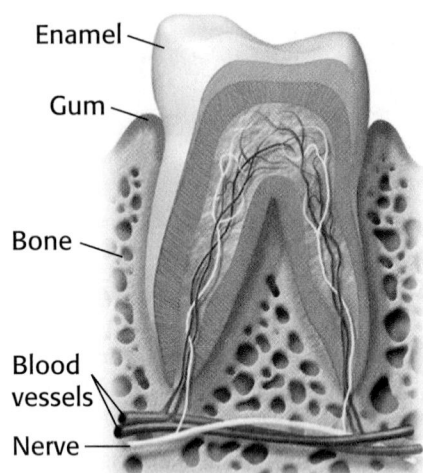

Figure 3 *A tooth, such as this molar, is made of many kinds of tissue.*

Enamel
Gum
Bone
Blood vessels
Nerve

esophagus a long, straight tube that connects the pharynx to the stomach

F.1.3.4 CS knows that the levels of structural organization for function in living things include cells, tissues, organs, systems, and organisms.

Digestion Begins in the Mouth

Chewing is important for two reasons. First, chewing creates small, slippery pieces of food that are easier to swallow than big, dry pieces are. Second, small pieces of food are easier to digest.

Teeth

Teeth are very important organs for mechanical digestion. With the help of strong jaw muscles, teeth break and grind food. *Enamel,* the outermost layer of a tooth, is the hardest material in the body. It protects nerves and softer material inside the tooth. **Figure 3** shows a cross section of a tooth.

Have you ever noticed that your teeth have different shapes? Look at **Figure 4** to locate the different kinds of teeth. The molars are well suited for grinding food. The *premolars* are perfect for mashing food. The *incisors* and *canines,* the sharp teeth at the front of your mouth, are for shredding food.

Saliva

As you chew, the food mixes with a liquid called *saliva.* Saliva is made in salivary glands located in the mouth. Saliva contains an enzyme that begins the chemical digestion of carbohydrates. Saliva changes complex carbohydrates into simple sugars.

Leaving the Mouth

Once the food has been reduced to a soft mush, the tongue pushes it into the throat, which leads to a long, straight tube called the **esophagus** (i SAHF uh guhs). The esophagus squeezes the mass of food with rhythmic muscle contractions called *peristalsis* (PER uh STAL sis). Peristalsis forces the food into the stomach.

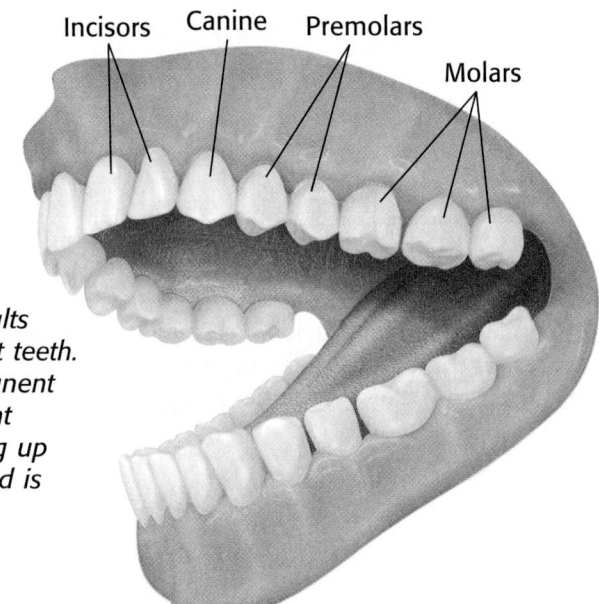

Incisors   Canine   Premolars   Molars

Figure 4 *Most adults have 32 permanent teeth. Each type of permanent tooth has a different function in breaking up food before the food is swallowed.*

Figure 5 **The Stomach**

The stomach squeezes and mixes food for hours before it releases the mixture into the small intestine.

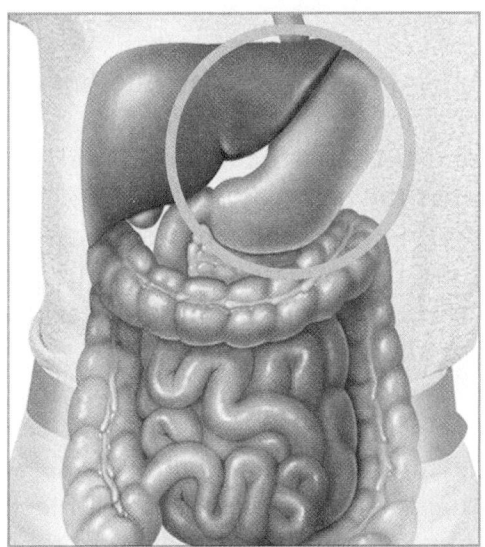

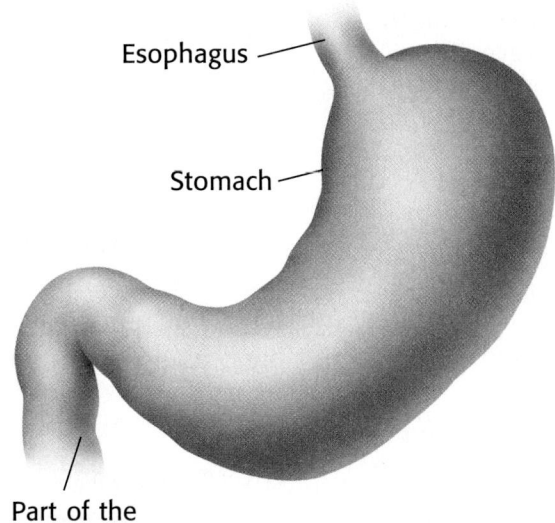

Esophagus

Stomach

Part of the small intestine

The Harsh Environment of the Stomach

The **stomach** is a muscular, saclike, digestive organ attached to the lower end of the esophagus. The stomach is shown in **Figure 5.** The stomach continues the mechanical digestion of your meal by squeezing the food with muscular contractions. While this squeezing takes place, tiny glands in the stomach produce enzymes and acid. The enzymes and acid work together to break food into nutrients. Stomach acid also kills most bacteria that you might swallow with your food. After a few hours of combined mechanical and chemical digestion, your peanut butter and jelly sandwich has been reduced to a soupy mixture called *chyme* (KIEM).

✔ **Reading Check** What is chyme?

Leaving the Stomach

The stomach slowly releases the chyme into the small intestine through a small ring of muscle that works like a valve. This valve keeps food in the stomach until the food has been thoroughly mixed with digestive fluids. Each time the valve opens and closes, it lets a small amount of chyme into the small intestine. Because the stomach releases chyme slowly, the intestine has more time to mix the chyme with fluids from the liver and pancreas. These fluids help digest food and stop the harsh acids in chyme from hurting the small intestine.

stomach the saclike, digestive organ that is between the esophagus and the small intestine and that breaks down food into a liquid by the action of muscles, enzymes, and acids

Tooth Truth

Young children get a first set of 20 teeth called *baby teeth*. These teeth usually fall out and are replaced by 32 permanent teeth. How many more permanent teeth than baby teeth does a person have? What is the ratio of baby teeth to permanent teeth? Be sure to express the ratio in its most reduced form.

Digestive Journey Describe the digestive process through the "eyes" of a piece of salt! Go to **go.hrw.com**, and type in the keyword **HL5BD3W**.

pancreas the organ that lies behind the stomach and that makes digestive enzymes and hormones that regulate sugar levels

small intestine the organ between the stomach and the large intestine where most of the breakdown of food happens and most of the nutrients from food are absorbed

CONNECTION TO Social Studies

WRITING SKILL **Parasites** Intestinal parasites are organisms such as roundworms and hookworms that infect people and live in the digestive tract. Worldwide, intestinal parasites infect more than 1 billion people. Some parasites can be deadly. Research intestinal parasites in a library or on the Internet. Then, write a report on a parasite, including how it spreads, what problems it causes, how many people have it, and what can be done to stop the spread of that parasite.

F.1.3.4 CS knows that the levels of structural organization for function in living things include cells, tissues, organs, systems, and organisms.

The Pancreas and Small Intestine

Most chemical digestion takes place after food leaves the stomach. Proteins, carbohydrates, and fats in the chyme are digested by the small intestine and fluids from the pancreas.

The Pancreas

The **pancreas** makes fluids that protect the small intestine from the acid in chyme as chyme leaves the stomach. The pancrease is an oval organ located between the stomach and small intestine. Chyme never enters the pancreas. Instead, pancreatic fluid enters the small intestine. This fluid has enzymes that chemically digest chyme and bicarbonate that neutralizes the acid. The pancreas also makes hormones to regulate blood sugar as a part of the endocrine system.

The Small Intestine

The **small intestine** is a muscular tube that is about 2.5 cm in diameter. The small intestine is really not very small. In fact, if you stretched the small intestine out, it would be 6 m long—longer than your height! If you flattened out the surface of the small intestine, it would be larger than a tennis court! How is this possible? The inside wall of the small intestine is covered with fingerlike projections called *villi*, shown in **Figure 6.** The surface area of the small intestine is very large because of the villi. The villi are covered with nutrient-absorbing cells. After the nutrients are absorbed, they enter the bloodstream.

Benchmark Check What is the most basic level of organization at which nutrients are absorbed: cells, tissues, or organs? **F.1.3.4 CS**

Figure 6 **The Small Intestine and Villi**

The highly folded lining of the small intestine has many fingerlike projections called *villi*.

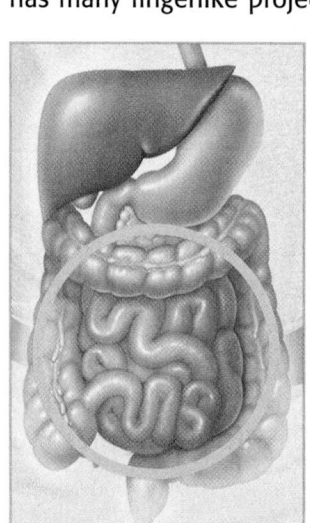
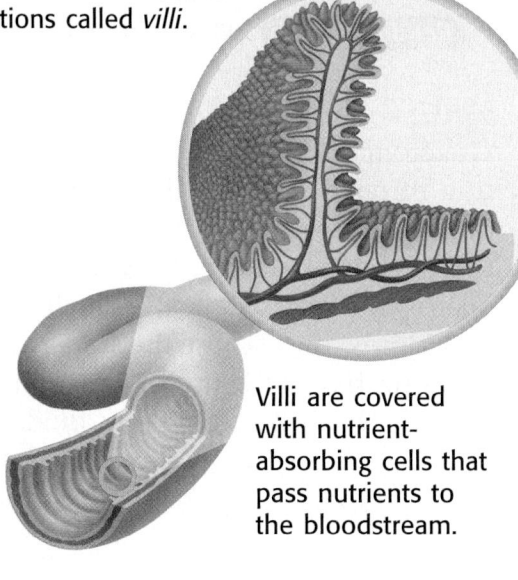

Villi are covered with nutrient-absorbing cells that pass nutrients to the bloodstream.

Figure 7 The Liver and the Gallbladder

Food does not move through the liver, gallbladder, and pancreas even though these organs are linked to the small intestine.

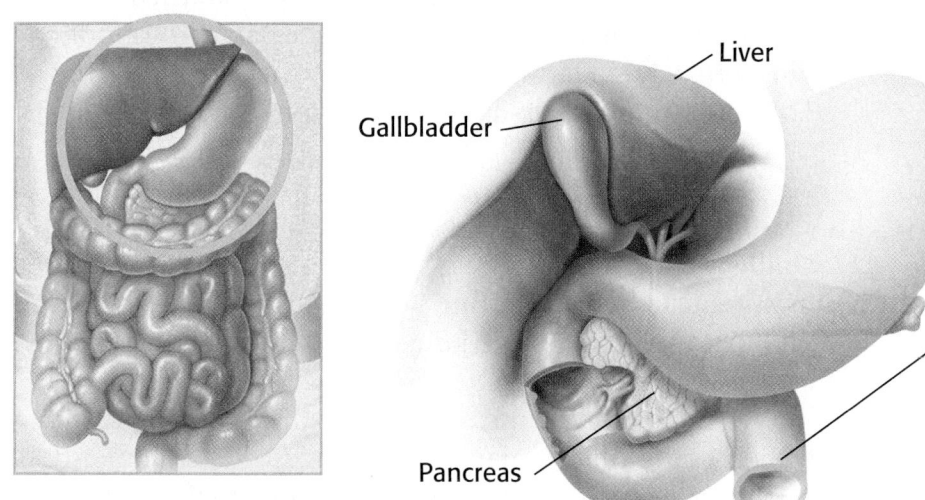

The Liver and Gallbladder

The **liver** is a large, reddish brown organ that helps with digestion. A human liver can be as large as a football. Your liver is located toward your right side, slightly higher than your stomach, as shown in **Figure 7.** The liver helps with digestion in the following ways:

- It makes bile to break up fat.
- It stores nutrients.
- It breaks down toxins.

Breaking Up Fat

Although bile is made by the liver, bile is temporarily stored in a small, saclike organ called the **gallbladder,** shown in **Figure 7.** Bile is squeezed from the gallbladder into the small intestine, where the bile breaks large fat droplets into very small droplets. This mechanical process allows more fat molecules to be exposed to digestive enzymes.

Reading Check How does bile help digest fat?

Storing Nutrients and Protecting the Body

After nutrients are broken down, they are absorbed into the bloodstream and carried throughout the body. Nutrients that are not needed right away are stored in the liver. The liver then releases the stored nutrients into the bloodstream as needed. The liver also captures and detoxifies many chemicals in the body. For instance, the liver produces enzymes that break down alcohol and many other drugs.

liver the largest organ in the body; it makes bile, stores and filters blood, and stores excess sugars as glycogen

gallbladder a sac-shaped organ that stores bile produced by the liver

SCHOOL to HOME

Bile Model
You can model the way that bile breaks down fat and oil by using dish soap. At home with a parent or guardian, put a small amount of water in a small jar. Then, add a few drops of vegetable oil to the water. Notice that the two liquids separate. Draw a picture of the jar and its contents. Next, add a few drops of dishwashing soap to the water, tighten the lid securely onto the jar, and shake the jar. What happened to the three liquids in the jar? Draw another picture of the jar and its contents.

The End of the Line

Material that cannot be absorbed into the blood is pushed into the large intestine. The **large intestine** is the organ of the digestive system that stores, compacts, and then eliminates indigestible material from the body. The large intestine, shown in **Figure 8,** has a larger diameter than the small intestine does. The large intestine is about 1.5 m long and has a diameter of about 7.5 cm.

In the Large Intestine

Undigested material enters the large intestine as a soupy mixture. The large intestine absorbs most of the water in the mixture and changes the liquid into semisolid waste materials called *feces,* or *stool.*

Whole grains, fruits, and vegetables contain *cellulose,* a carbohydrate that humans cannot digest. We commonly refer to this material as *fiber.* Fiber keeps the stool soft and keeps material moving through the large intestine.

Reading Check How does eating fiber help digestion?

Leaving the Body

The *rectum* is the last part of the large intestine. The rectum stores feces until they can be expelled. Feces pass to the outside of the body through an opening called the *anus.* It has taken your sandwich about 24 hours to make this journey through your digestive system.

large intestine the wider and shorter portion of the intestine that removes water from mostly digested food and that turns the waste into semisolid feces, or stool

CONNECTION TO Environmental Science

Waste Away Feces and other human wastes contain microorganisms and other substances that can contaminate drinking water. Every time you flush a toilet, the water and wastes go through the sewer to a wastewater treatment plant. At the wastewater treatment plant, the disease-causing microorganisms are removed, and the clean water is released back to rivers, lakes, and streams. Find out where the wastewater treatment plants are in your area. Report to your classmates where their wastewater goes.

ACTIVITY

F.1.3.4 CS knows that the levels of structural organization for function in living things include cells, tissues, organs, systems, and organisms.

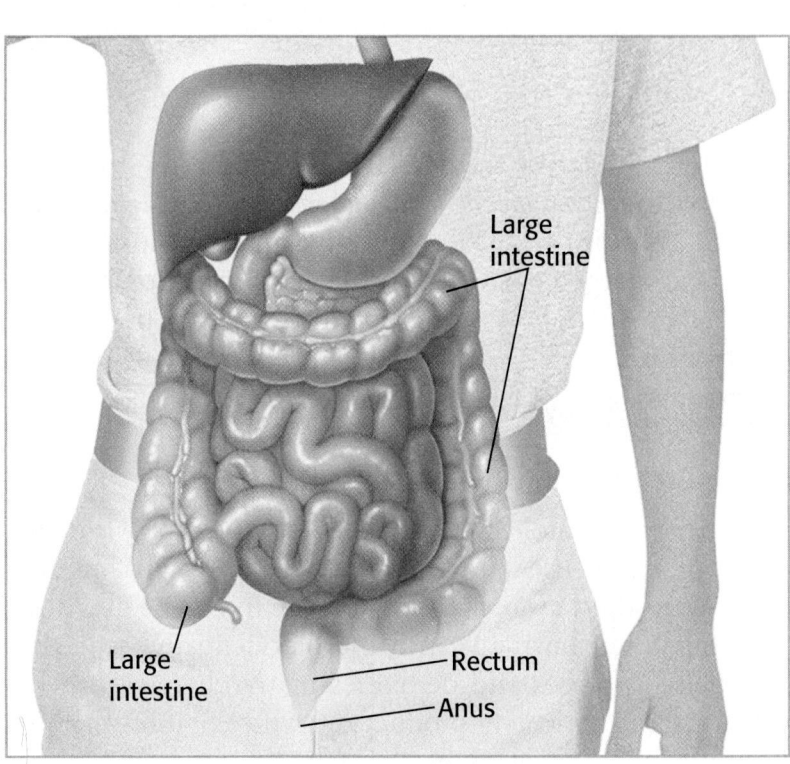

Figure 8 *The large intestine is the final organ of digestion.*

SECTION Review

Summary

- The digestive system is made up of a group of organs. These organs digest food so that the nutrients from food can be used to fuel the body's life functions. **F.I.3.1 AA, F.I.3.4 CS**

- The breaking and mashing of food is called *mechanical digestion*. Chemical digestion is the process that breaks large food molecules into simpler molecules.

- The stomach is an organ that mixes food with acid and enzymes that break down food. The mixture is called *chyme*. **F.I.3.4 CS**

- In the small intestine, pancreatic fluid and bile are mixed with chyme. **F.I.3.4 CS**

- From the small intestine, nutrients enter the bloodstream and are circulated to the cells of the body. **F.I.3.4 CS**

- The liver is an organ that makes bile, stores nutrients, and breaks down toxins. **F.I.3.4 CS**

- The large intestine is an organ that absorbs water and, changes liquid waste into semisolid stool, or feces. **F.I.3.4 CS**

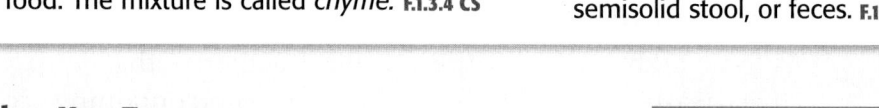

Using Key Terms

1. Use *digestive system, large intestine,* and *small intestine* in separate sentences. **F.I.3.4 CS**

Understanding Key Ideas

2. Which of the following is NOT a function of the digestive system? **F.I.3.1 AA**
   a. to digest food
   b. to remove wastes
   c. to break down nutrients
   d. to get oxygen

3. What is the difference between mechanical digestion and chemical digestion?

4. Describe the role of the liver, gallbladder, and pancreas in digestion.

5. Put the following steps of digestion in order.
   a. Teeth are used to chew food.
   b. Water is absorbed by the large intestine.
   c. Food is reduced to chyme in the stomach.
   d. Food moves down the esophagus.
   e. Nutrients are absorbed by the small intestine.
   f. The pancreas releases enzymes.

Critical Thinking

6. **Evaluating Conclusions** Explain the following statement: "Digestion begins in the mouth."

7. **Identifying Relationships** How would the inability to make saliva affect digestion?

FCAT Preparation

8. The body needs energy to perform life functions, such as reproduction, growth, maintenance, and regulation. How does the digestive system help the body meet its energy needs? **F.I.3.1 AA**
   A. by breaking down food
   B. by breaking down wastes
   C. by changing food to release enzymes
   D. by changing wastes into enzymes

9. The organs of the digestive system help the body maintain itself. The digestive system not only provides an immediate supply of nutrients for the body but it also stores some of the excess nutrients. **F.I.3.1 AA, F.I.3.4 CS**

   PART A Under what conditions might your body need to use stored nutrients?

   PART B Name the part of the digestive system that stores nutrients. Is it a cell, tissue or organ?

SCI**LINKS** NSTA
Developed and maintained by the
National Science Teachers Association

For a variety of links related to this chapter, go to www.scilinks.org

Topic: The Digestive System
SciLinks code: HSM0409

The Urinary System

As blood travels through the tissues, it picks up waste produced by the body's cells. Your blood is like a train that comes to town to drop off supplies and take away garbage. If the waste is not removed, your body can be poisoned.

Excretion is the process of removing waste products from the body. Excretion is an important part of maintaining the body. Three of the major body systems function in excretion. Your integumentary system releases waste products and water when you sweat. Your respiratory system releases carbon dioxide and water when you exhale. Finally, your **urinary system** removes waste products from your blood.

Cleaning the Blood

As your body performs the chemical activities that keep you alive, waste products, including nitrogen-containing compounds, are made. The urinary system, shown in **Figure 1,** removes nitrogen-containing compounds and other waste products from blood to keep you healthy.

Benchmark Check What is the function of the urinary system, and why is this function important? **F.1.3.1 AA**

urinary system the organs that make, store, and eliminate urine

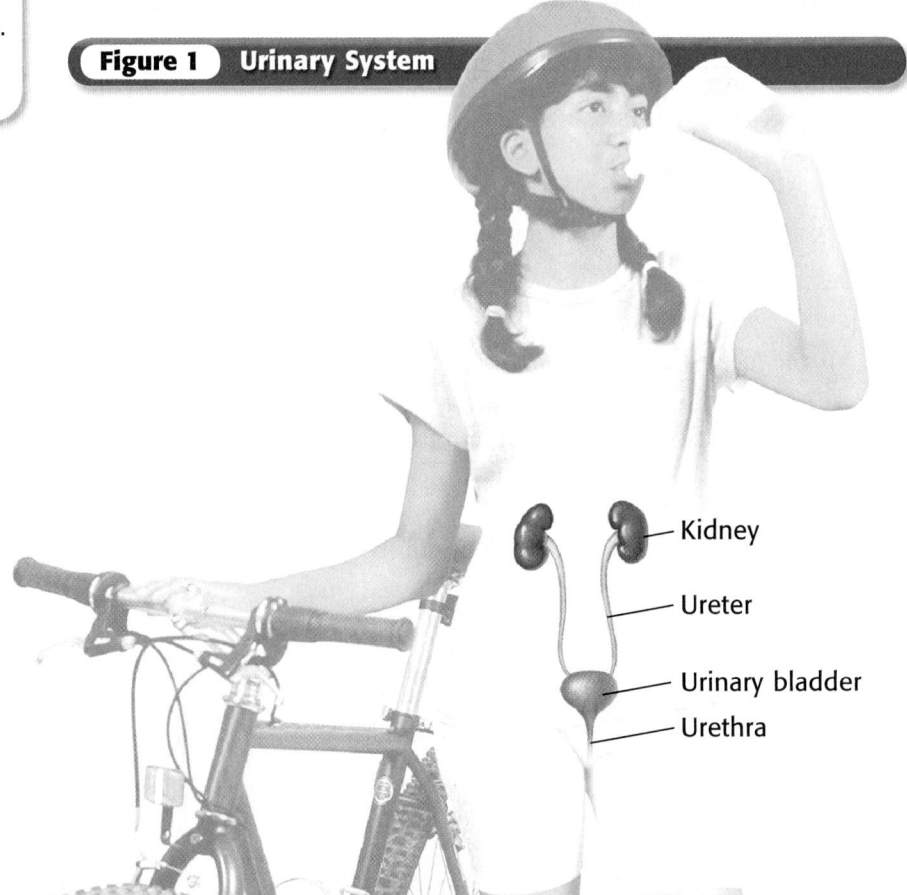

Figure 1 Urinary System

Kidney

Ureter

Urinary bladder

Urethra

F.1.3.1 AA understands that living things are composed of major systems that function in reproduction, growth, maintenance, and regulation.

The Kidneys as Filters

The **kidneys** are a pair of organs that constantly clean the blood. Your kidneys filter about 2,000 L of blood each day. Your body holds only 5.6 L of blood, so your blood cycles through your kidneys about 350 times per day!

Inside each kidney, shown in **Figure 2,** are more than 1 million nephrons. **Nephrons** are microscopic filters in the kidney that remove wastes from the blood. Nephrons remove many harmful substances. One of the most important substances removed by nephrons is urea (yoo REE uh), which contains nitrogen and is formed when cells use protein for energy.

Reading Check How are nephrons related to kidneys?

kidney one of the pair of organs that filter water and wastes from the blood and that excrete products as urine

nephron the unit in the kidney that filters blood

Figure 2 How the Kidneys Filter Blood

1 A large artery brings blood into each kidney.

2 Tiny blood vessels branch off the main artery and pass through part of each nephron.

3 Water and other small substances, such as glucose, salts, amino acids, and urea, are forced out of the blood vessels and into the nephrons.

4 As these substances flow through the nephrons, most of the water and some nutrients are moved back into blood vessels that wrap around the nephrons. A concentrated mixture of waste materials is left behind in the nephrons.

5 The cleaned blood, which has slightly less water and much less waste material, leaves each kidney in a large vein to recirculate in the body.

6 The yellow fluid that remains in the nephrons is called *urine.* Urine leaves each kidney through a slender tube called the *ureter* and flows into the *urinary bladder,* where urine is stored.

7 Urine leaves the body through another tube, called the *urethra. Urination* is the process of expelling urine from the body.

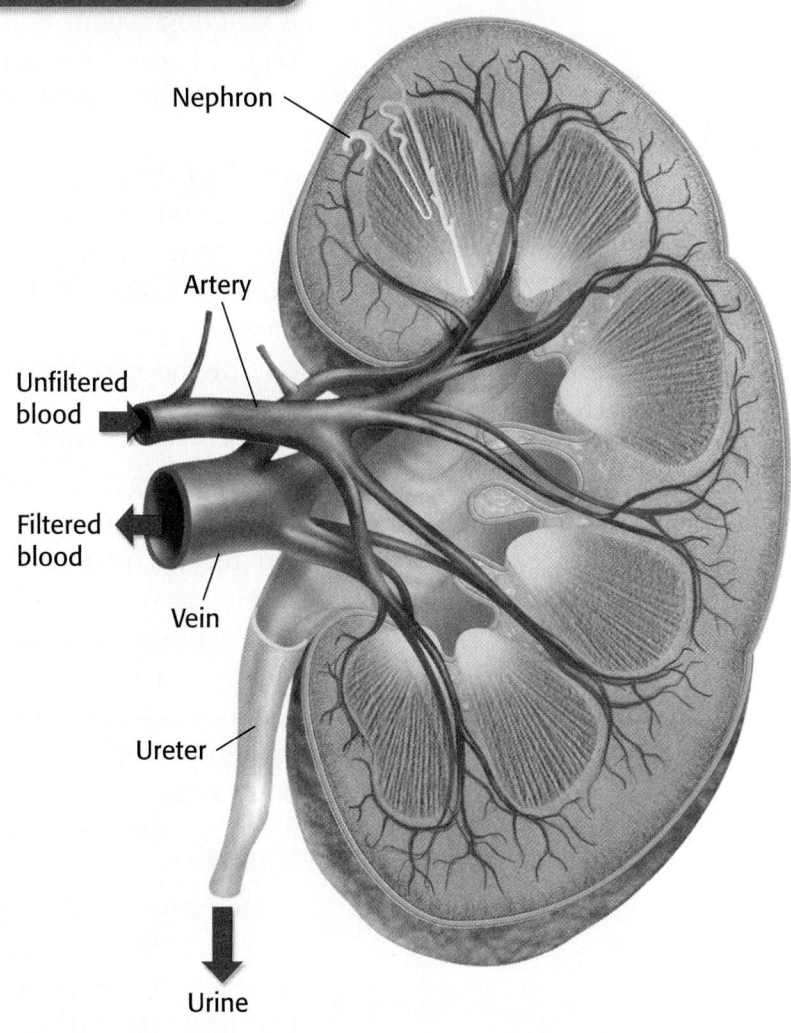

Nephron

Artery

Unfiltered blood

Filtered blood

Vein

Ureter

Urine

Figure 3 *Drinking water when you exercise helps replace the water that you lose when you sweat.*

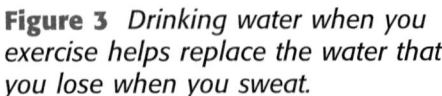
Water In, Water Out

You drink water every day. You lose water every day in sweat and urine. You need to get rid of as much water as you drink. If you don't, your body will swell up. So, how does your body keep the water levels in balance? The balance of fluids is controlled by chemical messengers in the body called *hormones*.

Sweat and Thirst

When you are too warm, as the boy in **Figure 3** is, you lose a lot of water in the form of sweat. The evaporation of water from your skin cools you down. As the water content of the blood drops, the salivary glands produce less saliva. This is one of the reasons you feel thirsty.

Antidiuretic Hormone

When you get thirsty, other parts of your body react to the water shortage, too. A hormone called *antidiuretic hormone* (AN tee DIE yoo RET ik HAWR MOHN), or ADH, is released. ADH signals the kidneys to take water from the nephrons. The nephrons return the water to the bloodstream. Thus, the kidneys make less urine. When your blood has too much water, small amounts of ADH are released. The kidneys react by allowing more water to stay in the nephrons and leave the body as urine.

Diuretics

Some beverages contain caffeine, which is a *diuretic* (DIE yoo RET ik). Diuretics cause the kidneys to make more urine, which decreases the amount of water in the blood. When you drink a beverage that contains water and caffeine, the caffeine increases fluid loss. So, your body gets to use less of the water from the caffeinated beverage than from a glass of water.

✓ Reading Check What are diuretics?

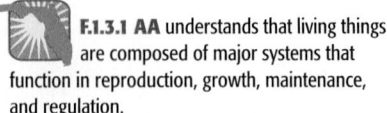
F.1.3.1 AA understands that living things are composed of major systems that function in reproduction, growth, maintenance, and regulation.

Urinary System Problems

The urinary system regulates body fluids and removes wastes from the blood. Any problems with water regulation can become dangerous for your body. Some common urinary system problems are described below.

- **Bacterial Infections** Bacteria can get into the bladder and ureters through the urethra and can cause painful infections. Infections should be treated early, before they spread to the kidneys. Infections in the kidneys can permanently damage the nephrons.

- **Kidney Stones** Sometimes, salts and other wastes collect inside the kidneys and form kidney stones like the one in **Figure 4.** Some kidney stones interfere with urine flow and cause pain. Most kidney stones pass naturally from the body, but sometimes they must be removed by a doctor.

- **Kidney Disease** Damage to nephrons can prevent normal kidney functioning and can lead to kidney disease. If a person's kidneys do not function properly, a kidney machine can be used to filter waste from the blood.

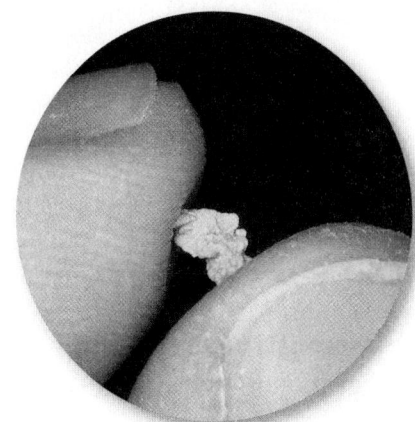

Figure 4 *This kidney stone had to be removed from a patient's urinary system.*

SECTION Review

Summary

- The integumentary, respiratory, and urinary systems excrete wastes from the body. F.I.3.1 AA
- The urinary system excretes waste in urine. Urine passes through the ureter, the bladder, and the urethra. F.I.3.1 AA
- Kidneys filter wastes from blood through nephrons. F.I.3.1 AA
- Hormones control the balance of body fluids.
- Urinary system disorders include infections, kidney stones, and kidney disease.

Using Key Terms

1. Write an original definition for *urinary system*.

Understanding Key Ideas

2. Name three body systems that excrete waste. F.I.3.1 AA

3. How does the body balance water levels?

4. How do kidneys filter blood?

5. Describe three disorders of the urinary system.

Math Skills

6. If a boy drinks 34 oz of soda per day, how many 12 oz cans of soda does he drink in a week?

Critical Thinking

7. **Applying Concepts** Which of the following contains more water: the blood going into a kidney or the blood leaving it?

FCAT Preparation

8. Excreting wastes is one way that the body maintains good health. What could happen to the body if the urinary system stopped functioning? F.I.3.1 AA

   A. Nutrients could build up and harm the body.

   B. The body could sweat a lot.

   C. Wastes could build up and harm the body.

   D. The body could absorb a lot of food.

Developed and maintained by the National Science Teachers Association

For a variety of links related to this chapter, go to www.scilinks.org
Topic: The Urinary System; Urinary System Ailments
SciLinks code: HSM1583; HSM1584

Skills Practice Lab

As the Stomach Churns

The stomach, as you know, performs not only mechanical digestion but also chemical digestion. As the stomach churns, which moves the food particles around, the digestive fluids—acid and enzymes—are added to begin protein digestion.

Commercially prepared meat tenderizers contain plant enzymes that break down, or digest, proteins. Two types of meat tenderizers are commonly available at grocery stores. One type of tenderizer contains an enzyme called *papain,* which is from papaya. Another type of tenderizer contains an enzyme called *bromelain,* which is from pineapple. In this lab, you will test the effects of these two types of meat tenderizers on beef stew meat.

OBJECTIVES

Demonstrate chemical digestion in the stomach.

Investigate three forms of chemical digestion.

MATERIALS

- beef stew meat, 1 cm cubes (3)
- eyedropper
- gloves, protective
- graduated cylinder, 25 mL
- hydrochloric acid, very dilute, 0.1 M
- measuring spoon, 1/4 tsp
- meat tenderizer, commercially prepared, containing bromelain
- meat tenderizer, commercially prepared, containing papain
- tape, masking
- test-tube marker
- test-tube rack
- test tubes (4)
- water

SAFETY

Ask a Question

❶ Determine which question you will answer through your experiment. That question may be one of the following: Which meat tenderizer will work faster? Which one will make the meat more tender? Will the meat tenderizers change the color of the meat or water? or What might these color changes, if any, indicate?

Form a Hypothesis

❷ Form a hypothesis from the question that you formed in step 1. **Caution:** Do not taste any of the materials in this activity.

Test the Hypothesis

❸ Identify all variables and controls present in your experiment. In your notebook, make a data table that includes these variables and controls. Use this data table to record your observations and results.

❹ Label one test tube with the name of one tenderizer, and label the other test tube with the name of the other tenderizer. Label the third test tube "Control." What will the test tube labeled "Control" contain?

5 Pour 20 mL of water into each test tube.

6 Use the eyedropper to add four drops of very dilute hydrochloric acid to each test tube. **Caution:** Hydrochloric acid can burn your skin. If any acid touches your skin, rinse the area with running water and tell your teacher immediately.

7 Use the measuring spoon to add 1/4 tsp of each meat tenderizer to its corresponding test tube.

8 Add one cube of beef to each test tube.

9 Record your observations for each test tube immediately, after 5 min, after 15 min, after 30 min, and after 24 h.

Analyze the Results

1 **Describing Events** Did you notice any immediate differences in the beef in the three test tubes? At what time interval did you notice a significant difference in the appearance of the beef in the test tubes? Explain the differences.

2 **Examining Data** Did one meat tenderizer perform better than the other? Explain how you determined which performed better.

Draw Conclusions

3 **Evaluating Results** Was your hypothesis supported? Explain your answer.

4 **Applying Conclusions** Many animals that sting have venom composed of proteins. Explain how applying meat tenderizer to the wound helps relieve the pain of such a sting.

Chapter Review

USING KEY TERMS

Use a term from the chapter to complete each sentence below.

1 The saclike organ at the end of the esophagus is called the ___. F.1.3.4 CS

2 The ___ is an organ that contains millions of nephrons. F.1.3.4 CS

3 The group of organs that remove waste from the blood is called the ___. F.1.3.4 CS

4 The ___ is made up of organs that work together to break down food. F.1.3.4 CS

UNDERSTANDING KEY IDEAS

Multiple Choice

5 Some hormones help maintain the body by signaling how the body should respond to changing conditions. When you do not drink enough water, the hormone ADH is released to balance the body's fluids. What does ADH make the kidneys do? F.1.3.1 AA *FCAT*

  a. ADH makes the kidneys make less urine.

  b. ADH makes the kidneys make less urea.

  c. ADH makes the kidneys make more urine.

  d. ADH makes the kidneys make more urea.

6 Which of the following organs aids digestion by producing bile? F.1.3.4 CS

  a. stomach   **c.** small intestine

  b. pancreas   **d.** liver

7 The part of the kidney that filters the blood is the

  a. artery.   **c.** nephron.

  b. ureter.   **d.** urethra.

8 Mechanical digestion includes

  a. digesting food with chemicals.

  b. crushing and mashing food.

  c. breaking molecules into nutrients.

  d. using enzymes to break nutrients into particles.

9 Removing wastes, such as urea, is an important part of maintaining the body. Urea is removed by which of the following body systems? F.1.3.1 AA *FCAT*

  a. respiratory system

  b. integumentary system

  c. urinary system

  d. digestive system

10 The stomach helps with

  a. the storage of food.

  b. chemical digestion.

  c. physical digestion.

  d. All of the above

11 The esophagus connects the

  a. pharynx to the stomach.

  b. stomach to the small intestine.

  c. kidneys to the nephrons.

  d. stomach to the large intestine.

12 Which of the following body parts is NOT a part of the digestive tract?

  a. kidney   **c.** stomach

  b. mouth   **d.** rectum

Short Answer

13 Describe how the digestive system aids in body functions such as growth and maintenance. **F.1.3.1 AA**

14 How does the structure of the small intestine help the small intestine absorb nutrients? **F.1.3.4 CS**

15 What is a kidney stone?

CRITICAL THINKING

Extended Response

16 Predicting Consequences How would digestion be affected if the liver were damaged?

17 Analyzing Processes When you put a piece of carbohydrate-rich food, such as bread, into your mouth, the food tastes bland. But if this food sits on your tongue for a while, the food will begin to taste sweet. What digestive process causes this change in taste?

18 Making Comparisons The recycling process for one kind of plastic begins with breaking the plastic into small pieces. Next, chemicals are used to break down the small pieces of plastic into its building blocks. Then, those building blocks are used to make new plastic. How is this process both like and unlike human digestion?

Concept Mapping

19 Use the following terms to create a concept map: *teeth, stomach, digestion, bile, saliva, mechanical digestion, gallbladder,* and *chemical digestion.*

INTERPRETING GRAPHICS

The bar graph below shows how long the average meal spends in each portion of your digestive tract. Use the graph below to answer the questions that follow.

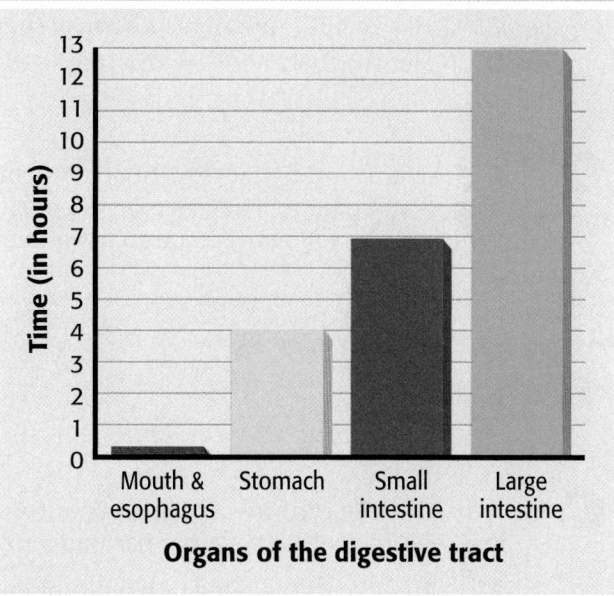

Length of Time in Digestive Organs

Time (in hours) / Organs of the digestive tract

20 In which part of your digestive tract does the food spend the longest amount of time?

21 On average, how much longer does food stay in the small intestine than in the stomach?

22 Which organ mixes food with special substances to make chyme? Approximately how long does food remain in this organ? **F.1.3.4 CS**

23 Bile breaks down large fat droplets into very small droplets. How long is the food in your body before it comes into contact with bile?

Standardized Test Preparation

For the following questions, write your answers on a separate sheet of paper.

1 Wei has been diagnosed with diabetes, so she has to be careful about eating too much sugar. Her body does not produce enough insulin to break down sugars and adequately regulate the amount of glucose in her blood. One of Wei's organs is not working well. Which of the following statements describes that organ?

    A.   Her pancreas is not making enough insulin.

    B.   Her salivary glands are breaking down the insulin too quickly.

    C.   Her smooth muscle tissue is not squeezing out enough insulin.

    D.   Her stomach acids are reacting with the insulin and neutralizing it.

2 Carlos has learned that the urinary system is an organ system that is made up of cells, tissues, and organs. The urinary system cleans blood and removes waste from the body. Which of the following is a urinary system organ that removes wastes from blood?

    F.   bladder

    G.   kidney

    H.   nephron

    I.   ureter

3 Jody has been running in a cross country race for the last hour. She has been sweating a lot and feels really thirsty. What has happened inside her body to make her feel thirsty?

    A.   Her liver is breaking down fat for energy to make more water.

    B.   Her kidneys are swelling with excess water because there is too much water.

    C.   Her sweat contains salt that has dried her skin because there is not enough water.

    D.   Her salivary glands are producing less saliva because the body is conserving water.

4 For the body to remain healthy, it requires energy and must get rid of wastes. How do the urinary system and the digestive system help perform these functions? How are these two systems different from each other?

5 Jamal's teacher has made a chart for the class describing the functions of organs of the digestive system. A section from the chart is shown below.

**COMPARING THE LIVER
AND THE PANCREAS**

	Liver	Pancreas
What the Organ Breaks Down	1. ___?___ 2. ___?___	Proteins Carbohydrates
What the Organ Produces	Bile	3. ___?___

What information belongs in the missing cells?

6 The digestive system, shown in the diagram below, is responsible for digesting food so that the body can absorb it. Digestion of food consists of mechanical and chemical digestion.

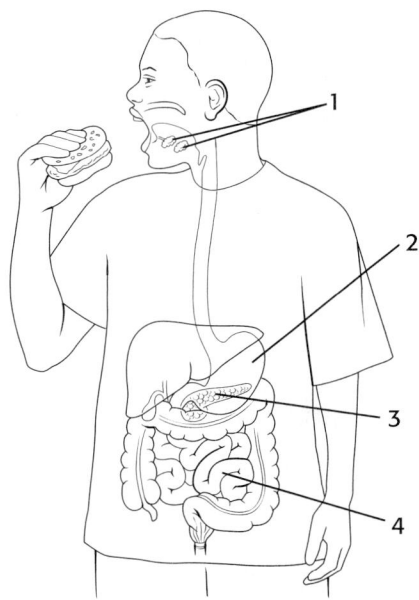

Which number indicates the organ that performs **most** of the chemical digestion of food?

F. 1
G. 2
H. 3
I. 4

Science in Action

Weird Science

Tapeworms

What would you do if you found out that you had a constant mealtime companion who didn't want just a bite but wanted it all? And what would you do if that companion never asked for your permission? This mealtime companion might be a tapeworm. Tapeworms are invertebrate flatworms. These flatworms are parasites. A parasite is an organism that obtains its food by living in or on another organism. A tapeworm doesn't have a digestive tract of its own. Instead, it absorbs the nutrients digested by the host. Some tapeworms can grow to be over 10 m long. Cooking beef, pork, and fish properly can help prevent people from getting tapeworms. People or animals who get tapeworms can be treated with medicines.

Science, Technology, and Society

Pill Cameras

Open wide, and say "Ahhhh." When you have a problem with your mouth or teeth, doctors can examine you pretty easily. But when people have problems that are farther down their digestive tract, examination becomes more difficult. So, some doctors have recently created a tiny, disposable camera that a patient can swallow. As the camera travels down the digestive tract, the camera takes pictures and sends them to a tiny recorder that the patient wears on his or her belt. The camera takes about 57,000 images during its trip. Later, doctors can review the pictures and see the pictures of the patient's entire digestive tract.

Social Studies

WRITING SKILL The World Health Organization and the Pan American Health Organization have made fighting intestinal parasites in children a high priority. Conduct library or Internet research on Worm Busters, which is a program for fighting parasites. Write a brief report of your findings.

Math ACTIVITY

If a pill camera takes 57,000 images while it travels through the digestive system and takes about two pictures per second, how many hours is the camera in the body?

Sarita Hleap-Faitelson

Medical Illustrator You have probably heard the familiar saying, "a picture is worth a thousand words." But as Sarita Hleap-Faitelson knows, pictures can also win court cases. Hleap is the president and director of Medical Illustration Services in Hallandale, Florida. Her company provides medical illustrations for the medical and legal communities. Hleap's illustrations are used as important evidence in court cases. Hleap has found that juries can better understand cases when they are shown illustrations as evidence.

Hleap creates many kinds of visual aids for trials. For example, she makes illustrations based on medical images, such as MRI scans, CT scans, and X rays, that need to be presented in court. If a concept is very complex, Hleap creates two-dimensional and three-dimensional computer animations. Hleap enjoys her job and says that she gets to use both sides of her brain. She enjoys researching medical reports to create illustrations. Even though Hleap needs to be very accurate, she can also be creative. She says that her greatest challenge is to interpret the medical reports and illustrate them clearly so that even a fourth-grade student can understand them.

Language Arts ACTiViTY

WRITING SKILL Pretend that you are going to publish an atlas of the human body. Write a classified advertisement to hire medical illustrators. Describe the job, and describe the qualities that the best candidates have. As you write the advertisement, remember that you are trying to persuade the best illustrators to contact you.

go.hrw.com

To learn more about these Science in Action topics, visit go.hrw.com and type in the keyword **HT6FBDFF**.

Current Science

Check out Current Science® articles related to this chapter by visiting go.hrw.com. Just type in the keyword HL5CS24.

Communication and Control

The Big Idea The human body has systems that respond to its internal and external environments.

About the PHOTO

This picture may look like it shows a flower garden or a coral reef. But it really shows something much closer to home. It shows the human tongue (magnified thousands of times, of course). Those round bumps are taste buds. You use taste and other senses to gather information about your surroundings.

PRE-READING ACTIVITY

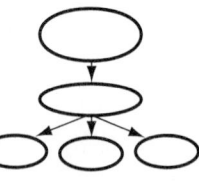
Graphic Organizer

Concept Map Before you read the chapter, create the graphic organizer entitled "Concept Map" described in the **Study Skills** section of the Appendix. As you read the chapter, fill in the concept map with details about each part or division of the nervous system. Include details about what each part or division does.

STARTUP ACTIVITY

Act Fast! F.1.3.7 CS

If you want to catch an object, your brain sends a message to the muscles in your arm. In this exercise, you will see how long sending that message takes.

Procedure

1. Sit in a **chair** with one arm in a "handshake" position. Your partner should stand facing you, holding a **meterstick** vertically. The stick should be positioned so that it will fall between your thumb and fingers.

2. Tell your partner to let go of the meterstick without warning you. Catch the stick between your thumb and fingers. Your partner should catch the meterstick if it tips over.

3. Record the number of centimeters that the stick dropped before you caught it. That distance represents your reaction time.

4. Repeat steps 1–3 three times. Calculate the average distance.

5. Repeat steps 1–4 with your other hand.

6. Trade places with your partner, and repeat steps 1–5.

Analysis

1. Compare the reaction times of your own hands. Why might one hand react more quickly than the other?

2. Compare your results with your partner's. Why might a person react more quickly than another?

The Nervous System

Which of the following activities do NOT involve your nervous system: eating, playing a musical instrument, reading a book, running, or sleeping?

This is a trick question. All of these activities involve your nervous system. In fact, your nervous system controls almost everything you do.

Two Systems Within a System

The nervous system acts as the body's central command post. It has two basic functions. First, it gathers and interprets information from inside your body and from outside your body. Then, the nervous system sends signals to the body to respond to that information appropriately. This process helps the body perform many activities such as maintenance and regulation.

The nervous system has two parts: the peripheral (puh RIF uhr uhl) nervous system and the central nervous system. The **peripheral nervous system** (PNS) is all of the parts of the nervous system except for the brain and the spinal cord. The PNS uses specialized structures, called *nerves*, to carry information between all the parts of your body and your central nervous system. The **central nervous system** (CNS) is the brain and spinal cord. The CNS processes and responds to all messages from the PNS. **Figure 1** shows the major divisions of the nervous system.

Benchmark Check What are the functions of the nervous system? **F.1.3.1 AA**

peripheral nervous system (PNS) all of the parts of the nervous system except for the brain and the spinal cord

central nervous system (CNS) the brain and the spinal cord

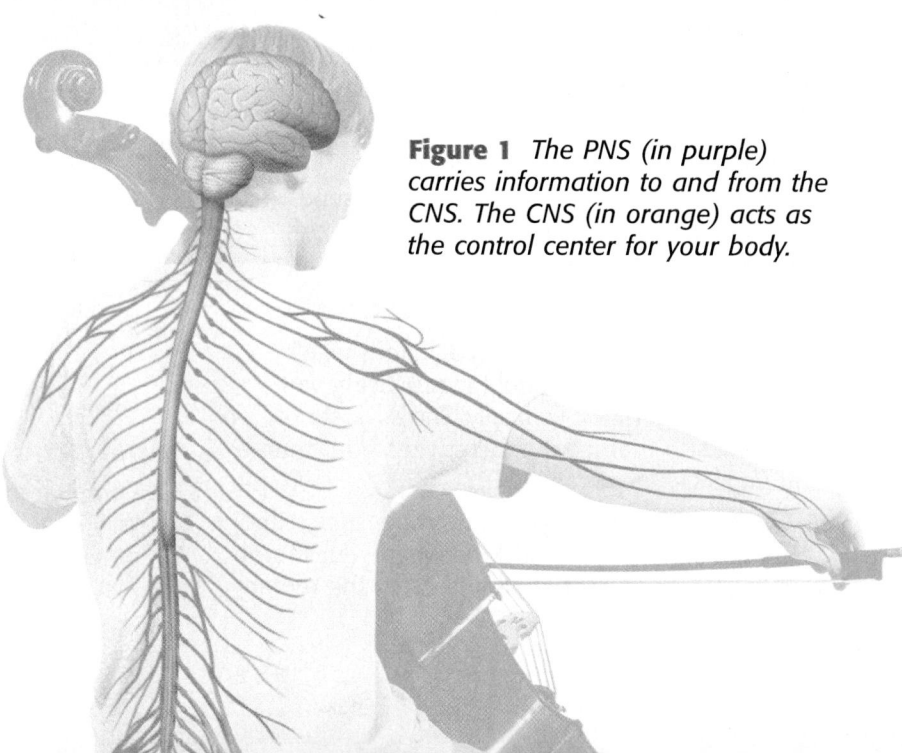

Figure 1 *The PNS (in purple) carries information to and from the CNS. The CNS (in orange) acts as the control center for your body.*

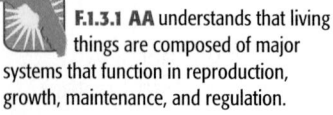
F.1.3.1 AA understands that living things are composed of major systems that function in reproduction, growth, maintenance, and regulation.

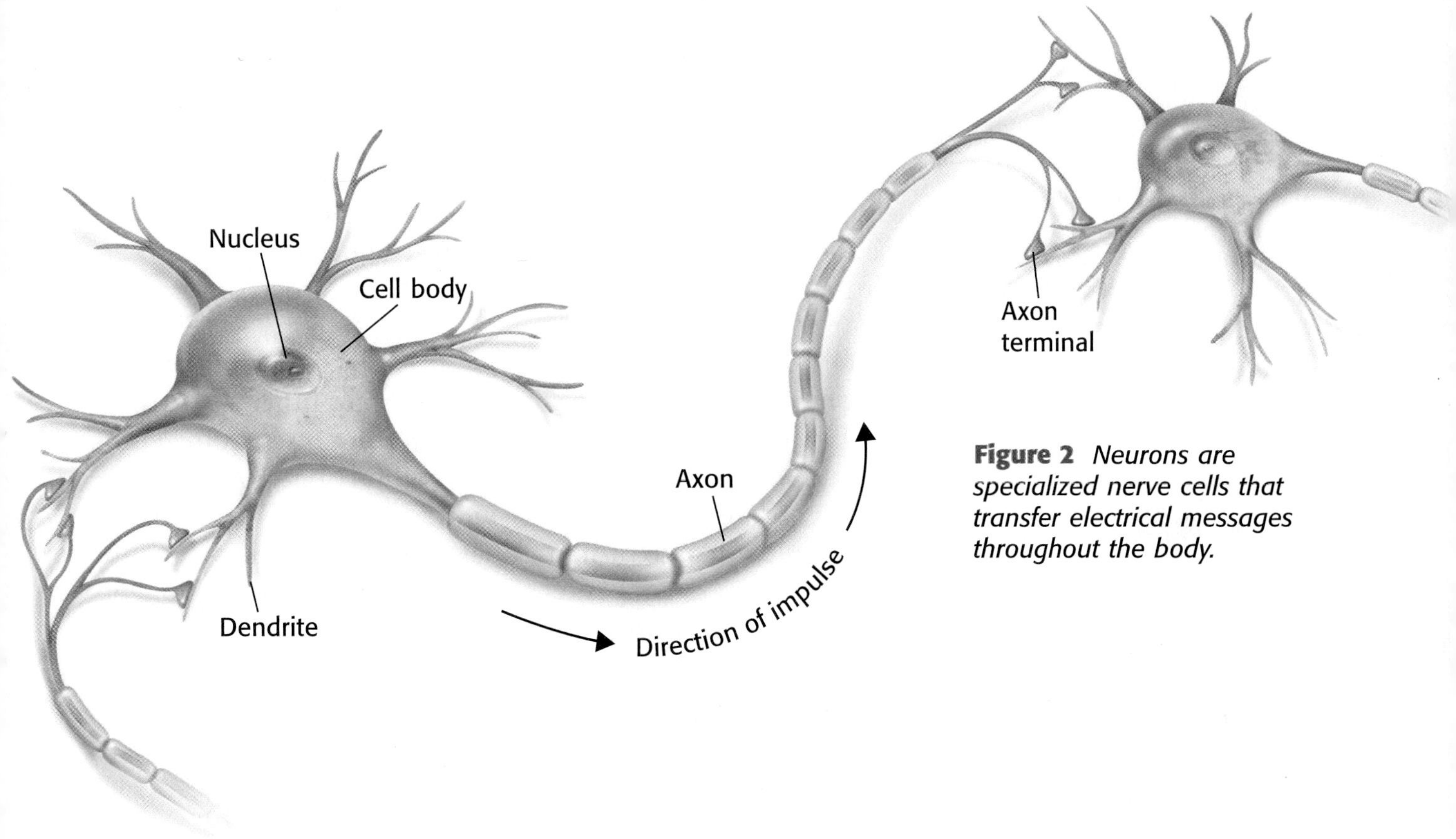

Figure 2 *Neurons are specialized nerve cells that transfer electrical messages throughout the body.*

Nucleus

Cell body

Axon
terminal

Axon

Direction of impulse

Dendrite

The Peripheral Nervous System

Messages about your environment travel through the nervous system along neurons. A **neuron** (NOO RAHN) is a specialized nerve cell that transfers messages in the form of fast-moving electrical energy. These electrical messages are called *impulses*. Impulses may travel as fast as 150 m/s or as slow as 0.2 m/s. **Figure 2** shows a typical neuron transferring an impulse.

Neuron Structure

A neuron has a large region in its center called the *cell body*. Like other cells, the cell body has a nucleus and cell organelles. But neurons also have special structures called *dendrites* and *axons*. Dendrites are usually short, branched extensions of the cell. Neurons receive information from other cells through their dendrites. A neuron may have many dendrites, which allow it to receive impulses from thousands of other cells.

Impulses are carried away from the cell body by axons. Axons are elongated extensions of a neuron. They can be very short or quite long. Some long axons extend almost 1 m from your lower back to your toes. The end of an axon often has branches that allow information to pass to other cells. The tip of each branch is called an *axon terminal*.

neuron a nerve cell that is specialized to receive and conduct electrical impulses

Time to Travel

To calculate how long an impulse takes to travel a certain distance, you can use the following equation:

$$time = \frac{distance}{speed}$$

If an impulse travels 100 m/s, about how long would it take an impulse to travel 10 m?

Information Collection

Remember that neurons are a type of nerve cell that carries impulses. Some neurons are *sensory neurons*. These neurons gather information about what is happening in and around your body. They have specialized nerve endings called *receptors*. Receptors detect changes inside and outside the body. For example, receptors in your eyes detect light. Sensory neurons then send this information to the CNS for processing.

Delivering Orders

Neurons that send impulses from the CNS to other systems are called *motor neurons*. When muscles get impulses from motor neurons, the muscles respond by contracting. For example, motor neurons cause muscles around your eyes to contract when you are in bright light. These muscles make you squint. Squinting lets less light enter the eyes. Motor neurons also send messages to your glands, such as sweat glands. These messages tell sweat glands to start or stop making sweat.

Benchmark Check Give an example of how your brain uses motor neurons to respond to the environment. **F.1.3.7 CS**

Nerves

The CNS is connected to the rest of your body by nerves. A **nerve** is a collection of axons bundled together with blood vessels and connective tissue. Most nerves have axons of both sensory neurons and motor neurons. Axons are parts of nerves, but nerves are more than just axons. **Figure 3** shows the structure of a nerve. The axon in this nerve transmits information from the spinal cord to muscle fibers.

nerve a collection of nerve fibers (axons) through which impulses travel between the central nervous system and other parts of the body

F.1.3.7 CS knows that behavior is a response to the environment and influences growth, development, maintenance, and reproduction.

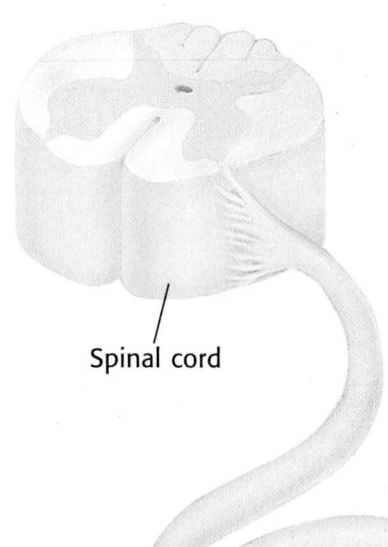

Spinal cord

Nerve

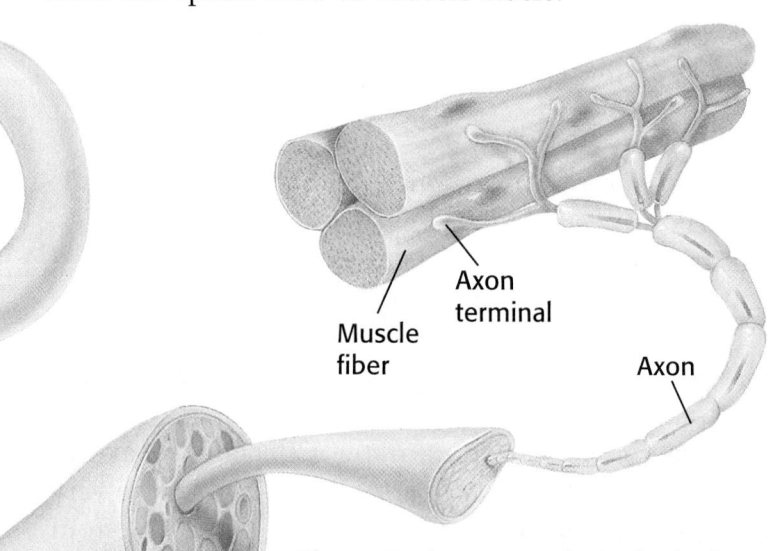

Muscle fiber

Axon terminal

Axon

Figure 3 *A message from the brain travels down the spinal cord, then along the axon of a motor neuron inside a nerve to the muscle. The message makes the muscle contract.*

Somatic and Autonomic Nervous Systems

Remember, the PNS connects your CNS to the rest of your body. And the PNS has two main parts—the sensory part (sensory neurons) and the motor part (motor neurons). You know that sensory nerves collect information from your senses and send that information to the CNS. You also know that motor nerves carry out the CNS's responses to that sensory information. To carry those responses, the motor part of the PNS has two kinds of nerves: somatic nerves and autonomic nerves.

Somatic Nervous System

Most of the neurons that are part of the *somatic nervous system* are under your conscious control. These are the neurons that stimulate skeletal muscles. They control voluntary movements, such as writing, talking, smiling, or jumping.

Autonomic Nervous System

Autonomic nerves do not need your conscious control. These neurons are part of the autonomic nervous system. The *autonomic nervous system* controls body functions that you do not think about, such as digestion and heart rate (the number of times your heart beats per minute).

The main job of the autonomic nervous system is to keep all of the body's functions in balance. Depending on the situation, the autonomic nervous system can speed up or slow down these functions. The autonomic nervous system has two divisions: the *sympathetic nervous system* and the *parasympathetic nervous system.* These two divisions work together to keep your internal environment stable, or maintain *homeostasis.* Some of these functions are shown in **Table 1.**

Benchmark Check Describe the function of the autonomic nervous system. F.I.3.1 AA

F.I.3.1 AA understands that living things are composed of major systems that function in reproduction, growth, maintenance, and regulation.

Table 1 Effects of the Autonomic Nervous System on the Body		
Organ	**Effect of sympathetic division**	**Effect of parasympathetic division**
Eyes	pupils dilate (grow larger; makes it easier to see objects)	pupils constrict (vision normal)
Heart	heart rate increases (increases blood flow)	heart rate slows (blood flow slows)
Lungs	bronchioles dilate (grow larger; increases oxygen in blood)	bronchioles constrict
Blood vessels	blood vessels dilate (increases blood flow except to digestion)	little or no effect
Intestines	digestion slows (reduces blood flow to stomach and intestines)	digestion returns to normal

The Central Nervous System

The central nervous system receives information from the sensory neurons. Then, the CNS responds by sending messages to the body through motor neurons in the PNS.

The Control Center

The largest organ in the nervous system is the brain. The **brain** is the main control center of the nervous system. Many processes that the brain controls happen automatically. These processes are called *involuntary*. For example, you could not stop digesting food even if you tried. On the other hand, some actions controlled by your brain are *voluntary*. When you want to move your arm, your brain sends signals along motor neurons to muscles in your arm. Then, the muscles contract, and your arm moves. The brain has three main parts—the cerebrum (suh REE bruhm), the cerebellum (SER uh BEL uhm), and the medulla (mi DUHL uh). Each part has its own job.

✓ *Reading Check* What is the difference between a voluntary action and an involuntary action?

The Cerebrum

The largest part of your brain is called the *cerebrum*. It looks like a mushroom cap. This dome-shaped area is where you think and where most memories are stored. It controls voluntary movements and allows you to sense touch, light, sound, odors, taste, pain, heat, and cold.

The cerebrum has two halves, called *hemispheres*. The left hemisphere directs the right side of the body, and the right hemisphere directs the left side of the body. **Figure 4** shows some of the activities that each hemisphere controls. However, most brain activities use both hemispheres.

brain the mass of nerve tissue that is the main control center of the nervous system

Brain Brochure Develop a brochure that discusses the structure and function of the human brain. Go to **go.hrw.com,** and type in the keyword **HL5BD4W.**

F.1.3.1 AA understands that living things are composed of major systems that function in reproduction, growth, maintenance, and regulation.

F.1.3.7 CS knows that behavior is a response to the environment and influences growth, development, maintenance, and reproduction.

Figure 4   The Cerebral Hemispheres

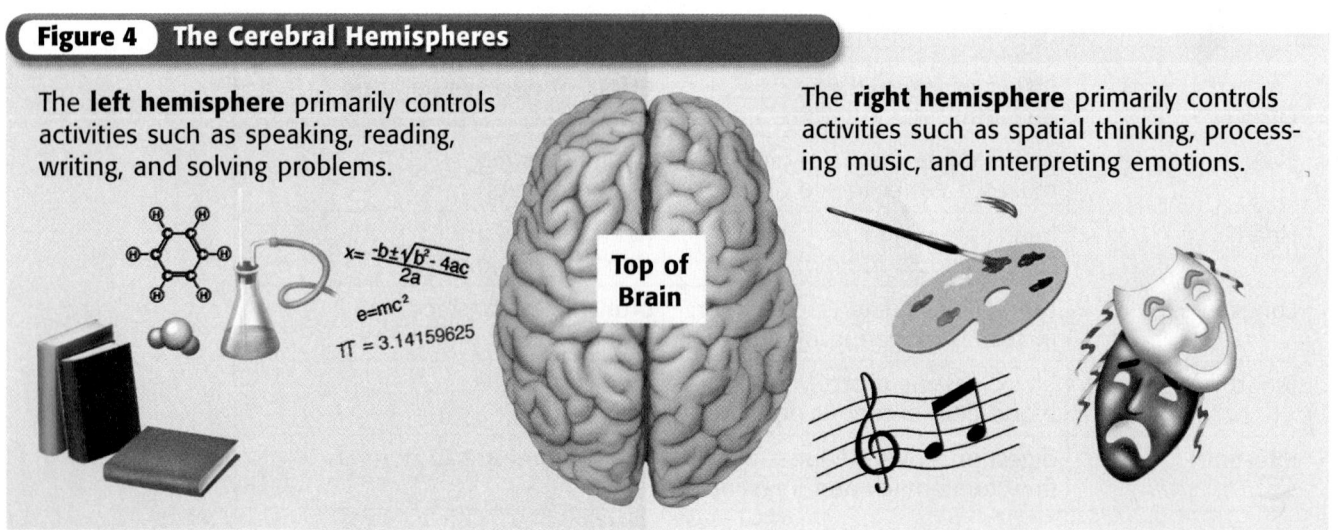

The **left hemisphere** primarily controls activities such as speaking, reading, writing, and solving problems.

The **right hemisphere** primarily controls activities such as spatial thinking, processing music, and interpreting emotions.

Top of Brain

$$x = \frac{-b \pm \sqrt{b^2 - 4ac}}{2a}$$

$$e = mc^2$$

$$\pi = 3.14159625$$

The Cerebellum

The second-largest part of your brain is the *cerebellum*. It lies beneath the back of the cerebrum. The cerebellum processes sensory information from your body, such as from skeletal muscles and joints. This allows the brain to keep track of your body's position. If you begin to lose your balance, the cerebellum sends impulses telling different skeletal muscles to contract. Those muscles shift a person's weight and keep a person, such as the girl in **Figure 5,** from losing her balance.

Figure 5 *Your cerebellum causes skeletal muscles to make adjustments so that you will stay upright.*

The Medulla

The *medulla* is the part of your brain that connects to your spinal cord. The medulla is about 3 cm long, and you cannot live without it. The medulla controls involuntary processes, which maintain and regulate your body, such as blood pressure, body temperature, heart rate, and involuntary breathing.

Your medulla constantly receives sensory impulses from receptors in your blood vessels. It uses this information to regulate your blood pressure. If your blood pressure gets too low, the medulla sends out impulses that tell blood vessels to tighten up. As a result, blood pressure rises. The medulla also sends impulses to the heart to make the heart beat faster or slower. **Figure 6** shows the location of the parts of the brain and some of the functions of each part.

Reading Check Explain why the medulla is important.

Figure 6 Areas of the Brain at Work

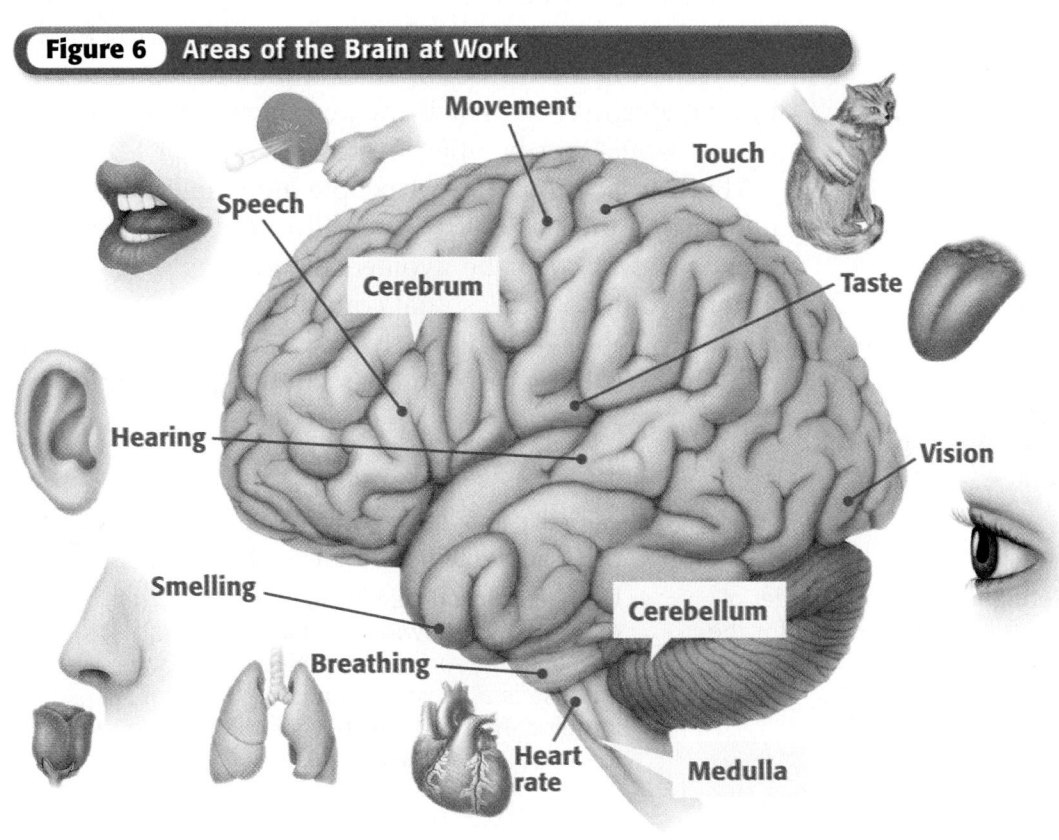

Movement
Touch
Speech
Cerebrum
Taste
Hearing
Vision
Smelling
Cerebellum
Breathing
Heart rate
Medulla

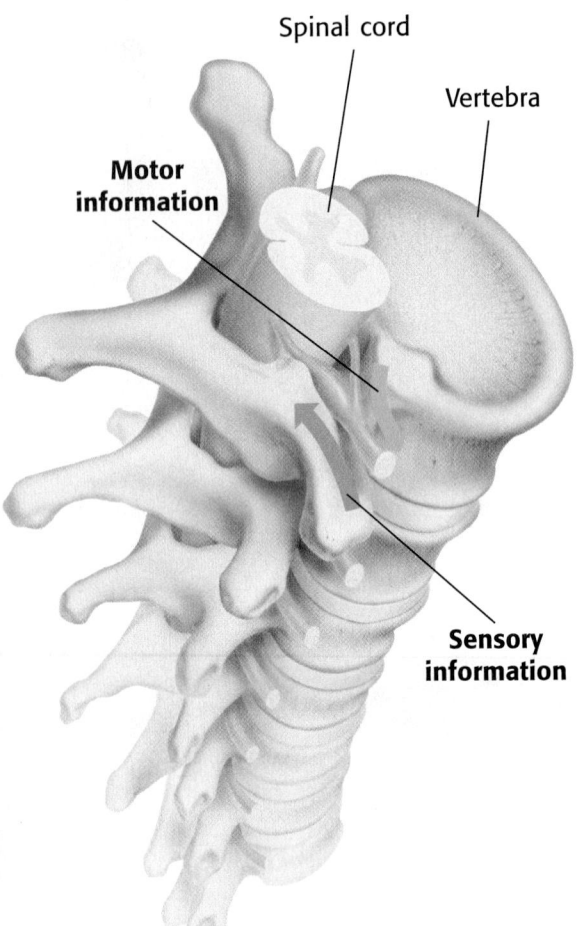

Spinal cord

Vertebra

Motor
information

Sensory
information

Figure 7 *The spinal cord carries information to and from the brain. Vertebrae protect the spinal cord.*

The Spinal Cord

Your spinal cord, which is part of your central nervous system, is about as big around as your thumb. The spinal cord is made of neurons and bundles of axons that pass impulses to and from the brain. As shown in **Figure 7,** the spinal cord is surrounded by protective bones called *vertebrae* (VUHR tuh BRAY).

The nerve fibers in your spinal cord allow your brain to communicate with your peripheral nervous system. Sensory neurons in your skin and muscles send impulses along their axons to your spinal cord. The spinal cord carries impulses to your brain. The brain interprets these impulses as pain, temperature, or other sensations. The brain then responds to the situation. Impulses moving from the brain down the spinal cord are relayed to motor neurons. Motor neurons carry the impulses along their axons to muscles and glands all over your body.

✓ **Reading Check** Describe the path of an impulse from the skin to the brain, and describe the path of the response.

Spinal Cord Injury

A spinal cord injury may block all information to and from the brain. Sensory information coming from below the injury may not get to the brain. For example, a spinal cord injury may block all sensory impulses from the feet and legs. A person with such an injury would not be able to sense pain, touch, or temperature with his or her feet. And motor commands from the brain to the injured area may not reach the peripheral nerves. So, the person would not be able to move his or her legs.

Each year, thousands of people are paralyzed by spinal cord injuries. Many of these injuries happen in car accidents and could be avoided by wearing a seat belt. Among young people, spinal cord injuries are sometimes related to sports or other activities. These injuries might be prevented by wearing proper safety equipment.

Building a Neuron

1. Your teacher will provide at least four different colors of **modeling clay.** Build a model of a neuron by using different-colored clay for the various parts of the neuron.

2. Use **tape** to attach your model neuron to a **piece of plain white paper.**

3. On the paper, label each part of the neuron. Draw an arrow from the label to the part.

4. Using a **colored pencil, marker,** or **crayon,** draw arrows showing the path of an impulse traveling in your neuron. Tell whether the impulse is a sensory impulse or a motor impulse. Then, describe what will happen when the impulse reaches its destination.

Summary

- The nervous system helps perform all activities and body functions, such as maintenance and regulation. **F.I.3.1 AA**

- The nervous system processes information and controls the body's reponse. **F.I.3.7 CS**

- The central nervous system (CNS) is made up of the brain and the spinal cord.

- The peripheral nervous system (PNS) is all the parts of the nervous system except the brain and spinal cord.

- The peripheral nervous system has nerves made up of axons of neurons.

- Sensory neuron receptors detect information from the body and its environment.

- Motor neurons carry messages from the brain and spinal cord to other parts of the body.

- The PNS has two types of motor nerves— somatic nerves and autonomic nerves.

- The cerebrum is the largest part of the brain and controls thinking, sensing, and voluntary movement. **F.I.3.7 CS**

- The cerebellum is the part of the brain that keeps track of the body's position and helps maintain balance. **F.I.3.1 AA**

- The medulla controls involuntary processes, such as heart rate, blood pressure, body temperature, and breathing. **F.I.3.1 AA**

Using Key Terms

1. Write an original definition for *neuron* and *nerve*.

2. Use *brain* and *peripheral nervous system* in the same sentence.

Understanding Key Ideas

3. Someone touches your shoulder, and you turn around. Which sequence do your impulses follow?

   a. motor neuron, sensory neuron, CNS response

   b. motor neuron, CNS response, sensory neuron

   c. sensory neuron, motor neuron, CNS response

   d. sensory neuron, CNS response, motor neuron

4. Describe one function of each part of the brain.

5. Compare the somatic nervous system with the autonomic nervous system.

Critical Thinking

6. **Applying Concepts** Some medications slow a person's nervous system. These drugs are often labeled "May cause drowsiness." Explain why a person would need to know this. **F.I.3.7 CS**

7. **Predicting Consequences** Explain how your life would change if your autonomic nervous system suddenly stopped working. **F.I.3.1 AA**

FCAT Preparation

8. Your nervous system senses information from your environment, processes that information, and then signals how your body should respond. Describe how the nervous system helps keep you cool when it is hot outside. **F.I.3.1 AA**

9. The milk you were about to drink did not smell right, so you chose not to drink it. Which of the following statements describes what happened? **F.I.3.7 CS**

   A. Your behavior was a response to the smell.

   B. Your behavior was an involuntary action.

   C. Your behavior was controlled only by your spinal cord.

   D. Your behavior was a response to what you saw.

SC**LINKS**

NSTA

Developed and maintained by the National Science Teachers Association

For a variety of links related to this chapter, go to www.scilinks.org

Topic: Nervous System

SciLinks code: HSM1023

Responding to the Environment

You feel a tap on your shoulder. Who tapped you? You turn to look, hoping to see a friend. Your senses are on the job!

The tap produces impulses in sensory receptors on your shoulder. These impulses travel to your brain. Once the impulses reach your brain, they create an awareness called a *sensation*. In this case, the sensation is of your shoulder being touched. But you still do not know who tapped you. So, you turn around. The sensory receptors in your eyes send impulses to your brain. Now, your brain recognizes your best friend.

Sense of Touch

Touch is what you feel when sensory receptors in the skin are stimulated. It is the sensation you feel when you shake hands or feel a breeze. As shown in **Figure 1,** skin has different kinds of receptors. Each kind of receptor responds mainly to one kind of stimulus. For example, *thermoreceptors* respond to temperature change. Each kind of receptor produces a specific sensation of touch, such as pressure, temperature, pain, or vibration. Skin is part of the integumentary (in TEG yoo MEN tuhr ee) system. The **integumentary system** protects the body from damage. It includes hair, skin, and nails.

✓ **Reading Check** List four conditions that your skin can detect.

READING WARM-UP

Objectives

● List four sensations to which you respond that are detected by receptors in the skin. F.1.3.7 CS

● Describe how a feedback mechanism works and helps you respond to your environment. F.1.3.7 CS

● Describe how light relates to sight.

● Describe how the senses of sight, hearing, taste, and smell work and how they help you respond to your environment. F.1.3.7 CS

Terms to Learn

integumentary system
reflex
feedback mechanism
retina
cochlea

READING STRATEGY

Reading Organizer As you read this section, create an outline of the section. Use the headings from the section in your outline.

integumentary system the organ system that forms a protective covering on the outside of the body

Figure 1 *Each type of receptor in your skin has its own structure and function.*

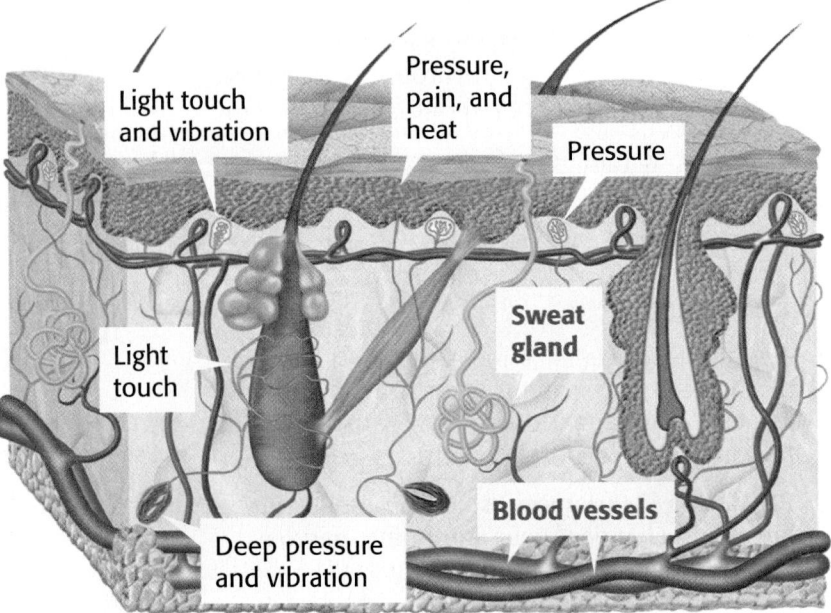

Light touch and vibration

Pressure, pain, and heat

Pressure

Light touch

Sweat gland

Blood vessels

Deep pressure and vibration

F.1.3.7 CS knows that behavior is a response to the environment and influences growth, development, maintenance, and reproduction.

Responding to Sensory Messages

When you step on something sharp, as the man in **Figure 2** did, pain receptors in your foot or toe send impulses to your spinal cord. Almost immediately, a message to move your foot travels back to the muscles in your leg and foot. Without thinking, you quickly lift your foot. This immediate, involuntary action is called a **reflex.** Your brain is not telling your leg to move. In fact, by the time the message reaches your brain, your leg and foot have already moved. If you had to wait for your brain to act, your toes might be seriously hurt!

Benchmark Check Why are reflexes important to the maintenance of your body's health? **F.1.3.7 CS**

Feedback Mechanisms

Most of the time, the brain processes information from skin receptors. For example, on a hot day, heat receptors in your skin detect an increase in your temperature. The receptors send impulses to the brain. Your brain responds by sending messages to your sweat glands to make sweat. As sweat evaporates, the body is cooled. Your brain also tells the blood vessels in your skin to dilate (open wider). Blood flow increases. Thermal energy from the blood in your skin moves to your surroundings. This process also cools your body. As your body cools, it sends messages to your brain. The brain responds by sending messages to sweat glands and blood vessels to reduce their activity.

This cooling process is one of your body's feedback mechanisms. A **feedback mechanism** is a cycle of events in which information from one step controls or affects a previous step. The temperature-regulating feedback mechanism helps keep your body temperature within safe limits. This cooling mechanism works like a thermostat on an air conditioner. Once a room reaches the right temperature, the thermostat sends a message to the air conditioner to stop blowing cold air.

reflex an involuntary and almost immediate movement in response to a stimulus

feedback mechanism a cycle of events in which information from one step controls or affects a previous step

Figure 2 *A reflex, such as lifting your foot when you step on something sharp, is one way your nervous system responds to your environment.*

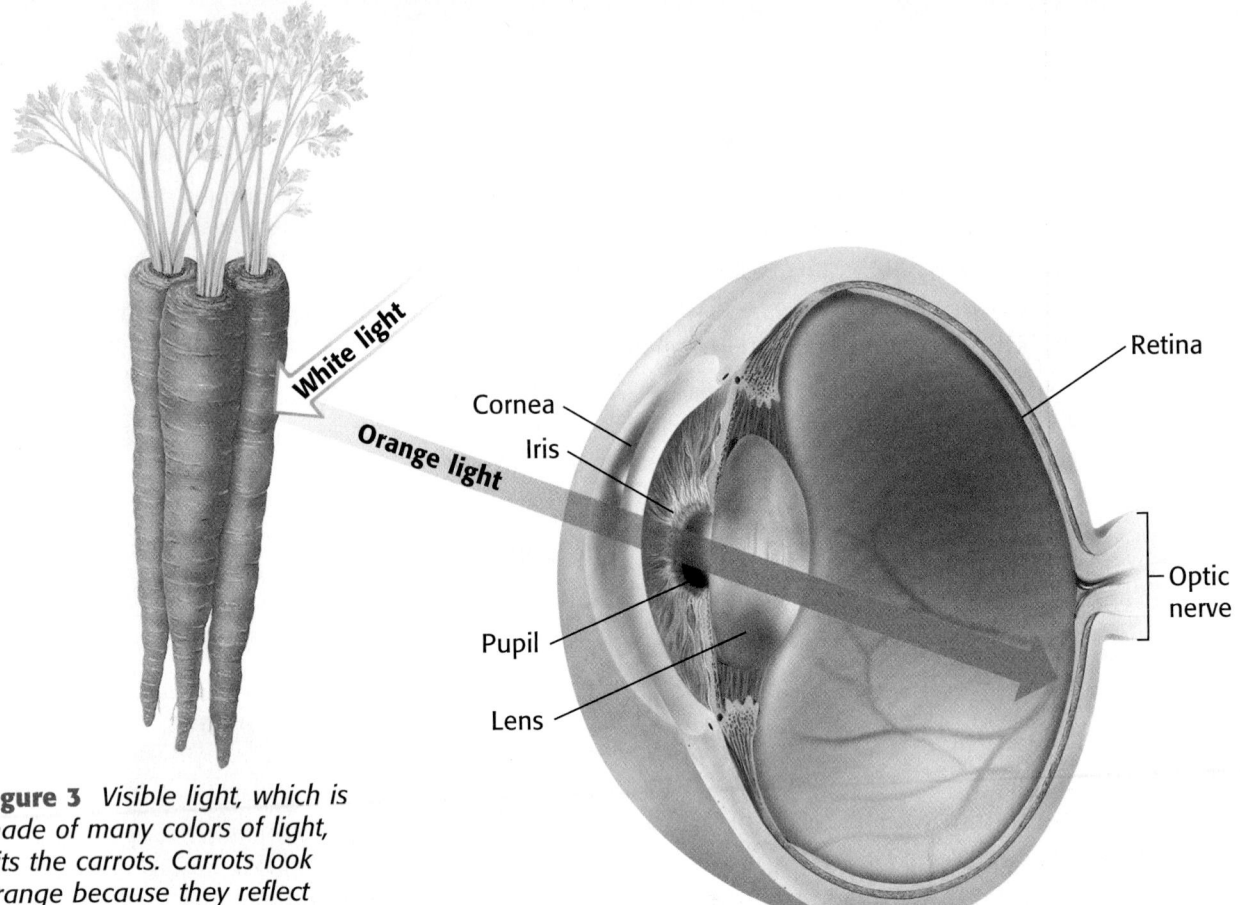

Figure 3 *Visible light, which is made of many colors of light, hits the carrots. Carrots look orange because they reflect orange light to your eyes.*

retina the light-sensitive inner layer of the eye, which receives images formed by the lens and transmits them through the optic nerve to the brain

F.1.3.7 CS knows that behavior is a response to the environment and influences growth, development, maintenance, and reproduction.

Sense of Sight

Sight is the sense that allows you to see the size, shape, motion, and color of objects around you. You see an object when it sends or reflects visible light toward your eyes. Your eyes detect this light, which enables your brain to form visual images.

Your eyes are complex sensory organs, as you can see in **Figure 3.** The front of the eye is covered by a clear membrane called the *cornea.* The cornea protects the eye but allows light to enter. Light from an object enters the front of your eye through an opening called the *pupil.* The light then travels through the lens to the back of the eye. There, the light strikes the **retina,** a layer of light-sensitive cells.

The retina is packed with photoreceptors. A *photoreceptor* is a special neuron that changes light into electrical impulses. The retina has two kinds of photoreceptors: rods and cones. Rods are very sensitive to dim light. They are important for night vision. Impulses from rods are interpreted as black-and-white images. Cones are very sensitive to bright light. Impulses from cones allow you to see fine details and colors.

Impulses from the rods and cones travel along axons. The impulses leave the back of each eye through an optic nerve. The optic nerve carries the impulses to your brain, where the impulses are interpreted as the images that you see.

Reading Check **Describe how light and sight are related.**

Reacting to Light

Your pupil looks like a black dot in the center of your eye. In fact, it is an opening that lets light enter the eye. The pupil is surrounded by the *iris,* a ring of muscle. The iris controls the amount of light that enters the eye and gives the eye its color. In bright light, the iris contracts, which makes the pupil smaller. A smaller pupil reduces the amount of light entering the eye and passing onto the retina. In dim light, the iris opens the pupil and lets in more light.

Reading Check How does your iris react to bright light?

Focusing the Light

Light travels in straight lines until it passes through the cornea and the lens. The *lens* is an oval-shaped piece of clear, curved material behind the iris. Muscles in the eye change the shape of the lens in order to focus light onto the retina. When you look at objects close to the eye, the lens becomes more curved. When you look at objects far away, the lens gets flatter.

Figure 4 shows some common vision problems. In some eyes, the lens focuses the light in front of the retina, which results in nearsightedness. If the lens focuses the light just behind the retina, the result is farsightedness. Glasses, contact lenses, or surgery can usually correct these vision problems.

Where's the Dot?

1. Hold your **book** at arm's length, and close your right eye. Focus your left eye on the black dot below.

2. Slowly move the book toward your face until the white dot disappears. You may need to try a few times to get this result. The white dot doesn't always disappear for every person.

3. Describe your observations.

4. Use the library or the Internet to research the optic nerve and to find out why the white dot disappears.

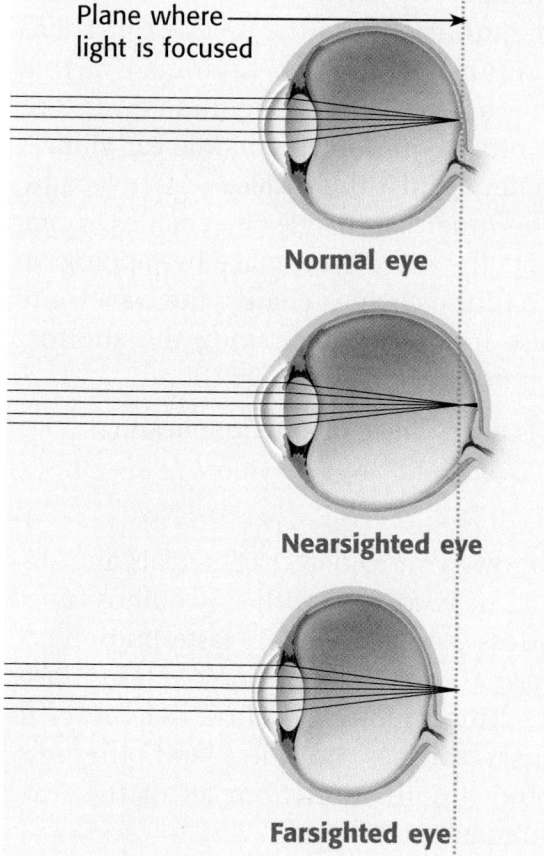

Normal eye

Nearsighted eye

Farsighted eye

Figure 4 *A concave lens bends light rays outward to correct nearsightedness. A convex lens bends light rays inward to correct farsightedness.*

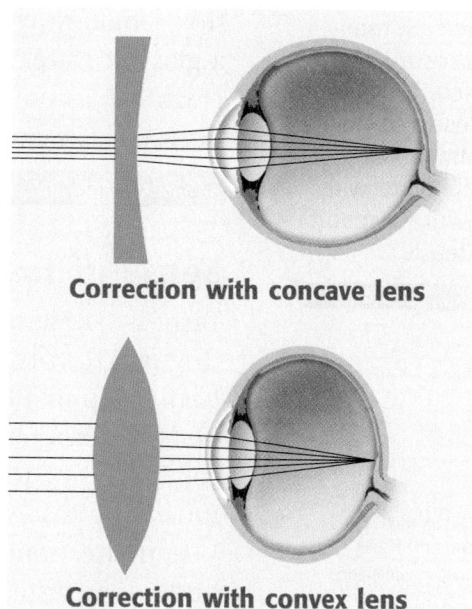

Correction with concave lens

Correction with convex lens

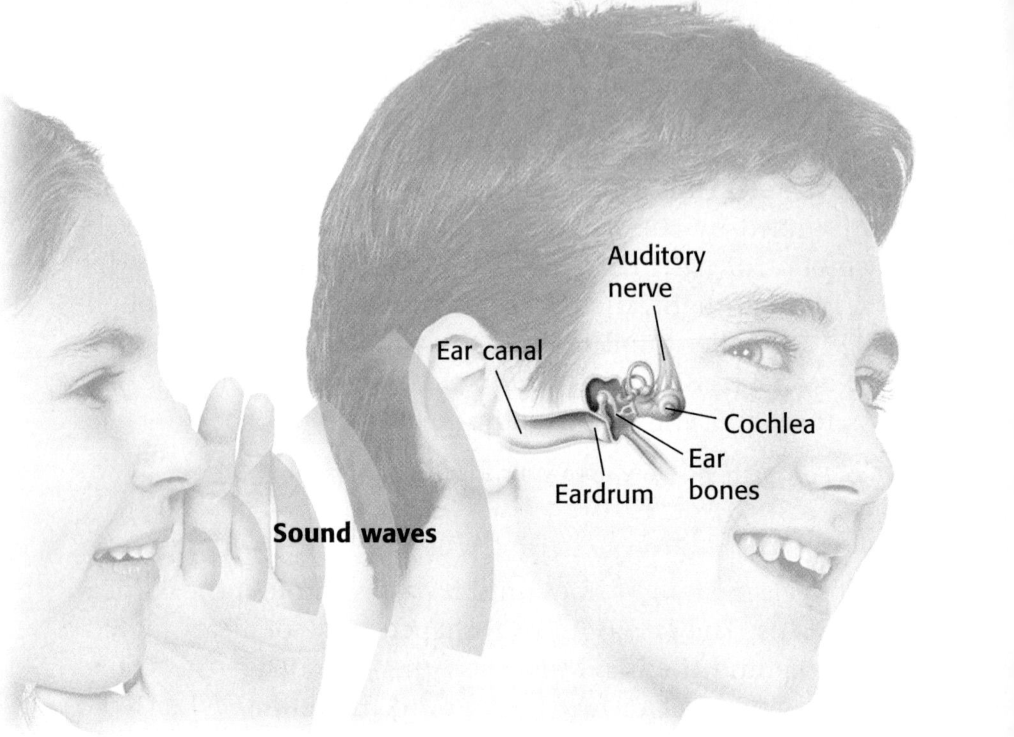

Figure 5 *A sound wave travels into the outer ear. It is converted into bone vibrations in the middle ear, then into liquid vibrations in the inner ear, and finally, into nerve impulses that travel to the brain.*

cochlea a coiled tube that is found in the inner ear and that is essential to hearing

CONNECTION TO Physics

WRITING SKILL **Elephant Talk** Sound is produced by vibrating objects. Some sounds, called *infrasonic sounds*, are too low for human ears to detect. Research how elephants use infrasonic sounds to communicate with each other, and write a report about what you learn.

F.1.3.7 CS knows that behavior is a response to the environment and influences growth, development, maintenance, and reproduction.

Sense of Hearing

Sound is produced when something, such as a drum, vibrates. Vibrations push on nearby air particles, which push on other air particles. The vibrations create waves of sound energy. Hearing is the sense that allows you to experience sound energy.

Ears are organs specialized for hearing, as shown in **Figure 5.** Each ear has an outer, middle, and inner portion. Sound waves reaching the outer ear are funneled into the middle ear. There, the waves make the eardrum vibrate. The eardrum is a thin membrane separating the outer ear from the middle ear. The vibrating eardrum makes tiny bones in the middle ear vibrate. One of these bones vibrates against the **cochlea** (KAHK lee uh), a fluid-filled organ of the inner ear. Inside the cochlea, vibrations make waves just like the waves you make by tapping on a glass of water. Neurons in the cochlea change the waves into electrical impulses. These impulses travel along the auditory nerve to the area of the brain that interprets sound.

✔ *Reading Check* **Why is the cochlea important to hearing?**

Sense of Taste

Taste is the sense that allows you to detect chemicals and distinguish flavors. Your tongue is covered with tiny bumps called *papillae* (puh PIL ee). Most papillae contain taste buds. Taste buds contain clusters of *taste cells,* the receptors for taste. Taste cells respond to dissolved food molecules. Taste cells react to four basic tastes: sweetness, sourness, saltiness, and bitterness. When the brain combines information from all of the taste buds, you taste a "combination" flavor.

Sense of Smell

As you can see in **Figure 6,** receptors for smell are located on *olfactory cells* in the upper part of your nasal cavity. An olfactory cell is a nerve cell that responds to chemical molecules in the air. You smell something when the receptors react to molecules that have been inhaled. The molecules dissolve in the moist lining of the nasal cavity and trigger an impulse. Olfactory cells send those impulses to the brain, which interprets the impulses as odors.

Taste buds and olfactory cells both detect dissolved molecules. Your brain combines information from both senses to give you sensations of flavor.

Figure 6 *Olfactory cells line the nasal cavity. These cells are sensory receptors that react to chemicals in the air.*

Brain

Olfactory cell

Nasal passage

SECTION Review

Summary

- Touch allows you to respond to temperature, pressure, pain, and vibration on the skin. **F.I.3.7 CS**
- Reflexes and feedback mechanisms help you respond to your environment. **F.I.3.7 CS**
- Sight allows you to respond to light energy. **F.I.3.7 CS**
- Hearing allows you to respond to sound energy. **F.I.3.7 CS**
- Taste allows you to distinguish and respond to flavors. **F.I.3.7 CS**
- Smell allows you to perceive and respond to different odors. **F.I.3.7 CS**

Using Key Terms

1. Write an original definition for *reflex* and *feedback mechanism.*

Understanding Key Ideas

2. Three sensations that receptors in the skin detect are
   a. light, smell, and sound.
   b. touch, pain, and odors.
   c. temperature, pressure, and pain.
   d. pressure, sound, and touch.

3. Explain how light and sight are related.

4. Describe how your senses of hearing, taste, and smell work.

5. Describe how the feedback mechanism that regulates body temperature works. **F.I.3.7 CS**

Critical Thinking

6. **Making Inferences** Why is it important for the human body to have reflexes? **F.I.3.7 CS**

7. **Applying Concepts** Rods help you detect objects and shapes in dim light. Explain why it is important for human eyes to have both rods and cones. **F.I.3.7 CS**

FCAT Preparation

8. While riding a bicycle, you see a tree branch lying in your path and ride around it. Your eye transmitted electrical impulses to our brain. Your brain then interpreted the information to help you respond. How does your sight help you? **F.I.3.7 CS**
   A. Sight helps you see and avoid dangers.
   B. Sight allows you to sense changes in pressure.
   C. Sight helps increase the speed of your reflexes.
   D. Sight allows you to sense changes in temperature.

SCiLINKS®

Developed and maintained by the National Science Teachers Association

For a variety of links related to this chapter, go to www.scilinks.org

Topic: The Senses; The Eye
SciLinks code: HSM1378; HSM0560

The Endocrine System

Have you ever heard of an epinephrine (EP uh NEPH rin) rush? You might have had one without realizing it. Exciting situations, such as riding a roller coaster or watching a scary movie, can cause your body to release epinephrine.

Epinephrine is one of the body's chemical messengers made by the endocrine system. Your endocrine system regulates body processes, such as fluid balance, growth, and development.

Hormones as Chemical Messengers

The **endocrine system** controls body functions by using chemicals that are made by the endocrine glands. A **gland** is a group of cells that make special chemicals for your body. Chemical messengers made by the endocrine glands are called *hormones*. A **hormone** is a chemical messenger made in one cell or tissue that causes a change in another cell or tissue in another part of the body. Hormones flow through the bloodstream to all parts of the body. Thus, an endocrine gland near your brain can control an organ that is somewhere else in your body.

Endocrine glands may affect many organs at one time. For example, in the situation shown in **Figure 1,** the adrenal glands release the hormone *epinephrine*, which is sometimes called *adrenaline*. Epinephrine increases your heartbeat and breathing rate. This response is called the "fight-or-flight" response. When you are frightened, angry, or excited, the "fight-or-flight" response prepares you to fight the danger or to run from it.

endocrine system a collection of glands and groups of cells that secrete hormones that regulate growth, development, and homeostasis

gland a group of cells that make special chemicals for the body

hormone a substance that is made in one cell or tissue and that causes a change in another cell or tissue in a different part of the body

Figure 1 *When you have to move quickly to avoid danger, your adrenal glands make more blood glucose available for energy.*

More Endocrine Glands

Your body has several other endocrine glands. Some of these glands have many functions. For example, your pituitary gland stimulates skeletal growth and helps the thyroid gland work properly. It also regulates the amount of water in the blood. And the pituitary gland stimulates the birth process in women.

Your thyroid gland is very important during infancy and childhood. Thyroid hormones control the secretion of growth hormones for normal body growth. Thyroid hormones also control the development of the central nervous system. And they control your metabolism. *Metabolism* is the sum of all the chemical processes that take place in an organism.

Your thymus gland is important to your immune system. Cells called *killer T cells* grow and mature in the thymus gland. These T cells help destroy or neutralize cells or substances that invade your body. The names and some of the functions of endocrine glands are shown in **Figure 2**.

Benchmark Check Describe the function and importance of an endocrine system gland that helps the body respond to a change in the environment. **F.1.3.1 AA, F.1.3.7 CS**

Benchmark Activity

WRITING SKILL **Fight or Flight?** Write a paragraph describing fight-or-flight experience you have had. Explain how your body felt and which of your organ systems helped you respond. Include how your behavior was a response to your environment and whether or not your response helped you stay healthy. **F.1.3.7 CS**

F.1.3.1 AA understands that living things are composed of major systems that function in reproduction, growth, maintenance, and regulation.

F.1.3.7 CS knows that behavior is a response to the environment and influences growth, development, maintenance, and reproduction.

Figure 2 **Endocrine Glands and Their Functions**

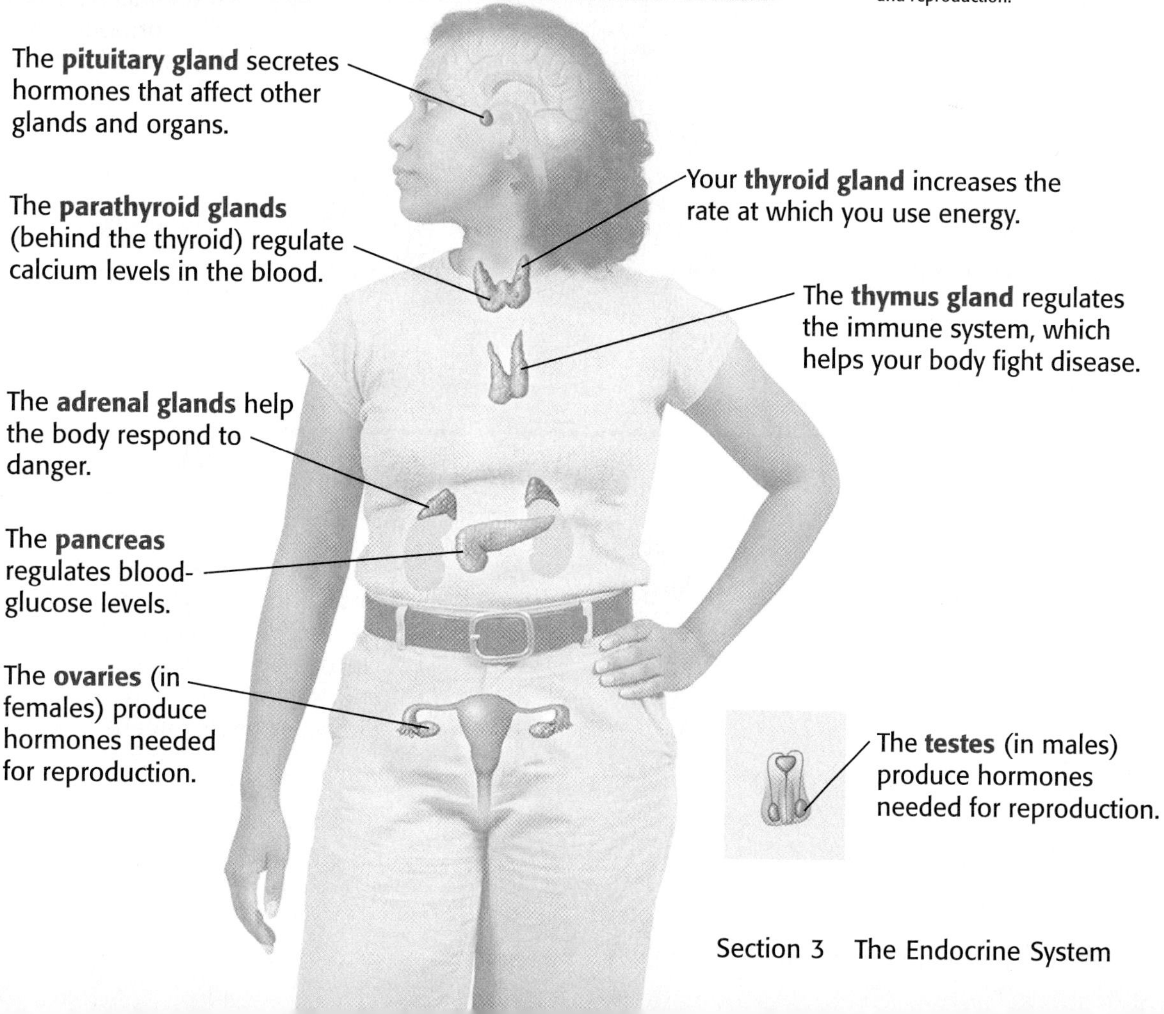

The **pituitary gland** secretes hormones that affect other glands and organs.

The **parathyroid glands** (behind the thyroid) regulate calcium levels in the blood.

The **adrenal glands** help the body respond to danger.

The **pancreas** regulates blood-glucose levels.

The **ovaries** (in females) produce hormones needed for reproduction.

Your **thyroid gland** increases the rate at which you use energy.

The **thymus gland** regulates the immune system, which helps your body fight disease.

The **testes** (in males) produce hormones needed for reproduction.

Controlling the Endocrine Glands

Do you remember the feedback mechanisms at work in the nervous system? Endocrine glands control similar feedback mechanisms. For example, the pancreas has specialized cells that make two different hormones, *insulin* and *glucagon*. As shown in **Figure 3,** these two hormones regulate and maintain the level of glucose in the blood. Insulin lowers blood-glucose levels by telling the liver to convert glucose into glycogen and to store glycogen for future use. Glucagon has the opposite effect. It tells the liver to convert glycogen into glucose and to release the glucose into the blood.

✓ Reading Check What does insulin do?

F.1.3.1 AA understands that living things are composed of major systems that function in reproduction, growth, maintenance, and regulation.

F.1.3.7 CS knows that behavior is a response to the environment and influences growth, development, maintenance, and reproduction.

Figure 3 **Blood-Glucose Feedback Control**

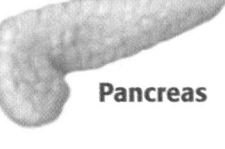

5b Sometimes, to raise your blood-glucose level, you must eat something.

1 Glucose is fuel for your body. Glucose is absorbed into the bloodstream from the small intestine.

5a If your blood-glucose falls too far, glucagon tells the liver to break down glycogen and release the glucose into your blood.

2 When the glucose level in the blood is high, such as after a meal, the pancreas releases the hormone insulin into the blood.

Pancreas

Pancreas

4 When the pancreas detects that your blood-glucose level has returned to normal, it stops releasing insulin.

3 Insulin signals the liver to take in glucose from the blood, convert the glucose into glycogen, and to store glycogen for future energy needs.

Liver

Hormone Imbalances

Occasionally, an endocrine gland makes too much or not enough of a hormone. For example, when a person's blood-glucose level rises, the pancreas secretes insulin. Insulin sends a message to the liver to convert glucose into glycogen. The liver stores glycogen for future use. But a person whose body does not use insulin properly or whose pancreas does not make enough insulin has a condition called *diabetes mellitus* (DIE uh BEET EEZ muh LIET uhs). A person who has diabetes may need daily injections of insulin to keep his or her blood-glucose levels within safe limits. Some patients, such as the woman in **Figure 4,** receive their insulin automatically from a small machine worn next to the body.

Another hormone imbalance is when a child's pituitary gland does not make enough growth hormone. As a result, the child's growth is stunted. Fortunately, if the problem is detected early, a doctor can prescribe growth hormone and monitor the child's growth. If the pituitary gland makes too much growth hormone, a child may grow taller than expected.

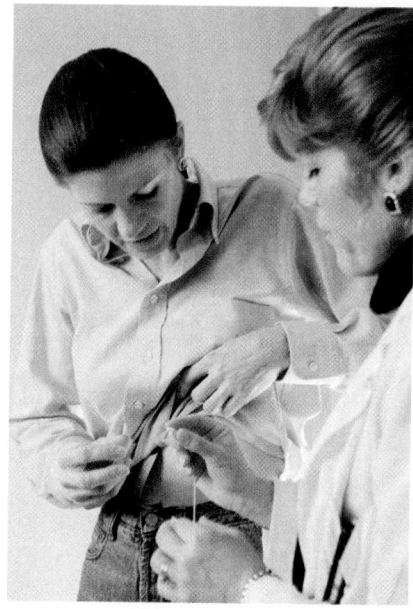

Figure 4 *This woman has diabetes and receives insulin from a device that also monitors her blood-glucose level.*

SECTION Review

Summary

- Glands in the endocrine system use chemical messengers called *hormones* to regulate and maintain homeostasis. **F.I.3.1 AA**

- Hormones help the body respond to the environment. **F.I.3.7 CS**

- Feedback mechanisms tell endocrine glands when to turn hormones on and off.

- A hormone imbalance is when a gland releases too much or too little of a hormone.

Using Key Terms

1. Use *endocrine system, glands,* and *hormone* in the same sentence.

Understanding Key Ideas

2. Identify five endocrine glands. Explain why their hormones are important to your body. **F.I.3.1 AA**

3. An insulin imbalance can cause
   a. allergies.
   b. diabetes.
   c. stunted growth.
   d. difficulty breathing.

4. How do feedback mechanisms control hormone production?

Critical Thinking

5. **Making Inferences** Glucose is a source of energy. Epinephrine can quickly increase the blood-glucose level when necessary. Why is epinephrine important in times of stress? **F.I.3.1 AA, F.I.3.7 CS**

FCAT Preparation

6. The endocrine system is composed of many glands that release hormones into the bloodstream. Under which of the following conditions would your adrenal glands release adrenaline to keep you safe? **F.I.3.1 AA, F.I.3.7 CS**

   A. when you are asleep
   B. when you are reading
   C. when you are painting
   D. when you are afraid

Developed and maintained by the National Science Teachers Association

For a variety of links related to this chapter, go to www.scilinks.org

Topic: Hormones; Endocrine System
SciLinks code: HSM0758; HSM0504

Skills Practice Lab

You've Gotta Lotta Nerve

Your skin has thousands of nerve receptors that detect sensations, such as temperature, pain, and pressure. Your brain is designed to filter out or ignore most of the input it receives from these skin receptors. If the brain did not filter input, simply wearing clothes would trigger so many responses that you couldn't function.

Some areas of the skin, such as the back of your hand, are more sensitive than others. In this activity, you will map the skin receptors for heat, cold, and pressure on the back of your hand.

OBJECTIVES

Locate areas on the skin that respond to certain stimuli.

Determine which areas on the skin are more sensitive to certain kinds of stimuli.

MATERIALS

- dissecting pin with a small piece of cork or a small rubber stopper covering the sharp end
- eyedropper, plastic
- paper, graphing
- pens or markers, washable, fine point
- ruler, metric
- tap water, hot
- water, very cold

SAFETY

Procedure

1. Form a group of three. One of you will volunteer the back of your hand for testing, one will do the testing, and the third will record the results.

2. Use a fine-point, washable marker or pen and a metric ruler to mark a 3 cm × 3 cm square on the back of one person's hand. Draw a grid within the area. Space the lines approximately 0.5 cm apart. You will have 36 squares in the grid when you are finished, as shown in the photograph below.

3. Mark off three 3 cm × 3 cm areas on a piece of graph paper. Make a grid in each area exactly as you did on the back of your partner's hand. Label one grid "Cold," another grid "Hot," and the third grid "Pressure."

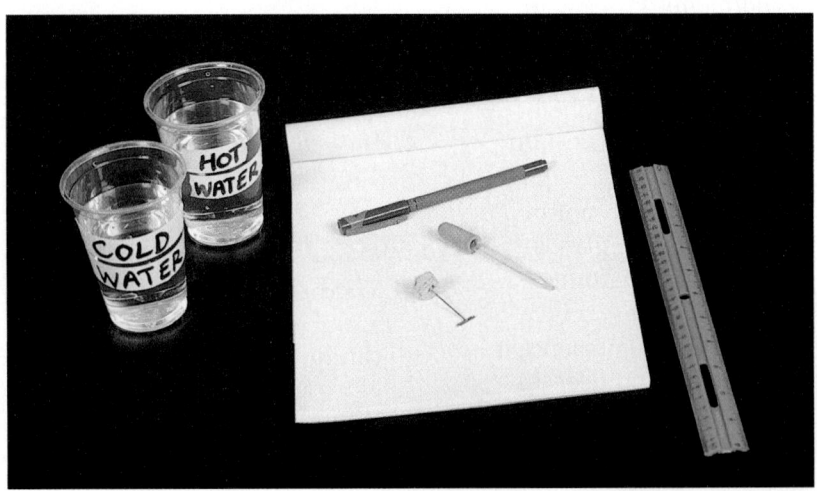

4. Use the eyedropper to apply one small droplet of cold water on each square in the grid on your partner's hand. Your partner should turn away while being tested. On your graph paper, mark an X on the "Cold" grid to show where your partner felt the cold droplet. Carefully blot the water off your partner's hand after several drops.

5. Repeat the test using hot-water droplets. The hot water should not be hot enough to hurt your partner. Mark an X on the "Hot" grid to indicate where your partner felt the hot droplet.

6. Repeat the test by using the head (not the point!) of the pin. Touch the skin to detect pressure receptors. Use a very light touch. On the graph paper, mark an X on the "Pressure" grid to indicate where your partner felt the pressure.

Analyze the Results

1. **Organizing Data** Count the number of Xs in each grid. How many heat receptor responses are there per 3 cm^2? How many cold receptor responses are there? How many pressure receptor responses are there?

2. **Explaining Events** Do you have areas on the back of your hand where the receptors overlap? Explain your answer.

3. **Recognizing Patterns** How do you think the results of this experiment would be similar or different if you mapped an area of your forearm? of the back of your neck? of the palm of your hand?

Draw Conclusions

4. **Interpreting Information** Prepare a written report that includes a description of your investigation and a discussion of your answers to items 1–3. What conclusions can you draw from your results?

Applying Your Data

Use the library or the Internet to research what happens if a receptor is continuously stimulated. Does the kind of receptor make a difference? Does the intensity or strength of the stimulus make a difference? Explain your answers.

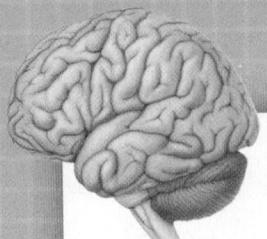

Chapter Review

USING KEY TERMS

Use a term from the chapter to complete each sentence below.

1 The two parts of the ___ are the brain and spinal cord.

2 Sensory receptors in the ___ detect light.

3 Epinephrine is a(n) ___ that triggers the fight-or-flight response.

4 A(n) ___ is an involuntary and almost immediate movement in response to a stimulus. **F.1.3.7 CS**

5 A(n) ___ is a specialized cell that receives and conducts electrical impulses.

UNDERSTANDING KEY IDEAS

Multiple Choice

6 Tina is hiking. She becomes frightened when she sees a snake on the trail, and her heart rate increases. What causes Tina's heart rate to increase? **F.1.3.7 CS** *FCAT*

a. the fluids in her inner ear
b. the brightness of the light
c. the fight-or-flight response
d. thermoreceptors in her skin

7 Which of the following have receptors for smelling?

a. cochlea cells
b. thermoreceptors
c. olfactory cells
d. optic nerves

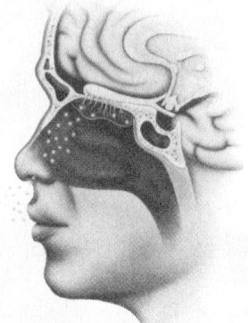

8 Which of the following allow you to see the world in color?

a. cones   c. lenses
b. rods   d. retinas

9 Sweat glands in your skin secrete more sweat when your body is hot. What causes sweat glands to do this? **F.1.3.1 AA** *FCAT*

a. Sweat glands produce sweat as a reflex.
b. Your brain signals the sweat glands to secrete sweat to cool your body.
c. Blood vessels in the skin dilate and push sweat out of sweat glands.
d. Skin muscles contract and squeeze sweat out of sweat glands.

10 The peripheral nervous system does NOT include

a. the spinal cord.
b. axons.
c. sensory receptors.
d. motor neurons.

11 Which part of the brain regulates blood pressure?

a. the right cerebral hemisphere
b. the left cerebral hemisphere
c. the cerebellum
d. the medulla

12 The process in which the endocrine system, the digestive system, and the cardiovascular system control the level of blood glucose is an example of

a. a reflex.
b. an endocrine gland.
c. the fight-or-flight response.
d. a feedback mechanism.

Short Answer

13 What is the difference between the somatic nervous system and the autonomic nervous system? Why are both systems important to the body? **F.1.3.1 AA**

14 Why is the endocrine system important to your body? **F.1.3.1 AA**

15 What is the relationship between the CNS and the PNS?

16 What is the function of the bones in the middle ear?

17 Describe two interactions between the endocrine system and the body that happen when a person is frightened. **F.1.3.7 CS**

18 Name the parts of the brain, and give a function of each part.

CRITICAL THINKING

Extended Response

19 **Making Comparisons** Compare a feedback mechanism with a reflex.

20 **Analyzing Ideas** Why is it important to have a lens that can change shape inside the eye?

21 **Applying Concepts** Why is it important that reflexes happen without a person thinking about them? **F.1.3.1 AA**

22 **Predicting Consequences** What would happen if you could not produce growth hormones or insulin? **F.1.3.1 AA**

23 **Making Comparisons** Compare the nervous system to the endocrine system.

Concept Mapping

24 Use the following terms to create a concept map: *nervous system, spinal cord, medulla, peripheral nervous system, brain, cerebrum, central nervous system,* and *cerebellum*.

INTERPRETING GRAPHICS

Use the diagram below to answer the questions that follow.

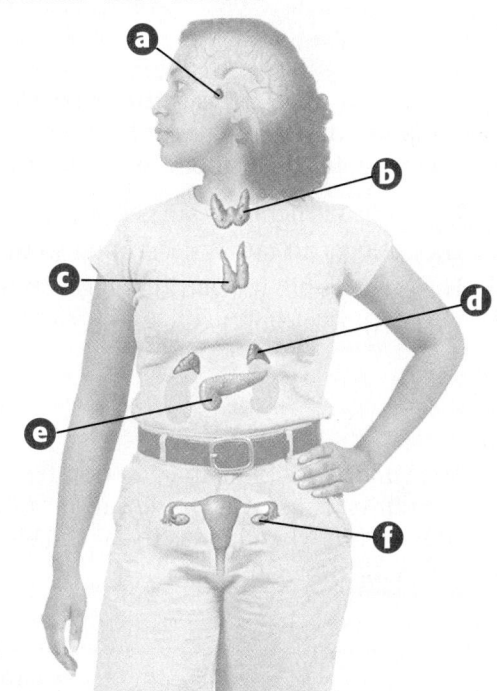

25 Which letter identifies the gland that regulates blood-glucose level?

26 Which letter identifies the gland that releases a hormone that stimulates the birth process?

27 Which letter identifies the gland that helps the body fight disease?

For the following questions, write your answers on a separate sheet of paper.

1 Sensory neurons gather information from the environment. A neuron is a cell that has specialized structures to carry out its function. A part of the cell gathers information and another part carries information to other parts of the body. Which part of the neuron gathers information from other cells?

A. long axon
B. small nucleus
C. short dendrite
D. large cell body

2 It is 10 P.M. and Paul is getting very sleepy. Paul's parasympathetic nervous system sends signals to different parts of his body to prepare it for sleep. What would you expect to find occurring inside his body as he turns out the light and gets into bed?

F. His bronchioles are getting larger to allow more oxygen into his blood.
G. His heart rate is decreasing so that blood flows more slowly through the body.
H. His pupils are getting bigger so that it becomes easier to see objects in the dark.
I. His digestion is slowing down so that his muscles can use the food they already have.

3 Your brain interprets information from the taste buds in your tongue and the olfactory cells in your nose to give you sensations of flavor. Jose doesn't like broccoli so he always holds his nose closed when he has to eat it. Describe why Jose finds it easier to eat brocolli when he holds his nose closed?

4 On Saturday, Gayle was skateboarding when her younger brother, Terry, decided to race her on his bicycle. He got in front of Gayle and suddenly stopped because he saw a rock in his path. Gayle immediately turned her skateboard so that she wouldn't crash into her little brother. Describe how Gayle's nervous system allowed her to avoid an accident. Make sure to mention which parts of her brain were involved during this sequence of events.

5 The flow chart below shows how the pituitary gland releases antidiuretic hormone (ADH), when the water level in blood is low. ADH signals the kidneys to reabsorb the water from the urine that is forming and return the water to blood.

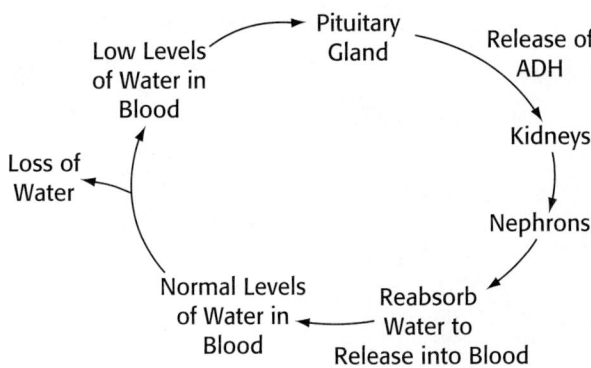

What do you think happens when water levels in the blood have returned to normal?

A. ADH is released into the blood stream.
B. The pituitary gland releases more ADH.
C. ADH is no longer released to the kidneys.
D. The kidneys continue reabsorbing water from forming urine.

6 Killer T cells that fight disease and infection, grow and mature in one of the glands shown in the diagram below. The gland and the killer T cells are a part of the body's immune system.

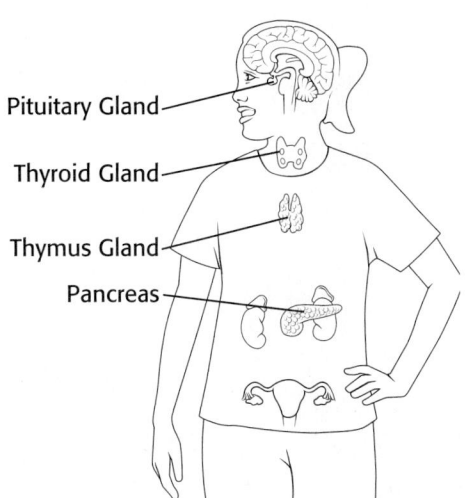

Which endocrine gland would help the body fight chicken pox?

F. pancreas
G. thyroid gland
H. thymus gland
I. pituitary gland

Science in Action

FOCUS ON FLORIDA

Scientific Discoveries

Seeing with Sound

The vOICe system allows blind people to 'hear' pictures. Moving from left to right, a computer program converts the lights and darks of the photo into loud and soft notes. The top of the photo is played on the highest frequencies you can hear. The lower part of the photo is played on the lowest frequencies. Using this program, a small camera, headphones, and a laptop computer, blind people have reported improved light perception. Using this new technology, Adam Shaible, a resident of Pompano Beach, Florida, was able to 'hear' a sunrise for the first time.

Social Studies ACTiViTY

Research schools for the blind and visually impaired near you. How do the students read? Do they study the same subjects you do? You could also find out whether there are programs that would allow you to sit in on some of their classes. Write a report on what you have learned.

Science, Technology, and Society

Robotic Limbs

For many years, science fiction has included cyborgs, or characters that are part human and part robot that usually have super-human strength and X-ray vision. The fact is that there are actual people who have lost the use of their arms and legs and could use some robot power. However, until recently, they have had to settle for clumsy mechanical limbs that were not very good substitutes for real arms or hands. Today, because of advances in technology, scientists are developing artificial limbs—and eyes and ears—that can be wired directly into the nervous system and can be controlled by the brain. In the near future, artificial limbs and some artificial organs will be much more like real organs.

Language Arts ACTiViTY

WRITING SKILL At the library or on the Internet, find examples of optical or visual illusions. Research how the brain processes visual information and how the brain "sees" and interprets these illusions. Write a report about why the brain seems to be fooled by visual tricks. How can understanding the brain's response to illusions help scientists create artificial vision?

Bertha Madras

Studying Brain Activity The brain is an amazing organ. Sometimes, though, drugs or disease keep the brain from working properly. Bertha Madras is a biochemist who studies drug addiction. Dr. Madras studies brain activity to see how substances, such as cocaine, target cells or areas in the brain. Using a variety of brain scanning techniques, Dr. Madras can observe a brain on drugs. She can see how a drug affects the normal activity of the brain. During her research, Dr. Madras realized that some of her results could be applied to Parkinson's disease and to attention deficit hyperactivity disorder (ADHD) in adults. Her research has led to new treatments for both problems.

Math ACTiViTY

Using a search engine on a computer connected to the Internet, search the Internet for "reaction time experiment." Go to one of the Web sites and take the response-time experiment. Record the time that it took you to respond. Repeat the test nine more times, and record your response time for each trial. Then, make a line graph or a bar graph of your response times. Did your response times change? In what way did they change?

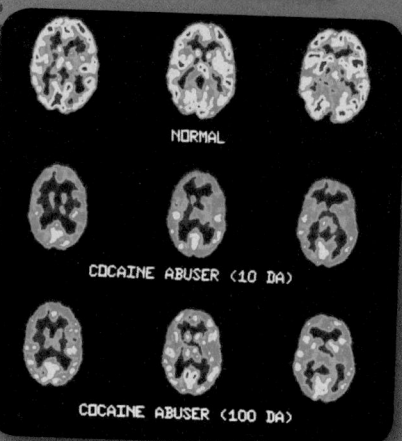

NORMAL

COCAINE ABUSER (10 DA)

COCAINE ABUSER (100 DA)

To learn more about these Science in Action topics, visit go.hrw.com and type in the keyword HT6FCCFF.

Current Science

Check out Current Science® articles related to this chapter by visiting go.hrw.com. Just type in the keyword HL5CS25.

Reproduction and Development

The Big Idea The human body has systems that function in reproduction and growth.

About the

If someone had taken your picture when your mother was about 13 weeks pregnant with you, that picture would have looked much like this photograph. You have changed a lot since then, haven't you? You started out as a single cell, and you became a complete person. And you haven't stopped growing and changing yet. In fact, you will continue to change for the rest of your life.

PRE-READING ACTIVITY

Graphic Organizer

Spider Map Before you read the chapter, create the graphic organizer entitled "Spider Map" described in the **Study Skills** section of the Appendix. Label the circle "Reproduction and development." Create a leg for each section title. As you read the chapter, fill in the map with details about reproduction and development from each section.

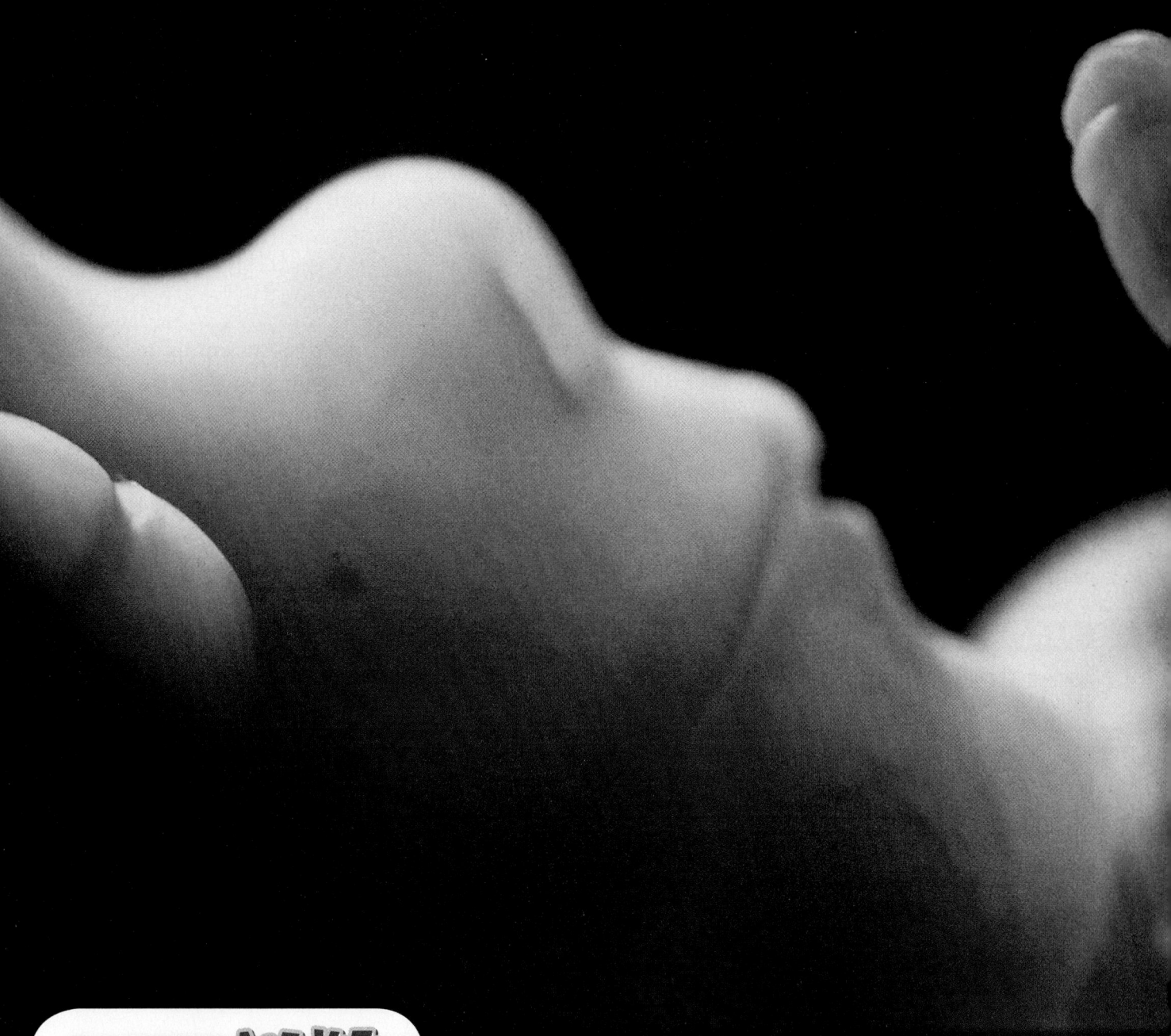

START-UP ACTIVITY

How Grows It?

As you read this paragraph, you are slowly aging. Your body is growing into the body of an adult. But does your body have the same proportions that an adult's body has? Complete this activity to find out.

Procedure

1. Have a classmate use a **tape measure** and **meterstick** to measure your total height, head height, and leg length. Your teacher will tell you how to take these measurements.

2. Use the following equations to calculate your head height–to–total body height proportion and your leg length-to-total body height proportion.

$$\text{head proportion} = \frac{\text{head height}}{\text{body height}} \times 100$$

$$\text{leg proportion} = \frac{\text{leg length}}{\text{body height}} \times 100$$

3. Your teacher will give you the head, body, and leg measurements of three adults. Calculate the head-body and leg-body proportions of each of the three adults. Record all of the measurements and calculations.

Analysis

1. Compare your proportions with the proportions of each of the three adults.

Human Reproduction

About nine months after a human sperm and egg combine and start to grow inside a woman, she gives birth to her baby. How does the human body make the sperm and egg?

READING WARM-UP

Objectives

● Identify the structures and functions of the male and female reproductive systems. **F.I.3.1 AA**

● Describe two reproductive system problems.

Terms to Learn

testes   uterus
penis   vagina
ovary

READING STRATEGY

Reading Organizer As you read this section, create an outline of the section. Use the headings from the section in your outline.

testes the primary male reproductive organs, which produce sperm and testosterone (singular, *testis*)

penis the male organ that transfers sperm to a female and that carries urine out of the body

The Male Reproductive System

The function of the male reproductive system is to make and deliver sperm to the female reproductive system. To perform this function, organs of the male reproductive system, shown in **Figure 1,** make sperm, hormones, and fluids. The **testes** (singular, *testis*) are a pair of organs that hang outside the body in the *scrotum,* a skin sac. Testes make sperm and testosterone (tes TAHS tuhr OHN), the main male sex hormone. Testosterone regulates sperm production and the development of male characteristics.

As sperm leave a testis, they are stored in the *epididymis* (EP uh DID i mis), a tube in which sperm mature. Another tube, a *vas deferens* (VAS DEF uh RENZ), passes from the epididymis into the body and through the *prostate gland*. As sperm move through the vas deferens, they mix with fluids from several glands, including the prostate gland. This mixture is *semen*.

Semen passes through the vas deferens into the *urethra* (yoo REE thruh), the tube that runs from the bladder through the penis. The **penis** is the external organ through which semen exits a male's body and can enter a female's body.

Benchmark Check Where is testosterone produced in males and what does testosterone do? **F.I.3.1 AA**

Figure 1   The Male Reproductive System

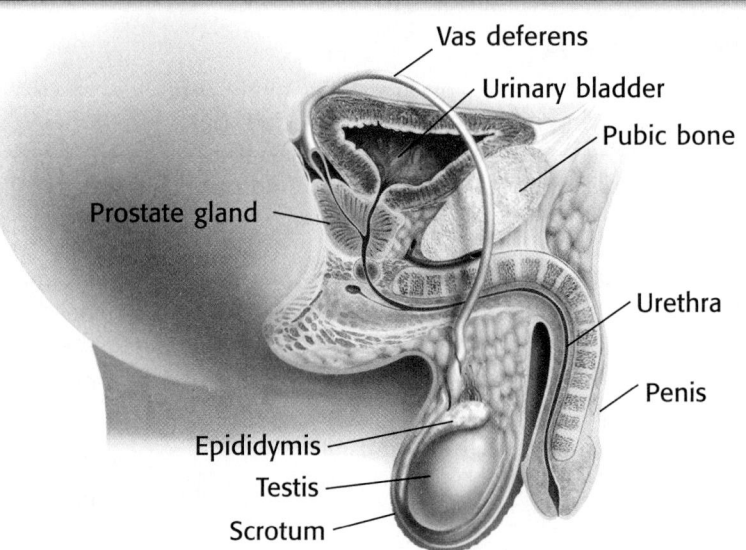

- Vas deferens
- Urinary bladder
- Pubic bone
- Prostate gland
- Urethra
- Penis
- Epididymis
- Testis
- Scrotum

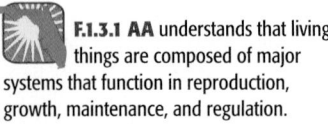

F.I.3.1 AA understands that living things are composed of major systems that function in reproduction, growth, maintenance, and regulation.

Figure 2 The Female Reproductive System

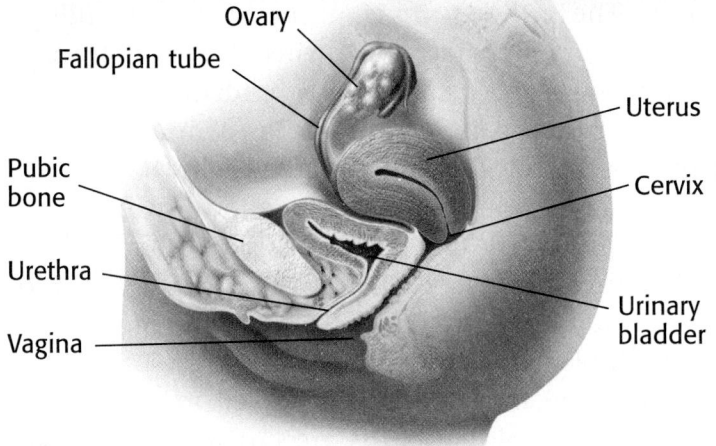

Ovary
Fallopian tube
Pubic bone
Urethra
Vagina
Uterus
Cervix
Urinary bladder

The Female Reproductive System

The female reproductive system, shown in **Figure 2,** produces eggs, nurtures fertilized eggs (zygotes), and gives birth. The two **ovaries** are the organs that make eggs. Ovaries also release estrogen (ES truh juhn) and progesterone (proh JES tuhr OHN), the main female sex hormones. These hormones regulate the release of eggs and development of female characteristics.

The Egg's Journey

During *ovulation* (AHV yoo LAY shuhn), an egg is released from an ovary and passes into a *fallopian tube* (fuh LOH pee uhn TOOB). A fallopian tube leads from each ovary to the uterus. The egg passes through the fallopian tube into the uterus. Fertilization usually happens in the fallopian tube. If the egg is fertilized, the resulting zygote enters the uterus. The zygote may become embedded in the thickened lining of the uterus. The **uterus** is the organ in which a zygote develops into a baby.

When a baby is born, he or she passes from the uterus through the vagina and emerges outside the body. The **vagina** is the canal between the outside of the body and the uterus.

Menstrual Cycle

From puberty through her late 40s or early 50s, a woman's reproductive system goes through the *menstrual cycle* (MEN struhl SIE kuhl), a monthly cycle of changes. This cycle of about 28 days prepares the body for pregnancy. The first day of *menstruation* (MEN STRAY shuhn), the monthly discharge of blood and tissue from the uterus, is counted as the first day of the cycle. Menstruation lasts about 5 days. When menstruation ends, the lining of the uterus thickens. Ovulation occurs on about the 14th day of the cycle. If the egg is not fertilized in a few days, menstruation begins and flushes the egg away.

ovary in the female reproductive system of animals, an organ that produces eggs

uterus in female mammals, the hollow, muscular organ in which a fertilized egg is embedded and in which the embryo and fetus develop

vagina the female reproductive organ that connects the outside of the body to the uterus

Counting Eggs

From about age 12 to about age 50, the average woman ovulates once each month. How many mature eggs could she produce from age 18 to age 50?

Multiple Births

In a multiple birth, a mother gives birth to two or more babies at a time. The birth of twins is the most common multiple birth. Have you ever seen identical twins? Identical twins develop from a single egg that split into two. Identical twins can be so similar that their parents cannot tell them apart. The boys in **Figure 3** are identical twins. Fraternal twins develop from two eggs and are more common than identical twins are. Fraternal twins can look very different from each other and can be of opposite sexes. In every 1,000 births, about 30 sets of twins are born. About one-third of twin births are of identical twins. Some multiple births are of triplets (three babies). In the United States, there are about two sets of triplets in every 1,000 births. Rarer types of multiple births are births of quadruplets (four babies) and quintuplets (five babies). Births of five or more babies happen only once in about 53,000 births.

✓ **Reading Check** What is the frequency of twin births?

Reproductive System Problems

Most of the time, the reproductive system functions well. But problems such as disease and infertility can cause it to fail.

Sexually Transmitted Diseases (STDs)

Chlamydia and herpes are common sexually transmitted diseases. A *sexually transmitted disease* (STD), is a disease that can pass from a person with an STD to another person during sexual contact. STDs are also called *sexually transmitted infections* (STIs). These diseases affect many people each year, as shown in **Table 1.** The STD *acquired immune deficiency syndrome* (AIDS) is caused by the *human immunodeficiency virus* (HIV). The STD *Hepatitis B,* is a liver disease that is also caused by a virus. Hepatitis B can be spread by sexual contact. In the United States, about 140,000 new hepatitis B cases occur each year.

Figure 3 *Identical twins have genes that are exactly the same. Many identical twins who are raised apart have similar personalities and interests.*

Twins and More

With an adult family member or guardian, discuss some challenges that are created by the birth of twins, triplets, quadruplets, or other multiples. Include financial, mental, emotional, and physical challenges.

Create a poster that shows these challenges. Include ways to meet each challenge.

If twins or other multiples are in your family, discuss how the individuals differ and how they are alike.

Table 1 The Spread of STDs in the United States	
STD	**Approximate number of new cases each year**
Chlamydia	3 to 10 million
Genital HPV (human papillomavirus)	5.5 million
Genital herpes	1 million
Gonorrhea	650,000
Syphilis	70,000
HIV/AIDS	40,000 to 50,000

Cancer

Sometimes, cancer happens in reproductive organs. *Cancer* is a disease in which cells grow at an uncontrolled rate. Cancer cells start out as normal cells. Then, something triggers uncontrolled cell growth. These triggers vary between types of cancer.

In men, the two most common reproductive system cancers are cancer of the testes and cancer of the prostate gland. In women, the two most common reproductive system cancers are breast cancer and cancer of the cervix. The *cervix* is the lower part, or neck, of the uterus. The cervix opens to the vagina.

Infertility

In the United States, about 15% of married couples have difficulty producing offspring. Many of these couples are *infertile,* or unable to have children. Men may be infertile if they do not produce enough healthy sperm. Women may be infertile if they do not ovulate normally.

Sexually transmitted diseases, such as gonorrhea and chlamydia, can lead to infertility in women. STD-related infertility occurs in men, but not as commonly as it does in women.

CONNECTION TO Social Studies

Understanding STDs Select an STD from **Table 1.** Make a poster or brochure that states the STD's cause, describes its symptoms, explains its effects on the body, and lists effective treatments of the STD. Include a bar graph that shows the number of cases per age group for several age groups.

ACTIVITY

F.I.3.1 AA understands that living things are composed of major systems that function in reproduction, growth, maintenance, and regulation.

SECTION Review

Summary

- The male reproductive system produces sperm and can deliver sperm to the female reproductive system. **F.I.3.1 AA**

- The female reproductive system produces eggs, nurtures zygotes, and gives birth. **F.I.3.1 AA**

- Humans usually have one child per birth, but some people have multiple births, such as twins or triplets.

- Human reproduction can be affected by infertility and diseases such as cancer.

Using Key Terms

1. Use *uterus* and *vagina* in the same sentence.

Understanding Key Ideas

2. Identify the structures and functions of the male and female reproductive systems. **F.I.3.1 AA**

3. Describe two reproductive system problems.

Math Skills

4. In one country, 7 out of 1,000 infants die before their first birthday. Convert this figure to a percentage.

Critical Thinking

5. **Applying Concepts** Twins can happen when a zygote splits in two or when two eggs are fertilized at the same time. How can these two ways of twin formation explain how identical twins differ from fraternal twins?

FCAT Preparation

6. In females, an egg travels to the uterus through a fallopian tube approximately once a month. However, untreated STDs in women can block the fallopian tubes. Which of the following occurs as a result? **F.I.3.1 AA**

   A. An egg cannot be fertilized.

   B. Ovulation does not occur.

   C. The urethra will become blocked.

   D. Menstruation will cease.

SCiLINKS **NSTA**

Developed and maintained by the National Science Teachers Association

For a variety of links related to this chapter, go to www.scilinks.org

Topic: Reproductive System Irregularities or Disorders

SciLinks code: HSM1298

Growth and Development

Every one of us started out as a single cell. How did that cell become a person made of trillions of cells?

A single cell divides many times and develops into a baby. But the development of a baby from a single cell is only the first stage of human development. Think about how you will change between now and when you become a grandparent!

From Fertilization to Embryo

Ordinarily, the process of human development starts when a man deposits millions of sperm into a woman's vagina. A few hundred sperm make it from the vagina through the uterus into a fallopian tube. There, a few sperm cover the protective outer coating of the egg. Usually, only one sperm gets through the outer coating of the egg. Penetration of the outer coating by a sperm triggers a response—the outer coating changes so that other sperm cannot go through it. When the sperm's nucleus joins with the egg's nucleus, the egg becomes fertilized.

The fertilized egg, or zygote, travels down the fallopian tube to the uterus. This journey takes 5 to 6 days. During the trip, the zygote undergoes cell division many times. By 11 to 12 days after fertilization, the zygote has become a tiny ball of cells called an **embryo.** Then, implantation occurs. *Implantation* is the embedding of the embryo in the thick, nutrient-rich lining of the uterus. **Figure 1** shows fertilization and implantation.

Benchmark Check Describe the processes of fertilization and implantation, including where they occur. **F.1.3.1 AA**

embryo a developing human, from fertilization through the first 8 weeks of development (the 10th week of pregnancy)

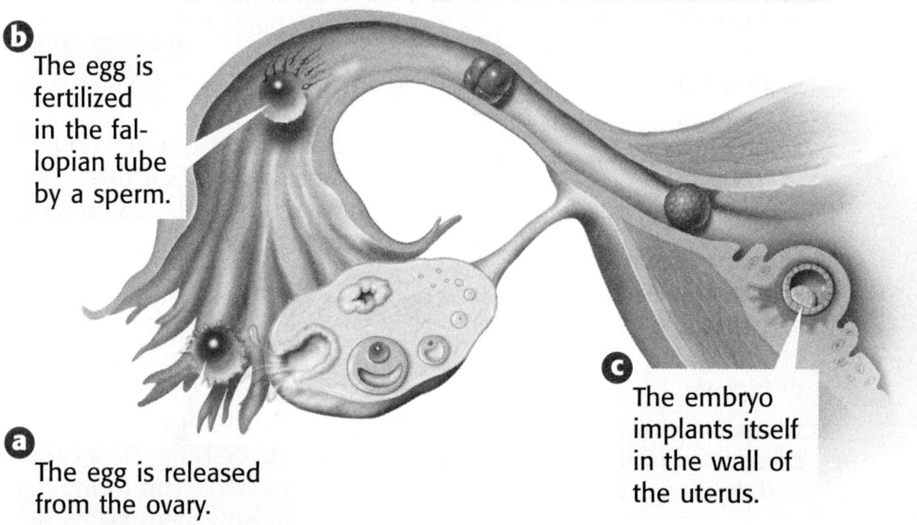

F.1.3.1 AA understands that living things are composed of major systems that function in reproduction, growth, maintenance, and regulation.

F.1.3.3 CS knows that in multicellular organisms cells grow and divide to make more cells in order to form and repair various organs and tissues.

Figure 1 Fertilization and Implantation

ⓑ The egg is fertilized in the fallopian tube by a sperm.

ⓒ The embryo implants itself in the wall of the uterus.

ⓐ The egg is released from the ovary.

From Embryo to Fetus

After implantation, the placenta (pluh SEN tuh) forms. The **placenta** is a special two-way exchange organ. The placenta's network of blood vessels provides the embryo with oxygen and nutrients from the mother's blood. The embryo's wastes move into the mother's blood through the placenta. The mother's body then excretes the wastes. In the placenta, the embryo's blood and the mother's blood flow near each other but usually do not mix.

Benchmark Check Describe what the placenta does. F.1.3.1 AA

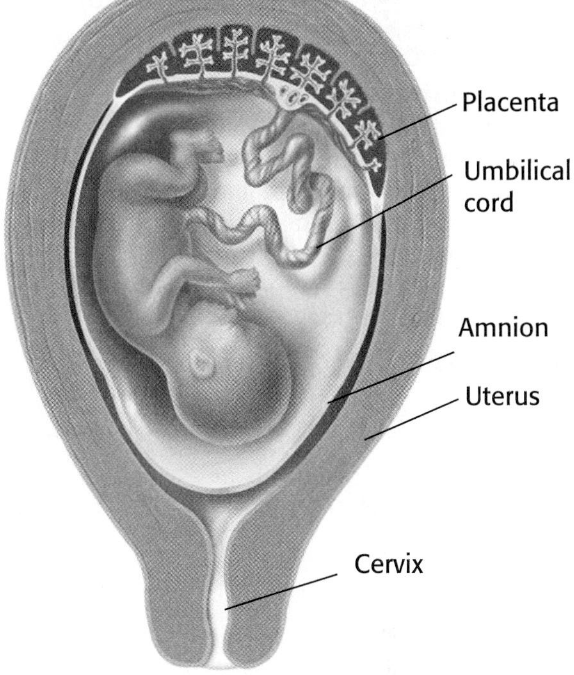

Weeks 1 and 2

Doctors commonly measure a woman's pregnancy as starting from the first day of her last menstrual period. On that day, fertilization has not yet taken place, but that day is an easy-to-recognize date from which to count. A normal pregnancy lasts about 280 days, or 40 weeks, from that day.

Weeks 3 and 4

Fertilization takes place at about the end of week 2. In week 3, after fertilization, the zygote moves to the uterus. As the zygote travels, it divides many times. It becomes a ball of cells that implants itself in the wall of the uterus. The zygote is now called an *embryo*. At the end of week 4, implantation is complete and the woman is pregnant. The embryo's blood cells begin to form. At this point, the embryo is about 0.2 mm long.

Weeks 5 to 8

Weeks 5 to 8 of pregnancy are weeks 3 to 6 of embryonic development. In this stage, a thin membrane called the *amnion* (AM nee AHN) surrounds the embryo. Amniotic fluid fills the amnion, which cushions and protects the growing embryo. In week 5, the umbilical cord forms. The **umbilical cord** (uhm BIL i kuhl KAWRD) connects the embryo to the placenta. **Figure 2** shows the umbilical cord, amnion, and placenta.

In this stage, the heart, brain, other organs, and blood vessels start to form and grow quickly. In weeks 5 and 6, eyes and ears form and the spinal cord begins to develop. In week 6, tiny limb buds that will become arms and legs appear. In week 8, muscles start to develop. Nerves in the shoulders and upper arms grow. Fingers and toes start to form. The embryo, now about 16 mm long, can swallow and blink.

Placenta

Umbilical cord

Amnion

Uterus

Cervix

Figure 2 *The placenta, amnion, and umbilical cord are the life support system for the fetus. This fetus is about 20 to 22 weeks old.*

placenta the partly fetal and partly maternal organ by which materials are exchanged between a fetus and the mother

umbilical cord the structure that connects an embryo and then the fetus to the placenta

Choose Your Parents
Introduce the animal contestants of a new game show called "Choose Your Parents!" Go to **go.hrw.com,** and type in the keyword **HL5BD5W.**

fetus a developing human from seven or eight weeks after fertilization until birth

F.1.3.1 AA understands that living things are composed of major systems that function in reproduction, growth, maintenance, and regulation.

Weeks 9 to 16

In this stage, the embryo changes as cells continue to form tissues and organs. At week 9, the embryo may make tiny movements. After week 10, the embryo is called a **fetus** (FEET uhs). At week 13, the fetus's face begins to look more human. Fetal muscle tissue grows stronger. As a result, the fetus can make a fist, and move. The fetus grows rapidly during this stage. Within a month, the size of the fetus doubles and then triples. For example, in week 10, the fetus is about 36 mm long. At week 16, the fetus is about 108 mm to 116 mm long. **Figure 3** shows changes that occur in the fetus as the fetus develops.

Benchmark Check Describe three changes that the fetus undergoes as cells form tissues and organs in weeks 9 to 16. **F.1.3.3 CS**

Weeks 17 to 24

By week 17, the fetus can make faces. Usually, in week 18, the fetus starts to make movements that the mother can feel. By week 18, the fetus can hear sounds through the mother's body and may even jump at loud noises. By week 23, fetal movements may be vigorous. A fetus that is born at week 24 might survive if given intensive medical care. In weeks 17 to 24, the fetus grows to between 25 cm and 30 cm in length.

Weeks 25 to 36

At about 25 or 26 weeks, the fetus's lungs are well developed but not fully mature. The fetus still gets oxygen from its mother through the placenta. The fetus will not take its first breath of air until it is born. By the 32nd week, the fetus's eyes can open and close. Studies of fetal heart rate and brain activity show that fetuses respond to light. Some scientists have observed brain activity and eye movements in sleeping fetuses that resemble those activities in sleeping children or adults. These scientists think that a sleeping fetus may dream. After 36 weeks, the fetus is almost ready to be born.

Birth

At 37 to 38 weeks, the fetus is fully developed. A full-term pregnancy usually lasts about 40 weeks. Typically, as birth begins, the mother's uterus begins a series of muscular contractions called *labor*. Usually, these contractions push the fetus through the mother's vagina, and the baby is born. The newborn is still connected to the placenta by its umbilical cord, which is tied and cut. All that will remain of the point where the umbilical cord was attached is the baby's navel. Soon, the mother expels the placenta, and labor is complete.

Figure 3   **Pregnancy Timeline**

Week

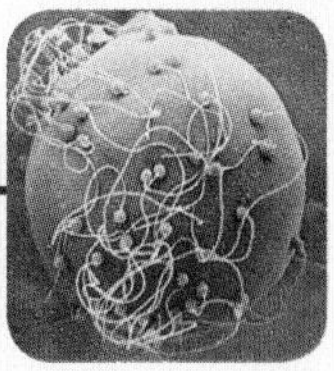

Fertilization takes place.

The fertilized egg becomes a ball of hundreds of cells.

2

4

Implantation is complete.

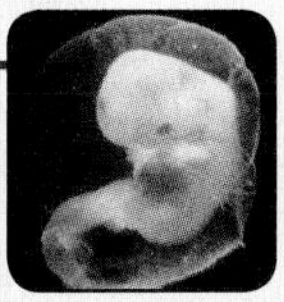

The spinal cord and brain begin to form.

6

8

Well-defined tiny fingers and toes become apparent.

The embryo may make tiny movements that may be detected by ultrasound.

10

The embryo is now called a *fetus*.

12

14

Bones and bone marrow continue to form.

16

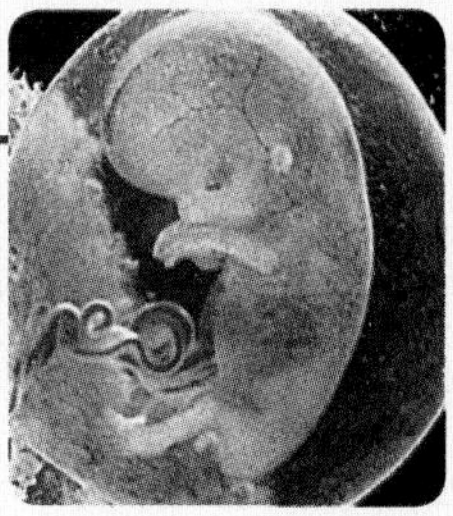

A layer of fat begins to form under the skin.

18

20

22

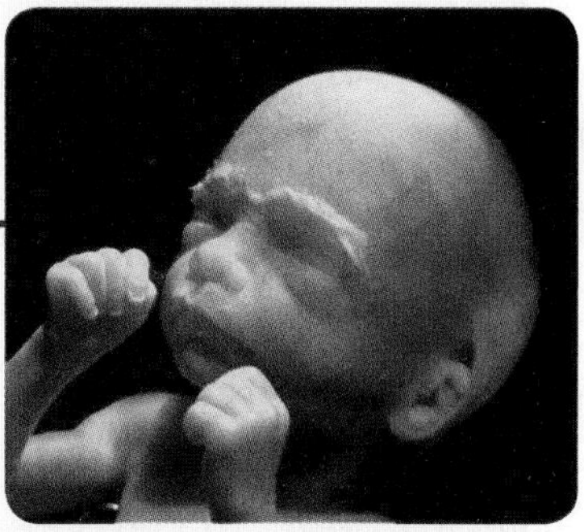

24

The fetus's lungs are almost ready to breathe air.

26

The fetus practice breathes and has brain wave activity.

28

The eyes of the fetus are open, and the fetus may turn toward a bright light.

30

32

The fetus is developing taste buds, and its brain is growing rapidly.

The fetus's skin turns from red to pink.

34

36

The fetus's skull has hardened.

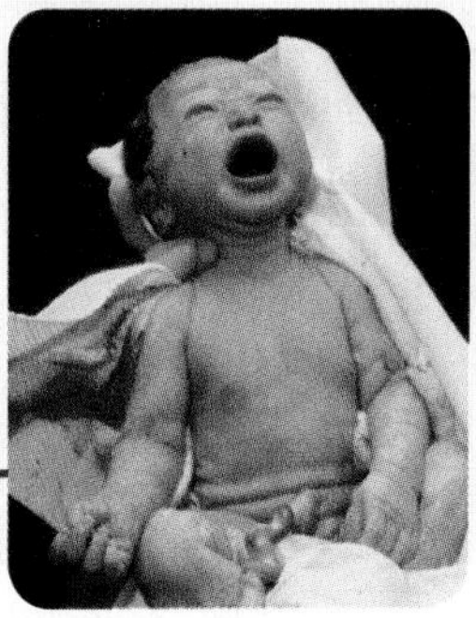

The baby is born.

38

40

Figure 4 Stages of Human Development

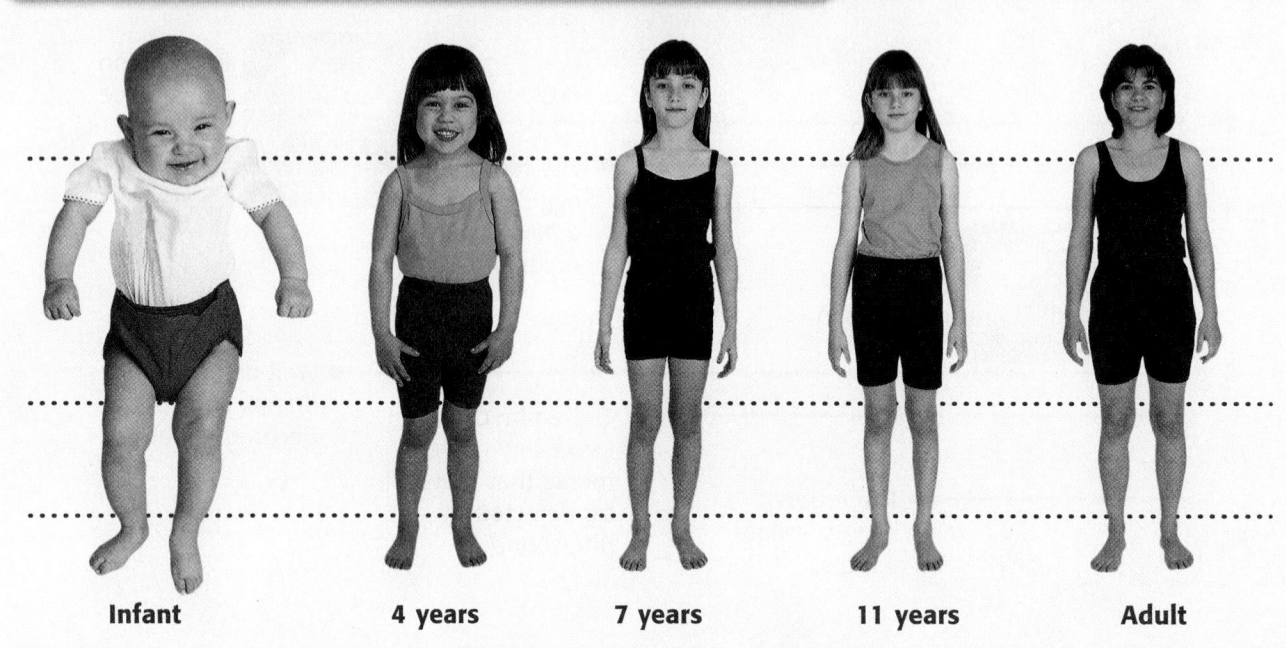

Infant   4 years   7 years   11 years   Adult

Life Grows On

Use **Figure 4** to complete this activity.

1. Use a **ruler** to measure the infant's head height. Then, measure the infant's entire height, including the head.

2. Calculate the ratio of the infant's head height to the infant's total height.

3. Repeat these measurements and calculations for the other people shown.

4. Does a baby's head grow faster or slower than the rest of the body? Why do you think this is so?

From Birth to Death

After birth, the human body goes through several stages of development. Some of those stages are shown in **Figure 4.**

Infancy and Childhood

Infancy is the stage from birth to age 2. During infancy, a person's body grows quickly. Baby teeth appear. As the nervous system and muscles develop, the person becomes more coordinated and starts to walk.

Childhood, another fast-growth period, lasts from age 2 to puberty. In childhood, permanent teeth grow in and replace the baby teeth. Nerve pathways in the brain mature, which enables the person to learn to read. Muscles become more coordinated, which allows the person to do things such as ride a bicycle.

Adolescence

The stage from puberty to adulthood is adolescence. During puberty, a person's reproductive system matures. In most boys, puberty takes place between the ages of 11 and 16. During this time, a male's body becomes more muscular, his voice becomes deeper, and body and facial hair appear. In most girls, puberty takes place between the ages of 9 and 14. During puberty in females, the amount of fat in the hips and thighs increases, the breasts enlarge, body hair appears, and menstruation begins.

✓ *Reading Check* Name an important change that takes place during adolescence.

Adulthood

From about age 20 to age 40 is the stage of young adulthood. Physical development is at its peak. Beginning around age 30, changes associated with aging begin. These changes are gradual and vary from person to person. Some early signs of aging include loss of muscle flexibility, deterioration of eyesight, increase in body fat, and some loss of hair.

The aging process continues in middle age, which occurs from age 40 to age 65. During this time, hair may turn gray, athletic abilities usually decline, and skin may wrinkle. A person who is more than 65 years old is considered an older adult. Although the aging process continues through the end of life, many older adults lead very active lives, as **Figure 5** shows.

Figure 5 *Many older adults can still enjoy activities that they enjoyed when they were younger.*

SECTION Review

Summary

- Fertilization occurs when a sperm from the male joins with an egg from the female.
- The embryo and fetus undergo many changes between implantation and birth. **F.1.3.3 CS**
- The first stage of human development lasts from fertilization to birth. **F.1.3.1 AA**
- After birth, a human goes through four more stages of growth and development.

Using Key Terms

1. Write an original definition for *umbilical cord*.

2. Use *embryo* and *fetus* in the same sentence.

Understanding Key Ideas

3. Describe the development of tissues and organs in an embryo and a fetus. **F.1.3.3 CS**

4. Summarize the processes of fertilization and implantation.

5. What are five stages of human development?

Math Skills

6. Alice is 80 years old, and she entered puberty when she was 12 years old. Calculate the percentage of her life that she has spent in each of the four stages of development after birth.

Critical Thinking

7. **Applying Concepts** Why does the egg's covering change after a sperm has entered the egg?

8. **Analyzing Ideas** Do you think that one stage of a human's life is more important than other stages are? Explain your answer.

FCAT Preparation

9. As embryonic cells grow to form organs and tissues, the embryo is supported by the placenta inside the uterus. Which of the following describes the role of the placenta? **F.1.3.1 AA**

   A. to protect the growing embryo from bumps

   B. to deliver oxygen and nutrition to the fetus

   C. to produce eggs when ovulation occurs

   D. to prepare the uterus for pregnancy

SCI**LINKS**® **NSTA**

Developed and maintained by the
National Science Teachers Association

For a variety of links related to this chapter, go to www.scilinks.org

Topic: Before Birth; Growth and Development

SciLinks code: HSM0140; HSM0700

Skills Practice Lab

OBJECTIVES

Construct a model of a human uterus protecting a fetus. F.1.3.1 AA

Compare the protection that a bird's egg gives a developing baby bird with the protection that a human uterus gives a fetus.

MATERIALS

- computer (optional)
- cotton, soft fabric, or other soft materials
- eggs, soft-boiled and in the shell (2 to 4)
- eggs, soft-boiled and peeled (3 or 4)
- gloves, protective
- mineral oil, cooking oil, syrup, or other thick liquid
- plastic bags, sealable
- water

SAFETY

F.1.3.1 AA understands that living things are composed of major systems that function in reproduction, growth, maintenance, and regulation.

It's a Comfy, Safe World!

Before birth, baby birds live inside a hard, protective shell until the baby has used up all of the food supply. Most mammal babies develop within their mother's uterus, in which they are surrounded by fluid and connected to a placenta, before they are born. Before human babies are born, they lead a comfy life. By the seventh month, they lie around sucking their thumb, blinking their eyes, and perhaps even dreaming.

Ask a Question

1. Inside which structure is a developing organism better protected from bumps and blows: the uterus of a placental mammal or the egg of a bird?

Form a Hypothesis

2. A placental mammal's uterus protects a developing organism from bumps and blows better than a bird's egg does.

Test the Hypothesis

3. Brainstorm ways to construct and test your model of a mammalian uterus. Then, use the materials provided by your teacher to build your model. A peeled, soft-boiled egg will represent the fetus inside your model uterus.

4. Make a data table similar to **Table 1** below. Test your model, examine the egg for damage, and record your results.

Table 1 First Test of Model Uterus	
Original model	**Modified model**
DO NOT WRITE	
IN BOOK	

5. Modify your model as necessary; test this modified model by using another peeled, soft-boiled egg; and record your results.

6 When you have completed the model's design, obtain another peeled, soft-boiled egg and an egg in the shell. The egg in the shell represents the baby bird inside the egg.

7 Make a data table similar to **Table 2** below. Test only the peeled egg inside the model. Test the egg in a shell as is. Examine the eggs for damage. Record the results in your data table.

Table 2 Final Test of Model Uterus	
	Test results
Model	DO NOT WRITE IN BOOK
Egg in shell	

Analyze the Results

1 **Explaining Events** Explain how the test results for the model differ from the test results for the egg in a shell.

2 **Analyzing Results** What modification to your model protected the "fetus" most effectively?

Draw Conclusions

3 **Evaluating Data** Review your hypothesis. Did your data support your hypothesis? Why or why not?

4 **Evaluating Models** What modifications to your model might make it more like a uterus?

Applying Your Data

Use the Internet or the library to find information about the development of monotremes, such as the echidna or the platypus, and the development of marsupials, such as the koala or the kangaroo. Then, using what you have learned in this lab, compare the development of placental mammals with that of marsupials and monotremes.

Chapter Review

USING KEY TERMS

For each pair of terms, explain how the meanings of the terms differ.

1 *embryo* and *fetus*

2 *testes* and *ovaries*

3 *uterus* and *vagina*

4 *fertilization* and *implantation*

5 *umbilical cord* and *placenta*

UNDERSTANDING KEY IDEAS

Multiple Choice

6 The human reproductive system helps perform functions such as reproduction and regulation. Which of the following is a function of the reproductive system? **FCAT** F.1.3.1 AA

   a. to produce all of the body's hormones

   b. to regulate body temperature

   c. to make hormones that fight disease

   d. to regulate the development of male and female characteristics

7 All of the following are sexually transmitted diseases EXCEPT

   a. chlamydia.

   b. AIDS.

   c. infertility.

   d. genital herpes.

8 Identical twins are the result of

   a. a fertilized egg splitting in two.

   b. the fertilization of two separate eggs.

   c. implantation.

   d. menstruation.

9 Tissues and organs develop as an embryo becomes a fetus. Humans grow in size as they become adults. How are cells responsible for these changes? **FCAT** F.1.3.3 CS

   a. through cell division

   b. through cell expansion

   c. through cell death

   d. through cell contraction

Short Answer

10 Which human reproductive organs produce sperm? Which produce eggs?

11 Explain how the fetus gets oxygen and nutrients and how the fetus gets rid of wastes. F.1.3.1 AA

12 What are four stages of human life that follow birth? Describe each stage.

13 Name three problems that can affect the human reproductive system, and explain why each is a problem.

14 Draw a diagram showing the structures of the male and female reproductive systems. Label each structure, and explain how each structure contributes to fertilization and implantation. F.1.3.1 AA

15 Describe the changes that occur in a zygote as it becomes a fetus. F.1.3.3 CS

Math Skills

16 Identical twin births happen once in 100 births. How many sets of identical twins might you expect at a school that has 2,700 students?

CRITICAL THINKING

Extended Response

17 Applying Concepts What is the function of the uterus? How is this function related to the menstrual cycle? **F.1.3.1 AA**

18 Making Inferences As the number of babies in a multiple birth increases, the type of multiple birth becomes less common. For example, the birth of twins is the most common type of multiple birth—30 sets of twins are born for every 1,000 births. But the birth of quintuplets is very rare—1 set of quintuplets is born in about 53,000 births. Why might multiple births in which a large number of babies are born be less common than multiple births in which a small number of babies are born?

19 Drawing Conclusions Menstruation is affected by a hormone called *estrogen*. A woman who produces very little estrogen may not have a menstrual cycle. In turn, the production of estrogen is affected by body fat. A woman who has very little body fat usually produces less estrogen. What might happen to the menstrual cycle of a female athlete who exercises a lot?

Concept Mapping

20 Use the following terms to create a concept map: *testes, penis, ovary, uterus, vagina, embryo, placenta, reproductive organs,* and *umbilical cord.*

INTERPRETING GRAPHICS

The following graph illustrates the cycles of the female hormone estrogen and the male hormone testosterone. The blue line shows the estrogen level in a female over 28 days. The red line shows the testosterone level in a male over the same amount of time. Use the graph below to answer the questions that follow.

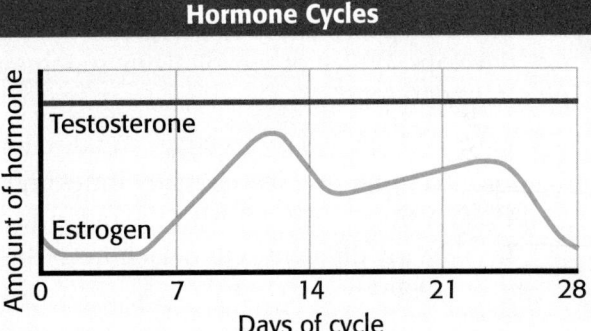

21 Over the 28 days, how do the day-to-day levels of testosterone differ from the day-to-day levels of estrogen?

22 What cycle do you think estrogen affects?

23 Why might the level of testosterone stay the same?

24 Do you think that the above estrogen cycle would change in a pregnant woman? Explain your answer.

247

For the following questions, write your answers on a separate sheet of paper.

1 A human develops from a single cell. Many tissues and organs are growing as the fetus develops in the uterus. Which of the following statements describes what cells undergo to allow the fetus to develop?

A. Cells are becoming larger.
B. Cells are becoming smaller.
C. Cells are growing and dividing.
D. Cells are dying and breaking down.

2 Melea's teacher taught her class that a fetus undergoes many changes in the uterus as it develops. Which of the following statements is a true description of what happens as the fetus develops?

F. A single cell grows larger and develops specialized features.
G. A single cell divides many times and forms specialized structures.
H. A single cell fuses with the placenta and grows from the mother's cells.
I. Many different cells detach from the uterus and join together, allowing the fetus to grow.

3 A baby girl already has all of the organs that she needs to have babies of her own when she is old enough. Many of these organs must undergo hormonal changes before she can reproduce. During what phase of human development does the reproductive system fully mature?

A. adolescence
B. adulthood
C. childhood
D. infancy

4 Both males and females have the hormones testosterone, estrogen, and progesterone. These hormones have many functions. One of these functions is to regulate the development of male and female characteristics. Which hormone is responsible for male characteristics? Describe two characteristics that are a result of this hormone in males.

5 As a fetus develops, it is dependent on the placenta to help it obtain nutrition and get rid of wastes. Which of the following statements about the placenta's function is true?

F. The placenta allows the exchange of materials between the fetus and the mother.

G. The placenta allows nutrition to move into the fetus and breaks down wastes from the fetus.

H. The placenta allows the mother's blood to mix with the blood of the fetus to allow the exchange of materials.

I. The placenta makes nutrition for the fetus and allows wastes from the fetus to move into the mother's blood so that her body can excrete them.

6 This is an illustration of the male reproductive system. The male reproductive system makes and regulates testoterone. The male reproductive system also makes and delivers sperm to the female reproductive system.

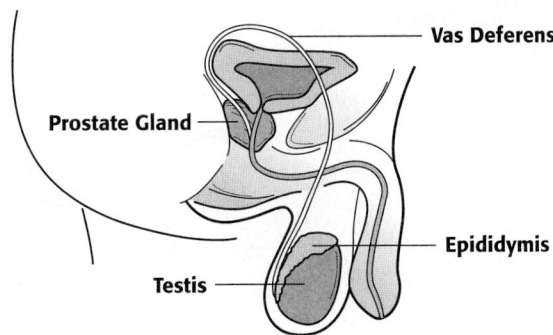

What could happen if the prostate gland were enlarged because of a disease?

A. Sperm would not be produced.

B. Testosterone could not be made.

C. Testosterone would not reach the rest of the body.

D. Sperm may not be delivered to the female reproductive system.

Science in Action

FOCUS ON
FLORIDA

Scientific Discoveries

Lasers and Acne

Many people think that acne affects only teenagers, but acne can strike at any age. Some acne is mild, but some is severe. Now, for some severe cases of acne, lasers may provide relief. That's right—lasers can be used to treat acne! Surgeons who specialize in the health and diseases of the skin use laser light to treat acne.

In addition, laser treatments may stimulate the skin cells that produce collagen. Collagen is a protein found in connective tissue. Increased production of collagen in the skin improves the skin's texture and helps smooth out acne scars.

Science, Technology, and Society

Aquaculture at Deland Middle School

Everyone can contribute to science! In Deland, Florida, students in the Deland Middle School Aquaculture Project are learning about aquaculture by raising Siberian sturgeon. Humans use aquaculture to raise aquatic organisms and products for human consumption. Students at Deland Middle School discovered that although Siberian sturgeon are naturally found in ice-covered waters, these fish grow faster in water at warmer temperatures, ranging from 16°C to 27°C. This discovery is an important contribution to the science of aquaculture.

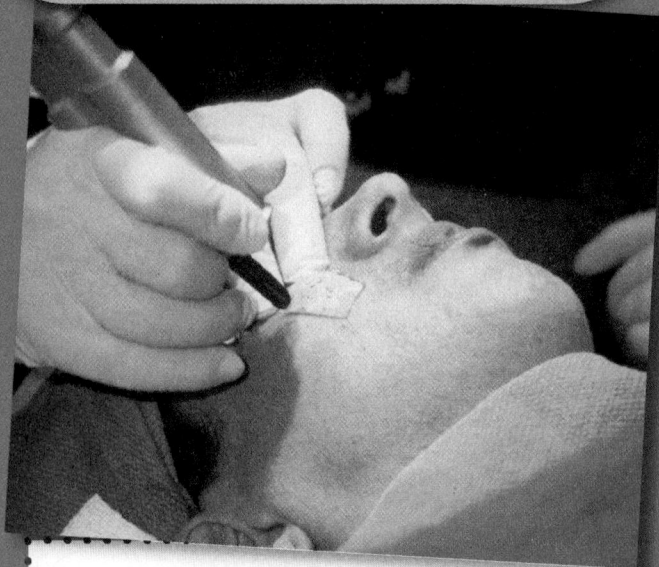

Language Arts ACTIVITY

WRITING SKILL Write a story about how a teen's life is affected by severe acne. Tell what happens when a doctor refers the teen to a specialist for laser treatment and how the successful treatment changes the teen's life.

Social Studies ACTIVITY

WRITING SKILL Many cultures have developed methods to raise aquatic organisms. Research which cultures practiced aquaculture and the organisms these cultures raised. On a poster, make a timeline of the development of aquaculture.

Reva Curry

Diagnostic Medical Sonographer Sounds are everywhere in our world. But only some of those sounds—such as your favorite music playing on the stereo or the dog barking next door—are sounds that we can hear. There are sound waves whose frequency is too high for us to hear. These high-pitched sounds are called *ultrasound*. Some animals, such as bats, use ultrasound to hunt and to avoid midair collisions.

Humans use ultrasound, too. Ultrasound machines can peer inside the human body to look at hearts, blood vessels, and fetuses. Diagnostic medical sonographers are people who use sonography equipment to diagnose medical problems. Diagnostic medical sonographers also use sonography to follow the growth and development of a fetus while the fetus is still in the uterus. One of the leading professionals in the field of diagnostic medical sonography is Dr. Reva Curry. Dr. Curry spent many years as a sonographer. Her primary job was to use high-tech ultrasound instruments to create images of parts of the body and interpret the images for other professionals. Today, Dr. Curry works with students as dean of a community college.

Math ACTIVITY

At 20°C, the speed of sound in water is 1,482 m/s, and the speed of sound in steel is 5,200 m/s. How long would it take a sound to travel 815.1 m in water? In that same amount of time, how far would a sound travel in a steel beam?

go.hrw.com

To learn more about these Science in Action topics, visit go.hrw.com and type in the keyword **HT6FRDFF**.

Current Science

Check out Current Science® articles related to this chapter by visiting go.hrw.com. Just type in the keyword **HL5CS26**.

10

Body Defenses and Disease

The Big Idea The human body has systems that protect the body from disease.

About the PHOTO

No, this photo is not from a sci-fi movie. This organism is not an alien insect soldier. This is, in fact, a greatly enlarged image of a house dust mite that is tinier than the dot of an *i*. Huge numbers of these creatures live in carpets, beds, and sofas in every home. Dust mites often cause problems for people who have asthma or allergies. The body's immune system fights diseases and foreign factors, such as dust mites, that cause allergies.

PRE-READING ACTIVITY

FOLDNOTES **Tri-Fold** Before you read the chapter, create the FoldNote entitled "Tri-Fold" described in the **Study Skills** section of the Appendix. Write what you know about the body's defenses in the column labeled "Know." Then, write what you want to know in the column labeled "Want." As you read the chapter, write what you learn about the body's defenses in the column labeled "Learn."

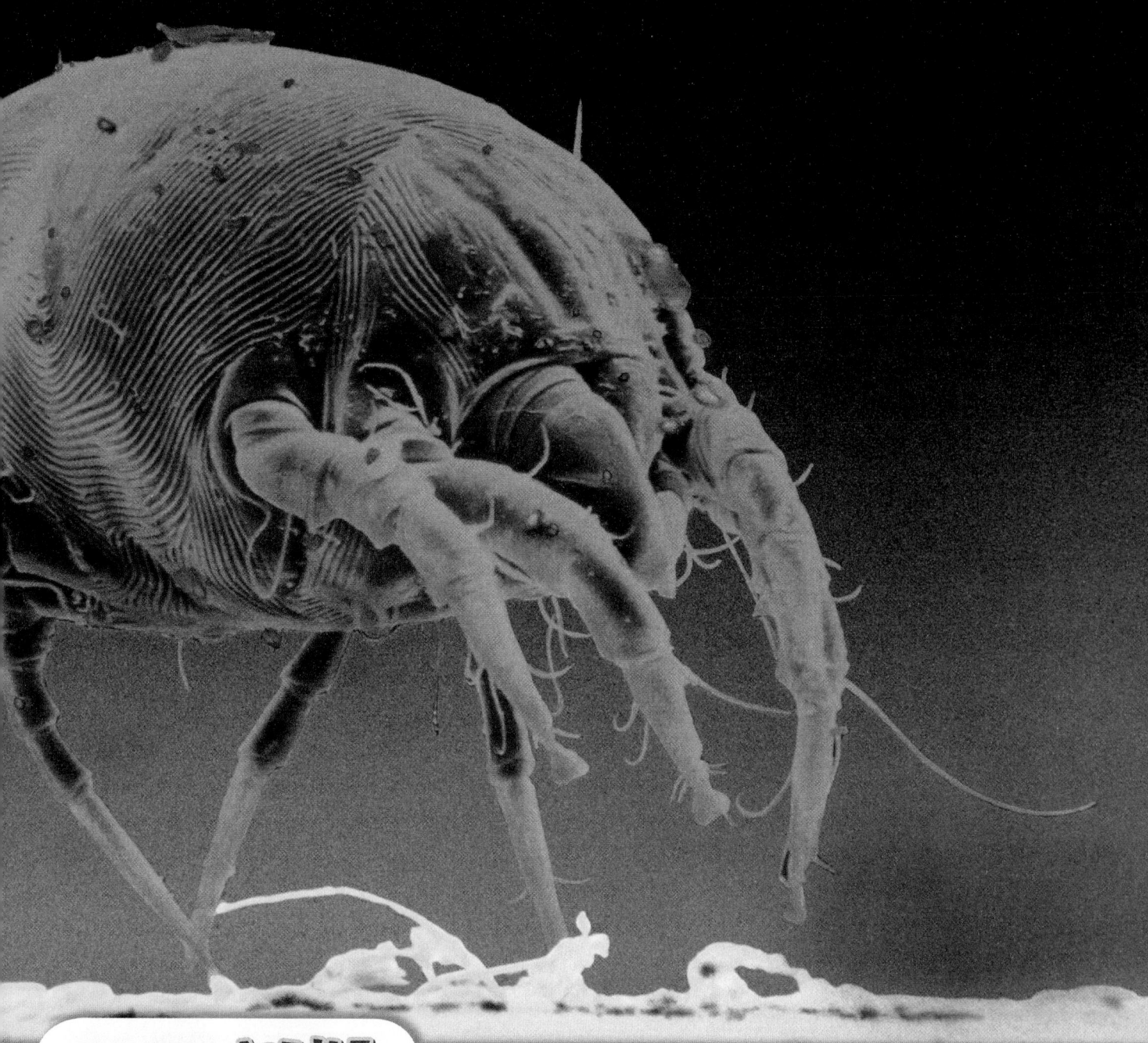

START-UP ACTIVITY

Invisible Invaders

In this activity, you will see tiny organisms grow.

Procedure

1. Obtain **two Petri dishes containing nutrient agar.** Label them "Washed" and "Unwashed."

2. Rub **two marbles** between the palms of your hands. Observe the appearance of the marbles.

3. Roll one marble in the Petri dish labeled "Unwashed."

4. Put on a pair of **disposable gloves.** Wash the other marble with **soap** and **warm water** for 4 min.

5. Roll the washed marble in the Petri dish labeled "Washed."

6. Secure the lids of the Petri dishes with **transparent tape.** Place the dishes in a warm, dark place. Do not open the Petri dishes after they are sealed.

7. Record changes in the Petri dishes for 1 week.

Analysis

1. How did the washed and unwashed marbles compare? How did the Petri dishes differ after several days?

2. Why is it important to wash your hands before eating?

Disease

You've probably heard it before: "Cover your mouth when you sneeze!" "Wash your hands!" "Don't put that in your mouth!"

What is all of the fuss about? When people say these things to you, they are concerned about the spread of disease.

Causes of Disease

When you have a *disease,* your normal body functions are disrupted. Some diseases, such as most cancers and heart disease, are not spread from one person to another. These diseases are called **noninfectious diseases.**

Noninfectious diseases can be caused by a variety of factors. For example, a genetic disorder causes the disease hemophilia (HEE moh FIL ee uh), in which a person's blood does not clot properly. Smoking, lack of physical activity, and a high-fat diet can greatly increase a person's chances of getting certain noninfectious diseases. Avoiding harmful habits may help you avoid noninfectious diseases.

A disease that can be passed from one living thing to another is an **infectious disease.** Infectious diseases are caused by agents called **pathogens,** such as a virus. **Viruses** are tiny, noncellular particles that depend on living things to reproduce. Some bacteria, fungi, protists, and worms may also cause diseases. **Figure 1** shows some enlarged images of common pathogens.

noninfectious disease a disease that cannot spread from one individual to another

infectious disease a disease that is caused by a pathogen and that can be spread from one individual to another

pathogen a virus, microorganism, or other organism that causes disease

virus a microscopic particle that gets inside a cell and often destroys the cell **FCAT** *VOCAB*

G.1.3.1 knows that viruses depend on other living things.

Figure 1 Pathogens

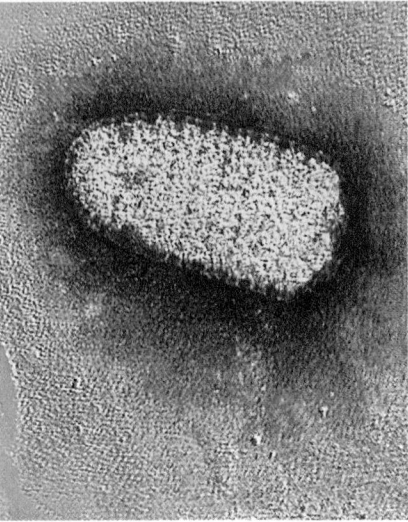

▲ This virus causes rabies.

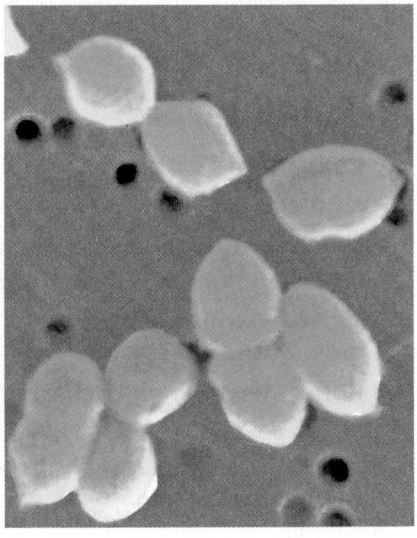
▲ *Streptococcus* bacteria can cause strep throat.

Pathways to Pathogens

There are many ways pathogens can be passed from one person to another. Being aware of them can help you stay healthy.

Air

Some pathogens travel through the air. For example, a single sneeze, such as the one shown in **Figure 2,** releases thousands of tiny droplets of moisture that can carry pathogens.

Contaminated Objects

You may already know that if you drink from a glass that an infected person has just used, you could become infected with a pathogen. A person who is sick may leave bacteria or viruses on many other objects, too. For example, contaminated doorknobs, keyboards, combs, and towels can carry pathogens that may be passed to a person.

Person to Person

Some pathogens are spread by direct person-to-person contact. For example, you can become infected with some illnesses by kissing, shaking hands, or touching the sores of an infected person.

Animals

Some pathogens are carried by animals. For example, humans can get a fungus called *ringworm* from handling an infected dog or cat. Also, ticks may carry bacteria that cause Lyme disease or Rocky Mountain spotted fever.

Food and Water

Drinking water in the United States is generally safe. But water lines can break, or treatment plants can become flooded. These problems may allow microorganisms to enter the public water supply. Bacteria growing in foods and beverages can cause illness, too. For example, meat, fish, and eggs that are not cooked enough can still contain dangerous bacteria or parasites. Even leaving food at room temperature can give bacteria, such as salmonella, the chance to grow and produce toxins in the food. Refrigerating foods can slow the growth of many of these pathogens. Because bacteria grow in food, washing all used cooking surfaces and tools is also important.

Reading Check Why must you cook meat and eggs thoroughly?

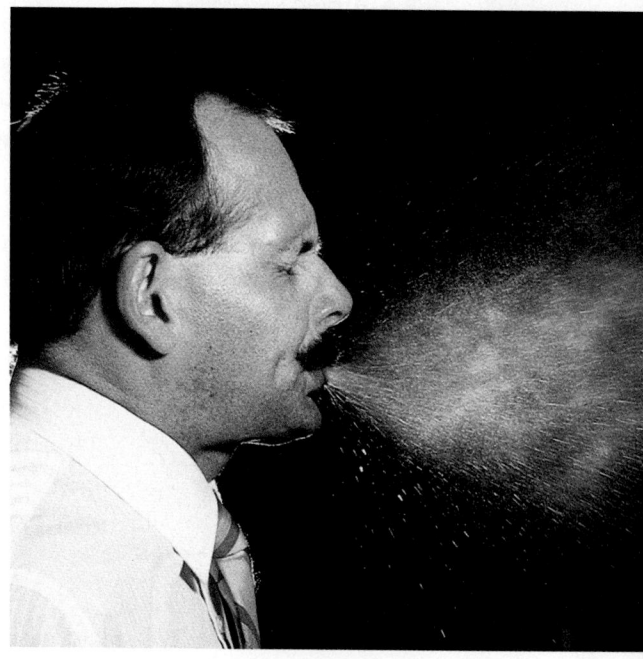

Figure 2 *A sneeze can force thousands of pathogen-carrying droplets out of your body at up to 160 km/h.*

CONNECTION TO Social Studies

Disease and History Many diseases have shaped history. For example, yellow fever, which is caused by a virus that is spread by mosquitoes, was one of the obstacles in building the Panama Canal. Only after people learned how to prevent the spread of the yellow fever virus could the canal be completed.

Use information from Internet and library research to create a poster describing how one infectious disease affected history.

ACTIVITY

Putting Pathogens in Their Place

Until the 20th century, surgery patients often died of bacterial infections. But doctors learned that simple cleanliness could help prevent the spread of some diseases. Today, hospitals and clinics use a variety of technologies to prevent the spread of pathogens. For example, ultraviolet radiation, boiling water, and chemicals are used to kill pathogens in health facilities.

Pasteurization

During the mid-1800s, Louis Pasteur, a French scientist, discovered that microorganisms cause wine to spoil. The uninvited microorganisms were bacteria. Pasteur devised a method of using heat to kill most of the bacteria in the wine. This method is called *pasteurization* (PAS tuhr i ZAY shuhn), and it is still used today. The milk that the girl in **Figure 3** is drinking has been pasteurized.

Vaccines and Immunity

In the late 1700s, no one knew what a pathogen was. During this time, Edward Jenner studied a disease called *smallpox*. He observed that people who had been infected with cowpox seemed to have protection against smallpox. These people had a resistance to the disease. The ability to resist or recover from an infectious disease is called **immunity.** Jenner's work led to the first modern vaccine. A *vaccine* is a substance that helps your body develop immunity to a disease.

Today, vaccines are used all over the world to prevent many serious diseases. Modern vaccines contain pathogens that are killed or specially treated so that they can't make you very sick. The vaccine is similar enough to the pathogen to allow your body to develop a defense against the disease.

SCHOOL to HOME

Label Check

At home or in a local store, find a product that has been pasteurized. In your **science journal,** write other safety information that you find on the label, including the product's refrigeration needs. Why do you think most products that require pasteurization also require refrigeration?

ACTIVITY

immunity the ability to resist an infectious disease

Figure 3 *Today, pasteurization is used to kill pathogens in many different types of food, including dairy products, shellfish, and juices.*

Antibiotics

Have you ever had strep throat? If so, you have had a bacterial infection. Bacterial infections can be a serious threat to your health. Fortunately, doctors can usually treat these kinds of infections with antibiotics. An *antibiotic* is a substance that can kill bacteria or slow the growth of bacteria. Antibiotics may also be used to treat infections caused by other microorganisms, such as fungi. You may take an antibiotic when you are sick. Always take antibiotics according to your doctor's instructions to ensure that all of the pathogens are killed.

Viruses, such as those that cause colds, are not affected by antibiotics. Antibiotics can kill only living things. Viruses are not considered to be alive because they do not have the ability to reproduce on their own. Therefore, viruses are dependent on other organisms to reproduce. In the past, the only way to destroy viruses in the body was to locate and kill the cells they had invaded. Today, although there are only a few, an increasing number of anti-viral medicines are being developed.

 Benchmark Check How do viruses depend on living things? G.1.3.1

 **Benchmark Activity**

Are Viruses Alive?

WRITING SKILL All living things are made of cells, respond to stimuli, reproduce themselves, grow and develop, and have DNA. Viruses do not have all of these characteristics. Research the characteristics of viruses and why they depend on living things. Write a short report on your findings. Include your opinion about whether viruses should be considered alive. You may also choose to illustrate your report. G.1.3.1

SECTION Review

Summary

- Noninfectious diseases cannot be spread from one person to another.
- Infectious diseases are caused by pathogens that are spread from one organism to another.
- Viruses depend on living organisms to reproduce. G.1.3.1
- Pathogens are spread by contact with infected organisms and through contaminated objects, food, water, or air.
- Cleanliness, antibiotics, pasteurization, vaccines, and anti-viral medicines help control diseases.

Using Key Terms

1. Write an original definition for *infectious disease, noninfectious disease,* and *immunity.*

Understanding Key Ideas

2. Vaccines contain
   a. treated pathogens.
   b. heat.
   c. antibiotics.
   d. pasteurization.

3. List five ways that you might come into contact with a pathogen.

4. Name five ways of avoiding and/or fighting pathogens.

Critical Thinking

5. **Identifying Relationships** Why might the risk of infectious disease be high in a community that has no water-treatment facility?

FCAT Preparation

6. Some viruses can cause disease. Unlike living things, viruses depend on organisms to multiply. Why are viruses not considered to be alive? G.1.3.1
   A. because they depend on living things for food
   B. because they depend on living things to reproduce
   C. because they respond to fungi
   D. because they respond to bacteria

SCiLINKS.

NSTA
Developed and maintained by the National Science Teachers Association

For a variety of links related to this chapter, go to www.scilinks.org

Topic: Pathogens; What Causes Diseases?
SciLinks code: HSM1118; HSM1653

Your Body's Defenses

Bacteria and viruses can be in the air, in the water, and on all of the surfaces around you.

Your body must constantly protect itself against pathogens that are trying to invade it. But how does your body do that? Luckily, your body has its own built-in defense system.

First Lines of Defense

For a pathogen to harm you, it must attack a part of your body. Usually, though, very few of the pathogens around you make it past your first lines of defense.

Many organisms that try to enter your eyes or mouth are destroyed by special enzymes. Pathogens that enter your nose are washed down the back of your throat by mucus. The mucus carries the pathogens to your stomach, where most are quickly digested.

Your skin is made of many layers of flat cells. The outermost layers are dead. As a result, many pathogens that land on your skin have difficulty finding a live cell to infect. As **Figure 1** shows, the dead skin cells are constantly dropping off your body as new skin cells grow from beneath. As the dead skin cells flake off, they carry away viruses, bacteria, and other microorganisms. In addition, glands secrete oil onto your skin's surface. The oil contains chemicals that kill many pathogens.

READING WARM-UP

Objectives
- Describe how your body keeps out pathogens.
- Explain how the immune system fights infections.
- Describe four challenges to the immune system.

Terms to Learn
immune system
macrophage
T cell
B cell
antibody
memory B cell
allergy
autoimmune disease
cancer

READING STRATEGY

Reading Organizer As you read this section, make a flowchart of the steps of how your body responds to a virus.

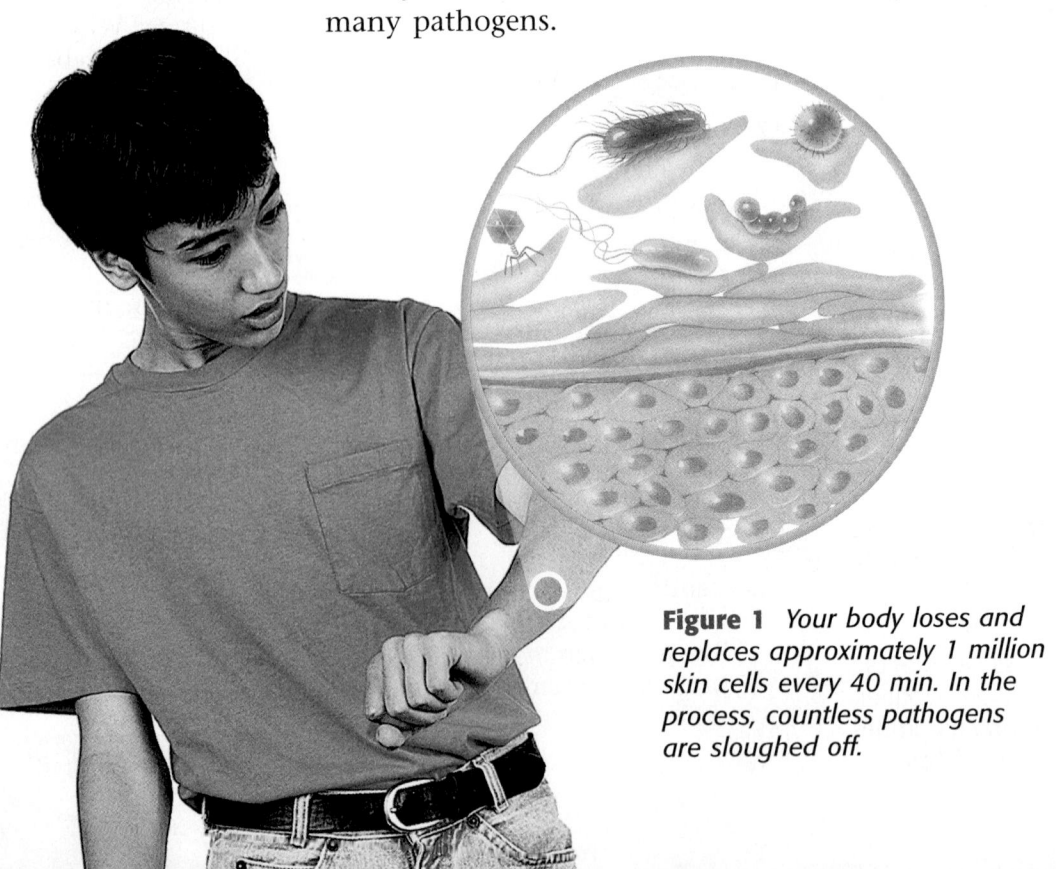

Figure 1 *Your body loses and replaces approximately 1 million skin cells every 40 min. In the process, countless pathogens are sloughed off.*

258

Failure of First Lines of Defense

Sometimes, skin is cut or punctured and pathogens can enter the body. The body acts quickly to keep out as many pathogens as possible. Blood flow to the injured area increases. Cell parts in the blood called *platelets* help seal the open wound so that no more pathogens can enter.

The increased blood flow also brings cells that belong to the **immune system,** the body system that fights pathogens. The immune system is not localized in one place in your body. It is not controlled by one organ, such as the brain. Instead, a team of individual cells, tissues, and organs work together to keep you safe from invading pathogens.

Cells of the Immune System

The immune system consists mainly of three kinds of cells. One kind is the macrophage (MAK roh FAYJ). **Macrophages** are immune system cells that engulf and digest many microorganisms or viruses that enter your body. If only a few microorganisms or viruses have entered a wound, the macrophages can easily stop them.

The other two main kinds of immune-system cells are T cells and B cells. **T cells** are immune system cells that coordinate the immune system and attack many infected cells. **B cells** are immune-system cells that make antibodies. **Antibodies** are proteins that attach to specific antigens, which are substances that stimulate an immune response. Your body is capable of making billions of different antibodies. Each antibody usually attaches to only one kind of antigen, as illustrated in **Figure 2.**

Reading Check How do macrophages help the body fight disease?

Only Skin Deep
1. Cut an **apple** in half.
2. Place **plastic wrap** over each half. The plastic wrap will act as skin.
3. Use **scissors** to cut the plastic wrap on one of the apple halves, and then use an **eyedropper** to drip **food coloring** on each apple half. The food coloring represents pathogens coming into contact with your body.
4. What happened to each apple half?
5. How is the plastic wrap similar to skin?
6. How is the plastic wrap different from skin?

immune system the cells and tissues that recognize and attack foreign substances in the body

macrophage an immune system cell that engulfs pathogens and other materials

T cell an immune system cell that coordinates the immune system and attacks many infected cells

B cell a white blood cell that makes antibodies

antibody a protein made by B cells that binds to a specific antigen

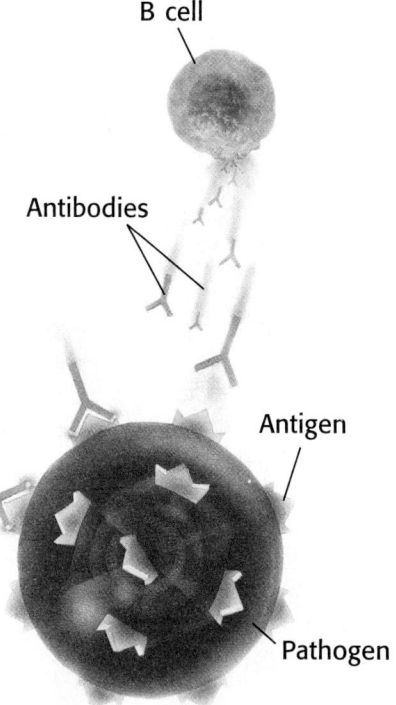

Figure 2 *An antibody's shape is very specialized. It matches an antigen like a key fits a lock.*

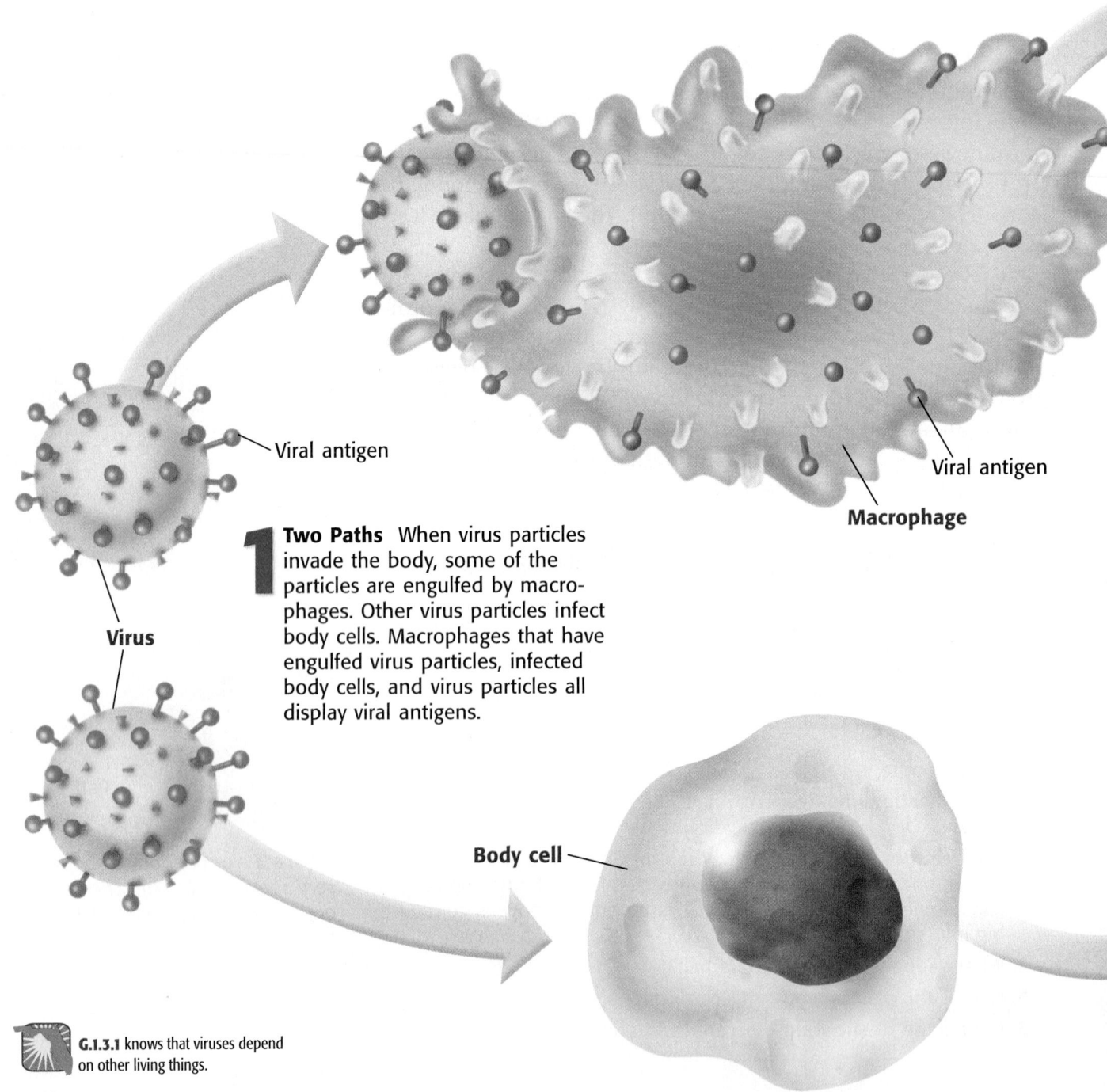
Responding to a Virus

If virus particles enter your body, only the particles that pass into body cells can begin to replicate. Other virus particles will be engulfed and broken up by macrophages. This process is just the beginning of the immune response. The process your immune system uses to fight an invading virus is summarized in the figure below.

✓ Reading Check What are two things that can happen to virus particles when they enter the body?

Viral antigen

Viral antigen

Macrophage

Virus

1 **Two Paths** When virus particles invade the body, some of the particles are engulfed by macrophages. Other virus particles infect body cells. Macrophages that have engulfed virus particles, infected body cells, and virus particles all display viral antigens.

Body cell

G.1.3.1 knows that viruses depend on other living things.

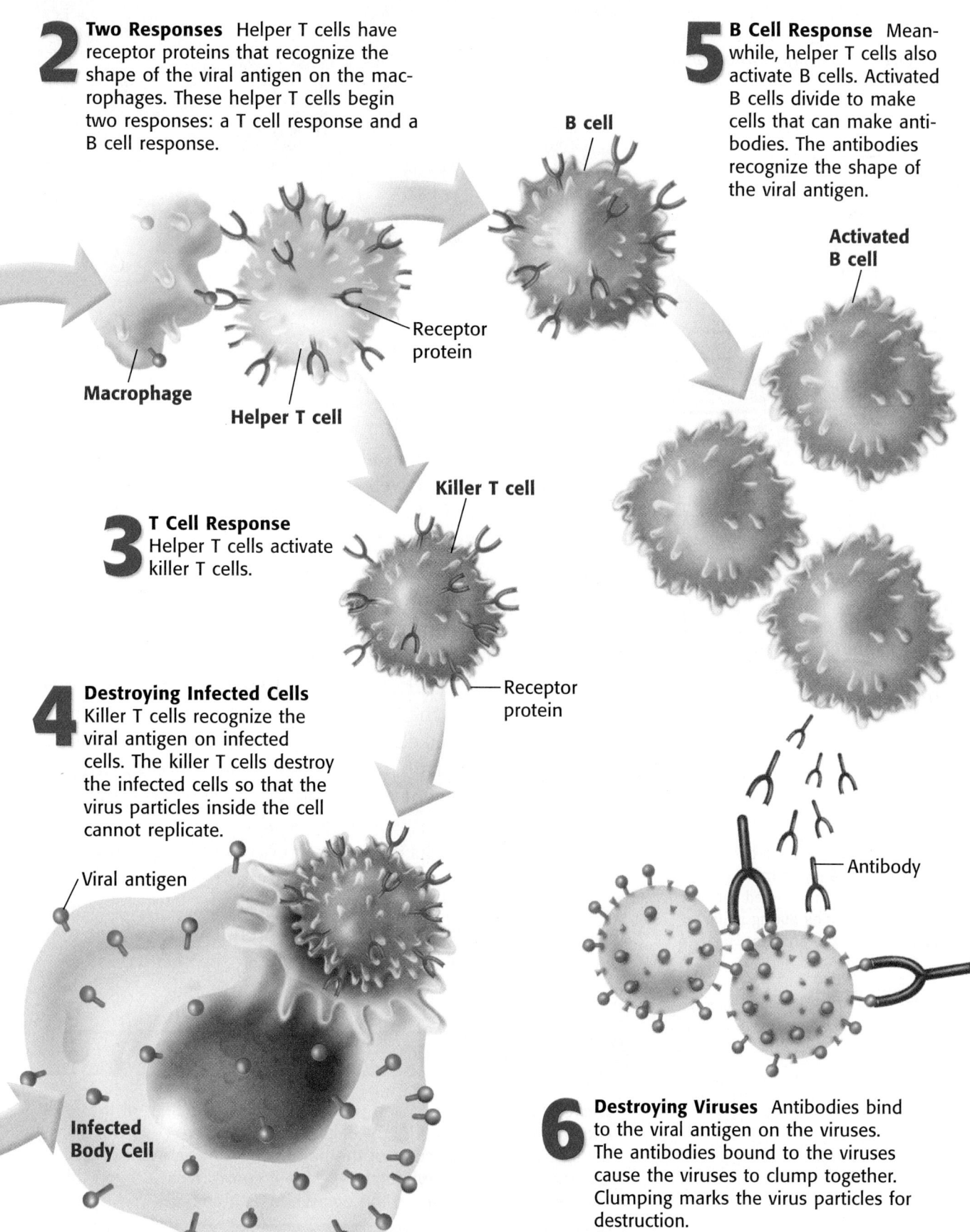

2 **Two Responses** Helper T cells have receptor proteins that recognize the shape of the viral antigen on the macrophages. These helper T cells begin two responses: a T cell response and a B cell response.

B cell

Receptor protein

Macrophage

Helper T cell

5 **B Cell Response** Meanwhile, helper T cells also activate B cells. Activated B cells divide to make cells that can make antibodies. The antibodies recognize the shape of the viral antigen.

Activated B cell

Killer T cell

3 **T Cell Response** Helper T cells activate killer T cells.

Receptor protein

4 **Destroying Infected Cells** Killer T cells recognize the viral antigen on infected cells. The killer T cells destroy the infected cells so that the virus particles inside the cell cannot replicate.

Viral antigen

Infected Body Cell

Antibody

6 **Destroying Viruses** Antibodies bind to the viral antigen on the viruses. The antibodies bound to the viruses cause the viruses to clump together. Clumping marks the virus particles for destruction.

Figure 3 *You may not feel well when you have a fever. But a fever is one way that your body fights infections.*

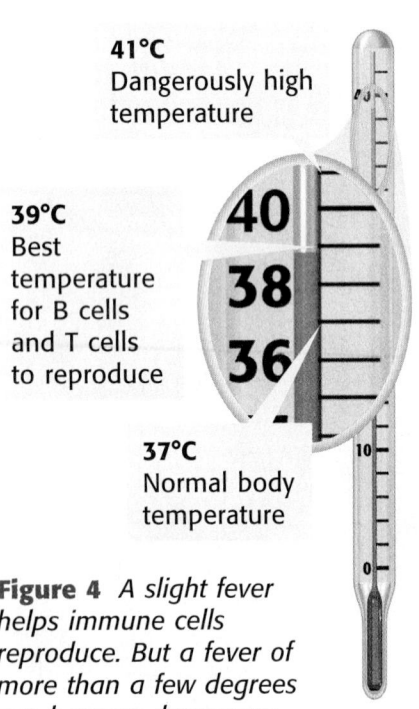

41°C
Dangerously high temperature

39°C
Best temperature for B cells and T cells to reproduce

37°C
Normal body temperature

Figure 4 *A slight fever helps immune cells reproduce. But a fever of more than a few degrees can become dangerous.*

memory B cell a B cell that responds to an antigen more strongly when the body is reinfected with an antigen than it does during its first encounter with the antigen

Fevers

The man in **Figure 3** is sick and has a fever. What is a fever? When macrophages activate the helper T cells, the helper T cells send a chemical signal that tells your brain to turn up the thermostat. In a few minutes, your body's temperature can rise several degrees. A moderate fever of one or two degrees actually helps you get well faster because it slows the growth of some pathogens. As shown in **Figure 4,** a fever also helps B cells and T cells multiply faster.

Memory Cells

Your immune system can respond to a second encounter faster than it can respond the first time. B cells must have had previous contact with a pathogen before they can make the correct antibodies. During the first encounter with a new pathogen, specialized B cells make antibodies that are effective against that particular invader. This process takes about 2 weeks, which is far too long to prevent an infection. Therefore, the first time you are infected, you usually get sick.

A few of the B cells become memory B cells. **Memory B cells** are cells in your immune system that "remember" how to make an antibody for a particular pathogen. If the pathogen shows up again, the memory B cells produce B cells that make enough antibodies in just 3 or 4 days to protect you.

CONNECTION TO
Chemistry

Bent out of Shape When you have a fever, the heat of the fever changes the shape of viral or bacterial proteins, which slows or prevents the reproduction of the pathogen. With an adult present, observe how an egg white changes as it cooks. What do you think happens to the protein in the egg white as it cooks?

ACTiViTY

Challenges to the Immune System

The immune system is a very effective body-defense system, but it is not perfect. The immune system is unable to deal with some diseases. There are also conditions in which the immune system does not work properly.

Allergies

Sometimes, the immune system overreacts to antigens that are not dangerous to the body. This inappropriate reaction is called an **allergy.** Allergies may be caused by many things, including certain foods and medicines. Many people have allergic reactions to pollen, shown in **Figure 5.** Symptoms of allergic reactions range from a runny nose and itchy eyes to more serious conditions, such as asthma.

Doctors are not sure why the immune system overreacts in some people. Scientists think allergies might be useful because the mucus draining from your nose carries away pollen, dust, and microorganisms.

Autoimmune Diseases

A disease in which the immune system attacks the body's own cells is called an **autoimmune disease.** In an autoimmune disease, immune-system cells mistake body cells for pathogens. One autoimmune disease is rheumatoid arthritis (ROO muh TOYD ahr THRIET IS), in which the immune system attacks the joints. A common location for rheumatoid arthritis is the joints of the hands, as shown in **Figure 6.** Other autoimmune diseases include type 1 diabetes, multiple sclerosis, and lupus.

✓ Reading Check Name four autoimmune diseases.

allergy a reaction to a harmless or common substance by the body's immune system

autoimmune disease a disease in which the immune system attacks the organism's own cells

Figure 5 *Pollen is one substance that can cause allergic reactions.*

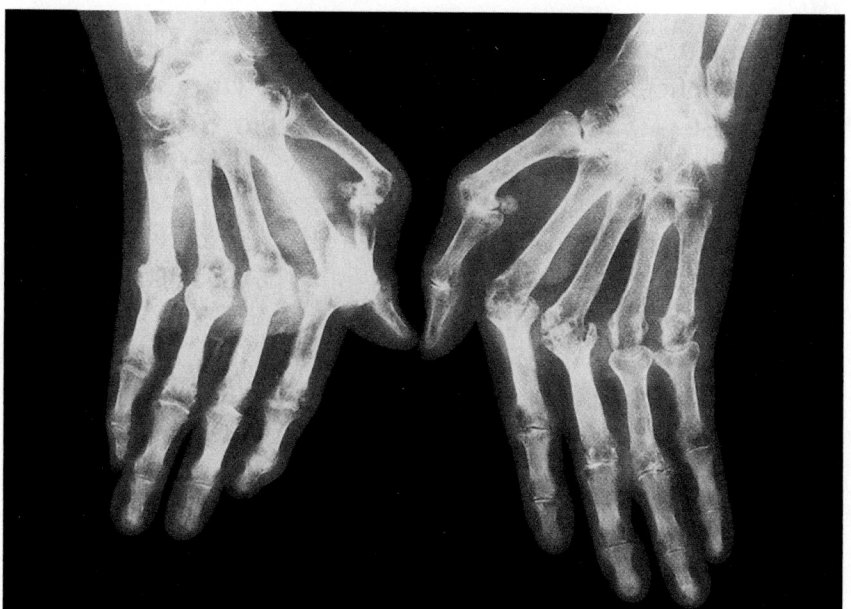

Figure 6 *In a person who has rheumatoid arthritis, immune-system cells cause joint-tissue swelling, which can lead to joint deformities.*

Figure 7 **Immune Cells Fighting Cancer**

❶ A killer T cell attacks an unregulated cell.

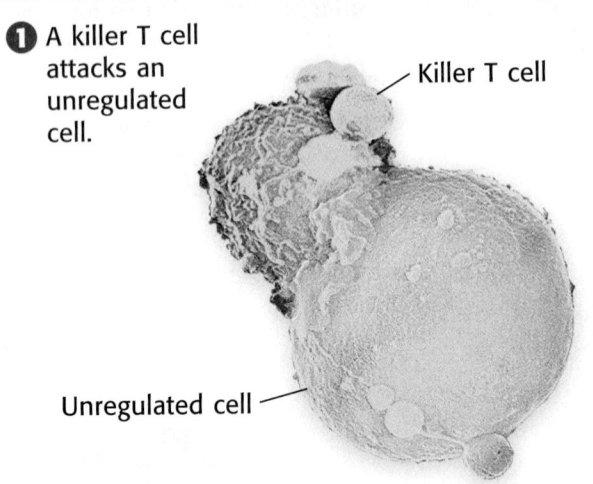

Killer T cell

Unregulated cell

❷ The cell's membrane ruptures as the cell dies.

Cancer

Healthy cells divide at a carefully regulated rate. Occasionally, a cell doesn't respond to the body's regulation and begins dividing at an uncontrolled rate. As can be seen in **Figure 7,** killer T cells destroy this type of cell. Sometimes, the immune system cannot control the division of these cells. **Cancer** is the condition in which cells divide at an uncontrolled rate.

cancer a tumor in which the cells begin dividing at an uncontrolled rate and become invasive

Many cancers will invade nearby tissues. They can also enter the cardiovascular system or lymphatic system. Cancers can then be transported to other places in the body. Cancers disrupt the normal activities of the organs they have invaded and sometimes lead to death. Today, though, there are many treatments for cancer. Surgery, radiation, and certain drugs can be used to remove or kill cancer cells or slow their division.

AIDS

The human immunodeficiency virus (HIV) causes acquired immune deficiency syndrome (AIDS). Most viruses infect cells in the nose, mouth, lungs, or intestines, but HIV is different. HIV infects the immune system itself by using helper T cells as factories to produce more viruses, which results in the destruction of the T cell. You can see HIV particles in **Figure 8.** Remember that the helper T cells put the B cells and killer T cells to work in fighting infection.

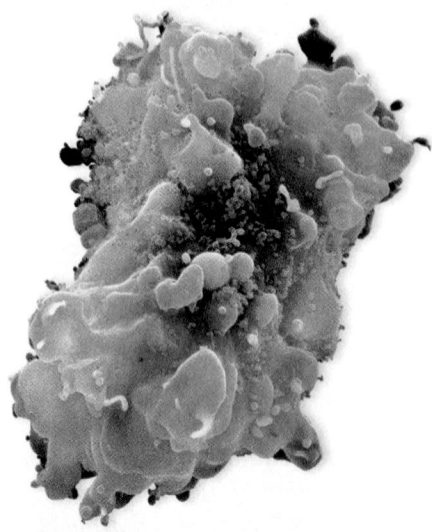

Figure 8 *The blue particles on this helper T cell are human immunodeficiency viruses. They replicated inside the T cell.*

People who have AIDS have very few helper T cells, so the B cells and killer T cells are not activated. Therefore, the immune system cannot attack HIV or any other pathogen. People who have AIDS do not usually die of AIDS itself. They die of other diseases that their immune systems are unable to fight.

✓ *Reading Check* What virus causes AIDS?

SECTION Review

Summary

- Macrophages engulf pathogens, display antigens on their surface, and activate helper T cells. The helper T cells put the killer T cells and B cells to work.
- Killer T cells kill infected cells. B cells make antibodies.
- Fever helps speed immune-cell growth and helps slow pathogen growth.
- Memory B cells remember how to make an antibody for a pathogen that the body had contact with.

- An allergy is the overreaction of the immune system to a harmless antigen.
- Autoimmune diseases are diseases that cause the immune system to attack healthy tissue.
- Cancer cells are cells that undergo uncontrolled division.
- AIDS is a disease that results when the human immunodeficiency virus kills helper T cells.

Using Key Terms

For each pair of terms, explain how the meanings of the terms differ.

1. *B cell* and *T cell*

2. *autoimmune disease* and *allergy*

Understanding Key Ideas

3. Your body's first line of defense against pathogens includes
   a. skin.
   b. macrophages.
   c. T cells.
   d. B cells.

4. List three ways your body defends itself against pathogens.

5. Name three different cells in the immune system, and describe how they respond to pathogens.

6. Describe four challenges to the immune system.

7. What characterizes a cancer cell?

Critical Thinking

8. **Identifying Relationships** Can your body make antibodies for pathogens that you have never been in contact with? Why or why not?

9. **Applying Concepts** If you had chickenpox at age 7, explain what might prevent you from getting chickenpox again at age 8.

FCAT Preparation

10. HIV is the virus that causes AIDS. Like any virus, HIV needs living things so that it can multiply. As shown in the graph below, the virus that causes AIDS uses T cells until the T cells are destroyed. The body uses T cells to fight infections.

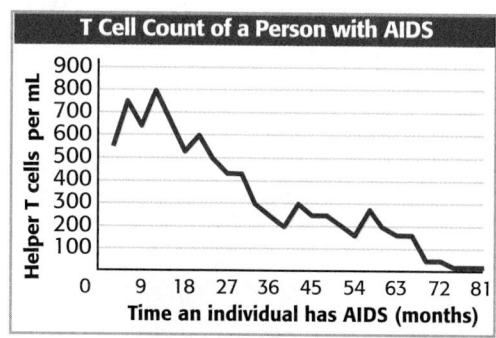

T Cell Count of a Person with AIDS

Helper T cells per mL

Time an individual has AIDS (months)

For what purpose does the virus that causes AIDS use the T cells, and why do people who have AIDS eventually become very sick? G.1.3.1

SCiLINKS®

NSTA
Developed and maintained by the
National Science Teachers Association

For a variety of links related to this chapter, go to www.scilinks.org

Topic: Body Defenses; Allergies
SciLinks code: HSM0181; HSM0048

265

Skills Practice Lab

OBJECTIVES

Investigate how diseases spread.

Analyze data about how diseases spread.

MATERIALS

- beaker or a cup, 200 mL
- eyedropper
- gloves, protective
- solution, unknown, 50 mL

SAFETY

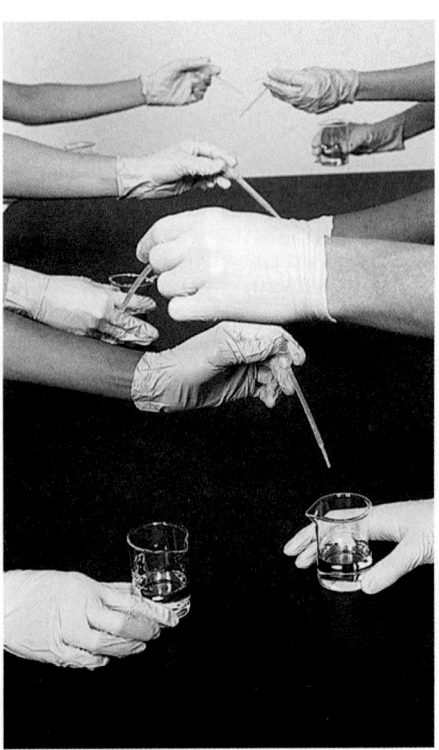

Passing the Cold

There are more than 100 viruses that cause the symptoms of the common cold. Any of the viruses can be passed from person to person—through the air or through direct contact. In this activity, you will track the progress of an outbreak in your class.

Ask a Question

1 With other members of your group, form a question about the spread of disease. For example "How are cold viruses passed from person to person?" or "How can the progress of an outbreak be modeled?"

Form a Hypothesis

2 Form a hypothesis based on the question you asked.

Test the Hypothesis

3 Obtain an empty cup or beaker, an eyedropper, and 50 mL of one of the solutions from your teacher. Only one student will have the "cold virus" solution. You will see a change in your solution when you have become "infected."

4 Your teacher will divide the class into two equal groups. If there is an extra student, that person will record data on the board. Otherwise, the teacher will act as the recorder.

5 The two groups should form straight lines, facing each other.

6 Each time your teacher says the word *mix,* fill your eyedropper with your solution, and place 10 drops of your solution in the beaker of the person in the line opposite you without touching your eyedropper to the other liquid.

7 Gently stir the liquid in your cup with your eyedropper. Do not put your eyedropper in anyone else's solution.

8 If your solution changes color, raise your hand so that the recorder can record the number of students who have been "infected."

9 Your teacher will instruct one line to move one person to the right. Then, the person at the end of the line without a partner should go to the other end of the line.

Results of Experiment			
Trial	Number of infected people	Total number of people	Percentage of infected people
1			
2			
3			
4			
5			
6			
7			
8			
9			
10			

DO NOT WRITE IN BOOK

10 Repeat steps 5–9 nine more times for a total of 10 trials.

11 Return to your desk, and create a data table in your notebook similar to the table above. The column with the title "Total number of people" will remain the same in every row. Enter the data from the board into your data table.

12 Find the percentage of infected people for the last column by dividing the number of infected people by the total number of people and multiplying by 100 in each line.

Analyze the Results

1 **Describing Events** Did you become infected? If so, during which trial did you become infected?

2 **Examining Data** Did everyone eventually become infected? If so, how many trials were necessary to infect everyone?

Draw Conclusions

3 **Interpreting Information** Explain at least one reason why this simulation may underestimate the number of people who might have been infected in real life.

4 **Applying Conclusions** Use your results to make a line graph showing the change in the infection percentage per trial.

Applying Your Data

Do research in the library or on the Internet to find out some of the factors that contribute to the spread of a cold virus. What is the best and easiest way to reduce your chances of catching a cold? Explain your answer.

Chapter Review

USING KEY TERMS

Use a term from the chapter to complete each sentence below.

1 A(n) ___ is caused by a pathogen.

2 Antibiotics can be used to kill a(n) ___.

3 Macrophages attract helper ___.

4 A(n) ___ binds to an antigen.

5 An immune-system overreaction to a harmless substance is a(n) ___.

6 The unregulated growth of cells is called ___.

UNDERSTANDING KEY IDEAS

Multiple Choice

7 Pathogens are
   a. all viruses and microorganisms.
   b. viruses and microorganisms that cause disease.
   c. noninfectious organisms.
   d. all bacteria that live in water.

8 Which of the following is an infectious disease?
   a. allergies
   b. rheumatoid arthritis
   c. asthma
   d. a common cold

9 A fever
   a. slows pathogen growth.
   b. helps B cells multiply faster.
   c. helps T cells multiply faster.
   d. All of the above

10 The skin keeps pathogens out by
   a. staying warm enough to kill pathogens.
   b. releasing killer T cells onto its surface.
   c. shedding dead cells and secreting oils.
   d. All of the above

11 Memory B cells
   a. kill pathogens.
   b. activate killer T cells.
   c. activate killer B cells.
   d. produce B cells that make antibodies.

12 Macrophages
   a. make antibodies.
   b. release helper T cells.
   c. live in the gut.
   d. engulf pathogens.

13 To multiply, a virus needs the cells of living things. Viruses are very small. Viruses can spread from person to person and cause diseases. Why are viruses not considered to be alive?
   G.1.3.1 **FCAT**
   a. because they need organisms to reproduce
   b. because they cause diseases
   c. because they spread on contact
   d. because they are very small

Short Answer

14 Explain how macrophages start an immune response.

15 Describe the role of helper T cells in responding to an infection.

16 Name two ways that you come into contact with pathogens.

Math Skills

17 You went to school with a cold and exposed five friends to your cold. The next day, each of those five friends passed the virus to five of their friends. If this pattern continues, how many people will have been exposed to the cold in five days?

CRITICAL THINKING

18 Identifying Relationships Why does the disappearance of helper T cells in people who have AIDS damage the immune systems of those people?

19 Predicting Consequences Many people take fever-reducing drugs as soon as their temperature exceeds 37°C. Why might it not be a good idea to reduce a fever immediately with drugs?

20 Evaluating Data The risk of dying from a whooping cough vaccine is about one in 1 million. In contrast, the risk of dying from whooping cough is about one in 500. Discuss the pros and cons of this vaccination.

Concept Mapping

21 Use the following terms to create a concept map: *macrophage, helper T cell, B cell, antibody, antigen, killer T cell,* and *memory B cell.*

INTERPRETING GRAPHICS

The graph below compares the concentration of antibodies in the blood the first time you are exposed to a pathogen with the concentration of antibodies the next time you are exposed to the pathogen. Use the graph below to answer the questions that follow.

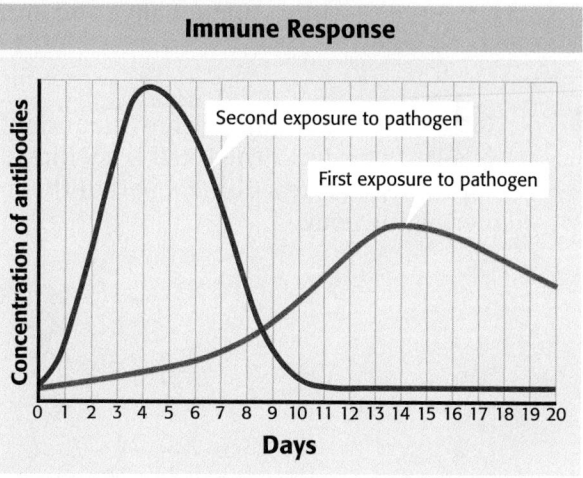

Immune Response

Second exposure to pathogen

First exposure to pathogen

Concentration of antibodies

0 1 2 3 4 5 6 7 8 9 10 11 12 13 14 15 16 17 18 19 20

Days

22 Are there more antibodies present during the first week of the first exposure or during the first week of the second exposure? Explain your answer.

23 What is the difference in recovery time between the first exposure and the second exposure? Why?

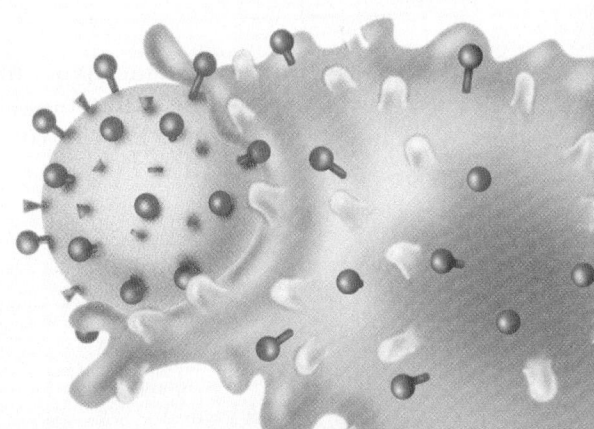

For the following questions, write your answers on a separate sheet of paper.

1 Antibiotics are substances that kill or slow the growth of bacteria. They can also be used to treat some infections caused by fungi and other microorganisms. Why are antibiotics unable to cure diseases caused by viruses?

    A. because viruses cause autoimmune diseases

    B. because viruses infect too many cells too quickly

    C. because viruses are too infectious to be treated by antibiotics

    D. because viruses are not alive and antibiotics kill only living things

2 As shown in the diagram below, an antibody's shape matches the shape of a viral antigen like a key fits a lock. The B cell is a white blood cell that makes antibodies in response to antigens. This reaction is a part of the immune system's response to foreign particles entering the body.

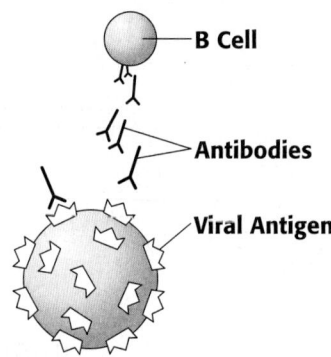

On which of the following are antigens found?

    F. antibiotics

    G. pathogens

    H. plasma

    I. platelets

3 Living things are made up of one or more cells, have DNA, reproduce themselves, grow and develop, can sense and respond to stimuli, and use energy. Should a virus be considered a living thing or not? Explain you answer.

READ
INQUIRE
EXPLAIN

4 During the late 1700s, a scientist named Edward Jenner observed that people who had been infected by cowpox seemed to have resistance to smallpox. This ability to resist disease is called immunity. Jenner's work led to the creation of substances that help people develop immunity to diseases. What are these substances called?

    A.   T cells
    B.   vaccines
    C.   antibiotics
    D.   antibodies

5 Viruses need the cells of living organisms to thrive and replicate. When viruses infect cells in the human body, the immune system responds by destroying infected cells. Which of the following describes the sequence of events that leads to the destruction of infected cells?

    F.   Killer B cells kill infected T cells, and helper T cells activate B cells, which divide and produce antibodies that bind viruses.
    G.   Killer T cells kill infected cells, and helper T cells activate B cells, which divide and produce antibodies that bind viruses.
    H.   Helper T cells kill infected cells, and killer T cells activate B cells, which divide and produce antibiotics that bind viruses.
    I.   Helper B cells kill infected T cells, and killer T cells activate B cells, which divide and produce antibiotics that bind viruses.

6 The illustration below shows one way in which the body's immune system responds to a virus. The sphere on the left represents a virus.

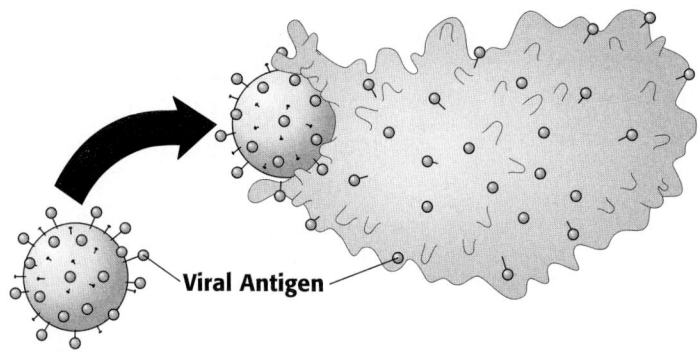

Viral Antigen

What is happening to the right of the arrow?

    A.   A virus is infecting a T cell.
    B.   A virus is infecting a B cell.
    C.   A platelet is absorbing a virus.
    D.   A macrophage is engulfing a virus.

FCAT Preparation

Science in Action

FOCUS ON FLORIDA

Weird Science

Frogs in the Medicine Cabinet?

Frog skin, mouse intestines, cow lungs, and shark stomachs are all being tested to make more effective medicines to combat harmful bacteria. In 1896, a biologist named Michael Zasloff was studying African clawed frogs. He noticed that cuts in the frogs' skin healed quickly and never became infected. Zasloff decided to investigate further. He found that when a frog was cut, its skin released a liquid antibiotic that killed invading bacteria. Furthermore, sand sharks, moths, pigs, mice, and cows also contain chemicals that kill bacteria and other microorganisms. These useful antibiotics are even found in the small intestines of humans!

Scientific Discoveries

Prions and Disease-Causing Proteins

What does a disease need to spread? Most scientists thought that infectious diseases required nucleic acid (DNA or RNA) in order to multiply and spread. However, some scientists thought that diseases could also be spread between organisms by proteins alone. Different kinds of proteins have unique folding patterns. According to the new hypothesis, proteins such as disease-causing *prions*, can change normally folded proteins into differently folded disease-causing proteins. Chih-Yen King and Ruben Diaz-Avalos, researchers at Florida State University (FSU), have been able to show that when prions come into contact with normal proteins, prions do indeed cause normal proteins to refold into new prions. Therefore prions can cause disease without DNA or RNA.

Social Studies ACTiViTY

Many medicines were discovered in plants or animals by people living near those plants or animals. Research the origin of one or two common medicines discovered this way. Make a poster showing a world map and the location of the medicines that you researched.

Math ACTiViTY

A prion can cause a healthy protein to change into a prion if the prion comes into contact with the protein. In a cycle, one prion causes a healthy protein to change into a new prion. In a second cycle, these two prions can cause two more healthy proteins to become prions. If you start with one prion, how many of these cycles will result in at least 1,000 prions?

Terrel Shepherd III

Nurse Terrel Shepherd III is a registered nurse (RN) at Texas Children's Hospital in Houston, Texas. RNs have many responsibilities. These responsibilities include giving patients their medications, assessing patients' health, and establishing intravenous access. Nurses also serve as a go-between for the patient and the doctor. Although most nurses work in hospitals or clinics, some nurses work for corporations. Pediatric nurses such as Shepherd work specifically with infants, children, and adolescents. The field of nursing offers a wide variety of job opportunities including home-care nurses, traveling nurses, and flight nurses. The hospital alone has many areas of expertise for nurses, including geriatrics (working with the elderly), intensive care, administration, and surgery. Traditionally, nursing has been considered to be a woman's career. However, since nursing began as a profession, men and women have practiced nursing. A career in nursing is possible for anyone who does well in science, enjoys people, and wants to make a difference in people's lives.

Language Arts ACTiViTy

WRITING SKILL Create a brochure that persuades people to consider a career in nursing. Describe nursing as a career, the benefits of becoming a nurse, and the education needed to be a nurse. Illustrate the brochure with pictures of nurses from the Internet or from magazines.

To learn more about these Science in Action topics, visit **go.hrw.com** and type in the keyword **HT6FBDFF.**

Current Science

Check out Current Science® articles related to this chapter by visiting go.hrw.com. Just type in the keyword **HL5CS27.**

UNIT 4

TIMELINE

Living Things and the Environment

What did you have for breakfast this morning? Your breakfast likely was the result of living things working together. For example, milk comes from a cow. The cow eats plants to get energy. Bacteria help the plants obtain nutrients from the soil. And the soil has nutrients because fungi break down dead trees.

All living things on Earth are interconnected. In this unit, you will study the interaction of living things. This timeline shows some of the ways that humans have studied and affected Earth.

1661

John Evelyn publishes a book condemning air pollution in London, England.

1771

In his experiments with plants, Joseph Priestley finds that plants use carbon dioxide and release oxygen.

1933

The Civilian Conservation Corps is established. The corps plants trees, fights forest fires, and builds dams to control floods.

1990

To save dolphins from being caught in fishing nets, U.S. tuna processors announce that they will not accept tuna caught in nets that can kill dolphins.

1851

The United States imports sparrows from Germany to defend against crop-damaging caterpillars.

1854

Henry David Thoreau's *Walden* is published. In it, Thoreau asserts that people should live in harmony with nature.

1872

The first U.S. national park, Yellowstone, is established by Congress.

1962

Rachel Carson's book *Silent Spring,* which describes the wasteful use of pesticides and their destruction of the environment, is published.

1970

The Environmental Protection Agency (EPA) is formed to set and enforce pollution-control standards in the United States.

1973

The United States Congress passes the Endangered Species Act.

1993

Americans recycle 59.5 billion aluminum cans (two out of every three cans).

1996

Gates at Glen Canyon Dam are opened, purposefully flooding the Grand Canyon. The flooding helps maintain ecological balance by restoring beaches and sandbars and rejuvenating marshes.

2002

The U.S. Fish and Wildlife Service installs red neon lights along the Florida coast to replace lights that distract baby sea turtles from finding the ocean when they hatch.

Adapting to the Environment

 **The Big Idea** Adaptations improve an organism's ability to survive and reproduce.

About the PHOTO

No, this thorny branch isn't part of a rose bush. The thorns on this tree branch are actually insects! Commonly known as thorn bugs, these insects are camouflaged as green thorns and are hard to notice unless they jump to another branch. These thorn bugs were photographed on Sanibel Island, Florida.

PRE-READING ACTIVITY

Graphic Organizer **Spider Map** Before you read the chapter, create the graphic organizer entitled "Spider Map" described in the **Study Skills** section of the Appendix. Label the circle "Adaptations." Create a leg for each type of plant or animal adaptation. As you read the chapter, fill in the map with details about each type of adaptation.

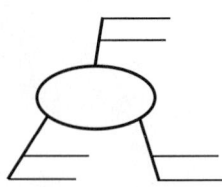

START-UP ACTIVITY

Go on a Safari!

You don't have to travel far to see interesting animals. If you look closely, you can find many animals, nearby. **Caution:** Always be careful around wild or unfamiliar animals, because they may bite or sting. Do not handle wild animals or any animals that are unfamiliar to you.

Procedure

1. Go outside, and find **two different kinds of animals** to observe.

2. Without disturbing the animals, watch them quietly for a few minutes from a distance. You may want to use **binoculars** or a **magnifying lens.**

3. Write down everything you notice about each animal. Do you know what kind of animal each is? Where did you find them? What do they look like? How big are they? What are they doing? You may want to draw a picture of them.

Analysis

1. Compare the two animals that you studied. Do they look alike? Do they have similar behaviors? Explain.

2. How do the animals move? Did you see them communicating with other animals or defending themselves? Explain.

3. Can you tell what each animal eats? What characteristics of each animal help it find or catch food?

SECTION 1

Animal Reproduction

The life span of some living things is short compared with ours. For example, a fruit fly lives only about 40 days. Other organisms live much longer than we do. For example, a giant tortoise can live as long as 177 years.

But all living things eventually die. For a species to survive, members of the species must reproduce.

READING WARM-UP

Objectives

- Describe the patterns and advantages of asexual reproduction in animals. **F.2.3.1 CS**
- Describe the patterns and advantages of sexual reproduction in animals. **F.2.3.1 CS**
- Explain how sexual reproduction is related to variation within a species. **F.2.3.2 AA**
- Explain the difference between external and internal fertilization.
- Identify the three different types of mammalian reproduction.

Terms to Learn

asexual reproduction *FCAT VOCAB*
sexual reproduction *FCAT VOCAB*
external fertilization
internal fertilization

READING STRATEGY

Prediction Guide Before reading this section, write the title of each heading in this section. Next, under each heading, write what you think you will learn.

Asexual Reproduction

Some animals reproduce asexually. In **asexual reproduction,** a single parent has offspring that are genetically identical to the parent. One advantage of asexual reproduction is that organisms can produce many offspring in a short amount of time. Another advantage of asexual reproduction is that organisms do not have to use energy to find a mate.

One pattern of asexual reproduction is called budding. *Budding* happens when a part of the parent organism pinches off and forms a new organism. The hydra, shown in **Figure 1,** reproduces by budding. The new hydra is genetically identical to its parent. Fragmentation is a second kind of asexual reproduction. In *fragmentation,* part of an organism breaks off and then new parts regenerate to form a new individual. Some organisms also have the ability to regenerate body parts. If an organism loses a body part, that part may develop into a new individual. A sea star, as shown in **Figure 2,** can regenerate body parts.

Benchmark Check What is an advantage of budding? **F.2.3.1 CS**

asexual reproduction reproduction that does not involve the union of sex cells and in which a single parent produces offspring that are genetically identical to the parent *FCAT VOCAB*

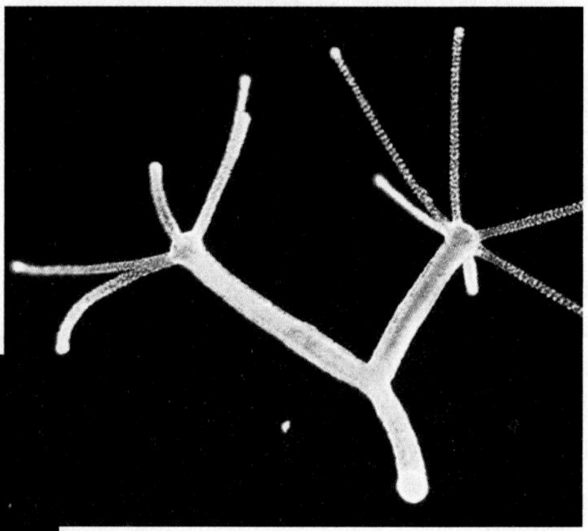

Figure 1 *The hydra bud will separate from its parent. Buds from other organisms, such as certain corals, remain attached to the parent.*

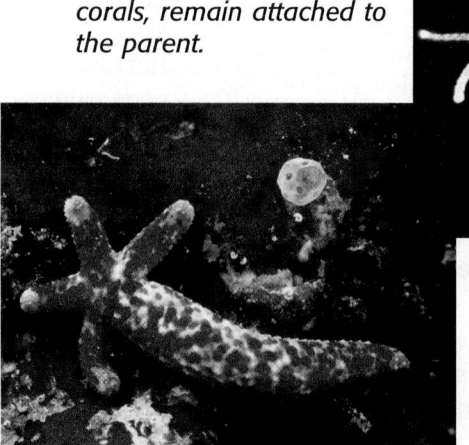

Figure 2 *The largest arm on this sea star was a fragment, from which a new sea star will be made. In time, all of the sea star's arms will grow to the same size.*

Sexual Reproduction

Most animals reproduce sexually. In **sexual reproduction,** offspring are formed when genetic information from more than one parent combines. Sexual reproduction in animals usually requires two parents—a male and a female. The female parent produces sex cells called *eggs*. The male parent produces sex cells called *sperm*. When an egg's nucleus and a sperm's nucleus join, a fertilized egg, called a *zygote* (ZIE GOHT), is created. This joining of an egg and sperm is known as *fertilization.*

Genetic information is found in *genes*. Genes are located on *chromosomes* (KROH muh SOHMZ) made of proteins and DNA. During fertilization, the egg and sperm each contribute chromosomes to the zygote. The combination of genes from the two parents results in a zygote that grows into a unique individual. This individual is not genetically identical to either of its parents. **Figure 3** shows how genes mix through three generations.

The combination of genes during sexual reproduction allows for variation within a population. Variation is an advantage of sexual reproduction and occurs in both plants and animals. The variation of genes allows a population to adapt to changes in the environment over time.

Benchmark Check How does variation occur during sexual reproduction? F.2.3.2 AA

sexual reproduction reproduction in which sex cells from two parents unite to produce offspring that share traits from both parents **FCAT** VOCAB

CONNECTION TO Language Arts

WRITING SKILL **Nature or Nurture?** Scientists debate whether genetics or upbringing is more important in shaping people. Use the Internet or library to research the issue of "nature versus nurture." Find information about identical twins who were raised apart. When you finish your research, write a persuasive essay supporting one side of the debate. Include evidence to support your argument.

Figure 3 **Inheriting Genes**

Eggs and sperm contain chromosomes. You inherit chromosomes— and the genes on them—from both of your parents. Your parents each inherited chromosomes from their parents.

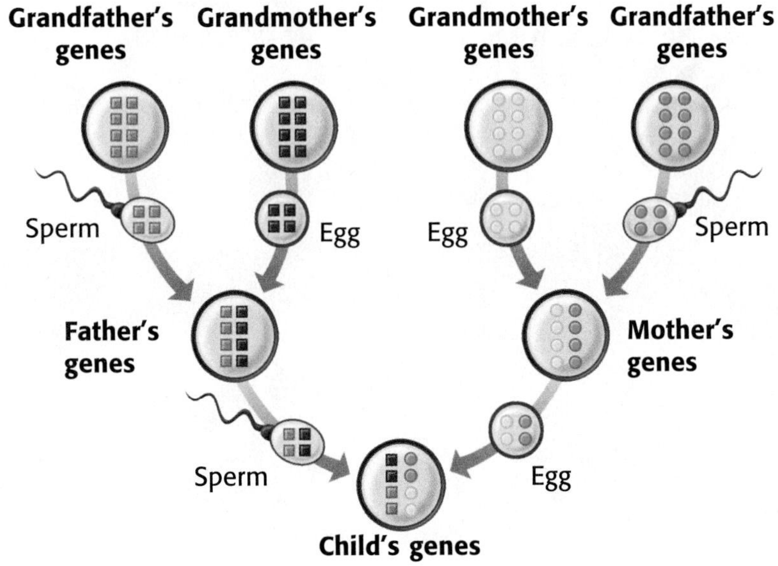

Grandfather's genes   Grandmother's genes   Grandmother's genes   Grandfather's genes

Sperm   Egg   Egg   Sperm

Father's genes   Mother's genes

Sperm   Egg

Child's genes

F.2.3.1 CS (partial) knows the patterns and advantages of sexual and asexual reproduction in plants and animals.

F.2.3.2 AA knows that the variation in each species is due to the exchange and interaction of genetic information as it is passed from parent to offspring.

Figure 4 *Some fish, such as these clownfish, fertilize their eggs externally. The eggs are the orange mass on the rock.*

external fertilization the union of sex cells outside the bodies of the parents

internal fertilization fertilization of an egg by sperm that occurs inside the body of a female

Internal and External Fertilization

Fertilization can happen either outside or inside the female's body. When the sperm fertilizes the eggs outside the female's body, the process is called **external fertilization.** External fertilization must take place in a moist environment so that the delicate zygotes will not dry out. Some fishes, such as those in **Figure 4,** reproduce by external fertilization.

Many amphibians, such as frogs, reproduce by external fertilization. For example, the female frog releases her eggs. At the same time, the male frog releases his sperm over the eggs to fertilize them. Frogs usually leave the zygotes to develop on their own. In about two weeks, the fertilized eggs hatch into tadpoles.

Internal Fertilization

When the egg and sperm join inside the female's body, the process is called **internal fertilization.** Internal fertilization allows the female animal to protect the developing egg inside her body. Reptiles, birds, mammals, and some fishes reproduce by internal fertilization. Many animals that reproduce by internal fertilization can lay fertilized eggs. Female chickens, for example, usually lay one or two eggs after internal fertilization has taken place. In most mammals, one or more fertilized eggs develop inside the mother's body. Many mammals give birth to young that are well developed. Young zebras, such as the one in **Figure 5,** can stand up and nurse almost immediately after birth.

✔ **Reading Check** What is the difference between external and internal fertilization?

Figure 5 *Within minutes of birth, this zebra is already able to stand. Within an hour of birth, he will be able to run.*

Mammals

All mammals reproduce sexually. All mammals nurture their young with milk. The following describes how monotremes, marsupials, and placental mammals reproduce:

- **Monotreme** *Monotremes* (MAHN oh TREEMZ) are mammals that lay eggs. After the eggs are incubated and hatch, the young are nourished by milk that oozes from pores on the mother's belly. Echidnas and platypuses are monotremes.

- **Marsupial** Mammals that give birth to partially developed live young, such as the kangaroo in **Figure 6,** are *marsupials* (mahr SOO pee uhlz). Most marsupials have pouches where their young continue to develop after birth. Opossums, koalas, wombats, and Tasmanian devils are marsupials.

- **Placental Mammal** There are more than 4,000 species of placental mammals, including armadillos, humans, and bats. Placental mammals are nourished inside their mother's body before birth. Newborn placental mammals are more developed than newborn monotremes or marsupials are.

Figure 6 *The red kangaroo is a marsupial. A young kangaroo, such as this one in its mother's pouch, is called a* joey.

SECTION Review

Summary

- In asexual reproduction, a single parent produces offspring that are genetically identical to the parent. F.2.3.1 CS

- In sexual reproduction, offspring receive a combination of genes from two parents. Combining genes allows for variation. Variation allows a population to adapt to changes. F.2.3.1 CS, F.2.3.2 AA

- Fertilization can be external or internal.

- All mammals reproduce sexually.

Understanding Key Ideas

1. Describe one advantage of asexual reproduction and one advantage of sexual reproduction. F.2.3.1 CS, F.2.3.2 AA

2. What is the difference between monotremes and marsupials?

3. List two patterns of asexual reproduction in animals. F.2.3.1 CS

4. How does sexual reproduction allow for variation to occur among a species? F.2.3.2 AA

Critical Thinking

5. **Making Comparisons** Compare the genetic information offspring receive as a result of asexual reproduction with the genetic information offspring receive as result of sexual reproduction. F.2.3.2 AA

6. **Applying Concepts** Describe one advantage of internal fertilization over external fertilization.

FCAT Preparation

7. Frogs reproduce sexually. Female frogs release their eggs in water. Male frogs release their sperm over the eggs to fertilize them. What is this process called? F.2.3.1 CS

   A. budding

   B. internal fertilization

   C. external fertilization

   D. regeneration

SC**L**INKS®

NSTA
Developed and maintained by the National Science Teachers Association

For a variety of links related to this chapter, go to www.scilinks.org

Topic: Reproduction
SciLinks code: HSM1293

Plant Reproduction

Imagine that you are walking through a lush forest filled with moss-covered rocks, ferns, tall trees, and wildflowers. Although each of these plants needs the same kinds of things to survive, each one reproduces differently.

Plants have two stages in their life cycle—the sporophyte (SPAWR uh FIET) stage and the gametophyte (guh MEET uh FIET) stage. During the sporophyte stage, plants make spores. A spore is a reproductive cell, which can grow into a gametophyte. During the gametophyte stage, female gametophytes produce eggs and male gametophytes produce sperm. For plants to reproduce sexually, a sperm must fertilize an egg.

READING WARM-UP

Objectives

● Describe the pattern and advantages of sexual reproduction in nonvascular plants. F.2.3.1 CS

● Describe the pattern and advantages of sexual reproduction in seedless vascular plants. F.2.3.1 CS

● Describe the pattern and advantage of sexual reproduction in seed plants. F.2.3.1 CS

● Identify the advantage of asexual reproduction and three kinds of asexual reproduction in plants. F.2.3.1 CS

Terms to Learn

pollination

READING STRATEGY

Reading Organizer As you read this section, make a table comparing sexual reproduction and asexual reproduction in plants.

Reproduction in Nonvascular Plants

Nonvascular plants include mosses, liverworts, and hornworts. During the sporophyte stage, nonvascular plants produce a large number of spores. This is an advantage because the greater the number of spores produced is, the greater the chance that some will grow into gametophytes. Spores can be carried by wind or water. Gametophytes of nonvascular plants must be covered by a film of water for fertilization to occur. Eggs and sperm form in separate structures, which are often on separate plants. Gametophytes of nonvascular plants grow very close together in clumps. The green parts of the moss in **Figure 1** are gametophytes. When water covers the gametophytes, sperm swim to the female gametophytes and fertilize the eggs.

 **Benchmark Check** Explain how nonvascular plants reproduce. F.2.3.1 CS

Reproduction in Seedless Vascular Plants

Vascular plants have tissues that deliver materials from one part of the plant to another part of the plant. Some vascular plants are seedless. Seedless vascular plants also produce a lot of spores and need water in order to reproduce. However, in most species of seedless vascular plants, both eggs and sperm are produced on the same plant. Gametophytes of seedless vascular plants are usually very small and develop on or below the surface of soil, on rocks, or on tree bark.

Figure 1 *Moss is an example of a nonvascular plant.*

Reproduction in Seed Plants

The two types of seed plants are *gymnosperms* and *angiosperms*. Gymnosperms are trees and shrubs that do not have flowers or fruit. Angiosperms have flowers and seeds that are protected by fruit. Most seed plants can reproduce sexually without water, which allows them to live in many places.

Reproduction in Gymnosperms

Most gymnosperms have reproductive structures called *cones*. A cone-bearing gymnosperm, as shown in **Figure 2,** has two kinds of cones—male cones and female cones. Male gametophytes are *pollen*. Pollen contain sperm. Female gametophytes produce eggs. Wind transfers pollen from the male cone to the female cone during **pollination.** Sperm from pollen fertilize the eggs of the female cone. The fertilized egg develops into a seed, and eventually develops into a young plant.

Reproduction in Angiosperms

In angiosperms, gametophytes develop within flowers. Pollen is produced in the male reproductive structures called *anthers*. Pollination happens when pollen is moved from anthers to stigmas. *Stigmas* are the female reproductive structures in flowers. Usually, wind or animals move pollen from one flower to another flower. After pollen lands on the stigma, a tube grows from each pollen grain. The pollen tube grows through the style to an ovule. Ovules are found inside the ovary. Each ovule contains an egg. Sperm from the pollen grain move down the pollen tube and into an ovule. Fertilization happens when a sperm fuses with the egg inside an ovule. **Figure 3** shows the process of pollination and fertilization in angiosperms.

Figure 2 *A gymnosperm, such as the spruce shown in the photo above, has reproductive structures called cones.*

F.2.3.1 CS (partial) knows the patterns and advantages of sexual and asexual reproduction in plants and animals.

pollination the transfer of pollen from the male reproductive structures to the female structures of seed plants

Figure 3   **Pollination and Fertilization in Angiosperms**

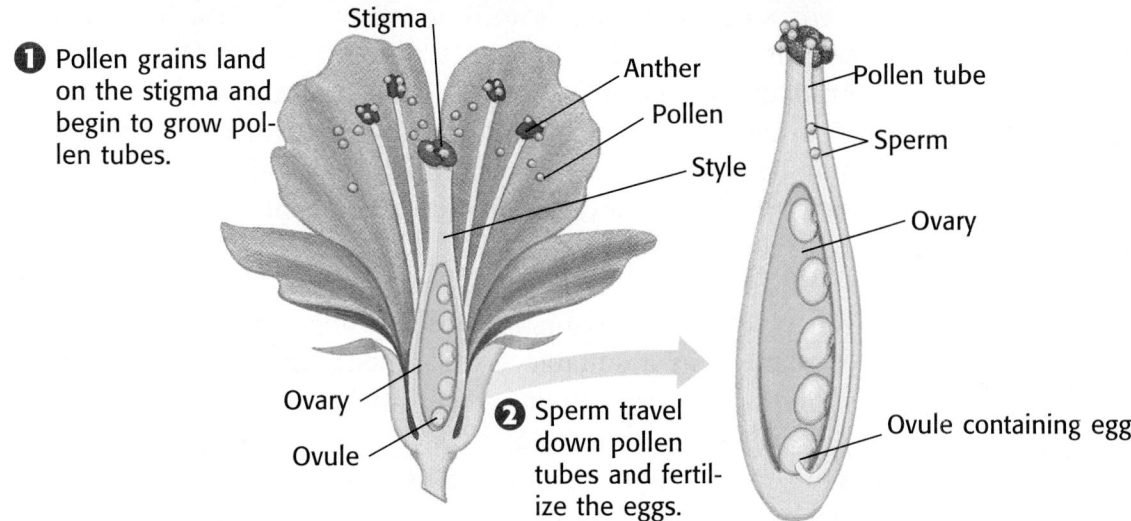

❶ Pollen grains land on the stigma and begin to grow pollen tubes.

Stigma

Anther

Pollen

Style

Ovary

Ovule

❷ Sperm travel down pollen tubes and fertilize the eggs.

Pollen tube

Sperm

Ovary

Ovule containing egg

Figure 4 Seed Production in Angiosperms

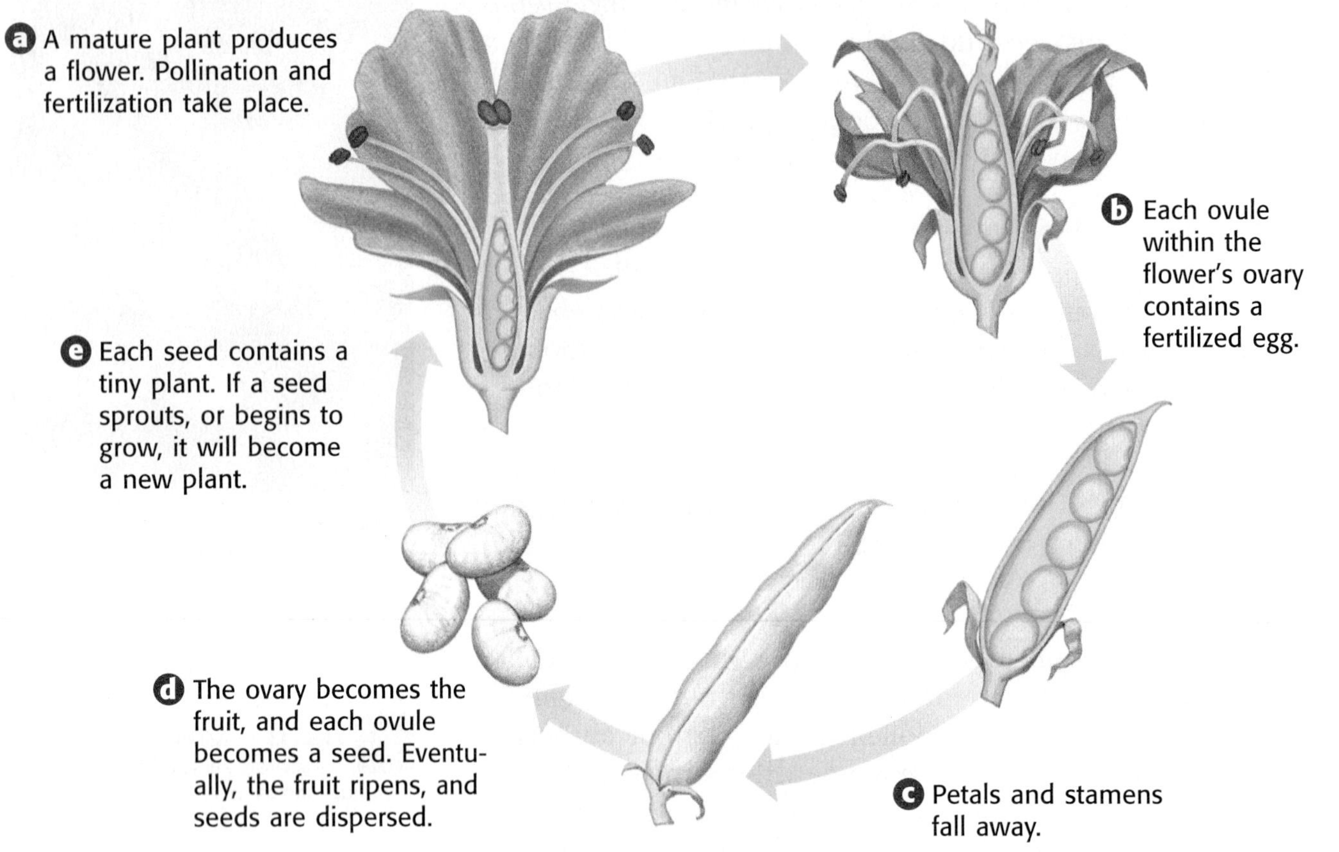

a A mature plant produces a flower. Pollination and fertilization take place.

b Each ovule within the flower's ovary contains a fertilized egg.

c Petals and stamens fall away.

d The ovary becomes the fruit, and each ovule becomes a seed. Eventually, the fruit ripens, and seeds are dispersed.

e Each seed contains a tiny plant. If a seed sprouts, or begins to grow, it will become a new plant.

Quick Lab

Thirsty Seeds

1. Fill a **Petri dish** two-thirds full of **water,** and add **six dry bean seeds.** Using a **wax pencil,** label the dish "Water."

2. Add **six dry bean seeds** to a dry **Petri dish.** Label this dish "Control."

3. The next day, compare the size of the two sets of seeds. Record your observations.

4. What caused the size of the seeds to change? Why is this change important to the seed's survival?

From Flower to Fruit

After fertilization takes place in angiosperms, the ovule develops into a seed. The seed contains a young plant. The ovary surrounding the ovule becomes a fruit, as shown in **Figure 4.** As a fruit swells and ripens, it protects the developing seeds. Some seeds, such as dandelion seeds, are dispersed by the wind. Fruits can also help a plant spread its seeds. Many fruits are edible. Animals may eat these fruits. Then, the animals discard the seeds away from the parent plant. Other fruits, such as burrs, may become caught in an animal's fur. And the animal may drop these fruits away from the parent plant.

From Seed to Plant

When seeds from gymnosperms and angiosperms are dropped or planted in a suitable environment, the seeds sprout and young plants begin to grow. To sprout, most seeds need water, air, and warm temperatures. Each plant species has an ideal temperature at which most of its seeds begin to grow.

Other Methods of Reproduction

Angiosperms may also reproduce asexually. The advantage of asexual reproduction is that these plants do not depend on other plants to reproduce. Instead, part of a plant produces a new plant. The following are three structures plants use to reproduce asexually:

- **Plantlets** Tiny plants grow along the edges of a plant's leaves. These plantlets fall off and grow on their own.
- **Tubers** Underground stems, or tubers, can produce new plants after a dormant season.
- **Runners** Above-ground stems from which new plants can grow are called *runners*.

The potato in **Figure 5** is an example of a tuber. A strawberry plant produces runners, or stems that grow horizontally along the ground. Buds along the runners grow into new plants.

Benchmark Check List the advantage of asexual reproduction, and list three kinds of asexual reproduction in plants. F.2.3.1 CS

Figure 5 *A potato is a tuber, or underground stem. The "eyes" of potatoes are buds that can grow into new plants.*

F.2.3.1 CS (partial) knows the patterns and advantages of sexual and asexual reproduction in plants and animals.

SECTION Review

Summary

- Most gametophytes of nonvascular plants and seedless vascular plants need water to reproduce. F.2.3.1 CS
- Some seed plants do not need water to reproduce. During fertilization, wind and animals can transfer pollen from cone to cone or from flower to flower. F.2.3.1 CS
- Some plants use plantlets, tubers, or runners to reproduce asexually. F.2.3.1 CS

Understanding Key Ideas

1. Differentiate between gymnosperms and angiosperms. F.2.3.1 CS

2. Describe one kind of asexual reproduction in plants. What is an advantage of this kind of asexual reproduction? F.2.3.1 CS

3. Compare the patterns of sexual reproduction in nonvascular plants and the patterns in seedless vascular plants. F.2.3.1 CS

4. Which part of a flower develops into a fruit? into a seed?

Critical Thinking

5. **Making Inferences** When might asexual reproduction be important for the survival of some angiosperms? F.2.3.1 CS

6. **Analyzing Ideas** Sexual reproduction results in more genetic variation than asexual reproduction does. Why is variation important? F.2.3.1 CS

FCAT Preparation

7. Angiosperms can reproduce asexually. One type of asexual reproduction produces stems that grow horizontally along the ground, take root, and grow into new plants. What are these stems called? F.2.3.1 CS
   - **A.** runners
   - **B.** tubers
   - **C.** plantlets
   - **D.** spores

Animal Behavior

Suppose that you look out a window and see a bird flying away from a tree. Is the bird leaving a nest in search of food? Or is the bird escaping from danger?

Though the bird's purpose may not be clear, the bird is flying away for a specific reason. Animals run from enemies, search for food, battle for territory, and build homes. All of these activities are known as *behavior*.

Kinds of Behavior

How do animals know when a situation is dangerous? How do they know where to find food? Sometimes, animals instinctively know how to behave, but sometimes they learn how.

Innate Behavior

Behavior that does not depend on learning or experience is known as **innate behavior.** Innate behaviors are inherited through genes. Puppies inherit the tendency to chew, and bees inherit the tendency to fly. The male bird in **Figure 1** inherited the tendency to collect colorful objects for its nest. Some innate behaviors are present at birth. Newborn whales have the innate ability to swim. Other innate behaviors develop months or years after birth. For example, walking is innate for humans. But we do not walk until we are about one year old.

Learned Behavior

Innate behaviors can be modified. Animals can use learning to change a behavior. **Learned behavior** is behavior that has been learned from experience or from observing other animals. Humans inherit the tendency to speak. But the language we use is not inherited. We might learn English, Spanish, or sign language. Humans are not the only animals that change behaviors through learning. All animals can learn.

Figure 1 *The male bowerbird collects colorful objects for its nest to attract a female bowerbird to be his mate.*

Figure 2 *Chimpanzees make and use tools to get ants and other food out of hard-to-reach places.*

Survival Behavior

Animals use their behaviors to survive. To stay alive, an animal has to do many things. It must avoid being eaten, and it must find food, water, and a place to live.

Finding Food

Animals find food in many ways. Bees fly from flower to flower collecting nectar. Koala bears climb trees to get eucalyptus leaves. Some animals, such as the chimpanzee shown in **Figure 2,** use tools to get food. Many animals hunt for their food. For example, owls hunt mice.

Animals that eat other animals are known as *predators*. The animal being eaten is the *prey*. Animals that are predators can also be the prey for another animal. For example, a frog eats insects. So, the frog is a predator. But a frog may be eaten by a snake. In this case, the frog is the prey.

Marking Territory

Sometimes, members of the same species must compete for food and mates. Some animals claim territories to save energy by avoiding this competition. A **territory** is an area that is occupied by one animal or by a group of animals that do not allow other members of the species to enter. Some birds mark a territory by singing. The song lets other birds know not to enter the area. If other birds do enter the area, the bird that has marked the territory may chase them away. Animals use their territories for mating, raising young, and finding food.

Benchmark Check Explain how marking territory is a survival behavior. **F.2.3.3 CS**

innate behavior an inherited behavior that does not depend on the environment or experience

learned behavior a behavior that has been learned from experience

territory an area that is occupied by one animal or a group of animals that do not allow other members of the species to enter

F.2.3.3 CS knows that generally organisms in a population live long enough to reproduce because they have survival characteristics.

Defensive Action

Defensive behavior allows animals to protect resources, including territories, from other animals. Animals defend food, mates, and offspring. Have you ever heard a pet dog growl when a person approached while it was eating? Many male animals, such as lions, fight violently to defend mates. Some birds use distraction to defend their young. When a predator is near, a mother killdeer may pretend to have a broken wing and move away from her young. This action distracts the predator's attention from the young so that they will remain safe.

Defensive behavior also helps animals protect themselves from predators. One way animals avoid predators is to make themselves hard to see. For example, a rabbit often stands still so that its color blends into a background of shrubs or grass. But once a predator is aware of its prey, the prey needs another way to defend itself. Rabbits also try to outrun predators. As seen in **Figure 3,** skunks spray irritating chemicals at predators. Has an animal ever defended itself against you?

Benchmark Check What are two ways a rabbit can defend itself? F.2.3.3 CS

Courtship

Animals need to find mates to reproduce. Reproduction is essential for the survival of an individual's genes. Animals have special behaviors that help them find a mate. These behaviors are referred to as *courtship.* Some birds and fish build nests to attract a mate. Other animals use special movements and sounds to attract a mate. **Figure 4** shows two cranes performing a courtship display.

Figure 3 *Skunks spray irritating chemicals at attackers to protect themselves.*

Figure 4 *These Japanese ground cranes use an elaborate courtship dance to tell each other when they are ready to mate.*

Figure 5 *Adult killer whales teach their young how to hunt in the first years of life.*

Parenting

Some animals, such as caterpillars, begin life with the ability to take care of themselves. But many young animals depend on their parents for survival. Some adult birds bring food to their young because they cannot feed themselves when they hatch. Other animals, such as the killer whales in **Figure 5,** spend years teaching their young how to hunt for food.

F.1.3.7 CS knows that behavior is a response to the environment and influences growth, development, maintenance, and reproduction.

F.2.3.3 CS knows that generally organisms in a population live long enough to reproduce because they have survival characteristics.

Seasonal Behavior

Humans bundle up when it is cold outside. Many other animals have to deal with bitter cold during the winter, too. Frogs hide from the cold by burrowing in mud. Other animals may face winter food shortages. Squirrels store food to prepare for winter. Seasonal behaviors help animals adapt to the environment.

Migration

Many animals avoid cold weather by traveling to warmer places. These animals migrate to find food, water, or safe nesting grounds. To *migrate* is to travel from one place to another. Whales, salmon, bats, and even chimpanzees migrate. Each winter, the monarch butterflies shown in **Figure 6** migrate to central Mexico from all over North America. And each fall, birds in the Northern Hemisphere fly south thousands of kilometers. In the spring, they return north to nest.

If you were planning a trip, you would probably use a map. But how do animals know which way to go when they migrate? For short trips, many animals use landmarks to find their way. *Landmarks* are fixed objects that an animal uses to find its way. Birds use landmarks such as mountain ranges, rivers, and coastlines to find their way.

Figure 6 *When monarch butterflies gather in Mexico for the winter, there can be as many as 4 million butterflies per acre!*

Figure 7 *Bears slow down for the winter, but they do not enter deep hibernation.*

Benchmark Activity

Do Not Disturb Many bats avoid food shortages during winter by hibernating in caves. Visiting a cave of hibernating bats may sound like fun, but people can endanger the bats by visiting their caves. The bats sleep with a lowered heart rate that allows them to save their energy until food is available. When people visit the caves, the bats may wake up. Waking up requires a lot of energy and makes it harder for the bats to survive until spring to find more food. If the bats lose too much energy, they can die. Make a poster that explains how people can help bats survive winters by avoiding their caves. **F.1.3.7 CS**

hibernation a period of inactivity and lowered body temperature that some animals undergo in winter as a protection against cold weather and lack of food

estivation a period of inactivity and lowered body temperature that some animals undergo in summer as a protection against hot weather and lack of food

F.1.3.7 CS knows that behavior is a response to the environment and influences growth, development, maintenance, and reproduction.

Slowing Down

Some animals deal with food and water shortages by hibernating. **Hibernation** is a period of inactivity and decreased body temperature that some animals experience in winter. Hibernating animals survive on stored body fat. Many animals hibernate, including mice, squirrels, and skunks. While an animal hibernates, its temperature, heart rate, and breathing rate drop. Some hibernating animals drop their body temperature to a few degrees above freezing and do not wake for weeks at a time. Other animals, such as the bear in **Figure 7,** slow down but do not enter deep hibernation. Also, bears hibernate for shorter periods of time than other hibernating animals do.

Winter is not the only time that resources can be hard to find. Many desert squirrels and mice experience a similar internal slowdown in the hottest part of the summer, when they cannot easily find water and food. This period of reduced activity in the summer is called **estivation.**

Benchmark Check Give an example of how a food shortage can affect the behavior of an animal. **F.1.3.7 CS**

A Biological Clock

Animals need to keep track of time so that they know when to store food and when to migrate. The internal control of an animal's natural cycles is called a *biological clock*. Animals may use clues such as the length of the day and the temperature to set their clocks. Some biological clocks keep track of daily cycles. These daily cycles are called *circadian rhythms*. Most animals wake up and get sleepy at about the same time each day and night. This is an example of a circadian rhythm.

Cycles of Change

Some biological clocks control long cycles. Seasonal cycles are nearly universal among animals. Many animals hibernate at certain times of the year and reproduce at other times. Reproducing during a particular season takes advantage of environmental conditions that help the young survive. Migration patterns are also controlled by seasonal cycles.

Biological clocks also control cycles of internal changes. For example, treehoppers, such as the one in **Figure 8,** go through several stages in life. They begin as an egg, then hatch as a nymph, and then develop into an adult. Finally, the adult emerges from the skin of its nymph form.

Figure 8 *The treehopper's biological clock signals the animal to shed the skin of its nymph form and emerge as an adult.*

SECTION Review

Summary

- Behavior may be classified as innate or learned. The potential for innate behavior is inherited. Learned behavior depends on experience.

- Behaviors that help animals survive include finding food, marking a territory, defensive action, courtship, and parenting. **F.2.3.3 CS**

- Seasonal behaviors, such as hibernation and estivation can help animals adapt to the environment. **F.1.3.7 CS, F.2.3.3 CS**

Understanding Key Ideas

1. An animal that lives in a hot, dry environment might spend the summer **F.1.3.7 CS**

    a. hibernating.

    b. estivating.

    c. migrating to a warmer climate.

    d. None of the above

2. Do bears hibernate? **F.1.3.7 CS**

3. What is the difference between innate and learned behaviors? **F.1.3.7 CS**

4. Name five behaviors that help animals survive. **F.2.3.3 CS**

Critical Thinking

5. **Applying Concepts** People who travel to different time zones often suffer from *jet lag*. Jet lag makes people have trouble waking up and going to sleep at appropriate times. Why do you think people experience jet lag?

6. **Making Inferences** Many children are born with the tendency to make babbling sounds. But few adults make these sounds. How could you explain this change in an innate behavior? **F.1.3.7 CS**

FCAT Preparation

7. During the winter season, animals travel to warmer places to find food, water, or safe nesting grounds. What is this seasonal behavior called? **F.1.3.7 CS**

    A. estivation

    B. migration

    C. courtship

    D. hibernation

8. Bees, ants, and wasps inject a powerful acid into their predators. What is this survival behavior called? **F.2.3.3 CS**

    F. defensive behavior

    G. slowing down

    H. parenting

    I. territorial behavior

SCI**LINKS**

NSTA
Developed and maintained by the
National Science Teachers Association

For a variety of links related to this chapter, go to www.scilinks.org
Topic: Animal Behavior;
    Rhythms of Life
SciLinks code: HSM0069; HSM1311

Adaptations and Survival

Sea turtles are strong swimmers because they have flippers. Sea turtles are also excellent divers. Leatherback sea turtles can dive to depths of more than 1,000 m!

The characteristics described above are called *adaptations*. An **adaptation** is a characteristic that improves an individual's ability to survive and reproduce in a particular environment. The abilities to swim fast and to dive to great depths can help sea turtles escape their predators and search for food. Although sea turtles lay their eggs on land, sea turtles are aquatic animals. Therefore, sea turtles have adaptations for an aquatic environment and could not survive in only a land environment.

Adaptations for Obtaining Food

Similar to the adaptations that some sea turtles have to be able to dive to great depths to find food, almost all other organisms have adaptations to help them obtain food. For example, the chameleon in **Figure 1** uses its long, fast-moving tongue to catch unsuspecting insects. The strong, sharply-pointed beak of the woodpecker in **Figure 1** is also an adaptation. The woodpecker could not drill into a tree to search for insects without its special beak. Even humans have adaptations for obtaining food. Because of the shape and function of our hands and fingers, humans are able to do things such as pick and peel fruit and open jars.

Benchmark Check Give an example of an adaptation that helps an organism obtain the food it needs to survive. **G.1.3.2 CS**

adaptation a characteristic that improves an individual's ability to survive and reproduce in a particular environment

Figure 1 *The chameleon (above) catches an insect with its long tongue. The woodpecker (right) uses its strong beak to drill holes into trees to find insects.*

Figure 2 *The protective quills of the porcupine (left) keep predators away. The pattern of black, red, and yellow on the coral snake (right) is a warning sign to predators.*

Predator-Prey Adaptations

Many organisms have adaptations that serve as a defense against predators. Some organisms, such as the porcupine in **Figure 2,** have a protective covering. Bright markings also warn potential predators to leave an organism alone. Patterns with black stripes and red, orange, or yellow markings are common in many species of bees, wasps, skunks, snakes, and poisonous frogs. For example, the venomous coral snake in **Figure 2** has bright markings.

Another adaptation that helps both predators and prey is called *camouflage*. An organism that is camouflaged is disguised so that it is hard to see even when the organism is in view. An organism's camouflage usually disguises the organism's recognizable features. For example, the eyes are usually the most recognizable part of an organism. Therefore, some organisms have black stripes around their eyes for disguise. Some predators use their environment as camouflage. These predators often do not chase their prey. Instead, they wait for the prey to come close enough to be caught. For example, the alligator in **Figure 3** is camouflaged by duckweed. Because the alligator blends with its environment, the alligator's prey may not notice it waiting to attack.

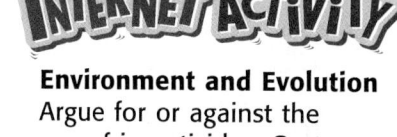

Environment and Evolution
Argue for or against the use of insecticides. Go to **go.hrw.com,** and type in the keyword **HL5EVOW.**

F.2.3.3 CS knows that generally organisms in a population live long enough to reproduce because they have survival characteristics.

G.1.3.2 CS knows that biological adaptations include changes in structures, behaviors, or physiology that enhance reproductive success in a particular environment.characteristics.

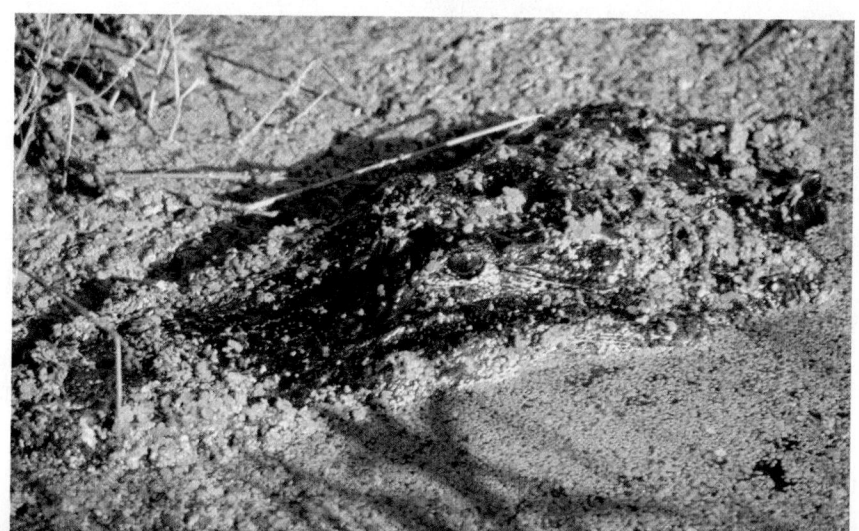

Figure 3 *Camouflaged by duckweed, this alligator can hide and wait for its prey.*

Figure 4 *The Hawaiian honeycreeper uses its curved beak to sip nectar from a lobelia flower.*

Adaptations to Interactions

Two species can also adapt to interact with one another. For example, the honeycreeper and the lobelia (loh BEEL yuh) plant in **Figure 4,** have adapted to each other. The honeycreeper has a long, curved beak, which lets it reach the nectar at the base of the long, curved lobelia flower. As the bird sips nectar from the flower, the bird gets pollen on its head. When the bird moves to another flower, some of the pollen will rub off. Therefore, the honeycreeper helps lobelia plants reproduce. Adaptations that allow close interactions between organisms usually occur between organisms that live close together. But these adaptations happen over a very long period of time.

Natural Selection

natural selection the process by which individuals that are better adapted to their environment survive and reproduce more successfully than less well adapted individuals do

As you have learned, adaptations help organisms survive. Organisms inherit adaptations and other characteristics from their parents. However, inherited characteristics in populations can change over time. The change in the inherited characteristics of a population over time can be explained by *natural selection*. **Natural selection** is the process by which individuals that are better adapted to their environment survive and reproduce more successfully than less well adapted individuals do. For example, only a small percentage of the baby sea turtles from the nest in **Figure 5** will survive to reproduce. Inherited characteristics and environmental factors, such as predation and food availability, may influence which baby sea turtles reach adulthood and which do not.

Figure 5 *Female sea turtles can lay from 50 to 160 eggs in one nest. Because of natural selection, only some baby sea turtles from each nest will survive to adulthood.*

Four Parts of Natural Selection

Natural selection affects how a population changes in response to its environment. Because of natural selection, a population will tend to be well adapted to its environment. But if the environment changes, only those individuals that have characteristics suited to the new environment are likely to survive and reproduce. The four parts of natural selection are illustrated in **Figure 6.**

Benchmark Check What is the relationship between the process of natural selection and survival? **F.2.3.3 CS**

F.2.3.2 AA knows that the variation in each species is due to the exchange and interaction of genetic information as it is passed from parent to offspring.

F.2.3.3 CS knows that generally organisms in a population live long enough to reproduce because they have survival characteristics.

G.1.3.2 CS knows that biological adaptations include changes in structures, behaviors, or physiology that enhance reproductive success in a particular environment.

Figure 6 **Natural Selection in Four Steps**

1. Overproduction
More offspring are born than will live to become adults.

2. Genetic Variation Within a Population
The individuals in a population are different from one another. Some of the different characteristics improve the chances that the individual will survive and reproduce. Others lower these chances. For example, rabbits that are stronger or faster are more likely to survive and reproduce than weaker or slower rabbits.

3. Struggle to Survive
An environment might not have enough food or water for every individual born. Many individuals are killed by other organisms. And others cannot find mates. Only some individuals survive and reproduce.

4. Successful Reproduction
Successful reproduction is the key to natural selection. The individuals that have better adaptations for living in their environment and for finding mates are more likely to reproduce. Those that are not well adapted to their environment are more likely to die early or to have few offspring.

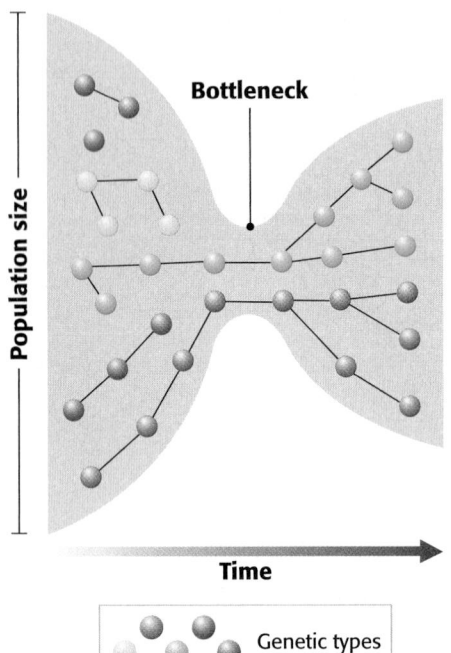

Figure 7 *When a population is reduced to a few members, a genetic bottleneck occurs and genetic variation decreases.*

Changes in Genetic Variation

Over time, a population will be made up of more individuals with characteristics that help them survive. And for natural selection to continue, individuals within the population must be genetically different. However, if a population decreases rapidly, many characteristics may be lost entirely from a population because all of the individuals with those characteristics died. This reduced number of characteristics within a population is called a *genetic bottleneck,* as shown in **Figure 7.** If the population is able to increase again, inbreeding will cause the individuals to be genetically similar. These genetic similarities may make a population more susceptible to birth defects and genetic diseases. And many individuals would likely be affected by the same disease.

The Florida panther population is an example of a population that has experienced a genetic bottleneck. Because of isolation from other populations of panthers, habitat loss, and an overall decrease in population size, the genetic variation within the Florida panther population has decreased. As a result, many of the panthers that survived have become genetically similar. This similarity has caused inbreeding to occur within the population. Inbreeding in panthers can result in heart defects, the failure of reproductive organs, and low birth rates. However, there is a recovery program in place for the Florida panther. The program includes protecting and enlarging the panther's habitat as well as monitoring the health of the population, as shown in **Figure 8.**

Benchmark Check How can a decrease in genetic variation within a population affect the population? **F.2.3.2 AA**

Figure 8 *These biologists have taken DNA samples from a tranquilized Florida panther. Monitoring the health of the Florida panther population is part of a program to increase the genetic variation within the population.*

F.2.3.2 AA knows that the variation in each species is due to the exchange and interaction of genetic information as it is passed from parent to offspring.

F.2.3.3 CS knows that generally organisms in a population live long enough to reproduce because they have survival characteristics.

Insecticide Resistance

Insecticide resistance is also a result of natural selection. Insecticides are used to kill insects. However, some individual insects within a population may be resistant to certain insecticides. These insects survive because they have genes that make them resistant to the insecticide. These survivors then reproduce and pass the insecticide-resistance genes to their offspring. Each time the insect population is sprayed with the same insecticide, the insect population changes to include more resistant members. The European corn borer in **Figure 9** is an example of an insect that is resistant to some insecticides.

Figure 9 *The European corn borer can destroy crops of corn. It is resistant to some insecticides.*

SECTION Review

Summary

- A strong beak, bright colors, and camouflage are adaptations that can help an organism survive. F.2.3.3 CS, G.1.3.2 CS

- The four parts of natural selection are overproduction, genetic variation, competition for resources, and successful reproduction. F.2.3.3 CS, G.1.3.2 CS

- Variation is due to the exchange of genetic information as it is passed from parent to offspring. F.2.3.2 AA

- Genetic variation allows a population to adapt to changes in the environment over time.

- When a population of insects is resistant to an insecticide, survival rates can increase. F.2.3.3 CS

Using Key Terms

1. Use *adaptation* and *natural selection* in separate sentences.

Understanding Key Ideas

2. How can a population of insects become resistant to an insecticide? F.2.3.3 CS

3. Give an example of two species that have special adaptations that allow them to interact with one another. G.1.3.2 CS

4. Describe the four steps of natural selection. F.2.3.3 CS, G.1.3.2 CS

5. What is a genetic bottleneck?

Critical Thinking

6. **Evaluating Conclusions** Why is genetic variation important to the survival of a population? Why is it important to increase the genetic variation within the Florida panther population? F.2.3.2 AA

7. **Making Comparisons** Compare the adaptations of two organisms described in this section. Describe how the adaptations help increase the chances that each organism will survive and reproduce. F.2.3.3 CS, G.1.3.2 CS

8. **Analyzing Processes** Many rats have become resistant to rat poison. Based on what you know about how insects become resistant to insecticides, how might rats become resistant to poisons? F.2.3.3 CS

FCAT Preparation

9. An adaptation improves an organism's ability to survive and reproduce. A chameleon can change the color of its skin to blend in with its environment. This adaptation helps it hide from predators. What is this adaptation called? G.1.3.2 CS

A. camouflage

B. resistance

C. natural selection

D. warning coloration

SCiLINKS®

NSTA
Developed and maintained by the National Science Teachers Association

For a variety of links related to this chapter, go to www.scilinks.org

Topic: Species and Adaptation
SciLinks code: HSM1433

Model-Making Lab

Adaptation: It's a Way of Life

Since the beginning of life on Earth, species have had special characteristics called *adaptations* that have helped them survive changes in environmental conditions. Changes in a species' environment include climate changes, habitat destruction, or the extinction of prey. These changes can cause a species to die out unless the species has a characteristic that helps it survive. For example, a species of bird may have an adaptation for eating sunflower seeds and ants. If the ant population dies out, the bird can still eat seeds and can therefore survive.

In this activity, you will explore several adaptations and design an organism with adaptations you choose. Then, you will describe how these adaptations help the organism survive.

OBJECTIVES

Design an organism with adaptations you choose.

Describe how these adaptations help the organism survive.

MATERIALS

- arts-and-crafts materials, various
- markers, colored
- magazines for cutouts
- poster board
- scissors

SAFETY

Procedure

1 Study the chart below. Choose one adaptation from each column. For example, an organism might be a scavenger that burrows underground and has spikes on its tail!

Adaptations		
Diet	**Type of transportation**	**Special adaptation**
carnivore	flies	uses sensors to detect heat
herbivore	glides through the air	is active only at night and has excellent night vision
omnivore	burrows underground	changes colors to match its surroundings
scavenger	runs fast	has armor
decomposer	swims	has horns
	hops	can withstand extreme temperature changes
	walks	secretes a terrible and sickening scent
	climbs	has poison glands
	floats	has specialized front teeth
	slithers	has tail spikes
		stores oxygen in its cells so it does not have to breathe continuously
		one of your own invention

2 Design an organism that has the three adaptations you have chosen. Use poster board, colored markers, picture cutouts, or craft materials to create your organism.

3 Write a caption on your poster describing your organism. Describe its appearance, its habitat, its niche, and the way its adaptations help it survive. Give your organism a two-part "scientific" name that is based on its characteristics.

4 Display your creation in your classroom. Share with classmates how you chose the adaptations for your organism.

Analyze the Results

1 **Organizing Data** What does your imaginary organism eat?

2 **Organizing Data** In what environment or habitat would your organism be most likely to survive—in the desert, tropical rain forest, plains, icecaps, mountains, or ocean? Explain your answer.

3 **Analyzing Data** Is your creature a mammal, a reptile, an amphibian, a bird, or a fish? What modern organism (on Earth today) or ancient organism (extinct) is your imaginary organism most like? Explain the similarities between the two organisms. Do some research outside the lab, if necessary, to find out about a real organism that may be similar to your imaginary organism.

Draw Conclusions

4 **Evaluating Data** If there were a sudden climate change, such as daily downpours of rain in a desert, would your imaginary organism survive? What adaptations for surviving such a change does it have?

 F.2.3.3 CS knows that generally organisms in a population live long enough to reproduce because they have survival characteristics.

G.1.3.2 CS knows that biological adaptations include changes in structures, behaviors, or physiology that enhance reproductive success in a particular environment.

Applying Your Data

Call or write to an agency such as the U.S. Fish and Wildlife Service to get a list of endangered species in your area. Choose an organism on that list. Describe the organism's niche and any special adaptations it has that help it survive. Find out why it is endangered and what is being done to protect it.

Examine the illustration of the animal at right. Based on its physical characteristics, describe its habitat and niche. Is this a real animal?

Chapter Review

USING KEY TERMS

For each pair of terms, explain how the meanings of the terms differ.

1 *asexual reproduction* and *sexual reproduction* **FCAT VOCAB**

2 *external fertilization* and *internal fertilization*

3 *innate behavior* and *learned behavior*

4 *hibernation* and *estivation*

5 *adaptation* and *natural selection*

UNDERSTANDING KEY IDEAS

Multiple Choice

6 The sea star reproduces asexually. When part of a sea star breaks off, the part can develop into a new individual. What is this pattern of asexual reproduction called? **F.2.3.1 CS FCAT**

a. fragmentation

b. budding

c. external fertilization

d. internal fertilization

7 Which is NOT a pattern of asexual reproduction in plants? **F.2.3.1 CS**

a. producing runners

b. producing tubers

c. producing flowers

d. producing plantlets

8 A biological clock controls

a. circadian rhythms.

b. defensive behavior.

c. learned behavior.

d. being a consumer.

9 Which of the following statements is true about migration? **F.1.3.7 CS**

a. It occurs only in birds.

b. It helps animals escape cold and food shortages in winter.

c. It always refers to moving southward for the winter.

d. It helps animals defend themselves.

10 Most gymnosperms have reproductive structures called *cones*. Gymnosperms have male and female cones. Where are male gametophytes found? **F.2.3.1 CS FCAT**

a. in soil

b. in eggs

c. in seeds

d. in pollen

11 Many desert animals experience an internal slowdown in the hottest part of the summer. When the availability of water and food is scarce, these animals undergo a period of inactivity and lowered body temperature. What is this seasonal behavior called? **F.1.3.7 CS FCAT**

a. hibernation

b. estivation

c. parenting

d. circadian rhythm

Short Answer

12 Choose an organism, and describe the adaptations that help it survive. **F.2.3.3 CS, G.1.3.2 CS**

13 What is the relationship between natural selection and reproduction? **F.2.3.3 CS, G.1.3.2 CS**

14 What is a territory? Give an example of a territory from your environment.

15 What is pollination? **F.2.3.1 CS**

CRITICAL THINKING

Extended Response

16 Identifying Relationships The environment in which organisms live may change over time. For example, a wet, swampy area may gradually become a grassy area with a small pond. Explain how sexual reproduction may give species that live in a changing environment a survival advantage. F.2.3.1 CS, F.2.3.2 AA

17 Applying Concepts During fertilization, an egg's nucleus and a sperm's nucleus join and a zygote is created. Is the zygote genetically identical to either of its parents? Explain your answer. F.2.3.2 AA FCAT

18 Analyzing Processes What is the relationship between genetic variation and the term *genetic bottleneck*? What can happen to a population when it experiences a genetic bottleneck? F.2.3.2 AA

19 Analyzing Ideas People have internal biological clocks. However, people are used to keeping track of time by using clocks and calendars. Why do you think people use these tools if they have internal clocks?

Concept Mapping

20 Use the following terms to create a concept map: *asexual reproduction, external fertilization, fragmentation, reproduction, internal fertilization, budding,* and *sexual reproduction.* F.2.3.1 CS

INTERPRETING GRAPHICS

Germinate means "to sprout," or "grow." The graph below shows percentages of seed germination for different seed companies. Use the graph below to answer the questions that follow.

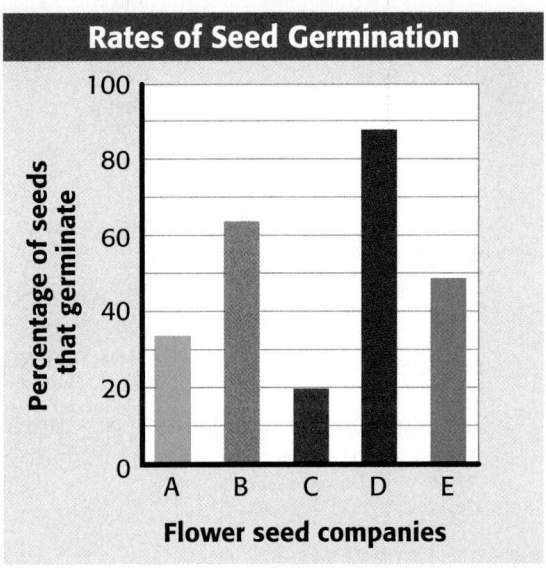

Rates of Seed Germination

Percentage of seeds that germinate

Flower seed companies

21 Which seed company had the highest percentage of seed germination? the lowest percentage of seed germination?

22 Which seed companies had percentages of seed germination higher than 50%?

23 If Elaine wants to buy seeds that had a germination percentage higher than 60%, which seed companies would she buy seeds from? Why might Elaine want to buy seeds that have a higher percentage of germination?

For the following questions, write your answers on a separate sheet of paper.

1

In sexual reproduction, offspring are formed when genetic information from more than one parent combines. The diagram below shows how genes mix through three generations. The child inherited genetic information from both of its parents. The child's parents inherited genetic information from their parents.

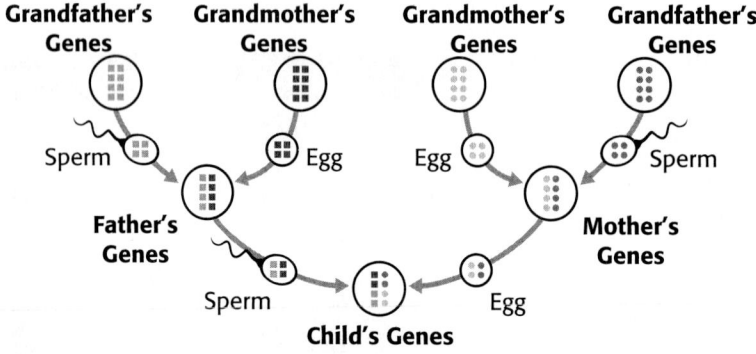

INHERITING GENES

What is an advantage of genetic variation? If the size of a population decreases drastically, how might this affect the genetic variation within a population?

2 An area that is occupied by one animal or a group of animals that do not allow other members of the species to enter is called a territory. Which of the following **best** describes why establishing a territory is a survival behavior?

A. Establishing a territory is not a survival behavior.

B. Establishing a territory makes it harder for an animal to find a mate.

C. Establishing a territory decreases the genetic variation of a population.

D. Establishing a territory makes it easier for an animal to raise young and find food.

3 A variety of behaviors helps animals survive. Some behaviors are innate. An innate behavior is inherited through genes. Some behavior is learned. A learned behavior is a type of behavior that is learned through observation. Which one of the following is an example of learned behavior?

F. the ability of humans to walk

G. the courtship behavior of birds

H. the use of tools by chimpanzees

I. the tendency of puppies to chew

4 In nonvascular plants, such as moss, reproduction begins when female gametophytes produce eggs and male gametophytes produce sperm. The sperm must fertilize an egg for the reproductive process to be complete. What other conditions are necessary for fertilization to take place in nonvascular plants?

A. The plants must be in a warm, dry environment.
B. The plants must be in a environment in which wind can carry the sperm to the eggs.
C. The plants must be covered with a film of water so that sperm can swim to the female gametophyte.
D. The male gametophytes from surrounding plants must grow large enough to get close to the female gametophytes.

5 The picture below shows an ocean-dwelling animal called a hydra. It reproduces through a pattern called *budding.* The new organism is genetically identical to its parent.

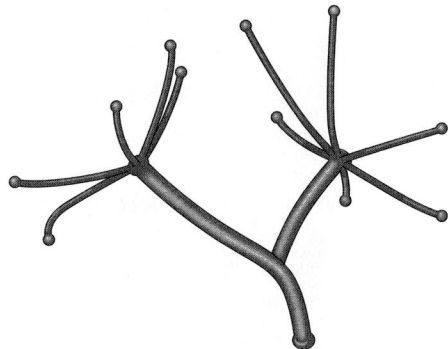

What pattern of reproduction is budding?

F. fragmentation
G. external fertilization
H. internal fertilization
I. asexual reproduction

6 An alligator is camouflaged by duckweed in a swamp. How is this an example of an adaptation?

A. This is not an example of an adaptation.
B. The duckweed helps the alligator swim faster.
C. The duckweed keeps the alligator cool during the summer.
D. The alligator can blend in with the duckweed and sneak up on its prey.

Science in Action

Scientific Discoveries

Pythons and the Florida Everglades

The tourists stopped and stared. The water churned as a giant Burmese python tried to squeeze and suffocate an alligator. Then, the alligator rolled over and swam off with the snake clamped in its jaw. Strangely, this scene is becoming familiar to park rangers at Everglades National Park. Burmese pythons are native to Burma, Vietnam, southern China, Thailand, and Indonesia. But, in the past 10 years, park staff members have captured more than 68 pythons that were released illegally by pet owners. Burmese pythons can grow more than 7 m long. The giant snakes have easily adapted to the environment of the Everglades because they are excellent swimmers. Many rangers and biologists fear that the pythons will threaten native wildlife.

Weird Science

What's That Smell?

Imagine that you are walking through a tropical rain forest. You're surrounded by green—green leaves, green vines, and green trees. You can hear monkeys and birds calling to each other. When you touch the plants nearby, they are wet from a recent rain shower. But what's that horrible smell? You don't see any rotting garbage around, but you do see a huge flower spike. As you get closer, the smell gets stronger. Then, you realize the flower is what smells so bad! The flower is called a *corpse flower*. The corpse flower is just one plant that uses bad odors to attract pollinators.

Math ACTiViTY

A corpse flower sprouts and grows to a maximum height of 2.35 m in 28 days. In centimeters, what is the average growth of the corpse flower per day?

Social Studies ACTiViTY

Find Burma (also called Myanmar) on a map. Compare its latitude with the latitude of southern Florida. How does the latitude of southern Florida relate to how well Burmese pythons have adapted to the Everglades?

George Archibald

Dancing with Cranes Imagine a man flapping his arms in a dance with a whooping crane. Does this sound funny? When Dr. George Archibald danced with a crane named Tex, he wasn't joking around. To help this endangered species survive, Archibald wanted cranes to mate in captivity so that he could release cranes into the wild. But the captive cranes wouldn't do their courtship dance. Archibald's cranes had imprinted on the humans that raised them. *Imprinting* is a process in which birds learn to recognize their species by looking at their parents. The birds saw humans as their own species, and could only reproduce if a human did the courtship dance. So, Archibald decided to dance. His plan worked! After some time, Tex hatched a baby crane.

After that, Archibald found a way to help the captive cranes imprint on other cranes. He and his staff now feed baby cranes with hand puppets that look like crane heads. They play recordings of real crane sounds for the young cranes. They even wear crane suits when they are near older birds. These cranes are happy to do their courtship dance with each other instead of with Archibald.

Language Arts ACTIVITY

WRITING SKILL Imagine that you are a wildlife biologist taking care of captive cranes. Write a journal entry describing your daily responsibilities and observations of the cranes that are under your care.

To learn more about these Science in Action topics, visit **go.hrw.com** and type in the keyword **HT6FSRFF.**

Current Science

Check out Current Science® articles related to this chapter by visiting **go.hrw.com.** Just type in the keyword **HL5CS14.**

12

Interactions of Living Things

The Big Idea Organisms interact with each other and with the nonliving parts of their environment.

About the

This baby loggerhead sea turtle has left its nest on Palm Beach, FL and is about to taste its first meal—seaweed. Only one of every 1,000 baby loggerheads survives to adulthood. One reason for this low survival rate is that in the first two years of its life, a baby loggerhead is preyed upon by land predators such as raccoons, skunks, and foxes and by sea predators such as sea birds, crabs, and fish.

PRE-READING ACTIVITY

FOLDNOTES **Tri-Fold** Before you read the chapter, create the FoldNote entitled "Tri-Fold" described in the **Study Skills** section of the Appendix. Write what you know about the interactions of living things in the column labeled "Know." Then, write what you want to know in the column labeled "Want." As you read the chapter, write what you learn about the interactions of living things in the column labeled "Learn."

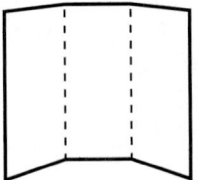

START-UP ACTIVITY

Who Eats Whom?

In this activity, you will learn how organisms interact when they are finding (or becoming) the next meal. **G.2.3.2 CS, G.2.3.3 CS**

Procedure

1. On **five index cards,** one name per card, print the organism names *killer whale, cod fish, krill shrimp, algae,* and *leopard seal.*

2. On your desk, arrange the cards in a chain to show who eats whom.

3. Record the order of your cards.

4. In nature, which organism, killer whales or cod fish, would likely have the greater number of individuals in a group? Arrange the cards in order of the number of individuals in an organism group, from most numerous to fewest.

Analysis

1. What might happen to the other four types of organisms in the chain if algae were removed from the chain? What might happen if the killer whales were removed from the chain?

2. Do any of the five types of organisms eat more than one kind of food? (Hint: What else might a seal, a fish, or a killer whale eat?) How could the card order show this information? How could you use pieces of string to show these relationships?

Everything Is Connected

An alligator drifts in a weedy Florida river, watching a long, thin fish called a gar. The gar swims too close to the alligator. Then, in a rush of murky water, the alligator swallows the gar whole and slowly swims away.

Organisms have many interactions other than that of "who eats whom." For example, alligators dig underwater holes to escape the heat. After the alligators abandon these holes, fish and other aquatic organisms live in the holes during the winter.

Studying the Web of Life

All living things are connected in a web of life. Scientists who study the web of life specialize in the science of ecology. **Ecology** is the study of the interactions of organisms with one another and with their environment.

The Two Parts of an Environment

An environment can be divided into two parts. All of the organisms that live and interact with one another within the environment make up the **biotic** part of the environment. The **abiotic** part of the environment consists of the nonliving factors, such as water, soil, light, and temperature. All biotic and abiotic factors of an environment are interrelated. For example, an alligator, shown in **Figure 1,** needs to live near water in order to catch its food. The alligator also needs the environmental temperature to stay within a range that it can tolerate.

Benchmark Check How are biotic factors and abiotic factors interrelated? G.2.3.2 CS

READING WARM-UP

Objectives

- Identify how biotic and abiotic factors of the environment are interrelated. G.2.3.2 CS
- Describe the five levels of environmental organization.
- Describe how the availability of an abiotic factor can affect a biotic factor. G.2.3.2 CS

Terms to Learn

ecology
biotic **FCAT** VOCAB
abiotic **FCAT** VOCAB
population
community
ecosystem **FCAT** VOCAB
biosphere

READING STRATEGY

Reading Organizer As you read this section, create an outline of the section. Use the headings from the section in your outline.

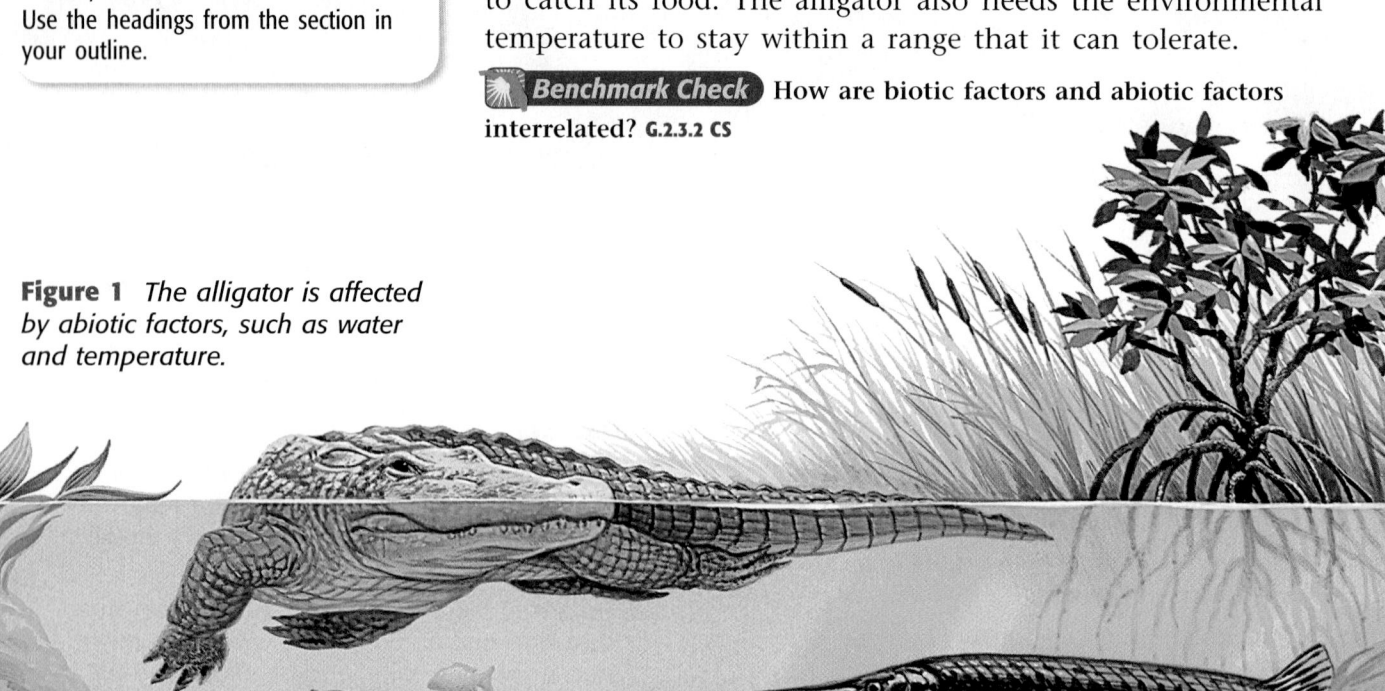

Figure 1 *The alligator is affected by abiotic factors, such as water and temperature.*

Organization in the Environment

The environment may seem disorganized. However, the environment can be arranged into levels, as shown in **Figure 2.** The first level is the level of the individual organism. The second level is larger and is the level of a group of individual organisms, which form a population. The third level is the level of various populations, which form a community. The fourth level is the level of a community and its abiotic environment, which form an ecosystem. The fifth and final level is the level that contains all ecosystems, which form the biosphere.

ecology the study of the interactions of living organisms with one another and with their environment

biotic describes living factors in the environment *FCAT VOCAB*

abiotic describes the nonliving part of the environment, including water, rocks, light, and temperature *FCAT VOCAB*

Figure 2 The Five Levels of Environmental Organization

Biosphere

Ecosystem

Community

Population

Organism

Populations

A salt marsh, such as the one shown in **Figure 3,** is a coastal area where grasslike plants grow. Animals live in the salt marsh. Each animal is a part of a **population,** or a group of individuals of the same species that live together. For example, all of the seaside sparrows that live in the same salt marsh are members of a population. The individuals in the population often compete with one another for food, nesting space, and mates.

Communities

A **community** consists of all of the populations of species that live and interact in an area. The animals and plants that you see in **Figure 3** form a salt-marsh community. The populations in a community depend on each other for things that are necessary to survival, such as food and shelter.

population a group of organisms of the same species that live in a specific geographical area

community all of the populations of species that live in the same habitat and interact with each other

G.2.3.2 CS knows that all biotic and abiotic factors are interrelated and that if one factor is changed or removed, it impacts the availability of other resources within the system.

Figure 3 *Examine the picture of a salt marsh. Try to find examples of each level of organization in this environment.*

Laughing gull

Egret

Cordgrass

Seaside sparrows eat insects, spiders, and small crabs. A male sparrow and his mate weave a nest of cordgrass.

Heron

Juvenile sea croaker

The little marsh crab eats cordgrass and tiny shrimp.

Jellyfish

Some animals eat cordgrass and the microscopic algae that grow on the surface of cordgrass leaves and stems.

The periwinkle snail eats the algae that grow on the cordgrass. And the periwinkle snail uses the cordgrass as a place to hide from predators.

Ecosystems

An **ecosystem** is made up of a community of organisms and the abiotic factors of the community. An ecologist studying the ecosystem could examine how organisms interact and how temperature, precipitation, and soil characteristics affect the organisms. For example, the rivers that empty into the salt marsh carry nutrients, such as nitrogen, from the land. These nutrients affect the growth of the cordgrass and algae.

Benchmark Check How can the amount of nutrients in water affect the growth of cordgrass and algae? G.2.3.2 CS

The Biosphere

The **biosphere** is the part of Earth where life exists. It extends from the deepest parts of the ocean to high in the air where plant spores drift. Ecologists study the biosphere to learn how organisms interact with the abiotic environment—Earth's atmosphere, water, soil, and rock. The water in the abiotic environment includes fresh water, salt water, and water that is frozen in polar icecaps and glaciers.

ecosystem a community of organisms and their abiotic, or nonliving, environment *FCAT VOCAB*

biosphere the part of Earth where life exists

SECTION Review

Summary

- Biotic and abiotic factors are interrelated. Living things depend on abiotic factors, such as water, soil, light, and temperature, in order to survive. G.2.3.2 CS

- The five levels of environmental organization are the organism level, population level, community level, ecosystem level, and biosphere level.

- The availability of an abiotic factor, such as nitrogen, can directly affect the growth of plants. G.2.3.2 CS

Using Key Terms

1. Write an original definition for *ecosystem*. *FCAT VOCAB*

2. Use *biotic* and *abiotic* in the same sentence. *FCAT VOCAB*

Understanding Key Ideas

3. What is the most complex level of environmental organization?

4. Give two examples of how abiotic factors can affect biotic factors in an ecosystem. G.2.3.2 CS

Critical Thinking

5. **Analyzing Relationships** What would happen to the other organisms in the salt-marsh ecosystem if the cordgrass suddenly died? G.2.3.2 CS

6. **Identifying Relationships** Explain in your own words what people mean when they say that everything is connected.

FCAT Preparation

7. Ecosystems can change over time. Which of the following changes in an ecosystem's abiotic factors would most likely cause more trees to grow in a grassland ecosystem? G.2.3.2 CS

A. an increase in soil depth

B. a decrease in precipitation

C. a decrease in carbon dioxide in the air

D. a decrease in the average amount of sunlight

SCILINKS

NSTA
Developed and maintained by the National Science Teachers Association

For a variety of links related to this chapter, go to www.scilinks.org

Topic: Biotic and Abiotic Factors; Florida's Environment

SciLinks code: HSM0164; HSMF06

Living Things Need Energy

Do you think that you could survive on only water and vitamins? Eating food satisfies your hunger because food provides something that you cannot live without—energy.

Living things need energy to survive. For example, black-tailed prairie dogs, which live in the grasslands of North America, eat grass and seeds to get the energy that they need. Everything that a prairie dog does requires energy. The same is true for plants that grow in the grasslands where the prairie dogs live.

The Energy Connection

Organisms, in a prairie or any ecosystem, can be divided into three groups based on how the organisms get energy. These groups are producers, consumers, and decomposers. Examine **Figure 1** to see how energy passes through an ecosystem.

Producers

Organisms that use sunlight directly to make food are *producers*. They make food by using a process called *photosynthesis*. Most producers are plants, but algae and some bacteria are also producers. Grasses are the main producers in a prairie ecosystem. Examples of producers in other ecosystems include cordgrass and algae in a salt marsh and trees in a forest. Algae called *phytoplankton* are the main producers in the ocean.

Energy Sunlight is the source of energy for almost all living things.

Figure 1 *Living things get their energy either from the sun or from eating other organisms.*

Consumer All of the prairie dogs in a colony watch for enemies, which include carnivores such as coyotes, hawks, and badgers. Often, coyotes kill and eat prairie dogs.

Consumer The black-tailed prairie dog, a herbivore, eats seeds and grass in the grasslands of western North America.

Producer Plants use the energy in sunlight to make food.

Consumers

Organisms that eat other organisms are called *consumers*. They cannot use the sun's energy to make food as producers can. Instead, consumers eat producers or other animals to obtain energy. There are several kinds of consumers. A consumer that eats only plants is called a **herbivore.** Herbivores found in the prairie include grasshoppers, prairie dogs, and bison. A **carnivore** is a consumer that eats animals. Carnivores in the prairie include coyotes, hawks, badgers, and owls. Consumers known as **omnivores** eat both plants and animals. The grasshopper mouse is an example of an omnivore. It eats insects, lizards, and grass seeds. *Scavengers* are omnivores that eat dead plants and animals. The turkey vulture is a scavenger in the prairie. A vulture will eat what is left after a coyote has killed and eaten an animal. Scavengers also eat animals and plants that have died from natural causes.

Decomposers

Organisms that get energy by breaking down dead organisms are called *decomposers*. Bacteria and fungi are examples of decomposers. These organisms remove stored energy from dead organisms. As decomposers break down matter, important nutrients are returned to the soil. Nutrients increase soil fertility and can stimulate plant growth. Decomposers also return important nutrients to water and the atmosphere.

Benchmark Check How can decomposers reshape the landscape? **D.1.3.2, D.1.3.4 AA**

herbivore an organism that eats only plants

carnivore an organism that eats animals

omnivore an organism that eats both plants and animals

D.1.3.2 (partial) knows that over the whole Earth, organisms are growing, dying, and decaying as new organisms are produced by the old ones.

D.1.3.4 AA (partial) knows the ways in which plants and animals reshape the landscape (e.g., bacteria, fungi, worms, rodents, and other organisms add organic matter to the soil, increasing the soil fertility, encouraging plant growth, and strengthening resistance to erosion).

G.1.3.4 AA knows that the interactions of organisms with each other and with the nonliving parts of their environments result in the flow of energy and the cycling of matter throughout the system.

Consumer A turkey vulture (scavenger) may eat some of the coyote's leftovers. A scavenger can pick bones completely clean.

Decomposer Any prairie dog remains that are not eaten by the turkey vulture or coyote are broken down by bacteria (decomposers) and fungi that live in soil.

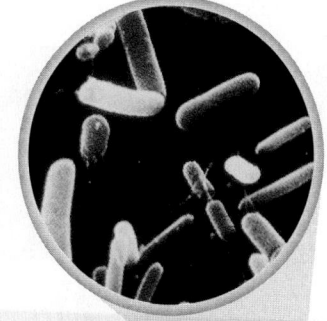

Food Chains and Food Webs

food chain the pathway of energy transfer through various stages as a result of the feeding patterns of a series of organisms

food web a diagram that shows the feeding relationships between organisms in an ecosystem

G.1.3.4 AA knows that the interactions of organisms with each other and with the nonliving parts of their environments result in the flow of energy and the cycling of matter throughout the system.

Figure 1 on the previous page shows a food chain. A **food chain** is a diagram that shows how energy in food flows from one organism to another. Because few organisms eat just one kind of food, simple food chains are rare.

Energy connections in nature are shown more accurately by a food web than by a food chain. A **food web** is a diagram that shows the feeding relationships between organisms in an ecosystem. **Figure 2** shows a simple food web. An arrow that starts at the prairie dog and points to the coyote shows that the prairie dog is food for the coyote. The prairie dog is food for the mountain lion, too. In a food web, as in a food chain, energy moves from one organism to the next in a one-way direction. Energy that is not immediately used by an organism is stored in the organism's tissues. Only energy that is stored in an organism's tissues can be used by the next consumer. Earth's main food webs are a land food web and an aquatic food web.

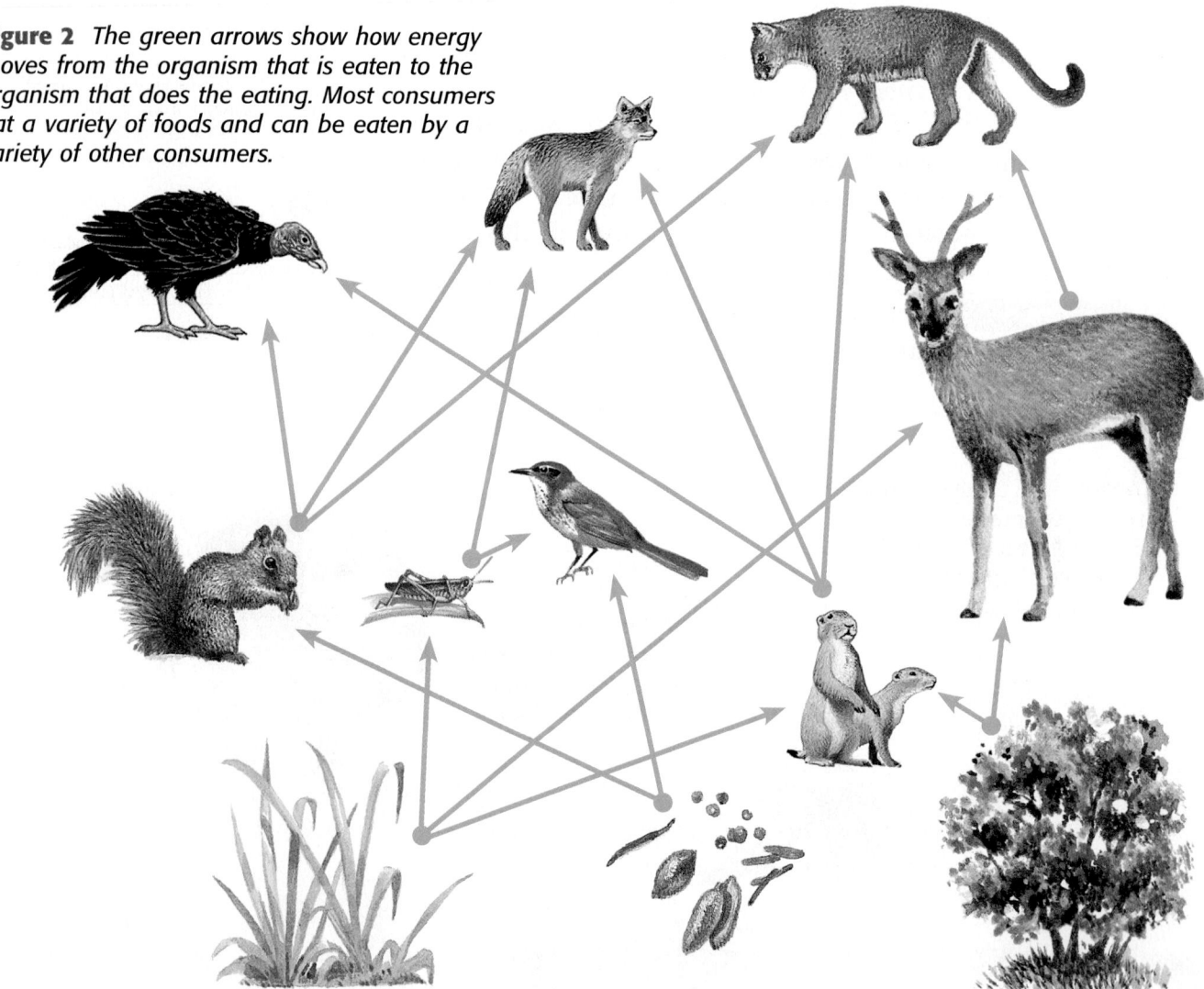

Figure 2 *The green arrows show how energy moves from the organism that is eaten to the organism that does the eating. Most consumers eat a variety of foods and can be eaten by a variety of other consumers.*

Decreasing number of organisms

Decreasing amount of energy

Figure 3 *The pyramid represents energy. As you can see, more energy is available at the pyramid's base than at its top.*

Energy Pyramids

Phytoplankton use most of the energy that they get from sunlight for their own life processes. But some of the energy is stored their cells. This energy is used by animals such as sea urchins. Sea urchins use most of the energy that they get from eating phytoplankton and store only a little in their tissues. Therefore, a population of sea urchins can support only a few large fish, which in turn can support only one shark. In an aquatic community, there must be more phytoplankton than sea urchins, more sea urchins than fish, and more fish than sharks. The energy at each level of the food chain can be seen in an energy pyramid. An **energy pyramid** is a diagram that shows an ecosystem's loss of energy. An example of an energy pyramid is shown in **Figure 3.** Less energy is available at higher levels because only energy that is stored in the tissues of an organism can be transferred to the next level.

energy pyramid a triangular diagram that shows an ecosystem's loss of energy, which results as energy passes through the ecosystem's food chain

Benchmark Check Explain how an energy pyramid represents the movement of energy through an ecosystem. **G.1.3.4 AA**

Figure 4 As the wilderness was settled, the gray wolf population in the United States declined.

Wolves and the Energy Pyramid

One species can be very important to the flow of energy in an environment. Gray wolves, which are shown in **Figure 4,** are consumers that control the populations of many other animals. Gray wolves' diet can include anything from a lizard to an elk. Because gray wolves are predators that prey on large animals, their place is at the top of the food pyramid.

Once common throughout much of the United States, gray wolves were almost wiped out as the wilderness was settled. Without wolves, some species, such as elk, were no longer controlled. The overpopulation of elk in some areas led to overgrazing. The overgrazing left too little grass to support the elk and other populations who depended on the grass for food. Soon, almost all of the populations in the area were affected by the loss of the gray wolves.

Benchmark Check How were other animals affected by the disappearance of the gray wolf? **G.2.3.3 CS**

Figure 5 In small wolf packs, only one female has pups. They are cared for by all of the males and females in the pack.

G.2.3.3 CS knows that a brief change in the limited resources of an ecosystem may alter the size of a population or the average size of individual organisms and that long-term change may result in the elimination of animal and plant populations inhabiting the Earth.

Gray Wolves and the Food Web

Gray wolves were brought back to Yellowstone National Park in 1995. The reintroduced wolves soon began to breed. **Figure 5** shows a wolf caring for pups. The U.S. Fish and Wildlife Service thinks that the wolves return will restore the natural energy flow in the area, bring populations back into balance, and help restore the natural integrity of the park's ecosystem.

But not everyone approves of the return of the wolves. Ranchers near Yellowstone are concerned for their livestock's safety. Cows and sheep are not wolves' natural prey, but wolves will eat cows and sheep if given the opportunity to do so.

Balance in Ecosystems

As wolves become reestablished in Yellowstone National Park, they kill the old, injured, and diseased elk. This process is reducing the number of elk. A smaller elk population allows more plants to grow. So, in Yellowstone, the number of animals that eat plants, such as snowshoe hares, and the number of animals that eat hares, such as foxes, are increasing.

All organisms in a food web are important for the health and balance of all other organisms in the food web. But the debate over the introduction of wolves to Yellowstone National Park will most likely continue for years to come.

Energy Pyramids

Draw an energy pyramid for a river ecosystem that contains four levels—aquatic plants, insect larvae, bluegill fish, and a large-mouth bass. The plants obtain 10,000 units of energy from sunlight. If each level uses 90% of the energy it receives from the previous level, how many units of energy are available to the bass?

SECTION Review

Summary

- Energy from sunlight passes through producers, consumers, and decomposers in an ecosystem. **G.1.3.4 AA**

- Decomposers can reshape the landscape by breaking down dead organisms and returning nutrients to the soil, water, and the atmosphere. **D.1.3.2, D.1.3.4 AA**

- Food chains, food webs, and energy pyramids represent how energy flows from one organism to another. **G.1.3.4 AA**

- All organisms are important to maintain the balance of energy in an ecosystem. **G.2.3.3 CS**

Using Key Terms

1. Use *herbivores, carnivores,* and *omnivores* in separate sentences.

2. Write an original definition for *food chain, food web,* and *energy pyramid.*

Understanding Key Ideas

3. Herbivores, carnivores, and scavengers are all examples of
   a. producers.   c. consumers.
   b. decomposers. d. omnivores.

4. Explain the importance of decomposers in an ecosystem. **D.1.3.2, D.1.3.4 AA**

5. Describe how producers, consumers, and decomposers are linked in a food chain. **G.1.3.4 AA**

6. Describe how energy flows through a food web. **G.1.3.4 AA**

Critical Thinking

7. **Applying Concepts** Are consumers found at the top or bottom of an energy pyramid? Explain your answer. **G.1.3.4 AA**

8. **Predicting Consequences** What would happen if a species disappeared from an ecosystem? **G.2.3.3 CS**

FCAT Preparation

9. Gardeners often use organic materials such as fruit skins and dead leaves to make a type of fertilizer called compost. Which organisms convert the organic materials into compost? **D.1.3.4 AA**

   A. consumers
   B. decomposers
   C. omnivores
   D. producers

10. Drought kills 70 percent of the plants in an ecosystem. How might this affect other organisms in the ecosystem? **G.2.3.3 CS**

    F. herbivores will starve
    G. producers will leave the area
    H. decomposers will starve
    I. scavengers will starve

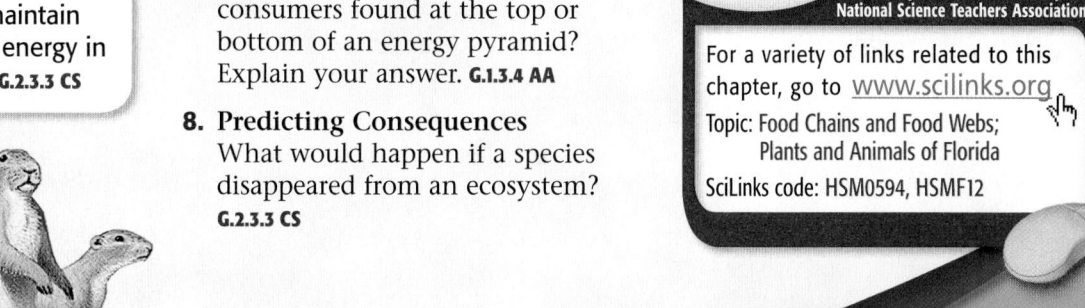

SCILINKS®

Developed and maintained by the
National Science Teachers Association

For a variety of links related to this chapter, go to www.scilinks.org

Topic: Food Chains and Food Webs;
        Plants and Animals of Florida
SciLinks code: HSM0594, HSMF12

Types of Interactions

Look at the seaweed forest shown in **Figure 1** *below. How many fish do you see? How many seaweed plants do you count? Why does the seaweed population have more members than the fish population has?*

In natural communities, population size can vary greatly between types of organisms. There is variation because all of the parts of the environment interact with each other. So, a change in one part, such as in a particular population, can cause a change in another part. Each population in an environment affects every other population in that environment.

Interactions with the Environment

Most living things have more offspring than will survive. For example, a frog might lay hundreds of eggs at once in a pond. But in a few months, the pond's frog population will be about the same size as it was before the eggs were laid. Why isn't the pond overrun with frogs? It is not overrun because frogs—as all organisms do—interact with the biotic and abiotic parts of the environment in a way that affects population size.

Limiting Factors

Populations cannot grow nonstop because the environment contains a limited amount of resources, such as food, water, and living space. A resource whose availability limits the size of a population is a *limiting factor*. Food is a limiting factor when there is not enough food available to feed the entire population. Any resource can be a limiting factor for population size.

READING WARM-UP

Objectives

● Explain the relationship between carrying capacity and limiting factors. **G.2.3.3 CS**

● Describe four ways that organisms interact with each other. **G.1.3.4 AA**

● Distinguish between mutualism, commensalism, and parasitism.

● Give an example of coevolution.

Terms to Learn

carrying capacity   mutualism
prey   commensalism
predator   parasitism
symbiosis   coevolution

READING STRATEGY

Reading Organizer As you read this section, make a concept map by using the terms above.

Figure 1 *This seaweed forest is home to a large number of interacting species. For example, sea otters prey on sea urchins.*

Carrying Capacity

The largest population that an environment can support is known as the **carrying capacity** of that environment. When a population grows larger than its carrying capacity, limiting factors in the environment cause individuals to die off or leave. As individuals die or leave, the population size decreases.

For example, after a rainy season, plants may produce a large crop of leaves and seeds. This large amount of food may allow a herbivore population to increase in size. If the next year has less rainfall, there won't be enough food to support the large herbivore population. This is one way in which a population can briefly become larger than the environment's carrying capacity. A limiting factor, such as the lack of food, will cause the population to die back. The population size will then decrease to a size that the environment can support.

Benchmark Check Explain how a brief change in the limited resources of an ecosystem can alter the size of a population. G.2.3.3 CS

carrying capacity the largest population that an environment can support at any given time

G.1.3.4 AA knows that the interactions of organisms with each other and with the nonliving parts of their environments result in the flow of energy and the cycling of matter throughout the system.

G.2.3.3 CS knows that a brief change in the limited resources of an ecosystem may alter the size of a population or the average size of individual organisms and that long-term change may result in the elimination of animal and plant populations inhabiting the Earth.

Interactions Between Organisms

Populations contain individuals of a single species that interact with one another, such as a group of rabbits feeding in the same area. Communities, such as a coral reef, contain many interacting populations, such as different species of corals and other organisms that live in the same area. Ecologists have described four main ways in which organisms affect each other: competition, predators and prey, symbiotic relationships, and coevolution.

Competition

Two or more individuals or populations trying to use the same resource, such as food, water, shelter, space, or sunlight, is called *competition*. Because resources are in limited supply in the environment, their use by one individual or population decreases the amount available to others.

Competition happens between individuals *within* a population. The elks in Yellowstone National Park are herbivores that compete with each other for the same food plants in the park. The competition becomes tougher in winter when many plants die.

Competition also happens *between* populations. The various species of trees in **Figure 2** are competing with each other for sunlight and space.

Figure 2 *Some of the trees in this forest grow tall to reach sunlight, which reduces the amount of sunlight available to shorter trees nearby.*

Predators and Prey

A common interaction between species is that of one organism eating another organism to get food and energy. This interaction transfers materials and energy between the organisms. The organism that is eaten is called the **prey.** The organism that eats the prey is called the **predator.** When a bird eats a worm, the worm is prey and the bird is the predator.

prey an organism that is killed and eaten by another organism

predator an organism that eats all or part of another organism

Benchmark Check **What is transferred from the predator to the prey in the predator-prey relationship? G.1.3.4 AA**

Predator Adaptations

To survive, predators must be able to catch prey. Predators use various methods and abilities to catch prey. For example, the cheetah runs very quickly to catch its prey. Its speed gives the cheetah an advantage over predators with which it competes for prey. Some predators, such as the goldenrod spider, ambush prey. As **Figure 3** shows, this spider blends in with the goldenrod flower. So, the spider simply waits for its insect prey to arrive, and then ambushes the insect.

Prey Adaptations

Prey use various methods and abilities to avoid being eaten. Prey can run away, stay in groups, or camouflage themselves. Some prey are poisonous. These prey may have bright colors that advertise their poison and warn predators to stay away. The fire salamander, shown in **Figure 4,** sprays a poison that burns. Predators learn to recognize the prey's *warning coloration.*

Many prey animals run from predators. Prairie dogs run to underground burrows when a predator approaches. Many fishes, such as anchovies, swim in groups called *schools.* Antelopes and buffaloes stay in herds. All members of the group watch, listen, and sniff for predators. These behaviors increase the likelihood that a predator is seen before it strikes the group.

Figure 3 *The goldenrod spider is difficult for its insect prey to see. Can you see the spider?*

Figure 4 *Many predators know better than to eat the fire salamander! This colorful animal will make a predator very sick.*

G.1.3.4 AA knows that the interactions of organisms with each other and with the nonliving parts of their environments result in the flow of energy and the cycling of matter throughout the system.

Camouflage

One way that animals avoid being eaten is by being hard to see. A rabbit often stays still so that its natural color blends into a background of shrubs or grass. Blending in with the background is called *camouflage*. Many animals mimic twigs, leaves, stones, bark, or other materials in their environment. One insect, called a walking stick, looks like a twig. Some walking sticks even sway a bit, as though a breeze were blowing.

✓ **Reading Check** What is camouflage, and how does it prevent an animal from being eaten?

Defensive Chemicals

The spines of a porcupine clearly signal trouble to a predator, but other animals' defenses may not be as obvious. Some animals defend themselves with chemicals. The skunk and the bombardier beetle both spray predators with irritating chemicals. Bees, ants, and wasps inject a powerful acid into their attackers. The skin of both the poison arrow frog and a bird called the *hooded pitohui* contain a deadly toxin. Any predator that eats, or tries to eat, one of these animals will likely die.

Warning Coloration

Animals that have a chemical defense often have a way to warn predators away. Often, prey animals that have chemical weapons have warning colors that advertise these weapons, as shown in **Figure 5.** Predators avoid animals that have colors and patterns that the predators associate with pain, illness, or unpleasant experiences. The most common warning colors are bright shades of red, yellow, orange, black, and white.

CONNECTION TO Environmental Science

Pretenders Some animals are pretenders. They do not have defensive chemicals. But they use warning coloration to their advantage. The Scarlet king snake has colored stripes that make it look like the poisonous coral snake. Even though the Scarlet king snake is harmless, predators see its bright colors and leave it alone. What might happen if there were more pretenders than there were animals that truly had defensive chemicals?

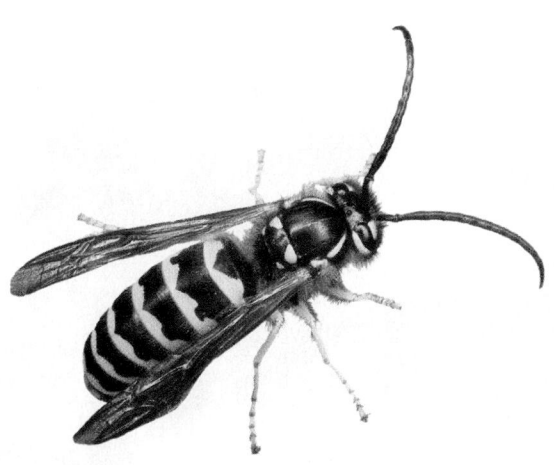

Figure 5 *Warning coloration warns predators that the yellow jacket (left) and the pitohui (above) are dangerous.*

Symbiosis

Some species have very close interactions with other species. **Symbiosis** is a close, long-term association between two or more species. The individuals in a symbiotic relationship can benefit from, be unaffected by, or be harmed by the relationship. Often, one species lives in or on the other species. The thousands of symbiotic relationships in nature are often classified into three groups: mutualism, commensalism, and parasitism.

symbiosis a relationship in which two different organisms live in close association with each other

mutualism a relationship between two species in which both species benefit

commensalism a relationship between two organisms in which one organism benefits and the other is unaffected

Mutualism

A symbiotic relationship in which both organisms benefit is called **mutualism** (MYOO choo uhl ɪz uhm). For example, you and a species of bacteria that lives in your intestines benefit each other. The bacteria get food from you, and you get vitamins that the bacteria produce.

Another example of mutualism is the relationship between corals and algae, as shown in **Figure 6.** Many types of corals and some types of algae form such relationships. The corals serve as a home for the algae. In turn, the algae give the coral some of the food that the algae make by photosynthesis. When a coral dies, other corals can grow on the skeleton of the dead coral. Over a long time, these skeletons form large structures called *reefs*.

Figure 6 *In the smaller photo above, you can see the gold-colored algae inside the coral.*

✓ *Reading Check* **Which organisms benefit in mutualism?**

Commensalism

A symbiotic relationship in which one organism benefits and the other is unaffected is called **commensalism.** An example of commensalism is the relationship between sharks and *remoras,* a small fish. **Figure 7** shows a shark that has a remora attached to it. Remoras "hitch a ride" and feed on the sharks' food scraps. Remoras benefit from this relationship; sharks are unaffected.

Figure 7 *The relationship between the remora and the shark benefits the remora and neither benefits nor harms the shark.*

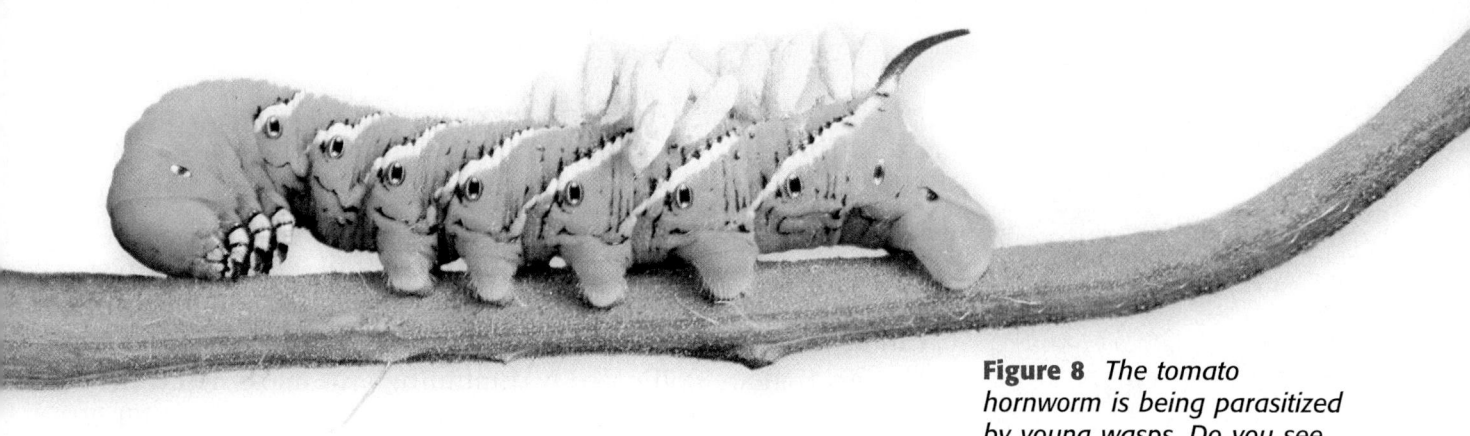

Figure 8 *The tomato hornworm is being parasitized by young wasps. Do you see their cocoons?*

Parasitism

A symbiotic association in which one organism benefits while the other is harmed is called **parasitism** (PAR uh SIT IZ uhm). The organism that benefits is called the *parasite*. The organism that is harmed is called the *host*. The parasite gets nutrients and energy from its host while the host is weakened or dies. Some parasites, such as ticks, live outside the host's body. Other parasites, such as tapeworms, live inside the host's body.

Figure 8 shows a bright green caterpillar called a *tomato hornworm*. A female wasp laid tiny eggs on the caterpillar. When the eggs hatch, each young wasp will burrow into the caterpillar's body. The young wasps will eat the caterpillar alive. In a short time, the caterpillar will be almost completely eaten and will die. When that happens, the wasps will have become adult wasps and will fly away.

In this example of parasitism, the host dies. Most parasites, however, do not kill their hosts. Most parasites don't kill their hosts because parasites depend on their hosts. If a parasite were to kill its host, the parasite would have to find a new host.

Benchmark Check Where do parasites get their energy and nutrients from? G.1.3.4 AA

parasitism a relationship between two species in which one species, the parasite, benefits from the other species, the host, which is harmed

coevolution the evolution of two species that is due to mutual influence, often in a way that makes the relationship more beneficial to both species

G.1.3.4 AA knows that the interactions of organisms with each other and with the nonliving parts of their environments result in the flow of energy and the cycling of matter throughout the system.

Coevolution

Relationships between organisms change over time. As the interactions change, the organisms change. When an inheritable change takes place in two species because of their close interactions with one another, the change is called **coevolution.**

The ant and the acacia tree shown in **Figure 9** have a mutualistic relationship. The ants protect the tree by attacking other organisms that come near the tree. The tree has special structures that make food for the ants. The ants and the acacia tree may have coevolved through interactions between the two species. Coevolution can take place between any organisms that live close together. But changes often happen over a very long period of time.

Figure 9 *Ants collect food from acacia trees and store the food in the shelter of the trees.*

CONNECTION TO
Social Studies

Rabbits in Australia In 1859, settlers released 12 rabbits in Australia. There was plenty of food and no natural predators of the rabbits. The rabbit population increased so fast that the country was soon overrun by rabbits. To control the rabbit population, the Australian government introduced a rabbit virus. The first time the virus was used, more than 99% of the rabbits died. The survivors reproduced, and the rabbit population grew large again. The second time the virus was used, about 90% of the rabbits died. Once again, the rabbit population increased. The third time the virus was used, only about 50% of the rabbits died. Suggest what changes might have occurred in the rabbits and the virus that made the virus increasingly ineffective.

INTERNET ACTIVITY

Prairie Play Write a play that describes all of the interactions that take place on the prairie. Go to **go.hrw.com,** and type in the keyword **HL5INTW.**

Coevolution and Flowers

A *pollinator* is an organism that carries pollen from one flower to another. In most plants, pollination is necessary for reproduction.

Flowers have changed over millions of years to attract pollinators. Pollinators, such as bees, bats, and hummingbirds, can be attracted to a flower because of its color, odor, or nectar. Flowers that are pollinated by hummingbirds make nectar that contains the right amount of sugar for the bird. Hummingbirds have long beaks, which help the birds drink the nectar.

Some types of bats, such as the type shown in **Figure 10,** changed over time to have long, thin tongues and noses that help them reach the nectar in flowers. As the bat feeds on the nectar, its nose becomes covered with pollen. So, the next flower that the bat eats from will be pollinated with the pollen from the previous flower. The long nose helps the bat feed and makes the bat a better pollinator.

Because flowers and pollinators have interacted so closely over millions of years, there are many examples of coevolution between them.

Reading Check Why do flowers need to attract pollinators?

Figure 10 *This bat is drinking nectar with its long, skinny tongue. The bat has coevolved with the flower over millions of years.*

Summary

- Limiting factors in the environment keep a population from growing without limit. **G.2.3.3 CS**

- Four ways in which organisms affect each other are competition, predator-prey relationships, symbiotic relationships, and coevolution. **G.1.3.4 AA**

- A predator is an organism that kills prey organisms so that it can eat all or part of those prey organisms. **G.1.3.4 AA**

- Prey have developed features such as camouflage, chemical defenses, and warning coloration that protect prey from predators.

- Symbiosis occurs when two organisms form a very close relationship with one another over time.

- Very long-term relationships can result in coevolution. For example, flowers and their pollinators have evolved traits that benefit both the flowers and the pollinators.

Understanding Key Ideas

1. Identify two things that organisms compete for.

2. Briefly describe the predator-prey relationship. Be sure to mention what is transferred between the predator and prey. **G.1.3.4 AA**

Critical Thinking

3. **Making Comparisons** Compare coevolution with symbiosis.

4. **Predicting Consequences** Predict what might happen if all of the ants were removed from an acacia tree. **G.2.3.3 CS**

Interpreting Graphics

The graph below shows the growth over 18 days of a population of paramecia (single-celled organisms) in a test tube. The test tube contained food. Use this graph to answer the questions that follow.

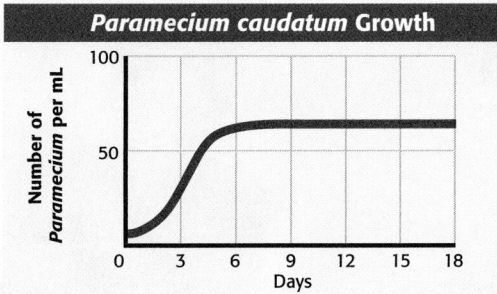

Paramecium caudatum Growth

5. What is the carrying capacity of the test tube when food is provided? **G.2.3.3 CS**

6. Predict what will happen if no additional food is provided. **G.2.3.3 CS**

FCAT Preparation

7. Organisms interact in many ways, including in competitive relationships, predator-prey relationships, and symbiotic relationships. Explain how these three types of interactions allow nutrients and energy to move through various organisms. **G.1.3.4 AA**

8. A pesticide is sprayed over a 100-acre area to kill insects that can harm the plants in that area. How might this pesticide affect the area's carrying capacity for insect-eating birds? **G.2.3.3 CS**

   A. The carrying capacity will fall because of a decrease in food supply.

   B. The carrying capacity will rise because of an increase in food supply.

   C. The carrying capacity will stay the same because the pesticides do not kill birds.

   D. The carrying capacity will stay the same because pesticides are rarely effective.

SCI LINKS®

NSTA
Developed and maintained by the
National Science Teachers Association

For a variety of links related to this chapter, go to www.scilinks.org

Topic: Predator/Prey; Coevolution
SciLinks code: HSM1205; HSM0309

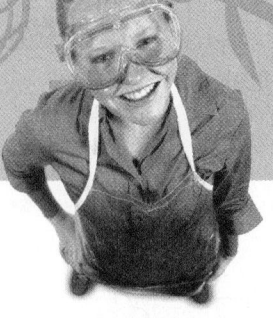

Skills Practice Lab

Capturing the Wild Bean

Estimate the size of a "population" of beans.

Calculate the difference between your estimation and the actual number of beans.

MATERIALS

- bag, paper lunch, small
- beans, pinto
- calculator (optional)
- marker, permanent

When wildlife biologists study a group of organisms in an area, they need to know how many organisms live there. Sometimes, biologists worry that a certain organism is outgrowing the environment's carrying capacity. Other times, scientists need to know if an organism is becoming rare so that steps can be taken to protect it. However, animals can be difficult to count because they can move around and hide. Because of this challenge, biologists have developed methods to estimate the number of animals in a specific area. One of these counting methods is called the *mark-recapture method*.

In this activity, you will enter the territory of the wild pinto bean to estimate the number of beans that live in the paper-bag habitat.

Procedure

❶ Prepare a data table like the one below.

Mark-Recapture Data Table				
Number of animals in first capture	Number of animals in recapture	Number of marked animals in recapture	Calculated estimate of population	Actual total population

❷ Your teacher will provide you with a paper bag containing an unknown number of beans. Carefully reach into the bag, and remove a handful of beans.

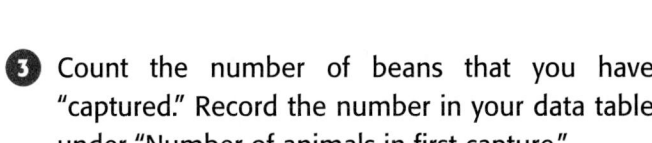

3. Count the number of beans that you have "captured." Record the number in your data table under "Number of animals in first capture."

4. Use the permanent marker to carefully mark each bean that you counted. Allow the marks to dry completely. When all of the marks are dry, place the marked beans back into the bag.

5. Mix the beans in the bag gently so that the marks won't rub off. Once again, reach into the bag. "Capture" and remove a handful of beans.

6. Count the number of beans in your "recapture." Record this number in your data table under "Total number of animals in recapture."

7. Count the beans in your recapture that have marks from the first capture. Record this number in your data table under "Number of marked animals in recapture."

8. Calculate your estimation of the total number of beans in the bag by using the following equation:

$$\frac{\text{number of beans in recapture} \times \text{number of beans marked}}{\text{number of marked beans in recapture}} = \begin{array}{l}\text{calculated estimate} \\ \text{of population}\end{array}$$

Enter this number in your data table under "Calculated estimate of population."

9. Place all of the beans in the bag. Then, empty the bag onto your work table. Be careful that no beans escape! Count each bean as you place the beans one at a time back into the bag. Record the number in your data table under "Actual total population."

Analyze the Results

1. **Evaluating Results** How close was your estimate to the actual number of beans?

Draw Conclusions

2. **Evaluating Methods** If your estimate was not close to the actual number of beans, how might you change your mark-recapture procedure? If you did not recapture any marked beans, what might be the cause?

Applying Your Data

How could you use the mark-recapture method to estimate the population of turtles in a small pond? Explain your procedure.

Chapter Review

USING KEY TERMS

1 Use *symbiosis*, *mutualism*, *commensalism*, and *parasitism* in separate sentences.

For each pair of terms, explain how the meanings of the terms differ.

2 *community* and *population*

3 *ecosystem* and *biosphere* FCAT VOCAB

4 *producers* and *consumers*

5 *biotic* and *abiotic* FCAT VOCAB

UNDERSTANDING KEY IDEAS

Multiple Choice

6 A tick sucks blood from a dog. In this relationship, the tick is the _____ and the dog is the _____.

  a. parasite, prey
  c. parasite, host
  b. predator, host
  d. host, parasite

7 A limiting factor is a resource that is so scarce that it limits the size of a population. When are resources such as water, food, or sunlight most likely to be limiting factors? G.2.3.3 CS FCAT

  a. when a population size is decreasing
  b. when predators eat their prey
  c. when a population is small
  d. when a population is approaching its habitat's carrying capacity

8 Nature's recyclers are D.1.3.2, D.1.3.4 AA

  a. predators.
  c. producers.
  b. decomposers.
  d. omnivores.

9 A beneficial association between coral and algae is an example of

  a. commensalism.
  c. mutualism.
  b. parasitism.
  d. predation.

10 Most plants need nitrogen to grow. What might happen to other resources in an ecosystem if all of its nitrogen were removed? G.2.3.2 CS FCAT

  a. Nothing, the soil alone will replenish the nitrogen.
  b. Nothing, other resources in the ecosystem will be unaffected.
  c. All of the consumers will survive, but the producers will die.
  d. Most of the producers, and thus the rest of the community, will die.

11 The base of an energy pyramid is the largest level and contains the largest number of organisms. Which type of organisms does the base of an energy pyramid represent? G.1.3.4 AA

  a. producer
  c. herbivore
  b. carnivore
  d. scavenger

12 Which of the following is the correct order in a food chain? G.1.3.4 AA

  a. sun→producers→herbivores→ scavengers→carnivores
  b. sun→consumers→predators→ parasites→hosts
  c. sun→producers→decomposers→ consumers→omnivores
  d. sun→producers→herbivores→ carnivores→scavengers

13 Remoras and sharks have a relationship that is best described as

  a. mutualism.
  c. predator and prey.
  b. commensalism.
  d. parasitism.

Short Answer

14 A food web is a diagram that shows the feeding relationships between organisms in an ecosystem. Describe how energy flows through a food web. G.1.3.4 AA FCAT

15 Explain how the park's food web changed when the gray wolf disappeared from Yellowstone National Park. G.2.3.3 CS

16 How are the competition between two trees of the same species and the competition between two different species of trees similar?

17 How do limiting factors affect the carrying capacity of an environment? G.2.3.3 CS

Extended Response

18 **Identifying Relationships** Could a balanced ecosystem contain producers and consumers but not decomposers? Why or why not? D.1.3.2, D.1.3.4 AA

19 **Predicting Consequences** Some biologists think that certain species, such as alligators and wolves, help maintain biological diversity in the species' ecosystems. Predict what would happen to other organisms, such as gar fish or herons, in the Florida Everglades if alligators were to become extinct. G.2.3.3 CS

20 **Expressing Opinions** Do you think that there is a carrying capacity for humans? Why or why not? G.2.3.3 CS

Concept Mapping

21 Use the following terms to create a concept map: *herbivores, organisms, producers, populations, ecosystems, consumers, communities, carnivores,* and *biosphere.*

INTERPRETING GRAPHICS

Use the energy pyramid below to answer the questions that follow.

22 According to this energy pyramid, which are more numerous, prairie dogs or plants?

23 What level has the most energy?

24 Would you expect such an energy pyramid to exist in nature? Why? G.1.3.4 AA

25 How could you change this pyramid to make it represent a real ecosystem? G.1.3.4 AA

Standardized Test Preparation

For the following questions, write your answers on a separate sheet of paper.

1 When living things die, they are recycled by other organisms in nature. Maggots that feed on the remains of dead organisms are a part of this recycling process. Maggots break down dead organisms so that bacteria and fungi can convert the matter into simpler materials, such as water and carbon dioxide. Other organisms can then use these materials. During this cycle, a maggot would be classified as which of the following?

A. a host
B. a predator
C. a herbivore
D. a decomposer

2 Jonquila finds an interesting lizard near a pond. Its tail is colored bright yellow and red. What type of defense against predators does this lizard **most** likely have?

F. camouflage
G. chemical
H. grouping
I. remoras

3 The characteristics of a praying mantis make it easy for it to be camouflaged by the green stems of plants. While camouflaged, a praying mantis can feed on other insects that inhabit or feed on a plant. If a praying mantis feeds on natural enemies of a plant, what type of relationship is occurring between the praying mantis and the plant?

A. camouflage
B. competition
C. mutualism
D. parasitism

4   The upper level of the ocean receives enough sunlight for algae to grow. Lower levels of the ocean receive little if any sunlight. Some parts of the ocean floor can be completely dark. The animals that live on the ocean floor get their food from dead organisms that float down from above. Where would you expect to find the greatest amount of stored energy in the ocean? Where would you find the least amount of stored energy? Explain where you would expect to find producers and consumers.

5 The diagram below shows the number of seaside sparrows and number of little marsh crabs in a small salt marsh habitat over a five year period. During this time period, there was a disease that killed off most of the cordgrass in the marsh.

TWO ANIMAL POPULATIONS IN A SALT MARSH HABITAT

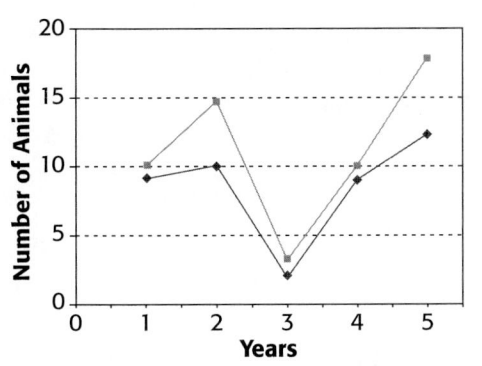

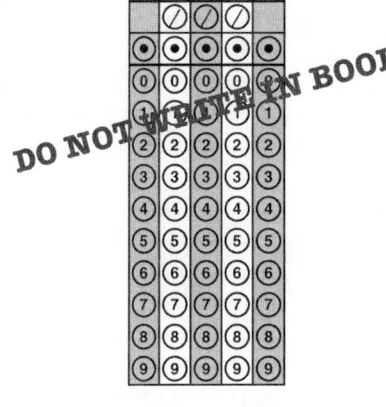

How many little marsh crabs were alive during the year that the disease occurred?

6 The diagram below shows a typical food chain in a grassland ecosystem. Notice that there is a missing entry in the food chain.

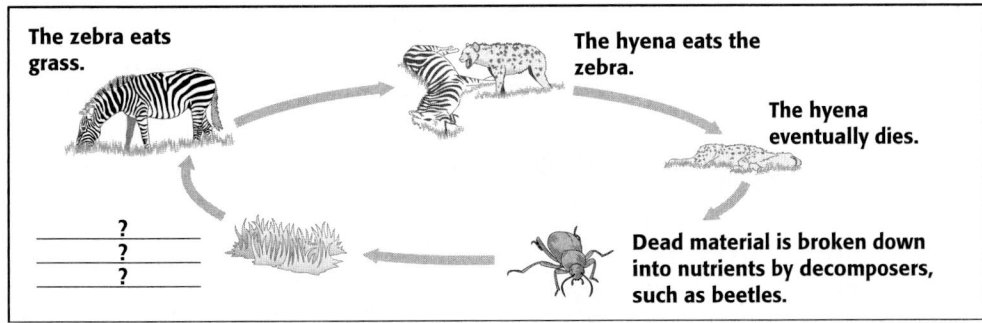

What description should go next to the drawing of grass to complete the food chain?

F. The zebra eats grass.

G. Scavengers, such as vultures, eat grass.

H. Grass is decomposed by sunlight and water.

I. Grass grows by absorbing nutrients from the soil.

FCAT Preparation

Science in Action

Scientific Debate

How Did Dogs Become Pets?

Did we humans change dogs from wild animals into the social and helpful pets that they are today? Or were dogs naturally social? Long ago, did dogs choose to move closer to our campfires? Or did we bring the dogs into our homes? We do not know how dogs became our friends, companions, and helpers. Some scientists think that contact with and training by humans socialized dogs. Other scientists think that dogs and humans formed their strong and unique bond by changing each other over time.

Science, Technology, and Society

Using DNA to Track Florida Black Bears

How would you count Florida black bears that are in the wild? Wildlife biologists use corn and donuts to help count! The food is left on a stand that is surrounded by barbed wire. To get to the food, a bear squeezes through the wires, which snag tufts of fur. Biologists collect and analyze the fur to see the bear's unique DNA pattern. This analysis allows biologists to safely identify and count the bears. Biologists use these data to map black bear habitats. Roads and buildings separate some Florida black bear populations, so such maps help biologists measure the genetic diversity of bears that remain in the wild.

Math ACTIVITY

Scientists have found dog fossils that are 15,000 years old. Generation time is the time between the birth of one generation and the birth of the next generation. If dogs' generation time is 1.5 years, how many generations are in 15,000 years?

Language Arts ACTIVITY

WRITING SKILL Imagine that you are a wildlife biologist studying Florida black bears. Write a creative story about your experiences studying bear behavior in the wild.

Dalton Dockery

Horticulture Specialist Did you know that instead of using pesticides to get rid of insects that are eating the plants in your garden, you can use other insects? "It is a healthy way of growing vegetables without the use of chemicals and pesticides, and it reduces the harmful effects pesticides have on the environment," says Dalton Dockery, a horticulture specialist in North Carolina. Some insects, such as ladybugs and praying mantises, are natural predators of many insects that are harmful to plants. They will eat other bugs but leave your precious plants in peace. Using bugs to drive off pests is just one aspect of natural gardening. Natural gardening takes advantage of relationships that already exist in nature and uses these interactions to our benefit. For Dockery, the best parts about being a horticultural specialist are teaching people how to preserve the environment, getting to work outside regularly, and having the opportunity to help people on a daily basis.

Social Studies ACTIVITY

WRITING SKILL Research gardening or farming techniques that are used in other cultures. Do other cultures use any of the aspects of natural gardening that horticultural specialists use? Write a short report describing your findings.

To learn more about these Science in Action topics, visit **go.hrw.com,** and type in the keyword **HT6FINFF.**

Current Science

Check out Current Science® articles related to this chapter by visiting go.hrw.com. Just type in the keyword **HL5CS18.**

Cycles in Nature

The Big Idea Ecosystems change over time and depend on the cycling of matter.

About the PHOTO

These penguins have a unique playground on this iceberg off the coast of Antarctica. Icebergs break off from glaciers and float out to sea. A glacier is a giant "river of ice" that slides slowly downhill. Glaciers form when snow piles up in mountains. Eventually, glaciers and icebergs melt and become liquid water. Water in oceans and lakes rises into the air and then falls as rain or snow. There is a lot of water on Earth, and most of it is constantly moving and changing form.

PRE-READING ACTIVITY

Pyramid Before you read the chapter, create the FoldNote entitled "Pyramid" described in the **Study Skills** section of the Appendix. Label the sides of the pyramid with "Water cycle," "Carbon cycle," and "Nitrogen cycle." As you read the chapter, define each cycle, and write the steps of each cycle on the appropriate pyramid side.

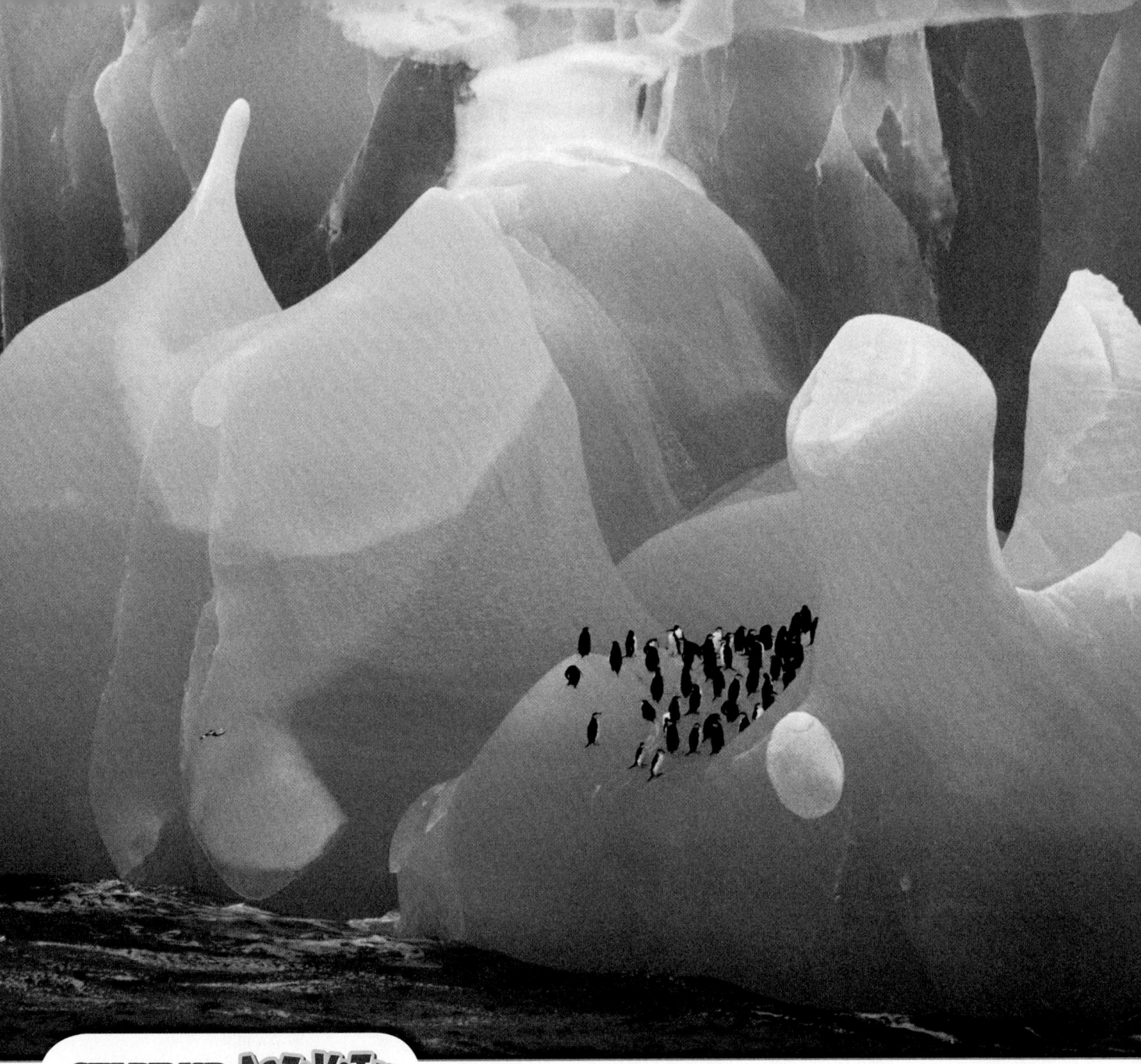

START-UP ACTIVITY

Making Rain

Do you have the power to make rain? Yes! On a small scale, you do. In this activity, you will cause water to change state in the same way that rain is formed. This process is one way that water is reused on Earth. G.1.3.4 AA

Procedure

1. Start with a **large, sealable, plastic freezer bag.** Be sure that the bag is clean and dry and has no leaks. Place a **small, dark-colored bowl** inside the bag. Position the bag with the opening at the top.

2. Fill the bowl halfway with water. Place a few drops of **red food coloring** in the water. Seal the bag.

3. Place the bowl and bag under a **strong, warm light source,** such as a lamp or direct sunlight.

4. Leave the bag in the light for as long as possible. Observe the bag at regular time intervals.

Analysis

1. Each time that you observe the bag, describe what you see. Explain what you think is happening inside the bag.

2. After observing the bag several times, carefully remove the bowl from the bag. Observe and describe any water that is now in the bag. Where did this water come from? How does it differ from the water in the bowl?

The Cycles of Matter

The matter in your body has been on Earth or in Earth's atmosphere since the planet formed billions of years ago!

Matter on Earth is limited, so the matter is used over and over again. Each kind of matter has a cycle. In such a cycle, matter moves between the organisms of an environment and the nonliving parts of that environment.

The Water Cycle

The movement of water between the oceans, atmosphere, land, and organisms is known as the *water cycle*. The parts of the water cycle are shown in **Figure 1.** The water cycle could not happen without energy from the sun. During **evaporation,** the sun's heat causes water to change from liquid to vapor. In the process of **condensation,** the water vapor cools and returns to a liquid state. The water that falls from the atmosphere to the land and oceans is **precipitation.** Rain, snow, sleet, and hail are forms of precipitation. Most precipitation falls into oceans. Precipitation that falls on land and flows into streams, rivers, and lakes is called *runoff*. Some precipitation is stored below the ground and is known as *groundwater*. Groundwater flows slowly back into the soil, streams, rivers, and oceans.

Benchmark Check Why is the sun an important part of the water cycle? **G.1.3.5**

evaporation the change of state from a liquid to a gas

condensation the change of state from a gas to a liquid

precipitation any form of water that falls to Earth's surface from the clouds

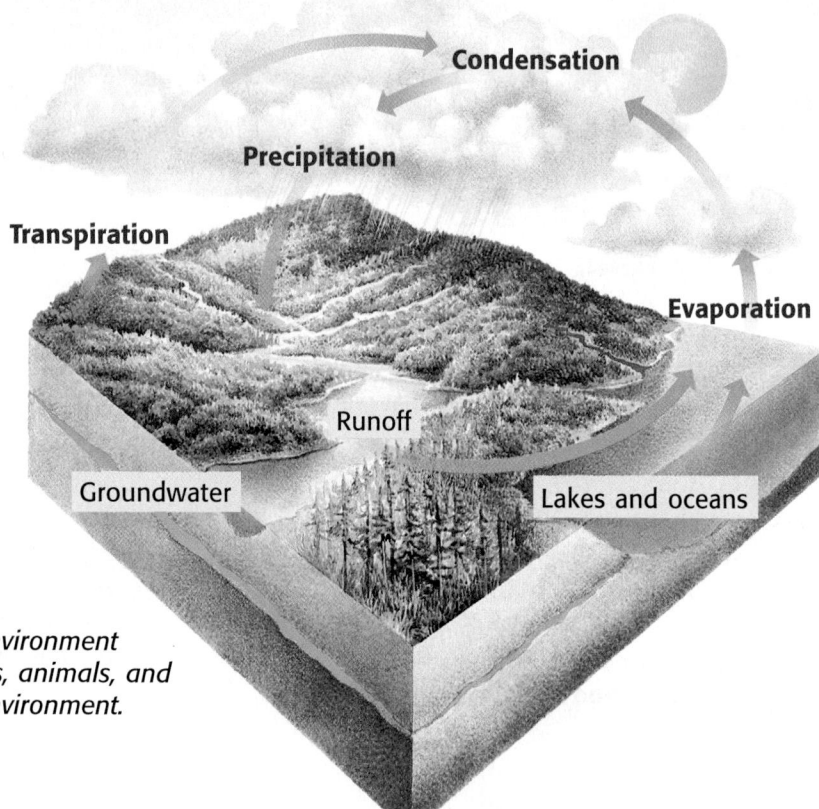

Figure 1 *Water in an environment moves through the plants, animals, and nonliving parts of that environment.*

Figure 2 *Mangrove trees (left) and animals, such as this blue heron (right), play a role in the water cycle.*

Water and Life

Without water, there would be no life on Earth. All organisms, from bacteria to the trees and blue heron shown in **Figure 2,** are composed mostly of water molecules. Water helps transport nutrients and wastes within an organism. Water also helps regulate body temperature. For example, when you sweat, water evaporates from your skin and cools your body. You must drink water to replace the water that you lose when you sweat.

Eventually, all of the water taken in by organisms is returned to the environment. For example, plants absorb liquid water from the ground through their roots. Plants then release a large amount of water vapor through the pores in their leaves. The process of releasing water vapor is called *transpiration*.

Benchmark Check How are organisms a part of the water cycle? **G.1.3.4 AA**

Global Water Use

You know that your body needs to take in water to survive. But humans use water in other ways. Humans use water for residential, agricultural, and industrial purposes. Activities such as drinking, washing, and cooking are residential uses of water. Water is used for agriculture mainly to water and irrigate crops. *Irrigation* is a method of watering plants with water from sources other than precipitation. Most of the water that humans use is used in agriculture. Industries use water to manufacture products, dispose of waste, and to generate power. The main source of water for all of these activities is groundwater. For example, 90% of Florida's drinking water comes from groundwater.

Benchmark Activity

Plants and the Water Cycle

1. Place a **small plant** in a **clear plastic cup.**
2. Seal the cup with **plastic wrap,** and place the cup in a sunny spot for at least two hours.
3. What appeared on the plastic wrap?
4. What part of the water cycle took place inside the sealed cup?
5. What can you infer about plants and their role in the water cycle?

G.1.3.4 AA

G.1.3.4 AA knows that the interactions of organisms with each other and with the nonliving parts of their environments result in the flow of energy and the cycling of matter throughout the system.

G.1.3.5 knows that life is maintained by a continuous input of energy from the sun and by the recycling of the atoms that make up the molecules of living organisms.

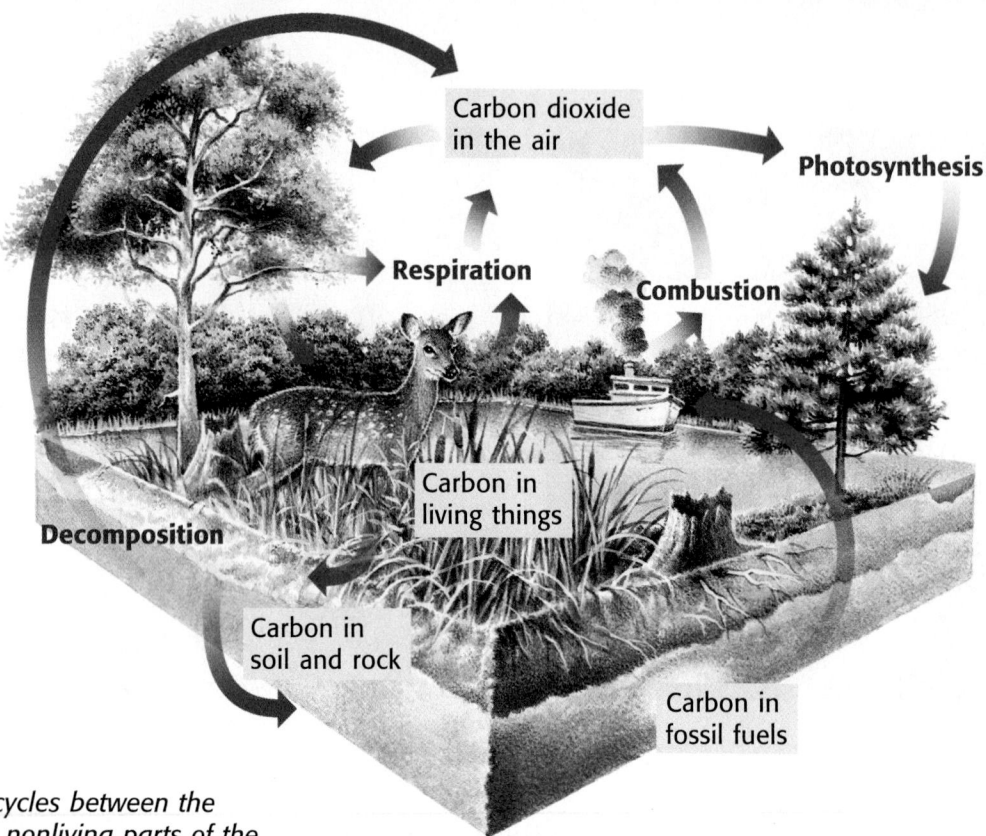

Figure 3 *Carbon cycles between the organisms and the nonliving parts of the environment.*

In the figure, labels read: Carbon dioxide in the air · Photosynthesis · Respiration · Combustion · Carbon in living things · Decomposition · Carbon in soil and rock · Carbon in fossil fuels

decomposition the breakdown of substances into simpler molecular substances

The Carbon Cycle

Besides water, the most common molecules in organisms are *organic molecules,* or molecules that contain carbon. The exchange of carbon between the organisms and the nonliving parts of the environment is known as the *carbon cycle,* shown in **Figure 3.**

Photosynthesis and Respiration

Photosynthesis is the basis of the carbon cycle. During photosynthesis, plants use carbon dioxide to make sugars. For most animals, the carbon that they need comes from plants, either directly or indirectly. So, how does carbon return to the environment? It returns when organic molecules break down to release energy. This process, called *respiration,* uses oxygen. Carbon dioxide and water are released as byproducts of respiration.

Decomposition and the Carbon Cycle

The breakdown of substances into simpler molecules is called **decomposition.** For example, when fungi and bacteria decompose organic matter, molecules of carbon dioxide and water are released into the soil. Carbon increases the fertility of soil and promotes plant growth. Over a very long period of time, these carbon-containing molecules can form deposits of fossil fuels, such as coal, oil, and natural gas.

Benchmark Check How can decomposers increase the fertility of soil? **D.1.3.4 AA**

Combustion and the Carbon Cycle

You may have witnessed another way that organic matter is broken down: by fire. **Combustion** is the process of burning a substance, such as wood or fossil fuels. Like decomposition, combustion of organic matter releases carbon dioxide into the atmosphere.

Humans and the Carbon Cycle

As you have learned, the burning of fossil fuels releases carbon dioxide into the atmosphere. Humans burn fossil fuels for transportation, as shown in **Figure 4.** Humans also burn fossil fuels for manufacturing products, for heating and cooling buildings, and for generating electricity. Evidence shows that the use of fossil fuels has increased the amount of carbon dioxide in the atmosphere. Carbon dioxide can cause the atmosphere to hold heat. A warming of the atmosphere could cause average global temperatures to rise. Some scientists think that this process, known as *global warming,* is happening.

Benchmark Check List one human activity that affects the carbon cycle. **G.2.3.4 AA, D.2.3.2**

Deforestation and the Carbon Cycle

Plants and trees take in carbon dioxide during the carbon cycle. However, because of *deforestation,* or the clearing of forest lands, less of the carbon dioxide in the atmosphere is absorbed. Thus, scientists think that deforestation may contribute to increasing the level of carbon dioxide in the atmosphere and to global warming, just as the burning of fossil fuels does.

combustion the burning of a substance

Combustion

1. Place a **candle** on a **jar lid,** and secure the candle with **modeling clay.** Have your teacher light the candle.

2. Hold the jar near the candle flame. Do not cover the flame with the jar. Describe the jar. Where did the substance on the jar come from?

3. Now, place the jar over the candle. What is deposited inside the jar? Where did this substance come from?

Figure 4 *Combining trips and carpooling can help reduce the amount of carbon dioxide that is released into the atmosphere.*

G.2.3.4 AA understands that humans are a part of an ecosystem and their activities may deliberately or inadvertently alter the equilibrium in ecosystems.

D.2.3.2 knows the positive and negative consequences of human action on the Earth's systems.

The Cycles of Matter   **339**

The Nitrogen Cycle

Like carbon, nitrogen is a substance that is important in life processes. Organisms need nitrogen to build proteins and to make DNA for new cells. The movement of nitrogen between the organisms and the nonliving parts of the environment is called the *nitrogen cycle*. This cycle is shown in **Figure 5.**

Converting Nitrogen Gas

About 78% of Earth's atmosphere is nitrogen gas, which most organisms cannot use directly. But bacteria in soil, lakes, and oceans can change this nitrogen gas into forms that plants can use. This process of change is called *nitrogen fixation*. After plants take in nitrogen by nitrogen fixation, other organisms get the nitrogen that they need by eating either plants or plant-eating organisms.

Decomposition and the Nitrogen Cycle

Decomposers break down remains of dead organisms. Decomposition releases into the soil a form of nitrogen that plants can use. This nitrogen makes soil more fertile. Certain soil bacteria convert nitrogen to a gas, which returns to the atmosphere.

D.1.3.4 AA knows the ways in which plants and animals reshape the landscape (e.g., bacteria, fungi, worms, rodents, and other organisms add organic matter to the soil, increasing soil fertility, encouraging plant growth, and strengthening resistance to erosion).

G.1.3.4 AA knows that the interactions of organisms with each other and with the nonliving parts of their environments result in the flow of energy and the cycling of matter throughout the system.

G.1.3.5 knows that life is maintained by a continuous input of energy from the sun and by the recycling of the atoms that make up the molecules of living organisms.

Figure 5 **The Nitrogen Cycle**

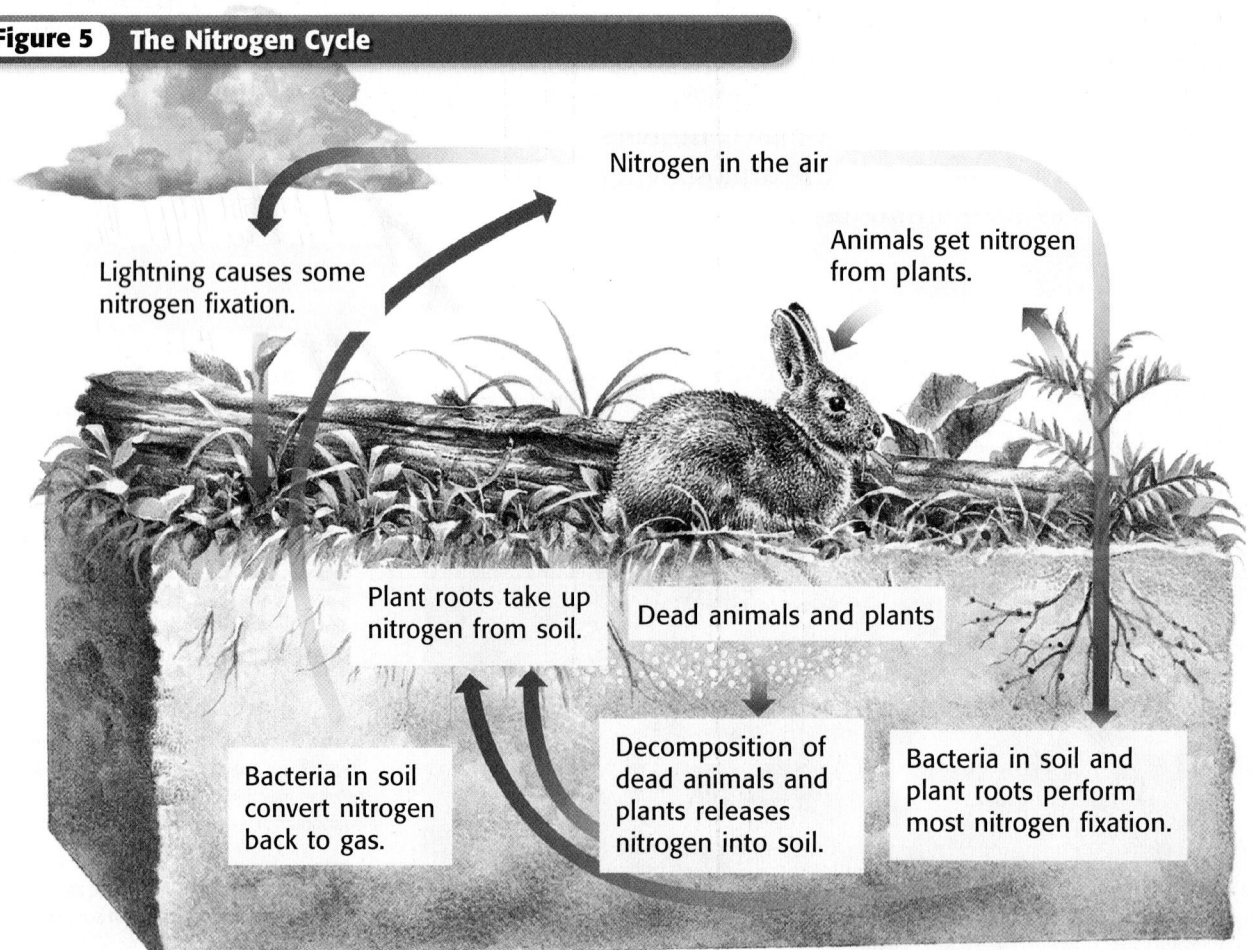

Nitrogen in the air

Lightning causes some nitrogen fixation.

Animals get nitrogen from plants.

Plant roots take up nitrogen from soil.

Dead animals and plants

Bacteria in soil convert nitrogen back to gas.

Decomposition of dead animals and plants releases nitrogen into soil.

Bacteria in soil and plant roots perform most nitrogen fixation.

Many Cycles

Many of the minerals that living cells need, such as calcium, phosphorus, and potassium, are cycled through the environment. When an organism dies, every substance in the organism's body is likely to be recycled or reused.

Each of the cycles is connected to the other cycles in many ways. For example, carbon cycles through the environment in the carbon cycle, and nitrogen cycles through the environment in the nitrogen cycle. But some forms of nitrogen and carbon are carried through the environment in water, which cycles between the organisms and the nonliving parts of the environment in the water cycle.

✓ **Reading Check** Give an example of a form of matter other than carbon, water, or nitrogen that is cycled on Earth.

SECTION Review

Summary

- Energy from the sun and the recycling of molecules maintains life on Earth. **G.1.3.5**

- Interactions between the organisms and the non-living parts of the environment result in the cycling of water, carbon, and nitrogen. **G.1.3.4 AA**

- All organisms need water. Humans use water for residential, agricultural, and industrial purposes.

- Organisms such as bacteria increase the fertility of soil by recycling matter. **D.1.3.4 AA**

- Humans affect the carbon cycle by burning fossil fuels, which adds carbon dioxide to the atmosphere. **G.2.3.4 AA , D.2.3.2**

Using Key Terms

1. Use *evaporation* and *condensation* in separate sentences.

2. Write an original definition for *decomposition*.

Understanding Key Ideas

3. Why is water essential to life on Earth?

4. What is the relationship between soil fertility and decomposers in the nitrogen cycle? **G.1.3.4 AA, D.1.3.4 AA**

5. Describe how molecules of carbon are cycled through the environment. Why is carbon important to organisms? **G.1.3.4 AA, G.1.3.5**

Critical Thinking

6. **Expressing Opinions** What do you think are effective ways to prevent the increase of carbon dioxide in the atmosphere?

7. **Predicting Consequences** Describe one negative way in which humans interact with the carbon cycle. How might increases in the amount of carbon dioxide in the atmosphere affect Earth? **G.2.3.4 AA, D.2.3.2**

FCAT Preparation

8. Deforestation is the clearing of forest lands. Humans clear forests to obtain rubber, grazing land, lumber for houses, and wood for paper. How can deforestation affect the carbon cycle? **G.2.3.4 AA**

9. Pond lilies grow in a pond ecosystem. What role do these organisms play in the pond ecosystem? **G.1.3.4 AA**

   A. They decompose dead organisms.

   B. They alter nitrogen through nitrogen fixation.

   C. They cause global warming.

   D. They provide carbon for other organisms and release water vapor into the air.

SCiLINKS®

NSTA
Developed and maintained by the
National Science Teachers Association

For a variety of links related to this chapter, go to www.scilinks.org

Topic: Cycles of Matter
SciLinks code: HSM0373

Ecological Succession

Imagine that you have a time machine that can take you back to the summer of 1988 in Yellowstone National Park. There, you would likely see fire all around you, because during that summer, fires raged throughout the park area.

By the end of that summer, large areas of the park were burned to the ground. When the fires were put out, a layer of gray ash blanketed the forest floor. Most of the trees were dead, although many of them were still standing.

Regrowth of a Forest

The following spring, the appearance of the "dead" forest began to change. **Figure 1** shows the changes after just one year. Some of the dead trees fell over, and small, green plants grew in large numbers. Within 10 years, scientists reported that many trees were growing and the forest community was coming back. A gradual development of a community over time, such as the regrowth of the burned areas of Yellowstone National Park, is called **succession.** Succession takes place in all communities, not just those affected by disturbances such as fire. Succession is important because it allows matter and nutrients to be recycled within a community.

Benchmark Check How is succession beneficial to a community? **G.1.3.4 AA**

READING WARM-UP

Objectives

- Explain how the process of succession results in the cycling of matter. **G.1.3.4 AA**
- Describe ways in which plants and animals reshape the landscape during succession. **D.1.3.4 AA**
- Contrast primary and secondary succession.
- Explain how mature communities develop.

Terms to Learn

succession
biodiversity **FCAT VOCAB**

READING STRATEGY

Reading Organizer As you read this section, make a table comparing primary succession and secondary succession.

succession the replacement of one type of community by another at a single location over a period of time

G.1.3.4 AA (partial) knows that the interactions of organisms with each other and with the nonliving parts of their environments result in the flow of energy and the cycling of matter throughout the system.

D.1.3.4 AA knows the ways in which plants and animals reshape the landscape (e.g., bacteria, fungi, worms, rodents, and other organisms add organic matter to the soil, increasing soil fertility, encouraging plant growth, and strengthening resistance to erosion).

Figure 1 *Huge areas of Yellowstone National Park were burned in 1988 (left). By the spring of 1989, regrowth was evident in the burned parts of the park (right).*

Primary Succession

Sometimes, a small community starts to grow in an area where organisms had not previously lived. There is no soil in such an area. And usually, there is nothing but bare rock. Over a very long time, a series of organisms live and die on the rock. As the organisms live and die, the rock is slowly transformed into soil. This process is called *primary succession,* as shown in **Figure 2.** The first organisms to live in an area are called *pioneer species.*

INTERNET ACTIVITY

Land Recovery Investigate the process of succession around Mount St. Helens. Go to **go.hrw.com,** and type in the keyword **HL5CYCW.**

Figure 2 An Example of Primary Succession

❶ A slowly retreating glacier exposes bare rock on which there are no living organisms, and primary succession begins.

❷ Most primary succession begins with lichens. Acids from the lichens begin breaking the rocks into small particles. These particles mix with the remains of dead lichens to start forming soil. Lichens are an example of a pioneer species.

❸ Years later, there is enough soil for mosses to grow. Over time, mosses replace lichens. Next, other organisms, such as insects, move in. As organisms die, their remains decompose and add nutrients to the soil.

❹ Over time, the soil deepens, and the mosses are replaced by ferns. The ferns may slowly be replaced by grasses and wildflowers. If there is enough soil, shrubs and small trees may grow.

❺ After hundreds or even thousands of years, plants and animals have changed the soil so much that it may be deep and stable enough to support a forest.

Secondary Succession

Sometimes, an existing community is destroyed by a disturbance that is a natural disaster, such as a fire or a flood. Other times, a community is affected by a type of disturbance that is caused by human activity. For example, a farmer might stop growing crops in an area that had been cleared. After either type of disturbance, if soil is left intact, the original community may regrow in a series of stages called *secondary succession*. **Figure 3** shows an example of secondary succession.

✓ **Reading Check** How does secondary succession differ from primary succession?

Figure 3 An Example of Secondary Succession

1 The first year after a farmer stops growing crops or the first year after some other major disturbance, weeds start to grow. In farming areas, crab grass is the weed that often grows first.

2 By the second year, new weeds appear. Their seeds may have been blown into the field by the wind or may have been carried into the field by insects. Horseweed is common during the second year.

3 In 5 to 15 years, small conifer trees may start growing among the weeds. The trees continue to grow, and after about 100 years, a forest may form.

4 As older conifers die, they may be replaced by hardwoods, such as oak or maple trees, if the climate can support the hardwoods.

Mature Communities and Biodiversity

In the early stages of succession, only a few species grow in an area. These species grow quickly and make many seeds that scatter easily. But all species are vulnerable to disease, disturbances, and competition. As a community matures, it may be dominated by well-adapted, slow-growing *climax species.*

As succession proceeds, more species may become established. The variety of species that are present in an area is referred to as **biodiversity.** A forest that has a high degree of biodiversity is less likely to be destroyed by an invasion of insects. Most plant-damaging insects prefer to attack only one species of plants. The presence of a variety of plants will lessen the impact and spread of invading insects. Not all mature communities are forests. A mature community is simply a community in which organisms are well adapted to living together in the community over time. For example, the plants of the Sonoran Desert, shown in **Figure 4,** are well adapted to the desert's conditions.

Benchmark Check How can an invasion of insects change the landscape of a community? **D.1.3.4 AA**

Figure 4 *This area of the Sonoran Desert in Arizona is a mature community.*

biodiversity the number and variety of organisms in a given area during a specific period of time
FCAT VOCAB

SECTION Review

Summary

● Succession results in the cycling of matter and nutrients. **G.1.3.4 AA**

● Organisms can reshape the landscape during succession. **D.1.3.4 AA**

● Primary succession occurs in an area where no soil is present. Secondary succession occurs in an area where soil is present.

● Mature communities develop slowly as organisms that are well adapted survive.

Using Key Terms

1. Write an original definition for *succession.*

Understanding Key Ideas

2. Describe how lichens can change the landscape of a community. **D.1.3.4 AA**

3. What is a mature community?

4. Contrast primary and secondary succession.

Critical Thinking

5. **Analyzing Ideas** Explain why soil formation is always the first stage of primary succession. Does soil formation ever stop? Explain your answer.

6. **Making Inferences** How are matter and nutrients cycled during succession? How can succession make a community's soil more fertile? **G.1.3.4 AA**

FCAT Preparation

7. Wind blew horseweed seeds into an abandoned cropland. How will the seeds change the cropland? **D.1.3.4 AA**

   A. No change will occur.

   B. Horseweeds will grow and will replace other weeds.

   C. Insects will destroy the cropland.

   D. Conifers will begin to grow.

SCI LINKS.

NSTA

Developed and maintained by the National Science Teachers Association

For a variety of links related to this chapter, go to www.scilinks.org

Topic: Succession
SciLinks code: HSM1475

Skills Practice Lab

Nitrogen Needs

The nitrogen cycle is one of several cycles that are vital to living organisms. Without nitrogen, organisms cannot make amino acids, the building blocks of proteins. Animals obtain nitrogen by eating nitrogen-containing plants and by eating animals that eat those plants. When animals die, nitrogen in their remains is returned to the soil by decomposers. Nitrogen enters soil in the form of *ammonia,* a nitrogen-containing chemical.

In this activity, you will set up the nitrogen cycle inside a closed system to investigate how decomposers return nitrogen to the soil.

Procedure

1 Fit a piece of filter paper into a funnel. Place the funnel inside a 50 mL beaker, and pour 5 g of soil into the funnel. Add 25 mL of distilled water to the soil.

2 Test the filtered water with pH paper, and record your observations.

3 Place enough soil in a jar to cover the bottom of the jar with about 5 cm of soil. Add 10 mL of distilled water to the soil.

4 Place the dead insects in the jar. Use the lid to seal the jar.

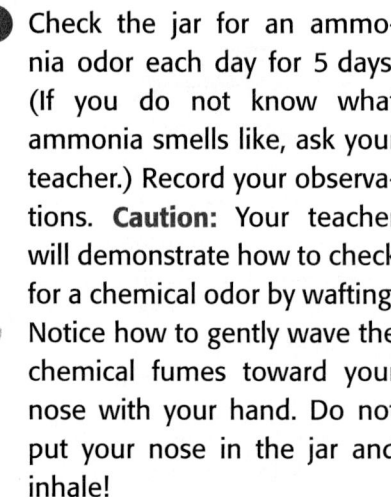

5 Check the jar for an ammonia odor each day for 5 days. (If you do not know what ammonia smells like, ask your teacher.) Record your observations. **Caution:** Your teacher will demonstrate how to check for a chemical odor by wafting. Notice how to gently wave the chemical fumes toward your nose with your hand. Do not put your nose in the jar and inhale!

OBJECTIVES

Investigate the nitrogen cycle inside a closed system. G.1.3.4 AA

Discover how decomposers return nitrogen to the soil.
D.1.3.4 AA

MATERIALS

- balance or scale
- beaker, 50 mL
- funnel
- gloves, protective
- graduated cylinder, 25 mL
- insects from home or schoolyard, large, dead (5)
- jar with lid, 1 pt (or 500 mL)
- paper, filter (2 pieces)
- pH paper
- soil, potting, commercially prepared without fertilizer
- water, distilled (60 mL)

SAFETY

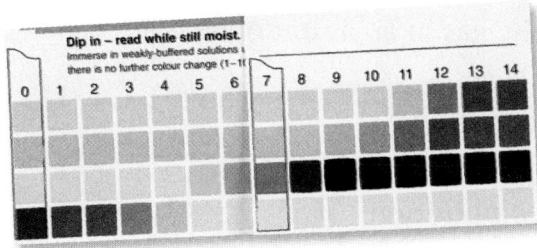

Dip in – read while still moist.
immerse in weakly-buffered solutions
there is no further colour change (1–1)

0 1 2 3 4 5 6 | 7 8 9 10 11 12 13 14

6 On the fifth day, place a second piece of filter paper into the funnel, and place the funnel inside a 50 mL beaker. Remove about 5 g of soil from the jar, and place it in the funnel. Add 25 mL of distilled water to the soil.

7 Once again, use pH paper to test the pH of the filtered water, and record your observations.

Analyze the Results

1 **Examining Data** What was the pH of the water in the beaker in the first trial? A pH of 7 indicates that the water is neutral. A pH below 7 indicates that the water is acidic, and a pH above 7 indicates that the water is basic. Was the water in the beaker neutral, acidic, or basic?

2 **Analyzing Data** What was the pH of the water in the beaker in the second trial? Explain the difference, if any, between the results of the first trial and the results of the second trial.

Draw Conclusions

3 **Drawing Conclusions** Based on your pH test results, which type of substance is ammonia: an acidic substance or a basic substance?

4 **Evaluating Results** On which days in your investigation were you able to detect an ammonia odor? Explain what caused the odor.

5 **Applying Conclusions** Describe the importance of decomposers in the nitrogen cycle.

Applying Your Data

Test the importance of nitrogen to plants. Fill two 12 cm flowerpots with commercially prepared potting soil and water. Be sure to use soil that does not contain fertilizer. Obtain a dozen tomato or radish seeds. Plant six seeds in each pot. Water your seeds so that the soil is constantly damp but not soaked. Keep your pots in a sunny window. Use a nitrogen-rich liquid plant fertilizer to fertilize one of the pots once a week. Dilute or mix the fertilizer with water according to the directions on the container. Water the other pot once a week with plain tap water.

1. After the seedlings appear, use a metric ruler to measure the growth of the plants in both pots. Measure the plants once a week, and record your results.

2. You may plant other seeds of your choice, but do not use legume (bean) seeds. Do research to find out why!

D.1.3.4 AA knows the ways in which plants and animals reshape the landscape (e.g., bacteria, fungi, worms, rodents, and other organisms add organic matter to the soil, increasing soil fertility, encouraging plant growth, and strengthening resistance to erosion).

G.1.3.4 AA (partial) knows that the interactions of organisms with each other and with the nonliving parts of their environments result in the flow of energy and the cycling of matter throughout the system.

Chapter Review

Complete each of the following sentences by choosing the correct term from the word bank.

evaporation	condensation
precipitation	decomposition
combustion	succession

1 The breakdown of dead materials into carbon dioxide and water is called ___.

2 The gradual development of a community over time is called ___.

3 During ___, heat causes water to change from liquid to vapor.

4 ___ is the process of burning a substance.

5 Water that falls from the atmosphere to the land and oceans is ___.

6 In the process of ___, water vapor cools and returns to a liquid state.

UNDERSTANDING KEY IDEAS

Multiple Choice

7 Clouds form in the atmosphere through the process of
- **a.** precipitation.
- **c.** condensation.
- **b.** respiration.
- **d.** decomposition.

8 Which of the following statements about groundwater is true?
- **a.** It stays underground for a few days.
- **b.** It is stored deep underground.
- **c.** It is salty like ocean water.
- **d.** It never reenters the water cycle.

9 Burning gas in an automobile is a type of
- **a.** combustion.
- **b.** respiration.
- **c.** decomposition.
- **d.** photosynthesis.

10 Nitrogen in the form of a gas can be used directly by some kinds of
- **a.** plants.
- **c.** bacteria.
- **b.** animals.
- **d.** fungi.

11 Bacteria play an important role in Earth's cycles. In which of the following processes are bacteria most important? **G.1.3.4 AA** *FCAT*
- **a.** combustion
- **c.** nitrogen fixation
- **b.** condensation
- **d.** evaporation

12 Pioneer species colonize bare rock and break the rock down to begin the formation of soil. Which of the following organisms are most likely to be a pioneer species? **D.1.3.4 AA** *FCAT*
- **a.** ferns
- **c.** mosses
- **b.** pine trees
- **d.** lichens

13 Which of the following is an example of primary succession?
- **a.** the recovery of Yellowstone National Park following the fires of 1988
- **b.** the appearance of lichens and mosses in an area where a glacier has recently melted away
- **c.** the growth of weeds in a field after a farmer stops using the field
- **d.** the growth of weeds in an empty lot that is no longer being mowed

Short Answer

⓮ How is the sun a part of the water, carbon, and nitrogen cycles? G.1.3.5

⓯ How does succession result in the cycling of matter and nutrients?

⓰ The carbon cycle could not occur without plants and animals. What role do plants and animals have in the carbon cycle? G.1.3.4 AA FCAT

⓱ What is the relationship between fossil fuels and humans? G.2.3.4 AA, D.2.3.2

⓲ Compare the two forms of succession.

CRITICAL THINKING

Extended Response

⓳ **Analyzing Ideas** Based on what you have learned, support the following statement: "The molecules in your body have been on Earth since the planet formed billions of years ago." G.1.3.5

⓴ **Analyzing Processes** Water exists in different forms and is found in many places on Earth. Describe three places where water might be found on Earth. For each item, state how the item is part of the water cycle. G.1.3.4 AA FCAT

㉑ **Forming Hypotheses** Predict what would happen if the water on Earth suddenly stopped evaporating.

㉒ **Forming Hypotheses** Why are bacteria important? Predict what would happen if all of the bacteria on Earth suddenly disappeared. D.1.3.4 AA

Concept Mapping

㉓ Use the following terms to create a concept map: *abandoned farmland, lichens, bare rock, soil formation, horseweed, succession, forest fire, primary succession, secondary succession,* and *pioneer species.*

INTERPRETING GRAPHICS

The graph below shows how water is used each day by an average household in the United States. Use the graph to answer the questions that follow.

Average Household Daily Water Use

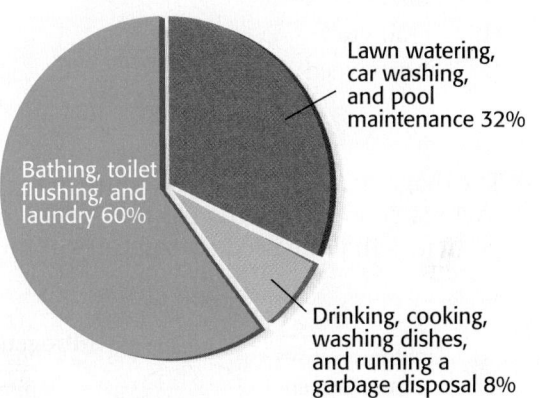

Lawn watering, car washing, and pool maintenance 32%

Bathing, toilet flushing, and laundry 60%

Drinking, cooking, washing dishes, and running a garbage disposal 8%

㉔ According to the graph, which of the following activities uses the greatest amount of water?

a. bathing

b. toilet flushing

c. washing laundry

d. There is not enough information to determine the answer.

㉕ An average family used 380 L of water per day until they stopped washing their car, stopped watering their lawn, and stopped using their pool. How much water per day do they use now?

Standardized Test Preparation

For the following questions, write your answers on a separate sheet of paper.

1 Arturo and his father are driving to school one morning in a very heavy fog. As they drive through the fog, Arturo's father uses the windshield wipers to clear water off of the windshield. Which part of the water cycle is responsible for the water on the windshield?

A. condensation

B. evaporation

C. respiration

D. transpiration

2 Adriana's father has not planted vegetables in their vegetable garden for several years. Recently, Adriana went to look at the garden and found that it was full of small pine trees. If Adriana lets the plot of land grow naturally, which of the following plants will begin to take root and grow next?

F. oaks

G. mosses

H. crab grass

I. horseweed

3 The diagram below shows the nitrogen cycle. During the nitrogen cycle, nitrogen-fixing bacteria change nitrogen gas into a form of nitrogen that can be used by plants. Some pesticides that are used on soil can kill these helpful bacteria.

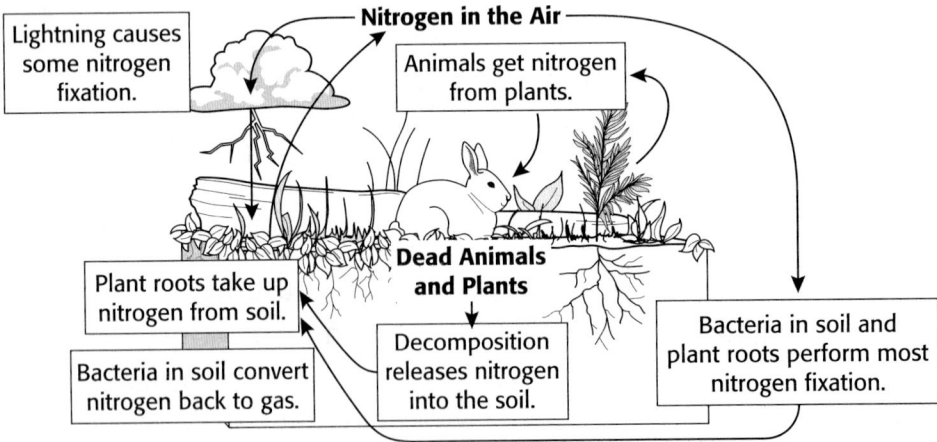

How would the nitrogen cycle be impacted if nitrogen-fixing bacteria were destroyed?

4 The diagram below shows the carbon cycle. During the carbon cycle, some carbon is released into the atmosphere and some carbon is released into the soil.

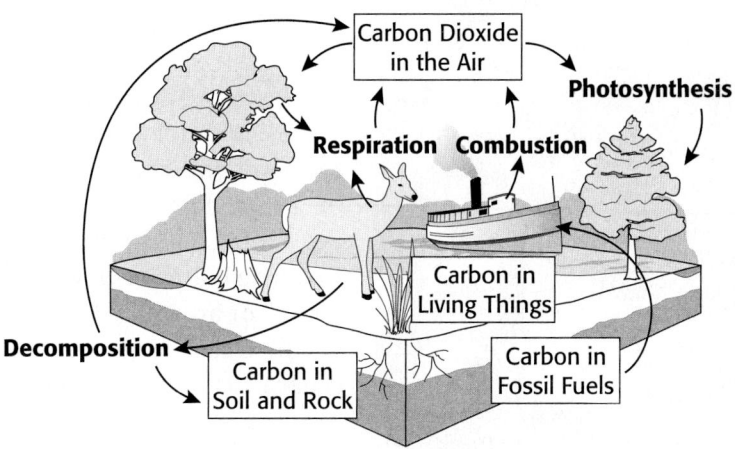

Which of the following processes is primarily involved in releasing carbon into the soil?

A. combustion
B. decomposition
C. photosynthesis
D. respiration

5 The movement of water between the oceans, atmosphere, land, and organisms is known as the water cycle. Without water, there would be no life on Earth. Describe three ways in which water is important to life on Earth.

6 Shauna and her friends are walking in a shady area. They notice a large rock that is covered with lichens. Lichens can live without soil. Which of the following processes explains how the lichens are able to grow on a rock?

F. global warming
G. nitrogen fixation
H. primary succession
I. secondary succession

FCAT Preparation

Science in Action

Science, Technology, and Society

Desalination

Scientists estimate that by the year 2025, almost a billion people will face water shortages. Only about 3% of the water on Earth is *fresh water*—the kind of water that we use for drinking and farming. And the human population is using and polluting Earth's fresh water more quickly than the water can be recycled. Most of the other 97% of Earth's water is in oceans. Ocean water is much too salty to use for drinking or farming.

Until recently, *desalination,* the process of filtering salt out of water, was very expensive and time-consuming. But new technologies are making desalination an affordable option for some areas.

Math ACTIVITY

You need to drink about 2 quarts of water each day. Imagine that you have a simple device that evaporates sea water and collects fresh, drinkable water at a rate of 6 mL/min. How long will the device take to collect enough drinking water for one day?

Scientific Debate

Florida's Mysterious Black Blob

Some people described it as a thick, slimy blob with spider webs floating in it. Others described it as "snotty water" or "sewer water." But what caused this black blob to form off the coast of Florida in the winter of 2001? People became concerned when the blob grew to the size of 1,000 km². At first, the black blob was described as a "dead zone," or an area where low levels of oxygen occur. Dead zones cause large numbers of organisms to die. But such numerous deaths did not happen. Also, scientists found that the blob did not have low oxygen levels. Then, scientists speculated that the blob might have been caused by chemical and sediment pollution. The mysterious blob eventually disappeared, but the blob's cause is still debated by scientists.

Language Arts ACTIVITY

WRITING SKILL Using the Internet or library resources, research the mysterious black blob that appeared near Florida. Write a short report describing what scientists thought about the blob and its possible causes.

The cause of the mysterious black blob off the coast of Florida is still under investigation.

Michael Fan

Wastewater Manager If you are concerned about clean water and like to work both in a laboratory and outdoors, you might like a career in wastewater management. The water cycle helps keep water in nature pure enough for most organisms to use. But *wastewater*—water that is produced when humans use water in houses, factories, and farms—is rarely pure enough for organisms to use. Wastewater is often produced faster than natural processes can clean it. To make the water safe for human use again, people use processes that imitate—and speed up—ways that water gets cleaned in nature.

Michael Fan is superintendent of wastewater operations at the Wastewater Treatment Plant of the University of California, Davis. This plant has one of the most advanced wastewater management systems in the country. Fan finds his job exciting. The plant operates 24 hours a day, and there are many tasks to manage. Running the plant requires skills in chemistry, physics, microbiology, and engineering. Many organisms in the Davis area depend on Fan to make sure that the water used by the university is safely returned to nature.

Social Studies ACTIVITY

Research the ways that the ancient Romans managed their wastewater. Make a poster that illustrates some of their methods and technologies.

go.hrw.com

To learn more about these Science in Action topics, visit **go.hrw.com** and type in the keyword **HT6FCYFF.**

Current Science

Check out Current Science® articles related to this chapter by visiting **go.hrw.com.** Just type in the keyword **HL5CS19.**

14

The Earth's Ecosystems

The Big Idea Earth's ecosystems are characterized by their living and nonliving parts.

About the

Why are these birds waiting in line? These willet birds aren't actually waiting, they're wading! Willet birds migrate south during the winter and can be seen probing for small crustaceans, mollusks, and fish in the waters of Florida's coastal ecosystems.

PRE-READING ACTIVITY

FOLDNOTES **Three-Panel Flip Chart**
Before you read the chapter, create the FoldNote entitled "Three-Panel Flip Chart" described in the **Study Skills** section of the Appendix. Label the flaps of the three-panel flip chart with "Land biomes," "Marine ecosystems," and "Freshwater ecosystems." As you read the chapter, write information you learn about each category under the appropriate flap.

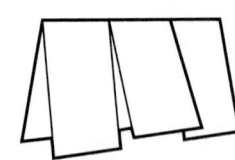

START-UP ACTIVITY

A Mini-Ecosystem

In this activity, you will build and observe a miniature ecosystem. G.2.3.2 CS

Procedure

1. Place a layer of **gravel** at the bottom of a **container,** such as a **large, wide-mouthed jar** or a **2 L soda bottle** with the top cut off. Then, add a layer of **soil.**

2. Add a variety of **plants** that need similar growing conditions. Choose small plants that will not grow too quickly.

3. Spray **water** inside the container to moisten the soil.

4. Loosely cover the container with a **lid** or **plastic wrap.** Place the container in indirect light.

5. Describe the appearance of your ecosystem.

6. Let your mini-ecosystem grow for 6 weeks. Add more water when the soil is dry.

7. Observe your mini-ecosystem every week. Record your observations.

Analysis

1. List the nonliving factors that make up the ecosystem that you built.

2. List the living factors that make up your ecosystem.

3. How is your mini-ecosystem similar to a real ecosystem? How is it different?

Land Biomes

What do you think of when you think of polar bears? You probably imagine them in a snow-covered setting. Why don't polar bears live in the desert?

Different ecosystems are home to different kinds of organisms. Polar bears don't live in the desert because they are adapted to cold environments.

Earth's Land Biomes

The ecosystem in which a polar bear lives is different from a desert ecosystem because of its abiotic (AY bie AHT ik) factors and biotic (bie AHT ik) factors. *Abiotic factors* are the nonliving parts of the environment, such as soil, water, and climate. Climate is the average weather conditions for an area over a long period of time. *Biotic factors* are the living parts of an environment, such as plants and animals. Areas that have similar abiotic factors usually have similar biotic factors. A **biome** (BIE OHM) is a large area characterized by its climate and the organisms that live in the area. Biomes can be used to classify living things because similar organisms live in a particular biome regardless of where the biome is located. For example, organisms that are adapted to extreme temperatures and little water live in deserts found throughout the world.

A biome is made up of many ecosystems. For example, a tropical rain forest biome contains treetop ecosystems and forest-floor ecosystems. **Figure 1** shows the major land biomes.

Benchmark Check How can biomes be used to classify living things? **G.1.3.3 CS**

biome a large region characterized by a specific type of climate and certain types of plant and animal communities

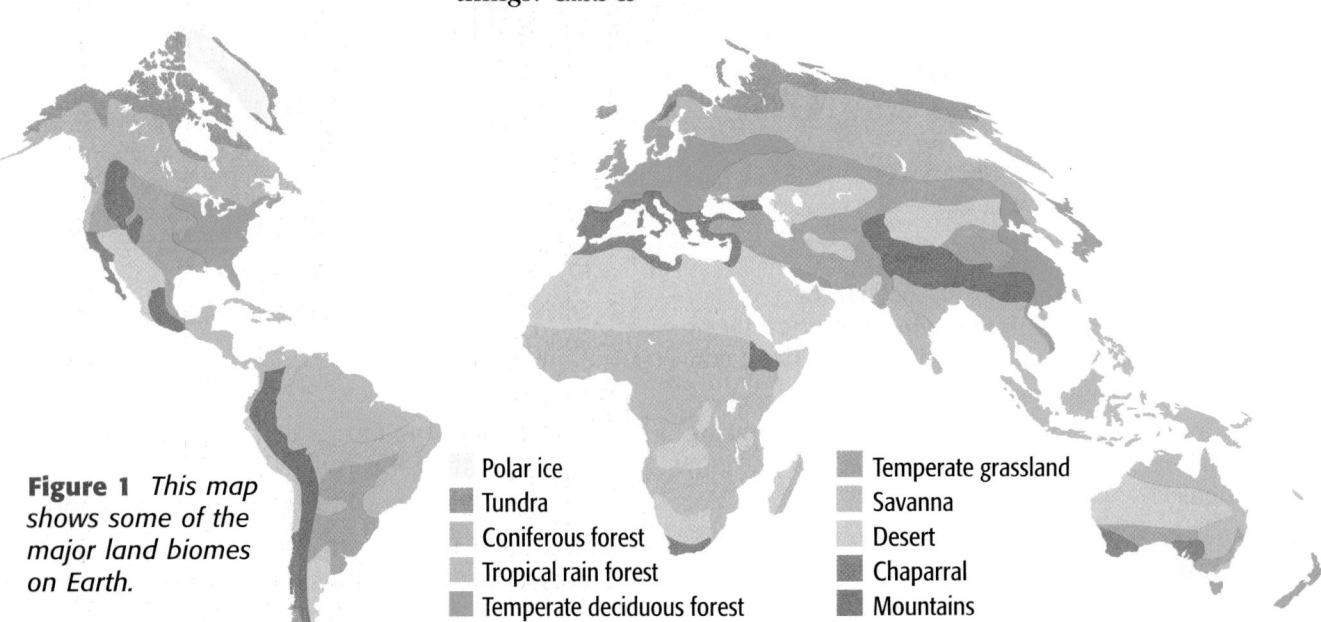

Figure 1 *This map shows some of the major land biomes on Earth.*

- Polar ice
- Tundra
- Coniferous forest
- Tropical rain forest
- Temperate deciduous forest
- Temperate grassland
- Savanna
- Desert
- Chaparral
- Mountains

In forests, plant growth happens in layers. The leafy tops of the trees reach high above the forest floor, where the leaves can get sunlight.

Woody shrubs catch the light that filters through the trees.

Ferns and mosses are scattered across the forest floor. Flowering plants often bloom in early spring, before the trees grow new leaves.

Temperate Deciduous Forest

- **Average Yearly Rainfall** 75 to 125 cm (29.5 to 49 in.)
- **Average Temperatures** Summer: 28°C (82°F) Winter: 6°C (43°F)

Figure 2 *In a temperate deciduous forest, mammals, birds, and reptiles thrive on the many leaves, seeds, nuts, and insects.*

Forests

Forest biomes are often found in areas that have mild temperatures and plenty of rain. The kind of forest biome that develops depends on an area's temperatures and rainfall. Three forest biomes are temperate deciduous (dee SIJ oo uhs) forests, coniferous (koh NIF uhr uhs) forests, and tropical rain forests.

Temperate Deciduous Forests

Have you seen leaves change colors in the fall? Have you seen trees lose all of their leaves? If so, you have seen trees that are deciduous. The word *deciduous* comes from a Latin word that means "to fall off." Deciduous trees shed their leaves to save water during the winter or during the dry season. As **Figure 2** shows, a variety of animals, such as bears, snakes, and woodpeckers, live in temperate deciduous forests.

Benchmark Check How does the availability of water, an abiotic factor, affect deciduous trees during the winter? G.2.3.2 CS

G.1.3.3 CS understands that the classification of living things is based on a given set of criteria and is a tool for understanding biodiversity and interrelationships.

G.2.3.2 CS (partial) knows that all biotic and abiotic factors are interrelated and that if one factor is changed or removed, it impacts the availability of other resources within the system.

Coniferous Forest

- **Average Yearly Rainfall**
  35 to 75 cm (14 to 29.5 in.)
- **Average Temperatures**
  Summer: 14°C (57°F)
  Winter: –10°C (14°F)

These conifer leaves are adapted to conserve water.

A coniferous forest is home to many insects and to birds that eat those insects.

Herbivores that live in the coniferous forest include deer, moose, porcupines, and squirrels.

Figure 3 *Many animals that live in a coniferous forest survive the harsh winters by hibernating or migrating to a warmer climate for the winter.*

Earth Biome Brochure
Create a brochure to help plants, animals, and people find the best place to live. Go to **go.hrw.com,** and type in the keyword **HL5ECOW.**

Coniferous Forests

Most of the trees in a coniferous forest are called *conifers*. Conifers produce seeds in cones. Conifers also have special leaves that are shaped like needles. The leaves have a thick, waxy coating. This waxy coating has three functions. First, it helps keep conifer leaves from drying out. Second, the waxy coating protects needles from being damaged by cold winter temperatures. Finally, the waxy coating allows most conifers to keep many of their leaves year-round. So, most conifers do not change very much from summer to winter. Trees that stay green all year and do not lose all of their leaves at one time are known as *evergreen trees*.

Figure 3 shows a coniferous forest and some of the animals that live there. Squirrels and insects live in coniferous forests. Birds, such as finches, chickadees, and jays, are common in these forests. Herbivores, such as porcupines, elk, and moose, also live in coniferous forests. The ground beneath large conifers is often covered by a thick layer of needles. Also, very little light reaches the ground. So, few large plants can grow beneath these trees.

✓ Reading Check What is another name for most conifers? What are some animals that live in coniferous forests?

Tropical Rain Forests

Tropical rain forests have more biological diversity than other places on Earth do. This means that rain forests have more kinds of plants and animals than any other land biome does. For example, more than 100 kinds of trees may grow in an area about one-fourth the size of a football field. Many animals live on the ground. But most animals live in the *canopy,* or the treetops. Many different animals live in the canopy. For example, nearly 1,400 species of birds live in the rain-forest canopy. **Figure 4** shows some of the diversity of the tropical rain forest.

Because of its diversity, the rain forest may seem to have nutrient-rich soil. But most of the nutrients in the tropical rain forest are found in the plants. The soil is actually very thin and poor in nutrients. Because the soil is so thin, many trees grow above-ground roots for extra support.

Figure 4 *Tropical rain forests have a greater variety of organisms than any other biome does.*

Trees form a continuous green roof, or canopy, that may extend 60 m above the forest floor.

Woody vines climb the tree trunks to reach sunlight.

Little light reaches the ground. Low-growing plants in the rain forest don't need a lot of light.

Tropical Rain Forest

- **Average Yearly Rainfall** up to 400 cm (157.5 in.)
- **Average Temperatures** Daytime: 34°C (93°F) Nighttime: 20°C (68°F)

Grasslands

Grasslands have many names, such as *steppes, prairies,* and *pampas.* Grasslands are found on every continent but Antarctica. Often, they are flat or have gently rolling hills.

Temperate Grasslands

Temperate grassland plants include grasses and other flowering plants. Temperate grasslands have few trees. Fires, drought, and grazing prevent the growth of trees and shrubs. Temperate grasslands support small seed-eating animals, such as prairie dogs and mice. Large grass eaters, such as the North American bison shown in **Figure 5,** also live in temperate grasslands.

Savannas

A grassland that has scattered clumps of trees and seasonal rains is called a **savanna.** Savannas are found in parts of Africa, India, and South America. During the dry season, savanna grasses dry out and turn yellow. But their deep roots survive for many months without water. The African savanna is home to many large herbivores, such as elephants, giraffes, zebras, and wildebeests. Some of these animals are shown in **Figure 6.**

✓ Reading Check What happens to grasses on a savanna during the dry season?

Temperate Grassland

- Average Yearly Rainfall
  25 to 75 cm (10 to 29.5 in.)
- Average Temperatures
  Summer: 30°C (86°F)
  Winter: 0°C (32°F)

Figure 5 *Bison once roamed North American temperate grasslands in great herds.*

savanna a grassland that often has scattered trees and that is found in tropical and subtropical areas where seasonal rains, fires, and drought happen

CONNECTION TO Environmental Science

WRITING SKILL **Mountains and Climate**

Mountains can affect the climate of the land around them. Research the ecosystems around a mountain range. In your **science journal,** write a report describing how the mountains affect the climate of the surrounding land.

Savanna

- Average Yearly Rainfall
  150 cm (59 in.)
- Average Temperatures
  Dry season: 34°C (93°F)
  Wet season: 16°C (61°F)

Figure 6 *In the African savanna, lions and leopards hunt zebras and wildebeests.*

Cactuses store water in their stems and roots.

Some flowering plants bloom, bear seeds, and die within a few weeks after a heavy rain.

Deep-rooted plants can reach groundwater as deep as 30 m.

Huge ears help jack rabbits get rid of body heat.

Kangaroo rats never need to drink. They recycle water from the foods that they eat.

Desert
- **Average Yearly Rainfall** less than 25 cm (10 in.)
- **Average Temperatures** Summer: 38°C (100°F) Winter: 7°C (45°F)

Figure 7 *The residents of the desert biome have special adaptations to survive in a dry climate.*

Deserts

Biomes that are very dry and often very hot are called **deserts.** Many kinds of plants and animals are found only in deserts. These organisms have special adaptations to live in a hot, dry climate. For example, plants grow far apart so that the plants won't have to compete with each other for water. Some plants have shallow, widespread roots that grow just under the surface. These roots let plants take up water during a storm. Other desert plants, such as cactuses, have fleshy stems and leaves. These fleshy structures store water. The leaves of desert plants also have a waxy coating that helps prevent water loss.

Animals also have adaptations for living in the desert. Most desert animals are active only at night, when temperatures are cooler. Some animals, such as the spadefoot toad, bury themselves in the ground and are dormant during the dry season. Doing so helps these animals escape the heat of summer. Animals such as desert tortoises eat flowers or leaves and store the water under their shells. **Figure 7** shows how some desert plants and animals live in the heat with little water.

✔ Reading Check What are some adaptations of desert plants?

desert an area that has little or no plant life, long periods without rain, and extreme temperatures; usually found in hot climates

Tundra

- Average Yearly Rainfall
  30 to 50 cm (12 to 20 in.)
- Average Temperatures
  Summer: 12°C (54°F)
  Winter: –26°C (–15°F)

Figure 8 *During winters in the tundra, caribou migrate to grazing grounds, where the supply of food is more plentiful.*

tundra a treeless plain found in the Arctic, in the Antarctic, or on the tops of mountains that is characterized by very low winter temperatures and short, cool summers

SCHOOL to HOME

WRITING SKILL **Local Ecosystems**

With a family member, explore the ecosystems around your home. What kinds of plants and animals live in your area? In your **science journal,** write a short essay describing the plants and animals in the ecosystems near your home.

Tundra

Imagine a place on Earth where it is so cold that trees do not grow. A biome that has very cold temperatures and little rainfall is called a **tundra.** Two types of tundra are polar tundra and alpine tundra.

Polar Tundra

Polar tundra is found near the North and South Poles. In polar tundra, the layer of soil beneath the surface soil stays frozen year-round. This layer is called *permafrost.* During the short, cool summers, only the surface soil thaws. The layer of thawed soil is too shallow for deep-rooted plants to live. So, shallow-rooted plants, such as grasses and small shrubs, are common. Mosses and lichens (LIE kuhnz) grow beneath these plants. The thawed soil above the permafrost becomes muddy. Insects, such as mosquitoes, lay eggs in the mud. Birds feed on these insects. Other tundra animals include musk oxen, wolves, and caribou, such as the one shown in **Figure 8.**

Alpine Tundra

Alpine tundra is similar to arctic tundra. Alpine tundra also has permafrost. But alpine tundra is found at the top of tall mountains. Above an elevation called the *tree line,* trees cannot grow on a mountain. Alpine tundra is found above the tree line. Alpine tundra gets plenty of sunlight and precipitation.

✓ **Reading Check** What is alpine tundra?

Summary

- A biome is characterized by abiotic factors and biotic factors. **G.2.3.2 CS**
- Biomes can be used to classify living things. **G.1.3.3 CS**
- Three forest biomes are temperate deciduous forests, coniferous forests, and tropical rain forests.
- Grasslands are areas where grasses are the main plants. Two kinds of grasslands are temperate grasslands and savannas.

- Deserts are very dry and often very hot. Desert plants and animals competing for the limited water supply have special adaptations for survival.
- Tundras are cold areas that have very little rainfall. Permafrost, the layer of frozen soil below the surface of arctic tundra, determines the kinds of plants and animals that live on the tundra.

Using Key Terms

1. Write an original definition for *savanna* and *desert*.

Understanding Key Ideas

2. If you visited a savanna, you would most likely see
   a. large herds of grazing animals, such as zebras, gazelles, and wildebeests.
   b. dense forests stretching from horizon to horizon.
   c. snow and ice throughout most of the year.
   d. trees that form a continuous green roof, called the *canopy*.

3. List seven land biomes that are found on Earth.

4. Compare the abiotic and biotic factors of tropical rain forests and deserts. **G.2.3.2 CS**

Critical Thinking

5. **Making Inferences** While excavating an area in the desert, a scientist discovers the fossils of very large trees and ferns. What might the scientist conclude about biomes in this area?

6. **Analyzing Ideas** Tundra receives very little rainfall. Could tundra accurately be called a *frozen desert*? Explain your answer.

7. **Making Inferences** Biomes can be used to classify organisms. How might this information be helpful to a biologist who is studying a newly-discovered tundra biome? **G.1.3.3 CS**

FCAT Preparation

8. Tropical rain forests have more kinds of plants than any other land biome does. Many trees grow above-ground roots for extra support. Which abiotic factor is the main cause of the growth of above-ground roots? **G.2.3.2 CS**
   A. water quality
   B. climate
   C. soil quality
   D. sunlight

9. A tree keeps its leaves year-round. Its leaves also have a waxy coating to protect them from cold temperatures. In which biome would this tree be classified? **G.1.3.3 CS**
   F. temperate rain forest
   G. coniferous forest
   H. tropical rain forest
   I. temperate deciduous forest

SCI**LINKS**

NSTA
Developed and maintained by the
National Science Teachers Association

For a variety of links related to this chapter, go to www.scilinks.org

Topic: Forests
SciLinks code: HSM0609

Marine Ecosystems

What covers almost three-fourths of Earth's surface? What holds both the largest animals and some of the smallest organisms on Earth?

If your answer to both questions is *oceans,* you are correct! Earth's oceans contain many kinds of ecosystems. Ecosystems in the ocean are called *marine ecosystems.*

Life in the Ocean

Marine ecosystems are affected by abiotic factors. These factors include water temperature, water depth, and the amount of sunlight that passes into the water. The animals and plants that live in the ocean come in all shapes and sizes. The largest animals on Earth—blue whales—live in the ocean. So do trillions of tiny plankton. **Plankton** are tiny organisms that float near the surface of the water. Many plankton are producers. They use photosynthesis to make their own food. Plankton form the base of the ocean's food chains. **Figure 1** shows plankton and an animal that relies on plankton for food.

✓ *Reading Check* What are plankton? How are they important to marine ecosystems?

READING WARM-UP

Objectives

- List three abiotic factors that affect marine ecosystems. G.2.3.2 CS
- Describe how water temperature can affect organisms. G.2.3.2 CS
- Describe how depth and sunlight affect life in the ocean. G.2.3.2 CS
- Describe four major ocean zones.
- Explain how conditions in one ocean zone can affect the conditions in another ocean zone. D.1.3.3 CS
- Describe five marine ecosystems.

Terms to Learn

plankton
estuary

READING STRATEGY

Prediction Guide Before reading this section, write the title of each heading in this section. Next, under each heading, write what you think you will learn.

plankton the mass of mostly microscopic organisms that float or drift freely in freshwater and marine environments

Figure 1 *Marine ecosystems support a broad diversity of life. Humpback whales rely on plankton for food.*

Temperature

The temperature of ocean water decreases as the depth of the water increases. However, the temperature change is not gradual. **Figure 2** shows the three temperature zones of ocean water. Notice that the temperature of the water is much warmer in the surface zone than it is in the rest of the ocean. Temperatures in the surface zone vary with latitude. Areas of the ocean along the equator are warmer than areas closer to the poles. Surface zone temperatures also vary with the time of year. During the summer, the Northern Hemisphere is tilted toward the sun. So, the surface zone is warmer than it is during the winter.

Temperature affects the animals that live in marine ecosystems. For example, fishes that live near the poles have adaptations to live in near-freezing water. In contrast, animals that live in coral reefs need warm water to live. Some animals, such as whales, migrate from cold areas to warm areas of the ocean to reproduce. Water temperature also affects whether some animals, such as barnacles, can eat. If the water is too hot or too cold, these animals may not survive.

Benchmark Check How might a change in water temperature affect barnacles? **G.2.3.2 CS**

Benchmark Activity

Coral Reefs and Water Temperature Coral reefs are delicate ecosystems because they need to live within a specific range of temperature to survive. Using library resources or the Internet, research the coral reefs in the Florida Keys. Find out the range of water temperature within which the coral reefs in the Florida Keys need to live. Then, find out how temperatures outside this range can affect the coral reefs and the other organisms that live in the reefs. Write a paragraph discussing your findings. **G.2.3.2 CS**

Figure 2 **Temperature Zones of Ocean Water**

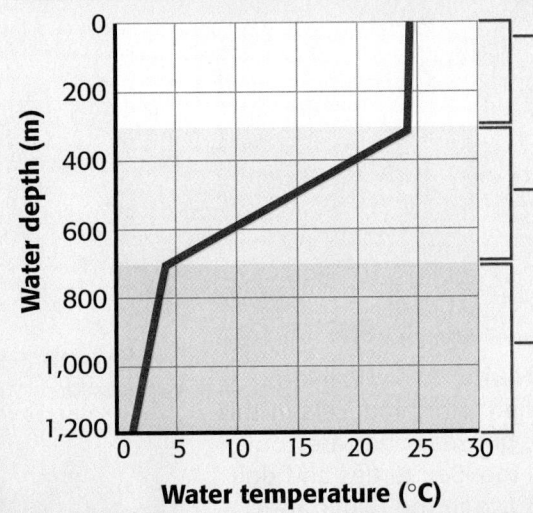

Surface Zone The surface zone is the warm, top layer of ocean water that extends to 300 m below sea level. Sunlight heats the top 100 m of the surface zone. Surface currents mix the heated water with cooler water below.

Thermocline The thermocline is a layer of water that extends from 300 m below sea level to about 700 m below sea level. In this zone, water temperature drops with increased depth faster than it does in the other two zones.

Deep Zone This bottom layer extends from the base of the thermocline to the bottom of the ocean. The temperature in this zone averages a chilling 2°C.

G.2.3.2 CS knows that all biotic and abiotic factors are interrelated and that if one factor is changed or removed, it impacts the availability of other resources within the system.

365

Depth and Sunlight

Life in the ocean is affected not only by water temperature but also by water depth and the amount of sunlight that passes into the water. The major ocean zones are shown in **Figure 3.**

The Intertidal Zone

The intertidal zone is the place where the ocean meets the land. This area is exposed to the air for part of the day. Waves are always crashing on the rock and sand. The animals that live in the intertidal zone have adaptations to survive exposure to air and to keep from being washed away by the waves.

The Neritic Zone

As you move farther away from shore, into the neritic zone (nee RIT ik ZOHN), the water becomes deeper. The ocean floor starts to slope downward. The water is warm and receives a lot of sunlight. Many interesting plants and animals, such as corals, sea turtles, fishes, and dolphins, live in this zone.

Figure 3 *The life in a marine ecosystem depends on water temperature, water depth, and the amount of sunlight that the area receives.*

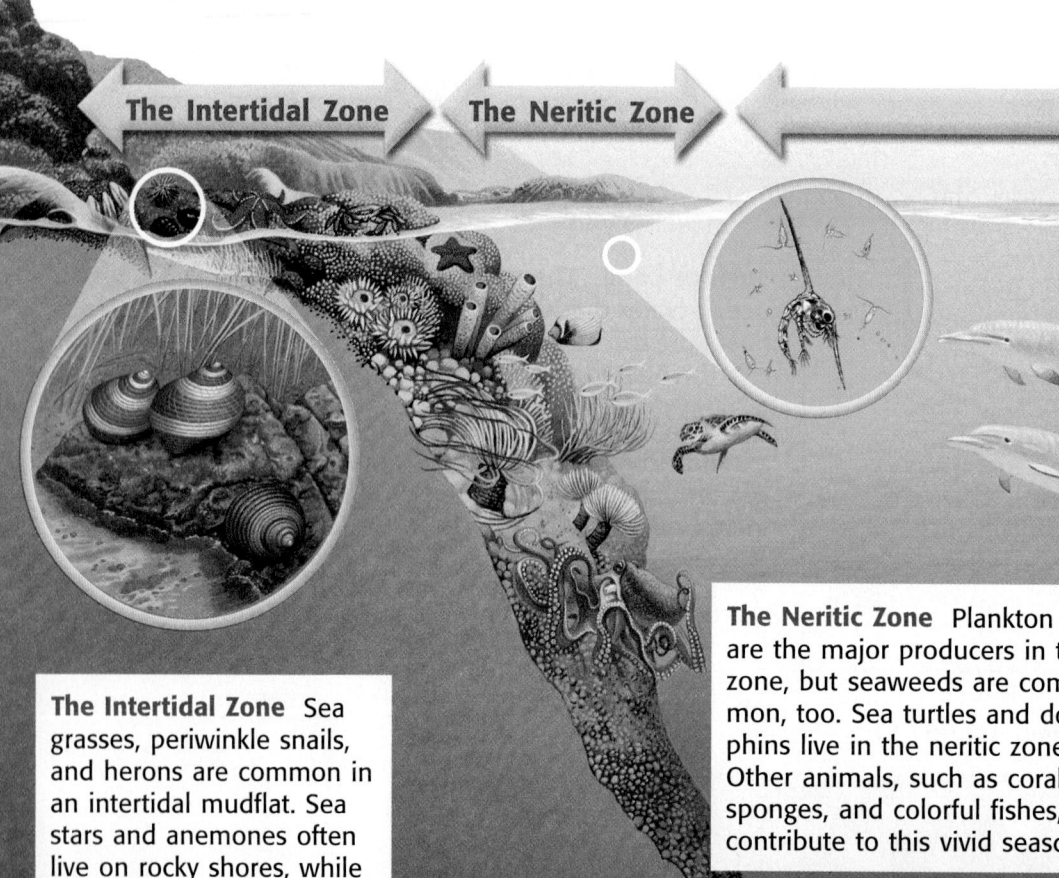

The Intertidal Zone Sea grasses, periwinkle snails, and herons are common in an intertidal mudflat. Sea stars and anemones often live on rocky shores, while clams, crabs, snails, and conchs are common on sandy beaches.

The Neritic Zone Plankton are the major producers in this zone, but seaweeds are common, too. Sea turtles and dolphins live in the neritic zone. Other animals, such as corals, sponges, and colorful fishes, contribute to this vivid seascape.

The Oceanic Zone

In the oceanic zone, the sea floor drops sharply. This zone contains the deep water of the open ocean. Plankton can be found near the water surface. Animals such as fishes, whales, and sharks are found in the oceanic zone. Some animals in this zone live in very deep water. These animals often get food from material that sinks down from the ocean surface.

The Benthic Zone

The benthic zone is the ocean floor. The deepest parts of the benthic zone do not get any sunlight. They are also very cold. Animals such as fishes, worms, and crabs have special adaptations to the deep, dark water. Many of these organisms get food by eating material that sinks from the oceanic zone. Some organisms, such as bacteria, get energy from chemicals that escape from thermal vents on the ocean floor. Thermal vents form at cracks in Earth's crust.

Benchmark Check How do conditions in the oceanic zone influence conditions in the benthic zone? **D.1.3.3 CS**

D.1.3.3 CS knows how conditions that exist in one system influence the conditions that exist in other systems.

G.2.3.2 CS knows that all biotic and abiotic factors are interrelated and that if one factor is changed or removed, it impacts the availability of other resources within the system.

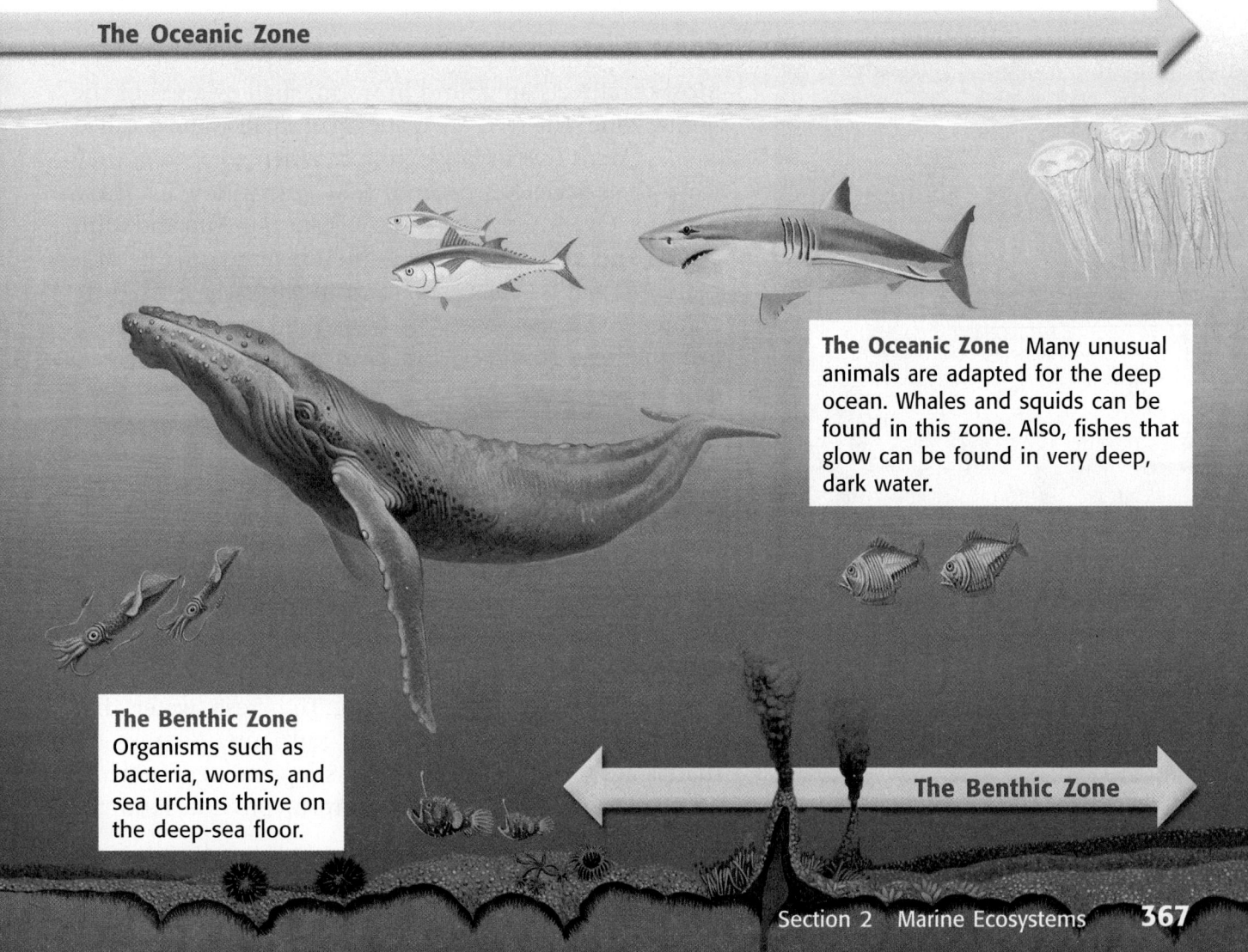

The Oceanic Zone

The Oceanic Zone Many unusual animals are adapted for the deep ocean. Whales and squids can be found in this zone. Also, fishes that glow can be found in very deep, dark water.

The Benthic Zone Organisms such as bacteria, worms, and sea urchins thrive on the deep-sea floor.

The Benthic Zone

A Closer Look

Life on Earth depends on the ocean. Through evaporation, the ocean provides most of the water that makes up Earth's precipitation. Ocean temperatures and currents can affect world climates and wind patterns. Humans and many animals depend on the ocean for food.

Many ecosystems exist in the ocean. Some of these ecosystems are found on or near the shore. Other ecosystems are found in the middle of the ocean or near the poles.

Intertidal Areas

Intertidal areas are found near the shore. These areas include mudflats, sandy beaches, and rocky shores. Intertidal organisms must be able to live both underwater and out of water. The organisms that live in mudflats include worms and crabs. Shorebirds feed on these animals. Organisms that live on sandy beaches include worms, clams, crabs, and plankton. On rocky shores, organisms have adaptations to keep from being swept away by crashing waves. Some organisms use rootlike structures called *holdfasts* to attach themselves to the rocks. Other organisms attach themselves to rocks by releasing a special glue.

estuary an area where fresh water from rivers mixes with salt water from the ocean

G.2.3.2 CS knows that all biotic and abiotic factors are interrelated and that if one factor is changed or removed, it impacts the availability of other resources within the system.

Coral Reefs

Most coral reefs are found in warm, shallow areas of the neritic zone. The reefs are made up of small animals called *corals*. Corals live in large groups. When corals die, they leave their skeletons behind. New corals grow on these remains. Over time, layers of skeletons build up and form a reef. This reef provides a home for many marine animals and plants. These organisms include algae, brightly colored fishes, sponges, sea stars, and sea urchins. An example of a coral reef is shown in **Figure 4.**

Reading Check How do coral reefs develop?

Estuaries

An area where fresh water from streams and rivers spills into the ocean is called an **estuary** (ES tyoo er ee). In estuaries, the fresh water from rivers and the salt water from the ocean are always mixing. Therefore, the amount of salt in the water is always changing. Plants and animals that live in estuaries must be able to survive the changing concentrations of salt. The fresh water that spills into an estuary is rich in nutrients. Because estuaries are so nutrient rich, they support large numbers of plankton. The plankton, in turn, provide food for many animals.

Figure 4 *A coral reef is one of the most biologically diverse ecosystems on Earth.*

The Sargasso Sea

An ecosystem called the *Sargasso Sea* (sahr GAS oh SEE) is found in the middle of the Atlantic Ocean. This ecosystem contains floating rafts of algae called *sargassums* (sahr GAS uhmz). Many of the animals that live in the Sargasso Sea are the same color as sargassums, which helps the animals hide from predators.

Polar Ice

The Arctic Ocean and the ocean around Antarctica make up another marine ecosystem. These icy waters are rich in nutrients, which support large numbers of plankton. Many fishes, birds, and mammals rely on the plankton for food. Animals such as polar bears and penguins live on the polar ice.

SECTION Review

Summary

- Abiotic factors that affect marine ecosystems are water temperature, water depth, and the amount of light that passes into the water. **G.2.3.2 CS**

- Four ocean zones are the intertidal zone, the neritic zone, the oceanic zone, and the benthic zone.

- Organisms in the benthic zone depend on organisms in the oceanic zone for food. **D.1.3.3 CS**

- Five marine ecosystems are intertidal areas, coral reefs, estuaries, the Sargasso Sea, and polar ice.

Using Key Terms

1. Use *plankton* and *estuary* in separate sentences.

Understanding Key Ideas

2. How does water temperature affect ocean organisms? **G.2.3.2 CS**

3. What are three abiotic factors that affect marine ecosystems? **G.2.3.2 CS**

4. Describe the intertidal zone.

5. Describe two marine ecosystems. For each ecosystem, list an organism that lives there.

6. How are the oceanic zone and the benthic zone related? **D.1.3.3 CS**

Critical Thinking

7. **Making Inferences** Animals in the Sargasso Sea hide from predators by blending in with the sargassums. Color is only one way to blend in. What is another way that animals can blend in with sargassums?

8. **Identifying Relationships** Many fishes and other organisms that live in the deep ocean produce light. What are two ways in which this light might be useful?

Freshwater Ecosystems

A brook bubbles over rocks. A mighty river thunders through a canyon. A calm swamp echoes with the sounds of frogs and birds. What do these places have in common?

Brooks, rivers, and swamps are examples of freshwater ecosystems. The water in brooks and rivers is often fast moving. In swamps, water moves very slowly. Also, water in swamps is often found in standing pools.

Stream and River Ecosystems

The water in brooks, streams, and rivers may flow from melting ice or snow. Or the water may come from a spring. A spring is a place where water flows from underground to Earth's surface. Each stream of water that joins a larger stream is called a *tributary* (TRIB yoo TER ee). As more tributaries join a stream, the stream contains more water. The stream becomes stronger and wider. A very strong, wide stream is called a *river*. **Figure 1** shows how a river develops.

Like the abiotic and biotic factors in other ecosystems, the abiotic and biotic factors in freshwater ecosystems are interrelated. One abiotic factor that affects organisms in freshwater ecosystems is how quickly water moves. Organisms that live in fast-moving water have adaptations to keep from being washed away. Some producers, such as algae and moss, are attached to rocks. Consumers, such as tadpoles, use suction disks to hold themselves to rocks. Other consumers, such as insects, live under rocks.

Benchmark Check How does the movement of water affect plants and animals in a freshwater ecosystem? **G.2.3.2 CS**

READING WARM-UP

Objectives

● Explain how abiotic and biotic factors in freshwater ecosystems are interrelated. **G.2.3.2 CS**

● Describe the three zones of a lake.

● Explain how conditions in the open-water zone affect conditions in the deep-water zone. **D.1.3.3 CS**

● Describe two wetland ecosystems.

● Explain how plants and animals reshape a lake as it becomes a wetland ecosystem. **D.1.3.4 AA**

Terms to Learn

littoral zone   wetland
open-water zone   marsh
deep-water zone   swamp

READING STRATEGY

Paired Summarizing Read this section silently. In pairs, take turns summarizing the material. Stop to discuss ideas that seem confusing.

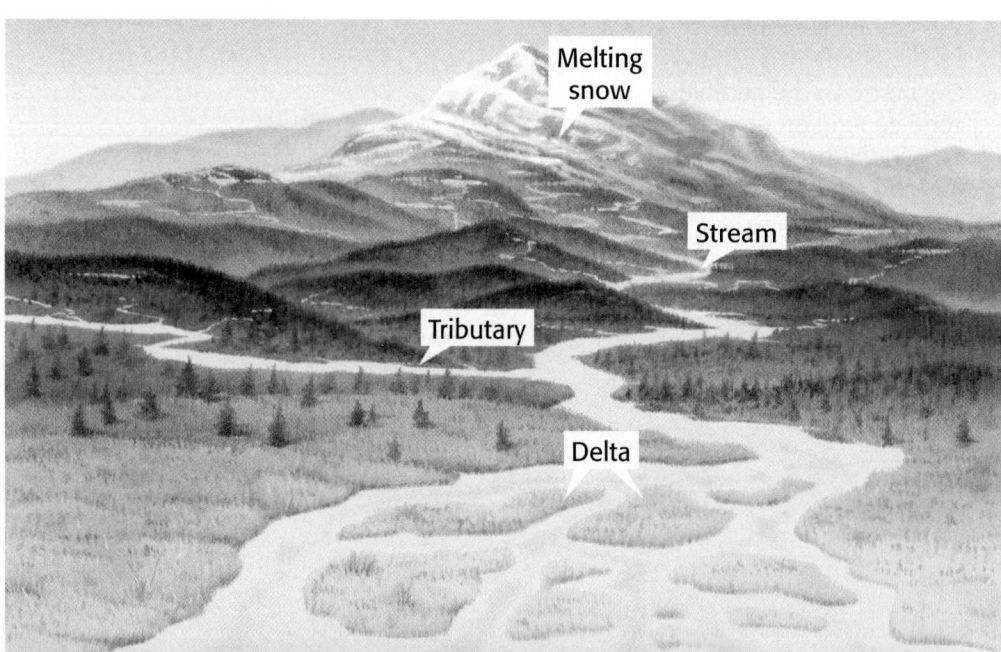

Figure 1 *Rivers become larger as more tributaries flow into them.*

Melting snow

Stream

Tributary

Delta

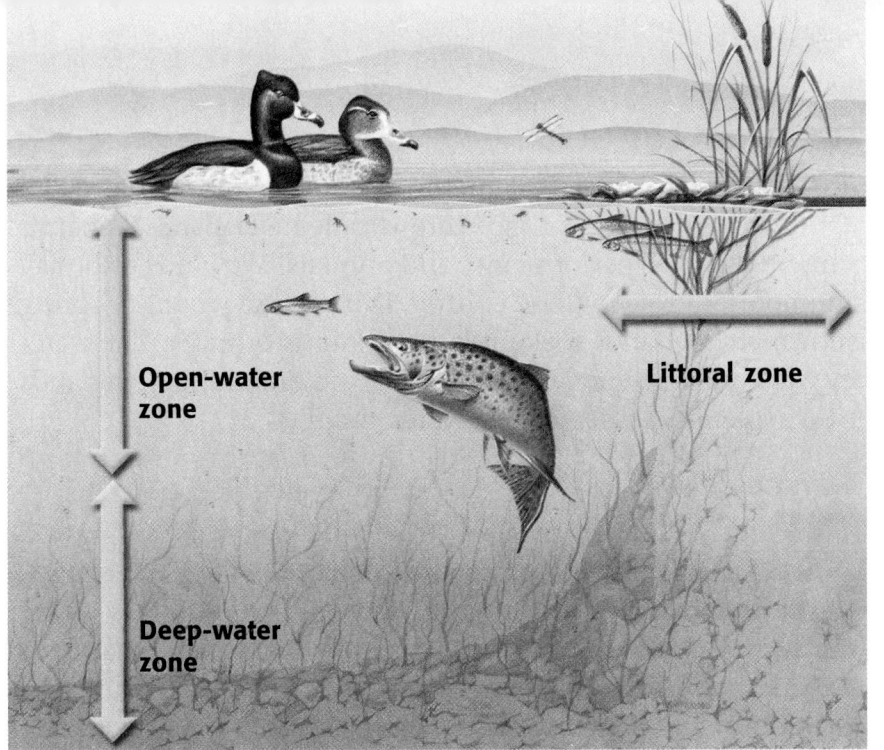

Open-water zone

Deep-water zone

Littoral zone

Figure 2 *Ponds and lakes can be divided into three zones. Each zone has different organisms and abiotic factors.*

Pond and Lake Ecosystems

Ponds and lakes have different ecosystems than streams and rivers do. **Figure 2** shows the zones of a typical lake.

Life near the Shore

The area of water closest to the edge of a lake or pond is called the **littoral zone** (LIT uh ruhl ZOHN). Sunlight reaches the bottom of the littoral zone. This sunlight makes it possible for algae and plants to grow in the littoral zone. Algae grow beneath the surface of the water in the littoral zone. Plants that grow near the shore include cattails and rushes. Floating leaf plants, such as water lilies, grow farther from the shore. The plants of the littoral zone are home to small animals, such as snails and insects. Clams and worms bury themselves in the mud. Frogs, salamanders, turtles, fish, and snakes also live in this zone.

Life Away from the Shore

The area of a lake or pond that extends from the littoral zone across the top of the water is called the **open-water zone.** The open-water zone goes as deep as sunlight can reach. This zone is home to bass, lake trout, and other fishes. Many photosynthetic plankton also live in this area. Beneath the open-water zone is the **deep-water zone,** where no sunlight reaches. Catfish, carp, worms, crustaceans, fungi, and bacteria live here. These organisms often feed on dead organisms that sink from the open-water zone.

Benchmark Check Describe how conditions in the open-water zone influence conditions in the deep-water zone. **D.1.3.3 CS**

Quick Lab

Pond-Food Relationships

1. On **index cards,** write the names of some of the plants and animals that live in a typical freshwater pond or small lake. Write one type of organism on each card.

2. Use **yarn** or **string** to connect each organism to its food sources.

3. Describe the food relationships in a pond.

littoral zone the shallow zone of a lake or pond where light reaches the bottom and nurtures plants

open-water zone the zone of a pond or lake that extends from the littoral zone and that is only as deep as light can reach

deep-water zone the zone of a lake or pond below the open-water zone, where no light reaches

D.1.3.3 CS knows how conditions that exist in one system influence the conditions that exist in other systems.

G.2.3.2 CS knows that all biotic and abiotic factors are interrelated and that if one factor is changed or removed, it impacts the availability of other resources within the system.

Figure 3 *This painted turtle suns itself on a log in a freshwater marsh.*

wetland an area of land that is periodically underwater or whose soil contains a great deal of moisture

marsh a treeless wetland ecosystem where plants such as grasses grow

swamp a wetland ecosystem in which shrubs and trees grow

CONNECTION TO Language Arts

Compound Words A compound word is a word made up of two or more single words. In your **science journal,** define the two words that make up the word *wetland.* Then, define three more compound words.

Figure 4 *The trunks of these Cypress trees in Everglades National Park are adapted to give the trees more support in the wet, soft soil.*

Wetland Ecosystems

An area of land that is sometimes underwater or whose soil contains a great deal of moisture is called a **wetland.** Wetlands support many types of plants and animals. Wetlands also play an important role in flood control. During heavy rains or spring snowmelt, wetlands soak up large amounts of water. The water in wetlands also moves deeper into the ground. So, wetlands help replenish underground water supplies.

Marshes

A treeless wetland ecosystem where plants, such as grasses, grow is called a **marsh.** A freshwater marsh is shown in **Figure 3.** Freshwater marshes are often found in shallow areas along the shores of lakes, ponds, rivers, and streams. The plants in a marsh vary depending on the depth of the water and the location of the marsh. Grasses, reeds, bulrushes, and wild rice are common marsh plants. Muskrats, turtles, frogs, and birds also live in marshes.

Swamps

A wetland ecosystem in which trees and vines grow is called a **swamp.** Everglades National Park, shown in **Figure 4,** is an example of a swamp. Swamps are found in low-lying areas and beside slow-moving rivers. Most swamps are flooded part of the year, depending on rainfall. Willows, bald cypresses, and oaks are common swamp trees. Vines, such as poison ivy, grow up tree trunks. Plants, such as orchids, may hang from tree branches. Water lilies and other plants grow in standing water. Many fishes, snakes, and birds also live in swamps.

Reshaping a Lake Ecosystem

Did you know that a lake can disappear? How can this happen? Water entering a standing body of water usually carries nutrients and sediment. These materials settle to the bottom of the lake. Dead leaves from overhanging trees and decaying plant and animal life also settle to the bottom of the lake. Then, bacteria decompose these materials. This process uses oxygen in the water. The loss of oxygen affects the kinds of animals that can survive in the lake. For example, many fishes would not be able to survive with less oxygen in the water.

Over time, the lake is filled with sediment. This sediment nourishes new plants as they begin to grow. First, plants grow in shallow areas. Then, plants slowly grow closer and closer to the center of the lake. What is left of the lake becomes a wetland, such as a marsh or a swamp. Eventually, as more changes occur, the wetland can become a forest.

D.1.3.4 AA knows the ways in which plants and animals reshape the landscape (e.g., bacteria, fungi, worms, rodents, and other organisms add organic matter to the soil, increasing soil fertility, encouraging plant growth, and strengthening resistance to erosion).

Benchmark Check How do plants reshape the landscape as a lake becomes a wetland? **D.1.3.4. AA**

SECTION Review

Summary

- Water movement affects biotic factors in freshwater ecosystems. **G.2.3.2 CS**

- A lake has a littoral zone, an open-water zone, and a deep-water zone.

- Conditions in the open-water zone affect conditions in the deep-water zone. **D.1.3.3 CS**

- Wetlands include marshes and swamps.

- A lake can become a wetland or a forest as plants and animals reshape the landscape. **D.1.3.4 AA**

Understanding Key Ideas

1. Explain how two organisms adapt to fast-moving water in freshwater ecosystems. **G.2.3.2 CS**

2. Describe the three zones of a lake.

3. Explain how plants and animals can affect the landscape of a lake over time. **D.1.3.4 AA**

4. Compare the abiotic and biotic factors of a marsh with those of a swamp.

Critical Thinking

5. **Applying Concepts** Imagine a steep, rocky stream. What kinds of adaptations might animals living in this stream have? Explain your answer. **G.2.3.2 CS**

6. **Predicting Consequences** What would happen to the organisms living in the deep-water zone if sunlight could no longer pass through the open-water zone? **D.1.3.3 CS**

FCAT Preparation

7. Animals in the deep-water zone of a lake live on dead organisms that sink from the open-water zone. Which of the following organisms influence the animals of the deep-water zone the greatest? **D.1.3.3 CS**

A. turtles at the edge of the lake

B. photosynthetic plankton

C. mud-dwelling clams

D. shoreline cattails

SCLINKS.

NSTA
Developed and maintained by the National Science Teachers Association

For a variety of links related to this chapter, go to www.scilinks.org
Topic: Freshwater Ecosystems; Florida's Freshwater
SciLinks code: HSM0621; HSMF07

Skills Practice Lab

Too Much of a Good Thing?

OBJECTIVES

Draw common pond-water organisms.

Observe the effect of fertilizer on pond-water organisms.

Describe how fertilizer affects the number and type of pond-water organisms over time.

MATERIALS

- beaker, 500 mL
- distilled water, 2.25 L
- eyedropper
- fertilizer
- gloves, protective
- graduated cylinder, 100 mL
- jars, 1 qt or 1 L (3)
- microscope
- microscope slides with coverslips
- pencil, wax
- plastic wrap
- pond water containing living organisms, 300 mL
- stirring rod

SAFETY

Plants need nutrients, such as phosphates and nitrates, to grow. Phosphates are often found in detergents. Nitrates are often found in animal wastes and fertilizers. When large amounts of these nutrients enter rivers and lakes, algae and plants grow rapidly and then die off. Microorganisms that decompose the dead matter use up oxygen in the water. Without oxygen, fish and other animals die. In this activity, you will observe the effect of fertilizers on organisms that live in pond water.

Procedure

1. Label one jar "Control," the second jar "Fertilizer," and the third jar "Excess fertilizer."

2. Pour 750 mL of distilled water into each jar. To the jar labeled "Fertilizer," add the amount of fertilizer recommended for 750 mL of water. To the jar labeled "Excess fertilizer," add 10 times the amount recommended for 750 mL of water. Stir the contents of each jar to dissolve the fertilizer.

3. Obtain a sample of pond water. Stir it gently to make sure that the organisms in it are evenly distributed. Pour 100 mL of pond water into each of the three jars.

4. Observe a drop of water from each jar under the microscope. Draw at least four of the organisms. Determine whether the organisms that you see are producers, which are usually green, or consumers, which are usually able to move. Describe the number and type of organisms in the pond water.

Common Pond-Water Organisms

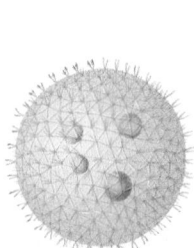

Volvox
(producer)

Spirogyra
(producer)

Daphnia
(consumer)

Vorticella
(consumer)

G.2.3.2 CS knows that all biotic and abiotic factors are interrelated and that if one factor is changed or removed, it impacts the availability of other resources within the system.

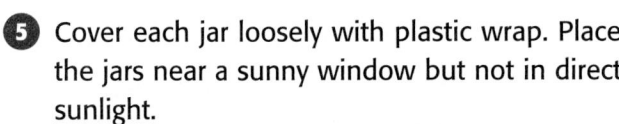

5 Cover each jar loosely with plastic wrap. Place the jars near a sunny window but not in direct sunlight.

6 Make a prediction about how the pond organisms will grow in each of the three jars.

7 Make three data tables. Title one table "Control," as shown below. Title another table "Fertilizer," and title the third table "Excess fertilizer."

Control			
Date	Color	Odor	Other observations
	DO NOT WRITE IN BOOK		

8 Observe the jars when you first set them up and once every 3 days for the next 3 weeks. Note the color, the odor, and the presence of organisms. Record your observations.

9 When organisms become visible in the jars, use an eyedropper to remove a sample from each jar. Observe the sample under the microscope. How have the number and type of organisms changed since you first looked at the pond water?

10 At the end of the 3-week period, observe a sample from each jar under the microscope. Draw at least four of the most abundant organisms, and describe how the number and type of organisms have changed since your last observation.

Analyze the Results

1 **Describing Events** After 3 weeks, which jar has the most abundant growth of algae?

2 **Analyzing Data** Did you observe any effects on organisms (other than algae) in the jar that had the most abundant growth of algae? Explain your answer.

Draw Conclusions

3 **Drawing Conclusions** What may have caused the growth of algae in the jars to increase?

4 **Evaluating Results** Did your observations match your predictions? Explain your answer.

5 **Interpreting Information** Decaying plant and animal life contribute to the filling of lakes and ponds. How might the rapid filling of lakes and ponds be prevented or slowed?

Chapter Review

USING KEY TERMS

1 Write an original definition for *biome* and *tundra*.

2 Use *intertidal zone*, *neritic zone*, and *oceanic zone* in separate sentences.

For each pair of terms, explain how the meanings of the terms differ.

3 *savanna* and *desert*

4 *open-water zone* and *deep-water zone*

5 *marsh* and *swamp*

UNDERSTANDING KEY IDEAS

Multiple Choice

6 Trees that lose their leaves in the winter are called
- **a.** evergreen trees.
- **b.** coniferous trees.
- **c.** deciduous trees.
- **d.** None of the above

7 An estuary is an area where fresh water from streams and rivers spills into the ocean. Which of the following statements best describes how plants and animals adapt to the abiotic factors in an estuary? **G.2.3.2 CS** *FCAT*
- **a.** They are able to live both underwater and out of water.
- **b.** They require warm, shallow water.
- **c.** They can survive changes in the concentration of salt.
- **d.** They have holdfasts that attach to rocks.

8 An abiotic factor that affects marine ecosystems is **G.2.3.2 CS**
- **a.** the temperature of the water.
- **b.** the depth of the water.
- **c.** the amount of sunlight that passes through the water.
- **d.** All of the above

9 After a small lake starts to fill with sediment, plants begin to grow around the edge of the lake. If more plants grow closer to the center of the lake, how will the lake ecosystem be affected? **D.1.3.4 AA** *FCAT*
- **a.** The lake will not change.
- **b.** The lake will become an estuary.
- **c.** The lake will be able to support more aquatic animals.
- **d.** The lake will become a wetland.

Short Answer

10 What are seven land biomes?

11 Explain how a small lake can become a forest. **D.1.3.4 AA**

12 How can biomes be used to classify living things? **G.1.3.3 CS**

13 Describe the three zones of a lake.

14 Name three abiotic factors in land biomes, three abiotic factors in marine ecosystems, and an abiotic factor in freshwater ecosystems. **G.2.3.2 CS**

Extended Response

15 **Making Inferences** Plankton use photosynthesis to make their own food. They need sunlight for photosynthesis. Which of the four major ocean zones can support the growth of plankton? Explain your answer.

16 **Predicting Consequences** Wetlands, such as marshes and swamps, play an important role in flood control. Wetlands also help replenish underground water supplies. Predict what might happen to other ecosystems if a wetland dries out. **D.1.3.3 CS**

17 **Applying Concepts** Imagine that you are a scientist. You are studying an area that gets about 100 cm of rain each year. The average summer temperatures are near 30°C. What biome are you in? What are some plants and animals that you will likely encounter? If you stayed in this area for the winter, what kind of preparations might you need to make?

18 **Identifying Relationships** Explain how the four zones of the ocean are related. How might a decrease in a population of fish in the neritic zone affect the other zones? **D.1.3.3 CS**

Concept Mapping

19 Use the following terms to create a concept map: *plants and animals, tropical rain forest, tundra, biomes, desert, permafrost, canopy,* and *abiotic factors.*

Use the graphs below to answer the questions that follow.

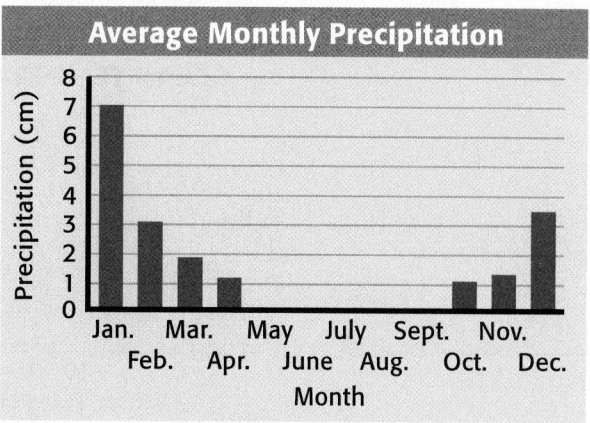

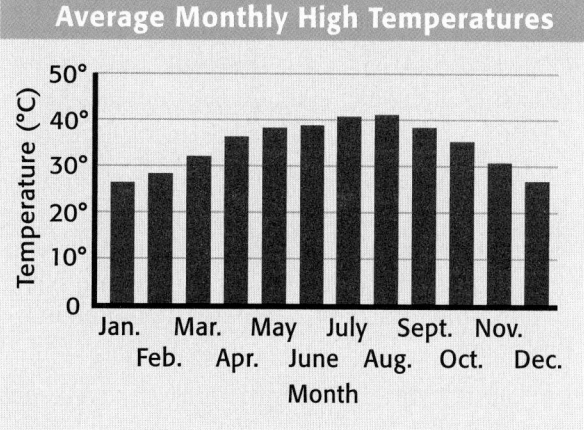

20 Which biome is most likely found in the region described by the graphs? Explain your answer.

21 How many centimeters of rain fell in the region during the course of the year?

22 Which month is the hottest in the region? Which month is the coolest in the region?

23 What is the average monthly precipitation for the month with the highest average monthly high temperature?

For the following questions, write your answers on a separate sheet of paper.

1 The diagram below shows the zones of the ocean by water depth in meters (m) and by temperature in degrees Celsius (°C). Wei-lin is studying the importance of sardines in ocean ecosystems. She learned that sardines can survive only in water that is between 14°C and 20°C.

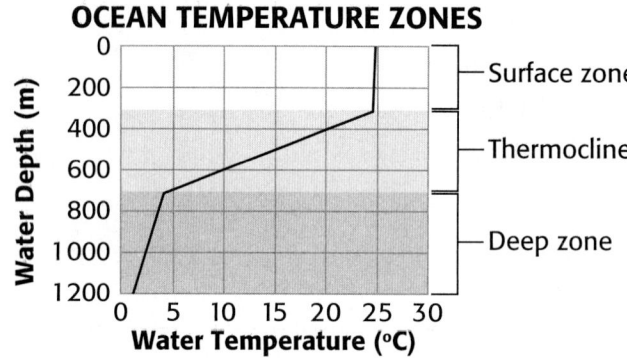

At what depth are sardines **most** likely found?

A.   between 200 and 300 meters

B.   between 400 and 500 meters

C.   between the surface and 100 meters

D.   between 100 meters and 200 meters

2 Biomes can be used to classify living systems because similar organisms live in a particular biome regardless of where the biome is located. Which of the following characterizes a temperate grassland?

F.   contains trees that grow above-ground roots

G.   contains grasses, flowering plants, and few trees

H.   contains trees that shed their leaves during the winter

I.   contains shallow-rooted plants, such as grasses and small shrubs

3 Similar to other fish that prefer oxygen-rich water, trout like to live in cool, fast-moving streams. Which of the following events might reduce the population of trout in a mountain stream?

A.   unusually heavy snowfall in the winter

B.   the flow of a tributary stream slows slightly

C.   the movement of a boulder forms a new waterfall

D.   ash and silt from a forest fire cover the surface of the stream

4 In a savanna, the average yearly rainfall is 150 centimeters. The average yearly rainfall in a desert is 25 centimeters. If a change in global climate causes the savanna's average yearly rainfall to reduce by 2 centimeters each year, in how many years will the savanna become a desert?

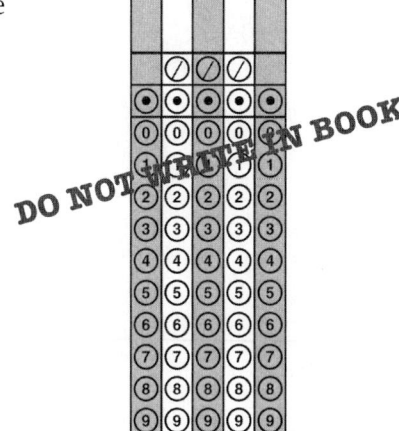

DO NOT WRITE IN BOOK

5 The map below shows the major land biomes on Earth. The biotic factors in a biome need water, an abiotic factor, to survive. The availability of water in a biome is dependent upon how much precipitation a biome receives. Some biomes receive less precipitation than other biomes do.

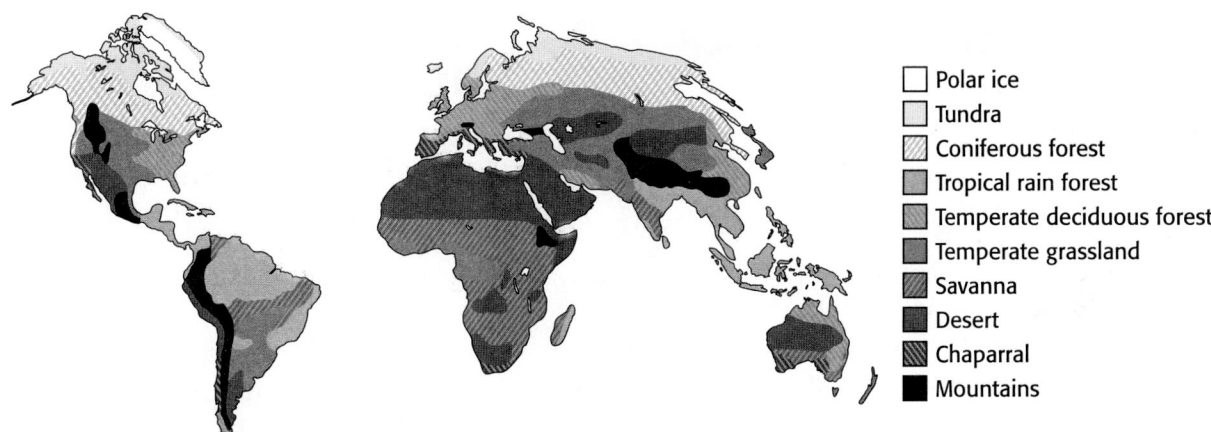

Polar ice
Tundra
Coniferous forest
Tropical rain forest
Temperate deciduous forest
Temperate grassland
Savanna
Desert
Chaparral
Mountains

In which land biome is water, an abiotic factor, in the scarcest supply?

F. desert
G. coniferous forest
H. tropical rain forest
I. temperate grassland

6 Over a long period of time, a lake ecosystem can become a forest ecosystem. The decomposition of dead plant and animal matter is a part of this process. Which of the following organisms would **most** likely be responsible for decomposing dead plant and animal matter in a lake?

A. bacteria
B. clams
C. fungi
D. snails

Science in Action

Scientific Debate

Developing Wetlands

Wetlands are home to many flowering plants, birds, and turtles. Wetlands also play important roles in controlling floods and maintaining water quality. However, as more people need homes, grocery stores, and other facilities, some wetlands are being developed for construction. State governments often regulate the development of wetlands. Development is not allowed on many environmentally sensitive wetlands. But it is sometimes allowed on wetlands that are less sensitive. However, some people think that all wetlands should be protected, regardless of how sensitive an area is.

Scientific Discoveries

Ocean Vents

Imagine the deepest parts of the ocean. There is no light at all, and it is very cold. Some of the animals that live here have found a unique place to live—vents on the ocean floor. Water seeps into Earth between plates on the ocean floor. The water is heated and absorbs sulfuric gases. When the water blasts up through ocean vents, it raises the temperature of the ocean hundreds of degrees! Bacteria use the gases from the ocean vents to survive. In turn, mussels and clams feed on the bacteria. Without ocean vents, it would be much more difficult for these organisms to survive.

Language Arts ACTiViTY

WRITING SKILL Research wetland development on your own. Then, write a letter in which you describe your opinion about the development of wetlands.

Math ACTiViTY

A thermal vent increases the temperature of the water around it to 360°C. If the temperature of the water was 2°C, what is the difference in temperature? By what percentage did the water temperature increase?

Friends of the Florida Panther

The Florida Panther Posse The Florida panther is one of the most endangered animals in the world. At one time, Florida panthers roamed the southern United States as far west as Texas. Today, most of the 80 panthers that remain in the wild live in Southwest Florida in the Florida Panther National Wildlife Refuge—an area more than 106 km^2. The refuge is off limits to the public, but some middle school students from Southwest Florida study the panthers that live there. These students belong to the Florida Panther Posse, a network of students who are trying to save Florida panthers. The students educate their school and community about the plight of Florida panthers. There are about 50 active posse programs throughout Florida.

Wildlife managers from the Florida Fish and Wildlife Conservation Commission give monthly reports on the movement of the panthers as well as other information to the Florida Panther Posse. Each posse is responsible for maintaining a school bulletin board that displays maps of the locations of collared panthers, information about the Florida Panther Refuge, photographs, and ways that an individual can help with the survival and protection of Florida panthers.

Social Studies ACTIVITY

Use library resources or the Internet to research the areas in which Florida panthers used to roam and currently roam. Draw two maps that illustrate the differences between the two areas.

To learn more about these Science in Action topics, visit **go.hrw.com** and type in the keyword **HT6FECFF**.

Current Science

Check out Current Science® articles related to this chapter by visiting go.hrw.com. Just type in the keyword HL5CS20.

Caring for Florida's Environment

The Big Idea Using Florida's natural resources wisely helps preserve them.

About the PHOTO

A researcher and a young manatee meet face to face in Florida's Crystal River National Wildlife Refuge. Every day, the Crystal River is fed by 600 million gallons of fresh water that flows from more than 30 springs. The refuge is an important habitat for Florida's endangered manatee population. Caring for Florida's land, freshwater, and ocean resources will help protect endangered animals such as manatees.

PRE-READING ACTIVITY

**Tri-Fold** Before you read the chapter, create the FoldNote entitled "Tri-Fold" described in the **Study Skills** section of the Appendix. Write what you know about Florida's environment in the column labeled "Know." Then, write what you want to know in the column labeled "Want." As you read the chapter, write what you learn about Florida's environment in the column labeled "Learn."

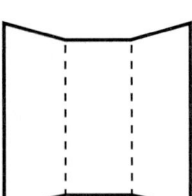

START-UP ACTIVITY

Florida Mapping Project D.1.3.3 CS

You live in Florida, but how well do you really know your home state? In this activity, you will work in groups to create a map of Florida's natural resources.

Procedure

1. Your teacher will display a **map of Florida** that is divided into different regions. As a class, brainstorm the features, such as rivers, parks, forestland, and cities, that you want to show on the map. Add these features to the map's key.

2. Form groups, and choose a region to map. Have each group member choose a feature to map.

3. As a group, begin drawing your map on a **large sheet of paper**.

4. When you finish your map, work as a class to join the the maps together. Use **tape** to produce a large classroom map. As you read this chapter, you can add features that you learn about.

Analysis

1. What did you learn about your region? What are the main natural resources in your region?

2. What did you learn about Florida? Where is the largest lake and the longest river?

3. In what ways are Florida's natural resources linked in a system? Are land resources linked to freshwater resources and ocean resources? How could human activity affect this system?

Florida's Land Resources

When Native Americans first reached Florida thousands of years ago, what do you think they saw?

They might have walked through vast forests of pine and oak and might have seen animals such as mastodons, giant sloths, panthers, and bears. Florida's environment has changed a lot in the past 10,000 years. In fact, the Everglades, the vast wetland area that covers much of South Florida, is only about 5,000 years old! **Figure 1** shows what Florida's landscape looks like today. Florida's environment is constantly changing, but living things still depend on Florida's natural resources to survive.

The Natural Landscape

Florida's land surface is about 36,000,000 acres. The major ecological communities found in Florida's landscape include woodland forests, dry prairies, wetlands, and beaches. Woodland forests are located mostly in northern Florida and include pine, oak, beech, hickory, and cabbage palms. Dry prairies with native grasses and shrubs are found mostly in Central Florida. Wetlands, such as the Everglades in South Florida, are lowland areas that are generally saturated with water. Florida's beaches are found on the shoreline and are sparsely vegetated. **Figure 2** describes Florida's main ecological communities in more detail. In which community do you live?

READING WARM-UP

Objectives

● Describe the natural, agricultural, and urban landscapes of Florida.

● Explain how Florida's land resources are managed to meet human needs and to protect the environment.
D.2.3.2, G.2.3.1 CS

● Identify four positive effects and four negative effects of human actions on Florida's ecosystems.
D.2.3.1, G.2.3.4 AA

Terms to Learn

sustainable agriculture
urban sprawl

READING STRATEGY

Prediction Guide Before reading this section, predict whether each of the following statements is true or false:

• Most agricultural land in Florida is used for ranching.

• The number of tourists that visit Florida each year is greater than the population of Florida.

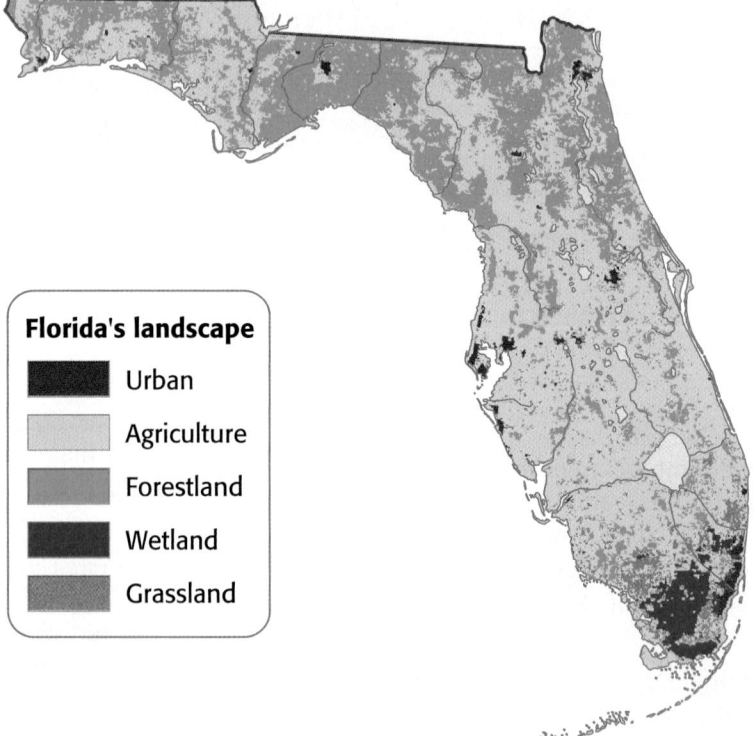

Florida's landscape

- ■ Urban
- ▨ Agriculture
- ▨ Forestland
- ■ Wetland
- ▨ Grassland

Figure 1 *Much of northern Florida is forestland. Large areas of Central Florida are used for farming. South Florida is dominated by a wetland area known as the Everglades.*

Figure 2 Florida's Ecological Communities

	Communities	Plants	Animals
	**Woodland forests** include pinelands, hardwood forests, and sand pine scrubs.	pine, beech, hickory, live oak, red maple, gumbo limbo, saw palmetto, sabal, and cabbage palm	black bear, deer, bobcats, raccoons, opossums, snakes, lizards, tortoises, and birds
	**Dry prairies** are treeless plains with large native grasses and shrubs that are maintained by recurrent fires.	palmetto shrub, scrub grass, wire grass, runner oak, blueberry, and fetterbush	sandhill cranes, burrowing owls, and tortoises
	**Wetlands** are lowland areas that are generally saturated with water and have plants that are uniquely adapted for watery ground.	saw grass, sweet bay, sweet gum, oak, elm, red maple, cypress, vines, and ferns	Florida panther, black bear, white-tailed deer, otters, alligators, fish, frogs, snakes, and wading birds
	**Beaches** are areas near the ocean that are sand covered and sparsely vegetated.	sea oats, sea grapes, beach morning glory, railroad vine, sea blite, sand spur, and saltwort	coquina clams, ghost crabs, laughing gulls, and sandpipers

Managing the Natural Landscape

Florida's land resources are important for their beauty and as habitat. But they also help support Florida's economy. More than 19 million people visit Florida's parks every year. Because Florida's natural resources are valued for many reasons, many individuals and organizations work to protect them. To protect public lands, Florida's State Park System manages 31 state forests. The National Park Service also manages eight national forests and parks.

Taking care of Florida's land is a lot of responsibility. Park managers educate the public, plant trees to control erosion, and set prescribed fires that help maintain an area's ecological balance. They remove invasive plants and animals that threaten ecosystems. Individuals also help protect Florida's public land. Every year, more than 7,000 people volunteer to help at Florida parks. You can volunteer by becoming a Junior Ranger at one of Florida's parks. Private landowners can also help protect land resources. For example, *The Florida Land Owners Incentive Program* works to restore natural habitats on private land.

✓ Reading Check How are Florida's public lands managed?

 G.2.3.1 CS knows that some resources are renewable and others are nonrenewable.

Agriculture in Florida

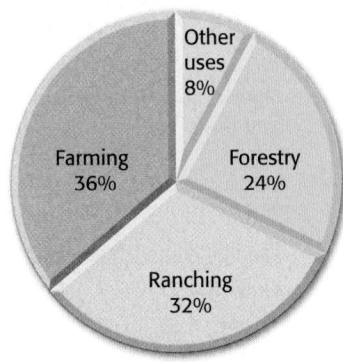

Figure 3 *Agricultural land is mainly used for growing crops, ranching, and forestry.*

The Agricultural Landscape

Agriculture is second only to tourism as a major contributor to Florida's economy. As shown in **Figure 3,** agricultural land use can be divided into three major categories: farming, ranching, and forestry. Because agriculture alters the environment to meet human needs, all forms of agriculture have positive and negative effects.

Farming

About 36% of Florida's land is farmed. Florida is a leading national producer of tomatoes, honey, strawberries, and ornamental plants. However, most of Florida's farmland is used to grow two major crops—sugar cane and citrus fruit. Sugar cane is grown in wetland areas that are part of the Everglades. Citrus trees, such as the ones in **Figure 4,** are grown mostly in Central and South Florida. Florida's 107 million citrus trees provide about $9 billion every year to Florida's economy.

Farming has many effects on Florida's environment. One major environmental effect of farming is pollution from agricultural chemicals. Water containing pesticides and herbicides can harm plants and animals. Fertilizers such as phosphates can flow from farmland into streams, rivers, and lakes. These pollutants encourage the growth of algae and invasive plants that can change the balance of ecosystems and affect habitat. Sugar cane and citrus farming also use large amounts of water. Diverting too much water from natural ecosystems can harm ecosystems.

Ranching and Forestry

About 32% of Florida's agricultural land is used for ranching. Much of Florida's ranchland is located in grassland ecosystems. Ranching provides many useful animal products such as beef, poultry, pork, and milk. However, if ranchland is not properly maintained, ranching can encourage the growth of invasive plants and damage freshwater resources.

About 24% of Florida land is used for forestry. Forestry lands are located in woodland ecosystems. About 90 percent of Florida's forested land is managed as commercial forests used to produce trees for lumber and paper.

Figure 4 *Citrus trees thrive in Florida's subtropical climate and sandy soil.*

Managing the Agricultural Landscape

Scientists and farmers are working to develop sustainable agriculture in Florida. **Sustainable agriculture** is the use of agricultural practices that limit negative environmental effects.

Protecting Water and Air

Many growers have developed *best management practices* to promote sustainable agriculture. For example, the citrus industry has developed irrigation systems that conserve water and reduce water pollution. Today, citrus farms use up to 88% less water than they used 20 years ago. Cooperatives in the sugar industry are also working to improve air and water quality. To reduce phosphate levels in farm runoff, sugar farms recycle water and have created marshes to filter pollutants. Sugar mills use filters to remove air pollutants from smokestack emissions. Sugar mills also use a byproduct of sugar cane processing called *bagasse* to generate steam and electricity. The use of bagasse saves about 31 million gallons of fossil fuel each year.

Reducing the Use of Chemicals

Some farmers and ranchers use natural predators rather than chemicals to control pests. For example, melaleuca (me luh Loo kuh) trees are an invasive species in the Everglades and in millions of acres of ranchland. The water-hungry trees were first introduced from Australia to drain the Everglades, but they soon became an invasive pest. Scientists are introducing the tree's natural parasite, the melaleuca weevil, shown in **Figure 5,** to control the invasive trees without the use of herbicides.

Benchmark Check Describe two ways that farmers are reducing the environmental effects of agriculture in Florida. **D.2.3.2, G.2.3.4 AA**

Figure 5 *The invasive melaleuca tree can be seen in this photo of the Everglades. Instead of using chemicals to control the tree, scientists are introducing the melaleuca weevil.*

sustainable agriculture the use of agricultural practices that limit negative environmental effects

D.2.3.2 knows the positive and negative consequences of human action on the Earth's systems.

G.2.3.4 AA understands that humans are a part of an ecosystem and their activities may deliberately or inadvertently alter the equilibrium in ecosystems.

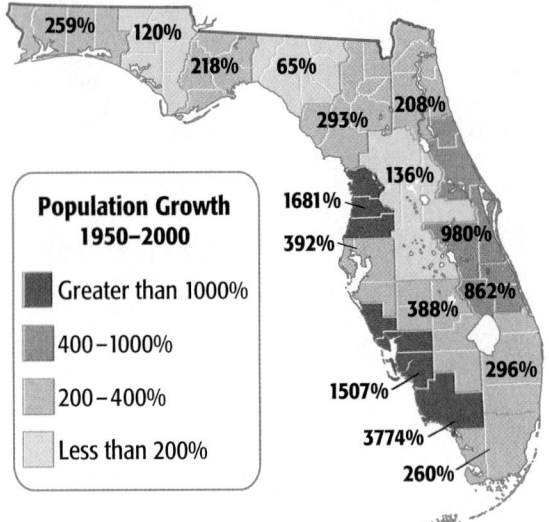

259% 120%
218% 65%
293% 208%
136%
1681% 980%
392%
862%
388%
296%
1507%
3774%
260%

Population Growth 1950–2000

- Greater than 1000%
- 400–1000%
- 200–400%
- Less than 200%

Figure 6 *The population of some regions in Florida has grown more than 3,000% in the past 50 years.*

urban sprawl the unplanned growth of urban areas

Figure 7 *Florida cities, such as St. Petersburg, have grown rapidly. Careful planning has helped preserve green spaces and the environment.*

The Urban Landscape

As shown in **Figure 6,** Florida's population has grown rapidly in the past 50 years. The population of Florida has increased from about 3 million people in 1950 to almost 17 million people today. And every year, tourists temporarily triple Florida's population. All of these people have an effect on Florida's natural resources. For example, Florida's population is concentrated on land that was once part of the Everglades and in cities near Florida's shore, as shown in **Figure 7.** Development in these areas has had an enormous impact on Florida's natural resources.

Urban Sprawl

If you live in the outskirts of a major city, you are probably familiar with the effects of urban sprawl. **Urban sprawl** is the unplanned growth of urban areas. The effects of urban sprawl include an increasing number of roads, parking lots, and shopping areas. This construction covers vegetation and soil and limits the amount of water that can enter the soil. Thus, freshwater supplies are reduced, and more pollutants flow directly into surface water. Urban sprawl can also increase air pollution and reduce the area of land available to grow food.

There are positive effects of urban growth. Urban areas can use land efficiently because many people live in a small area. When many people live close together, the energy needed to provide products and services is reduced. However, urban planning is needed to ensure that the urban landscape is livable and that environmental problems are reduced.

Managing the Urban Landscape

Most cities are developing plans for managing how they will grow. Growing cities face the problem of how to maintain freshwater resources and how to dispose of waste. Florida's cities are also trying to conserve and protect green spaces, such as parks. Many urban-planning efforts focus on the goal of smart growth. Smart growth involves ensuring that housing is affordable, that urban sprawl is reduced, and that cities have thriving centers. The goal of smart growth is to create urban spaces that are livable and that have a minimal effect on the environment.

 D.2.3.1 understands that quality of life is relevant to personal experience.

 D.2.3.2 knows the positive and negative consequences of human action on the Earth's systems.

 G.2.3.4 AA understands that humans are a part of an ecosystem and their activities may deliberately or inadvertently alter the equilibrium in ecosystems.

Benchmark Check Describe two positive and two negative effects of urban growth in Florida. **D.2.3.1, D.2.3.2**

SECTION Review

Summary

- Florida's natural landscape includes woodland forests, dry prairies, wetlands, and beaches.
- Florida's agricultural landscape is used for farming, ranching, and forestry.
- Florida's urban landscape has expanded greatly in the past 50 years.
- The park system, sustainable agriculture, and urban planning are all ways to manage Florida's land resources.
- Agriculture provides many benefits for Florida's economy and people. The environmental problems of agriculture include pollution and water consumption. **D.2.3.2, G.2.3.4 AA**
- Urban areas should be managed to reduce air and water pollution and to reduce urban sprawl. **D.2.3.1**

Understanding Key Ideas

1. Describe the major land ecosystems of Florida, and provide an example of a plant or an animal that lives in each ecosystem.

2. Describe agricultural land use in Florida, and list some of the positive and negative effects of agriculture. **D.2.3.2, G.2.3.4 AA**

3. Define urban sprawl, and list some positive and negative effects of urban growth. **D.2.3.1, G.2.3.4 AA**

Critical Thinking

4. **Predicting Consequences** An average of about 6,000 people move to Florida each week. List several effects that population growth has on land use. **G.2.3.1 CS**

5. **Analyzing Relationships** How does Florida's environmental health relate to its economy? Describe three examples of this relationship.

6. **Predicting Consequences** The melaleuca tree was brought to Florida to drain the Everglades. Now, the melaleuca weevil is being introduced to control the tree. What are some possible consequences of this program?

FCAT Preparation

7. The flow of energy in most ecosystems is balanced between producers, such as plants, and consumers, such as animals. Which of the following is an example of humans altering the flow of energy in the Everglades ecosystem? **G.2.3.4 AA**

A. Citrus farms use agricultural chemicals to increase their harvests.

B. Cranes consume fish in wetland ecosystems.

C. Urban planning preserves green spaces.

D. Fertilizer runoff causes the excessive growth of invasive water plants.

SCiLINKS **NSTA**
Developed and maintained by the National Science Teachers Association

For a variety of links related to this chapter, go to www.scilinks.org

Topic: Florida's Environment
SciLinks code: HSMF06

Florida's Freshwater Resources

Did you know that about 54 inches of rain fall on the state of Florida every year? This rainfall equals 150 billion gallons of water every day! Where does all this water go?

Most of the water evaporates or flows into the ocean. The rest becomes part of Florida's freshwater resources. We use this fresh water for many purposes. In Florida, about 42% of fresh water is used for agriculture, and 8% is used to generate electrical energy. The rest is used for industry and for residential needs such as watering lawns and providing drinking water.

Groundwater

One of Florida's most valuable resources is the water found underground. Groundwater is stored in formations called aquifers. An **aquifer** is an underground layer of rock or sediment that allows water to flow through it. Aquifers provide nearly 90% of Florida's drinking water. The Floridan aquifer underlies most of Florida and parts of three other states. It is one of the largest aquifers in the world! As shown in **Figure 1,** water in aquifers can rise to the surface to form springs. Every day, nearly 9 billion gallons of water flow from more than 700 springs in Florida. Testing the water from springs can indicate whether the groundwater in an area is polluted.

READING WARM-UP

Objectives

- Describe Florida's freshwater resources.
- Describe three threats to Florida's freshwater resources. **D.2.3.2, G.2.3.1 CS**
- Describe four ways that Florida's freshwater resources are managed to meet human needs and to protect the environment. **D.2.3.2, G.2.3.4 AA**
- Explain the importance of the Everglades to Florida's environment.
- Describe the Comprehensive Everglades Restoration Plan. **D.2.3.2, G.2.3.4 AA, H.3.3.4 CS**

Terms to Learn

aquifer
watershed

READING STRATEGY

Paired Summarizing Read this section silently. In pairs, take turns summarizing the material. Stop to discuss ideas that seem confusing.

aquifer a body of rock or sediment that stores groundwater and allows the flow of groundwater

Figure 1 *At Fern Hammock Springs in Ocala National Forest, groundwater rises to the surface to form springs.*

Figure 2 *Sinkholes, like this one in Plant City, Florida, can form when groundwater is removed faster than it can be replaced.*

Wells and Groundwater

How do we access water that is underground? Groundwater is usually pumped to the surface from wells drilled in Earth's crust. Wells that are deep enough can provide groundwater that is free of pollutants. The reason is that groundwater is filtered and purified as it flows through the rock and sediment that make up an aquifer.

Threats to Florida's Groundwater

In Florida, the main threats to groundwater are overwithdrawal, saltwater intrusion, and pollution. *Overwithdrawal* occurs when water is removed from an aquifer faster than it can be replaced. In some places in Florida, the level of groundwater has sunk more than 60 ft (18 m). In extreme cases, part of the aquifer collapses and forms a sinkhole, as shown in **Figure 2.** Overwithdrawal can also cause springs and streams to dry up.

Overwithdrawal in coastal aquifers can cause ocean water to flow into the aquifer. When fresh water is withdrawn too quickly, salt water flows into the aquifer and can pollute the groundwater. This process is called *saltwater intrusion.* Nearly 80% of Floridians live near the coast, and the increasing demand for groundwater has caused saltwater intrusion in many aquifers. Pollutants from the surface are another threat to groundwater. Once groundwater becomes polluted, it is very difficult to clean up. Major sources of groundwater pollution include agricultural and lawn-care chemicals and leaking underground fuel tanks.

Benchmark Check Describe three threats to the groundwater resources of Florida. **D.2.3.2, G.2.3.1 CS**

Quick Lab

Making an Aquifer Filter

1. Carefully cut off the bottom of an **empty 2 L soda bottle.**

2. Poke small holes in the **bottle's cap,** and screw the cap on.

3. Turn the bottle upside down, and add layers of **sand** and **gravel** until the bottle is 3/4 full. Add a layer of **potting soil** to fill the rest of the bottle.

4. Hold the bottle over a **500 mL beaker.**

5. Your teacher will provide several **water samples.** Pour the first sample into the bottle. Observe the water that comes out.

6. Repeat step 5, using each of the remaining samples.

7. Did the aquifer filter all of the samples? Explain.

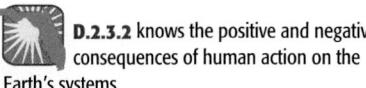**D.2.3.2** knows the positive and negative consequences of human action on the Earth's systems.

G.2.3.1 CS knows that some resources are renewable and others are nonrenewable.

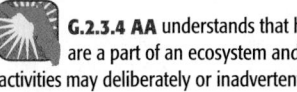**G.2.3.4 AA** understands that humans are a part of an ecosystem and their activities may deliberately or inadvertently alter the equilibrium in ecosystems.

Surface Water

Surface water is found in lakes, rivers, and springs. Florida has more than 50,000 miles of rivers and streams, some of which are shown in **Figure 3.** Florida also has more than 7,800 lakes. Lakes and rivers support complex food webs and provide habitat for many endangered species. Lakes and rivers are also an important source of drinking water, and they generate millions of dollars for Florida's fishing industry.

Surface water is found in areas of land that are called watersheds. A **watershed** is an area of land that is drained by a river system. Any human activity in a watershed can affect the surface water.

watershed the area of land that is drained by a river system

Threats to Florida's Surface Water

Any pollution in a watershed can affect the body of water into which the watershed drains. Pollutants can enter a watershed when runoff from roads, parking lots, and farms flows into rivers and lakes. Overuse of water also affects watersheds. In Florida, large amounts of surface water are used for agriculture. Diverting too much water from lakes and rivers can affect the organisms that depend on these water sources.

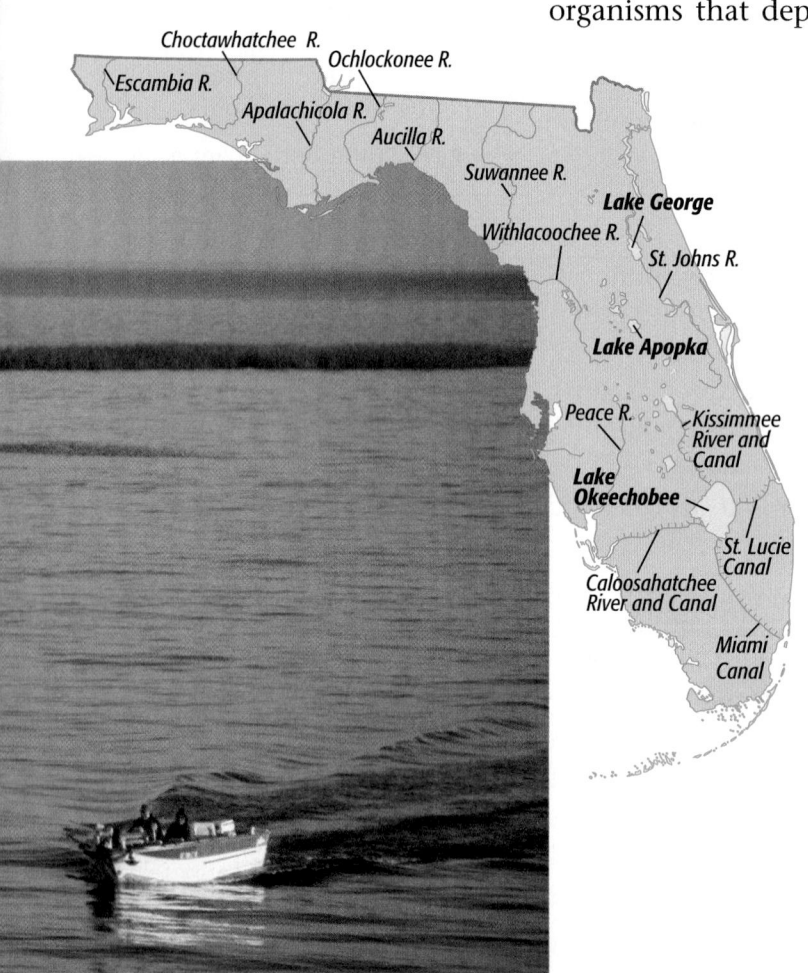

Figure 3 *Florida's surface water includes rivers, lakes, and springs. The St. Johns River is Florida's largest river, and Lake Okeechobee* (shown below) *is Florida's largest lake.*

Choctawhatchee R.
Escambia R.
Ochlockonee R.
Apalachicola R.
Aucilla R.
Suwannee R.
Lake George
Withlacoochee R.
St. Johns R.
Lake Apopka
Peace R.
Kissimmee River and Canal
Lake Okeechobee
St. Lucie Canal
Caloosahatchee River and Canal
Miami Canal

Managing Florida's Freshwater Resources

Florida has the highest water consumption per person in the United States, so all Floridians need to help protect Florida's fresh water. Several successful conservation programs help cities, golf courses, and homeowners in Florida use reclaimed water. *Reclaimed water* is wastewater that has been treated so that it is safe for watering lawns but not for drinking.

Another way that individuals can take steps to conserve water is to reduce water use. For example, more than 50% of water used in homes is used to water lawns. Planting native plants that require less water is a great way to conserve water. Also, if you water your lawn, do it in the evening so that less water evaporates. You can reduce water pollution by limiting the use of lawn chemicals and by reducing litter and other types of pollution in your watershed.

Figure 4 *The Everglades are formed by a shallow, slow-moving sheet of water that is as much as 50 mi (80 km) wide.*

The Everglades

The Florida Everglades, shown in **Figure 4,** are formed by an enormous, slow-moving sheet of water that flows south from Lake Okeechobee to the ocean. The Everglades are called the *River of Grass* because water flows slowly through large areas of native grasses such as saw grass. A system of connected rivers, lakes, and wetlands makes up the Everglades. The letters *KOE* can help you remember the main features of the Everglades system. KOE stands for the **Kissimmee River, Lake Okeechobee,** and the **Everglades wetlands.** The Everglades wetlands include Everglades National Park and Big Cypress Preserve.

History of the Everglades

For hundreds of years, the Everglades were considered too inhospitable for human settlement. In fact, until the 1950s, most of Central and South Florida was simply too wet for people to live in. In the 1950s, the Central and Southern Florida Project (CSFP) was started. This project was designed to control flooding in South Florida. The Army Corps of Engineers and the South Florida Water Management District created more than 1,000 miles of canals, levees, locks, and dams to change the flow of water in the Everglades. As a result, large areas of the Everglades became available for agriculture and development. Today, the Everglades are half the size they were before the CSFP began, and the environmental effects of the project are becoming clear. Efforts to restore the Everglades must be balanced with the needs of people living near this delicate, endangered ecosystem.

Benchmark Check How did the CSFP change Central and South Florida? **D.2.3.2, G.2.3.4 AA**

D.1.3.3 CS knows how conditions that exist in one system influence the conditions that exist in other systems.

D.2.3.2 knows the positive and negative consequences of human action on the Earth's systems.

G.2.3.4 AA understands that humans are a part of an ecosystem and their activities may deliberately or inadvertently alter the equilibrium in ecosystems.

The Importance of the Everglades

The Everglades system is important to Florida in many ways. It is a habitat for many unique plants and animals, and it functions as one of the largest water filters in the world. The Everglades are also a major storehouse of fresh water.

A Unique Habitat

The saw grass prairies, cypress swamps, and coastal lagoons and bays of the Everglades are home to a diversity of life. Nearly 50 mammal species and more than 350 bird species inhabit the Everglades. Alligators, wading birds, ducks, shore birds, bald eagles, ospreys, turtles, snakes, fishes, and insects are a few of the diverse animals that live in the Everglades. But the habitat that these animals live in changes throughout the year. The Everglades have a wet season in summer and a dry season in winter. The plants and animals that live in the Everglades are adapted to these cycles. In the dry season, thousands of migrating birds from different countries arrive in the Everglades and gather near water sources alongside native animals. During the wet season, which is shown in **Figure 5,** the water sources expand and animals move throughout the Everglades.

Filtering and Storing Water

The Everglades filter and store water. As water travels through the Everglades, it is filtered by the plants and soil. The slow movement of water through the River of Grass helps remove pollutants before they enter an aquifer or the ocean. The Everglades are one of the largest storehouses of surface water in Florida. During the wet season, the Everglades can limit flooding by storing excess surface water. During the dry season, fresh water is stored in the aquifers beneath the Everglades.

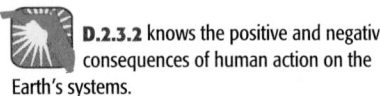

D.2.3.2 knows the positive and negative consequences of human action on the Earth's systems.

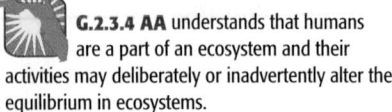

G.2.3.4 AA understands that humans are a part of an ecosystem and their activities may deliberately or inadvertently alter the equilibrium in ecosystems.

Figure 5 *Wading birds, such as this egret, hunt fish in the cypress swamps of the Everglades.*

Human Impact on the Everglades

People have changed the Everglades system in many ways. Two major effects of human activities in the Everglades are habitat change and pollution.

Habitat Change

Housing developments such as the one shown in **Figure 6** have created an imbalance in the Everglades system. Changing the water flow of the Everglades to allow development has resulted in the loss of habitat for many plants and animals. Now, 90% of the wading birds that once lived in the Everglades have disappeared. Developing the Everglades has also reduced the ability of the system to filter and store water. To balance the effects of development, developers are often required to construct wetlands to compensate for wetland areas that they have developed.

Pollution

Agricultural chemicals are a major source of pollution in the Everglades system. In many areas, large populations of cattails have replaced native saw grass. Cattails thrive in water that is polluted by phosphates from fertilizer. Lake Okeechobee is also threatened by high levels of phosphates. These pollutants cause the widespread growth of invasive plants. When the plants die, they use up much of the oxygen in the water. As the oxygen in the water decreases, fish and other animals can be killed.

Mercury is another pollutant that affects the Everglades. Even small levels of mercury are toxic to animals, including humans. In the 1980s, researchers found very high levels of mercury in fish and birds in the Everglades. Incinerators that burn trash were identified as a major source of this pollutant. Mercury levels decreased significantly after incinerators were required to install scrubbers on smokestacks. *Scrubbers* filter the incinerator smoke to remove mercury. In 2003, a study showed that the use of scrubbers had lowered mercury levels in wading birds by 70% in 10 years. Despite this success, scientists continue to monitor mercury in the Everglades.

Benchmark Check How have human activities altered the equilibrium of the Everglades? D.2.3.2, C.2.3.4 AA

Figure 6 *Housing developments such as this one were built on land reclaimed from the Everglades.*

Habitat Destruction Write a public service annoucement about the effects of habitat destruction. Go to **go.hrw.com,** and type in the keyword **HL5ENVW.**

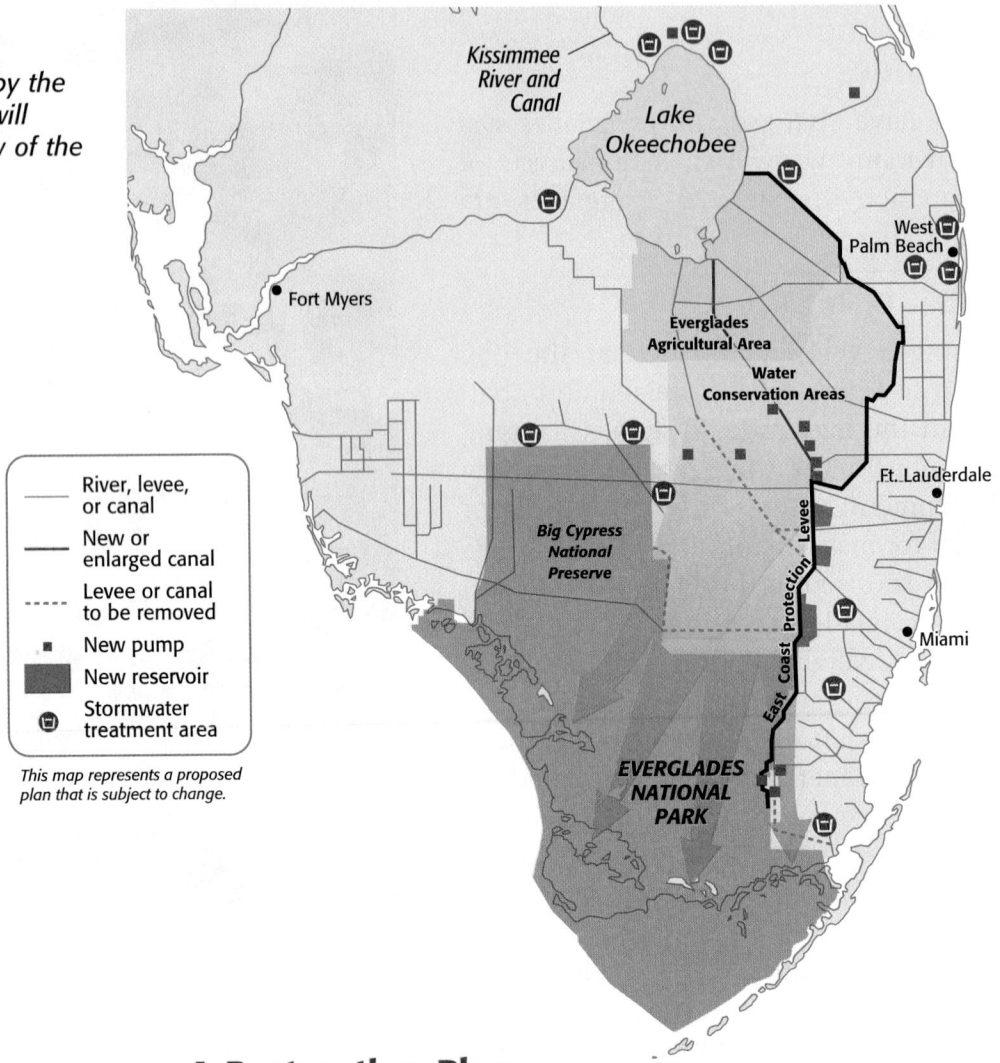

Figure 7 *As indicated by the blue arrows, the CERP will partially restore the flow of the Everglades system.*

Kissimmee River and Canal

Lake Okeechobee

Fort Myers

West Palm Beach

Everglades Agricultural Area

Water Conservation Areas

Ft. Lauderdale

Big Cypress National Preserve

East Coast Protection Levee

Miami

EVERGLADES NATIONAL PARK

River, levee, or canal

New or enlarged canal

Levee or canal to be removed

New pump

New reservoir

Stormwater treatment area

This map represents a proposed plan that is subject to change.

A Restoration Plan

The Comprehensive Everglades Restoration Plan (CERP), which is shown in **Figure 7,** is a large-scale plan to protect the Everglades. The plan began in 2000 and will take 30 years to complete. The goals of the plan are to partially restore the flow of the Everglades; to store water for cities, agriculture, and industry; and to control flooding.

Achieving all of the goals of the CERP will be a challenge because the needs of agriculture, cities, and the Everglades ecosystem are often in conflict. The plan will use storage reservoirs, wells, and artificial wetlands to store and filter some of the water that now flows out of the Everglades system into the ocean. This water will be redirected to farms, cities, and the Everglades at different times of the year.

Many of the CERP projects rely on untested technology, such as underground barriers to redirect groundwater and wells that pump surface water into aquifers. Some scientists have questioned whether the plan will restore the Everglades or will further harm the ecosystem. The CERP will continue to be revised with input from scientists, agencies, and the public.

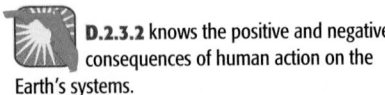

D.2.3.2 knows the positive and negative consequences of human action on the Earth's systems.

G.2.3.4 AA understands that humans are a part of an ecosystem and their activities may deliberately or inadvertently alter the equilibrium in ecosystems.

H.3.3.4 CS knows that technological design should require taking into account constraints such as natural laws, the properties of the materials used, and economic, political, social, ethical, and aesthetic values.

SECTION Review

Summary

- The major freshwater resources of Florida include rivers, lakes, and aquifers. The largest river in Florida is the St. Johns River, and the largest lake is Lake Okeechobee. The largest aquifer in Florida is the Floridan aquifer.

- The threats to Florida's freshwater resources include overwithdrawal, saltwater intrusion, and pollution. **D.2.3.2, G.2.3.1 CS**

- Florida's freshwater resources are managed to meet human needs and to protect the environment. **D.2.3.2, G.2.3.4 AA**

- The Everglades system includes the Kissimmee River, Lake Okeechobee, and the Everglades wetlands. Conditions in one system can affect the other systems. **D.1.3.3 CS**

- The Everglades are important because they are a habitat for unique plants and animals and because they store and filter fresh water.

- The CERP is a 30-year plan designed to restore part of the natural flow of the Everglades and to provide water to cities, farms, and industries. **D.2.3.2, G.2.3.4 AA, H.3.3.4 CS**

Understanding Key Ideas

1. Describe Florida's major freshwater resources. How does each resource benefit you?

2. Explain the threats to Florida's freshwater resources. Describe an example of how you can reduce each threat. **D.2.3.2, G.2.3.1 CS**

3. Outline the path taken by water as it flows through the Everglades system. How can conditions in one part of the Everglades system affect another part of the Everglades system? **D.1.3.3 CS**

4. What is a watershed? How does pollution in a watershed affect freshwater resources? **D.2.3.2**

5. How can excess phosphates be harmful to some organisms and helpful to other organisms? **D.2.3.2, G.2.3.4 AA**

Critical Thinking

6. **Analyzing Relationships** What does the presence of large populations of cattails in the Everglades indicate? **D.2.3.2, G.2.3.4 AA**

7. **Identifying Relationships** Describe the CERP, and identify three different values that affect the technological design of the project. **H.3.3.4 CS**

8. **Predicting Consequences** Describe some positive and negative effects of restoring the Everglades to a more natural state. **D.2.3.2, G.2.3.4 AA**

9. **Expressing Opinions** Are human needs always in conflict with the environment? Defend your opinion by using examples from this section.

FCAT Preparation

10. The Comprehensive Everglades Restoration Plan is designed to partially restore the flow of the Everglades and to provide water for farms and cities. Which of the following is an example of a natural constraint that affects the plan? **H.3.3.4 CS**

   A. A limited amount of fresh water is available in the Everglades system.

   B. Cities must implement water conservation plans to reduce their water consumption.

   C. Farms must use reclaimed water to reduce their water consumption.

   D. Implementing the project could protect communities from flooding.

11. A system of canals and levees redirected the flow of the Everglades. Explain how this is an example of how humans can alter the equilibrium in an ecosystem. **G.2.3.4 AA**

For a variety of links related to this chapter, go to www.scilinks.org

Topic: Florida's Freshwater
SciLinks code: HSMF07

Florida's Ocean Resources

Wherever you live in Florida, you are no more than 70 miles from the ocean. Floridians and millions of visitors every year depend on Florida's ocean resources for food, recreation, and other benefits.

Florida's coastal waters are home to a diversity of plants and animals. It is critical that we conserve these areas for their natural beauty, for their ecological importance, for the protection they offer against storms, and for Florida's economy.

Florida's Coastal and Marine Habitats

Florida's coastal and marine habitats include estuaries, beaches, mangroves, salt marshes, sea-grass meadows, and coral reefs. Some of these unique habitats are shown in **Figure 1.**

Estuaries

An **estuary** is a place where fresh water mixes with ocean water. Estuaries are called *the cradle of the ocean* because they are a nursery for many young fish, invertebrates, and mammals. In other words, many animals grow and develop in the protection of estuaries. When these animals grow larger, many will live in saltier ocean waters. More than 95% of Florida's recreationally and commercially important fish, crustaceans, and shellfish spend part of their lives in estuaries.

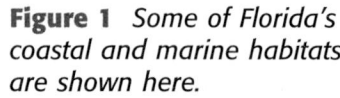 **Reading Check** Why are estuaries called *the cradle of the ocean*?

Figure 1 *Some of Florida's coastal and marine habitats are shown here.*

Mangroves ▶ are found along Florida's southern coastline.

◀ **Seagrass meadows** are found in Florida's bays, lagoons, and coastal waters.

Mangroves

Mangroves are trees that grow in environments that are flooded by tides. These trees provide habitat for fish, crustaceans, shellfish, and birds. People who live near the coastline benefit from mangroves because the trees remove pollutants, maintain water quality, and reduce erosion. Mangroves also protect homes from storm winds, waves, and floods.

Salt Marshes

Salt marshes are grassy coastal wetlands that are found in the zone between low and high tides. Salt marshes are nurseries for fish and shellfish and are habitat for shorebirds. Salt-marsh plants also prevent pollutants from entering estuary waters.

Sea-Grass Meadows

Sea-grass meadows are dense groups of flowering aquatic plants that grow in estuaries and bays. Manatees, green sea turtles, crabs, fish, skates, rays, and scallops live in sea-grass meadows. Sea grasses also improve water quality by trapping sediments and reducing erosion.

Coral Reefs

Coral reefs are unique habitats formed by tiny organisms that build rock like gardens underwater. Coral reefs are some of the most diverse ecosystems on Earth. Many specialized plants and animals are found only in coral-reef habitats. Because coral reefs are diverse habitats, they contribute greatly to Florida's tourism and fishing economy. Coral reefs also provide storm protection and help form sandy beaches.

estuary an area where fresh water mixes with salt water from the ocean

▼ **Coral reefs** are found off Florida's southern coast and in the Gulf of Mexico.

▼ **Salt marshes** are usually found upstream of estuaries or behind barrier islands.

Figure 2 *Some shrimp trawlers drag weighted nets across the sea floor to catch bottom-dwelling shrimp. Scientists are working to change this practice because it can destroy coral reefs.*

fishery an area of water that is managed to harvest commercially valuable fish and shellfish

Figure 3 *Turtle Excluder Devices help prevent endangered sea turtles from being caught in commercial fishing nets.*

Managing Ocean Resources

The diversity of Florida's marine habitats supports some of the world's most productive fisheries. **Fisheries** are areas of water that are managed to harvest commercially valuable fish and shellfish. Red drum, snapper, jack, tarpon, snook, sheepshead, mullet, oysters, and crabs are harvested in Florida's fisheries. Shrimp, which mature in Florida's coastal mangrove and sea-grass habitats, are another valuable ocean resource. Shrimp are harvested by trawlers such as the one shown in **Figure 2.** Managing fisheries in Florida involves balancing the needs of the commercial and recreational fishing industry while maintaining fish populations. To achieve this balance, fisheries management must consider the environmental problems of overfishing, habitat loss, and pollution.

Overfishing and Bycatch

Overfishing happens when fish or shellfish are harvested at a greater rate than the population is replaced by reproduction. Some of the species most vulnerable to overfishing are shark, red drum, snapper, grouper, and mackerel. To avoid overfishing, commercial fishing regulations restrict the size and number of fish of a particular species that can be caught.

Bycatch is another problem that the fishing industry is working to reduce. Bycatch refers to organisms that are accidentally caught in fishing boats. For example, sea turtles are often caught by fishing nets because they live in habitats where commercially valuable fish and shellfish are harvested. To avoid catching turtles, shrimp nets are fitted with Turtle Excluder Devices (TEDs), as shown in **Figure 3.**

Benchmark Check Describe two positive and two negative effects of human action on Florida's marine resources. D.2.3.2, G.2.3.4 AA

Habitat Loss

Although you may not think that activities on land affect the ocean, coastal development and urbanization are major causes of the loss of coastal and marine habitats. Coastal habitats are destroyed by the construction of sea walls and dredge-and-fill construction to create waterfront property. Dredge-and-fill construction involves digging sediment and rock from the ocean floor and using these materials to expand waterfront property. Sediments stirred up by these activities prevent sunlight, nutrients, and clean water from nourishing plants at the bottom of marine food webs.

The loss of mangrove, seagrass, salt marsh, and coral-reef habitats greatly affects Florida's economy. Many Florida estuaries have lost 80% of sea-grass habitat. As a result, the number of fish and shellfish that breed in this habitat has declined. Habitat loss also affects migratory shorebirds that rely on salt marshes and mangroves for food. Fishing practices such as bottom trawling, in which weighted nets are dragged across the ocean floor, are another cause of habitat loss. Although much habitat loss is due to human activities, natural events such as hurricanes also cause habitat loss.

Ocean Pollution

Pollution is another threat to Florida's ocean resources. About 80% of the pollutants in the oceans comes from activities on land. Pollutants from farms, roads, and lawns can wash into the ocean through rivers and storm drains. These pollutants can cause harmful algal blooms, or "red tides"; low oxygen areas, or "dead zones"; fish kills and the loss of sea grasses and coral reefs. Another source of ocean pollution is litter. Litter that ends up in the ocean can entangle and kill marine organisms, as shown in **Figure 4.**

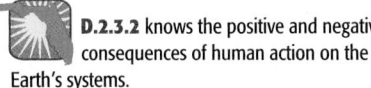

CONNECTION TO Environmental Science

Cruise-Ship Discharges

WRITING SKILL Thousands of cruise ships pass through Florida's waters every year. These ships can contain as many as 5,000 people—the population of a small town! Not surprisingly, cruise ships also generate as much waste as a small town. Much of this waste is dumped directly into the ocean. Find out about the effects of cruise-ship discharges on the environment, and report on how this practice is regulated.

D.2.3.2 knows the positive and negative consequences of human action on the Earth's systems.

G.2.3.1 CS knows that some resources are renewable and others are nonrenewable.

G.2.3.4 AA understands that humans are a part of an ecosystem and their activities may deliberately or inadvertently alter the equilibrium in ecosystems.

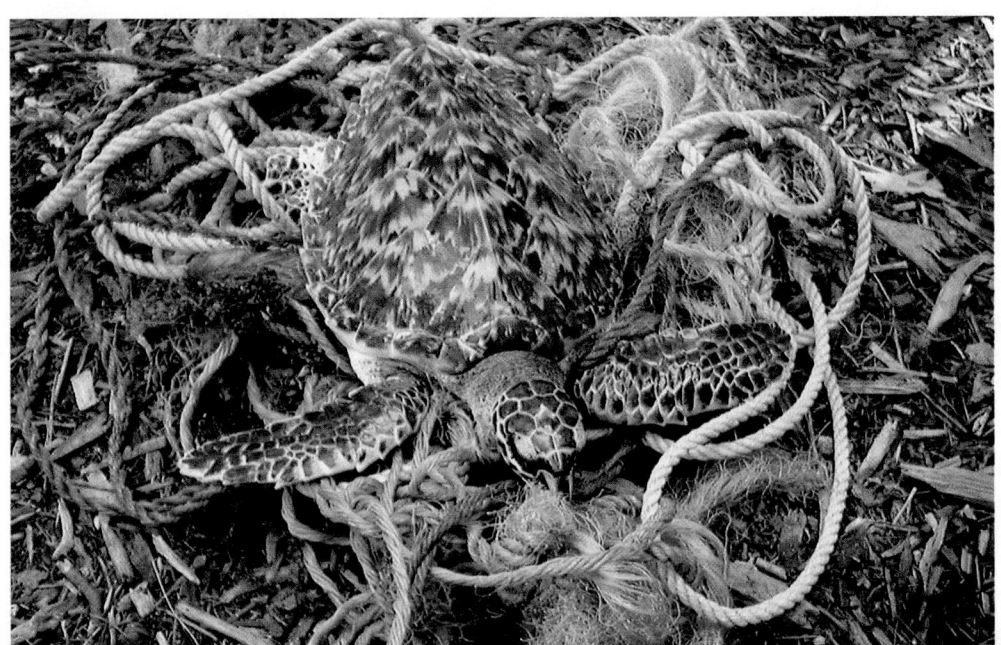

Figure 4 *Plastic waste is very dangerous for marine animals because it breaks down very slowly and can be mistaken for food. This turtle became entangled in discarded plastic rope.*

401

Figure 5 *These students in Miami are helping scientists gather green sea turtle eggs so that they can be incubated in a safe environment.*

Protecting Our Oceans

The choices that you make today will affect Florida's marine environment for years to come. There are many ways that you can help protect the oceans. For example, **Figure 5** shows some Miami students who volunteered to help protect sea turtles. Find out more about similar conservation efforts, such as Tampa Bay Watch, the Center for Marine Conservation, and the Adopt a Manatee Club. The Florida Fish and Wildlife Conservation Commission can also help you find out ways to help protect ocean resources.

Being an Environmentally Aware Consumer

One of the most important ways you can help protect Florida's marine environment is to make environmentally friendly choices when you shop. If you eat fish or shellfish, find out which species are threatened and which are harvested sustainably. Also, be aware that it is illegal to buy or sell most species of coral. There is also a thriving illegal trade in coral-reef fish. If you are shopping for aquarium fish, be sure to ask where the fish came from.

Restoring Habitat

Habitat restoration involves rebuilding habitat for native plants and animals. Find out about a habitat restoration project in your area. Habitat restoration can include planting sea oats on beaches, planting salt grass in wetland areas, or removing invasive species. Artificial reefs, made using "reef balls" or abandoned machinery, provides habitat for coral-reef organisms. Scientists are also researching habitat restoration for sea-grass meadows, oyster beds, salt marshes, and mangroves.

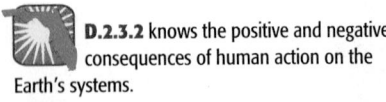

D.2.3.2 knows the positive and negative consequences of human action on the Earth's systems.

G.2.3.4 AA understands that humans are a part of an ecosystem and their activities may deliberately or inadvertently alter the equilibrium in ecosystems.

Reducing Pollution

One way to reduce pollution is to participate in International Coastal Cleanup Day. During Florida Coastal Cleanups, more than 250 tons of trash are collected every year. Carefully disposing of trash is an even better way to reduce pollution. For example, you should never discard fishing line in or near a body of water because it can kill or injure birds, marine mammals, turtles, and fish. Also, recreational activities such as boating can pollute the ocean. The Clean Boatyard Program reduces ocean pollution by helping people identify and use marinas that have adopted environmentally friendly practices.

Benchmark Check Identify three ways that you can help protect Florida's marine environment. **D.2.3.2, G.2.3.4 AA**

SCHOOL to HOME

Sustainable Seafood Guide

Many of the world's fish populations are threatened by habitat loss, pollution, and overfishing. Research the threats to fish populations. Find out which commercially available fish are most threatened. Then, work with a family member to create an illustrated sustainable seafood guide. **ACTIVITY**

SECTION Review

Summary

- Florida's coastal habitats include estuaries, beaches, mangroves, salt marshes, sea-grass meadows, and coral reefs.

- Florida's ocean resources provide food, reduce pollution and erosion, and provide habitat for many plants and animals. **G.2.3.1 CS**

- Fisheries are areas of water in which commercially valuable fish and shellfish are managed.

- Human activity has caused overfishing, habitat loss, and pollution in the ocean. **D.2.3.2, G.2.3.4 AA**

- Three ways to protect ocean resources are making environmentally aware purchases, restoring habitat, and reducing pollution. **D.2.3.2**

Understanding Key Ideas

1. Describe Florida's coastal habitats, and explain the benefits these habitats provide.

2. Describe three ways that human activities have affected the oceans. **D.2.3.2, G.2.3.4 AA**

3. Describe three solutions to the problems that threaten Florida's ocean resources. **D.2.3.2, G.2.3.1 CS**

4. Why are estuaries an important habitat?

5. How does habitat loss threaten marine resources? **D.2.3.2, G.2.3.4 AA**

Critical Thinking

6. **Analyzing Relationships** Why would the destruction of mangrove habitat affect people who live near the coast?

7. **Evaluating Assumptions** Evaluate the following statement: "Most pollution in the ocean comes from ships." **D.2.3.2**

8. **Analyzing Relationships** Many of the top predators in ocean food webs are threatened by overfishing. Why are these fish more endangered than other fish? **G.2.3.4 AA**

FCAT Preparation

9. "Dead zones" are areas of the ocean that contain high levels of agricultural pollutants, such as phosphates. These pollutants lead to the overgrowth of plankton, which use up oxygen in the water when they die. Very little life is found in dead zones. Which of the following best describes the formation of dead zones? **G.2.3.4 AA**

A. They are caused by red tides.

B. They are deliberately caused by human action.

C. They are inadvertently caused by human action.

D. They are caused by a lack of nutrients including phosphates.

SCILINKS

NSTA

Developed and maintained by the National Science Teachers Association

For a variety of links related to this chapter, go to www.scilinks.org

Topic: Florida's Coasts
SciLinks code: HSMF05

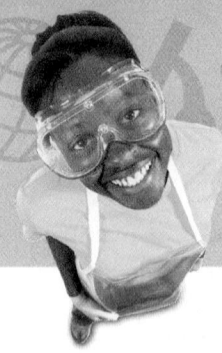

Skills Practice Lab

What's in an Ecosystem?

How well do you know the environment around your home or school? You may walk through it every day without noticing most of the living things it contains or thinking about how they survive. In this lab, you will play the role of an ecologist by closely observing part of your environment.

Procedure

1 Use a tape measure or meterstick to measure a 3 m X 3 m site to study. Place one stake at each corner of the site. Loop the string around each stake, and run the string from one stake to the next to form boundaries for the site.

2 Survey the site, and then prepare a site map of the physical features of the area on the poster board. For example, show the location of streams, sidewalks, trails, or large rocks, and indicate the direction of any noticeable slope.

3 Create a set of symbols to represent the organisms at your site. For example, you might use green triangles to represent trees, blue circles to represent insects, and brown squares to represent animal burrows or nests. At the bottom or side of the poster board, make a key for your symbols.

4 Draw your symbols on the map to show the location and relative abundance of each type of organism. In your notebook, describe the kinds of plants and animals you observed.

5 Record any observations of organisms in their environment. For example, note insects feeding on plants. Also, describe the following physical characteristics of your study area:

a. **Sunlight Exposure** How much of the area is exposed to sunlight?

b. **Soil** Is the soil mostly sand, silt, clay, or organic matter?

c. **Rain** When was the last rain recorded for this area? How much rain was received?

d. **Water Drainage** Is the area well drained?

e. **Vegetation Cover** How much of the soil is covered with vegetation?

6 After completing these observations, identify a 1 m X 1 m area that you would like to study in more detail. Stake out this area, and wrap the string around the stakes.

7 Use your hand lens to inspect the area, and record the insects you see. Be careful not to disturb the soil or the organisms. Then, record the types of insects and plants you see.

8 Collect a small sample of soil, and observe it with your hand lens. Record a description of the soil and the organisms that live in it.

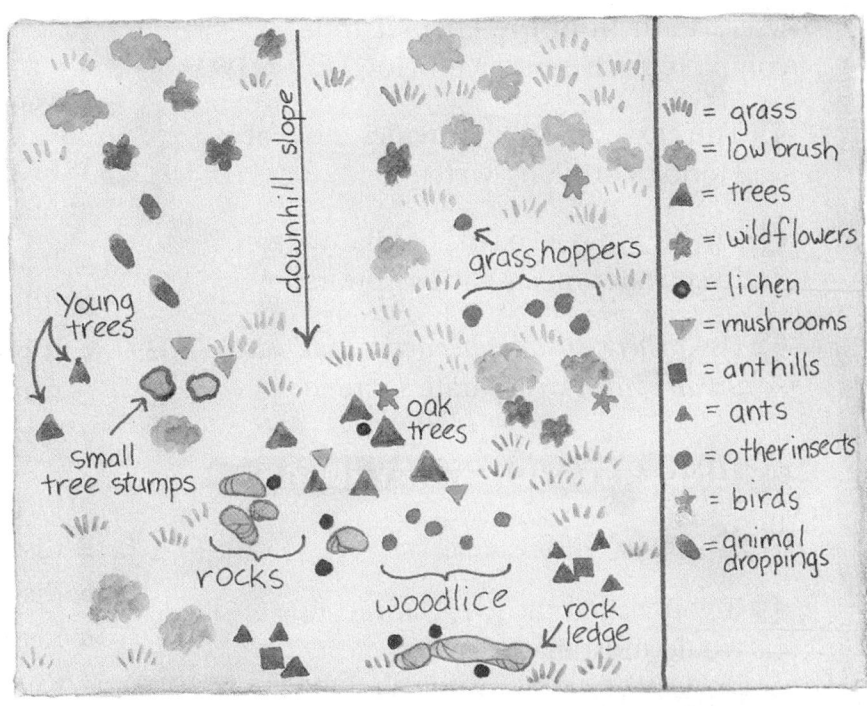

Analyze the Results

1 **Analyzing Data** Write one paragraph that describes the 3 m X 3 m site you studied.

2 **Analyzing Data** Describe the 1 m X 1 m site you studied. Is this site characteristic of the larger site?

Draw Conclusions

3 **Interpreting Conclusions** What are the differences between the areas that your classmates studied? Do different plants and animals live in different areas?

4 **Making Predictions** As the seasons change, the types of organisms that live in the area you studied may also change. Predict how your area might change in a different season or if a fire or flood occurred. If possible, return to the site at different times throughout the year, and record your observations.

Chapter Review

USING KEY TERMS

Use a term from the chapter to complete each sentence below.

1 The Floridan _____ provides most of Florida's drinking water.

2 A(n) _____ is a coastal habitat where fresh water mixes with salt water.

3 Use *fishery, sustainable agriculture,* and *urban sprawl* in separate sentences.

UNDERSTANDING KEY IDEAS

Multiple Choice

4 If you visited the Everglades, you would most likely see

a. dense forests of pine trees.

b. a sparsely vegetated area.

c. dense marsh grasses.

d. a treeless prairie.

5 Humans can deliberately or inadvertently alter the equilibrium in an ecosystem. Which of the following is an example of humans deliberately altering an ecosystem? **G.2.3.1 CS, G.2.3.4 AA** *FCAT*

a. Marine species are overfished.

b. Litter harms marine mammals.

c. Agricultural pollutants cause the excessive growth of algae.

d. Citrus groves are planted in a woodland ecosystem.

6 Groundwater rises to the surface to form

a. springs.　　c. estuaries.

b. reservoirs.　　d. aquifers.

7 In which year did the Comprehensive Everglades Restoration Plan begin?

a. 1950　　c. 2000

b. 1998　　d. 2003

8 Which of the following statements about groundwater is true?

a. It stays underground for a few days.

b. It is salty like ocean water.

c. It is difficult to clean pollutants from it.

d. It never reenters the water cycle.

9 What do the letters *KOE* represent?

a. Kissimmee, Ocean, Everglades

b. Kissimmee, Ochlockonee, Escambia

c. Kissimmee, Okeechobee, Everglades

d. Kissimmee, Ocean, Estuary

10 Florida's environment is composed of many systems. Conditions in one system can affect another system. If the Kissimmee River floods, how could it affect the Everglades? **D.1.3.3 CS** *FCAT*

a. The Everglades could experience saltwater intrusion.

b. The floodwaters will enter the Everglades.

c. Water in the Everglades will be overwithdrawn.

d. The Everglades will experience a drought.

11 Which of the following is an environmental problem that affects fresh water in Florida? **D.2.3.2, G.2.3.1 CS, G.2.3.4 AA**

a. the destruction of coral-reef habitat

b. overwithdrawal

c. underwithdrawal

d. the melaleuca weevil

Short Answer

12 Describe Florida's coastal and marine habitats.

13 How does pollution in a watershed enter groundwater? **D.2.3.2, G.2.3.4 AA** *FCAT*

14 Why does overwithdrawal cause the formation of sinkholes? **D.2.3.2, G.2.3.1 CS**

15 Explain how human population growth affects water resources. **D.2.3.2, G.2.3.1 CS**

16 What is the difference between urban growth and urban sprawl?

CRITICAL THINKING

Extended Response

17 **Applying Concepts** In which ecosystem is ranching mostly practiced? In which ecosystem is forestry mostly practiced?

18 **Making Inferences** Why do many marine animals live in estuaries when they are young?

19 **Analyzing Relationships** How is the environmental health of coastal ecosystems related to fisheries?

20 **Analyzing Ideas** Describe four ecological communities found in Florida's landscape. Give an example of how humans use land resources in each ecological community. **D.2.3.2, G.2.3.4 AA** *FCAT*

21 **Making Inferences** How does watering a lawn in the evening reduce water consumption? **D.2.3.2, G.2.3.1 CS**

Concept Mapping

22 Use the following terms to create a concept map: *estuary, mangrove, sea grass, salt marsh,* and *fishery*.

INTERPRETING GRAPHICS

The map below shows daily water use in Florida's five water management districts. Use the map to answer the questions that follow.

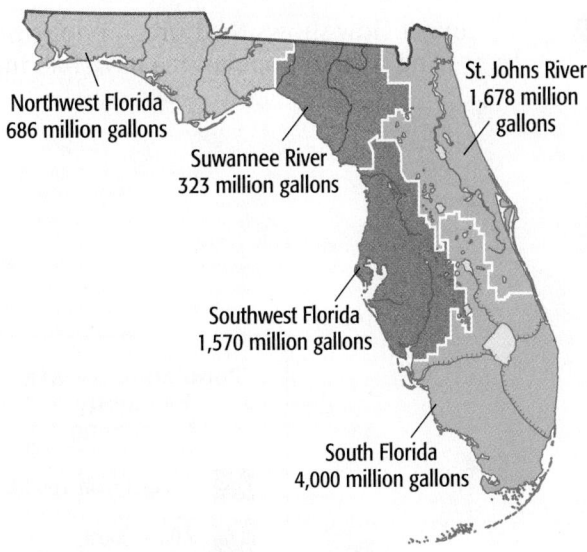

Northwest Florida
686 million gallons

St. Johns River
1,678 million gallons

Suwannee River
323 million gallons

Southwest Florida
1,570 million gallons

South Florida
4,000 million gallons

23 Make a bar graph that compares water use in each water management district.

24 What is Florida's total daily water use?

25 What percentage of Florida's total daily water use is South Florida responsible for?

26 What factors could explain the high levels of water use in South Florida?

27 If Florida's population is 17 million people, how many gallons of water are used per person in Florida every day?

Standardized Test Preparation

For the following questions, write your answers on a separate sheet of paper.

1 Two of the goals of the Comprehensive Everglades Restoration Plan (CERP) are to restore part of the Everglades ecosystem and to supply water to South Florida. The plan calls for water to be stored in reservoirs, wells, and artificial wetlands. The stored water will be redirected to farms, cities, and the Everglades. Which of the following is a concern about the CERP?

A. It will cause sinkholes to form.

B. It will cause widespread flooding.

C. Many of the projects in the plan rely on untested technology.

D. The plan only addresses the environmental problems in the Everglades.

2 The map below shows the human population increase in regions of Florida since 1950. Increasing human populations have had many effects on Florida's environment.

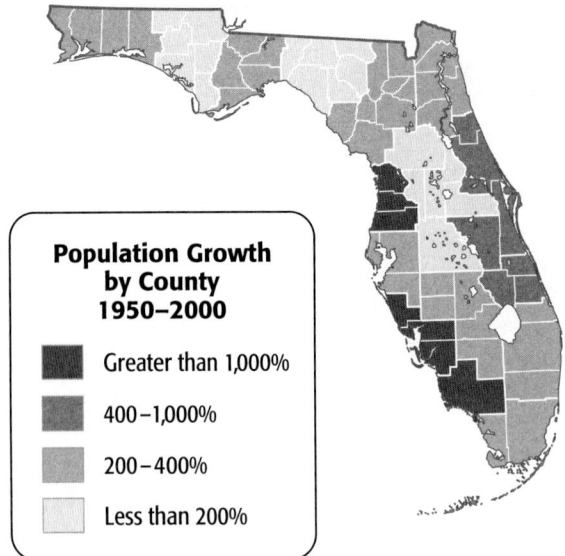

Population Growth by County 1950–2000

- Greater than 1,000%
- 400–1,000%
- 200–400%
- Less than 200%

How many counties have experienced a population increase of 400% or greater?

F. 3

G. 7

H. 14

I. 18

3 Florida is one of the leading agricultural producers in the United States. One of Florida's main crops is citrus fruit—there are about 107 million citrus trees in Florida. Farming provides many important benefits, but there are also environmental effects of farming.

Part A Describe two ways in which farming affects the environment.

Part B How can agricultural chemicals change the balance of Florida's ecosystems?

4 Florida has the highest water consumption rate per person in the United States. Which of the following are the main reasons that Florida has a high level of water consumption?

A. forestry

B. agriculture and fishing

C. the park system and melaleuca trees

D. agriculture and the size of Florida's population

5 Coastal development is a major cause of coastal and marine habitat loss. Dredge-and-fill construction removes sediment and rock from the ocean floor. This material is used to expand waterfront land. How can dredge-and-fill construction disrupt coastal habitats?

F. Pollution from building materials kills many plants and animals.

G. Stirred up sediments allow too much sunlight, nutrients, and water into coastal habitats.

H. Competition from new species drives organisms out of their coastal habitat and into the open ocean.

I. Stirred up sediments prevent sunlight, nutrients, and clean water from nourishing the plants in coastal habitats.

6  The construction of housing developments on land that was once part of the Everglades has resulted in the loss of habitat for many plants and animals. For example, 90 percent of the wading birds that once lived in the Everglades have disappeared. If 90 percent of 200,000 wading birds disappeared, how many wading birds would remain?

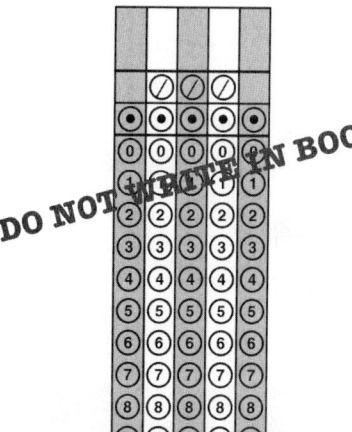

STOP

FCAT Preparation

Science in Action

Place to Visit

Busch Wildlife Sanctuary

Visiting the Busch Wildlife Sanctuary in Jupiter, Florida, is an exciting way to learn more about Florida's environment! The sanctuary helps injured animals, such as birds of prey, recover. If you visit the sanctuary, you can see researchers caring for injured animals and hike trails that wind through different Florida ecosystems. The sanctuary also has interactive exhibits and demonstrations that help you learn more about Florida's environment. If you want hands-on experience caring for injured animals, you can join the sanctuary's Junior Naturalist program.

Math ACTiViTY

The peregrine falcon is a bird of prey that can dive at speeds greater than 289 km/h. Convert this speed into ft/s.

Scientific Debate

Are Manatee Populations Increasing?

In the coldest months of the year, small planes can be heard buzzing overhead off Florida's coast. Every winter, biologists take to the air to estimate Florida's manatee population. The yearly estimate is part of an ongoing debate about how to help these endangered mammals recover. Manatees are endangered for many reasons, including the loss of sea-grass habitat. But they can also be injured or killed if they are struck by boats. Some populations of manatees have increased in recent years, but scientists are still debating whether the total manatee population is increasing. The debate will determine whether more boating restrictions will be implemented and whether expanding refuges would help manatees recover further.

Language Arts ACTiViTY

WRITING SKILL Find out more about the debate concerning manatee populations. Then, write a balanced essay that presents both sides of the debate.

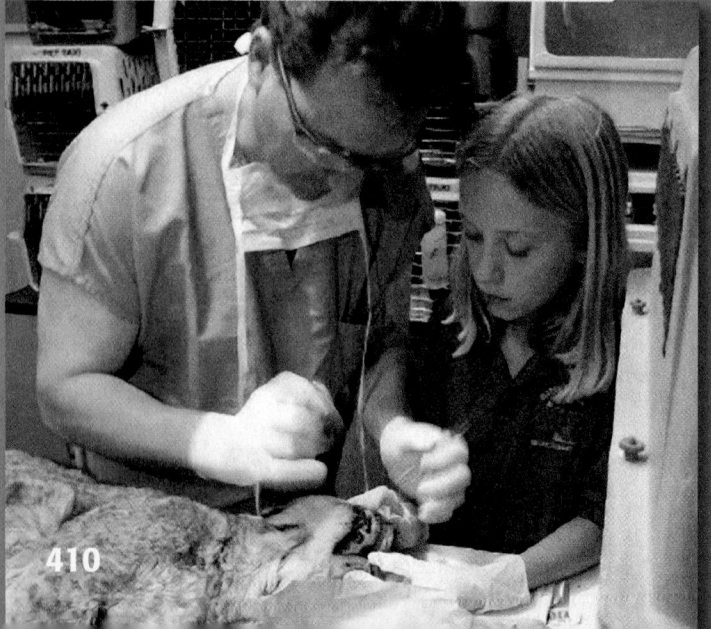

The Enviroteens of Manatee County

Building Artificial Reefs The Enviroteens of Manatee County are taking action to help protect Florida's environment. These students from Harllee Middle School read in a local newspaper that the Manatee County government needed help building artificial coral reefs. So, the students teamed up with a company called Reef Innovations in Sarasota that builds artificial "reef balls." Reef balls look like large concrete whiffle balls, but to marine organisms, they look just like home. When the reef balls are placed on the ocean floor, they serve as habitat for coral-reef organisms.

After the Enviroteens built and installed the reef balls, they began to monitor the artificial habitat with underwater cameras. When they realized that some of the reef balls were becoming clogged with trash, they formed a group called Reef Rakers. The Reef Rakers dive underwater to clean up the reef balls. In addition to building artificial reefs, the Enviroteens also restore habitat on land and remove exotic species from Florida's parks. If you want to find out what the Enviroteens are up to next, it's easy—they produce a television program, called METV, which has more than 15,000 viewers!

Social Studies ACTIVITY

Create a poster-board display about the importance of coral reefs in countries such as Thailand, Indonesia, Australia, and Belize. Include information about the threats to coral reefs, and describe how people are trying to preserve them.

To learn more about these Science in Action topics, visit go.hrw.com and type in the keyword **HT6FHIFF.**

Current Science

Check out Current Science® articles related to this chapter by visiting go.hrw.com. Just type in the keyword **HL5CS21.**

TIMELINE

Earth's Changing Surface

The movement of wind and water across Earth's surface affects the shape of the land. Over time, the movement of water can cut huge canyons or reshape a shoreline. In this unit, you will learn about the movement of water, erosion, and deposition. You will learn how these processes affect the landscape.

Because most of the water on Earth is found in the oceans, the oceans have immense power to reshape Earth's surface. This timeline shows some of the milestones in the exploration of the oceans.

1851
Herman Melville's novel *Moby Dick* is published.

1938
A coelacanth is discovered in the Indian Ocean near South Africa. Called a "fossil fish," the coelacanth was thought to have been extinct for 60 million years.

1978
Louise Brown, the first "test-tube baby," is born in England.

1986
Commercial whaling is temporarily stopped by the International Whaling Commission, but some whaling continues.

1872

The HMS *Challenger* begins its four-year voyage. Its discoveries lay the foundation for the science of oceanography.

1914

The Panama Canal, which links the Atlantic Ocean with the Pacific Ocean, is completed.

1927

Charles Lindbergh completes the first nonstop solo airplane flight over the Atlantic Ocean.

1943

Jacques Cousteau and Émile Gagnan invent the aqualung, a breathing device that allows divers to freely explore the silent world of the oceans.

Jacques Cousteau

1960

Jacques Piccard and Don Walsh dive to a record 10,916 m below sea level in their bathyscaph *Trieste*.

1977

Thermal vent communities of organisms that exist without sunlight are discovered on the ocean floor.

1994

The completion of the tunnel under the English Channel makes train and auto travel between Great Britain and France possible.

1998

Ben Lecomte of Austin, Texas, successfully swims across the Atlantic Ocean from Massachusetts to France, a distance of 5,980 km. His record-breaking feat takes 73 days.

2001

Researchers find that dolphins, like humans and the great apes, can recognize themselves in mirrors.

16

Rivers and Groundwater

The Big Idea Earth is rich in freshwater resources that should be used wisely.

About the PHOTO

A diver explores the clear, blue spring water that is mixing with the brown-stained waters of the Santa Fe River in north-central Florida. Seven springs located along the Santa Fe River discharge hundreds of millions of liters of spring water into the river each day.

PRE-READING ACTIVITY

Booklet Before you read the chapter, create the FoldNote entitled "Booklet" described in the **Study Skills** section of the Appendix. Label each page of the booklet with a main idea from the chapter. As you read the chapter, write what you learn about each main idea on the appropriate page of the booklet.

START-UP ACTiViTY

Stream Weavers D.1.3.1 CS

Do the following activity to learn how streams and river systems develop.

Procedure

1. Begin with enough **sand** and **gravel** to fill the bottom of a **rectangular plastic washtub.**

2. Spread the gravel in a layer at the bottom of the washtub. On top of the gravel, place a layer of sand that is 4 to 6 cm deep. Add more sand to one end of the washtub to form a slope.

3. Make a small hole in the bottom of a **paper cup.** Use a **clothespin** to attach the cup to the inside wall of the tub. The cup should be placed at the end that has more sand.

4. Fill the cup with **water,** and observe the water as it moves over the sand. Use a **magnifying lens** to observe features of the stream more closely.

5. Record your observations.

Analysis

1. At the start of your experiment, how did the moving water affect the sand?

2. As time passed, how did the moving water affect the sand?

3. Explain how this activity modeled the development of streams. In what ways was the model accurate? How was it inaccurate?

The Active River

If you fell asleep with your toes dangling in the Colorado River 6 million years ago and you did not wake up until today, your toes would be hanging about 1.6 km (about 1 mi) above the river!

The Colorado River carved the Grand Canyon, shown in **Figure 1,** by washing billions of tons of soil and rock from the canyon's riverbed. The Colorado River made the Grand Canyon by a process that can take millions of years.

Rivers: Agents of Erosion

Six million years ago, the area now known as the *Grand Canyon* was nearly as flat as a pancake. Over millions of years, the Colorado River cut down into the rock and formed the Grand Canyon through a process called erosion. **Erosion** is the process by which soil and sediment are transported from one location to another. Rivers are not the only agents of erosion. Wind, rain, ice, and snow can also cause erosion.

Because water has been eroding the Grand Canyon, the canyon is now about 1.6 km deep and 446 km long. In this section, you will learn about stream development, river systems, and the factors that affect the rate of stream erosion.

Benchmark Check Describe the process that created the Grand Canyon. **D.1.3.1 CS**

READING WARM-UP

Objectives

- Describe how moving water shapes the surface of Earth by the process of erosion. **D.1.3.1 CS**
- Explain how water moves through the water cycle.
- Describe a watershed.
- Explain three factors that affect the rate of stream erosion. **D.1.3.5 CS**
- Identify four ways that rivers are described.

Terms to Learn

erosion **FCAT VOCAB**   divide
water cycle   channel
tributary   load
watershed

READING STRATEGY

Reading Organizer As you read this section, create an outline of the section. Use the headings from the section in your outline.

D.1.3.1 CS knows that mechanical and chemical activities shape and reshape the Earth's land surface by eroding rock and soil in some areas and depositing them in other areas, sometimes in seasonal layers.

D.1.3.5 CS understands concepts of time and size relating to the interaction of Earth's processes.

Figure 1 *The Grand Canyon is located in northwestern Arizona. The canyon formed over millions of years as running water eroded the rock layers.*

The Water Cycle

Have you ever wondered how rivers keep flowing? Where do rivers get their water? Learning about the water cycle, shown in **Figure 2,** will help you answer these questions. The **water cycle** is the continuous movement of Earth's water from the ocean to the atmosphere, from the atmosphere to the land, and from the land back to the ocean. The water cycle is driven by energy from the sun.

erosion the process by which wind, water, ice, or gravity transports soil and sediment from one location to another **FCAT** *VOCAB*

water cycle the continuous movement of water between the atmosphere, the land, and the oceans

Figure 2 **The Water Cycle**

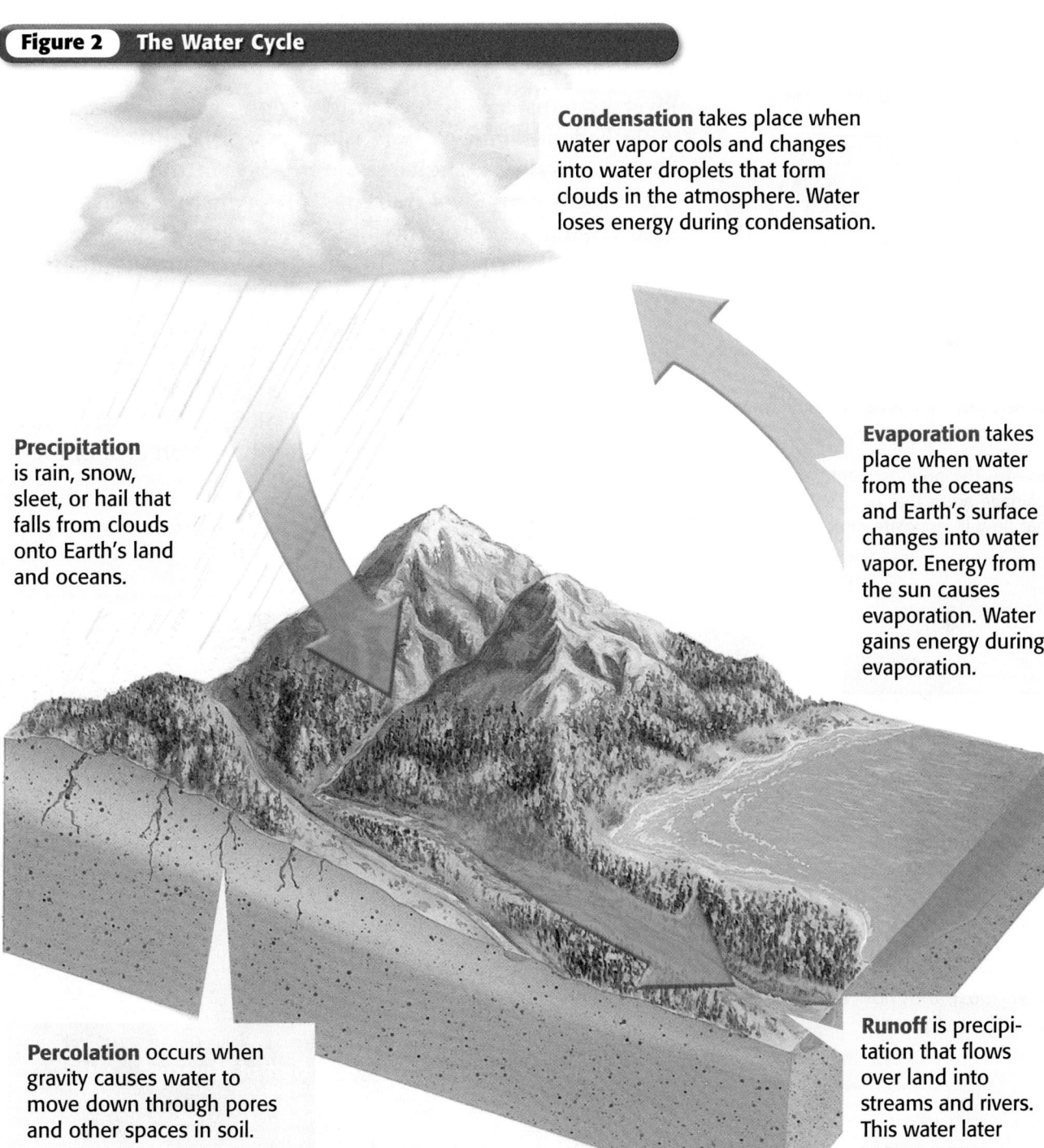

Condensation takes place when water vapor cools and changes into water droplets that form clouds in the atmosphere. Water loses energy during condensation.

Precipitation is rain, snow, sleet, or hail that falls from clouds onto Earth's land and oceans.

Evaporation takes place when water from the oceans and Earth's surface changes into water vapor. Energy from the sun causes evaporation. Water gains energy during evaporation.

Percolation occurs when gravity causes water to move down through pores and other spaces in soil.

Runoff is precipitation that flows over land into streams and rivers. This water later enters oceans.

School to Home

Floating down the River

At home, study a map of the United States with a family member. Imagine that you are planning a rafting trip down the Mississippi River. On the map, trace the route of your trip from Lake Itasca, Minnesota, to the Gulf of Mexico. What major tributaries would you pass? What cities would you pass? Mark them on the map. How many kilometers would you travel on this trip?

ACTIVITY

tributary a stream that flows into a lake or into a larger stream

watershed the area of land that is drained by a river system

divide the boundary between drainage areas that have streams that flow in opposite directions

River Systems

The next time you take a shower, notice that individual drops of water join together to become small streams. These streams join other small streams and form larger ones. Eventually, all of the water flows down the drain. Every time you shower, you create a model river system—a network of streams and rivers that drains an area of its runoff. Just as the shower forms a network of flowing water, streams and rivers form a network of flowing water on land. A stream that flows into a lake or into a larger stream is called a **tributary.**

Watersheds

River systems are divided into regions called *watersheds*. A **watershed,** or *drainage basin,* is the area of land that is drained by a river system. The largest watershed in the United States is the Mississippi River watershed. The Mississippi River watershed has hundreds of tributaries that extend from the Rocky Mountains, in the West, to the Appalachian Mountains, in the East.

The satellite image in **Figure 3** shows that the Mississippi River watershed covers more than one-third of the United States. Other major watersheds in the United States are the Columbia River, Rio Grande, and Colorado River watersheds. Watersheds are separated from each other by an area of higher ground called a **divide.**

Reading Check Describe the difference between a watershed and a divide.

Figure 3 *The Continental Divide runs through the Rocky Mountains. It separates the watersheds that flow into the Atlantic Ocean and the Gulf of Mexico from those that flow into the Pacific Ocean.*

Figure 4 *A mountain stream—such as the one at left, at Kenai Peninsula in Alaska—flows rapidly and has more erosive energy. A river on a flat plain—such as the Kuskokwim River in Alaska, shown below—flows slowly and has less erosive energy.*

Stream Erosion

As a stream forms, it erodes soil and rock to make a channel. A **channel** is the path that a stream follows. When a stream first forms, its channel is usually narrow and steep. Over time, the stream transports rock and soil downstream and makes the channel wider and deeper. When streams become longer and wider, they are called *rivers*. A stream's ability to erode is influenced by three factors: gradient, discharge, and load.

Benchmark Check Explain how a stream's channel changes with time. **D.1.3.5 CS**

Gradient

Figure 4 shows two photos of rivers that have very different gradients. *Gradient* is the measure of the change in elevation over a certain distance. A stream or river that has a high gradient has more energy to erode rock and soil. A river or stream that has a low gradient has less erosive energy.

Discharge

The amount of water that a stream or river carries in a given amount of time is called *discharge*. The discharge of a stream increases when a major storm occurs or when warm weather rapidly melts snow. As a stream's discharge increases, the erosive energy and speed of the stream and the amount of materials that the stream can carry also increase.

channel the path that a stream follows

Calculating a Stream's Gradient

If a stream starts at an elevation of 4,900 m and travels 450 km downstream to a lake that is at an elevation of 400 m, what is the stream's gradient? (Hint: Subtract the final elevation from the starting elevation, and divide by 450. Remember to keep track of the units.)

D.1.3.1 CS knows that mechanical and chemical activities shape and reshape the Earth's land surface by eroding rock and soil in some areas and depositing them in other areas, sometimes in seasonal layers.

D.1.3.5 CS understands concepts of time and size relating to the interaction of Earth's processes.

Load

load the materials carried by a stream

The materials carried by a stream are called the stream's **load.** The size of a stream's load is affected by the stream's speed. The faster a stream moves, the larger the particles that the stream can carry. Rocks and pebbles bounce and scrape along the bottom and sides of the stream bed. Thus, the size of a stream's load affects the stream's rate of erosion. The illustration below shows the three ways that a stream can carry its load.

A stream can bounce large materials, such as pebbles and boulders, along the stream bed. These rocks are called the **bed load.**

A stream can carry small rocks and soil in suspension. These materials, called the **suspended load,** make the river look muddy.

The **dissolved load** is material carried in solution, which means that the material is dissolved in the water. Sodium and calcium are some of the materials in the dissolved load.

The Stages of a River

In the early 1900s, William Morris Davis developed a model for the stages of river development. According to his model, rivers evolve from a youthful stage to an old-age stage. He thought that all rivers eroded in the same way and at the same rate.

Today, scientists support a different model, which considers factors of stream development that differ from those considered in Davis's model. For example, because different materials erode at different rates, one river may develop more quickly than another river does. Many factors—including climate, gradient, and load—influence the development of a river. Scientists no longer use Davis's model to explain river development, but they still use many of his terms to describe a river. These terms describe a river's general features, not a river's actual age.

CONNECTION TO Language Arts

Huckleberry Finn Mark Twain's famous book *The Adventures of Huckleberry Finn* describes the life of a boy who lived on the Mississippi River. Mark Twain's real name was Samuel Clemens. Do research to find out why Clemens chose to use the name Mark Twain and how the name relates to the Mississippi River.

Youthful Rivers

A youthful river, such as the one shown in **Figure 5,** erodes its channel deeper rather than wider. The river flows quickly because of its steep gradient. Its channel is narrow and straight. The river flows as rapids and waterfalls as it tumbles over rocks. Youthful rivers have very few tributaries.

Mature Rivers

A mature river, as shown in **Figure 6,** erodes its channel wider rather than deeper. The gradient of a mature river is not as steep as that of a youthful river. Also, a mature river has fewer falls and rapids. A mature river is fed by many tributaries. Because a mature river has good drainage, a mature river has more discharge than a youthful river does.

Benchmark Check Describe the characteristics of a mature river. **D.1.3.1 CS**

▲ **Figure 5** *This youthful river is located in Yellowstone National Park in Wyoming.*

◀ **Figure 6** *A mature river, such as this one in the Amazon basin of Peru, curves back and forth.*

D.1.3.1 CS knows that mechanical and chemical activities shape and reshape the Earth's land surface by eroding rock and soil in some areas and depositing them in other areas, sometimes in seasonal layers.

D.1.3.5 CS understands concepts of time and size relating to the interaction of Earth's processes.

Figure 7 *This old river is located in New Zealand.*

Old Rivers

An old river has a low gradient and little erosive energy. The river does not widen and deepen its channel but instead deposits rock and soil in and along the channel. Old rivers, such as the one in **Figure 7,** are characterized by valleys or wide, flat *floodplains* and by many bends. Also, an old river has fewer tributaries than a mature river does because the smaller tributaries have joined together.

Rejuvenated Rivers

A rejuvenated (ri JOO vuh NAYT ed) river is found where land is raised by tectonic activity. When land rises, the river's gradient becomes steeper and the river flows more quickly. The increased gradient of a rejuvenated river allows the river to cut more deeply into the valley floor. Steplike formations called *terraces* often form on both sides of a stream valley as a result of rejuvenation. Can you find the terraces in **Figure 8**?

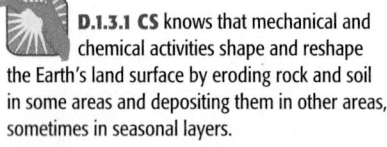 **D.1.3.1 CS** knows that mechanical and chemical activities shape and reshape the Earth's land surface by eroding rock and soil in some areas and depositing them in other areas, sometimes in seasonal layers.

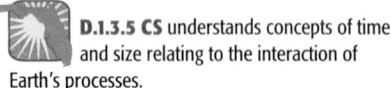 **D.1.3.5 CS** understands concepts of time and size relating to the interaction of Earth's processes.

Benchmark Check Explain why a rejuvenated river rapidly erodes into a valley floor. **D.1.3.5 CS**

Figure 8 *This rejuvenated river is located in Canyonlands National Park in Utah.*

Summary

- Rivers cause erosion by removing and transporting soil and rock from the riverbed. **D.1.3.1 CS**

- The water cycle is water's continuous passage through Earth's atmosphere, land, and oceans.

- A river system is made up of a network of streams and rivers.

- A watershed is a region that collects runoff water that then becomes part of a river or a lake.

- A stream that has a high gradient has more energy for eroding soil and rock. **D.1.3.1 CS**

- When a stream's discharge increases, the stream's erosive energy also increases. **D.1.3.1 CS**

- A stream with a load of large particles has a higher rate of erosion than a stream with a dissolved load does. **D.1.3.1 CS**

- A developing river can be described as youthful, mature, old, or rejuvenated.

Using Key Terms

1. Use *erosion, water cycle, tributary, watershed, divide, channel,* and *load* in separate sentences.
   FCAT VOCAB

Understanding Key Ideas

2. Which of the following drains a watershed?
   a. a divide
   b. a drainage basin
   c. a tributary
   d. a water system

3. Describe how the Grand Canyon formed. **D.1.3.1 CS, D.1.3.5 CS**

4. Draw the water cycle. In your drawing, label condensation, precipitation, and evaporation.

5. What are three factors that affect the rate of stream erosion? **D.1.3.1 CS, D.1.3.5 CS**

6. Which stage of river development is characterized by flat floodplains?

Critical Thinking

7. **Making Inferences** How does the water cycle help develop river systems?

8. **Making Comparisons** How do youthful rivers, mature rivers, and old rivers differ?

FCAT Preparation

9. Six million years ago, the area now known as the *Grand Canyon* was nearly as flat as a pancake. That area gradually changed as the Colorado River washed billions of tons of soil and rock from the riverbed to carve the Grand Canyon. The process of carving the Grand Canyon took millions of years. Before the Colorado River reaches the Grand Canyon, the Colorado River passes through Cataract Canyon in Canyonlands National Park in Utah. What process most likely formed Cataract Canyon? **D.1.3.1 CS**

   A. precipitation
   B. the water cycle
   C. erosion
   D. deposition

SCI LINKS

NSTA
Developed and maintained by the
National Science Teachers Association

For a variety of links related to this chapter, go to www.scilinks.org

Topic: Rivers and Streams
SciLinks code: HSM1316

Stream and River Deposits

If your job were to carry millions of tons of soil across the United States, how would you do it? You might use a bulldozer or a dump truck, but it would still take you a long time. Did you know that rivers do this job every day?

Rivers erode and move enormous amounts of material, such as soil and rock. Acting as liquid conveyor belts, rivers often carry fertile soil to farmland and wetlands. Although erosion is a serious problem, rivers also renew soils and form new land. As you will see in this section, rivers create some of the most impressive landforms on Earth.

Deposition in Water

You have learned how flowing water erodes Earth's surface. After rivers erode rock and soil, the rivers drop, or *deposit,* their load downstream. **Deposition** is the process in which material is laid down or dropped. Rock and soil deposited by streams are called *sediment.* Rivers and streams deposit sediment where the speed of the water current decreases. **Figure 1** shows this type of deposition.

Figure 1 *This photo shows erosion and deposition at a bend, or meander, of a river in Alaska.*

Deposition occurs along the inside bank of the bend, where the water flows slower.

Erosion occurs along the outside bank of the bend, where the water flows faster.

Placer Deposits

Sometimes, a river deposits heavy minerals at places where the current slows down. This kind of sediment is called a *placer deposit* (PLAS uhr dee PAHZ it). Some placer deposits contain gold. During the California gold rush, which began in 1849, many miners panned for gold in the placer deposits of rivers, as shown in **Figure 2.**

Delta

A river's current slows when the river empties into a large body of water, such as a lake or an ocean. As its current slows, a river often deposits its load in a fan-shaped pattern called a **delta.** An astronaut's view of the Nile Delta is shown in **Figure 3.** A delta usually forms on a flat surface and is made mostly of mud. These mud deposits form new land and cause the coastline to grow. The world's deltas are home to a rich diversity of plant and animal life.

If you look back at the map of the Mississippi River watershed, you will see that the Mississippi Delta formed where the Mississippi River flows into the Gulf of Mexico. Each of the fine mud particles in the delta began its journey far upstream. Parts of Louisiana are made up of particles that were transported from places as far away as Montana, Minnesota, Ohio, and Illinois!

Benchmark Check Describe the composition of deltas. **D.1.3.1 CS**

Figure 2 *In the 1850s, miners rushed to California to find gold. They often found gold in the bends of rivers in placer deposits.*

deposition the process in which material is laid down **FCAT VOCAB**

delta a fan-shaped mass of material deposited at the mouth of a stream

Mediterranean Sea

Nile Delta

Nile River

Egypt

Figure 3 *As sediment is dropped at the mouth of the Nile River in Egypt, a delta forms.*

D.1.3.1 CS knows that mechanical and chemical activities shape and reshape the Earth's land surface by eroding rock and soil in some areas and depositing them in other areas, sometimes in seasonal layers.

Figure 4 *An alluvial fan—such as this one in Death Valley, California—forms when an eroding stream rapidly changes into a depositing stream.*

Alluvial fan

River Brochure Investigate the characteristics of youthful, mature, and old rivers. Go to **go.hrw.com,** and type in the keyword **HZ5DEPW.**

alluvial fan a fan-shaped mass of material deposited by a stream when the slope of the land decreases sharply

floodplain an area along a river that forms from sediments deposited when the river overflows its banks

Deposition on Land

When a fast-moving mountain stream flows onto a flat plain, the stream slows down very quickly. As the stream slows down, it deposits sediment. The sediment forms an alluvial fan, such as the one shown in **Figure 4. Alluvial fans** are fan-shaped deposits that, unlike deltas, form on dry land.

Floodplains

During periods of high rainfall or rapid snowmelt, a sudden increase in the volume of water flowing into a stream can cause the stream's banks to overflow. When a river's banks overflow, sediment is deposited along the river to form an area called a **floodplain.** When a stream floods, a layer of sediment is deposited across the floodplain. Each flood adds another layer of sediment.

Floodplains are rich farming areas because periodic flooding brings new soil to the land. However, flooding can cause damage, too. When the Mississippi River flooded in 1993, farms were destroyed and entire towns were evacuated. **Figure 5** shows an area north of St. Louis, Missouri, that was flooded.

Figure 5 *The normal flow of the Mississippi River and Missouri River is shown in black. The area that was flooded when both rivers spilled over their banks in 1993 is shaded red.*

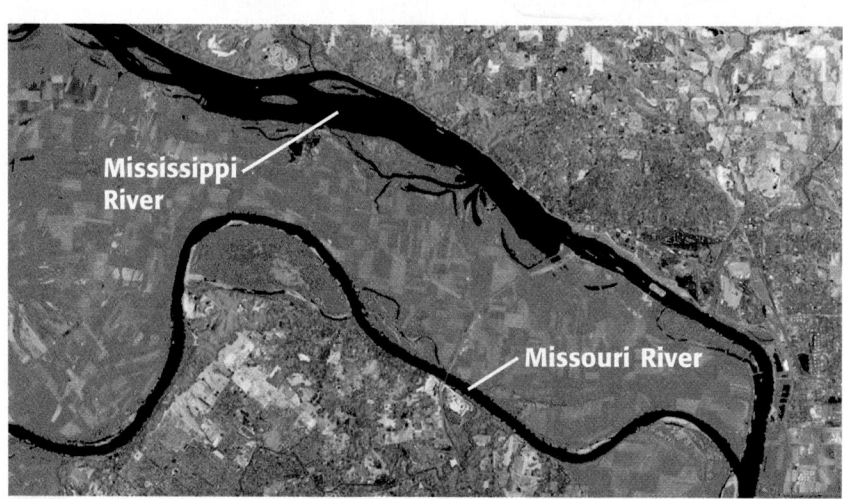

Mississippi River

Missouri River

D.1.3.1 CS knows that mechanical and chemical activities shape and reshape the Earth's land surface by eroding rock and soil in some areas and depositing them in other areas, sometimes in seasonal layers.

Flooding Dangers

The flooding of the Mississippi River in 1993 caused damage in nine states. But floods can damage more than property. Many people have lost their lives to powerful floods. As shown in **Figure 6,** flash flooding can take a driver by surprise. However, there are ways to control floods.

One type of barrier that can be built to help control flooding is called a *dam*. A dam is a barrier that can redirect the flow of water. A dam can prevent flooding in one area and create an artificial lake in another area. The water stored in the artificial lake can be used to irrigate farmland during droughts and to provide drinking water to local towns and cities. The stored water can also be used to generate electricity.

Overflow from a river can also be controlled by a barrier called a *levee*. A levee is the buildup of sediment deposited along the channel of a river. This buildup helps keep the river inside the banks of the river. People often use sandbags to build artificial levees to control water during serious flooding.

✓ **Reading Check** How do dams and levees prevent flooding?

Figure 6 *Floodwaters can easily carry cars on flooded roads down to deeper, more dangerous water.*

SECTION Review

Summary

- Sediment forms several types of deposits. **D.1.3.1 CS**
- Sediments deposited where a river's current slows are called *placer deposits*. **D.1.3.1 CS**
- A delta is a fan-shaped deposit of sediment where a river meets a body of water. **D.1.3.1 CS**
- Alluvial fans form when a river deposits sediment on land. **D.1.3.1 CS**
- Flooding brings rich soil to farmland but can also lead to property damage and death. **D.1.3.1 CS**

Using Key Terms

1. Write an original definition for *deposition*. **FCAT VOCAB**

Understanding Key Ideas

2. Which of the following can help prevent a flood?
   a. a placer deposit
   b. a delta
   c. a floodplain
   d. a levee

3. Where do alluvial fans form? **D.1.3.1 CS**

4. Explain why floodplains are both good and bad areas for farming.

Critical Thinking

5. **Identifying Relationships** What factors increase the likelihood that sediment will be deposited? **D.1.3.1 CS**

6. **Making Comparisons** How are alluvial fans and deltas similar?

FCAT Preparation

7. Rivers deposit sediment to create several kinds of landforms. Which of the following forms at places where the current of a river slows at the bend of the river? **D.1.3.1 CS**
   A. a placer deposit
   B. a delta
   C. a floodplain
   D. a levee

SCI LINKS®

NSTA
Developed and maintained by the National Science Teachers Association

For a variety of links related to this chapter, go to www.scilinks.org

Topic: Stream Deposits
SciLinks code: HSM1458

Water Underground

Imagine filling a glass not with water from a faucet but with water from a chunk of solid rock! This idea may sound crazy, but millions of people get their water from within rock that is underground.

Although you can see some of Earth's water in streams and lakes, you cannot see the large amount of water that flows underground. The water located within the rocks below Earth's surface is called *groundwater*. Groundwater not only is an important resource but also plays an important role in erosion and deposition.

The Location of Groundwater

Surface water seeps underground into the soil and rock. This underground area is divided into two zones. Rainwater passes through the upper zone, called the *zone of aeration*. Farther down, the water collects in an area called the *zone of saturation*. In this zone, the spaces between the rock particles are filled with water.

These two zones meet at a boundary known as the **water table,** shown in **Figure 1.** The water table rises during wet seasons and falls during dry seasons. In wet regions, the water table can be at or just beneath the soil's surface. In dry regions, such as deserts, the water table may be hundreds of meters beneath the ground.

Reading Check Describe where the zone of aeration is located.

water table the upper surface of underground water; the upper boundary of the zone of saturation

Figure 1 *The water table is the upper surface of the zone of saturation.*

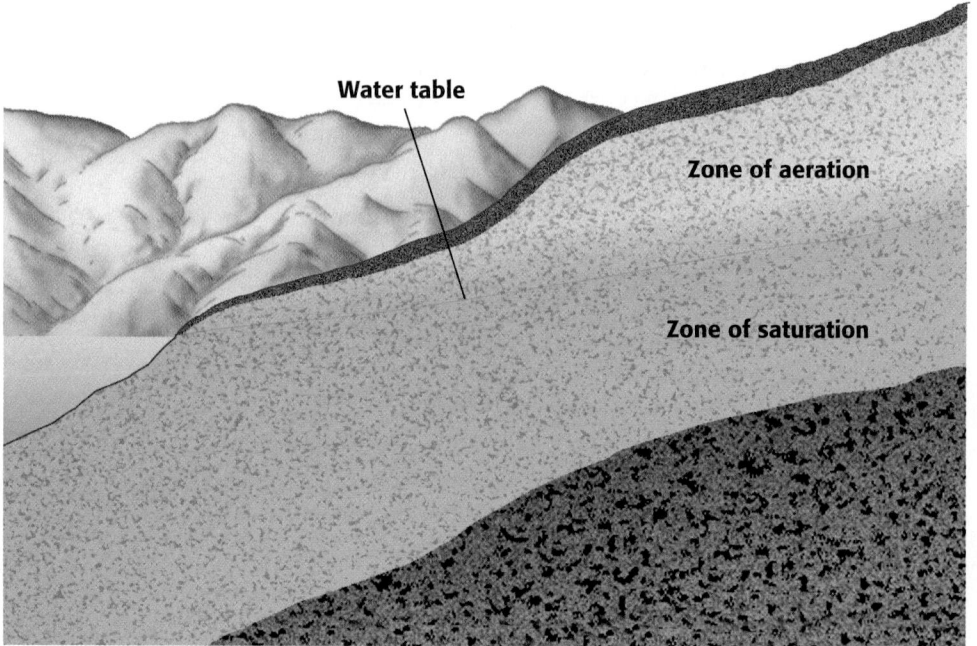

Water table

Zone of aeration

Zone of saturation

Aquifers

A rock layer that stores groundwater and allows the flow of groundwater is called an **aquifer.** An aquifer can be described by its ability to hold water and to allow water to pass freely through it.

Porosity

The more open spaces, or pores, between particles in an aquifer, the more water the aquifer can hold. The percentage of open space between individual rock particles in a rock layer is called **porosity.**

Porosity is influenced by the differences in the sizes of particles in a rock layer. If a rock layer contains particles of many sizes, the small particles will most likely fill the different-sized empty spaces between large particles. Therefore, a rock layer with particles of many sizes has a low percentage of open space between particles and has low porosity. On the other hand, a rock layer containing many particles of the same size has high porosity. This rock layer has high porosity because smaller particles are not present to fill the empty space between particles. So, there is more open space between particles.

Permeability

If the pores of a rock layer are connected, groundwater can flow through the rock layer. The ability of a rock to let water pass through the pores of the rock is called **permeability.** A rock that stops the flow of water is *impermeable*.

The larger the particles are, the more permeable the rock layer is. Because large particles have less surface area relative to their volume than small particles do, large particles cause less friction. *Friction* is a force that causes moving objects to slow down. Less friction allows water to flow more easily through the rock layer, as shown in **Figure 2.**

aquifer a body of rock or sediment that stores groundwater and allows the flow of groundwater

porosity the percentage of the total volume of a rock or sediment that consists of open spaces

permeability the ability of a rock or sediment to let fluids pass through its open spaces, or pores

Figure 2 *Large particles, shown at left, have less total surface area than small ones, shown at right, do. So, large particles cause less friction.*

Figure 3 *This map shows aquifers in the United States, excluding Alaska and Hawaii.*

Aquifers

recharge zone an area in which water travels downward to become part of an aquifer

G.2.3.4 AA understands that humans are a part of an ecosystem and their activities may deliberately or inadvertently alter the equilibrium in ecosystems.

Aquifer Geology and Geography

The best aquifers usually form in permeable materials, such as sandstone, limestone, or layers of sand and gravel. Some aquifers cover large underground areas and are an important source of water for cities and agriculture. The map in **Figure 3** shows the location of the major aquifers in the United States.

Recharge Zones

Like rivers, aquifers depend on the water cycle to maintain a constant flow of water. The ground surface where water enters an aquifer is called the **recharge zone.** The size of the recharge zone depends on how permeable rock is at the surface. If the surface rock is permeable, water can seep down into the aquifer. If the aquifer is covered by an impermeable rock layer, water cannot reach the aquifer. Construction of buildings on top of the recharge zone can also limit the amount of water that enters an aquifer.

Reading Check Explain the factors that affect the size of a recharge zone.

Springs and Wells

Groundwater movement is determined by the slope of the water table. Like surface water, groundwater tends to move downslope toward lower elevations. If the water table reaches Earth's surface, water will flow out from the ground and will form a *spring*. Springs are an important source of drinking water. In areas where the water table is higher than Earth's surface, lakes will form.

Artesian Springs

A sloping layer of permeable rock sandwiched between two layers of impermeable rock is called an *artesian formation*. The permeable rock is an aquifer, and the top layer of impermeable rock is called a *cap rock,* as shown in **Figure 4.** Artesian formations are the source of water for artesian springs. An **artesian spring** is a spring whose water flows from a crack in the cap rock of the aquifer. Sometimes, artesian springs are found in deserts, where they are often the only source of water.

Most springs have cool water. However, some springs have hot water. The water becomes hot when it flows deep within Earth, because Earth's temperature increases as depth increases. The temperature of some hot springs can reach 50°C!

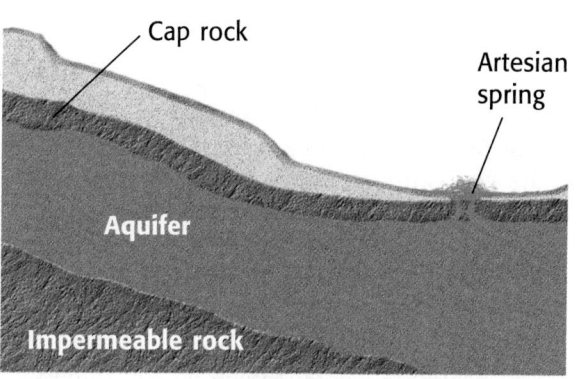

Figure 4 *Artesian springs form when water from an aquifer flows through cracks in the cap rock of an artesian formation.*

Wells

A human-made hole that is deeper than the level of the water table is called a *well*. If a well is not deep enough, as shown in **Figure 5,** it will dry up when the water table falls below the bottom of the well. Also, if an area has too many wells, groundwater can be removed too rapidly. If groundwater is removed too rapidly, the water table will drop and all of the wells will run dry.

artesian spring a spring whose water flows from a crack in the cap rock over the aquifer

Benchmark Check Explain how humans can cause a drop in a water table. **G.2.3.4 AA**

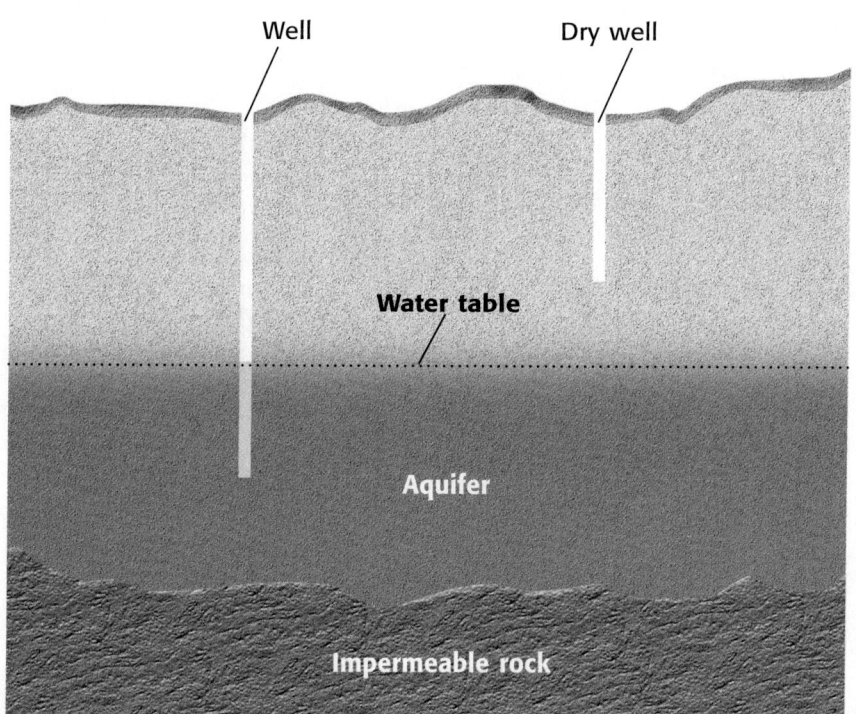

Benchmark Activity

When the Well Runs Dry
Fill a glass almost full with crushed ice, and then add cold water up to the top of the ice. Immerse one straw to the bottom of the glass and another straw halfway into the glass. Use the fully immersed straw to drink the water until the water is below the bottom of the other straw. Then, try drinking with the other straw. Describe how this model represents wells reaching into an aquifer. How could you add to the model to represent recharging the aquifer?
G.2.3.4 AA

Figure 5 *A well must be drilled deep enough so that the well still contains water when the water table drops.*

D.1.3.1 CS knows that mechanical and chemical activities shape and reshape the Earth's land surface by eroding rock and soil in some areas and depositing them in other areas, sometimes in seasonal layers.

D.1.3.5 CS understands concepts of time and size relating to the interaction of Earth's processes.

Underground Erosion and Deposition

You have learned that rivers cause erosion when water removes and transports rock and soil from the rivers' banks. Groundwater can also cause erosion. However, groundwater causes erosion by dissolving rock. Some groundwater contains weak acids that dissolve the rock, such as carbonic acid. Also, some types of rocks, such as limestone, dissolve more easily in groundwater than other types of rocks do.

When underground erosion happens, caves can form. Most of the world's caves formed over thousands of years as groundwater dissolved the limestone of the cave sites. Some caves, such as the one shown in **Figure 6,** reach spectacular proportions.

Cave Formations

Although caves are formed by erosion, they also show signs of deposition. Water that drips from a crack in a cave's ceiling leaves behind deposits of calcium carbonate. Sharp, icicle-shaped features that form on cave ceilings are known as *stalactites* (stuh LAK tiets). Water that falls to the cave's floor adds to cone-shaped features known as *stalagmites* (stuh LAG MIETS). If water drips long enough, the stalactites and stalagmites join to form a *dripstone column*.

Benchmark Check Describe the process that causes stalactites and stalagmites to form. **D.1.3.1 CS**

Figure 6 *At Carlsbad Caverns in New Mexico, underground passages and enormous "rooms" have been eroded below the surface of Earth.*

Stalactite

Stalagmite

Sinkholes

When the water table is lower than the level of a cave, the water underneath the cave no longer supports the cave. The roof of the cave can then collapse, which leaves a circular depression called a *sinkhole*. Surface streams can "disappear" into sinkholes and then flow through underground caves. Sinkholes often form lakes in areas where the water table is high. Central Florida is covered with hundreds of round sinkhole lakes. **Figure 7** shows how the collapse of an underground cave can affect a landscape.

Figure 7 *The damage to this city block shows the effects of a sinkhole in Winter Park, Florida.*

SECTION Review

Summary

- The water table is the boundary between the zone of aeration and the zone of saturation.
- Porosity describes an aquifer's ability to hold water, and permeability describes an aquifer's ability to allow water to flow through the aquifer.
- Springs are a natural way in which water reaches the surface.
- Humans can cause groundwater depletion. **G.2.3.4 AA**
- Caves and sinkholes form from the erosion of limestone by groundwater. **D.1.3.1 CS, D.1.3.5 CS**

Understanding Key Ideas

1. What is the water table?

2. Describe how particles affect the porosity of an aquifer.

3. Explain the difference between artesian springs and other springs.

4. Name a feature that is formed by underground erosion. **D.1.3.1 CS**

5. Name two features that are formed by underground deposition. **D.1.3.1 CS**

6. What type of weathering process causes underground erosion? **D.1.3.1 CS**

Critical Thinking

7. **Predicting Consequences** Explain how urban growth may affect the recharge zone of an aquifer. **G.2.3.4 AA**

8. **Making Comparisons** Explain the difference between a spring and a well.

9. **Analyzing Relationships** What is the relationship between the zone of aeration, the zone of saturation, and the water table?

FCAT Preparation

10. Sometimes, groundwater contains weak acids that erode limestone. Which of the following forms when groundwater erodes limestone? **D.1.3.1 CS**

    A. an aquifer
    B. a spring
    C. a well
    D. a cave

11. Some caves contain structures made by deposition. Which of the following is a structure made by the deposition of calcium carbonate on the floor of a cave? **D.1.3.1 CS**

    F. a sinkhole
    G. a dripstone column
    H. a stalactite
    I. a stalagmite

SCiLINKS®

NSTA
Developed and maintained by the
National Science Teachers Association

For a variety of links related to this chapter, go to www.scilinks.org

Topic: Water Underground
SciLinks code: HSM1633

Using Water Wisely

Did you know that you are almost 65% water? You depend on clean, fresh drinking water to maintain that 65% of you. But a limited amount of fresh water is available on Earth. Only 3% of Earth's water is drinkable.

And of the 3% of Earth's water that is drinkable, 75% is frozen in the polar icecaps. This frozen water is not readily available for our use. Practicing good stewardship of Earth's water supply helps preserve clean water for future generations.

Water Pollution

Surface water, such as the water in rivers and lakes, and groundwater can be polluted by waste from cities, factories, and farms. Pollution is the introduction of harmful substances into the environment. Water can become so polluted that it can no longer be used or can even be deadly.

Point-Source and Nonpoint-Source Pollution

Pollution that comes from one specific site is called **point-source pollution.** For example, wastewater that is released from a factory is point-source pollution. In most cases, this type of pollution can be controlled because its source can be identified.

  Nonpoint-source pollution is pollution that comes from many sources. This type of pollution is much more difficult to control because it does not come from a single source. Most nonpoint-source pollution reaches bodies of water by runoff. Some sources of nonpoint-source pollution in Florida include agricultural and urban runoff, land clearing, construction, and forestry. **Figure 1** shows an example of a source of nonpoint-source pollution.

Benchmark Check Identify which type of pollution is the hardest to control. D.2.3.2, G.2.3.4 AA

READING WARM-UP

Objectives

- Identify two forms of water pollution. D.2.3.2, G.2.3.4 AA
- Describe factors that can indicate poor water quality in a water system. G.2.3.2 CS
- Describe how water quality can affect animal and plant populations. G.2.3.2 CS, G.2.3.3 CS
- Describe two ways that wastewater can be treated. G.2.3.2 CS
- Describe how water is used and how water can be conserved in industry, in agriculture, and at home.

Terms to Learn

point-source pollution
nonpoint-source pollution
sewage treatment plant

READING STRATEGY

Paired Summarizing Read this section silently. In pairs, take turns summarizing the material. Stop to discuss ideas that seem confusing.

Figure 1 *The runoff from this irrigation system could collect pesticides and other pollutants. The result would be nonpoint-source pollution.*

Figure 2 *Waste from farm animals can seep into groundwater and cause nitrate pollution.*

Health of a Water System

You might not realize that water quality not only affects your quality of life but also affects other organisms that depend on water. Therefore, it is important to understand how the properties of water influence water quality.

Dissolved Oxygen

Just as you need oxygen to live, so do fish and other organisms that live in lakes and streams. The oxygen dissolved in water is called *dissolved oxygen,* or DO. Levels of DO that are below 4.0 mg/L in fresh water can cause stress and possibly death for organisms that live in the water. Pollutants such as sewage, fertilizer runoff, and animal waste can decrease DO levels.

Temperature

Temperature changes also affect DO levels. For example, cold water holds more oxygen than warm water does. Facilities such as nuclear power plants can increase the water temperature of lakes and rivers when the facilities use the water as a cooling agent. This kind of increase in water temperature is called *thermal pollution,* which causes a decrease in DO levels.

Nitrates

Nitrates are naturally occurring compounds of nitrogen and oxygen. Small amounts of nitrates in water are normal. However, elevated nitrate levels in water can be harmful to organisms. An excess of nitrates in lakes and rivers can also lower DO levels. As **Figure 2** shows, nitrate pollution can come from animal wastes that seep into groundwater.

point-source pollution pollution that comes from a specific site

nonpoint-source pollution pollution that comes from many sources rather than from a single, specific site

D.2.3.2 knows the positive and negative consequences of human action on the Earth's systems.

G.2.3.2 CS knows that all biotic and abiotic factors are interrelated and that if one factor is changed or removed, it impacts the availability of other resources within the system.

G.2.3.4 AA understands that humans are a part of an ecosystem and their activities may deliberately or inadvertently alter the equilibrium in ecosystems.

Quick Lab

Measuring pH

1. Identify two water sources from which to collect water samples.

2. Fill a **plastic cup** with water from one source. Fill a **second plastic cup** with water from the second source. Label each cup with its source.

3. Use a **pH test kit** to measure the pH of each sample. Follow the instructions in the test kit, and determine the pH of each of the two samples. Record your observations.

4. What did the results for the two samples indicate about the two sources?

5. Use **water test kits** to measure DO and nitrate levels in the two water samples, and discuss whether your results indicate a healthy or unhealthy environment.

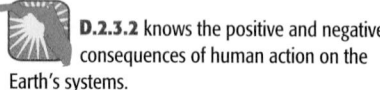

D.2.3.2 knows the positive and negative consequences of human action on the Earth's systems.

G.2.3.2 CS knows that all biotic and abiotic factors are interrelated and that if one factor is changed or removed, it impacts the availability of other resources within the system.

G.2.3.3 CS knows that a brief change in the limited resources of an ecosystem may alter the size of a population or the average size of an organism and that long-term change may result in the elimination of animal and plant populations inhabiting the Earth.

Figure 3 *This fish die-off in Brazil occurred as a result of thermal pollution, which decreased the level of dissolved oxygen in the water.*

pH

The pH of a body of water identifies the acid-base balance of the water. Normal pH in a healthy water system ranges from about 6.5 to 8.5. Chemicals dissolved in water that has a pH within this range are available as nutrients that aquatic organisms can use. However, a lower or higher pH may disrupt the availability of nutrients in a water system.

Turbidity

Another indicator of water quality is turbidity. *Turbidity* is a measure of the concentration of particles suspended in water. High turbidity reduces light penetration and visibility in the water. Common sources of turbidity are suspended sediments, such as silt and clay, wastewater discharge from industry, and abnormally high concentrations of microscopic plants, called *phytoplankton*. High concentrations of particles significantly reduce light penetration. A lack of light negatively affects the health of aquatic organisms and reduces photosynthesis.

Biological Indicators of Water Quality

Scientists use a variety of aquatic plants and animals as indicators of water quality. Among the most important biological indicators of the health of a water system are fishes. Fishes live in water their entire life and respond to chemical, physical, and biological changes in their environment in characteristic ways. The fishes shown in **Figure 3** are an obvious indicator of a change that has taken place in a body of water. This fish die-off is an indicator of thermal pollution. Other organisms that are used to indicate water quality are aquatic plants, aquatic insects, mussels, leeches, and worms.

Benchmark Check **Explain how changes in an environment can affect a population of organisms. G.2.3.2 CS, G.2.3.3 CS**

Figure 4 *Scientists monitor water quality in Florida to identify and correct problems in the water supply.*

Monitoring Water Quality

A number of government programs designed to monitor the quality of surface water and groundwater are currently being conducted in Florida. For example, the U.S. Geological Survey has a program to monitor water quality across southern Florida, an area that has changed dramatically over the last 100 years. Much of the water that once flowed from Lake Okeechobee to the Everglades has been diverted into canals. Development of agriculture, industry, and urban areas has created runoff that could contaminate surface water and groundwater in southern Florida.

Scientists, such as those in **Figure 4,** monitor water quality by looking for chemical and biological imbalances in a body of water. Detecting these imbalances can help scientists correct problems in a water supply. Chemical imbalances in water can be detected by measuring pH and the levels of dissolved oxygen and nitrates. Biological imbalances in an aquatic ecosystem can be measured by counting the relative numbers of biological indicator species. Finally, turbidity can be measured by instruments that indicate water clarity at various depths.

Water quality can also be monitored by instruments mounted aboard aircraft and satellites. These instruments measure biological activity, turbidity, and water temperature. For example, a satellite image of Lake Tahoe, located on the California-Nevada border, is shown in **Figure 5.**

Benchmark Check Explain the purpose of a water-quality monitoring program. **D.2.3.2, G.2.3.4 CS**

Figure 5 *This satellite photo helps scientists monitor the quality of the water in Lake Tahoe.*

Cleaning Polluted Water

When you flush the toilet or watch water go down the shower drain, where does the water go? If you live in a city or large town, the water flows through sewer pipes to a sewage treatment plant. **Sewage treatment plants** are facilities that remove the waste materials from water. These plants help protect the environment from water pollution. They also protect us from diseases that are easily transmitted through dirty water.

Primary Treatment

When water reaches a sewage treatment plant, it is cleaned in two ways. First, it goes through a series of steps known as *primary treatment*. In primary treatment, dirty water is passed through a large screen to catch solid objects, such as paper, rags, and bottle caps. Then, the water is placed in a large tank, where smaller particles, or sludge, can sink and be filtered out. These particles include things such as food, coffee grounds, and soil. Any floating oils and scum are skimmed off the surface.

Secondary Treatment

After undergoing primary treatment, the water is ready for *secondary treatment*. In secondary treatment, the water is sent to an aeration tank, where it is mixed with oxygen and bacteria. The bacteria feed on the wastes and use the oxygen. Then, the water is sent to another settling tank, where chlorine is added to disinfect the water. Finally, the water is released into a water source—a river, a lake, or the ocean. **Figure 6** shows the major components of a sewage treatment plant.

Economic and Environmental Trade-Offs In southern Florida, a system of canals has been created to drain water from the Everglades and to supply water to urban areas. This system has made new land available for agriculture, mining, and urban expansion. However, the drainage also has caused salt water to move inland from the coasts and has lowered water levels in the underlying aquifer. With your classmates, debate the economic and environmental trade-offs in this situation.

CONNECTION TO Social Studies

G.2.3.4 AA understands that humans are a part of an ecosystem and their activities may deliberately or inadvertently alter the equilibrium in ecosystems.

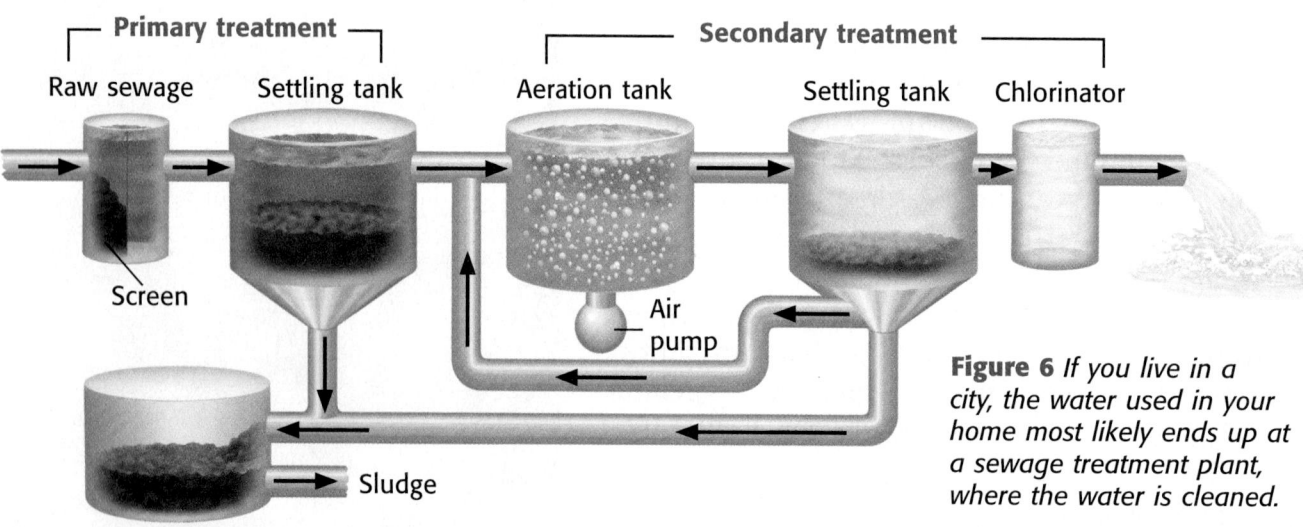

Primary treatment · Secondary treatment

Raw sewage · Settling tank · Aeration tank · Settling tank · Chlorinator

Screen

Air pump

Sludge

Figure 6 *If you live in a city, the water used in your home most likely ends up at a sewage treatment plant, where the water is cleaned.*

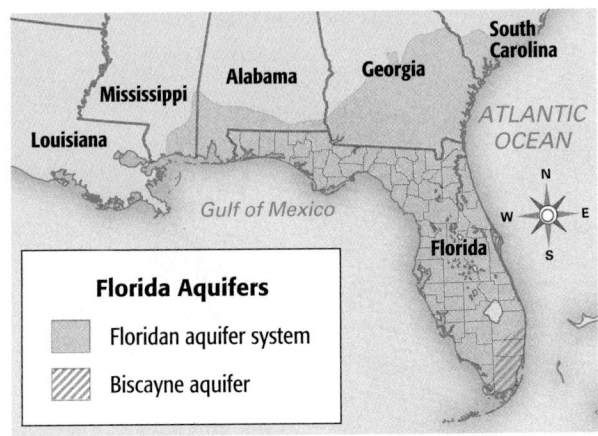

Figure 7 *Most residents of Florida obtain fresh water from the Floridan aquifer or the Biscayne aquifer.*

Florida Aquifers

Floridan aquifer system

Biscayne aquifer

Where the Water Comes From

The Floridan aquifer lies under most of Florida and extends into southern Georgia, Alabama, and South Carolina. This aquifer provides water to most of north Florida, including Jacksonville, Tallahassee, St. Petersburg, and Orlando. Residents of southeastern Florida, including Dade, Broward, and Palm Beach counties, get water from the smaller Biscayne aquifer. In addition, water from the Biscayne aquifer is sent from the mainland to the Florida Keys by pipeline.

sewage treatment plant a facility that cleans the waste materials found in water that comes from sewers or drains

Where the Water Goes

Think of some ways that you use water in your home. Do you water the lawn? Do you wash the dishes? The graph in **Figure 8** shows how an average household in the United States uses water. Notice that less than 8% of the water that we use in our homes is used for drinking. Most water is used for flushing toilets, doing laundry, bathing, and watering lawns and plants.

Using water in our homes is not the only way that water is used. More water is used in industry and agriculture than is used in homes.

Water in Agriculture

Most of the water that is lost during farming is lost through evaporation and runoff. High-pressure overhead sprinklers are particularly inefficient. Nearly half of the water released evaporates and never reaches plant roots. New technology, such as drip irrigation systems, has helped conserve water in agriculture. A drip irrigation system delivers small amounts of water directly to plant roots. This system allows plants to absorb the water before the water has a chance to evaporate or become runoff.

Figure 8 *The average household in the United States uses about 380 L of water per day. This pie graph shows some common uses of these 380 L.*

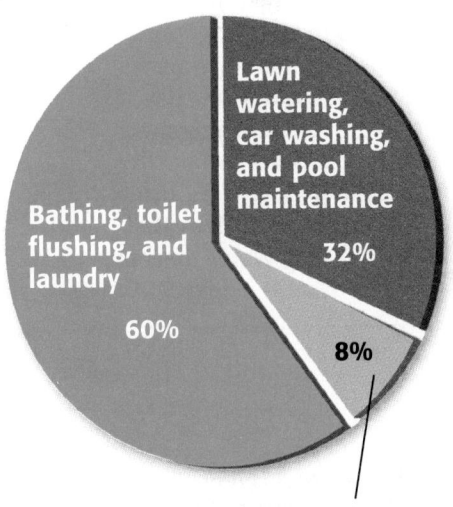

Lawn watering, car washing, and pool maintenance **32%**

Bathing, toilet flushing, and laundry **60%**

8%

Drinking, cooking, washing dishes, and running a garbage disposal

✓ Reading Check How does the drip irrigation system help conserve water?

Figure 9 *Running dishwashers and washing machines only when they are full conserves water.*

D.2.3.2 knows the positive and negative consequences of human action on the Earth's systems.

G.2.3.4 AA understands that humans are a part of an ecosystem and their activities may deliberately or inadvertently alter the equilibrium in ecosystems.

Water in Industry

About 19% of water used in the world is used for industrial purposes. Water is used to manufacture goods, cool power stations, clean industrial products, extract minerals, and generate energy for factories.

Because water resources have become expensive, many industries are trying to conserve, or use less, water. One way that industries conserve water is to recycle it. In the United States, most of the water used in factories is recycled at least once. At least 90% of this recycled water can be treated and returned to surface water.

Conserving Water at Home

There are many ways that people can conserve water at home. For example, many people save water by installing low-flow shower heads and low-flush toilets, because these items use much less water. To avoid watering lawns, some people plant only native plants in their yards. Native plants grow well in the local climate and don't need extra watering.

Your behavior can also help you conserve water. For example, you can take shorter showers. You can avoid running the water while brushing your teeth. And when you run the dishwasher or the washing machine, you can make sure that it is full, as **Figure 9** shows.

✓ **Reading Check** List ways in which you can conserve water in your home.

Summary

- Point-source pollution and nonpoint-source pollution are two kinds of water pollution. **D.2.3.2, G.2.3.4 AA**

- Pollutants can change pH, decrease oxygen levels, increase nitrate levels, and increase turbidity in water. These changes can harm plants, animals, and humans. **G.2.3.2 CS, G.2.3.3 CS**

- Certain organisms can be indicators of the health of a water system. **G.2.3.2 CS, G.2.3.3 CS**

- Wastewater can be treated by sewage treatment plants and septic systems.

- The purpose of water-quality monitoring programs is to detect imbalances that indicate poor water-system health. **D.2.3.2, G.2.3.4 AA**

- Water quality can be monitored by instruments aboard aircraft and satellites.

- Water can be conserved by using only the water that is needed, by recycling water, and by using drip irrigation systems.

- Many water conservation methods can be used in the home.

Using Key Terms

1. Write an original definition for *point-source pollution* and *nonpoint-source pollution*.

Understanding Key Ideas

2. Which of the following can help protect fish from acid rain? **G.2.3.2 CS, G.2.3.3 CS**
   a. dissolved oxygen
   b. nitrates
   c. balancing pH
   d. point-source pollution

3. Which kind of water pollution is often caused by the runoff of fertilizers? **D.2.3.2, G.2.3.4 AA**

4. Describe how water quality can affect animal and plant populations. **G.2.3.2 CS, G.2.3.3 CS**

5. What factors affect the level of dissolved oxygen in water? **G.2.3.2 CS**

6. List four water-monitoring methods that can indicate poor water quality in a water system.

7. What are some of the ways in which water can be conserved in the home?

Critical Thinking

8. **Making Inferences** How do bacteria help break down the waste in water treatment plants? **G.2.3.2 CS**

FCAT Preparation

Use the table below to answer the question that follows.

Daily Water Use in the United States (per person)	
Use	**Water (L)**
Lawn watering and pools	95
Toilet flushing	90
Bathing	70
Brushing teeth	10
Cleaning (inside and outside)	20
Cooking and drinking	10

9. How could all of this activity affect the ecosystem? **G.2.3.4 AA**

SCLINKS.

NSTA

Developed and maintained by the
National Science Teachers Association

For a variety of links related to this chapter, go to www.scilinks.org
Topic: Water Pollution and
        Conservation
SciLinks code: HSM1630

Model-Making Lab

Water Cycle—What Goes Up . . .

Why does a bathroom mirror fog up? Where does water go when it dries up? Where does rain come from? These questions relate to the major parts of the water cycle—condensation, evaporation, and precipitation. In this activity, you will make a model of the water cycle.

Procedure

1. Use the graduated cylinder to pour 50 mL of water into the beaker. Note the water level in the beaker.

2. Put on your safety goggles and gloves. Place the beaker securely on the hot plate. Turn the heat to medium, and bring the water to a boil.

3. While waiting for the water to boil, practice picking up and handling the glass plate or watch glass with the tongs. Hold the glass plate a few centimeters above the beaker, and tilt it so that the lowest edge of the glass is still above the beaker.

4. Observe the glass plate as the water in the beaker boils. Record the changes that you see in the beaker, in the air above the beaker, and on the glass plate held over the beaker. Write down any changes that you see in the water.

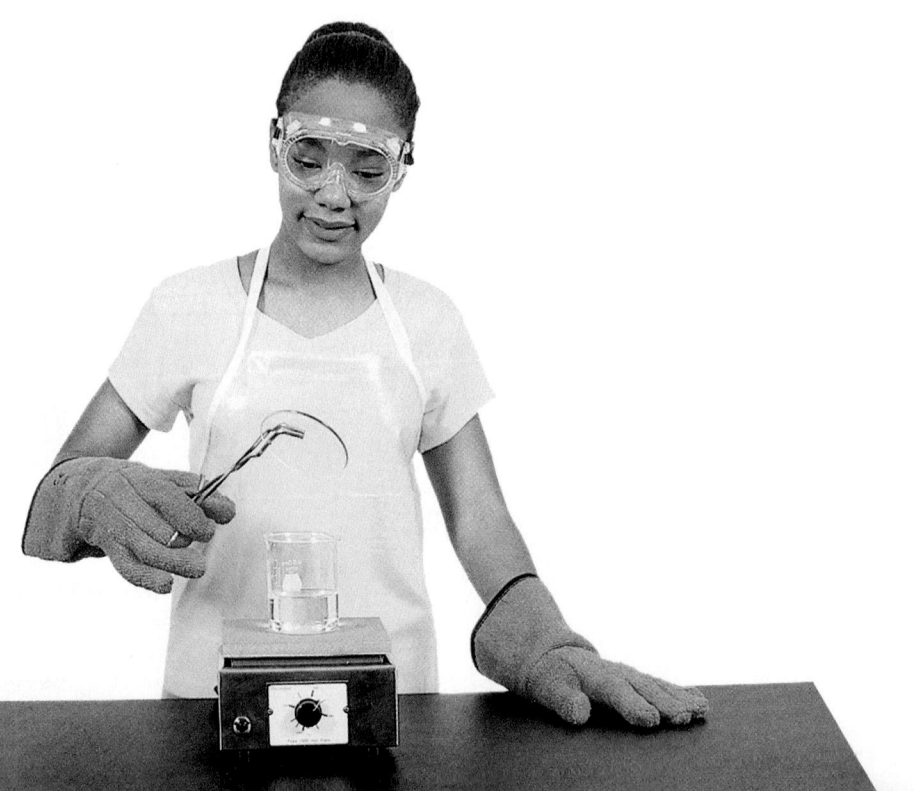

⑤ Continue until you have observed steam rising off the water, the glass plate becoming foggy, and water dripping from the glass plate.

⑥ Carefully set the glass plate on a counter or other safe surface as directed by your teacher.

⑦ Turn off the hot plate, and allow the beaker to cool. Move the hot beaker with gloves or tongs if your teacher directs you to do so.

Analyze the Results

① **Constructing Charts** Copy the illustration shown above. On your sketch, draw and label the water cycle as it happened in your model. Include arrows and labels for evaporation, condensation, and precipitation.

② **Analyzing Results** Compare the water level in the beaker now with the water level at the beginning of the experiment. Was there a change? Explain why or why not.

Draw Conclusions

③ **Making Predictions** If you had used a scale or a balance to measure the mass of the water in the beaker before and after this activity, would the mass have changed? Explain.

④ **Analyzing Charts** How is your model similar to Earth's water cycle? On your sketch of the illustration, label where the processes shown in the model reflect Earth's water cycle.

⑤ **Drawing Conclusions** When you finished this experiment, the water in the beaker was still hot. What stores much of the energy in Earth's water cycle?

Applying Your Data

As rainwater runs over the land, the water picks up minerals and salts. Do these minerals and salts evaporate, condense, and precipitate as part of the water cycle? Where do they go?

Chapter Review

USING KEY TERMS

Correct each statement by replacing the underlined term.

1 A stream that flows into a lake or into a larger stream is a <u>water cycle</u>.

2 The area along a river that forms from sediment deposited when the river overflows is a <u>delta</u>.

3 A rock's ability to let water pass through the rock is called <u>porosity</u>.

For each pair of terms, explain how the meanings of the terms differ.

4 *erosion* and *deposition* **FCAT VOCAB**

5 *artesian springs* and *wells*

6 *point-source pollution* and *nonpoint-source pollution*

UNDERSTANDING KEY IDEAS

Multiple Choice

7 Which of the following processes is NOT part of the water cycle?

a. evaporation

b. percolation

c. condensation

d. deposition

8 The features of a river change over time. Which features are common in youthful river channels? **D.1.3.5 CS** *FCAT*

a. meanders   c. rapids

b. floodplains   d. sandbars

9 Earth's features are changed by deposition. Which depositional feature is found at the coast? **D.1.3.1 CS** *FCAT*

a. delta   c. floodplain

b. alluvial fan   d. placer deposit

10 Caves are mainly a product of **D.1.3.1 CS**

a. erosion by rivers.

b. river deposition.

c. water pollution.

d. erosion by groundwater.

11 Sometimes, human activity can change an ecosystem. For example, human actions can pollute water and kill aquatic organisms. Which of the following factors is necessary for aquatic life to survive? **G.2.3.2 CS** *FCAT*

a. dissolved oxygen   c. nitrates

b alkalinity   d. silt

12 During primary treatment at a sewage treatment plant, **G.2.3.4 AA**

a. water is sent to an aeration tank.

b. water is mixed with bacteria and oxygen.

c. dirty water is passed through a large screen.

d. water is sent to a settling tank, where chlorine is added.

Short Answer

13 Identify and describe the location of the water table.

14 Explain how surface water enters an aquifer.

15 Why are caves usually found in limestone-rich regions? **D.1.3.1 CS**

The hydrograph below illustrates data collected on river flow during field investigations over a period of 1 year. The discharge readings are from the Yakima River in Washington. Use the hydrograph below to answer the questions that follow.

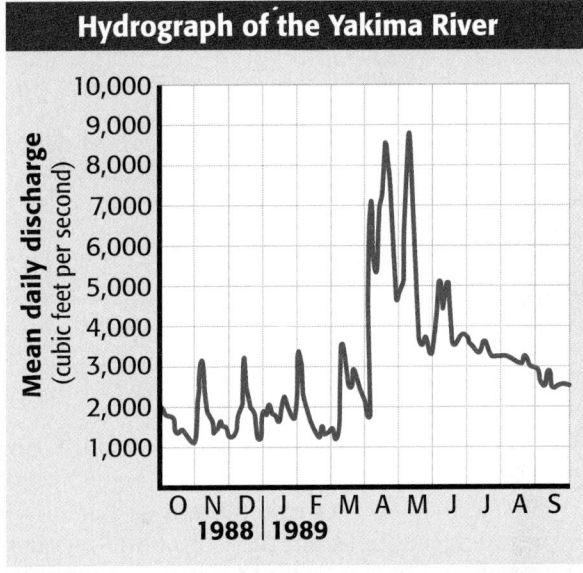

Hydrograph of the Yakima River

CRITICAL THINKING

Extended Response

16 Identifying Relationships What is water's role in erosion and deposition? D.1.3.1 CS

17 Analyzing Processes What are the features of a river channel that has a steep gradient?

18 Analyzing Processes How does human activity affect groundwater? Why is groundwater hard to clean? G.2.3.4 AA

19 Evaluating Conclusions How can water be considered both a renewable resource and a nonrenewable resource? Give an example of each case. G.2.3.1 CS

Concept Mapping

20 Use the following terms to create a concept map: *zone of aeration, zone of saturation, water table, permeability, porosity,* and *gravity*.

21 In which months is the river discharge the highest?

22 Why is the river discharge so high during these months?

23 What might cause the peaks in river discharge between November and March?

Chapter Review **445**

For the following questions, write your answers on a separate sheet of paper.

1 It took approximately six million years for the Colorado River to carve the Grand Canyon. The North Rim of the Grand Canyon is about 2440 meters above sea level, and the river is as much as 1830 meters lower than the North Rim. From this information, which of the following conclusions can you draw about the rate of erosion in the Grand Canyon?

    A. The rate of erosion by wind has been very fast.

    B. The rate of erosion by water has been very fast.

    C. The rate of erosion by wind has been comparatively slow.

    D. The rate of erosion by water has been comparatively slow.

2 Which one of the following kinds of deposits causes a continent's coastline to grow?

    F. a river delta

    G. an alluvial fan

    H. a placer deposit

    I. a river floodplain

3  Before the Glen Canyon Dam was built on the Colorado River, the Colorado River discharged approximately 182,500,000 tons of sediment each year. About how much sediment did the Colorado River deposit along its bed and in the Gulf of California each hour before the Glen Canyon Dam interrupted its flow?

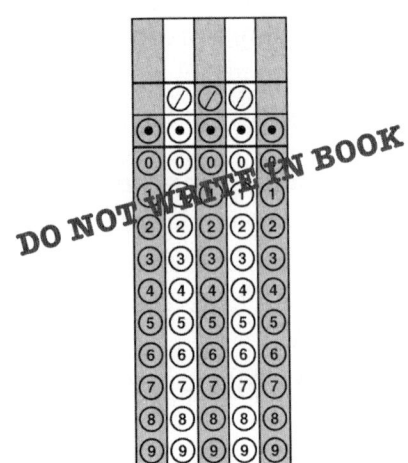

DO NOT WRITE IN BOOK

4 How do caves form in existing layers of limestone?

    A. by drops in the water table

    B. by the deposition of calcium carbonate

    C. by dissolution of limestone by weak acids in groundwater

    D. by the circulation of groundwater through an impermeable layer

5 The diagram below shows an artesian formation. Water in an artesian formation flows downhill through an aquifer under pressure. Where cracks occur in the overlying cap rock, water from the aquifer flows freely through the cracks, forming artesian springs.

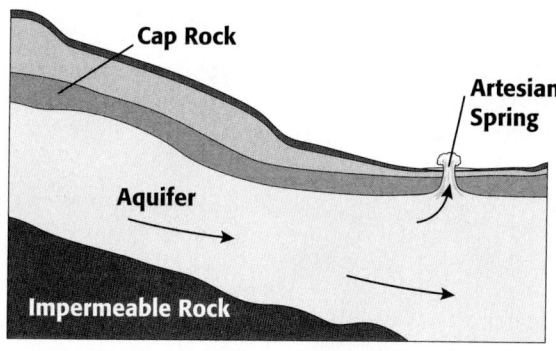

Artesian Springs

If a number of water wells were drilled into the aquifer, what would the **most likely** impact on the aquifer be?

   F.   Water pressure in the aquifer would increase.

   G.   The recharge zone of the aquifer would increase.

   H.   The water level in the aquifer would remain constant.

   I.   The rate of flow through the artesian spring would increase.

6 The table below shows the levels of dissolved oxygen in a lake in the northeastern United States over a period of 50 years. Since 1950, the dissolved oxygen level in the lake has been steadily decreasing, threatening the health of organisms living in the lake.

ANNUAL LEVELS OF DISSOLVED OXYGEN IN A LAKE

Year	Amount of Dissolved Oxygen (mg/l)
1950	8.1 mg/l
1960	7.6 mg/l
1970	7.0 mg/l
1980	6.4 mg/l
1990	5.8 mg/l
2000	5.0 mg/l

Between 1950 and 2000, the level of dissolved oxygen in the lake has decreased from 8.1 milligrams per liter to 5.0 milligrams per liter. What is the average decrease in the dissolved oxygen level per year (in milligrams per liter) in the lake over this 50-year period?

FCAT Preparation

Science in Action

Scientific Discoveries

Sunken Forests

Imagine having your own little secret forest. There are plenty of them in Ankarana National Park in Madagascar. Within the limestone mountain of the park, caves have formed from the twisting path of the flowing groundwater. In many places in the caves, the roof has collapsed to form a sinkhole. The light that now shines through the collapsed roof of the cave has allowed miniature sunken forests to grow. Each sunken forest has unique characteristics. Some have crocodiles. Others have blind cave fish. You can even find some species that can't be found anywhere else in the world!

Science, Technology, and Society

Mapping Wakulla Springs

The Wakulla Springs cave system is one of the world's largest and longest underwater caves and is located just 15 miles south of Tallahassee. Researchers don't even know how big the Wakulla Springs cave system is. To find out how big the cave system is, scientists have established Wakulla Springs mapping project. They hope to create a detailed three-dimensional map of the passageways and tunnels of the springs. Eventually, the project will create an interactive "virtual cave" for the public to explore. Scientists hope to make people aware of Florida's groundwater resources so that everyone can help protect these resources for the future. So far, researchers have explored more than 40,000 feet of the underwater passages, and there is much more to discover!

Social Studies ACTiViTY

Find out how Madagascar's geography contributes to the biodiversity of the island nation. Make a map of the island that highlights some of the unique forms of life found there.

Language Arts ACTiViTY

Create a treasure-mapping game. Write a story that explains how treasure came to be buried nearby. Then, write a series of clues that lead the players to a series of places and eventually to the treasure.

People in Science

Rita Colwell

A Water Filter for All Have you ever drunk a glass of water through a piece of cloth? Rita Colwell, former director of the National Science Foundation, has found that filtering drinking water through a cloth can decrease the number of disease-causing bacteria in the water. This discovery is very important for the people of Bangladesh, where deadly outbreaks of cholera are frequent. People are usually infected by the cholera bacteria by drinking contaminated water. Colwell knew that filtering the water would remove the bacteria. The water would then be safe to drink. Unfortunately, filters were too expensive for most of the people to buy. Colwell tried filtering the water with a sari. A sari is a long piece of colorful cloth that many women in Bangladesh wear as skirtlike clothing. Filtering the water with the sari did the trick. The amount of cholera bacteria in the water decreased. Fewer people contracted cholera, and many lives were saved!

Math

Using the cloth (sari) to filter water reduced the occurrence of cholera by 48%. If 125 people out of 100,000 contracted cholera before the cloth-filtering method was used, how many people per 100,000 contracted cholera after the cloth-filtering method was used?

To learn more about these Science in Action topics, visit go.hrw.com and type in the keyword **HT6FDEFF.**

Current Science

Check out Current Science® articles related to this chapter by visiting go.hrw.com. Just type in the keyword **HZ5CS11.**

17

Agents of Erosion and Deposition

The Big Idea Natural processes erode rock and soil and deposit them in other places.

About the PHOTO

The results of erosion can often be dramatic. For example, this sinkhole formed in a parking lot in Atlanta, Georgia, when water running underground eventually caused the surface of the land to collapse.

PRE-READING ACTIVITY

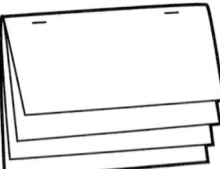

FOLDNOTES **Layered Book** Before you read the chapter, create the FoldNote entitled "Layered Book" described in the **Study Skills** section of the Appendix. Label the tabs of the layered book with "Shoreline erosion and deposition," "Wind erosion and deposition," and "Erosion and deposition by ice." As you read the chapter, write information you learn about each category under the appropriate tab.

START-UP ACTiViTY

Making Waves D.1.3.1 CS

Above or below ground, water plays an important role in the erosion and deposition of rock and soil. A shoreline is a good example of a place where water shapes Earth's surface by erosion and deposition. Did you know that shorelines are shaped by crashing waves? Build a model shoreline, and see for yourself!

Procedure

1. Make a shoreline by adding **sand** to one end of a **washtub.** Fill the washtub with **water** to a depth of 5 cm. Sketch the shoreline profile (side view), and label it "A."

2. Place a **block** at the end of the washtub opposite the beach.

3. Move the block up and down very slowly to create small waves for 2 min. Sketch the new shoreline profile, and label it "B."

4. Now, move the block up and down more rapidly to create large waves for 2 min. Sketch the new shoreline profile, and label it "C."

Analysis

1. Compare the three shoreline profiles. What is happening to the shoreline?

2. How does erosion of the shoreline by small waves differ from erosion by large waves?

Shoreline Erosion and Deposition

Think about the last time that you were at a beach. Where did all of the sand come from?

READING WARM-UP

Objectives

● Explain how energy from waves affects a shoreline.

● Identify six shoreline features created by wave erosion. **D.1.3.1 CS**

● Explain how wave deposits form beaches. **D.1.3.1 CS**

● Describe how sand moves along a beach. **D.1.3.1 CS**

Terms to Learn

shoreline
beach

READING STRATEGY

Reading Organizer As you read this section, create an outline of the section. Use the headings from the section in your outline.

Two ingredients are needed to make sand: rock and energy. Rock is usually available on the shore. Energy is provided by waves that travel through water. When waves crash into rock over long periods of time, the rock is broken down into smaller and smaller pieces until the pieces are so small that they are sand.

As you read on, you will learn how wave erosion and deposition shape the shoreline. A **shoreline** is simply the place where land and a body of water meet. Waves usually play a major role in building up and breaking down the shoreline.

Wave Energy

As wind moves across the ocean surface, it produces ripples called *waves*. The size of a wave depends on the strength of the wind and the time that the wind blows. The stronger the wind and the longer the wind blows, the bigger the wave.

Wind that results from summer hurricanes and severe winter storms produces large waves that cause dramatic shoreline erosion. Waves may travel hundreds or even thousands of kilometers from a storm before reaching the shoreline. Some of the largest waves to reach the California coast are produced by storms as far away as Australia. So, the California wave that the surfer in **Figure 1** is riding may have formed on the other side of the Pacific Ocean!

Figure 1 *Waves produced by storms on the other side of the Pacific Ocean propel this surfer toward a California shore.*

Wave Trains

When you drop a pebble into a pond, the pebble makes many ripples, not just one. Waves, like ripples, move in groups. As **Figure 2** shows, waves travel in groups called *wave trains*. As wave trains move away from their source, they travel uninterrupted through deep ocean water. But when a wave in a wave train reaches shallow water, the bottom of the wave drags against the sea floor, which slows the wave down. As a result, the top of the wave moves faster than the bottom of the wave does, and the wave gets taller. When the wave becomes so tall that it cannot support itself, it begins to curl and break. Breaking waves are known as *surf*. Now you know why people who ride the waves are called *surfers*. The waves in a wave train are separated by a period of time called the *wave period*. The wave period is the time interval between breaking waves. Most wave periods are 10 to 20 s long.

The Pounding Surf

Look at **Figure 3,** and you will get an idea of how sand is made. A tremendous amount of energy is released when waves break. A crashing wave can break solid rock and can throw broken rocks back against the shore. As the rushing water in breaking waves enters cracks in rock, the water helps break off large boulders and wash away fine grains of sand. The loose sand that is picked up by waves wears down and polishes coastal rocks. As a result of these actions, rock is broken down into smaller and smaller pieces that eventually become sand.

Benchmark Check Explain how waves help break rock down into sand. D.1.3.1 CS

Figure 2 *Because waves travel in wave trains, waves break at regular intervals.*

shoreline the boundary between land and a body of water

Benchmark Activity

Shifting Sands
Wave action moves sand along Florida's shores. Changes that affect waves affect beaches, too. Research how human activity, such as development, has changed the shape of local beaches. Then, make a diagram that shows how this activity alters waves and changes the beach. **D.1.3.1 CS**

Figure 3 *The energy of breaking waves is released when the waves crash against the rocky shore.*

Wave Erosion

Wave erosion produces a variety of features along a shoreline. *Sea cliffs* form when waves erode and undercut rock to produce steep slopes. Waves strike the base of the cliffs, which wears away the soil and rock and makes the cliffs steeper. The rate at which sea cliffs erode depends on the hardness of the rock and the energy of the waves. Sea cliffs made of hard rock, such as granite, erode very slowly. Sea cliffs made of soft rock, such as shale, erode more rapidly, especially during storms.

D.1.3.1 CS knows that mechanical and chemical activities shape and reshape the Earth's land surface by eroding rock and soil in some areas and depositing them in other areas, sometimes in seasonal layers.

Figure 4 **Coastal Landforms Created by Wave Erosion**

Sea stacks are offshore columns of resistant rock that were once connected to the mainland. Sea stacks form when waves erode the mainland and leave behind isolated columns of rock.

Sea arches form when wave action erodes sea caves until arches are cut through the caves.

Sea caves form when waves cut large holes into fractured or weak rock along the base of sea cliffs. Sea caves are common in cliffs that are composed of sedimentary rock.

Shaping a Shoreline

Much of the erosion responsible for landforms that you might see along the shoreline takes place during storms. Large waves generated by storms release far more energy than average-sized waves do. This energy is so powerful that it can remove huge chunks of rock. **Figure 4** shows some of the major landscape features that result from wave erosion.

Benchmark Check Explain why large waves are more capable of removing large chunks of rock from a shoreline than average-sized waves are. **D.1.3.1 CS**

Erosion Disasters

Sometimes, Earth changes very quickly. Research some of the dramatic results of such rapid change. Go to **go.hrw.com,** and type in the keyword **HZ5ICEW.**

Headlands are finger-shaped projections that form when cliffs of hard rock erode more slowly than the surrounding softer rock does. On many shorelines, hard rock forms headlands, and softer rock forms beaches or bays.

Wave-cut terraces form when a sea cliff is worn back from shore, which produces a nearly level platform beneath the water at the base of the cliff.

England

Florida

Hawaii

Figure 5 *Beaches are made of various types of materials deposited by waves.*

beach an area of the shoreline that is made up of deposited sediment

Wave Deposits

Waves carry a variety of materials, including sand, rock fragments, dead coral, and shells. Often, these materials are deposited on a shoreline, where they form a beach.

Beaches

You may think that all beaches are sandy places at the seashore. However, the technical definition of a **beach** is any area of shoreline that is made up of material deposited by waves. Some beach material is also deposited by rivers.

Notice that the color and texture of the beach materials shown in **Figure 5** vary between beaches. They vary because the source of the beach materials differs between beaches. The type of beach material depends on the material's source. Light-colored sand is the most common beach material. Much of this sand is made of the mineral quartz. Many Florida beaches are made of quartz sand. But not all beaches are made of light-colored sand. On many tropical islands, such as the Virgin Islands, sandlike beach material is made of finely ground white coral. Black sand beaches in Hawaii are made of eroded lava from Hawaiian volcanoes. In areas where stormy seas are common, beach material is made of pebbles and boulders.

Benchmark Check Identify different sources of materials that make up beaches. **D.1.3.1 CS**

Wave Angle and Sand Movement

The movement of sand along a beach depends on the angle at which waves strike the shore. Most waves approach the beach at a slight angle and retreat in a direction that is more perpendicular to the shore. This movement of water is a *longshore current*. A longshore current is a water current that moves sand in a zigzag pattern along the beach, as **Figure 6** shows.

Figure 6 *When waves strike the shoreline at an angle, sand migrates along the beach in a zigzag path.*

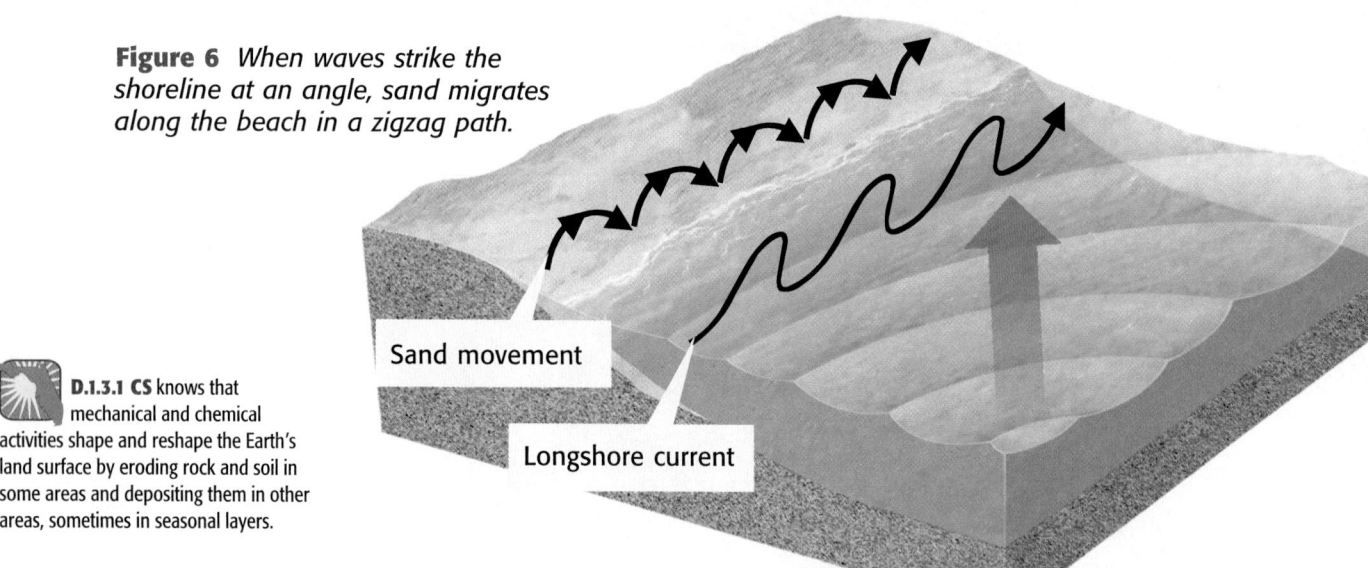

Sand movement

Longshore current

D.1.3.1 CS knows that mechanical and chemical activities shape and reshape the Earth's land surface by eroding rock and soil in some areas and depositing them in other areas, sometimes in seasonal layers.

Offshore Deposits

Waves moving at an angle to the shoreline push water along the shore and create longshore currents. When waves erode material from the shoreline, longshore currents can transport and deposit this material offshore, which creates landforms in open water. A *sandbar* is an underwater or exposed ridge of sand, gravel, or shell material. A *barrier spit* is an exposed sandbar that is connected to the shoreline. Cape Cod, Massachusetts, shown in **Figure 7,** is an example of a barrier spit. A barrier island is a long, narrow island usually made of sand that forms parallel to the shoreline a small distance offshore.

Figure 7 *A barrier spit, such as Cape Cod, Massachusetts, occurs when an exposed sandbar is connected to the shoreline.*

SECTION Review

Summary

- As waves break against a shoreline, their energy breaks rocks down into sand.

- Six shoreline features that are created by wave erosion are sea cliffs, sea stacks, sea caves, sea arches, headlands, and wave-cut terraces. **D.1.3.1 CS**

- Beaches are made from material deposited by waves. **D.1.3.1 CS**

- Longshore currents cause sand to move in a zigzag pattern along the shore. **D.1.3.1 CS**

Using Key Terms

Use a term from the section to complete each sentence below.

1. A(n) ___ is an area made up of material deposited by waves.

2. An area in which land and a body of water meet is a(n) ___.

Understanding Key Ideas

3. How do wave deposits affect a shoreline? **D.1.3.1 CS**

4. Describe how sand moves along a beach.

5. What are six shoreline features that are created by wave erosion? **D.1.3.1 CS**

6. How can the energy of water waves affect a shoreline?

Critical Thinking

7. **Applying Concepts** Which wave would have more energy: a small wave or a large wave? Explain your answer.

8. **Applying Concepts** Not all beaches are made from light-colored sand. Explain why this statement is true. **D.1.3.1 CS**

FCAT Preparation

9. Wave properties play an important role in shoreline erosion. How would an increase in wave period affect erosion of a rocky shoreline? **D.1.3.1 CS**

   A. More waves would hit the shore each day, which would increase erosion.

   B. Fewer waves would hit the shore each day, which would decrease erosion.

   C. Erosion of the rocky shoreline would not change.

   D. Wave trains would increase, which would cause more drag on the rocky shore and would increase erosion.

SCI**LINKS**®

NSTA
Developed and maintained by the
National Science Teachers Association

For a variety of links related to this chapter, go to www.scilinks.org

Topic: Wave Erosion
SciLinks code: HSM1638

Wind Erosion and Deposition

Have you ever been writing outside and had a gusty wind blow a stack of important papers all over the place?

Do you remember how fast and far the papers traveled and how long it took to pick them up? Every time that you caught up with them, they moved. If this has happened to you, you have seen how wind erosion works. In the same way that wind moved your papers, wind moves soil, sand, and rock particles from one place to another. When wind moves soil, sand, and rock particles, wind acts as an agent of erosion.

Some areas are more vulnerable to wind erosion than other areas are. An area that has sparse plant cover can be severely affected by wind erosion because the area lacks plant roots, which anchor sand and soil in place. Deserts and coastlines that are made of fine, loose rock material and that have sparse plant cover are shaped most dramatically by wind.

The Process of Wind Erosion

Wind moves material in different ways. In areas where strong winds occur, material is moved by saltation. **Saltation** is the skipping and bouncing movement of sand-sized particles in the direction that wind is blowing. As shown in **Figure 1,** wind causes the particles to bounce. When moving sand grains knock into one another, some grains bounce up in the air, fall forward, and strike other sand grains. These impacts cause other grains to roll and bounce forward.

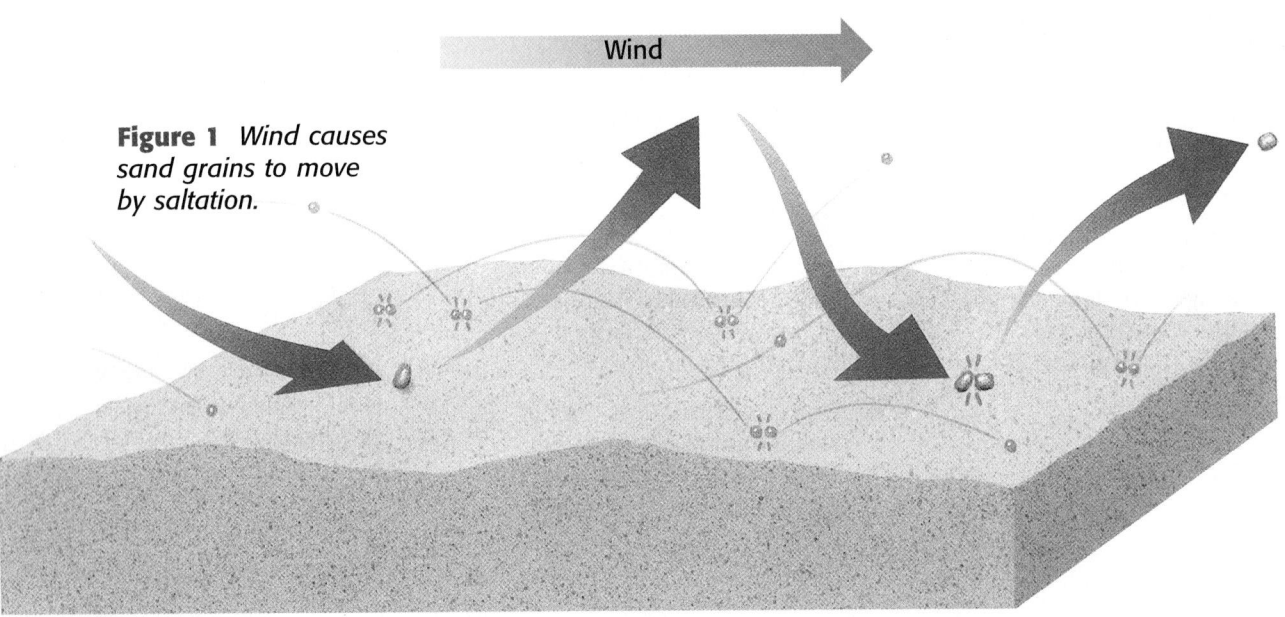

Wind

Figure 1 *Wind causes sand grains to move by saltation.*

Figure 2 *Desert pavement, such as that found in the Painted Desert in Arizona, forms when wind removes all of the fine materials.*

Deflation

The removal of fine sediment by wind is called **deflation.** During deflation, wind removes the top layer of fine sediment or soil and leaves behind rock fragments that are too heavy to be lifted by the wind. Deflation may cause the formation of *desert pavement*, which is a surface that is made of pebbles and small broken rocks. An example of desert pavement is shown in **Figure 2.**

Have you ever blown on a layer of dust on a shelf? If you have, you may have noticed not only that your face got dirty but also that a little scooped-out depression formed in the dust. Similarly, in areas where vegetation is scarce, the wind may scoop out depressions in the landscape. These depressions are called *deflation hollows*.

> **Benchmark Check** Explain how deflation hollows form. **D.1.3.1 CS**

saltation the movement of sand or other sediments by short jumps and bounces that is caused by wind or water

deflation a form of wind erosion in which fine, dry soil particles are blown away

abrasion the grinding and wearing away of rock surfaces through the mechanical action of other rock or sand particles

Abrasion

The grinding and wearing down of rock surfaces by other rock or by sand particles is called **abrasion.** Abrasion commonly happens in areas where there are strong winds, loose sand, and soft rocks. The blowing of millions of sharp sand grains creates a sandblasting effect. This effect helps erode, smooth, and polish rocks.

D.1.3.1 CS knows that mechanical and chemical activities shape and reshape the Earth's land surface by eroding rock and soil in some areas and depositing them in other areas, sometimes in seasonal layers.

Making Desert Pavement

1. Spread a mixture of **dust, sand,** and **gravel** on an **outdoor table.** The mixture represents sediment.

2. Place an **electric fan** at one end of the table.

3. Put on **safety goggles** and a **filter mask.** Aim the fan across the sediment. Set the fan on its lowest speed, and turn the fan on. Record your observations.

4. Set the fan on a medium speed. Record your observations.

5. Finally, set the fan on a high speed so that the fan imitates a desert windstorm. Record your observations.

6. What is the relationship between wind speed and the size of the sediment particles moved?

7. Does the remaining sediment fit the definition of *desert pavement*?

loess fine-grained sediments of quartz, feldspar, hornblende, mica, and clay deposited by the wind

dune a mound of wind-deposited sand that moves as a result of the action of wind

D.1.3.1 CS knows that mechanical and chemical activities shape and reshape the Earth's land surface by eroding rock and soil in some areas and depositing them in other areas, sometimes in seasonal layers.

Wind-Deposited Materials

In much the same way that rivers carry sediment, wind carries sediment. And just as rivers deposit their loads, wind eventually drops all of the material that it carries. The amount and size of the particles that wind can carry depend on wind speed. The faster wind blows, the more material and the heavier the particles that wind can carry. As wind speed slows, particles are deposited according to weight, from heaviest to lightest. So, heavy particles are deposited first.

Loess

Wind can deposit very fine-grained material. Thick deposits of windblown, fine-grained sediment are known as **loess** (LOH ES). Loess has the texture of talcum powder or cornstarch.

Because wind carries fine-grained material much higher and farther than it carries sand, loess deposits are often found far from the source of the loess. Many loess deposits came from glacial sources during the last ice age. In the United States, loess is found in the Midwest, along the eastern edge of the Mississippi Valley, and in eastern Oregon and Washington.

Dunes

When wind hits an obstacle, such as a plant or a rock, the wind slows down. As it slows, the wind deposits, or drops, on top of the obstacle the heaviest material that it is carrying. As the material builds up, the obstacle gets larger. This obstacle causes the wind to slow more and deposit more material, which forms a mound. Eventually, the original obstacle is buried. Mounds of wind-deposited sand are called **dunes.** Dunes are common in sandy deserts and along the sandy shores of lakes and oceans. **Figure 3** shows a large dune in a desert area.

Figure 3 *Dunes migrate in the direction of the wind.*

The Movement of Dunes

Generally, dunes move in the direction of strong winds. Wind conditions determine the shape and size of a dune. A dune usually has a gently sloped side and a steeply sloped side, or *slip face,* as shown in **Figure 4.** In most cases, the gently sloped side faces the wind. The wind is constantly transporting material up this side of the dune. As sand moves over the crest, or peak, of the dune, the sand slides down the slip face and creates a steep slope.

Benchmark Check Explain how dunes move. **D.1.3.1 CS**

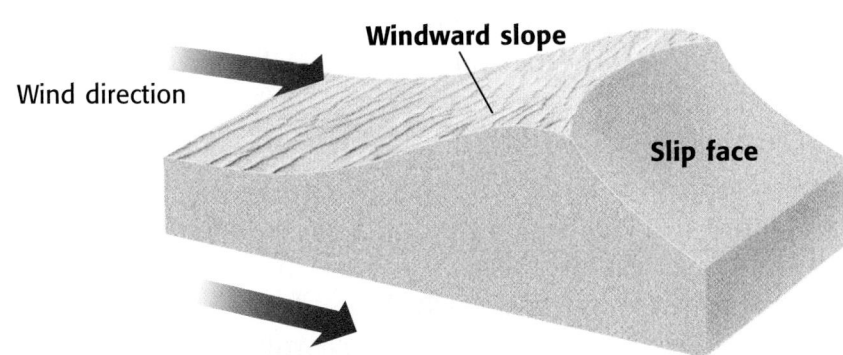

Wind direction

Windward slope

Slip face

Figure 4 *Dunes are formed from material deposited by wind.*

SECTION Review

Summary

● Areas that have sparse plant cover and desert areas that are covered with fine rock material are more vulnerable to wind erosion than other areas are. **D.1.3.1 CS**

● Saltation is the process in which sand-sized particles move in the direction of the wind.

● Desert pavement, deflation hollows, and dunes are landforms that are created by wind erosion and deposition. **D.1.3.1 CS**

● Dunes move in the direction of the wind.

Using Key Terms

1. Use *saltation, abrasion,* and *deflation* in separate sentences.

Understanding Key Ideas

2. Describe how material is moved in areas where strong winds blow. **D.1.3.1 CS**

3. Explain the process of abrasion. **D.1.3.1 CS**

4. Identify three landforms that result from wind erosion and deposition. **D.1.3.1 CS**

Critical Thinking

5. **Identifying Relationships** Explain the relationship between plant cover and wind erosion. **D.1.3.4 AA**

6. **Applying Concepts** If you climbed up the steep side of a sand dune, did you most likely travel in the direction that the wind was blowing? **D.1.3.1 CS**

FCAT Preparation

7. Wind erodes particles in one area and deposits them elsewhere. Which of the following materials would wind deposit farthest from the source of the material? **D.1.3.1 CS**

A. cobbles

B. desert pavement

C. sand

D. loess

Developed and maintained by the National Science Teachers Association

For a variety of links related to this chapter, go to www.scilinks.org

Topic: Wind Erosion
SciLinks code: HSM1669

Erosion and Deposition by Ice

Can you imagine an ice cube that is the size of a football stadium? Well, glaciers can be even bigger than that.

A **glacier** is an enormous mass of moving ice. Glaciers are very heavy and can move across Earth's surface. Because of this ability to move, glaciers can erode, move, and deposit large amounts of rock material. And while you are not likely to see a glacier floating in a punch bowl, you might visit some of the spectacular landscapes carved by glacial activity.

Glaciers—Rivers of Ice

Glaciers form in areas so cold that snow stays on the ground year-round. In polar regions and at high elevations, layers of snow build up year after year. Over time, the weight of the top layer causes the lower layers, which are deep-packed snow, to become packed ice. This packed ice eventually forms a giant ice mass. Because glaciers are massive, the pull of gravity has a noticeable affect on them. Gravity causes glaciers to flow—although slowly—like "rivers of ice." This section discusses two types of glaciers: alpine glaciers and continental glaciers.

Alpine Glaciers

Alpine glaciers form in mountainous areas. A common type of alpine glacier is a valley glacier. Valley glaciers form in valleys formed by stream erosion. As a valley glacier flows downhill, it widens and straightens its valley into a broad U shape, as **Figure 1** shows.

✓ Reading Check Where do alpine glaciers form?

glacier a large mass of moving ice

Figure 1 *Alpine glaciers start as snowfields in mountainous areas.*

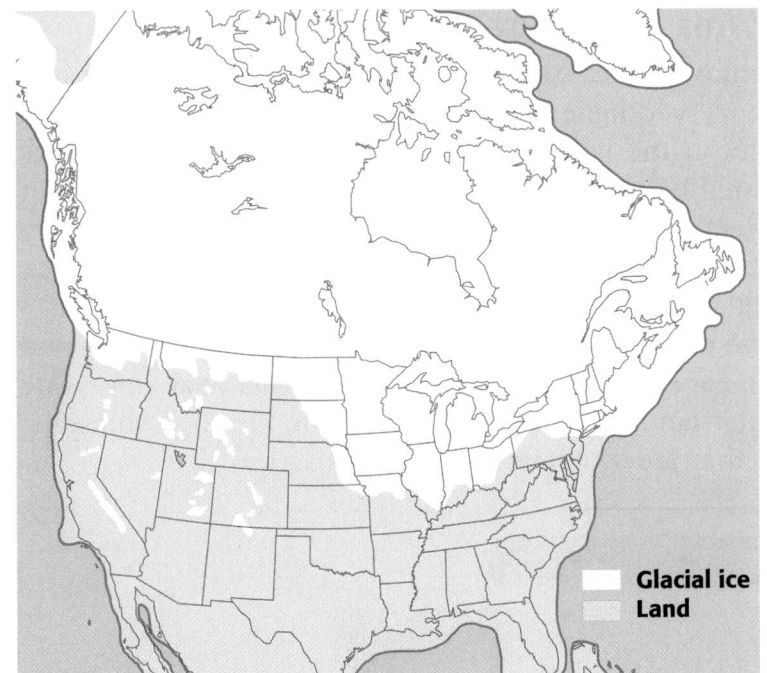

Figure 2 *Land that would become eleven U.S. states was covered by ice during the last glacial ice period. Because much of Earth's water was frozen in glaciers, sea levels fell. Blue lines show the coastline at that time.*

Glacial ice
Land

Continental Glaciers

Not all glaciers are "rivers of ice"; some glaciers spread across entire continents. These glaciers, called *continental glaciers,* are huge, continuous masses of ice. Earth's largest continental glacier covers almost all of Antarctica. This glacier covers approximately one and a half times the area of the United States. This ice sheet is so thick—more than 4,000 m in places—that it buries everything but the tallest mountain peaks.

Glaciers on the Move

When enough ice builds up on a slope, the ice begins to move downhill. Thick glaciers move faster than thin glaciers do, and the steeper the slope is, the faster the glaciers move. Glaciers move in two ways: by sliding and by flowing. A glacier slides when its weight causes the ice at the bottom of the glacier to melt. Much as the water from a melting ice cube causes the ice cube to slide across a table, the water from a melting glacier causes the glacier to move. A glacier also flows because the ice crystals of the glacier slip over each other. For example, when you tilt a table on which a deck of cards is placed, the top cards slide farther than the lower cards do. Similarly, the top of the glacier flows faster than the base does.

Glacier movement is affected by climate. As Earth cools, glaciers grow. About 10,000 years ago, a continental glacier covered most of North America, as shown in **Figure 2.** In some places, the glacial ice sheet was several kilometers thick.

WRITING SKILL **The *Titanic*** An area where an ice sheet rests on open water is an *ice shelf.* Pieces that break off of an ice shelf are *icebergs.* How far do you think the iceberg that struck the ship *Titanic* drifted before it met the ship on that fateful night in 1912? With a family member, plot on a map of the North Atlantic Ocean the route of the *Titanic* from Southampton, England, to New York. Then, plot a possible route of the drifting iceberg from Greenland to where the ship sank, which was south of Newfoundland, a Canadian island province. Describe your findings in your **science journal.**

Benchmark Check Explain why the top of a glacier flows faster than the base of a glacier does. **D.1.3.5 CS**

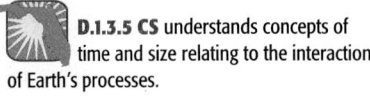

D.1.3.5 CS understands concepts of time and size relating to the interaction of Earth's processes.

Speed of a Glacier

An alpine glacier is moving toward a camp at a rate of 0.5 m per day. Calculate the number of days that the ice will take to reach the camp if the camp is 0.1 km from the glacier. (Hint: 1 km = 1,000 m) **D.1.3.5 CS**

Landforms Carved by Glaciers

Continental glaciers and alpine glaciers produce landscapes that are very different from one another. Continental glaciers smooth the landscape by scraping and eroding features that existed before the ice appeared. Alpine glaciers carve out rugged features in the mountain rocks through which they flow. **Figure 3** shows the very different landscapes that each type of glacier produces.

Alpine glaciers, such as those in the Rocky Mountains and the Alps, carve out large amounts of rock material and create spectacular landforms. **Figure 4** shows the kinds of landscape features that are sculpted by alpine glaciers.

Figure 3 **Landscapes Created by Glaciers**

◀ Continental glaciers smooth and flatten the landscape.

Alpine glaciers carved out this rugged landscape. ▶

Figure 4 **Landscape Features Carved by Alpine Glaciers**

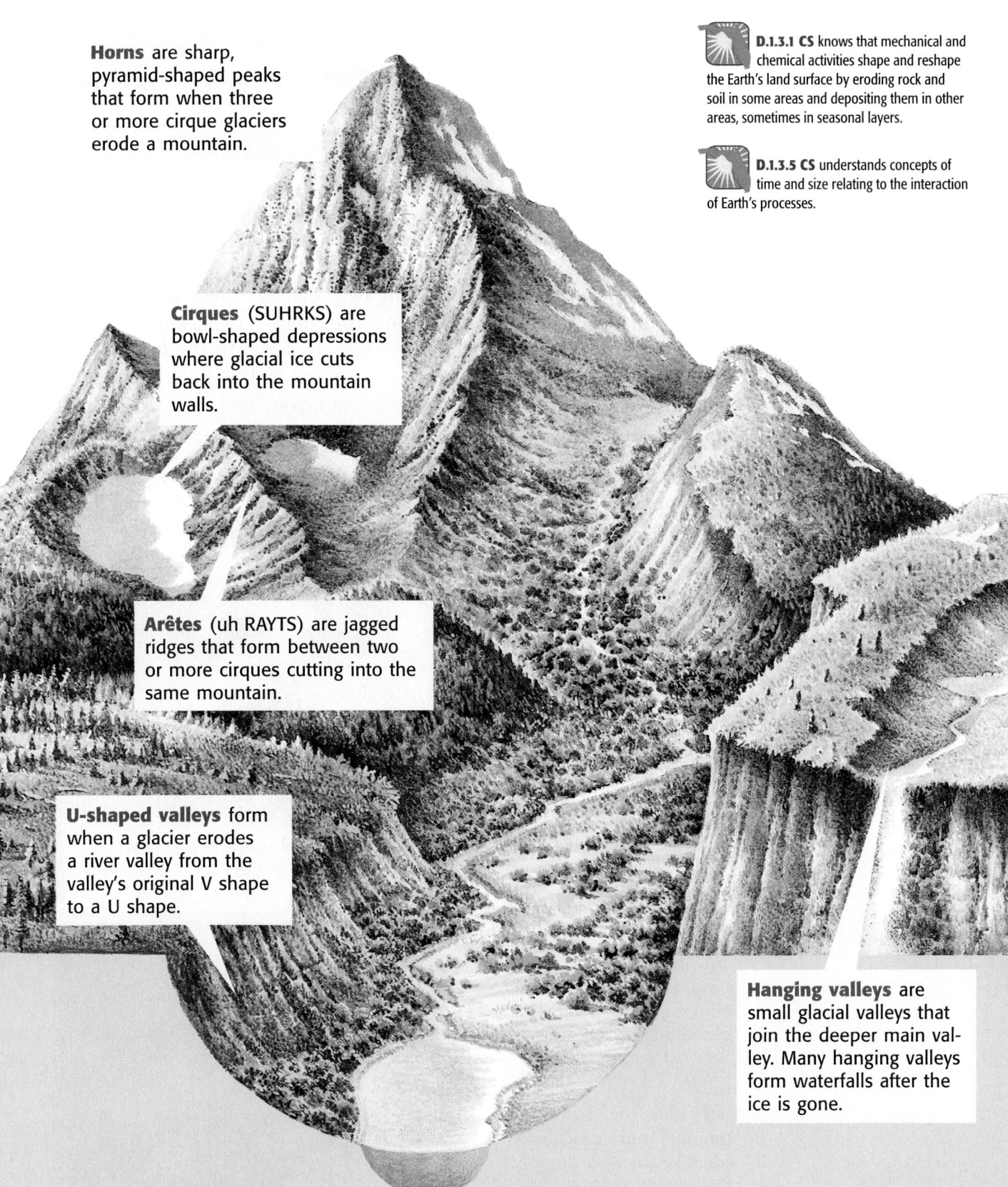

Horns are sharp, pyramid-shaped peaks that form when three or more cirque glaciers erode a mountain.

D.1.3.1 CS knows that mechanical and chemical activities shape and reshape the Earth's land surface by eroding rock and soil in some areas and depositing them in other areas, sometimes in seasonal layers.

D.1.3.5 CS understands concepts of time and size relating to the interaction of Earth's processes.

Cirques (SUHRKS) are bowl-shaped depressions where glacial ice cuts back into the mountain walls.

Arêtes (uh RAYTS) are jagged ridges that form between two or more cirques cutting into the same mountain.

U-shaped valleys form when a glacier erodes a river valley from the valley's original V shape to a U shape.

Hanging valleys are small glacial valleys that join the deeper main valley. Many hanging valleys form waterfalls after the ice is gone.

Section 3 Erosion and Deposition by Ice **465**

Types of Glacial Deposits

glacial drift the rock material carried and deposited by glaciers

till unsorted rock material that is deposited directly by a melting glacier

stratified drift a glacial deposit that has been sorted and layered by the action of streams or meltwater

D.1.3.1 CS knows that mechanical and chemical activities shape and reshape the Earth's land surface by eroding rock and soil in some areas and depositing them in other areas, sometimes in seasonal layers.

As a glacier melts, it drops all of the material that it is carrying. **Glacial drift** is the general term used to describe all material carried and deposited by glaciers. Glacial drift is divided into two main types, *till* and *stratified drift*.

Till Deposits

Unsorted rock material that is deposited directly by the ice when it melts is called **till.** *Unsorted* means that the till is made up of rock material of various sizes—from large boulders to fine sediment. When the glacier melts, the unsorted material is deposited on the surface of the ground.

The most common till deposits are *moraines*. Moraines generally form ridges along the edges of glaciers. Moraines are produced when glaciers carry material to the front of and along the sides of the ice. As the ice melts, the sediment and rock that the ice is carrying are dropped. This dropped material forms various types of moraines. The various types of moraines are shown in **Figure 5.**

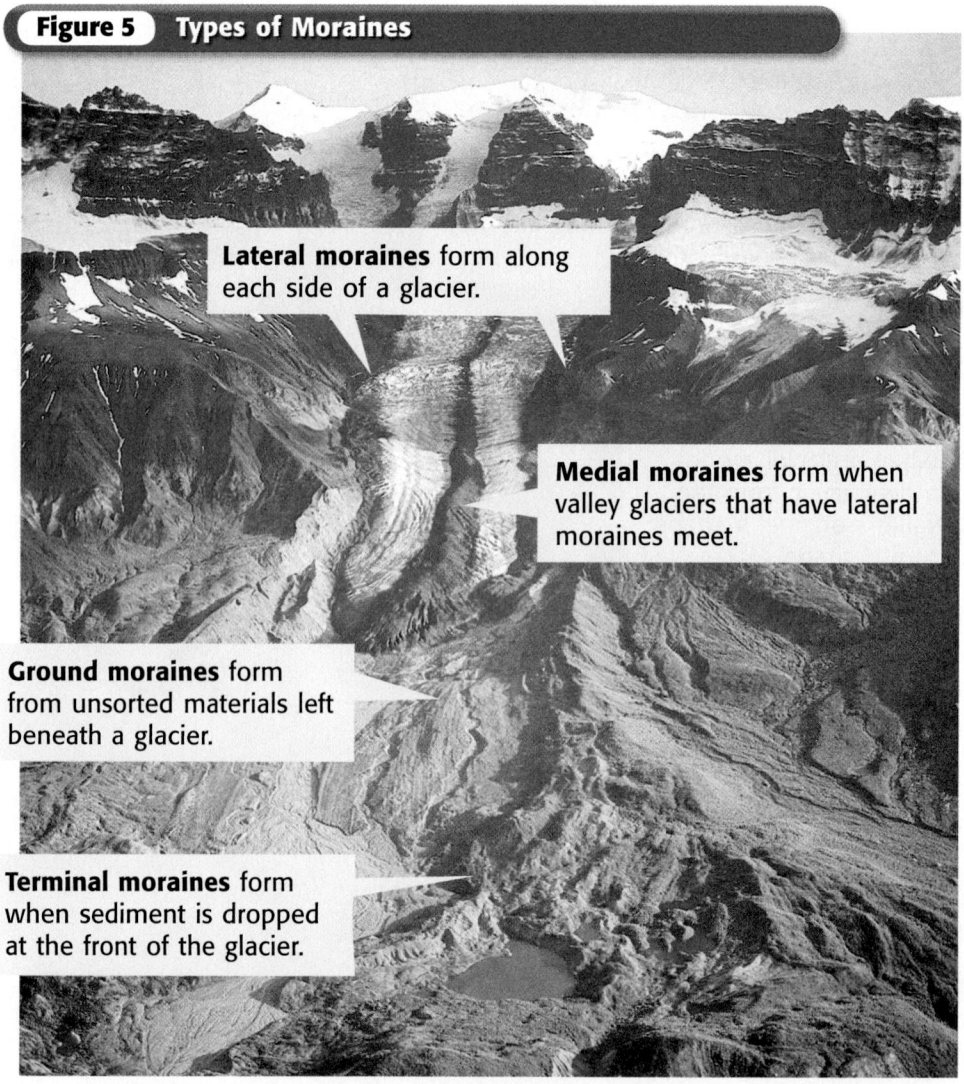

Figure 5 Types of Moraines

Lateral moraines form along each side of a glacier.

Medial moraines form when valley glaciers that have lateral moraines meet.

Ground moraines form from unsorted materials left beneath a glacier.

Terminal moraines form when sediment is dropped at the front of the glacier.

Stratified Drift

When a glacier melts, streams that carry rock material away from the shrinking glacier form. A glacial deposit that is sorted into layers based on the size of the rock material is called **stratified drift.** Streams carry sorted material and deposit it in front of the glacier in a broad area called an *outwash plain*. Sometimes, a block of ice is left in the outwash plain when a glacier retreats. As the ice melts, sediment builds up around the block of ice, and a depression called a *kettle* forms. Kettles commonly fill with water to form lakes or ponds, such as the lakes shown in **Figure 6.**

✔ **Reading Check** Explain what is meant by stratified drift.

Figure 6 *Kettle lakes form in outwash plains and are common in states such as Minnesota.*

SECTION Review

Summary

- Alpine glaciers form in mountainous areas. Continental glaciers spread across continents.
- Glaciers move by sliding or by flowing. **D.1.3.5 CS**
- Alpine glaciers can carve cirques, arêtes, horns, U-shaped valleys, and hanging valleys. **D.1.3.1 CS**
- Two types of glacial drift are till and stratified drift.
- Four types of moraines are lateral, medial, ground, and terminal moraines. **D.1.3.1 CS**

Using Key Terms

Use a term from the section to complete each sentence below.

1. A glacial deposit that is sorted into layers based on the size of the rock material is called ___.

2. ___ is all of the material carried and deposited by glaciers.

3. Unsorted rock material that is deposited directly by the ice when the ice melts is ___.

Understanding Key Ideas

4. Describe two ways in which glaciers move. **D.1.3.5 CS**

5. Name five landscape features formed by alpine glaciers. **D.1.3.1 CS**

6. Identify four types of moraines. **D.1.3.1 CS**

Critical Thinking

7. **Analyzing Ideas** Explain why continental glaciers smooth the landscape and alpine glaciers create a rugged landscape. **D.1.3.1 CS**

8. **Applying Concepts** Why are glaciers such effective agents of erosion and deposition? **D.1.3.1 CS**

FCAT Preparation

9. A glacier is a mass of moving ice. Because glaciers are very heavy and have the ability to move across Earth's surface, glaciers are capable of eroding, moving, and depositing large amounts of rock material. Which term describes the ridges that form as a glacier melts and deposits sediments on its sides? **D.1.3.1 CS**

   A. terminal moraine

   B. lateral moraine

   C. medial moraine

   D. ground moraine

SCiLINKS®

NSTA
Developed and maintained by the National Science Teachers Association

For a variety of links related to this chapter, go to www.scilinks.org

Topic: Glaciers
SciLinks code: HSM0675

Gravity's Effect on Erosion and Deposition

Did you know that the Appalachian Mountains may have once been almost five times as tall as they are now? Why are they now shorter than that? Part of the answer lies in the effect that gravity has on all objects on Earth.

Although you can't see it, the force of gravity is an agent of erosion and deposition. Gravity not only influences water and ice movement but also causes rocks and soil to move downslope. **Mass movement** is the movement of any material, such as rock, soil, or snow, downslope. Whether rapid or slow, mass movement plays a major role in shaping Earth's surface.

Angle of Repose

In a dry sand pile, sand in the pile moves downhill until the slope of the pile becomes stable, or unchanging. The *angle of repose* is the steepest angle, or slope, at which loose material no longer moves downslope. The angle of repose is demonstrated in **Figure 1.** The angle of repose varies with the type of surface material. Surface material characteristics, such as size, weight, shape, and moisture level, determine the angle of repose. If the slope of surface material is greater than the angle of repose, mass movement occurs.

mass movement the movement of a large mass of sediment or a section of land down a slope

Figure 1 *If the slope on which material rests is less than the angle of repose, the material will stay in place. If the slope is greater than the angle of repose, the material will move downslope.*

D.1.3.1 CS knows that mechanical and chemical activities shape and reshape the Earth's land surface by eroding rock and soil in some areas and depositing them in other areas, sometimes in seasonal layers.

Rapid Mass Movement

The most destructive mass movements happen suddenly and rapidly. Rapid mass movement can be very dangerous and can destroy everything in its path.

Rock Falls

While driving along a mountain road, you may have noticed signs along the road that warn of falling rocks. A **rock fall** happens when loose rocks fall down a steep slope. Steep slopes are sometimes created when a road is built through mountainous areas. Loosened and exposed rocks above the road tend to fall as a result of gravity. The rocks in a rock fall can range in size from small fragments to large boulders.

Landslides

Another type of rapid mass movement is a landslide. A **landslide** is the sudden and rapid movement of a large amount of material downslope. A *slump,* shown in **Figure 2,** is the most common type of landslide. Slumping occurs when a block of material moves downslope over a curved surface. Heavy rains, deforestation, construction on unstable slopes, and earthquakes increase the chances that a landslide will happen. **Figure 3** shows a landslide in India.

Benchmark Check Explain the cause of a slump. D.1.3.1 CS

Figure 2 *A slump is a type of landslide that occurs when a block of land becomes detached and slides downhill.*

rock fall the rapid mass movement of rock down a steep slope or cliff

landslide the sudden movement of rock and soil down a slope

Figure 3 *This landslide in Bombay, India, happened after heavy monsoon rains.*

Figure 4 *This photo shows one of the many mudflows that have occurred in California during rainy winters.*

mudflow the flow of a mass of mud or rock and soil mixed with a large amount of water

D.1.3.1 CS knows that mechanical and chemical activities shape and reshape the Earth's land surface by eroding rock and soil in some areas and depositing them in other areas, sometimes in seasonal layers.

D.1.3.5 CS understands concepts of time and size relating to the interaction of Earth's processes.

Mudflows

A rapid movement of a large mass of mud is a **mudflow.** Mudflows happen when a large amount of water mixes with soil and rock. The water causes the slippery mass of mud to flow rapidly downslope. Mudflows commonly happen in mountainous regions when a long dry season is followed by heavy rains. Deforestation and the removal of ground cover often result in devastating mudflows. As shown in **Figure 4,** a mudflow can carry trees, houses, cars, and other objects that lie in its path.

Lahars

Volcanic eruptions or heavy rains on volcanic ash can produce some of the most dangerous mudflows. Mudflows of volcanic origin are called *lahars*. Lahars can travel at speeds greater than 80 km/h and can be as thick as cement. On volcanoes that have snowy peaks, an eruption can suddenly melt a great amount of ice. The water from the ice liquefies the soil and volcanic ash to produce a hot mudflow that rushes downslope. **Figure 5** shows the effects of a massive lahar in Japan.

Benchmark Check How much time would a lahar whose speed is 80 km/h take to travel to a village that is 10 km away? D.1.3.5 CS

Figure 5 *This lahar overtook the city of Kyushu in Japan.*

Slow Mass Movement

Sometimes, mass movement is not noticeable. Although rapid mass movements are visible and dramatic, slow mass movements happen gradually. However, because slow mass movements occur more frequently than rapid mass movements do, over time slow mass movements move more material than rapid mass movements do.

Creep

Even though most slopes appear to be stable, they are actually undergoing slow mass movement, as shown in **Figure 6.** The extremely slow movement of material downslope is called **creep.** Many factors contribute to creep. Water loosens soil and allows the soil to move freely. In addition, plant roots act as wedges that force rocks and soil particles apart. Burrowing animals, such as gophers and groundhogs, also loosen rock and soil particles. In fact, all rock and soil on slopes travel slowly downhill.

Figure 6 *Bent tree trunks are evidence that creep is happening.*

creep the slow downhill movement of weathered rock material

Summary

- Gravity causes rocks and soil to move downslope. **D.1.3.1 CS**

- If the slope on which material rests is greater than the angle of repose, mass movement will occur. **D.1.3.1 CS**

- Four types of rapid mass movement are rock falls, landslides, mudflows, and lahars. **D.1.3.1 CS**

- Water, plant roots, and burrowing animals can cause creep. **D.1.3.1 CS**

Using Key Terms

Use a term from the section to complete each sentence below.

1. A(n) ___ occurs when a large amount of water mixes with soil and rock.

2. The extremely slow movement of material downslope is called ___. **D.1.3.5 CS**

Understanding Key Ideas

3. How is the angle of repose related to mass movement? **D.1.3.1 CS**

Critical Thinking

4. **Identifying Relationships** Which types of mass movement are most dangerous to humans? Explain your answer.

5. **Making Inferences** How does deforestation increase the likelihood of mudflows? **G.2.3.4 AA**

FCAT Preparation

7. Gravity can cause rapid mass movement of rocks and soil. Which situation would most likely cause the rapid fall of rocks down a mountainside? **D.1.3.1 CS**

   A. heavy rains
   B. deforestation
   C. volcanic eruption
   D. mountain road construction

SCI LINKS®

NSTA

Developed and maintained by the National Science Teachers Association

For a variety of links related to this chapter, go to www.scilinks.org

Topic: Mass Movements
SciLinks code: HSM0917

Model-Making Lab

Gliding Glaciers

A glacier is a large, moving mass of ice. Glaciers are responsible for shaping many of Earth's natural features. Glaciers are set in motion by the pull of gravity and by the gradual melting of the glacier. As a glacier moves, it changes the landscape by eroding the surface over which it passes.

Part A: Getting in the Groove

Procedure

The material that is carried by a glacier erodes Earth's surface by gouging out grooves called *striations*. Different materials have varying effects on the landscape. In this activity, you will create a model glacier with which to demonstrate the effects of glacial erosion by various materials.

1. Fill one margarine container with sand to a depth of 1 cm. Fill another margarine container with gravel to a depth of 1 cm. Leave the third container empty. Fill the containers with water.

2. Put the three containers in a freezer, and leave them there overnight.

3. Retrieve the containers from the freezer, and remove the three ice blocks from the containers.

4. Use a rolling pin to flatten the modeling clay.

5. Hold the ice block from the third container firmly with a towel, and press as you move the ice along the length of the clay. Do this three times. In a notebook, sketch the pattern that the ice block makes in the clay.

OBJECTIVES

Build a model of a glacier.

Demonstrate the effects of glacial erosion by various materials. **D.1.3.1 CS**

Observe the effect of pressure on the melting rate of a glacier.

MATERIALS

- brick (3)
- clay, modeling (2 lb)
- container, empty large margarine (3)
- freezer
- graduated cylinder, 50 mL
- gravel (1 lb)
- hand towel
- pan, aluminum rectangular (3)
- rolling pin, wood
- ruler, metric
- sand (1 lb)
- stopwatch
- water

D.1.3.1 CS knows that mechanical and chemical activities shape and reshape the Earth's land surface by eroding rock and soil in some areas and depositing them in other areas, sometimes in seasonal layers.

6 Using the ice block that contains sand, repeat steps 4 and 5.

7 Using the ice block that contains gravel, repeat steps 4 and 5.

Analyze the Results

1 **Describing Events** Did any material from the clay become mixed with the material in the ice blocks? Explain.

2 **Describing Events** Was any material from the ice blocks deposited on the clay surface? Explain.

3 **Examining Data** What glacial features are represented in your clay model?

Draw Conclusions

4 **Evaluating Data** Compare the patterns formed by the three model glaciers. Do the patterns look like features carved by alpine glaciers or by continental glaciers? Explain.

Part B: Melting Away

Procedure

As the layers of ice build up and a glacier gets larger, the glacier eventually begins to melt. The water from the melted ice allows a glacier to move forward. In this activity, you'll explore the effect of pressure on the melting rate of a glacier.

1 If possible, make three identical ice blocks without any sand or gravel in them. If that is not possible, use the ice blocks from Part A. Place one ice block upside down in each pan.

2 Place one brick on top of one of the ice blocks. Place two bricks on top of another ice block. Do not put any bricks on the third ice block.

3 After 15 min, remove the bricks from the ice blocks.

4 Using the graduated cylinder, measure the amount of water that has melted from each ice block.

5 Record your observations.

Analyze the Results

1 **Analyzing Data** Which ice block produced the most water?

2 **Explaining Events** What natural process, force, or event did the bricks represent?

3 **Analyzing Results** What part of the ice blocks melted first? Explain.

Draw Conclusions

4 **Interpreting Information** How could you relate this investigation to the melting rate of glaciers? Explain.

Applying Your Data

Replace the clay with various materials, such as soft wood or sand. How does each ice block affect each surface material? What type of surface does each of the materials represent?

Chapter Review

USING KEY TERMS

For each pair of terms, explain how the meanings of the terms differ.

1 *shoreline* and *longshore current*

2 *beaches* and *dunes*

3 *deflation* and *saltation*

4 *continental glacier* and *alpine glacier*

5 *stratified drift* and *till*

6 *mudflow* and *creep*

UNDERSTANDING KEY IDEAS

Multiple Choice

7 *Surf* refers to
   a. large storm waves in the open ocean.
   b. giant waves produced by hurricanes.
   c. breaking waves near the shoreline.
   d. small waves on a calm sea.

8 When waves cut completely through a headland, a ___ is formed.
   a. sea cave
   b. sea arch
   c. wave-cut terrace
   d. sandbar

9 A narrow strip of sand that is formed by wave deposition and is connected to the shore is called a
   a. barrier spit.
   b. sandbar.
   c. wave-cut terrace.
   d. headland.

10 Wind can shape Earth by deposition. Which of the following is a landform made by wind deposition? **D.1.3.1 CS FCAT**
   a. deflation hollow
   b. desert pavement
   c. dune
   d. dust bowl

11 Which of the following terms describes all types of glacial deposits?
   a. glacial drift
   b. dune
   c. till
   d. outwash

12 The activity of wind can shape and reshape Earth. Which of the following is a landform that is created by wind erosion? **D.1.3.1 CS FCAT**
   a. cirque   c. horn
   b. deflation hollow   d. arête

13 What is the term for a rapid mass movement that is of volcanic origin? **D.1.3.5 CS**
   a. lahar   c. creep
   b. slump   d. rock fall

14 Some Earth processes happen quickly, and some Earth processes happen slowly. Which of the following is the slowest to create change in the landscape? **D.1.3.5 CS FCAT**
   a. mudflow   c. creep
   b. landslide   d. rock fall

Short Answer

15 Why do waves break when they near the shore?

16 Why are some areas more affected by wind erosion than other areas are?

17 What kind of mass movement happens continuously? **D.1.3.5 CS**

18 In what direction do sand dunes move?

19 Describe the various types of glacial moraines.

Math Skills

20 If a glacier recedes at the rate of 0.18 km per year, how far will it recede in 3,000 years? **D.1.3.5 CS**

CRITICAL THINKING

Extended Response

21 **Making Inferences** How do humans increase the likelihood that wind erosion will occur? **G.2.3.4 AA**

22 **Identifying Relationships** If all of the large ice sheet covering Antarctica melted, what type of landscape would Antarctica likely have?

23 **Applying Concepts** You are a geologist who is studying rock to determine the direction of flow of an ancient glacier. What clues might help you determine the glacier's direction of flow?

Concept Mapping

24 Use the following terms to create a concept map: *strong wind, saltation, dune, deflation,* and *desert pavement.*

INTERPRETING GRAPHICS

The graph below illustrates coastal erosion and deposition at an imaginary beach over a period of 8 years. Use the graph below to answer the questions that follow.

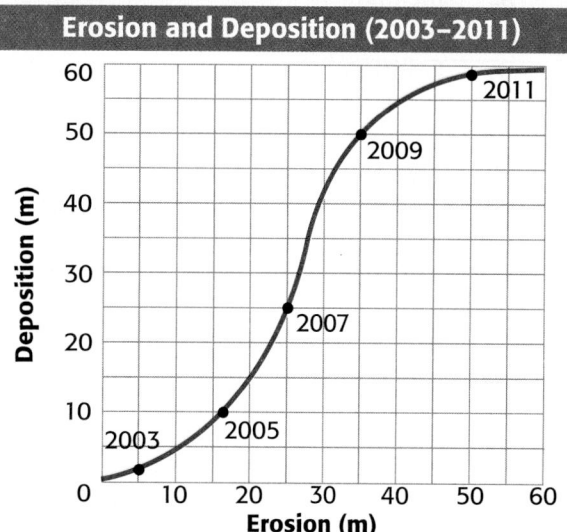

Erosion and Deposition (2003–2011)

25 What is happening to the beach over time? **D.1.3.5 CS**

26 In what year does the amount of erosion equal the amount of deposition?

27 Based on the erosion and deposition data for 2005, what might happen to the beach in the years that follow 2005?

Standardized Test Preparation

For the following questions, write your answers on a separate sheet of paper.

1 A mass movement is the movement of material, such as rock or soil, downslope. Mass movements may occur rapidly or slowly. Which of the following types of mass movements occurs at the **slowest** rate?

A. creep
B. rock fall
C. mudflow
D. landslide

2 The Outer Banks of North Carolina are a series of barrier islands that are located along the state's Atlantic coastline. They were formed by wave action over many centuries. Along the Outer Banks, the beaches that face east tend to erode away, and south-facing shorelines tend to grow. Explain how this pattern of shoreline erosion and deposition might occur.

3 Dunes are formed by wind. As wind deposits sediment, a dune can take on a distinctive shape.

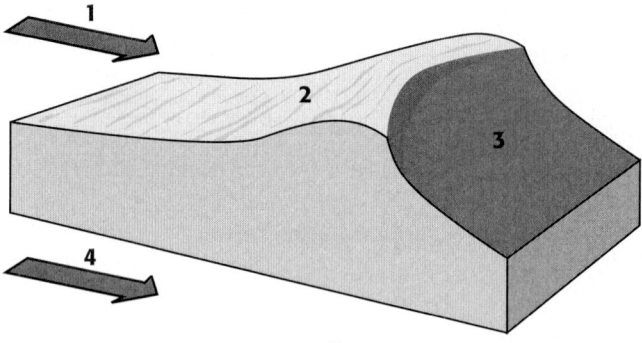

Dune Formation

In the diagram above, what is shown by the arrows marked 1 and 4?

F. The arrows indicate where the windward slope will form.
G. The arrows indicate wind direction and the slope of the ground.
H. The arrows indicate wind direction and the direction of dune movement.
I. The arrows indicate how particles are moved from the slip face to the windward slope.

4 Continental glaciers can be huge. Some continental glaciers may spread across entire landmasses, covering thousands of square kilometers with ice that is thousands of meters thick. During the last glacial period, glaciers extended as far south as the United States. What caused these continental glaciers to form?

A. the cooling of Earth and increased snowfall
B. the cooling of Earth and decreased snowfall
C. the warming of Earth and increased snowfall
D. the warming of Earth and decreased snowfall

5 Rashid and Maria are debating rates of erosion caused by wind, waves, rivers, and glaciers. They agree that all forms of erosion and deposition can produce spectacular landforms over thousands or millions of years. However, they disagree about which dramatic landforms can be produced in the shortest amount of time. Which one of the following landforms would form **most** rapidly?

F. a sand dune
G. an alpine horn
H. a hanging valley
I. a coastal headland

6 Marcus counted the number of waves that reached a beach per minute on the Oregon coastline. Three times in one day, he counted the number of waves that reached the shoreline and calculated the average wave period. He concluded that five waves struck the beach every minute. What is the wave period (in seconds) that Marcus recorded?

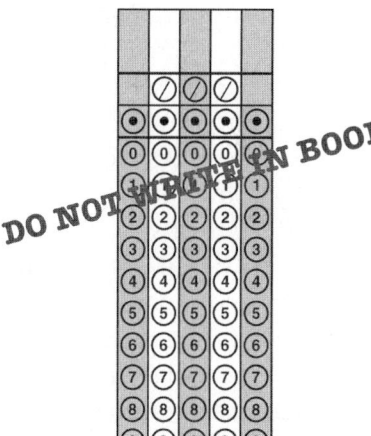

DO NOT WRITE IN BOOK

Science in Action

Scientific Discoveries

The Lost Squadron

During World War II, an American squadron of eight planes crash-landed on the ice of Greenland. The crew was rescued, but the planes were lost. After the war, several people tried to find the "Lost Squadron." Finally, in 1988, a team of adventurers found the planes by using radar. The planes were buried by 40 years of snowfall and had become part of the Greenland ice sheet! When the planes were found, they were buried under 80 m of glacial ice. Incredibly, the team tunneled down through the ice and recovered a plane. The plane is now named *Glacier Girl*, and it still flies today!

Language Arts ACTiViTY

WRITING SKILL The crew of the Lost Squadron had to wait 10 days to be rescued by dog sled. If you had been part of the crew, what would you have done to survive? Write a short story describing your adventure on the ice sheet of Greenland.

FOCUS ON FLORIDA

Weird Science

Florida's Sinkholes

It happens without warning. One moment, nothing is going on, and the next moment, the ground caves in! This caved-in place is a sinkhole, a circular slump created when sediments collapse into an underground cavity. Sinkholes are common in Florida because of Florida's bedrock. For eons, slightly acidic water has percolated through Florida's limestone and dolomite bedrock. This water has carved a network of channels and caves that make the bedrock resemble Swiss cheese. When a cave is too big or its ceiling is too thin to support the sediments above the cave, a sinkhole forms. Factors such as heavy rain, a fall in the water table, well drilling, and heavy construction trigger sinkholes.

Math ACTiViTY

A circular sinkhole has a diameter of 16 m. Calculate the sinkhole's perimeter.

Johan Reinhard

High-Altitude Anthropologist Imagine discovering the mummified body of a girl from 500 years ago! In 1995, while climbing Mount Ampato, one of the tallest mountains in the Andes, Johan Reinhard made an incredible discovery—the well-preserved mummy of a young Inca girl. The recent eruption of a nearby volcano had caused the snow on Mount Ampato to melt and uncover the mummy. The discovery of the "Inca Ice Maiden" gave scientists a wealth of new information about Incan culture. Today, Reinhard considers the discovery of the Inca Ice Maiden to be his most exciting moment in the field.

Johan Reinhard is an anthropologist. Anthropologists study the physical and cultural characteristics of human populations. Reinhard studied anthropology at the University of Arizona and at the University of Vienna in Austria. Early in his career, Reinhard worked on underwater archeology projects in Austria and Italy and on projects in the mountains of Nepal and Tibet. He soon made mountains and mountain peoples the focus of his career as an anthropologist. Reinhard spent 10 years in the Himalayas, the highest mountains on Earth. There, he studied the role of sacred mountains in Tibetan religions. Now, Reinhard studies the culture of the ancient Inca in the Andes of South America.

Social Studies ACTIVITY

Find out more about the Inca Ice Maiden or about Ötzi, a mummy that is more than 5,000 years old and that was found in a glacier in Italy. Create a poster that summarizes what scientists have learned from the discovery.

The Inca Ice Maiden was buried under ice and snow for more than 500 years.

To learn more about these Science in Action topics, visit go.hrw.com and type in the keyword **HT6FICFF**.

Current Science

Check out Current Science® articles related to this chapter by visiting go.hrw.com. Just type in the keyword **HZ5CS12**.

18
The Movement of Ocean Water

The Big Idea The ocean is a system of water that moves in constant, predictable patterns.

About the PHOTO

No, this isn't a traffic jam or the result of careless navigation. Hurricane Hugo is to blame for this major boat pile up. When Hurricane Hugo hit South Carolina's coast in 1989, the hurricane's strong winds created large ocean waves. These ocean waves carried these boats right onto the shore.

PRE-READING ACTIVITY

Graphic Organizer

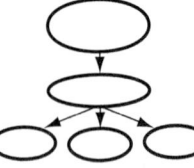

Concept Map Before you read the chapter, create the graphic organizer entitled "Concept Map" described in the **Study Skills** section of the Appendix. As you read the chapter, fill in the concept map with details about each type of ocean water movement.

START-UP ACTIVITY

When Whirls Collide D.1.3.3 CS

Some ocean currents flow in a clockwise direction, while other ocean currents flow in a counterclockwise direction. Sometimes these currents collide. In this activity, you and your lab partner will demonstrate how two currents flowing in opposite directions affect one another.

Procedure

1. Fill a large **tub** with **water** 5 cm deep.
2. Add **10 drops of red food coloring** to the water at one end of the tub.
3. Add **10 drops of blue food coloring** to the water at the other end of the tub.
4. Using a **pencil,** quickly stir the water at one end of the tub in a clockwise direction while your partner stirs the water at the other end in a counterclockwise direction. Stir both ends for 5 s.
5. Draw what you see happening in the tub immediately after you stop stirring. (Both ends should be swirling.)

Analysis

1. How did the blue water and the red water interact?
2. How does this activity relate to how ocean currents interact?

Currents

Imagine that you are stranded on a desert island. You stuff a distress message into a bottle and throw it into the ocean. Is there any way to predict where your bottle may land?

Actually, there is a way to predict where the bottle will end up. Ocean water contains streamlike movements of water called **ocean currents.** Currents are influenced by a number of factors, including weather, Earth's rotation, and the position of the continents. People can use knowledge of ocean currents to predict where objects in the open ocean will be carried.

Currents in the Global Ocean

Currents can be found within all divisions of Earth's global ocean. Earth's global ocean is divided by continents into four main oceans. These oceans are the Arctic Ocean, the Atlantic Ocean, the Indian Ocean, and the Pacific Ocean.

Two types of ocean currents exist. Surface currents flow at or near the surface of the global ocean. The waters of surface currents can be warm or cold. **Figure 1** shows surface currents off the coast of Florida. The other type of ocean current is called a *deep current*. As you may have guessed, deep currents flow far below the ocean surface. The waters of deep currents are cold.

Reading Check Describe the two types of ocean currents.

ocean current a movement of ocean water that follows a regular pattern

Figure 1 *This map shows currents off the coast of Florida. The Gulf Stream continues up the coast of North America.*

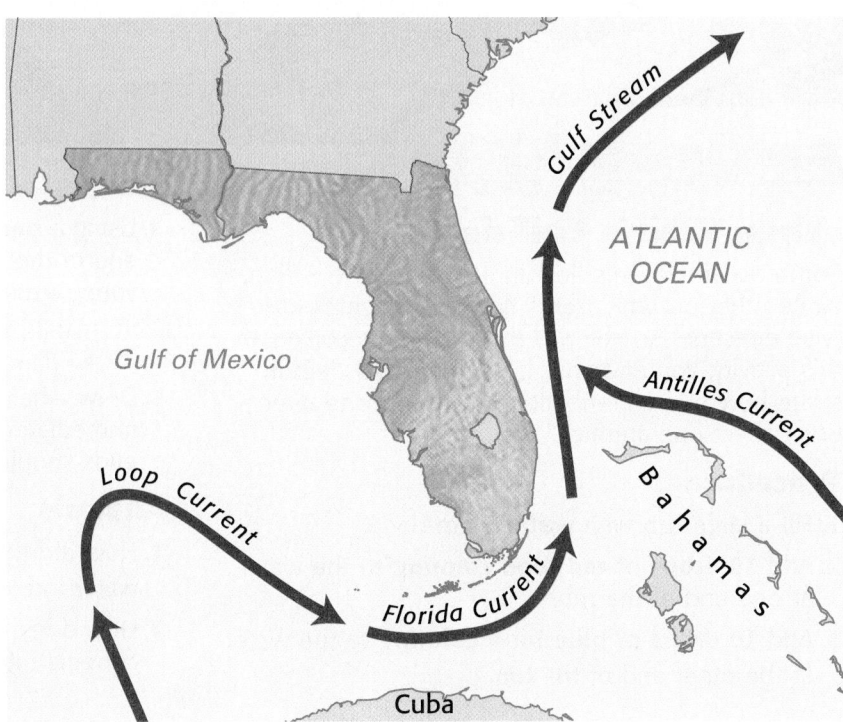

D.1.3.3. CS knows how conditions that exist in one system influence the conditions that exist in other systems.

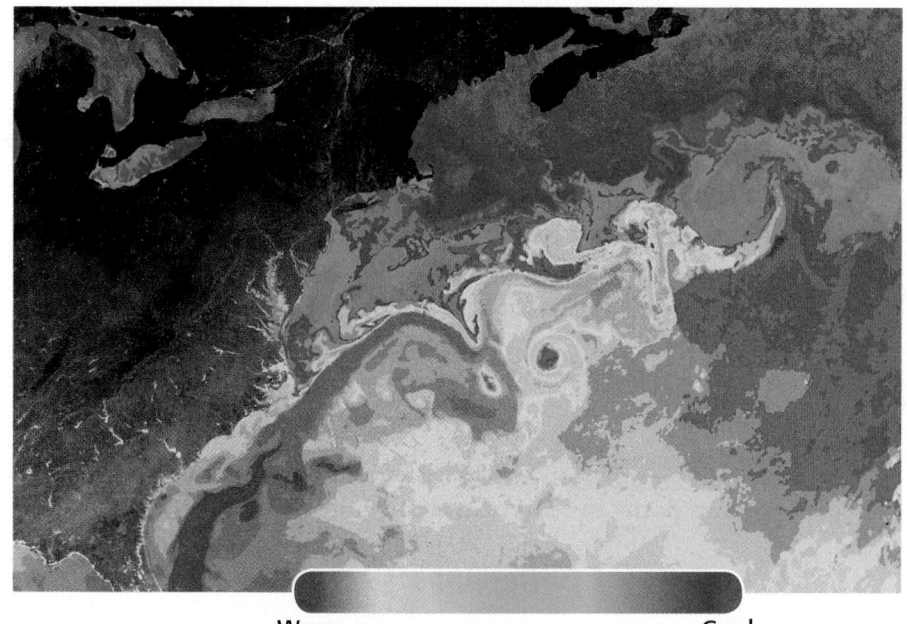

Figure 2 *This infrared satellite image shows the Gulf Stream current moving warm water from lower latitudes to higher latitudes.*

Warm   Cool

Surface Currents

Horizontal, streamlike movements of water that occur at or near the surface of the ocean are called **surface currents.** Surface currents can reach depths of several hundred meters and lengths of several thousand kilometers and can travel across oceans. The Gulf Stream, shown in **Figure 2,** is one of the longest surface currents—it transports 25 times more water than all of the rivers in the world.

Surface currents are controlled by three factors: global winds, the Coriolis effect, and continental deflections. These three factors keep surface currents flowing in distinct patterns around Earth.

surface current a horizontal movement of ocean water that is caused by wind and that occurs at or near the ocean's surface

Global Winds

Have you ever blown gently on a cup of hot chocolate? You may have noticed ripples moving across the surface, as in **Figure 3.** These ripples are caused by a tiny surface current created by your breath. In much the same way that you create ripples, winds that blow across Earth's surface create surface currents in the ocean.

Different winds cause currents to flow in different directions. Near the equator, the winds blow ocean water east to west, but closer to the poles, ocean water is blown west to east. Merchant ships often use these currents to travel more quickly back and forth across the oceans.

Figure 3 *Winds form surface currents in the ocean, much like blowing on a cup of hot chocolate forms ripples.*

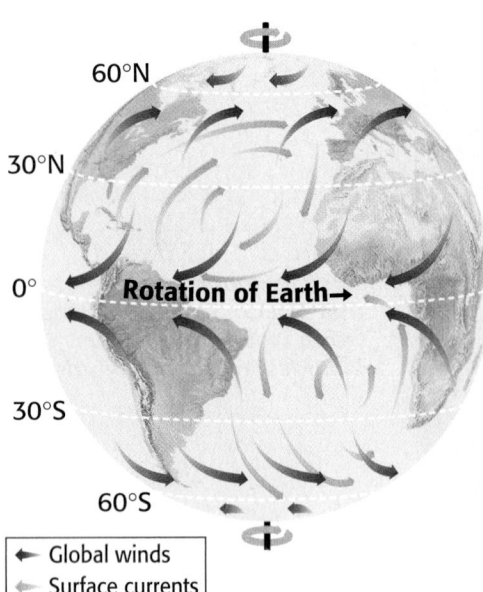

← Global winds
← Surface currents

Figure 4 *The rotation of the Earth causes surface currents (yellow arrows) and global winds (purple arrows) to curve as they move across Earth's surface.*

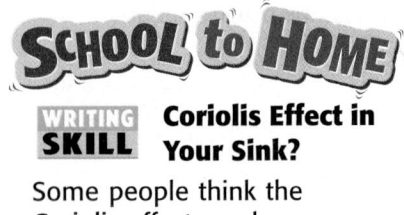

Coriolis Effect in Your Sink?

WRITING SKILL

Some people think the Coriolis effect can be seen in sinks. Does water draining from sinks turn clockwise in the Northern Hemisphere and counterclockwise in the Southern Hemisphere? Research this question at the library, on the Internet, and in your sink at home with a parent. Write what you learn in your **science journal.**

ACTIVITY

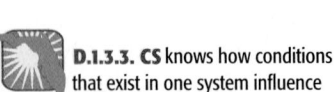
D.1.3.3. CS knows how conditions that exist in one system influence the conditions that exist in other systems.

The Coriolis Effect

Earth's rotation causes wind and surface currents to move in curved paths rather than in straight lines. The apparent curving of moving objects from a straight path due to Earth's rotation is called the **Coriolis effect.** To understand the Coriolis effect, imagine trying to roll a ball straight across a turning merry-go-round. Because the merry-go-round is spinning, the path of the ball will curve before it reaches the other side. **Figure 4** shows how the Coriolis effect causes surface currents in the Northern Hemisphere to turn clockwise and surface currents in the Southern Hemisphere to turn counterclockwise.

Benchmark Check What causes currents to move in curved paths instead of straight lines? **D.1.3.3 CS**

Continental Deflections

If Earth's surface were covered only with water, surface currents would travel freely across the globe in a very uniform pattern. However, you know that water does not cover the entire surface of Earth. Continents rise above sea level over roughly one-third of Earth's surface. When surface currents meet continents, the currents *deflect,* or change direction. Notice in **Figure 5** how the Brazil Current deflects southward as it meets the east coast of South America.

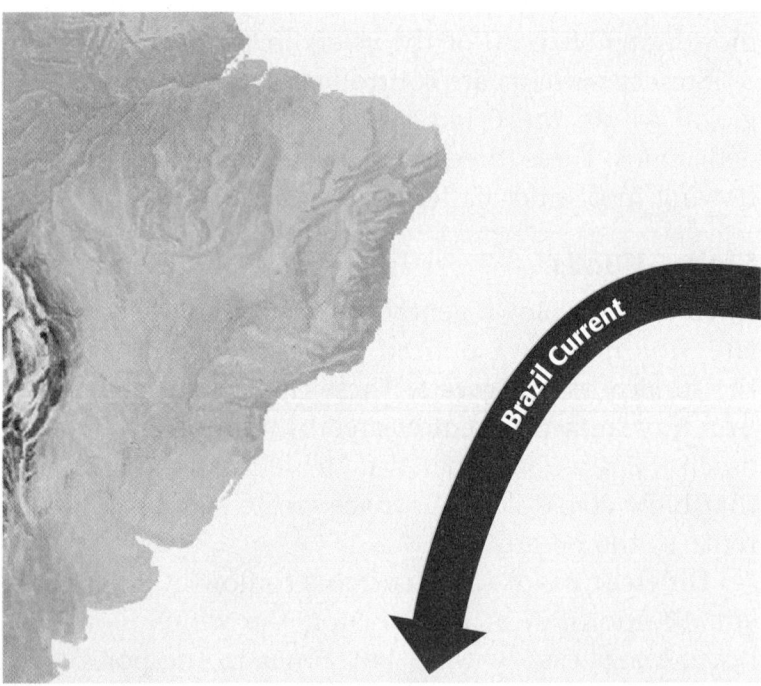

Figure 5 *If South America were not in the way, the Brazil Current would probably flow farther west.*

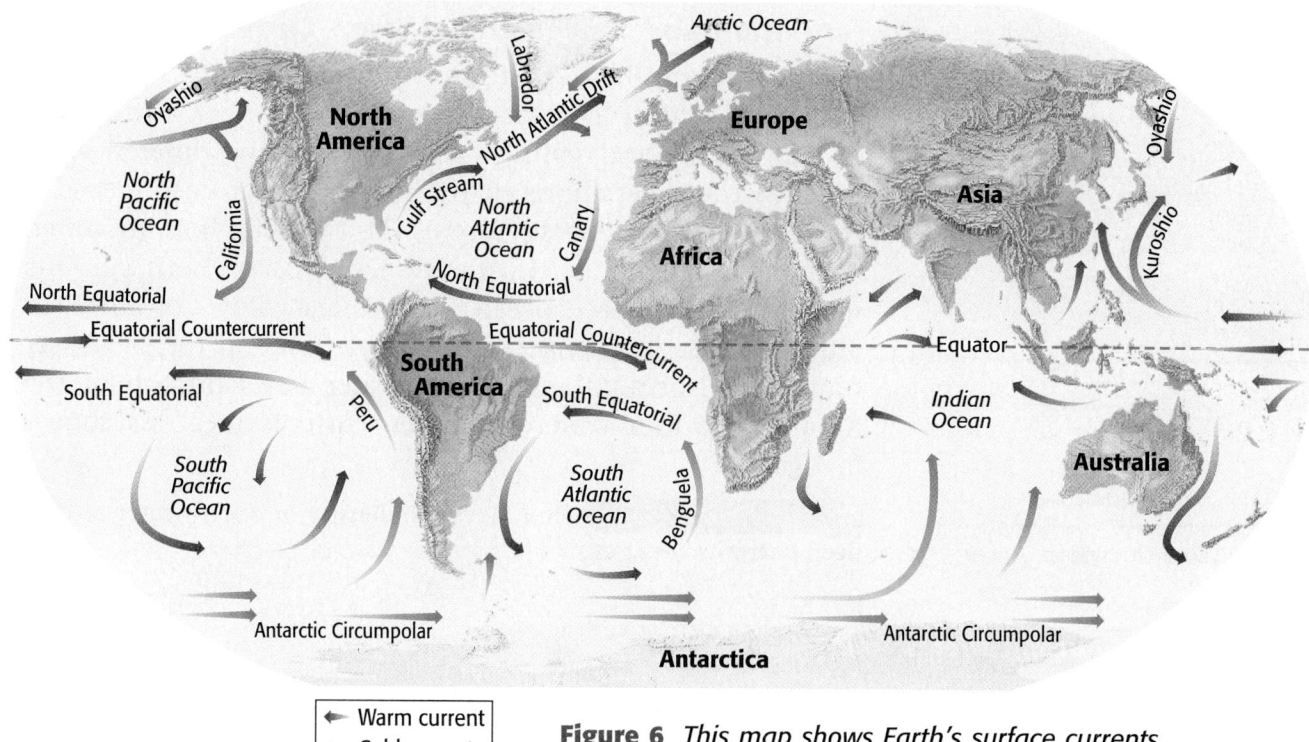

Warm current
Cold current

Figure 6 *This map shows Earth's surface currents. Warm-water currents are shown as red arrows, and cold-water currents are shown as blue arrows.*

Taking Temperatures

All three factors—global winds, the Coriolis effect, and continental deflections—work together to form a pattern of surface currents on Earth. But currents are also affected by the temperature of the water in which they form. Warm-water currents begin near the equator and carry warm water to other parts of the ocean. Cold-water currents begin closer to the poles and carry cool water to other parts of the ocean. As you can see on the map in **Figure 6,** all of the oceans are connected and both warm-water and cold-water currents travel from one ocean to another.

Benchmark Check What three factors form a pattern of surface currents on Earth? **D.1.3.3 CS**

Deep Currents

Streamlike movements of ocean water located far below the surface are called **deep currents.** Unlike surface currents, deep currents are not directly controlled by wind. Instead, deep currents form in parts of the ocean where water density increases. *Density* is the amount of matter in a given space, or volume. The density of ocean water is affected by temperature and *salinity*—a measure of the amount of dissolved salts or solids in a liquid. Both decreasing the temperature of ocean water and increasing the water's salinity increase the water's density.

CONNECTION TO Physics

Convection Currents While winds are often responsible for ocean currents, the sun is the initial energy source of the winds and currents. Because the sun heats Earth more in some places than in others, convection currents are formed. These currents transfer thermal energy. Which ocean currents do you think carry more thermal energy, currents located near the equator or currents located near the poles?

Coriolis effect the curving of the path of a moving object from an otherwise straight path due to the Earth's rotation

deep current a streamlike movement of ocean water far below the surface

Formation and Movement of Deep Currents

The relationship between the density of ocean water and the formation of deep currents is shown in **Figure 7.** Differences in temperature and salinity—and the resulting differences in density—cause variations in the movement of deep currents. For example, the deepest current, the Antarctic Bottom Water, is denser than the North Atlantic Deep Water. Both currents spread out across the ocean floor as they flow toward each other. Because less-dense water always flows on top of denser water, the North Atlantic Deep Water flows on top of the Antarctic Bottom Water when the currents meet, as shown in **Figure 8.**

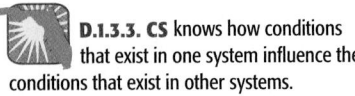 **D.1.3.3. CS** knows how conditions that exist in one system influence the conditions that exist in other systems.

Benchmark Check How does the density of ocean water affect deep currents? **D.1.3.3 CS**

Figure 7 How Deep Currents Form

Decreasing Temperature In Earth's polar regions, cold air chills the water molecules at the ocean's surface, which causes the molecules to slow down and move closer together. This reaction causes the water's volume to decrease. Thus, the water becomes denser. The dense water sinks and eventually travels toward the equator as a deep current along the ocean floor.

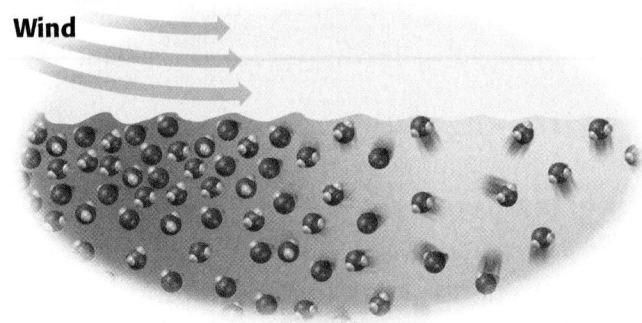
Wind

Increasing Salinity Through Freezing If the ocean water freezes at the surface, ice will float on top of the water because ice is less dense than liquid water. The dissolved solids are squeezed out of the ice and enter the liquid water below the ice. This process increases the salinity of the water. As a result of the increased salinity, the water's density increases.

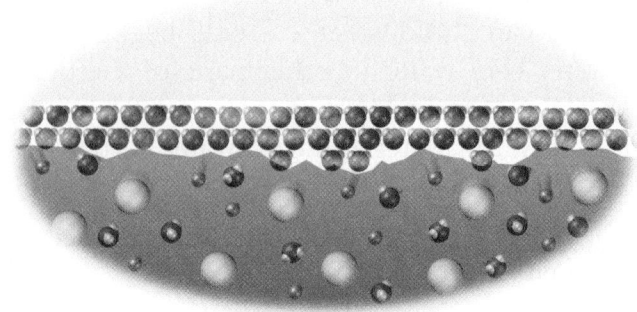

Increasing Salinity Through Evaporation Another way salinity increases is through evaporation of surface water, which removes water but leaves solids behind. This process is especially common in warm climates. Increasing salinity through freezing or evaporation causes water to become denser, to sink to the ocean floor, and to form a deep current.

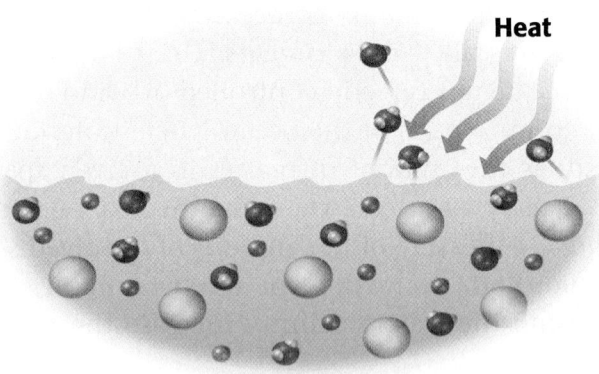
Heat

Figure 8 **Flow of Deep Currents**

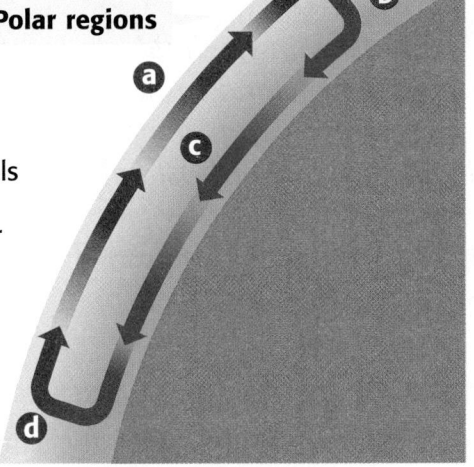

Polar regions

The warmer, less-dense water in surface currents cools and becomes the colder, denser water in deep currents.

Equatorial regions

ⓐ Surface currents carry the warmer, less-dense water from other ocean regions to polar regions.

ⓑ Warm water from surface currents replaces colder, denser water that sinks to the ocean floor.

ⓒ Deep currents carry colder, denser water along the ocean floor from polar regions to other ocean regions.

ⓓ Water from deep currents rises to replace water leaving surface currents.

SECTION Review

Summary

- Surface currents are streamlike movements of water at or near the surface of the ocean.

- Surface currents are controlled by three factors: global winds, the Coriolis effect, and continental deflections. **D.1.3.3 CS**

- Deep currents are streamlike movements of ocean water located far below the surface.

- Deep currents form where the density of ocean water increases. Water density depends on temperature and salinity. **D.1.3.3 CS**

Using Key Terms

Correct each statement by replacing the underlined term.

1. <u>Deep currents</u> are directly controlled by wind.

2. An increase in density in parts of the ocean can cause <u>surface currents</u> to form.

Understanding Key Ideas

3. List three factors that control surface currents. **D.1.3.3 CS**

4. How does a continent affect the movement of a surface current? **D.1.3.3 CS**

5. Explain how temperature and salinity affect the formation of deep currents. **D.1.3.3 CS**

Critical Thinking

6. **Evaluating Conclusions** If there were no land on Earth's surface, what would the pattern of surface currents look like? Explain your answer. **D.1.3.3 CS**

7. **Making Comparisons** Compare the factors that contribute to the formation of surface currents and deep currents. **D.1.3.3 CS**

FCAT Preparation

8. Two types of ocean currents exist. Surface currents flow at or near the surface of the global ocean. The waters of surface currents can be warm or cold. The other type of ocean current is called a *deep current*. Deep currents flow far below the ocean surface. The waters of deep currents are cold. A variety of conditions on Earth affect ocean currents. Which factor directly controls the movement of deep-ocean currents? **D.1.3.3 CS**

A. the Coriolis effect

B. the size of continents

C. global winds

D. density of water

SCILINKS.

NSTA
Developed and maintained by the National Science Teachers Association

For a variety of links related to this chapter, go to www.scilinks.org

Topic: Ocean Currents
SciLinks code: HSM1061

Currents and Climate

The Scilly Isles in England are located farther north than Prince Edward Island in northeast Canada. But the Scilly Isles experience warm temperatures almost all year long, while Prince Edward Island has long winters of frost and snow. How can two places at similar latitudes have completely different climates? This difference in climate is caused by surface currents.

READING WARM-UP

Objectives

● Explain how currents affect climate. **D.1.3.3 CS**

● Describe the effects of El Niño.

● Explain how scientists study and predict the pattern of El Niño.

Terms to Learn

upwelling
El Niño
La Niña

READING STRATEGY

Paired Summarizing Read this section silently. In pairs, take turns summarizing the material. Stop to discuss ideas that seem confusing.

D.1.3.3 CS knows how conditions that exist in one system influence the conditions that exist in other systems.

Surface Currents and Climate

Surface currents greatly affect the climate in many parts of the world. Some surface currents warm or cool coastal areas year-round. Other surface currents sometimes change their circulation pattern. Changes in circulation patterns cause changes in atmosphere that affect the climate in many parts of the world.

Warm-Water Currents and Climate

Although surface currents are generally much warmer than deep currents, the temperatures of surface currents do vary. Surface currents are classified as warm-water currents or cold-water currents. Warm-water currents create warmer climates in coastal areas that would otherwise be much cooler. **Figure 1** shows how the Gulf Stream carries warm water from the Tropics to the North Atlantic Ocean. The Gulf Stream flows to the British Isles and creates a relatively mild climate for land at such high latitude. The Gulf Stream is the same current that makes the climate of the Scilly Isles very different from the climate of Prince Edward Island.

Figure 1 **How Warm-Water Currents Affect Climate**

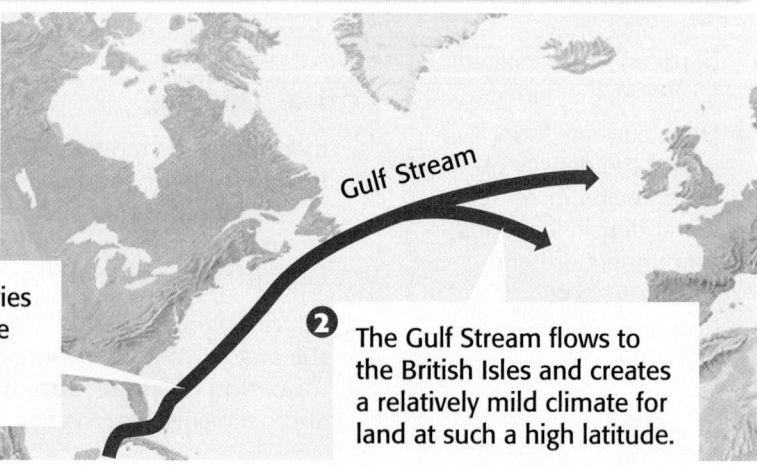

Warm-water currents, such as the Gulf Stream, can affect the climate of coastal regions.

❶ The Gulf Stream carries warm water from the Tropics to the North Atlantic Ocean.

❷ The Gulf Stream flows to the British Isles and creates a relatively mild climate for land at such a high latitude.

Figure 2 How Cold-Water Currents Affect Climate

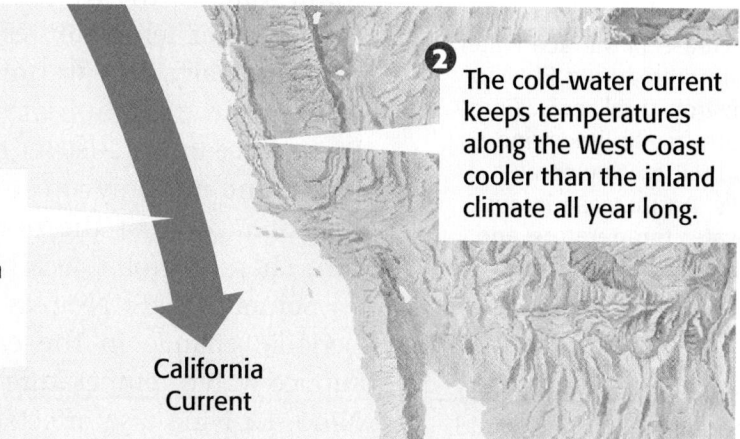

Cold-water currents, such as the California Current, can affect the climate of coastal regions.

① Cold water from the northern Pacific Ocean is carried south to Mexico by the California Current.

② The cold-water current keeps temperatures along the West Coast cooler than the inland climate all year long.

California Current

Cold-Water Currents and Climate

Cold-water currents also affect the climate of the land near where they flow. **Figure 2** shows how the California Current carries cold water from the North Pacific Ocean southward to Mexico. The cold-water California Current keeps the climate along the West Coast cooler than the inland climate year-round.

upwelling the movement of deep, cold, and nutrient-rich water to the surface

Benchmark Check How do cold-water currents affect coastal regions? **D.1.3.3 CS**

Upwelling

When local wind patterns blow along the northwest coast of South America, they cause local surface currents to move away from the shore. This warm water is then replaced by deep, cold water. This movement causes upwelling to occur in the eastern Pacific. **Upwelling** is a process in which cold, nutrient-rich water from the deep ocean rises to the surface and replaces warm surface water, as shown in **Figure 3.** The nutrients from the deep ocean are made up of elements and chemicals, such as iron and nitrate. When these chemicals are brought to the sunny surface, they help tiny plants grow through the process of photosynthesis.

The process of upwelling is extremely important to organisms. The nutrients that are brought to the surface of the ocean support the growth of phytoplankton and zooplankton. These tiny plants and animals support other organisms such as fish and seabirds.

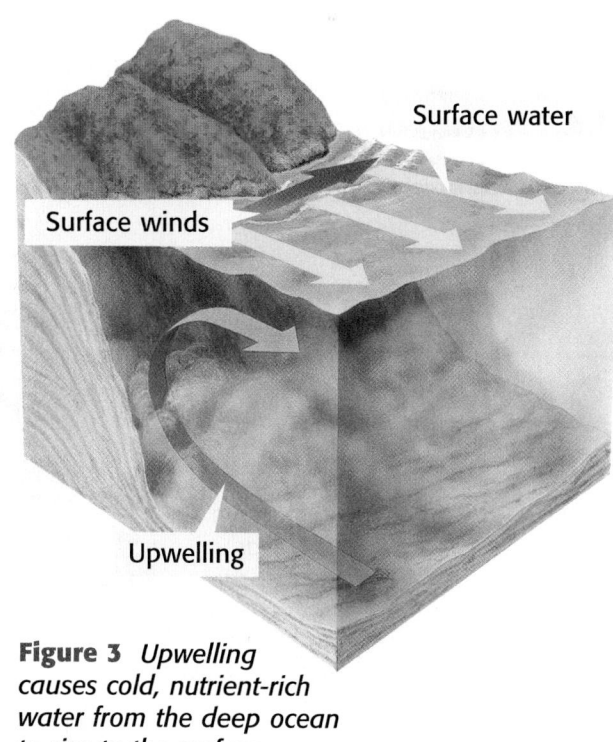

Surface water

Surface winds

Upwelling

Figure 3 *Upwelling causes cold, nutrient-rich water from the deep ocean to rise to the surface.*

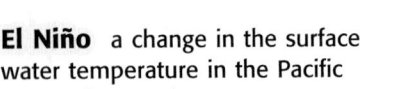
El Niño a change in the surface water temperature in the Pacific Ocean that produces a warm current

La Niña a change in the eastern Pacific Ocean in which the surface water temperature becomes unusually cool

D.1.3.3 CS knows how conditions that exist in one system influence the conditions that exist in other systems.

El Niño

Every 2 to 12 years, the South Pacific trade winds move less warm water to the western Pacific than they usually do. Thus, surface-water temperatures along the coast of South America rise. Gradually, this warming spreads westward. This periodic change in the location of warm and cool surface waters in the Pacific Ocean is called **El Niño.** El Niño can last for a year or longer and not only affects the surface waters but also changes the interaction of the ocean and the atmosphere, which in turn changes global weather patterns.

Sometimes, El Niño is followed by La Niña. **La Niña** is a periodic change in the eastern Pacific Ocean in which the surface-water temperature becomes unusually cool. Like El Niño, La Niña also affects weather patterns.

Benchmark Check Why does El Niño affect weather patterns around the world? **D.1.3.3 CS**

Effects of El Niño

El Niño alters weather patterns enough to cause disasters. These disasters include flash floods and mudslides in areas of the world that usually receive little rain, such as the southern half of the United States and Peru. **Figure 4** shows homes in Southern California that were destroyed by a mudslide caused by El Niño. While some regions flood, other regions may experience a *drought,* which is an unusually long period during which rainfall is below average. During El Niño, severe droughts can occur in Indonesia and Australia. Periods of severe drought can lead to crop failure.

During El Niño, the upwelling of nutrient-rich water does not occur off the coast of South America, which affects the organisms that depend on the nutrients for food.

Figure 4 *This damage in Southern California was the result of excessive rain caused by El Niño in 1997.*

Studying and Predicting El Niño

Because El Niño occurs every 2 to 12 years, studying and predicting it can be difficult. However, it is important for scientists to learn as much as possible about El Niño because of its effects on organisms and land.

One way scientists collect data to predict an El Niño is through a network of buoys operated by the National Oceanic and Atmospheric Administration (NOAA). The buoys, some of which are anchored to the ocean floor, are located along the Earth's equator. The buoys record data about surface temperature, air temperature, currents, and winds. The buoys transmit some of the data on a daily basis to NOAA through a satellite in space.

When the buoys report that the South Pacific trade winds are not as strong as they usually are or that the surface temperatures of the tropical oceans have risen, scientists can predict that an El Niño is likely to occur.

Reading Check What information do scientists use to predict when El Niño will occur?

INTERNET ACTIVITY

What Is El Niño? Explore the positive and negative effects of El Niño and La Niña. Go to **go.hrw.com,** and type in the keyword **HZ5H2OW.**

SECTION Review

Summary

- Surface currents affect the climate of the land near which they flow. **D.1.3.3. CS**
- Warm-water currents bring warmer climates to coastal regions. Cold-water currents bring cooler climates to coastal regions. **D.1.3.3. CS**
- El Niño can cause floods, mudslides, and drought in different areas around the world.
- Scientists monitor conditions in the ocean to predict El Niño.

Using Key Terms

1. Use *upwelling, El Niño,* and *La Niña* in separate sentences.

Understanding Key Ideas

2. Why is the climate in Scotland mild even though the country is at a high latitude? **D.1.3.3 CS**

3. Name two disasters caused by El Niño.

4. Explain how local wind patterns cause upwelling to occur.

5. What conditions do scientists monitor to predict El Niño? How do they gather this information?

Critical Thinking

6. **Applying Concepts** Many marine organisms depend on upwelling to bring nutrients to the surface. How might El Niño affect a fisher's way of life? **D.1.3.3. CS**

FCAT Preparation

7. El Niño and La Niña are local changes in the temperature of ocean waters that alter weather patterns around the world. Why do El Niño and La Niña have global effects? **D.1.3.3 CS**

   A. They alter deep-ocean current circulation.

   B. They change global surface currents.

   C. They last for many decades.

   D. They stop ocean circulation.

SCILINKS

Developed and maintained by the National Science Teachers Association

For a variety of links related to this chapter, go to www.scilinks.org

Topic: El Niño

SciLinks code: HSM0468

Waves

Have you ever seen a surfer riding waves? Did you ever wonder where the waves come from? And why are some waves big, while others are small?

We all know what ocean waves look like. Even if you have never been to the seashore, you have most likely seen waves on TV. But how do waves form and move? Waves are affected by a number of different factors. They can be formed by something as simple as wind or by something as violent as an earthquake. Ocean waves can travel through water slowly or incredibly quickly. Read on to discover the many forces that affect the formation and movement of ocean waves.

Anatomy of a Wave

Waves are made up of two main parts—crests and troughs. A **crest** is the highest point of a wave. A **trough** is the lowest point of a wave. Imagine a roller coaster designed with many rises and dips. The top of a rise on a roller-coaster track is similar to the crest of a wave, and the bottom of a dip in the track resembles the trough of a wave. The distance between two adjacent wave crests or wave troughs is a **wavelength.** The vertical distance between the crest and trough of a wave is called the *wave height*. **Figure 1** shows the parts of a wave.

Benchmark Check What are the two main parts of a wave? B.1.3.6 AA

crest the highest point of a wave *FCAT* VOCAB

trough the lowest point of a wave *FCAT* VOCAB

wavelength the distance from any point on a wave to an identical point on the next wave *FCAT* VOCAB

B.1.3.6 AA knows the properties of waves (e.g., frequency, wavelength, and amplitude); that each wave consists of a number of crests and troughs; and the effects of different media on waves.

Figure 1 Parts of a Wave

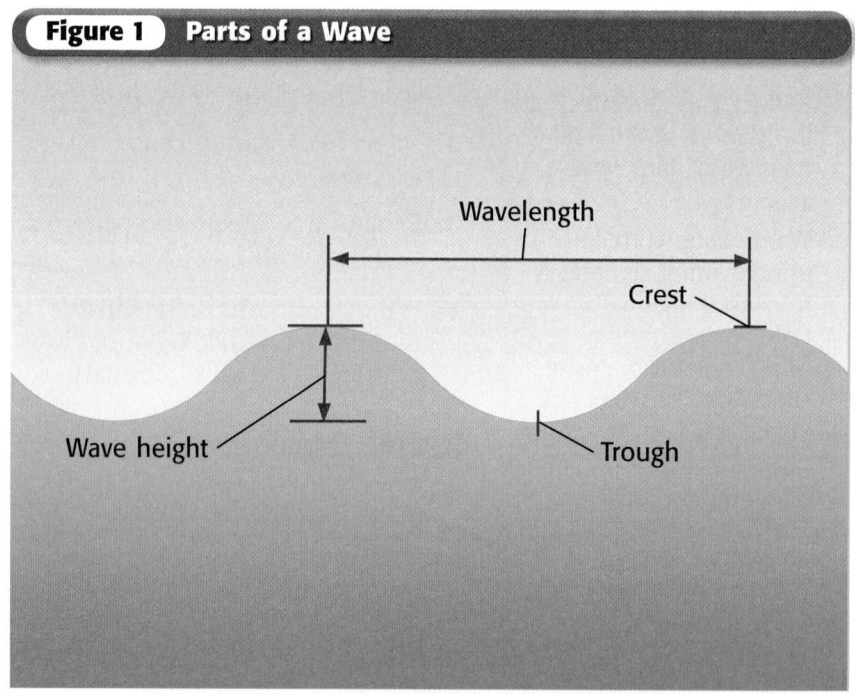

Wavelength

Crest

Wave height

Trough

Wave Formation and Movement

If you have watched ocean waves before, you may have noticed that water appears to move across the ocean's surface. However, this movement is only an illusion. Most waves form as wind blows across the water's surface and transfers energy to the water. As the energy moves through the water, so do the waves. But the water itself stays behind, rising and falling in circular movements. Notice in **Figure 2** that the floating bottle remains in the same spot as the waves travel from left to right. This circular motion gets smaller as the water depth increases, because wave energy decreases as the water depth increases. Wave energy reaches only a certain depth. Below that depth, the water is not affected by wave energy.

Specifics of Wave Movement

Waves not only come in different sizes but also travel at different speeds. To calculate wave speed, scientists must know the wavelength and the wave period. *Wave period* is the time between the passage of two wave crests (or troughs) at a fixed point, as shown in **Figure 3.** Dividing wavelength by wave period gives you wave speed, as shown below.

$$\frac{\text{wavelength (m)}}{\text{wave period (s)}} = \text{wave speed (m/s)}$$

For any given wavelength, an increase in the wave period will decrease the wave speed and a decrease in the wave period will increase the wave speed.

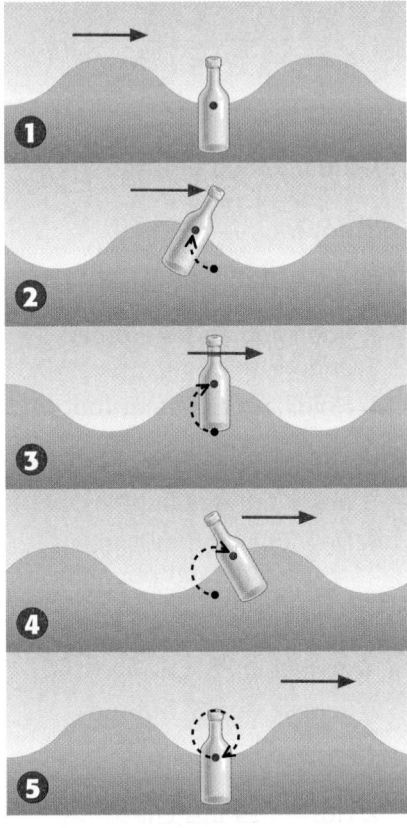

Figure 2 *Like the bottle, the water remains in the same place as waves travel through it.*

Figure 3   **Determining Wave Period**

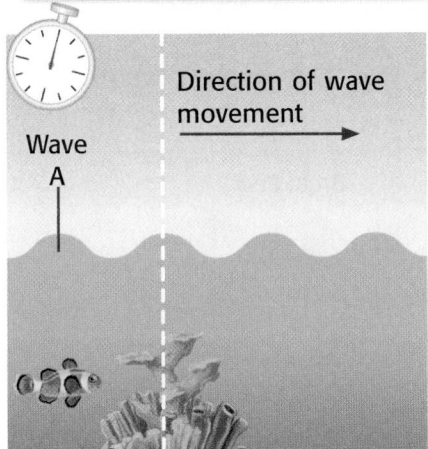

❶ Notice that the waves are moving from left to right.

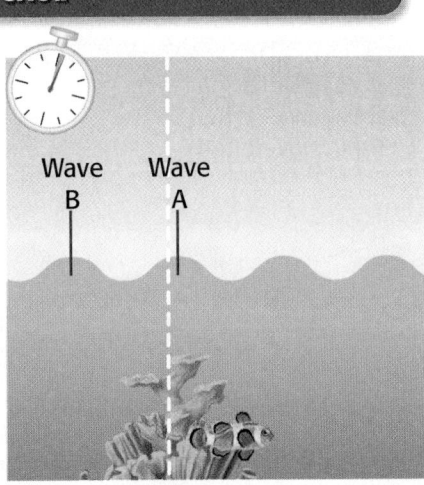

❷ The clock begins running as Wave A passes the reef's peak.

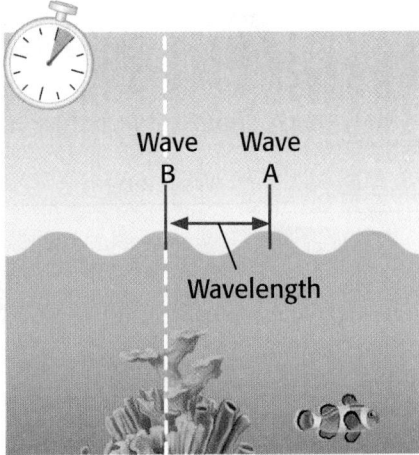

❸ The clock stops as Wave B passes the reef's peak. The time shown on the clock (5 s) represents the wave period.

Quick Lab

Doing the Wave

1. Tie one end of a **thin piece of rope** to a **doorknob.**

2. Tie a **ribbon** around the rope halfway between the doorknob and the other end of the rope.

3. Holding the rope at the untied end, quickly move the rope up and down and observe the ribbon.

4. How does the movement of the rope and ribbon relate to the movement of water and deep-water waves?

5. Repeat step 3, but move the rope higher and lower this time.

6. How does this affect the waves in the rope?

Types of Waves

As you learned earlier in this section, wind forms most ocean waves. Waves can also form by other mechanisms. Underwater earthquakes and landslides as well as impacts by cosmic bodies can form different types of waves. Most waves move in one way regardless of how they are formed. Depending on their size and the angle at which they hit the shore, waves can generate a variety of near-shore events, some of which can be dangerous to humans.

Deep-Water Waves and Shallow-Water Waves

Have you ever wondered why waves increase in height as they approach the shore? The answer has to do with the depth of the water. *Deep-water waves* are waves that move in water deeper than one-half their wavelength. When the waves reach water shallower than one-half their wavelength, they begin to interact with the ocean floor. These waves are called *shallow-water waves*. **Figure 4** shows how deep-water waves become shallow-water waves as they move toward the shore.

As deep-water waves become shallow-water waves, the water particles slow down and build up. This change forces more water between wave crests and increases wave height. Gravity eventually pulls the high wave crests down, which causes them to crash into the ocean floor as *breakers*. The area where waves first begin to tumble downward, or break, is called the *breaker zone*. Waves continue to break as they move from the breaker zone to the shore. The area between the breaker zone and the shore is called the *surf*.

Benchmark Check How do deep-water waves become shallow-water waves? **B.I.3.6 AA**

Figure 4   Deep-Water and Shallow-Water Waves

Deep-water waves become shallow-water waves when they reach depths of less than half of their wavelength.

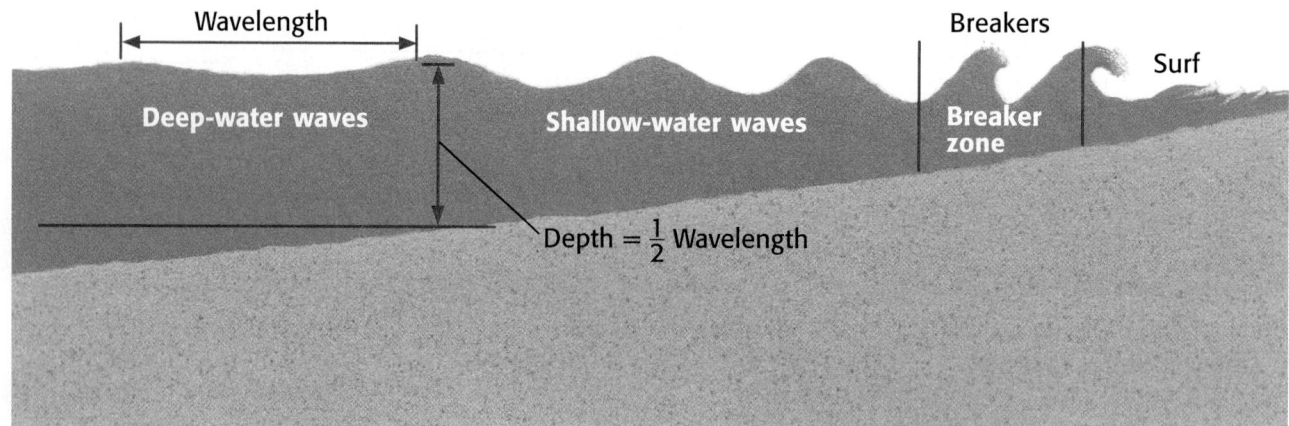

Figure 5 Formation of an Undertow

Head-on waves create an undertow.

Direction of wave movement

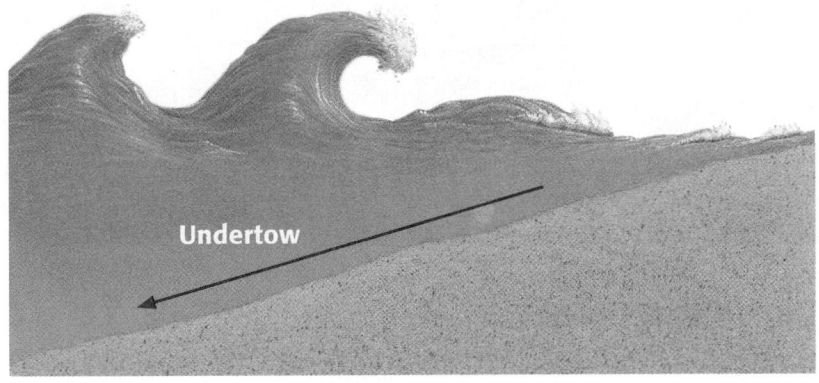

Undertow

Benchmark Activity

Watching Waves Go to the beach to observe how sand travels along the shore. Watch the waves to determine if they are hitting the shore head-on or at an angle. Toss one stick at a time in the ocean. Observe and record whether each stick moves directly away from the shore or along the coastline. Describe which type of current you are observing.
B.1.3.6 AA

Shore Currents

When waves crash on the beach head-on, the water they moved through flows back to the ocean underneath new incoming waves. This movement of water, which carries sand, rock particles, and plankton away from the shore, is called an **undertow. Figure 5** illustrates the back-and-forth movement of water at the shore.

Longshore Currents

When waves hit the shore at an angle, they cause water to move along the shore in a current called a **longshore current,** which is shown in **Figure 6.** Longshore currents transport most of the sediment in beach environments. This movement of sand and other sediment both tears down and builds up the coastline. Unfortunately, longshore currents also carry and spread trash and other types of ocean pollution along the shore.

undertow a subsurface current that is near shore and that pulls objects out to sea

longshore current a water current that travels near and parallel to the shoreline

B.1.3.6 AA knows the properties of waves (e.g. frequency, wavelength, and amplitude); that each wave consists of a number of crests and troughs; and the effects of different media on waves.

Figure 6 Longshore currents form where waves approach beaches at an angle.

Figure 7 *Whitecaps (left) break in the open ocean, while swells, (right), roll gently in the open ocean.*

whitecap the bubbles in the crest of a breaking wave

swell one of a group of long ocean waves that have steadily traveled a great distance from their point of generation

tsunami a giant ocean wave that forms after a volcanic eruption, submarine earthquake, or landslide

B.1.3.6 AA knows the properties of waves (e.g. frequency, wavelength, and amplitude); that each wave consists of a number of crests and troughs; and the effects of different media on waves.

Open-Ocean Waves

Sometimes, waves called *whitecaps* form in the open ocean. **Whitecaps** are white, foaming waves with very steep crests that break in the open ocean before the waves get close to the shore. These waves usually form during stormy weather, and they are usually short-lived. Winds that are far away from the shore form waves called *swells*. **Swells** are rolling waves that move steadily across the ocean. Swells have longer wavelengths than whitecaps and can travel for thousands of kilometers. **Figure 7** shows how whitecaps and swells differ.

Tsunamis

Professional surfers often travel to Hawaii to catch some of the highest waves in the world. But even the best surfers would not be able to handle a tsunami. **Tsunamis** are waves that form when a large volume of ocean water is suddenly moved up or down. This movement can be caused by underwater earthquakes, volcanic eruptions, landslides, underwater explosions, or the impact of a meteorite or comet. The majority of tsunamis occur in the Pacific Ocean because of the large number of earthquakes in that region. **Figure 8** shows how an earthquake can generate a tsunami.

Figure 8 *An upward shift in the ocean floor creates an earthquake. The energy released by the earthquake pushes a large volume of water upward, which creates a series of tsunamis.*

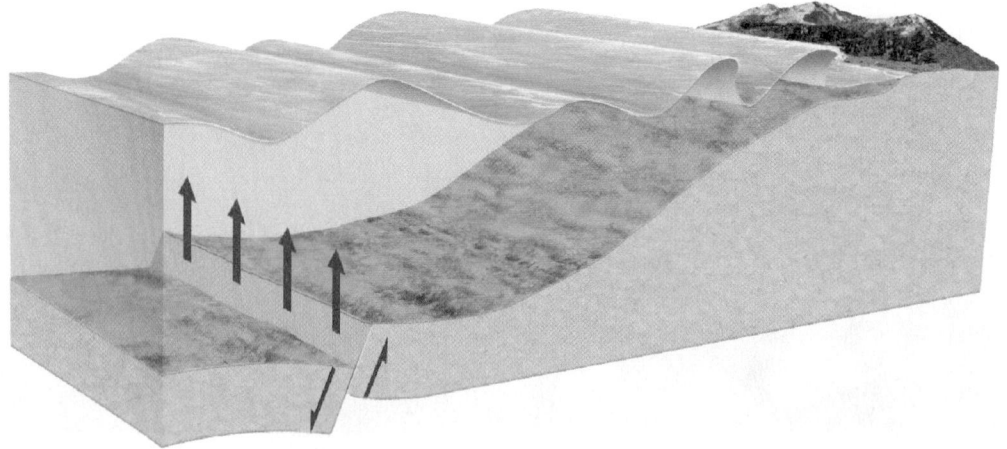

Storm Surges

A local rise in sea level near the shore that is caused by strong winds from a storm, such as a hurricane, is called a **storm surge.** Winds form a storm surge by blowing water into a big pile under the storm. As the storm moves onto shore, so does the giant mass of water beneath it. Storm surges often disappear as quickly as they form, which makes them difficult to study. Storm surges contain a lot of energy and can reach a height of about 8 m. Their size and power often make them the most destructive part of hurricanes.

storm surge a local rise in sea level near the shore that is caused by strong winds from a storm, such as those from a hurricane

✓ **Reading Check** What is a storm surge? Why are storm surges difficult to study?

SECTION Review

Summary

● Waves are made up of two main parts—crests and troughs. **B.1.3.6 AA**

● Crests and troughs travel through water near the water's surface, while the water itself rises and falls in circular movements. **B.1.3.6 AA**

● Waves are usually created by the transfer of the wind's energy across the surface of the ocean. **B.1.3.6 AA**

● Wind-generated waves are classified as deep-water or shallow-water waves.

● When waves hit the shore at certain angles, they can create either an undertow or a longshore current.

● Tsunamis are large waves that can damage coastal regions.

Using Key Terms

For each pair of terms, explain how the meanings of the terms differ.

1. *whitecap* and *swell*

2. *undertow* and *longshore current*

3. *crest* and *trough* **B.1.3.6 AA**
   FCAT VOCAB

Understanding Key Ideas

4. Where do deep-water waves become shallow-water waves? **B.1.3.6 AA**

5. Explain how water moves as waves travel through it. **B.1.3.6 AA**

6. Name five events that can cause a tsunami.

Critical Thinking

7. **Analyzing Processes** Describe the motion of a wave as it approaches the shore. **B.1.3.6 AA**

8. **Making Comparisons** How does the formation of an undertow differ from the formation of a longshore current? How is sand on the beach affected by undertow and by a longshore current?

FCAT Preparation

9. Waves have a number of measurable properties. How do you measure a wave's height? **B.1.3.6 AA**

   A. Find the distance between two crests.

   B. Find the vertical distance between the crest and trough.

   C. Calculate one-half of the wavelength.

   D. Divide the wavelength by the wave period.

10. You are on a dock watching waves. You notice that the crests of the waves are 10 m apart. Four seconds after a wave passes you on the dock, the next wave passes. Calculated the wave speed in m/s. **B.1.3.6 AA**

SCI**LINKS**®

NSTA
Developed and maintained by the National Science Teachers Association

For a variety of links related to this chapter, go to www.scilinks.org

Topic: Ocean Waves
SciLinks code: HSM1066

Tides

You are enjoying a sunny afternoon by the ocean. You spend hours building the best sand castle on the beach. When you started, the water was far away from you. But the water level is rising, and the ocean is moving closer to your sand castle!

The periodic rise and fall of the water level in the oceans is called the **tide.** *High tide* is when the water level is highest. *Low tide* is when the water level is lowest. The tide change is most noticeable at the beach. During high tide, the waves come farther up the beach than they do during low tide. **Figure 1** shows the Bay of Fundy in Canada, which is one place where the water level between high and low tide varies drastically.

The Causes of Tides

For thousands or years, people who lived by the coast could see the how the tides affected water levels. A Greek explorer named Pytheas was the first person to realize that the phases of the moon affected the tide. But for more than 1,500 years after Pytheas's discovery, no one could give a scientific explanation for the relationship between the moon and the tides.

Then, in the late 1600s, Isaac Newton identified the force that causes the rise and fall of tides. According to Newton's law of gravitation, the gravitational pull of the moon on Earth and on Earth's waters is the major cause of tides. The sun also causes tides, but those tides are smaller because the sun is so much farther from Earth than the moon is.

Benchmark Check How does the moon affect the oceans? E.1.3.1 AA

Figure 1 *These photos show the Bay of Fundy, in New Brunswick, Canada. The Bay of Fundy has the greatest variation in water levels on Earth.*

Low Tide

High Tide

Figure 2 *High Tide and Low Tide*

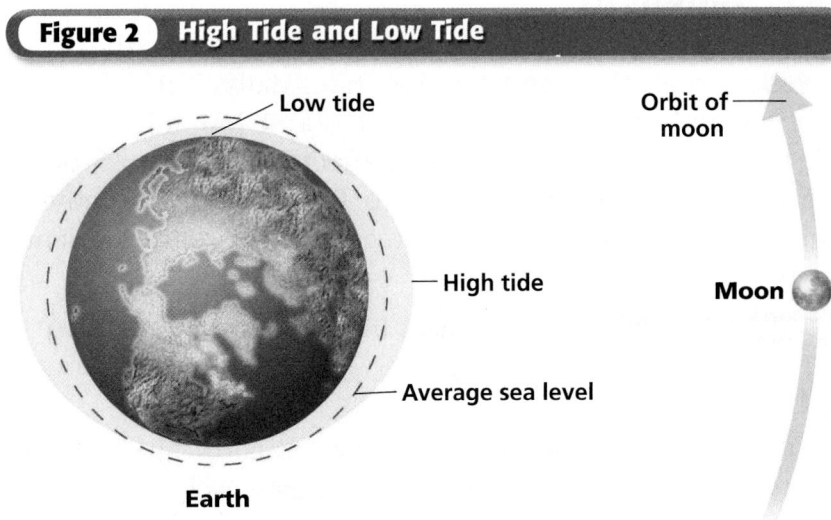

High tide occurs on the part of the earth closest to the moon. At the same time, high tide occurs on the opposite side of Earth. Low tide occurs because water flows toward the areas of high tide.

High Tide

But how does the gravitational pull of the moon cause a high tide on Earth? As the moon revolves around Earth, the moon exerts a gravitational pull on the entire Earth. The gravitational pull of the moon is strongest on the side of Earth that is nearest to the moon. As a result, the ocean on Earth's surface that faces the moon bulges slightly. This bulge causes a high tide within the area of the bulge.

At the same time, another tidal bulge forms on the opposite side of Earth. This tidal bulge forms because of the rotation of Earth and the motion of the moon around Earth. This tidal bulge is a smaller tidal bulge on the side of Earth that is farthest from the moon.

Low Tide

Low tides form halfway between the two high tides. Low tides form because as ocean water flows toward the areas of high tide, the water level in other areas of the oceans drops. **Figure 2** shows the Earth-moon system and the position of the moon in relation to the tidal bulges.

Timing the Tides

The moon is slowly orbiting Earth while Earth is rotating on its axis. Because of the rates that the moon and Earth move, all areas of the ocean pass under the moon every 24 h and 50 min. As seen from above the North Pole, Earth rotates counterclockwise and the tidal bulges appear to move westward around Earth. The times of high and low tides are about 50 minutes later each day, because the moon rises about 50 minutes later each day.

tide the periodic rise and fall of the water level in the oceans and other large bodies of water

E.1.3.1 AA understands the vast size of our Solar System and the relationship of the planets and their satellites.

Tidal Variations

Because there are two tidal bulges, most locations in the ocean have two high tides and two low tides daily. The difference in levels of ocean water at high tide and low tide is called the **tidal range.** The tidal range is affected by the position of the moon and the sun relative to Earth. The sun's gravitational force can strengthen or weaken the moon's influence on the tides.

 **Benchmark Check** What causes tidal ranges to vary? E.1.3.1 AA

Spring Tides

During the new moon and the full moon, Earth, the sun, and the moon are in a line, as shown in **Figure 3.** The combined gravitational pull of the sun and the moon results in higher high tides and lower low tides. So, the daily tidal range is greatest during the new moon and the full moon. During these two monthly periods, tides have an increased range and are called **spring tides.**

Neap Tides

During the first-quarter and third-quarter phases of the moon, the moon and the sun are at right angles to each other in relation to Earth, as shown in **Figure 3.** The gravitational forces of the sun and moon work against each other. As a result, the daily tidal range is small. Tides that occur during this time are of minimum range and are called **neap tides.**

Tidal Friction

As the tidal bulges move around Earth, friction between the water and the ocean floor slows Earth's rotation slightly. Scientists estimate that the average length of a day has increased by 10.8 min in the last 65 million years. How many years does it take for Earth's rotation to slow by 1 s?

tidal range the difference in levels of ocean water at high tide and low tide

spring tides a tide of increased range that occurs two times a month, at new and full moons FCAT VOCAB

neap tide a tide of minimum range that occurs during first and third quarters of the moon FCAT VOCAB

Figure 3 **Spring Tides and Neap Tides**

Tidal ranges vary because of the combined forces of the sun and moon on Earth. Tidal ranges are the largest during spring tides and are the smallest during neap tides.

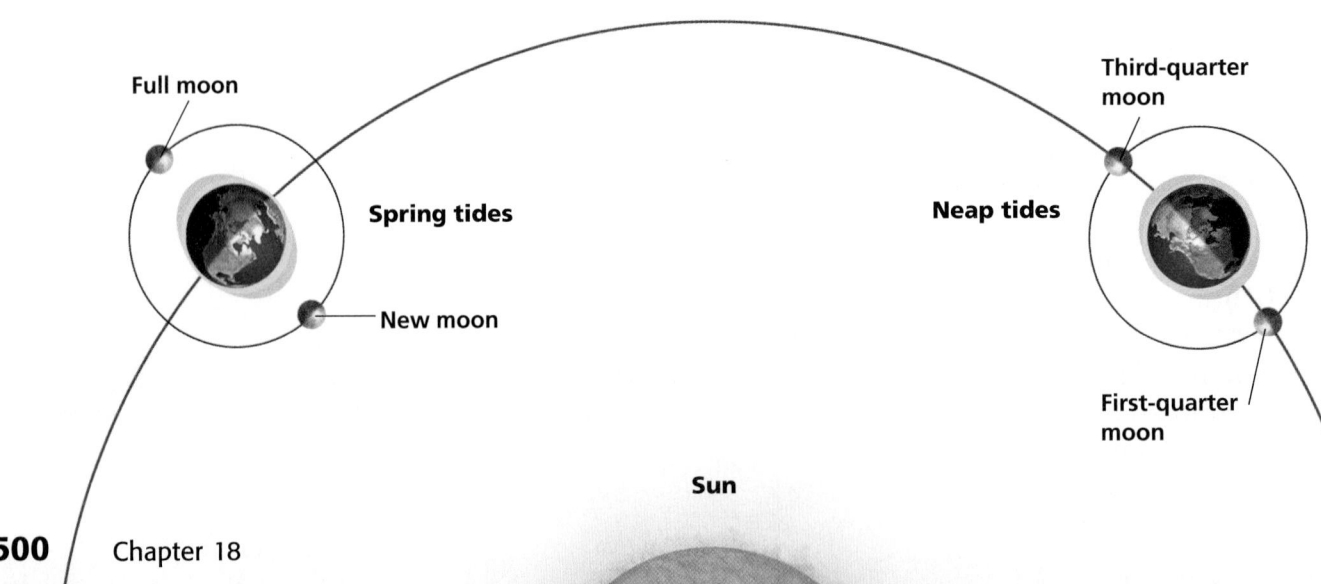

Full moon

Third-quarter moon

Spring tides

Neap tides

New moon

First-quarter moon

Sun

Tides and Land Formations

Land formations also affect tides. In some coastal areas that have narrow inlets, movements of water called tidal bores occur. A *tidal bore* is a surge of water that rushes up from the ocean and through a narrow bay or river channel. In some rivers, a tidal bore rushes upstream in the form of a wave that is up to 5 m high. **Figure 4** shows a tidal bore at an inlet in Alaska.

Tides and Ocean Basins

Continents and irregularities in the ocean floor divide the ocean into several basins. Tidal patterns are greatly influenced by the size, shape, depth, and location of the ocean basin in which the tides occur.

Along the Atlantic Coast of the United States, two high tides and two low tides occur each day and have a mostly regular tidal range. Along the shore of the Gulf of Mexico, however, one high tide and one low tide occur each day. Along the Pacific Coast, the tides follow a mixed pattern of tidal ranges.

Figure 4 *This photo shows a tidal bore in early spring at Turnagain Arm of Cook Inlet, Alaska.*

E.I.3.1 AA understands the vast size of our Solar System and the relationship of the planets and their satellites.

SECTION Review

Summary

● Tides are caused by the gravitational forces of the moon and sun on Earth. **E.I.3.1 AA**

● The moon's gravity is the main force behind the tides. **E.I.3.1 AA**

● The position of the sun and moon relative to the position of Earth causes tidal ranges.

● The four different types of tides are high tides, low tides, spring tides, and neap tides.

Using Key Terms

1. Write an original definition for *spring tide* and *neap tide*.

Understanding Key Ideas

2. How do land formations affect tides?

3. What causes tidal ranges? **E.I.3.1 AA**

Critical Thinking

4. **Applying Concepts** How many days pass between the minimum and the maximum of the tidal range in any given area? Explain your answer. **E.I.3.1 AA**

5. **Analyzing Processes** Explain how the position of the moon relates to the occurrence of high tides and low tides. **E.I.3.1 AA**

FCAT Preparation

6. The tidal range is determined by the position of the sun and the moon in relation to Earth. Which type of tide is formed when the sun and the moon are at right angles to Earth? **E.I.3.1 AA**

   A. a spring tide

   B. a high tide

   C. a neap tide

   D. a low tide

SCiLINKS

NSTA
Developed and maintained by the
National Science Teachers Association

For a variety of links related to this chapter, go to www.scilinks.org

Topic: Tides; Florida's Coasts
SciLinks code: HQ61525; HSMF05

Skills Practice Lab

Up from the Depths

Every year, the water in certain parts of the ocean "turns over." That is, the water at the bottom rises to the top and the water at the top falls to the bottom. This yearly change brings fresh nutrients from the bottom of the ocean to the fish living near the surface. However, the water in some parts of the ocean never turns over. By completing this activity, you will find out why not.

Keep in mind that some parts of the ocean are warmer at the bottom, and some are warmer at the top. And sometimes the saltiest water is at the bottom and sometimes not. As you complete this activity, you will investigate how these factors help determine whether the water will turn over.

Ask a Question

❶ Why do some parts of the ocean turn over and not others?

Form a Hypothesis

❷ Write a hypothesis that is a possible answer to the question above. Explain your reasoning.

Test the Hypothesis

❸ Label the beakers 1 through 5. Fill beakers 1 through 4 with tap water.

❹ Add a drop of blue food coloring to the water in beakers 1 and 2, and stir with the spoon.

❺ Place beaker 1 in the bucket of ice for 10 min.

❻ Add a drop of red food coloring to the water in beakers 3 and 4, and stir with the spoon.

❼ Set beaker 3 on a hot plate turned to a low setting for 10 min.

❽ Add one spoonful of salt to the water in beaker 4, and stir with the spoon.

OBJECTIVES

Demonstrate the effects of temperature and salinity on the density of water. D.1.3.3 CS

Describe why some parts of the ocean turn over, while others do not.

MATERIALS

- beakers, 400 mL (5)
- blue and red food coloring
- bucket of ice
- gloves, heat-resistant
- hot plate
- plastic wrap, 4 pieces, approximately 30 cm × 20 cm
- salt
- spoon
- tap water
- watch or clock

SAFETY

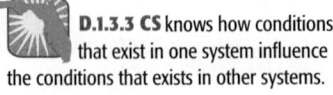 **D.1.3.3 CS** knows how conditions that exist in one system influence the conditions that exists in other systems.

9 While beaker 1 is cooling and beaker 3 is heating, copy the observations table below on a sheet of paper.

Observations Table	
Mixture of water	**Observations**
Warm water placed above cold water	
Cold water placed above warm water	DO NOT
Salty water placed above fresh water	WRITE IN BOOK
Fresh water placed above salty water	

10 Pour half of the water in beaker 1 into beaker 5. Return beaker 1 to the bucket of ice.

11 Tuck a sheet of plastic wrap into beaker 5 so that the plastic rests on the surface of the water and lines the upper half of the beaker.

12 Put on your gloves. Slowly pour half of the water in beaker 3 into the plastic-lined upper half of beaker 5 to form two layers of water. Return beaker 3 to the hot plate, and remove your gloves.

13 Very carefully, pull on one edge of the plastic wrap and remove it so that the warm, red water rests on the cold, blue water.
Caution: The plastic wrap may be warm.

14 Wait about 5 minutes, and then observe the layers in beaker 5. Did one layer remain on top of the other? Was there any mixing or turning over? Record your observations in your observations table.

15 Empty beaker 5, and rinse it with clean tap water.

16 Repeat the procedure used in steps 10–15. This time, pour warm, red water from beaker 3 on the bottom and cold, blue water from beaker 1 on top. (Use gloves when pouring warm water.)

17 Again, repeat the procedure used in steps 10–15. This time, pour blue tap water from beaker 2 on the bottom and red, salty water from beaker 4 on top.

18 Repeat the procedure used in steps 10–15 a third time. This time, pour red, salty water from beaker 4 on the bottom and blue tap water from beaker 2 on top.

Analyze the Results

1 **Analyzing Data** Compare the results of all four trials. Explain why the water turned over in some of the trials but not in all of them.

Draw Conclusions

2 **Evaluating Results** What is the effect of temperature and salinity on the density of water?

3 **Drawing Conclusions** What makes the temperature of ocean water decrease? What could make the salinity of ocean water increase?

4 **Drawing Conclusions** What reasons can you give to explain why some parts of the ocean do not turn over in the spring while some do?

Applying Your Data

Suggest a method for setting up a model that tests the combined effects of temperature and salinity on the density of water. Consider using more than two water samples and dyes.

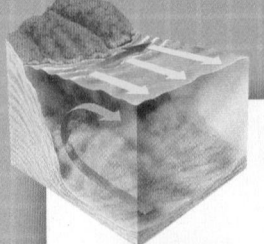

Chapter Review

USING KEY TERMS

For each pair of terms, explain how the meanings of the terms differ.

1 *surface current* and *deep current*

2 *El Niño* and *La Niña*

3 *spring tide* and *neap tide* **FCAT VOCAB**

4 *tide* and *tidal range*

UNDERSTANDING KEY IDEAS

Multiple Choice

5 Climate can affect the formation of deep-ocean currents. Which of the following statements describes how these currents form? **D.1.3.3 CS** **FCAT**

  a. Cold air decreases water density.

  b. Warm air increases water density.

  c. The ocean surface freezes, and solids from the water underneath are removed.

  d. Salinity increases.

6 The properties of waves change when they hit land. What happens to waves as they approach the shore? **B.1.3.6 AA** **FCAT**

  a. They speed up.

  b. They maintain their speed.

  c. Their wavelength increases.

  d. Their wave height increases.

7 Whitecaps break

  a. in the surf.

  b. in the breaker zone.

  c. in the open ocean.

  d. as their wavelength increases.

8 Tidal range is greatest during

  a. spring tide.

  b. neap tide.

  c. a tidal bore.

  d. the daytime.

9 The tides are affected by the gravitational forces of the sun and moon. Which object has a greater effect on tides? **E.1.3.1 AA** **FCAT**

  a. the sun has a greater effect because it is larger

  b. the moon has a greater effect because it is revolves faster

  c. the sun has a greater effect because it is farther away

  d. the moon has a greater effect because it is closer

10 During an El Niño event, an increase in surface-water temperature along the coast of South America can affect global weather patterns. El Niño can cause which of the following? **D.1.3.3 CS** **FCAT**

  a. droughts in Indonesia

  b. upwelling off the coast of South America

  c. heavy rains in Australia

  d. droughts in the southern half of the United States

Short Answer

11 Explain the relationship between upwelling and El Niño.

12 Waves have two parts. Identify the two parts of a wave and describe how these parts relate to wavelength and wave height. **B.1.3.6 AA** **FCAT**

13 Compare the relative positions of Earth, the moon, and the sun during the spring and neap tides. **E.1.3.1 AA**

14 Explain the difference between the breaker zone and the surf.

15 Describe how warm-water currents affect the climate in the British Isles. **D.1.3.3 CS**

16 Describe the factors that form deep currents. **D.1.3.3 CS**

CRITICAL THINKING

Extended Response

17 Identifying Relationships Why are tides more noticeable in Earth's oceans than on its land?

18 Expressing Opinions Why is it important to study El Niño and La Niña?

19 Identifying Relationships Describe how global winds, the Coriolis Effect, and continental deflections form a pattern of surface currents on Earth. **D.1.3.3 CS**

Concept Mapping

20 Use the following terms to create a concept map: *wind, deep current, sun's gravity, types of ocean-water movement, surface current, tide, increasing water density, wave,* and *moon's gravity.*

INTERPRETING GRAPHICS

The diagram below shows some of Earth's major surface currents that flow in the Western Hemisphere. Use the diagram to answer the questions that follow.

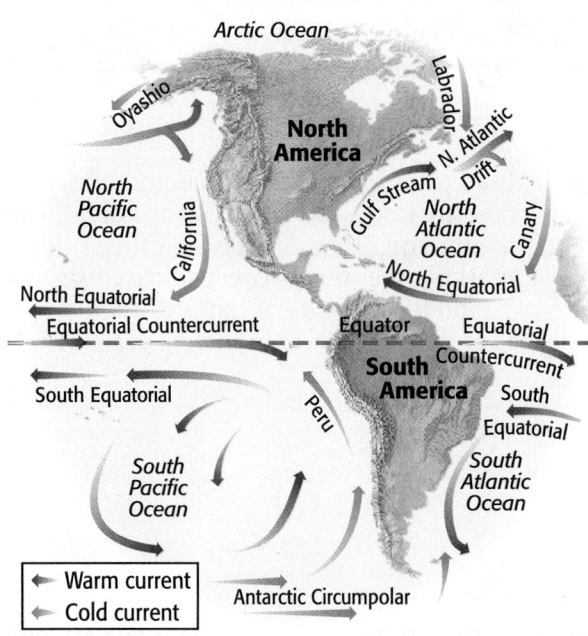

21 List two warm-water currents and two cold-water currents.

22 How do you think the Labrador Current affects the climate of Canada and Greenland? **D.1.3.3 CS, D.1.3.5 CS**

For the following questions, write your answers on a separate sheet of paper.

1 Surface currents are continual, long-term factors that influence the climate of the Earth. What causes the formation of surface currents?

    A.   global winds

    B.   water temperature

    C.   salinity differences

    D.   differences in density

2  Juan is out on a fishing boat and notices that the waves are coming faster and faster. He decides to time how fast the waves are moving. He estimates that the wavelength is 1.5 meters. By marking the time between wave crests he finds that the wave period is 5 seconds. What is the actual speed of the waves? Record your answer in meters per second.

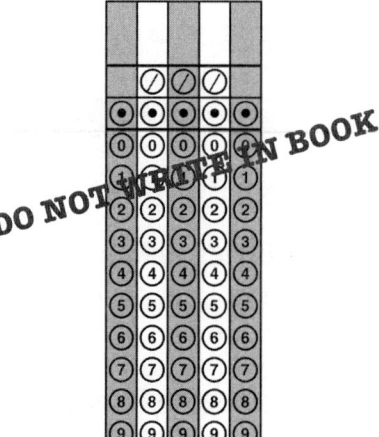

DO NOT WRITE IN BOOK

3 Chan has been studying the tidal variations near his home by charting the height of waters at high tide and again at low tide. He noticed that at certain times during the year the difference between the height of the water at high tide and at low tide was much less than the normal variations. Which of the following statements describes the relative positions of Earth, the Sun, and the Moon when Chan observed the smallest difference between high tide and low tide?

    F.   The Sun and Earth were at right angles to each other relative to the Moon.

    G.   The Sun and the Moon were at right angles to each other relative to Earth.

    H.   The Sun, the Moon, and Earth were aligned with the Moon between the Sun and Earth.

    I.   The Sun, the Moon, and Earth were aligned with Earth between the Moon and the Sun.

4 Brittany is on a cruise with her senior class. When the ship begins to reach shore she notices that the waves seem to be getting taller. What type of wave is Brittany looking at? Why are the waves near the shore taller than the waves farther away from the shore are?

5 Karla is going to search for clams and oysters during low tide. If she knows that low tide is at 3:00 P.M. today, how many minutes after 3:00 P.M. should she plan to go searching for shellfish tomorrow?

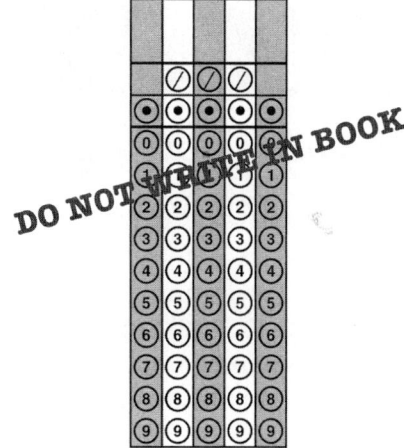

6 The diagram below shows a map of the ocean surface currents of Earth. Warm currents carry warm water from the equator. Cool currents carry cool water toward the equator. Hurricanes form where the ocean surface is warmest, when warm air flowing from the equator mixes with cooler air. Warm ocean currents provide the heat and moisture that a hurricane needs to develop and to stay fueled.

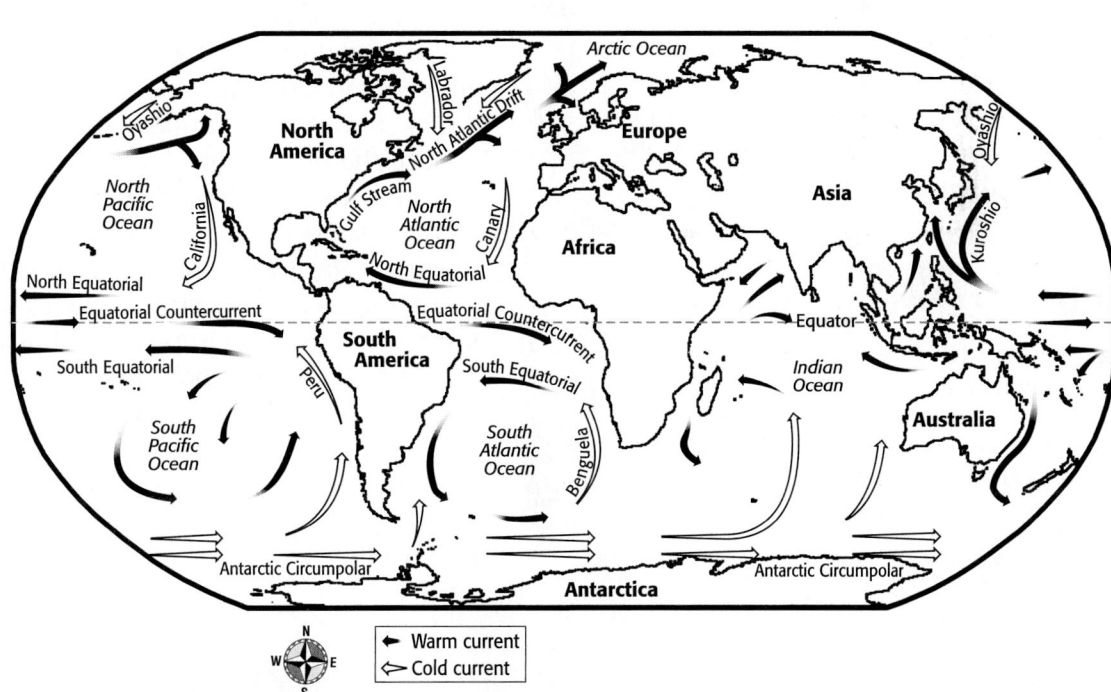

Based on the types of surface currents and the directions they flow, where would hurricanes **most** commonly form?

A. in the southern Indian Ocean

B. in the northwest Atlantic Ocean

C. off the western coast of Australia

D. along the western coast of South America

Science in Action

Weird Science

Using Toy Ducks to Track Ocean Currents

Accidents can sometimes lead to scientific discovery. For example, on January 10, 1992, 29,000 plastic tub toys spilled overboard when a container ship traveling northwest of Hawaii ran into a storm. In November of that year, those toys began washing up on Alaskan beaches. When oceanographers heard about this, they placed advertisements in newspapers along the Alaskan coast asking people who found the toys to call them. Altogether, hundreds of toys were recovered. Using recovery dates and locations and computer models, oceanographers were able to re-create the toys' drift and figure out which currents carried the toys. As for the remaining toys, currents may carry them to a number of different destinations. Some may travel through the Arctic Ocean and eventually reach Europe!

Math ACTiViTY

Between January 10, 1992, and November 16, 1992, some of the toys were carried approximately 3,220 km from the cargo-spill site to the coast of Alaska. Calculate the average distance traveled by these toys per day. (Hint: The year 1992 was a leap year.)

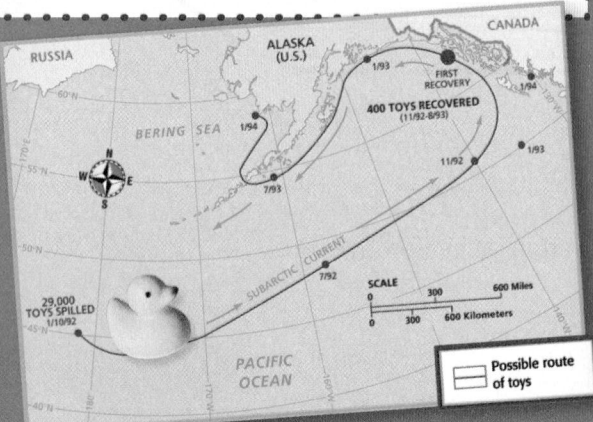

Science, Technology, and Society

Red Tides

Imagine going to the beach only to find that the ocean water has turned red and that a lot of fish are floating belly up. What could cause such damage to the ocean? It may surprise you to find that the answer is single-celled algae. When certain algae grow rapidly, they clump together on the ocean's surface in what are known as algal blooms. These algal blooms have been commonly called *red tides* because the blooms often turn the water red or reddish-brown. The term scientists use for these sudden explosions in algae growth is *harmful algal blooms* (HABs). The blooms are harmful because certain species of algae produce toxins that can poison fish, shellfish, and people who eat poisoned fish or shellfish. Toxic blooms can be carried hundreds of miles on ocean currents. HABs can ride into an area on an ocean current and cause fish to die and people who eat the poisoned fish or shellfish to become ill.

Social Studies ACTiViTY

Some scientists think that factors related to human activities, such as agricultural runoff into the ocean, are causing more HABs than occurred in the past. Other scientists disagree. Find out more about this issue, and have a class debate about the roles humans play in creating HABs.

Project Oceanography

Oceanographers in the Classroom *Project Oceanography* is a marine science television program for middle school students produced by The University of South Florida's College of Marine Science. Each week during the school year, you can learn about a variety of marine science topics right in your classroom. The program is viewed in more than 1,000 classrooms in seven countries every year! The programs are presented by real scientists and include an on-line question and answer session. By watching *Project Oceanography* on the Internet, on cable television, or on videotape, you will get to see scientists using high-tech equipment and science tools to explore the oceans. You can follow along as oceanographers describe the dangers, thrills, and excitement of exploring the oceans. Broadcasts have covered topics such as hurricanes, tsunamis, marine mammals, fish ecology, and deep sea organisms living near hydrothermal vents. Project Oceanography shows how real scientists investigate the oceans. You can follow along as oceanographers use submersibles to explore the deep-sea floor or use satellites to track currents.

You can watch *Project Oceanography* if you are interested in learning more about how researchers are unlocking the mysteries of the oceans!

Language Arts ACTiViTY

WRITING SKILL Research an ocean science topic that interests you. Write a script for a broadcast of *Project Oceanography* about that topic. Perform your broadcast for the class.

To learn more about these Science in Action topics, visit **go.hrw.com** and type in the keyword **HT6FH2FF.**

Current Science

Check out Current Science® articles related to this chapter by visiting go.hrw.com. Just type in the keyword **HZ5CS14.**

UNIT 6

TIMELINE

Earth and Space

In this section, you will learn about Earth and space. For centuries, people have been studying space from Earth. As a result, the number of objects in space that scientists could study was limited. In the last century, advances in technology have made space travel possible. Now, scientists can study the far reaches of space by using spacecraft, such as orbiting telescopes, human-made satellites, and probes. This timeline shows some of the events that have occurred as people have tried to understand the movement of Earth and other objects through space.

Around 250 BCE

Archimedes, a Greek mathematician, develops the principle that bears his name. The principle relates the buoyant force on an object in a fluid to the amount of fluid displaced by the object.

1764

In London, Wolfgang Amadeus Mozart composes his first symphony—at the age of 8.

1846

After determining that the orbit of Uranus is different from what is predicted by the law of universal gravitation, scientists discover Neptune, whose gravitational force causes Uranus's unusual orbit.

1947

While flying a Bell X-1 rocket-powered airplane, Chuck Yeager, an American pilot, becomes the first human to travel faster than the speed of sound.

Around 240 BCE

Chinese astronomers are the first to record a sighting of Halley's comet.

1519

Ferdinand Magellan, a Portuguese explorer, begins the first voyage around the world.

1687

Sir Isaac Newton, a British mathematician and scientist, publishes *Principia*, a book describing his laws of motion and the law of universal gravitation.

PHILOSOPHIÆ
NATURALIS
PRINCIPIA
MATHEMATICA.
Autore JS. NEWTON, Trin. Coll. Cantab. Soc. Matheseos Professore Lucasiano, & Societatis Regalis Sodali.

1905

While employed as a patent clerk, Albert Einstein, a German physicist, publishes his special theory of relativity. The theory states that the speed of light is constant no matter what the frame of reference is.

1921

Bessie Coleman becomes the first African American woman licensed to fly an airplane.

1971

Alan Shepard, an American astronaut, takes a break from gathering lunar data to play golf on the moon during the *Apollo 14* mission.

1990

The *Magellan* spacecraft begins orbiting Venus for a four-year mission to map the planet. By using the sun's gravitational forces, it propels itself to Venus without burning much fuel.

2003

NASA launches *Spirit* and *Opportunity,* two Mars Exploration Rovers, to study Mars.

Studying Space

The Big Idea Astronomy is the study of the universe.

About the PHOTO

This time-exposure photograph was taken at night at an observatory located high in the mountains of Chile. As the night passed, the photograph recorded the stars as they circled the southern celestial pole. Just as Earth's rotation causes the sun to appear to move across the sky during the day, Earth's rotation also causes the stars to appear to move across the night sky.

PRE-READING ACTIVITY

 **Three-Panel Flip Chart**
Before you read the chapter, create the FoldNote entitled "Three-Panel Flip Chart" described in the **Study Skills** section of the Appendix. Label the flaps of the three-panel flip chart with "Astronomy," "Telescopes," and "Mapping the stars." As you read the chapter, write information you learn about each category under the appropriate flap.

START-UP ACTIVITY

Making an Astrolabe

In this activity, you will make an astronomical device called an *astrolabe* (AS troh LAYB). Ancient astronomers used astrolabes to measure the location of stars in the sky. You will use the astrolabe to measure the angle, or altitude, of an object.

Procedure

1. Tie one end of a **piece of thread** that is 15 cm long to the center of the straight edge of a **protractor.** Tie a **paper clip** to the other end of the string.

2. Tape a **soda straw** lengthwise along the straight edge of the protractor. Your astrolabe is complete!

3. Go outside, and hold the astrolabe in front of you.

4. Look through the straw at a distant object, such as a treetop. The curve of the astrolabe should point toward the ground.

5. Hold the astrolabe still, and carefully pinch the string between your thumb and the protractor. Count the number of degrees between the string and the 90° marker on the protractor. This angle is the altitude of the object.

Analysis

1. What is the altitude of the object? How would the altitude change if you moved closer to the object?

2. Explain how you would use an astrolabe to find the altitude of a star. What are the advantages and disadvantages of this method of measurement?

Astronomy

Imagine that it is 5,000 years ago. Clocks and modern calendars have not been invented. How would you tell the time or know what day it is? One way to tell the time is to study the movement of stars, planets, and the moon.

People in ancient cultures used the seasonal cycles of the stars, planets, and the moon to mark the passage of time. For example, by observing these yearly cycles, early farmers learned the best times of year to plant and harvest various crops. Studying the movement of objects in the sky was so important to ancient people that they built observatories, such as the one shown in **Figure 1.** Over time, the study of the night sky became the science of astronomy. **Astronomy** is the study of the universe. Although ancient cultures did not fully understand how the planets, moons, and stars move in relation to each other, their observations led to the first calendars.

Our Modern Calendar

The years, months, and days of our modern calendar are based on the observation of bodies in our solar system. A **year** is the time required for Earth to orbit once around the sun. A **month** is roughly the amount of time required for the moon to orbit once around Earth. (The word *month* comes from the word *moon.*) A **day** is the time required for Earth to rotate once on its axis.

astronomy the scientific study of the universe

Figure 1 *This building is located at Chichén Itzá in the Yucatán, Mexico. It is thought to be an ancient Mayan observatory.*

H.1.3.1 AA knows that scientific knowledge is subject to modification as new information challenges prevailing theories and as a new theory leads to looking at old observations in a new way.

Who's Who of Early Astronomy

Astronomical observations have given us much more than the modern calendar that we use. The careful work of early astronomers helped people understand their place in the universe. The earliest astronomers had only oral histories to learn from. Almost everything they knew about the universe came from what they could discover with their eyes and minds. Not surprisingly, most early astronomers thought that the universe consisted of the sun, the moon, and the planets. They thought that the stars were at the edge of the universe. Claudius Ptolemy (KLAW dee uhs TAHL uh mee) and Nicolaus Copernicus (NIK uh LAY uhs koh PUHR ni kuhs) were two early scientists who influenced the way that people thought about the structure of the universe.

Ptolemy: An Earth-Centered Universe

In 140 CE, Ptolemy, a Greek astronomer, wrote a book that combined all of the ancient knowledge of astronomy that he could find. He expanded ancient theories with careful mathematical calculations in what was called the *Ptolemaic theory.* Ptolemy thought that Earth was at the center of the universe and that the other planets and the sun revolved around Earth. Although the Ptolemaic theory, shown in **Figure 2,** was incorrect, it predicted the motions of the planets better than any other theory at the time did. For more than 1,500 years in Europe, the Ptolemaic theory was the most popular theory for the structure of the universe.

Copernicus: A Sun-Centered Universe

In 1543, a Polish astronomer named Copernicus published a new theory that would eventually revolutionize astronomy. According to his theory, which is shown in **Figure 3,** the sun is at the center of the universe, and all of the planets—including Earth—orbit the sun. Although Copernicus correctly thought that the planets orbit the sun, his theory did not replace the Ptolemaic theory immediately. When Copernicus's theory was accepted, major changes in science and society called the *Copernican revolution* took place.

Reading Check What was Copernicus's theory?

year the time required for the Earth to orbit once around the sun

month a division of the year that is based on the orbit of the moon around the Earth

day the time required for Earth to rotate once on its axis

Figure 2 *According to the Ptolemaic theory, Earth is at the center of the universe.*

Figure 3 *According to Copernicus's theory, the sun is at the center of the universe.*

Tycho Brahe: A Wealth of Data

In the late-1500s, Danish astronomer Tycho Brahe (TIE koh BRAW uh) used several large tools, including the one shown in **Figure 4,** to make the most detailed astronomical observations that had been recorded so far. Brahe favored a theory of an Earth-centered universe that was different from the Ptolemaic theory. Brahe thought that the sun and the moon revolved around Earth and that the other planets revolved around the sun. While his theory was not correct, Brahe recorded very precise observations of the planets and stars that helped future astronomers.

Johannes Kepler: Laws of Planetary Motion

After Brahe died, his assistant, Johannes Kepler, continued Brahe's work. Kepler did not agree with Brahe's theory, but he recognized how valuable Brahe's data were. In 1609, after analyzing the data, Kepler announced that all of the planets revolve around the sun in elliptical orbits and that the sun is not in the exact center of the orbits. Kepler also stated three laws of planetary motion. These laws are still used today.

Figure 4 *Brahe (upper right) used a mural quadrant, which is a large quarter-circle on a wall, to measure the positions of stars and planets.*

Galileo: Turning a Telescope to the Sky

In 1609, Galileo Galilei became one of the first people to use a telescope to observe objects in space. Galileo discovered craters and mountains on Earth's moon, four of Jupiter's moons, sunspots on the sun, and the phases of Venus. These discoveries showed that the planets are not "wandering stars" but are physical bodies like Earth.

Isaac Newton: The Laws of Gravity

In 1687, a scientist named Sir Isaac Newton showed that all objects in the universe attract each other through gravitational force. The force of gravity depends on the mass of the objects and the distance between them. Newton's law of gravity explained why all of the planets orbit the most massive object in the solar system—the sun. Thus, Newton helped explain the observations of the scientists who came before him.

H.1.3.1 AA knows that scientific knowledge is subject to modification as new information challenges prevailing theories and as a new theory leads to looking at old observations in a new way.

Benchmark Check How did the work of Isaac Newton help explain the observations of earlier scientists? **H.1.3.1 AA**

Modern Astronomy

The invention of the telescope and the description of gravity were two milestones in the development of modern astronomy. In the 200 years following Newton's discoveries, scientists made many discoveries about our solar system. But they did not learn that our galaxy has cosmic neighbors until the 1920s.

Edwin Hubble: Beyond the Edge of the Milky Way

Before the 1920s, many astronomers thought that our galaxy, the Milky Way, included every object in space. In 1924, Edwin Hubble proved that other galaxies existed beyond the edge of the Milky Way. His data confirmed the beliefs of some astronomers that the universe is much larger than our galaxy. Today, larger and better telescopes on Earth and in space, new models of the universe, and spacecraft help astronomers study space. Computers, shown in **Figure 5,** help process data and control the movement of telescopes. These tools have helped answer many questions about the universe. Yet new technology has presented questions that were unthinkable even 10 years ago.

Figure 5 *Computers are used to control telescopes and process large amounts of data.*

SECTION Review

Summary

- Astronomy, the study of the universe, is one of the oldest sciences.
- The units of the modern calendar—days, months, and years—are based on observations of objects in space.
- Copernican theory states that the sun is at the center of the universe.
- Knowledge of the universe continually changes as new data are discovered and new theories are developed. **H.1.3.1 AA**

Using Key Terms

1. Use *year, day, month,* and *astronomy* in separate sentences.

Understanding Key Ideas

2. What happens in 1 year?
   a. The moon completes one orbit around Earth.
   b. The sun travels once around Earth.
   c. Earth revolves once.
   d. Earth completes one orbit around the sun.

3. What is the difference between the Ptolemaic and Copernican theories? Who was more accurate: Ptolemy or Copernicus?

Critical Thinking

4. **Analyzing Relationships** What advantage did Galileo have over earlier astronomers? **H.1.3.1 AA**

5. **Making Inferences** Why is astronomy such an old science?

FCAT Preparation

6. Kepler used data collected by Brahe to develop his theories. Which statement best describes the relationship between Brahe and Kepler? **H.1.3.1 AA**
   A. Brahe used Kepler's data.
   B. Brahe did not use Kepler's data.
   C. Brahe and Kepler did not share data.
   D. Kepler used Brahe's data to develop his theories.

SC*LINKS*. NSTA

Developed and maintained by the National Science Teachers Association

For a variety of links related to this chapter, go to www.scilinks.org

Topic: The Stars and Keeping Time; Early Theories in Astronomy

SciLinks code: HSM1449; HSM0444

Telescopes

What color are Saturn's rings? What is on the surface of the moon? To find out, look through a telescope.

For astronomers and modern stargazers, the telescope is the standard tool for observing the sky. A **telescope** is an instrument that gathers electromagnetic radiation from objects in space and concentrates it for better observation.

Optical Telescopes

Optical telescopes, which are the most common telescopes, are used to study visible light from objects in the universe. Before the invention of the telescope, astronomers knew relatively little about our solar system. They knew that the moon moved around Earth, but they did not know that other planets also had satellites. With the unaided eye, you can see about 3,000 stars in the night sky. Using an optical telescope, you can see millions of stars and other objects.

An optical telescope collects visible light and focuses it to a focal point. A *focal point* is the point where the rays of light that pass through a lens or that reflect from a mirror converge. The simplest optical telescope has two lenses. One lens, called the *objective lens,* collects light and forms an image at the back of the telescope. The second lens is located in the eyepiece and magnifies the image produced by the objective lens. **Figure 1** shows the moon as seen using an optical telescope.

Benchmark Check How did the invention of the telescope change our knowledge of the solar system? **E.1.3.1 AA**

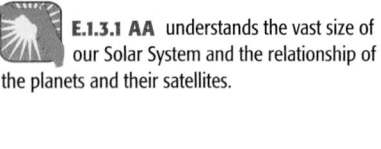

E.1.3.1 AA understands the vast size of our Solar System and the relationship of the planets and their satellites.

Figure 1 *By using telescopes, people can study objects such as the moon in greater detail.*

Figure 2 Refracting and Reflecting Telescopes

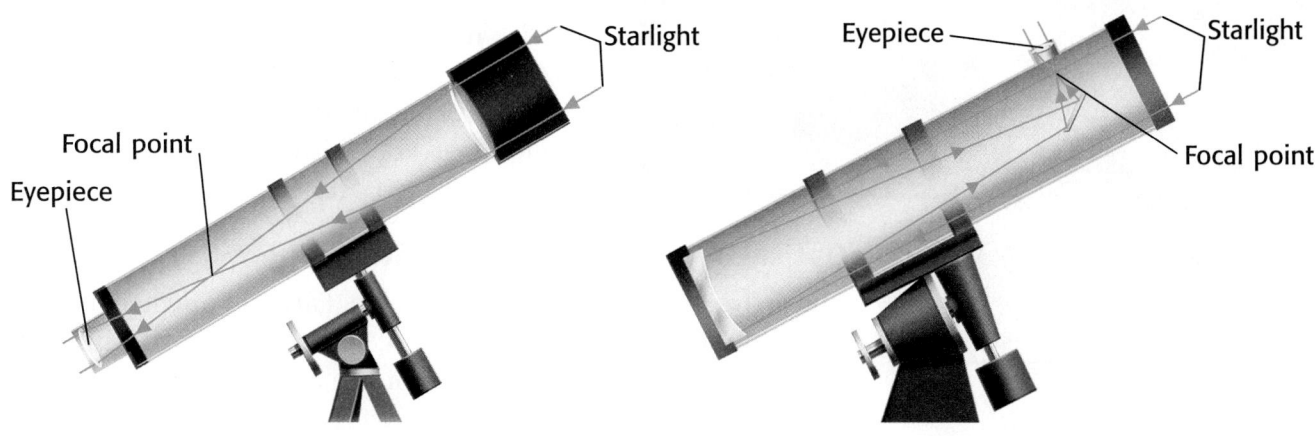

Refracting telescopes use lenses to gather and focus light.

Reflecting telescopes use mirrors to gather and focus light.

Refracting Telescopes

Telescopes that use lenses to gather and focus light are called **refracting telescopes.** As shown in **Figure 2,** a refracting telescope has an objective lens that bends light that passes through it and focuses the light to be magnified by an eyepiece. Refracting telescopes have two disadvantages. First, lenses focus different colors of light at slightly different distances, so images cannot be perfectly focused. Second, the size of a refracting telescope is also limited by the size of the objective lens. If the lens is too large, the glass sags under its own weight and images are distorted. These limitations are two reasons that most professional astronomers use reflecting telescopes.

Reflecting Telescopes

A telescope that uses a curved mirror to gather and focus light is called a **reflecting telescope.** Light enters the telescope and is reflected from a large, curved mirror to a flat mirror. As shown in **Figure 2,** the flat mirror focuses the image and reflects the light to be magnified by the eyepiece.

One advantage of reflecting telescopes is that the mirrors can be very large. Large mirrors allow reflecting telescopes to gather more light than refracting telescopes do. Another advantage is that curved mirrors are polished on their curved side, which prevents light from entering the glass. Thus, any flaws in the glass do not affect the light. A third advantage is that mirrors can focus all colors of light to the same focal point. Therefore, reflecting telescopes allow all colors of light from an object to be seen in focus at the same time.

telescope an instrument that collects electromagnetic radiation from the sky and concentrates it for better observation

refracting telescope a telescope that uses a set of lenses to gather and focus light from distant objects

reflecting telescope a telescope that uses a curved mirror to gather and focus light from distant objects

Very Large Reflecting Telescopes

In some very large reflecting telescopes, several mirrors work together to collect light and focus it in the same area. The Keck Telescopes in Hawaii, shown in **Figure 3,** are twin telescopes that each have 36 hexagonal mirrors that work together. Linking several mirrors allows more light to be collected and focused in one spot.

Figure 3 *The Keck Telescopes are in Hawaii. The 36 hexagonal mirrors in each telescope (shown in the inset) combine to form a light-reflecting surface that is 10 m across.*

Optical Telescopes and the Atmosphere

The light gathered by telescopes on Earth is affected by the atmosphere. Earth's atmosphere causes starlight to shimmer and blur because of the motion of the air above the telescope. Also, light pollution from large cities can make the sky look bright. As a result, an observer's ability to view faint objects is limited. Astronomers often place telescopes in dry areas to avoid moisture in the air. Mountaintops are also good locations for telescopes because the air is thinner at higher elevations. In addition, mountaintops generally have less air pollution and light pollution than other areas do.

✓ **Reading Check** How does the atmosphere affect the images produced by optical telescopes?

Optical Telescopes in Space

To avoid interference by the atmosphere, scientists have put telescopes in space. Although the mirror in the *Hubble Space Telescope,* shown in **Figure 4,** is only 2.4 m across, this optical telescope can detect very faint objects in space.

Figure 4 *The* Hubble Space Telescope *has produced very clear images of objects in deep space.*

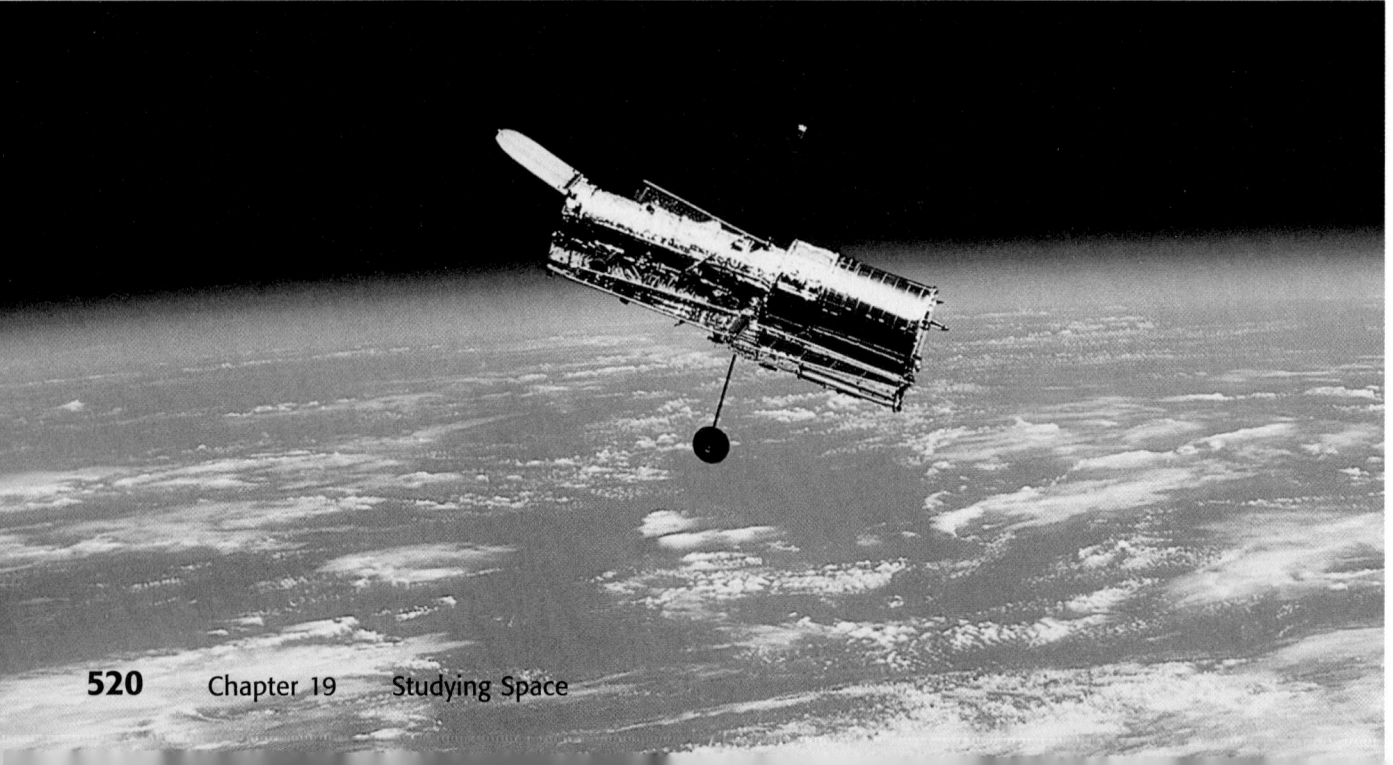

The Electromagnetic Spectrum

For thousands of years, humans have used their eyes to observe stars and planets. But scientists eventually discovered that visible light, the light that we can see, is not the only form of radiation. In 1852, James Clerk Maxwell proved that visible light is a part of the electromagnetic spectrum. The electromagnetic spectrum is made up of all of the wavelengths of **electromagnetic radiation.**

Detecting Electromagnetic Radiation

Each color of light is a different wavelength of electromagnetic radiation. Humans can see radiation from red light, which has a long wavelength, to blue light, which has a shorter wavelength. But visible light is only a small part of the electromagnetic spectrum, as shown in **Figure 5.** The rest of the electromagnetic spectrum—radio waves, microwaves, infrared light, ultraviolet light, X rays, and gamma rays—is invisible. Earth's atmosphere blocks most invisible radiation from objects in space. In this way, the atmosphere functions as a protective shield around Earth. Radiation that can pass through the atmosphere includes some radio waves, some microwaves, some infrared light, visible light, and some ultraviolet light.

electromagnetic radiation the radiation associated with an electric and magnetic field **FCAT** *VOCAB*

Figure 5 *Visible light is only a small band of the electromagnetic spectrum. Radio waves have the longest wavelengths, and gamma rays have the shortest wavelengths.*

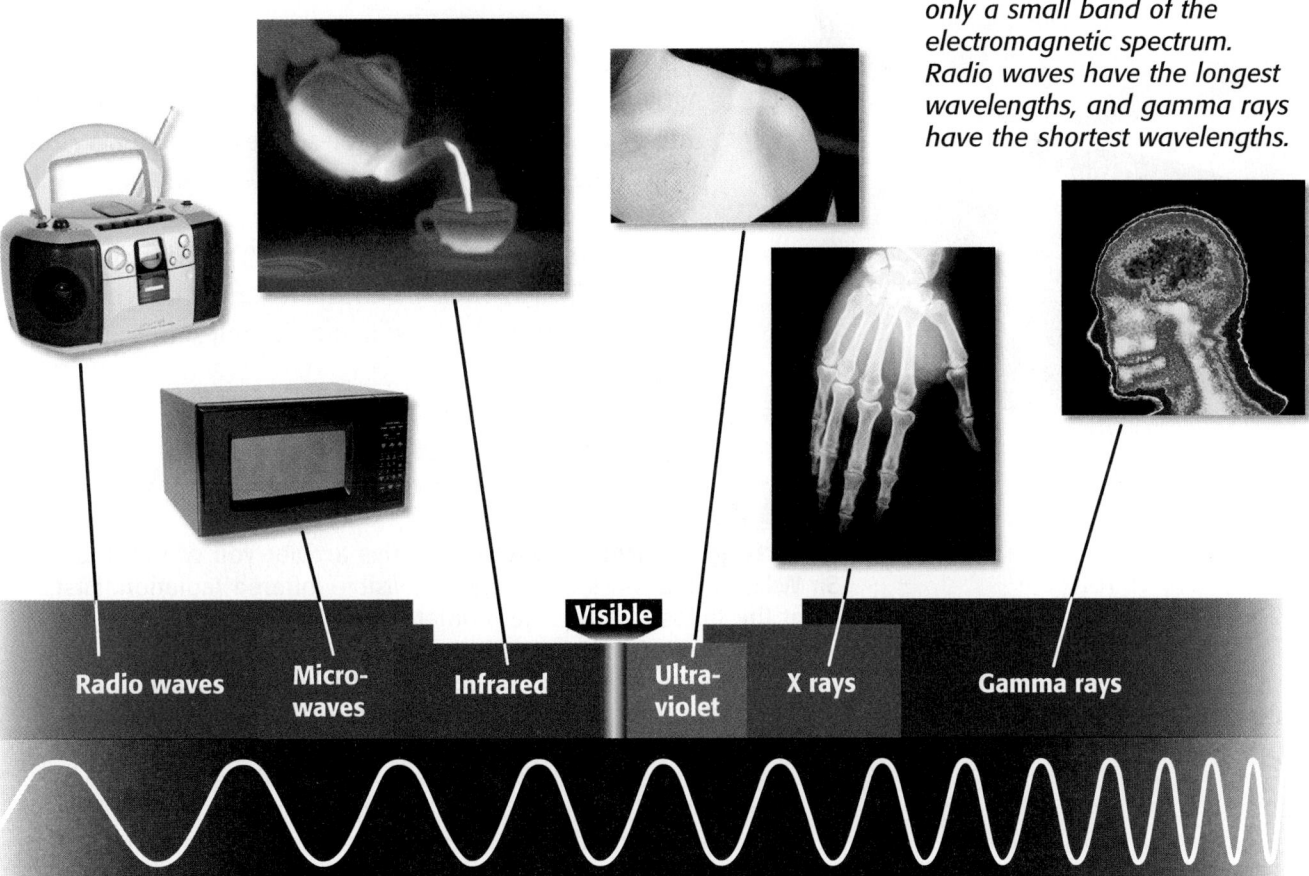

Radio waves | Micro-waves | Infrared | Visible | Ultra-violet | X rays | Gamma rays

Nonoptical Telescopes

To study invisible radiation, scientists use nonoptical telescopes. Nonoptical telescopes detect radiation that cannot be seen by the human eye. Astronomers study the entire electromagnetic spectrum because each type of radiation reveals different clues about an object. As **Figure 6** shows, our galaxy looks very different when it is observed at various wavelengths. A different type of telescope was used to produce each image. The "cloud" that goes across the image is the Milky Way galaxy.

Radio Telescopes

Radio telescopes detect radio waves. Radio telescopes have to be much larger than optical telescopes because radio wavelengths are about 1 million times longer than optical wavelengths. Most radio radiation reaches the ground and can be detected both during the day and night. The surface of radio telescopes does not have to be as flawless as the lenses and mirrors of optical telescopes. In fact, the surface of a radio telescope does not have to be solid.

Linking Radio Telescopes

Astronomers can get more detailed images of the universe by linking radio telescopes together. When radio telescopes are linked together, they work like a single giant telescope. For example, the Very Large Array (VLA) consists of 27 radio telescopes that are spread over 30 km. Working together, the telescopes function as a single telescope that is 30 km across!

Figure 6 *Each image shows the Milky Way as it would appear if we could see other wavelengths of electromagnetic radiation.*

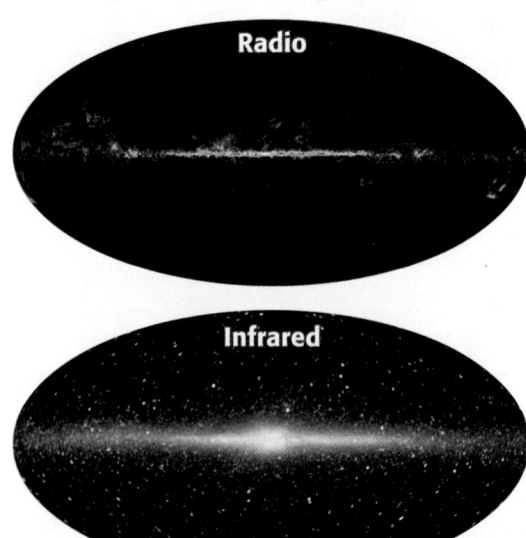

Radio

Infrared

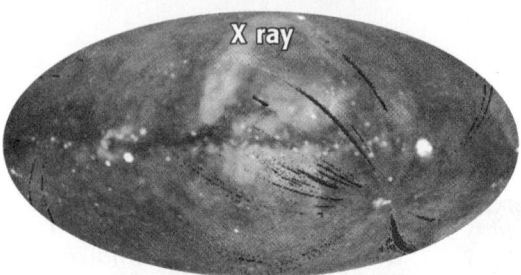

X ray

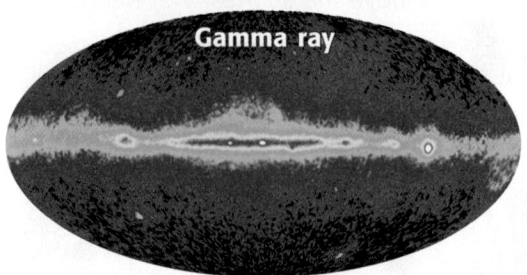

Gamma ray

CONNECTION TO Physics

Detecting Infrared Radiation In this activity, you will replicate Sir William Herschel's discovery of invisible infrared radiation. First, paint the bulbs of three thermometers black. Place a sheet of white paper inside a tall cardboard box. Tape the thermometers parallel to each other, and place them inside the box. Cut a small notch in the top of the box, and position a small glass prism so that a spectrum is projected inside the box. Arrange the thermometers so that one is just outside the red end of the spectrum, with no direct light on it. After 10 min, record the temperatures. Which thermometer recorded the highest temperature? Explain why.

ACTIVITY

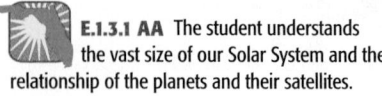

E.1.3.1 AA The student understands the vast size of our Solar System and the relationship of the planets and their satellites.

Nonoptical Telescopes in Space

Because most electromagnetic waves are blocked by Earth's atmosphere, scientists have placed ultraviolet telescopes, infrared telescopes, gamma-ray telescopes, and X-ray telescopes in space. The *Chandra X-Ray Observatory*, a space-based telescope that detects X rays, is illustrated in **Figure 7**. X-ray telescopes in space can be much more sensitive than optical telescopes. For example, NASA has tested an X-ray telescope that can detect an object that is the size of a frisbee on the surface of the sun. If an optical telescope had a similar power, it could detect a hair on the head of an astronaut on the moon!

✓ **Reading Check** Why are X-ray telescopes placed in space?

Figure 7 *The* Chandra X-Ray Observatory *can detect black holes and some of the most distant objects in the universe.*

SECTION Review

Summary

- Telescopes have extended our knowledge of the relationship between the planets and their satellites. **E.1.3.1 AA**

- Refracting telescopes use lenses to gather and focus light.

- Reflecting telescopes use mirrors to gather and focus light.

- Astronomers study all wavelengths of electromagnetic radiation.

- The atmosphere blocks most forms of electromagnetic radiation from reaching Earth. To overcome this limitation, astronomers place telescopes in space.

Using Key Terms

For each pair of terms, explain how the meanings of the terms differ.

1. *telescope* and *electromagnetic radiation* **FCAT VOCAB**

Understanding Key Ideas

2. How does the atmosphere affect astronomical observations?
   a. It focuses visible light.
   b. It blocks most electromagnetic radiation.
   c. It blocks all radio waves.
   d. It has no effect.

3. What advantages do reflecting telescopes have over refracting telescopes?

4. Arrange the types of electromagnetic radiation according to their wavelengths.

5. How did telescopes change our knowledge of the planets? **E.1.3.1 AA**

Critical Thinking

6. **Making Inferences** Why doesn't the surface of a radio telescope have to be as flawless as a mirror in an optical telescope?

FCAT Preparation

7. Galileo discovered Jupiter's four largest moons in 1610. Since that time, scientists have discovered that Jupiter has many more moons. Which of the following statements best describes Jupiter's moons? **E.1.3.1 AA**

   A. Jupiter has as many moons as Earth has.

   B. Jupiter's moons are the same size as Earth's moon.

   C. Jupiter's moons move in the same direction as Earth's moon.

   D. Jupiter has more moons than Earth has.

SCiLINKS®

NSTA
Developed and maintained by the National Science Teachers Association

For a variety of links related to this chapter, go to www.scilinks.org

Topic: Telescopes
SciLinks code: HSM1500

Mapping the Stars

Have you ever seen Orion the Hunter or the Big Dipper in the night sky? Ancient cultures linked stars together to form patterns that represented characters from myths and objects in their lives.

Today, we can see the same star patterns that people in ancient cultures saw. Modern astronomers still use many of the names given to stars centuries ago. But astronomers can now describe a star's location precisely. Advances in astronomy have led to a better understanding of how far away stars are and how big the universe is.

Patterns in the Sky

When people in ancient cultures connected stars in patterns, they named sections of the sky based on the patterns. These patterns are called *constellations*. **Constellations** are sections of the sky that contain recognizable star patterns. Understanding the location and movement of constellations helped people navigate and keep track of time.

Different civilizations had different names for the same constellations. For example, where the Greeks saw a hunter (Orion) in the northern sky, the Japanese saw a drum, as shown in **Figure 1.** Today, different cultures still interpret the sky in different ways, but astronomers have agreed on the names and locations of the constellations.

constellation a region of the sky that contains a recognizable star pattern and that is used to describe the location of objects in space

Figure 1 *The ancient Greeks saw Orion as a hunter, but the Japanese saw the same set of stars as a drum.*

Figure 2 *This sky map shows some of the constellations in the Northern Hemisphere at midnight in the spring. Ursa Major (the Great Bear) is a region of the sky that includes all of the stars that make up that constellation.*

Constellations Help Organize the Sky

When you think of constellations, you probably think of the stick figures made by connecting bright stars with imaginary lines. To an astronomer, however, a constellation is something more. As you can see in **Figure 2,** a constellation is a region of the sky. Each constellation shares a border with neighboring constellations. For example, in the same way that the state of Texas is a region of the United States, Ursa Major is a region of the sky. Every star or galaxy is located within 1 of 88 constellations.

Seasonal Changes

The sky map in **Figure 2** shows what the midnight sky in the Northern Hemisphere looks like in the spring. But as Earth revolves around the sun, the apparent locations of the constellations change from season to season. In addition, different constellations are visible in the Southern Hemisphere. Thus, a child in Chile can see different constellations than a child in the United States can. Therefore, the map in **Figure 2** is not accurate for the other three seasons or for the Southern Hemisphere. Sky maps for summer, fall, and winter in the Northern Hemisphere appear in the Appendix of this book.

Reading Check Why are different constellations visible in the Northern Hemisphere and Southern Hemisphere?

Using a Sky Map

1. Hold your **textbook** over your head with the cover facing upward. Turn the book so that the direction at the bottom of the sky map is the same as the direction you are facing

2. Notice the location to constellations in each other.

3. If you look up at night in you should se tioned on sky your e of how

4. Wh land maps?

the Stars

525

Sect

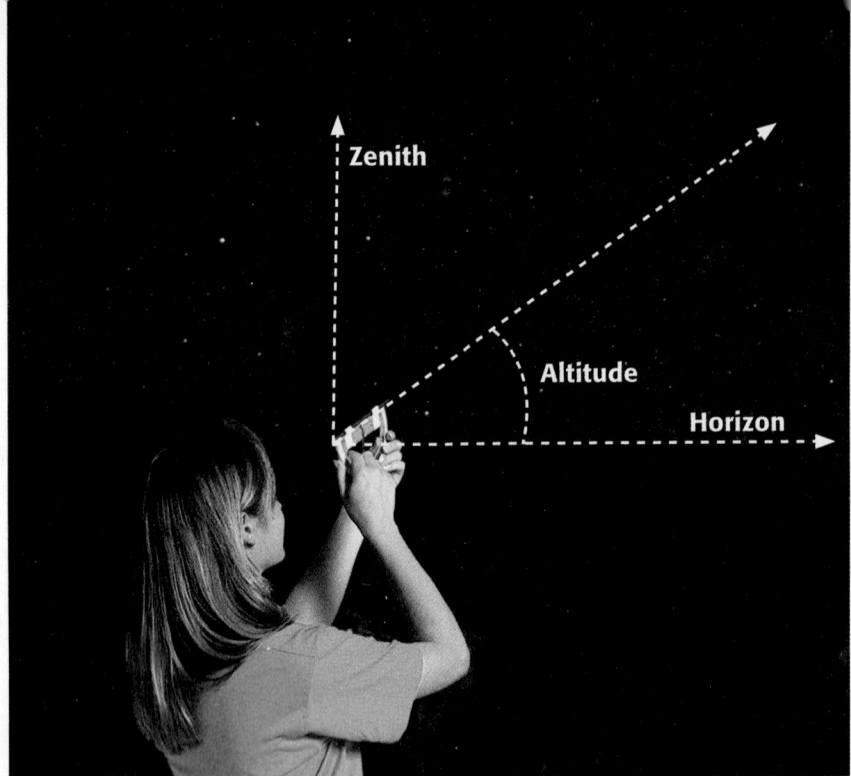

Figure 3 *Using an astrolabe, you can determine the altitude of a star by measuring the angle between the horizon and a star. The altitude of any object depends on where you are and when you look.*

Zenith

Altitude

Horizon

Finding Stars in the Night Sky

Have you ever tried to show someone a star by pointing to it? Did the person miss what you were seeing? If you use an instrument called an *astrolabe*, shown in **Figure 3,** you can describe the location of a star or planet. To use an astrolabe correctly, you need to understand the three points of reference shown in **Figure 4.** This method is useful to describe the location of a star relative to where you are. But if you want to describe a star's location in relation to Earth, you need to use the celestial sphere, which is shown in **Figure 5.**

zenith the point in the sky directly above an observer on Earth

altitude the angle between an object in the sky and the horizon

horizon the line where the sky and the Earth appear to meet

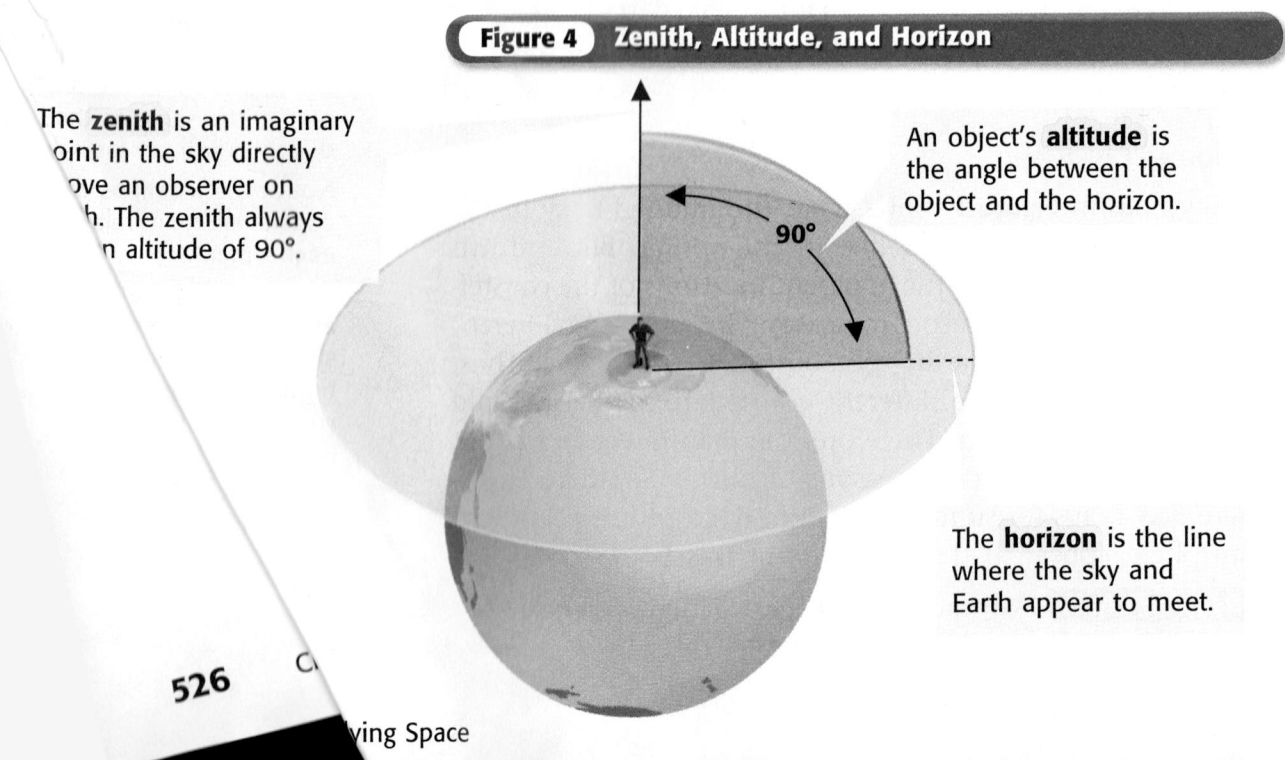

Figure 4 Zenith, Altitude, and Horizon

The **zenith** is an imaginary point in the sky directly above an observer on Earth. The zenith always [has] an altitude of 90°.

An object's **altitude** is the angle between the object and the horizon.

90°

The **horizon** is the line where the sky and Earth appear to meet.

Figure 5 **The Celestial Sphere**

To talk to each other about the location of a star, astronomers must have a common method of describing a star's location. The method that astronomers have invented is based on a reference system known as the *celestial sphere*. The celestial sphere is an imaginary sphere that surrounds Earth. Just as we use latitude and longitude to plot positions on Earth, astronomers use right ascension and declination to plot positions in the sky. *Right ascension* is a measure of how far east an object is from the *vernal equinox*, the location of the sun on the first day of spring. *Declination* is a measure of how far north or south an object is from the celestial equator.

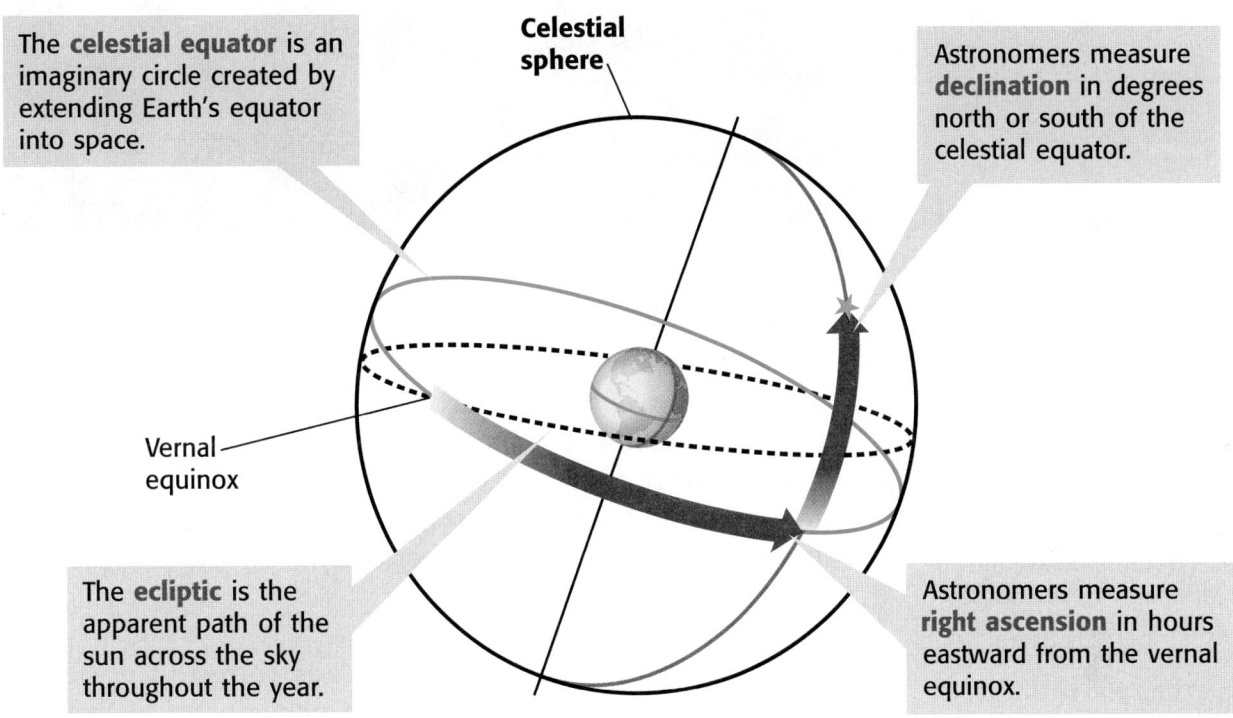

The **celestial equator** is an imaginary circle created by extending Earth's equator into space.

Celestial sphere

Astronomers measure **declination** in degrees north or south of the celestial equator.

Vernal equinox

The **ecliptic** is the apparent path of the sun across the sky throughout the year.

Astronomers measure **right ascension** in hours eastward from the vernal equinox.

The Path of Stars Across the Sky

Just as the sun appears to move across the sky during the day, most stars and planets rise and set throughout the night. This apparent motion is caused by Earth's rotation. As Earth spins on its axis, stars and planets appear to move. Near the poles, however, stars are circumpolar. *Circumpolar stars* are stars that can be seen at all times of year and all times of night. These stars never set, and they appear to circle the celestial poles. You also see different stars in the sky depending on the time of year. Why? The reason is that as Earth travels around the sun, different areas of the universe are visible.

Astronomer Biographies
Write a biography of an interesting astronomer. Go to **go.hrw.com,** and type in the keyword **HZ5OBSW.**

✓ Reading Check How is the apparent movement of the sun similar to the apparent movement of most stars during the night?

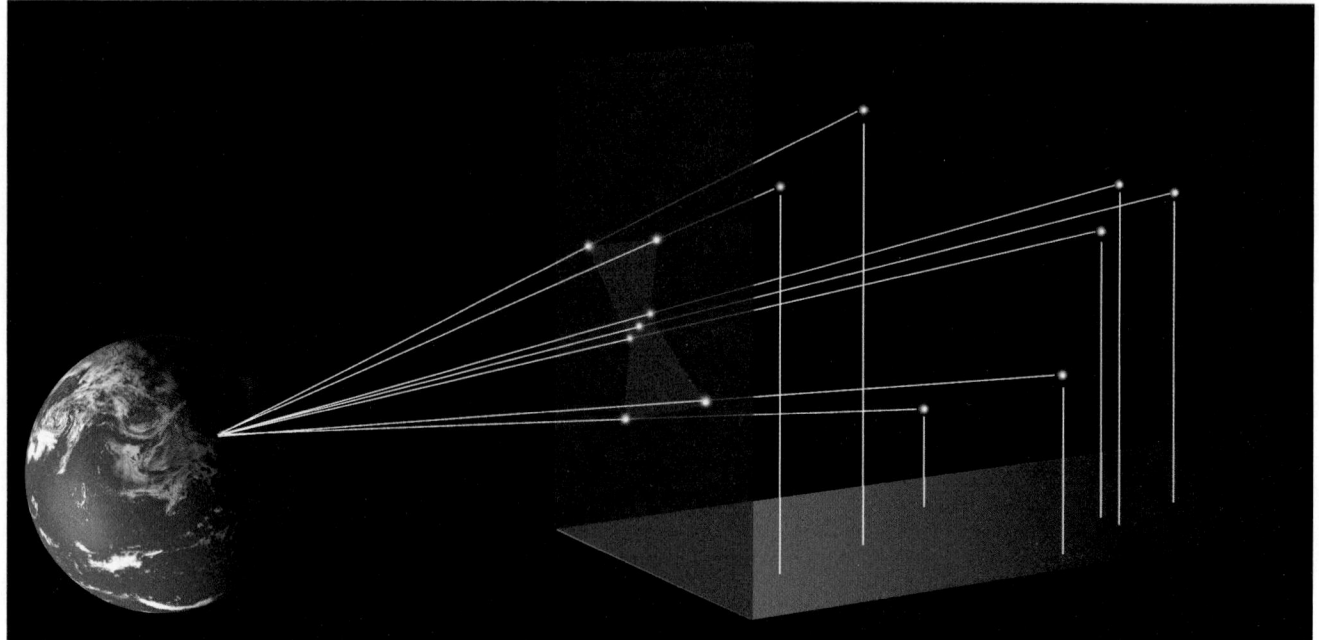

Figure 6 *While the stars in the constellation Orion appear to be near each other, they are actually very far apart.*

light-year the distance that light travels in one year; about 9.46 trillion kilometers

E.1.3.1 AA understands the vast size of our Solar System and the relationship of the planets and their satellites.

The Size and Scale of the Universe

Imagine looking out the window of a moving car. Nearby trees appear to move more quickly than farther trees do. The same principle applies to stars and planets. In the 1500s, Nicolaus Copernicus noticed that the planets appeared to move relative to each other but that the stars did not. Thus, he thought that the stars must be much farther away than the planets.

Measuring Distance in Space

Today, we know that Copernicus was correct. The stars are much farther from Earth than the planets are. In fact, stars are so distant that a new unit of length—the light-year—was created. A **light-year** is a unit of length that is equal to the distance that light travels in 1 year. One light-year is equal to about 9.46 trillion kilometers! The farthest objects we can observe are more than 10 billion light-years away. Although the stars may appear to be at similar distances from Earth, their distances vary greatly. **Figure 6** shows how far from Earth the stars that make up part of Orion are.

Considering Scale in the Universe

When you think about the universe and all of the objects it contains, you must consider scale. For example, stars appear to be very small in the night sky. But we know that most stars are much larger than Earth. **Figure 7** will help you understand the scale of objects in the universe.

Benchmark Check Why do stars larger than the sun appear small in the night sky? E.1.3.1 AA

Figure 7   From Home Plate to 10 Million Light-Years Away

1 Let's start with home plate in a baseball stadium. You are looking down from a distance of about 10 m.

2 At 1,000 m (1 km) away, you can see the baseball stadium and the surrounding neighborhood.

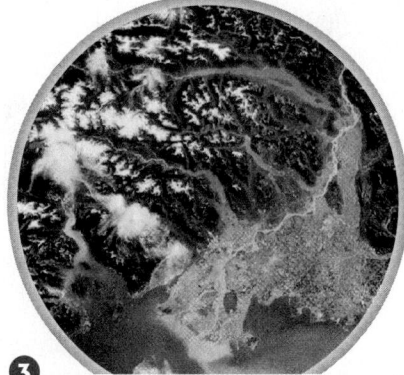

3 At 100 km away, you see the city that contains the stadium and the countryside around the city.

4 At 100,000 km away, you can see Earth and the moon.

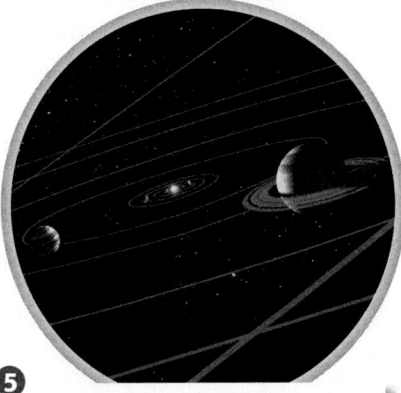

5 At 1,500,000,000 km (83 light-minutes) away, you can look back at the sun and the inner planets.

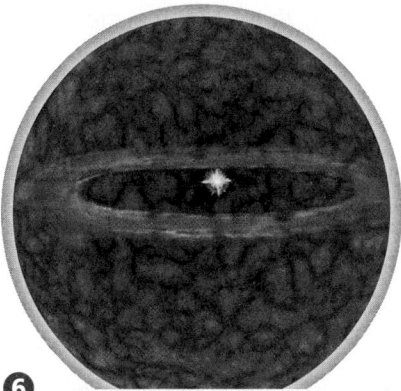

6 At 150 light-days, the solar system, surrounded by a cloud of comets and other icy debris, can be seen.

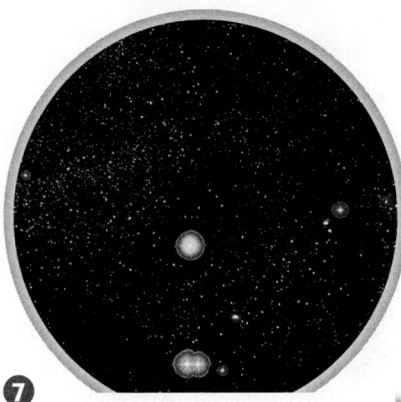

7 By the time you are 10 light-years away, the sun resembles any other star in space.

8 At 1 million light-years away, our galaxy looks like the Andromeda galaxy, a cloud of stars set in the blackness of space.

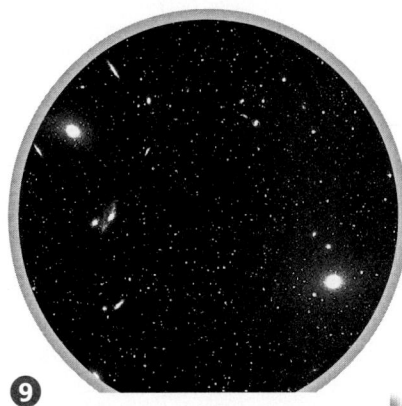

9 At 10 million light-years away, you can see a handful of galaxies called the *Local Group*.

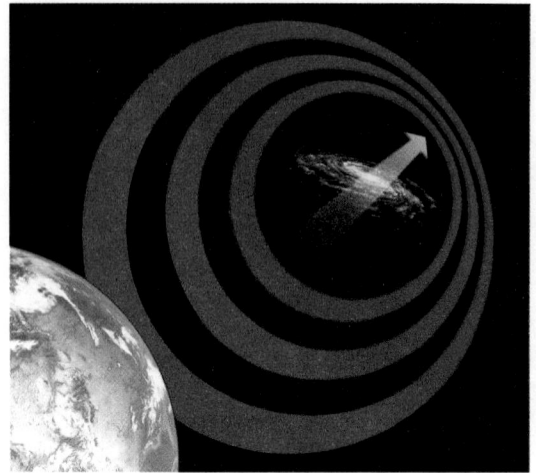

Figure 8 *As an object moves away from an observer at a high speed, the light from the object appears redder. As the object moves toward the observer, the light from the object appears bluer.*

The Doppler Effect

Have you ever noticed that when a driver in an approaching car blows the horn, the horn sounds higher pitched as the car approaches and lower pitched after the car passes? This effect is called the *Doppler effect*. As shown in **Figure 8,** the Doppler effect also occurs with light. If a light source, such as a star or galaxy, is moving quickly away from an observer, the light emitted looks redder than it normally does. This effect is called *redshift*. If a star or galaxy is moving quickly toward an observer, its light appears bluer than it normally does. This effect is known as *blueshift*.

An Expanding Universe

After discovering that the universe is made up of many other galaxies like our own, Edwin Hubble analyzed the light from galaxies and stars to study the general direction that objects in the universe are moving. Hubble soon made another startling discovery—the light from all galaxies except our close neighbors is affected by redshift. This means that galaxies are rapidly moving apart from each other. In other words, because all galaxies except our close neighbors are moving apart, the universe must be expanding. **Figure 9** shows evidence of redshift recorded by the *Hubble Space Telescope* in 2002.

Reading Check What logical conclusion could be made if the light from all of the galaxies were affected by blueshift?

Figure 9 *The galaxy that is cut off at the bottom of this image is moving away from Earth at a much slower speed than the other galaxies are. Distant galaxies are visible as faint disks.*

SECTION Review

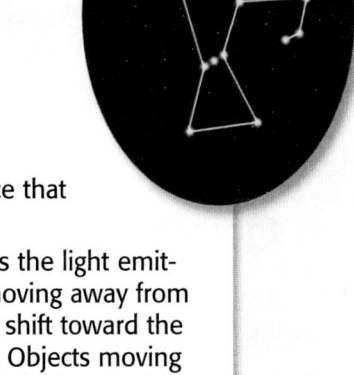

Summary

- Astronomers use constellations to organize the sky.

- The celestial sphere is an imaginary sphere that surrounds Earth. Using the celestial sphere, astronomers can accurately describe the location of an object without reference to an observer.

- The solar system is vast, but it is only a small part of the universe. **E.1.3.1 AA**

- A light-year is the distance that light travels in 1 year.

- The Doppler effect causes the light emitted by objects that are moving away from an observer to appear to shift toward the red end of the spectrum. Objects moving toward an observer are shifted to the blue end of the spectrum.

- Observations of redshift and blueshift indicate that the universe is expanding.

Using Key Terms

Correct the following statement by replacing the underlined term.

1. The distance that light travels in 1 year is called a <u>light-meter</u>.

Understanding Key Ideas

2. Stars appear to move across the night sky because of
   a. the rotation of Earth on its axis.
   b. the movement of the Milky Way galaxy.
   c. the movement of stars in the universe.
   d. the revolution of Earth around the sun.

3. How do astronomers use the celestial sphere to plot a star's exact position?

4. How do constellations relate to patterns of stars? How are constellations like states?

5. Describe the difference in scale between objects in our solar system and objects in the universe. **E.1.3.1 AA**

Critical Thinking

6. **Applying Concepts** Light from the Andromeda galaxy is affected by blueshift. What can you conclude about this galaxy?

7. **Making Comparisons** Explain how Copernicus concluded that stars were farther away than planets. Draw a diagram showing how this principle applies to another example.

FCAT Preparation

8. Stars in the Milky Way galaxy are light-years apart, but the planets are much closer. For example, it takes light from the sun about 43 minutes to reach Jupiter. What unit best describes distances between planets in our solar system? **E.1.3.1 AA**
   A. a light-second
   B. a light-minute
   C. a light-day
   D. a light-year

9. Which of the following bodies is farthest from Earth? **E.1.3.1 AA**
   F. the sun
   G. a star
   H. Earth's moon
   I. the planet Mars

For a variety of links related to this chapter, go to www.scilinks.org

Topic: Constellations; Space Science in Florida

SciLinks code: HSM0347; HSMF15

Skills Practice Lab

Through the Looking Glass

Have you ever looked toward the horizon or up into the sky and wished that you could see farther? Do you think that a telescope might help you see farther? Astronomers use huge telescopes to study the universe. You can build your own telescope to get a glimpse of how these enormous, technologically advanced telescopes help astronomers see distant objects.

OBJECTIVES

Construct a simple model of a refracting telescope.

Observe distant objects by using your telescope.

MATERIALS

- clay, modeling (1 stick)
- convex lens, 3 cm in diameter (2 of different focal length)
- lamp, desk
- paper, white (1 sheet)
- ruler, metric
- scissors
- tape, masking (1 roll)
- toilet-paper tube, cardboard
- wrapping paper tube, cardboard

SAFETY

Procedure

1 Use modeling clay to form a base that holds one of the lenses upright on your desktop. When the lights are turned off, your teacher will turn on a lamp at the front of the classroom. Rotate your lens so that the light from the lamp passes through the lens.

2 Hold the paper so that the light passing through the lens lands on the paper. To sharpen the image of the light on the paper, slowly move the paper closer to or farther from the lens. Hold the paper in the position in which the image is sharpest.

3 Using the metric ruler, measure the distance between the lens and the paper. Record this distance.

4 How far is the paper from the lens? This distance, called the *focal length,* is the distance that the paper has to be from the lens for the image to be in focus.

5 Repeat steps 1–4 using the other lens.

6 Measuring from one end of the long cardboard tube, mark the focal length of the lens that has the longer focal length. Place a mark 2 cm past this line toward the other end of the tube, and label the mark "Cut."

7 Measuring from one end of the short cardboard tube, mark the focal length of the lens that has the shorter focal length. Place a mark 2 cm past this line toward the other end of the tube, and label the mark "Cut."

8 Shorten the tubes by cutting along the marks labeled "Cut." Wear safety goggles when you make these cuts.

9 Tape the lens that has the longer focal length to one end of the longer tube. Tape the other lens to one end of the shorter tube. Slip the empty end of one tube inside the empty end of the other tube. Be sure that there is one lens at each end of this new, longer tube.

10 Congratulations! You have just constructed a telescope. To use your telescope, look through the short tube (the eyepiece) and point the long end at various objects in the room. You can focus the telescope by adjusting its length. Are the images right side up or upside down? Observe birds, insects, trees, or other outside objects. Record the images that you see. **Caution:** NEVER look directly at the sun! Looking directly at the sun could cause permanent blindness.

Analyze the Results

1 **Analyzing Results** Which type of telescope did you just construct: a refracting telescope or a reflecting telescope? What makes your telescope one type and not the other?

2 **Identifying Patterns** What factor determines the focal length of a lens?

Draw Conclusions

3 **Evaluating Results** How would you improve your telescope?

Chapter Review

USING KEY TERMS

1 Use *year*, *month*, *day*, *astronomy*, *electromagnetic radiation*, *constellation*, and *altitude* in separate sentences.
FCAT VOCAB

For each pair of terms, explain how the meanings of the terms differ.

2 *reflecting telescope* and *refracting telescope*

3 *zenith* and *horizon*

4 *year* and *light-year*

UNDERSTANDING KEY IDEAS

Multiple Choice

5 All objects in the solar system orbit the sun. Which of the following statements best describes the relationship between Jupiter, Jupiter's moons, and the sun? **E.1.3.1 AA** *FCAT*

a. Jupiter's moons orbit only Jupiter.
b. Jupiter's moons orbit only the sun.
c. Jupiter's moons orbit the sun and Jupiter.
d. Jupiter orbits its moons and the sun.

6 The length of a day is based on the amount of time that

a. Earth takes to orbit the sun one time.
b. Earth takes to rotate once on its axis.
c. the moon takes to orbit Earth one time.
d. the moon takes to rotate once on its axis.

7 Light from the sun takes about 6 minutes to reach Venus, which is the second planet from the sun. Earth is the third planet from the sun. Which of the following best describes how long it takes light from the sun to reach Earth? **E.1.3.1 AA** *FCAT*

a. less than 6 minutes
b. 6 minutes
c. more than 6 minutes
d. one light-year

8 According to ___, Earth is at the center of the universe.

a. the Ptolemaic theory
b. Copernicus's theory
c. Galileo's theory
d. None of the above

9 Many scientists have contributed to our growing knowledge of space. Which scientist was one of the first scientists to successfully use a telescope to observe the night sky? **H.1.3.1 AA** *FCAT*

a. Brahe
b. Galileo
c. Hubble
d. Kepler

10 Astronomers divide the sky into

a. galaxies.
b. constellations.
c. zeniths.
d. phases.

11 Which of the following determines which stars you see in the sky?

a. your latitude
b. the time of year
c. the time of night
d. All of the above

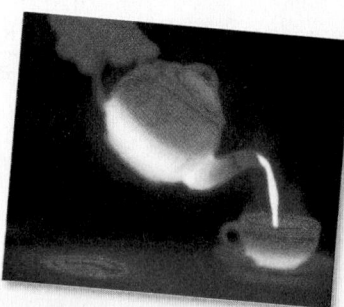

12 The altitude of an object in the sky is the object's angular distance

   a. above the horizon.

   b. from the north celestial pole.

   c. from the zenith.

   d. from the prime meridian.

13 Telescopes that work on Earth's surface include all of the following EXCEPT

   a. radio telescopes.

   b. refracting telescopes.

   c. X-ray telescopes.

   d. reflecting telescopes.

Short Answer

14 How are ascension and declination similar to latitude and longitude?

15 How does a reflecting telescope work?

16 Describe the size and scale of the solar system. E.1.3.1 AA *FCAT*

CRITICAL THINKING

Extended Response

17 **Making Inferences** Why was seeing objects in the sky easier for people in ancient cultures than it is for most people today?

18 **Making Inferences** Because many forms of radiation from space do not penetrate Earth's atmosphere, astronomers' ability to detect this radiation is limited. But how does the protection of the atmosphere benefit humans?

19 **Analyzing Ideas** Based on daily observations of the sun, explain why the Ptolemaic theory seems logical.

20 **Inferring Relationships**
How is the relationship between Earth and the moon similar to the relationship between Earth and the sun? E.1.3.1 AA *FCAT*

Concept Mapping

21 Use the following terms to create a concept map: *right ascension, declination, celestial sphere, degree, hour, celestial equator,* and *vernal equinox.*

INTERPRETING GRAPHICS

Use the sky map below to answer the questions that follow. (Example: The star Aldebaran is located at about 4 h, 30 min right ascension, and 16° declination.)

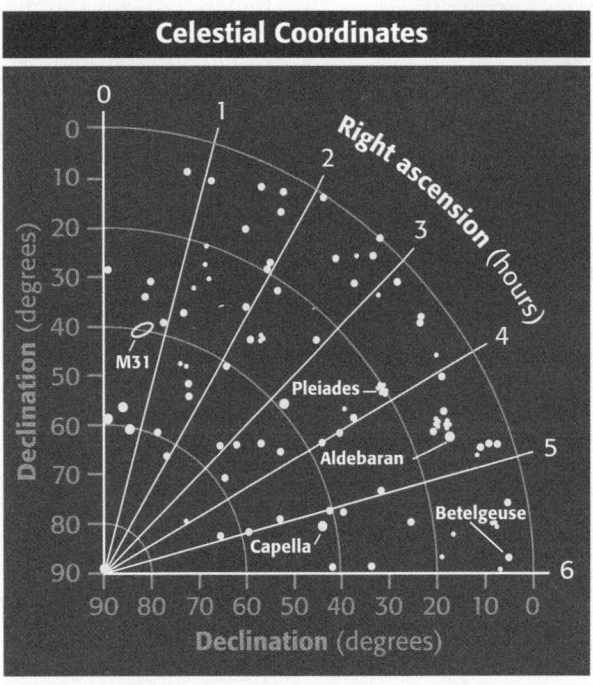

Celestial Coordinates

22 What object is located near 5 h, 55 min right ascension, and 7° declination?

23 What are the celestial coordinates for the Andromeda galaxy (M31)?

For the following questions, write your answers on a separate sheet of paper.

1   Rashad has been watching the stars and constellations in the sky and noticed that the Moon was visibly different every day that he made his observations. He knows that the Moon's appearance changes as it revolves around Earth. Approximately how many days does it take the Moon to complete one revolution around Earth?

2 Which ancient astronomer developed a theory that the Sun was the center of the universe?

A. Brahe
B. Copernicus
C. Kepler
D. Newton

3   Ancient cultures developed devices, such as sundials, to tell time. The Sun casts a shadow across the dial. The shadow falls on the dial on a mark that tells what time of day it is. What does the sundial actually record?

4   Dewanda has found a very bright star in the night sky. She is trying to explain to a friend exactly where it is located in the night sky. She tells her friend that it is 17 degrees less than the zenith. What is the altitude of the star Dewanda is looking at?

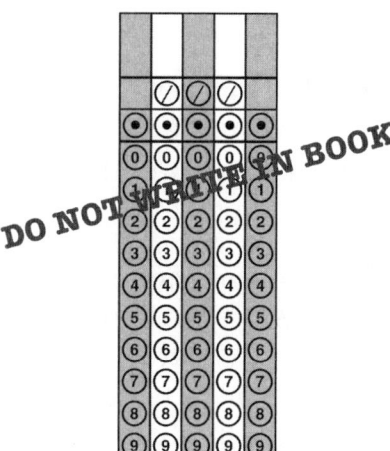

5 The diagram below shows Earth and its position relative to the constellations throughout the year. Many constellations can be seen on a clear night anytime of year. However, some constellations can be seen only during summer. Other constellations can be seen only during winter.

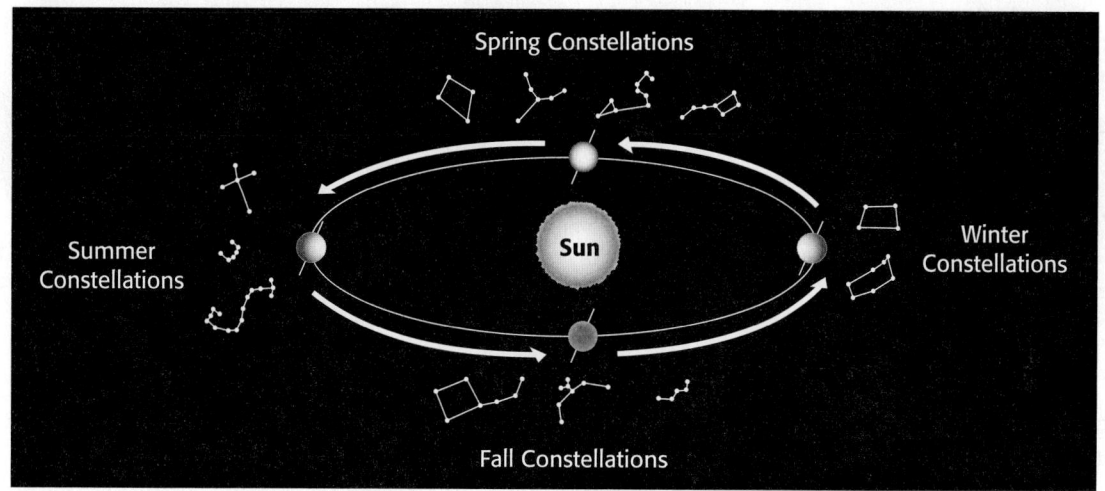

Which one of the following would explain why you can see certain constellations only at certain times of year?

F. the rotation of the galaxy around Earth
G. the distance between Earth and the stars
H. the location of Earth in its orbit around the Sun
I. the gravitational pull of the Sun and the Moon as they orbit Earth

6

READ
INQUIRE
EXPLAIN

Telescopes are made to detect electromagnetic radiation. The most sensitive and precise telescopes detect radiation that cannot be seen by the human eye. Some of this radiation is not able to penetrate Earth's atmosphere. Where would you expect to find telescopes that detect radiation that cannot penetrate Earth's atmosphere?

Science in Action

FOCUS ON
FLORIDA

Place to Visit

The Astronaut Memorial Planetarium and Observatory

Where can you take a tour of the universe with more than 200 fellow space tourists? The Astronaut Memorial Planetarium and Observatory in Cocoa, Florida, features state-of-the-art projectors and a powerful sound system to guide you on a journey through the stars. If you want to look at the planets in greater detail, the observatory has a 24-inch telescope that will help you zoom in on the moon, planets, and stars. You should also walk through the exhibit hall, which has a variety of displays, such as a telescope that shows a live image of the sun and scales that help you calculate your weight on other planets. Finally, stop by the International Hall of Space Explorers, which has a collection of souvenirs from every country that has sent an explorer into space!

Science, Technology, and Society

Light Pollution

When your parents were your age, they could look up at the night sky and see many more stars than you can now. In a large city, seeing more than 50 stars or planets in the night sky can be difficult. Light pollution is a growing—or you could say "glowing"—problem. If you have ever seen a white glow over the horizon in the night sky, you have seen the effects of light pollution. Most light pollution comes from outdoor lights that are excessively bright or misdirected. Light pollution not only limits the number of stars that the average person can see but also limits what astronomers can detect. Light pollution affects migrating animals, too. Luckily, there are ways to reduce light pollution. The International Dark Sky Association is working to reduce light pollution around the world. Find out how you can reduce light pollution in your community or home.

Social Studies ACTIVITY

WRITING SKILL Cultures have studied the planets, moons, and stars for thousands of years. Choose one culture, and write a report on the importance of astronomy in that culture.

Math ACTIVITY

A Virginia high school student named Jennifer Barlow started "National Dark Sky Week." If light pollution is reduced for 1 week each year, for what percentage of the year would light pollution be reduced?

Neil deGrasse Tyson

Star Writer When Neil deGrasse Tyson was nine years old, he visited a planetarium for the first time. Tyson was so affected by the experience he decided at that moment to dedicate his life to studying the universe. Tyson began studying the stars through a telescope on the roof of his apartment building. This interest led Tyson to attend the Bronx High School of Science, where he studied astronomy and physics. Tyson's passion for astronomy continued when he was a student at Harvard. However, Tyson soon realized that he wanted to share his love of astronomy with the public. So, today Tyson is America's best-known astrophysicist. When something really exciting happens in the universe, such as the discovery of evidence of water on Mars, Tyson is often asked to explain the discovery to the public. He has been interviewed hundreds of times on TV programs and has written several books. Tyson also writes a monthly column in the magazine *Natural History*. But writing and appearing on TV isn't even his day job! Tyson is the director of the Hayden Planetarium in New York—the same planetarium that ignited his interest in astronomy when he was nine years old!

Language Arts ACTiViTY

WRITING SKILL Be a star writer! Visit a planetarium or find a Web site that offers a virtual tour of the universe. Write a magazine-style article about the experience.

To learn more about these Science in Action topics, visit go.hrw.com and type in the keyword HT6FOBFF.

Current Science

Check out Current Science® articles related to this chapter by visiting go.hrw.com. Just type in the keyword HZ5CS18.

20

Exploring Space

The Big Idea The contributions of people from diverse backgrounds to the exploration of space have enriched our lives.

About the PHOTO

Although the astronauts in the photo appear to be motionless, they are orbiting the Earth at almost 28,000 km/h! The astronauts reached orbit—about 300 km above Earth's surface—in a space shuttle. Space shuttles are the first vehicles in a new generation of reusable spacecraft. They have opened an era of space exploration in which missions to space are more common than ever before.

PRE-READING ACTIVITY

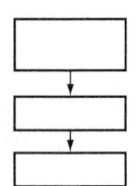

Graphic Organizer

Chain-of-Events Chart Before you read the chapter, create the graphic organizer entitled "Chain-of-Events Chart" described in the **Study Skills** section of the Appendix. As you read the chapter, fill in the chart with a timeline that describes the exploration of space from the theories of Konstantin Tsiolkovsky to the future of space exploration.

START-UP ACTIVITY

Balloon Rockets

In this activity, you will launch a balloon "rocket" to learn about how rockets move.

Procedure

1. Insert a **piece of thread** that is 2 m long through a **drinking straw.** Tie the thread between two objects that will not move, such as **chairs.** Make sure that the thread is tight.

2. Inflate a **large balloon.** Do not tie the neck of the balloon closed. Hold the neck of the balloon closed, and **tape** the balloon firmly to the straw, parallel to the thread.

3. Move the balloon to one end of the thread, and then release the neck of the balloon. Use a **meterstick** to record the distance the balloon traveled.

4. Repeat steps 2–3. This time, hold a piece of **poster board** behind the balloon.

Analysis

1. Did the poster board affect the distance that the balloon traveled? Explain your answer.

2. Newton's third law of motion states that for every action, there is an equal and opposite reaction. Apply this idea and your observations of the balloon to explain how rockets accelerate. Do rockets move by "pushing off" a launch pad? Explain your answer.

Rocket Science

If you could pack all of your friends in a car and drive to the moon, it would take about 165 days to get there. And that doesn't include stopping for gas or food!

The moon is incredibly far away, and years ago people could only dream of traveling into space. The problem was that no machine could generate enough force to overcome Earth's gravity and reach outer space. But about 100 years ago, a Russian high school teacher named Konstantin Tsiolkovsky (KAHN stuhn TEEN TSI uhl KAHV skee) proposed that machines called *rockets* could take people to outer space. A **rocket** is a machine that uses escaping gas to move. Tsiolkovsky stated, "The Earth is the cradle of mankind. But one does not have to live in the cradle forever." Rockets would become the key to leaving the cradle of Earth and starting the age of space exploration.

The Beginnings of Rocket Science

Tsiolkovsky's inspiration came from the imaginative stories of Jules Verne. In Verne's book *From the Earth to the Moon,* characters reached the moon in a capsule shot from an enormous cannon. Although this idea would not work, Tsiolkovsky proved—in theory—that rockets could generate enough force to reach outer space. He also suggested the use of liquid rocket fuel to increase a rocket's range. For his vision and careful work, Tsiolkovsky is known as the father of rocket theory.

Figure 1 *Robert Goddard is known as the father of modern rocketry.*

A Boost for Modern Rocketry

Although Tsiolkovsky proved scientifically that rockets could reach outer space, he never built any rockets himself. That task was left to American physicist and inventor Robert Goddard, shown in **Figure 1.** Goddard launched the first successful liquid-fuel rocket in 1926. Goddard tested more than 150 rocket engines, and by the time of World War II, his work began to interest the U.S. military. His work drew much attention because of a terrifying new weapon that the German army had developed.

✓ **Reading Check** How did Tsiolkovsky and Goddard contribute to the development of rockets?

From Rocket Bombs to Rocket Ships

Toward the end of World War II, Germany developed a new weapon known as the V-2 rocket. The V-2 rocket, shown in **Figure 2,** could deliver explosives from German military bases to London—a distance of about 350 km. The V-2 rocket was developed by a team led by Wernher von Braun, a young Ph.D. student whose research was supported by the German military. But in 1945, near the end of the war, von Braun and his entire research team surrendered to the advancing Americans. The United States thus gained 127 of the best German rocket scientists. With this gain, rocket research in the United States boomed in the 1950s.

Figure 2 *The V-2 rocket is the ancestor of all modern rockets.*

The Birth of NASA

The end of World War II marked the start of the *Cold War*—a long period of political tension between the United States and the Soviet Union. The Cold War was marked by an arms race and by competition in space technology. In response to Soviet advances in space, the U.S. government formed the National Aeronautics and Space Administration, or **NASA,** in 1958. NASA combined all of the rocket-development teams in the United States. The cooperation of these teams led to the development of many rockets, including those shown in **Figure 3.**

rocket a machine that uses escaping gas from burning fuel to move

NASA the **N**ational **A**eronautics and **S**pace **A**dministration

Figure 3　40 Years of NASA Rockets

A rocket's payload is the amount of material that the rocket is able to carry into space.

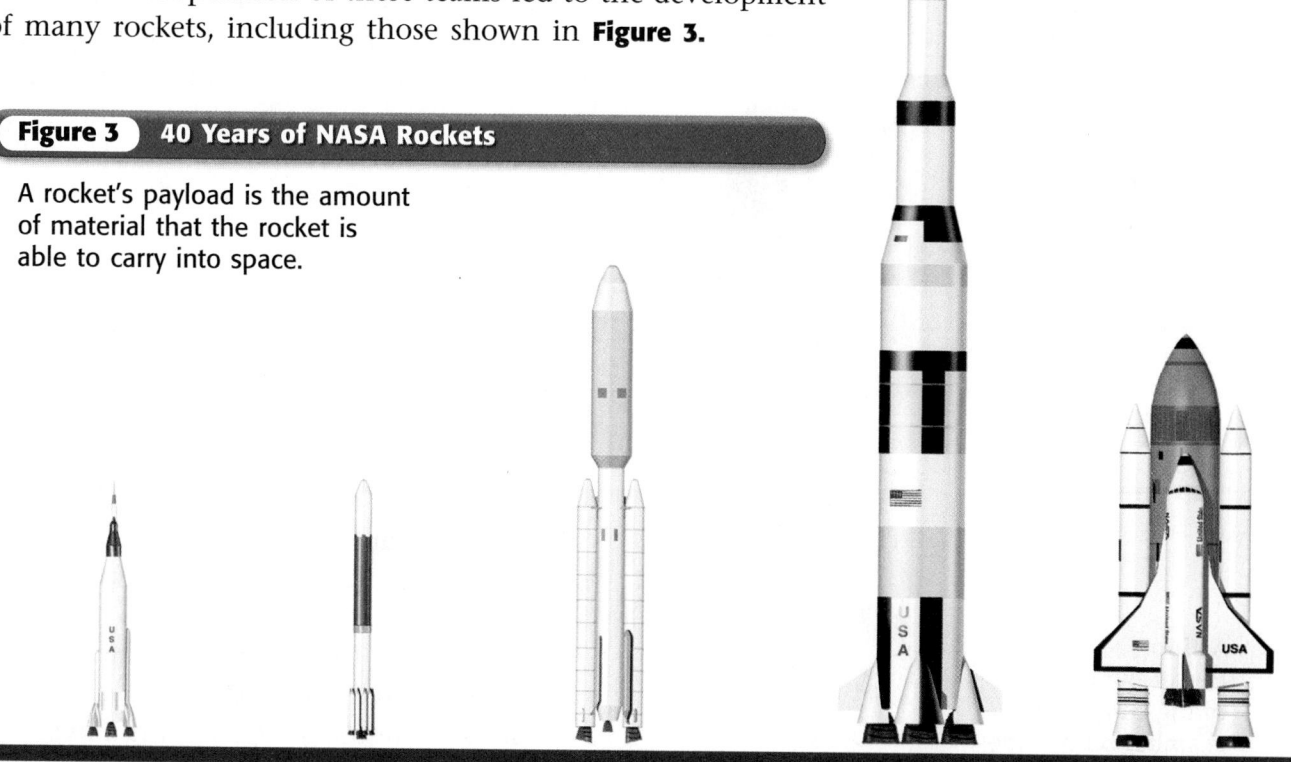

Mercury-Atlas	**Delta**	**Titan IV**	**Saturn V**	**Space shuttle and boosters**
Height: 29 m	**Height:** 36 m	**Height:** 62 m	**Height:** 111 m	**Height:** 56 m
Payload: 1,400 kg	**Payload:** 1,770 kg	**Payload:** 18,000 kg	**Payload:** 129,300 kg	**Payload:** 29,500 kg

How Rockets Work

If you are sitting in a chair that has wheels and you want to move, you would probably push away from a table or kick yourself along with your feet. Many people think that rockets move in a similar way—by pushing off a launch pad. But if rockets moved in this way, how would they accelerate in the vacuum of space, where there is nothing to push against?

thrust the pushing or pulling force exerted by the engine of an aircraft or rocket

Figure 4 *Rockets move according to Newton's third law of motion.*

For Every Action . . .

As you saw in the Start-up Activity, the balloon moved according to Newton's third law of motion. This law states that for every action, there is an equal and opposite reaction. For example, the air rushing backward from a balloon (the action) results in the forward motion of the balloon (the reaction). Rockets work in the same way. In fact, rockets were once called *reaction devices*.

However, in the case of rockets, the action and the reaction may not be obvious. The mass of a rocket—including all of the fuel that the rocket carries—is much greater than the mass of the hot gases that come out of the bottom of the rocket. But because the exhaust gases are under extreme pressure, they exert a huge amount of force. The force that accelerates a rocket is called **thrust.** Look at **Figure 4** to learn more about how rockets work.

Reaction
Gas at the top of the combustion chamber pushes the rocket upward.

Action
Gas at the bottom of the combustion chamber pushes the exhaust downward.

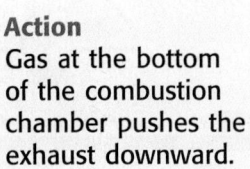

It Takes More Than Rocket Fuel

Rockets burn fuel to provide the thrust that propels them. In order for something to burn, oxygen must be present. Although oxygen is plentiful at the Earth's surface, there is little or no oxygen in the upper atmosphere and in outer space. For this reason, rockets that go into outer space must carry enough oxygen with them to be able to burn their fuel. The space shuttles, for example, carry hundreds of thousands of gallons of liquid oxygen. This oxygen is needed to burn their rocket fuel.

✓ Reading Check Why do rockets carry oxygen in addition to fuel?

How to Leave the Earth

The gravitational pull of the Earth is the main factor that a rocket must overcome. As shown in **Figure 5,** a rocket must reach a certain *velocity*, or speed and direction, to orbit or escape the Earth.

Orbital Velocity and Escape Velocity

To orbit the Earth, a rocket must have enough thrust to reach orbital velocity. *Orbital velocity* is the speed and direction that a rocket must travel in order to orbit a planet or moon. The lowest possible speed a rocket may go and still orbit Earth is about 8 km/s (17,927 mi/h). If the rocket goes any slower, it will fall back to Earth. For a rocket to travel beyond Earth orbit, the rocket must achieve escape velocity. *Escape velocity* is the speed and direction that a rocket must travel to completely break away from a planet's gravitational pull. The speed that a rocket must reach to escape the Earth is about 11 km/s (24,606 mi/h).

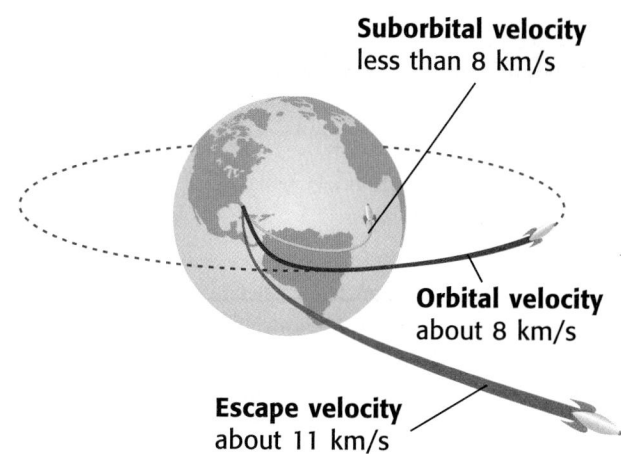

Suborbital velocity
less than 8 km/s

Orbital velocity
about 8 km/s

Escape velocity
about 11 km/s

Figure 5 *A rocket must travel very fast to escape the gravitational pull of the Earth.*

SECTION Review

Summary

- Tsiolkovsky and Goddard were pioneers of rocket science.

- The outcome of World War II and the political pressures of the Cold War helped advance rocket science.

- Rockets work according to Newton's third law of motion—for every action, there is an equal and opposite reaction.

- Rockets need to reach different velocities to attain orbit and to escape a planet's gravitational attraction.

Using Key Terms

1. Write an original definition for *thrust.*

Understanding Key Ideas

2. Use Newton's third law of motion to explain how rockets work.

3. Differentiate between orbital and escape velocity.

4. Outline the development of rocket technology.

5. How did the Cold War accelerate the U.S. space program?

6. Compare the contributions of Tsiolkovsky and Goddard to modern rocketry.

Critical Thinking

7. **Making Inferences** Analyze why escape velocity varies depending on the planet from which a rocket is launched.

FCAT Preparation

8. A NASA scientist conducted an experiment to test an invention that enables a rocket to control its thrust. The scientist was so surprised that he did not take notes during the experiment. Explain why the experiment would have been more successful if he had taken notes. **H.1.3.4 AA**

SCiLINKS

NSTA
Developed and maintained by the
National Science Teachers Association

For a variety of links related to this chapter, go to www.scilinks.org

Topic: Rocket Technology
SciLinks code: HSM1323

Artificial Satellites

artificial satellite any human-made object placed in orbit around a body in space

You are watching TV, and suddenly a weather bulletin interrupts your favorite show. There is a HURRICANE WARNING! You grab a cell phone and call your friend—the hurricane is headed straight for where she lives!

In the story above, the TV show, the weather bulletin, and perhaps even the phone call were all made possible by artificial satellites orbiting thousands of miles above Earth! An **artificial satellite** is any human-made object placed in orbit around a body in space.

There are many kinds of artificial satellites. Weather satellites provide continuous updates on the movement of gases in the atmosphere so that we can predict weather on Earth's surface. Communications satellites relay TV programs, phone calls, and computer data. Remote-sensing satellites monitor changes in the environment. Perhaps more than the exploration of space, satellites have changed the way we live.

The First Satellites

The first artificial satellite, *Sputnik 1,* was launched by the Soviets in 1957. **Figure 1** shows a model of *Sputnik 1,* which orbited for 57 days before it fell back to Earth and burned up in the atmosphere. Two months later, *Sputnik 2* carried the first living being into space—a dog named Laika. The United States followed with the launch of its first satellite, *Explorer 1,* in 1958. The development of new satellites increased quickly. By 1964, communications satellite networks were able to send messages around the world. Today, thousands of satellites orbit Earth, and more are launched every year.

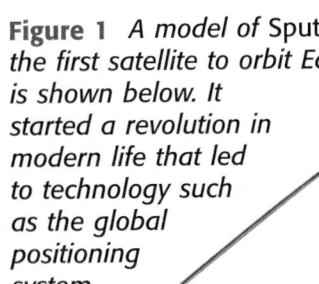

Figure 1 *A model of* Sputnik 1, *the first satellite to orbit Earth, is shown below. It started a revolution in modern life that led to technology such as the global positioning system.*

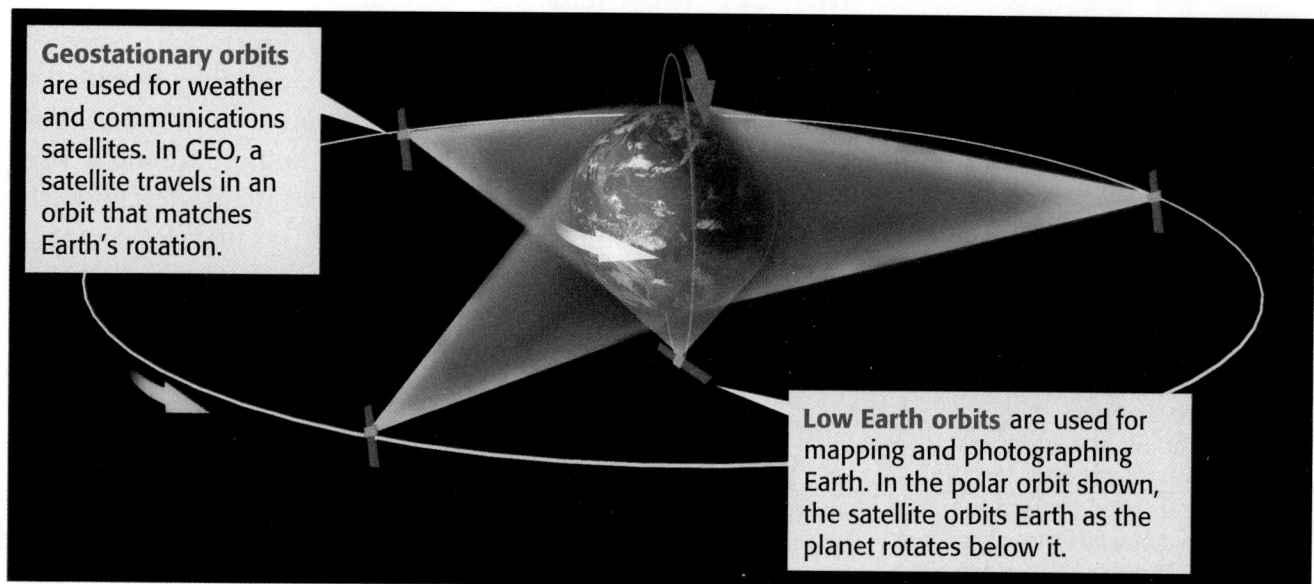

Geostationary orbits are used for weather and communications satellites. In GEO, a satellite travels in an orbit that matches Earth's rotation.

Low Earth orbits are used for mapping and photographing Earth. In the polar orbit shown, the satellite orbits Earth as the planet rotates below it.

Choosing Your Orbit

Satellites are placed in different types of orbits, as shown in **Figure 2.** All of the early satellites were placed in **low Earth orbit** (LEO), which is a few hundred kilometers above Earth's surface. A satellite in LEO moves around Earth very quickly and can provide clear images of Earth. However, this motion can place a satellite out of contact much of the time.

Most communications satellites and weather satellites orbit much farther from Earth. In this orbit, called a **geostationary orbit** (GEO), a satellite travels in an orbit that exactly matches Earth's rotation. Thus, the satellite is always above the same spot on Earth. Ground stations are in continuous contact with these satellites so that TV programs and other communications will not be interrupted.

✓ Reading Check What is the difference between GEO and LEO?

Figure 2 *Low Earth orbits are in the upper reaches of Earth's atmosphere, while geostationary orbits are about 36,000 km from Earth's surface.*

low Earth orbit an orbit that is less than 1,500 km above Earth's surface

geostationary orbit an orbit that is about 36,000 km above Earth's surface and in which a satellite is above a fixed spot on the equator

Modeling LEO and GEO

1. Use a **length of thread** to measure 300 km on the scale of a **globe**.

2. Use another **length of thread** to measure 36,000 km on the globe's scale.

3. Use the short thread to measure the distance of LEO from the surface of the globe and the long thread to measure the distance of GEO from the surface of the globe.

4. Your teacher will turn off the lights. One student will spin the globe, while other students will hold **penlights** at LEO and GEO orbits.

5. Was more of the globe illuminated by the penlights in LEO or GEO?

6. Which orbit is better for communications satellites? Which orbit is better for spy satellites?

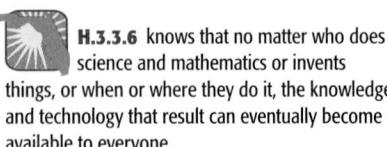

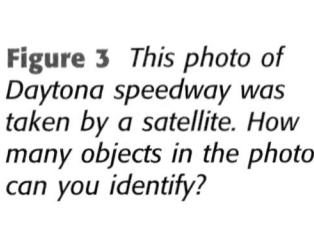

H.3.3.6 knows that no matter who does science and mathematics or invents things, or when or where they do it, the knowledge and technology that result can eventually become available to everyone.

Military Satellites

Some satellites placed in LEO are equipped with cameras that can photograph Earth's surface in amazing detail. It is possible to photograph objects as small as this book from LEO. While photographs taken by satellites are now used for everything from developing real estate to tracking the movements of dolphins, the technology was first developed by the military. Because satellites can take very detailed photos from hundreds of kilometers above Earth's surface, they are ideal for defense purposes. The United States and the Soviet Union developed satellites to spy on each other right up to the end of the Cold War. The Cold War is over, but the benefits of spy satellite technology have become available for commercial satellites. **Figure 3,** for example, is a photo of Daytona Speedway taken by the satellite *Quickbird* in 2003.

The Global Positioning System

In the past, people invented very complicated ways to keep from getting lost. Now, for less than $100, people can find out their exact location on Earth by using a global positioning system (GPS) receiver. GPS is another example of military satellite technology that has become a part of everyday life. The GPS consists of 27 solar-powered satellites that continuously send radio signals to Earth. From the amount of time it takes the signals to reach Earth, the hand-held receiver can calculate its distance from the satellites. Using the distance from four satellites, a GPS receiver can determine a person's location with great accuracy.

Figure 3 *This photo of Daytona speedway was taken by a satellite. How many objects in the photo can you identify?*

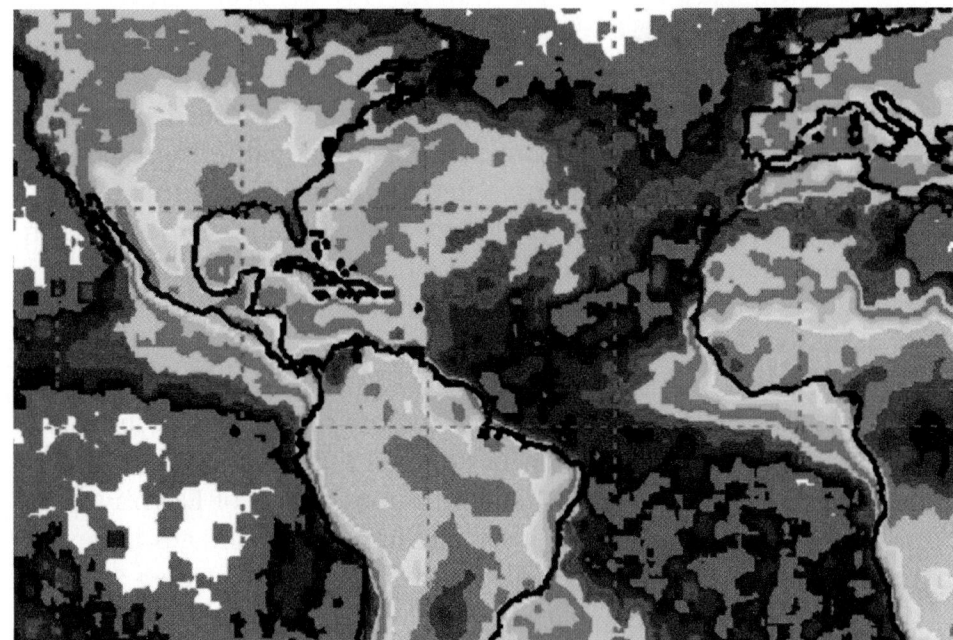

Figure 4 *This map shows average annual lightning strikes around the world. Red and black indicate a high number of strikes. Cooler colors, such as purple and blue, indicate fewer strikes.*

Weather Satellites

It is hard to imagine life without reliable weather forecasts. Every day, millions of people make decisions based on information provided by weather satellites. Weather satellites in GEO provide a big-picture view of Earth's atmosphere. These satellites constantly monitor the atmosphere for the "triggers" that lead to severe weather conditions. Weather satellites in GEO created the map of world lightning strikes shown in **Figure 4.** Weather satellites in LEO are usually placed in polar orbits. Satellites in polar orbits revolve around Earth in a north or south direction as Earth rotates beneath them. These satellites, which orbit between 830 and 870 km above Earth, provide a much closer look at weather patterns.

Communications Satellites

Many types of modern communications use radio waves or microwaves to relay messages. Radio waves and microwaves are ideal for communications because they can travel through the air. The problem is that the Earth is round, but the waves travel in a straight line. So how do you send a message to someone on the other side of the Earth? Communications satellites in GEO solve this problem by relaying information from one point on Earth's surface to another. The signals are transmitted to a satellite and then sent to receivers around the world. Communications satellites relay computer data, and some television and radio broadcasts.

SCHOOL to HOME

Tracking Satellites

A comfortable lawn chair and a clear night sky are all you need to track satellites. Just after sunset or before sunrise, satellites in LEO are easy to track. They look like slow-moving stars, and they generally move in a west-to-east direction. With a little practice, you should be able to find one or two satellites a minute. A pair of binoculars will help you get a closer look. Satellites in GEO are difficult to see because they do not appear to move. You and a parent can find out more about how to track specific satellites and space stations on the Internet.

ACTIVITY

Benchmark Check List three examples of how the benefits of satellite technology have become available to everyone. **H.3.3.6**

Remote Sensing and Environmental Change

Using satellites, scientists have been able to study Earth in ways that were never before possible. Satellites gather information by *remote sensing*. Remote sensing is the gathering of images and data from a distance. Remote-sensing satellites measure light and other forms of energy that are reflected from Earth. Some satellites use radar, which bounces high-frequency radio waves off Earth and measures the returned signal.

Landsat: Monitoring Earth from Orbit

One of the most successful remote-sensing projects is the Landsat program, which began in 1972 and continues today. It has given us the longest continuous record of Earth's surface as seen from space. Landsat satellites gather images in several wavelengths—from visible light to infrared. **Figure 5** shows Landsat images of part of the Mississippi Delta. One image was taken in 1973, and the other was taken in 2003. The two images reveal a pattern of environmental change over a 30-year period. The main change is a dramatic reduction in the amount of silt that is reaching the delta. A comparison of the images also reveals a large-scale loss of wetlands in the bottom left of the delta in 2003. The loss of wetlands affects plants and animals living on the delta and the fishing industry.

Figure 5 **The Loss of Wetlands in the Mississippi Delta**

Silt reaching the Mississippi Delta is shown in blue. The amount of silt reaching the delta was much greater in 1973 (left) than it was in 2003 (right). This reduction led to the rapid loss of wetlands, which are green in this image. Notice the lower left corner of the delta in both images. Areas of wetland loss are black.

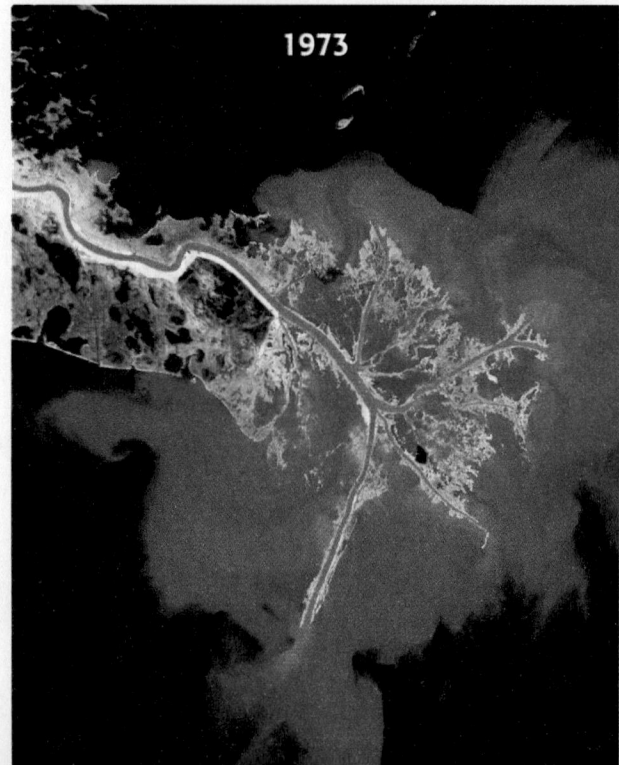
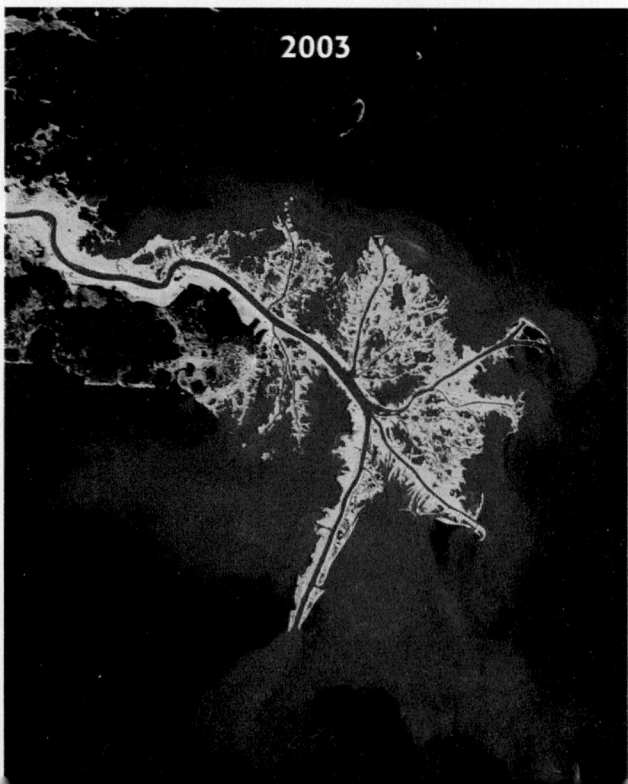

A New Generation of Remote-Sensing Satellites

The Landsat program has produced millions of images that are used to identify and track environmental change on Earth. Satellite remote sensing allows scientists to perform large-scale mapping, look at changes in patterns of vegetation growth, map the spread of urban development, and study the effect of humans on the global environment. In 1999, NASA launched *Terra 1*, the first satellite in NASA's Earth Observing System (EOS) program. Satellites in the EOS program are designed to work together so that they can gather integrated data on environmental change on the land, in the atmosphere, in the oceans, and on the icecaps.

✓ **Reading Check** What is unique about the EOS program?

SECTION Review

Summary

- *Sputnik 1* was the first artificial satellite. *Explorer 1* was the first U.S. satellite.

- Satellites in LEO are much closer to Earth than satellites in GEO are.

- The benefits of satellite technology include improved communication, navigation, and weather forecasting. **H.3.3.6**

- Satellites with remote-sensing technology have helped us understand Earth as a global system.

Using Key Terms

1. Use *artificial satellite, low Earth orbit*, and *geostationary orbit* in separate sentences.

Understanding Key Ideas

2. Describe how satellite technology benefits you. **H.3.3.6**

3. What was *Sputnik*?

4. Explain the differences between LEO and GEO satellites.

5. Explain how remote-sensing satellites help us study Earth as a global system.

Critical Thinking

6. **Applying Concepts** The *Hubble Space Telescope* is located in LEO. Does the telescope move faster or slower around Earth than a geostationary weather satellite does? Explain.

7. **Applying Concepts** To triangulate your location on a map, you need to know your distance from three points. If you knew your distance from two points on a map, how many places could you occupy?

FCAT Preparation

8. A research team is developing an experimental solar panel to power a satellite. The researchers test one design that is 3 m², and it generates 10 kW/h. They test another design under similar conditions, and it generates 30 kW/h.

   PART A Identify which variable is most likely to have changed in the experiments.

   PART B Predict what the outcome would be if the solar panels were tested at different times of day. **H.1.3.5 AA**

SC**LINKS**®

NSTA
Developed and maintained by the National Science Teachers Association

For a variety of links related to this chapter, go to www.scilinks.org

Topic: Artificial Satellites
SciLinks code: HSM0101

551

Space Probes

What does the surface of Mars look like? Does life exist anywhere else in the solar system?

To answer questions like these, scientists send space probes to explore the solar system. A **space probe** is an uncrewed vehicle that carries scientific instruments to planets or other bodies in space. Unlike satellites, which stay in Earth orbit, space probes travel away from Earth. Space probes are valuable because they can complete missions that would be very dangerous and expensive for humans to undertake.

Visits to the Inner Solar System

Because Earth's moon and the inner planets are much closer than the other planets and moons in the solar system, they were the first to be explored by space probes. Let's take a closer look at some missions to the moon, Venus, and Mars.

Luna and Clementine: Missions to the Moon

Luna 1, the first space probe, was launched by the Soviets in 1959 to fly past the moon. In 1966, *Luna 9* made the first soft landing on the moon's surface. During the next 10 years, the United States and the Soviet Union completed more than 30 lunar missions. Thousands of images of the moon's surface were taken. In 1994, the U.S. probe *Clementine* discovered that craters of the moon may contain water left by comet impacts. In 1998, the *Lunar Prospector* confirmed that frozen water exists on the moon. This ice would be very valuable to a human colony on the moon.

Space Probes

Investigate uncrewed space missions. Go to **go.hrw.com**, and type in the keyword **HZ5EXPW**.

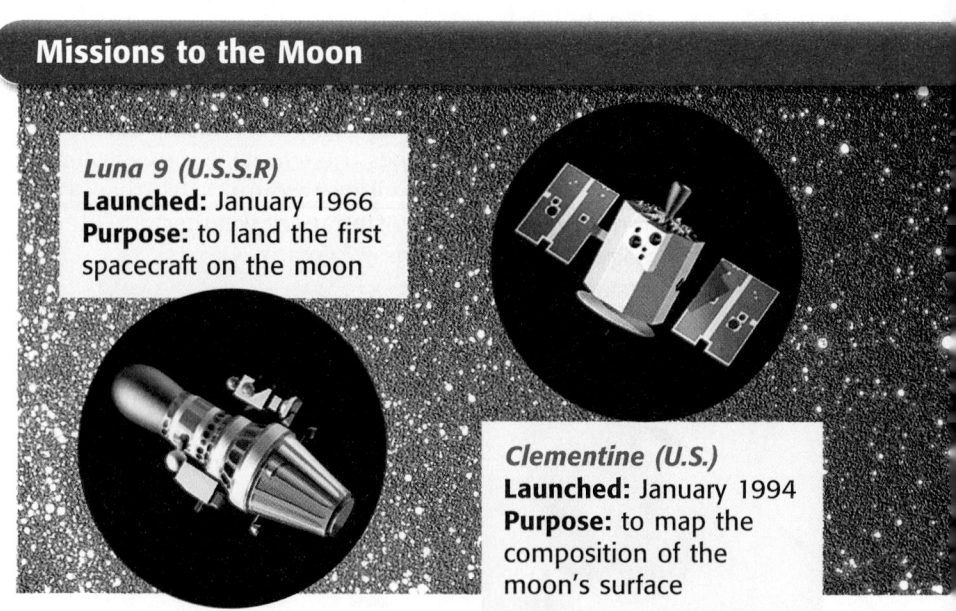

Missions to the Moon

Luna 9 (U.S.S.R)
Launched: January 1966
Purpose: to land the first spacecraft on the moon

Clementine (U.S.)
Launched: January 1994
Purpose: to map the composition of the moon's surface

Venera 9: The First Probe to Land on Venus

The Soviet probe *Venera 9* was the first probe to land on Venus. The probe parachuted into Venus's atmosphere and transmitted images of the surface to Earth. *Venera 9* found that the surface temperature and atmospheric pressure on Venus are much higher than on Earth. The surface temperature of Venus is an average of 464°C—hot enough to melt lead! *Venera 9* also found that the chemistry of the surface rocks on Venus is similar to that of Earth rocks. Perhaps most important, *Venera 9* and earlier missions revealed that Venus has a severe greenhouse effect. Scientists study Venus's atmosphere to learn about the effects of increased greenhouse gases in Earth's atmosphere.

The Magellan Mission: Mapping Venus

In 1989, the United States launched the *Magellan* probe, which used radar to map 98% of the surface of Venus. The radar data were transmitted back to Earth, where computers used the data to generate three-dimensional images like the one shown in **Figure 1.** The Magellan mission showed that the geology of Venus is similar to that of Earth in many ways. Venus has features that suggest plate tectonics occurs there, as it does on Earth. Venus also has volcanoes, and some of them may be active.

Benchmark Check What discoveries were made by *Magellan*? **E.1.3.2**

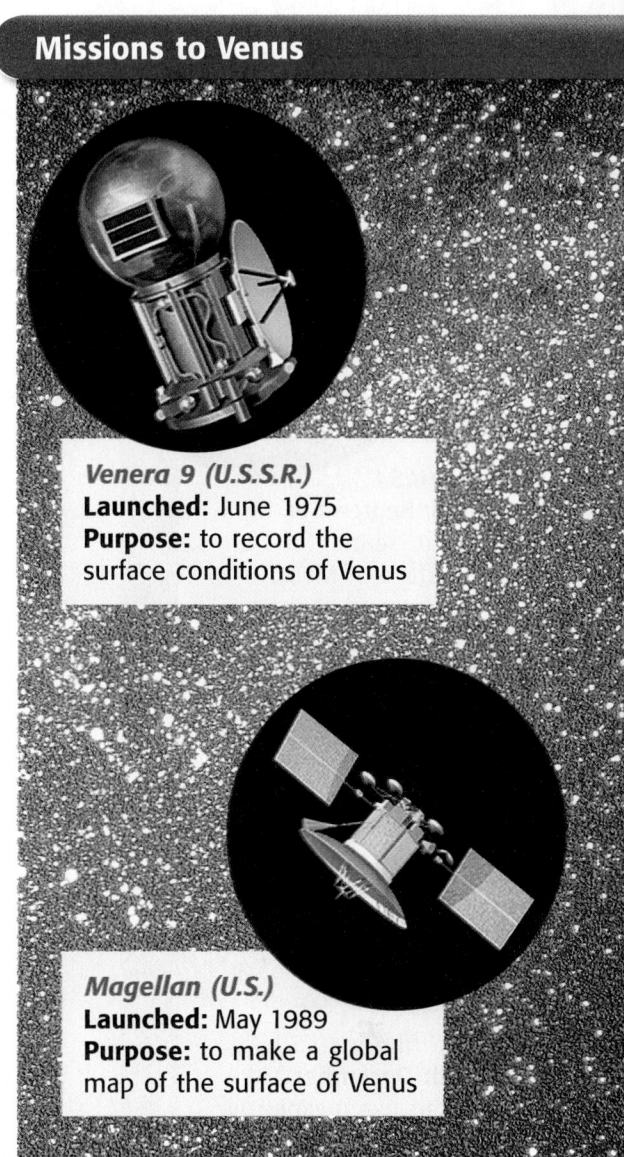

Missions to Venus

Venera 9 (U.S.S.R.)
Launched: June 1975
Purpose: to record the surface conditions of Venus

Magellan (U.S.)
Launched: May 1989
Purpose: to make a global map of the surface of Venus

Figure 1 *This false-color image of volcanoes on the surface of Venus was made with radar data transmitted to Earth by* Magellan.

Missions to Mars

Viking 2 (U.S.)
Launched: September 1975
Purpose: to search for life on the surface of Mars

Mars Pathfinder (U.S.)
Launched: December 1996
Purpose: to use inexpensive technology to study the surface of Mars

The Viking Missions: Exploring Mars

In 1975, the United States sent a pair of probes—*Viking 1* and *Viking 2*—to Mars. The surface of Mars is more like the surface of Earth than the surface of any other planet. For this reason, one of the main goals of the Viking missions was to look for signs of life. The probes contained instruments designed to gather soil and test it for evidence of life. However, no hard evidence was found. The Viking missions did find evidence that Mars was once much warmer and wetter than it is now. This discovery led scientists to ask even more questions about Mars. Did the Martian climate support life in the past? Why and when did the Martian climate change?

The Mars Pathfinder Mission: Revisiting Mars

More than 20 years later, in 1997, the surface of Mars was visited again by a NASA space probe. The goal of the Mars Pathfinder mission was to show that Martian exploration is possible at a much lower cost than the Viking missions. The probe sent back detailed images of dry water channels on the planet's surface. These images, such as the one shown in **Figure 2,** suggest that massive floods flowed across the surface of Mars relatively recently in the planet's past. The *Mars Pathfinder* successfully landed on Mars and deployed the *Sojourner* rover. *Sojourner* traveled across the surface of Mars for almost three months, collecting data and recording images. The European Space Agency and NASA have many more Mars missions planned for the near future. These missions will pave the way for a crewed mission to Mars that may occur in your lifetime!

Reading Check What discoveries were made by the Mars Pathfinder mission?

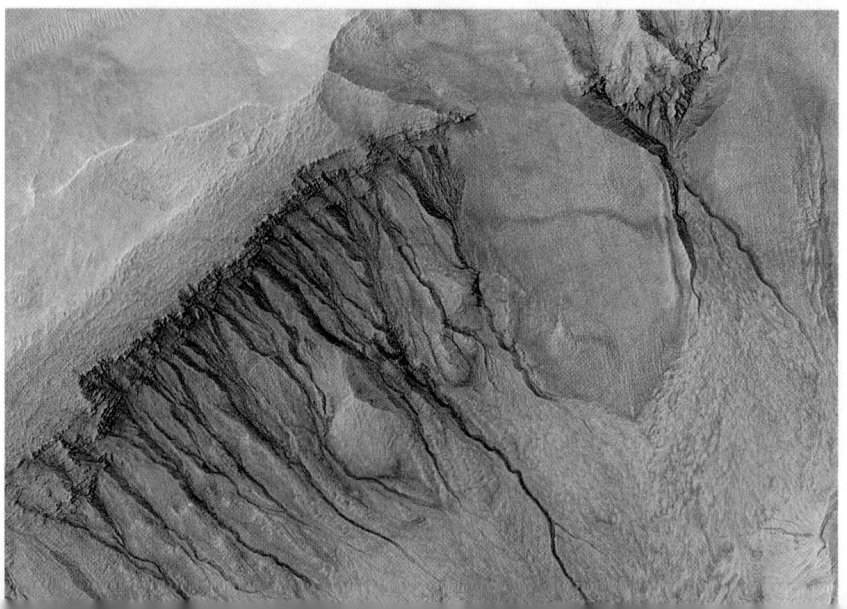

Figure 2 *The* Mars Pathfinder *took detailed photographs of the Martian surface. Photographs, such as this one, revealed evidence of massive flooding.*

Visits to the Outer Solar System

The planets in the outer solar system—Jupiter, Saturn, Uranus, Neptune, and Pluto—are very far away. Probes such as those described below can take 10 years or more to complete their missions.

Pioneer and Voyager: To Jupiter and Beyond

The *Pioneer 10* and *Pioneer 11* space probes were the first to visit the outer planets. Among other things, these probes sampled the *solar wind*—the flow of particles coming from the sun. The Pioneer probes also found that the dark belts on Jupiter provide deep views into Jupiter's atmosphere. In 1983, *Pioneer 10* became the first probe to travel past the orbit of Pluto, the outermost planet.

The Voyager space probes were the first to detect Jupiter's faint rings, and *Voyager 2* was the first probe to fly by the four gas giants—Jupiter, Saturn, Uranus, and Neptune. The paths of the Pioneer and Voyager space probes are shown in **Figure 3**. Today, they are near the solar system's edge and some are still sending back data.

The Galileo Mission: A Return to Jupiter

The *Galileo* probe arrived at Jupiter in 1995. While *Galileo* itself began a long tour of Jupiter's moons, it sent a smaller probe into Jupiter's atmosphere to measure its composition, density, temperature, and cloud structure. *Galileo* gathered data about the geology of Jupiter's major moons and Jupiter's magnetic properties. The moons of Jupiter proved to be far more exciting than the earlier Pioneer and Voyager images had suggested. *Galileo* discovered that two of Jupiter's moons have magnetic fields and that one of its moons, Europa, may have an ocean of liquid water under its icy surface.

Missions to the Outer Solar System

Pioneer 10 (U.S.)
Launched: March 1972
Purpose: to study Jupiter and the outer solar system

Galileo (U.S.)
Launched: October 1989
Purpose: to study Jupiter and its moons

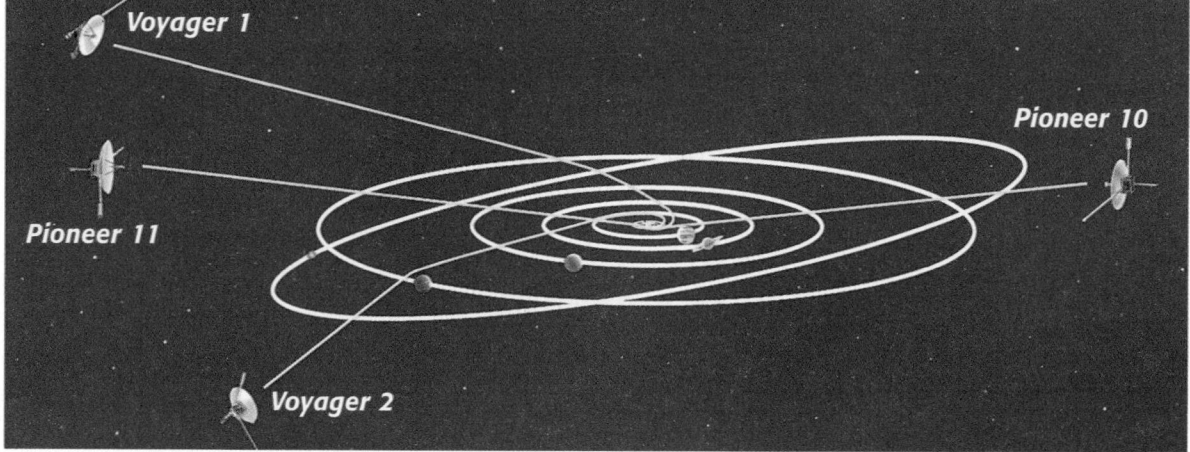

Figure 3 The Orbits of the *Pioneer* and *Voyager* Probes

Voyager 1

Pioneer 10

Pioneer 11

Voyager 2

Figure 4 *This artist's view shows the* Huygens *probe parachuting to the surface of Saturn's moon Titan.* Saturn *and* Cassini *are in the background.*

CONNECTION TO Social Studies

Cosmic Message in a Bottle
When the Voyager space probes were launched in 1977, they carried a variety of messages intended for alien civilizations that might find the messages. In addition to greetings spoken in 55 languages, various songs, nature sounds, photographs of life on Earth, and a diagram of the solar system were included. Find out more about the message carried by the Voyager missions, and then create your own cosmic message in a bottle.

ACTIVITY

The Cassini Mission: Exploring Saturn's Moons

In 1997, the *Cassini* space probe was launched on a seven-year journey to Saturn where it will make a grand tour of Saturn's moons. As shown in **Figure 4,** a smaller probe, called the *Huygens* probe, will detach itself from *Cassini* and descend into the atmosphere of Saturn's moon Titan. Scientists are interested in Titan's atmosphere because it may be similar to Earth's early atmosphere. Titan's atmosphere may reveal clues about how life developed on Earth.

Faster, Cheaper, and Better

The early space-probe missions were very large and costly. Probes such as *Voyager 2* and *Galileo* took years to develop. Now, NASA has a vision for missions that are "faster, cheaper, and better." One new program, called Discovery, seeks proposals for smaller science programs. The first six approved Discovery missions include sending small space probes to asteroids, landing on Mars again, studying the moon, and returning comet dust to Earth.

Stardust: Comet Detective

Launched in 1999, the *Stardust* space probe is the first probe to focus only on a comet. The probe will arrive at the comet in 2004 and gather samples of the comet's dust tail. It will return the samples to Earth in 2006. For the first time, pure samples from beyond the orbit of the moon will be brought back to Earth. The comet dust should help scientists better understand how the solar system formed.

Reading Check What is the mission of the *Stardust* probe?

Deep Space 1: Testing Ion Propulsion

Another NASA project is the New Millennium program. Its purpose is to test new technologies that can be used in the future. *Deep Space 1,* shown in **Figure 5,** is the first mission of this program. It is a space probe with an ion-propulsion system. Instead of burning chemical fuel, an ion rocket uses charged particles that exit the vehicle at high speed. An ion rocket follows Newton's third law of motion, but it does so using a unique source of propulsion. Ion propulsion is like sitting on the back of a truck and shooting peas out of a straw. If there were no friction, the truck would gradually accelerate to tremendous speeds.

Figure 5 Deep Space 1 *uses a revolutionary type of propulsion— an ion rocket.*

SECTION Review

Summary

- Exploration with space probes began with missions to the moon. Space probes then explored other bodies in the inner solar system.

- Space-probe missions to Mars have focused on the search for signs of water and life. **E.1.3.2**

- The Pioneer and Voyager programs explored the outer solar system.

- Space-probe missions have helped us understand Earth's formation and environment.

- NASA's new strategy of "faster, cheaper, and better" seeks to create space-probe missions that are smaller than the missions of the past.

Using Key Terms

Correct each statement by replacing the underlined term.

1. *Luna 1* discovered evidence of water on the moon. **E.1.3.2**

2. *Venera 9* helped map 98% of Venus's surface. **E.1.3.2**

Understanding Key Ideas

3. Describe five discoveries that have been made by space probes.

4. Explain how missions to Venus, Mars, and Titan help us understand Earth's environment.

Critical Thinking

5. **Making Inferences** Infer why space probes were used to discover water channels on Mars and evidence of ice on Europa.

6. **Expressing Opinions** Evaluate the advantages and disadvantages of NASA's Discovery program relative to the older space-probe missions.

7. **Applying Concepts** How would you explain how *Deep Space 1* uses Newton's third law of motion to accelerate?

FCAT Preparation

8. NASA's new policy of "faster, cheaper, and better" is very different from the policies that guided its earlier space missions. Earlier missions took much longer to plan and were very expensive. Which of the following values do you think are primary influences on NASA's new policy? **H.3.3.4 CS**

   A. aesthetic and recreational values

   B. economic and scientific values

   C. social and ethical values

   D. environmental and political values

SCLINKS.

NSTA

Developed and maintained by the National Science Teachers Association

For a variety of links related to this chapter, go to www.scilinks.org

Topic: Space Probes
SciLinks code: HSM1342

SECTION
4

READING WARM-UP

Objectives

● Summarize the history and future of human spaceflight.

● Explain the role of political and social values in the development of space exploration. **H.3.3.4 CS**

● Describe the *International Space Station,* and explain its value to science. **H.1.3.6**

● Identify five space-age spinoffs that are used in everyday life. **H.3.3.6**

Terms to Learn

space shuttle
space station

READING STRATEGY

Reading Organizer As you read this section, make a flowchart that shows the events of the space race.

H.3.3.4 CS knows that technological design should require taking into account constraints such as natural laws, the properties of the materials used, and economic, political, social, ethical, and aesthetic values.

People in Space

One April morning in 1961, a rocket stood on a launch pad in a remote part of the Soviet Union. Inside, a 27-year-old cosmonaut named Yuri Gagarin sat and waited. He was about to do what no human had done before—travel to outer space. No one knew if his brain would function in space or if he would be instantly killed by radiation.

On April 12, 1961, Yuri Gagarin, shown in **Figure 1,** became the first human to orbit Earth. The flight lasted 108 minutes. An old woman, her granddaughter, and a cow were the first to see Gagarin as he safely parachuted back to Earth, but the news of his success was quickly broadcast around the world.

The Race Is On

The Soviets were first once again, and the Americans were concerned that their rivals were winning the space race. Therefore, on May 25, 1961, President Kennedy announced, "I believe that the nation should commit itself to achieving the goal, before this decade is out, of landing a man on the moon and returning him safely to Earth. No single project in this period will be more impressive to mankind, or more important for the long range exploration of space."

Kennedy's speech took everyone—even NASA's leaders—by surprise. We are going to the moon? We had not even reached orbit yet! In response to Kennedy's challenge, a new spaceport called Kennedy Space Center was built in Florida, and Mission Control was established in Houston, Texas. In February 1962, John Glenn became the first American to orbit Earth.

Figure 1 *In 1961, Yuri Gagarin (left) became the first person in space. In 1962, John Glenn (right) became the first American to orbit Earth.*

"The Eagle Has Landed"

Seven years later, on July 20, 1969, Kennedy's challenge was met. The world watched on television as the *Apollo 11* landing module—the *Eagle,* shown in **Figure 2**—landed on the moon. Neil Armstrong became the first human to set foot on a world other than Earth. This moment forever changed the way we view ourselves and our planet. The Apollo missions also contributed to the advancement of science. *Apollo 11* returned moon rocks to Earth for study. Its crew also put devices on the moon to study moonquakes and the solar wind.

Benchmark Check How did political and social values influence the space race? **H.3.3.4 CS**

The Space Shuttle

The Saturn V rockets, which carried the Apollo astronauts to the moon, were huge and very expensive. They were longer than a football field, and each could be used only once. To save money, NASA began to develop the space shuttle program in 1972. A **space shuttle** is a reusable space vehicle that takes off like a rocket and lands like an airplane.

The Space Shuttle Gets off the Ground

Columbia, the first space shuttle, was launched on April 12, 1981. Since then, NASA has completed more than 100 successful shuttle missions. If you look at the shuttle *Endeavour* in **Figure 3,** you can see its main parts. The orbiter is about the size of an airplane. It carries the astronauts and payload into space. The liquid-fuel tank is the large red column. Two white solid-fuel booster rockets help the shuttle reach orbit. Then, they fall back to Earth along with the fuel tank. The booster rockets are reused; the fuel tank is not. After completing a mission, the orbiter returns to Earth and lands like an airplane.

Shuttle Tragedies

On January 28, 1986, the booster rocket on the space shuttle *Challenger* exploded just after takeoff, and all seven of the astronauts were killed. On board was Christa McAuliffe, who would have been the first teacher in space. Investigations found that cold weather on the morning of the launch had caused rubber gaskets in the solid-fuel booster rockets to stiffen and fail. The failure of the gaskets led to the explosion. The shuttle program resumed in 1988. In 2003, however, the space shuttle *Columbia* exploded as it reentered the atmosphere. All seven astronauts on board were killed. These disasters emphasize the dangers of space exploration that continue to challenge scientists and engineers.

Figure 2 *Neil Armstrong took this photo of Edwin "Buzz" Aldrin as Aldrin was about to become the second human to set foot on the moon.*

space shuttle a reusable space vehicle that takes off like a rocket and lands like an airplane

Figure 3 *The space shuttles are the first reusable space vehicles.*

Figure 4 *As this illustration shows, space planes may provide transportation to outer space and around the world.*

space station a long-term orbiting platform from which other vehicles can be launched or scientific research can be carried out

H.1.3.6 recognizes the scientific contributions that are made by individuals of diverse backgrounds, interests, talents, and motivations.

Space Planes: The Shuttles of the Future?

NASA is working to develop advanced space systems, such as a space plane. This craft will fly like a normal airplane, but it will have rocket engines for use in space. Once in operation, space planes, such as the one shown in **Figure 4,** may lower the cost of getting material to LEO by 90%. Private companies are also becoming interested in developing space vehicles for commercial use and in making space travel cheaper, easier, and safer.

Space Stations—People Working in Space

A long-term orbiting platform in space is called a **space station.** On April 19, 1971, the Soviets became the first to successfully place a space station in orbit. A crew of three Soviet cosmonauts conducted a 23-day mission aboard the station, which was called *Salyut 1.* By 1982, the Soviets had put up seven space stations. Because of this experience, the Soviet Union became a leader in space-station development and in the study of the effects of weightlessness on humans. The Soviets' discoveries will be important for future flights to other planets—journeys that will take years to complete.

Skylab and *Mir*

Skylab, the United States' first space station, was a science and engineering lab used to conduct a wide variety of scientific studies. These studies included experiments in biology and space manufacturing and astronomical observations. Three different crews spent a total of 171 days on *Skylab* before it was abandoned. In 1986, the Soviets began to launch the pieces for a much more ambitious space station called *Mir* (meaning "peace"). Astronauts on *Mir* conducted a wide range of experiments, made many astronomical observations, and studied manufacturing in space. After 15 years, *Mir* was abandoned, and it burned up in Earth's atmosphere in 2001.

The *International Space Station*

The *International Space Station* (*ISS*), the newest space station, is being constructed in LEO. Russia, the United States, and 14 other countries are designing and building different parts of the station. **Figure 5** shows what the *ISS* will look like when it is completed. The *ISS* is being built with materials brought up on the space shuttles and by Russian rockets. The United States is providing lab modules, the supporting frame, solar panels, living quarters, and a biomedical laboratory. The Russians are contributing a service module, docking modules, life-support and research modules, and transportation to and from the station. Other components will come from Japan, Canada, and several European countries.

Benchmark Check What contributions are the Americans and Russians making to the *ISS*? **H.1.3.6**

Research on the *International Space Station*

The *ISS* will provide many benefits, some of which we cannot predict. What scientists do know is that it will be a unique, space-based facility to perform space-science experiments and to test new technologies. Much of the space race involved political and military rivalry between the Soviet Union and the United States. Hopefully, the *ISS* will promote cooperation between countries while continuing the pioneering spirit of the first astronauts and cosmonauts.

CONNECTION TO
Social Studies

Oral Histories The exciting times of the Apollo moon missions thrilled the nation. Interview adults in your community about their memories of those times. Prepare a list of questions first, and have your questions and contacts approved by your teacher. If possible, use a tape recorder or video camera to record the interviews. As a class, create a library of your oral histories for future students.

ACTIVITY

Figure 5 *When the* International Space Station *is completed, it will be about the size of a soccer field and will weigh about 500 tons.*

Figure 6 *As this illustration shows, humans may eventually establish a colony on the moon or on Mars.*

To the Moon, Mars, and Beyond

We may eventually need resources beyond what Earth can offer. Space offers many such resources. The moon will be an important part of the further study and exploration of the solar system. For example, the far side of the moon can be 100 times as dark as any observatory site on Earth. A base on the moon similar to the one shown in **Figure 6** could be used to manufacture materials in low gravity or in a vacuum. A colony on the moon or on Mars could be an important link to bringing space resources to Earth. The key will be to make space missions economically worthwhile.

The Benefits of the Space Program

The exploration of space is a challenge to human courage and a quest for new knowledge of ourselves and the universe. We have visited the moon and spent decades exploring space. So, why should we continue to explore space? When exploring space, scientists not only learn more about space itself but also gain a large amount of knowledge from developing the missions to space. The information gained by developing these missions can be used to make our everyday lives better. For example, space missions required the development of new pumps. Later, this pump technology enabled scientists to develop artificial hearts. Computerized processes that were originally developed to manage launch preparations for the space shuttle are now used in businesses all over the world. NASA's aerogel, shown in **Figure 7,** may become an energy-saving replacement for windows in the future. The cost of space exploration is high, but the rewards are great.

Figure 7 *Aerogel is the lightest solid on Earth. Aerogel is only 3 times as heavy as air and has 39 times the insulating properties of the best fiberglass insulation.*

Space-Age Spinoffs

Technologies that were developed for the space programs but are now used in everyday life are called *space-age spinoffs*. There are dozens of examples of common items that were first developed for the space programs. Cordless power tools, such as the drill shown in **Figure 8,** were first developed for use on the moon by the Apollo astronauts. Hand-held cameras that were developed to study the heat emitted from the space shuttle are now used by firefighters to detect dangerous hot spots in fires. In addition to developing new, everyday technologies, the space program has created new tools for scientists to conduct future research.

 **Benchmark Check** What are space-age spinoffs? **H.3.3.6**

Spinoffs in Health and Medicine

Many people who have heart problems may rely on a pacemaker, which uses wireless technology developed by NASA. A pacemaker, shown in **Figure 9,** is a small machine that is inserted into a patient's body. The machine helps regulate the patient's heart rate.

You may be more familiar with another tool developed from space technology. The ear thermometer in **Figure 9** is used to measure a person's body temperature. The thermometer uses a special lens that detects infrared energy, which we feel as heat. The lens detects the infrared energy of the body. The lens used in this type of thermometer was originally developed to detect the birth of stars in space!

Figure 8 *Cordless power tools were originally developed for astronauts to drill samples from the moon.*

H.3.3.6 knows that no matter who does science and mathematics or invents things, or when or where they do it, the knowledge and technology that result can eventually become available to everyone.

Figure 9 **Space-Age Spinoffs in Medicine**

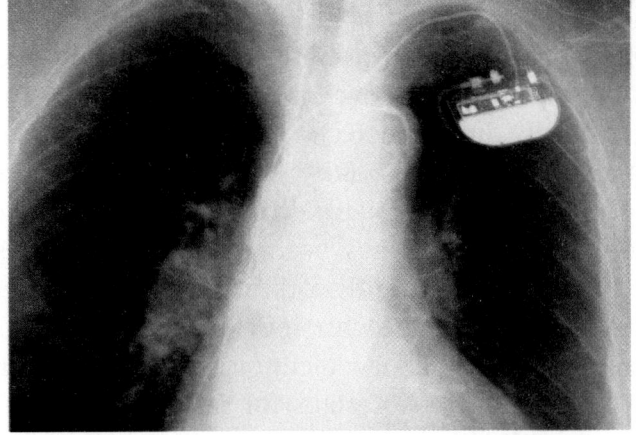

Doctors can program a patient's pacemaker wirelessly. This wireless technology was originally developed for the space program.

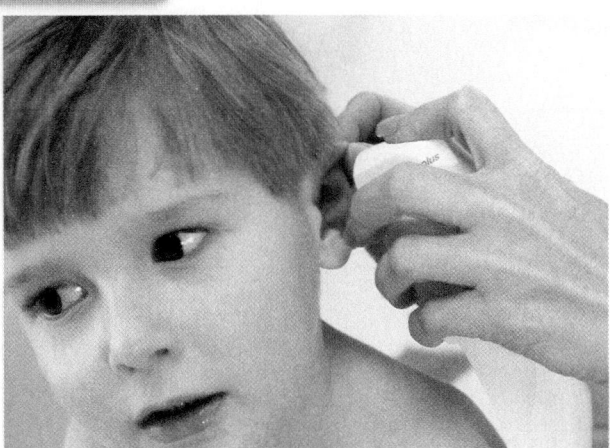

The technology that was developed to detect the birth of new stars in space is now used in ear thermometers to measure body temperature.

Figure 10   Materials from Space-Age Spinoffs

Chemicals invented by NASA were used to make this heat-resistant suit.

NASA's aircraft cushion material is now being used for shock-absorbing sports helmets.

Benchmark Activity

Pamphlet of Space-Age Spinoffs Research a space-age spinoff that interests you. You can research a spinoff described in the book, or you can find one on your own. Then, make a short pamphlet showing how the technology became available to everyone. H.3.3.6

Space-Age Materials

Several types of materials that we use every day were originally designed for use in space. Examples include fire-resistant and heat-resistant materials. The heat-resistant suit shown in **Figure 10** was made from chemically treated fabric. The chemicals were originally developed to treat fabrics for use in spacesuits and inside spacecraft.

What kind of common object would you expect to be made from material used for aircraft cushions? Protective helmets, of course! Material developed by NASA for aircraft passenger seats is now used in shock-absorbing helmets and shin guards, as shown in **Figure 10.** Space technology is also responsible for the scratch-resistant lenses that are used in eyeglasses.

Transportation and Safety Spinoffs

Spinoff technology has led to transportation and safety advancements, such as safer bridges, improved automobile designs, and storm-warning devices. Smoke detectors were originally used on the orbiting space station *Skylab* to detect toxic vapors. Material developed for the *Viking Lander* parachute shroud is 5 times as strong as steel and has been used to make tires. These new tires are very tough and work well in bad weather. Three types of NASA-developed technology are used to design and test school buses. With this new technology, manufacturers are able to test new school bus designs for safety before even making the school bus!

Benchmark Check What is an example of a transportation spinoff? H.3.3.6

H.3.3.6 knows that no matter who does science and mathematics or invents things, or when or where they do it, the knowledge and technology that result can eventually become available to everyone.

SECTION Review

Summary

- Political and social values influenced the development of space technology. **H.3.3.4 CS**

- In 1961, the Soviet cosmonaut Yuri Gagarin became the first person in space. In 1969, Neil Armstrong became the first person on the moon. **H.1.3.6**

- During the 1970s, the United States focused on developing the space shuttle, and the Soviets focused on developing space stations. **H.1.3.6**

- The United States, Russia, and 14 other countries are currently developing the *International Space Station*. **H.1.3.6**

- There have been many scientific, economic, and social benefits of the space programs. Space-age spinoffs are some examples of these benefits. **H.3.3.6**

Using Key Terms

1. Use *space shuttle* and *space station* in separate sentences.

Using Key Ideas

2. Differentiate between the space shuttles and other space vehicles.

3. Outline the history and future of human spaceflight. How was the race to explore space influenced by the Cold War? **H.3.3.4 CS**

4. Identify five space-age spinoffs. **H.3.3.6**

5. Articulate the differences between the U.S. and Soviet space programs in the 1970s.

6. What is the *International Space Station*? How will the space station benefit science?

Math Skills

7. When fueled, a space shuttle has a mass of about 2,000,000 kg. About 80% of that mass is fuel and oxygen. Calculate the mass of a space shuttle's fuel and oxygen.

Critical Thinking

8. **Making Inferences** Infer why the United States stopped sending people to the moon after the Apollo program ended.

9. **Expressing Opinions** Imagine that you are a U.S. senator reviewing NASA's proposed budget. Write a two-paragraph statement expressing your opinion about funding for NASA.

FCAT Preparation

10. When the Apollo astronauts returned from the first moon mission, they were held in quarantine for more than two weeks. The astronauts were not allowed to contact other people or leave the quarantine area. What was the primary reason for the quarantine? **H.3.3.1 CS**

    A. to allow the spacecraft to cool off

    B. to reduce risks to the mission payload

    C. to allow astronauts to study Earth

    D. to reduce risks to coworkers and the public

11. Many different values influenced the space race. Which of the following values had the greatest influence on the space race? **H.3.3.4 CS**

    F. political values

    G economic values

    H. aesthetic values

    I. ethical values

Developed and maintained by the National Science Teachers Association

For a variety of links related to this chapter, go to www.scilinks.org

Topic: Space Exploration and Space Stations

SciLinks code: HSM1430

Inquiry Lab

Water Rockets Save the Day!

OBJECTIVES

Predict which design features would improve a rocket's flight.

Design and build a rocket that includes your design features.

Test your rocket design, and evaluate your results.

MATERIALS

- bottle, soda, 2 L
- clay, modeling
- foam board
- rocket launcher
- scissors
- tape, duct
- watch or clock that indicates seconds
- water

SAFETY

Imagine that for the big Fourth of July celebration, you and your friends had planned a full day of swimming, volleyball, and fireworks at the lake. You've just learned, however, that the city passed a law that bans all fireworks within city limits. But you do not give up so easily on having fun. Last year at summer camp, you learned how to build water rockets. And you have kept the launcher in your garage since then. With a little bit of creativity, you and your friends are going to celebrate with a splash!

Ask a Question

1 What is the most efficient design for a water rocket?

Form a Hypothesis

2 Write a hypothesis that provides a possible answer to the question above.

Test the Hypothesis

3 Decide how your rocket will look, and then draw a sketch.

4 Using only the materials listed, decide how to build your rocket. Write a description of your plan, and have your teacher approve your plan. Keep in mind that you will need to leave the opening of your bottle clear. The bottle opening will be placed over a rubber stopper on the rocket launcher.

5 Fins are often used to stabilize rockets. Do you want fins on your water rocket? Decide on the best shape for the fins, and then decide how many fins your rocket needs. Use the foam board to construct the fins.

6 Your rocket must be heavy enough to fly in a controlled manner. Consider using clay in the body of your rocket to provide some additional weight and stability.

7 Pour water into your rocket until the rocket is one-third to one-half full.

8 Your teacher will provide the launcher and will assist you during blastoff. Attach your rocket to the launcher by placing the opening of the bottle on the rubber stopper.

9 When the rocket is in place, clear the immediate area and begin pumping air into your rocket. Watch the pump gauge, and take note of how much pressure is needed for liftoff. **Caution:** Be sure to step back from the launch site. You should be several meters away from the bottle when you launch it.

10 Use the watch to time your rocket's flight. How long was your rocket in the air?

11 Make small changes in your rocket design that you think will improve the rocket's performance. Consider using different amounts of water and clay or experimenting with different fins. You may also want to compare your design with those of your classmates.

Analyze the Results

1 **Describing Events** How did your rocket perform? If you used fins, do you think they helped your flight? Explain your answer.

2 **Explaining Results** What do you think propelled your rocket? Use Newton's third law of motion to explain your answer.

3 **Analyzing Results** How did the amount of water in your rocket affect the launch?

Draw Conclusions

4 **Drawing Conclusions** What modifications made your rocket fly for the longest time? How did the design help the rockets fly so far?

5 **Evaluating Results** Which group's rocket was the most stable? How did the design help the rocket fly straight?

6 **Making Predictions** How can you improve your design to make your rocket perform even better?

Chapter Review

USING KEY TERMS

For each pair of terms, explain how the meanings of the terms differ.

1 *geostationary orbit* and *low Earth orbit*

2 *space probe* and *space station*

3 *artificial satellite* and *moon*

Complete each of the following sentences by choosing the correct term from the chapter

4 The force that accelerates a rocket is called ___.

5 Rockets need ___ in order to burn fuel.

UNDERSTANDING KEY IDEAS

Multiple Choice

6 Whose rocket research team surrendered to the Americans at the end of World War II? **H.3.3.4 CS**

   a. Konstantin Tsiolkovsky's
   b. Robert Goddard's
   c. Wernher von Braun's
   d. Yuri Gargarin's

7 Rockets work according to Newton's

   a. first law of motion.
   b. second law of motion.
   c. third law of motion.
   d. law of universal gravitation.

8 The first artificial satellite to orbit the Earth was

   a. *Pioneer 4.*   **c.** *Voyager 2.*
   b. *Explorer 1.*   **d.** *Sputnik 1.*

9 Communications satellites are able to transfer TV signals between continents because communications satellites

   a. are located in LEO.
   b. relay signals past the horizon.
   c. travel quickly around Earth.
   d. can be used during the day and night.

10 GEO is a better orbit for communications satellites because satellites that are in GEO

   a. remain in position over one spot.
   b. have polar orbits.
   c. do not revolve around Earth.
   d. orbit a few hundred kilometers above Earth.

11 The political rivalry between the United States and the Soviet Union influenced the space programs of each nation. Which values were the main influence on the technological design of spacecraft during this period? **H.3.3.4 CS FCAT**

   a. aesthetic values
   b. political values
   c. economic values
   d. ethical values

12 When did humans first set foot on the moon?

   a 1959   **c.** 1969
   b. 1964   **d.** 1973

13 Based on space-probe data, which of the following is the most likely place in our solar system to find liquid water? **E.I.3.2**

   a. the moon   **c.** Europa
   b. Mercury   **d.** Venus

Short Answer

14 Describe the *International Space Station,* and explain why it is an example of international cooperation. **H.1.3.6**

15 What is one disadvantage that objects in LEO have?

16 Why did the United States develop the space shuttle? **H.3.3.4 CS**

17 How does data from satellites and space-probe missions help us understand Earth's environment? **H.3.3.6**

18 Describe the contributions made by individuals with diverse backgrounds to the exploration of space. **H.3.3.5**

CRITICAL THINKING

Extended Response

19 Expressing Opinions Describe the impact that space research has had on scientific thought, on society, and on the environment. **H.3.3.6**

20 Making Inferences Infer the difference between speed and velocity.

21 Applying Concepts Clarify why rockets that travel in outer space carry oxygen with them.

22 Applying Concepts Paraphrase how NASA's "faster, cheaper, and better" program relates to space probes.

23 Expressing Opinions Write a balanced essay that considers two points of view on the following statement: "The benefits of space exploration outweigh the expense." Include information about space age spinoffs in your essay. **H.3.3.6**

Concept Mapping

24 Use the following terms to create a concept map: *orbital velocity, thrust, LEO, artificial satellites, escape velocity, space probes, GEO,* and *rockets.*

INTERPRETING GRAPHICS

The diagram below illustrates suborbital velocity, orbital velocity, and escape velocity. Use the diagram below to answer the questions that follow.

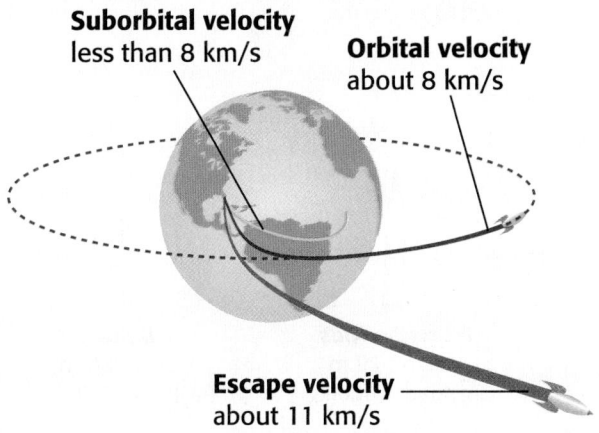

Suborbital velocity less than 8 km/s

Orbital velocity about 8 km/s

Escape velocity about 11 km/s

25 Could a rocket traveling at 6 km/s reach orbital velocity?

26 If a rocket traveled for 3 days at the minimum escape velocity, how far would the rocket travel?

27 How much faster would a rocket traveling in orbital velocity need to travel to reach escape velocity?

28 If the escape velocity for a planet was 9 km/s, would you assume that the mass of the planet was more or less than the mass of Earth?

For the following questions, write your answers on a separate sheet of paper.

1 The illustration below shows the development of rockets over several decades. A rocket's payload is the amount of material that the rocket is able to carry into space. Over time, the ratio of a rocket's payload to its size has increased. For example, the ratio of payload in kilograms (kg) to rocket height in meters (m) for the Mercury-Atlas rocket is 1400/29 or roughly 48 to 1 (or 48).

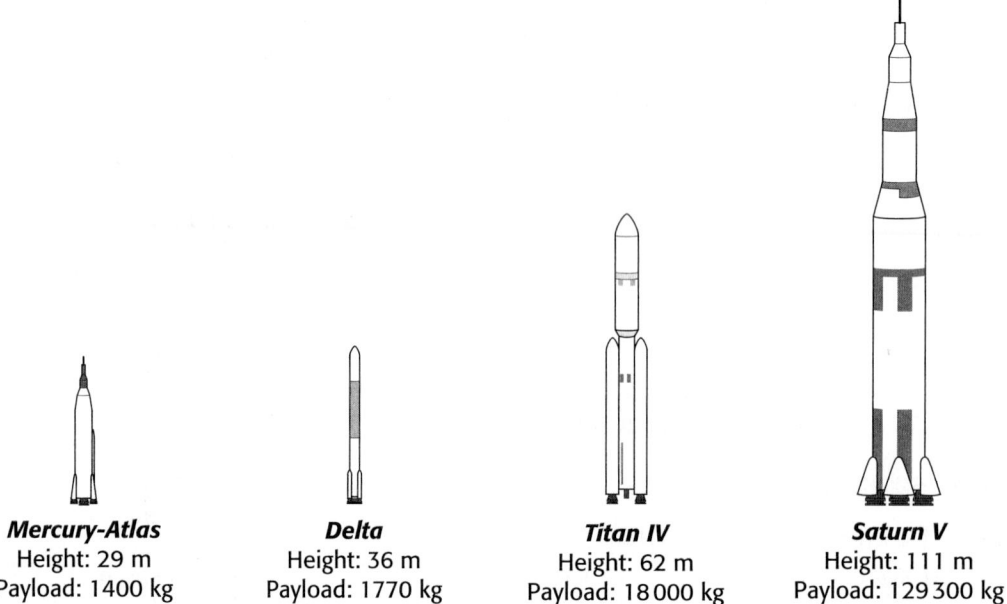

Mercury-Atlas
Height: 29 m
Payload: 1400 kg

Delta
Height: 36 m
Payload: 1770 kg

Titan IV
Height: 62 m
Payload: 18 000 kg

Saturn V
Height: 111 m
Payload: 129 300 kg

What was the approximate ratio of payload to height in the Saturn V rocket (expressed as a whole number)?

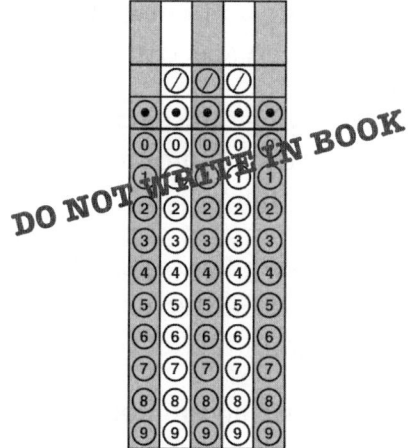

2 Maya is a very careful person. She always wears her seat belt when she rides in a car. She makes sure the clothes she wears are warm enough on cold days. Every time she rides her bicycle, she wears a helmet. She crosses major streets at stop lights and crosswalks instead of in the middle of the block. Which of the following items described above is a benefit of space program technology?

A. seat belts
B. stop lights
C. warm clothes
D. bicycle helmets

3 Before World War II, which two men contributed theory and practical engineering to the development of rockets?

F. Buzz Aldrin and Robert Goddard
G. Yuri Gagarin and Neil Armstrong
H. Yuri Gagarin and Konstantin Tsiolokovsky
I. Konstantin Tsiolokovsky and Robert Goddard

4 Space programs often involve international cooperation to share technology and protect participants. One such example is being designed and built by a team of scientists from the United States, Russia, and 14 other countries. What is it?

A. Skylab
B. Terra 1
C. the Global Positioning System
D. the International Space Station

5 Which of the following satellite technologies is a military spinoff?

F. Terra 1
G. weather satellites
H. the Landsat program
I. the Global Positioning System

6  The space shuttle carries hundreds of thousands of gallons of liquid oxygen. Imagine that you are a scientist working to reduce the mass of the space shuttle. Using a computer model, you experiment with reducing the amount of liquid oxygen that is carried by the space shuttle by half. What are some of the variables that you need to consider? How might changing these variables affect your experiment? What should you do to ensure the credibility of your experiment?

Science in Action

FLASHLINE MARS ARCTIC RESEARCH

Place to Visit

The Kennedy Space Center

NASA's launch headquarters, the Kennedy Space Center (KSC), is located south of Orlando. The outdoor "Rocket Garden" has rockets that are 10 stories high and historic space capsules that you can explore. At the U.S. Astronaut Hall of Fame, you can experience four "Gs" in a spaceflight simulator. (1 "G" is equal to the gravitational force you feel on Earth's surface.) You will also learn about the Mars missions, and you will have the chance to meet a real astronaut. Call ahead to find out if you can see a rocket launch, but don't worry if you miss a liftoff. The KSC has an I-Max theater that brings spaceflight to life on a screen that is 5 stories tall!

Weird Science

Flashline Mars Arctic Research Station

If you wanted to visit a place on Earth that is like the surface of Mars, where would you go? You might head to an impact crater on Devon Island, close to the Arctic circle. The rugged terrain and harsh weather there resemble what explorers will find on Mars, although Mars has no breathable air and is a lot colder. In the summer, volunteers from the Mars Society live in an experimental base in the crater and test technology that might be used on Mars. The volunteers try to simulate the experience of explorers on Mars. For example, the volunteers wear spacesuits when they go outside, and they use rovers to explore the landscape. They even communicate with the outside world by using types of technology likely to be used on Mars. These dedicated volunteers have already made discoveries that will help NASA plan a crewed mission to Mars!

Social Studies ACTIVITY

A Mars mission could require astronauts to endure nearly two years of extreme isolation. Research how NASA would prepare astronauts for the psychological pressures of a mission to Mars.

Language Arts ACTIVITY

WRITING SKILL Find out more about the exciting history of spaceflight, and write a short story based on a historical moment in the history of space exploration.

Franklin Chang-Diaz

Astronaut You have to wear a suit, but the commute is not too long. In fact, it is only about eight and a half minutes, and what a view you have on your way to work! Astronauts, such as Franklin Chang-Diaz, have one of the most exciting jobs on Earth—or in space. Chang-Diaz has flown on seven space shuttle missions and has completed three space walks. Since 1981, when he became an astronaut, Chang-Diaz has spent more than 1,601 hours (66 days) in space.

Chang-Diaz was born in San Jose, Costa Rica. He earned a degree in mechanical engineering in 1973 and received a doctorate in applied plasma physics from the Massachusetts Institute of Technology (MIT) in 1977. His work in physics attracted the attention of NASA, and he began training at the Johnson Space Center in Houston, Texas. In addition to doing research on the space shuttle, Chang-Diaz has worked on developing plasma propulsion systems for long space flights. He has also helped create closer ties between astronauts and scientists by starting organizations such as the Astronaut Science Colloquium Program and the Astronaut Science Support Group. If you want to find out more about what it takes to be an astronaut, look on NASA's Web site.

Math ACTIVITY

If 1 out of 120 people interviewed by NASA is selected for astronaut training, how many people will be selected for training if 10,680 people are interviewed?

As this mission patch shows, Chang-Diaz flew on the 111th space shuttle mission.

To learn more about these Science in Action topics, visit **go.hrw.com** and type in the keyword **HT6FEXFF.**

Current Science

Check out Current Science® articles related to this chapter by visiting go.hrw.com. Just type in the keyword **HZ5CS22.**

UNIT 7

TIMELINE

Matter, Forces, and Work

How are you like a hammer? Both you and a hammer are made up of matter. Matter is anything that has mass and takes up space. A hammer is a type of machine. It makes work easier by changing the size or direction of a force. In this unit, you will learn about matter, machines, work, and forces. This timeline shows some of the events that have occurred as people have learned about matter, machines, work, and forces.

Around 3000 BCE

The sail is used in Egypt. Sails use the wind rather than human power to move boats through the water.

1818

Baron Karl von Drais de Sauerbrun, a German inventor, exhibits the first two-wheeled, rider-propelled machine. Made of wood, this early machine paves the way for the invention of the bicycle.

1948

Maria Telkes, a Hungarian-born physicist, designs the heating system for the first solar-heated house.

1972

The first American self-service gas station opens.

Around 200 BCE

Under the Han dynasty, the Chinese become one of the first civilizations to use coal as fuel.

1656

Christiaan Huygens, a Dutch scientist, invents the pendulum clock.

1776

The American colonies declare their independence from Great Britain.

1893

The "clasp locker," an early zipper, is patented.

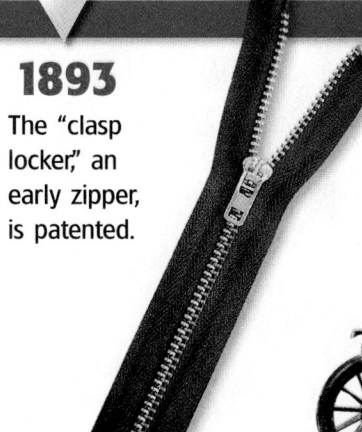

1908

The automobile age begins with the mass production of the Ford Model T.

1926

Robert Goddard, an American scientist, launches the first rocket powered by liquid fuel. The rocket reaches a height of 12.5 m and a speed of 97 km/h.

1988

A wind-powered generator begins generating electrical energy in Scotland's Orkney Islands.

2000

The 2000 Olympic Summer Games are held in Sydney, Australia.

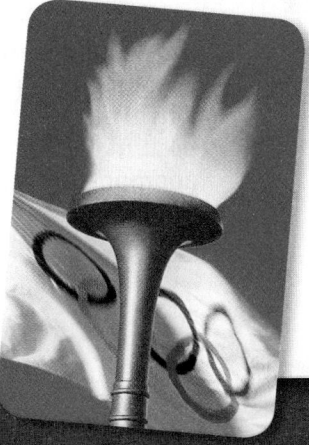

2001

A two-wheeled, battery-powered "people mover" is introduced. Gyroscopes and tilt sensors allow riders to guide the scooter-like transporter by leaning.

21

The Properties of Matter

The Big Idea Matter has properties that are observable and measurable.

About the PHOTO

This giant ice dragon began as a 1,700 kg block of ice! Making the blocks of ice takes six weeks. Then, the ice blocks are stored at −30°C until the sculpting begins. The artist has to work at −10°C to keep the ice from melting. An ice sculptor has to be familiar with the many properties of water, including its melting point.

PRE-READING ACTIVITY

 **FOLDNOTES** **Booklet** Before you read the chapter, create the FoldNote entitled "Booklet" described in the **Study Skills** section of the Appendix. Label each page of the booklet with a main idea from the chapter. As you read the chapter, write what you learn about each main idea on the appropriate page of the booklet.

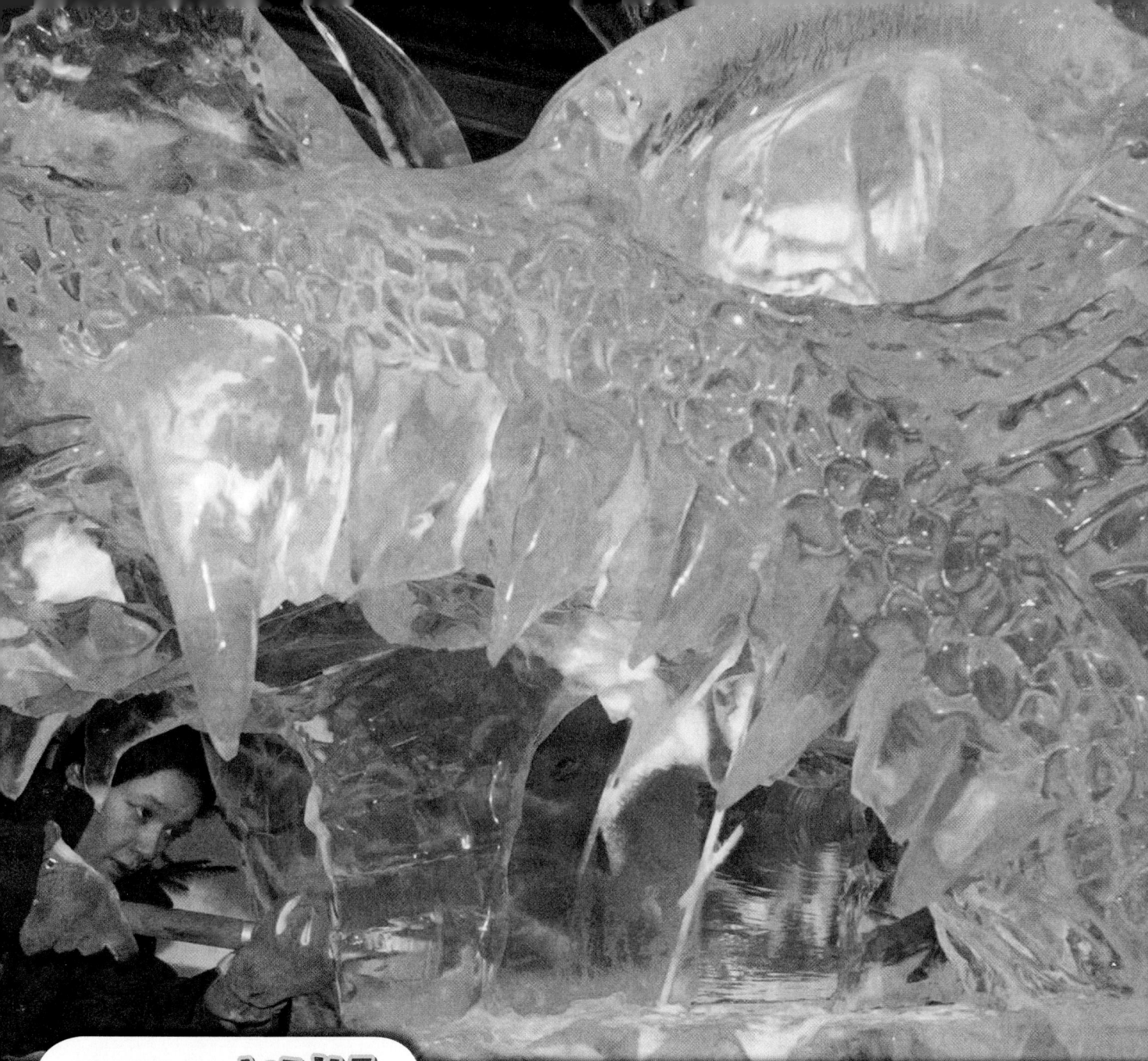

START-UP ACTIVITY

Sack Secrets A.1.3.1 AA

In this activity, you will test your skills in determining an object's identity based on the object's properties.

Procedure

1. You and two or three of your classmates will receive a **sealed paper sack** containing a **mystery object.** Do not open the sack!

2. For five minutes, make as many observations about the object as you can without opening the sack. You may touch, smell, shake, or listen to the object through the sack. Record your observations.

Analysis

1. At the end of five minutes, discuss your findings with your partners.

2. List the object's properties that you can identify. Make another list of properties that you cannot identify. Make a conclusion about the object's identity.

3. Share your observations, your list of properties, and your conclusion with the class. Then, open the sack.

4. Did you properly identify the object? If so, how? If not, why not? Record your answers.

The Nature of Matter

What do you have in common with a toaster, a steaming bowl of soup, or a bright neon sign?

You are probably thinking that this is a trick question. It is hard to imagine that a person has anything in common with a kitchen appliance, hot soup, or a glowing neon sign.

Matter

From a scientific point of view, you have at least one characteristic in common with all of these things. You, the toaster, the bowl, the soup, the steam, the glass tubing of a neon sign, and the glowing gas are made of matter. But exactly what is matter? **Matter** is anything that takes up space and has mass. It's that simple! Everything in the universe that you can see is made up of some type of matter.

Matter and Volume

All matter takes up space. The amount of space taken up, or occupied, by an object is known as the object's **volume.** Your fingernails, the continent of Africa, and a cloud have volume. And because these things have volume, they cannot share the same space at the same time. Even the tiniest speck of dust takes up space. Another speck of dust cannot fit into the same space without somehow bumping the first speck out of the way. **Figure 1** shows an example of how one object cannot share the same space with another object at the same time.

🔆 **Benchmark Check** What are two properties of all matter?
A.1.3.1 AA

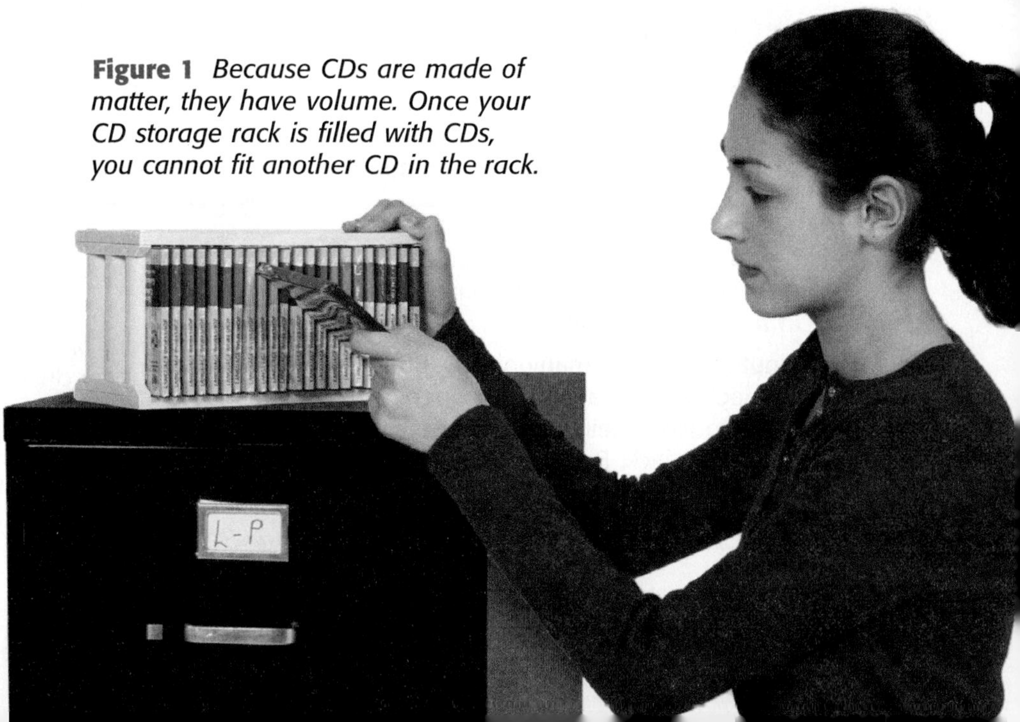

matter anything that has mass and takes up space

volume a measure of the size of a body or region in three-dimensional space

Figure 1 *Because CDs are made of matter, they have volume. Once your CD storage rack is filled with CDs, you cannot fit another CD in the rack.*

L - P

🔆 **A.1.3.1 AA** identifies various ways in which substances differ (e.g., mass, volume, shape, density, texture, and reaction to temperature and light).

Quick Lab

Space Case

1. Crumple a **piece of paper.** Fit it tightly in the bottom of a **clear plastic cup** so that it won't fall out.

2. Turn the cup upside down. Lower the cup straight down into a **bucket** filled halfway with **water.** Be sure that the cup is completely underwater.

3. Lift the cup straight out of the water. Turn the cup upright, and observe the paper. Record your observations.

4. Use the point of a **pencil** to punch a small hole in the bottom of the cup. Repeat steps 2 and 3.

5. How do the results show that air has volume? Explain your answer.

Liquid Volume

Lake Erie, the smallest of the Great Lakes, has a volume of approximately 483 trillion (that's 483,000,000,000,000) liters of water. Can you imagine that much water? Think of a 2-liter bottle of soda. The water in Lake Erie could fill more than 241 trillion 2-liter soda bottles. That's a lot of water! On a smaller scale, a can of soda has a volume of only 355 milliliters, which is about one-third of a liter. You can check the volume of the soda by using a large measuring cup from your kitchen.

Liters (L) and milliliters (mL) are the units used most often to express the volume of liquids. The volume of many liquids, from one raindrop to a can of soda to an entire ocean, can be expressed in these units or units derived from them, such as microliters.

meniscus the curve at a liquid's surface by which one measures the volume of the liquid

Reading Check What are two units used to measure volume?

Measuring the Volume of Liquids

In your science class, you'll probably use a graduated cylinder instead of a measuring cup to measure the volume of liquids. Graduated cylinders are used to measure the liquid volume when accuracy is important. The surface of a liquid in any container, including a measuring cup or a large beaker, is curved. The curve at the surface of the liquid is called the **meniscus** (muh NIS kuhs). To measure the volume of most liquids, such as water, you must look at the bottom of the meniscus, as shown in **Figure 2.** Note that you may not be able to see a meniscus in a large beaker. The meniscus looks flat because the liquid is in a wide container.

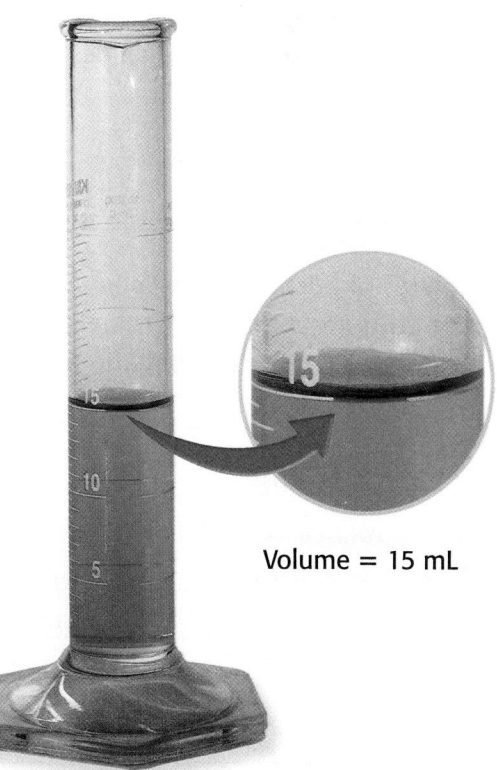

Volume = 15 mL

Figure 2 *To measure volume correctly, read the scale of the lowest part of the meniscus at eye level.*

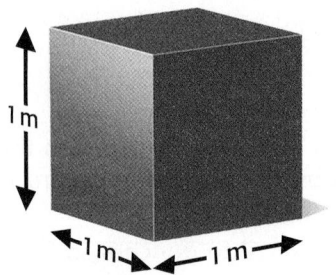

Figure 3 *A cubic meter (1 m³) is the volume of a cube that has a length, width, and height of 1 m.*

Volume of a Regularly Shaped Solid Object

The volume of any solid object is expressed in cubic units. The word *cubic* means "having three dimensions." In science, cubic meters (m^3) and cubic centimeters (cm^3) are the units most often used to express the volume of solid things. The 3 in these unit symbols shows that three quantities, or dimensions, were multiplied to get the final result. You can see the three dimensions of a cubic meter in **Figure 3.** There are formulas to find the volume of regularly shaped objects. For example, to find the volume of a cube or a rectangular object, multiply the length, width, and height of the object, as shown in the following equation:

$$volume = length \times width \times height$$

Volume of an Irregularly Shaped Solid Object

How do you find the volume of a solid that does not have a regular shape? For example, to find the volume of a 12-sided object, you cannot use the equation given above. But you can measure the volume of a solid object by measuring the volume of water that the object displaces. An object *displaces* water when the object takes up space once filled by water. **Figure 4** shows that when a 12-sided object is added to the water in a graduated cylinder, the water level rises. The volume of water displaced by the object is equal to the object's volume. Because 1 mL is equal to 1 cm^3, you can express the volume of the water displaced by the object in cubic centimeters. Although volumes of liquids can be expressed in cubic units, volumes of solids should not be expressed in liters or milliliters.

Figure 4 *The 12-sided object displaced 15 mL of water. Because 1 mL = 1 cm³, the volume of the object is 15 cm³.*

Reading Check Explain how you would measure the volume of an apple.

Volume of a Rectangular Solid What is the volume of a box that has a length of 5 cm, a width of 1 cm, and a height of 2 cm?

Step 1: Write the equation for volume.

$$volume = length \times width \times height$$

Step 2: Replace the variables with the measurements given to you, and solve.

$$volume = 5 \text{ cm} \times 1 \text{ cm} \times 2 \text{ cm} = 10 \text{ cm}^3$$

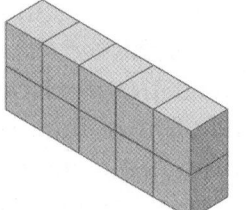

Now It's Your Turn

1. A book has a length of 25 cm, a width of 18 cm, and a height of 4 cm. What is its volume?
2. What is the volume of a suitcase that has a length of 95 cm, a width of 50 cm, and a height of 20 cm?
3. A CD case is 14.2 cm long, 12.4 cm wide, and 1 cm deep. What is its volume?

Matter and Mass

Another characteristic of all matter is mass. **Mass** is the amount of matter in an object. For example, you and a peanut are made of matter. But you are made of more matter than a peanut is, so you have more mass. The mass of an object is the same no matter where in the universe the object is located.

The Difference Between Mass and Weight

The terms *mass* and *weight* are often used as though they mean the same thing, but they don't. **Weight** is a measure of the gravitational (GRAV i TAY shuhn uhl) force exerted on an object. Gravitational force keeps objects on Earth from floating into space. The gravitational force between an object and the Earth depends partly on the object's mass. The more mass an object has, the greater the gravitational force on the object and the greater the object's weight. But an object's weight can change depending on its location in the universe. An object would weigh less on the moon than it does on Earth because the moon has less gravitational force than Earth does. **Figure 5** explains the differences between mass and weight.

Benchmark Check Describe how mass and weight are different. A.1.3.2

mass a measure of the amount of matter in an object *FCAT VOCAB*

weight a measure of the gravitational force exerted on an object; its value can change with the location of the object in the universe

 A.1.3.2 understands the difference between weight and mass.

Figure 5 Differences Between Mass and Weight

Mass

- Mass is a measure of the amount of matter in an object.
- Mass is always constant for an object no matter where the object is located in the universe.
- Mass is measured by using a balance (shown below).
- Mass is expressed in kilograms (kg), grams (g), or milligrams (mg).

Weight

- Weight is a measure of the gravitational force on an object.
- Weight varies depending on where the object is in relation to the Earth (or any large body in the universe).
- Weight is measured by using a spring scale (shown at right).
- Weight is expressed in newtons (N).

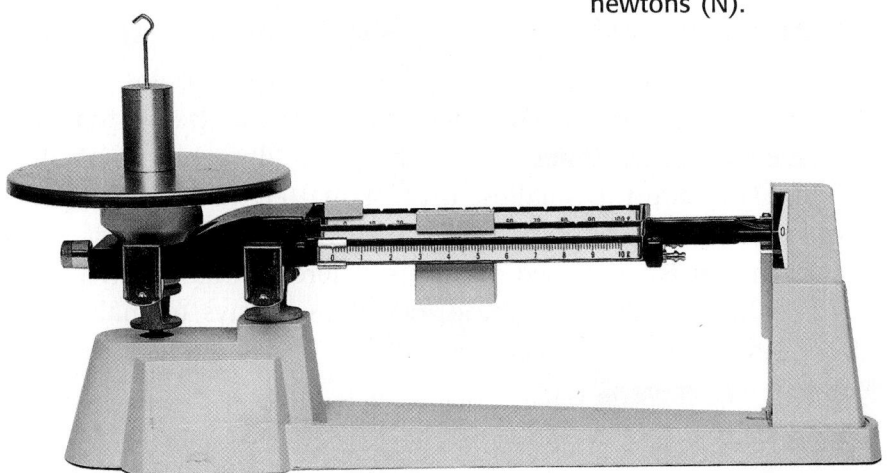

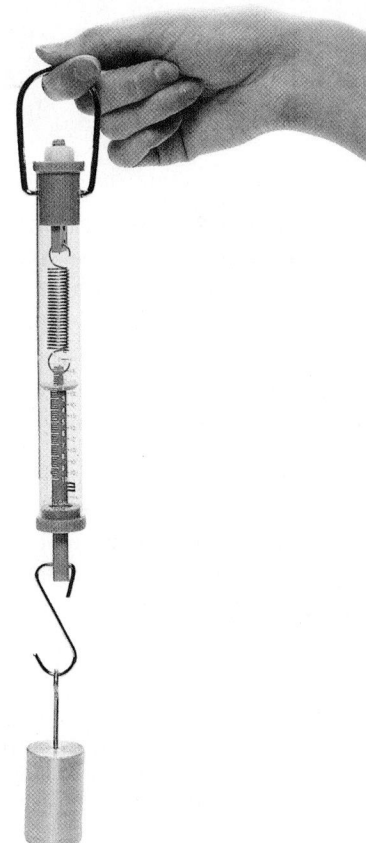

Converting Mass to Weight A student has a mass of 45,000 g. What is this student's weight in newtons? The weight of 100 g is about 1 N.

Step 1: Write the information given to you.

45,000 g

Step 2: Write the conversion factor to change grams into newtons.

1 N = 100 g

Step 3: Write the equation so that grams will cancel.

$$45{,}000 \text{ g} \times \frac{1 \text{ N}}{100 \text{ g}} = 450 \text{ N}$$

Now It's Your Turn

1. What is the weight of a car that has a mass of 1,362,000 g?
2. Your pair of boots has a mass of 850 g. If each boot has exactly the same mass, what is the weight of each boot?

Figure 6 *The brick and the sponge take up the same amount of space. But the brick has more matter in it, so its mass—and thus its weight—is greater.*

atom the smallest unit of an element that maintains the properties of that element

A.2.3.2 CS knows the general properties of the atom (a massive nucleus of neutral neutrons and positive protons surrounded by a cloud of negative electrons) and accepts that single atoms are not visible.

Measuring Mass and Weight

The brick and the sponge in **Figure 6** have the same volume. Because the brick has more mass, a greater gravitational force is exerted on the brick than on the sponge. As a result, the brick weighs more than the sponge.

The SI unit of mass is the kilogram (kg), but mass is often expressed in grams (g) or milligrams (mg). These units can be used to express the mass of any object in the universe.

Weight is a measure of gravitational force and is expressed in the SI unit of force, the *newton* (N). One newton is about equal to the weight of an object that has a mass of 100 g on Earth. On Earth, weight is a good estimate of the mass of an object because gravity doesn't change much on Earth.

Atoms: The Basic Building Blocks of Matter

You know that in order to be called matter, an object must have mass and volume. Another property of matter is that it is made of atoms. **Atoms** are the basic building blocks of all matter. They are the smallest unit of matter that has unique properties.

All matter is composed of atoms. There are many different kinds of atoms. They combine in different ways to make all the matter in the universe.

 **Benchmark Check** What is the smallest particle of matter?

A.2.3.2 CS

Table 1 Some Properties of Subatomic Particles

Particle	Mass	Charge and Location
Proton	1 amu	positive charge in nucleus
Neutron	1 amu	no charge in nucleus
Electron	0 amu	negative charge outside nucleus

Structure of Atoms

Atoms are very small. Your cells, which are too small to be seen with the unaided eye, are made of trillions of atoms. But atoms are made of even smaller parts called *subatomic particles,* listed in **Table 1.** An atom is composed of electrons, protons, and neutrons. Electrons are the smallest subatomic particles. They have a negative charge. Protons, which have a positive charge, and electrons are attracted to each other. Neutrons have no charge. Protons and neutrons are located in the nucleus of an atom. Electrons are located outside the nucleus. **Figure 7** shows these subatomic particles in a model of an atom.

Mass of Atoms

Although it's hard to imagine, atoms have a measurable mass. You can calculate the mass of an atom from the mass of certain subatomic particles. Because the mass of subatomic particles is so small, scientists created a new unit to describe their mass. This unit is called the *atomic mass unit* (amu).

Look at **Table 1.** Protons and neutrons have a mass of 1 amu, but the electron is so small that it is listed as 0 amu. So, to calculate the mass of an atom, you add the masses of the protons and neutrons in that atom.

Benchmark Activity

Democri-who?

People have always wondered about the objects that filled their world. As early as 350 BCE, people were talking about atoms. The Greek philosopher Democritus was among the first people to discuss atoms. Research how ideas about the structure of atoms have changed over time. Create a timeline that traces the history of the development of the atomic theory. To help you understand the time periods, include important historical events on your timeline.

A.2.3.2 CS

Figure 7 Model of a Helium Atom

This model shows a helium atom. Helium has two protons and two electrons. Many helium atoms contain two neutrons. The nucleus of an atom is very small and dense. An atom is mostly empty space.

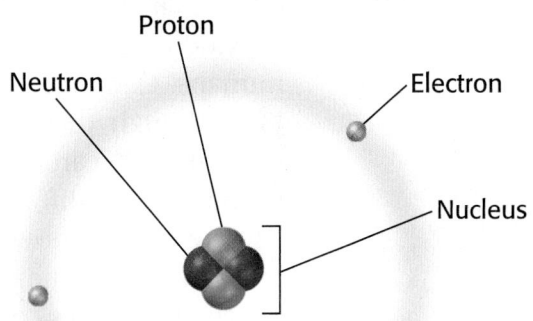

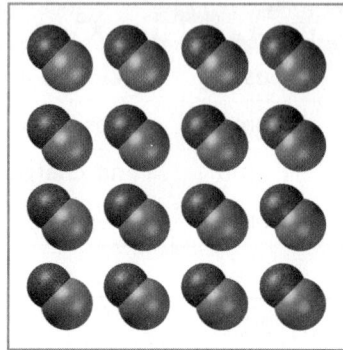

Figure 8 *Carbon dioxide and carbon monoxide have different properties even though they are made of the same kinds of atoms.*

Carbon dioxide, CO_2 Carbon monoxide, CO

Oxygen

Carbon

Identifying Atoms

Protons contribute to the mass of an atom. Protons are also important in identifying atoms. Although a single kind of atom may have different numbers of neutrons, the number of protons in an atom is always the same. For this reason, you can determine the identity of an atom from the number of protons it contains. The *atomic number* is equal to the number of protons in an atom's nucleus.

Atoms and the Properties of Matter

The properties of an atom are determined by the number of protons in the atom's nucleus and by its electrons. The electrons outside the nucleus can interact with the electrons of other atoms. Atoms, in turn, determine the properties of matter. The kind, number, and arrangement of atoms in a substance all determine the substance's properties.

Figure 8 shows two different substances made from carbon and oxygen atoms. Carbon dioxide is a colorless gas that we exhale. Carbon monoxide, with one carbon atom and one oxygen atom, is also a colorless gas. But, carbon monoxide and carbon dioxide differ in other properties. Carbon dioxide is used to smother fires and is harmless to humans. Carbon monoxide is toxic and flammable. Even though they are both composed of atoms of oxygen and carbon, carbon dioxide and carbon monoxide are different.

The water shown in **Figure 9** is composed of one oxygen atom and two hydrogen atoms. Water's unique properties come from the properties of these atoms and the way that they are arranged.

Benchmark Check Why do carbon dioxide and carbon monoxide have different properties? **A.2.3.2 CS**

Figure 9 *Water's properties are due to the kind, number, and arrangement of its atoms.*

A.2.3.2 CS knows the general properties of the atom (a massive nucleus of neutral neutrons and positive protons surrounded by a cloud of negative electrons) and accepts that single atoms are not visible.

Summary

- Two properties of matter are volume and mass. **A.1.3.1 AA**
- Volume is the amount of space taken up by an object.
- Mass is the amount of matter in an object.
- Weight is a measure of the gravitational force on an object, usually in relation to the Earth. It is different from mass. **A.1.3.2**

- Atoms are the building blocks of matter. They are made of protons, neutrons, and electrons. **A.2.3.2 CS**
- There are many different kinds of atoms. The kind, number, and arrangement of atoms determine a substance's properties.
- Atoms are made up of three subatomic particles: protons, neutrons, and electrons.

Understanding Key Ideas

1. Which of the following is matter?
   - **a.** dust
   - **b.** the moon
   - **c.** strand of hair
   - **d.** all of the above

2. A graduated cylinder is used to measure
   - **a.** volume.
   - **b.** weight.
   - **c.** mass.
   - **d.** inertia.

3. Which is a subatomic particle?
   - **a.** proton
   - **b.** neutron
   - **c.** electron
   - **d.** all of the above

4. The mass of an atom is mostly
   - **a.** in the nucleus.
   - **b.** in the electrons.
   - **c.** spread evenly in the atom.
   - **d.** not present.

5. Explain the relationship between mass and weight. **A.1.3.2**

Math Skills

6. A nugget of gold is placed in a graduated cylinder that contains 80 mL of water. The water level rises to 225 mL after the nugget is added to the cylinder. What is the volume of the gold nugget?

Critical Thinking

7. **Identifying Relationships** Do objects with large masses always have large weights? Explain.

8. **Applying Concepts** Would an elephant weigh more or less on the moon than it weighs on Earth? Explain your answer.

FCAT Preparation

9. Lynell has been asked to measure the volume of an unknown liquid. What tool should she use to accomplish this task? **A.1.3.1 AA**
   - **A.** a graduated cylinder
   - **B.** a scale
   - **C.** a computer
   - **D.** a thermometer

10. Atoms are composed of three different subatomic particles: electrons, protons, and neutrons. Based on the information in the table below, which two particles would be attracted to one another? **A.2.3.2 CS**

	Charge	Location	Mass (amu)
proton	positive	nucleus	1
neutron	neutral	nucleus	1
electron	negative	outside nucleus	0

   - **F.** protons and neutrons
   - **G.** neutrons and electrons
   - **H.** electrons and protons
   - **I.** All subatomic particles repel one another.

For a variety of links related to this chapter, go to www.scilinks.org

Topic: What Is Matter?
SciLinks code: HSM1662

Physical Properties

Have you ever played the game 20 Questions? The goal of this game is to figure out what object another person is thinking of by asking 20 or fewer yes-or-no questions.

If you can't figure out the object's identity after asking 20 questions, you may not be asking the right kinds of questions. What kinds of questions should you ask? You may want to ask questions about the physical properties of the object. Knowing the properties of an object can help you find out what it is.

Physical Properties

The questions in **Figure 1** help someone gather information about color, odor, mass, and volume. Each piece of information is a physical property of matter. A **physical property** of matter can be observed or measured without changing the matter's identity. For example, you don't have to change an apple's identity to see its color or to measure its volume.

Other physical properties, such as magnetism, the ability to conduct electric current, strength, and flexibility, can help someone identify how to use a substance. For example, think of a scooter with an electric motor. The magnetism produced by the motor is used to convert energy stored in a battery into energy that will turn the wheels.

Benchmark Check List four physical properties. **A.1.3.1 AA**

physical property a characteristic of a substance that does not involve a chemical change, such as density, color, or hardness

Could I hold it in my hand? **Yes.**
Does it have an odor? **Yes.**
Is it safe to eat? **Yes.**
Is it orange? **No.**
Is it yellow? **No.**
Is it red? **Yes.**
Is it an apple? **Yes!**

Figure 1 *Asking questions about the physical properties of an object can help you identify it.*

Figure 2 Examples of Physical Properties

Thermal conductivity (KAHN duhk TIV uh tee) is the rate at which a substance transfers heat. Plastic foam is a poor conductor.

State is the physical form in which a substance exists, such as a solid, liquid, or gas. Ice is water in the solid state.

Density is the mass-per-unit volume of a substance. Lead is very dense, so it makes a good sinker for a fishing line.

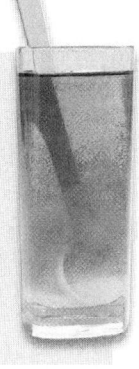

Solubility (SAHL yoo BIL uh tee) is the ability of a substance to dissolve in another substance. Flavored drink mix dissolves in water.

Ductility (duhk TIL uh tee) is the ability of a substance to be pulled into a wire. Copper is often used to make wiring because it is ductile.

Malleability (MAL ee uh BIL uh tee) is the ability of a substance to be rolled or pounded into thin sheets. Aluminum can be rolled into sheets to make foil.

Identifying Matter

You use physical properties every day. For example, physical properties help you determine if your socks are clean (odor), if your books will fit into your backpack (volume), or if your shirt matches your pants (color). **Figure 2** gives more examples of physical properties.

Density

Density is a physical property that describes the relationship between mass and volume. **Density** is the amount of matter in a given space, or volume. A golf ball and a table-tennis ball, such as those in **Figure 3,** have similar volumes. But a golf ball has more mass than a table-tennis ball does. So, the golf ball has a greater density.

density the ratio of the mass of a substance to the volume of the substance

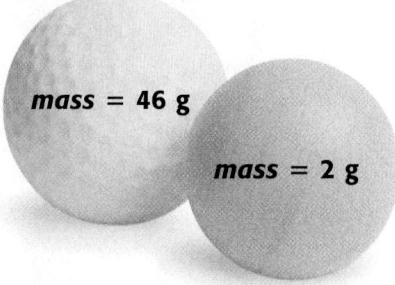

Figure 3 *A golf ball is denser than a table-tennis ball because the golf ball contains more matter in a similar volume.*

mass = 46 g

mass = 2 g

A.1.3.1 AA identifies various ways in which substances differ (e.g., mass, volume, shape, density, texture, and reaction to temperature and light).

Figure 4 *This graduated cylinder contains six liquids. From top to bottom, they are corn oil, water, shampoo, dish detergent, antifreeze, and maple syrup.*

Liquid Layers

What do you think causes the liquid in **Figure 4** to look the way it does? Is it trick photography? No, it results from differences in density! There are six liquids in the graduated cylinder. Each liquid has a different density. If the liquids are carefully poured into the cylinder, they can form six layers because of the differences in density. The densest layer is on the bottom. The least dense layer is on top. The order of the layers shows the order of increasing density. The yellow layer is the least dense, followed by the layers that are colorless red, blue, green, and brown (the densest).

Density of Solids

Which would you rather carry around all day, a kilogram of lead or a kilogram of feathers? At first, you might say feathers. But the feathers and the lead have the same mass, just as the cotton balls and the tomatoes shown in **Figure 5** have the same mass. So, the lead would be less awkward to carry around than the feathers would. The feathers are much less dense than the lead. So, it takes a lot of feathers to equal the same mass of lead.

Knowing the density of a substance can also tell you if the substance will float or sink in water. If the density of an object is less than the density of water, the object will float. Likewise, a solid object whose density is greater than the density of water will sink when the object is placed in water.

Reading Check What will happen to an object placed in water if the object's density is less than water's density?

Figure 5 *The cotton balls and the tomatoes have the same mass. But cotton is much less dense than the tomatoes.*

Solving for Density

To find an object's density (D), first measure its mass (m) and volume (V). Then, use the equation below.

$$D = \frac{m}{V}$$

Units for density consist of a mass unit divided by a volume unit. Some units for density are g/cm^3, g/mL, kg/m^3, and kg/L. Remember that the volume of a solid is often given in cubic centimeters or cubic meters. So, the density of a solid should be given in units of g/cm^3 or kg/m^3.

Using Density to Identify Substances

Density is a useful physical property for identifying substances. Each substance has a density that differs from the densities of other substances. And the density of a substance is always the same at a given temperature and pressure. Look at **Table 1** to compare the densities of several common substances.

Table 1 Densities of Common Substances*

Substance	Density* (g/cm^3)	Substance	Density* (g/cm^3)
Helium (gas)	0.00001663	Zinc (solid)	7.13
Oxygen (gas)	0.001331	Silver (solid)	10.50
Water (liquid)	1.00	Lead (solid)	11.35
Pyrite (solid)	5.02	Mercury (liquid)	13.55

*at 20°C and 1.0 atm

Calculating Density What is the density of an object whose mass is 25 g and whose volume is 10 cm^3?

Step 1: Write the equation for density.

$$D = \frac{m}{V}$$

Step 2: Replace m and V with the measurements given in the problem, and solve.

$$D = \frac{25 \text{ g}}{10 \text{ cm}^3} = 2.5 \text{ g/cm}^3$$

The equation for density can also be rearranged to find mass and volume, as shown.

$m = D \times V$ (Rearrange by multiplying by V.)

$V = \frac{m}{D}$ (Rearrange by dividing by D.)

Now It's Your Turn

1. Find the density of a substance that has a mass of 45 kg and a volume of 43 m^3. (Hint: Make sure your answer's units are units of density.)
2. Suppose that you have a lead ball whose mass is 454 g. What is the ball's volume? (Hint: Use **Table 1** above.)
3. What is the mass of a 15 mL sample of mercury?

Figure 6 Examples of Physical Changes

Changing from a solid to a liquid is a physical change. All changes of state are physical changes.

This aluminum can has gone through the physical change of being crushed. The properties of the can are the same.

Physical Changes

physical change a change of matter from one form to another without a change in chemical properties

A **physical change** is a change that affects one or more physical properties of a substance. Imagine that a piece of silver is pounded and molded into a heart-shaped pendant. This change is a physical one because only the shape of the silver has changed. The piece of silver is still silver. Its properties are the same. **Figure 6** shows more examples of physical changes.

Benchmark Check What is a physical change? Give one example to illustrate your answer. **A.1.3.5 CS**

Examples of Physical Changes

Freezing water to make ice cubes and sanding a piece of wood are examples of physical changes. These changes do not change the identities of the substances. Ice is still water, and sawdust is still wood. Another interesting physical change takes place when certain substances dissolve in other substances. For example, when you dissolve sugar in water, the sugar seems to disappear. But if you heat the mixture, the water evaporates. Then, you will see that the sugar is still there. The sugar went through a physical change when it dissolved.

CONNECTION TO Geology

WRITING SKILL **Erosion** Erosion of soil is a physical change. Soil erodes when wind and water move soil from one place to another. Research the history of the Grand Canyon. Write a one-page report about how erosion formed the Grand Canyon.

A.1.3.5 CS (partial) knows the difference between a physical change in a substance (i.e., altering the shape, form, volume, or density) and a chemical change (i.e., producing new substances with different characteristics).

Matter and Physical Changes

Physical changes do not change the identity of the matter involved. A stick of butter can be melted and poured over a bowl of popcorn, as shown in **Figure 7**. Although the shape of the butter has changed, the butter is still butter, so a physical change has occurred. In the same way, if you make a figure from a lump of clay, you change the clay's shape and cause a physical change. But the identity of the clay does not change. The properties of the figure are the same as those of the lump of clay.

Figure 7 *Melting butter for popcorn involves a physical change.*

SECTION Review

Summary

- Physical properties of matter can be observed without changing the identity of the matter.

- Examples of physical properties are conductivity, state, malleability, ductility, solubility, and density. **A.1.3.1 AA**

- Density is the amount of matter in a given space.

- Density is used to identify substances because the density of a substance is always the same at a given pressure and temperature.

- Examples of physical changes are freezing, cutting, bending, dissolving, and melting.

- When a substance undergoes a physical change, its identity stays the same. **A.1.3.5 CS**

Understanding Key Ideas

1. The units of density for a rectangular piece of wood are
   a. grams per milliliter.
   b. cubic centimeters.
   c. kilograms per liter.
   d. grams per cubic centimeter.

2. Describe what happens to a substance when it goes through a physical change. **A.1.3.5 CS**

3. Name six physical properties. **A.1.3.1 AA**

4. List six physical changes that matter can undergo. **A.1.3.5 CS**

Math Skills

5. What is the density of an object that has a mass of 350 g and a volume of 95 cm³?

Critical Thinking

6. **Applying Concepts** How can you determine that a coin is not pure silver if you know the mass and volume of the coin?

7. **Identifying Relationships** What physical property do the following substances have in common: water, oil, mercury, and alcohol?

FCAT Preparation

8. The density of an object is 5 g/cm³, and the volume of the object is 10 cm³. What is the mass of the object? **A.1.3.1 AA**
   A. 0.5 g
   B. 2 g
   C. 5 g
   D. 50 g

9. Which of the following is a valid example of a physical change? **A.1.3.5 CS**
   F. rusting metal
   G. digesting food
   H. freezing water
   I. burning paper

Chemical Properties

How would you describe a piece of wood before and after it is burned? Has it changed color? Does it have the same texture? The original piece of wood changed, and physical properties alone can't describe what happened to it.

chemical property a property of matter that describes a substance's ability to participate in chemical reactions

Chemical Properties

Physical properties are not the only properties that describe matter. **Chemical properties** describe matter based on its ability to change into new matter that has different properties. For example, when wood is burned, ash and smoke are created. These new substances have very different properties than the original piece of wood had. Wood has the chemical property of flammability. *Flammability* is the ability of a substance to burn. Ash and smoke cannot burn, so they have the chemical property of *nonflammability*.

Another chemical property is reactivity. *Reactivity* is the ability of two or more substances to combine and form one or more new substances. The photo of the old car in **Figure 1** illustrates reactivity and nonreactivity.

Benchmark Check How are reactivity and chemical properties related? **A.1.3.1 AA**

Figure 1 **Reactivity with Oxygen**

The iron used in this old car has the chemical property of **reactivity with oxygen**. When iron is exposed to oxygen, it rusts.

The bumper on this car still looks new because it is coated with chromium. Chromium has the chemical property of **nonreactivity with oxygen**.

Figure 2 Physical Versus Chemical Properties

Physical Property	Chemical Property

Shape Bending an iron nail will change its shape.

Reactivity with Oxygen An iron nail can react with oxygen in the air to form iron oxide, or rust.

State Rubbing alcohol is a clear liquid at room temperature.

Flammability Rubbing alcohol is able to burn easily.

A.1.3.1 AA identifies various ways in which substances differ (e.g., mass, volume, shape, density, texture, and reaction to temperature and light).

Comparing Physical and Chemical Properties

How do you tell a physical property from a chemical property? You can observe physical properties without changing the identity of the substance. For example, you can find the density and hardness of wood without changing anything about the wood.

Chemical properties, however, aren't as easy to observe. For example, you can see that wood is flammable only while it is burning. And you can observe that gold is nonflammable only when it won't burn. But a substance always has chemical properties. A piece of wood is flammable even when it's not burning. **Figure 2** shows examples of physical and chemical properties.

Characteristic Properties

The properties that are most useful in identifying a substance are *characteristic properties*. These properties are always the same no matter what size the sample is. Characteristic properties can be physical properties, such as density and solubility, as well as chemical properties, such as flammability and reactivity. Scientists rely on characteristic properties to identify and classify substances.

CONNECTION TO Social Studies

WRITING SKILL **The Right Stuff** When choosing materials to use in manufacturing, you must make sure that their properties are suitable for their uses. For example, false teeth can be made from acrylic plastic, porcelain, or gold. According to legend, George Washington wore false teeth made of wood. Do research, and find out what Washington's false teeth were really made of. In your **science journal**, write a paragraph about what you have learned. Include information about the advantages of the materials used in modern false teeth.

Chemical Changes and New Substances

A **chemical change** happens when one or more substances are changed into new substances that have new and different properties. Chemical changes and chemical properties are not the same. Chemical properties of a substance describe which chemical changes will occur and which chemical changes will not occur. Chemical change is the process by which substances actually change into new substances. You can learn about the chemical properties of a substance by looking at the chemical changes that take place.

You see chemical changes more often than you may think. For example, a chemical reaction happens every time a battery is used. When the chemicals fail to react, a dead battery results. Chemical changes also take place within your body when the food you eat is digested. **Figure 3** describes other examples of chemical changes.

Reading Check How does a chemical change differ from a chemical property?

Figure 3 **Examples of Chemical Changes**

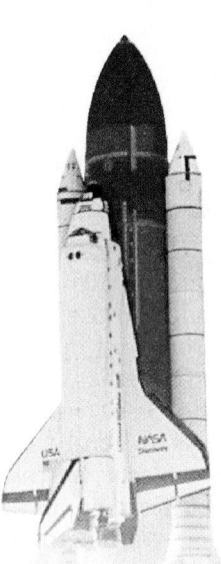

Soured milk smells bad because bacteria have formed new substances in the milk.

Effervescent tablets bubble when the citric acid and baking soda in them react in water.

The **hot gas** formed when hydrogen and oxygen join to make water helps blast the space shuttle into orbit.

The **Statue of Liberty** is made of orange-brown copper but looks green because the metal has interacted with moist air. New copper compounds formed, and these chemical changes made the statue turn green over time.

Figure 4 *Each of the original ingredients has different physical and chemical properties than the final product, the cake, does!*

What Happens During a Chemical Change?

A fun way to see what happens during chemical changes is to bake a cake. You combine eggs, flour, sugar, and other ingredients, as shown in **Figure 4.** When you bake the batter, you end up with something completely different. The heat of the oven and the interaction of the ingredients cause a chemical change. The result is a cake that has properties that differ from the properties of the ingredients.

Signs of Chemical Changes

Look back at **Figure 3.** In each picture, at least one sign indicates a chemical change. Other signs that indicate a chemical change include a change in color or odor, production of heat, fizzing and foaming, and sound or light being given off.

In the cake example in **Figure 4,** you would smell the cake as it baked. You would also see the batter rise and begin to brown. When you cut the finished cake, you would see the air pockets made by gas bubbles that formed in the batter. These signs show that chemical changes have happened.

Matter and Chemical Changes

Chemical changes alter the identity of the matter involved. So, most of the chemical changes that occur in your daily life, such as a cake baking, would be hard to reverse. Imagine trying to unbake a cake. However, some chemical changes can be reversed by more chemical changes. For example, the water formed in the space shuttle's rockets could be split into hydrogen and oxygen by using an electric current.

chemical change a change that occurs when one or more substances change into entirely new substances with different properties

Physical Scientist Biographies Write a biography about a physical scientist. Go to **go.hrw.com,** and type in the keyword **HP5STAW.**

Figure 5 Physical and Chemical Changes

Change in Texture Grinding baking soda into a fine, powdery substance is a physical change.

Reactivity with Vinegar Gas bubbles are produced when vinegar is poured into baking soda.

Physical Versus Chemical Changes

The most important question to ask when trying to decide if a physical or chemical change has happened is, Did the composition change? The *composition* of an object is the type of matter that makes up the object and the way that the matter is arranged in the object. **Figure 5** shows both a physical and a chemical change.

A Change in Composition

Physical changes do not change the composition of a substance. For example, water is made of two hydrogen atoms and one oxygen atom. Whether water is a solid, liquid, or gas, its composition is the same. But chemical changes do alter the composition of a substance. For example, through a process called *electrolysis,* water is broken down into hydrogen and oxygen gases. The composition of water has changed, so you know that a chemical change has taken place.

CONNECTION TO Environmental Science

Acid Rain When fossil fuels are burned, a chemical change takes place. Sulfur from fossil fuels and oxygen from the air combine to produce sulfur dioxide, a gas. When sulfur dioxide enters the atmosphere, it undergoes another chemical change by interacting with water and oxygen. Research this chemical reaction. Make a poster describing the reaction and showing how the final product affects the environment.

ACTIVITY

Physical or Chemical Change?

1. Watch as your teacher places a burning **wooden stick** into a **test tube.** Record your observations.

2. Place a mixture of **powdered sulfur** and **iron filings** on a **sheet of paper.** Place a **bar magnet** underneath the paper, and try to separate the iron from the sulfur.

3. Drop an **effervescent tablet** into a **beaker of water.** Record your observations.

4. Identify whether each change is a physical change or a chemical change. Explain your answers.

A.1.3.5 CS knows the difference between a physical change in a substance (i.e., altering the shape, form, volume, or density) and a chemical change (i.e., producing new substances with different characteristics).

Reversing Changes

Many physical changes are easily reversed. They do not change the composition of a substance. For example, if an ice cube melts, you could freeze the liquid water to make another ice cube. But composition does change in a chemical change. So, most chemical changes are not easily reversed. Look at **Figure 6.** The chemical changes that happen when a firework explodes would be almost impossible to reverse, even if you collected all of the materials made in the chemical changes.

Benchmark Check What is the difference between a chemical and a physical change? **A.1.3.5 CS**

Figure 6 *This display of fireworks in Miami represents many chemical changes happening at the same time.*

SECTION Review

Summary

- Chemical properties describe a substance based on its ability to change into a new substance that has different properties. **A.1.3.1 AA**

- Chemical properties can be observed only when a chemical change might happen.

- Examples of chemical properties are flammability and reactivity.

- New substances form as a result of a chemical change.

- Unlike a chemical change, a physical change does not alter the identity of a substance. **A.1.3.5 CS**

Using Key Terms

1. Write an original definition for *chemical property* and *chemical change*.

Understanding Key Ideas

2. Write two examples of chemical properties, and explain what they are. **A.1.3.1 AA**

3. The Statue of Liberty was originally a copper color. After being exposed to the air, the statue turned a greenish color. What kind of change happened? Explain your answer.

4. Explain how to tell the difference between a physical and a chemical property.

Critical Thinking

5. **Making Comparisons** Describe the difference between physical and chemical changes in terms of what happens to the matter involved in each kind of change. **A.1.3.5 CS**

6. **Applying Concepts** Identify two physical properties and two chemical properties of a bag of microwave popcorn before popping and after popping.

FCAT Preparation

7. Rebecca and Joaquim are studying chemical and physical changes. Following the procedures in their lab manual, they make several observations. What observation would best verify that a chemical change has taken place? **A.1.3.5 CS**

   A. The amount of the substance has changed.

   B. The shape of the substance has changed.

   C. A new substance has formed.

   D. The substance has changed from a liquid to a gas.

SCILINKS®

NSTA
Developed and maintained by the National Science Teachers Association

For a variety of links related to this chapter, go to www.scilinks.org

Topic: Chemical Changes
SciLinks code: HSM0266

Interactions of Matter

It's a clear day in the Everglades, and you're surrounded by clumps of grass. But when you step down, your foot sinks into the moist ground and water seeps into your shoe!

Clearly, no average vehicle is going to transport you through this wetland. To get around the Everglades, people use airboats like the one shown in **Figure 1.** Airboats convert the chemical energy stored in gasoline into mechanical energy that moves the boat forward.

Energy

Like the airboat, you rely on energy. Without energy, you wouldn't be able to move, blink, breathe, or live! **Energy** is the ability to do work. Energy is not a form of matter, because it does not have mass or volume. However, energy is involved in every interaction of matter.

Energy has many forms and effects. For example, you know that energy in the form of heat caused the ice cream in **Figure 2** to melt. The law of **conservation of energy** states that energy cannot be created or destroyed. Energy can only be changed from one form to another or transferred. As the ice cream melts, energy is not destroyed. The heat energy is converted into energy of motion as the molecules in ice cream move faster and the ice cream turns from a solid into a liquid.

Benchmark Check What is the law of conservation of energy?
B.2.3.1 AA

energy the capability to do work

conservation of energy the law that states that energy cannot be created or destroyed but can be changed from one form to another *FCAT VOCAB*

B.2.3.1 AA knows that most events in the universe involve some form of energy transfer and that these changes almost always increase the total disorder of the system and its surroundings, reducing the amount of useful energy.

Figure 1 *Airboats, like most vehicles, convert chemical energy into mechanical energy in order to move.*

Role of Energy in Physical Change

There are many forms of energy. **Potential energy** is the energy an object has as a result of its position, shape, or condition. The textbook sitting on your desk has potential energy because of its position above the ground. If the textbook were to fall, it would have **kinetic energy**, the energy of motion.

Even objects that seem perfectly still have some kinetic energy. The atoms or molecules that make up a substance are in constant motion. The combined kinetic energy of all atoms or molecules in a substance is that substance's **thermal energy.** Thermal energy is an important factor in how matter undergoes physical change.

Energy and Changes of State

An object's thermal energy helps to determine its physical state. The three most common states of matter are solid, liquid, and gas. A substance can change from one physical state to another when its thermal energy changes. The ice cream in **Figure 2** melted as it sat in the sunlight. The sunlight caused the thermal energy of the ice cream to increase. **Figure 3** shows how the physical state of water changes as the temperature increases. Thermal energy is often measured as temperature. As the temperature of water increases, water changes from solid (ice) to liquid and then to gas (steam). When you add thermal energy to an ice cube, you increase the movement of its water molecules. As the molecules move faster and faster, they move farther apart from one another. At a certain point, the molecules are moving fast enough that a physical change of state occurs. Remember that no new substances are formed as water changes physical state.

Figure 2 *Energy is involved in the physical change that takes place when ice cream melts.*

potential energy the energy that an object has because of the position, shape, or condition of the object **FCAT** *VOCAB*

kinetic energy the energy of an object that is due to the object's motion

thermal energy the kinetic energy of a substance's atoms **FCAT** *VOCAB*

Figure 3 **Changing the State of Water**

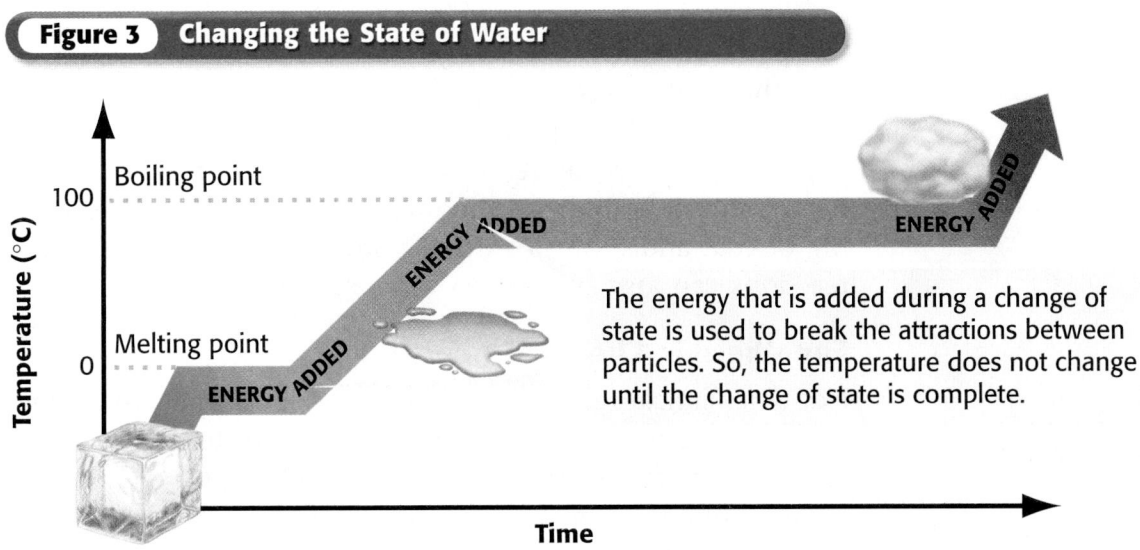

The energy that is added during a change of state is used to break the attractions between particles. So, the temperature does not change until the change of state is complete.

Figure 4 **Energy and Chemical Change**

The instant cold pack in this picture becomes cold when an endothermic reaction occurs inside. The *endothermic reaction* absorbs energy.

As the fuel in this blowtorch is burned, heat and light are released. A change that releases energy is called an *exothermic reaction*.

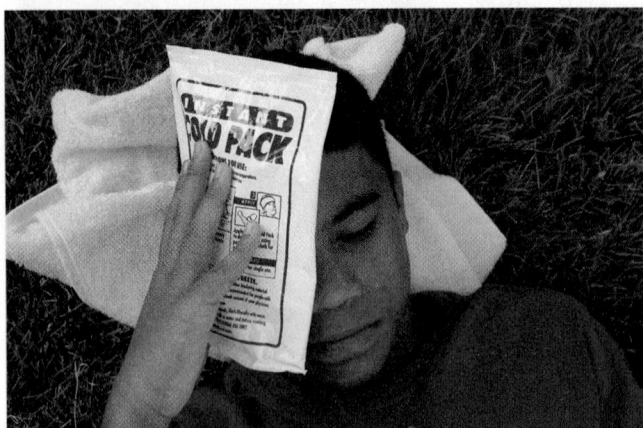

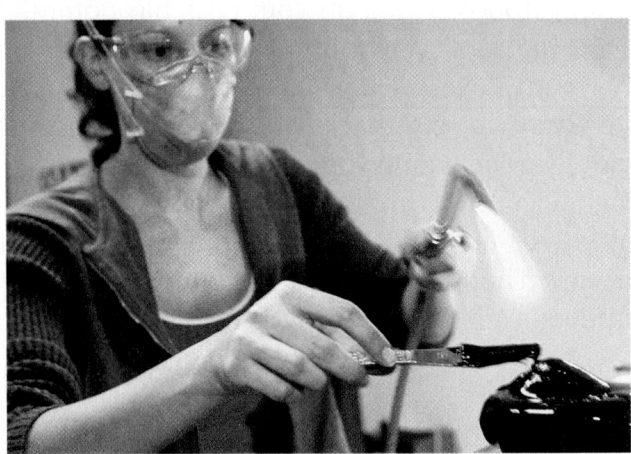

Role of Energy in Chemical Change

Energy plays a role in all changes. In a physical change, no new substance is formed. Chemical changes are different. In a chemical change, or *reaction*, energy is involved in the rearrangement of atoms. New substances are formed in a chemical reaction. For example, in **Figure 4,** the blue flame is evidence of a chemical reaction. In the ignited blowtorch, fuel and oxygen undergo a chemical reaction. During the reaction, the atoms in both substances are rearranged and energy is released in the form of light and heat. This energy was not created. It was released as the fuel reacted with oxygen and the energy that had been stored in the chemical bonds changed form.

entropy a measure of the randomness or disorder of a system
FCAT VOCAB

Benchmark Check Describe the difference between a physical and a chemical change in terms of how energy is used. **A.1.3.5 CS**

Exothermic Chemical Reaction

The chemical reaction that occurs in a blowtorch is an *exothermic reaction* because it releases energy. The energy released during an exothermic reaction can take many forms, such as heat, light, or sound. Exothermic reactions such as the burning of coal and other fossil fuels provide us with heat. These reactions can also be used to generate electricity.

Endothermic Chemical Reaction

Not all chemical reactions release energy. Some absorb energy. A chemical reaction that absorbs energy is called an *endothermic reaction*. The cold pack, shown in **Figure 4,** relies on an endothermic reaction between two chemicals to work. Photosynthesis, a reaction in plants, is an endothermic reaction.

A.1.3.5 CS knows the difference between a physical change in a substance (i.e., altering the shape, form, volume, or density) and a chemical change (i.e., producing new substances with different characteristics).

Change, Energy, and Disorder

So far, you've learned that energy is involved in the interactions of matter. You've also learned that energy is never created or destroyed, but it can be transferred from one form to another. Even though energy cannot be destroyed, energy can sometimes be transferred into a form that cannot be used to do work. Some of the thermal energy generated by the lawn mower in **Figure 5** cannot be used to do work. Instead, this energy is lost as noise and heat.

Most processes result in an increase in randomness or disorder. Think about a sparkler, a hand-held firework. Once lit, the sparkler releases its stored energy as light and heat. Small, dark flakes and smoke are given off as it burns. No matter how hard you try, you cannot use the sparkler again nor can you put the sparkler back together again. **Entropy** is a measure of randomness or disorder. The sparkler's entropy increases as it burns.

 **Benchmark Check** What is entropy? **B.2.3.1 AA**

Figure 5 *The heat and noise released by the chemical reaction in this lawn mower cannot be used to do work.*

B.2.3.1 AA knows that most events in the universe involve some form of energy transfer and that these changes almost always increase the total disorder of the system and its surroundings, reducing the amount of useful energy.

SECTION Review

Summary

- Energy is never created or destroyed but it can be transferred. **B.2.3.1 AA**
- Energy is involved in most interactions of matter. **B.2.3.1 AA**
- During a change of physical state, the thermal energy of a substance changes. **A.1.3.5 CS**
- Energy is involved in the rearrangement of atoms in a chemical change. **A.1.3.5 CS**

Understanding Key Terms

1. Use *conservation of energy*, *thermal energy*, and *entropy* in separate sentences. **FCAT VOCAB**

2. Write an original definition for *potential energy*. **FCAT VOCAB**

Understanding Key Ideas

3. How is energy involved in the physical change of liquid water to ice? **B.2.3.1 AA**

4. How is energy involved in a physical change? **B.2.3.1 AA**

Critical Thinking

5. **Analyzing Ideas** Energy cannot be created or destroyed. Where does the light and heat from burning wood come from?

6. **Identifying Relationships** Compare the role of energy in a chemical change to the role of energy in a physical change. **A.1.3.5 CS**

FCAT Preparation

7. In an engine, fuel and oxygen chemically react and release energy. What happens to the energy not used by the engine? **B.2.3.1 AA**

   A. It has been destroyed.

   B. It is lost in the form of heat and sound.

   C. It remains stored in the chemical bonds of the fuel.

   D. It is converted into methane.

SCi LINKS®

NSTA
Developed and maintained by the National Science Teachers Association

For a variety of links related to this chapter, go to www.scilinks.org

Topic: What Is Energy?
SciLinks code: HSM1660

Skills Practice Lab

White Before Your Eyes

OBJECTIVES

Describe the physical properties of four substances. A.1.3.1 AA

Identify physical and chemical changes. A.1.3.5 CS

Classify four substances by their chemical properties.

You have learned how to describe matter based on its physical and chemical properties. You have also learned some signs that can help you determine whether a change in matter is a physical change or a chemical change. In this lab, you'll use what you have learned to describe four substances based on their properties and the changes that they undergo.

Procedure

1 Copy Table 1 and Table 2, shown on the next page. Be sure to leave plenty of room in each box to write down your observations.

2 Using a spatula, place a small amount of baking powder into three cups of your egg carton. Use just enough baking powder to cover the bottom of each cup. Record your observations about the baking powder's appearance, such as color and texture, in the "Unmixed" column of Table 1.

MATERIALS

- baking powder
- baking soda
- carton, egg, plastic-foam
- cornstarch
- eyedroppers (3)
- iodine solution
- spatulas (4)
- stirring rod
- sugar
- vinegar
- water

SAFETY

A.1.3.1 AA identifies various ways in which substances differ (e.g., mass, volume, shape, density, texture, and reaction to temperature and light).

A.1.3.5 CS knows the difference between a physical change in a substance (i.e., altering the shape, form, volume, or density) and a chemical change (i.e., producing new substances with different characteristics).

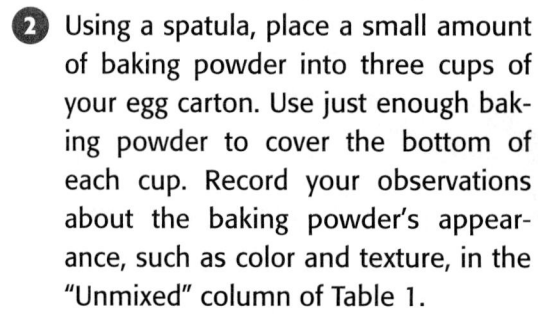

3 Use an eyedropper to add 60 drops of water to the baking powder in the first cup. Stir with the stirring rod. Record your observations in Table 1 in the column labeled "Mixed with water." Clean your stirring rod.

4 Use a clean dropper to add 20 drops of vinegar to the second cup of baking powder. Stir. Record your observations in Table 1 in the column labeled "Mixed with vinegar." Clean your stirring rod.

5 Use a clean dropper to add 5 drops of iodine solution to the third cup of baking powder. Stir. Record your observations in Table 1 in the column labeled "Mixed with iodine solution." Clean your stirring rod. **Caution:** Be careful when using iodine. Iodine will stain your skin and clothes.

6 Repeat steps 2–5 for each of the other substances (baking soda, cornstarch, and sugar). Use a clean spatula for each substance.

Analyze the Results

1 **Examining Data** What physical properties do all four substances share?

2 **Analyzing Data** In Table 2, write the type of change—physical or chemical—that you observed for each substance. State the property that the change demonstrates.

Draw Conclusions

3 **Evaluating Results** Classify the four substances by the chemical property of reactivity. For example, which substances are reactive with vinegar (acid)?

Table 1 Observations				
Substance	Unmixed	Mixed with water	Mixed with vinegar	Mixed with iodine solution
Baking powder				
Baking soda		DO NOT WRITE IN BOOK		
Cornstarch				
Sugar				

Table 2 Changes and Properties						
	Mixed with water		Mixed with vinegar		Mixed with iodine solution	
Substance	Change	Property	Change	Property	Change	Property
Baking powder						
Baking soda		DO NOT WRITE IN BOOK				
Cornstarch						
Sugar						

Chapter Review

USING KEY TERMS

For each pair of terms, explain how the meanings of the terms differ.

1 *mass* and *weight* **FCAT** VOCAB

2 *proton* and *electron* **FCAT** VOCAB

3 *volume* and *density*

UNDERSTANDING KEY IDEAS

Multiple Choice

4 Which of the following properties is NOT a chemical property?

a. reactivity with oxygen
b. malleability
c. flammability
d. reactivity with acid

5 The volume of a liquid can be expressed in all of the following units EXCEPT **A.1.3.1 AA**

a. grams.
b. liters.
c. milliliters.
d. cubic centimeters.

6 The best way to measure the volume of an irregularly shaped solid is to **A.1.3.1 AA**

a. use a ruler to measure the length of each side of the object.
b. weigh the solid on a balance.
c. use the water displacement method.
d. use a spring scale.

7 Which of the following statements about weight is true? **A.1.3.2**

a. Weight is a measure of the gravitational force on an object.
b. Weight varies depending on where the object is located in relation to the Earth.
c. Weight is measured by using a spring scale.
d. All of the above

8 Which of the following statements does NOT describe a physical property of a piece of chalk?

a. Chalk is a solid.
b. Chalk can be broken into pieces.
c. Chalk is white.
d. Chalk will bubble in vinegar.

9 Density is an important physical property of matter. It is used to distinguish one kind of matter from another. Which of the following statements about density is true? **A.1.3.1 AA** *FCAT*

a. Density is expressed in grams.
b. Density is mass-per-unit volume.
c. Density is expressed in milliliters.
d. Density is a chemical property.

10 Entropy is a measure of randomness or disorder. When energy transfers occur during physical and chemical changes, what typically happens to the amount of entropy? **B.2.3.1 AA** *FCAT*

a. Entropy increases.
b. Entropy decreases.
c. Entropy remains the same.
d. Entropy increases and then returns to normal.

Short Answer

11 In one or two sentences, explain how the process of measuring the volume of a liquid differs from the process of measuring the volume of a solid.

12 What is the difference between potential and kinetic energy? *FCAT VOCAB*

13 List three characteristic properties of matter.

Math Skills

14 What is the volume of a book that has a width of 10 cm, a length that is 2 times the width, and a height that is half the width? Remember to express your answer in cubic units. **A.1.3.1 AA** *FCAT*

15 A jar contains 30 mL of glycerin (whose mass is 37.8 g) and 60 mL of corn syrup (whose mass is 82.8 g). Which liquid is on top? Show your work, and explain your answer.

CRITICAL THINKING

Extended Response

16 Applying Concepts Develop a set of questions that would be useful when identifying an unknown substance. The substance may be a liquid, a gas, or a solid. **A.1.3.1 AA**

17 Analyzing Processes You are making breakfast for your friend Filbert. When you take the scrambled eggs to the table, he asks, "Would you please poach these eggs instead?" What scientific reason do you give Filbert for not changing his eggs?

18 Analyzing Ideas You may sometimes hear on the radio or on TV that astronauts are weightless in space. Explain why this statement is not true. **A.1.3.2**

Concept Mapping

19 Use the following terms to create a concept map: *matter, mass, inertia, volume, milliliters, cubic centimeters, weight,* and *gravity.*

INTERPRETING GRAPHICS

Use the photograph below to answer the questions that follow.

20 List three physical properties of this aluminum can.

21 When this can was crushed, did it undergo a physical change or a chemical change? **A.1.3.5 CS**

22 How does the density of the metal in the crushed can compare with the density of the metal before the can was crushed?

23 Describe the role of energy in the change that occurred when the can was crushed. **B.2.3.1 AA**

For the following questions, write your answers on a separate sheet of paper.

1 Fish require liquid water to survive. In northern climates, cold weather makes rivers freeze. In spite of this, fish are able to find running water underneath the ice. What property of water causes ice to float on top of liquid water?

    A. Its volume increases as it boils.

    B. Its volume increases as it freezes.

    C. Its temperature increases as it melts.

    D. Its temperature increases as energy is added.

2 Different atoms of an element that have nuclei with different masses are isotopes. The isotope of uranium used as a fuel to generate electrical energy is less dense than the main uranium isotope found in natural ores. What is the main difference between uranium isotopes?

    F. number of atoms

    G. number of protons

    H. number of neutrons

    I. number of electrons

3 Allison put some ice in her hot tea. After the ice melted, she was able to drink her tea. What describes the change that took place?

    A. The usable energy of the system increased.

    B. A new substance formed as the ice changed.

    C. The average density of the system decreased.

    D. A physical change occurred as the ice melted.

4 Chemical and physical changes are continuously occurring. One kind of change which humans rely on for many things is combustion. Combustion is occurring when a log burns in a fireplace. Which of the following statements about the process of combustion is true?

    F. Combustion is an endothermic reaction.

    G. The entropy of the system increases as the log burns.

    H. The energy released by the log's combustion is gradually destroyed.

    I. The mass of all products of the combustion is less than that of the log.

5  Some thermometers contain mercury. A particular thermometer contains 0.68 grams (g) of mercury. The density of mercury at a given temperature is 13.6 grams per cubic centimeter (g/cm^3). What is the volume of mercury inside the thermometer at this temperature? Express your answer in cubic centimeters (cm^3).

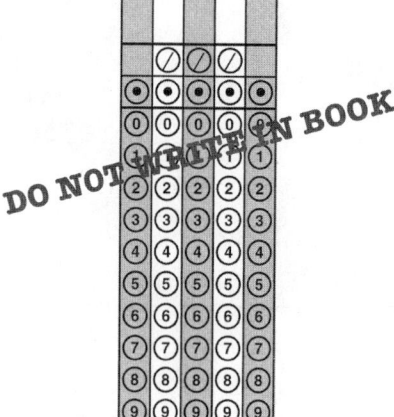

6 A lunar rover is a little car that transports astronauts on the surface of the Moon. Much less effort is needed to lift the rover on the Moon than is needed to lift the rover on Earth. Explain what is different about the rover on the Moon and what stays the same.

7 In most events in the universe, energy is transformed or converted. For example, a car's engine burns fuel in order to power the car. Is all of the energy generated by the car's engine used to do work? Explain your answer.

Science in Action

Weird Science

Diamonds from the Lab

Imagine making diamonds from your pencil! Gemesis Corporation grows gem-quality diamonds from graphite, the form of carbon commonly found in pencils. The company combines a small amount of graphite, a seed diamond, and a catalyst into a small pill. This capsule is placed in a huge pressure cooker and subjected to intense pressure. A process that takes millions of years in nature is accomplished in five days in the Lakewood Ranch, Florida laboratory. Each month, roughly 150 yellow diamonds are made. The yellow color is caused by the presence of a few atoms of nitrogen.

Language Arts ACTiViTY

WRITING SKILL Research how natural diamonds form. Write a short story about a diamond that traces all the experiences the gem has had since it was made.

Science, Technology, and Society

Building a Better Body

Have you ever broken a bone? If so, you probably wore a cast while the bone healed. But what happens if the bone is too damaged to heal? Sometimes, a false bone made from titanium can replace the damaged bone. Titanium appears to be a great bone-replacement material. It is a lightweight but strong metal. It can attach to existing bone and resists chemical changes. But, friction can wear away titanium bones. Research has found that implanting a form of nitrogen on the titanium makes the metal last longer.

Social Studies ACTiViTY

Do some research on bone-replacement therapy. Make a poster that shows a timeline of events leading up to current technology.

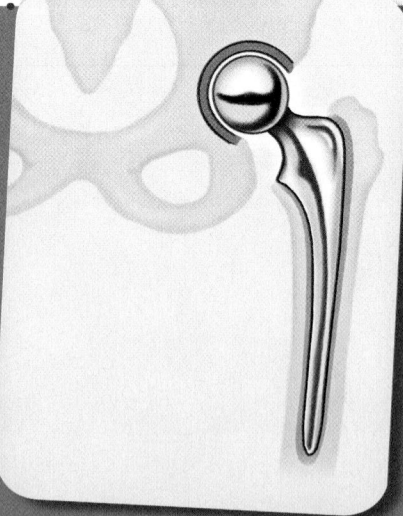

Mimi So

Gemologist and Jewelry Designer A typical day for gemologist and jewelry designer Mimi So involves deciding what materials to work with. When she chooses a gemstone for a piece of jewelry, she must consider the size, hardness, color, grade, and cut of the stone. When choosing a metal to use as a setting for a stone, she must look at the hardness, melting point, color, and malleability of the metal. She needs to choose a metal that not only looks good with a particular stone but also has physical properties that will work with that stone. For example, Mimi So says that emeralds are soft and fragile. A platinum setting would be too hard and could damage the emerald. So, emeralds are usually set in a softer metal, such as 18-karat gold.

The chemical properties of stones must also be considered. Heating can burn or discolor some gemstones. Mimi So says, "If you are using pearls in a design that requires heating the metal, the pearl is not a stone, so you cannot heat the pearl, because it would destroy the pearl."

Math ACTiViTY

Pure gold is 24 karats (24K). Gold that contains 18 parts gold and 6 parts other metals is 18-karat gold. The percentage of gold in 18K gold is found by dividing the amount of gold by the total amount of the material and then multiplying by 100%. For example, (18 parts gold)/(24 parts total) = 0.75 × 100% = 75% gold. Find the percentage of gold in 10K and 14K gold.

To learn more about these Science in Action topics, visit **go.hrw.com** and type in the keyword **HT6FMF7F**.

Current Science

Check out Current Science® articles related to this chapter by visiting go.hrw.com. Just type in the keyword HP5CS02.

22

Forces and Work

 **The Big Idea** A machine is a device that makes work easier by changing the size or direction of a force.

About the PHOTO

"One, two, stroke!" shouts the coach as the team races to the finish line. These paddling teams are competing in Hong Kong's annual Dragon Boat Races. The Dragon Boat Festival is a 2,000-year-old Chinese tradition that commemorates Qu Yuan, a national hero. The contestants are using paddles to move their boats forward. Even though they are celebrating by racing their dragon boats, these paddlers are, in scientific terms, doing work.

PRE-READING ACTIVITY

FOLDNOTES **Booklet** Before you read the chapter, create the FoldNote entitled "Booklet" described in the **Study Skills** section of the Appendix. Label each page of the booklet with a main idea from the chapter. As you read the chapter, write what you learn about each main idea on the appropriate page of the booklet.

START-UP ACTIVITY

C'mon, Lever a Little! C.2.3.4 CS

In this activity, you will use a simple machine, a lever, to make your task a little easier.

Procedure

1. Stack **two books,** one on top of the other, on a **table.**

2. Slide your index finger underneath the edge of the bottom book. Using only the force of your finger, try to lift one side of the books 2 or 3 cm off the table. Is it hard to do so? Write your observations.

3. Slide the end of a **wooden ruler** underneath the edge of the bottom book. Then, slip a **large pencil eraser** or similar object under the ruler.

4. Again, using only your index finger, push down on the edge of the ruler and try to lift the books. Record your observations. **Caution:** Push down slowly to keep the ruler and eraser from flipping.

Analysis

1. Which was easier: lifting the books with your finger or lifting the books with the ruler? Explain your answer.

2. In what way did the direction of the force that your finger applied on the books differ from the direction of the force that your finger applied on the ruler?

Forces

A hockey player's stick slaps a puck into the net. A train's engine pulls 200 cars of coal. A magnet attracts an iron nail. A leaf falls from a tree. What do these events have in common? They are examples of how forces result in motion.

Anytime you see a change in an object's motion, you have observed a force in action. Sometimes, the cause of a force is clear, such as when you kick a soccer ball. Other times, the cause of a force cannot be seen, such as when a leaf falls to the ground.

What Is a Force?

A **force** is a push or a pull. Forces can cause an object to move or change its speed or direction. The SI unit of force is called the *newton* (N). One newton of force is equal to the force exerted by Earth's gravity on an object that has a mass of 100 g. One newton is about one-fifth of a pound.

Forces can be organized into two types. One type of force involves direct contact. This type of force is called a *contact force*. In **Figure 1,** the wind is exerting a contact force on the sailboats. The other type of force acts at a distance. For example, in **Figure 1,** the Earth's gravitational force is pulling down on the sailboats.

force a push or a pull exerted on an object in order to change the motion of the object; force has size and direction

Figure 1 *Wind is exerting a contact force on the sail of each sailboat. Gravity is acting at a distance to hold the sailboats at Earth's surface.*

Figure 2 Contact Forces

This soccer player is exerting a contact force on the soccer ball.

This skydiver is affected by air resistance, which is a form of friction.

Contact Forces

A *contact force* is a force that results from physical contact between two objects. Contact forces happen only between objects that are touching. Two examples of contact forces are the force that a bat exerts on a baseball and the force that a car's tires exert on a road. Some other examples of contact forces are shown in **Figure 2.**

Friction, Tension, and Buoyant Force

Three important contact forces are friction, tension, and buoyant force. *Friction* is a force that opposes motion between two surfaces that are touching. For example, when you push a heavy box across the floor, friction opposes the motion of the box. So, you have to push the box even harder to move it. *Tension* is another contact force. Tension occurs when a force pulls against the materials that make up an object. For example, the cables on a bridge exert tension on the supports of the bridge. This tension makes the bridge strong. *Buoyant force* is an upward force exerted on an object by a fluid that the object is in. When the buoyant force pushing up on an object is equal to the force of gravity pulling down on the object, the object will float. If the force of gravity on the object is greater than the buoyant force on the object, the object will sink.

C.2.3.2 knows common contact forces.

C.2.3.1 CS knows that many forces (e.g., gravitational, electrical, and magnetic) act at a distance (i.e., without contact).

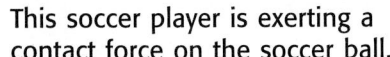 **Benchmark Check** Describe friction, tension, and buoyant force. **C.2.3.2**

Forces That Act at a Distance

When a force acts at a distance, objects do not have to touch each other to exert the force. Gravity, electric force, and magnetic force are examples of forces that can act at a distance.

Gravity, Magnetic Force, and Electric Force

Gravity is a force of attraction between objects that is due to the masses of the objects. Gravity between the sun and the planets holds the planets in orbit around the sun. Magnetic force is the force exerted by magnetized objects. A compass needle aligns with Earth's magnetic field because magnetic force acts at a distance. Electric force is the force of attraction or repulsion between charged particles. For example, if you rub a balloon with a piece of wool, you can see how electric force causes the balloon to be attracted to objects.

 **Benchmark Check** Describe forces that act at a distance. **C.2.3.1 CS**

Forces Acting in the Same Direction

When more than one force acts on an object, predicting how the object will be affected can be difficult. To calculate the effect of many forces, scientists use the concept of net force. **Net force** is the combination of all of the forces that act on an object. Calculating the net force when forces act in the same direction is easy. In this case, you add up the forces that are acting on the object. For example, the kids in **Figure 3** are trying to move a sofa. If the girl is pushing with a force of 450 N to the right and the boy is pulling with a force of 400 N to the right, the net force is 850 N to the right.

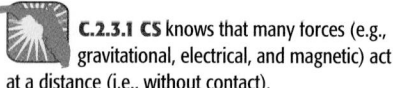 **net force** the combination of all of the forces acting on an object

C.2.3.1 CS knows that many forces (e.g., gravitational, electrical, and magnetic) act at a distance (i.e., without contact).

Figure 3 *When forces act in the same direction, the net force is the sum of the forces.*

Opposing Forces

When forces act in opposite directions, they are called *opposing forces.* Opposing forces can be balanced or unbalanced. To calculate net force when forces are opposing, subtract the smaller force from the larger force. The net force is in the direction of the larger force.

Balanced Forces

When the net force on an object is 0 N, the forces on the object are balanced. When forces are balanced, the motion of an object does not change. For example, **Figure 4** shows an example of two forces that are acting on an object in opposite directions. If the force of the boy pulling on the remote control is equal to the force of the girl pulling on the remote control, the forces are balanced and the net force is 0 N.

Unbalanced Forces

When the net force on an object is greater than 0 N, the forces are unbalanced. Imagine that the boy in **Figure 4** is pulling on the remote control with a force of 200 N to the right. But the girl is pulling on the remote control with a force of 250 N to the left. When you subtract the smaller force from the larger force, the result is 50 N to the left. Because the girl is pulling with a larger force, the remote control moves toward her.

Benchmark Check How is net force calculated when forces act on an object in opposite directions? **C.2.3.6 AA**

Benchmark Activity

Identifying Balanced and Unbalanced Forces

When two forces act on an object, the result can be a balanced or unbalanced force. Look in newspapers and magazines to find photographs that show balanced and unbalanced forces. Cut out the photographs, and paste them to a piece of poster board. Use a marker to draw arrows that indicate the forces in each photograph. **C.2.3.3, C.2.3.6 AA**

C.2.3.3 knows that if more than one force acts on an object, then the forces can reinforce or cancel each other, depending on their direction and magnitude.

C.2.3.6 AA explains and shows the ways in which a net force (i.e., the sum of all acting forces) can act on an object.

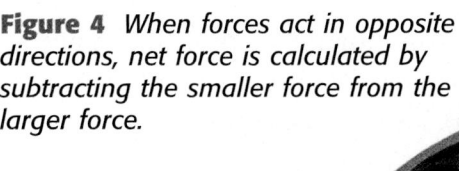

Figure 4 *When forces act in opposite directions, net force is calculated by subtracting the smaller force from the larger force.*

Figure 5 *Because the bowling ball has more inertia than the bowling pins do, the bowling ball will knock over the pins.*

inertia the tendency of an object to resist being moved or, if the object is moving, to resist a change in speed or direction until an outside force acts on the object FCAT VOCAB

C.2.3.5 understands that an object in motion will continue at a constant speed and in a straight line until acted upon by a force and that an object at rest will remain at rest until acted upon by a force.

Inertia and Motion

If you have ever stubbed your toe, you have experienced inertia. If the object you stubbed your toe on didn't move, then the object had more inertia than your foot did. **Inertia** is the tendency of an object to resist any change in motion. An object's inertia is related to the object's mass. The greater an object's mass is, the greater the object's inertia is. As **Figure 5** shows, inertia affects objects that are moving and objects that are not moving. The bowling ball is moving, and the bowling pins are not moving. The ball and the pins are affected by inertia.

Objects at Rest

Objects that are not moving, such as bowling pins, are said to be at rest. Because of inertia, the bowling pins will remain at rest until an unbalanced force acts on them. In other words, objects will not move unless an unbalanced push or pull is exerted on them.

Objects in Motion

An object that is in motion, such as a bowling ball, will stay in motion without changing its speed or direction until an unbalanced force acts on the object. As a bowling ball rolls down the lane, it has a lot of inertia. Therefore, the direction and speed of the bowling ball changes very little. When the bowling ball strikes the bowling pins, it will knock down the bowling pins because the bowling ball has more inertia than the bowling pins do. However, when the bowling ball reaches the back of the lane, an unbalanced force causes the bowling ball to stop moving.

Inertia and Friction

If inertia causes moving objects to stay in motion, why does a ball that is rolling on the ground eventually stop even if the ball does not hit anything? The ball stops because the unbalanced force of friction acts on the ball. The force of friction acts on nearly all moving objects. For example, the baseball player in **Figure 6** relies on friction to slow him down as he slides into a base. It is important to consider the force of friction when designing any machine that has moving parts.

Benchmark Check How do friction and inertia affect moving objects? **C.2.3.5**

Figure 6 *Friction slows this baseball player as he slides into the base.*

SECTION Review

Summary

- Three common contact forces are friction, tension, and buoyant force. **C.2.3.2**
- Gravity, electrical force, and magnetic force are three forces that act at a distance. **C.2.3.1 CS**
- When forces are acting in the same direction, net force can be calculated by adding the forces. **C.2.3.3, C.2.3.6 AA**
- When forces are acting in opposite directions, net force can be calculated by subtracting the smaller force from the larger force. **C.2.3.3, C.2.3.6 AA**
- If the net force is 0, forces are balanced. If the net force is greater than 0, the forces are unbalanced. **C.2.3.3**
- Inertia is the tendency of an object to resist any change in motion. **C.2.3.5**

Using Key Terms

1. Use *inertia, force,* and *net force* in separate sentences. **FCAT VOCAB**

Understanding Key Ideas

2. Describe three common contact forces, and list examples of each force. **C.2.3.2**

3. Describe three forces that act at a distance, and list examples of each force. **C.2.3.1 CS**

4. What are balanced forces and unbalanced forces? **C.2.3.3**

5. How do you calculate net force when forces are acting in the same direction? **C.2.3.6 AA**

6. How do you calculate net force when forces are acting in opposite directions? **C.2.3.6 AA**

Critical Thinking

7. **Making Inferences** Do objects in orbit have inertia? Explain why or why not. **C.2.3.5**

8. **Predicting Consequences** How can three forces act on an object and result in a balanced force? **C.2.3.6 AA**

FCAT Preparation

9. During a tug of war, a team of students pulls with a force of 1,000 N to the right. Another team pulls with a force of 1,200 N to the left. What is the net force on the rope? **C.2.3.6 AA**

A. 2,200 N to the left

B. 200 N to the left

C. 200 N to the right

D. 2,200 N to the right

10. Many forces act at a distance. Which of the following is a force that acts at a distance? **C.2.3.1 CS**

F. buoyant force

G. electrical force

H. friction

I. tension

Developed and maintained by the National Science Teachers Association

For a variety of links related to this chapter, go to www.scilinks.org

Topic: Forces
SciLinks code: HSM0604

Work and Power

Your science teacher has just given you tonight's homework assignment. You have to read an entire chapter by tomorrow! That sounds like a lot of work!

Actually, in the scientific sense, you won't be doing much work at all! How can that be? In science, **work** is done when a force causes an object to move in the direction of the force. In the example above, you may have to put a lot of mental effort into doing your homework, but you won't be using force to move anything. So, in the scientific sense, you will not be doing work—except the work to turn the pages of your book!

What Is Work?

The student in **Figure 1** is having a lot of fun, isn't she? But she is doing work even though she is having fun. She is doing work because she is applying a force to the bowling ball and making the ball move through a distance. However, she is doing work on the ball only as long as she is touching it. The ball will keep moving away from her after she releases it. But she will no longer be doing work on the ball because she will no longer be applying a force to it.

Transfer of Energy

Examine the girl with the bowling ball in **Figure 1.** One way that you can tell that the bowler has done work on the bowling ball is that the ball now has *kinetic energy.* This means that the ball is moving. The bowler has transferred energy to the ball.

Differences Between Force and Work

Applying a force doesn't always result in work being done. Suppose that you help push a stalled car. You push and push, but the car doesn't budge. The pushing may have made you tired. But you haven't done any work on the car, because the car hasn't moved.

You do work on the car as soon as the car moves. Whenever you apply a force to an object and the object moves in the direction of the force, you have done work on the object.

✓ **Reading Check** Is work done every time a force is applied to an object? Explain.

Figure 1
You might be surprised to find out that bowling is work!

Force and Motion in the Same Direction

Suppose that you are in an airport and are late for a flight. You have to run through the airport carrying a heavy suitcase. Because you are making the suitcase move, you are doing work on it, right? Wrong! For work to be done on an object, the object must move in the *same direction* as the force. You are applying a force to hold the suitcase up, but the suitcase is moving forward. So, no work is done on the suitcase. But work *is* done on the suitcase when you lift it off the ground.

Work is done on an object if two things happen: (1) the object moves as a force is applied and (2) the direction of the object's motion is the same as the direction of the force. The pictures and arrows in **Figure 2** will help you understand when work is being done on an object.

work the transfer of energy to an object by using a force that causes the object to move in the direction of the force

Figure 2 Work or Not Work?

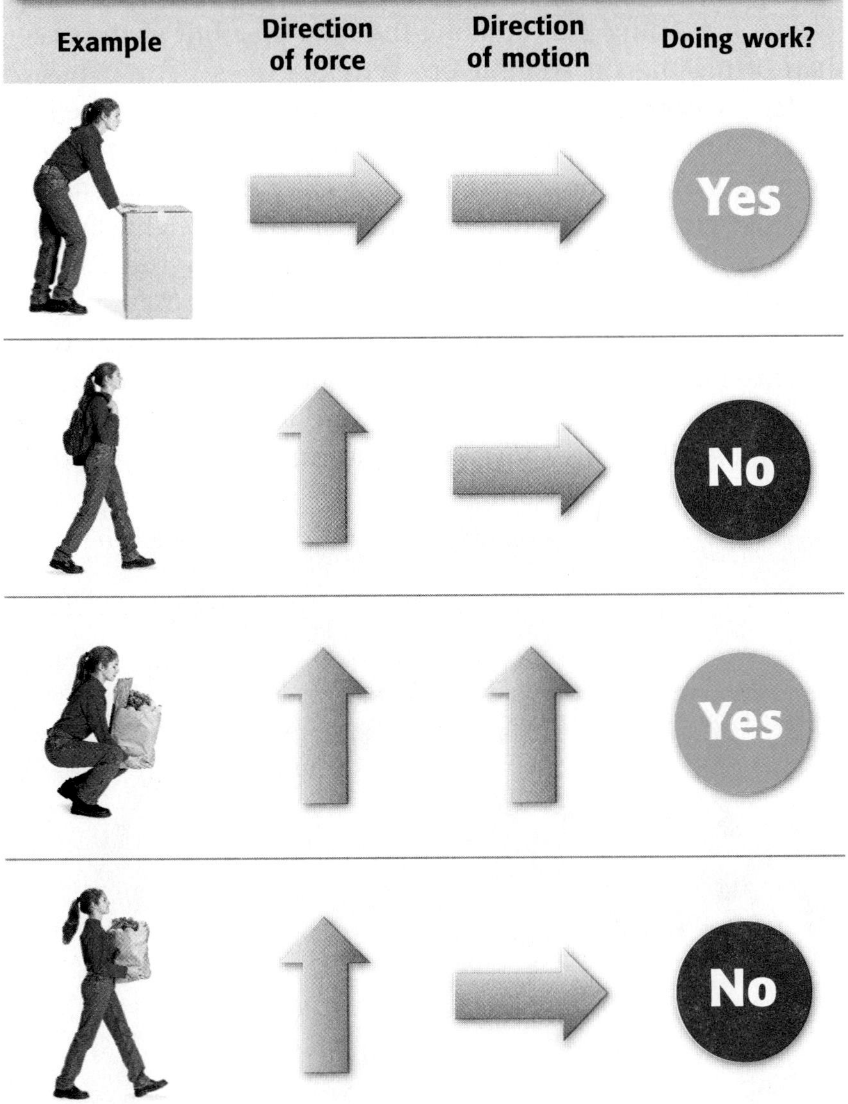

Example	Direction of force	Direction of motion	Doing work?
	→	→	Yes
	↑	→	No
	↑	↑	Yes
	↑	→	No

CONNECTION TO Biology

WRITING SKILL **Work in the Human Body**

You may not be doing any work on a suitcase if you are just holding it in your hands, but your body will still get tired from the effort because you are doing work on the muscles inside your body. Your muscles can contract thousands of times in just a few seconds while you try to keep the suitcase from falling. What other situations can you think of that might involve work being done somewhere inside your body? Describe these situations in your **science journal**.

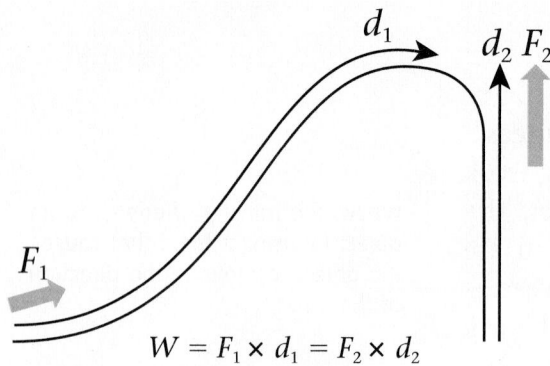

$$W = F_1 \times d_1 = F_2 \times d_2$$

Figure 3 *For each path, the same work is done to move the car to the top of the hill, although distance and force along the two paths differ.*

How Much Work?

Would you do more work on a car by pushing it up a long road to reach the top of a hill or by using a cable to raise the car up the side of a cliff to the top of the same hill? You would certainly need different amounts of force. Common use of the word *work* may make you think that different amounts of work would be done in the two cases, too.

Same Work, Different Forces

You may be surprised to learn that the amount of work done to push the car up a road is the same as the amount of work done to raise the car up the cliff. Look at **Figure 3.** A certain amount of energy is needed to move the car from the bottom to the top of the hill. Because the car ends up at the same place either way, the work done on the car is the same. However, pushing the car along the road up a hill seems easier than lifting the car straight up. Why?

The reason is that work depends on distance as well as force. Consider a mountain climber who reaches the top of a mountain by climbing straight up a cliff, as in **Figure 4.** She must use enough force to overcome her entire weight. But the distance that she travels up the cliff is shorter than the distance traveled by hikers who reach the top of the same mountain by walking up a slope. In both cases, the same amount of work is done. But the hikers going up a slope don't need to use as much force as they would if they were to go straight up the side of the cliff. This shows how you can use less force to do the same amount of work.

Figure 4 *Climbers going to the top of a mountain do the same amount of work whether they hike up a slope or go straight up a cliff.*

Calculating Work

To calculate the amount of work (W) done in moving an object, such as the barbell in **Figure 5,** you multiply the force (F) applied to the object by the distance (d) through which the force is applied, as shown in the following equation:

$$W = F \times d$$

Force is expressed in newtons, and the meter is the basic SI unit for length or distance. Therefore, the unit used to express work is the newton-meter (N × m), which is more simply called the **joule.** Because work is the transfer of energy to an object, the joule (J) is also the unit used to express energy.

joule the unit used to express energy; equivalent to the amount of work done by a force of 1 N acting through a distance of 1 m in the direction of the force (symbol, J)

✓ **Reading Check** How is work calculated?

Figure 5 **Force Times Distance**

W = 80 N × 1 m = 80 J

The force needed to lift an object is equal to the gravitational force on the object—in other words, the object's weight.

W = 160 N × 1 m = 160 J

If you increase the weight, an increased force is needed to lift the object. This increases the amount of work done.

W = 80 N × 2 m = 160 J

Increasing the distance also increases the amount of work done.

Get to Work!

1. Use a **loop of string** to attach a **spring scale** to a **weight.**

2. Slowly pull the weight across a **table** by dragging the spring scale. Record the amount of force that you exerted on the weight.

3. Use a **metric ruler** to measure the distance that you pulled the weight.

4. Now, use the spring scale to slowly pull the weight up a **ramp.** Pull the weight the same distance that you pulled it across the table.

5. Calculate the work that you did on the weight for both trials.

6. How were the amounts of work and force affected by the way you pulled the weight? What other ways of pulling the weight could you test?

Power: How Fast Work Is Done

power the rate at which work is done or energy is transformed

watt the unit used to express power; equivalent to a joule per second (symbol, W)

Like the term *work,* the term *power* is used a lot in everyday language but has a very specific meaning in science. **Power** is the rate at which energy is transferred.

Calculating Power

To calculate power (*P*), you divide the amount of work done (*W*) by the time (*t*) that it takes to do that work, as shown in the following equation:

$$P = \frac{W}{t}$$

Power is expressed in joules per second (J/s), also called **watts** (W). One watt is equal to 1 J/s. So, if you do 50 J of work in 5 s, your power is 10 J/s, or 10 W.

Power measures how fast work happens, or how quickly energy is transferred. When more work is done in a given amount of time, the power output is greater. Power output is also greater when the time that it takes to do a certain amount of work is decreased, as **Figure 6** shows.

Reading Check How is power calculated?

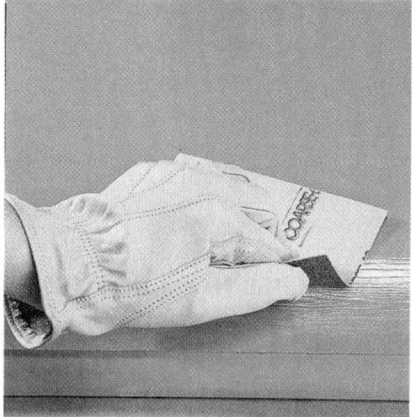 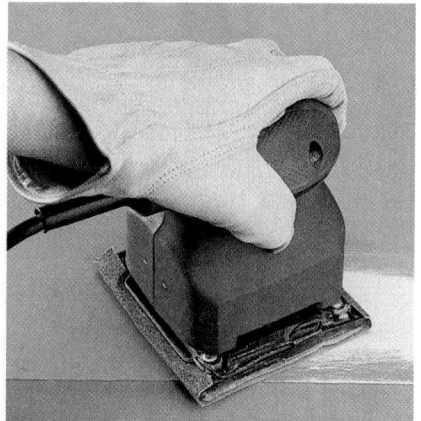

Figure 6 *No matter how fast you can sand by hand, an electric sander can do the same amount of work faster. Therefore, the electric sander has more power.*

More Power to You A stage manager at a play raises the curtain by doing 5,976 J of work on the curtain in 12 s. What is the power output of the stage manager?

Step 1: Write the equation for power.

$$P = \frac{W}{t}$$

Step 2: Replace *W* and *t* with work and time.

$$P = \frac{5,976\,\text{J}}{12\,\text{s}} = 498\ \text{W}$$

Now It's Your Turn

1. If it takes you 10 s to do 150 J of work on a box to move the box up a ramp, what is your power output?
2. A light bulb is on for 12 s. During that time, it uses 1,200 J of electrical energy. What is the wattage (power) of the light bulb?

Increasing Power

It may take you longer to sand a wooden shelf by hand than by using an electric sander, but the amount of energy needed is the same in each case. Only the power output is lower when you sand the shelf by hand (although your hand may get more tired). You could also dry your hair with a fan, but it would take a long time! A hair dryer is more powerful. It can give off energy more quickly than a fan does, so your hair dries faster.

Car engines are usually rated with a certain power output. The more powerful the engine is, the more quickly the engine can move a car. And for a given speed, a more powerful engine can move a heavier car than a less powerful engine can.

CONNECTION TO Language Arts

Horsepower The unit of power most commonly used to rate car engines is the horsepower (hp). Look up *horsepower* in a dictionary. How many watts are equal to 1 hp? Do you think that all horses output exactly 1 hp? Why or why not? Write your answers in your **science journal.**

SECTION Review

Summary

- In scientific terms, *work* is done when a force causes an object to move in the direction of the force.
- Work is calculated as force times distance. The unit of work is the newton-meter, or joule.
- *Power* is a measure of how fast work is done.
- Power is calculated as work divided by time. The unit of power is the joule per second, or watt.

Using Key Terms

For each pair of terms, explain how the meanings of the terms differ.

1. *work* and *joule*
2. *power* and *watt*

Understanding Key Ideas

3. How is work calculated?
   a. force times distance
   b. force divided by distance
   c. power times distance
   d. power divided by distance

4. What is the difference between work and power?

Math Skills

5. Using a force of 10 N, you push a shopping cart 10 m. How much work did you do?

6. If you did 100 J of work in 5 s, what was your power output?

Critical Thinking

7. **Analyzing Processes** Work is done on a ball when a pitcher throws the ball. Is the pitcher still doing work on the ball as it flies through the air? Explain.

FCAT Preparation

8. Most events in the universe involve the transfer of energy. However, energy transfer is never completely efficient and almost always increases the total disorder of a system. This disorder reduces the amount of useful energy in a system. Which of the following is an example of this idea? **B.2.3.1 AA**

   A. Power is the rate at which work is done.

   B. A car engine burns gasoline and becomes hot after running for several hours.

   C. A watt is a unit of power.

   D. A more powerful engine can move a heavier car than a less powerful engine can.

SCiLINKS.

NSTA
Developed and maintained by the National Science Teachers Association

For a variety of links related to this chapter, go to www.scilinks.org

Topic: Work and Power
SciLinks code: HSM1675

What Is a Machine?

You are in the car with your mom on the way to a party when suddenly—KABLOOM hisssss—a tire blows out. "Now I'm going to be late!" you think as your mom pulls over to the side of the road.

You watch as your mom opens the trunk and gets out a jack and a tire iron. Using the tire iron, she pries the hubcap off and begins to unscrew the lug nuts from the wheel. She then puts the jack under the car and turns the jack's handle several times until the flat tire no longer touches the ground. After exchanging the flat tire with the spare, she lowers the jack and puts the lug nuts and hubcap back on the wheel.

"Wow!" you think, "That wasn't as hard as I thought it would be." As your mom drops you off at the party, you think how lucky it was that she had the right equipment to change the tire.

Machines: Making Work Easier

Now, imagine changing a tire without the jack and the tire iron. Would it have been easy? No, you would have needed several people just to hold up the car! Sometimes, you need the help of machines to do work. A **machine** is a device that makes work easier by changing the size or direction of a force.

When you think of machines, you might think of things such as cars, big construction equipment, or even computers. But not all machines are complicated. In fact, you use many simple machines in your everyday life. **Figure 1** shows some examples of machines.

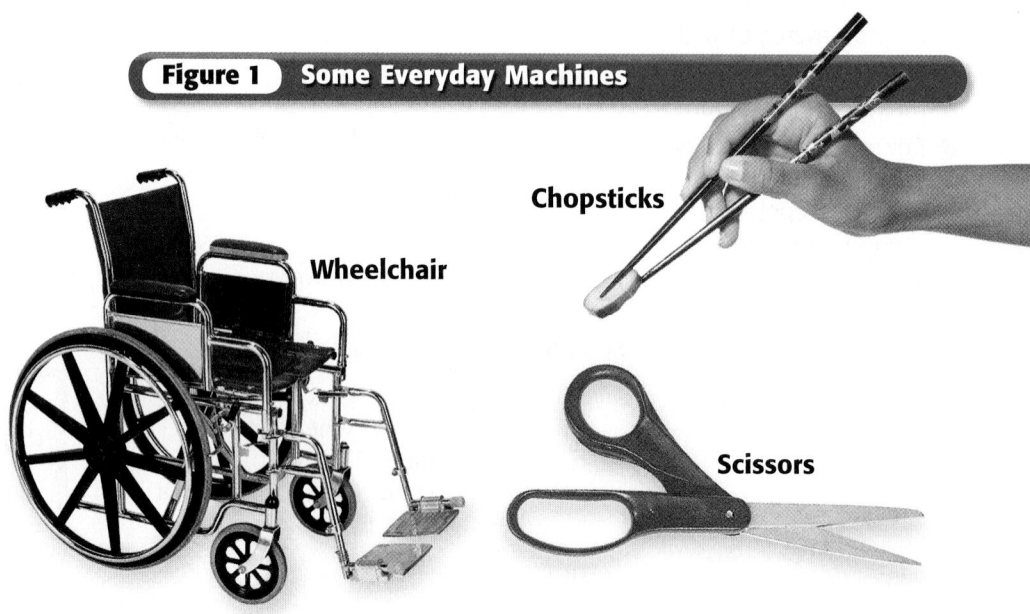

Figure 1 Some Everyday Machines

Wheelchair

Chopsticks

Scissors

Work In, Work Out

Suppose that you need to get the lid off a can of paint. What do you do? One way to pry the lid off is to use a common machine known as a *lever*. **Figure 2** shows a screwdriver being used as a lever. You place the tip of the screwdriver under the edge of the lid and then push down on the screwdriver's handle. The tip of the screwdriver lifts the lid as you push down. In other words, you do work on the screwdriver, and the screwdriver does work on the lid.

Work is done when a force is applied through a distance. Look again at **Figure 2.** The work that you do on a machine is called **work input.** You apply a force, called the *input force,* to the machine through a distance. The work done by the machine on an object is called **work output.** The machine applies a force, called the *output force,* through a distance.

How Machines Help

You might think that machines help you because they increase the amount of work done. But that's not true. If you multiplied the forces by the distances through which the forces are applied in **Figure 2** (remember that $W = F \times d$), you would find that the screwdriver does not do more work on the lid than you do on the screwdriver. Work output can never be greater than work input. Machines allow force to be applied over a greater distance, which means that less force will be needed for the same amount of work.

Reading Check How do machines make work easier?

machine a device that helps do work by either overcoming a force or changing the direction of the applied force

work input the work done on a machine; the product of the input force and the distance through which the force is exerted

work output the work done by a machine; the product of the output force and the distance through which the force is exerted

Output force

Input force

Figure 2 *When you use a machine, you do work on the machine and the machine does work on something else.*

C.2.3.4 CS knows that simple machines can be used to change the direction or size of a force.

Same Work, Different Force

Machines make work easier by changing the size or direction (or both) of the input force. When a screwdriver is used as a lever to open a paint can, both the size and direction of the input force change. Remember that using a machine does not change the amount of work that you will do. As **Figure 3** shows, the same amount of work is done with or without the ramp. The ramp decreases the size of the input force needed to lift the box but increases the distance over which the force is exerted. So, the machine allows a smaller force to be applied over a longer distance.

The Force-Distance Trade-Off

When a machine changes the size of the force, the distance through which the force is exerted must also change. Force or distance can increase, but both cannot increase. When one increases, the other must decrease.

Figure 4 shows how machines change force and distance. Whenever a machine changes the size of a force, the machine also changes the distance through which the force is applied. **Figure 4** also shows that some machines change only the direction of the force, not the size of the force or the distance through which the force is exerted.

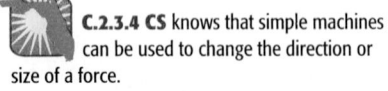

C.2.3.4 CS knows that simple machines can be used to change the direction or size of a force.

Benchmark Check What is the relationship between force and distance when a machine does work? **C.2.3.4 CS**

Figure 3 **Input Force and Distance**

Lifting this box straight up requires an input force equal to the weight of the box.

$$W = 450\ N \times 1 = 450\ J$$

Using a ramp to lift the box requires an input force less than the weight of the box, but the input force must be exerted over a greater distance than if you didn't use a ramp.

$$W = 150\ N \times 3\ m = 450\ J$$

Figure 4 Machines Change the Size and/or Direction of a Force

Input force

Output force

A nutcracker *increases* the force but applies it over a *shorter* distance.

A hammer *decreases* the force but applies it over a *greater* distance.

Output force

Input force

A simple pulley changes the *direction* of the input force, but the size of the output force is the same as the input force.

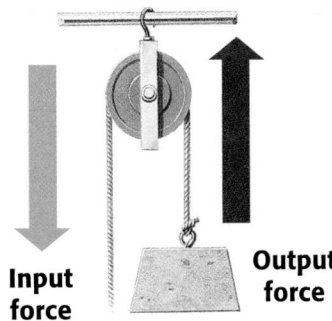

Input force

Output force

When a screwdriver is used as a lever, it *increases* the force and *decreases* the distance over which the force is applied.

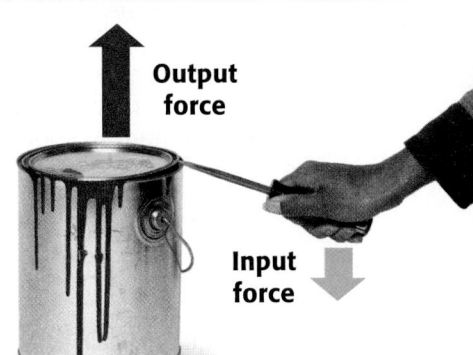

Output force

Input force

Mechanical Advantage

Some machines make work easier than others do because they can increase force more than other machines can. A machine's **mechanical advantage** is the number of times that the machine multiplies force. In other words, the mechanical advantage compares the input force with the output force.

mechanical advantage a number that tells how many times a machine multiplies force

Calculating Mechanical Advantage

You can find mechanical advantage by using the following equation:

$$mechanical\ advantage\ (MA) = \frac{output\ force}{input\ force}$$

For example, imagine that you had to push a 500 N weight up a ramp and only needed to push with 50 N of force the entire time. The mechanical advantage of the ramp would be calculated as follows:

$$MA = \frac{500\ N}{50\ N} = 10$$

A machine that has a mechanical advantage that is greater than 1 can help move or lift heavy objects because the output force is greater than the input force. A machine that has a mechanical advantage that is less than 1 will reduce the output force but can increase the distance that an object moves. **Figure 4** shows an example of such a machine—a hammer.

Finding the Advantage

A grocer uses a handcart to lift a heavy stack of canned food. Suppose that he applies an input force of 40 N to the handcart. The cart applies an output force of 320 N to the stack of canned food. What is the mechanical advantage of the handcart?

efficiency a quantity, usually expressed as a percentage, that measures the ratio of work output to work input *FCAT VOCAB*

mechanical efficiency a quantity, usually expressed as a percentage, that measures the ratio of work output to work input in a machine

B.1.3.4 CS knows that energy conversions are never 100% efficient (i.e., some energy is transformed to heat and is unavailable for further useful work).

Mechanical Efficiency

Comparing a system's work input with its work output can determine the **efficiency** of the system. The work output of a machine is always less than the work input. Why? Some of the work done by the machine is used to overcome the friction created by the use of the machine. But keep in mind that no work is lost. The work output plus the work done to overcome friction is equal to the work input.

The less work that a machine has to do to overcome friction, the more efficient the machine is. **Mechanical efficiency** (muh KAN i kuhl e FISH uhn see) is a comparison of a machine's work output with its work input.

Calculating Efficiency

A machine's mechanical efficiency is calculated by using the following equation:

$$mechanical\ efficiency = \frac{work\ output}{work\ input} \times 100$$

The 100 in this equation means that mechanical efficiency is expressed as a percentage. Mechanical efficiency tells you what percentage of the work input gets converted into work output.

Figure 5 shows a machine that is used to drill holes in metal. Some of the work input is used to overcome the friction between the metal and the drill. This energy cannot be used to do work on the steel block. Instead, it heats up the steel and the machine itself.

Benchmark Check Is the machine that is shown in Figure 5 100% efficient? **C.2.3.4 CS**

Figure 5 *In this machine, some of the work input is converted into sound and heat energy.*

Perfect Efficiency?

An *ideal machine* would be a machine that had 100% mechanical efficiency. An ideal machine's useful work output would equal the work done on the machine. Ideal machines are impossible to build, because every machine has moving parts. Moving parts always use some of the work input to overcome friction. But new technologies help increase efficiency so that more energy is available to do useful work. The train in **Figure 6** is floating on magnets, so there is almost no friction between the train and the tracks. Other machines use lubricants, such as oil or grease, to lower the friction between their moving parts, which makes the machines more efficient.

Figure 6 *There is very little friction between this magnetic levitation train and its tracks, so it is highly efficient.*

SECTION Review

Summary

- A machine makes work easier by changing the size or direction (or both) of a force. **C.2.3.4 CS**
- A machine can increase force or distance, but not both.
- Mechanical advantage tells how many times a machine multiplies force.
- Mechanical efficiency is a comparison of a machine's work output with its work input.
- Machines are not 100% efficient, because some of the work done is used to overcome friction. **B.1.3.4 CS**

Using Key Terms

For each pair of terms, explain how the meanings of the terms differ.

1. *work input* and *work output*

2. *mechanical advantage* and *efficiency* **FCAT VOCAB**

Understanding Key Ideas

3. Explain how using a ramp makes work easier. **C.2.3.4 CS**

4. Give a specific example of a machine, and describe how its mechanical efficiency might be calculated.

5. Why can't a machine be 100% efficient? **B.1.3.4 CS**

Critical Thinking

6. **Making Inferences** For a machine that has a mechanical advantage of 3, how does the distance through which the output force is exerted differ from the distance through which the input force is exerted?

7. **Analyzing Processes** Describe the effect of friction on a machine's mechanical efficiency. How do lubricants increase a machine's mechanical efficiency?

FCAT Preparation

8. A lever is a simple machine that is used to do work. Machines such as levers change the size and direction of a force. When a lever is used to open a paint can, the lever increases the force used. How does the distance over which the force is applied change? **C.2.3.4 CS**

A. The distance over which the force is applied increases.

B. The distance over which the force is applied decreases.

C. The distance over which the force is applied remains the same.

D. The distance over which the force is applied becomes 0 m.

Developed and maintained by the National Science Teachers Association

For a variety of links related to this chapter, go to www.scilinks.org

Topic: Mechanical Efficiency
SciLinks code: HSM0929

Types of Machines

Imagine that it's a hot summer day. You have a whole ice-cold watermelon in front of you. It would taste cool and delicious—if only you had a machine that could cut it!

The machine that you need is a knife. But how is a knife a machine? A knife is actually a very sharp wedge, which is one of the six simple machines. The six simple machines are the lever, the inclined plane, the wedge, the screw, the pulley, and the wheel and axle. All machines are made from one or more of these simple machines.

Levers

Have you ever used the claw end of a hammer to remove a nail from a piece of wood? If so, you were using the hammer as a lever. A **lever** is a simple machine that has a bar that pivots at a fixed point, called a *fulcrum*. Levers are used to apply a force to a load. There are three classes of levers, which are based on the locations of the fulcrum, the load, and the input force.

First-Class Levers

With a first-class lever, the fulcrum is between the input force and the load, as shown in **Figure 1.** First-class levers always change the direction of the input force. And depending on the location of the fulcrum, first-class levers can be used to increase force or to increase distance.

Figure 1 **Examples of First-Class Levers**

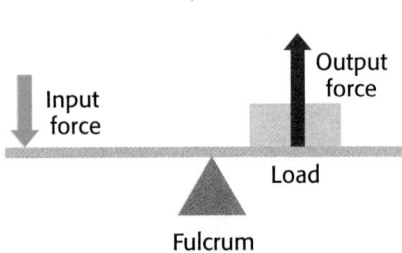

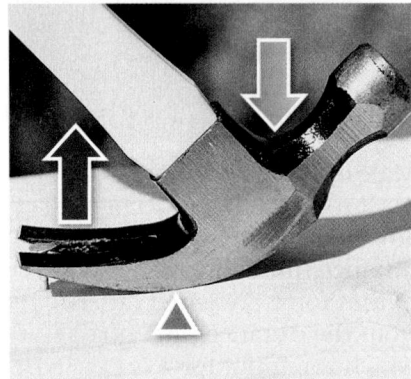

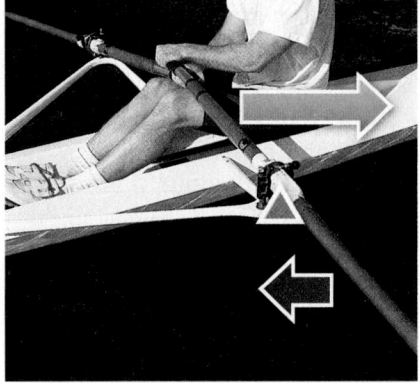

When the fulcrum is closer to the load than to the input force, the lever has a **mechanical advantage of greater than 1.** The output force increases because it is exerted over a shorter distance.

When the fulcrum is exactly in the middle, the lever has a **mechanical advantage of 1.** The output force does not increase because the input force's distance does not increase.

When the fulcrum is closer to the input force than to the load, the lever has a **mechanical advantage of less than 1.** Although the output force is less than the input force, distance increases.

Figure 2 Examples of Second-Class Levers

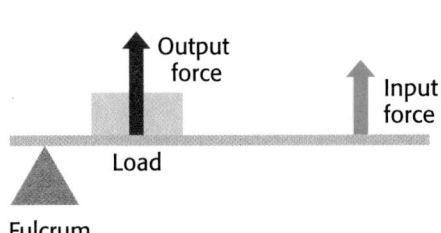
Output force
Input force
Load
Fulcrum

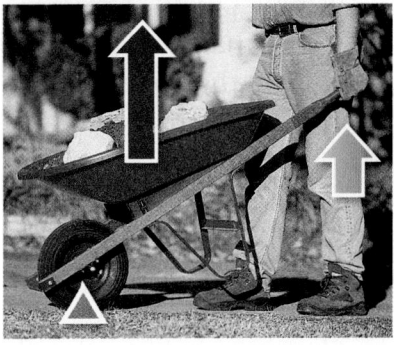

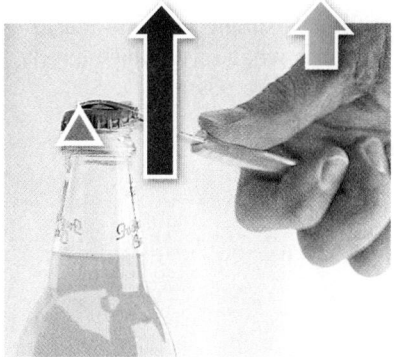

In a **second-class lever,** the output force, or load, is between the input force and the fulcrum.

Using a second-class lever results in a **mechanical advantage of greater than 1.** The closer the load is to the fulcrum, the greater the increase in the force and the greater the mechanical advantage.

Second-Class Levers

The load of a second-class lever is between the fulcrum and the input force, as shown in **Figure 2.** Second-class levers do not change the direction of the input force. But they allow you to apply less force than the force exerted by the load. Because the output force is greater than the input force, you must exert the input force over a greater distance.

lever a simple machine that consists of a bar that pivots at a fixed point called a *fulcrum*

Third-Class Levers

The input force in a third-class lever is between the fulcrum and the load, as shown in **Figure 3.** Third-class levers do not change the direction of the input force. In addition, they do not increase the input force. Therefore, the output force is always less than the input force.

Benchmark Check How do the three types of levers differ from one another? **C.2.3.4 CS**

C.2.3.4 CS knows that simple machines can be used to change the direction or size of a force.

Figure 3 Examples of Third-Class Levers

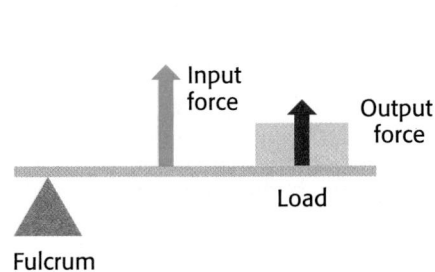
Input force
Output force
Load
Fulcrum

In a **third-class lever,** the input force is between the fulcrum and the load.

Using a third-class lever results in a **mechanical advantage of less than 1** because force decreases. But third-class levers increase the distance through which the output force is exerted.

Pulleys

pulley a simple machine that consists of a wheel over which a rope, chain, or wire passes

When you open window blinds by pulling on a cord, you're using a pulley. A **pulley** is a simple machine that has a grooved wheel that holds a rope or a cable. A load is attached to one end of the rope, and an input force is applied to the other end. Types of pulleys are shown in **Figure 4.**

Fixed Pulleys

A fixed pulley is attached to something that does not move. By using a fixed pulley, you can pull down on the rope to lift the load up. The pulley changes the direction of the force. Elevators make use of fixed pulleys.

Movable Pulleys

Unlike fixed pulleys, movable pulleys are attached to the object being moved. A movable pulley does not change a force's direction. Movable pulleys do increase force, but they also increase the distance over which the input force must be exerted.

Block and Tackles

When a fixed pulley and a movable pulley are used together, the pulley system is called a *block and tackle*. The mechanical advantage of a block and tackle depends on the number of rope segments.

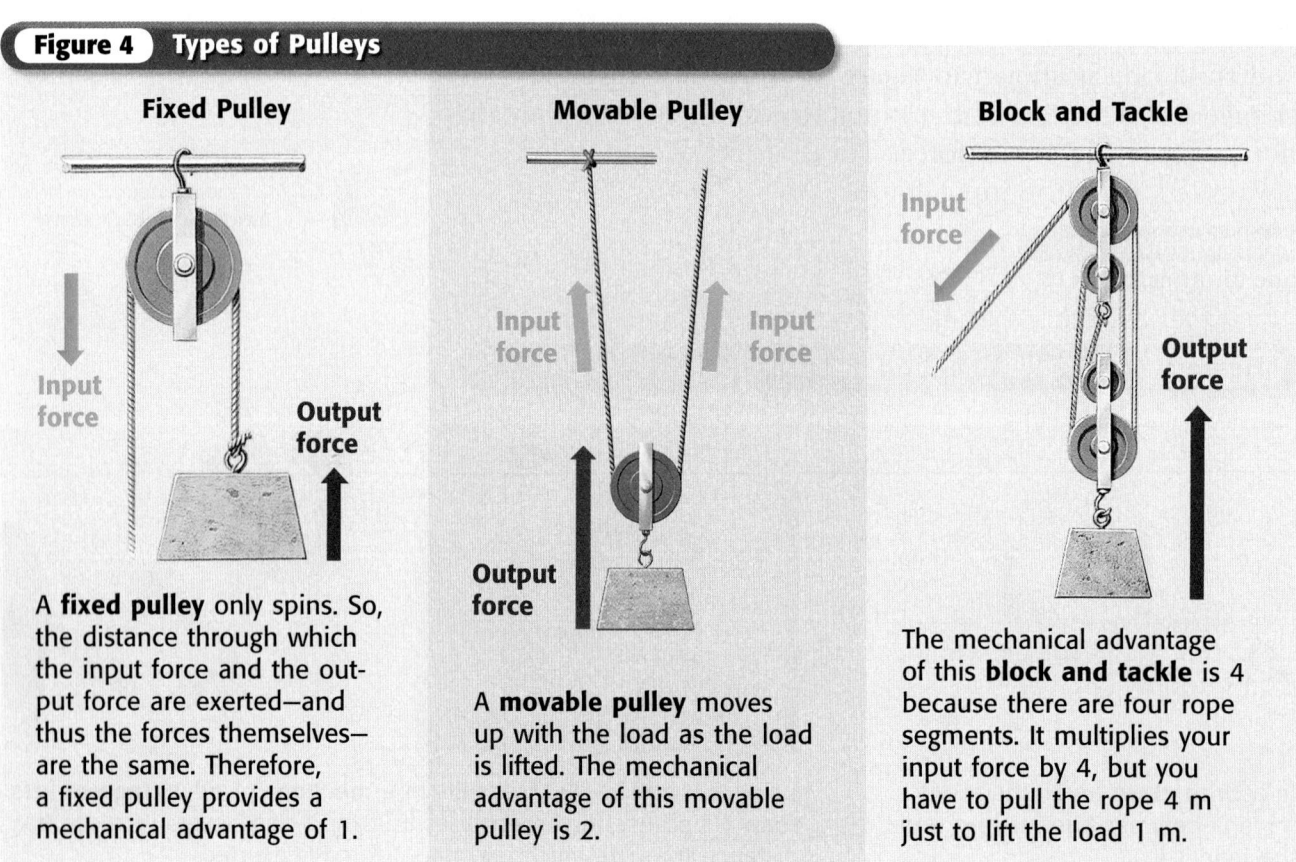

Figure 4   Types of Pulleys

Fixed Pulley

Input force

Output force

A **fixed pulley** only spins. So, the distance through which the input force and the output force are exerted—and thus the forces themselves—are the same. Therefore, a fixed pulley provides a mechanical advantage of 1.

Movable Pulley

Input force   Input force

Output force

A **movable pulley** moves up with the load as the load is lifted. The mechanical advantage of this movable pulley is 2.

Block and Tackle

Input force

Output force

The mechanical advantage of this **block and tackle** is 4 because there are four rope segments. It multiplies your input force by 4, but you have to pull the rope 4 m just to lift the load 1 m.

Figure 5 How a Wheel and Axle Works

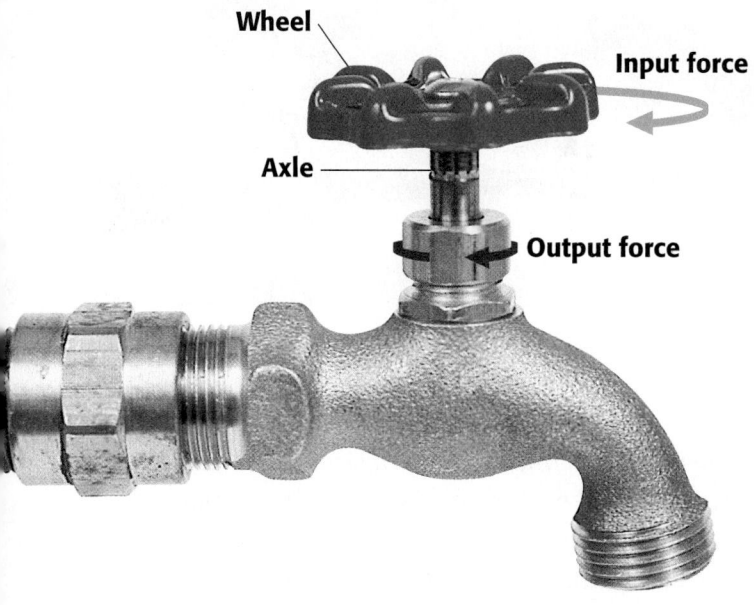

Wheel

Axle

Input force

Output force

a When a small input force is applied to the wheel, the wheel rotates through a circular distance.

b As the wheel turns, so does the axle. But because the axle is smaller than the wheel, it rotates through a smaller distance, which makes the output force larger than the input force.

Wheel and Axle

Did you know that a faucet is a machine? The faucet shown in **Figure 5** is an example of a **wheel and axle,** a simple machine consisting of two circular objects of different sizes. Doorknobs, wrenches, and steering wheels use a wheel and axle. **Figure 5** shows how a wheel and axle works.

wheel and axle a simple machine consisting of two circular objects of different sizes; the wheel is the larger of the two circular objects
FCAT VOCAB

Mechanical Advantage of a Wheel and Axle

The mechanical advantage (*MA*) of a wheel and axle can be found by dividing the *radius* (the distance from the center to the edge) of the wheel by the radius of the axle, as shown in **Figure 6.** Turning the wheel results in a mechanical advantage of greater than 1 because the radius of the wheel is larger than the radius of the axle.

Reading Check How is the mechanical advantage of a wheel and axle calculated?

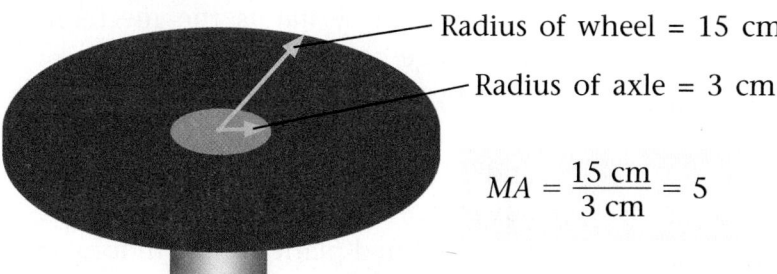

Radius of wheel = 15 cm

Radius of axle = 3 cm

$$MA = \frac{15 \text{ cm}}{3 \text{ cm}} = 5$$

Figure 6 *The mechanical advantage of a wheel and axle is the radius of the wheel divided by the radius of the axle.*

C.2.3.4 CS knows that simple machines can be used to change the direction or size of a force.

Figure 7 *The work you do on the piano to roll it up the ramp is the same as the work you would do to lift the piano straight up. An inclined plane simply allows you to apply a smaller force over a greater distance.*

$$MA = \frac{3\text{ m}}{0.6\text{ m}} = 5$$

Inclined Planes

One of the machines used by the Egyptians to build pyramids was the **inclined plane.** An *inclined plane* is a simple machine that is a straight, slanted surface. A ramp is an inclined plane.

Using an inclined plane to load a piano into a truck, as **Figure 7** shows, is easier than lifting the piano into the truck. Rolling the piano along an inclined plane requires a smaller input force than is needed to lift the piano into the truck. The same work is done on the piano, just over a longer distance.

inclined plane a simple machine that is a straight, slanted surface, which facilitates the raising of loads; a ramp

Benchmark Check How does an inclined plane change the size and distance of a force? **C.2.3.4 CS**

Mechanical Advantage of Inclined Planes

The greater the ratio of an inclined plane's length to its height is, the greater the mechanical advantage is. The mechanical advantage of an inclined plane is calculated by dividing the plane's *length* by the *height* to which the load is lifted. The inclined plane in **Figure 7** has an *MA* of 3 m/0.6 m = 5.

C.2.3.4 CS knows that simple machines can be used to change the direction or size of a force.

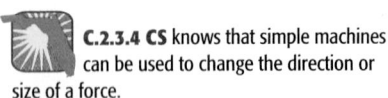 

Mechanical Advantage of an Inclined Plane A heavy box is pushed up a ramp whose incline is 4.8 m long and 1.2 m high. What is the mechanical advantage of the ramp?

Step 1: Write the equation for the mechanical advantage of an inclined plane.

$$MA = \frac{l}{h}$$

Step 2: Replace *l* and *h* with length and height.

$$MA = \frac{4.8\text{ m}}{1.2\text{ m}} = 4$$

Now It's Your Turn

1. A wheelchair ramp is 9 m long and 1.5 m high. What is the mechanical advantage of the ramp?

2. As a pyramid is built, a stone block is dragged up a ramp that is 120 m long and 20 m high. What is the mechanical advantage of the ramp?

3. If an inclined plane were 2 m long and 8 m high, what would its mechanical advantage be?

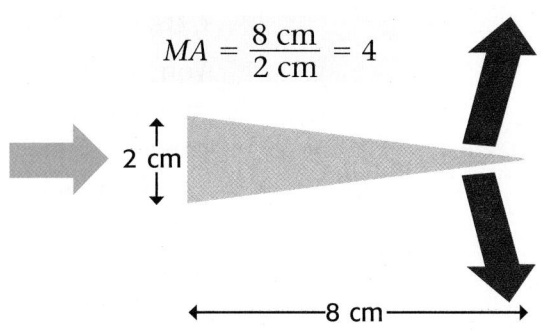

$$MA = \frac{8\ cm}{2\ cm} = 4$$

2 cm

8 cm

Figure 8 *A knife is a common example of a wedge, a simple machine consisting of two inclined planes back to back.*

Wedges

Imagine trying to cut a melon in half with a spoon. It wouldn't be easy, would it? A knife is much more useful for cutting because it is a **wedge.** A *wedge* is a pair of inclined planes that move. A wedge applies an output force that is greater than your input force, but you apply the input force over a greater distance. For example, a knife is a common wedge that can easily cut into a melon and push apart its two halves, as shown in **Figure 8.** Other useful wedges include doorstops, plows, ax heads, and chisels.

Mechanical Advantage of Wedges

The longer and thinner the wedge is, the greater its mechanical advantage is. That's why axes and knives cut better when you sharpen them—you are making the wedges thinner. Therefore, less input force is required. The mechanical advantage of a wedge can be found by dividing the length of the wedge by the wedge's greatest thickness, as shown in **Figure 8.**

Screws

A **screw** is an inclined plane that is wrapped in a spiral around a cylinder, as **Figure 9** shows. When a screw is turned, a small force is applied over the long distance along the inclined plane of the screw. Meanwhile, the screw applies a large force through the short distance that the screw is pushed. Screws are used most commonly as fasteners.

Mechanical Advantage of Screws

If you could unwind the inclined plane of a screw, you would see that the plane is long and has a gentle slope. Recall that the greater the length relative to the height of an inclined plane is, the greater the mechanical advantage of the plane. Similarly, the longer the spiral on a screw is and the closer together the threads are, the greater the mechanical advantage of the screw. A jar lid is a screw with a large mechanical advantage.

wedge a simple machine that is made up of two inclined planes and that moves; often used for cutting **FCAT VOCAB**

screw a simple machine that consists of an inclined plane wrapped around a cylinder **FCAT VOCAB**

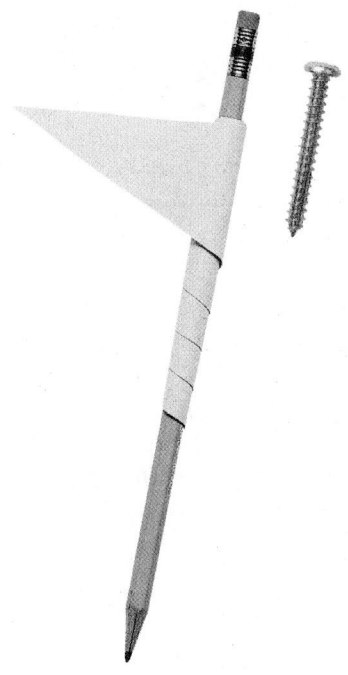

Figure 9 *If you could unwind a screw, you would see that it is actually a very long inclined plane.*

Compound Machines

You are surrounded by machines. You even have machines in your body! But most of the machines in your world are **compound machines,** machines that are made of two or more simple machines. You have already seen one example of a compound machine: a block and tackle. A block and tackle consists of two or more pulleys.

Figure 10 shows a common compound machine. A can opener may seem simple, but it is actually a combination of three machines. It consists of a second-class lever, a wheel and axle, and a wedge. When you squeeze the handle, you are making use of a second-class lever. The blade of the can opener acts as a wedge as it cuts into the can's top. The knob that you turn to open the can is a wheel and axle.

Mechanical Efficiency of Compound Machines

The mechanical efficiency of most compound machines is low. The efficiency is low because compound machines have more moving parts than simple machines do. Thus, there is more friction to overcome. Compound machines, such as automobiles and airplanes, can be made up of many simple machines. It is very important to reduce friction as much as possible, because too much friction can damage the simple machines that make up the compound machine. Friction can be lowered by using lubrication and other techniques.

Benchmark Check Why is the mechanical efficiency of most compound machines low? **B.1.3.4 CS**

compound machine a machine made of more than one simple machine

Everyday Machines

With a parent, think of five simple or compound machines that you encounter each day. In your **science journal,** list them and indicate what type of machine each is. Include at least one compound machine and one machine that is part of your body.

B.1.3.4 CS (partial) knows that energy conversions are never 100% efficient (i.e., some energy is transformed to heat and is unavailable for further useful work).

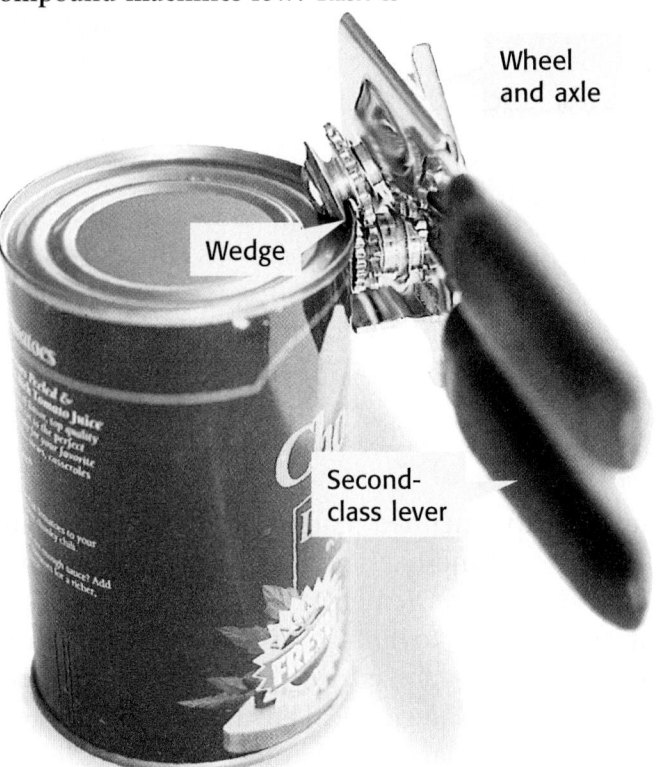

Wheel and axle

Wedge

Second-class lever

Figure 10 *A can opener is a compound machine. The handle is a second-class lever, the knob is a wheel and axle, and a wedge is used to open the can.*

SECTION Review

Summary

- Simple machines change the direction or size of a force to accomplish work. **C.2.3.4 CS**

- In a first-class lever, the fulcrum is between the force and the load. In a second-class lever, the load is between the force and the fulcrum. In a third-class lever, the force is between the fulcrum and the load.

- The mechanical advantage of a wheel and axle is the radius of the wheel divided by the radius of the axle.

- The mechanical advantage of an inclined plane is the length of the plane divided by the height of the plane.

- A wedge's mechanical advantage is its length divided by its greatest thickness.

- Types of pulleys include fixed pulleys, movable pulleys, and block and tackles.

- Compound machines have low mechanical efficiencies because they have more moving parts and therefore more friction to overcome. **B.1.3.4 CS**

Using Key Terms

1. Write an original definition for *wheel and axle*. **FCAT VOCAB**

2. Use the following terms in separate sentences: *inclined plane, wedge,* and *screw.* **FCAT VOCAB**

Understanding Key Ideas

3. Give an example of each of the following simple machines: first-class lever, second-class lever, third-class lever, inclined plane, wedge, and screw. Then, explain how each machine changes the direction or size of a force to do work. **C.2.3.4 CS**

Math Skills

4. A ramp is 0.5 m high and has a slope that is 4 m long. What is its mechanical advantage?

5. The radius of the wheel of a wheel and axle is 4 times the radius of the axle. What is the mechanical advantage of the wheel and axle?

Critical Thinking

6. **Applying Concepts** A third-class lever has a mechanical advantage of less than 1. Explain why it is useful for some tasks.

7. **Making Inferences** Which compound machine would you expect to have the lower mechanical efficiency: a can opener or a pair of scissors? Explain your answer.

FCAT Preparation

8. Thomas removes a screw that was used to fasten two boards together. He finds that the screw is very warm. Which of the following explanations describes why the screw became warm? **B.1.3.4 CS**

    A. Some of the energy used to create the screw was converted into heat energy.

    B. Some of the energy used to insert the screw was converted into heat energy.

    C. Some of the energy used to remove the screw was converted into heat energy.

    D. None of the energy was converted.

9. Which of the following is an advantage of simple machines? **C.2.3.4 CS**

    F. They can change the size and direction of a force.

    G. They are not 100% efficient.

    H. They can create energy.

    I. They have many moving parts.

Developed and maintained by the
National Science Teachers Association

For a variety of links related to this chapter, go to www.scilinks.org

Topic: Simple Machines;
    Compound Machines

SciLinks code: HSM1395; HSM0331

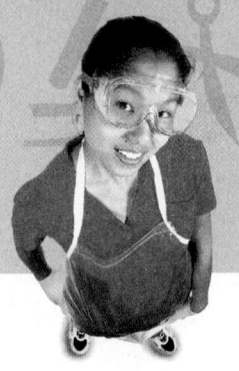

Skills Practice Lab

OBJECTIVES

Calculate the work and power used to climb a flight of stairs.

Compare your work and power with the work and power of a 100 W light bulb.

MATERIALS

- flight of stairs
- ruler, metric
- stopwatch

A Powerful Workout

Does the amount of work that you do depend on how fast you do it? No! But the amount of time in which you do work does affect your power—the rate of work done. In this lab, you'll calculate your work and power for climbing a flight of stairs at different speeds. Then, you'll compare your power with the power of an ordinary household object—a 100 W light bulb.

Ask a Question

1. How does your power in climbing a flight of stairs compare with the power of a 100 W light bulb?

Form a Hypothesis

2. Write a hypothesis that answers the question in step 1. Explain your reasoning.

Data Collection Table				
Height of step (cm)	Number of steps	Height of stairs (m)	Time for slow walk (s)	Time for quick walk (s)

DO NOT WRITE IN BOOK

Test the Hypothesis

3. Copy the Data Collection Table onto a separate sheet of paper.

4. Use a metric ruler to measure the height of one stair step. Record the measurement in your Data Collection Table. Be sure to include units for all measurements.

5. Count the number of stairs, including the top step, and record this number in your Data Collection Table.

6. Calculate the height of the climb by multiplying the number of steps by the height of one step. Record your answer in meters. (You will need to convert your answer from centimeters to meters.)

7. Use a stopwatch to measure how many seconds you take to walk slowly up a flight of stairs. Record your measurement in your Data Collection Table.

8. Now, measure how many seconds you take to walk quickly up a flight of stairs. Be careful not to overexert yourself. You are not racing to see who can get the fastest time!

Analyze the Results

1. **Constructing Tables** Copy the Calculations Table below onto a separate sheet of paper.

Calculations Table			
Weight (N)	Work (J)	Power for slow walk (W)	Power for quick walk (W)
	DO NOT WRITE IN BOOK		

2. **Examining Data** Determine your weight in newtons, and record it in your Calculations Table. Your weight in newtons is your weight in pounds (lb) multiplied by 4.45 N/lb.

3. **Examining Data** Calculate and record your work done in climbing the stairs by using the following equation:

$$work = force \times distance$$

(Hint: If you are having trouble determining the force exerted, remember that force is measured in newtons.)

4. **Examining Data** Calculate and record your power output by using the following equation:

$$power = \frac{work}{time}$$

The unit for power is the watt (1 watt = 1 joule per second).

Draw Conclusions

5. **Evaluating Methods** In step 3 under the head "Analyze the Results," you were asked to calculate your work done in climbing the stairs. Why weren't you asked to calculate your work for each trial (slow walk and quick walk)?

6. **Drawing Conclusions** Look at your hypothesis. Was your hypothesis correct? Now that you have measured your power, write a statement that describes how your power compares with the power of a 100 W light bulb.

7. **Applying Conclusions** The work done to move one electron in a light bulb is very small. Write down two reasons that the power used is large. (Hint: How many electrons are in the filament of a light bulb? How did you use more power in trial 2?)

Communicating Your Data

Your teacher will provide a class data table on the board. Add your average power to the table. Then, calculate the average power from the class data. How many students would it take to create power equal to the power of a 100 W bulb?

Chapter Review

USING KEY TERMS

For each pair of terms, explain how the meanings of the terms differ.

1 *power* and *efficiency* **FCAT VOCAB**

2 *screw* and *inclined plane* **FCAT VOCAB**

3 *wheel and axle* and *wedge* **FCAT VOCAB**

UNDERSTANDING KEY IDEAS

Multiple Choice

4 Work is being done when

  a. you apply a force to an object.

  b. an object is moving after you applied a force to it.

  c. you exert a force that moves an object in the direction of the force.

  d. you do something that is difficult.

5 When a machine is used to do work, some of the energy is lost as heat. Which of the following statements best describes the efficiency of machines? **B.1.3.4 CS FCAT**

  a. Machines are 100% efficient.

  b. Machines are more than 100% efficient.

  c. Machines are less than 100% efficient.

  d. Machines are about 100% efficient.

6 A machine can increase **C.2.3.4 CS**

  a. distance by decreasing force.

  b. force by decreasing distance.

  c. neither distance nor force.

  d. Either (a) or (b)

7 What is power?

  a. the strength of someone or something

  b. the force that is used

  c. the work that is done

  d. the rate at which work is done

8 If a moving object is acted upon by an unbalanced force, its speed and direction will change. Which example best illustrates this point? **C.2.3.5**

  a. A rocket rests on the launch pad.

  b. A bowling ball has inertia.

  c. A moving ball stops because of friction.

  d. A lever is used to open a can.

Short Answer

9 Identify the two simple machines that make up a pair of scissors.

10 Why is the work output of a machine always less than the work input? **B.1.3.4 CS**

11 What does the mechanical advantage of a first-class lever depend on? Describe how it can be changed. **C.2.3.4 CS**

12 Does every object have inertia? Explain why or why not. **C.2.3.5**

13 Describe three contact forces that affect you in your life. **C.2.3.2**

14 Describe three forces that act at a distance. **C.2.3.1 CS**

15 How is net force calculated? If the net force is 0, are the forces balanced or unbalanced? **C.2.3.3, C.2.3.6 AA FCAT**

16 Is it possible for a machine to be 100% efficient? Explain. **B.1.3.4 CS**

CRITICAL THINKING

Extended Response

17 **Analyzing Ideas** Explain why levers usually have a greater mechanical efficiency than other simple machines do. C.2.3.4 CS

18 **Making Inferences** The amount of work done on a machine is 300 J, and the machine does 50 J of work. What can you say about the amount of friction that the machine has while operating? B.1.3.4 CS

19 **Applying Concepts** The winding road shown below is a series of inclined planes. Describe how a winding road makes it easier for vehicles to travel up a hill. C.2.3.4 CS

20 **Making Comparisons** How does the way that a wedge's mechanical advantage is determined differ from the way that a screw's mechanical advantage is determined? C.2.3.4 CS

21 **Identifying Relationships** If the mechanical advantage of a machine is greater than 1, what can you say about how the input force and distance are related to the output force and distance? C.2.3.4 CS

Concept Mapping

22 Use the following terms to create a concept map: *work*, *force*, *distance*, *machine*, and *mechanical advantage*.

INTERPRETING GRAPHICS

For each of the images below, identify the class of lever used and calculate the mechanical advantage of the lever.

23

Output force 120 N

Input force 40 N

Fulcrum

24

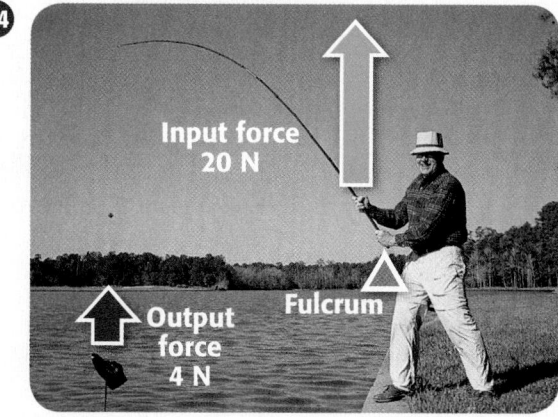

Input force 20 N

Output force 4 N

Fulcrum

Standardized Test Preparation

For the following questions, write your answers on a separate sheet of paper.

1 Asha and her friends are competing against each other to see how far they can each throw a football. Asha throws the ball 23 meters by applying force to the football to make it fly through the air. Friction from the air slows the ball's flight through direct contact. What other force changes the ball's flight without making direct contact with the ball?

A. inertia

B. gravity

C. magnetism

D. buoyant force

2 The diagram below shows the relationship between work, force, and distance. In the diagram, W stands for work, F stands for force, and d stands for distance. Work is equal to force multiplied by distance.

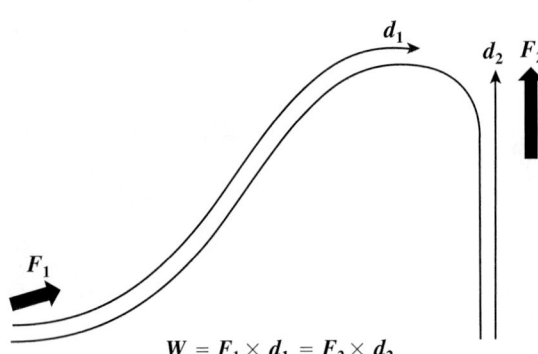

$$W = F_1 \times d_1 = F_2 \times d_2$$

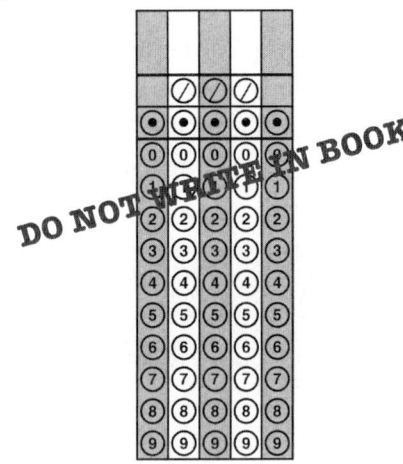

Let's say you wanted to ride your bicycle to the top of a hill that looks like the curve in the diagram. If F_1 is 2000 newtons (N) and d_1 is 60 meters (m), the work of riding the bike up the hill is 120000 joules. If d_2 is 30 meters, what is F_2 in newtons?

3 If a machine has a lot of moving parts, its mechanical efficiency is low. Why is this?

F. Most of the parts will not fit together well, so the efficiency of the machine decreases.

G. Each part needs to be lubricated, and this reduces the overall efficiency of the machine.

H. Every moving part has friction to overcome, and the energy it takes to overcome friction is usually lost as heat energy.

I. Manufacturing all of the small parts that make up the machine cause the machine's overall efficiency to be very low.

4 The picture below shows a wheel and axle, a common simple machine. The mechanical advantage of a machine is the number of times that the machine multiplies force. A machine's mechanical advantage is a comparison between its input force and its output force.

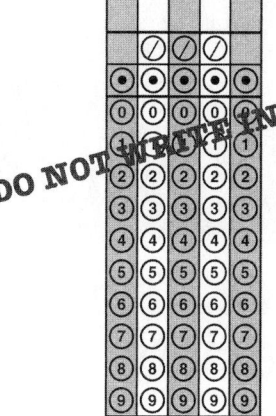

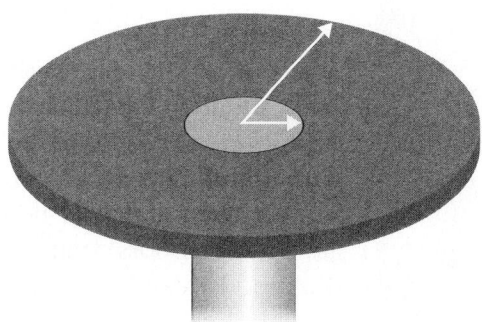

If the radius of the wheel is 48 centimeters and the radius of the axle is 12 centimeters, what is the mechanical advantage of this machine?

5 Simple machines can be used to change the size or direction of a force. Which of the following answers lists some examples of simple machines?

A. pen, pencil, paper

B. screw, lever, wedge

C. hammer, nail, saw

D. paper clip, staple, thumb tack

6   You and your friend each roll a ball at the same time. Your friend's ball hits your ball and changes its path. Describe the forces that are applied to your ball from the moment you rolled it to the moment it stops rolling.

FCAT Preparation

Science in Action

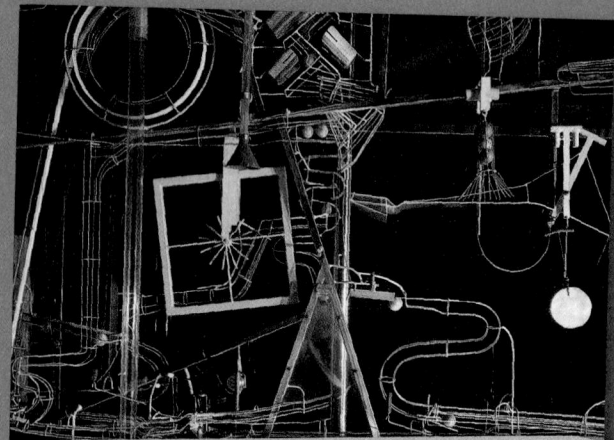

Science, Technology, and Society

Kinetic Sculpture

The collection of tubes, tracks, balls, and blocks of wood shown in the photo is an audio-kinetic sculpture. A conveyor belt lifts the balls to a point high on the track, and the balls wind their way down as they are pulled by the force of gravity and pushed by various other forces. They twist through spirals, drop straight down tubes, and sometimes go up and around loops as if on a roller coaster. All of this movement is made possible by the artist's applications of principles of kinetic energy, the energy of motion.

Math ACTIVITY

A conveyor belt on a kinetic sculpture lifts a ball to a point 0.8 m high. As it does so, it exerts 0.05 N of force. How much work does the conveyor belt do on the ball?

Weird Science

Nanomachines

The technology of making things smaller and smaller keeps advancing. Powerful computers can now be held in the palm of your hand. But what can motors that are smaller than grains of pepper do? How can gnat-sized robots that can swim through the bloodstream be used? One possible field in which very small machines, called *nanomachines*, can be used is in medicine.

Some scientists are looking into the possibility of creating cell-sized machines called *nanobots*. These tiny robots may have many uses in medicine if they can be injected into a person's bloodstream.

Language Arts ACTIVITY

WRITING SKILL Write a short story in which nanobots are used to save someone's life. Describe the machines that the nanobots use in destroying deadly bacteria, clearing blood clots, or delivering medicine.

Mike Hensler

The Surf Chair Mike Hensler was a lifeguard at Daytona Beach, Florida, when he realized that it was next to impossible for someone in a wheelchair to come onto the beach. Although he had never invented a machine before, Hensler decided to build a wheelchair that could be driven across sand without getting stuck. He began spending many evenings in his driveway with a pile of lawn-chair parts, designing the chair by trial and error.

The result of Hensler's efforts looks very different from a conventional wheelchair. With huge rubber wheels and a thick frame of white PVC pipe, the Surf Chair not only moves easily over sandy terrain but also is weather resistant and easy to clean. The newest models of the Surf Chair come with optional attachments, such as a variety of umbrellas, detachable armrests and footrests, and even places to attach fishing rods.

Social Studies ACTIVITY

List some simple and compound machines that are used as access devices for people who are disabled. Research how these machines came to be in common use.

go.hrw.com

To learn more about these Science in Action topics, visit **go.hrw.com** and type in the keyword **HT6FWKFF**.

Current Science

Check out Current Science® articles related to this chapter by visiting **go.hrw.com**. Just type in the keyword **HP5CS08**.

Forces in Fluids

The Big Idea The forces of fluids are describable and predictable.

About the PHOTO

As you race downhill on your bicycle, the air around you pushes on your body and slows you down. "What a drag!" you say. Well, actually, it is a drag. When designing bicycle gear and clothing, manufacturers consider more than just looks and comfort. They also try to decrease drag, a fluid force that opposes motion. This photo shows cyclists riding their bikes in a wind tunnel in a study of how a fluid—air—affects their ride.

PRE-READING ACTIVITY

FOLDNOTES **Booklet** Before you read the chapter, create the FoldNote entitled "Booklet" described in the **Study Skills** section of the Appendix. Label each page of the booklet with a main idea from the chapter. As you read the chapter, write what you learn about each main idea on the appropriate page of the booklet.

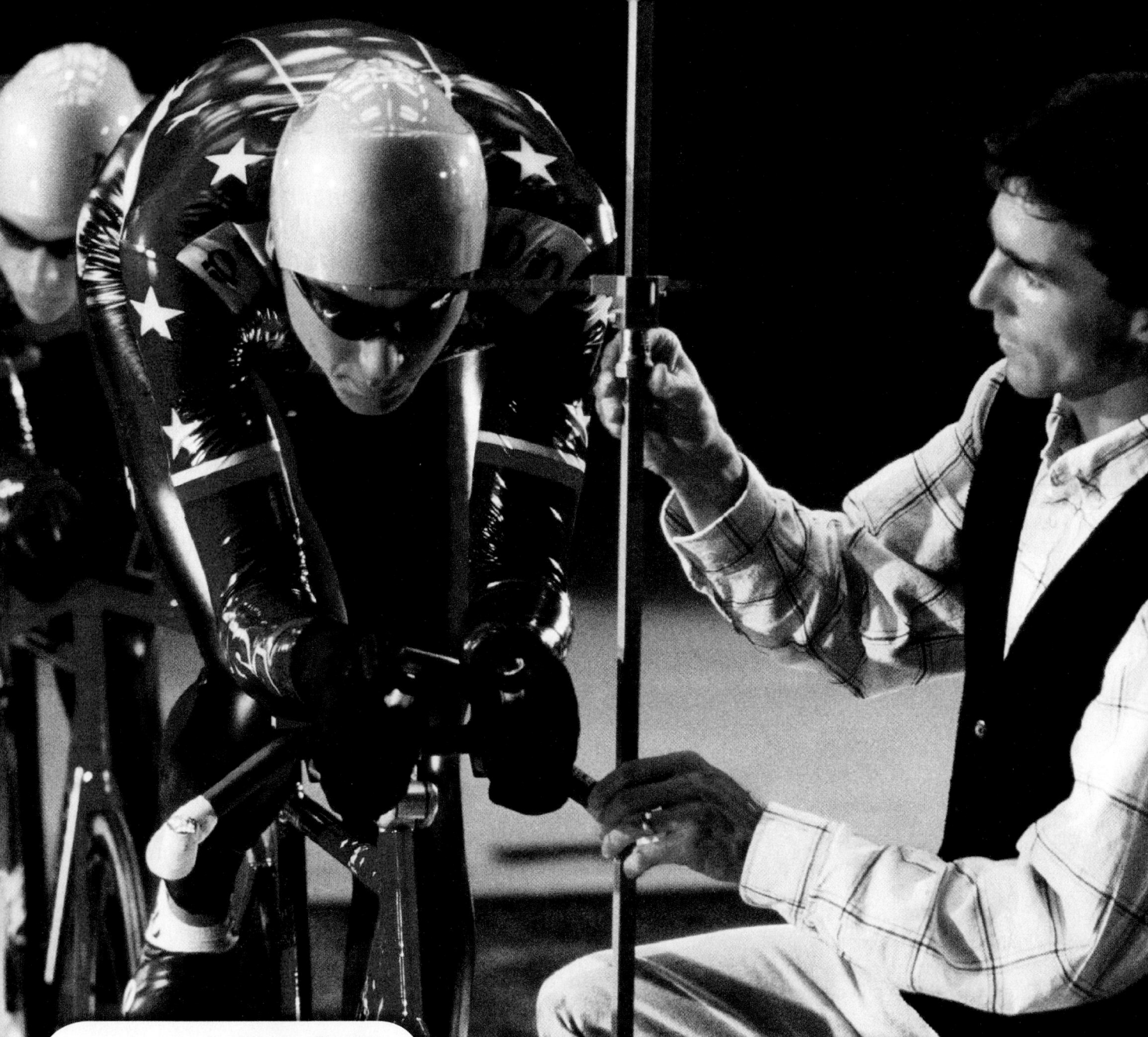

START-UP ACTIVITY

Taking Flight H.1.3.5 AA

In this activity, you will build a model airplane to learn how wing size affects flight.

Procedure

1. Fold a **sheet of paper** in half lengthwise. Then, open it. Fold the top corners toward the center crease. Keep the corners folded down, and fold the entire sheet in half along the center crease.

2. With the plane on its side, fold the top front edge down so that it meets the bottom edge. Fold the top edge down again so that it meets the bottom edge. Turn the plane over, and repeat.

3. Raise the wings so that they are perpendicular to the body.

4. Point the plane slightly upward, and gently throw it. Repeat several times. Describe what you see.

5. Make the wings smaller by folding them one more time. Gently throw the plane. Repeat several times. Describe what you see.

6. Using the smaller wings, try to achieve the same flight path you saw when the wings were bigger.

Analysis

1. What happened to the plane's flight when you reduced the size of its wings? What did you have to do to achieve the same flight path as when the wings were bigger?

2. What gave your plane its forward motion?

Forces in Fluids **647**

Fluids and Pressure

What does a dolphin have in common with a sea gull? What does a dog have in common with a fly? What do you have in common with all these living things?

One answer to these questions is that you and all these other living things spend a lifetime moving through fluids. A **fluid** is any material that can flow and that takes the shape of its container. Fluids include liquids and gases. Fluids can flow because the particles in fluids move easily past each other.

Fluids Exert Pressure

You probably have heard the terms *air pressure* and *water pressure*. Air and water are fluids. All fluids exert pressure. So, what is pressure? **Pressure** is the amount of force exerted on a given area. Think about this example. When you pump up a bicycle tire, you push air into the tire. And like all matter, air is made of tiny particles that are constantly moving.

Look at **Figure 1.** Inside the tire, the air particles collide with each other and with the walls of the tire. Together, these collisions create a force on the tire.

Calculating Pressure

Pressure can be calculated by using the following equation:

$$pressure = \frac{force}{area}$$

The SI unit for pressure is the **pascal.** One pascal (1 Pa) is the force of one newton exerted over an area of one square meter (1 N/m^2).

fluid a nonsolid state of matter in which the atoms or molecules are free to move past each other, as in a gas or liquid

pressure the amount of force exerted per unit area of a surface *FCAT VOCAB*

pascal the SI unit of pressure (symbol, Pa)

atmospheric pressure the pressure caused by the weight of the atmosphere

Air particles

Figure 1 *The force of the air particles hitting the inner surface of the tire creates pressure, which keeps the tire inflated.*

Pressure, Force, and Area What is the pressure exerted by a book that has an area of 0.2 m² and a weight of 10 N?

Step 1: Write the equation for pressure.

$$pressure = \frac{force}{area}$$

Step 2: Replace *force* and *area* with the values given, and solve. (Hint: Weight is a measure of gravitational force.)

$$pressure = \frac{10 \text{ N}}{0.2 \text{ m}^2} = 50 \text{ N/m}^2 = 50 \text{ Pa}$$

The equation for pressure can be rearranged to find force or area, as shown below.

$force = pressure \times area$ *(Rearrange by multiplying by area.)*

$area = \dfrac{force}{pressure}$ *(Rearrange by multiplying by area and then dividing by pressure.)*

Now It's Your Turn

1. Find the pressure exerted by a 3,000 N crate that has an area of 2 m².
2. Find the weight of a rock that has an area of 10 m² and that exerts a pressure of 250 Pa.

Pressure and Bubbles

When you blow a soap bubble, you blow in only one direction. So, why does the bubble get rounder instead of longer as you blow? The shape of the bubble partly depends on an important property of fluids: Fluids exert pressure evenly in all directions. The air you blow into the bubble exerts pressure evenly in all directions. So, the bubble expands in all directions to create a sphere.

Atmospheric Pressure

The *atmosphere* is the layer of nitrogen, oxygen, and other gases that surrounds Earth. Earth's atmosphere is held in place by gravity, which pulls the gases toward Earth. The pressure caused by the weight of the atmosphere is called **atmospheric pressure.**

Atmospheric pressure is exerted on everything on Earth, including you. At sea level, the atmosphere exerts a pressure of about 101,300 N on every square meter, or 101,300 Pa. So, there is a weight of about 10 N (about 2 lbs) on every square centimeter of your body. Why don't you feel this crushing pressure? Like the air inside a balloon, the fluids inside your body exert pressure. **Figure 2** can help you understand why you don't feel the pressure.

✓ Reading Check Name two gases in the atmosphere.

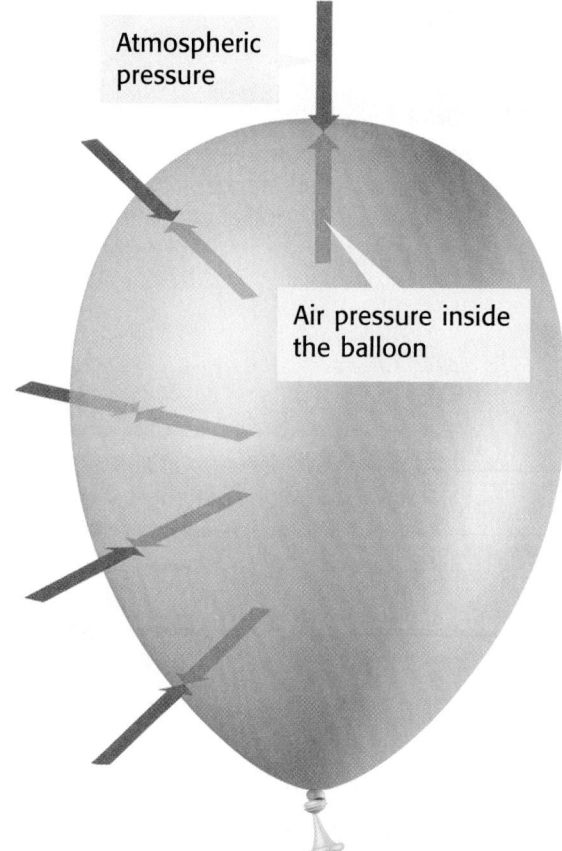

Atmospheric pressure

Air pressure inside the balloon

Figure 2 *The air inside a balloon exerts pressure that keeps the balloon inflated against atmospheric pressure. Similarly, fluid inside your body exerts pressure that works against atmospheric pressure.*

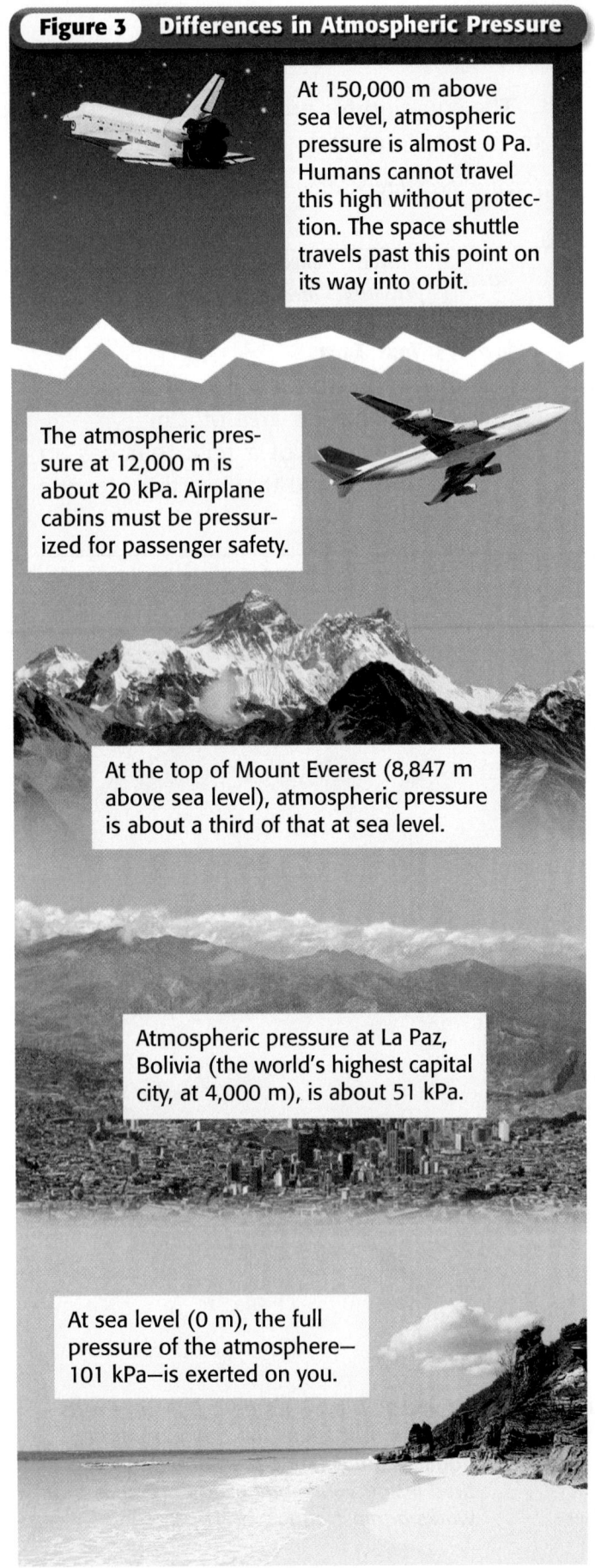

Figure 3 Differences in Atmospheric Pressure

At 150,000 m above sea level, atmospheric pressure is almost 0 Pa. Humans cannot travel this high without protection. The space shuttle travels past this point on its way into orbit.

The atmospheric pressure at 12,000 m is about 20 kPa. Airplane cabins must be pressurized for passenger safety.

At the top of Mount Everest (8,847 m above sea level), atmospheric pressure is about a third of that at sea level.

Atmospheric pressure at La Paz, Bolivia (the world's highest capital city, at 4,000 m), is about 51 kPa.

At sea level (0 m), the full pressure of the atmosphere—101 kPa—is exerted on you.

Variation of Atmospheric Pressure

The atmosphere stretches about 150 km above Earth's surface. However, about 80% of the atmosphere's gases are found within 10 km of Earth's surface. At the top of the atmosphere, pressure is almost nonexistent. The pressure is close to 0 Pa because the gas particles are far apart and rarely collide. Mount Everest in south-central Asia is the highest point on Earth. At the top of Mount Everest, atmospheric pressure is about 33,000 Pa, or 33 kilo-pascals (33 kPa). (Remember that the prefix *kilo-* means 1,000. So, 1 kPa is equal to 1,000 Pa.) At sea level, atmospheric pressure is about 101 kPa.

Atmospheric Pressure and Depth

Take a look at **Figure 3.** Notice how atmospheric pressure changes as you travel through the atmosphere. The further down through the atmosphere you go, the greater the pressure is. In other words, the pressure increases as the atmosphere gets "deeper." An important point to remember about fluids is that pressure varies depending on depth. At lower levels of the atmosphere, there is more fluid above that is being pulled by Earth's gravitational force. So, there is more pressure at lower levels of the atmosphere.

Reading Check Describe how pressure changes with depth.

Pressure Changes and Your Body

So, what happens to your body when atmospheric pressure changes? If you travel to higher or lower points in the atmosphere, the fluids in your body have to adjust to maintain equal pressure. You may have experienced this adjustment if your ears have "popped" when you were in a plane taking off or in a car traveling down a steep mountain road. The "pop" happens because of pressure changes in pockets of air behind your eardrums.

Water Pressure

Water is a fluid. So, it exerts pressure like the atmosphere does. Water pressure also increases as depth increases, as shown in **Figure 4.** The deeper a diver goes in the water, the greater the pressure is. The pressure increases because more water above the diver is being pulled by Earth's gravitational force. In addition, the atmosphere presses down on the water, so the total pressure on the diver includes water pressure and atmospheric pressure.

Water Pressure and Depth

Like atmospheric pressure, water pressure depends on depth. Water pressure does not depend on the total amount of fluid present. A swimmer would feel the same pressure swimming at 3 m below the surface of a small pond and at 3 m below the surface of an ocean. Even though there is more water in the ocean than in the pond, the pressure on the swimmer in the pond would be the same as the pressure on the swimmer in the ocean.

Density Making a Difference

Water is about 1,000 times more dense than air. *Density* is the amount of matter in a given volume, or mass per unit volume. Because water is more dense than air, a certain volume of water has more mass—and weighs more—than the same volume of air. So, water exerts more pressure than air.

For example, if you climb a 10 m tree, the decrease in atmospheric pressure is too small to notice. But if you dive 10 m underwater, the pressure on you increases to 201 kPa, which is almost twice the atmospheric pressure at the surface!

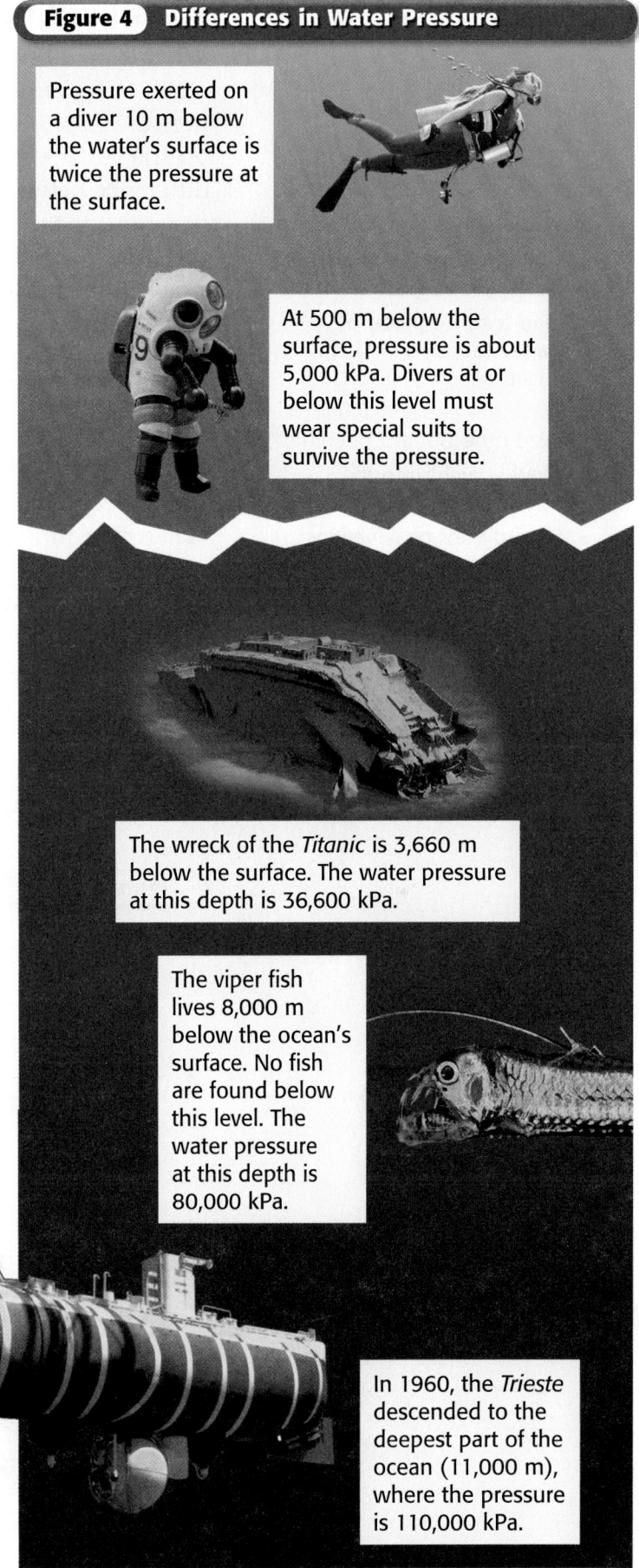

Figure 4 Differences in Water Pressure

Pressure exerted on a diver 10 m below the water's surface is twice the pressure at the surface.

At 500 m below the surface, pressure is about 5,000 kPa. Divers at or below this level must wear special suits to survive the pressure.

The wreck of the *Titanic* is 3,660 m below the surface. The water pressure at this depth is 36,600 kPa.

The viper fish lives 8,000 m below the ocean's surface. No fish are found below this level. The water pressure at this depth is 80,000 kPa.

In 1960, the *Trieste* descended to the deepest part of the ocean (11,000 m), where the pressure is 110,000 kPa.

Pressure Differences and Fluid Flow

When you drink through a straw, you remove some of the air in the straw. Because there is less air inside the straw, the pressure in the straw is reduced. But the atmospheric pressure on the surface of the liquid remains the same. Thus, there is a difference between the pressure inside the straw and the pressure outside the straw. The outside pressure forces the liquid up the straw and into your mouth. So, just by drinking through a straw, you can observe an important property of fluids: Fluids flow from areas of high pressure to areas of low pressure.

Reading Check When you drink through a straw, how do you decrease the pressure inside the straw?

Pressure Differences and Breathing

Take a deep breath—fluid is flowing from high to low pressure! When you inhale, a muscle increases the space in your chest and gives your lungs room to expand. This expansion decreases the pressure in your lungs. The pressure in your lungs becomes lower than the air pressure outside your lungs. Air then flows into your lungs—from high to low pressure. This air carries oxygen that you need to live. **Figure 5** shows how exhaling also causes fluids to flow from high to low pressure. You can see a similar flow of fluid when you open a carbonated beverage or squeeze toothpaste onto your toothbrush.

Figure 5 Exhaling, Pressure, and Fluid Flow

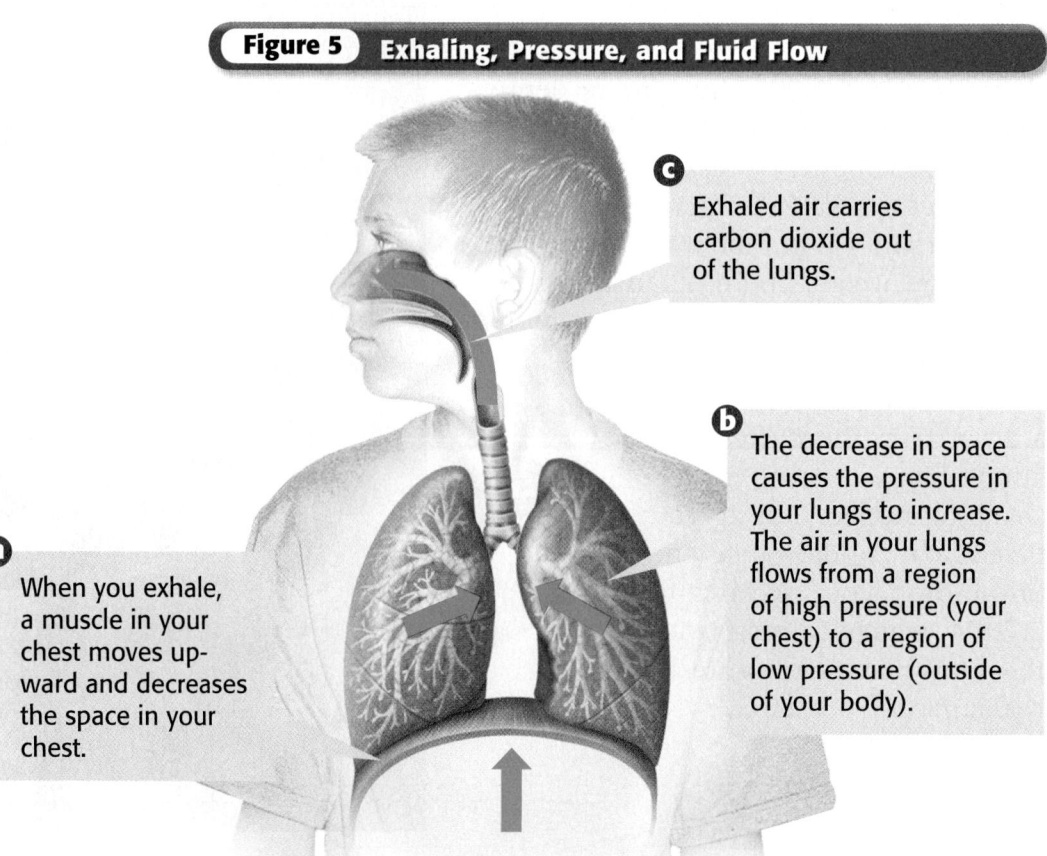

c Exhaled air carries carbon dioxide out of the lungs.

b The decrease in space causes the pressure in your lungs to increase. The air in your lungs flows from a region of high pressure (your chest) to a region of low pressure (outside of your body).

a When you exhale, a muscle in your chest moves upward and decreases the space in your chest.

Pressure Differences and Tornadoes

Look at the tornado in **Figure 6.** Some of the damaging winds caused by tornadoes are the result of pressure differences. The air pressure inside a tornado is very low. Because the air pressure outside of the tornado is higher than the pressure inside, air rushes into the tornado. The rushing air causes the tornado to be like a giant vacuum cleaner—objects are pushed into the tornado. The winds created are usually very strong and affect the area around the tornado. So, objects, such as trees and buildings, can be severely damaged by wind even if they are not in the direct path of a tornado.

Figure 6 *Tornadoes are like giant vacuum cleaners because of pressure differences.*

SECTION Review

Summary

- A fluid is any material that flows and takes the shape of its container.
- Pressure is force exerted on a given area.
- Moving particles of matter create pressure by colliding with one another and with the walls of their container.
- The pressure caused by the weight of the atmosphere is called *atmospheric pressure.*
- Fluid pressure increases as depth increases.
- As depth increases, water pressure increases faster than atmospheric pressure does because water is denser than air.
- Fluids flow from areas of high pressure to areas of low pressure.

Using Key Terms

1. Write an original definition for *fluid* and *atmospheric pressure*.

2. Use *pressure* and *pascal* in the same sentence.

Understanding Key Ideas

3. How do fluids exert pressure?

4. What is the relationship between depth, density, and water pressure?

5. Explain why atmospheric pressure changes as depth changes.

6. Give three examples of fluids flowing from high pressure to low pressure in everyday life.

Critical Thinking

7. **Identifying Relationships** Mercury is a liquid that has a density of 13.5 g/mL. Water has a density of 1.0 g/mL. Equal volumes of mercury and water are in identical containers. What would you conclude about the pressures exerted on the bottoms of the containers? Explain.

8. **Making Inferences** Why do you think airplanes need to be pressurized for safety when flying high in the atmosphere?

FCAT Preparation

9. A student wants to find out how air pressure in a basketball affects the ball's ability to bounce. The student pumps air into the ball, measures the air pressure, drops the ball from a certain height, measures the height of the first bounce of the ball, and counts the number of bounces. In the experiment, what is the independent variable? **H.I.3.5 AA**

A. air pressure inside the ball

B. height from which the ball is dropped

C. height of the first bounce

D. number of bounces

Developed and maintained by the
National Science Teachers Association

For a variety of links related to this chapter, go to www.scilinks.org

Topic: Fluids and Pressure
SciLinks code: HSM0586

Buoyant Force

Why does an ice cube float on water? Why doesn't it sink to the bottom of your glass?

Imagine that you use a straw to push an ice cube underwater. Then, you release the cube. A force pushes the ice back up. The force, called **buoyant force** (BOY uhnt FAWRS), is the upward, contact force that fluids exert on all matter.

Buoyant Force and Fluid Pressure

Look at **Figure 1.** Water exerts fluid pressure on all sides of an object. The pressure exerted horizontally on one side of the object is equal to the pressure exerted on the opposite side. These equal pressures cancel one another. So, the only fluid pressures affecting the net force on the object are at the top and at the bottom. Pressure increases as depth increases. So, the pressure at the bottom of the object is greater than the pressure at the top. The water exerts a net upward force on the object. This upward force is buoyant force.

Determining Buoyant Force

Archimedes (AHR kuh MEE DEEZ), a Greek mathematician who lived in the third century BCE, discovered how to determine buoyant force. **Archimedes' principle** states that the buoyant force on an object in a fluid is an upward force equal to the weight of the fluid that the object takes the place of, or displaces. Suppose the object in **Figure 1** displaces 250 mL of water. The weight of that volume of displaced water is about 2.5 N. So, the buoyant force on the object is 2.5 N. Notice that only the weight of the displaced fluid determines the buoyant force on an object. The weight of the object does not affect buoyant force.

READING WARM-UP

Objectives

● Explain how fluid pressure and buoyant force are related. **C.2.3.2, C.2.3.3**
● Predict whether an object will float or sink in a fluid.
● Analyze the role of density in an object's ability to float.
● Explain how the overall density of an object can be changed.

Terms to Learn

buoyant force
Archimedes' principle

READING STRATEGY

Discussion Read this section silently. Write down questions that you have about this section. Discuss your questions in a small group.

buoyant force the upward force that keeps an object immersed in or floating on a liquid

Archimedes' principle the principle that states that the buoyant force on an object in a fluid is an upward force equal to the weight of the volume of fluid that the object displaces

Figure 1 *There is more pressure at the bottom of an object because pressure increases with depth. This results in an upward buoyant force on the object.*

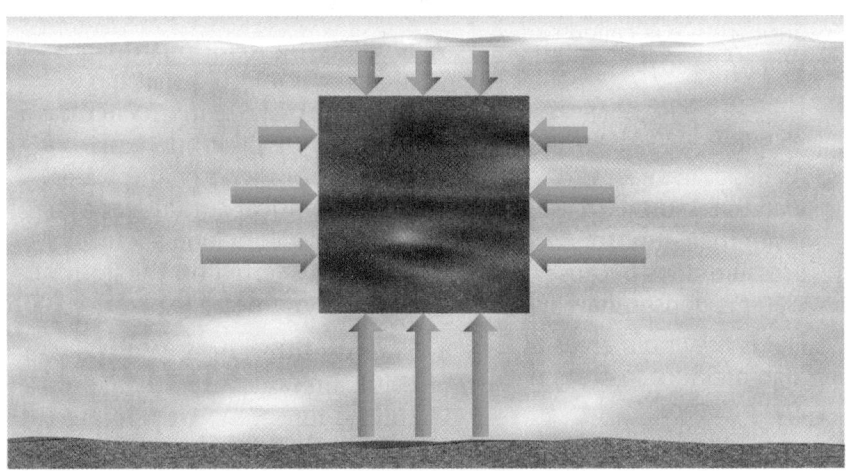

Weight Versus Buoyant Force

An object in a fluid will sink if its weight is greater than the buoyant force (the weight of the fluid it displaces). An object floats only when the buoyant force on the object is equal to the object's weight.

Sinking

The rock in **Figure 2** weighs 75 N. It displaces 5 L of water. Archimedes' principle says that the buoyant force is equal to the weight of the displaced water—about 50 N. The rock's weight is greater than the buoyant force. So, the rock sinks.

Floating

The fish in **Figure 2** weighs 12 N. It displaces a volume of water that weighs 12 N. Because the fish's weight is equal to the buoyant force, the fish floats in the water. In fact, the fish is suspended in the water as it floats. Now, look at the duck. The duck does not sink. So, the buoyant force on the duck must be equal to the duck's weight. But the duck isn't all the way underwater! Only the duck's feet, legs, and stomach have to be underwater to displace 9 N of water, which is equal to the duck's weight. So, the duck floats on the surface of the water.

Buoying Up

If the duck dove underwater, it would displace more than 9 N of water. So, the buoyant force on the duck would be greater than the duck's weight. When the buoyant force on an object is greater than the object's weight, the object is *buoyed up* (pushed up) in water. An object is buoyed up until the part of the object underwater displaces an amount of water that equals the object's entire weight. Thus, an ice cube pops to the surface when it is pushed to the bottom of a glass of water.

 Benchmark Check What causes an object to buoy up?
C.2.3.2, C.2.3.3

Figure 2 *Will an object sink or float? That depends on whether the buoyant force is less than or equal to the object's weight.*

Weight = 12 N
Buoyant force = 12 N
Fish floats and is suspended in the water.

Weight = 9 N
Buoyant force = 9 N
Duck floats on the surface.

Weight = 75 N
Buoyant force = 50 N
Rock sinks.

Floating, Sinking, and Density

Think again about the rock in the lake. The rock displaces 5 L of water. But volumes of solids are measured in cubic centimeters (cm^3). Because 1 mL is equal to 1 cm^3, the volume of the rock is 5,000 cm^3. But 5,000 cm^3 of rock weighs more than an equal volume of water. So, the rock sinks.

Because mass is proportional to weight, you can say that the rock has more mass per volume than water has. Mass per unit volume is density. The rock sinks because it is more dense than water is. The duck floats because it is less dense than water is. The density of the fish is equal to the density of the water.

More Dense Than Air

Why does an ice cube float on water but not in air? An ice cube floats on water because it is less dense than water. But most substances are *more* dense than air. So, there are few substances that float in air. The ice cube is more dense than air, so the ice cube doesn't float in air.

Less Dense Than Air

One substance that is less dense than air is helium, a gas. In fact, helium has one-seventh the density of air under normal conditions. A given volume of helium displaces an equal volume of air that is much heavier than itself. So, helium floats in air. Because helium floats in air, it is used in parade balloons, such as the one shown in **Figure 3**.

✓ **Reading Check** Why do helium balloons float in air?

Figure 3 *Helium in a balloon floats in air for the same reason an ice cube floats on water—helium is less dense than the surrounding fluid.*

Finding Density Find the density of a rock that has a mass of 10 g and a volume of 2 cm^3.

Step 1: Write the equation for density. Density is calculated by using this equation:

$$density = \frac{mass}{volume}$$

Step 2: Replace *mass* and *volume* with the values in the problem, and solve.

$$density = \frac{10 \text{ g}}{2 \text{ cm}^3} = 5 \text{ g/cm}^3$$

Now It's Your Turn

1. What is the density of a 20 cm^3 object that has a mass of 25 g?
2. A 546 g fish displaces 420 mL of water. What is the density of the fish? (Note: 1 mL = 1 cm^3)
3. A beaker holds 50 mL of a slimy green liquid. The mass of the liquid is 163 g. What is the density of the liquid?

Changing Overall Density

Steel is almost 8 times denser than water. And yet huge steel ships cruise the oceans with ease. But hold on! You just learned that substances that are more dense than water will sink in water. So, how does a steel ship float?

Changing Shape

The secret of how a ship floats is in the shape of the ship. What if a ship were just a big block of steel, as shown in **Figure 4**? If you put that block into water, the block would sink because it is more dense than water. So, ships are built with a hollow shape. The amount of steel in the ship is the same as in the block. But the hollow shape increases the volume of the ship. Remember that density is mass per unit volume. So, an increase in the ship's volume leads to a decrease in the ship's density. Thus, ships made of steel float because their *overall density* is less than the density of water.

Most ships are built to displace more water than is necessary for the ship to float. Ships are made this way so that they won't sink when people and cargo are loaded on the ship.

CONNECTION TO Geology

Floating Rocks The rock that makes up Earth's continents is about 15% less dense than the molten (melted) mantle rock below it. Because of this difference in density, the continents are floating on the mantle. Research the structure of Earth, and make a poster that shows Earth's interior layers.

ACTIVITY

Figure 4 **Shape and Overall Density**

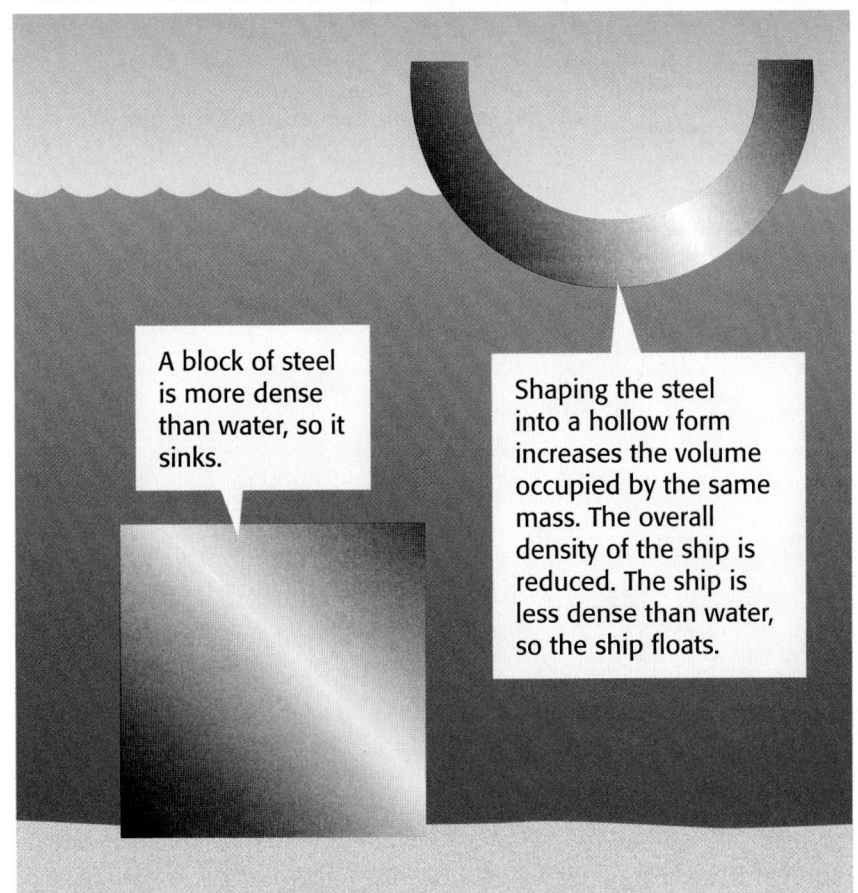

A block of steel is more dense than water, so it sinks.

Shaping the steel into a hollow form increases the volume occupied by the same mass. The overall density of the ship is reduced. The ship is less dense than water, so the ship floats.

INTERNET ACTIVITY

Trapped with No Bottle
You are stranded on a desert island and want to send a distress message in a bottle. The problem is that there are no bottles! Go to **go.hrw.com**, and type in the keyword **HP5FLUW**.

Quick Lab

Ship Shape

1. Roll a **piece of clay** into a ball the size of a golf ball, and drop it into a **container of water.** Record your observations.

2. With your hands, flatten the ball of clay until it is a bit thinner than your little finger, and press it into the shape of a bowl or canoe.

3. Place the clay boat gently in the water. How does the change of shape affect the buoyant force on the clay? How is that change related to the overall density of the clay boat? Record your answers.

Changing Mass

A submarine is a special kind of ship that can travel both on the surface of the water and underwater. Submarines have *ballast tanks* that can be opened to allow sea water to flow in. As water is added, the submarine's mass increases, but its volume stays the same. The submarine's overall density increases so that it can dive under the surface. Crew members control the amount of water taken in. In this way, they control how dense the submarine is and how deep it dives. Compressed air is used to blow the water out of the tanks so that the submarine can rise. Study **Figure 5** to learn how ballast tanks work.

✓ **Reading Check** How do crew members control the density of a submarine?

Figure 5 **Controlling Density Using Ballast Tanks**

When a submarine is floating on the ocean's surface, its ballast tanks are filled mostly with air.

Vent holes on the ballast tanks are opened to allow the submarine to dive. Air escapes as the tanks fill with water.

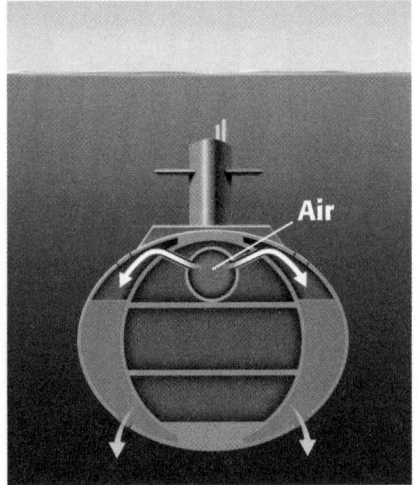

Vent holes are closed, and compressed air is pumped into the ballast tanks to force the water out, so the submarine rises.

Changing Volume

Like a submarine, some fish adjust their over-all density to stay at a certain depth in the water. Most bony fishes have an organ called a *swim bladder,* shown in **Figure 6.** This swim blad-der is filled with gases produced in a fish's blood. The inflated swim bladder increases the fish's volume and thereby decreases the fish's overall density, which keeps the fish from sinking in the water. The fish's nervous system controls the amount of gas in the bladder. Some fish, such as sharks, do not have a swim bladder. These fish must swim constantly to keep from sinking.

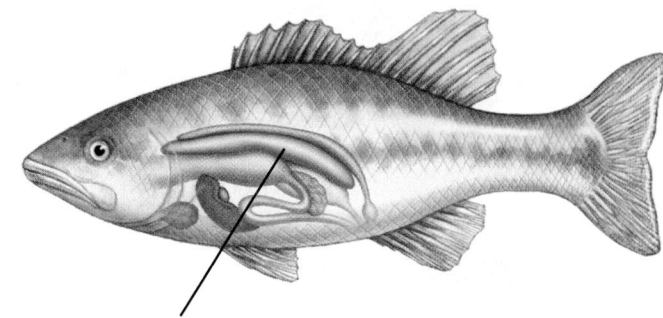

Swim bladder

Figure 6 *Most bony fishes have an organ called a* swim bladder *that allows them to adjust their overall density.*

SECTION
Review

Summary

- All fluids exert an upward force called *buoyant force.* **C.2.3.2**

- Buoyant force is caused by differences in fluid pressure. **C.2.3.3**

- Archimedes' principle states that the buoyant force on an object is equal to the weight of the fluid displaced by the object.

- Any object that is more dense than the sur-rounding fluid will sink. An object that is less dense than the sur-rounding fluid will float.

- The overall density of an object can be changed by changing the object's shape, mass, or volume.

Using Key Terms

1. Use *buoyant force* and *Archimedes' principle* in the same sentence.

Understanding Key Ideas

2. Explain how differences in fluid pressure create buoyant force on an object. **C.2.3.2, C.2.3.3**

3. How does an object's density determine whether the object will sink or float in water?

4. Name three methods that can be used to change the overall density of an object.

Critical Thinking

5. **Applying Concepts** An object weighs 20 N. It displaces a vol-ume of water that weighs 15 N.

   a. What is the buoyant force on the object?

   b. Predict what would happen if this object were placed in a tank of water. Explain your answer.

6. **Predicting Consequences** Iron has a density of 7.9 g/cm^3. Mercury is a liquid that has a density of 13.5 g/cm^3. Will iron float or sink in mercury? Justify your conclusion.

FCAT Preparation

7. Buoyant force is an upward force that fluids exert on matter. Gravity is a downward force that is exerted on all matter. When an object is placed in water, both buoyant force and gravity act on the object. What must be true if an object sinks in water? **C.2.3.6 AA**

   A. Buoyant force is equal to gravity.

   B. Buoyant force is greater than gravity.

   C. Buoyant force is less than gravity.

   D. Buoyant force does not act against gravity.

SCiLINKS® NSTA
Developed and maintained by the
National Science Teachers Association

For a variety of links related to this chapter, go to www.scilinks.org

Topic: Buoyant Force
SciLinks code: HSM0202

Fluids and Motion

Hold two sheets of paper so that the edges are hanging in front of your face about 4 cm apart. The flat faces of the paper should be parallel to each other. Now, blow as hard as you can between the two sheets of paper.

What's going on? You can't separate the sheets by blowing between them. In fact, the sheets move closer together the harder you blow. You may be surprised that the explanation for this unusual occurrence also includes how wings help birds and planes fly and how pitchers throw screwballs.

Fluid Speed and Pressure

The strange reaction of the paper is caused by a property of moving fluids. This property was first described in the 18th century by Daniel Bernoulli (ber NOO lee), a Swiss mathematician. **Bernoulli's principle** states that as the speed of a moving fluid increases, the fluid's pressure decreases. In the case of the paper, air speed between the two sheets increased when you blew air between them. Because air speed increased, the pressure between the sheets decreased. Thus, the higher pressure on the outside of the sheets pushed them together.

Science in a Sink

Bernoulli's principle is at work in **Figure 1.** A table-tennis ball is attached to a string and swung into a stream of water. Instead of being pushed out of the water, the ball is held in the water. Why? The water is moving faster than the air around it, so the water has a lower pressure than the surrounding air. The higher air pressure pushes the ball into the area of lower pressure—the water stream. Try this at home to see for yourself!

READING WARM-UP

Objectives

● Describe the relationship between pressure and fluid speed.

● Analyze the roles of lift, thrust, and wing size in flight. **C.2.3.3, C.2.3.6 AA**

● Describe drag, and explain how it affects lift. **C.2.3.3, C.2.3.6 AA**

● Explain Pascal's principle.

Terms to Learn

Bernoulli's principle
lift
thrust
drag
Pascal's principle

READING STRATEGY

Reading Organizer As you read this section, create an outline of the section. Use the headings from the section in your outline.

Bernoulli's principle the principle that states that the pressure in a fluid decreases as the fluid's velocity increases

Figure 1 *This ball is pushed by the higher pressure of the air into an area of reduced pressure—the water stream.*

Figure 2 Wing Design and Lift

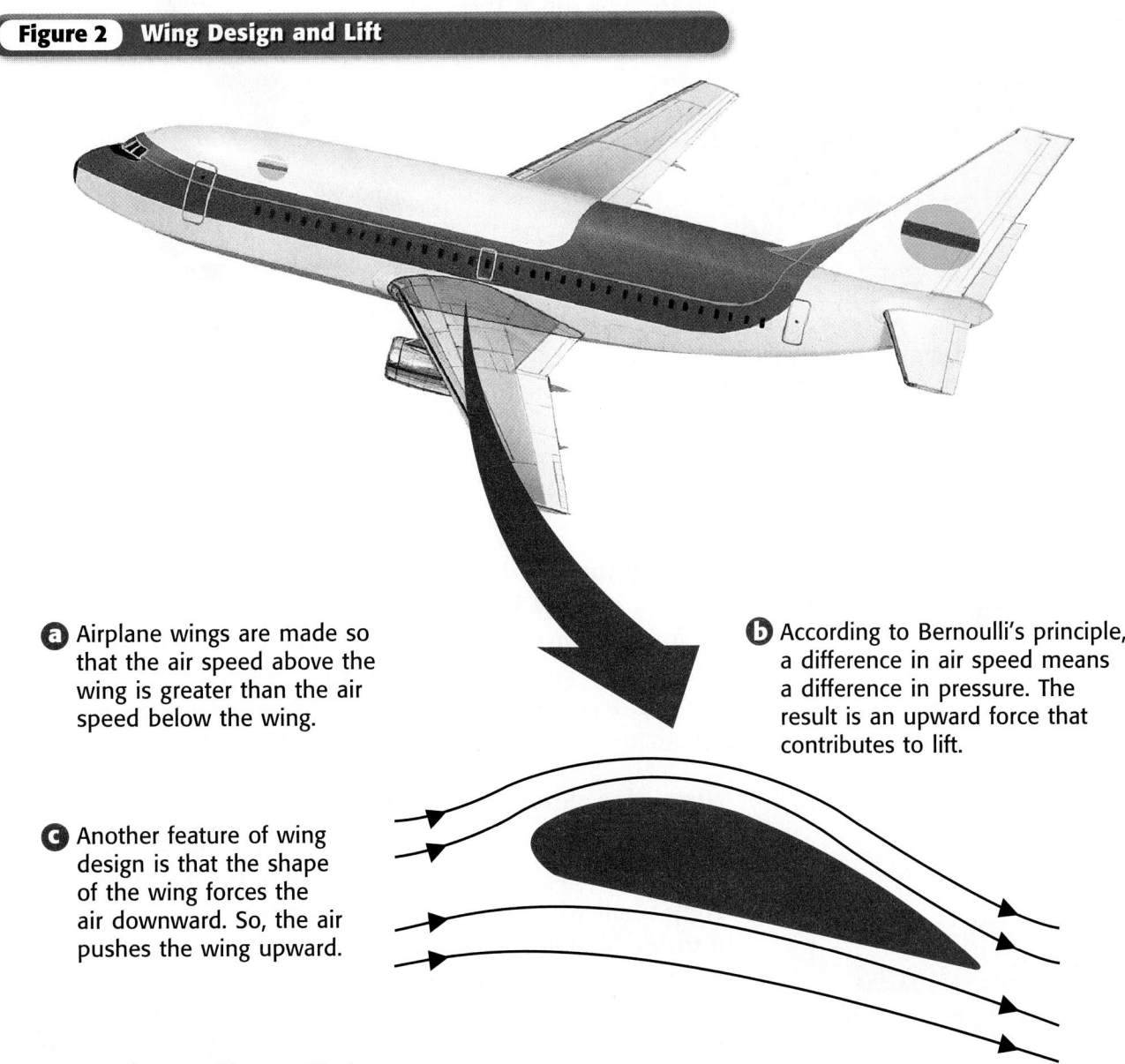

a Airplane wings are made so that the air speed above the wing is greater than the air speed below the wing.

b According to Bernoulli's principle, a difference in air speed means a difference in pressure. The result is an upward force that contributes to lift.

c Another feature of wing design is that the shape of the wing forces the air downward. So, the air pushes the wing upward.

Factors That Affect Flight

A common commercial airplane in the skies today is the Boeing 737 jet. Even without passengers, the plane weighs 350,000 N. How can something so big and heavy get off the ground and fly? Wing shape plays a role in helping these big planes—as well as smaller planes and birds—achieve flight, as shown in **Figure 2.**

According to Bernoulli's principle, the fast-moving air above the wing exerts less pressure than the slow-moving air below the wing. The greater pressure below the wing exerts an upward force. This upward force, known as **lift,** pushes the wings (and the rest of the airplane or bird) upward against the downward pull of gravity.

Benchmark Check What is the relationship between lift and gravity? **C.2.3.3, C.2.3.6 AA**

lift an upward force on an object that moves in a fluid

C.2.3.3 knows that if more than one force acts on an object, then the forces can reinforce or cancel each other, depending on their direction and magnitude.

C.2.3.6 AA explains and shows the ways in which a net force (i.e., the sum of all acting forces) can act on an object.

Section 3 Fluids and Motion **661**

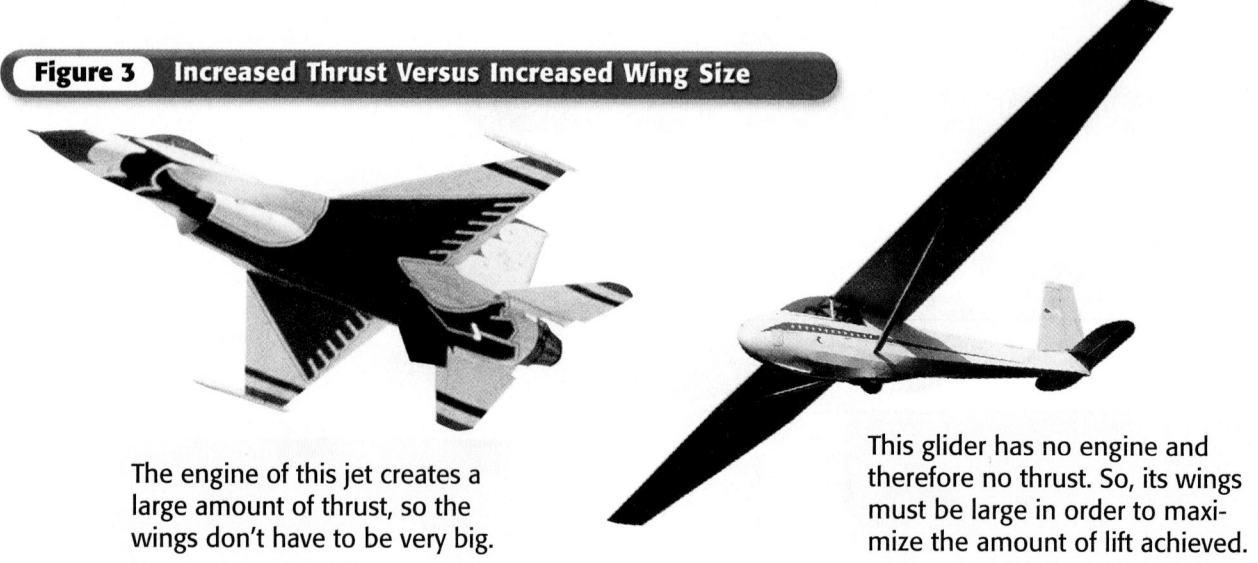

Figure 3 Increased Thrust Versus Increased Wing Size

The engine of this jet creates a large amount of thrust, so the wings don't have to be very big.

This glider has no engine and therefore no thrust. So, its wings must be large in order to maximize the amount of lift achieved.

thrust the pushing or pulling force exerted by the engine of an aircraft or rocket

Thrust and Lift

The amount of lift created by a plane's wing is determined partly by the speed at which air travels around the wing. The speed of a plane is determined mostly by its thrust. **Thrust** is the forward force produced by the plane's engine. In general, a plane with a large amount of thrust moves faster than a plane that has less thrust does. This faster speed means air travels around the wing at a higher speed, which increases lift.

Wing Size, Speed, and Lift

The amount of lift also depends partly on the size of a plane's wings. Look at the jet plane in **Figure 3.** It can fly with a relatively small wing size because its engine gives a large amount of thrust. This thrust pushes the plane through the sky at great speeds. So, the jet creates a large amount of lift with small wings by moving quickly through the air. Smaller wings keep a plane's weight low, which also helps the plane move faster.

Compared with the jet, the glider in **Figure 3** has a large wing area. A glider is an engineless plane. It must be towed up into the air and rides rising air currents to stay in flight. Without engines, gliders produce no thrust and move more slowly than many other kinds of planes. Thus, a glider must have large wings to create the lift it needs to stay in the air.

Bernoulli and Birds

Birds don't have engines, so birds must flap their wings to push themselves through the air. A small bird must flap its wings at a fast pace to stay in the air. But a hawk flaps its wings only occasionally because it has larger wings than the small bird has. A hawk uses its large wings to fly with very little effort. Fully extended, a hawk's wings allow the hawk to glide on wind currents and still have enough lift to stay in the air.

CONNECTION TO Social Studies

The First Flight The first successful flight of an engine-driven machine that was heavier than air happened in Kitty Hawk, North Carolina, in 1903. Orville Wright was the pilot. The plane flew only 37 m (about the length of a 737 jet) before landing, and the entire flight lasted only 12 s. Research another famous pilot in the history of flight. Make a poster that includes information about the pilot as well as pictures of the pilot and his or her airplane.

ACTiViTY

Figure 4 Bernoulli's Principle and the Screwball

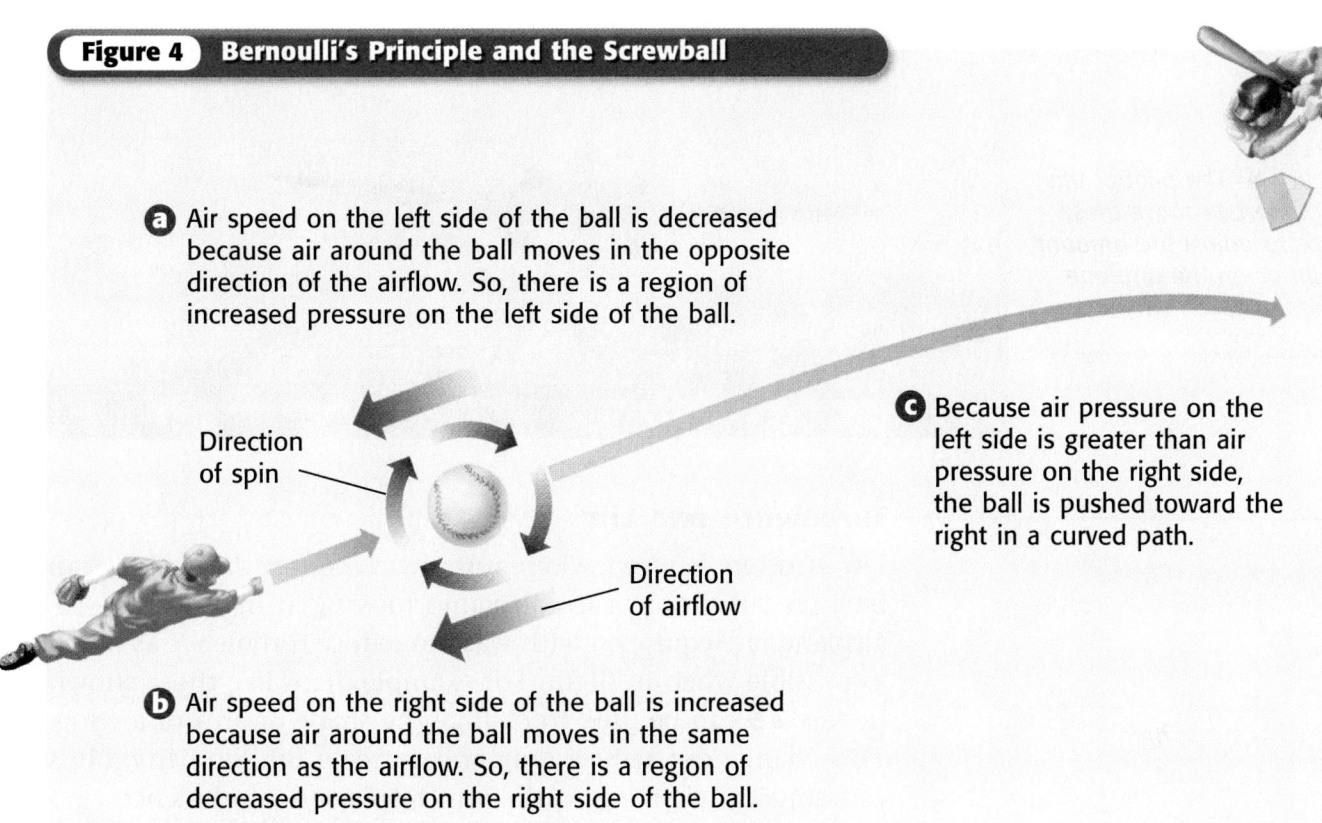

a Air speed on the left side of the ball is decreased because air around the ball moves in the opposite direction of the airflow. So, there is a region of increased pressure on the left side of the ball.

Direction of spin

Direction of airflow

c Because air pressure on the left side is greater than air pressure on the right side, the ball is pushed toward the right in a curved path.

b Air speed on the right side of the ball is increased because air around the ball moves in the same direction as the airflow. So, there is a region of decreased pressure on the right side of the ball.

Bernoulli and Baseball

You don't have to look up at a bird or a plane flying through the sky to see Bernoulli's principle in your world. Any time fluids are moving, Bernoulli's principle is at work. **Figure 4** shows how a baseball pitcher can take advantage of Bernoulli's principle to throw a confusing screwball that is difficult for a batter to hit.

Drag and Motion in Fluids

Have you ever walked into a strong wind and noticed that the wind seemed to slow you down? It may have felt like the wind was pushing you backward. Fluids exert a force that opposes the motion of objects moving through the fluids. The force that opposes or restricts motion in a fluid is called **drag.**

In a strong wind, air "drags" on your body and makes it difficult for you to move forward. Drag also works against the forward motion of a plane or bird in flight. Drag is usually caused by an irregular flow of air. An irregular or unpredictable flow of fluids is known as *turbulence.*

Benchmark Check How does drag affect the motion of a plane in flight? **C.2.3.6 AA**

drag a force parallel to the velocity of the flow; it opposes the direction of an aircraft and, in combination with thrust, determines the speed of the aircraft

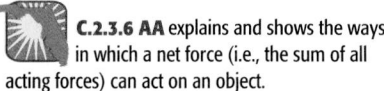
C.2.3.6 AA explains and shows the ways in which a net force (i.e., the sum of all acting forces) can act on an object.

Figure 5 *The pilot of this airplane can move these flaps to adjust the amount of lift when the airplane lands or takes off.*

Turbulence and Lift

Lift is often reduced when turbulence causes drag. Drag can be a serious problem for airplanes moving at high speeds. So, airplanes are equipped with ways to reduce turbulence as much as possible when in flight. For example, flaps like those shown in **Figure 5** can be used to change the shape or area of a wing. This change can reduce drag and increase lift. Similarly, birds can adjust their wing feathers in response to turbulence.

✓ *Reading Check* **Why do airplanes need to reduce turbulence?**

Pascal's Principle

Imagine that the water-pumping station in your town increases the water pressure by 20 Pa. Will the water pressure be increased more at a store two blocks away or at a home 2 km away?

Believe it or not, the increase in water pressure will be the same at both locations. This equal change in water pressure is explained by Pascal's principle. **Pascal's principle** states that a change in pressure at any point in an enclosed fluid will be transmitted equally to all parts of that fluid. This principle was discovered by the 17th-century French scientist Blaise Pascal.

Pascal's principle the principle that states that a fluid in equilibrium contained in a vessel exerts a pressure of equal intensity in all directions

Pascal's Principle and Motion

Hydraulic (hie DRAW lik) devices use Pascal's principle to move or lift objects. Liquids are used in hydraulic devices because liquids cannot be easily compressed, or squeezed, into a smaller space. Cranes, forklifts, and bulldozers have hydraulic devices that help them lift heavy objects.

Hydraulic devices can multiply forces. Car brakes are a good example. In **Figure 6,** a driver's foot exerts pressure on a cylinder of liquid. This pressure is transmitted to all parts of the liquid-filled brake system. The liquid moves the brake pads. The pads press against the wheels, and friction stops the car. The force is multiplied because the pistons that push the brake pads are larger than the piston that is pushed by the brake pedal.

Figure 6 *Because of Pascal's principle, the touch of a foot can stop tons of moving metal.*

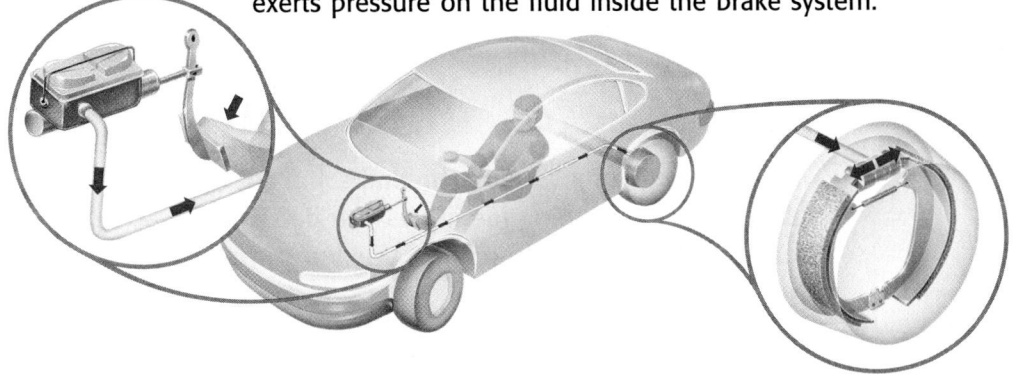

1 When the driver pushes the brake pedal, a small piston exerts pressure on the fluid inside the brake system.

2 The change in pressure is transmitted to the large pistons that push on the brake pads.

SECTION Review

Summary

● Bernoulli's principle states that fluid pressure decreases as the speed of the fluid increases.

● Wing shape allows airplanes to take advantage of Bernoulli's principle to achieve flight. **C.2.3.3, C.2.3.6 AA**

● Lift on an airplane is determined by wing size and thrust.

● Drag opposes motion through fluids. **C.2.3.6 AA**

● Pascal's principle states that a change in pressure in an enclosed fluid is transmitted equally to all parts of the fluid.

Using Key Terms

For each pair of terms, explain how the meanings of the terms differ.

1. *Bernoulli's principle* and *Pascal's principle*

2. *thrust* and *drag*

Understanding Key Ideas

3. How are pressure and fluid speed related?

4. What is Pascal's principle?

5. What force opposes motion through a fluid? How does this force affect lift? **C.2.3.6 AA**

6. How do thrust, lift, and wing size apply to an airplane's flight? **C.2.3.3, C.2.3.6 AA**

Critical Thinking

7. **Applying Concepts** Air moving around a speeding race car can create lift. Upside-down wings, or spoilers, are mounted on the rear of race cars. Use Bernoulli's principle to explain how spoilers reduce the number of accidents.

8. **Making Inferences** When you squeeze a balloon, where is the pressure inside the balloon increased the most? Explain.

FCAT Preparation

9. Gravity is a force that pulls objects toward Earth. Lift is an upward force on an object that moves in a fluid. Lift is the force that keeps airplanes aloft. Lift on a plane can be increased by increasing the plane's speed. Predict the motion of a plane if the lift on the plane is greater than the force of gravity on the plane.
C.2.3.6 AA

A. The plane will move forward.

B. The plane will move backward.

C. The plane will move upward.

D. The plane will move downward.

Skills Practice Lab

Fluids, Force, and Floating

Why do some objects sink in fluids but others float? In this lab, you'll get a sinking feeling as you determine that an object floats when its weight equals the buoyant force exerted by the surrounding fluid.

OBJECTIVES

Calculate the buoyant force on an object. C.2.3.2

Compare the buoyant force on an object with its weight.

MATERIALS

- balance
- mass set
- pan, rectangular baking
- paper towels
- ruler, metric
- tub, plastic, large rectangular
- water

SAFETY

Procedure

① Copy the table shown below.

Measurement	Trial 1	Trial 2
Length (l), cm		
Width (w), cm		
Initial height (h_1), cm		
Initial volume (V_1), cm³ $V_1 = l \times w \times h_1$		
New height (h_2), cm	*DO NOT WRITE IN BOOK*	
New total volume (V_2), cm³ $V_2 = l \times w \times h_2$		
Displaced volume (ΔV), cm³ $\Delta V = V_2 - V_1$		
Mass of displaced water, g $m = \Delta V \times 1 \text{ g/cm}^3$		
Weight of displaced water, N (buoyant force)		
Weight of pan and masses, N		

② Fill the tub half full with water. Measure (in centimeters) the length, width, and initial height of the water. Record your measurements in the table.

③ Using the equation given in the table, determine the initial volume of water in the tub. Record your results in the table.

④ Place the pan in the water, and place masses in the pan, as shown on the next page. Keep adding masses until the pan sinks to about three-quarters of its height. Record the new height of the water in the table. Then, use this value to determine and record the new total volume of water plus the volume of water displaced by the pan.

C.2.3.2 knows common contact forces.

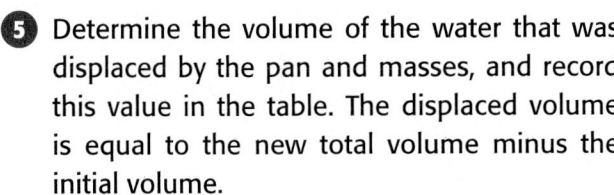

5 Determine the volume of the water that was displaced by the pan and masses, and record this value in the table. The displaced volume is equal to the new total volume minus the initial volume.

6 Determine the mass of the displaced water by multiplying the displaced volume by its density (1 g/cm^3). Record the mass in the table.

7 Divide the mass by 100. The value you get is the weight of the displaced water in newtons (N). This is equal to the buoyant force. Record the weight of the displaced water in the table.

8 Remove the pan and masses, and determine their total mass (in grams) using the balance. Convert the mass to weight (N), as you did in step 7. Record the weight of the masses and pan in the table.

9 Place the empty pan back in the tub. Perform a second trial by repeating steps 4–8. This time, add masses until the pan is just about to sink.

Analyze the Results

1 **Identifying Patterns** Compare the buoyant force (the weight of the displaced water) with the weight of the pan and masses for both trials.

2 **Examining Data** How did the buoyant force differ between the two trials? Explain.

Draw Conclusions

3 **Drawing Conclusions** Based on your observations, what would happen if you were to add even more mass to the pan than you did in the second trial? Explain your answer in terms of the buoyant force.

4 **Making Predictions** What would happen if you put the masses in the water without the pan? What difference does the pan's shape make?

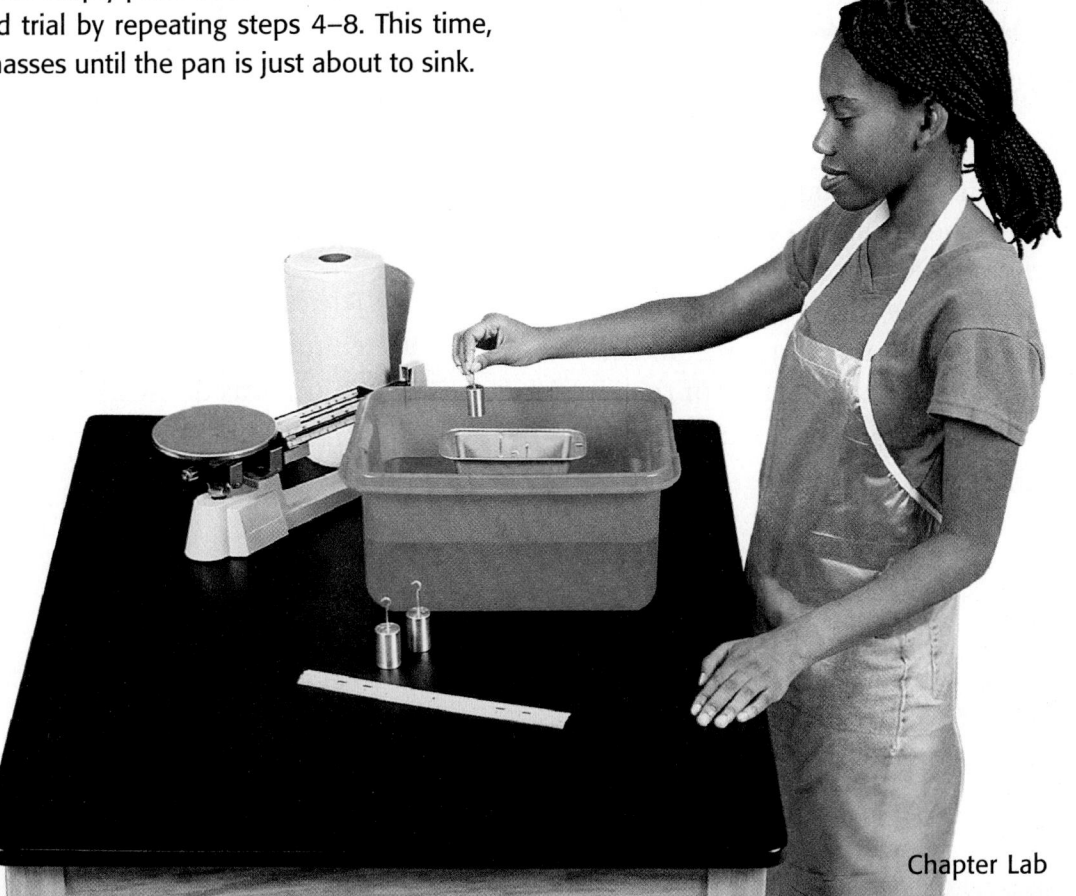

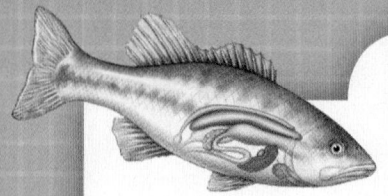

Chapter Review

USING KEY TERMS

In each of the following sentences, replace the incorrect term with the correct term from the word bank.

thrust
pressure FCAT VOCAB
drag
fluid
Pascal's principle
Bernoulli's principle

1 Lift increases with the depth of a fluid.

2 A plane's engines produce drag to push the plane forward.

3 A pascal can be a liquid or a gas.

4 A hydraulic device uses Archimedes' principle to lift or move objects.

UNDERSTANDING KEY IDEAS

Multiple Choice

5 Water pressure increases as depth increases. So, if you place an object in water, the water will exert more pressure on the bottom of an object than it will on the top of the object. The result is a net upward force on the object. What is the name of this net upward force? C.2.3.6 AA FCAT

a. drag
b. lift
c. buoyant force
d. water force

6 Fluid pressure is always directed

a. up.　　　　**c.** sideways.
b. down.　　　**d.** in all directions.

7 An object surrounded by a fluid will displace a volume of fluid that is

a. equal to its own volume.
b. less than its own volume.
c. greater than its own volume.
d. denser than itself.

8 An object weighs 50 N. When the object is placed in water, the object displaces a volume of water that weighs 10 N. What is the buoyant force on the object? C.2.3.6 AA FCAT

a. 60 N　　　**c.** 40 N
b. 50 N　　　**d.** 10 N

9 A helium-filled balloon will float in air because

a. there is more air than helium.
b. helium is less dense than air.
c. helium is as dense as air.
d. helium is denser than air.

10 Materials that can flow to fit their containers include

a. gases.
b. liquids.
c. both gases and liquids.
d. gases, liquids, and solids.

Short Answer

11 Where is water pressure greater, at a depth of 1 m in a large lake or at a depth of 2 m in a small pond? Justify your conclusion.

12 Why are tornadoes like giant vacuum cleaners?

Math Skills

13 Calculate the area of a 1,500 N object that exerts a pressure of 500 Pa (500 N/m^2). Then, calculate the pressure exerted by the same object over twice that area.

CRITICAL THINKING

Extended Response

14 **Forming Hypotheses** Gases can be easily compressed into smaller spaces. Hypothesize a reason for why this property of gases makes gases less useful than liquids in hydraulic brakes.

15 **Applying Concepts** What would happen if the force of gravity on a plane is greater than the lift on the plane? At what point during a plane's flight would a pilot want gravity to be greater than lift? **C.2.3.6 AA** *FCAT*

16 **Evaluating Hypotheses** A 600 N girl on stilts talks to two 600 N boys who are sitting on the ground. She says that she is exerting over twice as much pressure as the two boys are exerting together. Could her statement be true? Explain your reasoning.

17 **Making Comparisons** Will a ship that is loaded with beach balls float higher or lower in the water than an empty ship? Explain your reasoning.

Concept Mapping

18 Use the following terms to create a concept map: *fluid, pressure, depth, density,* and *buoyant force.*

INTERPRETING GRAPHICS

Use the diagram of an iceberg below to answer the questions that follow.

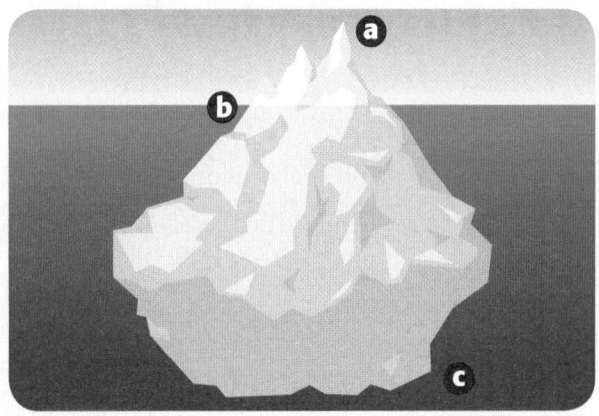

19 At what point (a, b, or c) is water pressure greatest on the iceberg?

20 How much of the iceberg has a weight that is equal to the buoyant force? **C.2.3.3, C.2.3.6 AA**

a. all of the iceberg

b. the section from a to b

c. the section from b to c

d. None of the above

21 Compare the density of ice with the density of water.

22 Why do you think icebergs are dangerous to passing ships?

For the following questions, write your answers on a separate sheet of paper.

1 The image below shows a type of thermometer that was invented by Galileo. The hearts move up and down as the temperature changes. You read the temperature by looking at the labeled coin hanging from the lowest floating heart. The heart shown in close-up to the right of the thermometer is suspended in the fluid inside the thermometer.

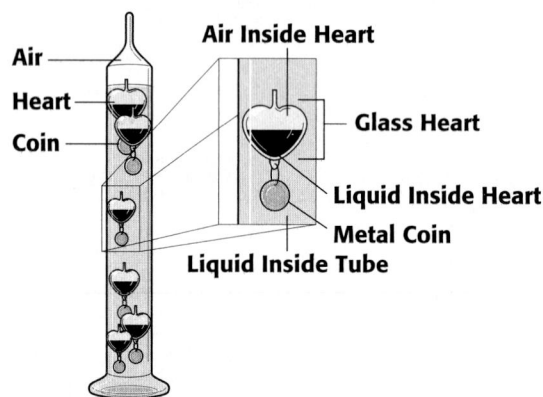

Galileo Thermometer

Which four forces acting on this suspended heart are balanced?

A. the weight of the metal coin, the weight of the glass heart, the pressure of the air inside the tube, and the buoyancy of the air inside the heart

B. the buoyancy of the heart and coin, the weight of the contents of the heart, the weight of the metal coin, and the weight of the glass heart

C. the pressure of the air inside the tube, the buoyancy of the heart and coin, the weight of the contents of the heart, and the weight of the metal coin

D. the weight of the glass heart, the pressure of the air inside the tube, the buoyancy of the air inside the heart, and the weight of the liquid inside the heart

2 Veronica is flying a kite. The kite weighs 1.4 newtons, the kite string weighs 0.2 newtons, and the kite has a tail weighing 0.5 newtons. The wind is pushing the kite up with a force of 7.5 newtons. How much force (in newtons) does Veronica need to exert to keep the kite from flying away?

DO NOT WRITE IN BOOK

3 The image below shows the forces acting on an airplane in flight.

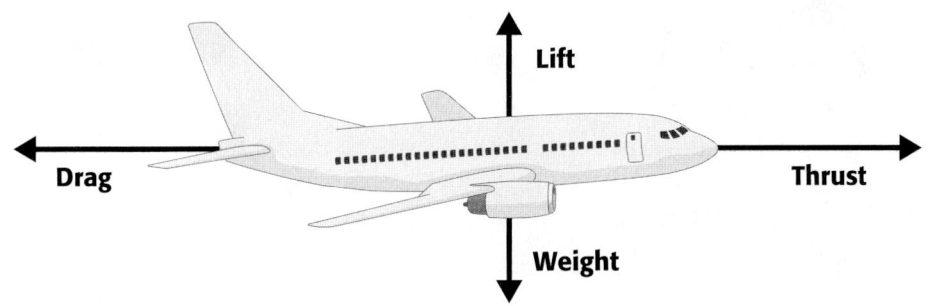

Which two forces balance each other when the airplane flies at a constant altitude?

F. lift and drag
G. thrust and lift
H. weight and lift
I. thrust and weight

4 The image below shows a human-powered vehicle. The vehicle and rider are fully enclosed.

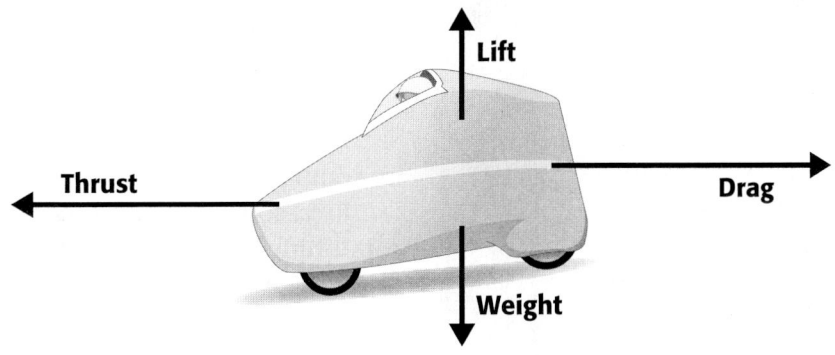

Which force is **most** reduced by putting the enclosure around the vehicle and rider?

A. drag
B. lift
C. thrust
D. weight

5 Sky divers jump out of airplanes at high altitudes. Before the parachute opens, a sky diver can adjust his or her speed by changing body position. Explain why a sky diver accelerates downward after jumping out of the plane and how changing body position can adjust speed during the fall.

READ
INQUIRE
EXPLAIN

STOP

Science in Action

Weird Science

Kiteboarding

If you go to any beach in Florida and look out over the water you might see something strange—someone who appears to be flying a giant kite over the ocean! No, a person has not been accidentally blown out to sea. It is someone who is participating in a new, popular water sport called *kiteboarding*.

The idea behind kiteboarding is simple. A person straps his or her feet to a small board and uses a large, controllable kite to propel himself or herself across the water and into the air. The kites create lift as the strong ocean breezes blow around them. This lift is large enough to send a person soaring through the air for short periods of time.

Math **Activity**

A person who is kiteboarding is moving at a speed of 12 m/s. How much time is needed for the person to travel 60 m?

Science Fiction

"Wet Behind the Ears"
by Jack C. Haldeman II

Willie Joe Thomas cheated to get a swimming scholarship. Now, he is faced with a major swim meet, and his coach told him that he has to swim or be kicked off the team. Willie Joe could lose his scholarship.

One day, Willie Joe's roommate, Frank, announces that he has developed a new "sliding compound." And Frank also said something about using the compound to make ships go faster. So, Willie Joe thought, if it works for ships, it might work for swimming.

See what happens when Willie Joe tries to save his scholarship by using Frank's compound at the swim meet. Read "Wet Behind the Ears," by Jack C. Haldeman II in the *Holt Anthology of Science Fiction*.

Language Arts **Activity**

Analyze the story structure of "Wet Behind the Ears." In your analysis, identify the introduction, the rising action, the climax, and the denouement. Summarize your analysis in a chart.

Alisha Bracken

Scuba Instructor Alisha Bracken first started scuba diving in her freshman year of college. Her first dives were in a saltwater hot spring near Salt Lake City, Utah. "It was awesome," Bracken says. "There were nurse sharks, angelfish, puffer fish and brine shrimp!" Bracken enjoyed her experience so much that she wanted to share it with other people. The best way to do that was to become an instructor and teach other people to dive.

Bracken says one of the biggest challenges of being a scuba instructor is teaching people to adapt and function in a foreign environment. She believes that learning to dive properly is important not only for the safety of the diver but also for the protection of the underwater environment. She relies on science principles to help teach people how to control their movements and protect the natural environment. "Buoyancy is the foundation of teaching people to dive comfortably," she explains. "Without it, we cannot float on the surface or stay off the bottom. Underwater life can be damaged if students do not learn and apply the concepts of buoyancy."

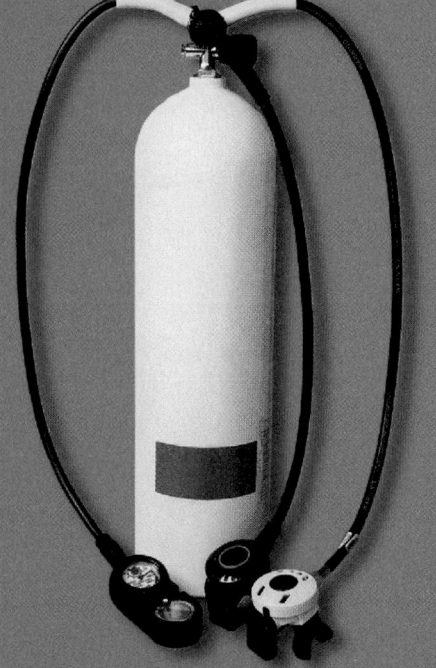

Social Studies ACTiViTY

Scuba divers and other underwater explorers sometimes investigate shipwrecks on the bottom of the ocean. Research the exploration of a specific shipwreck. Make a poster showing what artifacts were retrieved from the shipwreck and what was learned from the exploration.

To learn more about these Science in Action topics, visit **go.hrw.com** and type in the keyword **HT6FFLFF.**

Current Science

Check out Current Science® articles related to this chapter by visiting go.hrw.com. Just type in the keyword HP5CS07.

Contents

Skills Practice Lab

Exploring the Unseen

Your teacher will give you a box in which a special divider has been created. Your task is to describe this divider as precisely as possible—without opening the box! Your only aid is a marble that is also inside the box. This task will allow you to demonstrate your understanding of the scientific method. Good luck!

Ask a Question

❶ Record the question that you are trying to answer by doing this experiment. (Hint: Read the introductory paragraph again if you are not sure what your task is.)

Form a Hypothesis

❷ Before you begin the experiment, think about what's required. Do you think you will be able to easily determine the shape of the divider? Can you determine its texture or color? Write a hypothesis that states how much you think you will be able to determine about the divider during the experiment. (Remember that you can't open the box!)

Test the Hypothesis

❸ Using all the methods you can think of (except opening the box), test your hypothesis. Make careful notes about your testing and observations.

Analyze the Results

❶ What characteristics of the divider were you able to identify? Draw or write your best description of the interior of the box.

❷ Do your observations support your hypothesis? Explain. If your results do not support your hypothesis, write a new hypothesis, and test it.

❸ With your teacher's permission, open the box, and look inside. Record your observations.

Draw Conclusions

❹ Write a paragraph summarizing your experiment. Be sure to include what methods you used, whether your results supported your hypothesis, and how you could improve your methods.

Skills Practice Lab

Graphing Data

When performing an experiment, you usually need to collect data. To understand the data, you can often organize them into a graph. Graphs can show trends and patterns that you might not notice in a table or list. In this exercise, you will practice collecting data and organizing the data into a graph.

Procedure

1 Pour 200 mL of water into a 400 mL beaker. Add ice to the beaker until the waterline is at the 400 mL mark.

2 Place a Celsius thermometer into the beaker. Use a thermometer clip to prevent the thermometer from touching the bottom of the beaker. Record the temperature of the ice water.

3 Place the beaker and thermometer on a hot plate. Turn the hot plate on medium heat, and record the temperature every minute until the water temperature reaches 100°C.

4 Using heat-resistant gloves, remove the beaker from the hot plate. Continue to record the temperature of the water each minute for 10 more minutes. **Caution:** Don't forget to turn off the hot plate.

5 On a piece of graph paper, create a graph similar to the one below. Label the horizontal axis (the x-axis) "Time (min)," and mark the axis in increments of 1 min as shown. Label the vertical axis (the y-axis) "Temperature (°C)," and mark the axis in increments of 10° as shown.

6 Find the 1 min mark on the x-axis, and move up the graph to the temperature you recorded at 1 min. Place a dot on the graph at that point. Plot each temperature in the same way. When you have plotted all of your data, connect the dots with a smooth line.

MATERIALS

- beaker, 400 mL
- clock (or watch) with a second hand
- gloves, heat-resistant
- hot plate
- ice
- paper, graph
- thermometer, Celsius, with a clip
- water, 200 mL

SAFETY

Analyze the Results

1 Examine your graph. Do you think the water heated faster than it cooled? Explain.

2 Estimate what the temperature of the water was 2.5 min after you placed the beaker on the hot plate. Explain how you can make a good estimate of temperature between those you recorded.

Draw Conclusions

3 Explain how a graph may give more information than the same data in a table.

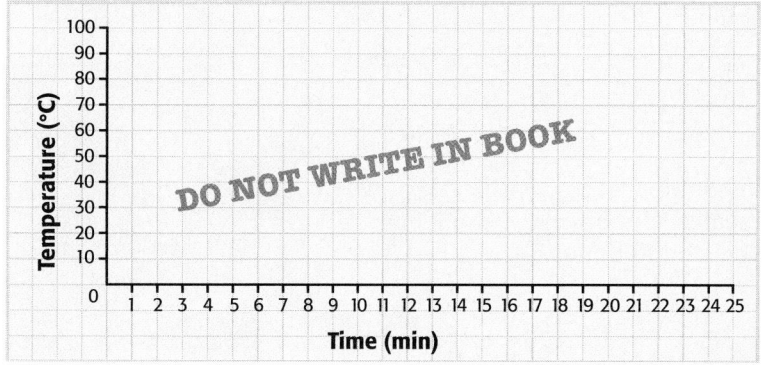

Model-Making Lab

A Window to a Hidden World

Have you ever noticed that objects underwater appear closer than they really are? The reason is that light waves change speed when they travel from air into water. Anton van Leeuwenhoek, a pioneer of microscopy in the late 17th century, used a drop of water to magnify objects. That drop of water brought a hidden world closer into view. How did Leeuwenhoek's microscope work? In this investigation, you will build a model of it to find out.

MATERIALS

- eyedropper
- hole punch
- newspaper
- plastic wrap, clear
- poster board, 3 cm × 10 cm
- tape, transparent
- water

Procedure

1. Punch a hole in the center of the poster board with a hole punch, as shown in (a) at right.

2. Tape a small piece of clear plastic wrap over the hole, as shown in (b) at right. Be sure the plastic wrap is large enough so that the tape you use to secure it does not cover the hole.

3. Use an eyedropper to put one drop of water over the hole. Check to be sure your drop of water is dome-shaped (convex), as shown in (c) at right.

4. Hold the microscope close to your eye and look through the drop. Be careful not to disturb the water drop.

5. Hold the microscope over a piece of newspaper, and observe the image.

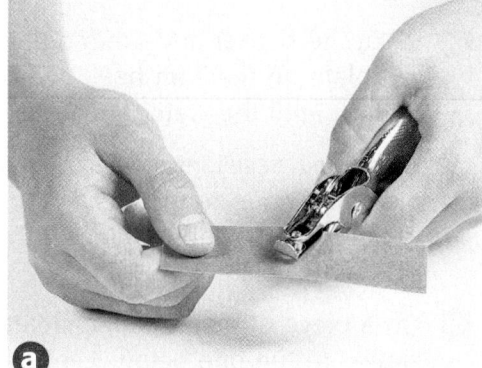
a

Analyze the Results

1. Describe and draw the image you see. Is the image larger than or the same size as it is without the microscope? Is the image clear or blurred? Is the shape of the image distorted?

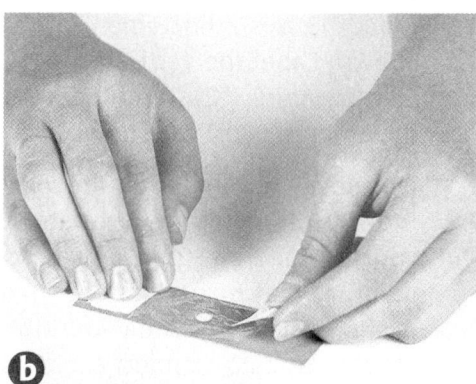
b

Draw Conclusions

2. How do you think your model could be improved?

Applying Your Data

Robert Hooke and Zacharias Janssen contributed much to the field of microscopy. Research one of them, and write a paragraph about his contributions.

c

Inquiry Lab

Save the Cube!

The biggest enemy of an ice cube is the transfer of thermal energy—heat. Energy can be transferred to an ice cube in three ways: conduction (the transfer of energy through direct contact), convection (the transfer of energy by the movement of a liquid or gas), and radiation (the transfer of energy through matter or space). Your challenge in this activity is to design a way to protect an ice cube as much as possible from all three types of energy transfer.

MATERIALS

- bag, plastic, small
- balance, metric
- cup, plastic or paper, small
- ice cube
- milk carton, empty, half-pint
- assorted materials provided by your teacher

Ask a Question

1 What materials prevent energy transfer most efficiently?

Form a Hypothesis

2 Design a system that protects an ice cube against each type of energy transfer. Describe your proposed design.

Test the Hypothesis

3 Use a plastic bag to hold the ice cube and any water if the ice cube melts. You may use any of the materials to protect the ice cube. The whole system must fit inside a milk carton.

4 Find the mass of the empty cup, and record it. Then, find and record the mass of an empty plastic bag.

5 Find and record the mass of the ice cube and cup together.

6 Quickly wrap the bag (and the ice cube inside) in its protection. Remember that the package must fit in the milk carton.

7 Place your ice cube in the "thermal zone" set up by your teacher. After 10 min, remove the ice cube from the zone.

8 Open the bag. Pour any water into the cup. Find and record the mass of the cup and water together.

9 Find and record the mass of the water by subtracting the mass of the empty cup from the mass of the cup and water.

10 Use the same method to determine the mass of the ice cube.

11 Using the following equation, find and record the percentage of the ice cube that melted:

$$\% \ melted = \frac{mass \ of \ water}{mass \ of \ ice \ cube} \times 100$$

Analyze the Results

1 Compared with other designs in your class, how well did your design protect against each type of energy transfer? How could you improve your design?

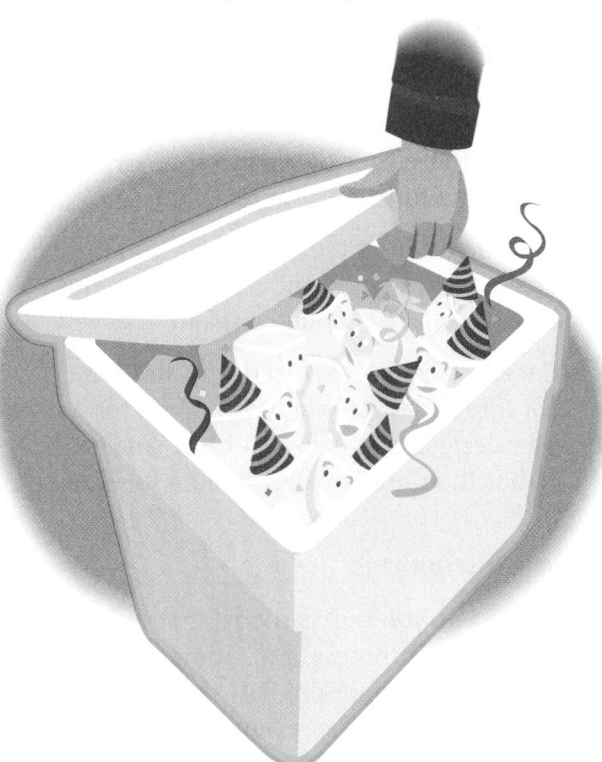

Model-Making Lab

Off to the Races!

Scientists often use models—representations of objects or systems. Physical models, such as a model airplane, are generally a different size than the objects they represent. In this lab, you will build a model car, test its design, and then try to improve the design.

MATERIALS

- board
- clothes-hanger wire, 16 cm
- eraser, pink rubber, or small wood block
- glue
- paper, typing (2 sheets)
- pliers (or wire cutters)
- ruler, metric
- stopwatch
- textbooks

SAFETY

Procedure

1. Using the materials listed, design and build a car that will carry the load (the eraser or block of wood) down the ramp as quickly as possible. Your car must be no wider than 8 cm, it must have room to carry the load, and it must roll.

2. As you test your design, do not be afraid to rebuild or re-design your car. Improving your methods is an important part of scientific progress.

3. When you have a design that works well, measure the time required for your car to roll down the ramp. Record this time. Test your car with this design several times for accuracy.

4. Try to improve your model. Find one thing that you can change to make your model car roll faster down the ramp. Write a description of the change.

5. Test your model again as you did in step 3 and make additional improvements if needed.

Analyze the Results

1. Why is it important to have room in the model car for the eraser or wood block? (Hint: Think about the function of a real car.)

2. Before you built the model car, you created a design for it. Do you think this design is also a model? Explain.

3. Based on your observations in this lab, list three reasons why it is helpful for automobile designers to build and test small model cars rather than immediately build a full-size car.

Draw Conclusions

4. In this lab, you built a model that was smaller than the object it represented. Some models are larger than the objects they represent. List three examples of larger models that are used to represent objects. Why is it helpful to use a larger model in these cases?

Skills Practice Lab

Stayin' Alive!

Every second of your life, your body's trillions of cells take in, use, and store energy. They repair themselves, reproduce, and get rid of waste. Together, these processes are called *metabolism.* Your cells use the food that you eat to provide the energy you need to stay alive.

Your Basal Metabolic Rate (BMR) is a measurement of the energy that your body needs to carry out all the basic life processes while you are at rest. These processes include breathing, keeping your heart beating, and keeping your body's temperature stable. Your BMR is influenced by your gender, your age, and many other things. Your BMR may be different from everyone else's, but it is normal for you. In this activity, you will find the amount of energy, measured in Calories, you need every day in order to stay alive.

MATERIALS

- bathroom scale
- tape measure

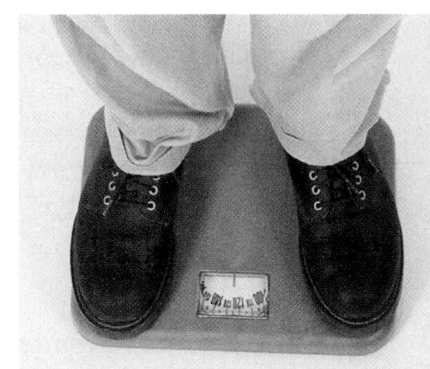

Procedure

1. Find your weight on a bathroom scale. If the scale measures in pounds, you must convert your weight in pounds to your mass in kilograms. To convert your weight in pounds (lb) to mass in kilograms (kg), multiply the number of pounds by 0.454.

Example: If Carlos weighs 125 lb, his mass in kilograms is:

$$\begin{array}{r} 125 \text{ lb} \\ \times\ 0.454 \\ \hline 56.75 \text{ kg} \end{array}$$

2. Use a tape measure to find your height. If the tape measures in inches, convert your height in inches to height in centimeters. To convert your height in inches (in.) to your height in centimeters (cm), multiply the number of inches by 2.54.

If Carlos is 62 in. tall, his height in centimeters is:

$$\begin{array}{r} 62 \text{ in.} \\ \times\ 2.54 \\ \hline 157.48 \text{ cm} \end{array}$$

3 Now that you know your height and mass, use the appropriate formula below to get a close estimate of your BMR. Your answer will give you an estimate of the number of Calories your body needs each day just to stay alive.

Calculating Your BMR	
Females	**Males**
65 + (10 × your mass in kilograms)	66 + (13.5 × your mass in kilograms)
+ (1.8 × your height in centimeters)	+ (5 × your height in centimeters)
− (4.7 × your age in years)	− (6.8 × your age in years)

4 Your metabolism is also influenced by how active you are. Talking, walking, and playing games all take more energy than being at rest. To get an idea of how many Calories your body needs each day to stay healthy, select the lifestyle that best describes yours from the table at right. Then multiply your BMR by the activity factor.

Activity Factors	
Activity lifestyle	**Activity factor**
Moderately inactive (normal, everyday activities)	1.3
Moderately active (exercise 3 to 4 times a week)	1.4
Very active (exercise 4 to 6 times a week)	1.6
Extremely active (exercise 6 to 7 times a week)	1.8

Analyze the Results

1 In what way could you compare your whole body to a single cell? Explain.

2 Does an increase in activity increase your BMR? Does an increase in activity increase your need for Calories? Explain your answers.

Draw Conclusions

3 If you are moderately inactive, how many more Calories would you need if you began to exercise every day?

Applying Your Data

The best energy sources are those that supply the correct amount of Calories for your lifestyle and also provide the nutrients you need. Research in the library or on the Internet to find out which kinds of foods are the best energy sources for you. How does your list of best energy sources compare with your diet?

List everything you eat and drink in 1 day. Find out how many Calories are in each item, and find the total number of Calories you have consumed. How does this number of Calories compare with the number of Calories you need each day for all your activities?

Inquiry Lab

Muscles at Work

Have you ever exercised outside on a cold fall day wearing only a thin warm-up suit or shorts? How did you stay warm? The answer is that your muscle cells contracted, and when contraction takes place, some energy is used to do work, and the rest is converted to thermal energy. This process helps your body maintain a constant temperature in cold conditions. In this activity, you will learn how the release of energy can cause a change in your body temperature.

MATERIALS

- clock (or watch) with a second hand
- thermometer, small, hand held
- other materials as approved by your teacher

Ask a Question

1 Write a question that you can test about how activity affects body temperature.

Form a Hypothesis

2 Form a group of four students. In your group, discuss several exercises that can produce a change in body temperature. Write a hypothesis that could answer the question you asked.

Test the Hypothesis

3 Develop an experimental procedure that includes the steps necessary to test your hypothesis. Be sure to get your teacher's approval before you begin.

4 Assign tasks to individuals in the group, such as note taking, data recording, and timing. What observations and data will you be recording? Design your data tables accordingly.

5 Perform your experiment as planned by your group. Be sure to record all observations in your data tables.

Analyze the Results

1 How did you determine if muscle contractions cause the release of thermal energy? Was your hypothesis supported by your data? Explain your results in a written report. Describe how you could improve your experimental method.

Applying Your Data

Why do humans shiver in the cold? Do all animals shiver? Find out why shivering is one of the first signs that your body is becoming too cold.

Model-Making Lab

Build a Lung

When you breathe, you actually pull air into your lungs because your diaphragm muscle causes your chest to expand. You can see this is true by placing your hands on your ribs and inhaling slowly. Did you feel your chest expand?

In this activity, you will build a model of a lung by using some common materials. You will see how the diaphragm muscle works to inflate your lungs. Refer to the diagrams at right as you construct your model.

MATERIALS

- bag, trash, small plastic
- balloon, small
- bottle, top half, 2 L
- clay, golf-ball-sized piece
- rubber bands (2)
- ruler, metric
- straw, plastic
- tape, transparent

Procedure

1. Attach the balloon to the end of the straw with a rubber band. Make a hole through the clay, and insert the other end of the straw through the hole. Be sure at least 8 cm of the straw extends beyond the clay. Squeeze the ball of clay gently to seal the clay around the straw.

2. Insert the balloon end of the straw into the neck of the bottle. Use the ball of clay to seal the straw and balloon into the bottle.

3. Turn the bottle gently on its side. Place the trash bag over the cut end of the bottle. Expand a rubber band around the bottom of the bottle to secure the bag. You may wish to reinforce the seal with tape. Before the plastic is completely sealed, gather the excess material of the bag into your hand, and press toward the inside of the bottle slightly. (You may need to tie a knot about halfway up from the bottom of the bag to take up excess material.) Use tape to finish sealing the bag to the bottle with the bag in this position. The excess air will be pushed out of the bottle.

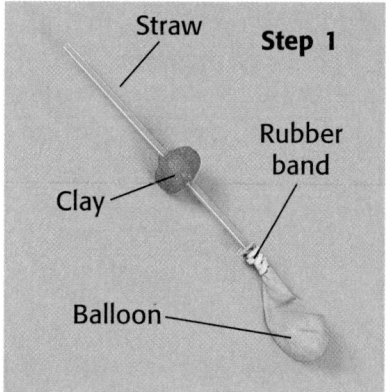

Straw · Step 1 · Rubber band · Clay · Balloon

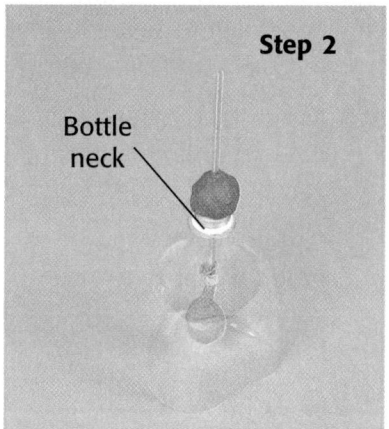

Step 2 · Bottle neck

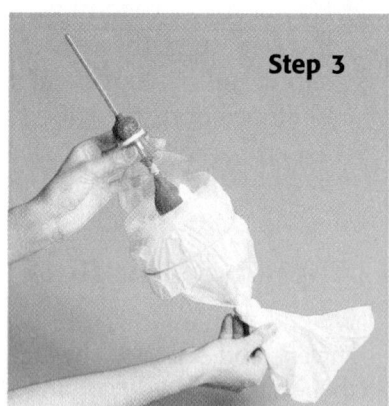

Step 3

Analyze the Results

1. What can you do with your model to make the "lung" inflate?

2. What do the balloon, the plastic wrap, and the straw represent in your model?

3. Using your model, demonstrate to the class how air enters the lung and how air exits the lung.

Applying Your Data

Do some research to find out what an "iron lung" is and why it was used in the past. Research and write a report about what is used today to help people who have difficulty breathing.

Skills Practice Lab

Enzymes in Action

You know how important enzymes are in the process of digestion. This lab will help you see enzymes at work. Hydrogen peroxide is continuously produced by your cells. If it is not quickly broken down, hydrogen peroxide will kill your cells. Luckily, your cells contain an enzyme that converts hydrogen peroxide into two nonpoisonous substances. This enzyme is also present in the cells of beef liver. In this lab, you will observe the action of this enzyme on hydrogen peroxide.

Procedure

1 Draw a data table similar to the one below. Be sure to leave enough space to write your observations.

MATERIALS

- beef liver, 1 cm cubes (3)
- gloves, protective
- graduated cylinder, 10 mL
- hydrogen peroxide, fresh (4 mL)
- mortar and pestle (or fork and watch glass)
- plate, small
- spatula
- test tube (3)
- test-tube rack
- tweezers
- water

SAFETY

Data Table

Size and condition of liver	Experimental liquid	Observations
1 cm cube beef liver	2 mL water	
1 cm cube beef liver	2 mL hydrogen peroxide	DO NOT WRITE IN BOOK
1 cm cube beef liver (mashed)	2 mL hydrogen peroxide	

2. Get three equal-sized pieces of beef liver from your teacher, and use your forceps to place them on your plate.

3. Pour 2 mL of water into a test tube labeled "Water and liver."

4. Using the tweezers, carefully place one piece of liver in the test tube. Record your observations in your data table.

5. Pour 2 mL of hydrogen peroxide into a second test tube labeled "Liver and hydrogen peroxide."
Caution: Do not splash hydrogen peroxide on your skin. If you do get hydrogen peroxide on your skin, rinse the affected area with running water immediately, and tell your teacher.

6. Using the tweezers, carefully place one piece of liver in the test tube. Record your observations of the second test tube in your data table.

7. Pour another 2 mL of hydrogen peroxide into a third test tube labeled "Ground liver and hydrogen peroxide."

8. Using a mortar and pestle (or fork and watch glass), carefully grind the third piece of liver.

9. Using the spatula, scrape the ground liver into the third test tube. Record your observations of the third test tube in your data table.

Analyze the Results

1. What was the purpose of putting the first piece of liver in water? Why was this a necessary step?

2. Describe the difference you observed between the liver and the ground liver when each was placed in the hydrogen peroxide. How can you account for this difference?

Applying Your Data

Do plant cells contain enzymes that break down hydrogen peroxide? Try this experiment using potato cubes instead of liver to find out.

Skills Practice Lab

My, How You've Grown!

MATERIALS

• paper, graph
• pencils, colored

In humans, the process of development that takes place between fertilization and birth lasts about 266 days. In 4 weeks, the new individual grows from a single fertilized cell to an embryo whose heart is beating and pumping blood. All of the organ systems and body parts are completely formed by the end of the seventh month. During the last 2 months before birth, the baby grows, and its organ systems mature. At birth, the average mass of a baby is about 33,000 times as much as that of an embryo at 2 weeks of development! In this activity, you will discover just how fast a fetus grows.

Procedure

1. Using graph paper, make two graphs—one entitled "Length" and one entitled "Mass." On the length graph, use intervals of 25 mm on the y-axis. Extend the y-axis to 500 mm. On the mass graph, use intervals of 100 g on the y-axis. Extend this y-axis to 3,300 g. Use 2-week intervals for time on the x-axes for both graphs. Both x-axes should extend to 40 weeks.

2. Examine the data table at right. Plot the data in the table on your graphs. Use a colored pencil to draw the curved line that joins the points on each graph.

Analyze the Results

1. Describe the change in mass of a developing fetus. How can you explain this change?

2. Describe the change in length of a developing fetus. How does the change in mass compare to the change in length?

Increase of Mass and Length of Average Human Fetus		
Time (weeks)	Mass (g)	Length (mm)
2	0.1	1.5
3	0.3	2.3
4	0.5	5.0
5	0.6	10.0
6	0.8	15.0
8	1.0	30.0
13	15.0	90.0
17	115.0	140.0
21	300.0	250.0
26	950.0	320.0
30	1,500.0	400.0
35	2,300.0	450.0
40	3,300.0	500.0

Applying Your Data

Using the information in your graphs, estimate how tall a child would be at age 3 if he or she continued to grow at the same average rate that a fetus grows.

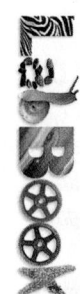

Model-Making Lab

Antibodies to the Rescue

Some cells of the immune system, called *B cells,* make antibodies that attack and kill invading viruses and microorganisms. These antibodies help make you immune to disease. Have you ever had chickenpox? If you have, your body has built up antibodies that can recognize that particular virus. Antibodies will attach themselves to the virus, tagging it for destruction. If you are exposed to the same disease again, the antibodies remember that virus. They will attack the virus even quicker and in greater number than they did the first time. This is the reason that you will probably never have chickenpox more than once.

In this activity, you will construct simple models of viruses and their antibodies. You will see how antibodies are specific for a particular virus.

MATERIALS

- craft materials, such as buttons, fabric scraps, pipe cleaners, and recycled materials
- paper, colored
- scissors
- tape (or glue)

Procedure

1 Draw the virus patterns shown on this page on a separate piece of paper, or design your own virus models from the craft supplies. Remember to design different receptors on each of your virus models.

2 Write a few sentences describing how your viruses are different.

3 Cut out the viruses, and attach them to a piece of colored paper with tape or glue.

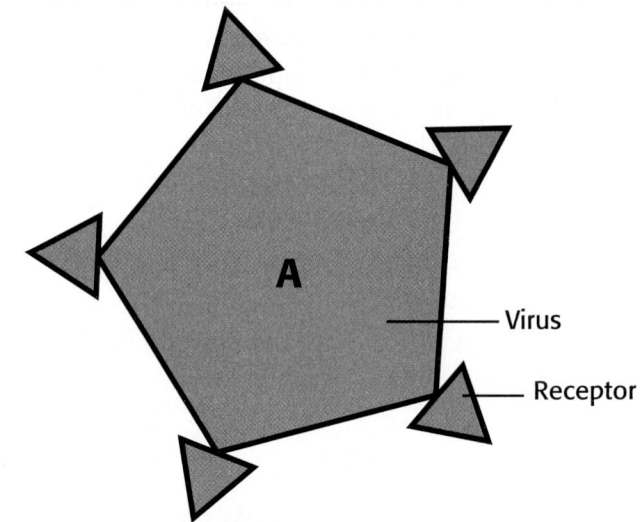

A — Virus — Receptor

Viruses

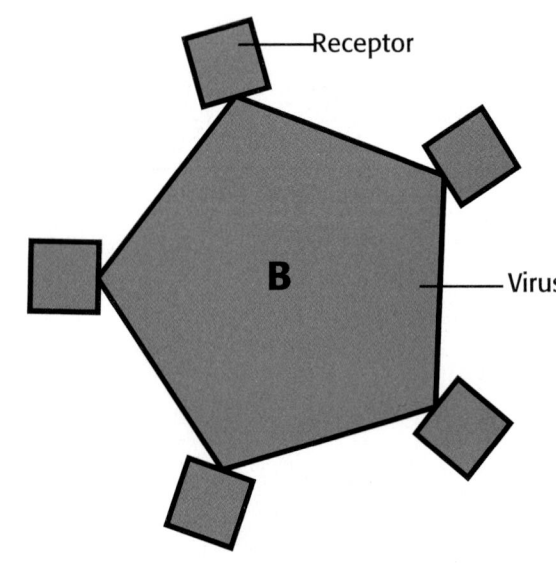

Receptor — B — Virus

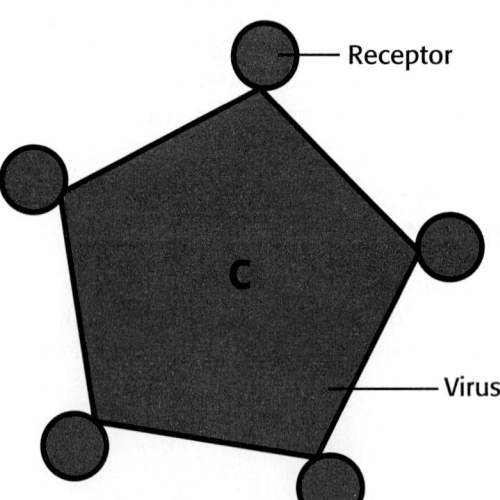

Receptor — C — Virus

4 Select the antibodies drawn below, or design your own antibodies that will exactly fit on the receptors on your virus models. Draw or create each antibody enough times to attach one to each receptor site on the virus.

Antibodies

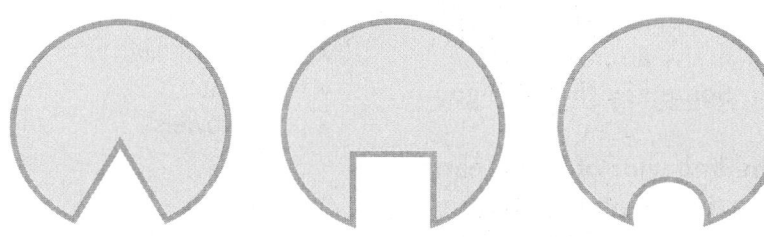

5 Cut out the antibodies you have drawn. Arrange the antibodies so that they bind to the virus at the appropriate receptor. Attach them to the virus with tape or glue.

Analyze the Results

1 Explain how an antibody "recognizes" a particular virus.

2 After the attachment of antibodies to the receptors, what would be the next step in the immune response?

3 Many vaccines use weakened copies of the virus to protect the body. Use the model of a virus and its specific antibody to explain how vaccines work.

Draw Conclusions

4 Use your model of a virus to demonstrate to the class how a receptor might change or mutate so that a vaccine would no longer be effective.

Applying Your Data

Research in the library or on the Internet to find information about the discovery of the Salk vaccine for polio. Include information on how polio affects people today.

Research in the library or on the Internet to find information and write a report about filoviruses. What do they look like? What diseases do they cause? Why are they especially dangerous? Is there an effective vaccine against any filovirus? Explain.

Skills Practice Lab

Wet, Wiggly Worms!

Earthworms have been digging in the Earth for more than 100 million years! Earthworms fertilize the soil with their waste and loosen the soil when they tunnel through the moist dirt of a garden or lawn. Worms are food for many animals, such as birds, frogs, snakes, rodents, and fish. Some say they are good food for people, too!

In this activity, you will observe the behavior of a live earthworm. Remember that earthworms are living animals that deserve to be handled gently. Be sure to keep your earthworm moist during this activity. The skin of the earthworm must stay moist so that the worm can get oxygen. If the earthworm's skin dries out, the worm will suffocate and die. Use a spray bottle to moisten the earthworm with water.

MATERIALS

- celery leaves
- clock
- dissecting pan
- earthworm, live
- flashlight
- paper towels
- probe
- ruler, metric
- shoe box, with lid
- soil
- spray bottle
- water

SAFETY

Procedure

1 Place a wet paper towel in the bottom of a dissecting pan. Put a live earthworm on the paper towel, and observe how the earthworm moves. Record your observations.

2 Use the probe to carefully touch the anterior end (head) of the worm. Gently touch other areas of the worm's body with the probe. Record the kinds of responses you observe.

3 Place celery leaves at one end of the pan. Record how the earthworm responds to the presence of food.

4 Shine a flashlight on the anterior end of the earthworm. Record the earthworm's reaction to the light.

5 Line the bottom of the shoe box with a damp paper towel. Cover half of the shoe box with the box top.

6 Place the worm on the uncovered side of the shoe box in the light. Record your observations of the worm's behavior for 3 min.

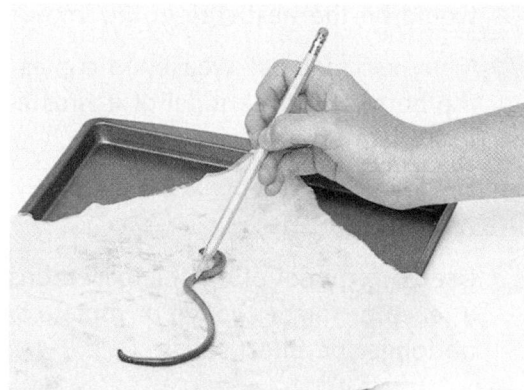

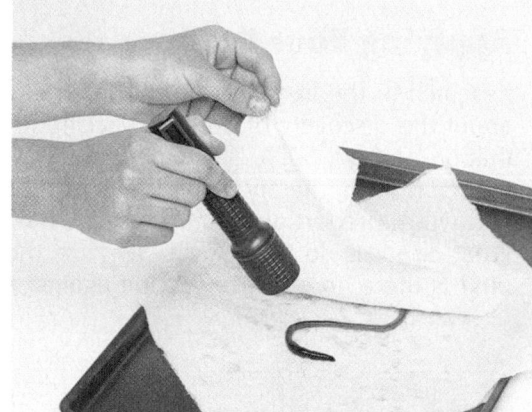

7 Place the worm in the covered side of the box. Record your observations for 3 min.

8 Repeat steps 6–7 three times.

9 Spread some loose soil evenly in the bottom of the shoe box so that the soil is about 4 cm deep. Place the earthworm on top of the soil. Observe and record the earthworm's behavior for 3 min.

10 Dampen the soil on one side of the box, and leave the other side dry. Place the earthworm in the center of the box between the wet and dry soil. Cover the box, and wait 3 min. Uncover the box, and record your observations. Repeat this procedure three times. (You may need to search for the worm!)

Analyze the Results

1 How did the earthworm respond to being touched? Were some areas more sensitive than others?

2 How did the earthworm respond to the presence of food?

Draw Conclusions

3 How is the earthworm's behavior influenced by light? Based on your observations, describe how an animal's response to a stimulus might provide protection for the animal.

4 When the worm was given a choice of wet or dry soil, which did it choose? Explain this result.

Communicating Your Data

Based on your observations of an earthworm's behavior, prepare a poster showing where you might expect to find earthworms. Draw a picture with colored markers, or cut out pictures from magazines. Include all the variables that you used in your experiment, such as soil or no soil, wet or dry soil, light or dark, and food. Write a caption at the bottom of your poster describing where earthworms might be found in nature.

Model-Making Lab

A Passel o' Pioneers

Succession is the natural process of the introduction and development of living things in an area. The area could be one that has never supported life before and has no soil, such as a recently cooled lava flow from a volcano. In an area where there is no soil, the process is called *primary succession.* In an area where soil already exists, such as an abandoned field or a forest after a fire, the process is called *secondary succession.*

In this investigation, you will build a model of secondary succession using natural soil.

MATERIALS

- balance
- graduated cylinder, 250 mL
- large fishbowl
- plastic wrap
- protective gloves
- soil from home or schoolyard, 500 g
- water, 250 mL

Procedure

1. Place the natural soil you brought from home or the schoolyard into the fishbowl, and dampen the soil with 250 mL of water. Cover the top of the fishbowl with plastic wrap, and place the fishbowl in a sunny window.
   Caution: Do not touch your face, eyes, or mouth during this activity. Wash your hands thoroughly when you are finished.

2. For 2 weeks, observe the fishbowl for any new growth. Describe and draw any new organisms you observe. Record these and all other observations.

3. Identify and record the names of as many of these new organisms as you can.

Analyze the Results

1 What kinds of plants sprouted in your model of secondary succession? Were they tree seedlings, grasses, or weeds?

2 Were the plants that sprouted in the fishbowl unusual or common for your area?

Draw Conclusions

3 Explain how the plants that grew in your model of secondary succession can be called pioneer species.

Applying Your Data

Examine each of the photographs on this page. Determine whether each area, if abandoned forever, would undergo primary or secondary succession. You may decide that an area will not undergo succession at all. Explain your reasoning.

Bulldozed land

Eutrophic pond

Mount St. Helens volcano

Shipping port parking lot

Life in the Desert

Organisms that live in the desert have some unusual methods for conserving water. Conserving water is a special challenge for animals that live in the desert. In this activity you will invent a water-conserving "adaptation" for a desert animal, represented by a piece of sponge. You will protect your wet desert sponge so it will dry out as little as possible over a 24 h period.

Ask a Question

1 How can an animal conserve water in the desert?

Form a Hypothesis

2 Plan a method for keeping your "desert animal" from drying out. Your "animal" must be in the open for at least 4 h during the 24 h period. Real desert animals expose themselves to the dry desert heat to search for food. Write your plan and predictions about the outcome of your experiment.

3 Design and draw data tables, if necessary. Have your teacher approve your plan before you begin.

Test the Hypothesis

4 Soak two pieces of sponge in water until they begin to drip. Place each piece on a balance, and record its mass.

5 Immediately protect one sponge according to your plan. Place both pieces in an area where they will not be disturbed. You should take your protected "animal" out for feeding for a total of at least 4 h.

6 At the end of 24 h, place each piece of sponge on the balance again, and record its mass.

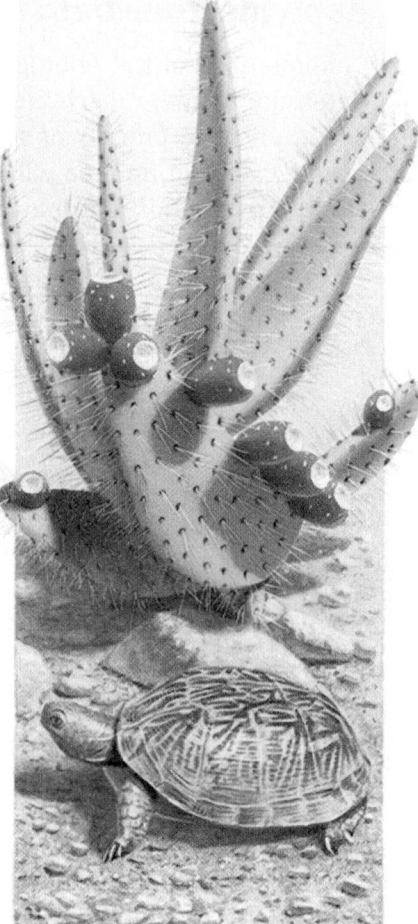

Analyze the Results

1 Describe the adaptation you used to help your "animal" survive. Was it effective? Explain.

2 What was the purpose of leaving one of the sponges unprotected? How did the water loss in each of your sponges compare?

Communicating Your Data

Conduct a class discussion about other adaptations and results. How can you relate these invented adaptations to adaptations for desert survival among real organisms?

Inquiry Lab

Discovering Mini-Ecosystems

In your study of ecosystems, you learned that a biome is a very large ecosystem that includes a set of smaller, related ecosystems. For example, a coniferous forest biome may include a river ecosystem, a wetland ecosystem, and a lake ecosystem. Each of those ecosystems may include several other smaller, related ecosystems. Even cities have mini-ecosystems! You may find a mini-ecosystem on a patch of sidewalk, in a puddle of rainwater, under a leaky faucet, in a shady area, or under a rock. In this activity, you will design a method for comparing two different mini-ecosystems found near your school.

MATERIALS

- items to be determined by the students and approved by the teacher

SAFETY

Ask a Question

1 Examine the grounds around your school, and select two different areas you wish to investigate. Decide what you want to learn about your mini-ecosystems. For example, you may want to know what kind of living things each area contains. Be sure to get your teacher's approval before you begin.

Form a Hypothesis

2 For each mini-ecosystem, make data tables for recording your observations.

Test the Hypothesis

3 Observe your mini-ecosystem according to your plan at several different time points throughout the day. Record your observations.

4 Wait 24 h and observe your mini-ecosystem again at the same times that you observed it the day before. Record your observations.

5 Wait 1 week, and observe your mini-ecosystem again at the same times. Record your observations.

Analyze the Results

1 What factors determine the differences between your mini-ecosystems? Identify the factors that set each mini-ecosystem apart from its surrounding area.

2 How do the populations of your mini-ecosystems compare?

3 Identify some of the adaptations that the organisms living in your two mini-ecosystems have. Describe how the adaptations help the organisms survive in their environment.

Draw Conclusions

4 Write a report describing and comparing your mini-ecosystems with those of your classmates.

Skills Practice Lab

Clean Up Your Act

When you wash dishes, the family car, the bathroom sink, or your clothes, you wash them with water. But have you ever wondered how water gets clean? Two major methods of purifying water are filtration and evaporation. In this activity, you will use both of these methods to test how well they remove pollutants from water. You will test detritus (decaying plant matter), soil, vinegar, and detergent. Your teacher may also ask you to test other pollutants.

Form a Hypothesis

1 Form a hypothesis about whether filtration and evaporation will clean each of the four pollutants from the water and how well they might do it. Then, use the procedures below to test your hypothesis.

Part A: Filtration

Filtration is a common method of removing various pollutants from water. Filtration requires very little energy—gravity pulls water down through the layers of filter material. See how well this energy-efficient method works to clean your sample of polluted water.

Test the Hypothesis

2 Put on your gloves and goggles. Use scissors to carefully cut the bottom out of the empty soda bottle.

3 Using a small nail and hammer, carefully punch four or five small holes through the plastic cap of the bottle. Screw the plastic cap onto the bottle.

4 Turn the bottle upside down, and set its neck in a ring on a ring stand, as shown on the next page. Put a handful of gravel into the inverted bottle. Add a layer of activated charcoal, followed by thick layers of sand and gravel. Place a 400 mL beaker under the neck of the bottle.

5 Fill each of the large beakers with 1,000 mL of clean water. Set one beaker aside to serve as the control. Add three or four spoonfuls of each of the following pollutants to the other beaker: detritus, soil, household vinegar, and dishwashing detergent.

6 Copy the table on the next page, and record your observations for each beaker in the columns labeled "Before cleaning."

7 Observe the color of the water in each beaker.

8 Use a hand lens to examine the water for visible particles.

MATERIALS

Part A
- charcoal, activated
- goggles
- gravel
- hammer and small nail
- sand
- scissors
- soda bottle, plastic, with cap, 2 L

Part B
- bag, plastic sandwich, sealable
- flask, Erlenmeyer
- gloves, heat-resistant
- hot plate
- ice
- stopper, rubber, one-hole, with a glass tube
- tubing, plastic, 1.5 m

Parts A and B
- beaker, 400 mL
- beaker, 1,000 mL (2)
- detergent, dishwashing
- detritus (grass and leaf clippings)
- hand lens
- pH test strips
- ring stand with ring
- soil
- spoons, plastic (2)
- vinegar, household
- water, 2,000 mL

SAFETY

9. Smell the water, and note any unusual odors.

10. Stir the water in each beaker rapidly with a plastic spoon, and check for suds. Use a different spoon for each sample.

11. Use a pH test strip to find the pH of the water.

12. Gently stir the clean water, and then pour half of it through the filtration device.

13. Observe the water in the collection beaker for color, particles, odors, suds, and pH. Be patient. It may take several minutes for the water to travel through the filtration device.

14. Record your observations in the appropriate "After filtration" column in your table.

15. Repeat steps 12–14 using the polluted water.

Analyze the Results

1. How did the color of the polluted water change after the filtration? Did the color of the clean water change?

2. Did the filtration method remove all of the particles from the polluted water? Explain.

3. How much did the pH of the polluted water change? Did the pH of the clean water change? Was the final pH of the polluted water the same as the pH of the clean water before cleaning? Explain.

	Results Table					
	Before cleaning (clean water)	Before cleaning (polluted water)	After filtration (clean water)	After filtration (polluted water)	After evaporation (clean water)	After evaporation (polluted water)
Color						
Particles						
Odor			DO NOT WRITE IN BOOK			
Suds						
pH						

Part B: Evaporation

Cleaning water by evaporation is more expensive than cleaning water by filtration. Evaporation requires more energy, which can come from a variety of sources. In this activity, you will use an electric hot plate as the energy source. See how well this method works to clean your sample of polluted water.

Form a Hypothesis

1 Write a hypothesis about which method you think will work better for water purification. Explain your reasoning.

Test the Hypothesis

2 Fill an Erlenmeyer flask with about 250 mL of the clean water, and insert the rubber stopper and glass tube into the flask.

3 Wearing goggles and gloves, connect about 1.5 m of plastic tubing to the glass tube.

4 Set the flask on the hot plate, and run the plastic tubing up and around the ring and down into a clean, empty 400 mL collection beaker.

5 Fill the sandwich bag with ice, seal the bag, and place the bag on the ring stand. Be sure the plastic bag and the tubing touch, as shown below.

6 Bring the water in the flask to a slow boil. As the water vapor passes by the bag of ice, the vapor will condense and drip into the collection beaker.

7 Observe the water in the collection beaker for color, particles, odor, suds, and pH. Record your observations in the "After evaporation" column in your data table.

8 Repeat steps 2–7 using the polluted water.

Analyze the Results

1 How did the color of the polluted water change after evaporation? Did the color of the clean water change after evaporation?

2 Did the evaporation method remove all of the particles from the polluted water? Explain.

3 How much did the pH of the polluted water change? Did the pH of the final clean water change? Was the final pH of the polluted water the same as the pH of the clean water before it was cleaned? Explain.

Draw Conclusions: Parts A and B

4 Which method—filtration or evaporation—removed the most pollutants from the water? Explain your reasoning.

5 Describe any changes that occurred in the clean water during this experiment.

6 What do you think are the advantages and disadvantages of each method?

7 Explain how you think each material (sand, gravel, and charcoal) used in the filtration system helped clean the water.

8 List areas of the country where you think each method of purification would be the most and the least beneficial. Explain your reasoning.

Applying Your Data

Do you think either purification method would remove oil from water? If time permits, repeat your experiment using several spoonfuls of cooking oil as the pollutant.

Filtration is only one step in the purification of water at water treatment plants. Research other methods used to purify public water supplies.

Model-Making Lab

Dune Movement

Wind moves the sand by a process called *saltation*. The sand skips and bounces along the ground in the same direction as the wind is blowing. As sand is blown across a beach, the dunes change. In this activity, you will investigate the effect wind has on a model sand dune.

Procedure

1 Use the marker to draw and label vertical lines 5 cm apart along one side of the box.

2 Fill the box about halfway with sand. Brush the sand into a dune shape about 10 cm from the end of the box.

3 Use the lines you drew along the edge of the box to measure the location of the dune's peak to the nearest centimeter.

4 Slide the box into the paper bag until only about half the box is exposed, as shown below.

5 Put on your safety goggles and filter mask. Hold the hair dryer so that it is level with the peak of the dune and about 10–20 cm from the open end of the box.

6 Turn on the hair dryer at the lowest speed, and direct the air toward the model sand dune for 1 min.

7 Record the new location of the model dune.

8 Repeat steps 5 and 6 three times. After each trial, measure and record the location of the dune's peak.

Analyze the Results

1 How far did the dune move during each trial?

2 How far did the dune move overall?

Draw Conclusions

3 How might the dune's movement be affected if you were to turn the hair dryer to the highest speed?

MATERIALS

- bag, paper, large enough to hold half the box
- box, cardboard, shallow
- hair dryer
- marker
- mask, filter
- ruler, metric
- sand, fine

SAFETY

Applying Your Data

Flatten the sand. Place a barrier, such as a rock, in the sand. Position the hair dryer level with the top of the sand's surface. How does the rock affect the dune's movement?

Skills Practice Lab

Creating a Kettle

As glaciers recede, they leave huge amounts of rock material behind. Sometimes receding glaciers form moraines by depositing some of the rock material in ridges. At other times, glaciers leave chunks of ice that form depressions called *kettles*. As the ice melts, these depressions may form ponds or lakes. In this activity, you will discover how kettles are formed by creating your own.

> **MATERIALS**
> - ice, cubes of various sizes (4–5)
> - ruler, metric
> - sand
> - tub, small

Ask a Question

1. How are kettles formed?

Form a Hypothesis

2. Write a hypothesis that could answer the question above.

Test the Hypothesis

3. Fill the tub three-quarters full with sand.

4. Describe the size and shape of each ice cube.

5. Push the ice cubes to various depths in the sand.

6. Put the tub where it won't be disturbed overnight.

7. Closely observe the sand around the area where you left each ice cube.

8. What happened to the ice cubes?

9. Use a metric ruler to measure the depth and diameter of the indentation left by each ice cube.

Analyze the Results

1. How does this model relate to the size and shape of a natural kettle?

2. In what ways are your model kettles similar to real ones? How are they different?

Draw Conclusions

3. Based on your model, what can you conclude about the formation of kettles by receding glaciers?

Skills Practice Lab

The Sun's Yearly Trip Through the Zodiac

During the course of a year, the sun appears to move through a circle of 12 constellations in the sky. The 12 constellations make up a "belt" in the sky called the *zodiac.* Each month, the sun appears to be in a different constellation. The ancient Babylonians developed a 12-month calendar based on the idea that the sun moved through this circle of constellations as it revolved around the Earth. They believed that the constellations of stars were fixed in position and that the sun and planets moved past the stars. Later, Copernicus developed a model of the solar system in which the Earth and the planets revolve around the sun. But how can Copernicus's model of the solar system be correct when the sun appears to move through the zodiac?

MATERIALS

- ball, inflated
- box, cardboard, large
- cards, index (12)
- chairs (12)
- tape, masking (1 roll)

Ask a Question

1 If the sun is at the center of the solar system, why does it appear to move with respect to the stars in the sky?

Form a Hypothesis

2 Write a possible answer to the question above. Explain your reasoning.

Test the Hypothesis

3 Set the chairs in a large circle so that the backs of the chairs all face the center of the circle. Make sure that the chairs are equally spaced, like the numbers on the face of a clock.

4 Write the name of each constellation in the zodiac on the index cards. You should have one card for each constellation.

5 Stand inside the circle with the masking tape and the index cards. Moving counterclockwise, attach the cards to the backs of the chairs in the following order: Aries, Taurus, Gemini, Cancer, Leo, Virgo, Libra, Scorpio, Sagittarius, Capricorn, Aquarius, and Pisces.

6 Use masking tape to label the ball "Sun."

7 Place the large, closed box in the center of the circle. Set the roll of masking tape flat on top of the box.

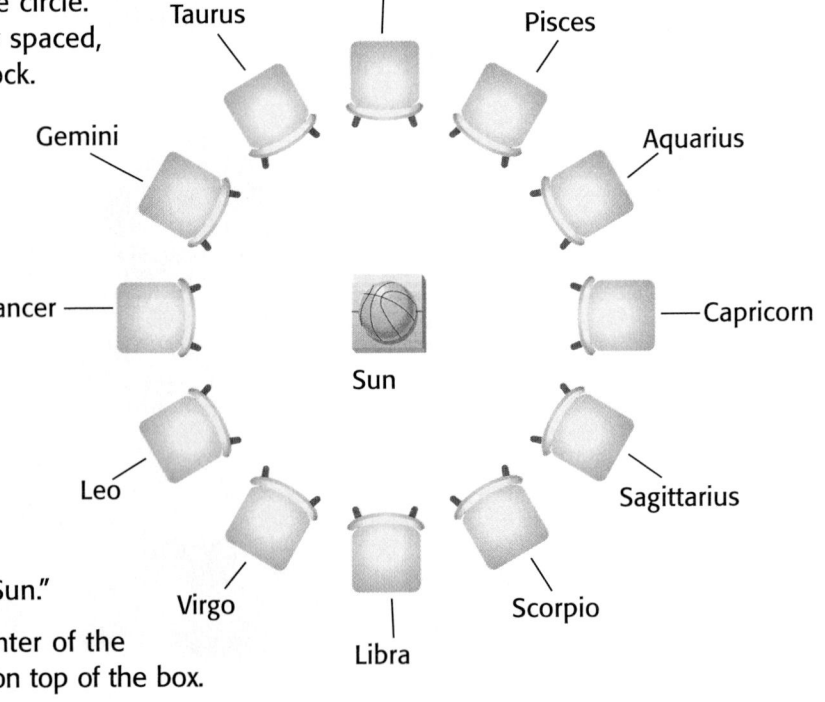

8 Place the ball on top of the roll of masking tape so that the ball stays in place.

9 Stand inside the circle of chairs. You will represent the Earth. As you move around the ball, you will model the Earth's orbit around the sun. Notice that even though only the "Earth" is moving, as seen from the Earth, the sun appears to move through the entire zodiac!

10 Stand in front of the chair labeled "Aries." Look at the ball representing the sun. Then, look past the ball to the chair at the opposite side of the circle. Where in the zodiac does the sun appear to be?

11 Move to the next chair on your right (counterclockwise). Where does the sun appear to be? Is it in the same constellation? Explain your answer.

12 Repeat step 10 until you have observed the position of the sun from each chair in the circle.

Analyze the Results

1 Did the sun appear to move through the 12 constellations, even though the Earth was orbiting around the sun? How can you explain this apparent movement?

Draw Conclusions

2 How does Copernicus's model of the solar system explain the apparent movement of the sun through the constellations of the zodiac?

Model-Making Lab

Reach for the Stars

Have you ever thought about living and working in space? Well, in order for you to do so, you would have to learn to cope with the new environment and surroundings. At the same time that astronauts are adjusting to the topsy-turvy conditions of space travel, they are also dealing with special tools used to repair and build space stations. In this activity, you will get the chance to model one tool that might help astronauts work in space.

MATERIALS

- ball, plastic-foam
- box, cardboard
- hole punch
- paper brads (2)
- paper clips, jumbo (2)
- ruler, metric
- scissors
- wire, metal

SAFETY

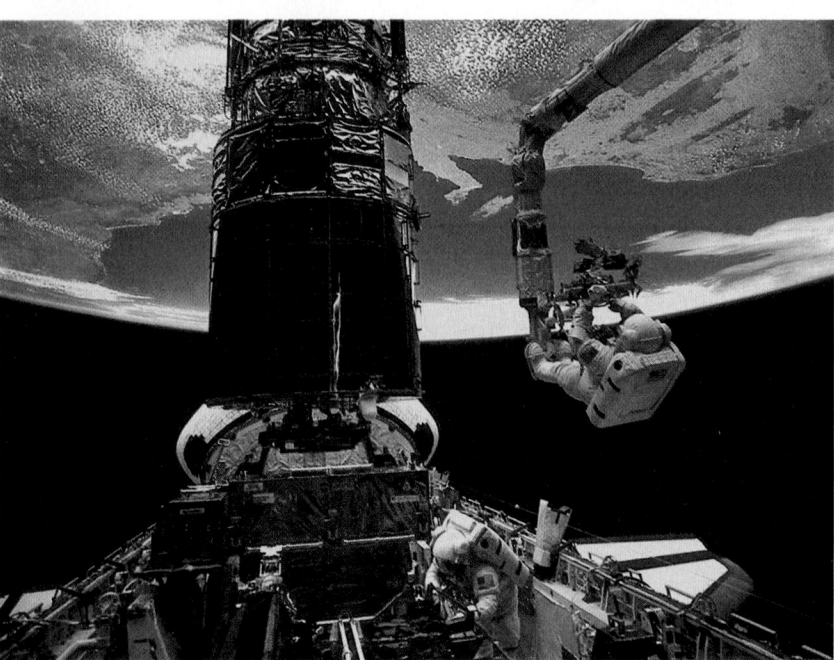

Ask a Question

1. How can I build a piece of equipment that models how astronauts work in space?

Form a Hypothesis

2. Write a possible answer for the question above. Describe a possible tool that would help astronauts work in space.

Test the Hypothesis

3. Cut three strips from the cardboard box. Each strip should be about 5 cm wide. The strips should be at least 20 cm long but not longer than 40 cm.

4 Punch holes near the center of each end of the three cardboard strips. The holes should be about 3 cm from the end of each strip.

5 Lay the strips end to end along your table. Slide the second strip toward the first strip so that a hole in the first strip lines up with a hole in the second strip. Slip a paper brad through the holes, and bend its ends out to attach the cardboard strips.

6 Use another brad to attach the third cardboard strip to the free end of the second strip. Now, you have your mechanical arm. The paper brads create joints where the cardboard strips meet.

7 Straighten the wire, and slide it through the hole in one end of your mechanical arm. Bend about 3 cm of the wire in a 90° angle so that it will not slide back out of the hole.

8 Now, try to move the arm by holding the free ends of the cardboard and wire. The arm should bend and straighten at the joints. If it is difficult to move your mechanical arm, adjust the design. Consider loosening the brads, for example.

9 Your mechanical arm now needs a hand. Otherwise, it won't be able to pick things up! Straighten one paper clip, and slide it through the hole where you attached the wire in step 7. Bend one end of the paper clip to form a loop around the cardboard and the other end to form a hook. You will use this hook to pick things up.

10 Bend a second paper clip into a U shape. Stick the straight end of this paper clip into the foam ball. Leave the ball on your desk.

11 Move your mechanical arm so that you can lift the foam ball. The paper-clip hook on the mechanical arm will have to catch the paper clip on the ball.

Analyze the Results

1 Did you have any trouble moving the mechanical arm in step 8? What adjustments did you make?

2 Did you have trouble picking up the foam ball? What might have made picking up the ball easier?

Draw Conclusions

3 What improvements could you make to your mechanical arm that might make it easier to use?

4 How would a tool like this one help astronauts work in space?

Applying Your Data

Adjust the design for your mechanical arm. Can you find a way to lift objects other than the foam ball? For example, can you lift heavier objects or objects that do not have a loop attached? How?

Research the tools that astronauts use on space stations and on the space shuttle. How do their tools help them work in the special conditions of space?

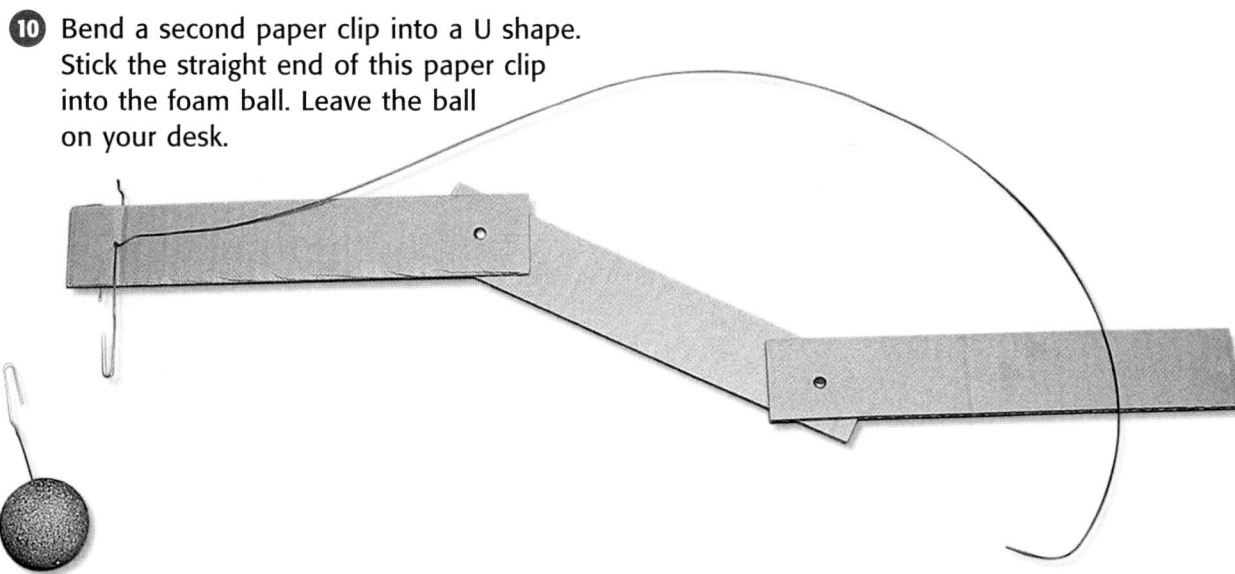

Skills Practice Lab

Coin Operated

All pennies are exactly the same, right? Probably not! After all, each penny was made in a certain year at a specific mint, and each has traveled a unique path to reach your classroom. But all pennies are similar. In this lab, you will investigate differences and similarities among a group of pennies.

MATERIALS

- balance, metric
- graduated cylinder, 100 mL
- paper, notebook (10 sheets)
- paper towels
- pennies (10)
- water

SAFETY

Procedure

1 Write the numbers 1 through 10 on a page, and place a penny next to each number.

2 Use the metric balance to find the mass of each penny to the nearest 0.1 g. Record each measurement next to the number of that penny.

3 On a table that your teacher will provide, make a mark in the correct column of the table for each penny you measured.

4 Separate your pennies into piles, based on the class data. Place each pile on its own sheet of paper.

5 Measure and record the mass of each pile. Write the mass on the paper you are using to identify the pile.

6 Fill a graduated cylinder halfway with water. Carefully measure the volume in the cylinder, and record it.

7 Carefully place the pennies from one pile into the graduated cylinder. Measure and record the new volume.

8 Carefully pour out the water into the sink, and remove the pennies from the graduated cylinder. With a paper towel, dry off the pile of pennies.

9 Repeat steps 6 through 8 for each pile of pennies.

Analyze the Results

1 Determine the volume of the displaced water by subtracting the initial volume from the final volume. This amount is equal to the volume of the pennies. Record the volume of each pile of pennies.

2 Calculate the density of each pile. To make this calculation, divide the total mass of the pennies by the volume of the pennies. Record the density.

3 What differences, if any, did you note in the mass, volume, and density of the pennies?

Draw Conclusions

4 If you noted differences, what do you think might be the cause of these differences?

5 How is it possible for the pennies to have different densities?

6 What clues might allow you to separate the pennies into the same groups without experimentation? Explain.

Skills Practice Lab

Wheeling and Dealing

A crank handle, such as that used in pencil sharpeners, ice-cream makers, and water wells, is one kind of wheel and axle. In this lab, you will use a crank handle to find out how a wheel and axle helps you do work. You will also determine what effect the length of the handle has on the operation of the machine.

MATERIALS

- C-clamps (2)
- handles(4)
- mass, large
- meterstick
- spring scale
- string, 0.5 m
- wheel-and-axle assembly

SAFETY

Ask a Question

1 What effect does the length of a handle have on the operation of a crank?

Form a Hypothesis

2 Write a possible answer to the question above.

Test the Hypothesis

3 Copy Table 1.

4 Measure the radius (in meters) of the large dowel in the wheel-and-axle assembly. Record this in Table 1 as the axle radius, which remains constant throughout the lab. (Hint: Measure the diameter, and divide by 2.)

5 Using the spring scale, measure the weight of the large mass. Record this in Table 1 as the output force, which remains constant throughout the lab.

6 Use two C-clamps to secure the wheel-and-axle assembly to the table, as shown.

7 Measure the length (in meters) of handle 1. Record this length as a wheel radius in Table 1.

8 Insert the handle into the hole in the axle. Attach one end of the string to the large mass and the other end to the screw in the axle. The mass should hang down, and the handle should turn freely.

9 Turn the handle to lift the mass off the floor. Hold the spring scale upside down, and attach it to the end of the handle. Measure the force (in newtons) as the handle pulls up on the spring scale. Record this as the input force.

Table 1 Data Collection

Handle	Axle radius (m)	Output force (N)	Wheel radius (m)	Input force (N)
1				
2				
3		*DO NOT WRITE IN BOOK*		
4				

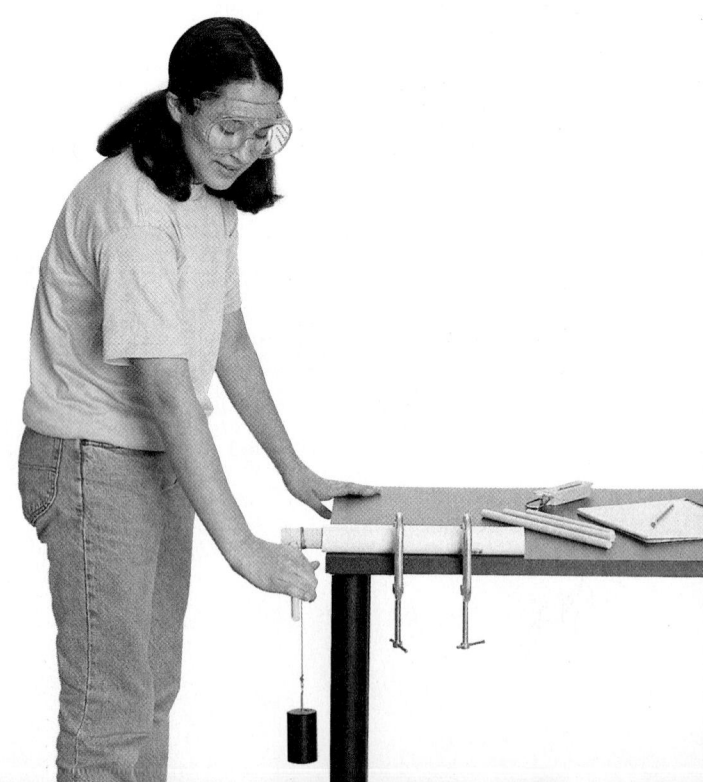

10 Remove the spring scale, and lower the mass to the floor. Remove the handle.

11 Repeat steps 7 through 10 with the other three handles. Record all data in Table 1.

Analyze the Results

1 Copy Table 2.

Table 2 Calculations						
Handle	Axle distance (m)	Wheel distance (m)	Work input (J)	Work output (J)	Mechanical efficiency (%)	Mechanical advantage
1						
2						
3						
4						

DO NOT WRITE IN BOOK

2 Calculate the following for each handle, using the equations given. Record your answers in Table 2.

a. *Distance axle rotates =*
$2 \times \pi \times$ *axle radius*

Distance wheel rotates =
$2 \times \pi \times$ *wheel radius*

(Use 3.14 for the value of π.)

b. *Work input =*
input force × *wheel distance*

Work output =
output force × *axle distance*

c. *Mechanical efficiency =*
$\dfrac{work\ output}{work\ input} \times 100$

d. *Mechanical advantage =*
$\dfrac{wheel\ radius}{axle\ radius}$

Draw Conclusions

3 What happens to work output and work input as the handle length increases? Why?

4 What happens to mechanical efficiency as the handle length increases? Why?

5 What happens to mechanical advantage as the handle length increases? Why?

6 What will happen to mechanical advantage if the handle length is kept constant and the axle radius gets larger?

7 What factors were controlled in this experiment? What was the variable?

Inquiry Lab

Building Machines

You are surrounded by machines. Some are simple machines, such as ramps for wheelchair access to a building. Others are compound machines, such as elevators and escalators, that are made of two or more simple machines. In this lab, you will design and build several simple machines and a compound machine.

Ask a Question

1 How can simple machines be combined to make compound machines?

Form a Hypothesis

2 Write a possible answer to the question above.

Test the Hypothesis

3 Use the listed materials to build a model of each simple machine: inclined plane, lever, wheel and axle, pulley, screw, and wedge. Describe and draw each model.

4 Design a compound machine by using the materials listed. You may design a machine that already exists, or you may invent your own machine. Be creative!

5 After your teacher approves your design, build your compound machine.

Analyze the Results

1 List a possible use for each of your simple machines.

2 How many simple machines are in your compound machine? List them.

3 Compare your compound machine with those created by your classmates.

4 What is a possible use for your compound machine? Why did you design it as you did?

5 A compound machine is listed in the materials list. What is it?

Applying Your Data

Design a compound machine that has all the simple machines in it. Explain what the machine will do and how it will make work easier. With your teacher's approval, build your machine.

MATERIALS

- bottle caps
- cardboard
- clay, modeling
- craft sticks
- glue
- paper
- pencils
- rubber bands
- scissors
- shoe boxes
- stones
- straws
- string
- tape
- thread spools, empty
- other materials available in your classroom that are approved by your teacher

SAFETY

Skills Practice Lab

Density Diver

Crew members of a submarine can control the submarine's density underwater by allowing water to flow into and out of special tanks. These changes in density affect the submarine's position in the water. In this lab, you'll control a "density diver" to learn for yourself how the density of an object affects its position in a fluid.

MATERIALS

- bottle, plastic, with screw-on cap, 2 L
- dropper, medicine
- water

SAFETY

Ask a Question

1 How does the density of an object determine whether the object floats, sinks, or maintains its position in a fluid?

Form a Hypothesis

2 Write a possible answer to the question above.

Test the Hypothesis

3 Completely fill the 2 L plastic bottle with water.

4 Fill the diver (medicine dropper) approximately halfway with water, and place it in the bottle. The diver should float with only part of the rubber bulb above the surface of the water. If the diver floats too high, carefully remove it from the bottle, and add a small amount of water to the diver. Place the diver back in the bottle. If you add too much water and the diver sinks, empty out the bottle and diver, and go back to step 3.

5 Put the cap on the bottle tightly so that no water leaks out.

6 Apply various pressures to the bottle. Carefully watch the water level inside the diver as you squeeze and release the bottle. Record what happens.

7 Try to make the diver rise, sink, or stop at any level. Record your technique and your results.

Analyze the Results

1 How do the changes inside the diver affect its position in the surrounding fluid?

2 What relationship did you observe between the diver's density and the diver's position in the fluid?

Draw Conclusions

3 Explain how your density diver is like a submarine.

4 Explain how pressure on the bottle is related to the diver's density. Be sure to include Pascal's principle in your explanation.

Contents

FCAT Study Guide

FCAT Glossary

A

abiotic describes the nonliving part of the environment, including water, rocks, light, and temperature, that is not associated with the actions of organisms

acceleration the rate at which velocity changes over time; an object accelerates if its speed, direction, or both change; usually expressed in meters per second per second (m/s^2)

air resistance the force that opposes the motion of objects through air

allele one of the alternative forms of a gene that governs a characteristic, such as hair color

amplitude the maximum distance that the particles of a wave's medium vibrate from their rest position; the maximum variation of any periodic function

asexual reproduction reproduction that does not involve the union of sex cells, or gametes, and in which one parent produces offspring that are genetically identical to the parent

B

biodiversity the number and variety of organisms in a given area during a specific period of time

biotic describes living factors in the environment; related to, caused by, or produced by organisms

C

calorie the amount of energy needed to raise the temperature of 1 g of water 1°C at 1 standard atmosphere; the Calorie used to indicate the energy content of food is a kilocalorie; a unit of energy

chemical weathering the process by which rocks break down as a result of chemical reactions

circuit a complete path of an electric current formed from interconnected electrical elements

conduction the transfer of energy as heat through a material without movement of the material

conservation of energy the law that states that energy cannot be created or destroyed but can be changed from one form to another

convection the transfer of thermal energy by the circulation or movement of a liquid or gas

crest the highest point of a wave

crust the thin and solid outermost layer of the Earth above the mantle

D

dependent variable in an experiment, the factor that changes as a result of manipulation of one or more other factors (the independent variables)

deposition the process in which material is laid down after being carried by wind, rain, or water

diffraction a change in the direction of a wave when the wave finds an obstacle or an edge, such as an opening

dominance the tendency of certain (dominant) alleles to mask the expression of their corresponding (recessive) alleles

E

ecosystem a community of organisms and their abiotic, or nonliving, environment

efficiency a quantity, usually expressed as a percentage, that measures the ratio of work output to work input; used to describe the relative effectiveness of a system or device

electromagnetic radiation the radiation associated with an electric and magnetic field; it varies periodically and travels at the speed of light; includes radio waves, visible light, ultraviolet light, microwaves, X rays, and gamma rays

electron a subatomic particle that has a negative charge; found around the nucleus

entropy a measure of the randomness or disorder of a system

erosion the process by which wind, water, ice, or gravity transports soil and sediment from one location to another

F

fossil fuel a nonrenewable energy resource formed from the remains of organisms that lived long ago; includes natural gas, oil, and coal

frequency the number of waves produced in a given amount of time

G

gene one set of instructions for an inherited trait; in a DNA sequence or as a part of a chromosome

H

heterozygous describes an individual that has two different alleles for a trait

homozygous describes an individual that has identical alleles for a trait on both homologous chromosomes

I

independent variable in an experiment, the factor that is deliberately manipulated in order to examine how the dependent variable is affected

inertia the tendency of an object, as a result of its mass, to resist being moved or, if the object is moving, to resist a change in speed or direction until an outside force acts on the object

M

magnetic field a region where a magnetic force can be detected near electric currents or magnets

mass a measure of the amount of matter in an object

meiosis a process in cell division during which the number of chromosomes decreases to half the original number by two divisions of the nucleus, which results in the production of sex cells (gametes or spores)

mitosis in eukaryotic cells, a process of cell division that forms two new nuclei, each of which has the same number of chromosomes

N

neap tide a tide of minimum range that occurs during the first and third quarters of the moon; occurs when the positions of Earth, the moon, and the sun form a right angle

neutral lacking a net charge; can be applied to particles, objects, or systems

neutron a subatomic particle that has no charge and that is located in the nucleus of an atom

nucleus in physical science, an atom's central region, which is made up of protons and neutrons; also, in a eukaryotic cell, a membrane-bound organelle that contains the cell's DNA and that has a role in processes such as growth, metabolism, and reproduction

O

ocean basin the area of Earth that is covered by oceans

P

plate tectonics the theory that explains how large pieces of the Earth's outermost layer, called tectonic plates, move and change shape which results in seismic activity where the plates meet

potential energy the energy that an object has because of the position, shape, or condition of the object

pressure the amount of force exerted per unit area of a surface

prism in optics, a system that consists of two or more plane surfaces of a transparent solid at an angle with each other; used to separates white light into its colors

proton a subatomic particle that has a positive charge and that is located in the nucleus of an atom; the number of protons of the nucleus is the atomic number, which determines the identity of an element

Punnett square a graphic used to predict the results of a genetic cross

R

radiation the transfer of energy as electromagnetic waves

recessive describes an allele that will be masked unless the organism is homozygous for the trait

S

screw a simple machine that consists of an inclined plane wrapped around a cylinder

sexual reproduction reproduction in which the sex cells, or gametes, from two parents unite to produce offspring that share traits from both parents

spectroscope an instrument that splits white light into a band of colors

speed the distance traveled divided by the time interval during which the motion occurred; also, the rate at which a process occurs

spring tide a tide of increased range that occurs two times a month, at the new and full moons

T

thermal energy the kinetic energy of a substance's atoms

tropism growth of all or part of an organism in response to an external stimulus, such as light

trough the lowest point of a wave

V

variable a factor that changes in an experiment in order to test a hypothesis

velocity the speed of an object in a particular direction; found by dividing displacement by time

vibration a repetitive, back-and-forth motion of an object around its rest, or equilibrium, position

virus a microscopic particle that gets inside a cell and often destroys the cell; it replicates using its host's genetic material and often causes disease

W

wavelength the distance from any point on a wave to an identical point on the next wave (for example, from one crest to the next crest)

wedge a simple machine that is made up of two inclined planes and that moves; often used for cutting

wheel and axle a simple machine consisting of two circular objects of different sizes; the wheel is the larger of the two circular objects; the mechanical advantage is the ratio of the wheel's radius to the axle's radius

 Science Reference Sheet

Acceleration

Average **acceleration** is the rate at which velocity changes over time. An object accelerates if its speed, its direction, or both change.

$$\textit{average acceleration} = \frac{\textit{change in velocity (m/s)}}{\textit{time it takes to change velocity (s)}} = \frac{\textit{final velocity} - \textit{starting velocity}}{\textit{time it takes to change velocity}}$$

Example: Calculate the average acceleration of an Olympic 100 m dash sprinter who reaches a velocity of 20 m/s south at the finish line. The race was in a straight line and lasted 10 s.

$$\textit{average acceleration} = \frac{20 \text{ m/s} - 0 \text{ m/s}}{10 \text{ s}} = 2 \text{ m/s}^2$$

The sprinter's average acceleration is 2 m/s² south.

Average Speed

Most of the time, objects do not travel at a constant speed. So, it is useful to calculate average speed. **Average speed** is the total distance traveled divided by the total time interval during which the motion occurred.

$$\textit{average speed} = \frac{\textit{total distance}}{\textit{total time}}$$

Example: A bicycle messenger traveled a distance of 136 km in 8 h. What was the messenger's average speed?

$$\textit{average speed} = \frac{136 \text{ km}}{8 \text{ h}} = 17 \text{ km/h}$$

The messenger's average speed was 17 km/h.

Density

The ratio of the mass of a substance to the volume of the substance is **density**. An object's density is a measurement of the amount of matter packed in a given volume.

$$\textit{density} = \frac{\textit{mass (g)}}{\textit{volume (cm}^3\textit{)}}$$

Example: Calculate the density of a sponge that has a mass of 10 g and a volume of 40 cm³.

$$\textit{density} = \frac{10 \text{ g}}{40 \text{ cm}^3} = 0.25 \text{ g/cm}^3$$

The density of the sponge is 0.25 g/cm³.

Percent Efficiency

The **percent efficiency** is found by dividing the work output by the work input and then multiplying the answer by 100. Percent efficiency is also known as *mechanical efficiency.* Percent efficiency tells you what percentage of the work input is converted to work output.

$$\textbf{percent efficiency} = \frac{\textbf{work out (J)}}{\textbf{work in (J)}} \times \textbf{100}$$

Example: A hand-crank drill requires 3,540 J to complete 2,480 J of work. What is the efficiency of the drill?

$$\textbf{percent efficiency} = \frac{\textbf{2,480 J}}{\textbf{3,540 J}} \times \textbf{100} = \textbf{70.0\%}$$

The hand-crank drill has a percent efficiency of 70.0%.

Force in Newtons

A **force** is a push or a pull in a particular direction. Force is calculated by multiplying the mass of the object being acted on and the acceleration of the object. The unit of force is the newton (N). One newton is equivalent to 1 kg•m/s^2.

$$\textbf{force in newtons} = \textbf{mass (kg)} \times \textbf{acceleration (m/s}^2\textbf{)}$$

Example: A toy car whose mass is 0.03 kg has an acceleration of 0.5 m/s^2. Calculate the force that is acting on the toy car.

$$\textbf{force in newtons} = \textbf{0.03 kg} \times \textbf{0.5 m/s}^2 = \textbf{0.15 kg} \times \textbf{m/s}^2 = \textbf{0.15 N}$$

The force acting on the toy car is 0.15 N.

Frequency in Hertz

The number of events produced in a given amount of time is the **frequency.** Frequency (f) is usually expressed in hertz (Hz). For waves, one hertz equals one wave per second.

$$\textbf{frequency in hertz} = \frac{\textbf{number of events}}{\textbf{time (s)}}$$

Example: Joseph is floating in a wave pool. He observes two waves pass by a stationary point in 10 s. What is the frequency of the waves in Joseph's pool?

$$\textbf{frequency in hertz} = \frac{\textbf{2 waves}}{\textbf{10 s}} = \textbf{0.2 waves per second} = \textbf{0.2 Hz}$$

The frequency of the waves is 0.2 Hz.

Momentum

The **momentum (ρ)** of an object depends on the object's mass and velocity. The more momentum an object has, the harder it is to stop the object or change its direction. Momentum is calculated by multiplying an object's mass by its velocity.

$$momentum = mass \text{ (kg)} \times velocity \text{ (m/s)}$$

Example: What is the momentum of a 6 kg bowling ball that is moving at 10 m/s down the alley toward the pins?

$$momentum = 6 \text{ kg} \times 10 \text{ m/s} = 60 \text{ kg} \times \text{m/s}$$

The momentum of the bowling ball is 60 kg × m/s.

Pressure

The amount of force exerted on a given surface area is called **pressure (p).** Pressure can be calculated by dividing the force acting on the surface by the area of the surface being acted on. The unit that scientists use to express pressure is the pascal (Pa). One pascal is equal to 1 N/m².

$$pressure = \frac{force \text{ (N)}}{area \text{ (m}^2\text{)}}$$

Example: A waterbed has an area of 3.75 m². If the waterbed is exerting a force of 1,025 N on the floor beneath, what pressure is the bed exerting on the floor?

$$pressure = \frac{1{,}025 \text{ N}}{3.75 \text{ m}^2} = 273 \text{ N/m}^2 = 273 \text{ Pa}$$

The pressure on the floor is 273 Pa.

Wavelength

A **wavelength (λ)** is the distance from any point on a wave to an identical point on the next wave. Wavelength can be calculated by dividing the velocity of the wave by the frequency of waves.

$$wavelength = \frac{velocity \text{ (m/s)}}{frequency \text{ (Hz)}}$$

Example: A wave has a frequency of 5 Hz and a wave speed of 18 m/s. What is its wavelength?

$$wavelength = \frac{18 \text{ m/s}}{5 \text{ Hz}} = 3.6 \text{ m/(s} \times \text{Hz)} = 3.6 \text{ m}$$

The wavelength is 3.6 m.

Work

Work is done by exerting a force through a distance. Work has units of joules (J), which are equivalent to newton-meters (N × m). Work is calculated by multiplying force by distance.

$$\textbf{\textit{Work}} = \textbf{\textit{force}} \textbf{ (N)} \times \textbf{\textit{distance}} \textbf{ (m)}$$

Example: Calculate the amount of work done by a man who lifts a 100 N toddler 1.5 m off the floor.

$$\textbf{\textit{Work}} = \textbf{100 N} \times \textbf{1.5 m} = \textbf{150 N} \times \textbf{m} = \textbf{150 J}$$

The work done by the man is 150 J.

Power

Power is the rate at which work is done. Power is measured in watts (W), which are equivalent to joules per second (J/s).

$$\textbf{\textit{power}} = \frac{\textbf{\textit{Work}} \textbf{ (J)}}{\textbf{\textit{time}} \textbf{ (s)}}$$

Example: Calculate the power of a weightlifter who raises a 300 N barbell 2.1 m off the floor in 1.25 s.

$$\textbf{\textit{power}} = \frac{\textbf{(300 N} \times \textbf{2.1 m)}}{\textbf{1.25 s}} = \textbf{504 W}$$

The power of the weightlifter is 504 W.

Concentration

Concentration is a measure of the amount of a particular substance in a given quantity of a mixture, solution, or ore. One way to find concentration is by dividing the mass of the solute (the dissolved substance) by the volume of the solvent (the substance in which the solute dissolves).

$$\textbf{\textit{concentration}} = \frac{\textbf{\textit{mass of solute}}}{\textbf{\textit{volume of solvent}}}$$

Example: Calculate the concentration of a solution in which 10 g of sugar is dissolved in 125 mL of water.

$$\textbf{\textit{concentration}} = \frac{\textbf{10 g of sugar}}{\textbf{125 mL of water}} = \textbf{0.08 g/mL}$$

The concentration of sugar in the solution is 0.08 g/mL.

Net Force

There are many situations where multiple forces act on a single object. **Net force** is the combination of all forces acting on an object.

Forces in the Same Direction

When forces are in the same direction, add the forces together to determine net force.

net force = force + force

Example: Calculate the net force on a stalled car that is being pushed by two people. One person is pushing with a force of 13 N northwest, and the other person is pushing with a force of 8 N in the same direction.

net force = **13 N + 8 N = 21 N northwest**

The net force on the stalled car is 21 N northwest.

Forces in Opposite Directions

When forces are in opposite directions, subtract the smaller force from the larger force to determine the net force. The net force will be in the direction of the larger force.

net force = larger force − smaller force

Example: Calculate the net force on a rope that is being pulled on each end. One person is pulling on one end of the rope with a force of 12 N south. Another person is pulling on the opposite end of the rope with a force of 7 N north.

net force = **12 N − 7 N = 5 N south**

The net force on the rope is 5 N south.

The Periodic Table

Each square on the table includes an element's name, chemical symbol, atomic number, and atomic mass.

The color of the chemical symbol indicates the physical state at room temperature. Carbon is a solid.

6	— Atomic number
C	— Chemical symbol
Carbon	— Element name
12.0	— Atomic mass

The background color indicates the type of element. Carbon is a nonmetal.

Period 1

1
H
Hydrogen
1.0

Group 1	Group 2

Period 2

3	4
Li	**Be**
Lithium	Beryllium
6.9	9.0

Period 3

11	12
Na	**Mg**
Sodium	Magnesium
23.0	24.3

		Group 3	Group 4	Group 5	Group 6	Group 7	Group 8	Group 9

Period 4

19	20	21	22	23	24	25	26	27
K	**Ca**	**Sc**	**Ti**	**V**	**Cr**	**Mn**	**Fe**	**Co**
Potassium	Calcium	Scandium	Titanium	Vanadium	Chromium	Manganese	Iron	Cobalt
39.1	40.1	45.0	47.9	50.9	52.0	54.9	55.8	58.9

Period 5

37	38	39	40	41	42	43	44	45
Rb	**Sr**	**Y**	**Zr**	**Nb**	**Mo**	**Tc**	**Ru**	**Rh**
Rubidium	Strontium	Yttrium	Zirconium	Niobium	Molybdenum	Technetium	Ruthenium	Rhodium
85.5	87.6	88.9	91.2	92.9	95.9	(98)	101.1	102.9

Period 6

55	56	57	72	73	74	75	76	77
Cs	**Ba**	**La**	**Hf**	**Ta**	**W**	**Re**	**Os**	**Ir**
Cesium	Barium	Lanthanum	Hafnium	Tantalum	Tungsten	Rhenium	Osmium	Iridium
132.9	137.3	138.9	178.5	180.9	183.8	186.2	190.2	192.2

Period 7

87	88	89	104	105	106	107	108	109
Fr	**Ra**	**Ac**	**Rf**	**Db**	**Sg**	**Bh**	**Hs**	**Mt**
Francium	Radium	Actinium	Rutherfordium	Dubnium	Seaborgium	Bohrium	Hassium	Meitnerium
(223)	(226)	(227)	(261)	(262)	(263)	(264)	(265)†	(268)†

A row of elements is called a *period*.

A column of elements is called a *group* or *family*.

Values in parentheses are the mass numbers of those radioactive elements' most stable or most common isotopes.

† Estimated from currently available IUPAC data.

These elements are placed below the table to allow the table to be narrower.

Lanthanides

58	59	60	61	62
Ce	**Pr**	**Nd**	**Pm**	**Sm**
Cerium	Praseodymium	Neodymium	Promethium	Samarium
140.1	140.9	144.2	(145)	150.4

Actinides

90	91	92	93	94
Th	**Pa**	**U**	**Np**	**Pu**
Thorium	Protactinium	Uranium	Neptunium	Plutonium
232.0	231.0	238.0	(237)	(244)

FCAT Study Guide

Background

Metals

Metalloids

Nonmetals

Chemical symbol

Solid

Liquid

Gas

Topic: **Periodic Table**
Go To: **go.hrw.com**
Keyword: **HN0 PERIODIC**
Visit the HRW Web site for updates on the periodic table.

This zigzag line reminds you where the metals, nonmetals, and metalloids are.

	Group 13	Group 14	Group 15	Group 16	Group 17	Group 18
						2 **He** Helium 4.0
	5 **B** Boron 10.8	6 **C** Carbon 12.0	7 **N** Nitrogen 14.0	8 **O** Oxygen 16.0	9 **F** Fluorine 19.0	10 **Ne** Neon 20.2
	13 **Al** Aluminum 27.0	14 **Si** Silicon 28.1	15 **P** Phosphorus 31.0	16 **S** Sulfur 32.1	17 **Cl** Chlorine 35.5	18 **Ar** Argon 39.9

Group 10	Group 11	Group 12	Group 13	Group 14	Group 15	Group 16	Group 17	Group 18
28 **Ni** Nickel 58.7	29 **Cu** Copper 63.5	30 **Zn** Zinc 65.4	31 **Ga** Gallium 69.7	32 **Ge** Germanium 72.6	33 **As** Arsenic 74.9	34 **Se** Selenium 79.0	35 **Br** Bromine 79.9	36 **Kr** Krypton 83.8
46 **Pd** Palladium 106.4	47 **Ag** Silver 107.9	48 **Cd** Cadmium 112.4	49 **In** Indium 114.8	50 **Sn** Tin 118.7	51 **Sb** Antimony 121.8	52 **Te** Tellurium 127.6	53 **I** Iodine 126.9	54 **Xe** Xenon 131.3
78 **Pt** Platinum 195.1	79 **Au** Gold 197.0	80 **Hg** Mercury 200.6	81 **Tl** Thallium 204.4	82 **Pb** Lead 207.2	83 **Bi** Bismuth 209.0	84 **Po** Polonium (209)	85 **At** Astatine (210)	86 **Rn** Radon (222)
110 **Ds** Darmstadtium (269)†	111 **Uuu** Unununium (272)†	112 **Uub** Ununbium (277)†		114 **Uuq** Ununquadium (285)†				

The names and three-letter symbols of elements are temporary. They are based on the atomic numbers of the elements. Official names and symbols will be approved by an international committee of scientists.

63 **Eu** Europium 152.0	64 **Gd** Gadolinium 157.2	65 **Tb** Terbium 158.9	66 **Dy** Dysprosium 162.5	67 **Ho** Holmium 164.9	68 **Er** Erbium 167.3	69 **Tm** Thulium 168.9	70 **Yb** Ytterbium 173.0	71 **Lu** Lutetium 175.0
95 **Am** Americium (243)	96 **Cm** Curium (247)	97 **Bk** Berkelium (247)	98 **Cf** Californium (251)	99 **Es** Einsteinium (252)	100 **Fm** Fermium (257)	101 **Md** Mendelevium (258)	102 **No** Nobelium (259)	103 **Lr** Lawrencium (262)

FCAT Study Guide

Annually Assessed Benchmark Focus

Benchmark

 A.1.3.1 The student identifies various ways in which substances differ (e.g., mass, volume, shape, density, texture, and reaction to temperature and light).

Tutorial

All objects are made up of one or more substances and have properties such as mass, shape, and volume. Substances have properties such as density and texture. Properties of substances are determined by gathering data from experiments. Properties of objects can usually be measured directly. The tables below show some of the properties of objects and substances.

PROPERTIES OF OBJECTS

Property	Description
Shape	Form of an object
Volume	Amount of space an object takes up
Weight	A measure of the pull of gravity on an object
Mass	A measure of the amount of matter in an object

PROPERTIES OF SUBSTANCES

Property	Description
Density	The ratio of the mass of a substance to the volume of the substance
Response to heat	The increased movement of particles when temperature is increased
Response to light	Whether light passes through a substance
Texture	The quality of the surface of a substance

Sample Problem

1. Hernando is finding the weight of a package in ounces (oz). He tests what happens when he tips the scale about 25°. The figures below show the results.

A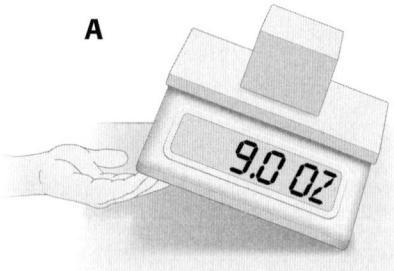

B

Why does Figure B show a different reading?

A. The mass of the package increased.

B. More gravitational pull was detected.

C. The volume of the package increased.

D. More magnetic attraction was detected.

Answer

Answer B is the correct choice. The mass and volume of the package are the same in both figures. Magnetic attraction does not affect weight. Because Hernando tipped the scale, only part of the pull of gravity is detected by the scale in Figure A. If you had difficulty with this question, review gravity.

Mini-Assessment

1. The sketch below shows the dimensions in centimeters (cm) of a piece of bronze whose mass is 534 grams (g).

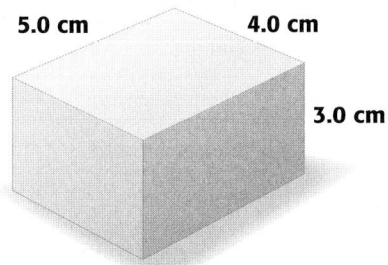

Cube of Casting Bronze

   Calculate the density of the bronze in grams per cubic centimeter (g/cm³).

2. Gravity on Earth is 2.65 times as great as gravity on Mercury. If Beatrice weighs 450.5 newtons (N) on Earth, calculate her weight in newtons on Mercury.

Enrichment

Making shadow puppets is a popular hobby. The sketch below shows how puppeteers create shadow puppets by using a cutout shape to cast a shadow onto a screen. The audience sees the shadow, not the puppet.

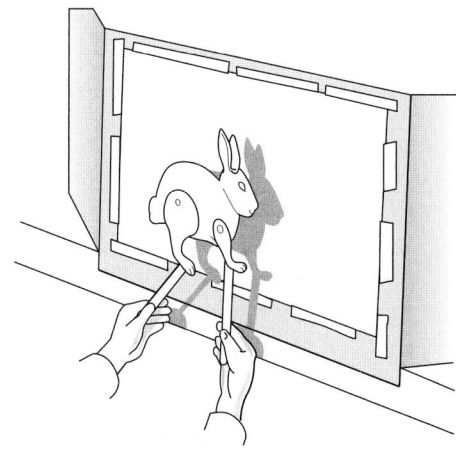

Try making shadow puppets of your own from different materials, such as cardboard or clear plastic. Identify the properties of the materials used to make the puppets. Explain how the different materials respond to light.

Benchmark

B.1.3.1 The student identifies forms of energy and explains that they can be measured and compared.

Tutorial

Energy is neither created nor destroyed. It is simply converted from one form to another. Some forms of energy are described in the table at right. Two main forms of energy are kinetic energy and potential energy. Kinetic energy is the energy of motion. The kinetic energy of an object can be measured using the object's mass and speed. An object's kinetic energy increases as the object's mass, speed, or both increase. Potential energy is the energy that an object has because of its position. Gravitational potential energy of an object can be measured by using the object's weight and height above a surface. An object's gravitational potential energy increases as the object's weight, height, or both increase. Although kinetic energy and potential energy are different forms of energy, they can be converted into one another. When an object is in motion, you can compare its kinetic energy and potential energy at different time intervals. Often, you will see that one form of energy increases as the other form decreases.

Chemical energy and nuclear energy are examples of potential energy. Electrical energy, electromagnetic energy, sound energy, and thermal energy are examples of kinetic energy.

DESCRIPTION OF SOME FORMS OF ENERGY

Energy	Description and Example
Chemical energy	Chemical bonds; natural gas
Electrical energy	Moving charges; circuits
Gravitational potential energy	Objects at a height; car parked on a hill
Kinetic energy	Moving objects; rolling car
Electromagnetic energy	Vibrating electric and magnetic fields; visible light, microwaves, X rays
Nuclear energy	Changes in atomic nuclei; fission in a nuclear power plant
Sound energy	Vibrating matter; music
Thermal energy	Random particle motion; air in a hot oven

Sample Problem

1. The picture below shows a lit candle.

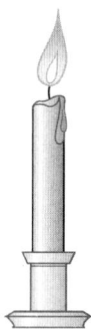

What conversion of energy takes place after the candle is lit?

A. the conversion from thermal energy into kinetic energy and electromagnetic energy

B. the conversion of electromagnetic energy into kinetic energy and chemical energy

C. the conversion of chemical energy into thermal energy and electromagnetic energy

D. the conversion of kinetic energy into thermal energy and chemical energy

Answer

Answer C is the correct answer. The wax stores chemical energy, which is released as heat (thermal energy) and visible light (electromagnetic energy) when the candle is lit. If you had difficulty with this question, review energy conversions.

Mini-Assessment

1. The picture below shows the inside of a music box. By turning the crank, you wind a spring inside the box, which rotates a barrel. Protruding pins on the barrel strike a comb that has tuned teeth, and a tune is played.

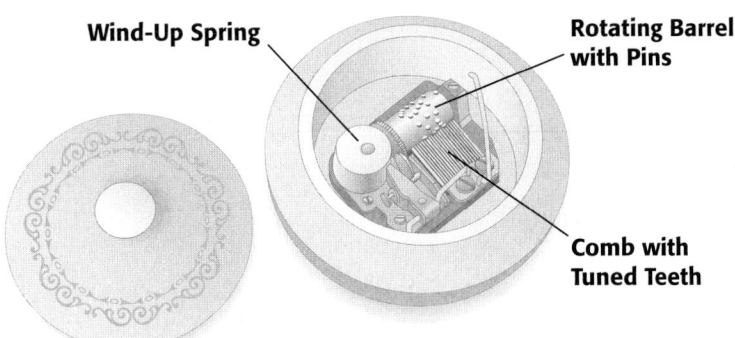

Wind-Up Spring

Rotating Barrel with Pins

Comb with Tuned Teeth

Inside of a Music Box

What type of energy conversion takes place when a music box plays?

A. the conversion of potential energy into kinetic energy

B. the conversion of chemical energy into thermal energy

C. the conversion of kinetic energy into electromagnetic energy

D. the conversion of electromagnetic energy into chemical energy

2. Humans generate heat even when they are sitting still. In fact, they generate so much heat that busy places, such as movie theaters, often turn on cooling systems to compensate for crowded conditions. From which form of energy is heat converted in the human body?

F. kinetic energy

G. chemical energy

H. gravitational energy

I. electromagnetic energy

Enrichment

Put some loose tea in a clear glass mug. If you have only tea bags available, simply open one and empty the contents into the mug. Make tea by pouring hot water into the mug over the loose tea. **Caution:** Be careful when handling hot water because it can cause burns. Observe how the tea leaves move in the mug as you add the water. Why do the leaves move in this way? Make a sketch of the entire system, including the materials that you used to heat the water, and trace the conversions of energy from the original heat source to the final product.

Benchmark

B.1.3.6 The student knows the properties of waves (e.g., frequency, wavelength, and amplitude), that each wave consists of a number of crests and troughs, and the effects of different media on waves.

Tutorial

A *wave* is any disturbance that transmits energy through matter or empty space. There are two main types of waves:

- **Mechanical Waves** Mechanical waves are waves, such as sound, water, and seismic waves, that must pass through a medium (a gas, a liquid, or a solid). Mechanical waves can be transverse, longitudinal, or a combination of both (as surface waves are). Mechanical waves cannot pass through a vacuum.

- **Electromagnetic Waves** Electromagnetic waves are waves that pass through both empty space and media. Examples include visible light, infrared light, and microwaves. Electromagnetic waves consist of changing electric and magnetic fields. Electromagnetic waves are transverse waves.

Transverse waves consist of crests and troughs. The height of the wave is related to the amplitude of the wave. Amplitude is the maximum distance that the particles of the medium through which a wave is passing move. All waves have a velocity, a wavelength, and a frequency. The following equation can be used to solve for any of these three variables:

$$Wavelength = \frac{Velocity}{Frequency}$$

Waves behave differently in different media. A wave can bounce off a barrier (reflection), bend as it passes from one medium into another (refraction), or bend around a barrier or through an opening (diffraction).

Sample Problems

1. The picture below shows an ultrasound image of a pancreas. This image was made by a machine that emits high-frequency sound waves.

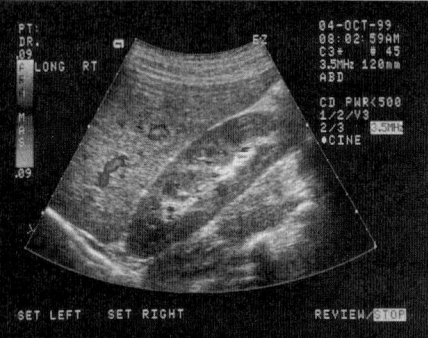

Which of the following statements **best** describes the property of sound waves that is most important to ultrasound imaging?

A. Sound waves reflect off a barrier.

B. Sound waves are longitudinal waves.

C. Sound waves travel slower than light waves.

D. Sound waves do not travel through a vacuum.

> ## Answer
>
> **Answer A** is the correct choice. By reflecting or refracting at medium boundaries, sound waves can create images of internal organs. The characteristics described in Answers B, C, and D do not aid in making images of internal organs. If you found this question difficult, review the definitions of *refraction, reflection,* and *diffraction*.

2. Middle C is a musical note. It has a frequency of 262 waves per second (Hz). If a pianist strikes middle C in a room where the speed of sound is 340.6 meters per second (m/s), what is the wavelength of the sound waves in meters (m)?

Mini-Assessment

1. Trains sound their horns at road intersections. A driver waiting for a train to pass notices that the horn's pitch gets lower as the train passes her car. What is the reason for this change in pitch?

A. The amplitude of the sound waves increases.

B. The wavelength of the sound waves decreases.

C. The vibration source moves closer to the driver.

D. The frequency of the vibration source increases.

Enrichment

The photos below show two satellite views of Baton Rouge, Louisiana, taken with different cameras. The image on the left shows reflected visible light, and the image on the right shows reflected infrared radiation.

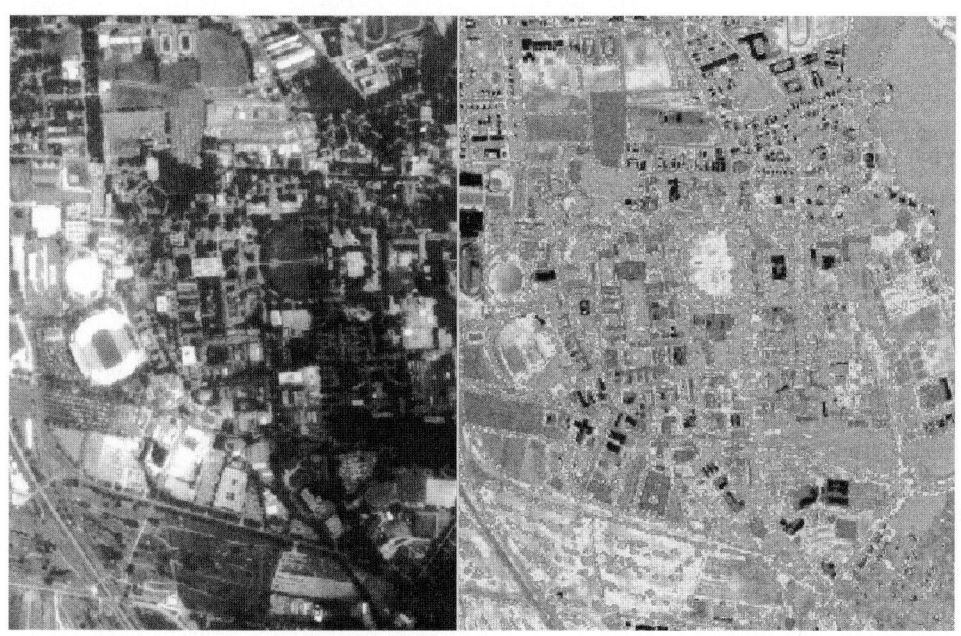

Identify the differences between visible light and infrared radiation shown in these images, and explain how each form of radiation reacts when it reaches a medium.

Benchmark

B.2.3.1 The student knows that most events in the universe (e.g., weather changes, moving cars, and the transfer of a nervous impulse in the human body) involve some form of energy transfer and that these changes almost always increase the total disorder of the system and its surroundings, reducing the amount of useful energy.

Tutorial

Energy drives all systems. Every time that energy is transferred or converted, the amount of useful energy is reduced. Therefore, the energy output of any energy conversion is less than the input of energy. Efficiency is the ratio of energy output to energy input. Use the equation shown to the right to solve for efficiency, energy output, or energy input.

The law of conservation of energy states that energy is neither created nor destroyed. Useful energy, however, is always reduced in transfers and conversions. A decrease in useful energy results in an increase in the disorder of the system. Energy that is lost during a conversion is often in the form of heat that radiates into space.

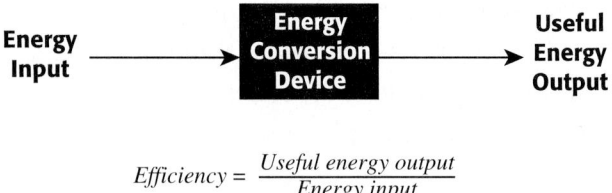

$$Efficiency = \frac{Useful\ energy\ output}{Energy\ input}$$

Sample Problem

1. The table below shows the energy input and light output of incandescent and compact fluorescent light bulbs.

ENERGY IN DIFFERENT LIGHT BULBS

Bulb Type	Energy Used Per Hour in Kilojoules (kJ)	Light Output Per Hour in Kilojoules (kJ)
Incandescent	216	4.3
Fluorescent	54	4.8

Which of the following statements **best** explains why the incandescent light bulb uses more energy and produces less light than a fluorescent light bulb does?

A. The incandescent bulb generates more heat.

B. The fluorescent bulb glows in the dark more.

C. The incandescent bulb produces more electricity.

D. The fluorescent bulb absorbs more ultraviolet rays.

Answer

Answer A is correct. Heat is a byproduct of inefficient energy conversions. The incandescent bulb requires more energy because so much energy is wasted as heat. Answers B and D are incorrect. While fluorescent bulbs can glow in the dark and absorb ultraviolet radiation, these characteristics do not affect efficiency. Answer C is incorrect. Incandescent bulbs do not produce electricity. If you had difficulty with this question, review the loss of heat during energy conversions.

FCAT Study Guide

Mini-Assessment

1. The sketch below shows how the amount of available energy changes as energy moves through an ecosystem.

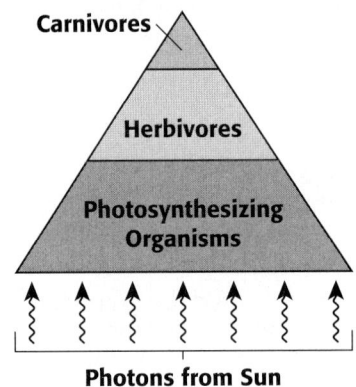

Movement of Energy Through an Ecosystem

Which of the following statements explains why less energy is available at the top of the pyramid than at the bottom?

A. Energy that exists in one form cannot be converted into other forms.

B. Every time that energy is converted, some of the energy is destroyed.

C. Every time that energy is converted, the amount of useful energy is reduced.

D. Energy that exists in one form cannot be transferred from one organism to another.

Enrichment

The sketches below illustrate how energy is used in an electric stove, a microwave oven, and a gas stove.

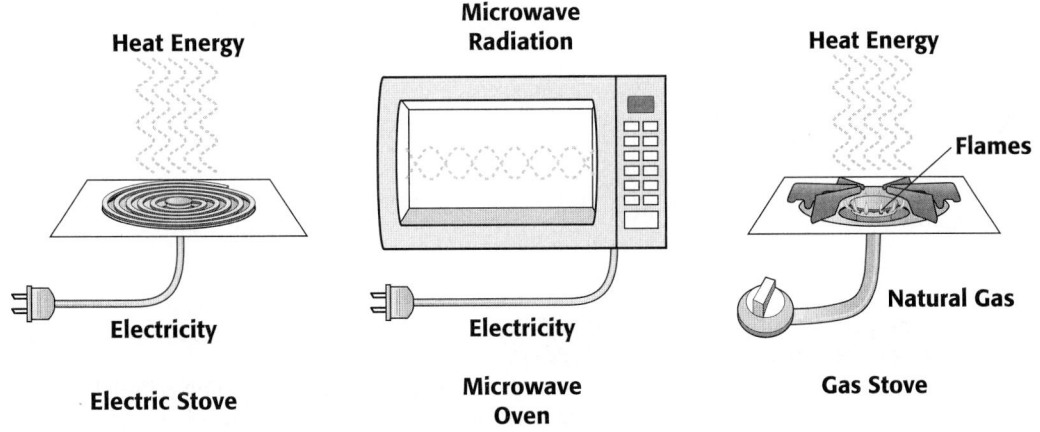

For each device, identify any energy conversions that occur, trace the energy from its original source to the food, and discuss where useful energy is reduced.

Benchmark

C.2.3.6 The student explains and shows the ways in which a net force (i.e., the sum of all acting forces) can act on an object (e.g., speeding up an object traveling in the same direction as the net force, slowing down an object traveling in the direction opposite of the net force).

Tutorial

When an unbalanced force acts on an object, the object will accelerate in the direction in which the force is being exerted. More than one force can act on an object at one time. The net force on an object is the combination of all of the forces acting on the object and is the force that causes objects to accelerate.

Gravitational force causes objects on Earth to accelerate toward the ground. A motionless object exerts a downward force on the ground. At the same time, the ground exerts an upward force of equal magnitude. As a result, the net force on the object is 0.

A falling object accelerates as it moves toward the ground. Resistance in the air (drag) slows the object down until the upward force of the air cancels the downward force of gravity. The object has then reached its terminal velocity.

Touching objects exert contact forces on one another. These forces include friction, tension, air resistance, buoyancy, and applied force. Objects can exert many contact forces at one time.

Sample Problem

1. The image below shows a soccer player preparing to kick a ball.

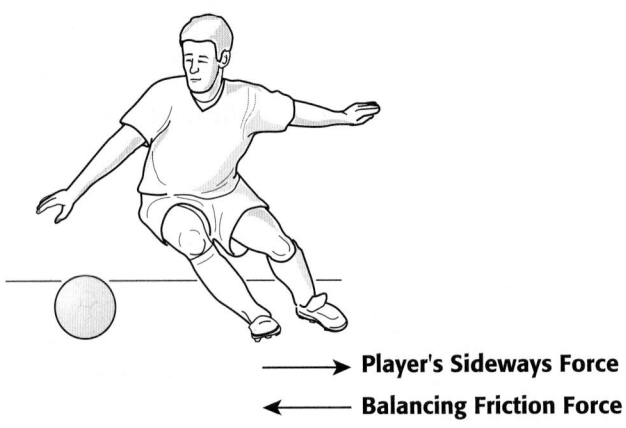

→ **Player's Sideways Force**

← **Balancing Friction Force**

What will happen to the player if the friction force of his foot is less than his sideways force?

A. He will slide forward.

B. He will fall backward.

C. He will move to the left.

D. He will slide to the right.

> **Answer**
>
> **Answer D** is correct. If the force of friction is less than the player's sideways force, the two forces will not balance each other and the player will slide to the right. Answers A and B are incorrect. Because the two forces are acting to the left and to the right, the player will move left or right if the forces do not balance. The player will move to the left if his sideways force is less than the force of friction, so Answer C is incorrect. If you had difficulty with this question, practice calculating net force.

Mini-Assessment

1. The image below shows a car with a mass of 2000 kilograms (kg) parked on a hill. A strong wind exerts a force of 240 newtons (N) downhill on the car.

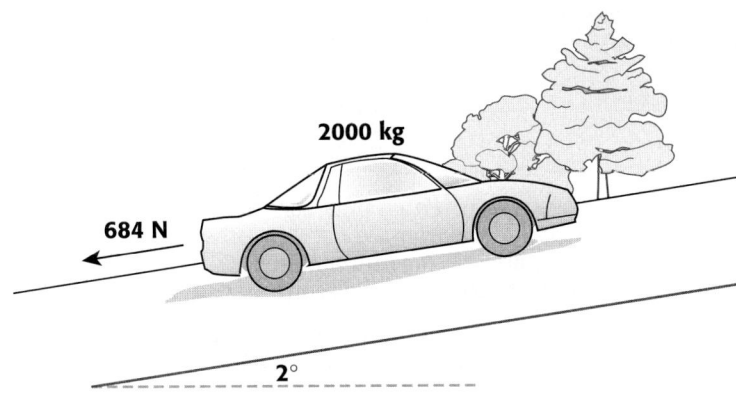

2000 kg

684 N

2°

Car Parked on a Hill

How much force in newtons (N) will the parking brake need to exert uphill to keep the car from rolling down the hill?

Enrichment

1. The sketch below shows a fishing trawler dragging nets through the water.

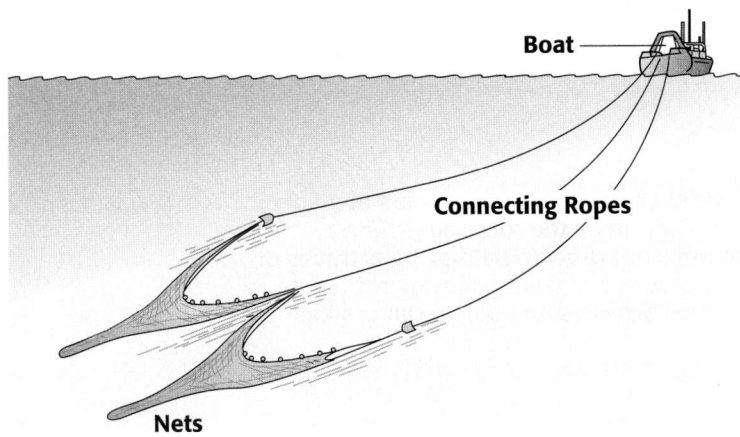

Boat

Connecting Ropes

Nets

Identify the primary forces acting on the ropes, including the direction in which each force acts.

2. Friction prevents cars from using all of the energy that they generate. Friction acts on most moving parts, including the engine and wheels, and thus decreases efficiency. Identify one way to reduce friction in a car.

Benchmark

D.1.3.4 The student knows the ways in which plants and animals reshape the landscape (e.g., bacteria, fungi, worms, rodents, and other organisms add organic matter to the soil, increasing soil fertility, encouraging plant growth, and strengthening resistance to erosion).

Tutorial

Every organism exchanges materials with its ecosystem. When an organism dies, for example, its body is broken down into molecules that either are used by other organisms or are incorporated into the rocks, water, and air. If this material is added to the soil, the fertility of the soil increases and plant growth is encouraged.

The image below shows how carbon cycles through Earth's systems. Every living thing is part of these recycling processes. For example, fungi return nutrients to the soil.

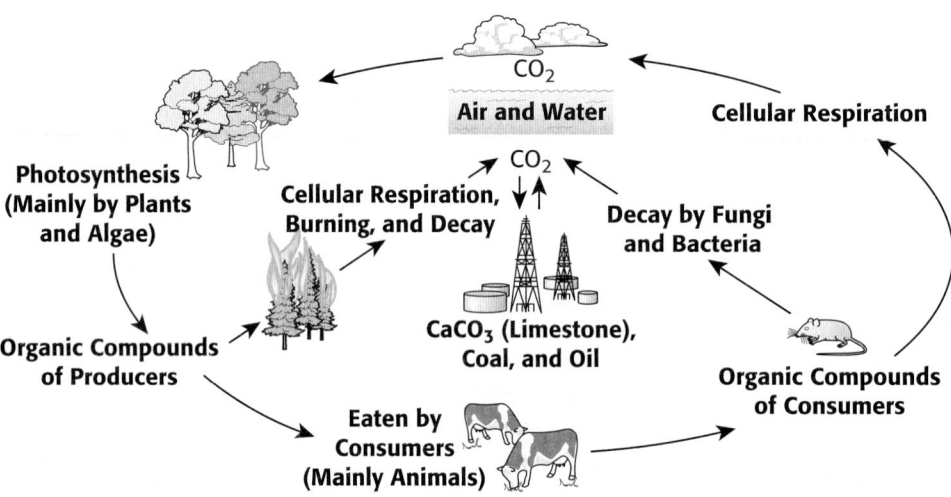

Plants and animals are also important agents of weathering. The roots of plants can expand cracks in rocks and eventually may break the rocks apart. The roots of plants may also anchor soil in place and prevent erosion. The digging activities of burrowing animals also cause weathering of rock and soil by moving rock material and by mixing soil with water and air. Animal activities and plants can dramatically affect the landscape over a long period of time.

Sample Problem

1. Debris from the tides collects in mudflat communities along the coast. People often dig for clams in these communities. Clams are organisms that have two shells and dig through the sand. Which of the following resources does the mudflat ecosystem get from clams' activities?

   A. bacteria and soil

   B. water and sediment

   C. oxygen and organic material

   D. inorganic minerals and erosion prevention

Answer

Answer C is correct. As clams dig through the sand, holes form. These holes can become filled with air, which allows oxygen to enter the ground. The clams provide organic materials in the form of wastes. In addition, dead clams provide organic material that other organisms consume. If you had difficulty with this question, review the carbon cycle.

FCAT Study Guide

Mini-Assessment

1. Corals are organisms that use calcium from ocean water to build a hard skeleton. The picture below shows corals living together.

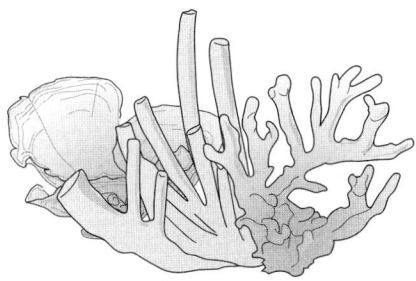

Which of the following statements **best** describes how corals reshape the ocean floor?

A. They remove minerals from the water.

B. They move sand to the ocean's surface.

C. They convert ocean minerals into structures.

D. They make minerals available to other organisms.

Enrichment

The picture below shows a beaver dam.

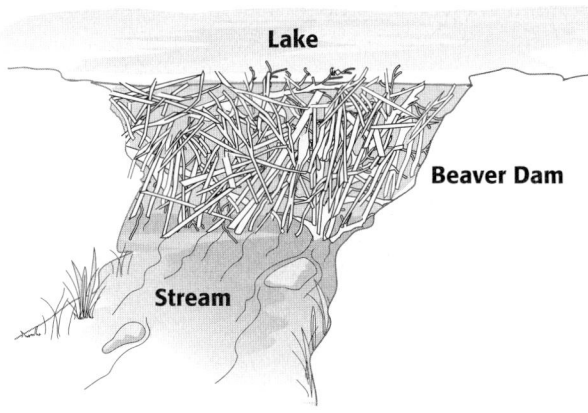

Explain how the dam affects the soil, water table, stream flow, and surrounding terrain. Describe how plant and animal life may have been affected by the near-elimination of beavers in the early 1900s.

Benchmark

E.1.3.1 The student understands the vast size of our solar system and the relationship of the planets and their satellites.

Tutorial

Our solar system is very large. If you made a scale model of the solar system in which Earth was the size of a peppercorn, your model would be 1 kilometer long! Even though the solar system includes the Sun, nine planets, and various smaller bodies, the solar system is made up mostly of empty space.

The Sun is a huge ball of hot gas that consists primarily of hydrogen and helium. The Sun and planets formed billions of years ago from a cloud of dust and gas. Because the Sun's gravity pulls on the planets, they orbit the Sun. The time that a planet takes to complete its orbit depends on the planet's distance from the Sun.

The solar system includes the inner planets and the outer planets. The inner planets—Mercury, Venus, Earth, and Mars—are closest to the Sun. The outer planets, which are farthest from the Sun, are Jupiter, Saturn, Uranus, Neptune, and Pluto. Rocky bodies called *asteroids* also orbit the Sun. Most of these asteroids orbit between Mars and Jupiter in an area called the *asteroid belt*. Comets, which are small bodies of rock and ice, also orbit the Sun. Comets come from the Oort cloud, which surrounds the solar system, and from the Kuiper belt, which lies outside the orbit of Neptune. In addition, nearly every planet in the solar system is orbited by one or more smaller bodies. These natural satellites are called *moons*.

Because everything in the solar system is constantly moving, eclipses sometimes occur. Solar eclipses occur when the Moon comes between Earth and the Sun and the shadow, or umbra, of the Moon falls on part of Earth. During a total solar eclipse, the Moon blocks the entire disk of the Sun in the areas of the world onto which the umbra falls, but the Sun's corona is still visible. People living farther away from the umbra and are in the penumbra and will see a partial eclipse.

Lunar eclipses occur when Earth passes between the Sun and Moon. During a lunar eclipse, sunlight is bent around Earth through Earth's atmosphere. Blue light is filtered out by particles in the atmosphere, causing mainly red light to reach the Moon. As a result, the Moon appears red. Lunar eclipses are more common than solar eclipses are.

The Moon controls Earth's tides. Its gravitational pull causes the oceans to bulge on the side of Earth that is nearest to the Moon. This bulge also occurs on the opposite side of Earth. These bulges are called *high tides*. Low tides occur in the areas where water is drawn away between the bulges. There are two high tides and two low tides each day.

The Sun also contributes to tides. However, because the Sun is so far away, its influence on tides is less powerful than the Moon's influence. When the Sun, Earth, and Moon are aligned, a spring tide occurs. A spring tide has the largest tidal range of all tides. When the Sun, Earth, and Moon form a 90° angle, a neap tide occurs. Neap tides are tides that have the smallest daily range.

Sample Problem

1. Early scientists believed that the Sun revolved around Earth instead of the other way around. What evidence in the night sky contributed to the idea that Earth revolves around the Sun?

Answer

Early scientists noticed that the constellations seemed to move across the sky as the seasons changed. They also noticed that some constellations were visible only during certain times of the year. Scientists recorded the apparent movement of the stars and found an orderly pattern. From the pattern, the scientists concluded that Earth changed positions relative to the stars and therefore was revolving around the Sun. If Earth did not revolve, the stars would always remain in the same positions.

Mini-Assessment

1. The Moon, like Earth, has gravity. While Earth's gravity keeps the Moon in orbit, the Moon's gravity pulls on Earth and causes the water in Earth's oceans to move, as shown in the illustration below. High tides and low tides are the result of this gravitational pull; they occur around the same time every day.

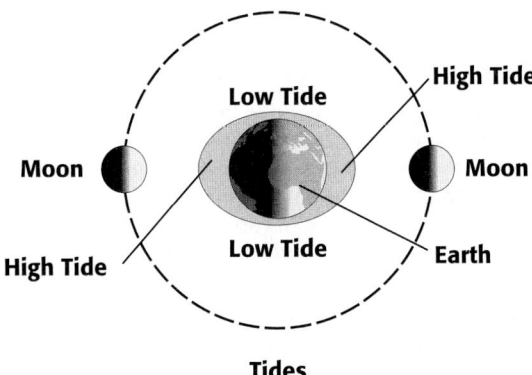

Tides

What two characteristics of Earth and the Moon are responsible for the regularity of the tides?

Enrichment

Study the diagram of a solar eclipse below.

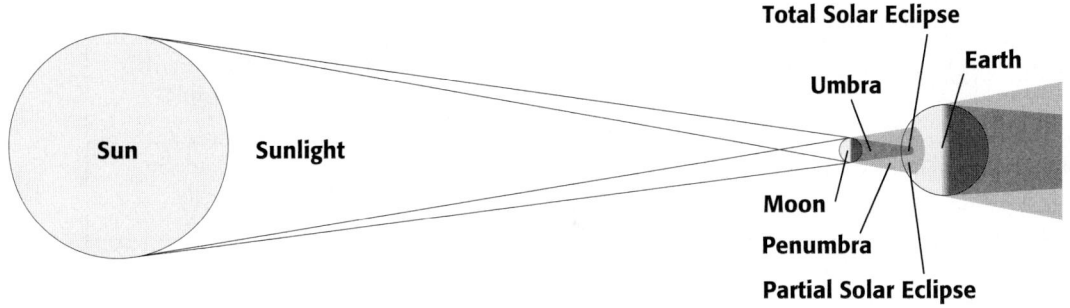

Solar Eclipse

Create a poster or model that illustrates the positions of the Sun, the Moon, and Earth during a lunar eclipse, and summarize how the orbits of the Moon and Earth allow both solar and lunar eclipses to occur.

Benchmark

F.1.3.1 The student understands that living things are composed of major systems that function in reproduction, growth, maintenance, and regulation.

Tutorial

All living organisms are made up of cells. Some organisms are made up of one cell, while other organisms are made up of many cells. In a single-celled organism, one cell must function in reproduction, growth, maintenance, and regulation. In multicellular organisms, a single cell is not required to perform all of these functions. Instead, cells are specialized for a specific function. Cells are organized into tissues, which are organized into organs. Organs are organized into organ systems, in which two or more organs work together to perform a function.

Like most other multicellular organisms, the human body is made up of specialized cells that work together to form tissues, organs, and organ systems. Use the table below to study the 11 human organ systems, their organs, and their major functions.

BODY SYSTEMS

Organ System	Major Organs	General Functions
Cardiovascular system	Heart, veins, arteries, capillaries, and blood	Carries oxygen and nutrients to cells, removes wastes, and helps fight infection
Digestive system	Salivary glands, esophagus, stomach, gallbladder, liver, pancreas, small intestine, and large intestine	Breaks down food into nutrients that can be used by cells
Endocrine system	Glands, includes the pituitary gland	Controls growth, helps maintain homeostasis and other body functions, and plays a role in reproduction
Integumentary system	Skin, hair, and nails	Protects the body, allows for sense of touch, regulates body temperature, and removes some wastes
Lymphatic system	Spleen, lymph nodes, thymus, and tonsils	Fights infection and returns leaked fluids to blood vessels
Muscular system	Muscles and tendons	Allows movement
Nervous system	Brain, spinal cord, and nerves	Senses internal and external environment, sends electrical signals throughout the body, and controls responses to stimuli
Reproductive system	Male: penis, testes, epididymis, vas deferens, and prostate gland Female: vagina, cervix, uterus, fallopian tubes, and ovaries	Male: produces and delivers sperm Female: produces eggs and nourishes and protects the fetus
Respiratory system	Lungs, bronchus, pharynx, larynx, trachea, and diaphragm	Absorbs oxygen from the air and expels carbon dioxide wastes
Skeletal system	Bones, cartilage, and ligaments	Supports and protects the body, allows movement, stores minerals, and produces blood cells
Urinary system	Kidneys, ureters, and urinary bladder	Removes wastes from body and regulates body fluids

Sample Problem

1. Shara is studying cells under a microscope. She knows that the shape of a cell helps determine the function of the cell. A diagram of the cell that Shara is examining appears below.

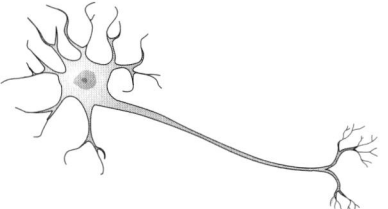

What type of cell is Shara studying?

A. a nerve cell

B. a muscle cell

C. a red blood cell

D. an epithelial cell

Answer

Answer A is correct. Shara is looking at a nerve cell. Nerve cells have long branches that allow the cells to receive information and send messages. Muscle cells are long, thin cells that form strands, which enable movement, so Answer B is incorrect. Answer C is incorrect. Because red blood cells are disk shaped, they can carry oxygen to other body cells. Answer D is incorrect because epithelial cells are compact cells that form a protective layer. If you had difficulty with this question, review the four kinds of tissues.

Mini-Assessment

1. The human digestive system breaks down the food that people eat into molecules that cells in the body can use. The image below shows the human digestive system.

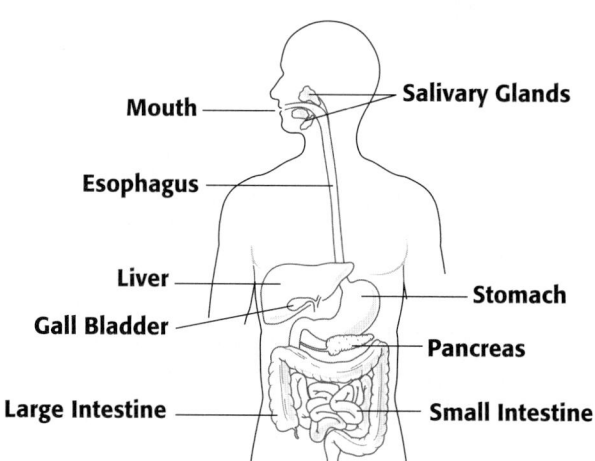

Which organ of the digestive system stores nutrients for future use? What other important function does this organ perform?

Enrichment

1. Several organs in the human body are part of more than one organ system. Identify one such organ. Describe its function in each of the organ systems of which it is a part.

2. Research how skin wounds, such as cuts and scrapes, heal. Make a timeline that shows all of the steps in the healing process, and describe which organ systems are involved in each step.

Benchmark

 F.2.3.2 The student knows that the variation in each species is due to the exchange and interaction of genetic information as it is passed from parent to offspring.

Tutorial

Sexual reproduction happens in many species in both plants and animals. In plants, the male and female reproductive systems often are on the same plant. Sometimes, this characteristic results in offspring that have traits that are identical to the parent if the parent plant self-pollinates. Two parent plants, or cross-pollinating plants, produce offspring that have traits from both parents.

Traits and characteristics are passed from parents to offspring through genes. Each individual has two *alleles*, or forms of the same gene. One allele comes from each parent. The combination of these two alleles is the organism's *genotype*. Genotype determines an organism's appearance, or *phenotype*. Often, alleles are either dominant or recessive. A dominant allele is expressed in the offspring's phenotype. Recessive alleles determine the phenotype of offspring if both parents contribute the recessive allele.

In humans, an egg and a sperm, each of which carries 23 chromosomes, join during sexual reproduction to form a zygote that has 23 pairs of chromosomes, or 46 chromosomes. Body cells also contain 46 chromosomes. Sex cells, or eggs and sperm, contain only 23 chromosomes as a result of division by meiosis, which produces cells that carry one-half of each pair of chromosomes.

Populations adapt over time to better survive in an environment. These adaptations are passed on to offspring and may eventually result in new species. In speciation, a population changes over time until the individuals in that population can no longer reproduce with individuals from the original species.

Sample Problem

1. The table below shows the number of bear cubs born to a pair of adult bears over a period of four years. The table lists whether the cubs had brown fur or white fur. Brown fur (*B*) is the dominant trait, and white fur (*b*) is the recessive trait.

BEAR CUB BIRTHS OVER FOUR YEARS

Year	Total Cubs Born	Cubs with Brown Fur	Cubs with White Fur
1	2	2	0
2	3	3	0
3	1	1	0
4	2	2	0

If both parents have brown fur, what genotype must at least one parent have to produce these offspring?

A. *bb*

B. *bB*

C. *Bb*

D. *BB*

Answer

Answer D is correct. At least one parent would have to carry two dominant alleles (*BB*) for fur color to produce only brown-furred cubs. Answers A, B, and C are incorrect. One parent can have the recessive allele (*Bb* or *bb*), but if both parents carry the recessive gene, some of the cubs will have white fur. In addition, the problem states that both parents have brown fur; a parent with *bb* genotype will have white fur. If you had difficulty with this question, use Punnett squares to examine different crosses.

FCAT Study Guide

Mini-Assessment

1. The table below shows some characteristics of three lizard species. The climate of an ecosystem has changed over time. The ecosystem was once very wet, but it is now very dry and resembles a desert biome.

CHARACTERISTICS OF THREE LIZARDS

	Characteristics
Lizard A	Stores fat in its tail, has coloring that indicates that it is poisonous, often feeds at night
Lizard B	Loses its tail when trapped by predators, has suckers on its toes for climbing, feeds mostly on insects
Lizard C	Changes color to blend in with the environment, has independently movable eyes, uses long tongue to capture insects

Which of these lizard species could survive and continue to reproduce in the new ecosystem? What adaptations would be passed along to future offspring?

Enrichment

Sometimes, offspring lack a sex chromosome, have an incomplete sex chromosome, or have extra sex chromosomes. These abnormalities can cause severe physical and emotional problems as a person grows and develops. The table below shows normal sex chromosomes and some sex chromosome abnormalities. LOVE if

SEX CHROMOSOMES AND ABNORMALITIES

Description	Chromosomes
Normal female	XX
Normal male	XY
Turner's Syndrome	X chromosome with an incomplete or missing second X chromosome
Klinefelter's Syndrome	XXY, XXXY, XXXXY, XXYY, XXXYY
XYY Syndrome	XYY
Triple-X Syndrome	XXX

Choose one sex chromosome abnormality from the table to research. Identify the cause of the abnormality and the gender affected by the abnormality. Describe some of the physical and emotional characteristics of people who have the abnormality, and present your findings in a table or in an outline.

Benchmark

G.1.3.4 The student knows that the interactions of organisms with each other and with the nonliving parts of their environments result in the flow of energy and the cycling of matter throughout the system.

Tutorial

Energy is neither created nor destroyed. In an ecosystem, energy is transferred from one organism to another. This cycle begins with producers. Producers, such as plants, convert light energy into chemical energy during photosynthesis. Other organisms—the consumers—obtain this chemical energy by eating plants or by eating organisms that have eaten plants. Food chains and food webs show how energy is transferred through an ecosystem. Any energy that is not used for an organism's life functions or lost as heat is stored in the organism's body tissue. This stored energy is transferred to the organism that eats the organism. Consequently, less energy is available farther up the food chain.

If a species is removed from a food web, the rest of the ecosystem may be affected. The number of consumers in an ecosystem depends on the amount of energy that is available. Over time, organisms must evolve and adapt to better compete for this limited supply of energy.

Like energy, nonliving matter cycles through an ecosystem. For example, matter, such as nitrogen, can move from the atmosphere into the soil and from organism to organism until the matter returns to the atmosphere to begin the cycle again. Water, carbon, nitrogen, and oxygen are the most commonly cycled materials on Earth.

Sample Problem

1. The food web below shows some of the interactions between the organisms in an ecosystem.

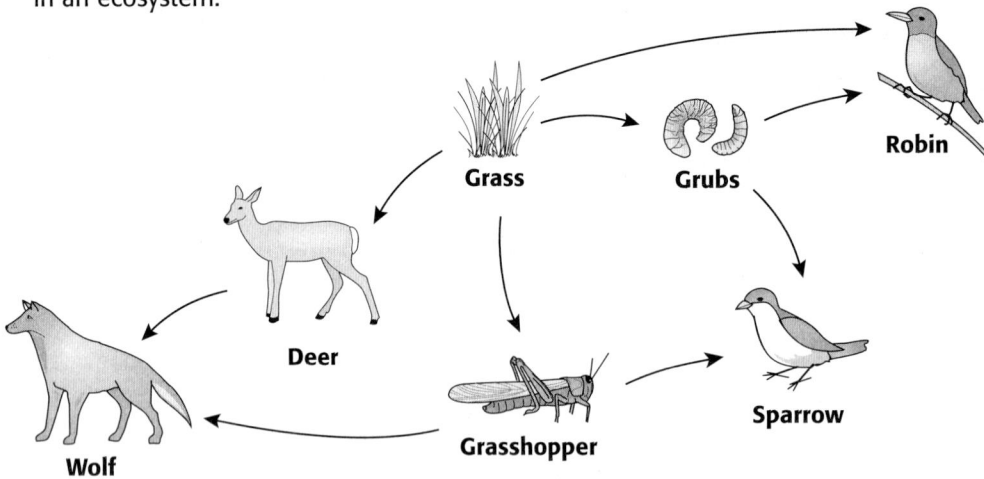

Grass · Grubs · Robin · Deer · Grasshopper · Sparrow · Wolf

What is the **best** way to increase the total amount of energy available in this ecosystem?

A. eliminate the wolf population

B. increase the number of grubs

C. increase the sheep population

D. decrease the number of grasshoppers

Answer

Answer D is correct. Decreasing the number of grasshoppers would increase the amount of grass (and energy) in the system. Increasing the number of consumers of grass would decrease the amount of energy in the system. Eliminating wolves would increase populations of consumers that eat grass. If you had difficulty with this question, review food webs and energy pyramids.

Mini-Assessment

1. Many nonliving materials are cycled through ecosystems. Among these materials are carbon and nitrogen. Study the diagrams of the carbon and nitrogen cycles shown below.

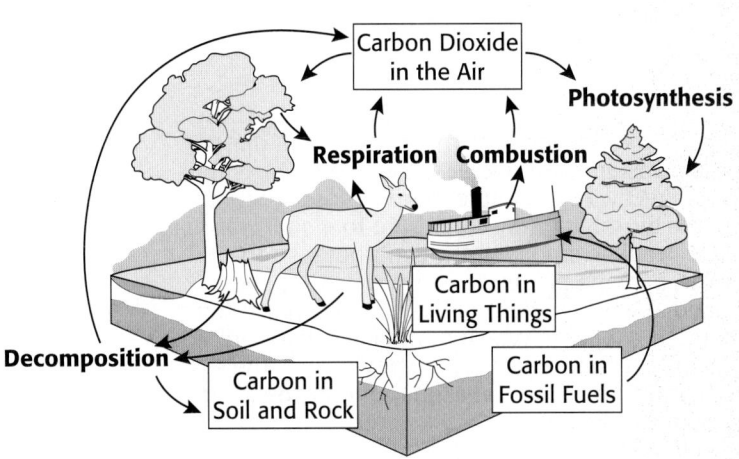

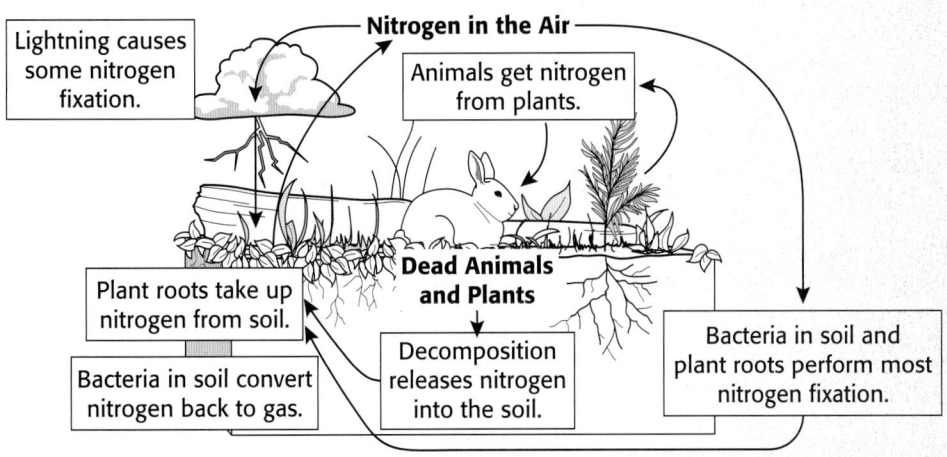

What role do decomposers play in these cycles? What function do bacteria serve in the nitrogen cycle?

Enrichment

1. Many parasites, such as ringworm and tapeworms, attack both humans and animals. Research a parasite that can live in both human and animal hosts. Create a graphic that shows the way in which the parasite infects the host and the type of damage that the parasite can produce.

2. Acid rain can develop when certain chemicals enter the water cycle. Make a flowchart that shows the process in which these chemicals form acid rain and the damage that they can cause in an environment.

Benchmark

G.2.3.4 The student understands that humans are a part of an ecosystem and their activities may deliberately or inadvertently alter the equilibrium in ecosystems.

Tutorial

Human activities affect other organisms in the environment. Sometimes, these activities are deliberate. For example, clearing land for construction can directly damage the habitats of other organisms and can decrease biodiversity. Humans may also harm the environment indirectly. For example, burning fossil fuels can increase carbon dioxide levels in the air, which may contribute to global warming. The burning of fossil fuels can also produce smog, which contributes to the formation of acid rain. Acid rain can damage plants, soil, and water supplies. When these resources are damaged, the equilibrium of the affected ecosystems may be altered. Another example of the ways in which human activities indirectly affect Earth systems is the use of certain chemicals that destroy ozone. The destruction of ozone in the upper atmosphere has weakened the ozone layer that protects Earth from harmful ultraviolet radiation.

Often, humans can have a positive effect on an ecosystem. Many natural areas are set aside and protected. Humans also restore some habitats and protect endangered organisms. Through these deliberate actions, people hope to restore equilibrium in an area. For example, scientists have been working to restore wetlands by flooding areas that have been drained. Scientists have also reintroduced wolves into several areas around the United States. By restoring these predators, scientists hope to restore the natural food web of an area.

Sample Problem

1. Scientists can make predictions about air quality in certain areas. Study the map of an air-quality forecast shown below.

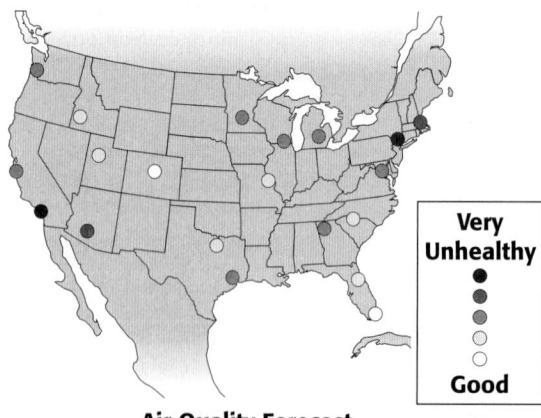

Air Quality Forecast

What is being measured to determine air quality?

A. ozone

B. pollen

C. humidity

D. barometric pressure

Answer

Answer A is the correct answer. Air quality is a measure of how much ozone or smog is present in the atmosphere. If you had difficulty with this question, research the difference between ozone in the lower atmosphere and ozone in the ozone layer.

Mini-Assessment

1. Humans rely on power plants to provide electricity. However, power plants can have a negative effect on the environment. Study the illustration of a power plant shown below.

Describe some of the ways that a power plant can pollute an ecosystem. What are two ways to decrease the amount of pollution that a power plant generates?

Enrichment

Many people confuse global warming with the destruction of the ozone layer. Create a table that summarizes each process clearly. What factors contribute to each process? What are the effects of each process?

Benchmark

H.1.3.1 The student knows that scientific knowledge is subject to modification as new information challenges prevailing theories and as a new theory leads to looking at old theories in a new way.

Tutorial

All scientific inquiry begins with asking questions, recording observations, and conducting research. Often, scientists examine what other scientists have studied and learned. By studying the work of other scientists, people can develop new theories and test these theories by using scientific methods.

Many early astronomers developed their theories about Earth's movements based on the conclusions of previous astronomers. For example, even though Ptolemy's theory that Earth was the center of the solar system was incorrect, his mathematical observations helped future astronomers develop accurate descriptions of planetary motion.

The current theory of plate tectonics was developed in the same way. Alfred Wegener theorized that all of the continents were once one mass and drifted apart over many years. Many scientists did not believe Wegener's theory. As scientists collected new evidence, they discovered that Wegener was partly right. Several of his ideas now form the basis of the current theory of plate tectonics.

The ideas of Gregor Mendel and Charles Darwin have had a great influence on the modern study of heredity and evolution. Gregor Mendel used pea plants to develop hypotheses about genetics and trait inheritance. However, Mendel's ideas were not accepted until long after his death. Charles Darwin, on the other hand, modified his theory of evolution several times throughout his lifetime and incorporated the influences and ideas of other scientists into his theories.

The development of increasingly powerful tools is another way that scientists can use old theories to help explain new observations. Isaac Newton's study of gravity and the attraction of planets, for example, explained previous astronomers' observations of the sky. Now, with tools such as satellites, telescopes, and robotics, who knows what future scientists may discover and which theories they may disprove!

Sample Problem

1. Imagine that you are a scientist investigating hair loss. Your theory currently states that men are more prone to hair loss than women are. Your next step is to research new developments in the field. While conducting your research, you discover that women who have high levels of testosterone experience more hair loss than men do. How should you treat this new information? Explain how you would reexamine your own research and possibly rethink your theory.

Answer

Science is always building on new discoveries. The discovery that women who have high levels of testosterone experience more hair loss than men do indicates that gender may not determine hair loss. So, a scientist would likely examine the results of his or her research to see whether testosterone levels, rather than gender, are the primary factor in hair loss.

Mini-Assessment

1. Hibiscus plants are flowering plants that thrive in Florida but are not known to survive where temperatures drop below freezing. The table below shows the average low temperatures in degrees Celsius (°C) of cities where hibiscus plants are grown. Two of these cities have below-freezing temperatures.

AVERAGE LOW TEMPERATURES FOR FOUR CITIES

City	Average Low Temperature (°C)
Atlanta, Georgia	0
Little Rock, Arkansas	−1.61
Nashville, Tennessee	−3.05
Santa Barbara, California	−4.5

How should a scientist react to this information?

A. A scientist should disregard this information.

B. A scientist should believe that the new information is true.

C. A scientist should decide that the new information is false.

D. A scientist should conduct additional research by using other sources.

Enrichment

1. For years, scientists have researched a number of serious diseases. These diseases include cancer, AIDS, Alzheimer's disease, tuberculosis, and Parkinson's disease. Choose a specific disease, and chart how theories about the cause of the disease have developed through history. Present your findings in a timeline.

2. Scientists often use the work of other scientists to help them develop new theories. Doing so allows scientists to look at problems in a new way. Choose a scientific problem that interests you, and describe how you would use the work of other scientists to help you conduct your own research.

Benchmark

H.1.3.4 The student knows that accurate record keeping, openness, and replication are essential to maintaining an investigator's credibility with other scientists and society.

Tutorial

Science begins with direct observations of the world around us. When conducting research, scientists must use standard tools to measure and record data. Doing so allows scientists from different countries or different fields of science to share and compare data.

Scientists must keep accurate and detailed records of their observations and procedures. All observations, procedures, and data must be made available for other scientists to review. This practice allows other scientists to replicate an investigation and confirm or deny the results of any experiment. Other scientists should be able to repeat an investigation in the same way that the original investigation was conducted. Experiments that explore theories and laws in science must be replicated by other scientists several times before the results can be accepted.

When scientists repeat an investigation and obtain different results, they should thoroughly examine the reasons for the differences in the results. Scientists must determine whether the procedures of the experiment are flawed. They also must determine if they made an incorrect measurement or procedural error. If an error has not occurred, scientists must determine if the differences in the data are great enough to suggest another explanation for the results.

Sample Problem

1. Zach has a hypothesis about the commercials that are shown on TV during Saturday morning cartoons. He thinks that most of the commercials advertise cereals and trendy toys. Zach decides to watch some commercials to test his hypothesis. When should Zach conduct his experiment? How should he record his observations? Keep in mind that Zach must provide enough information for someone else to be able to repeat the experiment.

Answer

Zach should watch commercials at different times of the day and night as well as on different days. He should record the times that he watches TV. He should also record the number of commercials and the products that the commercials advertise during each time period. After Zach makes his observations, he should compare commercials shown on Saturday mornings with commercials shown at other times and then draw conclusions.

Mini-Assessment

1. Sheila surveyed two eighth-grade classes to determine whether eighth-grade students like pizza, hamburgers, or tacos best. Her results are shown in the table below.

FAVORITE FOODS FOR TWO
CLASSES OF EIGHTH GRADERS

	Students in Class A	Students in Class B
Pizza	15	16
Hamburgers	5	10
Tacos	8	5

What should Sheila do to ensure that her results are reliable?

A. She should publish her results.

B. She should repeat her survey in another class.

C. She should interview a local restaurant owner.

D. She should research food choices in the library.

Enrichment

Antonio's class is studying the characteristics of different animals. The students recorded the environmental temperature in an area and the body temperatures of two different animals in the area during different times of the year. Their results are shown in degrees Celsius (°C) in the table below.

BODY TEMPERATURES OF TWO ANIMALS
AT DIFFERENT TIMES OF THE YEAR

Outdoor Temperature (°C)	Body Temperature (°C) of Animal A	Body Temperature (°C) of Animal B
−5.0	−3.0	38.1
4.5	4.0	38.3
37.8	39.0	38.6
15.5	14.5	39.1

What information is missing from the collected data? What additional information about the experiment or the data should people interested in replicating the experiment know?

Benchmark

 H.1.3.5 The student knows that a change in one or more variables may alter the outcome of an investigation.

Tutorial

When scientists begin an investigation, they start by using reputable and reliable sources to research what is known about their subject. When their research is complete, scientists can make predictions and form hypotheses for their own experiments. Hypotheses are tested through scientific methods, which can include recording observations and making measurements. To test hypotheses, scientists design experiments that have variables that are related to the subject being investigated. They look at how differences in these variables affect the outcome.

Scientists use controlled experiments, or experiments in which only one variable is tested at a time, to test their hypotheses. They set up both experimental groups and a control group. A control group is a group that serves as a standard of comparison with experimental groups. The control group is identical to the experimental groups except for one factor—the variable. The variable that scientists purposefully change is known as the *independent variable*. Changes in the independent variable may cause changes in another variable. The *dependent variable* is a variable that changes as a result of a change in the independent variable. For example, in an experiment in which a scientist is studying how different concentrations of a chemical affect plant height, the chemical concentration would be the independent variable and plant height would be the dependent variable.

When scientists design an experiment, they try to test as many subjects as they can. They do so to make sure that any differences in the results between the control group and the experimental groups are caused by the independent variable and not by another factor. Scientists often replicate their experiments to verify their results. After concluding their experiments, they analyze the results and draw conclusions. They also must decide whether the results support the hypothesis.

Sample Problem

1. Sheri has prepared three pitchers of iced tea to find out which recipe makes the sweetest drink. The volume of tea in milliliters (ml) and the mass of sugar in grams (g) that she put in each pitcher are recorded in the table below.

COMPARISON OF TEA MIXTURES

	Tea (ml)	Sugar (g)
Pitcher A	250	62
Pitcher B	450	62
Pitcher C	650	62

Which pitcher has the sweetest tea? How will the results change if Sheri doubles the amount of sugar in Pitcher B? What does this result reveal about the investigation?

Answer

Pitcher A has the sweetest tea. It has the highest concentration of sugar per volume. If Sheri doubles the amount of sugar in Pitcher B, the tea in Pitcher B will be the sweetest because it will have the greatest concentration of sugar. This investigation shows that changing one variable in a study affects the outcome of the study.

Mini-Assessment

1. Jorge wants to grow corn to sell at the farmer's market. He thinks that coffee grounds would be a good fertilizer, so he designs an experiment to test his hypothesis. First, Jorge plants one corn plant in each of two pots. He then adds coffee grounds to one of the pots. He measures the height of each plant in centimeters (cm). His results are recorded in the table below.

EFFECT OF COFFEE GROUNDS ON CORN PLANT GROWTH

Week	Height of Plant with No Fertilizer (cm)	Height of Plant with Coffee Grounds (cm)
0	10	10
1	11	20
2	15	26
3	21	34
4	26	42

What is the independent variable in this experiment? What is the dependent variable in this experiment? How does the dependent variable change in the presence of the independent variable?

Enrichment

Dr. Vet is developing new puppy-food formulas. She performs an experiment to see which of her three formulas causes the greatest increase in mass. She feeds a different formula to each of three puppies. Each puppy receives the same amount of food. Each puppy's mass in grams (g) at the end of each week are recorded in the table below.

MASS IN GRAMS OF FOUR PUPPIES OVER FIVE WEEKS

Week	Mass of Puppy A (g)	Mass of Puppy B (g)	Mass of Puppy C (g)
1	454	454	454
2	681	772	863
3	772	908	999
4	863	999	1226
5	954	1090	1544

Identify the independent and dependent variables. According to the data in Dr. Vet's table, which formula causes the greatest increase in mass? What changes in the design of this experiment would have made the experiment better?

Contents

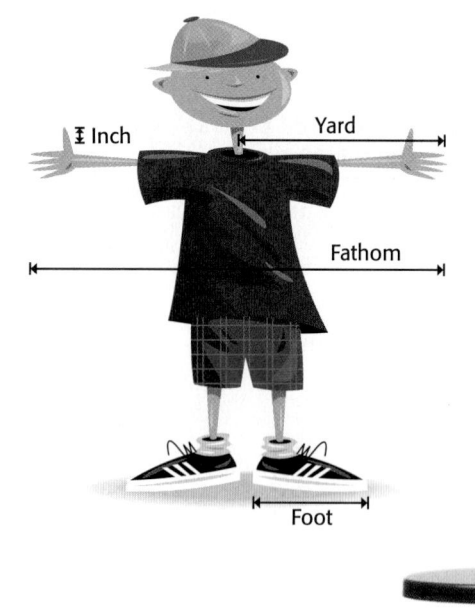

Study Skills

FoldNote Instructions

Have you ever tried to study for a test or quiz but didn't know where to start? Or have you read a chapter and found that you can remember only a few ideas? Well, FoldNotes are a fun and exciting way to help you learn and remember the ideas you encounter as you learn science!

FoldNotes are tools that you can use to organize concepts. By focusing on a few main concepts, FoldNotes help you learn and remember how the concepts fit together. They can help you see the "big picture." Below you will find instructions for building 10 different FoldNotes.

Pyramid

1. Place a sheet of paper in front of you. Fold the lower left-hand corner of the paper diagonally to the opposite edge of the paper.

2. Cut off the tab of paper created by the fold (at the top).

3. Open the paper so that it is a square. Fold the lower right-hand corner of the paper diagonally to the opposite corner to form a triangle.

4. Open the paper. The creases of the two folds will have created an X.

5. Using scissors, cut along one of the creases. Start from any corner, and stop at the center point to create two flaps. Use tape or glue to attach one of the flaps on top of the other flap.

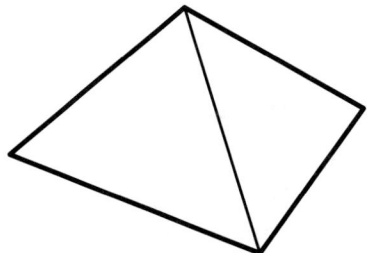

Double Door

1. Fold a sheet of paper in half from the top to the bottom. Then, unfold the paper.

2. Fold the top and bottom edges of the paper to the crease.

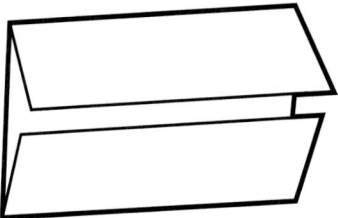

Booklet

1. Fold a sheet of paper in half from left to right. Then, unfold the paper.

2. Fold the sheet of paper in half again from the top to the bottom. Then, unfold the paper.

3. Refold the sheet of paper in half from left to right.

4. Fold the top and bottom edges to the center crease.

5. Completely unfold the paper.

6. Refold the paper from top to bottom.

7. Using scissors, cut a slit along the center crease of the sheet from the folded edge to the creases made in step 4. Do not cut the entire sheet in half.

8. Fold the sheet of paper in half from left to right. While holding the bottom and top edges of the paper, push the bottom and top edges together so that the center collapses at the center slit. Fold the four flaps to form a four-page book.

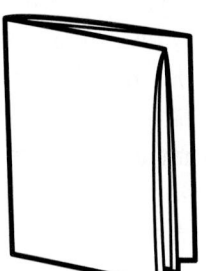

Layered Book

1. Lay one sheet of paper on top of another sheet. Slide the top sheet up so that 2 cm of the bottom sheet is showing.

2. Hold the two sheets together, fold down the top of the two sheets so that you see four 2 cm tabs along the bottom.

3. Using a stapler, staple the top of the FoldNote.

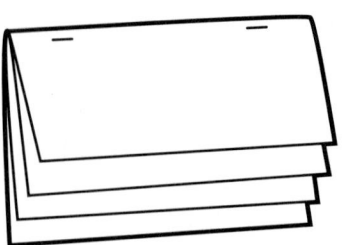

Key-Term Fold

1. Fold a sheet of lined notebook paper in half from left to right.

2. Using scissors, cut along every third line from the right edge of the paper to the center fold to make tabs.

Four-Corner Fold

1. Fold a sheet of paper in half from left to right. Then, unfold the paper.

2. Fold each side of the paper to the crease in the center of the paper.

3. Fold the paper in half from the top to the bottom. Then, unfold the paper.

4. Using scissors, cut the top flap creases made in step 3 to form four flaps.

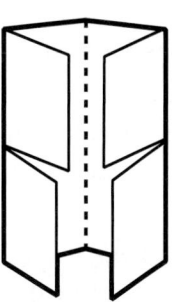

Three-Panel Flip Chart

1. Fold a piece of paper in half from the top to the bottom.

2. Fold the paper in thirds from side to side. Then, unfold the paper so that you can see the three sections.

3. From the top of the paper, cut along each of the vertical fold lines to the fold in the middle of the paper. You will now have three flaps.

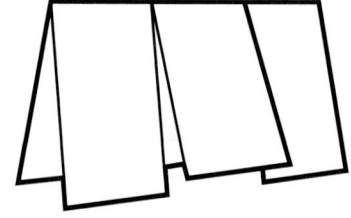

Table Fold

1. Fold a piece of paper in half from the top to the bottom. Then, fold the paper in half again.

2. Fold the paper in thirds from side to side.

3. Unfold the paper completely. Carefully trace the fold lines by using a pen or pencil.

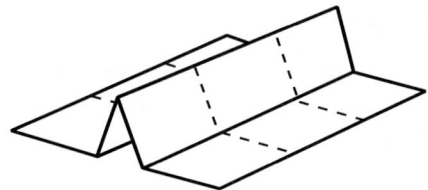

Two-Panel Flip Chart

1. Fold a piece of paper in half from the top to the bottom.

2. Fold the paper in half from side to side. Then, unfold the paper so that you can see the two sections.

3. From the top of the paper, cut along the vertical fold line to the fold in the middle of the paper. You will now have two flaps.

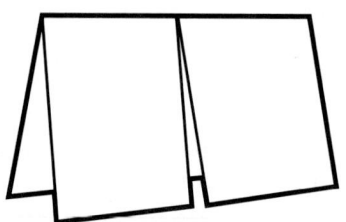

Tri-Fold

1. Fold a piece a paper in thirds from the top to the bottom.

2. Unfold the paper so that you can see the three sections. Then, turn the paper sideways so that the three sections form vertical columns.

3. Trace the fold lines by using a pen or pencil. Label the columns "Know," "Want," and "Learn."

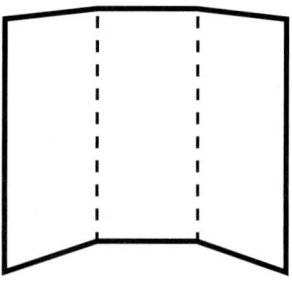

Graphic Organizer Instructions

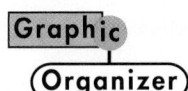 Have you ever wished that you could "draw out" the many concepts you learn in your science class? Sometimes, being able to *see* how concepts are related really helps you remember what you've learned. Graphic Organizers do just that! They give you a way to draw or map out concepts.

All you need to make a Graphic Organizer is a piece of paper and a pencil. Below you will find instructions for four different Graphic Organizers designed to help you organize the concepts you'll learn in this book.

Spider Map

1. Draw a diagram like the one shown. In the circle, write the main topic.

2. From the circle, draw legs to represent different categories of the main topic. You can have as many categories as you want.

3. From the category legs, draw horizontal lines. As you read the chapter, write details about each category on the horizontal lines.

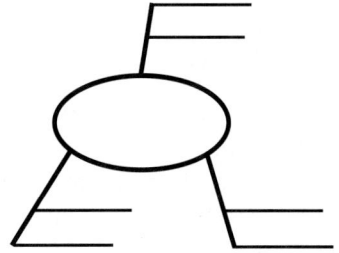

Comparison Table

1. Draw a chart like the one shown. Your chart can have as many columns and rows as you want.

2. In the top row, write the topics that you want to compare.

3. In the left column, write characteristics of the topics that you want to compare. As you read the chapter, fill in the characteristics for each topic in the appropriate boxes.

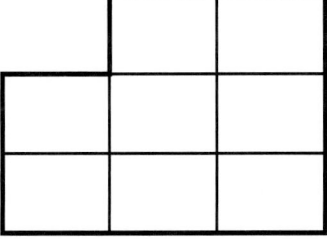

Appendix

Chain-of-Events-Chart

1. Draw a box. In the box, write the first step of a process or the first event of a timeline.

2. Under the box, draw another box, and use an arrow to connect the two boxes. In the second box, write the next step of the process or the next event in the timeline.

3. Continue adding boxes until the process or timeline is finished.

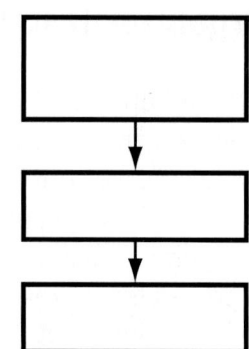

Concept Map

1. Draw a circle in the center of a piece of paper. Write the main idea of the chapter in the center of the circle.

2. From the circle, draw other circles. In those circles, write characteristics of the main idea. Draw arrows from the center circle to the circles that contain the characteristics.

3. From each circle that contains a characteristic, draw other circles. In those circles, write specific details about the characteristic. Draw arrows from each circle that contains a characteristic to the circles that contain specific details. You may draw as many circles as you want.

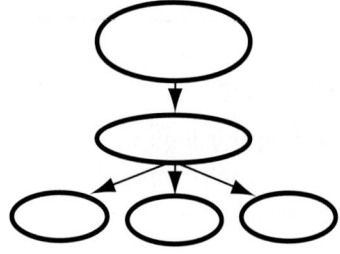

Appendix

Physical Science Refresher

Atoms and Elements

Every object in the universe is made up of particles of some kind of matter. **Matter** is anything that takes up space and has mass. All matter is made up of elements. An **element** is a substance that cannot be separated into simpler components by ordinary chemical means. This is because each element consists of only one kind of atom. An **atom** is the smallest unit of an element that has all of the properties of that element.

Atomic Structure

Atoms are made up of small particles called subatomic particles. The three major types of subatomic particles are **electrons, protons,** and **neutrons.** Electrons have a negative electric charge, protons have a positive charge, and neutrons have no electric charge. The protons and neutrons are packed close to one another to form the **nucleus.** The protons give the nucleus a positive charge. Electrons are most likely to be found in regions around the nucleus called **electron clouds.** The negatively charged electrons are attracted to the positively charged nucleus. An atom may have several energy levels in which electrons are located.

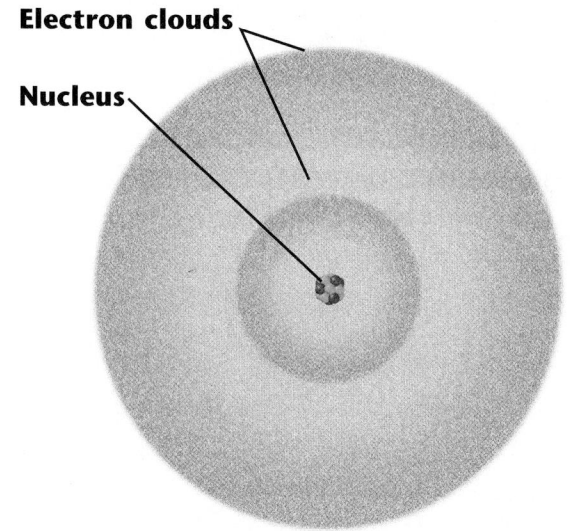

Electron clouds

Nucleus

Atomic Number

To help in the identification of elements, scientists have assigned an **atomic number** to each kind of atom. The atomic number is the number of protons in the atom. Atoms with the same number of protons are all the same kind of element. In an uncharged, or electrically neutral, atom there are an equal number of protons and electrons. Therefore, the atomic number equals the number of electrons in an uncharged atom. The number of neutrons, however, can vary for a given element. Atoms of the same element that have different numbers of neutrons are called **isotopes.**

Periodic Table of the Elements

In the periodic table, the elements are arranged from left to right in order of increasing atomic number. Each element in the table is in a separate box. An uncharged atom of each element has one more electron and one more proton than an uncharged atom of the element to its left. Each horizontal row of the table is called a **period.** Changes in chemical properties of elements across a period correspond to changes in the electron arrangements of their atoms. Each vertical column of the table, known as a **group,** lists elements with similar properties. The elements in a group have similar chemical properties because their atoms have the same number of electrons in their outer energy level. For example, the elements helium, neon, argon, krypton, xenon, and radon all have similar properties and are known as the noble gases.

Molecules and Compounds

When two or more elements are joined chemically, the resulting substance is called a **compound.** A compound is a new substance with properties different from those of the elements that compose it. For example, water, H_2O, is a compound formed when hydrogen (H) and oxygen (O) combine. The smallest complete unit of a compound that has the properties of that compound is called a **molecule.** A chemical formula indicates the elements in a compound. It also indicates the relative number of atoms of each element present. The chemical formula for water is H_2O, which indicates that each water molecule consists of two atoms of hydrogen and one atom of oxygen. The subscript number after the symbol for an element indicates how many atoms of that element are in a single molecule of the compound.

Acids, Bases, and pH

An ion is an atom or group of atoms that has an electric charge because it has lost or gained one or more electrons. When an acid, such as hydrochloric acid, HCl, is mixed with water, it separates into ions. An **acid** is a compound that produces hydrogen ions, H+, in water. The hydrogen ions then combine with a water molecule to form a hydronium ion, H_3O^+. A **base,** on the other hand, is a substance that produces hydroxide ions, OH^-, in water.

To determine whether a solution is acidic or basic, scientists use pH. The **pH** is a measure of the hydronium ion concentration in a solution. The pH scale ranges from 0 to 14. The middle point, pH = 7, is neutral, neither acidic nor basic. Acids have a pH less than 7; bases have a pH greater than 7. The lower the number is, the more acidic the solution. The higher the number is, the more basic the solution.

Chemical Equations

A chemical reaction occurs when a chemical change takes place. (In a chemical change, new substances with new properties are formed.) A chemical equation is a useful way of describing a chemical reaction by means of chemical formulas. The equation indicates what substances react and what the products are. For example, when carbon and oxygen combine, they can form carbon dioxide. The equation for the reaction is as follows: $C + O_2 \rightarrow CO_2$.

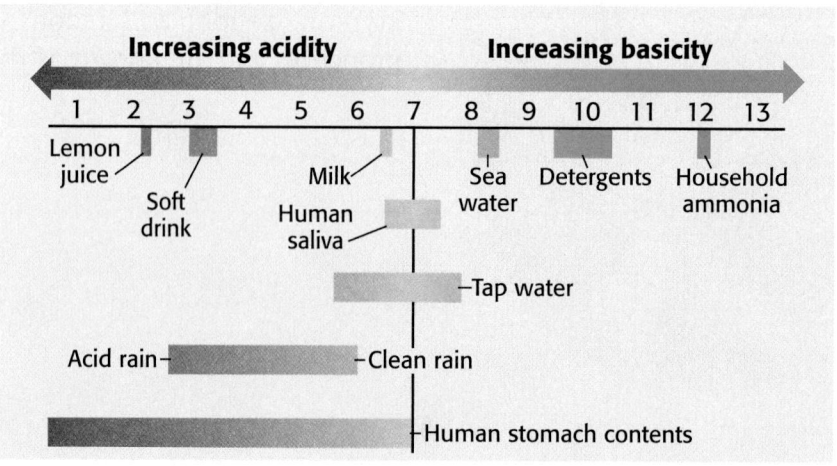

Math Refresher

Science requires an understanding of many math concepts. The following pages will help you review some important math skills.

Averages

An **average,** or **mean,** simplifies a set of numbers into a single number that *approximates* the value of the set.

Example: Find the average of the following set of numbers: 5, 4, 7, and 8.

Step 1: Find the sum.
$$5 + 4 + 7 + 8 = 24$$

Step 2: Divide the sum by the number of numbers in your set. Because there are four numbers in this example, divide the sum by 4.
$$\frac{24}{4} = 6$$

The average, or mean, is **6.**

Ratios

A **ratio** is a comparison between numbers, and it is usually written as a fraction.

Example: Find the ratio of thermometers to students if you have 36 thermometers and 48 students in your class.

Step 1: Make the ratio.
$$\frac{36 \text{ thermometers}}{48 \text{ students}}$$

Step 2: Reduce the fraction to its simplest form.
$$\frac{36}{48} = \frac{36 \div 12}{48 \div 12} = \frac{3}{4}$$

The ratio of thermometers to students is **3 to 4,** or $\frac{3}{4}$. The ratio may also be written in the form 3:4.

Proportions

A **proportion** is an equation that states that two ratios are equal.
$$\frac{3}{1} = \frac{12}{4}$$

To solve a proportion, first multiply across the equal sign. This is called *cross-multiplication.* If you know three of the quantities in a proportion, you can use cross-multiplication to find the fourth.

Example: Imagine that you are making a scale model of the solar system for your science project. The diameter of Jupiter is 11.2 times the diameter of the Earth. If you are using a plastic-foam ball that has a diameter of 2 cm to represent the Earth, what must the diameter of the ball representing Jupiter be?
$$\frac{11.2}{1} = \frac{x}{2 \text{ cm}}$$

Step 1: Cross-multiply.
$$\frac{11.2}{1} \diagup\!\!\!\!\diagdown \frac{x}{2}$$
$$11.2 \times 2 = x \times 1$$

Step 2: Multiply.
$$22.4 = x \times 1$$

Step 3: Isolate the variable by dividing both sides by 1.
$$x = \frac{22.4}{1}$$
$$x = 22.4 \text{ cm}$$

You will need to use a ball that has a diameter of **22.4** cm to represent Jupiter.

Appendix

Percentages

A **percentage** is a ratio of a given number to 100.

Example: What is 85% of 40?

Step 1: Rewrite the percentage by moving the decimal point two places to the left.

0.85

Step 2: Multiply the decimal by the number that you are calculating the percentage of.

0.85 × 40 = 34

85% of 40 is **34.**

Decimals

To **add** or **subtract decimals,** line up the digits vertically so that the decimal points line up. Then, add or subtract the columns from right to left. Carry or borrow numbers as necessary.

Example: Add the following numbers: 3.1415 and 2.96.

Step 1: Line up the digits vertically so that the decimal points line up.

$$3.1415$$
$$+ 2.96$$

Step 2: Add the columns from right to left, and carry when necessary.

$$\overset{1\ \ 1}{3.1415}$$
$$+ 2.96$$
$$\overline{6.1015}$$

The sum is **6.1015.**

Fractions

Numbers tell you how many; **fractions** tell you *how much of a whole.*

Example: Your class has 24 plants. Your teacher instructs you to put 5 plants in a shady spot. What fraction of the plants in your class will you put in a shady spot?

Step 1: In the denominator, write the total number of parts in the whole.

$$\frac{?}{24}$$

Step 2: In the numerator, write the number of parts of the whole that are being considered.

$$\frac{5}{24}$$

So, $\frac{5}{24}$ of the plants will be in the shade.

Reducing Fractions

It is usually best to express a fraction in its simplest form. Expressing a fraction in its simplest form is called *reducing* a fraction.

Example: Reduce the fraction $\frac{30}{45}$ to its simplest form.

Step 1: Find the largest whole number that will divide evenly into both the numerator and denominator. This number is called the *greatest common factor* (GCF).

Factors of the numerator 30:
1, 2, 3, 5, 6, 10, **15,** 30

Factors of the denominator 45:
1, 3, 5, 9, **15,** 45

Step 2: Divide both the numerator and the denominator by the GCF, which in this case is 15.

$$\frac{30}{45} = \frac{30 \div 15}{45 \div 15} = \frac{2}{3}$$

Thus, $\frac{30}{45}$ reduced to its simplest form is $\frac{2}{3}$.

Appendix

Adding and Subtracting Fractions

To **add** or **subtract fractions** that have the **same denominator,** simply add or subtract the numerators.

Examples:

$$\frac{3}{5} + \frac{1}{5} = ? \text{ and } \frac{3}{4} - \frac{1}{4} = ?$$

Step 1: Add or subtract the numerators.

$$\frac{3}{5} + \frac{1}{5} = \frac{4}{} \text{ and } \frac{3}{4} - \frac{1}{4} = \frac{2}{}$$

Step 2: Write the sum or difference over the denominator.

$$\frac{3}{5} + \frac{1}{5} = \frac{4}{5} \text{ and } \frac{3}{4} - \frac{1}{4} = \frac{2}{4}$$

Step 3: If necessary, reduce the fraction to its simplest form.

$\frac{4}{5}$ cannot be reduced, and $\frac{2}{4} = \frac{1}{2}$.

To **add** or **subtract fractions** that have **different denominators,** first find the least common denominator (LCD).

Examples:

$$\frac{1}{2} + \frac{1}{6} = ? \text{ and } \frac{3}{4} - \frac{2}{3} = ?$$

Step 1: Write the equivalent fractions that have a common denominator.

$$\frac{3}{6} + \frac{1}{6} = ? \text{ and } \frac{9}{12} - \frac{8}{12} = ?$$

Step 2: Add or subtract the fractions.

$$\frac{3}{6} + \frac{1}{6} = \frac{4}{6} \text{ and } \frac{9}{12} - \frac{8}{12} = \frac{1}{12}$$

Step 3: If necessary, reduce the fraction to its simplest form.

The fraction $\frac{4}{6} = \frac{2}{3}$, and $\frac{1}{12}$ cannot be reduced.

Multiplying Fractions

To **multiply fractions,** multiply the numerators and the denominators together, and then reduce the fraction to its simplest form.

Example:

$$\frac{5}{9} \times \frac{7}{10} = ?$$

Step 1: Multiply the numerators and denominators.

$$\frac{5}{9} \times \frac{7}{10} = \frac{5 \times 7}{9 \times 10} = \frac{35}{90}$$

Step 2: Reduce the fraction.

$$\frac{35}{90} = \frac{35 \div 5}{90 \div 5} = \frac{7}{18}$$

Dividing Fractions

To **divide fractions,** first rewrite the divisor (the number you divide by) upside down. This number is called the *reciprocal* of the divisor. Then multiply and reduce if necessary.

Example:

$$\frac{5}{8} \div \frac{3}{2} = ?$$

Step 1: Rewrite the divisor as its reciprocal.

$$\frac{3}{2} \rightarrow \frac{2}{3}$$

Step 2: Multiply the fractions.

$$\frac{5}{8} \times \frac{2}{3} = \frac{5 \times 2}{8 \times 3} = \frac{10}{24}$$

Step 3: Reduce the fraction.

$$\frac{10}{24} = \frac{10 \div 2}{24 \div 2} = \frac{5}{12}$$

Scientific Notation

Scientific notation is a short way of representing very large and very small numbers without writing all of the place-holding zeros.

> **Example:** Write 653,000,000 in scientific notation.

Step 1: Write the number without the place-holding zeros.

$$653$$

Step 2: Place the decimal point after the first digit.

$$6.53$$

Step 3: Find the exponent by counting the number of places that you moved the decimal point.

$$6.53000000$$

The decimal point was moved eight places to the left. Therefore, the exponent of 10 is positive 8. If you had moved the decimal point to the right, the exponent would be negative.

Step 4: Write the number in scientific notation.

$$\mathbf{6.53 \times 10^8}$$

Area

Area is the number of square units needed to cover the surface of an object.

Formulas:

area of a square = side × side
area of a rectangle = length × width
area of a triangle = $\frac{1}{2}$ × base × height

Examples: Find the areas.

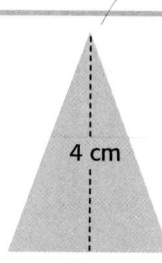

Triangle

$area = \frac{1}{2} \times base \times height$

$area = \frac{1}{2} \times 3\ cm \times 4\ cm$

$area = \mathbf{6\ cm^2}$

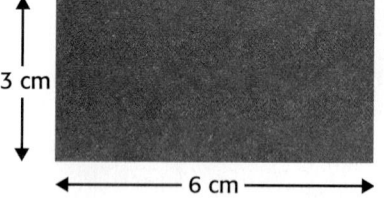

Rectangle

$area = length \times width$

$area = 6\ cm \times 3\ cm$

$area = \mathbf{18\ cm^2}$

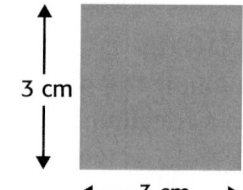

Square

$area = side \times side$

$area = 3\ cm \times 3\ cm$

$area = \mathbf{9\ cm^2}$

Volume

Volume is the amount of space that something occupies.

Formulas:

volume of a cube = side × side × side

volume of a prism = area of base × height

Examples:

Find the volume of the solids.

Cube

$volume = side \times side \times side$

$volume = 4\ cm \times 4\ cm \times 4\ cm$

$volume = \mathbf{64\ cm^3}$

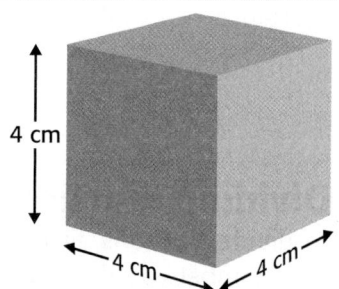

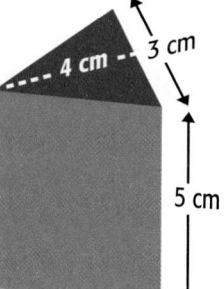

Prism

$volume = area\ of\ base \times height$

$volume = (area\ of\ triangle) \times height$

$volume = (\frac{1}{2} \times 3\ cm \times 4\ cm) \times 5\ cm$

$volume = 6\ cm^2 \times 5\ cm$

$volume = \mathbf{30\ cm^3}$

Appendix

Making Charts and Graphs

Pie Charts

A pie chart shows how each group of data relates to all of the data. Each part of the circle forming the chart represents a category of the data. The entire circle represents all of the data. For example, a biologist studying a hardwood forest in Wisconsin found that there were five different types of trees. The data table at right summarizes the biologist's findings.

Wisconsin Hardwood Trees	
Type of tree	Number found
Oak	600
Maple	750
Beech	300
Birch	1,200
Hickory	150
Total	3,000

How to Make a Pie Chart

1 To make a pie chart of these data, first find the percentage of each type of tree. Divide the number of trees of each type by the total number of trees, and multiply by 100.

$$\frac{600 \text{ oak}}{3,000 \text{ trees}} \times 100 = 20\%$$

$$\frac{750 \text{ maple}}{3,000 \text{ trees}} \times 100 = 25\%$$

$$\frac{300 \text{ beech}}{3,000 \text{ trees}} \times 100 = 10\%$$

$$\frac{1,200 \text{ birch}}{3,000 \text{ trees}} \times 100 = 40\%$$

$$\frac{150 \text{ hickory}}{3,000 \text{ trees}} \times 100 = 5\%$$

2 Now, determine the size of the wedges that make up the pie chart. Multiply each percentage by 360°. Remember that a circle contains 360°.

$20\% \times 360° = 72°$ $25\% \times 360° = 90°$

$10\% \times 360° = 36°$ $40\% \times 360° = 144°$

$5\% \times 360° = 18°$

3 Check that the sum of the percentages is 100 and the sum of the degrees is 360.

$20\% + 25\% + 10\% + 40\% + 5\% = 100\%$

$72° + 90° + 36° + 144° + 18° = 360°$

4 Use a compass to draw a circle and mark the center of the circle.

5 Then, use a protractor to draw angles of 72°, 90°, 36°, 144°, and 18° in the circle.

6 Finally, label each part of the chart, and choose an appropriate title.

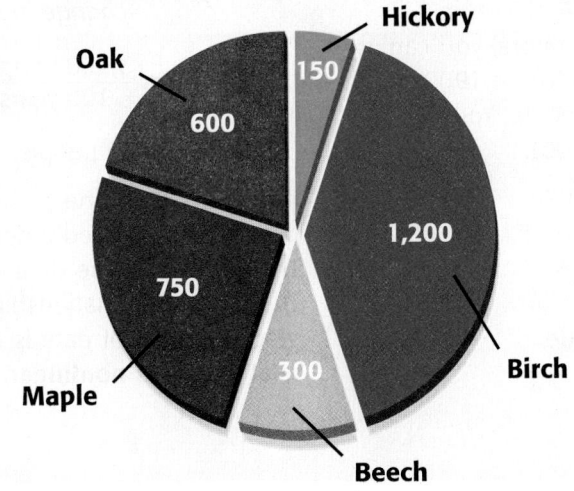

A Community of Wisconsin Hardwood Trees

Appendix

Line Graphs

Line graphs are most often used to demonstrate continuous change. For example, Mr. Smith's students analyzed the population records for their hometown, Appleton, between 1900 and 2000. Examine the data at right.

Because the year and the population change, they are the *variables*. The population is determined by, or dependent on, the year. Therefore, the population is called the **dependent variable,** and the year is called the **independent variable.** Each set of data is called a **data pair.** To prepare a line graph, you must first organize data pairs into a table like the one at right.

Population of Appleton, 1900–2000	
Year	Population
1900	1,800
1920	2,500
1940	3,200
1960	3,900
1980	4,600
2000	5,300

How to Make a Line Graph

1 Place the independent variable along the horizontal (*x*) axis. Place the dependent variable along the vertical (*y*) axis.

2 Label the *x*-axis "Year" and the *y*-axis "Population." Look at your largest and smallest values for the population. For the *y*-axis, determine a scale that will provide enough space to show these values. You must use the same scale for the entire length of the axis. Next, find an appropriate scale for the *x*-axis.

3 Choose reasonable starting points for each axis.

4 Plot the data pairs as accurately as possible.

5 Choose a title that accurately represents the data.

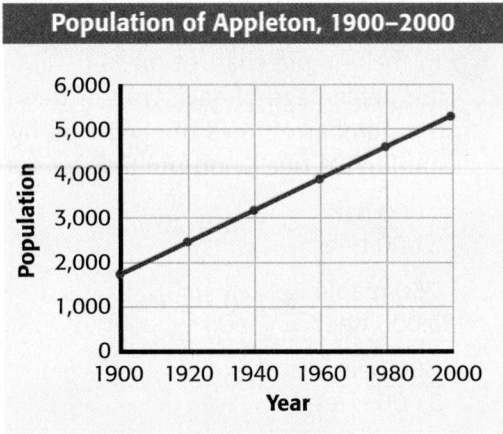

How to Determine Slope

Slope is the ratio of the change in the *y*-value to the change in the *x*-value, or "rise over run."

1 Choose two points on the line graph. For example, the population of Appleton in 2000 was 5,300 people. Therefore, you can define point *a* as (2000, 5,300). In 1900, the population was 1,800 people. You can define point *b* as (1900, 1,800).

2 Find the change in the *y*-value.
(*y* at point *a*) − (*y* at point *b*) =
5,300 people − 1,800 people =
3,500 people

3 Find the change in the *x*-value.
(*x* at point *a*) − (*x* at point *b*) =
2000 − 1900 = 100 years

4 Calculate the slope of the graph by dividing the change in *y* by the change in *x*.

$$slope = \frac{change\ in\ y}{change\ in\ x}$$

$$slope = \frac{3,500\ people}{100\ years}$$

$$slope = 35\ people\ per\ year$$

In this example, the population in Appleton increased by a fixed amount each year. The graph of these data is a straight line. Therefore, the relationship is **linear.** When the graph of a set of data is not a straight line, the relationship is **nonlinear.**

Using Algebra to Determine Slope

The equation in step 4 may also be arranged to be

$$y = kx$$

where y represents the change in the y-value, k represents the slope, and x represents the change in the x-value.

$$slope = \frac{change\ in\ y}{change\ in\ x}$$

$$k = \frac{y}{x}$$

$$k \times x = \frac{y \times x}{x}$$

$$kx = y$$

Bar Graphs

Bar graphs are used to demonstrate change that is not continuous. These graphs can be used to indicate trends when the data cover a long period of time. A meteorologist gathered the precipitation data shown here for Hartford, Connecticut, for April 1–15, 1996, and used a bar graph to represent the data.

Precipitation in Hartford, Connecticut April 1–15, 1996			
Date	Precipitation (cm)	Date	Precipitation (cm)
April 1	0.5	April 9	0.25
April 2	1.25	April 10	0.0
April 3	0.0	April 11	1.0
April 4	0.0	April 12	0.0
April 5	0.0	April 13	0.25
April 6	0.0	April 14	0.0
April 7	0.0	April 15	6.50
April 8	1.75		

How to Make a Bar Graph

1 Use an appropriate scale and a reasonable starting point for each axis.

2 Label the axes, and plot the data.

3 Choose a title that accurately represents the data.

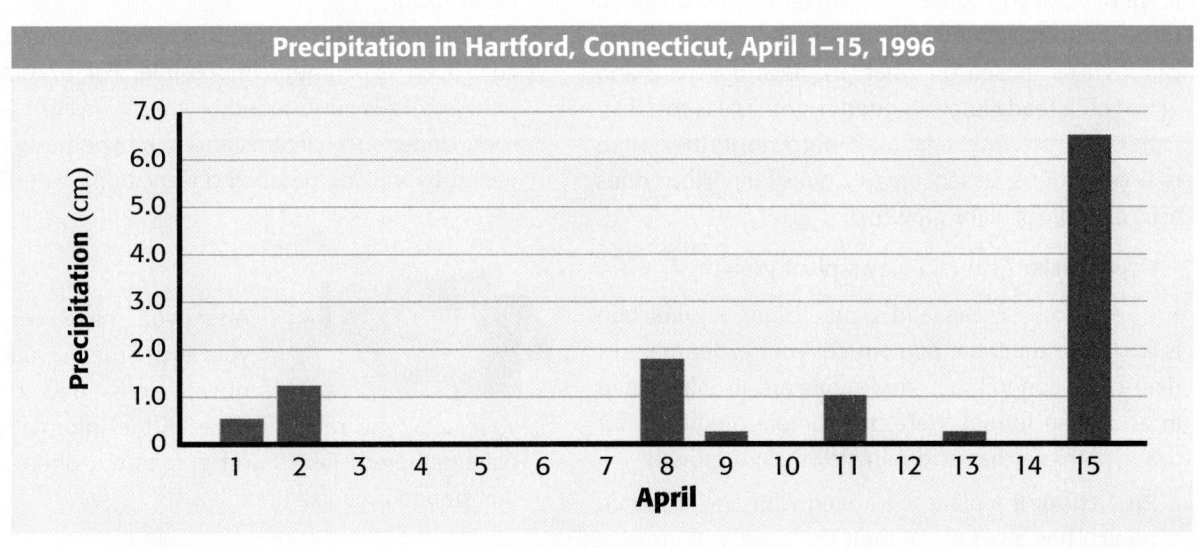

Precipitation in Hartford, Connecticut, April 1–15, 1996

Scientific Methods

The ways in which scientists answer questions and solve problems are called **scientific methods.** The same steps are often used by scientists as they look for answers. However, there is more than one way to use these steps. Scientists may use all of the steps or just some of the steps during an investigation. They may even repeat some of the steps. The goal of using scientific methods is to come up with reliable answers and solutions.

Six Steps of Scientific Methods

1 Ask a Question

Good questions come from careful **observations.** You make observations by using your senses to gather information. Sometimes, you may use instruments, such as microscopes and telescopes, to extend the range of your senses. As you observe the natural world, you will discover that you have many more questions than answers. These questions drive investigations.

Questions beginning with *what, why, how,* and *when* are important in focusing an investigation. Here is an example of a question that could lead to an investigation.

> **Question:** How does acid rain affect plant growth?

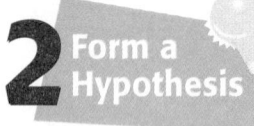
2 Form a Hypothesis

After you ask a question, you need to form a **hypothesis.** A hypothesis is a clear statement of what you expect the answer to your question to be. Your hypothesis will represent your best "educated guess" based on what you have observed and what you already know. A good hypothesis is testable. Otherwise, the investigation can go no further. Here is a hypothesis based on the question, "How does acid rain affect plant growth?"

> **Hypothesis:** Acid rain slows plant growth.

The hypothesis can lead to predictions. A prediction is what you think the outcome of your experiment or data collection will be. Predictions are usually stated in an if-then format. Here is a sample prediction for the hypothesis that acid rain slows plant growth.

> **Prediction:** If a plant is watered with only acid rain (which has a pH of 4), then the plant will grow at half its normal rate.

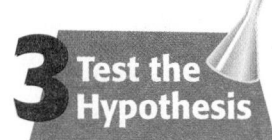
3 Test the Hypothesis

After you have formed a hypothesis and made a prediction, your hypothesis should be tested. One way to test a hypothesis is with a controlled experiment. A **controlled experiment** tests only one factor at a time. In an experiment to test the effect of acid rain on plant growth, the **control group** would be watered with normal rain water. The **experimental group** would be watered with acid rain. All of the plants should receive the same amount of sunlight and water each day. The air temperature should be the same for all groups. However, the acidity of the water will be a variable. In fact, any factor that is different from one group to another is a **variable.** If your hypothesis is correct, then the acidity of the water and plant growth are *dependant variables.* The amount a plant grows is dependent on the acidity of the water. However, the amount of water each plant receives and the amount of sunlight each plant receives are *independent variables.* Either of these factors could change without affecting the other factor.

Sometimes, the nature of an investigation makes a controlled experiment impossible. For example, the Earth's core is surrounded by thousands of meters of rock. Under such circumstances, a hypothesis may be tested by making detailed observations.

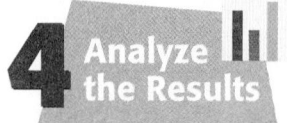
4 Analyze the Results

After you have completed your experiments, made your observations, and collected your data, you must analyze all the information you have gathered. Tables and graphs are often used in this step to organize the data.

5 Draw Conclusions

After analyzing your data, you can determine if your results support your hypothesis. If your hypothesis is supported, you (or others) might want to repeat the observations or experiments to verify your results. If your hypothesis is not supported by the data, you may have to check your procedure for errors. You may even have to reject your hypothesis and make a new one. If you cannot draw a conclusion from your results, you may have to try the investigation again or carry out further observations or experiments.

6 Communicate Results

After any scientific investigation, you should report your results. By preparing a written or oral report, you let others know what you have learned. They may repeat your investigation to see if they get the same results. Your report may even lead to another question and then to another investigation.

Scientific Methods in Action

Scientific methods contain loops in which several steps may be repeated over and over again. In some cases, certain steps are unnecessary. Thus, there is not a "straight line" of steps. For example, sometimes scientists find that testing one hypothesis raises new questions and new hypotheses to be tested. And sometimes, testing the hypothesis leads directly to a conclusion. Furthermore, the steps in scientific methods are not always used in the same order. Follow the steps in the diagram, and see how many different directions scientific methods can take you.

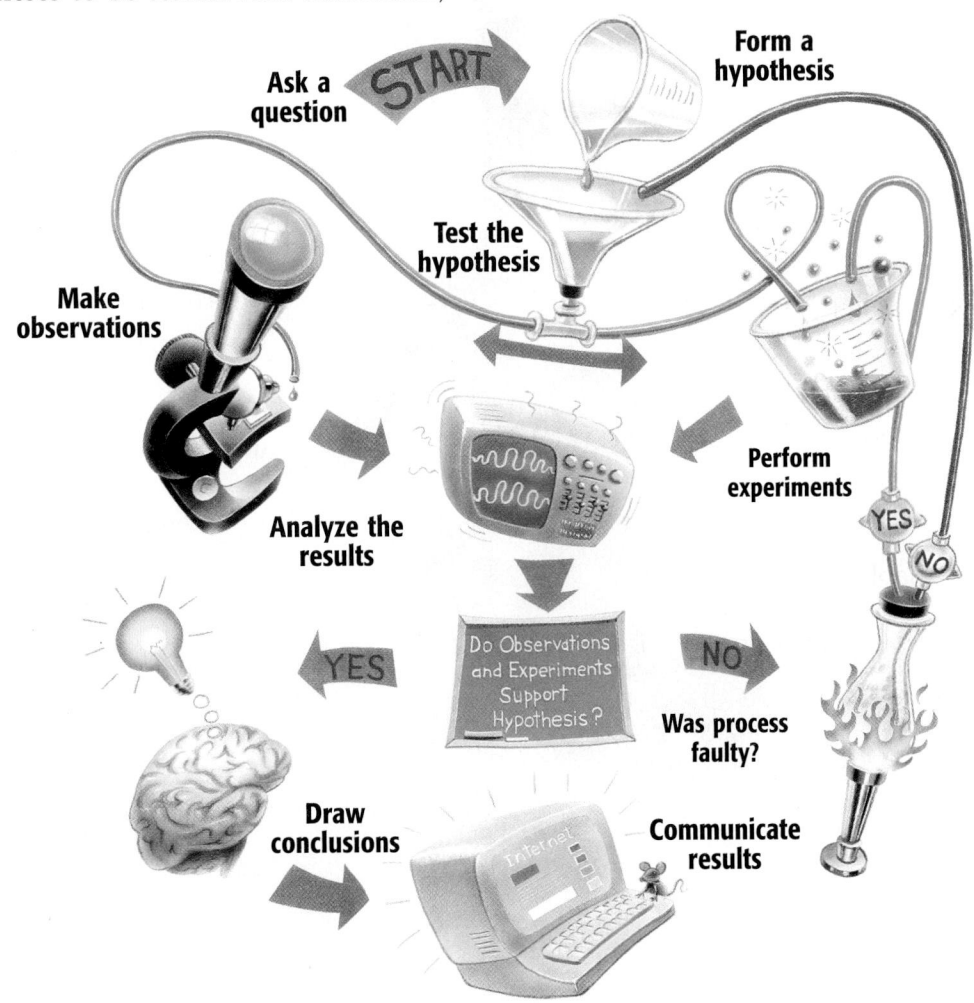

Using the Microscope

Parts of the Compound Light Microscope

- The **ocular lens** magnifies the image 10×.
- The **low-power objective** magnifies the image 10×.
- The **high-power objective** magnifies the image either 40× or 43×.
- The **revolving nosepiece** holds the objectives and can be turned to change from one magnification to the other.
- The **body tube** maintains the correct distance between the ocular lens and objectives.
- The **coarse-adjustment knob** moves the body tube up and down to allow focusing of the image.

- The **stage** supports a slide.
- **Stage clips** hold the slide in place for viewing.
- The **diaphragm** controls the amount of light coming through the stage.
- The light source provides a **light** for viewing the slide.
- The **arm** supports the body tube.
- The **base** supports the microscope.

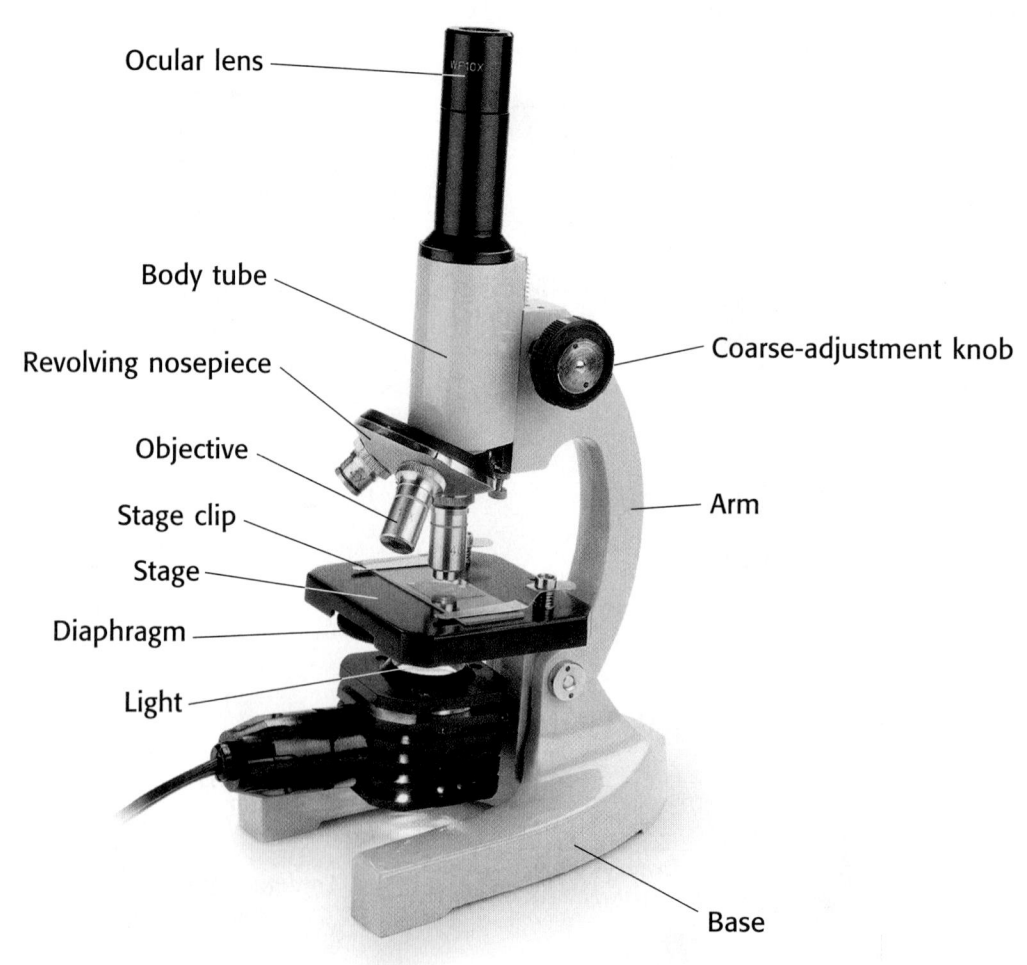

Ocular lens

Body tube

Revolving nosepiece

Objective

Stage clip

Stage

Diaphragm

Light

Coarse-adjustment knob

Arm

Base

Appendix

Proper Use of the Compound Light Microscope

1. Use both hands to carry the microscope to your lab table. Place one hand beneath the base, and use the other hand to hold the arm of the microscope. Hold the microscope close to your body while carrying it to your lab table.

2. Place the microscope on the lab table at least 5 cm from the edge of the table.

3. Check to see what type of light source is used by your microscope. If the microscope has a lamp, plug it in and make sure that the cord is out of the way. If the microscope has a mirror, adjust the mirror to reflect light through the hole in the stage. **Caution:** If your microscope has a mirror, do not use direct sunlight as a light source. Direct sunlight can damage your eyes.

4. Always begin work with the low-power objective in line with the body tube. Adjust the revolving nosepiece.

5. Place a prepared slide over the hole in the stage. Secure the slide with the stage clips.

6. Look through the ocular lens. Move the diaphragm to adjust the amount of light coming through the stage.

7. Look at the stage from eye level. Slowly turn the coarse adjustment to lower the objective until the objective almost touches the slide. Do not allow the objective to touch the slide.

8. Look through the ocular lens. Turn the coarse adjustment to raise the low-power objective until the image is in focus. Always focus by raising the objective away from the slide. Never focus the objective downward. Use the fine adjustment to sharpen the focus. Keep both eyes open while viewing a slide.

9. Make sure that the image is exactly in the center of your field of vision. Then, switch to the high-power objective. Focus the image by using only the fine adjustment. Never use the coarse adjustment at high power.

10. When you are finished using the microscope, remove the slide. Clean the ocular lens and objectives with lens paper. Return the microscope to its storage area. Remember to use both hands when carrying the microscope.

Making a Wet Mount

1. Use lens paper to clean a glass slide and a coverslip.

2. Place the specimen that you wish to observe in the center of the slide.

3. Using a medicine dropper, place one drop of water on the specimen.

4. Hold the coverslip at the edge of the water and at a 45° angle to the slide. Make sure that the water runs along the edge of the coverslip.

5. Lower the coverslip slowly to avoid trapping air bubbles.

6. Water might evaporate from the slide as you work. Add more water to keep the specimen fresh. Place the tip of the medicine dropper next to the edge of the coverslip. Add a drop of water. (You can also use this method to add stain or solutions to a wet mount.) Remove excess water from the slide by using the corner of a paper towel as a blotter. Do not lift the coverslip to add or remove water.

Sky Maps

Spring

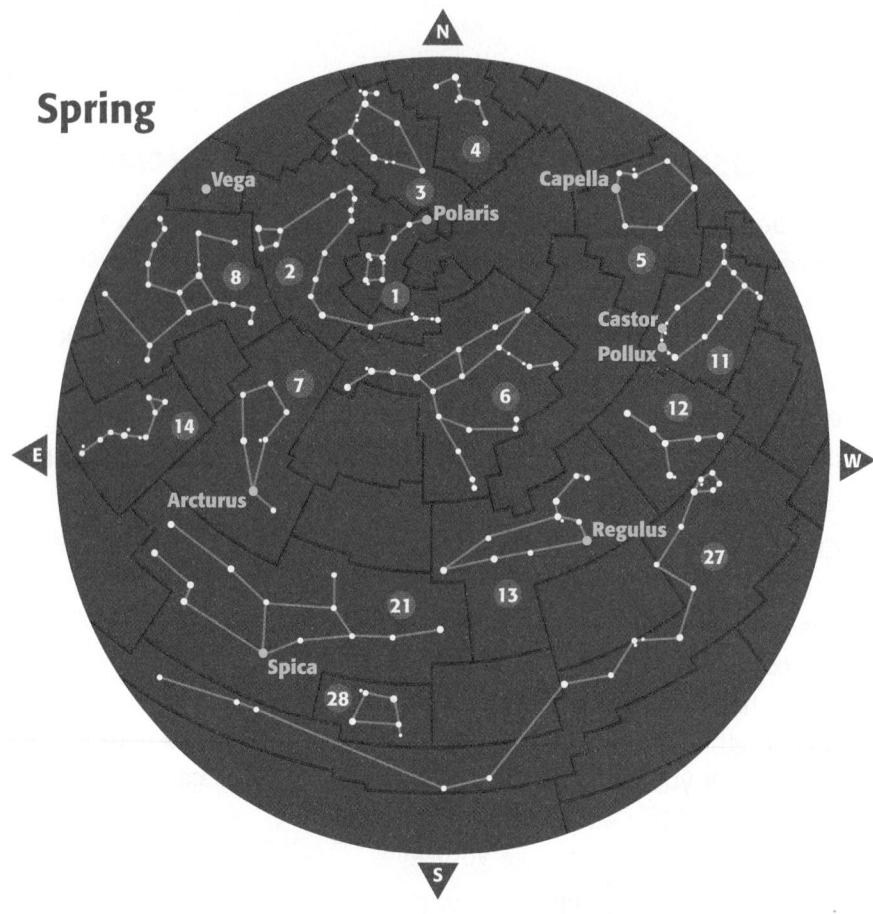

Summer

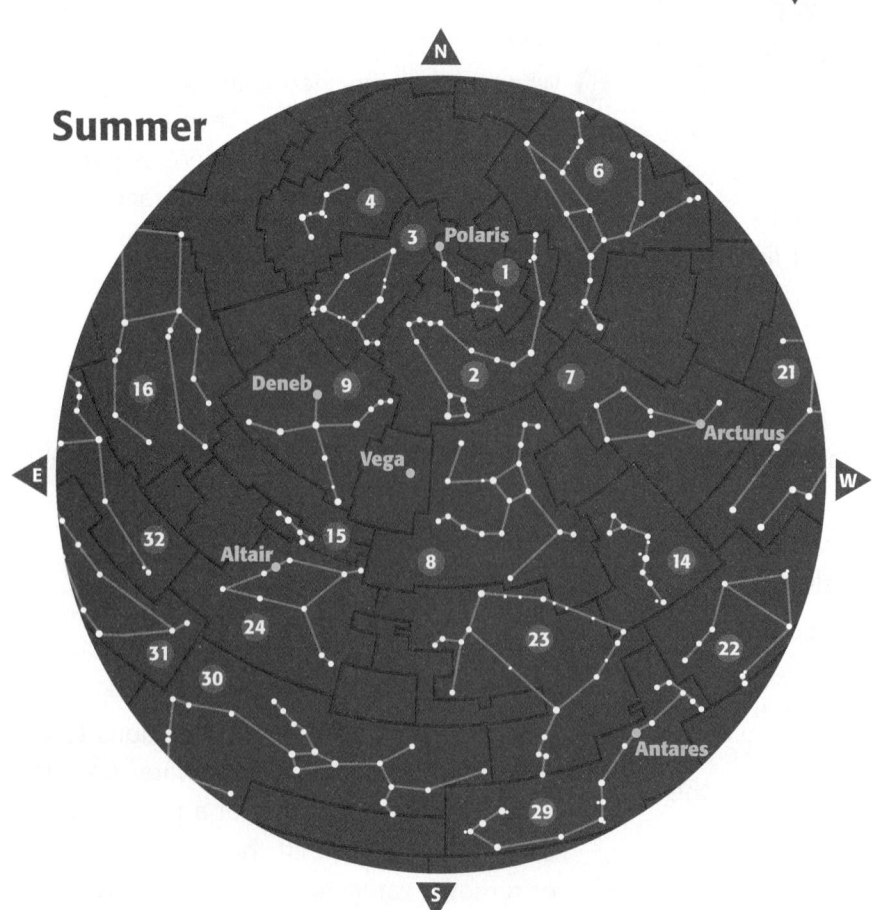

Constellations

1 **Ursa Minor**
2 **Draco**
3 **Cepheus**
4 **Cassiopeia**
5 **Auriga**
6 **Ursa Major**
7 **Boötes**
8 **Hercules**
9 **Cygnus**
10 **Perseus**
11 **Gemini**
12 **Cancer**
13 **Leo**
14 **Serpens**
15 **Sagitta**
16 **Pegasus**
17 **Pisces**

Appendix

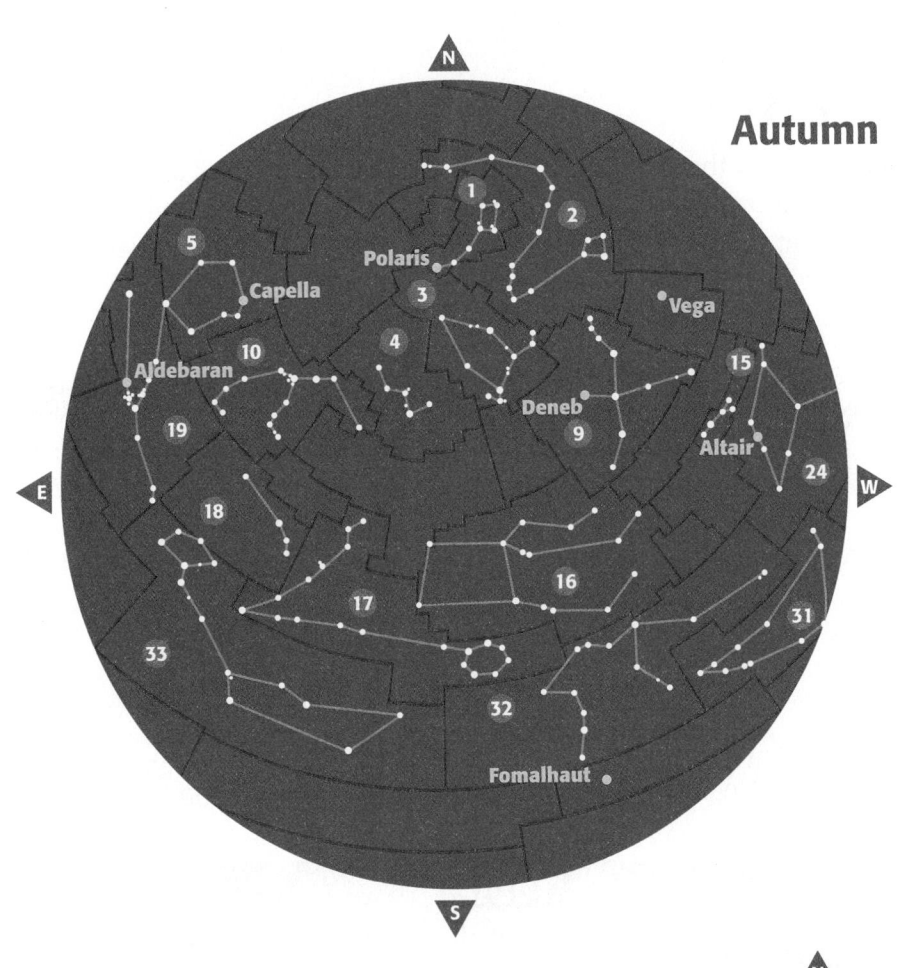

Autumn

Constellations

Winter

Appendix

SI Measurement

The International System of Units, or SI, is the standard system of measurement used by many scientists. Using the same standards of measurement makes it easier for scientists to communicate with one another.

SI works by combining prefixes and base units. Each base unit can be used with different prefixes to define smaller and larger quantities. The table below lists common SI prefixes.

SI Prefixes

Prefix	Symbol	Factor	Example
kilo-	k	1,000	kilogram, 1 kg = 1,000 g
hecto-	h	100	hectoliter, 1 hL = 100 L
deka-	da	10	dekameter, 1 dam = 10 m
		1	meter, liter, gram
deci-	d	0.1	decigram, 1 dg = 0.1 g
centi-	c	0.01	centimeter, 1 cm = 0.01 m
milli-	m	0.001	milliliter, 1 mL = 0.001 L
micro-	μ	0.000 001	micrometer, 1 μm = 0.000 001 m

SI Conversion Table

SI units	From SI to English	From English to SI
Length		
kilometer (km) = 1,000 m	1 km = 0.621 mi	1 mi = 1.609 km
meter (m) = 100 cm	1 m = 3.281 ft	1 ft = 0.305 m
centimeter (cm) = 0.01 m	1 cm = 0.394 in.	1 in. = 2.540 cm
millimeter (mm) = 0.001 m	1 mm = 0.039 in.	
micrometer (μm) = 0.000 001 m		
nanometer (nm) = 0.000 000 001 m		
Area		
square kilometer (km^2) = 100 hectares	1 km^2 = 0.386 mi^2	1 mi^2 = 2.590 km^2
hectare (ha) = 10,000 m^2	1 ha = 2.471 acres	1 acre = 0.405 ha
square meter (m^2) = 10,000 cm^2	1 m^2 = 10.764 ft^2	1 ft^2 = 0.093 m^2
square centimeter (cm^2) = 100 mm^2	1 cm^2 = 0.155 $in.^2$	1 $in.^2$ = 6.452 cm^2
Volume		
liter (L) = 1,000 mL = 1 dm^3	1 L = 1.057 fl qt	1 fl qt = 0.946 L
milliliter (mL) = 0.001 L = 1 cm^3	1 mL = 0.034 fl oz	1 fl oz = 29.574 mL
microliter (μL) = 0.000 001 L		
Mass		
kilogram (kg) = 1,000 g	1 kg = 2.205 lb	1 lb = 0.454 kg
gram (g) = 1,000 mg	1 g = 0.035 oz	1 oz = 28.350 g
milligram (mg) = 0.001 g		
microgram (μg) = 0.000 001 g		

Measuring Skills

Using a Graduated Cylinder

When using a graduated cylinder to measure volume, keep the following procedures in mind:

1 Place the cylinder on a flat, level surface before measuring liquid.

2 Move your head so that your eye is level with the surface of the liquid.

3 Read the mark closest to the liquid level. On glass graduated cylinders, read the mark closest to the center of the curve in the liquid's surface.

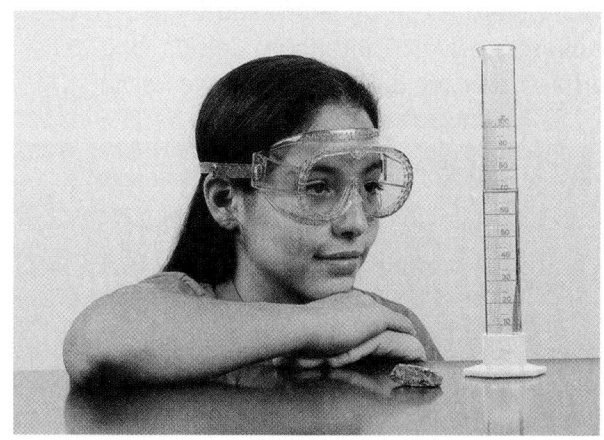

Using a Meterstick or Metric Ruler

When using a meterstick or metric ruler to measure length, keep the following procedures in mind:

1 Place the ruler firmly against the object that you are measuring.

2 Align one edge of the object exactly with the 0 end of the ruler.

3 Look at the other edge of the object to see which of the marks on the ruler is closest to that edge. (Note: Each small slash between the centimeters represents a millimeter, which is one-tenth of a centimeter.)

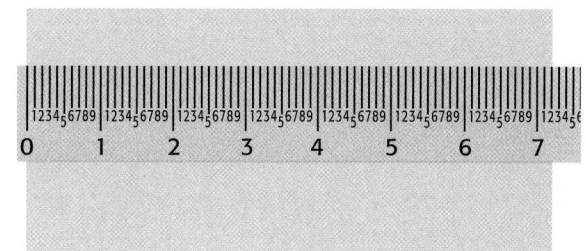

Using a Triple-Beam Balance

When using a triple-beam balance to measure mass, keep the following procedures in mind:

1 Make sure the balance is on a level surface.

2 Place all of the countermasses at 0. Adjust the balancing knob until the pointer rests at 0.

3 Place the object you wish to measure on the pan. **Caution:** Do not place hot objects or chemicals directly on the balance pan.

4 Move the largest countermass along the beam to the right until it is at the last notch that does not tip the balance. Follow the same procedure with the next-largest countermass. Then, move the smallest countermass until the pointer rests at 0.

5 Add the readings from the three beams together to determine the mass of the object.

6 When determining the mass of crystals or powders, first find the mass of a piece of filter paper. Then, add the crystals or powder to the paper, and remeasure. The actual mass of the crystals or powder is the total mass minus the mass of the paper. When finding the mass of liquids, first find the mass of the empty container. Then, find the combined mass of the liquid and container. The mass of the liquid is the total mass minus the mass of the container.

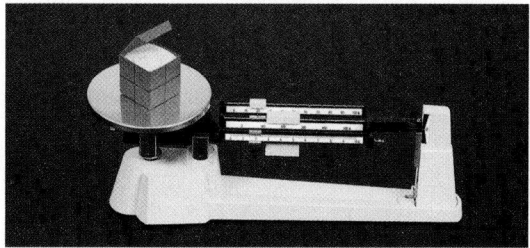

Temperature Scales

Temperature can be expressed by using three different scales: Fahrenheit, Celsius, and Kelvin. The SI unit for temperature is the kelvin (K).

Although 0 K is much colder than 0°C, a change of 1 K is equal to a change of 1°C.

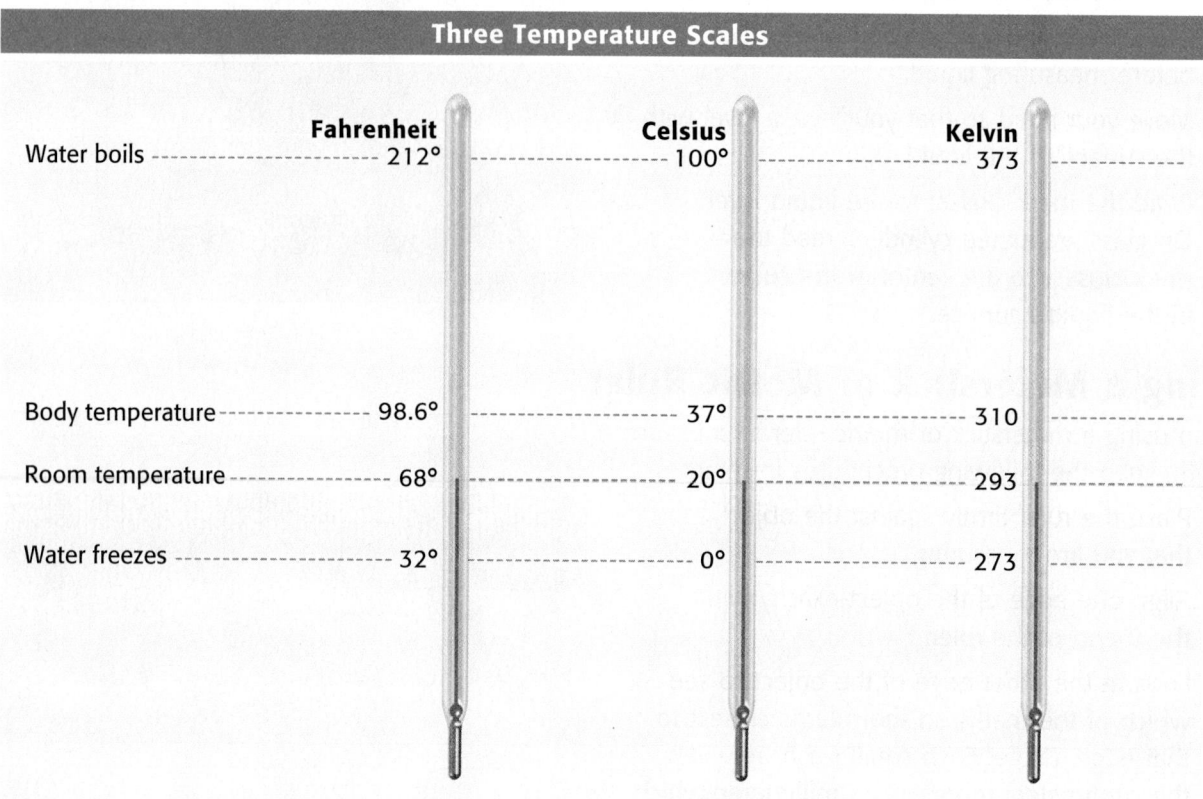

Three Temperature Scales			
	Fahrenheit	**Celsius**	**Kelvin**
Water boils	212°	100°	373
Body temperature	98.6°	37°	310
Room temperature	68°	20°	293
Water freezes	32°	0°	273

Temperature Conversions Table		
To convert	**Use this equation:**	**Example**
Celsius to Fahrenheit °C → °F	$°F = \left(\dfrac{9}{5} \times °C\right) + 32$	Convert 45°C to °F. $°F = \left(\dfrac{9}{5} \times 45°C\right) + 32 = 113°F$
Fahrenheit to Celsius °F → °C	$°C = \dfrac{5}{9} \times (°F - 32)$	Convert 68°F to °C. $°C = \dfrac{5}{9} \times (68°F - 32) = 20°C$
Celsius to Kelvin °C → K	$K = °C + 273$	Convert 45°C to K. $K = 45°C + 273 = 318 \ K$
Kelvin to Celsius K → °C	$°C = K - 273$	Convert 32 K to °C. $°C = 32K - 273 = -241°C$

Appendix

Glossary

A

abiotic describes the nonliving part of the environment, including water, rocks, light, and temperature (308) *FCAT VOCAB*

abrasion the grinding and wearing away of rock surfaces through the mechanical action of other rock or sand particles (459)

active transport the movement of substances across the cell membrane that requires the cell to use energy (108)

adaptation a characteristic that improves an individual's ability to survive and reproduce in a particular environment (293)

allergy a reaction to a harmless or common substance by the body's immune system (263)

alluvial fan a fan-shaped mass of material deposited by a stream when the slope of the land decreases sharply (426)

altitude the angle between an object in the sky and the horizon (526)

alveoli any of the tiny air sacs of the lungs where oxygen and carbon dioxide are exchanged (171)

antibody a protein made by B cells that binds to a specific antigen (259)

aquifer a body of rock or sediment that stores groundwater and allows the flow of groundwater (390, 429)

Archimedes' principle the principle that states that the buoyant force on an object in a fluid is an upward force equal to the weight of the volume of fluid that the object displaces (654)

area a measure of the size of a surface or a region (22)

artery a blood vessel that carries blood away from the heart to the body's organs (158)

artesian spring a spring whose water flows from a crack in the cap rock over the aquifer (431)

artificial satellite any human-made object placed in orbit around a body in space (546)

asexual reproduction reproduction that does not involve the union of sex cells and in which one parent produces offspring that are genetically identical to the parent (278) *FCAT VOCAB*

astronomy the scientific study of the universe (514)

atmospheric pressure the pressure caused by the weight of the atmosphere (649)

atom the smallest unit of an element that maintains the properties of that element (582)

autoimmune disease a disease in which the immune system attacks the organism's own cells (263)

axis an imaginary straight line running through the Earth from pole to pole (50)

B

B cell a white blood cell that makes antibodies (259)

beach an area of the shoreline that is made up of deposited sediment (456)

Bernoulli's principle the principle that states that the pressure in a fluid decreases as the fluid's velocity increases (660)

biodiversity the number and variety of organisms in a given area during a specific period of time (345) *FCAT VOCAB*

biome a large region characterized by a specific type of climate and certain types of plant and animal communities (356)

biosphere the part of Earth where life exists (311)

biotic describes living factors in the environment (308) *FCAT VOCAB*

blood the fluid that carries gases, nutrients, and wastes through the body and that is made up of platelets, white blood cells, red blood cells, and plasma (162)

blood pressure the force that blood exerts on the walls of the arteries (164)

brain the mass of nerve tissue that is the main control center of the nervous system (210)

bronchus one of the two tubes that connect the lungs with the trachea (171)

buoyant force the upward force that keeps an object immersed in or floating on a liquid (654)

C

cancer a tumor in which the cells begin dividing at an uncontrolled rate and become invasive (264)

Glossary

capillary a tiny blood vessel that allows an exchange between blood and cells in tissue (158)

cardiovascular system a collection of organs that transport blood throughout the body; the organs in this system include the heart, the arteries, and the veins (156)

carnivore an organism that eats animals (313)

carrying capacity the largest population that an environment can support at any given time (319)

cell in biology, the smallest unit that can perform all life processes; cells are covered by a membrane and contain DNA and cytoplasm (76)

cell cycle the life cycle of a cell (114)

cell membrane a phospholipid layer that covers a cell's surface and acts as a barrier between the inside of a cell and the cell's environment (79)

cellular respiration the process by which cells use oxygen to produce energy from food (111)

cell wall a rigid structure that surrounds the cell membrane and provides support to the cell (84)

central nervous system the brain and the spinal cord; its main function is to control the flow of information in the body (206)

channel the path that a stream follows (419)

chemical change a change that occurs when one or more substances change into entirely new substances with different properties (594)

chemical property a property of matter that describes a substance's ability to participate in chemical reactions (592)

chromosome in a eukaryotic cell, one of the structures in the nucleus that are made up of DNA and protein; in a prokaryotic cell, the main ring of DNA (114)

cochlea a coiled tube that is found in the inner ear and that is essential to hearing (218)

coevolution the evolution of two species that is due to mutual influence, often in a way that makes the relationship more beneficial to both species (323)

combustion the burning of a substance (339)

commensalism a relationship between two organisms in which one organism benefits and the other is unaffected (322)

community all of the populations of species that live in the same habitat and interact with each other (310)

compound machine a machine made of more than one simple machine (636)

computer an electronic device that can accept data and instructions, follow the instructions, and output the results (48)

condensation the change of state from a gas to a liquid (336)

constellation a region of the sky that contains a recognizable star pattern and that is used to describe the location of objects in space (524)

controlled experiment an experiment that tests only one factor at a time by using a comparison of a control group with an experimental group (16)

Coriolis effect the curving of the path of a moving object from an otherwise straight path due to the Earth's rotation (485)

creep the slow downhill movement of weathered rock material (471)

crest the highest point of a wave (492) *FCAT VOCAB*

cytokinesis the division of the cytoplasm of a cell (116)

D

day the time required for Earth to rotate once on its axis (514)

decomposition the breakdown of substances into simpler molecular substances (338)

deep current a streamlike movement of ocean water far below the surface (485)

deep-water zone the zone of a lake or pond below the open-water zone, where no light reaches (371)

deflation a form of wind erosion in which fine, dry soil particles are blown away (459)

delta a fan-shaped mass of material deposited at the mouth of a stream (425)

density the ratio of the mass of a substance to the volume of the substance (24, 587)

dependent variable in an experiment, the factor that changes as a result of manipulation of one or more other factors (the independent variables) (49) *FCAT VOCAB*

deposition the process in which material is laid down (424) *FCAT VOCAB*

dermis the layer of skin below the epidermis (143)

desert an area that has little or no plant life, long periods without rain, and extreme temperatures; usually found in hot climates (361)

diffusion the movement of particles from regions of higher density to regions of lower density (106)

digestive system the organs that break down food so that it can be used by the body (184)

divide the boundary between drainage areas that have streams that flow in opposite directions (418)

drag a force parallel to the velocity of the flow; it opposes the direction of an aircraft and, in combination with thrust, determines the speed of the aircraft (663)

dune a mound of wind-deposited sand that moves as a result of the action of wind (460)

E

ecology the study of the interactions of living organisms with one another and with their environment (308)

ecosystem a community of organisms and their abiotic, or nonliving, environment (311) *FCAT VOCAB*

efficiency a quantity, usually expressed as a percentage, that measures the ratio of work output to work input (628) *FCAT VOCAB*

electromagnetic radiation the radiation associated with an electric and magnetic field; it varies periodically and travels at the speed of light (521) *FCAT VOCAB*

El Niño a change in the surface water temperature in the Pacific Ocean that produces a warm current (490)

embryo a developing human, from fertilization through the first 8 weeks of development (the 10th week of pregnancy) (238)

endocrine system a collection of glands and groups of cells that secrete hormones that regulate growth, development, and homeostasis; includes the pituitary, thyroid, parathyroid, and adrenal glands, the hypothalamus, the pineal body, and the gonads (220)

endocytosis the process by which a cell membrane surrounds a particle and encloses the particle in a vesicle to bring the particle into the cell (108)

endoplasmic reticulum a system of membranes that is found in a cell's cytoplasm and that assists in the production, processing, and transport of proteins and in the production of lipids (87)

energy the capacity to do work (598)

energy pyramid a triangular diagram that shows an ecosystem's loss of energy, which results as energy passes through the ecosystem's food chain (315)

entropy a measure of the randomness or disorder of a system (601) *FCAT VOCAB*

epidermis the surface layer of cells on a plant or animal (143)

erosion the process by which wind, water, ice, or gravity transports soil and sediment from one location to another (416) *FCAT VOCAB*

esophagus a long, straight tube that connects the pharynx to the stomach (186)

estimate a rough or approximate calculation (44)

estivation a period of inactivity and lowered body temperature that some animals undergo in summer as a protection against hot weather and lack of food (290)

estuary an area where fresh water mixes with salt water from the ocean (368, 398)

eukaryote an organism made up of cells that have a nucleus enclosed by a membrane; eukaryotes include protists, animals, plants, and fungi but not archaea or bacteria (82)

evaporation the change of state from a liquid to a gas (336)

exocytosis the process in which a cell releases a particle by enclosing the particle in a vesicle that then moves to the cell surface and fuses with the cell membrane (109)

external fertilization the union of sex cells outside the bodies of the parents (280)

F

feedback mechanism a cycle of events in which information from one step controls or affects a previous step (215)

fermentation the breakdown of food without the use of oxygen (111)

fetus a developing human from seven or eight weeks after fertilization until birth (240)

first aid emergency medical care for someone who has been hurt or who is sick (31)

fishery an area of water that is managed to harvest commercially valuable fish and shellfish (400)

floodplain an area along a river that forms from sediments deposited when the river overflows its banks (426)

fluid a nonsolid state of matter in which the atoms or molecules are free to move past each other, as in a gas or liquid (648)

food chain the pathway of energy transfer through various stages as a result of the feeding patterns of a series of organisms (314)

food web a diagram that shows the feeding relationships between organisms in an ecosystem (314)

force a push or a pull exerted on an object in order to change the motion of the object; force has size and direction (612)

function the special, normal, or proper activity of an organ or part (95)

G

gallbladder a sac-shaped organ that stores bile produced by the liver (189)

geostationary orbit an orbit that is about 36,000 km above Earth's surface and in which a satellite is above a fixed spot on the equator (547)

glacial drift the rock material carried and deposited by glaciers (466)

glacier a large mass of moving ice (462)

gland a group of cells that make special chemicals for the body (220)

Golgi complex a cell organelle that helps make and package materials to be transported out of the cell (89)

H

herbivore an organism that eats only plants (313)

hibernation a period of inactivity and lowered body temperature that some animals undergo in winter as a protection against cold weather and lack of food (290)

homeostasis the maintenance of a constant internal state in a changing environment (130)

homologous chromosomes chromosomes that have the same sequence of genes and the same structure (115)

horizon the line where the sky and the Earth appear to meet (526)

hormone a substance that is made in one cell or tissue and that causes a change in another cell or tissue in a different part of the body (220)

hypothesis a testable idea or explanation that leads to scientific investigation (14)

I

immune system the cells and tissues that recognize and attack foreign substances in the body (259)

immunity the ability to resist an infectious disease (256)

inclined plane a simple machine that is a straight, slanted surface, which facilitates the raising of loads; a ramp (634)

independent variable in an experiment, the factor that is deliberately manipulated (49) **FCAT** VOCAB

inertia the tendency of an object to resist being moved or, if the object is moving, to resist a change in speed or direction until an outside force acts on the object (616) **FCAT** VOCAB

infectious disease a disease that is caused by a pathogen and that can be spread from one individual to another (254)

innate behavior an inherited behavior that does not depend on the environment or experience (287)

integumentary system the organ system that forms a protective covering on the outside of the body (142, 214)

internal fertilization fertilization of an egg by sperm that occurs inside the body of a female (280)

J

joint a place where two or more bones meet (136)

joule the unit used to express energy; equivalent to the amount of work done by a force of 1 N acting through a distance of 1 m in the direction of the force (symbol, J) (621)

K

kidney one of the pair of organs that filter water and wastes from the blood and that excrete products as urine (193)

kinetic energy the energy of an object that is due to the object's motion (599)

L

landslide the sudden movement of rock and soil down a slope (469)

La Niña a change in the eastern Pacific Ocean in which the surface water temperature becomes unusually cool (490)

Glossary

large intestine the wider and shorter portion of the intestine that removes water from mostly digested food and that turns the waste into semi-solid feces, or stool (190)

larynx the area of the throat that contains the vocal cords and produces vocal sounds (171)

law of conservation of energy the law that states that energy cannot be created or destroyed but can be changed from one form to another (598)

learned behavior a behavior that has been learned from experience (286) **FCAT** *VOCAB*

lever a simple machine that consists of a bar that pivots at a fixed point called a *fulcrum* (630)

lift an upward force on an object that moves in a fluid (661)

light-year the distance that light travels in one year; about 9.46 trillion kilometers (528)

littoral zone the shallow zone of a lake or pond where light reaches the bottom and nurtures plants (371)

liver the largest organ in the body; it makes bile, stores and filters blood, and stores excess sugars as glycogen (189)

load the materials carried by a stream (420)

loess fine-grained sediments of quartz, feldspar, hornblende, mica, and clay deposited by the wind (460)

longshore current a water current that travels near and parallel to the shoreline (495)

low Earth orbit an orbit that is less than 1,500 km above Earth's surface (547)

lymph the fluid that is collected by the lymphatic vessels and nodes (166)

lymphatic system a collection of organs whose primary function is to collect extracellular fluid and return it to the blood; the organs in this system include the lymph nodes and the lymphatic vessels (166)

lymph node an organ that filters lymph and that is found along the lymphatic vessels (167)

lysosome a cell organelle that contains digestive enzymes (90)

M

machine a device that helps do work by either overcoming a force or changing the direction of the applied force (624)

macrophage an immune system cell that engulfs pathogens and other materials (259)

marsh a treeless wetland ecosystem where plants such as grasses grow (372)

mass a measure of the amount of matter in an object (23, 581) **FCAT** *VOCAB*

mass movement the movement of a large mass of sediment or a section of land down a slope (468)

matter anything that has mass and takes up space (578)

mean the number obtained by adding up the data for a given characteristic and dividing this sum by the number of individuals (56)

mechanical advantage a number that tells how many times a machine multiplies force (627)

mechanical efficiency a quantity, usually expressed as a percentage, that measures the ratio of work output to work input in a machine (628)

median the value of the middle item when data are arranged in order by size (57)

memory B cell a B cell that responds to an antigen more strongly when the body is reinfected with an antigen than it does during its first encounter with the antigen (262)

meniscus the curve at a liquid's surface by which one measures the volume of the liquid (579)

meter the basic unit of length in the SI (symbol, m) (22)

mitochondrion in eukaryotic cells, the cell organelle that is surrounded by two membranes and that is the site of cellular respiration (88)

mitosis in eukaryotic cells, a process of cell division that forms two new nuclei, each of which has the same number of chromosomes (115) **FCAT** *VOCAB*

mode the most frequently occurring value in a data set (57)

model a pattern, plan, representation, or description designed to show the structure or workings of an object, system, or concept (58)

month a division of the year that is based on the orbit of the moon around the Earth (514)

mudflow the flow of a mass of mud or rock and soil mixed with a large amount of water (470)

muscular system the organ system whose primary function is movement and flexibility (138)

mutualism a relationship between two species in which both species benefit (322)

NASA the National Aeronautics and Space Administration (543)

natural selection the process by which individuals that are better adapted to their environment survive and reproduce more successfully than less well adapted individuals do; a theory to explain the mechanism of evolution (294)

neap tide a tide of minimum range that occurs during the first and third quarters of the moon (500) FCAT VOCAB

nephron the unit in the kidney that filters blood (193)

nerve a collection of nerve fibers through which impulses travel between the central nervous system and other parts of the body (208)

net force the combination of all of the forces acting on an object (614)

neuron a nerve cell that is specialized to receive and conduct electrical impulses (207)

noninfectious disease a disease that cannot spread from one individual to another (254)

nonpoint-source pollution pollution that comes from many sources rather than from a single, specific site (434)

nucleus in a eukaryotic cell, a membrane-bound organelle that contains the cell's DNA and that has a role in processes such as growth, metabolism, and reproduction (79) FCAT VOCAB

observation the process of obtaining information by using the senses (43)

ocean current a movement of ocean water that follows a regular pattern (482)

omnivore an organism that eats both plants and animals (313)

open-water zone the zone of a pond or lake that extends from the littoral zone and that is only as deep as light can reach (371)

organ a collection of tissues that carry out a specialized function of the body (93, 131)

organelle one of the small bodies in a cell's cytoplasm that are specialized to perform a specific function (79)

organism a living thing; anything that can carry out life processes independently (94)

organ system a group of organs that work together to perform body functions (94)

osmosis the diffusion of water through a semipermeable membrane (107)

ovary in the female reproductive system of animals, an organ that produces eggs (235)

pancreas the organ that lies behind the stomach and that makes digestive enzymes and hormones that regulate sugar levels (188)

parasitism a relationship between two species in which one species, the parasite, benefits from the other species, the host, which is harmed (323)

pascal the SI unit of pressure (symbol, Pa) (648)

Pascal's principle the principle that states that a fluid in equilibrium contained in a vessel exerts a pressure of equal intensity in all directions (664)

passive transport the movement of substances across a cell membrane without the use of energy by the cell (108)

pathogen a virus, microorganism, or other organism that causes disease (254)

penis the male organ that transfers sperm to a female and that carries urine out of the body (234)

peripheral nervous system all of the parts of the nervous system except for the brain and the spinal cord (206)

permeability the ability of a rock or sediment to let fluids pass through its open spaces, or pores (429)

pharynx in flatworms, the muscular tube that leads from the mouth to the gastrovascular cavity; in animals with a digestive tract, the passage from the mouth to the larynx and esophagus (171)

photosynthesis the process by which plants, algae, and some bacteria use sunlight, carbon dioxide, and water to make food (110)

physical change a change of matter from one form to another without a change in chemical properties (590)

physical property a characteristic of a substance that does not involve a chemical change, such as density, color, or hardness (586)

placenta the partly fetal and partly maternal organ by which materials are exchanged between a fetus and the mother (239)

Glossary

plankton the mass of mostly microscopic organisms that float or drift freely in freshwater and marine environments (364)

point-source pollution pollution that comes from a specific site (434)

pollination the transfer of pollen from the male reproductive structures to the female structures of seed plants (283)

population a group of organisms of the same species that live in a specific geographical area (310)

porosity the percentage of the total volume of a rock or sediment that consists of open spaces (429)

potential energy the energy that an object has because of the position, shape, or condition of the object (599) *FCAT VOCAB*

power the rate at which work is done or energy is transformed (622)

precipitation any form of water that falls to Earth's surface from the clouds (336)

predator an organism that eats all or part of another organism (320)

pressure the amount of force exerted per unit area of a surface (648) *FCAT VOCAB*

prey an organism that is killed and eaten by another organism (320)

prokaryote a single-celled organism that does not have a nucleus or membrane-bound organelles; examples are archaea and bacteria (80)

pulley a simple machine that consists of a wheel over which a rope, chain, or wire passes (632)

pulmonary circulation the flow of blood from the heart to the lungs and back to the heart through the pulmonary arteries, capillaries, and veins (159)

Q

qualitative observation descriptive information that is not expressed as a number (43)

quantitative observation information that is expressed in terms of quantity of numbers (43)

R

recharge zone an area in which water travels downward to become part of an aquifer (430)

reflecting telescope a telescope that uses a curved mirror to gather and focus light from distant objects (519)

reflex an involuntary and almost immediate movement in response to a stimulus (215)

refracting telescope a telescope that uses a set of lenses to gather and focus light from distant objects (519)

respiration in biology, the exchange of oxygen and carbon dioxide between living cells and their environment; includes breathing and cellular respiration (170)

respiratory system a collection of organs whose primary function is to take in oxygen and expel carbon dioxide; the organs of this system include the lungs, the throat, and the passageways that lead to the lungs (170)

retina the light-sensitive inner layer of the eye, which receives images formed by the lens and transmits them through the optic nerve to the brain (216)

ribosome a cell organelle composed of RNA and protein; the site of protein synthesis (87)

rocket a machine that uses escaping gas from burning fuel to move (542)

rock fall the rapid mass movement of rock down a steep slope or cliff (469)

S

saltation the movement of sand or other sediments by short jumps and bounces that is caused by wind or water (458)

savanna a grassland that often has scattered trees and that is found in tropical and subtropical areas where seasonal rains, fires, and drought happen (360)

science the knowledge obtained by observing natural events and conditions in order to discover facts and formulate laws or principles that can be verified or tested (6)

scientific ethics the principles and values of proper scientific conduct (47)

scientific methods a series of steps followed to solve problems (12)

screw a simple machine that consists of an inclined plane wrapped around a cylinder (635) *FCAT VOCAB*

sewage treatment plant a facility that cleans the waste materials found in water that comes from sewers or drains (438)

Glossary

sexual reproduction reproduction in which the sex cells from two parents unite to produce offspring that share traits from both parents (279) **FCAT**VOCAB

shoreline the boundary between land and a body of water (453)

skeletal system the organ system whose primary function is to support and protect the body and to allow the body to move (134)

small intestine the organ between the stomach and the large intestine where most of the breakdown of food happens and most of the nutrients from food are absorbed (188)

space probe an uncrewed vehicle that carries scientific instruments into space to collect scientific data (552)

space shuttle a reusable space vehicle that takes off like a rocket and lands like an airplane (559)

space station a long-term orbiting platform from which other vehicles can be launched or scientific research can be carried out (560)

spleen the largest lymphatic organ in the body; serves as a blood reservoir, disintegrates old red blood cells, and produces lymphocytes and plasmids (168)

spring tide a tide of increased range that occurs two times a month, at the new and full moons (500) **FCAT**VOCAB

stomach the saclike, digestive organ that is between the esophagus and the small intestine and that breaks down food by the action of muscles, enzymes, and acids (187)

storm surge a local rise in sea level near the shore that is caused by strong winds from a storm, such as those from a hurricane (497)

stratified drift a glacial deposit that has been sorted and layered by the action of streams or meltwater (467)

structure the arrangement of parts in an organism (95)

succession the replacement of one type of community by another at a single location over a period of time (342)

surface current a horizontal movement of ocean water that is caused by wind and that occurs at or near the ocean's surface (483)

sustainable agriculture the use of agricultural practices that limit negative environmental effects (387)

swamp a wetland ecosystem in which shrubs and trees grow (372)

swell one of a group of long ocean waves that have steadily traveled a great distance from their point of generation (496)

symbiosis a relationship in which two different organisms live in close association with each other (322)

systemic circulation the flow of blood from the heart to all parts of the body and back to the heart (159)

T

T cell an immune system cell that coordinates the immune system and attacks many infected cells (259)

technology the application of science for practical purposes; the use of tools, machines, materials, and processes to meet human needs (60)

telescope an instrument that collects electromagnetic radiation from the sky and concentrates it for better observation (518)

temperature a measure of how hot (or cold) something is; specifically, a measure of the average kinetic energy of the particles in an object (24)

territory an area that is occupied by one animal or a group of animals that do not allow other members of the species to enter (287)

testes the primary male reproductive organs, which produce sperm cells and testosterone (singular, *testis*) (234)

thermal energy the kinetic energy of a substance's atoms (599) **FCAT**VOCAB

thrust the pushing or pulling force exerted by the engine of an aircraft or rocket (544, 662)

thymus the main gland of the lymphatic system; it releases mature T lymphocytes (167)

tidal range the difference in levels of ocean water at high tide and low tide (500)

tide the periodic rise and fall of the water level in the oceans and other large bodies of water (498)

timbre the musical quality of a tone resulting from the combination of all of the harmonics associated with the fundamental frequency (466)

tissue a group of similar cells that perform a common function (93, 130)

tonsils organs that are small, rounded masses of lymphatic tissue located in the pharynx and in the passage from the mouth to the pharynx (169)

trachea in insects, myriapods, and spiders, one of a network of air tubes; in vertebrates, the tube that connects the larynx to the lungs (171)

tributary a stream that flows into a lake or into a larger stream (418)

trough the lowest point of a wave (492)
*FCAT*VOCAB

tsunami a giant ocean wave that forms after a volcanic eruption, submarine earthquake, or landslide (496)

tundra a treeless plain found in the Arctic, in the Antarctic, or on the tops of mountains that is characterized by very low winter temperatures and short, cool summers (362)

U

umbilical cord the structure that connects an embryo and then the fetus to the placenta and through which blood vessels pass (239)

undertow a subsurface current that is near shore and that pulls objects out to sea (495)

upwelling the movement of deep, cold, and nutrient-rich water to the surface (489)

urban sprawl the unplanned growth of urban areas (388)

urinary system the organs that make, store, and eliminate urine (192)

uterus in female mammals, the hollow, muscular organ in which a fertilized egg is embedded and in which the embryo and fetus develop (235)

V

vagina the female reproductive organ that connects the outside of the body to the uterus (235)

variable a factor that changes in an experiment in order to test a hypothesis (16) *FCAT*VOCAB

vein in biology, a vessel that carries blood to the heart (158)

vesicle a small cavity or sac that contains materials in a eukaryotic cell; forms when part of the cell membrane surrounds the materials to be taken into the cell or transported within the cell (89)

virus a microscopic particle that gets inside a cell and often destroys the cell (254) *FCAT*VOCAB

volume a measure of the size of a body or region in three-dimensional space (23, 578)

W

water cycle the continuous movement of water between the atmosphere, the land, and the oceans (417)

watershed the area of land that is drained by a river system (418, 392)

water table the upper surface of underground water; the upper boundary of the zone of saturation (428)

watt the unit used to express power; equivalent to a joule per second (symbol, W) (622)

wavelength the distance from any point on a wave to an identical point on the next wave (492)
*FCAT*VOCAB

wedge a simple machine that is made up of two inclined planes and that moves; often used for cutting (635) *FCAT*VOCAB

weight a measure of the gravitational force exerted on an object; its value can change with the location of the object in the universe (581)

wetland an area of land that is periodically underwater or whose soil contains a great deal of moisture (372)

wheel and axle a simple machine consisting of two circular objects of different sizes; the wheel is the larger of the two circular objects (633)
*FCAT*VOCAB

whitecap the bubbles in the crest of a breaking wave (496)

work the transfer of energy to an object by using a force that causes the object to move in the direction of the force (618)

work input the work done on a machine; the product of the input force and the distance through which the force is exerted (625)

work output the work done by a machine; the product of the output force and the distance through which the force is exerted (625)

Y

year the time required for the Earth to orbit once around the sun (514)

Z

zenith the point in the sky directly above an observer on Earth (526)

Spanish Glossary

A

abiotic/abiótico término que describe la parte sin vida del ambiente, incluyendo el agua, las rocas, la luz y la temperatura (308) **FCAT** *VOCAB*

abrasion/abrasión proceso por el cual las superficies de las rocas se muelen o desgastan por medio de la acción mecánica de otras rocas y partículas de arena (459)

active transport/transporte activo el movimiento de sustancias a través de la membrana celular que requiere que la célula gaste energía (108)

adaptation/adaptación una característica que mejora la capacidad de un individuo para sobrevivir y reproducirse en un determinado ambiente (293)

allergy/alergia una reacción del sistema inmunológico del cuerpo a una sustancia inofensiva o común (263)

alluvial fan/abanico aluvial masa de materiales rocosos en forma de abanico, depositados por un arroyo cuando la pendiente del terreno disminuye bruscamente (426)

altitude/altitud el ángulo que se forma entre un objeto en el cielo y el horizonte (526)

alveoli/alveolos las diminutas bolsas de aire de los pulmones, en donde ocurre el intercambio de oxígeno y dióxido de carbono (171)

antibody/anticuerpo una proteína producida por las células B que se une a un antígeno específico (259)

aquifer/acuífero un cuerpo rocoso o sedimento que almacena agua subterránea y permite que fluya (390, 429)

Archimedes' principle/principio de Arquímedes el principio que establece que la fuerza flotante de un objeto que está en un fluido es una fuerza ascendente cuya magnitud es igual al peso del volumen del fluido que el objeto desplaza (654)

area/área una medida del tamaño de una superficie o región (22)

artery/arteria un vaso sanguíneo que transporta sangre del corazón a los órganos del cuerpo (158)

artesian spring/manantial artesiano un manantial en el que el agua fluye a partir de una grieta en la capa de rocas que se encuentra sobre el acuífero (431)

artificial satellite/satélite artificial cualquier objeto hecho por los seres humanos y colocado en órbita alrededor de un cuerpo en el espacio (546)

asexual reproduction/reproducción asexual reproducción que no involucra la unión de células sexuales, en la que un solo progenitor produce descendencia que es genéticamente igual al progenitor (278) **FCAT** *VOCAB*

astronomy/astronomía el estudio científico del universo (514)

atmospheric pressure/presión atmosférica la presión producida por el peso de la atmósfera (649)

atom/átomo la unidad más pequeña de un elemento que conserva las propiedades de ese elemento (582)

autoimmune disease/enfermedad autoinmune una enfermedad en la que el sistema inmunológico ataca las células del propio organismo (263)

axis/eje una línea recta imaginaria que va de polo a polo, atravesando el centro de la Tierra (50)

B

B cell/célula B un glóbulo blanco de la sangre que fabrica anticuerpos (259)

beach/playa un área de la costa que está formada por sedimento depositado (456)

Bernoulli's principle/principio de Bernoulli el principio que establece que la presión de un fluido disminuye a medida que la velocidad del fluido aumenta (660)

biodiversity/biodiversidad el número y la variedad de organismos que se encuentran en un área determinada durante un período específico de tiempo (345) **FCAT** *VOCAB*

biome/bioma una región extensa caracterizada por un tipo de clima específico y ciertos tipos de comunidades de plantas y animales (356)

biosphere/biosfera la parte de la Tierra donde existe la vida (311)

biotic/biótico término que describe los factores vivientes del ambiente (308) **FCAT** *VOCAB*

blood/sangre el líquido que lleva gases, nutrientes y desechos por el cuerpo y que está formado por plaquetas, glóbulos blancos, glóbulos rojos y plasma (162)

blood pressure/presión sanguínea la fuerza que la sangre ejerce en las paredes de las arterias (164)

brain/encéfalo la masa de tejido nervioso que es el centro principal de control del sistema nervioso (210)

bronchus/bronquio uno de los dos tubos que conectan los pulmones con la tráquea (171)

buoyant force/fuerza boyante la fuerza ascendente que hace que un objeto se mantenga sumergido en un líquido o flotando en él (654)

C

cancer/cáncer un tumor en el cual las células comienzan a dividirse a una tasa incontrolable y se vuelven invasivas (264)

capillary/capilar diminuto vaso sanguíneo que permite el intercambio entre la sangre y las células de los tejidos (158)

cardiovascular system/aparato cardiovascular un conjunto de órganos que transportan la sangre a través del cuerpo; los órganos de este sistema incluyen al corazón, las arterias y las venas (156)

carnivore/carnívoro un organismo que se alimenta de animales (313)

carrying capacity/capacidad de carga la población más grande que un ambiente puede sostener en cualquier momento dado (319)

cell/célula en biología, la unidad más pequeña que puede realizar todos los procesos vitales; las células están cubiertas por una membrana y tienen ADN y citoplasma (76)

cell cycle/ciclo celular el ciclo de vida de una célula (114)

cell membrane/membrana celular una capa de fosfolípidos que cubre la superficie de la célula y funciona como una barrera entre el interior de la célula y el ambiente de la célula (79)

cellular respiration/respiración celular el proceso por medio del cual las células utilizan oxígeno para producir energía a partir de los alimentos (111)

cell wall/pared celular una estructura rígida que rodea la membrana celular y le brinda soporte a la célula (84)

central nervous system/sistema nervioso central el cerebro y la médula espinal; su principal función es controlar el flujo de información en el cuerpo (206)

channel/canal el camino que sigue un arroyo (419)

chemical change/cambio químico un cambio que ocurre cuando una o más sustancias se transforman en sustancias totalmente nuevas con propiedades diferentes (594)

chemical property/propiedad química una propiedad de la materia que describe la capacidad de una sustancia de participar en reacciones químicas (592)

chromosome/cromosoma en una célula eucariótica, una de las estructuras del núcleo que está hecha de ADN y proteína; en una célula procariótica, el anillo principal de AND (114)

cochlea/cóclea un tubo enrollado que se encuentra en el oído interno y es esencial para poder oír (218)

coevolution/coevolución la evolución de dos especies que se debe a su influencia mutua, a menudo de un modo que hace que la relación sea más beneficiosa para ambas (323)

combustion/combustión fenómeno que ocurre cuando una sustancia se quema (339)

commensalism/comensalismo una relación entre dos organismos en la que uno se beneficia y el otro no es afectado (322)

community/comunidad todas las poblaciones de especies que viven en el mismo hábitat e interactúan entre sí (310)

compound machine/máquina compuesta una máquina hecha de más de una máquina simple (636)

computer/computadora un aparato electrónico que acepta información e instrucciones, sigue instrucciones y produce una salida para los resultados (48)

condensation/condensación el cambio de estado de gas a líquido (336)

constellation/constelación una región del cielo que contiene un patrón reconocible de estrellas y que se utiliza para describir la ubicación de los objetos en el espacio (524)

controlled experiment/experimento controlado un experimento que prueba sólo un factor a la vez, comparando un grupo de control con un grupo experimental (16)

Coriolis effect/efecto de Coriolis la desviación de la trayectoria recta que experimentan los objetos en movimiento debido a la rotación de la Tierra (485)

creep/arrastre el movimiento lento y descendente de materiales rocosos desgastados (471)

crest/cresta el punto más alto de una onda (492)
FCAT VOCAB

cytokinesis/citocinesis la división del citoplasma de una célula (116)

D

day/día el tiempo que se requiere para que la Tierra rote una vez sobre su eje (514)

decomposition/descomposición la desintegración de sustancias en sustancias moleculares más simples (338)

deep current/corriente profunda un movimiento del agua del océano que es similar a una corriente y ocurre debajo de la superficie (485)

deep-water zone/zona de aguas profundas la zona de un lago o laguna debajo de la zona de aguas abiertas, a donde no llega la luz (371)

deflation/deflación una forma de erosión del viento en la que se mueven partículas de suelo finas y secas (459)

delta/delta un depósito de materiales rocosos en forma de abanico ubicado en la desembocadura de un río (425)

density/densidad la relación entre la masa de una sustancia y su volumen (24, 587)

dependent variable/variable dependiente en un experimento, el factor que cambia como resultado de la manipulación de uno o más factores (las variables independientes) (49) *FCAT VOCAB*

deposition/deposición el proceso por medio del cual un material se deposita (424) *FCAT VOCAB*

dermis/dermis la capa de piel que está debajo de la epidermis (143)

desert/desierto una región con poca vegetación o sin vegetación, largos períodos sin lluvia y temperaturas extremas; generalmente se ubica en climas calientes (361)

diffusion/difusión el movimiento de partículas de regiones de mayor densidad a regiones de menor densidad (106)

digestive system/aparato digestivo los órganos que descomponen la comida de modo que el cuerpo la pueda usar (184)

divide/división el límite entre áreas de drenaje que tienen corrientes que fluyen en direcciones opuestas (418)

drag/resistencia aerodinámica una fuerza paralela a la velocidad del flujo; se opone a la dirección de un avión y, en combinación con el empuje, determina la velocidad del avión (663)

dune/duna un montículo de arena depositada por el viento que se mueve como resultado de la acción de éste (460)

E

ecology/ecología el estudio de las interacciones de los seres vivos entre sí mismos y entre sí mismos y su ambiente (308)

ecosystem/ecosistema una comunidad de organismos y su ambiente abiótico o no vivo (311) *FCAT VOCAB*

efficiency/eficiencia una cantidad, generalmente expresada como un porcentaje, que mide la relación entre el trabajo de entrada y el trabajo de salida (628) *FCAT VOCAB*

electromagnetic radiation/radiación electromagnética la radiación asociada con un campo eléctrico y magnético; varía periódicamente y se desplaza a la velocidad de la luz (521) *FCAT VOCAB*

El Niño/El Niño un cambio en la temperatura del agua superficial del océano Pacífico que produce una corriente caliente (490)

embryo/embrión un ser humano desde la fecundación hasta las primeras 8 semanas de desarrollo (décima semana del embarazo) (238)

endocrine system/sistema endocrino un conjunto de glándulas y grupos de células que secretan hormonas que regulan el crecimiento, el desarrollo y la homeostasis; incluye las glándulas pituitaria, tiroides, paratiroides y suprarrenal, el hipotálamo, el cuerpo pineal y las gónadas (220)

endocytosis/endocitosis el proceso por medio del cual la membrana celular rodea una partícula y la encierra en una vesícula para llevarla al interior de la célula (108)

endoplasmic reticulum/retículo endoplásmico un sistema de membranas que se encuentra en el citoplasma de la célula y que tiene una función en la producción, procesamiento y transporte de proteínas y en la producción de lípidos (87)

energy/energía la capacidad de realizar un trabajo (598)

energy pyramid/pirámide de energía un diagrama triangular que muestra la pérdida de energía en un ecosistema, producida a medida que la energía pasa a través de la cadena alimenticia del ecosistema (315)

entropy/entropía una medida del grado de aleatoriedad o desorden de un sistema (601) *FCAT VOCAB*

epidermis/epidermis la superficie externa de las células de una planta o animal (143)

erosion/erosión el proceso por medio del cual el viento, el agua, el hielo o la gravedad transporta tierra y sedimentos de un lugar a otro (416) *FCAT VOCAB*

esophagus/esófago un conducto largo y recto que conecta la faringe con el estómago (186)

estimate/estimación un cálculo aproximado (44)

estivation/estivación un período de inactividad y menor temperatura corporal por el que pasan algunos animales durante el verano para protegerse del calor y la falta de alimento (290)

estuary/estuario un área donde el agua dulce de los ríos se mezcla con el agua salada del océano (368, 398)

eukaryote/eucariote un organismo cuyas células tienen un núcleo contenido en una membrana; entre los eucariotes se encuentran protistas, animales, plantas y hongos, pero no arqueas ni bacterias (82)

evaporation/evaporación el cambio de estado de líquido a gas (336)

exocytosis/exocitosis el proceso por medio del cual una célula libera una partícula encerrándola en una vesícula que luego se traslada a la superficie de la célula y se fusiona con la membrana celular (109)

external fertilization/fecundación externa la unión de células sexuales fuera del cuerpo de los progenitores (280)

F

feedback mechanism/mecanismo de retroalimentación un ciclo de sucesos en el que la información de una etapa controla o afecta a una etapa anterior (215)

fermentation/fermentación la descomposición de los alimentos sin utilizar oxígeno (111)

fetus/feto un ser humano en desarrollo de las semanas siete a ocho después de la fecundación hasta el nacimiento (240)

first aid/primeros auxilios atención médica de emergencia para una persona que se lastimó o está enferma (31)

fishery/zona de pesca un área de agua que se explota para obtener peces y mariscos con valor comercial (400)

floodplain/llanura de inundación un área a lo largo de un río formada por sedimentos que se depositan cuando el río se desborda (426)

fluid/fluido un estado no sólido de la materia en el que los átomos o moléculas tienen libertad de movimiento, como en el caso de un gas o un líquido (648)

food chain/cadena alimenticia la vía de transferencia de energía través de varias etapas, que ocurre como resultado de los patrones de alimentación de una serie de organismos (314)

food web/red alimenticia un diagrama que muestra las relaciones de alimentación entre los organismos de un ecosistema (314)

force/fuerza una acción de empuje o atracción que se ejerce sobre un objeto con el fin de cambiar su movimiento; la fuerza tiene magnitud y dirección (612)

function/función la actividad especial, normal o adecuada de un órgano o parte (95)

G

gallbladder/vesícula biliar un órgano que tiene la forma de una bolsa y que almacena la bilis producida por el hígado (189)

geostationary orbit/órbita geoestacionaria una órbita que está a aproximadamente 36,000 km de la superficie terrestre, en la que un satélite permanece sobre un punto fijo en el ecuador (547)

glacial drift/deriva glaciar el material rocoso que es transportado y depositado por los glaciares (466)

glacier/glaciar una masa grande de hielo en movimiento (462)

gland/glándula un grupo de células que elaboran ciertas sustancias químicas para el cuerpo (220)

Golgi complex/aparato de Golgi un organelo celular que ayuda a hacer y a empacar los materiales que serán transportados al exterior de la célula (89)

H

herbivore/herbívoro un organismo que sólo come plantas (313)

hibernation/hibernación un período de inactividad y disminución de la temperatura del cuerpo que algunos animales experimentan en invierno como protección contra el tiempo frío y la escasez de comida (290)

homeostasis/homeostasis la capacidad de mantener un estado interno constante en un ambiente en cambio (130)

homologous chromosomes/cromosomas homólogos cromosomas con la misma secuencia de genes y la misma estructura (115)

horizon/horizonte la línea donde parece que el cielo y la Tierra se unen (526)

hormone/hormona una sustancia que es producida en una célula o tejido, la cual causa un cambio en otra célula o tejido ubicado en una parte diferente del cuerpo (220)

hypothesis/hipótesis una idea o explicación que conlleva a la investigación científica y que se puede probar (14)

I

immune system/sistema inmunológico las células y tejidos que reconocen y atacan sustancias extrañas en el cuerpo (259)

immunity/inmunidad la capacidad de resistir una enfermedad infecciosa (256)

inclined plane/plano inclinado una máquina simple que es una superficie recta e inclinada, que facilita el levantamiento de cargas; una rampa (634)

independent variable/variable independiente en un experimento, el factor que se manipula deliberadamente (49) *FCAT VOCAB*

inertia/inercia la tendencia de un objeto a no moverse o, si el objeto se está moviendo, la tendencia a resistir un cambio en su rapidez o dirección hasta que una fuerza externa actúe en el objeto (616) *FCAT VOCAB*

infectious disease/enfermedad infecciosa una enfermedad que es causada por un patógeno y que puede transmitirse de un individuo a otro (254)

innate behavior/conducta innata una conducta heredada que no depende del ambiente ni de la experiencia (287)

integumentary system/sistema integumentario el sistema de órganos que forma una cubierta de protección en la parte exterior del cuerpo (142, 214)

internal fertilization/fecundación interna fecundación de un óvulo por un espermatozoide, la cual ocurre dentro del cuerpo de la hembra (280)

J

joint/articulación un lugar donde se unen dos o más huesos (136)

joule/joule la unidad que se usa para expresar energía; equivale a la cantidad de trabajo realizada por una fuerza de 1 N que actúa a través de una distancia de 1 m en la dirección de la fuerza (símbolo: J) (621)

K

kidney/riñón uno de los dos órganos que filtran el agua y los desechos de la sangre y excretan productos en fomra de orina (193)

kinetic energy/energía cinética la energía de un objeto debido al movimiento del objeto (599)

L

landslide/derrumbamiento el movimiento súbito hacia abajo de rocas y suelo por una pendiente (469)

La Niña/La Niña un cambio en el océano Pacífico oriental por el cual el agua superficial se vuelve más fría que de costumbre (490)

large intestine/intestino grueso la porción más ancha y más corta del intestino, que elimina el agua de los alimentos casi totalmente digeridos y convierte los desechos en heces semisólidas o excremento (190)

larynx/laringe el área de la garganta que contiene las cuerdas vocales y que produce sonidos vocales (171)

law of conservation of energy/ley de la conservación de la energía la ley que establece que la energía ni se crea ni se destruye, sólo se transforma de una forma a otra (598) *FCAT VOCAB*

learned behavior/conducta aprendida una conducta que se ha aprendido por experiencia (286)

lever/palanca una máquina simple formada por una barra que gira en un punto fijo llamado *fulcro* (630)

lift/propulsión una fuerza hacia arriba en un objeto que se mueve en un fluido (661)

light-year/año luz la distancia que viaja la luz en un año; aproximadamente 9.46 trillones de kilómetros (528)

littoral zone/zona litoral la zona poco profunda de un lago o una laguna donde la luz llega al fondo y nutre a las plantas (371)

liver/hígado el órgano más grande del cuerpo; produce bilis, almacena y filtra la sangre, y almacena el exceso de azúcares en forma de glucógeno (189)

load/carga los materiales que lleva un arroyo (420)

loess/loess sedimentos de grano fino de cuarzo, feldespato, hornablenda, mica y arcilla depositados por el viento (460)

longshore current/corriente de ribera una corriente de agua que se desplaza cerca de la costa y paralela a ella (495)

low Earth orbit/órbita terrestre baja una órbita ubicada a menos de 1,500 km sobre la superficie terrestre (547)

lymph/linfa el fluido que es recolectado por los vasos y nodos linfáticos (166)

lymphatic system/sistema linfático un conjunto de órganos cuya función principal es recolectar el fluido extracelular y regresarlo a la sangre; los órganos de este sistema incluyen los nodos linfáticos y los vasos linfáticos (166)

lymph node/nodo linfático un órgano que filtra la linfa y que se encuentra a lo largo de los vasos linfáticos (167)

lysosome/lisosoma un organelo celular que contiene enzimas digestivas (90)

M

machine/máquina un aparato que ayuda a realizar un trabajo, ya sea venciendo una fuerza o cambiando la dirección de la fuerza aplicada (624)

macrophage/macrófago una célula del sistema inmunológico que envuelve a los patógenos y otros materiales (259)

marsh/pantano un ecosistema pantanoso sin árboles, donde crecen plantas tales como el pasto (372)

mass/masa una medida de la cantidad de materia que tiene un objeto (23, 581) **FCAT**VOCAB

mass movement/movimiento masivo el movimiento hacia abajo por una pendiente de una gran masa de sedimento o una sección de terreno (468)

matter/materia cualquier cosa que tiene masa y ocupa un lugar en el espacio (578)

mean/media el número que se obtiene al sumar los datos de una característica determinada y dividir esta suma entre el número de individuos (56)

mechanical advantage/ventaja mecánica un número que dice cuántas veces una máquina multiplica una fuerza (627)

mechanical efficiency/eficiencia mecánica una cantidad, generalmente expresada como un porcentaje, que mide la relación entre el trabajo de entrada y el trabajo de salida en una máquina (628)

median/mediana el valor del elemento medio cuando los datos están ordenados según su tamaño (57)

memory B cell/célula B de memoria una célula B que responde con mayor eficacia a un antígeno cuando el cuerpo vuelve a infectarse con él que cuando lo encuentra por primera vez (262)

meniscus/menisco la curva que se forma en la superficie de un líquido, la cual sirve para medir el volumen de un líquido (579)

meter/metro la unidad fundamental de longitud en el sistema internacional de unidades (símbolo: m) (22)

mitochondrion/mitocondria en las células eucarióticas, el organelo celular rodeado por dos membranas que es el lugar donde se lleva a cabo la respiración celular (88)

mitosis/mitosis en las células eucarióticas, un proceso de división celular que forma dos núcleos nuevos, cada uno de los cuales posee el mismo número de cromosomas (115) **FCAT**VOCAB

mode/moda el valor más frecuente en un conjunto de datos (57)

model/modelo un diseño, plan, representación o descripción cuyo objetivo es mostrar la estructura o funcionamiento de un objeto, sistema o concepto (58)

month/mes una división del año que se basa en la órbita de la Luna alrededor de la Tierra (514)

mudflow/flujo de lodo el flujo de una masa de lodo o roca y suelo mezclados con una gran cantidad de agua (470)

muscular system/sistema muscular el sistema de órganos cuya función principal es permitir el movimiento y la flexibilidad (138)

mutualism/mutualismo una relación entre dos especies en la que ambas se benefician (322)

N

NASA/NASA la Administración Nacional de Aeronáutica y del Espacio (543)

natural selection/selección natural el proceso por medio del cual los individuos que están mejor adaptados a su ambiente sobreviven y se reproducen con más éxito que los individuos menos adaptados; una teoría que explica el mecanismo de la evolución (294)

neap tide/marea muerta una marea que tiene un rango mínimo, la cual ocurre durante el primer y el tercer cuartos de la Luna (500) **FCAT**VOCAB

nephron/nefrona la unidad del riñón que filtra la sangre (193)

nerve/nervio un conjunto de fibras nerviosas a través de las cuales se desplazan los impulsos entre el sistema nervioso central y otras partes del cuerpo (208)

net force/fuerza neta la combinación de todas las fuerzas que actúan sobre un objeto (614)

neuron/neurona una célula nerviosa que está especializada en recibir y transmitir impulsos eléctricos (207)

noninfectious disease/enfermedad no infecciosa una enfermedad que no se contagia de una persona a otra (254)

nonpoint-source pollution/contaminación no puntual contaminación que proviene de muchas fuentes, en lugar de provenir de un solo sitio específico (434)

nucleus/núcleo en una célula eucariótica, un organelo cubierto por una membrana, el cual contiene el ADN de la célula y participa en procesos tales como el crecimiento, metabolismo y reproducción (79) **FCAT**VOCAB

O

observation/observación el proceso de obtener información por medio de los sentidos (43)

ocean current/corriente oceánica un movimiento del agua del océano que sigue un patrón regular (482)

omnivore/omnívoro un organismo que come tanto plantas como animales (313)

open-water zone/zona de aguas abiertas la zona de un lago o una laguna que se extiende desde la zona litoral y cuya profundidad sólo alcanza hasta donde penetra la luz (371)

organ/órgano un conjunto de tejidos que desempeñan una función especializada en el cuerpo (93, 131)

organelle/organelo uno de los cuerpos pequeños del citoplasma de una célula que están especializados para llevar a cabo una función específica (79)

organism/organismo un ser vivo; cualquier cosa que pueda llevar a cabo procesos vitales independientemente (94)

organ system/aparato (o sistema) de órganos un grupo de órganos que trabajan en conjunto para desempeñar funciones corporales (94)

osmosis/ósmosis la difusión del agua a través de una membrana semipermeable (107)

ovary/ovario en el aparato reproductor femenino de los animales, un órgano que produce óvulos (235)

P

pancreas/páncreas el órgano que se encuentra detrás del estómago y que produce las enzimas digestivas y las hormonas que regulan los niveles de azúcar (188)

parasitism/parasitismo una relación entre dos especies en la que una, el parásito, se beneficia de la otra, el huésped, que resulta perjudicada (323)

pascal/pascal la unidad de presión del sistema internacional de unidades (símbolo: Pa) (648)

Pascal's principle/principio de Pascal el principio que establece que un fluido en equilibro que esté contenido en un recipiente ejerce una presión de igual intensidad en todas las direcciones (664)

passive transport/transporte pasivo el movimiento de sustancias a través de una membrana celular sin que la célula tenga que usar energía (108)

pathogen/patógeno un virus, microorganismo u otra sustancia que causa enfermedades (254)

penis/pene el órgano masculino que transfiere espermatozoides a una hembra y que lleva la orina hacia el exterior del cuerpo (234)

peripheral nervous system/sistema nervioso periférico todas las partes del sistema nervioso, excepto el encéfalo y la médula espinal (206)

permeability/permeabilidad la capacidad de una roca o sedimento de permitir que los fluidos pasen a través de sus espacios abiertos o poros (429)

pharynx/faringe en los gusanos planos, el tubo muscular que va de la boca a la cavidad gastrovascular; en los animales que tienen tracto digestivo, el conducto que va de la boca a la laringe y al esófago (171)

photosynthesis/fotosíntesis el proceso por medio del cual las plantas, las algas y algunas bacterias utilizan la luz solar, el dióxido de carbono y el agua para producir alimento (110)

physical change/cambio físico un cambio de materia de una forma a otra sin que ocurra un cambio en sus propiedades químicas (590)

physical property/propiedad física una característica de una sustancia que no implica un cambio químico, tal como la densidad, el color o la dureza (586)

placenta/placenta el órgano parcialmente fetal y parcialmente materno por medio del cual se intercambian materiales entre el feto y la madre (239)

plankton/plancton la masa de organismos en su mayoría microscópicos que flotan o se encuentran a la deriva en ambientes de agua dulce o marina (364)

point-source pollution/contaminación puntual contaminación que proviene de un lugar específico (434)

pollination/polinización la transferencia de polen de las estructuras reproductoras masculinas a las estructuras femeninas de las plantas con semillas (283)

population/población un grupo de organismos de la misma especie que viven en un área geográfica específica (310)

porosity/porosidad el porcentaje del volumen total de una roca o sedimento que está formado por espacios abiertos (429)

potential energy/energía potencial la energía que tiene un objeto debido a su posición, forma o condición (599) *FCAT VOCAB*

power/potencia la tasa a la que se realiza un trabajo o a la que se transforma la energía (622)

precipitation/precipitación cualquier forma de agua que cae de las nubes a la superficie de la Tierra (336)

predator/depredador un organismo que se alimenta de otro organismo o de parte de él (320)

pressure/presión la cantidad de fuerza ejercida en una superficie por unidad de área (648) *FCAT VOCAB*

prey/presa un organismo al que otro organismo mata para alimentarse de él (320)

prokaryote/procariote un organismo unicelular que no tiene núcleo ni organelos cubiertos por una membrana, por ejemplo, las arqueas y las bacterias (80)

pulley/polea una máquina simple formada por una rueda sobre la cual pasa una cuerda, cadena o cable (632)

pulmonary circulation/circulación pulmonar el flujo de sangre del corazón a los pulmones y de vuelta al corazón a través de las arterias, los capilares y las venas pulmonares (159)

Q

qualitative observation/observación cualitativa información descriptiva que no se expresa con números (43)

quantitative observation/observación cuantitativa información que se expresa en términos de cantidad o con números (43)

R

recharge zone/zona de recarga un área en la que el agua se desplaza hacia abajo para convertirse en parte de un acuífero (430)

reflecting telescope/telescopio reflector un telescopio que utiliza un espejo curvo para captar y enfocar la luz de objetos lejanos (519)

reflex/reflejo un movimiento involuntario y prácticamente inmediato en respuesta a un estímulo (215)

refracting telescope/telescopio refractante un telescopio que utiliza un conjunto de lentes para captar y enfocar la luz de objetos lejanos (519)

respiration/respiración en biología, el intercambio de oxígeno y dióxido de carbono entre células vivas y su ambiente; incluye la respiración y la respiración celular (170)

respiratory system/aparato respiratorio un conjunto de órganos cuya función principal es tomar oxígeno y expulsar dióxido de carbono; los órganos de este aparato incluyen a los pulmones, la garganta y las vías que llevan a los pulmones (170)

retina/retina la capa interna del ojo, sensible a la luz, que recibe imágenes formadas por el lente ocular y las transmite al cerebro por medio del nervio óptico (216)

ribosome/ribosoma un organelo celular compuesto de ARN y proteína; el sitio donde ocurre la síntesis de proteínas (87)

rocket/cohete un aparato que para moverse utiliza el gas de escape que se origina a partir de la combustión (542)

rock fall/desprendimiento de rocas el movimiento rápido y masivo de rocas por una pendiente empinada o un precipicio (469)

S

saltation/saltación el movimiento de la arena u otros sedimentos por medio de saltos pequeños y rebotes debido al viento o al agua (458)

savanna/sabana una región de pastizales que, a menudo, tiene árboles dispersos; se encuentra en áreas tropicales y subtropicales donde se producen lluvias, incendios y sequías estacionales (360)

science/ciencia el conocimiento que se obtiene por medio de la observación natural de acontecimientos y condiciones con el fin de descubrir hechos y formular leyes o principios que puedan ser verificados o probados (6)

scientific ethics/ética científica los principios y valores que caracterizan la conducta científica adecuada (47)

scientific methods/métodos científicos una serie de pasos que se siguen para solucionar problemas (12)

screw/tornillo una máquina simple formada por un plano inclinado enrollado a un cilindro (635) *FCAT VOCAB*

sewage treatment plant/planta de tratamiento de residuos una instalación que limpia los materiales de desecho que se encuentran en el agua procedente de cloacas o alcantarillas (438)

sexual reproduction/reproducción sexual reproducción en la que se unen las células sexuales de los dos progenitores para producir descendencia que comparte caracteres de ambos progenitores (279) *FCAT VOCAB*

shoreline/costa el límite entre la tierra y una masa de agua (453)

skeletal system/sistema esquelético el sistema de órganos cuya función principal es sostener y proteger el cuerpo y permitir que se mueva (134)

small intestine/intestino delgado el órgano que se encuentra entre el estómago y el intestino grueso en el cual se produce la mayor parte de la descomposición de los alimentos y se absorben la mayoría de los nutrientes (188)

space probe/sonda espacial un vehículo no tripulado que lleva instrumentos científicos al espacio con el fin de recopilar información científica (552)

space shuttle/transbordador espacial un vehículo espacial reutilizable que despega como un cohete y aterriza como un avión (559)

space station/estación espacial una plataforma orbital de largo plazo desde la cual pueden lanzarse otros vehículos o en la que pueden realizarse investigaciones científicas (560)

spleen/bazo el órgano linfático más grande del cuerpo; funciona como depósito para la sangre, desintegra los glóbulos rojos viejos y produce linfocitos y plásmidos (168)

spring tide/marea viva una marea de mayor rango que ocurre dos veces al mes, durante la luna nueva y la luna llena (500) **FCAT** VOCAB

stomach/estómago el órgano digestivo con forma de bolsa, ubicado entre el esófago y el intestino delgado, que descompone la comida por la acción de músculos, enzimas y ácidos (187)

storm surge/marea de tempestad un levantamiento local del nivel del mar cerca de la costa, el cual es resultado de los fuertes vientos de una tormenta, como por ejemplo, los vientos de un huracán (497)

stratified drift/deriva estratificada un depósito glacial que ha formado capas debido a la acción de los arroyos o de las aguas de ablación (467)

structure/estructura el orden y distribución de las partes de un organismo (95)

succession/sucesión el reemplazo de un tipo de comunidad por otro en un mismo lugar a lo largo de un período de tiempo (342)

surface current/corriente superficial un movimiento horizontal del agua del océano que es producido por el viento y que ocurre en la superficie del océano o cerca de ella (483)

sustainable agriculture/agricultura sustentable la aplicación de prácticas agrícolas que reducen los efectos negativos en el ambiente (387)

swamp/ciénaga un ecosistema de pantano en el que crecen arbustos y árboles (372)

swell/mar de leva un grupo de olas oceánicas grandes que se han desplazado una gran distancia desde el punto en el que se originaron (496)

symbiosis/simbiosis una relación en la que dos organismos diferentes viven estrechamente asociados uno con el otro (322)

systemic circulation/circulación sistémica el flujo de sangre del corazón a todas las partes del cuerpo y de vuelta al corazón (159)

T

T cell/célula T una célula del sistema inmunológico que coordina el sistema inmunológico y ataca a muchas células infectadas (259)

technology/tecnología la aplicación de la ciencia con fines prácticos; el uso de herramientas, máquinas, materiales y procesos para satisfacer las necesidades de los seres humanos (60)

telescope/telescopio un instrumento que capta la radiación electromagnética del cielo y la concentra para mejorar la observación (518)

temperature/temperatura una medida de qué tan caliente (o frío) está algo; específicamente, una medida de la energía cinética promedio de las partículas de un objeto (24)

territory/territorio un área que está ocupada por un animal o por un grupo de animales que no permiten que entren otros miembros de la especie (287)

testes/testículos los principales órganos reproductores masculinos, los cuales producen espermatozoides y testosterona (234)

thermal energy/energía térmica la energía cinética de los átomos de una sustancia (599) **FCAT** VOCAB

thrust/empuje la fuerza de empuje o arrastre ejercida por el motor de un avión o cohete (544, 662)

thymus/timo la glándula principal del sistema linfático; libera linfocitos T maduros (167)

tidal range/rango de marea la diferencia en los niveles del agua del océano entre la marea alta y la marea baja (500)

tide/marea el ascenso y descenso periódico del nivel del agua en los océanos y otras masas grandes de agua (498)

timbre/timbre la calidad musical de un tono, la cual resulta debido a la combinación de todos los sonidos armónicos relacionados con la frecuencia fundamental (466)

tissue/tejido un grupo de células similares que llevan a cabo una función común (93, 130)

tonsils/amígdalas órganos que son masas pequeñas y redondas de tejido linfático, ubicadas en la faringe y en el paso de la boca a la faringe (169)

trachea/tráquea en los insectos, miriápodos y arañas, uno de los conductos de una red de conductos de aire; en los vertebrados, el conducto que une la laringe con los pulmones (171)

tributary/afluente un arroyo que fluye a un lago o a otro arroyo más grande (418)

trough/seno el punto más bajo de una onda (492) *FCAT VOCAB*

tsunami/tsunami una ola gigante del océano que se forma después de una erupción volcánica, terremoto submarino o desprendimiento de tierras (496)

tundra/tundra una llanura sin árboles situada en la región ártica o antártica o en la cumbre de las montañas; se caracteriza por temperaturas muy bajas en el invierno y veranos cortos y frescos (362)

U

umbilical cord/cordón umbilical la estructura que une al embrión y después al feto con la placenta, a través de la cual pasan vasos sanguíneos (239)

undertow/resaca un corriente subsuperficial que está cerca de la orilla y que arrastra los objetos hacia el mar (495)

upwelling/surgencia el movimiento de las aguas profundas, frías y ricas en nutrientes hacia la superficie (489)

urban sprawl/derrame urbano el crecimiento no planeado de las áreas urbanas (388)

urinary system/sistema urinario los órganos que producen, almacenan y eliminan la orina (192)

uterus/útero en los mamíferos hembras, el órgano hueco y muscular en el que se incrusta el óvulo fecundado y en el que se desarrollan el embrión y el feto (235)

V

vagina/vagina el órgano reproductivo femenino que conecta la parte exterior del cuerpo con el útero (235)

variable/variable un factor que se modifica en un experimento con el fin de probar una hipótesis (16) *FCAT VOCAB*

vein/vena en biología, un vaso que lleva sangre al corazón (158)

vesicle/vesícula una cavidad o bolsa pequeña que contiene materiales en una célula eucariótica; se forma cuando parte de la membrana celular rodea los materiales que van a ser llevados al interior la célula o transportados dentro de ella (89)

virus/virus una partícula microscópica que se introduce en una célula y a menudo la destruye (254) *FCAT VOCAB*

volume/volumen una medida del tamaño de un cuerpo o región en un espacio de tres dimensiones (23, 578)

W

water cycle/ciclo del agua el movimiento continuo del agua entre la atmósfera, la tierra y los océanos (417)

watershed/cuenca hidrográfica el área del terreno que es drenada por un sistema de ríos (418, 392)

water table/capa freática el nivel más alto del agua subterránea; el límite superior de la zona de saturación (428)

watt/watt (o vatio) la unidad que se usa para expresar potencia; es equivalente a un joule por segundo (símbolo: W) (622)

wavelength/longitud de onda la distancia entre cualquier punto de una onda y un punto idéntico en la onda siguiente (492) *FCAT VOCAB*

wedge/cuña una máquina simple que está formada por dos planos inclinados y que se mueve; normalmente se usa para cortar (635) *FCAT VOCAB*

weight/peso una medida de la fuerza gravitacional ejercida sobre un objeto; su valor puede cambiar en función de la ubicación del objeto en el universo (581)

wetland/pantano un área de tierra que está periódicamente bajo el agua o cuyo suelo contiene una gran cantidad de humedad (372)

wheel and axle/rueda y eje una máquina simple que está formada por dos objetos circulares de diferente tamaño; la rueda es el mayor de los dos objetos circulares (633) *FCAT VOCAB*

whitecap/cabrillas las burbujas de la cresta de una ola rompiente (496)

work/trabajo la transferencia de energía a un objeto mediante una fuerza que hace que el objeto se mueva en la dirección de la fuerza (618)

work input/trabajo de entrada el trabajo realizado en una máquina; el producto de la fuerza de entrada por la distancia a través de la que se ejerce la fuerza (625)

work output/trabajo de salida el trabajo realizado por una máquina; el producto de la fuerza de salida por la distancia a través de la que se ejerce la fuerza (625)

Y

year/año el tiempo que se requiere para que la Tierra le dé la vuelta al Sol una vez (514)

Z

zenith/cenit el punto del cielo situado directamente sobre un observador en la Tierra (526)

Index

Index

Index

Index

Index

ecological communities in, 384–385, **384, 385**
Enviroteens of Manatee County, 411, **411**
Everglades National Park, 304, 372, 384, 387, 393–396
fisheries, 400–401, **400, 401**
forestry, 386, **386**
Gemesis Corporation, 608
groundwater in, 390–391, **390, 391,** 439
Kennedy Space Center, 572
kiteboarding, 672, **672**
Lake Okeechobee, **392,** 395
mapping project, 383
Mote's Pigeon Key Marine Research Center, 152
mystery blob on beach, 102, **102**
ocean currents around, 482, **482**
panthers in, 296, **296,** 381, **381**
population growth in, 388, **388**
Project Oceanography, USF, 509
sinkholes in, 433, **433,** 478, **478**
springs in, 390, **390,** 414–415
State and National Park Systems in, 385
surface water resources, 392, **392**
Surf Chair invention, 645, **645**
urban landscape in, 388–389, **388**
Wakulla Springs, 448, **448**
water-quality monitoring in, 437
Florida Coastal Cleanups, 403
Florida Land Owners Incentive Program, 385
Floridan Aquifer, 390
Florida Panther Posse, 381, **381**
flowers
coevolution with pollinators, 324, **324**
reproduction in, 283–284, **283**
fluids, 646–673
atmospheric pressure, 649–650, **649, 650**
Bernoulli's principle, 660–663, **660, 661, 662, 663**
buoyant force, 654–659, **654, 655, 657, 658, 659**
definition of, 648
density layers, 588, **588**
drag, 663–664, **664**
flow of, 652–653, **652, 653**
lab on, 666–667
Pascal's principle, 664, **665**
pressure and, 648–649, **648**
volume of, 579, **579**
water pressure, 651, **651**

focal point, 518, **519**
FoldNote instructions, 751–754, **751, 752, 753, 754**
food, pathogens in, 255
food chains and webs, 314, **314**
forces, 612–617
balanced vs. unbalanced, 615
buoyant, 654–659, **654, 655, 657, 658, 659**
contact, 612–613, **613**
definition of, 612
electric, 614
friction, 429, 501, 613, 617, 628
gravitational, 498–499, **499,** 581–582, **581,** 614
inertia, 616–617, **616, 617**
input vs. output, 625–626, **625, 626, 627**
machines and, 625–626, **625, 626, 627**
magnetic, 614
net, 614, **614, 615**
opposing, 615
pressure and, 649
that act at a distance, 614
units of, 612
work and, 618–619, **619**
Forde, Evan, 71, **71**
forensic detectives, 46, **46,** 64–65
forest biomes, 357–359, **357, 358, 359**
forest fires, 38, **38**
forestry, in Florida, 386, **386**
formulas, 758
fossil fuels, **338,** 339
four-corner fold instructions (FoldNote), 753, **753**
fractions, 760–761
fragmentation, 278, **278**
fraternal twins, 236
freezing, salinity increases through, **486**
freshwater ecosystems, 370–373, **370, 371, 372**
friction, 429, 501, 613, 617, 628
frogs, **4–5,** 12–18, **16, 17,** 272
fuels, 124, **338,** 339
fulcrum, 630–631, **630, 631**
function, structure and, 95, **95**
fungi, as decomposers, 313

G

Gagarin, Yuri, 558, **558**
Galileo, 516
Galileo mission, 555, **555**
gallbladder, 189, **189**

gametophytes, 282, **282**
gamma rays, **522**
GCF (greatest common factor), 760
Gemesis Corporation, 608
gemologists, 609, **609**
genes, 279, **279**
genetic bottlenecks, 296, **296**
genetic variability, 294–296, **295, 296**
genital herpes, 236, **236**
genital HPV, 236, **236**
geochemists, 10, **10**
geostationary orbits (GEO), 547, **547**
glacial drift, 466
glaciers, 462–467
alpine, 462, **462**
continental, 463, **463**
deposition from, 466–467, **466, 467**
icebergs, **334–335**
kettle formation from, 701
lab on, 472–473
landforms from, 464, **464–465**
"Lost Squadron" in, 478, **478**
movement of, 463
glands, 220
Glenn, John, 558, **558**
global positioning system (GPS), 548
global warming, 339
glucagon, 222–223, **222**
glucose, 110, **110**
Goddard, Robert, 542, **542**
gold, 425, **425,** 609
goldenrod spider, 320, **320**
Golgi complex, 89, **89, 90**
gonorrhea, 236, **236**
GPS (global positioning system), 548
gradient, stream, 419
graduated cylinders, **20,** 55, 579, **579,** 773
Grand Canyon, 416, **416**
Graphic Organizer instructions, 755–756
graphs, 50–52, **50, 51, 52,** 677, 763–765
grasses as producers, 312, **312**
grasslands, 360, **360**
gravitational force
definition of, 614
mass and, 581–582, **581**
Newton on, 516
tides and, 498–500, **499, 500**
gray wolves, 316–317, **316**
greatest common factor (GCF), 760
greenhouse effect, on Venus, 553
ground moraines, **466**

Index

Index

Index

Index

mini-ecosystems, 695
Miquelle, Dale, **9**
Mir, 560
Mississippi River
    flooding from, 426–427, **426, 427**
    Mississippi Delta, 425, **425**, 550, **550**
    watershed, 418, **418**
mitochondria
    respiration in, 111, **111, 112**
    structure and function of, 88, **88, 90**
mitosis, 115–116, **116–117**
mode, 57, **57**
model airplanes, 647
models, 58–59, **58**, 680
molecules, 758
monotremes, 281
months, 514
moon
    effect on tides, 498–499, **499**
    exploration of, 552, **552**, 562, **562**
moraines, 466, **466**
mosses, 282, **282**
Mote's Pigeon Key Marine Research Center, Florida, 152
motion
    escape velocity, 545, **545**
    inertia and, 616–617, **616, 617**
    orbits, 547, **547**
    work and, 619, **619**
motor neurons, 208-209, **208**
mouth, 186, **186**
movable pulleys, 632, **632**
mucus, 258, 263
mudflows, 470, **470**
multicellular organisms, 82, 92
multiple births, 236, **236**
multiple sclerosis, 263
multiplying fractions, 761
mural quadrant, **516**
muscle tissue, **131, 208**
muscular system, 138–141, **138, 139**
mutualism, 322, **322**

N

nails, 144, **144**, 146–147
nanobots, 644
nanomachines, 644
National Aeronautics and Space Administration (NASA), 551

National Oceanic and Atmospheric Association (NOAA), 71, 491
natural landscape, in Florida, 384–385, **384, 385**
natural selection, 294–295, **294, 295**
"nature vs. nurture" debate, 279
neap tides, 500, **500**
nearsightedness, 217, **217**
nephrons, 193–194, **193**
neritic zone, 366, **366**
nerves, 206, **207**, 208
nervous system, 206–212
    autonomic, 209, **209**
    central, 206, **206**, 210–212, **210, 211, 212**
    labs on, 129, 224–225
    nerves, 206, **207**, 208
    peripheral, 206–208, **206, 207**
    somatic, 209
    spinal cord, 212, **212**
nervous tissue, **130**
net forces, 614, **614, 615**
neurons, 207–208, **207**
    motor, 208-209, **208**
    sensory, 208-209
neutrons, 583, **583**, 757
New Millennium program, 557
Newton, Isaac, 498, 516
newton-meters, 621
newtons (N), 582, 612
Nile Delta, **425**
nitrate pollution, 435, **435**
nitrogen cycle, 340, **340**, 346–347
nitrogen fixation, 340, **340**
NOAA (National Oceanic and Atmospheric Association), 71, 491
noninfectious diseases, 254
nonlinear graphs, 52, **52**, 764
nonpoint-source pollution, 434
nonvascular plants, reproduction in, 282, **282**
North Atlantic Deep Water, 486
nose, **170**, 171, 219, 219, 258
nucleolus, 86, **86**
nucleus, atomic, 583, **583**, 757
nucleus, cell, 79, **79**, 86, **86, 90**
nurses, 273, **273**
nutcrackers, work and, **627**
nymph stage, **104–105**

O

objective lenses, 518, **519**

observations, importance of, 7, 13, 42–43, **43**, 766
observatories
    Astronaut Memorial Planetarium and Observatory, 538, **538**
    Chandra X-Ray Observatory, 523, **523**
    Chichén Itzá observatory, **514**
ocean currents, 482–491
    climate and, 488–491, **488, 489**
    Coriolis effect, 484, **484**
    deep currents, 485–486, **486, 487**
    El Niño, 490–491, **490**
    global currents, 482, **482**
    labs on, 481, 502–503
    salinity and, 485, **486**
    surface currents, 483–485, **483, 484, 485, 487**
    temperature and, 485, **485**
    toy duck tracking of, 508, **508**
oceanic zone, 367, **367**
oceanographers, 10, 71, **71**
oceans. *See also* ocean currents; ocean waves
    basins, 501
    climate and, 488–491, **488, 489**
    currents, 482–486, **483, 484, 485, 486**
    dead zones, 352
    depth and sunlight in, 366–367, **366–367**
    El Niño, 490–491, **490**
    estuaries, 368
    fisheries, 400–401, **400, 401**
    four main, 482, **482**
    lab on, 502–503
    marine ecosystems, 364–369, **365, 366–367**, 398–399, **398–399**
    pollution of, 401, **401**
    protecting, 402–403, **402**
    salinity, 485, **486**
    shoreline erosion, 452–457, **454–455, 456**
    temperature of, 365, **365**, 486, **487**
    tides, 498–501, **498, 499, 500**
    upwelling in, 489, **489**, 502–503
ocean vents, 380, **380**
ocean waves, 492–496
    circular motion in, 493, **493**
    deep-water and shallow-water, 494, **494**
    deposition from, 456–457, **456, 457**
    energy in, 452, **452**

Index

of groundwater, 391
lab on, 374–375
light, 538, **538**
mercury, 395
of oceans, 401, **401,** 403
point-source vs. nonpoint-source, 434
of surface water, 386, 392, 395, 434
thermal, 435, 436
water treatment and, 696–699
pond ecosystems, 371, **371,** 374–375
populations. *See also* interactions of living things
carrying capacity, 319
competition and, 319, **319**
definition, **309,** 310, **310**
Florida Black Bear, 332
human, in Florida, 388, **388**
limiting factors in, 318–319
mark-recapture method of estimating, 326–327
porosity, 429, **429**
potential energy, 599
power, 622–623, **622,** 638–639
prairie dogs, 312, **312,** 315
prairie ecosystem, 312–313, **312–313,** 360, **360**
precipitation, in the water cycle, 335, 336, **336,** 417, **417**
predator-prey adaptations, 293, **293,** 320, **320**
predators
adaptations, 320, **320**
energy pyramid and, 307, 315, **315**
gray wolves, 316–317, **316**
predator-prey adaptations, 293, **293,** 320, **320**
survival behavior in, 287
use in gardening, 333
predictions, 15, **15**
prefixes, unit, 772
pregnancy
birth, 240
from fertilization to embryo, 238, **238**
fetus growth during, 239–240, **239, 241,** 687, **687**
lab on, 244–245
multiple births, 236, **236**
placenta formation, 239, **239**
timeline, **241**
premolars, 186, **186**
pressure
atmospheric, 649–650, **649, 650**

Bernoulli's principle and, 660–663, **660, 661, 662, 663**
blood, 158, 160, 164, 211
breathing and, 652, **652**
definition of, 648
fluid, 648–649, **648**
water, 651, **651,** 664
pretenders, 321
prey
adaptations of, 293, **293,** 320–321, **320, 321**
predators as, 287
primary succession, 343, **343**
primary treatment, 438, **438**
prions, 272
prism, volume of, 762
producers, 312, **312**
progesterone, 235
Project Oceanography, 509
prokaryotes, 80–81, **80, 81,** 114, **114**
proportions, 233, 242, **242,** 759
prostate gland, 234, **234,** 237
prostheses, 152, **152,** 230
proteins
digestion of, 185, **185**
enzymes, 185, **185,** 196–197, 685–686
prions, 272
from ribosomes, 87
protists, 77, **77**
protons, 583–584, **583,** 757
Ptolemaic theory, 515, **515**
Ptolemy, Claudius, 515
puberty, 242
pulleys, **627,** 632, **632**
pulmonary circulation, 159, **159**
pulp, in spleen
red, 168, **168**
white, 168, **168**
pulse, 158, 160
pupils, 216–217, **216**
pyramid instructions (FoldNote), 751, **751**
Pytheas, 498
pythons, 304, **304**

Q

qualitative observations, 43, **43**
quantitative observations, 43, **43**

R

rabbits in Australia, 324, **324**

radiation
electromagnetic, 521, **521**
energy transfer through, 679
infrared, 522, **522**
ultraviolet, 16–18, 142
radiation oncologists, 125, **125**
radio telescopes, 522, **522**
ramps, **626,** 627
ranching, in Florida, 386, **386**
range, data, 50
ratios, 759
RBCs (red blood cells), **154–155,** 162, **162,** 164, 168
reaction, in rockets, 544, **544**
reaction devices, 544
reactivity, 592, **592, 593**
receptor proteins, **261**
receptors, 208. *See also* sensory system
recharge zones, 430
reciprocals, 761
reclaimed water, 392
rectangle, area of, 762
rectangular solids, volume of, 580
rectum, 190, **190**
recycling, 8, **8**
red blood cells (RBCs), **154–155,** 162, **162,** 164, 168
red pulp, 168, **168**
redshifts, 530, **530**
red tides, 401, 508, **508**
reducing fractions, 760
reef balls, 411, **411**
Reef Rakers, 411, **411**
reflecting telescopes, 519–520, **519, 520**
reflexes, 205, 215, **215**
refracting telescopes, 519, **519**
registered nurses (RNs), 273, **273**
rehabilitation, 153
Reinhard, Johan, 479, **479**
rejuvenated rivers, 422, **422**
remoras, 322, **322**
remote-sensing satellites, 550–551, **550**
replications, 17
reproduction
asexual, 278, **278,** 285
birth, 240
cancer and, 237
fertilization, 279–280, **279**
human reproductive systems, 234–235, **234, 235**
infertility, 237
lab on, 244–245
in mammals, 281
multiple births, 236, **236**

Index

Index

tributaries, 370, **370**, 418
triceps muscle, 139, **139**
tri-fold instructions (FoldNote), 754,
    754
triple-beam balances, 773, **773**
triplets, 236
tropical rain forests, 359, **359**
trough, wave, 492, **492**
Tsiolkovsky, Konstantin, 542
tsunamis, 496, **496**
tubers, 285, **285**
tundra, 362, **362**
turbidity, 436
turbulence, 663–664, **664**
turkey vultures, 313, **313**
Turtle Excluder Devices (TEDs), 400,
    400
turtles, sea, **41–42, 306–307,** 400,
    400, 402
Tutorials, Annually Assessed
    Benchmark, 722–749
twenty questions, 589
twins, 236, **236**
two-panel flip chart instructions
    (FoldNote), 754, **754**
Tyson, Neil deGrasse, 539, **539**

U

ultrasound, 240, 251, **251**
ultraviolet light
    frog deformities and, **4–5,** 16–
        18, **16, 17, 18**
    melanin and, 142
umbilical cord, 239, **239**
undertow, 495, **495**
unicellular organism, 94
units
    conversion table, 772
    of force, 612
    of mass, 772
    prefixes for, 772
    of pressure, 648
    SI, 21–24, **21, 23, 24,** 772
    of volume, 579–580, 772
    of weight, 582
    of work, 621
universal donors, **165**
universe, 528, **529,** 530
upwelling, 489, **489,** 502–503
urban landscape, in Florida, 388–
    389, **388**
urban sprawl, 388
urea, 193
ureters, **193**
urethra, **193,** 234, **234**

urinary bladder, **193**
urinary infections, 195
urinary system, 192–195, **192, 193,**
    195
urination, **193**
urine, **193**
Ursa Major, 525, **525**
U-shaped valleys, **465**
uterus, 235, **235,** 244–245

V

V-2 rockets, 543, **543**
vaccines, 256
vacuoles, 90, **90**
vagina, 235, **235**
valves, 157, **157**
variables
    in controlled experiments, 16,
        16, 766
    in data tables, 49, **49**
    in graphs, 764
vas deferens, 234, **234**
veins, 158, **158**
velocity
    escape, 545, **545**
    orbital, 545, **545**
    suborbital, 545, **545**
Venera 9, 553, **553**
ventricle, 157, **157**
Venus, exploration of, 553, **553**
vernal equinox, **527**
vertebrae, 212, **212**
Very Large Array (VLA), 522
vesicles, 108, **108**
Viking missions, 554, **554**
villi, 188, **188**
Virchow, Rudolf, 77
viruses
    antibiotics and, 257
    coevolution of, 324
    common cold, 266–267
    diseases from, 254, **254,** 266–
        267
    immune system response to,
        260, **260–261**
visible light, 521, **521**
vision, 216–217, **216, 217**
VLA (Very Large Array), 522
vocal cords, 171
vOICe system, 230
volcanoes
    lahars from, 470, **470**
    on Venus, 553, **553**
volcanologist, 11, **11**

volume, 578–580
    formulas for, 762
    liquid, 579, **579**
    matter and, 578
    measurement of, **21,** 23, 579–
        580, **579, 580**
    of solids, 580, **580**
    unit conversions for, 772
voluntary muscle action, 138
voluntary processes, 210
von Braun, Wernher, 543
Voyager missions, 555–556, **555**

W

wading birds, 394–395, **394**
Wakulla Springs, Florida, 448, **448**
warm-water currents, 485, **485,**
    488, **488**
warning coloration, 321, **321**
Washington, George, 593
wasps, 323, **323**
wastewater managers, 353, **353**
wastewater treatment, 190
water. *See also* groundwater
    conservation of, 392, 440, **440**
    dead zones, 352
    desalination, 352
    drinking, 194
    in the Everglades, 394
    global use of, 337
    labs on, 442–443, 696–697
    on the moon, 552
    osmosis, 107, **107**
    phase change of, 599, **599**
    pollution of, 374–375, 386, 395,
        434
    pressure, 651, **651,** 664
    quality, 435–437, **436, 437**
    reclaimed, 392
    treatment, 392, 438, **438,** 449,
        696–697
    usage, 439–440, **439**
water cycle, 336–337, **336,** 417, **417,**
    442–443
water filtration, 449, **449,** 696–697
water pressure, 651, **651,** 664
water rockets, 566–567
watersheds, 392, 418, **418**
water table, 428, **428, 430**
water treatment
    evaporation, 698–699
    filtration, 449, **449,** 696–697
    lab on, 696–697
    primary and secondary, 438, **438**
    reclaimed water from, 392

X

Y

Z

Acknowledgments *continued from page ii*

Florida Teacher Consultants *continued*

Patricia Soto
Science Department Chair
George Washington
  Carver Middle School
Coral Gables, Florida

ZoEllen Warren
Science Teacher
Oak View Middle School
Archer, Florida

Angie Williams
Science Teacher
Riversprings Middle
  School
Crawfordville, Florida

Inclusion and Special Needs Consultants

Karen Clay
Inclusion Consultant
Boston, Massachusetts

Ellen McPeek Glisan
Special Needs Consultant
San Antonio, Texas

Safety Reviewer

Jack Gerlovich, Ph.D.
Associate Professor
School of Education
Drake University
Des Moines, Iowa

Academic Reviewers

Glenn Adelson, Ph.D.
Instructor
Department of Organismic
  and Evolutionary
  Biology
Harvard University
Cambridge, Massachusetts

Carl Beaver, Ph.D.
Research Scientist
Florida Fish and Wildlife
  Commission
St. Petersburg, Florida

Kenneth H. Brink, Ph.D.
*Senior Scientist and Physical
  Oceanography Director*
Coastal Ocean Institute
  and Rinehart Coastal
  Research Center
Woods Hole
  Oceanographic
  Institution
Woods Hole,
  Massachusetts

John Brockhaus, Ph.D.
*Professor of Geospatial
  Information Science and
  Director of Geospatial
  Science Information
  Program*
Department of Geography
  and Environmental
  Engineering
United States Military
  Academy
West Point, New York

Howard L. Brooks, Ph.D.
*Professor of Physics &
  Astronomy*
DePauw University
Greencastle, Indiana

Dan Bruton, Ph.D.
Associate Professor
Department of Physics
  and Astronomy
Stephen F. Austin State
  University
Nacogdoches, Texas

Wesley N. Colley, Ph.D.
Lecturer
Department of Astronomy
University of Virginia
Charlottesville, Virginia

Joe W. Crim, Ph.D.
*Professor and Head of
  Cellular Biology*
Department of Cellular
  Biology
University of Georgia
Athens, Georgia

Scott Darveau, Ph.D.
*Assistant Professor of
  Chemistry*
Chemistry Department
University of Nebraska at
  Kearney
Kearney, Nebraska

Jim Denbow, Ph.D.
*Associate Professor of
  Archaeology*
Department of
  Anthropology and
  Archaeology
University of Texas
Austin, Texas

William E. Dunscombe, Ph.D.
Chairman
Biology Department
Union County College
Cranford, New Jersey

Simonetta Frittelli, Ph.D.
Associate Professor
Department of Physics
Duquesne University
Pittsburgh, Pennsylvania

Linda K. Gaul, Ph.D., MPH
Epidemiologist
Texas Department of State
  Health Services
Austin, Texas

William Grisham, Ph.D.
Lecturer
Psychology Department
University of California,
  Los Angeles
Los Angeles, California

P. Shiv Halasyamani, Ph.D.
*Associate Professor of
  Chemistry*
Department of Chemistry
University of Houston
Houston, Texas

Mary Kay Hemenway, Ph.D.
*Research Associate and
  Senior Lecturer*
Department of Astronomy
University of Texas
Austin, Texas

David Hershey, Ph.D.
Education Consultant
Hyattsville, Maryland

Steven A. Jennings, Ph.D.
Associate Professor
Department of Geography
  & Environmental
  Studies
University of Colorado
Colorado Springs,
  Colorado

Ping H. Johnson, M.D., Ph.D., CHES
*Assistant Professor of Health
  Education*
Department of Health,
  Physical Education and
  Sport Science
Kennesaw State University
Kennesaw, Georgia

John Krenz, Ph.D.
Associate Professor
Biological Sciences
Minnesota State
  University
Mankato, Minnesota

David Lamp, Ph.D.
*Associate Professor of
  Physics*
Physics Department
Texas Tech University
Lubbock, Texas

Madeline Micceri Mignone, Ph.D.
Assistant Professor
Natural Science
Dominican College
Orangeburg, New York

Richard F. Niedziela, Ph.D.
*Assistant Professor of
  Chemistry*
Department of Chemistry
DePaul University
Chicago, Illinois

Eva Oberdoerster, Ph.D.
Lecturer
Department of Biology
Southern Methodist
  University
Dallas, Texas

Academic Reviewers

continued

Kate Queeney, Ph.D.
Assistant Professor of Chemistry
Chemistry Department
Smith College
Northampton, Massachusetts

Michael H. Renfroe, Ph.D.
Professor of Biology
Department of Biology
James Madison University
Harrisonburg, Virginia

Lisa Robbins, Ph.D.
Chief Scientist
U.S. Geological Survey
   Center for Coastal and
   Watershed Studies
St. Petersburg, Florida

Laurie Santos, Ph.D.
Assistant Professor
Department of Psychology
Yale University
New Haven, Connecticut

Patrick K. Schoff, Ph.D.
Research Associate
Natural Resources
   Research Institute
University of Minnesota at
   Duluth
Duluth, Minnesota

Fred Seaman, Ph.D.
Retired Research Associate
College of Pharmacy
The University of Texas at
   Austin
Austin, Texas

**H. Michael Sommermann,
Ph.D.**
Professor of Physics
Physics Department
Westmont College
Santa Barbara, California

John D. Wehr, Ph.D.
Associate Professor
Department of Biological
   Sciences
Fordham University
Bronx, New York

Dale Wheeler
*Associate Professor of
   Chemistry*
A. R. Smith Department of
   Chemistry
Appalachian State
   University
Boone, North Carolina

Kim Withers, Ph.D.
Research Scientist
Center for Coastal Studies
Texas A&M University at
   Corpus Christi
Corpus Christi, Texas

Teacher Reviewers

Barbara Gavin Akre
*Teacher of Biology,
   Anatomy-Physiology, and
   Life Science*
Duluth Independent
   School District
Duluth, Minnesota

Laura Buchanan
*Science Teacher and
   Department Chair*
Corkran Middle School
Glen Burnie, Maryland

Sarah Carver
Science Teacher
Jackson Creek Middle
   School
Bloomington, Indiana

Robin K. Clanton
Science Department Head
Berrien Middle School
Nashville, Georgia

Hilary Cochran
Science Teacher
Indian Crest Junior High
   School
Souderton, Pennsylvania
Karen Dietrich, S.S.J., Ph.D.
*Principal and Biology
   Instructor*
Mount Saint Joseph
   Academy
Flourtown, Pennsylvania

Trisha Elliott
*Science and Mathematics
   Teacher*
Chain of Lakes Middle
   School
Orlando, Florida

Liza M. Guasp
Science Teacher
Celebration K-8 School
Celebration, Florida

Meredith Hanson
Science Teacher
Westside Middle School
Rocky Face, Georgia

Denise Hulette
Science Teacher
Conway Middle School
Orlando, Florida

M. R. Penny Kisiah
*Science Teacher and
   Department Chair*
Fairview Middle School
Tallahassee, Florida

Laura Kitselman
*Science Teacher and
   Coordinator*
Loudoun Country Day
   School
Leesburg, Virginia

Debra S. Kogelman, MAed.
Science Teacher
University of Chicago
   Laboratory Schools
Chicago, Illinois

Jennifer L. Lamkie
Science Teacher
Thomas Jefferson Middle
   School
Edison, New Jersey

Rebecca Larsen
Science Teacher
Fernandina Beach Middle
   School
Fernandina Beach, Florida

Sally M. Lesley
ESL Science Teacher
Burnet Middle School
Austin, Texas

Augie Maldonado
Science Teacher
Grisham Middle School
Round Rock, Texas

Lab Testing

Barry L. Bishop
*Science Teacher and
   Department Chair*
San Rafael Junior High
   School
Ferron, Utah

Paul Boyle
Science Teacher
Perry Heights Middle
   School
Evansville, Indiana

Yvonne Brannum
*Science Teacher and
   Department Chair*
Hine Junior High School
Washington, D.C.

Gladys Cherniak
Science Teacher
St. Paul's Episcopal School
Mobile, Alabama

James Chin
Science Teacher
Frank A. Day Middle
   School
Newtonville,
   Massachusetts

Randy Christian
Science Teacher
Stovall Junior High School
Houston, Texas

Kenneth Creese
Science Teacher
White Mountain Junior
   High School
Rock Springs, Wyoming

Alonda Droege
Biology Teacher
Evergreen High School
Seattle, Washington

Susan Gorman
Science Teacher
North Ridge Middle
School
North Richland Hills,
Texas

C. John Graves
Science Teacher
Monforton Middle School
Bozeman, Montana

Janel Guse
*Science Teacher and
Department Chair*
West Central Middle
School
Hartford, South Dakota

Norman Holcomb
Science Teacher
Marion Elementary School
Marion, Ohio

Kerry A. Johnson
Science Teacher
Isbell Middle School
Santa Paula, California

M. R. Penny Kisiah
*Science Teacher and
Department Chair*
Fairview Middle School
Tallahassee, Florida

Michael E. Kral
Science Teacher
West Hardin Middle
School
Cecilia, Kentucky

Kathy LaRoe
Science Teacher
East Valley Middle School
East Helena, Montana

Jason P. Marsh
Biology Teacher
Montevideo High School
& Montevideo Country
School
Montevideo, Minnesota

Edith C. McAlanis
*Science Teacher and
Department Chair*
Socorro Middle School
El Paso, Texas

Kevin McCurdy, Ph.D.
Science Teacher
Elmwood Junior High
School
Rogers, Arkansas

Alyson Mike
Science Teacher
East Valley Middle School
East Helena, Montana

Joseph Price
*Science Teacher and
Department Chair*
H. M. Browne Junior High
School
Washington, D.C.

Terry J. Rakes
Science Teacher
Elmwood Junior High
School
Rogers, Arkansas

Bert J. Sherwood
Science Teacher
Socorro Middle School
El Paso, Texas

David M. Sparks
Science Teacher
Redwater Junior High
School
Redwater, Texas

Larry Tackett
*Science Teacher and
Department Chair*
Andrew Jackson Middle
School
Cross Lanes, West Virginia

Christopher Wood
Science Teacher
Western Rockingham
Middle School
Madison, North Carolina

Sharon L. Woolf
Science Teacher
Langston Hughes Middle
School
Reston, Virginia

Gordon Zibelman
Science Teacher
Drexel Hill Middle School
Drexel Hill, Pennsylvania

Maureen Martin
Green Team Science Teacher
Jackson Creek Middle
School
Bloomington, Indiana

Magdalena F. Molledo
Science Department Chair
DeLaura Middle School
Satellite Beach, Florida

Jean Pletchette
Health Educator
Winterset Community
Schools
Winterset, Iowa

Nancy Poage-Nixon
Science Teacher
Covington Middle School
Austin, Texas

Elizabeth J. Rustad
Science Department Chair
Coronado Elementary
Gilbert, Arizona

Helen P. Schiller
Instructional Coach
The School District of
Greenville County
Greenville, South Carolina

Stephanie Snowden
Science Teacher
Canyon Vista Middle
School
Austin, Texas

Marci L. Stadiem
Science Department Chair
Cascade Middle School
Seattle, Washington

Martha Tedrow
Science Teacher
Thomas Jefferson Middle
School
Winston-Salem, North
Carolina

Sherrye Valenti
Curriculum Leader
Science Department
Wildwood Middle School
Wildwood, Missouri

Florence Vaughan
Science Teacher
Science Department
University of Chicago
Laboratory Schools
Chicago, Illinois

Angie Williams
Classroom Teacher
Riversprings Middle
School
Crawfordville, Florida

Contributing Writers
Karin Akre
William J. Barlow
Bill Burnside
David Gilbert
Eric Kincaid
Eileen Nehme
Catherine Podeszwa
Marjorie Roueché
Daniel Sharp
Larry Ward
Molly Frohlich
  Wetterschneider

Answer Checking
Marie Amato
Bronx, New York

Alyson Mike
East Helena, Montana

Staff Credits

Editorial

Leigh Ann García,
   Executive Editor
Kelly Rizk, *Senior Editor*
David Westerberg,
   Senior Editor
Laura Zapanta, *Senior Editor*

Editorial Development Team
Monica Brown
Jen Driscoll
Michael Mazza
Kristen McCardel
Laura Prescott
Bill Rader
Jim Ratcliffe
Betsy Roll
Roshan Strong
Tam Voynick
David Wisnieski

Copyeditors
Dawn Marie Spinozza,
   Copyediting Manager
Simon Key
Jane A. Kirschman
Kira J. Watkins

Editorial Support Staff
Debbie Starr,
   Managing Editor
Soojinn Choi

Online Products
Bob Tucek, *Executive Editor*
Wesley M. Bain

Design

Book Design
Kay Selke
Peter Reid
Sally Bess
Sonya Mendeke
Mercedes Newman
Holly Whittaker
Lisa Woods

Media Design
Richard Metzger
Chris Smith

Ancillary Design
Jeff Robinson

Image Acquisitions
Curtis Riker
Jeannie Taylor
Angela Boehm
Andy Christiansen
Michelle Dike

Cover Design
Kay Selke

Graphic Services
Cathy Murphy
Nanda Patel

Publishing Services

Technology Services
Juan Baquera
Sarah Buller
Laura Likon
Margaret Sanchez
Patty Zepeda

eMedia

Melanie Baccus
Lydia Doty
Cathy Kuhles
Marsh Flournoy
Tara F. Ross
Ed Blake
Kimberly Cammerata
Michael Rinella

Production

Eddie Dawson,
   Senior Production Manager
Sherry Sprague, *Project
   Manager*
Dustin Ognowski, *Production
   Assistant*

Credits

Abbreviations used: (t) top, (c) center, (b) bottom, (l) left, (r) right, (bkgd) background

PHOTOGRAPHY

Cover (owl), Kim Taylor/Bruce Coleman, Inc, ; (tl), Mike Powell/Getty Images; (tr), Dennis Kunkel Microscopy, Inc; (br), John Pontier/Animals Animals/Earth Scenes; (bl), Jeff Greenberg/age footstock.

Table of Contents Page iii (t), Joe McBride/Stone/Getty Images; iii (b), Sam Dudgeon/HRW; iv (b), NASA, vii, © David Madison/Getty Images/Stone; viii (t), John Langford/HRW; x, Jeff Greenberg/PhotoEdit; xi, © Eunice Harris/Index Stock Imagery, Inc.; xiii (l), Peter Van Steen/HRW; xv, Bruno P. Zehnder/Peter Arnold, Inc..

Unit One 2 (tl), O.S.F./Animals Animals; 2 (c), Hulton Archive/Getty Images; 2 (bl), Digital Image copyright © 2006 PhotoDisc; 3 (cl), University of Pennsylvania/Hulton Getty; 3 (t), National Portrait Gallery, Smithsonian Institution/Art Resource; 3 (br), © National Geographic Image Collection/O. Louis Mazzatenta; 3 (cr), Digital Image copyright © 2006 PhotoDisc.

Chapter One 4-5, Craig Line/AP/Wide World Photos; 6, 7 (t),Peter Van Steen/HRW; 7 (b), Sam Dudgeon/HRW; 8 (b), Peter Van Steen/HRW; 8 (t), Hank Morgan/Photo Researchers, Inc.; 9, © National Geographic Image Collection/Dale Miquelle; 10 (b), John Langford/HRW; 10 (t), © NC: Science VU/PNNL/Visuals Unlimited; 11, Jeremy Bishop/Science Photo Library/Photo Researchers, Inc.; 13 (t), Peter Van Steen/HRW; 13 (b), 14, Sam Dudgeon/HRW; 16, John Mitchell/Photo Researchers, Inc.; 18, Sam Dudgeon/HRW; 19, John Mitchell/Photo Researchers, Inc.; 20 (l), Sam Dudgeon/HRW; 20 (bl, tc, r, c, bc), Victoria Smith/HRW; 22, David Austen/Stock Boston/Picture Quest; 23 (r, l), Peter Van Steen/HRW; 2-3 (bl & br), Peter Veit/DRK Photo; 24 (tl), © Tony Freeman/PhotoEdit; 24 (r), Victoria Smith/HRW; 24 (bl), © Royalty Free/CORBIS; 26-27 (tl), John Langford/HRW; 26, 27 (r), 28, 29, Sam Dudgeon/HRW; 30 (t, bc), Victotria Smith/HRW; 31, 32, 33, Sam Dudgeon/HRW; 34 (t), John Mitchell/Photo Researchers, Inc.; 34 (b), Peter Van Steen/HRW; 35, Sam Dudgeon/HRW; 38 (r), marinethemes.com/Kelvin Aitken; 38 (l), Craig Fugii/©1988 The Seattle Times; 39 (t), NASA; 39 (b), NASA.

Chapter Two 40-41, © Mark Conlin/USFWS/FWC/SeaPics.com; 42 (tl), John Langford/HRW; 42 (br), Corbis Images; 42, © Peter Johnson/CORBIS; 43, © Photodisc/gettyimages; 44 (b), Sam Dudgeon/HRW; 44 (t), © Yann Arthus-Bertrand/CORBIS; 44 (bl), Erich Lessing/Art Resource, NY; 44 (br), The Granger Collection, New York; 45 (r), David Zalubowski/AP/Wide World Photos; 45 (l), © Photodisc/gettyimages; 45 (c), Sam Dudgeon/HRW; 46 (t), Richard Megna/Fundamental Photographs; 46, Bob Daemmrich/The Image Works; 50, © Farrell Grehan/CORBIS; 53, © Paul Barton/CORBIS; 54 (br), Scaled Composites/Photo Researchers, Inc.; 54 (bl), Scaled Composites/Photo Researchers, Inc.; 56, © Jeff Greenberg/PhotoEdit; 58, ©Tom Pantages/Phototake; 59, © Jeff Greenberg/PhotoEdit; 60, © James Strawser/Grant Heilman Photography, Inc.; 61 (l), AP/Wide World Photos; 61 (c), Science Museum, London/Topham-HIP/The Image Works; 61 (r), © Kim Kulish/CORBIS; 62, Joe Brockert/AP/Wide World Photos; 63, © Jason Reed/Reuters/CORBIS; 64, Victoria Smith/HRW; 70 (l), © National Geographic Image Collection/Michael K. Nichols; 70 (r), U.S. Navy, Brien Aho, HO/AP/Wide World Photos; 71, Photo Courtesy of NOAA.

Unit Two 72 (t), © Bettman/CORBIS; 72 (cr), Don W. Fawcett/Photo Researchers, Inc.; 72 (b), David McCarthy/Photo Researchers, Inc.; 73 (tl), Omikron/Photo Researchers, Inc.; 73 (tr), Scimat/Photo Researchers, Inc.; 73 (c), SPL/Photo Researchers, Inc.; 73 (cr), SPL/Photo Researchers, Inc.; 73 (b), Dr. Tim Evans/Photo Researchers, Inc..

Chapter Three 74-75, Dennis Kunkel/Phototake; 76 (r), Visuals Unlimited/Kevin Collins; 76 (l), Leonard Lessin/Peter Arnold; 77 (bkgd), © Stephen Frink/CORBIS; 77 (tl), VVG/SPL/Photo Researchers, Inc.; 77 (tc), Andrew Syred/SPL/Photo Researchers, Inc.; 77 (t), © Mark Farmer, University of Georgia; 78, Photodisc, Inc.; 79 (t), William Dentler/BPS/Stone/Getty Images; 79 (b), Dr. Gopal Murti/Science Photo Library/Photo Researchers, Inc.; 81, Wolfgang Baumeister/Science Photo Library/Photo Researchers, Inc.; 82 (l), Biophoto Associates/Photo Researchers, Inc.; 83, M.I. Walker/Photo Researchers, Inc.; 86 (l), Dr. Peter Dawson/ Science Photo Library/Photo Researchers, Inc.; 86 (br), Don Fawcett/Visuals Unlimited; 87 (r), R. Bolender-D. Fawcett/Visuals Unlimited; 88 (cl), Don Fawcett/Visuals Unlimited; 88 (bl), Newcomb & Wergin/BPS/Getty Images; 89 (br), Garry T Cole/BPS/Getty Images; 90 (cl), Dr. Jeremy Burgess/Science PhotoLibrary/Science Source/Photo Researchers, Inc.; 90 (t), Dr. Gopal Murti/Science Photo Library/Photo Researchers, Inc.; 92, Quest/Science Photo Library/Photo Researchers, Inc.; 93, Manfred Kage/Peter Arnold, Inc. ; 96 (b), Sam Dudgeon/HRW; 102 (r), Photo Van Lockwood, Archives Saint-Augustine Historical Society; 102 (l), Science Photo Library/Photo Researchers, Inc.; 103 (b), Artville/gettyimages; 103 (t), Courtesy Caroline Schooley.

Chapter Four 104-105, © Michael & Patricia Fogden/CORBIS; 106, Sam Dudgeon/HRW; 108 (br), Photo Researchers, Inc.; 109 (tr), Birgit H. Satir; 110 (l), Runk/Schoenberger/Grant Heilman; 111 (r), John Langford/HRW; 113, Corbis Images; 114, CNRI/SPL/Photo Researchers, Inc. ; 115 (t), L. Willatt, East Anglian Regional Genetics Service/Science Photo Library/Photo Researchers, Inc..; 115 (b), Biophoto Associates/Photo Researchers, Inc.; 116 (b), Visuals Unlimited/R. Calentine; 116 (c, cl, cr), Ed Reschke/Peter Arnold, Inc.; 117 (cl), Ed Reschke/Peter Arnold, Inc.; 117 (c), Biology Media/Photo Researchers, Inc.; 117 (cr), Biology Media/Photo Researchers, Inc.; 118, 119 Sam Dudgeon/HRW; 121 (cl, cr), Biophoto Associates/Science Source/Photo Researchers, Inc.; 121 (br), John Langford/HRW; 124 (l), Lee D. Simons/Science Souce/Photo Researchers, Inc.; 125 (t), Reproduced with permission from the University of Florida Department of Radiation Oncology; 125 (b), BSIP, Raguet/SPL/Photo Researchers, Inc..

Unit Three 126 (t), Geoffrey Clifford/Woodfin Camp; 126 (c), J & L Weber/Peter Arnold; 126 (b), AP/Wide World Photos; 127 (cl), Brown Brothers; 127 (cr), SuperStock; 127 (tl), Gamma-Liaison/Getty News Images; 127 (bl), Enrico Ferorelli; 127 (tr), Sheila Terry/SPL/Photo Researchers, Inc.; 127 (br), © CORBIS.

Chapter Five 128-129, AFP/CORBIS; 130-131 (b-bkgd), © David Madison/Getty Images/Stone; 132, Sam Dudgeon/HRW; 134, Sam Dudgeon/HRW; 136 (l), SP/FOCA/HRW; 136 (r), HRW by Sergio Purtell/FOCA; 136 (c), HRW by Sergio Purtell/FOCA; 137, Scott Camazine/Photo Researchers, Inc.; 138 (bkgd), © Bob Torrez/Getty Images/Stone; 138 (tl-inset), © G.W. Willis/Biological Photo Service; 138 r-inset Manfred Kage/Peter Arnold, Inc. ; 138 (bl-inset), Dr. E.R. Degginger; 140 (l), Chris Hamilton; 140 (r), 142, Sam Dudgeon/HRW; 144 (bkgd, r), Peter Van Steen/HRW; 144 (l), Dr. Robert Becker/Custom Medical Stock Photo; 147, 148, Sam Dudgeon/HRW; 149, Sam Dudgeon/HRW; 152 (t), © Mote Marine Laboratory; 152 (r), Reuters/David Gray/NewsCom; 153 (t), Photo courtesy of Dr. Zahra Beheshti; 153 (b), Creatas/PictureQuest.

Chapter Six 154-155, © Nih /Science Source/Photo Researchers, Inc.; 158 (l), (r), O. Meckes/Nicole Ottawa/Photo Researchers, Inc.; 160, © John Bavosi /Photo Researchers, Inc.; 162, Susumu Nishinaga/SPL/Photo Researchers, Inc.; 163 (b), Don Fawcett/Photo Researchers, Inc.; 165, © Getty Images/The Image Bank; 168, © Collection CNRI/Phototake Inc./Alamy Photos; 173 (l, r), Matt Meadows/Peter Arnold, Inc.; 174, 175, Sam Dudgeon/HRW; 176 (bl), Susumu Nishinaga/SPL/Photo Researchers, Inc 180 (l), Richard T. Nowitz/Phototake; 180 (r), © Paul A. Souders/CORBIS; 181 (b), Al Giddings/Al Giddings Images, Inc.; 181 (t), Natalie B. Fobes/National Geographic Image Collection.

Chapter Seven 182-183, © ISM/Phototake; 191, Victoria Smith/HRW; 194, Getty Images/The Image Bank; 195, Stephen J. Krasemann/DRK Photo; 196, 197, Sam Dudgeon/HRW; 202 (l), J.H. Robinson/Photo Researchers, Inc.; 202 (r), REUTERS/David Gray/NewsCom; 203 (t), Mabel Nino/HRW.

Chapter Eight 204-205, Omikron/Photo Researchers, Inc.; 211 (t), Sam Dudgeon/HRW; 212 (bl), © Galen Rowell/CORBIS; 215, 222 (c), Sam Dudgeon/HRW; 223, Will & Deni McIntyre/Photo Researchers, Inc.; 224 (l, r), 225, Sam Dudgeon/HRW; 226 (tr), Lisa Davis/HRW; 227 (t), Sam Dudgeon/HRW; 230 (l), © Susan Stocker/South-Florida Sun-Sentinel; 230 (r), Mike Derer/AP/Wide World Photos; 231 (t), Photo courtesy of Dr. Bertha Madras; 231 (b), SPL/Photo Researchers, Inc..

Chapter Nine 232-233, Photo Lennart Nilsson/Albert Bonniers Forlag AB, A Child Is Born, Dell Publishing Company; 236, Chip Henderson; 237 (bl), Digital Image copyright © 2006 PhotoDisc; 241 (tl), Petit Format/Nestle/Science Source/Photo Researchers, Inc.; 241 (cl, cr), Photo Lennart Nilsson/Albert Bonniers Forlag AB, A Child Is Born, Dell Publishing Company; 241 (br), Keith/Custom Medical Stock Photo; 241 (tr), David M. Phillips/Photo Researchers, Inc.; 242 (l, cl, c, cr, r), Peter Van Steen/HRW; 243, © Mark Harmel/Getty Images/FPG International; 245, PhotoDisc/gettyimages; 246, Peter Van Steen/HRW; 247, Chip Henderson; 250 (l), Mabel Nino/HRW; 250 (r), Jim Tunell/Zuma Press/NewsCom; 251 (l), ZEPHYR/Science Photo Library/Photo Researchers, Inc.; 251 (r), Salem Community College.

Chapter Ten 252-253 (t), © K. Kjeldsen/Photo Researchers, Inc.; 254 (r), CNRI/Science Photo Library/Photo Researchers, Inc.; 254 (l), Tektoff-RM/CNRI/SPL/Photo Researchers, Inc.; 255, Kent Wood/Photo Researchers, Inc.; 256, 258 (l), Peter Van Steen/HRW ; 262 (t), John Langford/HRW; 263 (t), SuperStock; 263 (b), Clinical Radiology Dept., Salisbury District Hospital/SPL/Photo Researchers, Inc.; 264 (tl), Dr. A. Liepins/SPL/Photo Researchers, Inc.; 264 (tr), Dr. A. Liepins/SPL/Photo Researchers, Inc.; 264 (b), Photo Lennart Nilsson/Albert Bonniers Forlag AB; 266, Sam Dudgeon/HRW; 272 (r), Michele Edmunds/FSU Photo Lab; 272 (l), E. R. Degginger/Bruce Coleman; 273 (t), Peter Van Steen/HRW; 273 (b), Corbis Images.

Unit Four 274 (t), Carr Clifton/Minden Pictures; 274 (c), Getty Images/FPG International; 274 (b), Tom Brakefield/Corbis; 275 (tr), Photo Researchers, Inc.; 275 (cr), SuperStock; 275 (bl), © David Young Wolff/Getty Images/Stone; 275 (cl), Alfred Eisenstaedt/ Life Magazine © Time Inc./ 275 (br), © James Watt/Visuals Unlimited; 275 (tl), © Tony Hamblin/CORBIS.